PRINCIPLES OF MACROECONOMICS

FOR B.A. AND B.COM. STUDENTS

Based on UGC Model Curriculum and Syllabi of Several Indian Universities

Dr. H.L. AHUJA
M.A., Ph.D. (DSE)
Formerly, Senior Reader
Department of Economics
Zakir Husain Delhi College
University of Delhi, Delhi.

AMIT AHUJA

S. CHAND
PUBLISHING
empowering minds

S. CHAND & COMPANY PVT. LTD.

(AN ISO 9001: 2008 COMPANY)

RAM NAGAR, NEW DELHI-110 055

S. CHAND & COMPANY PVT. LTD.

S. CHAND PUBLISHING
empowering minds

(An ISO 9001:2008 Company)

Head Office: 7361, RAM NAGAR, NEW DELHI - 110 055
Phone: 23672080-81-82, 9899107446, 9911310888 Fax: 91-11-23677446
www.schandpublishing.com; e-mail: helpdesk@schandpublishing.com

Branches

Ahmedabad	:	Ph: 27541965, 27542369, ahmedabad@schandpublishing.com
Bengaluru	:	Ph: 22268048, 22354008, bangalore@schandpublishing.com
Bhopal	:	Ph: 4274723, 4209587, bhopal@schandpublishing.com
Chandigarh	:	Ph: 2625356, 2625546, chandigarh@schandpublishing.com
Chennai	:	Ph: 28410027, 28410058, chennai@schandpublishing.com
Coimbatore	:	Ph: 2323620, 4217136, coimbatore@schandpublishing.com (Marketing Office)
Cuttack	:	Ph: 2332580, 2332581, cuttack@schandpublishing.com
Dehradun	:	Ph: 2711101, 2710861, dehradun@schandpublishing.com
Guwahati	:	Ph: 2738811, 2735640, guwahati@schandpublishing.com
Hyderabad	:	Ph: 27550194, 27550195, hyderabad@schandpublishing.com
Jaipur	:	Ph: 2219175, 2219176, jaipur@schandpublishing.com
Jalandhar	:	Ph: 2401630, 5000630, jalandhar@schandpublishing.com
Kochi	:	Ph: 2378740, 2378207-08, cochin@schandpublishing.com
Kolkata	:	Ph: 22367459, 22373914, kolkata@schandpublishing.com
Lucknow	:	Ph: 4026791, 4065646, lucknow@schandpublishing.com
Mumbai	:	Ph: 22690881, 22610885, mumbai@schandpublishing.com
Nagpur	:	Ph: 6451311, 2720523, 2777666, nagpur@schandpublishing.com
Patna	:	Ph: 2300489, 2302100, patna@schandpublishing.com
Pune	:	Ph: 64017298, pune@schandpublishing.com
Raipur	:	Ph: 2443142, raipur@schandpublishing.com (Marketing Office)
Ranchi	:	Ph: 2361178, ranchi@schandpublishing.com
Siliguri	:	Ph: 2520750, siliguri@schandpublishing.com (Marketing Office)
Visakhapatnam	:	Ph: 2782609, visakhapatnam@schandpublishing.com (Marketing Office)

First Edition 2014
Reprint 2016

ISBN : 978-93-8374-693-4 **Code** 1008 257

This book is for sale in India & other SAARC countries only.

PRINTED IN INDIA

By Vikas Publishing House Pvt. Ltd., Plot 20/4, Site-IV, Industrial Area Sahibabad, Ghaziabad-201010 and published by S.Chand & Company Pvt. Ltd., 7361, Ram Nagar, New Delhi -110 055.

To
Prem and Shaifali
With
Love and Affection

Preface

Since I published my book on '**Macroeconomics : Theory and Policy**' for postgraduate classes, there has been a request from fellow teachers from several Indian Universities to write a book on macroeconomics meant for B.A. and B.Com. (Pass and Honours) classes. Due to growing importance of macroeconomics, a separate paper on macroeconomics is presently prescribed by the several Indian universities for B.A. and B.Com. classes. We have therefore decided to bring out the present book on '**Principles of Macroeconomics**' for the students of B.A. and B.Com. classes as a companion volume to our book on '**Principles of Microeconomics**'.

Like our book on *Principles of Microeconomics*, this book on macroeconomics is also mainly based on UGC Model Curriculum. However, several Indian universities in their prescribed syllabi for B.A. and B.Com. have added some topics such as demand and supply of money, theories of money and prices, theories of demand for money and inflation, IS-LM curves model (which integrates money market with goods market), Philips curve concept of trade-off between inflation and unemployment and balance of payments and foreign exchange which are not covered in UGC Model Curriculum. Therefore, to cater to the needs of the students of B.A. and B.Com. classes of these universities we have incorporated the study of these topics as well in this book.

The first six parts of the book form core of macroeconomics and are common in various Indian Universities. In Part–I of the book, apart from the introductory subjects such as nature and scope of macroeconomics, circular flow of income and expenditure, concepts of national income and their measurement, classical and Keynesian theories of income and employment and their associated topics of consumption function, investment demand and theory of income multiplier have been explained. It is worthwhile to note that in this part we have confined ourselves not only to Keynes's AD-AS model with fixed price level but also newly developed Keynesian AD-AS model with price flexibility.

In Part–II, we have briefly explained the post-Keynesian developments, namely, IS-LM curves model which integrates money market with goods market and Phillips curve concept which is concerned with inflation-unemployment trade-off.

In Part–III we have explained the determination of money supply and theories of demand for money, namely, Keynes's liquidity preference theory, Baumol's inventory approach to transactions demand for money and Friedman's demand for money. Besides, in this Part–III, we have explained the roles of commercial banks and central bank in the determination of money supply. Further, we have briefly discussed the objectives and instruments of monetary policy.

Part–IV of the book is devoted to the explanation of relation between money supply and general price level. In this regard we have critically examined quantity theory of money (both Fishers' transactions and Cambridge cash-balance approaches), Keynes's theory of money and prices and Friedman's restatement of the quantity theory of money. Besides, we have discussed the demand-pull and cost-push theories of inflation and effects of unanticipated inflation on distribution and growth of the economy.

In Part–V, we have not only critically examined in detail the theories of business cycles but also fiscal and monetary policies for controlling business cycles and achieving economic stabilisation. Part–VI of the book deals with the study of **open economy macroeconomics** in which we have explained the determination of national income in the open economy and foreign trade multiplier. Besides, we have explained the determinants of balance of payments and foreign exchange.

It is important to note that some universities have not included the topic on '***Economic Growth***, in their syllabi of B.A. and B.Com. classes. Since other universities strictly follow UGC model curriculum we have included the important topic on 'Economic Growth' accordingly the last Part–VIII of the book deals with the brief analysis of determinants of economic growth, important growth models, sources of growth. The students of those universities which have not prescribed the subject on economic growth in their syllabi can skip the last Part–VIII concerned with the analysis of economic growth.

Likewise, some universities do not include the study of *Public Finance and Fiscal Policy* of the Government in their course on macroeconomics. Since several universities such as Bombay include the study of this important topic in their syllabi for B.A. and B.Com., Part–VII of this book deals with this subject.

It is worth mentioning that in this book we have confined ourselves not only to Classical and Keynesian theories of macroeconomics but have tried to incorporate Post-Keynesian developments in various subjects of macroeconomics. Thus we have briefly explained and critically evaluated the post-Keynesian theories of consumption function namely, Kuznets' consumption function, Modigliani's life cycle hypothesis. Duesenberry's relative income hypothesis, Friedman's permanent consumption theory of investment demand, namely, accelerator theory of investment. In theory of money and prices in addition to the old quantity theory we have discussed Keynes's theory of money and prices and Friedman's restatement of quantity theory of money.

Similarly, post-Keynesian explanations of business cycles such as Samuelson's interaction of multiplier and accelerator and Hicks' trade cycle theory. Besides, post-Keynesian theories of demand for money such as Tobin's portfolio approach of demand for money, Banmol's transactions demand for money and Friedman's theory of demand for money have been briefly explained and critically evaluated in Appendix to Chapter 20. Similarly, with a view to update our macroeconomic analysis in Appendix to Chapter 10, we have explained not only Keynesian and monetarist explanations of causes of depression but also explained what caused recent '*global financial crisis*' (*2007-09*) which causes recession or economic slowdown all over the world.

Lastly, throughout the book our efforts have been to explain wherever considered necessary the *relevance and applicability of various macroeconomic theories for the developing countries*. In this connection mention may be made of the inclusion of relevance and limitations of Keynesian theory of investment multiplier, theories of nature and causes of unemployment in developing countries and how they are different from Keynesian demand deficiency theory of cyclical unemployment and the relevance of Harrod-Domar and Neoclassical growth models for the developing countries. Further, we have explained the roles of monetary and fiscal policies for economic growth in developing countries. Further, to make the subject of economic growth both interesting and relevant for Indian students in Appendix to Part–VIII we have critically examined the ***ongoing debate between two eminent Indian economists, Amartya Sen and Ja dish Bhagwati, about economic growth, poverty and redistribution***.

We hope the book will be useful for the students of B.A., B.Com., and business economics. Suggestions for further improvement of the book from fellow teachers will be heartly welcomed.

Dr. H.L. AHUJA
AMIT AHUJA

69, Vaishali, Pitampura
Delhi - 110 034
e-mail : drhlahuja@gmail.com

UGC Model Curriculum

B.A. (Pass & Honours)

MACROECONOMICS

PREAMBLE

On account of the growing influence and involvement of the State in economic field macroeconomics has become a major area of economic analysis in terms of theoretical, empirical as well as policy-making issues. Macroeconomics has an extensive, substantive as well as methodological content. It deals with the functioning of the economy as a whole, including how economy's total output of goods and services and employment of resources is determined what causes these totals to fluctuate. The canvass of the study is the whole rather than the parts because what is true of parts is not necessarily true of the whole.

The Paper entitled "*Macroeconomics*" is designed to make an undergraduate student aware of basic theoretical framework underlying the field of macroeconomics.

Module 1 : National Income and Social Accounts

Concept and measurement of national income; National income identities with government and international trade; Incorporation of environmental concerns in national accounts – Green accounting.

Module 2 : Output and Employment

Say's law of markets and the classical theory of employment; Keynes' objection to the class theory; Aggregate demand and aggregate supply functions; The principle of effective demand-Consumption function – Average and marginal propensity to consume; Factors influencing consumption spending; The investment multiplier and its effectiveness in LDCs: Theory of investment – Autonomous and induced investment; Marginal efficiency of capital; Savings and investment, ex-post and ex-ante, Equality and equilibrium.

Module 3 : Rate of Interest

Classical, Neo-classical and Keynesian theories of interest.

Module 4 : Trade Cycles

Nature and characteristics: Hawtrey's monetary theory; Hayek's over-investment theory; Keynes' view of trace cycle; The concept of accelerator; Samuelson and Hicks multiplier-accelerator interaction model; Control of trade cycles.

Module 5 : Economic Growth

Sources of growth; Growth model — Harrod and Domar; Instability of equilibrium; Neo-classical growth models—Solow; Economic growth and technical progress.

CONTENTS

PART – I

MACROECONOMICS : THEORY OF INCOME AND EMPLOYMENT

PART – II
IS-LM MODEL, INFLATION–UNEMPLOYMENT TRADE-OFF : PHILLIPS CURVE

PART – III
MONETARY DEMAND AND SUPPLY

PART – IV
MONEY, PRICES AND INFLATION

PART – V
BUSINESS CYCLES AND MACROECONOMIC POLICY

PART – VI
OPEN ECONOMY MACROECONOMICS

PART – VII

GOVERNMENT AND THE MACROECONOMY : PUBLIC FINANCE AND FISCAL POLICY

PART – VIII
ECONOMIC GROWTH

PART – I

MACROECONOMICS : THEORY OF INCOME AND EMPLOYMENT

- Nature and Scope of Macroeconomics
- Circular Flow of Income and Expenditure
- National Income and its Measurement
- Classical Theory of Income and Employment : Full Employment Model
- Keynes's Theory of Employment : An Outline
- Determination of National Income : Keynes's Simple Two-Sector Model
- Determination Of National Income in a Three Sector Economy With Government
- Consumption Function
- Investment Demand
- Theory of Investment Multiplier
- Aggregate Demand - Aggregate Supply Model (with Variable Prices)
- Unemployment, Full Employment and Wage-Price Flexibility

CHAPTER 1

Nature and Scope of Macroeconomics

In the first volume of this book we have studied microeconomics which is concerned with the behaviour of individual consumers, factor owners, firms and individual industries and markets. It is through their interaction that microeconomic theory explains how prices of products and factors are determined and how resources are allocated between various products. In microeconomic theory it is assumed that full employment of resources such as labour and capital prevails and analyses how they are allocated among different products. Further, it explains whether resource allocation achieved is economically efficient. In this second volume we will study macroeconomic theory and its applications to the formulation of economic policies. In this chapter we shall briefly explain what macroeconomics is about and why the British economist J.M. Keynes laid stress on macroeconomic analysis as a separate study from microeconomic analysis. Besides, we shall explain the various issues that are studied in macroeconomics. In the end we shall briefly explain the various post-Keynesian developments in macroeconomics. We shall also discuss the importance of the study of macroeconomics.

What is Macroeconomics?

Whereas microeconomics deals with the analysis of small individual units of an economy such as individual consumers, individual firms, individual industries and markets and explains how prices of products and factors are determined. On the basis of these prices microeconomics explains how resources are allocated among various products and how income distribution among factors is determined. On the other hand, *macroeconomics is concerned with the analysis of the behaviour of the economic system in totality. Thus, macroeconomics studies how the large aggregates such as total employment, national product or national income of an economy and the general price level are determined. Macroeconomics is therefore a study of aggregates. Besides, macroeconomics explains how the productive capacity and national income of the country increase over time in the long run.*

Professor Gardner Ackley makes the distinction between macroeconomics and microeconomics more clearly when he says, "macroeconomics concerns itself with such variables as the aggregate volume of the output of an economy, with the extent to which its resources are employed, with the size of the national income, with the 'general price level'. Microeconomics, on the other hand, deals with the division of total output among industries, products and firms and the allocation of resources among competing uses. It considers problem of income distribution. Its interest is in relative prices of particular goods and services."[1]

It is evident from above that the subject matter of macroeconomics is to explain what *determines the level of total economic activity* (that is, the size of the national income and employment) and fluctuations (*i.e.*, ups and downs) in it in the short run. It also explains what causes the general price level to rise and determines the rate of inflation in the economy. Besides, modern macroeconomics analyses those factors which determine the increase in productive capacity and national income in the long run. The problem of increasing productive capacity and national income over time in the long run is called the problem of *economic growth*. Thus, what determines rate of growth of an economy is also the concern of macroeconomics.

Thus, why is national income higher today than it was in 1950? Why does rate of unemployment in a free market economy go up in a period and fall in another period? Why do some countries

1. Gardner Ackley, *Macroeconomic Theory*, 1961, p. 4.

have high rates of inflation, while others maintain price stability? What causes alternating periods of depression and boom (generally described as business cycles)? Why should government intervene in the economy and what policy it should adopt to check inflation, control business cycles, raise level of national income, reduce unemployment and restore equilibrium in the balance of payments are some of the important questions which macroeconomics seeks to answer.

The Origin and Roots of Macroeconomics

The Great Depression. Beginning in late 1929, capitalist economies of the world experienced a severe depression which created a lot of involuntary unemployment and also a sharp fall in their GDP. This depression was caused by drastic decline in private investment. For example, in the United States in 1929, 1.5 million workers were unemployed. After four years in 1933 this unemployment of labour rose to 13 million people out of labour force of 51 million, that is, around 25 per cent of labour force became unemployed. GDP, that is, national income of the US declined from $ 312 billion in 1929 to $ 222 billion in 1933–$93 billion or 28 per cent fall in just four-year period. In October 1929 when stock prices crashed on Wall Street billions of dollars of the US investors were washed away. This resulted in gloomy economic environment for investors resulting in fall in investment from $ 56 billion in 1929 to just $ 8.5 billion in 1933. The rate of unemployment in the US remained over 14 per cent of labour force until 1940 and it was feared that unless some effective measures were taken by the government the capitalist system would collapse. The similar situation prevailed in Britain and other capitalist countries. This depression spurred a great deal of controversy among economists about the causes of this depression and the policies to overcome it and restore full employment. It was at this time that a noted British economist J.M. Keynes (1883-1946) challenged the view of classical economists who applied microeconomic models to explain depression and involuntary unemployment. By emphasising that the prevailing depression and large-scale involuntary unemployment was due to lack of aggregate effective demand resulting from a fall in private investment he laid the foundation of modern macroeconomics. In his theory he showed that a free market economy was not self-correcting and therefore there was a need for the government to intervene and take appropriate fiscal measures to restore full employment in the economy.

The Classical Economists and Say's Law of Markets. Classical and neoclassical economists[2] assumed that full employment of labour and other resources always prevailed in the economy and concentrated mainly upon explaining how the resources were allocated to the production of various goods and services and how the relative prices of products and factors were determined. It is mainly because of their full-employment assumption that they concentrated on the problem of determination of prices, outputs and resource employment in the individual industries. They believed that if there were departures from full employment, a free market economy would automatically work in way that would restore full employment of resources. They argued that involuntary unemployment and underutilisation of the productive capacity could not occur in capitalist economies if market mechanism were allowed to work freely without any interference by the trade unions. Thus, according to them, even when deficiency of aggregate demand arises as it happens during the times of recession or depression, prices and wages would quickly change in such a way that employment, output and national income would not decline. The belief of classical economists that full employment of labour and capital stock will always exist was based on *Say's Law of Markets*. According to Say's Law, ***supply creates its own demand*** and, therefore, the problem of lack of demand for supply of goods and services does not arise. Factors which produce goods and services for supply in the market get rewards (wages, interest and rent) for their contributions to the production of goods and services produced. Thus, incomes earned by them become expenditure made on goods and services. Therefore, the problem of deficiency of demand does not arise. They thus could not provide adequate explanation of the occurrence of huge unemployment that prevailed during depression of 1930s in the capitalist economies. What is worse,

2. Note that Keynes called all those economists who preceded him as classical economists. Thus, neoclassical economists are included in the term classical economists as used by Keynes.

the classical economists, particularly A.C. Pigou, tried to apply the economic laws that hold good in the case of an individual industry to the case of the behaviour of the whole economic system and macroeconomic variables.

The classical economists believed that when the economy went into recession resulting in fall in output, this would cause a shift in the demand curve for labour to the left. As a result, at the given wage rate, excess supply of labour would emerge which, under the competitive conditions, will quickly drive wages down so that in the new equilibrium in the labour market all those who are willing to work at the lower wage rate will get employment. Those who are not willing to work at the lower wages would remain unemployed but classical economists called them ***voluntarily unemployed***. Classical economists believed that despite the existence of this voluntary unemployment of some workers at new lower wages full employment of labour prevailed. It is the *involuntary unemployment,* according to them, that cannot persist for long in a free market economy. They believed that with adjustment in wages and prices quickly output and employment will increase and recession would come to end. Thus, classical economists believed that **recessions were self-correcting.** However, during the Great Depression of 1930s the high rate of unemployment persisted for a long period and did not seem to be self-correcting as classical economists believed. This showed the failure of classical model to explain the existence of involuntary unemployment for a long time that what we now call macroeconomics was born in 1930s and it was J.M. Keynes who put forward a new macroeconomic model that successfully explained the causes of involuntary unemployments and depression and provided a rationale for intervention of the Government to adopt expansionary fiscal policy to lift the economy out of recession and restore full employment.

Keynsian Revolution. It may be noted that the Great Depression of 1930s unemployed remained at a high level for nearly 10 years. At that time, an eminent British economist A.C. Pigou asserted that involuntary unemployment existing at the time of depression in the 1930s was due to the obstacles put up by trade unions and government which prevented wages from falling and further that this involuntary unemployment could be eliminated and employment expanded by cutting down the wages. A noted British economist J.M. Keynes challenged this classical viewpoint during the early nineteen thirties when severe depression took place in the capitalist countries such as Britain and the U.S.A. According to him, while the cut in wages may expand employment in an individual industry, the reduction in wages throughout the economy will result in fall in incomes of the working classes and is likely to cause decrease in the level of aggregate demand. The fall in aggregate demand will tend to lower the level of employment rather than expand it.

Though there were pre-Keynesian theories of business cycles and the general price level that were "macro" in nature, but it was J.M. Keynes, an eminent British economist, who laid stress on macroeconomic analysis and put forward a general theory of income and employment in his revolutionary book, "*A General Theory of Employment, Interest and Money*" published in 1936. Keynes' theory made a genuine break from the classical and neo-classical economics and produced such a fundamental and drastic change in economic thinking that his macroeconomic analysis has earned the names '*Keynesian Revolution*' and *'New Economics'*. Keynes in his analysis made a frontal attack on the classical '*Say's Law of Markets*' which was the basis of full-employment assumption of classical view that involuntary unemployment could not prevail in a free private enterprise economy. According to Keynes, it is not wages and prices that determine the level of employment as classical economists thought *but aggregate demand for goods and services*. Much of what we now call macroeconomics has roots in Keynes's analysis of determination of national income (GDP), employment and inflation. He showed how the equilibrium level of national income and employment was determined by aggregate demand and aggregate supply and further that due to lack of aggregate effective demand equilibrium level of income and employment might well be established at far less than full-employment level in a free-market capitalist economy. This causes involuntary unemployment of labour on the one hand and excess productive capacity (*i.e.* underutilisation of the existing capital stock) on the other. His macroeconomic model reveals how consumption function, investment function, liquidity preference function, conceived in aggregate terms, interact to determine the level of national income and employment.

Further, the fall in employment in the Great Depression of 1930s and emergence of huge unemployment of labour which in some countries went up to 25 per cent of labour force gives unmistakable evidence that aggregate demand is not always large enough to ensure full employment of labour and full use of productive capacity.

After Keynes, there has been significant developments in macroeconomics. Apart from what determines the level of employment of labour and use of productive capacity, modern macroeconomics is concerned with many more issues such as the problems of inflation, economic growth, business cycles, stagflation and the balance of payments and the exchange rate. The analysis of these six major issues describes the scope of macroeconomics. We shall be explaining all these six issues of macroeconomics in detail in later chapters. Here we shall explain only briefly what these problems are.

THE MAJOR ISSUES AND CONCERNS OF MACROECONOMICS

As explained above, Keynes in his book *'Theory of Employment, Interest and Money'* explained how levels of income and employment were determined in a free market economy. During the Second World War period, he extended his macro-theory to explain inflation. However, after Keynes, economists have further developed and extended macroeconomics. We briefly explain below the main issues of macroeconomics.

The Problem of Unemployment. The first major issue in macroeconomics is to explain what determines the level of employment and national income in an economy and therefore what causes involuntary unemployment. Why is level of national income and employment very low in times of depression as in 1930s in various capitalist countries of the world. This will explain the cause of huge unemployment that emerged in these countries. As mentioned above, classical economists denied that there could be involuntary unemployment of labour and other resources for a long time. They thought that with quickly changes in wages and prices, unemployment would be automatically removed and full employment established. But this did not appear to be so at the time of depression in the thirties and after. Keynes explained that level of employment and national income is determined by aggregate demand and aggregate supply. With aggregate supply curve remaining unchanged in the short run, it is the deficiency of aggregate demand that causes underemployment equilibrium with the emergence of involuntary unemployment. According to him, it is the changes in private investment that causes fluctuations in aggregate demand and is, therefore, responsible for the problems of cyclical unemployment. We will explain Keynes's theory of employment in detail in the subsequent chapters.

Recession and Determination of Actual Level of National Income (or GNP). National income is the value of all final goods and services produced in a country in a year. Level of national income or what is called Gross National Product (GNP) shows the performance of the economy in a year and determines the *overall living standards of the people* of a country. Recession in the economy not only results in involuntary unemployment but also fall in the actual level of national income below its **potential level**. Given the state of technology, when all resources in an economy are being employed for production, the size of national income generated is called *potential* GNP or full-employment level of income. The classical economists believed that there could be only temporary departures from potential GNP at times of recession or depression and **through adjustment in prices and wages quickly, the economy** would be automatically lifted out of recession. According to them, when national income of the economy is less than its potential level, it is in state of disequilibrium and the equilibrium at potential GNP or at full-employment level is restored quickly through changes in prices and wages. On the other hand, Keynes believed that wages and prices were rigid and if at all they change, they do so only very slowly. According to him, recession or fall in level of GNP below its potential level occurs due to decline in aggregate demand which results form fall in private investment because of firm's bleak profit expectations for the future. Keynes argued that in such circumstances unless the government intervenes and increases its expenditure financed by borrowing from the Central Bank (that is, getting more money printed) recession and unemployment will persist for long. Given the technology used for production, the magnitude of employment goes hand-in-hand with the change in size of national output. The fluctuations in economic activity primarily manifest themselves in changes in national income and employment. In a free market economy, the changes in aggregate demand cause divergence of national income from the level of potential GNP in the short run.

It is however important to note that in a developing country such as India it is not a mere level of aggregate demand that determines national income. In it the ***supply-side factors*** such as availability of physical capital, human capital (skills and education of people), material resources, the technology used for production in agriculture and industries that play a more important role in the determination of national income.

Problem of Inflation. Another macroeconomic issue is to explain the problem of inflation. Inflation has been a major problem faced by both the developed and developing countries in the last fifty years. Classical economists thought that it was the quantity of money in the economy that determined the general price level in the economy and, according to them, rate of inflation depended on the growth of money supply in the economy. Keynes criticised the `*Quantity Theory of Money*' and showed that expansion in money supply did not always lead to inflation or rise in price level. Keynes who before the Second World War explained that involuntary unemployment and depression were due to the deficiency of aggregate demand, during the war period when prices rose very high he explained in a booklet '*How to Pay for War*' that just as unemployment and depression were caused by the deficiency of aggregate demand, inflation was due to the excessive aggregate demand. Thus, Keynes put forward what is now called ***demand-pull theory of inflation***. After Keynes, theory of inflation has been further developed and many theories of inflation depending upon various causes have been put forward. *Cost-push* and *structuralist* theories of inflation have been put forward. To analyse the problem of inflation is an important issue of macroeconomics.

Business Cycles. Throughout history market economies have experienced what are called business cycles. Business cycles refer to fluctuations in output and employment with alternating periods of boom and recession. In boom periods both output and employment are at high levels, whereas in recession periods both output and employment fall and as a consequence large unemployment comes to exist in the economy. When these recessions are extremely severe, they are called depressions. What are the causes of these business cycles or ups and downs in market economies is an important macroeconomic issue which has been highly controversial. The objective of macroeconomic policy is to achieve economic stability with equilibrium at full employment level of output and income. We shall discuss various theories of business cycles and also monetary and fiscal policies to control business cycles and achieve economic stability.

Stagflation. How to control business cycles and achieve economic stability has been a very difficult problem for the economies to solve. But during the decade of 1970s and in some later times in the subsequent decades market economies have experienced a still more intricate problem which has been described as stagflation. While in business cycles, recession or depression is accompanied by high unemployment and falling prices, *in the seventies recession or stagnation was accompanied by not only high unemployment but also high inflation. Since in that period high unemployment and recession (or stagnation) co-existed with high inflation, this problem was given the name* ***stagflation***. In the Indian context stagflation is often used in the sense of slow economic growth along with high inflation. This stagflation could not be explained with the Keynesian theory which focuses on the demand side. Therefore, a new economic thought which is called ***Supply-side Economics*** emerged which explained stagflation by laying stress on the supply side of economic activity. Stagflation is an important issue of modern macroeconomics. Stagflation along with supply-side economics will be explained in a later chapter.

Economic Growth. Another important issue in macroeconomics is to explain what determines economic growth in a country. Economic growth means *sustained* increase in national income (GNP) or per capita income over a sufficiently long period of time. Given the availability of natural resources, economic growth of a country depends on the growth of physical capital, human capital and progress in technology. The growth of all these factors requires saving and investment. The growth rate can therefore the stepped up by raising the rates of saving and investment. The expansion in these factors determines the increase in productive capacity. To ensure full use of the rising productive capacity aggregate to demand for output must be increasing sufficiently.

Theory of economic growth or what is simply called *growth economics* has been recently developed a good deal and is an important branch of macroeconomics. The problem of growth is a long-run problem and Keynes did not deal with it. In fact, Keynes is said to have once remarked that "in the long run we are all dead". From this remark of Keynes it should not be understood that he thought long run to be quite unimportant. By this remark he simply emphasized the importance of short-run problem of fluctuations in the level of economic acitivity (involuntary cyclical unemployment, depression). It was Harrod[3] and Domar[4] who extended the Keynesian analysis to the long-run problem of growth with stability. They laid stress on the dual role of investment—one of *income-generating*, which Keynes considered, and the second of *capacity-creating* which Keynes ignored because of his preoccupation with the short run. In view of the fact that an investment adds to the productive capacity (*i.e.*, capital stock), then if growth with stability (*i.e.*, without stagnation or inflation) is to be achieved, income or demand must be increasing at a rate large enough to ensure the full utilisation of the increasing capacity. Thus, macroeconomic models of Harrod and Domar have explained the rate of growth of income that must take place if the steady growth of the economy is to be achieved. These days growth economics has been further developed and extended a good deal and new theories of growth have been put forward by Solow, Meade, Kaldor and Joan Robinson and recently by Romer.

It is important to note that in the context of developing countries, *economic growth* has been distinguished from *economic development*. Economic development is a more inclusive concept than economic growth. Economic development is generally understood to mean that apart from increase in national income or per capita income, poverty, unemployment and inequality must also be declining in the growth process. Besides, according to Amartya Sen, winner of Nobel Prize in economics, freedom to improve the quality of life of the poor, their freedom from undernourishment, freedom from illiteracy, freedom from illness are essential requirements of economic development. *It is the building up capabilities of the poor and enlargement of the opportunities for them to gain freedom in these respects* that Amartya Sen calls development[5]. The macroeconomics for developing countries must therefore concern itself with not only economic growth but also econnomic developemnt.

Since the above growth theories apply particularly to the present-day developed economies, special theories which explain the causes of underdevelopment and poverty in less developed countries (LDCs) and which also suggest strategies for initiating and accelerating growth in them have also been propounded. These special growth theories relating to less developed countries (LDCs) are generally known as *Economics of Development*.

Balance of Payments and Exchange Rate. Balance of payments is the record of economic transactions of the residents of a country with the rest of the world during a period. The aim to prepare such a record is to present an account of all receipts on account of goods and services exported, and capital received by the residents of a country from foreign countries and the payments made for goods and services imported received and capital transferred to other countries by residents of a country.

3. R.F. Harrod, *Towards a Dynamic Economics* (1948).
4. E.D. Domar, "Expansion and Employment", *American Economic Review* (March 1947).
5. Amartya Sen, *Development as Freedom*, Oxford University Press, 2000.

There may be deficit or surplus in balance of payments. Both create problems for an economy. An important effect is that the transactions in balance of payment are influenced by the exchange rate. The exchange rate is the rate at which a country's currency is exchanged for foreign currencies. The instability in exchange rate has been a major problem in recent years that has given rise to serious balance of payments problems. During the 23 years period (1991-2013), Indian rupee has depreciated to a large extent in terms of US dollar giving rise to serious problems. In the year 2013, the Indian rupee started depreciating rapidly against the US dollar so much its value fell to ₹ 68.85 to a US dollar on Aug, 28, 2013. As a result of certain steps taken by RBI rupee gained and its value remained in the range of ₹ 61.50 to a US dollar in the months of October, November and December 2013. During the two years 1997 and 1998, currencies of many South-East Asian countries and Japan rapidly depreciated in terms of US dollar. This creates the situation of economic crisis which needs to be overcome. Both interrelated problems of balance of payments and instability of foreign exchange rate will be analysed in a separate part of this book.

THE ROLE OF GOVERNMENT IN THE MACROECONOMY

In modern macroeconomics, the intervention by the government to influence economic activity is well recognised. It is now widely believed that instability is inherent in a free-market economy and further that there is no any self-correcting mechanism to ensure stability at full employment level and sustained economic growth. There are three types of economic policy that are used by the government to influence the working of macroeconomy:

1. Fiscal Policy
2. Monetary Policy
3. Supply-Side Policies

We will discuss these three policy instruments in detail in the subsequent chapters. However, we briefly explain them below and indicate what they are concerned with.

Fiscal Policy. An important way the government affects the economy is through the adoption of appropriate fiscal policy. The fiscal policy refers to taxation and expenditure decisions of the government. Before Keynes it was believed that the government budget should preferabily be balanced, that is, revenue collected through taxes should be equal to the expenditure made by the government. Keynes showed that balanced budget is not good under all circumstances. He advocated that at times of depression, *deficit budget* should be made to get the economy out of it and to eliminate involuntary unemployment. In case of deficit budget the government expenditure exceeds revenue collected through taxes. The budget deficit arises when the government increases its expenditure without raising taxes or it arises when taxes are reduced without cutting back on expenditure. Therefore, the policy of budget deficit represents expansionary fiscal policy. The budget deficit raises aggregate demand and leads to the increase in national income and employment.

To meet the budget deficit, the government borrows from the banks and the public and pays interest to them. This raises debt burden of the government. The borrowing by the government increases the demand for loanable funds and leads to rise in rate of interest. The higher interest rate discourages private investment. It is therefore claimed that government borrowing to finance budget deficit *crowds out* some private investment so that net effect of budget deficit on expansion in output and employment is small. We will explain in detail in a subsequent chapter how far this crowding-out effect is significant.

However, to avoid borrowing and rise in public debt, the alternative way to finance the budget deficit is printing of money by the government. The danger of financing budget deficit through printing of money is that it may lead to inflation in the economy. The implications of different ways of financing budget deficit will be discussed in detail in a later chapter.

On the contrary, when there is high inflation in the economy the government can check it by reducing its expenditure or raising taxes and in this way make a surplus budget or reduce its budget deficit. This will tend to reduce aggregate demand which will help in controlling inflation. Thus fiscal policy is an important instrument used by the government to change the level of aggregate demand and thereby affect income, employment and prices.

Monetary Policy

Monetary policy is another important instrument which the government (or Central Bank of the country) uses to achieve the objectives of price stability, full employment and economic growth. Monetary policy refers to the policies regarding growth of money supply, availability of credit and interest or cost of credit. Monetary policy is an important tool of controlling inflation in the economy. It is generally believed that large expansion in money supply causes rise in general increase price level. To check inflation ***tight monetary policy*** is adopted wherein rate of interest is raised and availability of credit is reduced. When interest rate rises, businessmen and households find it more costly to borrow. This discourages demand for credit and leads to the contraction of money supply in the economy. Besides, to discourage the creation of excess credit by the banks for investment and consumption purposes, cash reserve ratio of the banks is raised or Government bonds and securities are sold to the banks and the public. The decrease in credit for investment and consumption will cause decline in aggregate demand which will exert downward pressure on prices.

On the contrary, to get the economy out of recession, ***expansionary monetary policy*** is adopted. The increase in money supply lowers the rate of interest. The credit from banks becomes cheaper which encourages investment. At lower interest rate households also tend to borrow more for consumption and therefore demand for home loans, car loans from banks increases. As a result, aggregate demand in the economy increases which raises levels of output and employment. However, it may be noted that Keynes was not optimistic about the efficacy of monetary policy to tackle the problem of depression and unemployment. He argued that demand for money at the time of depression is highly interest-elastic and therefore expansion in money supply will not lead to lowering of interest rate significantly. Besides, according to him, investment demand is not much interest-elastic so that even smaller interest rate will not stimulate investment.

In a developing country such as India the right monetary policy can play a useful role for achieving the objectives of higher economic growth with price stability. For example, in India the Reserve Bank of India ensures that while genuine demand for credit for investment purposes by the firms must be met, the excessive growth in money supply and credit be avoided. The Reserve Bank of India has been often adjusting its monetary policy to suit the changing economic situation.

Supply-Side Policies

Money economists doubt the efficacy of fiscal and monetary policies to eliminate the fluctuations in the economic activity through *demand management* (that is, influencing the level of aggregate demand). A school of economic thought known as ***supply-side economics*** argues that focus of government policy should shift from demand management to stimulation of aggregate supply of output. For example, in the seventies when the USA and Britain experienced the problem of ***stagflation***, some economists suggested that instead of demand management the government should reduce taxes to increase the incentives to work, save and invest more. More labour supply and more investment will increase the supply of goods and services. As a result, price level will fall and at the same time output will rise. India is also experiencing inflation in recent years (2011–14) which has arisen due to the supply-side factors preventing adequate in output of certain essential food items to meet the rising demand for them. This has resulted demand for them, this has resulted in demand-supply unbalances and led to high *food-inflation* of over even 15 per cent per annum this high food inflation is responsible for rapid rise in consumer price index number (CPI) which in November 2013 rose to more than per cent on annual basis it is important to note that this supply-side inflation cannot solved by tight monetary policy. The proper solution for this supply-side inflation is to increase the output of goods in short-supply and make suitable reforms in the market system to prevent the tendency to board them the policies to reduce inflation through expansion in supply of output are generally described as *supply-side policies*.

Besides, for promotion of growth, especially in developing countries, the government adopts appropriate fiscal and monetary policies. It is generally believed that higher economic growth in the developing countries will lead to the reduction in a poverty and unemployment. To raise the rate of saving and investment the government must take appropriate fiscal and monetary measures. Recently, it has been found that policy of moderate taxes generates more revenue through greater tax compliance and at the same time it provides incentives to save and invest more. In developing countries in order to speed up economic growth the government should increase its expenditure on infrastructure such as irrigation projects, roads and highways, power, telecommunication, ports etc. Besides, as has been emphasised by Prof. Amartya Sen, for accelerating growth and removal of poverty the government must invest more in social sector consisting of education, health, literacy and under nourishment. It is important to note that a developing country cannot rely on private sector investment alone which is governed and guided by profit motive. Therefore, to supplement the private sector investment the government itself should directly undertake investment especially in infrastructure projects, to promote and accelerate economic growth.

WHY A SEPARATE STUDY OF MACROECONOMICS

Now an important question which arises is why a separate study of the economic system as a whole or its large aggregates is necessary. Can't we generalise about the behaviour of the economic system as a whole or about the behaviour of large aggregates such as aggregate consumption, aggregate saving, aggregate investment from the economic laws governing the behaviour patterns of the individual units found by microeconomics? In other words, can't we obtain the laws governing the macroeconomic variables such as total national product, total employment and total income, general price level, etc by simply adding up, multiplying or averaging the results obtained from the behaviour of the individual firms and industries? The answer to this question is the behaviour of the economic system as a whole or the macroeconomic aggregates is not merely a matter of addition or multiplication or averaging of what happens in the various individual parts of the whole. As a matter of fact, in the economic system what is true of parts is not necessarily true of the whole. Therefore, the application of micro-approach to generalise about the behaviour of the economic system as a whole or macroeconomic aggregates is incorrect and may lead to misleading conclusions. Therefore, a separate macro-analysis is needed to study the behaviour of the economic system as a whole in respect of various macroeconomic aggregates. When laws or generalisations are true of constituent individual parts but untrue and invalid in case of the whole economy, paradoxes seem to exist. Boulding has called these paradoxes as ***macro-economic paradoxes***. It is because of the existence of these macro-economic paradoxes that there is a justification for making macro-analysis of the behaviour of the whole economic system or its large economic aggregates. Thus Professor Boulding rightly remarks, "*It is these paradoxes more than any other factor, which justify the separate study of the system as a whole, not merely as an inventory or list of particular items, but as a complex of aggregates.*[6]

Professor Boulding further elaborates his point by comparing the economic system with a forest and the individual firms or industries with the trees in the forest. Forest, he says, is the aggregation of trees but it does not reveal the same properties and behaviour pattern as those of the individual trees. It will be misleading to apply the rules governing the individual trees to generalise about the behaviour of the forest.

Various examples of macro-paradoxes (that is, what is true of parts is not true of the whole) can be given from the economic field. We shall give two such examples of savings and wages on the

---

6. K.E. Boulding, *A Reconstruction of Economics* (1952), p. 173

basis of which Keynes laid stress on evolving and applying macroeconomic analysis as separate and distinct approach from microeconomic analysis.

Paradox of Thrift. Savings are generally good for individuals. People save for some motives in view. They save for meeting their needs in old age, for education of their children, for purchasing durable goods such as houses and cars and thereby raise their standards of living. Further, they save for making investment or deposits in banks which raise their income in future years. But an interesting paradox of thrift arises which shows the importance of macroeconomic analysis as distinct from microeconomic analysis. *The paradox of thrift arises because it so happens that when all people in a society try to save more but they are actually unable to do so.* Not only that, the attempt to save more by *all people* causes their income or standard of living to decline. Keynes's macroeconomic analysis helps to explain this paradox. Keynes pointed out that efforts to save more, especially at times of depression, will lower the consumption demand of the people and will therefore adversely affect aggregate demand in the economy. *The decline in aggregate demand will cause national output and income to fall and unemployment to increase.* At the lower level of national income, savings will fall to the original level but the consumption of the people will be less than before which implies that people would become worse off as a result of their decision of saving more. Thus decision to save more will deepen the economic depression. It goes to the credit of Keynes's theory of effective demand as determinant of national income and his multiplier theory (which shows that income and employment fall more than the original rise in saving) that paradox of thrift has been resolved. It clearly shows at times of depression, more savings deepen the economic crisis.

Wage-Employment Paradox. Another common example to prove that what is true for the individual may not be true for the society as a whole is the wage-employment relationship. As pointed out above, classical and neo-classical economists, especially A.C. Pigou, contended that the cut in money wages at times of depression and unemployment would lead to the increase in employment and thereby eliminate unemployment and depression. Now, it is true that a cut in money wages in an individual industry will lead to more employment in that industry. This is quite commonplace conclusion of microeconomic theory that, given the demand curve for labour, at a lower wage rate more men will be employed. But for the society or economy as a whole this is highly misleading. If the wages are cut all round in the economy, as was suggested by Pigou and others on the basis of wage-employment relationship in an individual industry, the aggregate demand for goods and services in the society will decline since wages are incomes of the workers which constitute majority in the society. The decline in aggregate demand will mean the decrease in demand for goods of many industries. Because the demand for labour is a derived demand, *i.e.*, derived from the demand for goods, the fall in aggregate demand for goods will result in the decline in demand for labour which will create more unemployment rather than reduce it.

Fallacy of Composition

We thus see that the laws or generalisations which hold good for the behaviour of an individual consumer, firm or industry may be quite invalid and misleading when applied to the behaviour of the economic system as a whole. There is thus *a fallacy of composition*. This is so because what is true of individual components is not true of the collective whole. As mentioned above, these are called macroeconomic paradoxes and it is because of these paradoxes that a separate study of the economic system as a whole is essential.

Macroeconomic analysis takes account of many relationships which are not applicable to individual parts at all. For instance, an individual may save more than that he invests or he may invest more than he saves, but for economy as a whole it is one of the important principles of Keynesian macroeconomics that actual savings are always equal to actual investment. Likewise, for an individual or a group of individuals, expenditure may be more or less than the income but the national expenditure of the economy must be equal to the national income. In fact, the national expenditure and national income are two identical things. Similarly, in the case of full employment, an individual industry may increase its output and employment by bidding away the workers from other industries, but the economy cannot increase its output and employment in this way. Thus what applies to an individual industry, does not do so in case of the economic system as a whole.

We therefore conclude that a separate and distinct macroeconomic analysis is essential if we want to understand the true working of the economic system as a whole. From this it should not be understood that microeconomic theory is worthless and should be abandoned. As a matter of fact, *microeconomics and macroeconomics are complementary to each other rather than being competitive.* The two types of theories deal with different subjects, one deals mainly with the explanation of relative prices of goods and factors and the other mainly with the short-run determination of income and employment of the society and its long-run economic growth. The study of both micro and macroeconomics is therefore necessary. Professor Samuelson rightly says, "There is really no opposition between micro and macro-economics. Both are absolutely vital. And you are only half-educated if you understand the one while being ignorant of the other."[7]

IMPORTANCE OF MACROECONOMICS

To Understand the Working of Macroeconomy : Macroeconomic Paradoxes. The study of macroeconomics is important in its own sake, as it tells us how the economy as a whole works. We cannot obtain and derive the laws governing macroeconomic variables such as national income, total employment, general price level by studying the microeconomic decisions of individual consumers, firms and industries. This is because what is true and valid in case of an individual firm or industry may not be valid for the economy as a whole. Boulding has pointed out several *macroeconomic paradoxes* which reveal that results obtained from the study of the behaviour of individual firms or industries may lead us to *misleading conclusions about the working of the macroeconomy*. Boulding compared it to the case of a forest and its trees. According to him, it will be misleading to apply the rules governing the individual trees to generalise about the behaviour of the forest.

Two examples of macroeconomic paradoxes will make it clear why the study of macroeconomic analysis separate from microeconomics is important. Take the case of wages. A neoclassical economist A.C. Pigou suggested all-round cut in wage rates to promote employment and thereby to solve the problem of unemployment that prevailed in times of Great Depression. We know from the marginal productivity theory of distribution of microeconomics that in the case of an individual firm or industry, it is quite valid that at a lower wage rate, an individual firm or industry will employ more labour. But this does not apply to the whole economy. This is because wages are not only cost for a firm or industry, they represent incomes of the workers who constitute a majority in a society. Fall in wages means decline in their incomes which would lead to a fall in aggregate demand for goods and services. This fall in aggregate demand will cause national output and employment to decline. Thus, from the viewpoint of the economy as a whole cut in wages will increase unemployment of labour rather than reducing it.

The second important example of a macroeconomic paradox relates to saving. When an individual saves more he is able to invest more and the higher investment yields bring more income for him in the future. But this result does not necessarily apply to the case when a society saves more. Suppose the economy is in the grip of recession and a society as a whole decides to save more. This may not only fail to increase national income but ultimately even saving may not rise as well. This is called *paradox of thrift*. This happens because more saving than before leads to the decrease in aggregate demand for goods and services. The fall in aggregate demand will cause the level of national income to decline and at the lower level of national income, less saving will be done. Thus, the initial increase in saving will not only lead to lower national income and output but eventually even saving of the society may not rise.

7. Paul A. Samuelson, *Economics*, 10th edition, 1976.

The above two examples of macroeconomic paradoxes clearly reveal that a *separate macroeconomic analysis is important to understand the working of the economy as a whole*.

Important Nature of Macroeconomic Issues. Macroeconomics is concerned with the study of issues and problems which are of vital importance for determining well-being of the people. Macroeconomic problems such as unemployment, inflation, instability of foreign exchange rate cause a lot of human suffering. Unemployment creates a lot of misery for the unemployed workers and gives rise to many social evils. Unemployment involves waste of economic resources and loss of potential output. Inflation erodes real incomes or purchasing power of the people. It redistributes national income in favour of rich and thus creates more income inequalities. Inflation sends more people under the poverty line and thus accentuates the problem of poverty. Similarly, depreciation of domestic currency encourages flight of capital from an economy and increases the prices of imports and thereby adds to the inflationary pressures in the economy. Macroeconomics explains the causes of such important problems and helps in formulating economic policies to tackle them.

Importance of Macroeconomics for Accelerating Economic Growth. Macroeconomics explains the factors which determine economic growth and brings out what causes slowdown in productivity growth. Every community wants to grow economically because economic growth helps to raise the standards of living of the people. Moreover, higher rate of economic growth helps in solving the problems of poverty and unemployment in the developing countries like India. Macroeconomic models of Harrod-Domar and Solow reveal that increase in the rate of saving and investment (or capital formation) and improvement in technology are the important factors determining economic growth. Macroeconomic theories also reveal that lack of growth in aggregate effective demand may serve as constraint to the growth process of an economy. Thus, macroeconomics provides us knowledge as to how to achieve self-sustained economic growth.

Understanding Business Cycles. Business cycles have been the biggest ailment of market economies. Though there is no unanimity in macroeconomic theory about the proper explanation of business cycles, significant advances have been made in bringing out the causes which lead to them. Fluctuations in aggregate demand due to volatile nature of investment demand, as explained by Keynes, together with the interaction of multiplier and accelerator provides an adequate explanation of business cycles. It is because of this understanding about business cycles that has helped to adopt proper fiscal and monetary policies to control business cycles and also due to these policies that the severity of business cycles in recent years has greatly reduced. This shows the important contribution made by macroeconomics in controlling business cycles.

Formulating Government's Macroeconomic Policies. Understanding how the economy works which is obtained from macroeconomics has a practical value in the formulation of government's fiscal and monetary policies. With the knowledge of the causes of recession and inflation brought out by macroeconomics, governments formulate proper fiscal and monetary policies to tackle them. During recession, expansionary fiscal and monetary policies are adopted to lift the economy out of recession. On the other hand, inflation has been checked quite successfully by tight monetary policy and contractionary fiscal policy. Besides, the understanding about the factors which determine economic growth, fiscal and monetary policies have been so designed as to raise saving and investment and also to promote technological improvement of the production process. Further, with the knowledge furnished by macroeconomics about fluctuations in market economies, central bank often intervenes to achieve foreign exchange rate stability.

Individual Decision-Making. The understanding about the working of the economy as a whole helps the individuals to take better decisions. For example, the knowledge about macroeconomics helps them to assess the impact of government's economic policies. If on the basis of certain Government's economic policy they predict that inflation rate will increase, they may decide to act in the present in a way to ward off the adverse effects of inflation. The knowledge of macroeconomics tells them that inflation will erode their real incomes, will lower the real rate of interest, will make exports dearer than before. Keeping in view these impacts of inflation arising out of government's policy they will make decisions so as to save themselves from the undesirable consequencies of inflation. Similarly, people's decisions about whether or not to buy a house, or a new car, give loans to others at present would be governed by their predictions about the likely state of the economy. These predictions, it may be noted, are based by the individuals on their understanding of macroeconomics.

Importance in Business Decisions. The understanding of macroeconomics also helps a good deal to businesses or their managers who are faced with various decision-making problems. Business firms do not work in vacuum. The level of overall economic activity (*i.e.*, national income and employment), aggregate demand conditions, government's policies (both fiscal and monetary) the rate of inflation affect business firms. These aggregates of the economy make up overall *business environment* which affects decisions of managers. Forecasts of future demand and investment decisions by managers are especially based on the state of the economy and its growth process.

QUESTIONS FOR REVIEW

1. What is macroeconomics ? How will you distinguish it from microeconomics ?
2. What are the important problems that constitute the subject matter of macroeconomics ? Briefly explain them.
3. What is say's law of markets? How does it show that there cannot be deficiency of aggregate demand.
4. In what sense did Keynes bring about a revolution in economics ?
5. Macroeconomics has been described as a study of aggregates. Name some important 'aggregates' or variables whose behaviour is analysed in macroeconomics. Explain them briefly.
6. Why is there a need for a separate theory of macroeconomics ? Explain.
7. What is involuntary unemployment ? Why did classical economists believe that involuntary unemployment cannot exist in a free market economy ?
8. What are the major issues that have been the concern of macroeconomics ? Explain them briefly.
9. What is potential GNP ? What can cause equilibrium of national income below it ?
10. Explain briefly the meaning of the following:
    1. Business Cycles
    2. Economic Growth
    3. Stagflation
    4. Inflation
11. What are macroeconomic paradoxes ? Explain any two of them. Explain how these paradoxes limit the applicability of microeconomic theories to explain the behaviour of the economy as a whole.
12. Name which of the following problems fall within the purview of macroeconomics ?
    1. How is general price level determined ?
    2. Determination of output of a cotton textile industry.
    3. How is wage rate of computer engineer determined ?
    4. The problem of unemployment in the economy.
    5. On what factors does economic growth of a country depend ?
    6. How is level of national income determined ?
    7. Deficit in the balance of payments of a country
13. Explain the importance of the study of macroeconomics.
14. What policy instruments are available with the government to achieve full employment, price stability and economic growth ? Explain them briefly.

CHAPTER 2 Circular Flow of Income and Expenditure

Introduction

National income measures the flow of market value of final goods and services produced in a year. The production of these goods and services generates flows of income in the form of wages, rent, interest and profit to the households who supply the services of their factors for the production of goods and services. These incomes are then spent by households for purchase of goods and services. These three aspects of national income, namely, 'the market value of all final goods and services produced and sold', 'the sum of factor incomes generated for the households' and the 'expenditure made on purchases of goods and services by households' generate circular flow of money. The relation between these three aspects of national income is best understood by circular flow of money income and expenditure. In the modern economy, money is used in the process of exchange. Money has facilitated the process of exchange and has removed the difficulties of the barter system. Money acts a medium of exchange. The households supply the economic resources or factors to the productive firms and receive in return the payments in terms of money. It is thus clear that, in the monetary economy, there will be flows of money corresponding to the flows of economic resources and the flows of goods and services. We explain below the circular flow of income and expenditure.

Circular Income Flow in a Two-Sector Economy

To begin with, to explain the circular flow of income and expenditure we assume that all incomes which households receive are spent on consumer goods and services and thus, there is no saving by them. Similarly, we assume there is no investment by business firms. Real flows of resources, goods and services have been shown in Fig. 2.1. Initially, ignore the '*Financial Market*' represented within the circle where savings are deposited and from which funds are borrowed for investment by business firms. In the upper loop of this figure, the resources such as land, capital and entrepreneurial ability flow from households to business firms as indicated by the arrow mark. In opposite direction to this, money flows from business firms to the households as factor payments such as wages, rent, interest and profits. In the lower part of the figure, money flows from households to firms as consumption expenditure made by the households on the goods and services produced by the firms, while the flow of goods and services is in opposite direction from business firms to households. Thus we see that money flows from business firms to households as factor payments and then it flows from households to firms as expenditure made by them on goods and services produced by the firms. Thus there is, in fact, *a circular flow of money or income*. This circular flow of money will continue indefinitely week by week and year by year. This is how the economy functions.

It may, however, be pointed out that this flow of money income will not always remain the same in volume. In other words, the flow of money income will not always continue at a constant level. In years of depression, the circular flow of money income will contract, *i.e.*, will become lesser in volume, and in years of prosperity it will expand, *i.e.*, will become greater in volume. This is so because the flow of money is a measure of national income and will, therefore, change with changes in the national income. In years of depression, when national income is low, the volume of the flow of money will be small and in years of prosperity when the level of national income is quite high, the flow of money will be large.

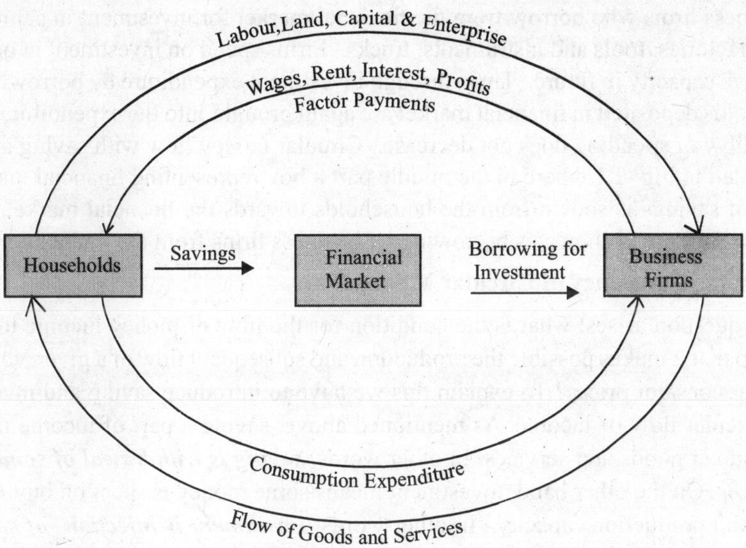

Fig. 2.1. *Circular Flow of Income in a Simple Two-Sector Economy*

In order to make our analysis simple and to explain the central issues involved, we take many assumptions. In the first place, we assume that neither the households save from their incomes, nor the firms save from their profits. We further assume that the government does not play any part in the national economy. In other words, the government does not receive any money from the people by way of taxes, nor does the government spend any money on the goods and services produced by the firms or on the resources and services supplied by the households. Thirdly, we assume that the economy neither imports goods and services, nor exports anything. In other words, in our above analysis we have not taken into account the role of foreign trade. In fact we have explained above the flow of money that occurs in the functioning of a closed economy with no savings and no role of government.

Circular Money Flow with Saving and Investment

In our above analysis of the circular flow of money we have assumed that all income which the households receive, they spend it on consumer goods and services. As a result, circular flow of money spending and income remains undiminished. We will now explain if households save a part of their income, how their savings will affect money flows in the economy. When households save, their expenditure on goods and services will decline to that extent and as a result money flow to the business firms will contract. With reduced money receipts, firms will hire fewer workers (or lay off some workers) or reduce the factor payments they make to the suppliers of factors such as workers. This will lead to the fall in total incomes of the households. Thus, savings reduce the flow of money expenditure to the business firms and will cause a fall in economy's total income. *Economists therefore call savings a leakage from the money expenditure flow.*

But savings by households need not lead to reduced aggregate spending and income if they find their way back into flow of expenditure. In free market economies there exists a set of institutions such as banks, insurance companies, financial houses, stock markets where households deposit their savings. All these institutions together are called financial institutions or financial market. We assume that all the savings of household come in the financial market. We further assume that there are no inter-households borrowings.

It is business firms who borrow from the financial market for investment in capital goods such as machines, factories, tools and instruments, trucks. Firms spend on investment in order to expand their productive capacity in future. Thus, through investment expenditure by borrowing the savings of the households deposited in financial market are again brought into the expenditure stream and as a result total flow of spending does not decrease. Circular money flow with saving and investment is also illustrated in Fig. 2.1 where in the middle part a box representing financial market is drawn. Money flow of savings is shown from the households towards the financial market. Then flow of investment expenditure is shown as borrowing by business firms from the financial market[1].

Condition for the Constancy of Circular Money Flow

Now the question arises: what is the condition for the flow of money income to continue at a steady level so that it makes possible the production and subsequent flow of a given volume of goods and services at constant prices? To explain this we have to introduce saving and investment in the analysis of circular flow of income. As mentioned above, saving a part of income means it is not spent on consumer goods and services. In other words, ***saving is withdrawal of some money from the income flow***. On the other hand, investment means some money is spent on buying new capital goods to expand production capacity. In other words, ***investment is injection of some money in circular flow of income***. For the circular flow of income to continue unabated, the withdrawal of money from the income stream by way of saving must equal injection of money by way of investment expenditure. Therefore, planned savings must be equal to planned investment if the constant money income flow in an economy is to be obtained. Now, what will happen if planned investment expenditure falls short of the planned savings? As a result of fall in planned investment expenditure, income, output and employment will fall and therefore the flow of money will contract. If the equality between planned savings and planned investment is disturbed by increase in savings, then the immediate effect will be that the stocks of goods lying in the shelves of the shops will increase (as some of the goods will not be sold due to the fall in consumption *i.e.,* increase in savings). Owing to the deficiency of demand for goods and the accumulation of stocks, retailers will place small orders with the wholesalers. Consequently, smaller amount of goods will be produced and therefore fewer capital goods like machinery will be needed with the result that fixed investment will tend to fall. Thus the ultimate effect of either the fall in planned investment or the increase in planned savings is the same, namely, the fall in income, output, employment and prices with the result that the flow of money will contract.

On the other hand, if the equality between planned savings and planned investment is disturbed by the increase in investment demand, the result will be increase in income, output and employment. Consequently, the flow of money income will expand.

It is thus clear from the above analysis that the *flow of money income will continue at a constant level only when the condition of equality between planned saving and investment is satisfied*. It was believed by classical economists that financial market provides a mechanism which coordinates the savings of households and the investment expenditure by the firms. Rate of interest, which is the price for the use of savings, is determined by saving and investment. If savings exceed investment expenditure, rate of interest falls so that, at a lower rate of interest, investment increases and both become equal. On the contrary, if investment expenditure is greater than savings, rate of interest will rise so that at a higher rate of interest savings increase and become equal to planned investment expenditure.

1. It may be noted that business firms also save when they do not distribute among shareholders all the profits made by them and keep the undistributed profits as reserves. We are ignoring them in our money flow analysis as firms themselves use their savings for buying machinery and making other investment expenditure.

However, an eminent British economist J.M. Keynes refuted the above argument that changes in rate of interest will cause saving and investment to become equal. According to him, since in a free market capitalist economy, investment is made by business enterprises and savings are mostly done by households and for different reasons, there is no guarantee that planned investment will be equal to planned savings and thus fluctuations in income, output and employment are inevitable. As a result, circular flow of income does not continue at a steady level in a free-enterprise capitalist economy unless certain corrective and preventive steps are taken by the government to maintain stability in the economy.

Saving-Investment Identity in National Income Accounts

Despite the fact that people who save are different from the business firms which primarily invest, in national income accounts savings are identical or always equal to investment in a simple two-sector economy having no roles of Government and foreign trade. This is a basic identity in national income accounts which needs to be carefully understood. Of course, in our above analysis of circular flow of income, we explained that planned investment by business firms can differ from savings by household. But in that analysis we referred to *planned or intended* investment and savings which often differ and affect the flow of national income. However, **in national income accounts we are concerned with *actual saving* and *actual investment*.** It is these actual or realised saving and investment that are identical in national income accounts. We can prove their identity in the following way.

In a simple economy which has neither government, nor foreign trade, the value of *output produced* which we denote by Y is equal to the value of *output sold*. Since the value of output sold in a simple two-sector economy is equal to the sum of consumption expenditure and investment expenditure, we have

$$Y \equiv C + I \qquad ...(i)$$

where Y = Value of aggregate output, C = Consumption expenditure and I = Investment expenditure.

A pertinent question which arises here is what happens to the unsold output. The unsold output leads to the *increase in the inventories of goods* and in national income accounting increase in inventories of goods is treated as a part of actual investment. This may be considered as the firms selling the goods to themselves to add to their inventories. Thus, gross national product (GNP) produced is used either for consumption or for investment.

Now, look at the gross national product or income in the simple economy from the viewpoint of its allocation between consumption and saving. Since national income (which is equal to GNP) can be either consumed or saved,[2] we have

$$Y \equiv C + S \qquad ...(ii)$$

From the identities (*i*) and (*ii*) we get

$$C + I \equiv Y \equiv C + S \qquad ...(iii)$$

The left-hand side of the identity (*iii*), namely $C + I = Y$ shows the components of aggregate demand (that is, aggregate expenditure on goods and services produced) and the right-hand side of the identitiy (*iii*) namely $Y = C + S$ shows the allocation of national income to either consumption or saving. Thus, the identity (*iii*) shows that the value of output produced or sold is equal to the total income received. It is income received that is spent on goods and services produced.

Now subtracting the consumption (C) from both sides of the identity (*iii*) we have

$$I = S$$

Thus, in *our two-sector simple economy with neither government, nor foreign trade, investment is identically equal to saving.*

---

2. Note that decisions about saving are made both by households and business firms. In national income accounts they are generally put together and referred to as private sector savings.

Circular Income Flow in a Three-Sector Economy with Government Sector

In our above analysis of money flow, we have ignored the existence of government for the sake of making our circular flow model simple. This is quite unrealistic because government absorbs a good part of the incomes earned by households. Government affects the economy in a number of ways. Here we will concentrate on its taxing, spending and borrowing roles. Government purchases goods and services just as households and firms do. Government expenditure takes many forms including spending on capital goods and infrastructure (highways, power, communication), on defence goods, and on education and public health and so on. These add to the money flows which are shown in Fig. 2.2 where a box representing Government has been drawn. It will be seen that government purchases of goods and services from firms and households are shown as flow of money spending on goods and services.

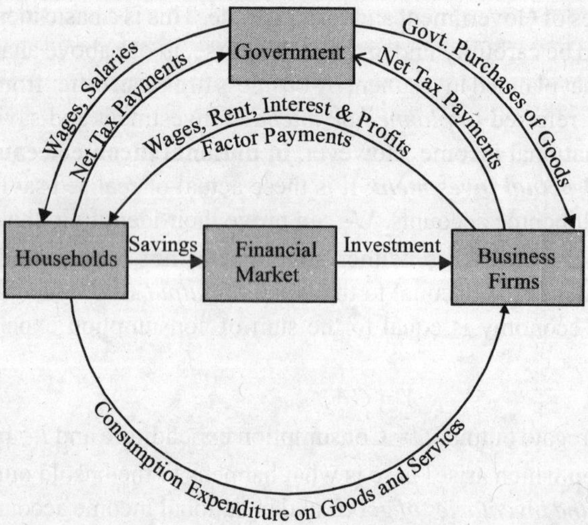

Fig. 2.2. *Circular Money Flow Model with Government*

Government expenditure may be financed through taxes, out of assets or by borrowing. The money flow from households and business firms to the government is labelled as tax payments in Fig. 2.2. This money flow includes all the tax payments made by households less transfer payments received from the Government. Transfer payments are treated as negative tax payments.

Another method of financing Government expenditure is borrowing from the financial market. This can be represented by the money flow from the financial market to the Government and is labelled as Government borrowing (To avoid confusion we have not drawn this money flow from financial market to the Government). Government borrowing increases the demand for credit which causes rate of interest to rise. The government borrowing through its effect on the rate of interest affects the behaviour of firms and households. Business firms consider the interest rate as cost of borrowing and the rise in the interest rate as a result of borrowing by the Government lowers private investment. However, households who view the rate of interest as return on savings feel encouraged to save more.

It follows from above that the inclusion of the Government sector significantly affects the overall economic situation. Total expenditure flow in the economy is now the sum of consumption expenditure (denoted by C), investment expenditure (I) and Government expenditure (denoted by G). Thus

$$\text{Total expenditure } (E) = C + I + G \qquad \ldots (i)$$

Total income (Y) received is allocated to consumption (C), savings (S) and taxes (T). Thus

$$Y = C + S + T \qquad \ldots (ii)$$

Since expenditure(E) made must be equal to the income received (Y), from equations (i) and (ii) above we have

$$C + I + G = C + S + T \quad \ldots (iii)$$

Since C occurs on both sides of the equation (*iii*) and will therefore be cancelled out, we have

$$I + G = S + T \quad \ldots (iv)$$

By rearranging we obtain

$$G - T = S - I \quad \ldots (v)$$

Equation (*v*) is very significant as it depicts what would be the consequences if government budget is not balanced. If Government expenditure (G) is greater than the tax revenue (T), that is, $G > T$, the government will have a budget deficit. To finance the budget deficit, the Government will borrow from the financial market. For this purpose, then private investment (I) by business firms must be less than the savings(S) of the households. Thus Government borrowing reduces private investment in the economy. In other words, Government borrowing *crowds out* private investment.

Another important conclusion that can be drawn from national income account identity incorporating Government expenditure relates to the condition for equilibrium in the financial market. National income identity with government expenditure is

$$Y = C + I + G$$

or

$$Y - C - G = I \quad \ldots (vi)$$

In the expression (*vi*), the left hand side ($Y - C - G$) represents national saving or simply saving (S). Note that in this National Income Identity all government expenditure is treated as consumption expenditure. To understand the identity (*vi*), we break up its left hand side representing national saving into two parts, namely, (1) *private saving* ($Y - T - C$) and (2) *public saving* (*i.e.* saving of the government ($T - G$). Thus

$$S = (Y - T - C) + (T - G) = Y - C - G$$

(Note that $Y - T$ is disposable income)

If the economy is to remain in a steady state, the *flows into* the financial market (*i.e.* private saving and public saving) must balance the *flows out of* the financial market. Thus, for the economy to remain in a steady state

$$Y - T - C + (T - G) = I$$

That is, for the economy to remain in a steady state, the sum of private saving and public saving must equal investment.

Money Flows in the Four-Sector Open Economy : Adding Foreign Sector

We now turn to explain the money flows that are generated in an open economy, that is, economy which have trade relations with foreign countries. Thus, the inclusion of the foreign sector will reveal to us the interaction of the domestic economy with foreign countries. Foreigners interact with the domestic firms and households through exports and imports of goods and services as well as through borrowing and lending operations through financial market. Goods and services produced within the domestic territory which are sold to the foreigners are called exports.

On the other hand, purchases of foreign-made goods and services by domestic households are called imports. Figure 2.3 illustrates additional money flows that occur in the open economy when exports and imports also exist in the economy. In our analysis, we assume it is only the business firms of the domestic economy that interact with foreign countries and therefore export and import goods and services. A flow of money spending on imports has been shown to be occurring from the domestic business firms to the foreign countries (*i.e.*, rest of the world) . On the contrary, flow of money expenditure on exports of a domestic economy has been shown to be taking place from foreign countries to the business firms of the domestic economy. If exports are equal to the imports, then there exists a balance of trade. Generally, exports and imports are not equal to each other. If value of exports exceeds the value of imports, *trade surplus* occurs. On the other hand, if value of imports exceeds value of exports of a country, *trade deficit* occurs.

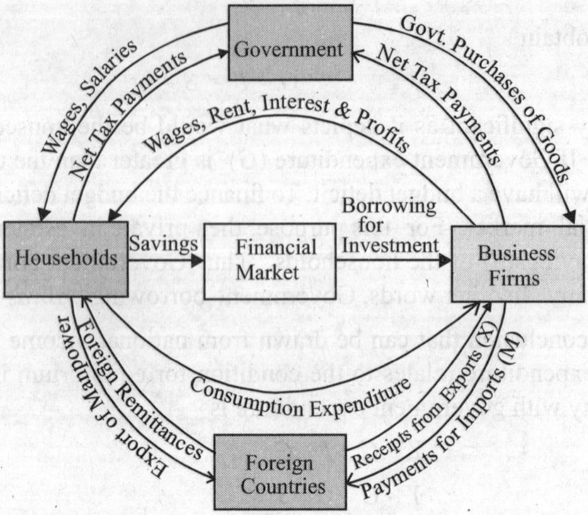

Fig. 2.3. *Circular Flow of Income in an Open Economy with Government and Foreign Sector*

In the open economy there is interaction between countries not only through exports and imports of goods and services but also through borrowing and lending funds or what is also called financial market. These days financial markets around the world have become well integrated. When there is a trade surplus in the economy, that is, when exports (X) exceed imports (M), *net capital outflow* will take place. By net capital outflow we mean foreigners will borrow from domestic savers to finance their purchases of our exports. In this way as a result of net capital outflow domestic savers will lend to foreigners, that is, acquire foreign financial assets.

On the contrary, in case of import surplus, that is, when imports are greater than exports, trade deficit will occur. Therefore, in case of trade deficit, domestic consumer households and business firms will borrow from abroad to finance their excess of imports over exports. This means there will be capital inflow in our economy. As a result, foreigners will acquire domestic financial assets.

Saving-Investment Identity in the Open Economy

From the circular flows that occur in the open economy the national income must be measured by aggregate expenditure that includes net of exports, that is, $X–M$ where X represents exports and M represents imports. Imports must be subtracted from the total expenditure made by foreigners on our domestically produced goods and services exported to them to get the value of net exports. Thus, in the open economy

$$\text{National Income} = C + I + G + NX$$

where NX represents net exports, $X–M$.

Since national income can be either consumed, saved or paid as taxes to the Government, we have

$$C + I + G + NX = C + S + T$$

Since C is common on both sides of the above equation, we have

$$I + G + NX = S + T \qquad \ldots (vi)$$

The above equation (*vi*) shows that in the open economy sum of private investment (I), Government expenditure (G) and net exports (NX) is equal to the sum of savings and tax revenue.

Relation of Aggregate Domestic Output and Expenditure with Trade Balance. The national income account identity of the open economy can be used further to show how aggregate domestic output (Y) and aggregate expenditure ($C + I + G$) and net exports (*i.e.* trade balance) are related. Rearranging the national income of the open economy ($Y = C + I + G + NX$), we have

$$NX = Y - (C + I + G)$$

where $C + I + G$ is aggregate domestic expenditure. Thus

Net Exports = National Domestic Product (Y) – Aggregate Domestic Expenditure

From above it follows that in an open economy aggregate domestic expenditure need not be equal to the aggregate domestic output of goods and services (*i.e. Y*). If aggregate domestic output (*Y*) exceeds aggregate domestic expenditure ($C + I + G$), there is *export surplus* and we export the excess of domestic output, that is, net exports (*NX*) are positive ($NX > 0$). On the other hand, if domestic output is less than domestic expenditure, we import this shortfall (i.e. $NX < 0$).

Foreign Capital Flows and Trade Balance

As in the case of a closed economy goods market is intimately related to the financial market in the open economy. To show this, let us rearrange the national income accounts identity ($Y = C + I + G + NX$) of the open economy.

$$Y - C - G = I + NX \qquad \ldots (vii)$$

The left-hand side of the above equation (*i.e.* $Y - C - G$) represents national saving (*S*). Note that all Government expenditure is here treated as consumption expenditure. Thus, it follows from above that

$$S = I + NX$$

or

$$S - I = NX \qquad \ldots (viii)$$

The national income identity of expression (*viii*) shows that the *economy's net exports (NX) must always be equal to the difference between saving and investment. The net exports are also called trade balance because it shows the difference between exports and imports of an economy*. The trade balance (*NX*) may be positive or negative. If exports exceed imports, trade balance (*NX*) is positive and if exports fall short of imports, the trade balance (*NX*) is negative.

But the important result that follows from national income identity of the open economy relates to the link between *international capital flows* and the *goods market*. If $S - I$ in (*viii*) is positive, that is, if the economy's national saving exceeds domestic investment, it will be lending the excess funds to foreigners, that is, there will be *net capital outflow* from the economy. On the other hand, if $S - I$ is negative, that is, if domestic investment exceeds domestic saving, the economy will be borrowing from abroad to finance the excess investment. That is, there will be *net capital inflow* into the economy to finance higher capital formation in the economy.

It follows from above that net capital flows ($S - I$) always equal the trade balance or to *current account balance* which is the broader term that includes *invisibiles* (that is, exports and imports of services) also.

NATIONAL INCOME AND NATIONAL PRODUCT

The sum of all incomes of the people of a country is called national income. This national income is greatly related to the national product. In fact in a two-sector economy without the Government and its imposition of indirect taxes and grant of subsidies and also assuming no depreciation national income and national product are one and the same thing. The incomes which different people of the society get are obtained by them for their contribution of labour, land, capital and entrepreneurial services to the national production. Hence the income which the labourers get are wages for the productive services which labourers lend to the various firms which undertake the work of production. Similarly, the owners of land get income as rent because of their contribution of land to the productive firms; the capitalists get interest for lending their money capital to the entrepreneurs for undertaking any work of production or business. The entrepreneurs get profits for starting and organising the work of production and bearing risk and uncertainty involved in it. It is thus clear that the different individuals of a country obtain their income either as wages of their labour, or as interest on their money capital, or as rent for their land, or as profits for their enterprise. The sum of incomes obtained as wages, rent, interest and profits is the national income of the country.

Various households obtain their income from the productive firms or businesses which utilise their labour, land, capital and other services for the production of goods and services. The incomes earned by the various households and individuals from the work of production are in fact costs of production of the goods produced. The total value of all final goods and services produced by various productive firms or businesses in a year is known as national product. Therefore, the national product of a country can be estimated by multiplying the total output of final goods and services with their market prices.

Hence the total national product in terms of rupees or value which is produced by various productive firms in a year will be distributed among the various productive factors which have contributed to its production. Therefore, out of this national production (in value terms) wages will be paid to those households which have sold their labour to the productive firms. Out of this total value of the national product, land owners would get rent for the contribution of the services of land and capitalists would get interest for lending money capital to the productive firms. After the payment of wages, rent, interest, what is left is the profits of the entrepreneurs who set up productive firms, organise their work and bear risk and uncertainty and because of these services they get profits. It is thus clear the national product (value of total output of final goods and services in a year of a country) is distributed among wages, rents, interests and profits. As we have stated above, the sum of total wages, total interest, total rents and total profits is national income. Hence national product will be equal to he national income. The above conclusion that in a two-sector economy without Government and foreign trade national inocme equals national product can be expressed in the form of the following equation:

$$\text{National Product} = \begin{bmatrix} \text{Value of Final} \\ \text{Goods and Services} \\ \text{Produced} \end{bmatrix} = \left\{ \begin{array}{c} \text{Wages} \\ + \\ \text{Rent} \\ + \\ \text{Interest} \\ + \\ \text{Profits} \end{array} \right\} = \text{National Income}$$

From the above analysis it is evident that national income and national product are one and the same thing. Professor J.R. Hicks rightly writes, "*The value of the net social product of the community and the sum of the incomes of its members are exactly equal. The net social product and the social income are one and the same thing.*"[3]

It needs to be emphasised that the above conclusion regarding equality of national product and national income is valid only in our simple two-sector economy where we have assumed no depreciation funds are kept and also no role of Government (and therefore no indirect taxes collected by it and no subsidies granted by it). In case of a real economy, firms keep a part of some value created as depreciation allowance which therefore do not become a part of the income of the factors. When role of Government is brought into our analysis, a part of the value of output is taken away by the Government as indirect taxes and therefore the incomes of factor owners are reduced to that extent. Thus, only in the absence of depreciation funds and net indirect taxes, national product will be equal to national income. In our simple economy we assume away these depreciation funds and net indirect taxes levied by the Government on business firms to emphasise the point that national income does not come out of thin air, it is in fact generated by the production of goods and services. Therefore, growth in national income can be achieved by the increase in production of goods and services.

3. J. R. Hicks *The Social Framework*.

QUESTIONS FOR REVIEW

1. Explain the circular flow of income in an economy. What does it measure ?
2. Describe the circular flow of income in a two-sector economy with households and business firms. What determines the magnitude of circular flow of income and expenditure ?
3. What is meant by saving and investment ? How do they affect circular flow of income in a free market economy ?
4. Despite the fact that motives to save are different from the motives of business men to invest, in national income accounts savings are always equal to investment. Explain
5. How does the addition of Government in a two-sector economy affect circular flow of income? If Government's budget is deficit, how will it affect circular flow of income ?
6. Show with a circular income flow model of a *two-sector economy* that national product equals national income.
7. In a three-sector model (with firms, households and Government) show that financing of budget deficit by borrowing from the market *crowds out* private investment.
8. What are withdrawals from and injections into the income flow? How do they affect the size of circular flow of income.
9. If investment by business firms falls short of savings, how will it affect the circular flow of income.
10. In open economy, explain with a circular flow model that the sum of investment, government expenditure and net exports must equal the sum of savings and taxes (that is, $I + G + NX = S + T$).
11. Show that in a two-sector economy (with households and business firm) saving and investment are identical.
12. Show that the difference between investment and saving always equal trade deficit (*i.e.*, current account deficit).
13. Explain how foreign capital flows are related to domestic saving and investment.
14. Show that for the economy with government expenditure and taxes, for the economy to remain in steady state the sum of private saving and public saving must equal investment.
15. Show that in a two-sector economy, the value of net national product, and the sum of the incomes of its members are exactly equal.

CHAPTER

3

National Income and its Measurement

Introduction

The labour and capital of a country acting on its natural resources produce annually a certain amount **of final goods and services**. This is called **Gross Domestic Product (GDP)** of a country. It is the same thing as **Gross National Income** if we ignore net factor income earned by the residents of a country from abroad. It is important to note that for calculating gross domestic product (GDP) or national income of a country accurately all goods and services produced in any given year must be counted only once, and not more than once. Most of the goods go through a series of production stages before reaching a market. As a result, parts or components of many goods are bought and sold many times. Hence, in order to avoid counting several times the parts of goods that are sold and resold, national income only includes the market value of all *final goods and services* only and ignores the transactions involving *intermediate goods*.

The above way of explaining gross domestic product (GDP) is only one way of interpreting it. In fact, the concept of GDP or Gross National Income has three aspects. It represents a flow of total value of output (as explained above), it represents a flow of total receipts or incomes, and it represents a flow of total expenditure. It is an obvious fact that every expenditure is at the same time a receipt. In other words, amount spent is equal to amount received. But if goods and services are valued at their market prices, we have three-fold identity, namely, that the value received equals the value paid equals the value of goods and services produced and sold.

To explain the above idea, let us take an economy where there are only two agents: households and firms. Firms are required to produce goods. To produce them, they require services of factors of production from households. Factors of production are paid the rewards for their contribution to the production of goods. Thus, incomes of these factors arise in the course of production. The sales value of net production of goods and services must equal the sum total of payments made by the firms to the factors of production used in the process of production. The sales value of net production must equal the sum total of payments made by the firms to the factors of production in the form of wages, rents, interest and profits. These incomes in turn become the sources of expenditure. Thus income flows from the firms to the households in exchange for productive services. This income again returns to the firms when expenditure is made by the households on the goods and services produced by the firms.

From above it follows that:

National Income = National Product = National Expenditure.

In other words, there are three types of flows concerning national income of a country. They are:

(*a*) the flow of total values of all final goods and services produced;

(*b*) the flow of all incomes, in cash and kind, accruing to factors of production in a year; and

(*c*) the flow of total expenditure, consisting of consumers' expenditure, private investment expenditure and government expenditure on goods and services.

Sum of all income, sum of values of all final production, and sum of all expenditures will be the same, but the significance of each arises from the fact that they reflect the three basic activities of the nation's economy, viz., production, distribution and expenditure.

CONCEPTS OF NATIONAL INCOME

There are various concepts of national income which we study below one by one.

Gross Domestic Product (GDP)

This is the basic national accounting measure of the total output or aggregate supply of goods and services. *Gross Domestic Product is defined as the total market value of all final goods and services produced in a year in the domestic territory of a country.* Six things must be noted in regard to gross domestic product. First, it measures the **market value** of output of all final goods and services produced in a country in a year. In other words, GDP is a *monetary measure*. There is no other way of adding up the different sorts of goods and services produced in a year except in terms of their money prices. But in order to know accurately the changes in physical output, the figure for gross domestic product is adjusted for price changes. Secondly, it is important to note that the goods, both consumer and capital goods, that are produced in the domestic territory of a country but are exported to other countries form part of the gross domestic product (GDP) of a country. Besides, the goods that are imported from other countries in a year for either consumption or production purposes generate incomes in other countries are excluded from gross domestic product (GDP). Therefore, it is only **net exports,** that is, exports minus imports that are included in GDP.

Thirdly, for calculating gross domestic product accurately, all goods and services produced in any given year must be counted once, and not more than once. Most of the goods go through a series of production stages before reaching a market. As a result, parts or components of many goods are bought and sold many times. Hence to avoid counting several times the parts of goods that are sold and resold, gross domestic product includes the market value of only *final goods and services* and ignores the transactions involving *intermediate goods*.

Final Goods and Intermediate Goods. What do we mean by *final goods*? Final goods are those goods which are purchased for final use and *not for resale or further processing.* Intermediate goods, on the other hand, are those goods which are purchased for further processing or for resale. The sale of intermediate goods is excluded from gross national product. Why? Because the value of final goods includes the value of all intermediate goods used in their production. *The inclusion of intermediate goods would involve double counting and would therefore give an exaggerated estimate of gross domestic product.* An example will clarify this point. Suppose in our economy only two things are being produced, raw cotton worth Rs. 1000 and cotton cloth worth Rs. 2000. Now what will be the measure of gross national product? For finding it, if we add up the sales value of cloth and cotton, there is clearly an element of *double counting* in the sense that we have added the value of cotton *twice*—one as the sales value of cotton and secondly when we added to it the value of cloth. Actually, the value of cloth includes also the value of cotton which having been accounted for in the value of cloth should not be added second time.

Fourth, it is worth noting that Gross Domestic Product (GDP) includes only *newly* or *currently produced* goods and services in a year. It is a *flow measure* of output of goods and services per time period, say in a year. In it only goods and services currently produced in a particular year are included. Market transactions involving goods produced in previous periods such as old houses, cars, factories built in earlier years are not included in gross domestic product of the current year. Similarly, purchase and sale of assets such as stock and bonds do not involve current production of goods and are therefore excluded from GDP of the year.

Fifth, Gross Domestic Product (GDP) refers to the value of goods and services currently produced by *normal residents of a country*. These residents may be national or non-national companies. Thus, many foreign companies have set up plants in India. They are owned by non-nationals but work to produce goods and services within the domestic territory of India and generate incomes for the Indian people employed in them. These foreign companies can only send back to their home countries profits earned by them.

Lastly, gross domestic product (GDP) of a country does not include net factor incomes (wages, rent, interest and profits) *earned from abroad* (*i.e.,* from foreign countries). Net factor income earned from abroad by Indian nationals is arrived at by calculating receipts of factor incomes from the rest of the world and subtracting from them the factor incomes paid to the rest of the world. We will explain the net factor income earned from abroad when we explain Gross National Product (GNP), another important national income aggregate.

Gross domestic product (GDP) has the following components :

1. Value of *final consumer goods and services* produced in a year and consumed by the households which is denoted by *consumption* (*C*) by households.
2. Value of *new capital goods produced and addition to the inventories of goods* such as raw materials, unfinished goods and consumer goods produced but not sold during a year. This is called *Gross Private Investment* (*I*).
3. Value of output of General Government which is taken to be equal to the value of *purchases of goods and services by the Government* which we denote by *G*.
4. Net Exports (*NX*) which is equal to value of goods *exported* (*X*) *minus* the value of goods *imported* (*M*) in a year.

Thus, we can obtain Gross Domestic Product (GDP) by adding up the four items listed above.

$$GDP = C + I + G + NX$$

where $NX = (X - M)$

Gross National Product (GNP)

Another important concept of national income is gross national product (GNP). Gross national product is the money value of all final goods and services produced *in the domestic territory of a country and also includes net factor income earned from abroad.* Thus difference between gross domestic product (GDP) and gross national product (GNP) at market prices arises due to the existence of *'net factor income earned from abroad'*. Gross domestic product does not include net factor income from abroad, whereas gross national product includes it. Therefore,

Gross National Product (at market prices) or

$$GNP_{MP} = GDP_{MP} + \textit{Net factor income from abroad}$$

Let us explain net factor income earned from abroad. Net factor income from abroad means the receipts of factor incomes such as wages, rent, interest and profits by the Indian nationals from which we subtract factor incomes *paid to foreign nationals* for their factor services rendered by them for our country.

For example, non-residents (*i.e.*, foreigners) work in the domestic territory of India and earn wages and salary. Thus, foreign individuals and companies from the USA, Great Britain and other countries have acquired property such as factories, offices, buildings, and have also acquired financial assets such as bonds and shares of Indian companies. They generate incomes in the form of rent and interest to them. In addition to this, foreign residents—individuals and companies—have set up industrial plants and factories producing goods and services from which they earn profits.

On the other hand, Indians go abroad and work in the territories of other countries and earn wages and salaries. Likewise, some Indian individuals and corporate companies have acquired assets such as buildings, factories, commercial space, and have also invested in bonds, bank deposits of foreign countries and thus receive rent and interest. Some Indian companies have set up factories abroad and earn profits.

We have graphically depicted GNP_{MP} and GDP_{MP} in Figure 3.1.

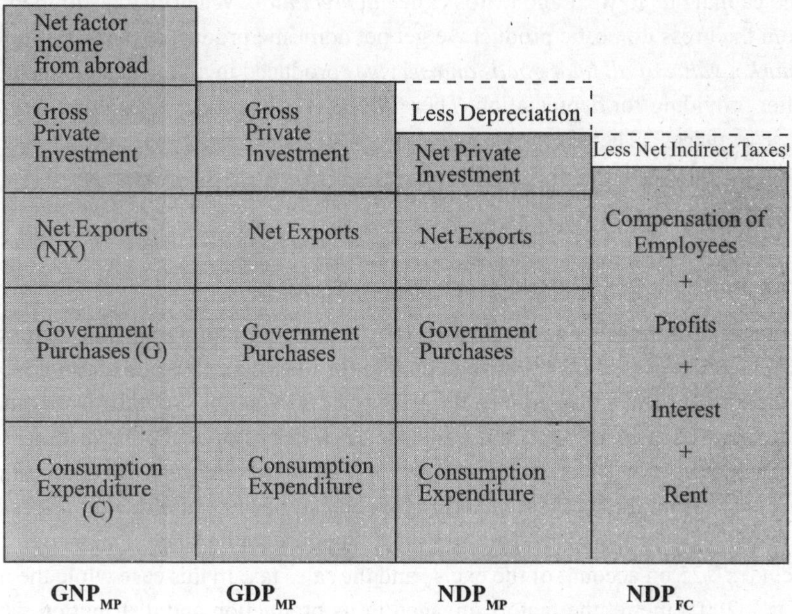

Fig. 3.1. *Various Concepts of National Product*

(Note: By adding Net Factor Income from Abroad to NDP_{MP} and NDP_{FC} we will get NNP_{MP} and NNP_{FC} (respectively).

Now, the *net factor income from abroad is the difference between factor incomes received from abroad by normal residents of India for rendering factor services in other countries on the one hand and the factor incomes paid to the foreign residents for factor services rendered by them in the domestic territory of India on the other.*

Net factor income earned from abroad have therofore the following three components:

1. *Net* compensation of employees, that is, wages and salaries.
2. *Net* income from property *i.e.*, rent, interest and income from entrepreneurship (that is, profits and dividends).
3. *Net* retained earnings of the Indian companies working in foreign countries.

(Note that '*Net*' in the above means the difference between the relevant income of normal residents earned from abroad and the same type of incomes paid to non-residents working in the domestic territory of a country)

It should however be noted that net factor income from abroad should not be confused with income from *net exports* which are a part of both gross national product (GNP) and gross domestic product (GDP). Net exports equal total exports minus imports. Gross exports are the total value of domestically produced goods and services sold to foreign buyers in a year and are therefore a part of Gross Domestic Product (GDP) and not a factor income from abroad. On the other hand, imports are the value of imported goods and services pruchased by the domestic buyers. Therefore, imports do not form a part of GDP or GNP. In national income accounting, we subtract the value of imports from the value of exports to arrive at net exports which are a part of GDP and therefore also of GNP. Thus, earnings from *net exports* are quite distinct from net factor income from abroad.

Net Domestic Product at Market Prices (NDP_{MP})

The third important concept of national income is that of net domestic product (NDP_{MP}). In the production of gross domestic product of a year, we consume or use up some fixed capital *i.e.*, equipment, machinery, etc. The capital goods, like machinery, wear out or fall in value as a result of its consumption or use in the production process. This consumption of fixed capital or fall in the value of fixed capital due to wear and tear is called *depreciation.* When charges for depreciation are deducted from the gross domestic product we get net domestic product at market prices. Clearly, it means the *market value of all final goods and services* produced in a year in a domestic territory of a country after providing for depreciation. Therefore, it is also called '*net domestic product or net income at market prices*'. Therefore,

$$\left.\begin{array}{l}\text{Net Domestic Product}\\ \text{at Market Prices}\end{array}\right\} = \text{Gross Domestic Product} - \text{Depreciation}$$

$$NDP_{MP} = GDP_{MP} - Depreciation$$

Net Domestic Product at Factor Cost (NDP_{FC}). Net Domestic Product at factor cost means the sum of all incomes earned by resource suppliers for their contributions of land, labour, capital and entrepreneurial ability which go into the year's net production. In other words, net domestic product at factor cost shows how much it costs society in terms of economic resources to produce net output. The difference between Net Domestic Product at factor cost and net domestic product at market prices arises from the fact that *indirect taxes* and *subsidies* cause market prices of output to be different from the factor incomes resulting from it. Suppose for instance, a metre of mill cloth sold for ₹ 200 includes ₹ 25 on account of the excise and the sales tax. In this case while the market price of the cloth is ₹ 200 a metre, the factors engaged in its production and distribution would receive ₹175 a metre. The value of cloth at factor cost would thus be equal to its value at market price less the indirect taxes on it. On the other hand, a subsidy causes the market price to be less than the factor cost. Suppose handloom cloth is subsidised at the rate of ₹ 10 per metre and it sells at ₹ 90 per metre. Then while the consumer pays ₹ 90 per metre, the factors engaged in the production and distribution of such cloth will receive ₹ 100 per metre (₹ 90 + 10 = ₹ 100). The value of handloom cloth at factor cost would thus be equal to its market price plus the subsidies paid on it. It follows, therefore, that the net domestic product at factor cost (NDP_{FC}) (or net domestic income at factor cost) is equal to net domestic product at market prices minus indirect taxes plus subsidies.

$$\left.\begin{array}{l}\text{Net Domestic Product}\\ \text{at Factor Cost } (NDP_{FC})\end{array}\right\} = \text{Net Domestic Product at Market Prices } (NDP_{MP}) - \text{Indirect Taxes} + \text{Subsidies}$$

Net of indirect taxes and subsidies is called Net Indirect Taxes. Therefore,

Net Domestic Product at Factor Cost = Net Domestic Product at Market prices – Net Indirect Taxes.

$$NDP_{FC} = NDP_{MP} - Net\ Indirect\ Taxex.$$

National Income and NDP_{FC}

An important thing to understanu is how the concept of GDP related to what we generally call **national income.** National income, as is generally understood, is the same thing as **Net National Product at factor cost** (NNP_{FC}). Now, when we obtain net domestic product at factor cost (NDP_{FC}) from GDP at market prices as explained above, then net national product at factor cost (NNP_{FC}) which is simply called *national income* can be measured by adding '*net factor income from abroad*' to NDF_C.

Thus, $NNP_{FC} = NDP_{FC} + Net\ Factor\ Income\ from\ abroad.$

Net National Product (NNP) or Net National Income at Market Prices

The other important concept of national income is that of net national product (NNP). In the production of gross national product of a year, we consume or use up some fixed capital *i.e.*, equipment, machinery, etc. As explained above, the capital goods, like machinery, wear out or fall in value as a result of its consumption or use in the production process. This consumption of fixed capital or fall in the value of fixed capital due to wear and tear is called *depreciation* or *consumption of fixed capital*. Alternatively, net natural product can be obtained from *adding net factor income from abroad to* NDM_{MP}. When charges for depreciation are deducted from the gross national product we get net national product. Clearly, it means the *market value of all final goods and services* after providing for depreciation. Therefore, it is also called '*national income at market prices*'. Therefore,

Net National Product at Market Prices or Net National Income at Market Prices } = Gross National Product – Depreciation

National Income (NI) or National Income at Factor Cost (NNP_{FC})

National Income at factor cost which is also simply called *national income* means the sum of all incomes earned by resource suppliers for their contribution of land, labour, capital and entrepreneurial ability which go into the year's net production. In other words, national income (or national income at factor cost) shows how much it costs society in terms of economic resources to produce net output. It is really the national income at factor cost for which we use the term National Income. The difference between national income (or national income at factor cost) and net national product (Net national income) at market prices arises from the fact that *indirect taxes* and *subsidies* cause market prices of output to be different from the factor incomes resulting from it. It follows, therefore, that the national income (or national income at factor cost) is equal to net national product minus indirect taxes plus subsidies.

National Income or National Income at Factor Cost } = Net National Product (Net National Income at Market Prices) – Indirect Taxes + Subsidies

Net of indirect taxes and subsidies is called *Net Indirect Taxes*. Therefore,
National Income = Net National Product – Net Indirect Taxes

Alternatively, national income or net national product at factor cost (NNP_{FC}) can be obtained by adding net factor income from abroad to NDP at factor cost.

Personal Income (PI)

Personal Income is the sum of all incomes actually received by all individuals or households during a given year. National income, that is, total incomes earned and personal income, that is, total incomes received must be different because some incomes which are earned such as social security contributions, corporate income taxes and undistributed corporate profits are not actually received by households, and conversely, some incomes which are received like transfer payments are not currently earned (examples of transfer payments are old-age pensions, unemployment compensation, relief payments, interest payments on the public debt, etc.). Obviously, in moving from national income as an indicator of income earned to personal income as an indicator of income actually received, we must subtract from national income those three types of income which are earned but not received and add those incomes which are received but currently not earned. Therefore,

Personal Income = National Income — Social Security Contributions — Corporate Income Taxes —Undistributed Corporate Profits + Transfer Payments.

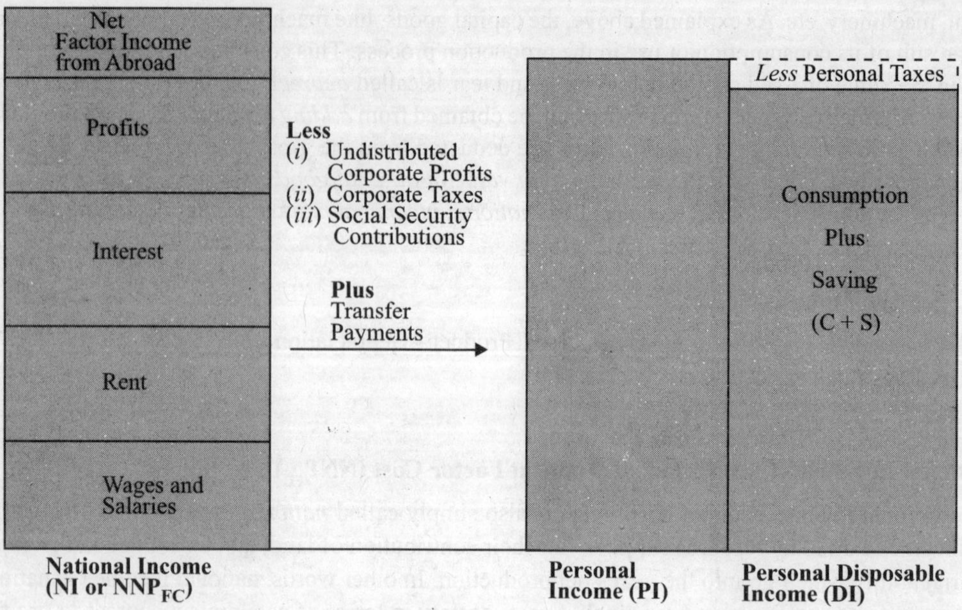

Fig. 3.2. *From National Income to Personal Disposable Income*

Personal Disposable Income (PDI)

Even whole of the incomes which are actually received by the people are not available to them for consumption. This is because governments levy some personal taxes such as income tax, personal property taxes. Therefore, after a part of personal income is paid to government in the form of *personal taxes* like income tax, personal property taxes, etc., what remains of personal income is called *personal disposable income*. Therefore,

Personal Disposable Income = Personal Income – Personal Taxes.

Personal Disposable Income can either be either consumed or saved. Hence,

Personal Disposable Income = Consumption + Saving.

How do we get personal income and disposable income from national income is illustrated in Figure 3.2.

MEASUREMENT OF NATIONAL INCOME

Since factor *incomes* arise from the production of goods and services, and since incomes are spent on goods and services produced, three alternative methods of measuring national income are possible.

1. Value Added Method

This is also called *output method or production method.* In this method the contribution of each enterprise to the generation of flow of goods and services is measured. Under this method, the economy is divided into different industrial sectors such as agriculture, fishing, mining, construction, manufacturing, trade and commerce, transport, communication and other services. Then, the net value added at factor cost (NVA_{FC}) by each productive enterprise as well as by each industry or sector is estimated. Measuring net value added at factor cost (NVA_{FC}) by each industry requires first to find out the value of output.

Let us explain how we arrive at net value added at factor cost (NVA_{FC}) from value of output step by step. An important estimate which we have to make in this method is to find out the value of various goods and services produced by enterprises in the domestic territory of a country. *The quantity of goods and services produced by a particular enterprise multiplied by their market prices is called value of output*. By summing up the value of output of all producing enterprises in a given industry or a sector we can obtain the value of output of that industry or sector. A major part of output of a firm or enterprise is sold in the market and termed as *sales*. The remaining part of output which is *not sold* in the accounting year is added to the stock of goods or inventories. Thus.

Value of output of an enterprise = Sales + Change in Stocks

Gross Value Added at Market Prices (GVA_{MP}). Gross value added measures the contribution to the value of output of a product produced during a year. As mentioned above, value of output is estimated by multiplying the quantity of output with the market prices. Therefore, gross value added at market prices by a production unit is obtained by deducting the value of intermediate consumption (that is, the value of intermediate goods such as raw materials used from the value of output (at market prices) produced. Thus.

Gross value added at market prices (GVA_{MP}) *= Value of Output – Intermediate Consumption*

A firm disposes of its value added at market prices (GVA_{MP}) among the three items : (1) making depreciation provision for consumption of fixed capital during the year, (2) making payments of indirect taxes such as excise duties, sales tax, import duty to the government, and (3) making factor payments suhc as wages, interest and profits to the factors of production whose services have been used for the production of a good.

Net Value Added at Market Prices (NVA_{MP}). When from gross value added at market prices we deduct depreciation on account of consumption of fixed capital during the production process of a good during the year, we get Net Value Added at market prices (NVA_{MP}). Thus

$NVA_{MP} = GVA_{MP}$ – Consumption of Fixed Capital i.e. Depreciation

Thus net value added is net of depreciation or consumption of fixed capital.

Net Value Added at Factor Cost (NVA_{FC}). When adjustment is made in net value added at market prices (NVA_{MP}) for the payment of *net indirect taxes*, (that is, indirect taxes such as sales tax, excise duty, customs duties to the government minus subsidies received from the government) we get Net Value Added at Factor Cost (NVA_{FC}) This is because after the subtraction of depreciation amount and net indirect taxes what remains is used for making payments to factors of production such as wages to labour, interest on capital borrowed, rent for land and building hired from others and profits and dividends to entrepreneur. In other words, NVA_{FC} measures the value of factor cost a firm has to incur.

Summing up the net values added at factor cost (NVA_{FC}) by all productive enterprises of an industry or sector gives us the net value added at factor cost of each industry or sector. We then add up net values added at factor cost by all industries or sectors to get *net domestic product at factor cost* (NDP_{FC}). Lastly, to the net domestic product we add the *net factor income from abroad* to get *net national product at factor cost* (NNP_{FC}) which is also called national income. Thus,

NI or $NNP_{FC} = NDP_{FC}$ + Net factor income from abroad

This method of calculating national income can be used where there exists a census of production for the year. In many countries, the data of production of only important industries are known. Hence this method is employed along with other methods to arrive at the national income. The one great advantage of this method is that it reveals the relative importance of the different sectors of the economy by showing their respective contributions to the national income.

Precautions. The following precautions should be taken while measuring national income of a country through value added method:

1. *Imputed rent values* of self-occupied houses should be included in the value of output. Though these payments are not made to others, their values can be easily estimated from prevailing values in the market.
2. Sale and purchase of *second-hand goods* should not be included in measuring value of output of a year because their values were counted in the year of output of the year of their

production. Of course, commission or brokerage earned in their sale and purchase has to be included because this is a new service rendered in the current year.

3. *Value of production for self-consumption* are be counted while measuring national income. In this method, the production for self-consumption should be valued at the prevailing market prices.
4. *Value of services of housewives* are not included because it is not easy to find out correctly the value of their services.
5. Value of intermediate goods *must not* be counted while measuring value added because this will amount to double counting.

2. Income Method

This method approaches national income from distribution side. In other words, this method measures national income at the phase of distribution and appears as income paid and or received by individuals of the country. Thus, under this method, *national income is obtained by summing up of the incomes of all individuals of a country*. Individuals earn incomes by contributing their own services and the services of their property such as land and capital to the national production. Therefore, national income is calculated by adding up the rent of land, wages and salaries of employees, interest on capital, profits of entrepreneurs (including undistributed corporate profits) and incomes of self-employed people. This method of estimating national income has the great advantage of indicating the distribution of national income among different income groups such as landlords, owners of capital, workers, entrepreneurs. Measurement of national income through income method involves the following main steps:

1. Like the value added method, the first step in income method is also to *identify* the productive enterprises and then *classify* them into various industrial sectors such as agriculture, fishing, forestry, manufacturing, transport, trade and commerce, banking, etc.

2. The second step is to classify *the factor payments*. The factor payments are classified into the following groups:

1. *Compensation of employees* which includes wages and salaries, employers' contribution to social security schemes.
2. *Rent and also royalty*, if any.
3. *Interest.*
4. *Profits*: Profits are divided into three sub-groups:
   (*i*) Dividends
   (*ii*) Undistributed profits
   (*iii*) Corporate income tax

5. *Mixed income of the self-employed*: In India as in other developing countries there is fifth category of factor income which is termed as *mixed income of self-employed*. In India a good number of people are engaged in household industries, in family farms and other unorganised enterprises. Because of self-employment nature of the business it is difficult to separate wages for the work done by the self-employed from the surplus or profits made by them. Therefore, the incomes earned by them are mix of wages, rent, interest and profit and are, therefore, called *mixed income of the self-employed.*

3. The third step is to *measure factor payments*. Income paid out by each enterprise can be estimated by gathering information about the number of units of each factor employed and the income paid out to each unit of every factor. Price paid out to each factor multiplied by the number of units of each factor employed would give us the factor's income.

4. The *adding up of factor payments* by all enterprises belonging to an industrial sector would give us the incomes paid out to various factors by a *particular* industrial sector.

5. By summing up the incomes paid out by *all industrial sectors* we will obtain domestic factor income which is also called net domestic product at factor cost (NDP_{FC}).

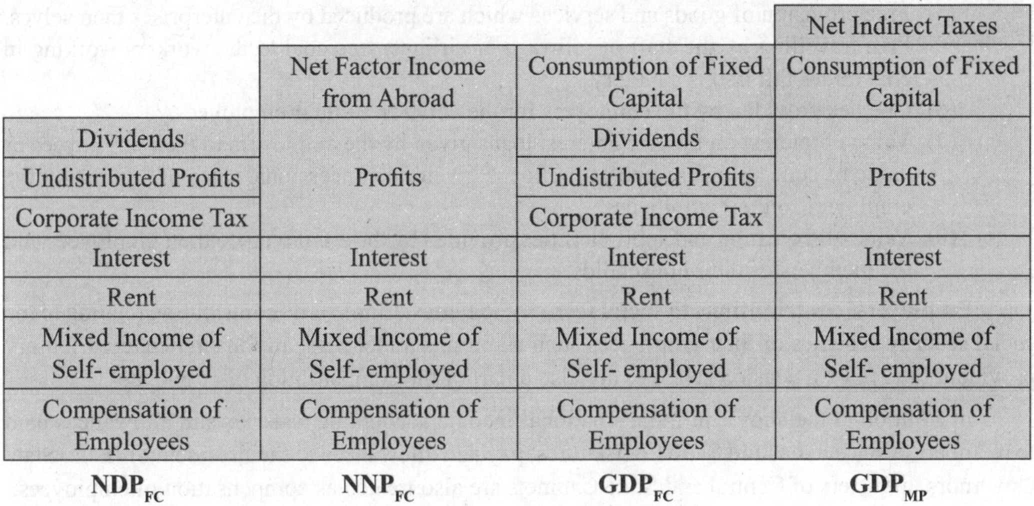

Fig. 3.3. *Income Approach to National Income*

6. Finally, by adding net factor income earned from abroad to domestic factor income or NDP$_{FC}$ we get net national product at factor cost (NNP$_{FC}$) which is also called *national income*.

Income approach to measurement of national income is shown through bar diagrams in Figure 3.3

Compensation of Employees

From the above items of income categories compensation of employees require further explanation. Compensation of employees by the producers is the sum of wages and salaries, paid both in cash and kind, and contribution to social security schemes of the employees made by the employers. Thus, it has the following components:

Wages and Salaries: These include all payments made by the employers to their employees, both in cash and kind, for the services they render to their employers.

Wages and Salaries Payable in Cash. They include the following:

(1) Wages and salaries received in cash by the employees from their employers.
(2) Payments received by the employees for overtime work done by them.
(3) Travelling allowance received by the employees for going to and coming home from their work-places.
(4) Bonuses, if any, receivable by the workers.
(5) Dearness allowance paid to the employees to neutralise the rise in cost of living.
(6) Vacation allowance and sick leave allowance.
(7) Leave travelling allowance (LTC).
(8) Commission provided, if any, to the sales staff on the sales.

Wages and Salaries in kind. These are the remuneration in kind received in the form of goods and services by the employees for their use by themselves or by the members of their households. The following are some important types of remuneration received in kind.

(1) Housing accommodation provided free of cost.
(2) Free meals and drinks (such as tea, coffee, cold drinks) provided free to the employees when they are on duty.
(3) Uniforms and special clothing, if any, received free of cost by the employer.
(4) The free services of vehicles (cars, scooters, vans etc.) provided by the employers to their employees.

(5) Free provision of goods and services which are produced by the enterprises themselves. Free travelling by the staff of railways or airlines, free coal to the workers working in coal mines fall in this category.
(6) Creches provided by the employers for the children of their employees.
(7) Value of interest on the free-interest loans given by the employers to their employees or value of concessions in interest on loans given on concessional rates of interest by the employers to their employees.
(8) Value of recreation and sport facilities provided by the employers to their employees and the members of their households.

Employers' contributions to social security schemes. Employers' contribution relating to the social security schemes of their employees such as life insurance, casualty insurance, contributory provident fund (CPF), pension schemes are also a part of the compensation of employees.

In addition to the above, in India's national income accounting, salaries and allowances paid to members of Parliament and State Legislatures, pay and allowances to the President of India, State Governors, ministers of Central and State Cabinets are also treated as compensation of employees.

Precautions. While estimating national income through income method the following precautions should be taken:

1. *Transfer payments* are not included in estimating national income through this method.

2. *Imputed rent* of self-occupied houses are included in national income as these houses provide services to those who occupy them and its value can be easily estimated from the market value data.

3. *Illegal money* such as *hawala money, money earned through smuggling* etc. are not included as they cannot be easily estimated.

4. *Windfall gains* such as prizes won, lotteries are also not included.

5. Corporate profit tax (that is, tax on income of the companies) should not be separately included as it has already been included as a part of profits.

6. *Death duties, gift tax, wealth tax, tax on lotteries*, etc., are paid from past savings or wealth and not from current income. Therefore, they should not be treated as a part of national income of a year.

7. The receipts from the *sale of second-hand goods* should not be treated as a part of national income. This is because the sale of second-hand goods does not create new flows goods and services in the current year.

8. Income equal to the *value of production used for self-consumption* should be estimated and included in the measure of national income.

Expenditure Method

Expenditure method arrives at national income by adding up all expenditures made on goods and services during a year. Income can be spent either on consumer goods or capital goods. Again, expenditure can be made by private individuals and households or by government and business enterprises. Further, people of foreign countries spend on the goods and services which a country exports to them. Similarly, people of a country spend on imports of goods and services from other countries. We add up the following types of expenditure by households, government and by productive enterprises to obtain national income.

1. Expenditure on consumer goods and services by individuals and households. This is called *final private consumption expenditure*, and is denoted by C.

2. Government's expenditure on goods and services to satisfy collective wants. This is called *government's final consumption expenditure*, and is denoted by G.

3. The expenditure by productive enterprises on capital goods and inventories or stocks. This is called *gross domestic capital formation*, or gross domestic investment and is denoted by I or GDCF. Gross domestic capital formation is divided into two parts:
   (*i*) Gross fixed capital formation
   (*ii*) Addition to the stocks or inventories of goods
4. The expenditure made by foreigners on goods and services of a country exported to other countries which are called exports and are denoted by *X*. We deduct from exports (*X*) the expenditure by people, enterprises and government of a country on imports (*M*) of goods and services from other countries. That is, we have to estimate net exports (that is, exports –imports) or (*X*—*M*).

Thus, we add up the above four types of expenditure to get final expenditure on gross domestic product at market prices (GDP_{MP}). Thus,

GDP_{MP} = Private final consumption expenditure + Government's final consumption expenditure + Gross domestic capital formation + Exports – Imports or

$$GDP_{MP} = C + G + I + (X - M)$$
$$= C + G + I + NX$$

On deducting consumption of fixed capital (*i.e.*, depreciation) from gross domestic product at market prices (GDP_{MP}) we get net domestic product at market prices (NDP_{MP}).

In this method, we then subtract net indirect taxes (that is, indirect taxes – subsidies) to arrive at net domestic product at factor cost (NDP_{FC}),

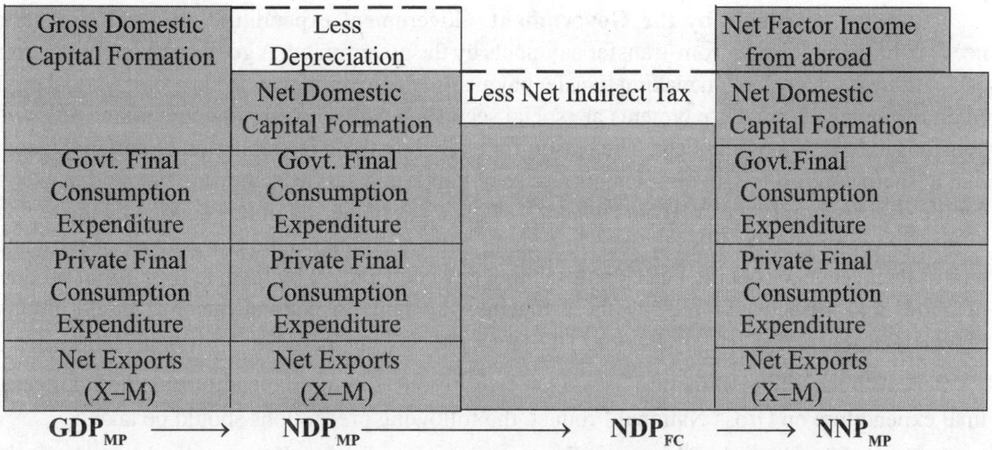

Fig. 3.4. *Expenditure Approach to National Income Concepts*

(**Note:** To any concept of the domestic product, if we add '*Net Income from Abroad*' we will get corresponding National Product)

Lastly, we add 'net factor income from abroad' to obtain net national product at factor cost (NNP_{FC}), which is called national income. Thus,

NNP_{FC} = GDP_{MP} – Consumption of Fixed capital - Net Indirect taxes + Net Factor Income from Abroad.

Expenditure approach to national income is shown through bar diagram in Figure 3.4.

Government's expenditure on goods and services need explanation in some detail.

Government's Final Consumption Expenditure on Goods and Services

The general government provides services such as defence, law and order, public health, education, cultural services, etc., to satisfy collective wants of its citizens. The government purchases various goods and services from others for providing its services to the people and incurs cost on them.

This cost of goods and services purchased by the government to provide its services to the people to satisfy collective wants is called intermediate consumption. Further, the government employs several persons, such as soldiers, policemen, other official clerks, secretaries in various departments and pays them wages and salaries. Thus, compensation to employees (that is wages, salaries, etc.), both in cash and in kind, is another type of cost incurred by the Government. Since government generally *does not sell* its services and instead provides them free of cost or sells them at a price much lower than production cost, the value of services provided by the government are valued at their cost to the government. The cost is the sum of (1) expenditure on intermediate consumption incurred by Government and (2) compensation to employees (wages and salaries etc.).

However, the government also sells some goods and services, though at nominal prices, such as hospital fees, tuition fees charged from the students in Government institutions. In order to find out the cost of government services, proceeds from sales of some goods and services, if any, by the government must be deducted.

Thus, the Government's final consumption expenditure on goods and services includes the following items.

1. Compensation of employees
2. Intermediate consumption expenditure by the General Government which refers to purchases of goods and services by the Government *less* sales of some goods by it.
3. Consumption of fixed capital.

Transfer Payments by the Government. Government expenditure on goods and services needs to be distinguished from transfer payments by the government. A good amount of Government expenditure is undertaken on making transfer payments which is not included in gross national product. Main examples of transfer payments are social security benefits, unemployment allowance, old age pensions, interest on public debt. The reason for excluding them in estimation of national income is that in sharp contrast to Government purchases of goods and services, they are not paid in exchange for the *contribution to the current production of goods* or rendering of any service by the recipients to the Government in the current year. In making transfer payments the Government just transfers a part of its revenue to specific individuals without any contribution by them to the current production of goods and services. To include these transfer payments in national income would amount to overestimate current year's production. Therefore, they are not included in national income of a year.

Precautions. While estimating Gross Domestic Product through expenditure method or measuring final expenditure on Gross National Product, the following precautions should be taken:

1. *Second-hand goods*: The expenditure made on second-hand goods should not be included because this does not contribute to the current year production of goods and services.

2. *Purchase of shares and bonds*. Expenditure on purchase of old shares and bonds from other people and from business enterprises should not be included while estimating Gross Domestic Product through expenditure method. This is because bonds and shares are mere financial claims and do not represent expenditure on currently produced goods and services.

3. *Expenditure on transfer payments by government* such as unemployment benefits, old-age pension should also not be included because no goods or productive services are produced in exchange by the recipients of these payments.

4. *Expenditure on intermediate goods* such as fertilisers and seeds by the farmers and wool, cotton and yarn by manufacturers of garments should also be excluded. This is because we have to avoid double counting. Therefore, for estimating Gross Domestic Product we have to include only *expenditure on final goods* and services.

DIFFICULTIES IN THE MEASUREMENT OF NATIONAL INCOME

There are many difficulties in measuring national income of a country accurately. The difficulties involved are both conceptual and statistical in nature. Some of these difficulties or problems involved in the measurement of national income are enumerated below.

1. **Treatment of non-monetary transactions.** The first problem relates to the *treatment of non-monetary transactions* such as the services of housewives to the members of their families and farm output consumed at home. On this point, the general agreement is *to exclude the services of housewives while to include the value of farm output consumed at home in the estimate of national income*. This, however, gives rise to certain anomalies. For example, if a man employs a maid-servant for household work, payment to her will appear as a positive item in national income. If the next day the man were to marry the maid-servant, she would be performing the same services as before but without payments. In this event the value of national income would go down though the real amount of goods and services performed remains the same as before.

2. **Treatment of Government activities in national income accounts.** The second difficulty arises with regard to the treatment of the government in national income accounts. On this point the general viewpoint is that as regards the administrative functions of the government like justice, administration and defence are concerned they should be treated as giving rise to final consumption of such services by the community as a whole so that contribution of general government activities will be equal to the amount of wages and salaries paid by the government. As regards capital formation by the government, this is treated as par with capital formation by private enterprises.

3. **Treatment of income generated by foreign firms.** The third major problem arises with regard to the treatment of income arising out of activities of the foreign firms in a country. Should their income form a part of the national income of the country in which they are located or should it belong to the national income of the country owning the firms? On this point, the IMF viewpoint which is generally accepted is that production and income arising from a foreign enterprise should be ascribed to the country in which production takes place. However, profits earned by foreign companies are credited to the parent country.

Difficulties of Measuring National Income in India

In developing countries like India, we face some special difficulties in estimating national income. Some of these difficulties are given below:

1. A great difficulty in estimating national income in the developing countries like India arises because of the *prevalence of non-monetised transactions in such countries* so that a considerable part of the output does not come into the market at all. Agriculture still being largely in the nature of subsistence farming in these countries, a major part of output is consumed at the farm itself. The national statistician, therefore, has to face the problem of finding a suitable measure of value for this part of national output.

2. Because of illiteracy in the developing countries most producers have no idea of the quantity and value of their output and do not follow the practice of keeping regular accounts. This makes the task of getting reliable information from a large number of petty producers all the more difficult."

3. Because of underdevelopment, *occupational specialisation is still incomplete*, so that there is a lack of differentiation in economic functioning. An individual may receive income partly from farm ownership, partly from manual work in industry in the slack season, etc. This makes the task of estimating national income very difficult.

4. Another difficulty in measuring national income in the developing countries arises because *production, both agricultural and industrial, is unorganised* and scattered in these countries. This does not admit of easy calculation. In India, agriculture, cottage industries and indigenous banking are some

of the production sectors which are unorganised and scattered. An assessment of output produced by self-employed agriculturists, small producers and owners of household enterprises in the unorganised sectors requires an element of guess work which makes the figure for national income unreliable.

5. The greatest difficulty in the measurement of national income in the developing countries is general *lack of adequate statistical data*. Inadequacy, non-availability and unreliability of statistics is a great handicap in measuring national income in these countries. As stated above, statistical information regarding agriculture and allied occupations, and household enterprises is not available. Even the statistical information regarding the enterprises in the organised sector is sketchy and unreliable. There is no accurate information available regarding consumption, investment expenditure and savings of either rural or urban population.

NOMINAL GNP AND REAL GNP

Nominal GNP, as explained above, is the money value of all final goods and services produced in a year. This money value is obtained using current year market prices of final goods and services produced. However, Nominal GNP does not truly indicate the real performance or economic growth of a country over time if prices are changing. While nominal GNP may be increasing due to rise in price level, the quantity of goods and services produced may remain constant. Therefore, in order to estimate to what extent the amount of final goods and services produced has increased we have to eliminate the effect of change in prices on the nominal value of GNP in the current year. To do so the economists evaluate the output of final goods and services produced in a year using the market prices that prevaited in a certain chosen year, called as the *base year*. Estimates of India's real GNP which were made using 1993-94 as the base year has now been changed to the year 1999-2000. Thus, in India now market prices of the year 1999-2000 are used to estimate the real GNP which is also called *national income at constant prices*.

How this valuation is done using the market prices of a base year can be illustrated through a simple numerical example. Suppose an imaginary economy produces only four final goods, namely, wheat, standard cloth, milk and computers whose prices in the current year 2006-07 and the base year (i.e., 1999-2000) are given in column 3 and 5 of Table–1. The amounts of final goods, wheat, cloth, milk and computers in the current year 2006-07 are given in column 2.

Table – 1. Estimation of Real GNP

Final Goods	*Quantities produced in 2006-07*	*Market Prices in 2006-07* (₹)	*Value of Final Goods at Current market Prices of 2006-07*	*Market Price in base year* (1999-2000)	*Value of Final Goods at base year (1999-2000) prices*
1	2	3	4	5	6
Wheat (quintals)	650	700 per quintal	4,55,000	550	3,57,500
Standard cloth (metres)	345	120 per metre	41,400	100	34,500
Milk (litres)	520	15 per litre	7,800	12	6,240
Computers (Nos.)	200	2500 per unit	50,00,000	18000	3,66,0000
			5504200		3998240

In order to obtain the *nominal GNP* for the current year 2006-07 we multiply the quantities of four final commodities by the market prices of the current year 2006-07 and the results are given in column 4. By adding up the market values of all the final goods at current prices we get the total value equal to ₹ 5504200 for the year 2006-07 ₹ 5504200 is the nominal GNP for the current year 2006-07.

For obtaining the value of *real GNP* for the current year 2006-07 we multiply the outputs of final goods produced in the current year 2006-07 by the prices of the base year (1999-2000), and record the estimates in column 6. Summing up the values of four final goods evaluated at base-year prices we get the total estimate of ₹ 3998240 which is the real GNP (or gross national income at constant prices) for the current year 2006-07.

It may be noted that real GNP and nominal GNP for the base year will be the same.

It will noticed from Table–1 that for the current year 2006-07, whereas the value of nominal GNP is equal to ₹ 5504200, the real GNP is only ₹ 3998240. This is because market prices have risen between the base year (1999-2000) and the current year 2006-07.

The calculation of real GNP helps us to know whether the availability of real goods and services in the economy has increased over time. *Besides, by calculating the percentge change of real GNP in a year enables us to measure rate of economic growth in a year*. Further, it is real GNP that is often used for making comparisons of international standards of living and rates of economic growth of various countries.

Finally, with the help of nominal GNP and real GNP we can measure rate of inflation that has taken place over time. This measure of rate of inflation is known as **GNP deflator**. This is calculated as follows :

$$\text{GNP Deflator} = \frac{\text{Nominal GNP of a year}}{\text{Real GNP of the year}} \times 100$$

LIMITATIONS OF GDP CONCEPT AS A MEASURE OF SOCIAL WELFARE

National income, or GNP, as explained in the last chapter, measures the value of aggregate output of goods and services produced in a year. Since goods and services satisfy the wants of the people, national income or GNP has often been used as a measure of satisfaction or economic welfare of the people. The greater the magnitude of national income, the greater the level of economic welfare. Besides, economic progress or what is now generally called economic growth has been measured in terms of increase in national income (that is, increase in GNP or NNP) in terms of total or per capita income. In recent years doubts have been expressed about the validity of national income or gross national product (GNP) as a measure and index of economic welfare.

It has been asserted by several modern economists that national income as it is usually defined is not a satisfactory measure of economic welfare. According to them, in order to obtain a true measure of economic welfare, some adjustments both in the form of additions and subtractions have to be made in the aggregate of national income. National income, as it is usually conceived and measured, includes some things that do not increase welfare of the people. Therefore, such things ought to be excluded in order to get a true measure of economic welfare. This true measure of economic welfare is now often called "*Net Economic Welfare*" or simply *NEW*. On the other hand, the usual concept of national income excludes some goods and services which increase satisfaction of the people and therefore ought to be included in any good index of Net Economic Welfare.

As regards the things that ought to be added to obtain the index of Net Economic Welfare (NEW), the first important thing is the *value of satisfaction that people derive from leisure*. The usual concept of national income (or GNP) does not attach any significance to the amount of leisure people enjoy. However, the individuals derive satisfaction not only from the consumption of goods and services but also from leisure they have. Therefore, for constructing any index of net economic welfare, the value of leisure which the people enjoy must also be included. For example, if the average working hours are reduced, this is likely to reduce national production or national income but may raise welfare of the people by enabling them to enjoy more leisure.

The other important items that ought to be added to obtain a true measure of welfare are the *non-marketed personal services* (that is, the personal services which are not sold and purchased in the market) which also greatly raise the satisfaction and welfare of the people. For instance, services rendered by the housewives to the family members greatly add to their welfare but they are not recorded in national income accounting. Likewise, personal services rendered by the individuals to themselves such as gardening, painting one's own house significantly raise their welfare but do not get registered in the national income or GNP. Hence in order to get any true index of economic welfare, the value of non-market activities such as personal services which increase welfare ought to be incorporated.

As regards the items that have to be deducted from the national income, mention may be made of those harmful effects which result from increase in output. As is well known, the production of modern industries pollutes the environment such as polluting air, water and calmness which significantly reduce welfare of the people. Though modern industrialization has greatly increased national income of the countries but by causing *air pollution, water pollution and noise* has tended to reduce the welfare of the people. Therefore, for preparing a measure of net welfare, negative values ought to be assigned to the *environment pollution* that results from the production of goods and services. The various forms of pollution of environment have often been referred to as *costs of economic growth*, which like other costs, have to be deducted to obtain the index of net economic welfare.

Apart from environment pollution, certain other deductions on account of wasteful and non-productive expenditure such as Government expenditure on police and law courts so as to maintain law and order and on defence to protect the country from external aggression. These have been called "*regrettable costs*", because economists consider them regrettable necessities expenditure on which does not lead to increase in welfare of the people. Hence expenditure on them should be excluded from GNP to arrive at the measure of net economic welfare.

To sum up, the relation between national income (GNP) and Net Economic Welfare (NEW) can be represented as follows:

Real GNP
– Depreciation
+ Value of leisure
+ Value of non-market activities (*i.e.*, services of housewives and personal services)
– Environment pollution
– Regrettable costs
= Net Economic Welfare

But it is worth-mentioning that even the measure of Net Economic Welfare (NEW) as defined above does not truly indicate the welfare enjoyed by the people. There are other things which play a significant role in determining welfare of a nation and which do not get registered in national income or in Net Economic Welfare. Thus, *composition of national output* as between wage goods and luxuries and also the *distribution of goods between individuals* determine welfare to a great extent. If with the increase in total national income and per capita income, the rich are getting richer and the poor getting poorer, then this growth in national income and per capita income cannot be said to promote welfare. Professor Hicks rightly remarks, "*the national income only measure the total volume of goods and services at the disposal of the community during the year; it can tell us nothing, for example, about the way in which the national income is divided up between rich and poor.*"[1]

Further national income and per capita income are also not true measures of welfare because they do not consider the composition of output. A country's national income and per capita income may be very high but the well-being of the people may be very low because the national output consist of a larger quantity of war material. This is a very important factor because it is well known fact that various countries are spending quite a large part of national budgets on the manufacture of

1. J.R. Hicks, *The Social Framework*.

war materials and the greater the expenditure on the defence forces, the smaller will be the actual well-being of the people, given the size of national and per capita income.

Similarly, the well-being of the people also depends upon the relative proportions of wage-goods (necessities) and luxuries in the composition of national product. It may be noted that in a country if luxuries are being produced in relatively greater quantities than the wage-goods, then in that case while the few rich will be rolling in luxuries, the poor will be deprived of even sufficient quantities of necessities of life. Likewise, national and per capita income do not accurately reflect improvements in the quality of products. This is a shortcoming because improvements in the quality of products affect the economic welfare of the people as much as the increase in quantities of goods.

Lastly, the increase in national income does not truly indicate the increase in welfare of the people because it does not take into account *how the national income is being produced and how the increase in it has been brought about*. If increase is national income has been brought about by making workers work longer hours which impair their health and efficiency, then this increase in national income will not promote welfare but will adversely affect it. Similarly, if the increase in national income has been obtained by introducing labour-saving machinery throwing out a large number of workers out of employment, this growth in national income which increases unemployment and therefore cannot lead to the increase in social welfare.

Accounting for Environment Pollution and Natural Resource Depletion in National Income Accounting: The Concept of Green GNP

We have explained above the limitations of GDP or GNP as a measure of welfare. In recent years the economists have realised that in national income accounting two aspects or costs of producing GDP need to be incorporated in estimating GDP or national income so that it should truly reflect welfare of the people. These real costs are of two types. First, *when producing GDP firms pollute the air and water which adversely affects the welfare of the people*. Thus, it has been found that while producing goods the firms pollute the river water by dumping their wasters in local rivers. Similarly, the factories in the urban areas using oil and coal emit smoke and gas that pollute the air which harms those who live in the surrounding area. Therefore, in estimating real GDP or national income the costs of pollution of air and water by the firms in the production process of goods must be subtracted to arrive at what has been called ***green* GDP or green *GNP*.**

Another important aspect of producing GDP which requires adjustment for calculating green GDP is **depletion of natural resources** such as oil, forests, coal and natural gas resources. Conventional national income accounting does not take into account the depletion of natural resources. For example, when oil drilling machines pump out oil from an underground field, it leads to the depletion of the non-renewable resources but no deduction is made to account for the *depletion of oil reserves* in national income accounting. In fact, the depletion of natural resources should be treated as a type of *negative inventory investment* which if accounted for in national income accounting would tend to lower the GDP estimates, other things remaining the same. Likewise, measuring the true cost of timber from cutting trees of the forests which causes not only destruction of forests–a natural resource–but also soil erosion. The damage caused by cutting trees and thereby destroying forests and causing soil erosion be assessed and evaluated and accordingly proper deduction be made on this count in estimation of real GDP. In this connection the loss due to destruction of forests can be better understood from the damage and devastation caused by floods and landslides in May 2013 in Uttarakhand in India which was the result of cutting of trees in the forests nearby the rivers passing through them. It follows from above that "*ideal accounting system, the economic costs of environment degradation would be subtracted in the calculation of a firm's contribution to output and all activities that improve the environment because they provide real economic benefits to the people be added to output.*"[2]

In this regard some western economists have pointed out that some developing countries in their attempt to speed up economic growth and raising their GDP as rapidly as possible have overexploited

2. Andrew B. Abel, Ben S. Bernanke and Dean Croushore, *Macroeconomics*, 7th edition, Pearson, 2011, p. 29.

the natural resources and caused a good deal of environment pollution and natural resources degradation, they therefore suggest that costs of environment pollution and natural resources degradation are incorporated in their estimates of growth of GDP and their growth policies need to be modified. However, in our view this is not entirely correct to blame the developing countries who want higher GDP growth rate to reduce poverty in their countries. As a matter of fact, it is the developed countries who in the past for achieving rapid industrial growth have contributed a lot to the emission of harmful gases such as carbon dioxide that have significantly contributed to the global warming affecting the welfare of the poor people of developing countries. As a matter of fact, they should not only provide financial assistance to the developing countries for the harm done to the global environment in their growth process in the past but also transfer technology that ensures protection of environment from the growth processes in poor developing countries.

SOME EXAMPLES OF NATIONAL INCOME CALCULATION

We solve below some numerical problems of calculation of national income by three methods, namely, expenditure method, income method and value added method.

Problem 1. *Calculate (1) GDP at market prices and (2) national income from the following information.*

	₹
Personal consumption expenditure	***6,500***
Indirect taxes less subsidies	***150***
State government consumption and investment expenditure	***500***
Central government consumption and investment expenditure	***2,000***
Change in business inventories	***100***
Gross private domestic fixed investment	***1,200***
Exports	***900***
Net factor payments to rest of the world	***– 100***
Imports	***1,200***
Depreciation	***200***

DU BA(Hons.) 2006

Solution.

(*i*) GDP_{MP} = (Private Consumption Expenditure + Gross private investment (both fixed and inventories) + Gov. Expenditure (both State and Central) + Net exports (X–M))

= 6500 + (1200 + 100) + (500 + 2000) + (900 – 1200)

= 6500 + 1300 + 2500 – 300

= 10,000

(*ii*) *National Income*. National income is net national product at factor cost (NNP_{FC}). Therefore, to find out *net* domestic product at factor cost we have to deduct depreciation and net indirect taxes from GDP_{MP} and to get *national* income we have to deduct net factor payments to the rest of the world. Thus

NI or $NNP_{FC} = GDP_{MP}$ – Depreciation – net Indirect taxes (*i.e.* indirect taxes less subsidies) – net factor payments to the rest of the world.

NI = 10,000 – 200 – 150 – 100

= 9550

Problem 2. *Calculate the national income and personal disposable income from the following information* :

GDP_{MP}	***6,000***
Receipts of factor income from the rest of the world	***150***
Payments of factor income to the rest of the world	***225***

Depreciation	***800***
Indirect taxes minus subsidies	***700***
Corporate Profits	***1,200***
Dividend	***600***
Transfer payments to persons	***1,300***
Personal Taxes	***1,500***

D.U. BA (Hons.) 2007

Solution.

(*i*) National Income is Net National Product at factor cost

NI or NNP_{FC} = GDP_{MP} – Depreciation – Net Indirect taxes + Net Factor income from abroad

= 6000 – 800 – 700 + (150 – 225)

= 6000 –1500 – 75

= 6000 – 1575

= 4425

(*ii*) Personal Disposable income = National Income – Retained Corporate Profits + Transfer Payments to Persons – Personal taxes

PDI = 4425 – (1200 – 600) + 1300 – 1500

= 4425 – 600 + 1300 – 1500

= 3625

(Note: Retained corporate profits equals corporate profits minus dividends paid to shareholders)

Problem 3. *Calculate (1) Net Domestic Product at market Prices and (2) National Income from the following date of all the enterprises in an economy.*

		₹ in Crore
(i)	***Subsidies***	***10***
(ii)	***Sales***	***1000***
(iii)	***Closing stock***	***100***
(iv)	***Indirect taxes***	***50***
(v)	***Intermediate Consumption***	***300***
(vi)	***Opening stock***	***200***
(vii)	***Consumption of fixed capital***	***150***
(viii)	***Net factor income from abroad***	***10***

Solution.

NDP_{MP} and National Income be obtained through *value added method.* Net Domestic Product at Market Prices is the sum of net value added by all enterprises in the economy.

Value of output = Sales + Change in stock

= 1000 + (Closing Stock – Opening Stock)

= 1000 + (100 – 200)

= 900 crore

$\Sigma NVA_{MP} = NDP_{MP}$ = Value of output–Intermediate Consumption – Consumption of fixed capital

= 900 – 300 – 150

= 450 crore

National Income (NNP_{FC}) = NDP_{MP} – Net Indirect taxes + Net factor income from abroad

$= 450 - (50 - 10) + 10$

$= 450 - 40 + 10$

$= 420$ crore

Problem 4. *On the basis of the following data about the economy which consists of only two firms, finds out:*

(*a*) *Value added by firms A and B.*

(*b*) *Gross Domestic Product at market prices and factor cost*

		₹ *in Crore*
(i)	***Sales by firm A***	***200***
(ii)	***Purchases from B by firm A***	***80***
(iii)	***Purchases from A by firm B***	***120***
(iv)	***Sales by firm B***	***400***
(v)	***Closing stock of firm A***	***40***
(vi)	***Closing stock of firm B***	***70***
(vii)	***Opening stock of firm A***	***50***
(viii)	***Opening stock of firm B***	***90***
(ix)	***Indirect taxes paid by both firms***	***60***

Solution.

Firms	**Output**		**Intermediate cost**	**Value added**
Firm A:	Sale	= 200	Purchases From B = 80	190 – 80 = 110
	Change in stock	= 40 – 50 = –10		
	Total Value of Output	= 200 – 10 = 190		
Firm B:	Sales	= 400	Purchases From A = 120	380 – 120 = 260
	Change in stock	= 70 – 90 = –20		
	Total Value of Output	= 400 + (–20) = 380		

Gross domestic product at market prices (GDP_{MP}) $= \Sigma GVA = 110 + 260 = 370$ crore

GDP_{MP} is sum total of GVA_{MP} of all firms

Gross domestic product at factor cost (GDP_{FC}) $= GDP_{MP}$ – Net Indirect taxes

$= 370 - 60$

$= 310$ crore

Problem 5. *Calculate Gross Domestic Product at Market Prices and Net National Product at Factor Cost and Gross Domestic Product at Factor Cost from the following data:*

		₹ *in Crore*
(i)	***Net indirect taxes***	***38***
(ii)	***Consumption of fixed capital***	***34***
(iii)	***Net factor income from abroad***	***(–) 3***
(iv)	***Rent***	***100***
(v)	***Profits***	***125***

(vi)	***Interest***	***20***
(vii)	***Mixed Income of self employed***	***120***
(viii)	***Wages and salaries***	***170***
(ix)	***Employers' contribution to social security schemes***	***30***

Solution.

Note that (*viii*) wages and salaries and (*ix*) Employer's contribution to social security schemes together constitute compensation of employees

Net national product at factor cost (NNP_{FC}) = Wages and salaries + Employers' contribution to social security schemes + Rent + Profit + Interest + Mixed Income of Self employed + Net factor income from abroad

$= 170 + 30 + 100 + 125 + 20 + 120 - 3$

$= 562$ crore

GDP_{MP} = NNP_{FC} + Net Indirect taxes + Consumption of fixed capital – Net factor income from abroad

$= 562 + 38 + 34 - (-3)$

$= 562 + 38 + 34 + 3$

$= 637$ crore

GDP_{FC} = GDP_{MP} – Net Indirect Taxes

$= 637 - 38 = 599$ crore

Problem 6. *Calculate gross domestic product at market prices (GDP_{MP}), gross domestic product at factor cost (GDP_{FC}) and net national product at factor cost (NNP_{FC}) from the following data:*

		₹ in Crore
(i)	***Private final consumption expenditure***	***290***
(ii)	***Government's final consumption expenditure***	***50***
(iii)	***Subsidies***	***20***
(iv)	***Gross domestic fixed capital formation***	***105***
(v)	***Indirect taxes***	***70***
(vi)	***Depreciation (i.e., Consumption of Fixed Capital)***	***45***
(vii)	***Net factor income from abroad***	***(–) 5***
(viii)	***Net addition to stock***	***15***
(ix)	***Net exports***	***(–) 5***

Solution :

Gross domestic product at market prices (GDP_{MP}) = Private final consumption expenditure + Government's final consumption expenditure + Gross domestic fixed capital formation + Change in stock + Net exports

$= 290 + 50 + (105 + 15) + (-5)$

$= 290 + 50 + 105 + 15 - 5$

$= 455$ crore

GDP_{FC} = GDP_{MP} – Net Indirect Taxes

$= 455 -$ (Indirect Taxes – Subsidies)

$$= 455 - (70 - 20) = 405 \text{ crore}$$

$$NNP_{MP} = GDP_{MP} - \text{Depreciation}$$
$$= 455 - 45$$
$$= 410 \text{ crore}$$

$$NDP_{FC} = NDP_{MP} - \text{Indirect taxes} + \text{Subsides}$$
$$= 410 - 70 + 20$$
$$= 360 \text{ crore}$$

$$NNP_{FC} = NDP_{FC} + \text{Net factor income from abroad}$$
$$= 360 + (-5)$$
$$= 360 - 5$$
$$= 355 \text{ crore}$$

QUESTIONS FOR REVIEW

1. Define gross domestic product? Are value of exports and imports included in it?
2. Distinguish between final goods and intermediate goods. Why are intermediate goods not included in gross domestic product of a country?
3. What are the components of gross domestic product? Explain them briefly.
4. Distinguish between gross national product (GNP) and gross domestic product (GDP. In this connection explain 'net factor income from abroad'.
5. Define *'national income'*. How is it different from gross domestic product (GDP)? Explain.
6. Distinguish between Net Domestic Product at Market Prices (NDP_{MP}) and Net Domestic Product at Factor Cost (NDP_{FC}).
7. What is meant by *'value added'*? Explain how national income is measured by value added method.
8. Explain the following terms:
   (*i*) Net value added
   (*ii*) Net factor income from abroad
   (*iii*) Transfer Payments by the Government
9. Distinguish between *nominal* GDP and *Real* GDP. Which concept is used for measuring economic growth of a country?
10. Explain how national income is measured through expenditure method. What types of expenditure are included in measuring national income of a country?
11. Explain 'income method' of measuring national income. Which of the following terms will be included while calculating national income of a country through income method?
    (*i*) Transfer Payments by the government to individuals in a year
    (*ii*) Imputed rent of self-occupied houses
    (*iii*) Hawala money
    (*iv*) Windfall gains
    (*v*) The receipts from the sale of second-hand goods.
12. Is gross domestic product (GDP) a true indicator of welfare of the society? Explain.
13. What is meant by *net economic welfare?* How is it derived or obtained from the estimate of GNP?
14. On the basis of the following data about an economy which consists of only two firms, find out:
    (*a*) Value added by Firms A and B.
    (*b*) Gross domestic product at market prices.

		₹ *in Crore*
(i)	***Exports by Firm A***	***40***
(ii)	***Imports by Firm A***	***100***
(iii)	***Sales to households by Firm A***	***180***
(iv)	***Sales to Firm B by Firm A***	***80***
(v)	***Sales to Firm A by Firm B***	***60***
(vi)	***Sales to households by Firm B***	***120***

(**Hint.** Note that value of exports by firm A will be a part of value of output, whereas imports by it will be a part of intermediate cost of production.)

(**Ans.** GDP_{MP} = 240 crore)

15. From the following data calculate Gross National Product and Net National Product at market prices by (*i*) income method, and (*ii*) expenditure method.

		₹ *in Crore*
(i)	***Mixed income of self-employed***	***400***
(ii)	***Compensation of employees***	***500***
(iii)	***Private final consumption expenditure***	***900***
(iv)	***Net factor income from abroad***	***(–)20***
(v)	***Net direct taxes***	***100***
(vi)	***Consumption of fixed capital***	***120***
(vii)	***Net domestic capital formation***	***280***
(viii)	***Net Exports***	***(–)30***
(ix)	***Profits***	***350***
(x)	***Rent***	***100***
(xi)	***Government final consumption expenditure***	***300***

CHAPTER 4

Classical Theory of Income and Employment : Full Employment Model

Economy in the Long Run : The Classical Full-Employment Model

Before explaining the Keynesian macrotheory of income and employment, it will be in the fitness of things to explain classical theory regarding income and employment determination. The study of classical theory of income and employment is essential because some of the aspects of classical theory are more relevant to the conditions prevailing in the developing countries and this theory highlights those factors which govern income and employment in these countries. While the Keynesian theory emphasises the role of effective demand in the determination of income and employment, classical economists believed that in a free-market economy there was always a tendency towards the establishment of full employment of labour and there was sufficient demand for the output produced. Note that Keynes called all economists who preceded him (including Marshall and Pigou) as classical economists.

CLASSICAL THEORY OF INCOME EMPLOYMENT : AN INTRODUCTORY ANALYSIS

Classical theory of employment and output is based on the following two basic notions:

1. Say's Law of Markets
2. Wage-price flexibility

We explain below these two notions of classical theory

Say's Law of Markets

According to the classical theory propounded by Ricardo and Adam Smith, levels of income and employment are governed by fixed capital stock on the one hand and wage-goods fund on the other. It may be noted in the beginning that the classical theory believes in full employment or near full employment prevailing in the economy. This belief of classical theory regarding the existence of full employment in the economy is based on *Say's Law of Markets* put forward by a French economist J.B. Say. According to Say's law, *"Supply creates its own demand"*. This implies that every increase in production made possible by the increase in the productive capacity or the stock of fixed capital will be sold in the market and there will be no problem of lack of demand. Thus, classical economists rule out the possibility of overproduction, there being no problem in selling the output produced. According to Say's Law, greater production automatically leads to the greater money incomes which create the market for the greater flow of goods produced. Thus, deficiency in demand being no problem, the process of capital accumulation and expansion of productive capacity will continue till all people are employed and there is no reason why the productive capacity created remains unutilized or underutilized. According to this theory, the income which is not spent on consumer goods and thus saved will become investment expenditure. Therefore, investment equals saving. Thus, the leakage in the income flow caused by the saving is made up by the investment expenditure. In this way, a given productive capacity continues to be fully utilized and no problem of deficiency of demand arises.

Classical economists thought that if price mechanism in a capitalist economy is allowed to work freely without any interference by the Government, there is a tendency towards full-employment in it. Of course, they admitted that in advanced capitalist economies often certain circumstances arise due to which they are not in full-employment equilibrium. But they firmly believed that there was always a tendency towards full-employment in the economy and certain economic forces automatically operate so as to move the economy towards full employment. Therefore, according to the classical economists, whenever there are lapses from full-employment level, these are removed automatically by the working of free price mechanism. The modern economists do not regard this aspect of classical theory of employment as valid and correct description of the real world. J.M. Keynes bitterly criticised the classical theory of automatic establishment of full-employment.

The classical model of employment was based upon two basic assumptions. The first assumption is that there is always enough expenditure or aggregate demand to purchase the total production at full-employment level of resources. In other words, in this theory the classical economists disregarded the problem of deficiency of demand for purchasing goods produced at full-employment level of resources. The second assumption is that even when deficiency of aggregate expenditure or demand arises, the ***prices, wages and interest would adjust quickly*** so that equilbrium is restored at full-employment level of output.

The classical view that there was no problem of deficiency of expenditure and demand was based upon Say's law of markets. J.B. Say has been a famous French economist of the 19th century. Say's law is based upon the fact that every production of goods also creates incomes equal to the value of goods produced and these incomes are spent on purchasing these goods. In other words, production of goods itself creates its own purchasing power, that is, demand for buying them. Therefore, Say's law is expressed as "***supply creates its own demand***", that is, the supply of goods produced creates demand for it equal to its own value with the result that the problem of general overproduction does not arise. In this way in Say's law, the possibility of lack of aggregate demand has not been visualised.

Say's law expresses an important fact about the working of a free-enterprise economy. The fact is that the source of demand for goods is the incomes earned by the various factors of production employed for their production. All unemployed and idle labourers and other resources when employed for production, create their own demand because the total incomes which they earn create equal market demand for the goods produced by their employment. When a new entrepreneur employs some factors of production and pays them their monetary rewards, he not only increases the supply of goods but also at the same time creates the demand for them. Therefore, it is the production which creates market or demand for goods. Production is the only source of demand. Dillard rightly writes that *"Say's Law of Markets is the denial of the possibility of deficiency of aggregate demand. Therefore, employment of more resources will always be profitable and will take place to the point of full-employment, subject to the limitation that the contributors of the resources are willing to accept rewards no greater than their physical productivity justifies. There could be no general unemployment, according to this view, if workers will account what they are worth."*[1]

We thus see that according to Say's law aggregate expenditure or demand will always be such that all resources are fully employed. The factors which participate in productive activity and earn incomes from it, they spend a good part of their incomes on consumer goods and some part they save. But, according to classical economists, the savings by the individuals are actually spent on investment or capital goods. *Since saving when invested also becomes expenditure or demand, in classical theory the whole income is spent, partly on consumption and partly on investment.* There is thus no reason for any leakage in the income stream and hence supply creates its own demand. Now, a question arises as to how in classical theory saving becomes equal to investment expenditure. According to the classical theory, it is the rate of interest which makes investment equal to saving. When savings of the people increase, the rate of interest declines. As a result of fall in the rate of interest, demand for investment rises and in this way investment becomes equal to the increased

1. D. Dillard, *Economics of J.M. Keynes*.

savings. Hence, according to the classical economists, it is the interest rate changes that bring about equality between saving and investment and, therefore, Say's law applies in spite of saving by the people. This guarantees full employment in the economy. In other words, it is changes in the rate of interest due to which the withdrawal of some money from the income stream as a result of savings automatically comes back to it in the form of investment expenditure and therefore income flow continues unchanged and supply goes on creating its own demand.

Wage-Price Flexibility and Full-Employment

The classical economists also proved the validity of the assumption of full-employment with another fundamental logic. According to them, the amount of production which the business firms can supply does not depend only on aggregate demand or expenditure but also on the prices of products. When aggregate demand for goods and services decline due to the fall in investment, the economy will still remain at full-employment level of output. According to them, this happens because product prices fall quickly so that quantity demanded increases to restore equilibrium at full-employment level of output. In this way, they expressed the view that in spite of the decline in aggregate demand caused by the decline in investment, the real output, income and employment will not fall because the fall in prices of products brings about balance between demand and supply at full-employment level of output.

Classical economists thought that a free-market capitalist economy is self-correcting. Owing to the intense competition between the sellers of products as a consequence of the fall in demand, the prices will decline. This is because when aggregate expenditure on goods or demand for them declines, the various sellers and producers reduce the prices of their products so as to avoid the excessive accumulation of stocks of goods with them. Hence, according to the classical logic, decline in demand will bring down the prices of products and not the amount of production and employment. But now a question arises as to what extent the sellers or producers will tolerate the decline in prices. However, to make their business profitable they will have to reduce the prices of the factors of production such as labour. When due to the decrease in demand for output, demand for labour declines, this will cause a fall in wages quickly so that labour demanded increases to restore labour-market equilibrium at full-employment. Thus, a fall in wages of labour ensures that all workers will get employment. If some workers do not want to work at reduced wages, they will not get any job or employment and therefore will remain unemployed. But, according to classical economists, those workers who do not want to work at lower wages and thus remain unemployed are only *voluntarily unemployed*. This voluntary unemployment is not real unemployment. According to the classical thought, it is ***involuntary unemployment*** which is not possible in a free-market capitalist economy. All those workers who want to work at the going wage rate determined by market forces will get employment. That is, full employment of labour continues to prevail due to quick adjustment of wages.

During the period 1929-33 when there was a great depression in capitalist economies, a renowned neoclassical economist Pigou suggested a cut in wage rates in order to remove huge and widespread unemployment prevailing at that time. According to him, the cause of depression or unemployment was that the Government and trade unions of workers were preventing the free working of the capitalist economies and were artificially keeping the wage rates at high levels. He expressed the view that if the wage rates were cut down, demand for labour would increase so that all would get employment. It is important to mention here what has been called *Pigou effect* or *real balance effect*. Pigou pointed out that all-round cut in wages will cause price level to fall. The fall in price level will lead to the increase in real value of money assets such as stock of money, deposits in banks, bonds of government or private companies held by them. This implies that due to fall in price level, the purchasing power of their money assets will increase. As a result, they would feel *better off* or richer which will lead to the increase in their consumption demand for goods and services which will prevent the fall in any aggregate demand due to all-round cut in wages. Later D. Patinkin supported Pigou's view about favourable effect of reduction in wages on fall in price level which according to him will lead to what he calls increase in *real money balances*. This increase in real money balances, as pointed out above, will have a favourable effect on demand for goods. However, critics have pointed out that the effect of increase in real money balances on consumes' demand for goods and services is quantitatively insignificant and therefore one cannot rely on this to create enough demand to counteract the fall in demand for goods and services as a result of all-round cut in wages. J.M. Keynes challenged the classical theory and put forward a new theory of income and employment. He brought about a fundamental change in economic thought regarding the determination of income and employment in a free-market capitalist economy. Therefore, it is often said that *Keynes brought about a revolution in our economic theory and laid the foundation of macroeconomic theory*.

THE CLASSICAL MODEL OF EMPLOYMENT AND OUTPUT (INCOME) : A DETAILED ANALYSIS

Classical economists such as Adam Smith and Ricardo maintained that the growth of income and employment depends on the growth of the stock of fixed capital and inventories of wage goods. But, in the short run, the stock of fixed capital and wage goods inventories are given and constant. According to them, even in the short run full-employment of labour force would tend to prevail as the economy would not experience any problem of deficiency of demand. On the basis of their theory they denied the possibility of the existence of *involuntary unemployment* in the economy. The short-run classical theory of income and employment can be explained through the following three stages:

1. *Determination of income and employment when there is no saving and* investment;
2. *Determination of income and employment in an economy with saving and investment; and*
3. *Determination of income and employment : Role of money and prices.*

Determination of Income and Employment in the Short Run Without Saving and Investment

According to the classical theory, the magnitude of national income and employment depends on the aggregate production function and the supply and demand for labour. To show this let us assume that the economy produces one homogeneous and divisible good, say corn. Let symbol Y stand for output of this good. To produce this good we require two factors of production : (1) labour which we denote by N and (2) capital which we denote by K. Thus we have the following aggregate prodcution function

$$Y = F(N, K, T) \qquad ...(i)$$

In the short run the stock of capital (i.e. plant and equipment) is assumed to be fixed. The state of technology is also assumed to be constant in the short run. Thus, rewritting the aggregate production function we have

$$Y = F(N, \bar{K}, \bar{T}) \qquad ...(ii)$$

The bar over the symbol K and T for capital and technology indicates that stock of capital and technology is fixed. It is worth noting that changes in capital stock and technology will cause a shift in the production function.

Therefore, with a fixed capital stock and a given and constant technology, the output Y (or what is also the real income) would increase only when employment of labour N increases. That is, employment of labour and output (income) rise or fall together. Now, according to classical theory, with a fixed capital stock and given technology as employment of labour increases, marginal product of labour would diminish. This is the famous law of diminishing returns of the classical economists.

Labour Market Equilibrium

In the classical model wages and employment are determined by demand for and supply of labour. In this model the demand for labour is derived from this short-run production function, that is, diminishing marginal product of labour. The classical theory assumes perfect competition in both the factor and product markets . Further, assuming that the firms which undertake the task of production attempt to maximise profits, they will employ labour until the marginal product of labour is equal to the given real wage rate. It may be noted that real wage rate is given by nominal wage rate divided by the general price level, that is, real wage rate $= \frac{W}{P}$ where W is the nominal or money wage rate and P is the average price level. Thus, a firm will employ so much labour at which

$$\frac{W}{P} = MP_N$$

where MP_N stands for marginal product of labour.

At a lower real wage rate, more labour will be demanded or employed by the firms and *vice versa*. Thus, the demand curve for labour is derived from the marginal product curve of labour. In fact, the former coincides with the latter. Thus demand function for labour can be written as

$$N^d = f\left(\frac{W}{P}\right) \quad \ldots (iii)$$

This shows that demand for labour (N^d) is a function of real wage $\left(\frac{W}{P}\right)$.

Consider Fig. 4.1 where *MP* curve depicts the diminishing marginal product of labour with a given stock of fixed capital and a given state of technology. As explained just above, marginal product (*MP*) curve of labour also represents the demand curve of labour (N^d).

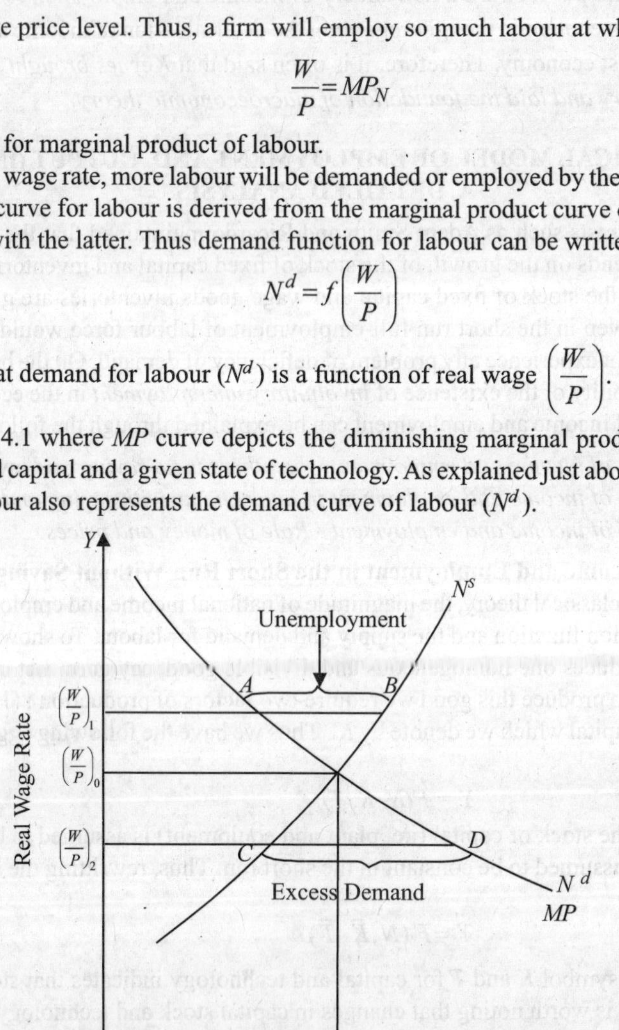

Fig. 4.1. *Labour-Market Equilibrium : Determination of Employment and Wages*

On the other hand, the *supply of labour by the households in the economy depends on their pattern of preference between income and leisure*. The classical theory assumes that in the short run when population does not vary, supply curve of labour slopes upward. Now, what is the rationale behind the upward-sloping supply curve of labour. This is based on the assumption that households or individual workers maximise their utility or satisfaction in their choice of work (which yields them income) and leisure. When real wage rate rises, two effects work in opposite direction. It may be noted that real wage is the opportunity cost or relative price of lesiure. When real wage rate rises leisure becomes relatively more expensive, that is, opportunity cost or price of leisure in terms of income forgone by not working goes up. This induces the individual to work more (*i.e.,* supply more labour hours) and thereby substitutes income for leisure. This is the substitution effect. On the other hand, with a rise in real wage rate individuals become relatively richer than before, and this induces them to consume more of all commodities (including leisure which is regarded as a normal commodity). This is income effect of the rise in real wage rate which tends to increase leisure and reduce labour-hours supplied. The classical economists believed that substitution effect is larger than income effect of the rise in real wage rate and as a result supply of labour increases with the rise in wage rate. Thus the supply function of labour can be written as

$$N^S = g\left(\frac{W}{P}\right) \qquad \ldots (iv)$$

The above equation (*iv*) shows that supply of labour is a function of real wage rate $\left(\frac{W}{P}\right)$. At a higher real wage rate, more labour would be supplied and *vice versa*. It will be seen from Fig. 4.1 that supply and demand for labour are in equilibrium at the real wage rate $\left(\frac{W}{P}\right)_0$. Hence, given the supply and demand curves, the real wage rate $\left(\frac{W}{P}\right)_0$ is determined. It will be seen that ON_F labour is employed in this equilibrium situation. Thus, *in classical theory level of employment is determined by labour market equilibrium*. This *equilibrium between supply and demand for labour at the real wage rate* $\left(\frac{W}{P}\right)_0$ *implies that all those who offer their labour services at this wage rate are in fact employed.* There is neither excess supply of labour, nor excess demand for labour. In other words, there is no involuntary unemployment of labour in this equilibrium situation and full employment of labour prevails.

If somehow real wage rate in the labour market is higher than this equilibrium wage rate $\left(\frac{W}{P}\right)_0$, say it is equal to $\left(\frac{W}{P}\right)_1$, then it will be observed from Fig. 4.1 that excess supply of labour equal to *AB* would emerge. In other words, at real wage rate $\left(\frac{W}{P}\right)_1$, *AB* workers will be unemployed.

But given the competition among workers, the excess supply of labour at wage rate $\left(\frac{W}{P}\right)_1$ would cause the wage rate to fall to the equilibrium level $\left(\frac{W}{P}\right)_0$ at which the labour market is cleared. On the contrary, if somehow real wage rate in the labour market is $\left(\frac{W}{P}\right)_2$, the firms would demand more labour than is offered at this real wage rate. As a result of the competition among the firms to hire labour desired by them, the wage rate would go up to the equilibrium level $\left(\frac{W}{P}\right)_0$. At $\left(\frac{W}{P}\right)_0$ to repeat, all those who offer their labour services are in fact demanded and employed. *It therefore follows that at the real wage* $\left(\frac{W}{P}\right)_0$, *there is no involuntary unemployment, or, in other words, full-*

employment of labour prevails. Thus, it is the wage flexibility (i.e., quick adjustment in wage rate) which brings about this full-employment situation.

The Classical View of Self-Correction by a Free Market Economy

It will be relevant here to explain the classical view about the self-correction by the economy. When due to depression unemployment occurs in the economy, then through quick adjustment in wages full employment of labour is restored. The aggregate output increases to potential GDP level and thus economy comes out of slump. This is illustrated in Fig 4.2 where initially the labour market is in equilibrium at point E_0 at which demand curve for labour N^d intersects the supply curve of labour N^s and thereby determines N_0 level of employment and real wage rate $\frac{W_0}{P_0}$. Now suppose depression occurs in the economy and due to fall in aggregate output demand for labour decreases causing a shift in the demand curve for labour to the left (Fig. 4.2) where following the decrease in aggregate demand for output labour demand curve shifts to the left to $N_1{}^d$, supply curve of labour N^s remaining the same. At the initial wage rate $\frac{W_0}{P_0}$ fewer workers will be demanded than the number of workers who are willing to supply their labour at this wage rate. As a result (as is seen from Fig. 4.2) the excess supply of labour equal to KE_0 will emerge at this initial real wage rate $\frac{W_0}{P_0}$. However, in the classical full-employment model this excess supply of labour (*i.e.*, unemployment of workers) will cause real wage rate to fall to $\frac{W_0}{P_0}$ (where $W_1 < W_0$) at which new equilibrium between demand for and supply of labour is again established at point E_1. Note that even in this new labour market equilibrium at lower real wage rate $\frac{W_1}{P_0}$ full employment of labour prevails as all those who are willing

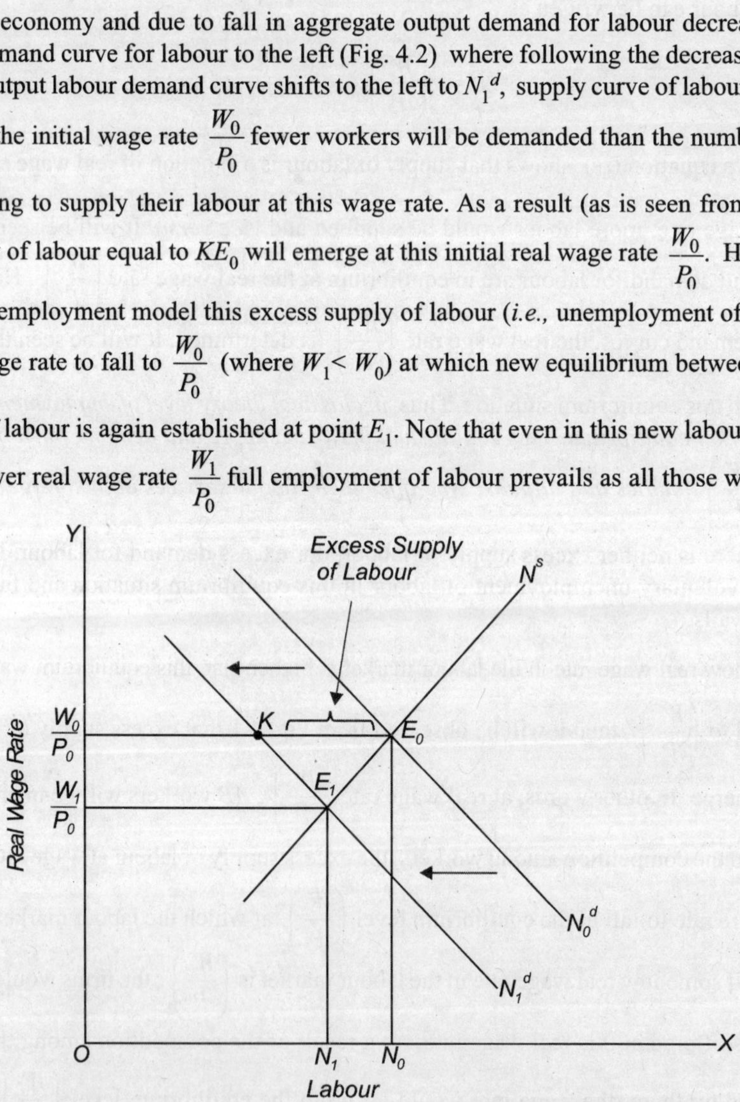

Fig. 4.2. *Adjustment of Real Wage Rate when Depression Occurs.*

to work at this real wage rate find employment. of course, N_0N_1 workers have voluntarily withdrawn themselves from labour force and therefore no one remains involuntarily unemployed.

Similarly, when due to depression demand for output declines, in the product market demand curve for output will shift to the left and given the supply curve of output, price of output will fall, say from P_0 to P_1 ($P_1 < P_0$) the real wage rate will rise to $\frac{W_1}{P_1}$ which in equilibrium will become equal to $\frac{W_0}{P_0}$ $\left(\text{that is, } \frac{W_1}{P_1} = \frac{W_0}{P_0}\right)$ and thereby equilibrium is established at the initial equilibrium point E_0 and thus full employment is restored. Thus *it is evident that in the classical model when depression or recession occurs then through quick adjustment of wages and prices* the economy corrects itself to attain full-employment equilibrium again.

Determination of Aggregate Output (GDP)

How much output will be produced in this full-employment situation can be readily known from the short-run aggregate production function *OY* drawn in the lower part of Fig. 4.2, which shows the relationship between employment of labour (*N*) and total output (*Y*), given the stock of fixed capital (*i.e.*, a set of machines, equipment and buildings) and given the technology. This short-run production function *OY* shows that as more workers are employed, output increases but at a diminishing rate, that is, there are *diminishing returns to labour*. It will be seen from the lower panel of Fig. 4.3 that, *given the stock of fixed capital and the state of technology*, full employment of labour ON_F produces OY_F output. This output OY_F of output will constitute the real income of the society and will be distributed between wages and profits. Thus sum of wages as reward for labour and total profits as reward for capital would constitute the total income of the society and would be equal to the national output OY_F produced.

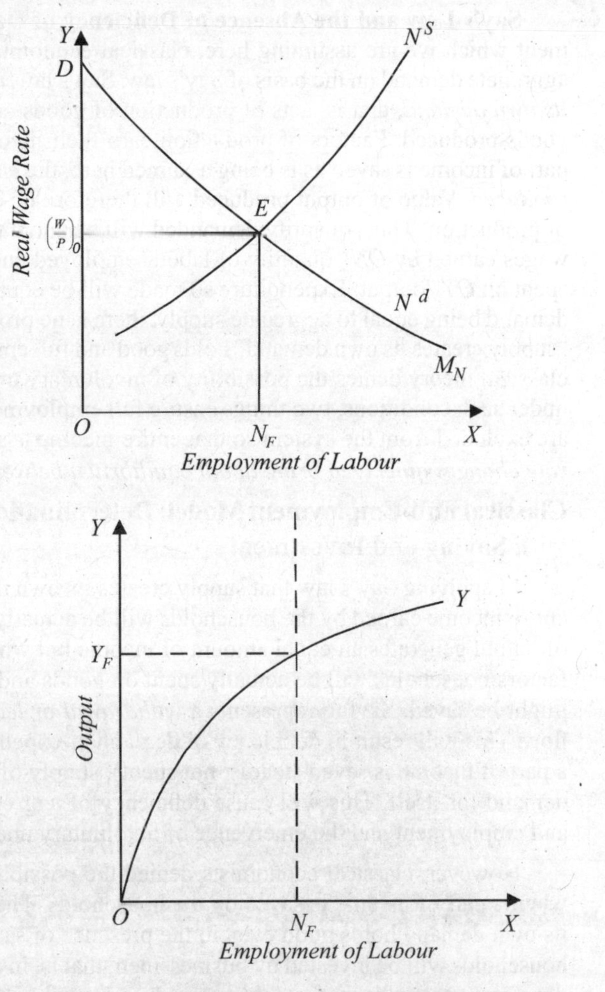

Fig. 4.3. *Classical Theory : Determination of Employment and Output*

It follows from above that the quick changes in the real wage rate upward or downward ensures that neither excess supply of labour, nor excess demand for labour will persist and thus equilibrium will be reached with full employment of labour in the economy. Further, given the stock of capital and the state of technology with this full employment of labour, total output or income of the economy equal to OY_F is determined. **The level of output OY_F is referred to as full-employment level of output or potential GDP** of the economy. This is also often called **aggregate supply.** The potential GDP or full-employment level of output is the amount of goods and services that producers are willing to produce, given their stock of fixed capital (machines, equipment and buildings) and the given technology, when labour market is in equilibrium and all workers who want the work at the going wage rate find employment. It will be seen from Fig. 4.3 that full employment of labour as determined by labour market equilibrium is N_F and given the short-run production function OY, potential GDP or full-employment output is Y_F (See lower part of Fig. 4.3). To conclude, *potential GDP or full-employment output is the level of output when with adjustment of wages labour market is in equilibrium and all workers who want to work at the going wage rate find employment and firms are using their plant and equipment at normal rates of their utilisation.*

Now, an important question to enquire is what guarantees that output produced by the full employment level of labour and capital (assumed as fixed in the short run) will be actually demanded. If this does not happen, then the problem of insufficient demand for output will emerge which will ultimately lead to reduction in output and employment and hence to the emergence of involuntary unemployment.

Say's Law and the Absence of Deficiency of Demand. In the absence of saving and investment which we are assuming here, classical economists ruled out the possibility of deficiency of aggregate demand on the basis of Say's law. Say's law, as mentioned above, states that *supply creates its own demand*, that is, acts of production of goods create demand equal to the value of output of goods produced. Factors of production earn their incomes during the process of production. If no part of income is saved as is being assumed here, the *entire income will be spent on consumer goods produced.* Value of output produced will therefore be equal to the income generated in the process of production. Thus, quantity demanded will be equal to the supply of output produced. In Fig. 4.3, wages earned by ON_F quantity of labour employed and profits earned by the entrepreneurs will be spent on OY_F output. Expenditure so made will be equal to the value of output produced. Aggregate demand being equal to aggregate supply, there is no problem of deficiency of demand. Say's law that "supply creates its own demand" holds good and full employment of labour is guaranteed. In this way classical theory denies the possibility of involuntary unemployment. It needs to be emphasised that under such conditions, two things ensure full employment. First, it is because saving and investment are excluded from the system so that entire income is spent on consumer goods. Second, *real wage rate changes quickly to bring about equilibrium between demand for and supply of labour.*

Classical Full-Employment Model: Determination of Income (Output) and Employment with Saving and Investment

In applying Say's law that supply creates its own demand an invalid assumption was made that entire income earned by the households will be actually spent. Although it is correct that production of output generates an equal amount of income but what is the guarantee that all income earned by factors/households will be actually spent on goods and services produced. In fact, a part of income might be saved. Saving represents a *withdrawal or leakage* of some income from the expenditure flow. This will result in deficiency of demand or expenditure on output of goods produced. Thus, if a part of income is saved (that is, not spent), supply of output produced would not create sufficient demand for itself. This will cause deficiency of aggregate demand which will cause fall in output and employment and the emergence of involuntary unemployment.

However, classical economists denied the possibility of deficiency of aggregate demand even when a part of income is saved by the households. They showed that Say's law that supply creates its own demand holds good even in the presence of saving. They argued that every rupee saved by households will be invested by businessmen, that is, investment expenditure will be equal to savings done by households. In fact, output produced consists of consumer goods and capital goods. Income earned from production will be partly spent on consumer goods and partly on investment in capital goods: When at full employment level of output what is not spent on consumer goods is saved and investment expenditure on capital goods made by businessmen equals this saving. Therefore, there is no deficiency of demand or expenditure and circular flow of income goes on undisturbed. Thus, when investment equals saving at full employment level of output, supply goes on creating its own demand to maintain full employment. Now, in bringing about equality between saving and investment, capital market plays a crucial role.

Capital-Market Equilibrium : Determination of Interest

Now, the pertinent question is what is the guarantee that investment expenditure will be equal to savings of the households. *According to classical economists, it is changes in the rate of interest that bring about equality between saving and investment.* Further, according to them, rate of interest is determined in the capital market by supply of savings and demand for investment. The investment demand is stipulated to be decreasing function of the rate of interest. At the lower rate of interest, more would be borrowed for investment. On the other hand, the savings of the people are taken to be the increasing function of the rate of interest, that is,the higher the rate of interest, the larger the savings and *vice versa.* The capital market will be in equilibrium at the rate of interest at which the demand for investment is equal to the supply of savings. The changes in rate of interest would cause investment and supply of savings to become equal. This is illustrated in Fig. 4.4. It will be seen that intersection of investment demand cuve *II* and the supply of savings curve *SS* determines the rate of interest i_0. At a higher rate of interest i_2, the investment demand is less than the intended supply of savings. Due to the excess supply of savings, rate of interest would fall to i_0. On the contrary, at a lower rate of interest, say i_1, the demand for investment exceeds the supply of savings. Now, due to the excess demand for investment in the capital market rate of interest would go up. Thus, it is at rate of interest i_0 that capital market is in equilibrium, *i.e.*, investment is equal to savings ($I = S$).

Now an important thing to know about classical theory is when due to decline in profit expectations of business firms investment falls as it happens in times of recession or depression, how it then explains that demand deficiency problem would not arise and equilibrium will continue to remain at full employment level. This is illustrated in Figure 4.5, where initially saving and investment are in equilibrium at rate of interest i_0. Now suppose that due to fall in profit expectations investment by business firms decreases by ΔI or *EK* causing a shift in the investment curve to the left to the new position *I′I′*. With this at the initial rate of interest i_0, supply of savings exceeds investment by *KE*. This excess supply of savings will put downward pressure on rate of interest and as a result interest will fall to i_1 at which saving and investment are again equal. According to classical theory, the lower interest induces more investment and therefore as a result of fall in interest to i_1, investment increases from OT_2 to OT_1. Besides, with the fall in interest rate from i_0 to i_1, savings decline by T_0T_1,

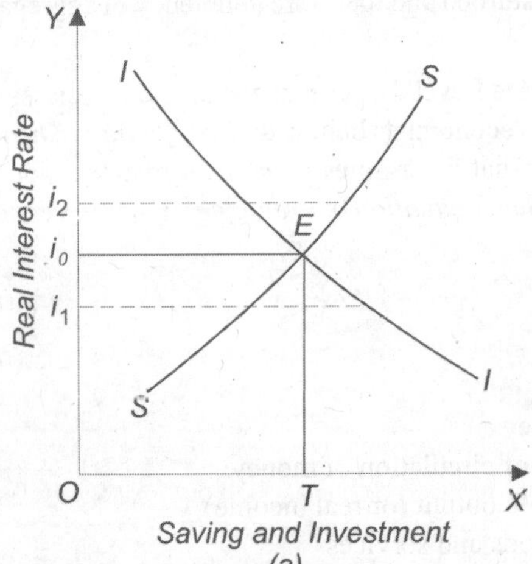

Fig. 4.4. *Capital-Market Equilibrium: Determination of Interest Rate*

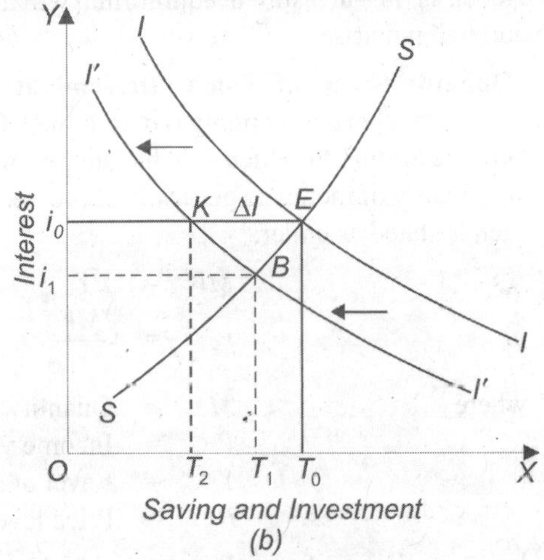

Fig. 4.5. *Decrease in investment demand does not disturb full-employment equilibrium.*

which implies consumption demand will increase by T_0T_1. Thus, *shift in investment demand curve to the left results in lowering of rate of interest which leads to more investment and consumption demand so that aggregate demand is not affected.* It is thus clear that due to adjustment in interest rate even decline in investment does not give rise to demand deficiency problem and full-employment continues to prevail.

It follows from above that capital market equilibrium (that is, equality between investment and saving) brought about by changes in the rate of interest would guarantee that aggregate demand for output would be equal to aggregate supply of output. Thus, the problem of deficiency of aggregate demand would not be faced and full employment of labour will prevail.

Now an important thing to explain is how capital market equilibrium ensures equality between saving and investment at full-employment level of output. It is easy to understand how equilibrium between saving and investment in the capital market ensures equilibrium at full-employment output with the help of circular flow of income. *Savings by households are leakages of money from the income flow, while investment expenditure is injection of money into it.* Given the full employment level of output as determined by labour market equilibrium and short-run aggregate production function, if the *leakage* (*i.e.,* saving) from income flow that measures full-employment output (income) is equal to *injection* (investment) into it, the aggregate expenditure (*i.e.,* aggregate demand for goods and services) would equal full employment level of output (income). Thus, the product market will continue to be in equilibrium and money flow will continue undisturbed at full employment level of income.

Classical Model of Income and Employment : Money, Prices and Inflation

Now, we shall examine how full employment of labour is assured in the classical theory even when money is introduced in the system. The introduction of money does not affect the result of the classical theory that problem of deficiency of aggregate demand would not be experienced by the free-market system and therefore full employment of labour is guaranteed. *The quantity of money, according to the classical theory, determines only the price level of output and in no way affects the real magnitudes of saving and investment. Further, since quantity of money determines the price level of output, it also affects real wage rate,* that is, the ratio of money wages to the price level, or $\frac{W}{P}$. But with increase in money supply, money wages and price level change in such a way that real wage rate in the equilibrium situation remains constant and equilibrium in the labour market is automatically restored. Besides, with the increase in money supply and consequent change in the price level, saving-investment equilibrium will not be disturbed and therefore deficiency of aggregate demand will not arise.

Quantity Theory of Money : Determination of Price Level. Let us first explain how in classical theory price level in the economy is determined. Classical economists believed in the *Quantity Theory of Money* according to which it is the supply of money that determines price level in an economy. Quantity theory of money is generally expressed by *Fisher's equation of exchange*[2], income version of which is stated as under:

$$MV = PY \qquad ...(i)$$

or

$$P = \frac{MV}{Y} \qquad ...(ii)$$

where M = Quantity of money
V = Income velocity of circulation of money
Y = Level of aggregate output (or real income)
P = Price level of goods and services

Income velocity of money is defined as the number of times a unit of money is used for purchase of final goods and services in a period, say during a year. In classical theory velocity is assumed to be constant. Besides, in classical theory level of aggregate output is determined by the supply of productive resources, (*i.e.*, capital stock, availability of labour, land etc.) and the state of technology

2. Quantity theory of money and Fisher's Equation of Exchange will be explained and critically examined in detail in a separate chapter.

which do not change in the short run. Further, due to operation of Say's law and wage-price flexibility full employment of resources occurs in the economy. Thus, with a given amount of productive resources such as labour and capital stock and constant technology and with further assumption that they are fully utilised and employed, the aggregate output (Y) is held constant at full-employment level of output in the short run.

Now, with velocity of money (V) and aggregate output (Y) remaining constant, price level is determined by the money supply (M) and increases in money supply brings about rise in price level in the same proportion. The supply of money is fixed by the monetary policy of the Government or its Central Bank (e.g. Reserve Bank of India). The important question is what determines the demand for money. In the classical theory the function of money is to serve as medium of exchange and therefore demand for money is determined by the *money value of transactions* occurring in the economy. The aggregate output (Y) multiplied by the price level (i.e. PY) indicates the total money value of goods and services transacted (*i.e.,* sold and purchased). Now, since a unit of money is used to make transactions of goods and services more than once in a year as measured by the velocity of money (V), a given amount of money can be used to make transactions of a larger amount of goods and services constituting GDP transacted during a period. PY is the nominal value of GDP and MV is the demand for money. Now the quantity theory of money assumes that the level of national income or GDP (*i.e.,* Y in equation (*ii*)) remains constant as they believe that full employment prevails in the economy. Further they also assume velocity of circulation of money does not change as it depends on modes of wage payment and habits of the people. With Y and V remaining constant, increase in money supply will cause proportionate increase in price level (P). Thus, *according to classical economists, there is direct and proportionate relationship between the quantity of money and the price level.*

CLASSICAL AGGREGATE SUPPLY CURVE

Aggregate supply curve describes the relationship between aggregate supply of output with price level. Classical theory regards aggregate supply curve to be perfectly inelastic. Now, an important question is why in classical model, aggregate supply curve is perfectly inelastic. As explained above, aggregate output Y_F is determined by the equilibrium level of employment N_F given the aggregate production function, Equilibrium level of employment along with real wage rate is determined by labour-market equilibrium, that is, equilibrium between demand for and supply of labour. Thus, in classical theory aggregate supply curve is determined by supply-side factors, namely, preferences of households or individuals regarding work and leisure, the stock of capital (and other factor endowments), the state of technology. Supply of labour, as seen above, is determined by indvidual preferences between work and leisure and demand curve for labour is determined by marginal product of labour.

Thus in classical model aggregate supply curve reflects supply-determined nature of output and does not depend on the aggregate demand and price level. The classical aggregate supply curve is shown in Fig. 4.6. The pertinent question is how with changes in price level, which in the classical theory depends on the quantity of money, leaves levels of employment and output remain unaffected. The reason for this is that *changes in price level causes equal proportionate changes in money wage rate* with the result that the equilibrium real wage rate which is given by $\frac{W}{P}$ remains constant and therefore equilibrium level of employment does not get affected. The adjustment process works in the following way.

If due to the increase in supply of money *price level rises*, with a given money wage rate (W), real wage rate, which is equal to $\frac{W}{P}$, will fall. At a real wage rate lower than the equilibrium real wage rate, the quantity demanded of labour will exceed the supply of labour. This disequilibrium between labour demand and supply will cause money wage rate to rise to a level so that original real wage rate determined by labour market equilibrium is restored. Suppose that in labour-market equilibrium money wage rate is W_1 and, given the price level equal to P_1, the equilibrium real wage rate will be $\frac{W_1}{P_1}$. Now, if price level is doubled to $2P_1$ money wage rate rises to $2W_1$, then the equilibrium real wage rate will become equal to $\frac{2W_1}{2P_1} = \frac{W_1}{P_1}$. Thus, with equal proportionate increase in money wage rate as a result of rise in price level, equilibrium real wage rate and level of employment will remain unaffected. Thus, with rise in price level, the level of employment remains unchanged and, therefore, given the aggregate production function, level of output will remain constant. This implies that aggregate supply curve of output is perfectly inelastic. Thus whatever the price level, money wage rate changes in such a way that equilibrium real wage rate, level of employment and therefore output will remain constant. Thus in classical theory aggregate supply of output is determined by supply-side real variables such as labour supply, stock of fixed capital and state of technology and does not depend on money and prices.

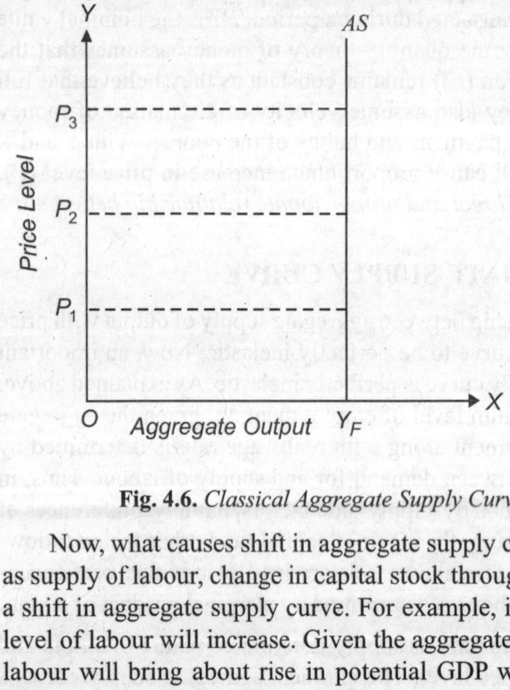

Fig. 4.6. *Classical Aggregate Supply Curve*

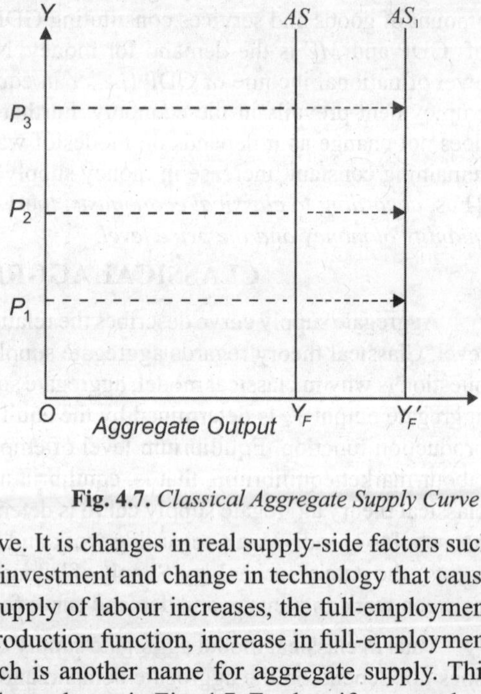

Fig. 4.7. *Classical Aggregate Supply Curve*

Now, what causes shift in aggregate supply curve. It is changes in real supply-side factors such as supply of labour, change in capital stock through investment and change in technology that cause a shift in aggregate supply curve. For example, if supply of labour increases, the full-employment level of labour will increase. Given the aggregate production function, increase in full-employment labour will bring about rise in potential GDP which is another name for aggregate supply. This will cause shift in aggregate supply curve to the right as shown in Fig. 4.7. Further, if as a result of investment capital stock (K) increases, short-run aggregate production function will shift upward and, therefore, with a given supply of labour, potential GDP or aggregate supply will increase leading to the rightward shift in aggregate supply curve. Similarly, introduction of new technology that raises productivity of workers will cause an upward shift in the short-run aggregate production function and with a given supply of labour will raise potential GDP or aggregate supply.

CLASSICAL DICHOTOMY AND NEUTRALITY OF MONEY

An important conclusion which follows from the classical theory of output and employment is what is called *classical dichotomy. Classical dichotomy means that the real variables such as real GDP (that is, output of goods and services produced), the level of labour employment, real wage rate* $\left(\frac{W}{P}\right)$, *real interest rate are determined by real factors such as stock of capital, state of technology and marginal physical product of labour, households' preference between work and leisure which underlies supply of labour and are not affected by the changes in quantity of money* that determines only the price level. *Changes in the quantity of money affect only nominal variables (i.e. money wages, nominal interest rate, nominal GNP, money balances), and have no influence whatsoever on the real variables of the economy* such as real GNP (*i.e.* output of goods and services produced), level of employment (*i.e.* number of labour-hours or number of workers employed), real wage rate (*i.e.* wage rate in terms of its purchasing power).

Actually, as seen above in Fig. 4.7, according to classical full-employment model, the nominal variables move in proportion to changes in the quantity of money, while real variables such as GNP, employment, real wage rate, real rate of interest remain unaffected. Classical economists explained that real variables such as GNP, employment, real wage rate are determined by real factors such as stock of capital, the state of technology, marginal physical product of labour, households' preferences regarding work and leisure. On the other hand, in the classical model based on flexibility of prices and wages, changes in money supply only affect the price level and *nominal* magnitudes (*i.e.*, money wages, nominal interest rate), while the real variabiles such as levels of labour employment and output, saving and investment, real wages, real rate of interest remain unaffected. That is, *money is neutral in its effect on the real variables of the economy*. **Thus, in the classical theory real variables such as levels of output and employment, real wages, real rate of interest, as mentioned above, depend on the stock of capital (*K*), supply of labour (*N*) and the state of technology (*T*) and are not affected by changes money supply.** Thus the *nominal* variables and the *real* variables are determined by two different sets of factors. *The independence of real variables from changes in money supply and nominal variables is called classical dichotomy.*

The classical dichotomy and the neutrality of money can be graphically illustrated from Fig. 4.8. Suppose, to begin with, the stock of money in the economy is equal to M_0. With this, as will be seen from panel (*d*) of Figure 4.8, aggregate demand curve for output is AD_0 which with interaction with aggregate supply curve *AS* determines price level P_0. Given the price level P_0, labour-market equilibrium determines money wage rate W_0 (*i.e.* real wage rate $\frac{W_0}{P_0}$) and level of employment N_F (see panel (*a*) of Fig. 4.8). The level of employment N_F, given the production function, determines aggregate output Y_F in panel (*b*) of Fig. 4.8.

Now suppose there is expansion in money supply from M_0 to M_1 which causes an upward shift in the aggregate demand curve AD_0 to AD_1 [see panel (*d*) of Fig. 4.8]. As a result of this upward shift in the aggregate demand curve from AD_0 to AD_1, price level rises from P_0 to P_1. Now, as will be seen from panel (*a*) of Fig. 4.8, with money wage rate W_0 and the higher price level equal to P_1, real wage rate falls to $\frac{W_0}{P_1}$ at which demand for labour exceeds supply of labour. This will cause, according to classical theory, money wage rate to rise to W_1 *in equal proportion to the rise in price level* so that real wage is restored to the original level $\left(\frac{W_1}{P_1}=\frac{W_0}{P_0}\right)$ and labour-market equilibrium determines the original level of employment N_F. With the same level of labour employment aggregate output (*i.e.* GNP) will not be affected. Thus, we see that with the expansion in money supply, nominal wage rate and price level have risen, but real wage rate, level of employment and output remain constant. *Hence it shows that money is neutral in its effect on real variables.*

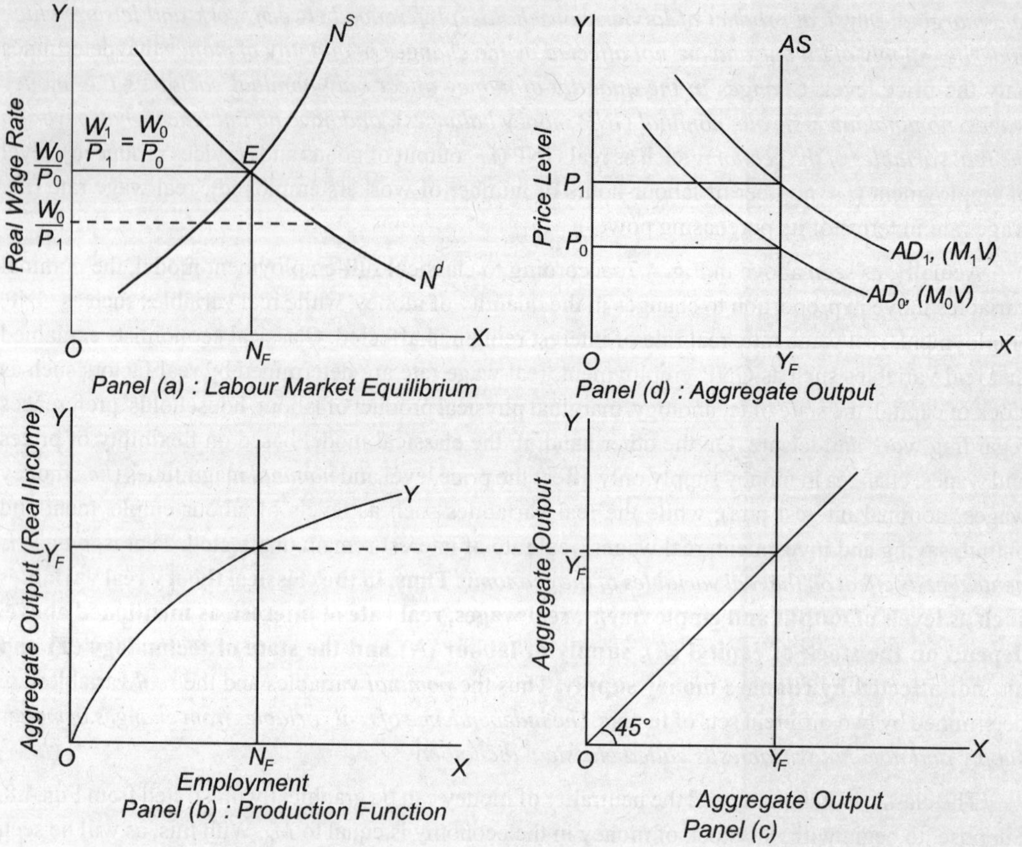

Fig. 4.8. *Classical Dichotomy and Neutrality of Money*

In sharp contrast to the classical model *Keynes in his model integrated money market with goods market* through changes in interest rate. He explains that rate of interest is determined by demand for money (which he calls *liquidity preference*) and the supply of money. The rate of interest along with expected rate of profit (which he calls *marginal efficiency of capital*) determines level of investment. Level of investment plays a significant role in the determination of levels of real GDP and employment. Thus, it is through the effect of changes in rate of interest, determined in the money market, on level of investment that Keynes succeeded in establishing the link between the money market and goods market.

A serious limitation of the classical concept of neutrality of money may be noted. As seen above, *the neutrality of money is a basic result reached in the classical full-employment model based on flexibility of prices and wages*. If increase in money supply and consequent rise in prices has no real effects, then inflation would not be a matter of concern. However, we know that inflation is a matter of serious concern as it lowers standards of living of the people and also adversely affects economic growth. Inflation affects the distribution of income in a society. It hurts the poor most. Therefore, efforts are made to control inflation and achieve price stability in the economy.

KEYNES'S CRITIQUE OF CLASSICAL THEORY

Keynes in his renowned book "*General Theory*" severely criticised the classical theory of employment. We explain below various criticisms of classical theory made by Keynes.

Keynes challenged Say's Law. Keynes criticised Say's Law and proved that it was quite invalid. As we have said above, according to Say's Law, every supply or production creates its own demand and therefore problems of over-production and unemployment do not arise. It is, of course, true that supply creates demand for goods because the various factors which are employed in a productive activity earn incomes from it, which in turn are spent on goods. For example, when factors of production are employed in producing cloth, then the incomes in the form of wages, rent, interest and profits accrue to them which they spend on various goods. But from this it does not follow that the supply of production will create its own entire demand. The incomes earned by the various factors of production are equal to the value of output produced, but this does not mean that the whole income received by the factors of production will be spent on goods and services. A part of the income is saved and the saved part does not necessarily create demand for goods and services. If entrepreneurs do not invest equal to the desired savings, then aggregate demand which, without government intervation, consists of demand for consumer goods and capital goods, will not be enough to purchase the available supply of output. Hence, if aggregate demand is not sufficient to purchase the available supply, the producers would be unable to sell their whole output due to which their profits would decline and as a result they would reduce their level of production giving rise to involuntary unemployment in the economy.

In a given period, consumers spend a part of their income on consumption and the rest they save. Likewise, in a period, the entrepreneurs plan to spend on factories and machines, that is, they plan to invest. Aggregate demand is the sum of consumption demand and investment demand. But in a free market capitalist economy, the persons who save are often different from those who invest and further that the factors that determine savings are different from the factors that determine investment by the entrepreneurs. People save to provide for their old age, to accumulate money for education and marriage of their children and also save and hold money balances for speculative motive, that is, to buy stocks and bonds to earn profits in future. But investment by entrepreneurs depends upon marginal efficiency of capital (that is, expected rate of profit), rate of interest, population growth and technological progress. Keynes also explained that the equality between saving and investment cannot be brought about by changes in interest rate as saving mainly depends on income and it is changes in income that bring about equality between saving and investment rather than changes in rate of interest. But classical economists ignored the changes in level of income because of their assumption of full-employment.

To conclude, savers and investors are different people with different motives. Much of the economy's saving is done by households while investment is mostly done by business firms on the basis of profit expectations and the amount of investment they want to make fluctuates widely from year to year and is unlikely to be equal to savings which households want to do. This affects aggregate demand and causes fluctuations in income, output and employment in capitalist economies. We thus see that there is no any mechanism in a free market economy which guarantees that investments made by the entrepreneurs are equal to the saving by the people. If the desired investment by entrepreneurs falls short of the amount of saving at full-employment level of income, the equilibrium of the economy will be at less than full employment level and as a result involuntary unemployment will emerge in the economy. In this way, according to Keynes, there is no reason that sum of consumption expenditure and investment expenditure is necessarily equal to the value of output produced. In other words, there is no guarantee that aggregate demand will be equal to aggregate forthcoming at full-employment level of resources. Hence, it is not necessary that the economy will be in equilibrium at the level of full employment. This invalidates Say's law, since according to it over-production and unemployment cannot occur.

Keynes proved Pigou's view that cut in money wages will restore full-employment as fallacious. Keynes also criticised Pigou's view that a general fall in wages and prices in times of depression will remove unemployment and automatically restore full empooyment in the economy if market mechanism is allowed to work freely without any obstruction by trade unions and Government. According to Keynes, a general fall in wages will not bring about increase in employment because the reduction in wages will reduce aggregate demand for goods. Keynes put forward the view that *wages are not only the cost of production, they are also incomes of the workers* which constitute the majority of the population of a country. As a result of a *general fall* in wages, the incomes of the workers will fall due to which aggregate demand will decline. As a result of decline in aggregate demand, level of production will have to be reduced and less labour will be employed than before. This will create more unemployment rather than reducing it. No doubt, as a result of a general cut in wages, cost of production of industries will fall but with the fall in costs, the demand for the products will not increase because due to the *all-round cut in wages,* purchasing power of the working class will decrease. Hence all-round cut in wages will reduce the level of employment by reducing aggregate demand and will thus deepen the depression.

There is a fundamental difference between Keynes and Pigou in respect of the relationship between wages and employment. Pigou thought that level of employment in an economy depends upon the level of money wages and therefore reduction in money wages will promote employment. On the other hand, Keynes thought that the level of employment depends upon the aggregate demand and aggregate demand declines as a result of an all-round cut in money wages.

Classical economists thought that a general cut in wages would reduce the cost of production of various industries but they ignored the fact that a general cut in wages will also reduce the incomes of the workers. In view of the fall in incomes and aggregate demand, how will manufacturers be able to sell their whole output? It is the sales of output that makes the wheel of trade, output and employment going. However, note that the classical theory is valid in case of an individual industry. With the decline in wages, the cost of the industry decreases and as a result the price of its product falls. The industry will be able to sell a larger amount of output at a lower price because it is not necessary that the goods produced by the industry are to be purchased by the workers employed in that industry whose wages have been reduced. But in the case of the economy as a whole, this is not valid because a general cut in wages will reduce the incomes of the working class and as a result enough demand will not be there for the output produced by the whole economy. This deficiency in demand will reduce demand for workers as a result of which unemployment will spread among them. Although it is true that a reduction in real wages (*i.e.,* money wages relative to the general price level, $\frac{W}{P}$) in a single firm or industry is not likely to affect the *overall demand* for that product, it is quite wrong to assume that a *general economy-wide reduction in wages* of *all workers* have no effect on aggregate demand. Pigou and other classical economists *committed a logical fallacy* in their thinking by applying the analysis which is true for a particular firm or industry to the economy as a whole. Thus, the fundamental flaw in Pigou and other classical economists is that they applied partial equilibrium analysis, which is valid in the case of an individual industry, to the determination of income and employment in the whole economy. The determination of the level of aggregate income and employment in the economy should be explained with the aid of general equilibrium analysis rather than with partial or particular equilibrium analysis of microeconomics.

Sticky Wages and Unemployment : A basic idea of classical economists is that in a free market economy full employment is the normal state of affairs and any deviation from it will be automatically corrected through quick adjustment in prices and wages. As explained above, when during the period of great depression, 25 per cent of labour force in the USA was unemployed A.C. Pigeon wrote, "With perfectly free competition, there will always be a strong tendency toward full employment. Such *unemployment as exists at any time is due wholly to the frictional resistances that prevent the appropriate wage and price adjustments being made instantaneously.*"[3]

3. A.C. Pigou, *The Theory of Unemployment*, 1933 (Italics added)

On the contrary, Keynes explained that unemployment that prevailed during depression was due to fall in aggregate demand and argued that prices and wages were inflexible downward (*i.e.* sticky) and fall in aggregate demand causes decline in real output and employment. As a result, involuntary unemployment emerges.

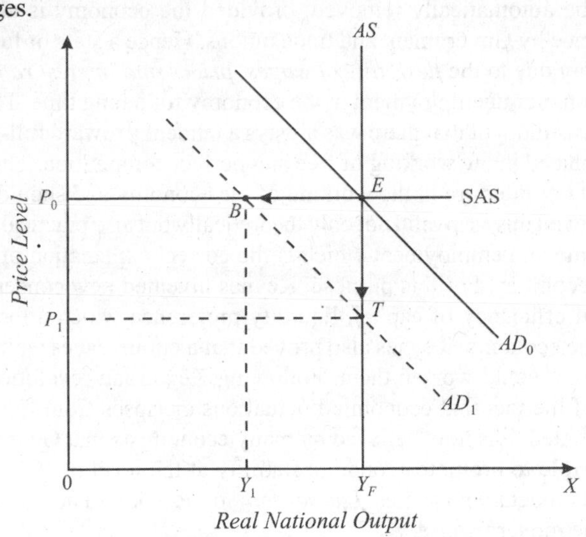

Fig. 4.9. *Wage-Price Flexibility Keynes vs Classics*

The Classical and Keynesian viewpoints are illustrated in Fig. 4.9 through *AS-AD* model. According to classical economists, aggregate supply curve is vertical at full employment output Y_F and is represented by *AS*. Keynes's short run aggregate supply curve is given by the horizontal line *SAS*. Suppose, to begin with, aggregate demand curve is AD_0 which intersects aggregate supply curve *AS* at point *E* with price level equal to P_0. Now suppose that aggregate demand declines due to the fall in investment demand or due to the contraction in money supply and as a result aggregate demand curve shifts leftward to the new position AD_1 (dotted). *According to the classical economists, prices and wages would adjust quickly so that equilibrium will be achieved at point T at the lower price level P_1, level of national output remaining unchanged at full-employment output level Y_F.* Thus, in the classical framework, if market system is allowed to work freely, even with the fall in aggregate demand, full employment tends to prevail and no involuntary unemployment can exist.

On the other hand, according to Keynes, *prices and wages are sticky* and therefore Keynes's short-run aggregate supply curve is flat as is represented by *SAS* in Fig. 4.9. Therefore, when there is leftward shift in aggregate demand due to decline in desired investment, the real national output will fall by *EB* or Y_FY_1, price level and money wages remaining unchanged.[4] We shall discuss in detail in a later chapter the Keynesian and Classical theories regarding wage-price flexibility and employment.

Because of the above-mentioned shortcomings of the classical theory, there was a need for development of a new theory which could provide a correct explanation of the determination of income and employment in the economy. A capitalist economy cannot automatically attain a state of full employment. Keynes in his famous work "*General Theory of Employment, Interest and Money*" not only criticised the classical theory but also propounded a new one which is still regarded as substantially valid and correct.

Conclusion

We have discussed above Say's law of classical economics. This is a basic law of the classical economics. In brief this law states that supply creates its own demand. From this, it has been concluded

4. Note that modern Keynesians consider the short-run aggregate supply curve to be gently sloping upward. Therefore, when aggregate demand falls, there is a small fall in price but a large fall in real national output and employment.

that in a free-enterprise capitalist economy, there is always a tendency towards full employment. According to them, if sometimes unemployment appears in the economy, then wages would decline, the rate of interest and prices would also fall. As a result, employment of labour would increase and unemployment will be automatically removed, provided the economy is allowed to work freely without any interference by Government and trade unions. Hence a state of full employment will be established. In this way due to the *flexibility of wages, prices and interest rate*, there can neither be general overproduction, nor unemployment in the economy for a long time. Therefore, classical and neoclassical economists thought that there was always a tendency toward full-employment provided no restrictions were placed in the working of free and perfect competition. Thus, according to them, the Government need not interfere in the working of the economy and should follow a *laissez faire policy*. But Keynes proved this as invalid not only theoretically but also practically. Keynes put forward a new theory of income and employment which is the correct explanation of the phenomenon in a developed capitalist economy. For this purpose, Keynes invented new concepts such as propensity to consume, marginal efficiency of capital, liquidity preference which affect the level of income and employment in the economy. Keynes also proved that a cut in wages would not cure depression and unemployment, but would worsen them. Following Keynesian revolution in economic theory and the recognition of the fact that economic fluctuations or lapses from full-employment will not be automatically corrected, it is now believed by many economists that Government should play an active and important role to promote economic stability at the level of full-employment by taking appropriate fiscal and monetary measures. *Laissez faire* policy should not, therefore, be followed by the Government in the modern world.

QUESTIONS FOR REVIEW

1. What is Say's Law ? How did classical economists use this law to show that there could not be involuntary unemployment in the economy ?
2. "The supply creates its own demand." How did classical economists justify this argument ? How did Keynes challenge its validity ?
3. Explain briefly classical theory of income and employment. How does this theory show that a free market economy *automatically* adjusts to full-employment level ?
4. What is meant by wage-price flexibility ? How does classical full-employment model show that in a free enterprise competitive economic system flexibility of wages and prices always ensures full employment ?
5. Explain how Keynes showed that money wage cut would fail to increase employment.
6. What is aggregate demand ? How classical economists showed that there would always be sufficient aggregate demand even when there is saving by the households ?
7. What is meant by *neutrality of money* ? How did classical economists explain that money had no effect on real income, output and employment ?

   OR

   Why are only the price level and money wages affected by a change in the money supply in the classical full-employment model ? *DU BA (Hons.) 2009*
8. How is the level of output determined in a classical full-employment model ? What will happen to output if investment demand falls due to the decline in profit expectations of business firms ?
9. How are saving and investment balanced ? Why will demand and supply in the product market be equal if saving and investment are equal ?
10. What are the main factors according to Keynes that may prevent the attainment of full-employment when wages and prices are flexible ?
11. Explain briefly Keynes's critique of classical theory of income and employment
12. What mechanism in classical theory of output and employment ensures equality between saving and investment at full employment ? How did Keynes prove it as fallacious?

13. What is meant by neutrality of money ? Show why money is neutral in the classical model of output and employment.
14. What determines the economy's productive capacity or potential GDP. (*i.e.* long-run aggregate supply) ? How does it change when (a) labour supply increases, (b) capital stock increases as a result of net investment, (c) technology improves ?
15. In a full-employment model where all prices are flexible, explain how the financial capital market reaches its equilibrium. When investment falls, how in a free market economy in this model equilibrium at full-employment level of output is restored ? *DU BA (Hons.) 2007*
16. How are leakages and injections balanced in a free market economy ? Why will demand and supply in the product market be equal if leakages and injections are equal ?
17. In classical full-employment model, how is price level determined ? How is the rate of inflation related to the rate of growth of the money supply ?
18. Why is long-run classical aggregate supply a vertical straight line ? What determines the aggregate demand for goods in the classical theory of output and employment ? How does interaction between the two determine the general price level ?

CHAPTER 5

Keynes's Theory of Employment : an Outline

Introduction : Keynesian Revolution

Classical economists were of the view that there is always full employment in the economy or there is always a tendency towards full-employment in the economy. This view of them was based upon their belief in *Say's Law of Markets*. They thought that when there was unemployment in the economy, then, given the free and perfect competition in the economy, certain economic forces automatically operate in such a way that the condition of full-employment is restored. During the period 1929-33, there occurred great depression in the capitalist countries which caused huge unemployment of labour and other resources in those countries and as a result level of national income fell down. Due to this depression many factories were closed in these countries and factories which were working were also not being used to their full productive capacity. In other words, there appeared a good deal of excess productive capacity in these economies. As a result of unemployment, low income and production created by depression, people had to undergo a good deal of sufferings. This condition of depression and unemployment did not seem to disappear automatically. Therefore, people's belief in the classical economic thought regarding the tendency to full-employment was shaken. Thus, the classical theory of full employment was proved empirically wrong. In this background, Keynes wrote his book "*General Theory of Employment. Interest and Money*" in which he challenged the validity of the classical theory of employment. Not only did he criticise the classical theory of full-employment and proved it wrong but also presented a new theory of income and employment which is generally believed to be correct and valid by modern economists. Keynes brought about such a fundamental and important change in our economic thought at that time that the Keynesian theory is generally known as *new economics*. By being impressed by the fundamental and revolutionary nature of change in our economic theory by Keynes, many economists called his "*General Theory of Employment, Interest and Money*" as the *Keynesian Revolution*. We explain below the outline of the Keynes's theory of employment.

We have critically examined the classical theory of employment and Say's Law of Markets on which the classical theory is based. Keynes in his eminent work "*General Theory of Employment, Interest and Money*" not only criticised the classical Say's law but also propounded a new theory of income and employment. Keynes in his work put forward a more systematic and realistic analysis of the determinants of employment in an advanced capitalist economy and the factors which lead to unemployment. Keynes tried to prove that full-employment is not a normal feature of an advanced capitalist economy and that underemployment equilibrium is its normal feature. Keynes also invented new tools and concepts of economic analysis in terms of which he propounded his theory of income and employment. These new tools and concepts are propensity to consume, multiplier, marginal efficiency of capital and liquidity preference. We will explain these concepts in detail in later chapters. Here we will explain only the outline of the Keynesian theory of income and employment.

It is important to note that Keynesian theory of income and employment is a short-run theory because Keynes assumes that the amount of capital, the size of population and labour force, technology, efficiency of labourers, etc., do not change. That is why, in Keynesian theory, the amount of employment depends upon the level of national income and production. This is because, given the amount of capital, technology and labour efficiency, increase in income and output can be obtained by employment of more labour. Therefore, in the Keynesian short run, the higher the level of national income, the greater the amount of employment; and lower the level of national income, the lower the amount of employment. Hence Keynes's theory of employment determination is also Keynes's theory of income determination. But, for the simplicity, in this chapter we shall explain the Keynesian theory in terms of employment and all the diagrams we will draw will show explicitly the determination of employment. In the next chapter, we will explain Keynesian theory in terms of national income through *income-expenditure analysis* and the diagrams which we will draw they will explicitly show income determination. But it is important to note that the factors that determine the level of income are the same as those that determine the level of employment; only the diagrams used to show their determination are different. It is important to note that *Keynes thought that prices and wages do not adjust quickly to balance demand and supply*. Therefore, in his theory of income and employment he ***assumes that wages and prices remain constant***.

KEYNES'S THEORY OF EMPLOYMENT: PRINCIPLE OF EFFECTIVE DEMAND

At the outset, it may be noted that in Keynesian theory of income and employment determination, principle of effective demand occupies a significant place. In an advanced capitalist economy, the level of employment depends upon the level of aggregate effective demand, the greater the level of effective demand, the greater the amount of employment in the economy. How many men will be employed by an individual firm depends upon the number of persons employed which give it maximum profits. Likewise, in the whole economy, how many men will be employed by firms or entrepreneurs in the economy depends upon the fact that they give them profits. In the whole economy, the amount of employment is determined by aggregate supply and aggregate demand. We will now discuss below these concepts of aggregate supply and aggregate demand functions and will show how they determine the equilibrium level of employment.

Aggregate Supply Function

When entrepreneurs employ some people they incur some cost of production. If the proceeds obtained from the sale of output produced by a certain number of people employed is greater than the cost of production incurred, it will be wrothwhile to employ them. The cost of production incurred on the employment of a certain number of labourers must be recovered by the entrepreneurs, otherwise they will not produce and provide employment to labour. At any given level of employment of labour, *aggregate supply price is the total amount of money which all the entrepreneurs in the economy taken together must expect to receive from the sale of the output produced* by the given number of labourers employed. In other words, *aggregate supply price is the total cost of production* incurred by employing a certain given number of labourers. It is obvious that if the cost of production incurred by the entrepreneur in employing a certain number of labourers is not recovered, they will reduce the amount of employment offered. As the amount of employment of labour increases, the total cost of production will also increase. Therefore, aggregate supply price will rise as more labour is employed to produce goods and services. *Keynes's aggregate supply function (curve) shows the relationship between the number of workers employed and the receipts which all firms in the economy must get if it is just worth employing them, prices remaining constant.* In other words, Keynes's aggregate supply function (curve) shows the relationship between the number of workers employed and the aggregate supply price. Thus we can construct a schedule or *curve of aggregate supply showing aggregate supply price at different levels of employment.*

Let us now explain in detail the factors on which aggregate supply curve depends. *The aggregate supply curve depends ultimately on the physical and technical conditions of production* (that is, capital stock, the state of technology and the nature of production function). However, physical and technical conditions remain constant in the short-run. Hence, given these technical conditions, the level of output can be increased only by increasing employment of labour. But, when output and employment are increased, more cost of production is incurred. Whether production is subject to the law of increasing, diminishing or constant returns, when more workers are employed to increase production, more cost has to be incurred since additional workers are to be paid wages. Hence, more workers will be employed only if the entrepreneurs *must expect to receive* greater revenue so as to cover the rise in cost incurred. Therefore, the aggregate supply curve slopes upward to the right.

The *slope* of the aggregate supply curve (function) depends on the physical or technical conditions of production. If the technical conditions are such that with the increase in output, marginal cost of production does not rise, the aggregate supply curve will be a straight line. On the other hand, if technical conditions are such that diminishing returns occur with the increase in employment of labour, marginal cost of production will rise with the increase in the level of output. This will make the slope of aggregate supply curve to increase with the increase in employment of labour. Besides, if with the increase in employment of labour, wage rate of labour rises, the slope of aggregate supply curve will increase with the employment of more labour. It is however worth noting that Keynes thought in conditions of depression/recession when huge unemployment of labour prevailed in the economy, with the increase in employment of labour to produce more, wage rate will remain constant. Assuming that marginal cost of production rises with the increase in employment of labour, upward sloping aggregate supply curve *AS* with increasing slope as more labour is employed is shown in Fig. 5.1. This aggregate supply curve (function) depicts rising aggregate supply price at various levels of labour employment.

We have said that the aggregate supply is determined by the physical and technical conditions prevailing in the economy, that is, the quantity and quality of labour, stock of capital and raw materials available in the economy and the state of technology. As these changes, or as production technology is improved, *AS* curve will also change. But in the analysis of the determination of employment in the advanced capitalist economies in the short run aggregate supply curve can be assumed to be given and constant. This is for the simple reason that in times of depression the main problem of advanced capitalist economies is how to employ idle manpower and capital resources to increase production by raising demand and not that how the productive capacity be raised by augmenting the stock of capital or by improving the techniques of production. That is why Keynes assumed the *AS* curve to be constant and paid greater attention to the factors determining aggregate demand. The need of the moment in times of recession is to increase aggregate demand so that the equilibrium be achieved at full-employment level. When aggregate demand is increased, the aggregate demand curve will shift upward and it will intersect the *AS* curve more on the right, *i.e.*, the number of men employed will increase.

When the full-employment level has been reached, then, given the stock of fixed capital and the prevailing technology, output and employment cannot be further increased by increasing aggregate demand. Under such conditions increase in aggregate demand will only result in inflation. In such a situation, it becomes necessary to cause a rightward shift in the aggregate supply curve by making addition to the stock of capital and effecting improvements in production technology. This will contain the inflationary pressures. In other words, efforts should be made to increase aggregate supply when full-employment level has already been achieved and the economy is in the grip of inflation.

The curve of aggregate supply price *AS* starts from the point of origin and slopes upward to the right. In the beginning aggregate supply price curve *AS* rises slowly, afterwards it rises rapidly. This curve *AS* shows that as the number of men employed is increased, the aggregate supply price rises slowly in the beginning and rapidly afterwards. This is because cost of production rises as more people are employed and further due to the operation of law of diminishing returns total cost of production increases at an increasing rate. Once all the men willing to get employment are employed, then we have a state of full employment. When the state of full employment is reached further increases in aggregate demand or expenditure will be unable to increase employment further since output of goods and services cannot be increased further as no more labour is available for production after full-employment level is reached. Therefore, aggregate supply curve assumes a vertical shape after full-employment level is reached. In Fig. 5.1, ON_F is the level of full-employment at which aggregate supply curve assumes a vertical shape.

Aggregate Demand Function

It is aggregate demand function which plays a more important role in the determination of employment. Aggregate demand function (curve) shows for each possible level of employment the total sum of money (proceeds) which all the firms or entrepreneurs in the economy *actually expect to receive* from the sale of output produced by the workers employed in the economy. *The amount of expenditure actually expected by the firms when a given number of workers are employed to produce goods and services is called aggregate demand price.* Like the aggregate supply price, aggregate demand price also varies at different levels of employment. This is because at different levels of employment different income levels would be generated and at different income levels, expenditure, especially consumption expenditure, would be different. Aggregate demand has the following four components : (1) *Consumption demand,* (2) *Investment demand,* (3) *Government expenditure, and* (4) *Net Exports (that is, exports–imports).* In this introduction to the theory of employment, we confine ourselves to the consumption demand and investment demand and will introduce Government expenditure and net exports in later chapters of this book.

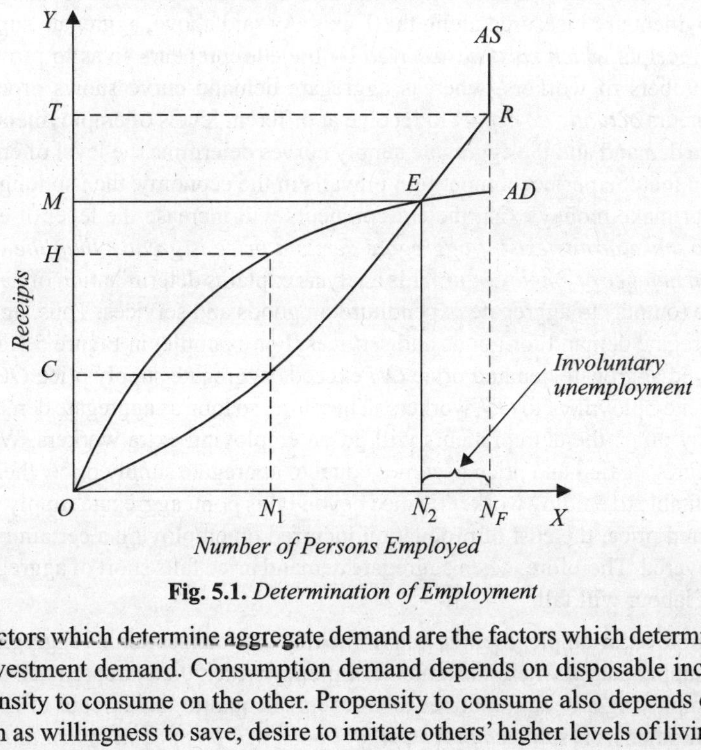

Fig. 5.1. *Determination of Employment*

Thus the factors which determine aggregate demand are the factors which determine consumption demand and investment demand. Consumption demand depends on disposable income on the one hand and propensity to consume on the other. Propensity to consume also depends on some subjective factors such as willingness to save, desire to imitate others' higher levels of living and objective factors such as price level, taxation policy of the Government, rate of interest. Given these factors, changes in which cause a shift in the entire consumption function, the higher the level of disposable income, the greater the amount of consumption demand. As regards investment demand, according to Keynes, it is determined by rate of interest on the one hand and marginal efficiency of capital on the other. While rate of interest is more or less sticky, it is changes in *marginal efficiency of capital* (*i.e., expected rate of return*) that cause frequent changes in inducement to invest. Marginal efficiency of capital means expected rate of profit by the entrepreneurs from the investment they propose to undertake. When prospects for profit-making in future are bright, there will be more investment. If investors become pessimistic about profit earning in future, they will undertake less new investment.

But what are the factors on which business expectations about opportunities of making profits depend. The expected rate of profits (which Keynes calls marginal efficiency of capital) of business men depends on their estimates of consumer demand for goods, taxation policy of the Government, expectations regarding changes in technology. It is worth noting that it is due to the frequent changes in business expectations that investment demand is volatile. When business men become pessimistic about profit earning, investment declines which lowers aggregate demand. On the other hand, when entrepreneurs become bullish or optimistic, they undertake new investment on a large scale which raises the level of aggregate demand of the economy. On the other hand, *consumption function*, according to Keynes, remains stable in the short run. However, *amount of consumption demand* increases as the income of the people rises in the short run. Therefore, we can construct a schedule or curve of aggregate demand showing different aggregate demand prices at different levels of employment. The curve of aggregate demand is shown by the curve *AD* in Fig. 5.1. The aggregate demand curve also rises from left to right. It will be seen in Fig. 5.1 that when ON_1 number of men are employed, the aggregate demand price is *OH* and when ON_2 men are employed, aggregate demand price is *OM*.

Determination of the Equilibrium Level of Employment by Effective Demand

In Fig. 5.1 we have shown together aggregate supply curve and aggregate demand curve. The amount of employment is measured along the *X*-axis and the receipts or proceeds obtained at various levels of employment are measured along the *Y*-axis. As said above, aggregate supply curve shows the revenue or receipts *which must be received* by the entrepreneurs so as to provide employment to different numbers of workers, whereas aggregate demand curve shows proceeds or receipts which entrepreneurs *actually do expect* to receive at different levels of employment and production. These aggregate demand and the aggregate supply curves determine the level of employment in the economy. Given that the perfect competition prevails in the economy, then so long as opportunities to earn profits or make money exist, the entrepreneurs will increase the level of employment. *The opportunities to make profits exist if aggregate demand price is greater than the aggregate supply price for a given number of employment.* This analysis explains determination of national income by relating income (output) to aggregate expenditure on goods and services. Thus, aggregate expenditure shows aggregate demand for goods and services. For example, in Figure 5.1 at ON_1 number of persons employed aggregate demand price *OH* exceeds aggregate supply price *OC*. Therefore, it is profitable to offer employment to ON_1 workers. Therefore, so long as aggregate demand price exceeds aggregate supply price, the entrepreneurs will go on employing extra workers. When at a level of employment aggregate demand price becomes equal to aggregate supply price, then after this it will be no more profitable to employ workers. Since beyond this point aggregate supply price will exceed aggregate demand price, the cost of production incurred on employing a certain number of people will not be recovered. Therefore, when aggregate demand price falls short of aggregate supply price, employment of labour will fall.

Equilibrium level of employment is determined by the intersection of aggregate demand curve and aggregate supply curve, where the amount of money which the entrepreneurs actually expect to receive from employing a certain number of workers is equal to the amount of money which they must receive. In other words, *the employment of labour will be in equilibrium at the level at which aggregate demand price equals aggregate supply price*. It will be seen from Fig. 5.1 that aggregate supply curve and aggregate demand curve intersect at point *E* and therefore ON_2 level of employment is determined. It will be noticed that *at less than* ON_2 level of employment, aggregate demand curve *AD* lies above the aggregate supply curve *AS* showing that it is profitable to expand the amount of employment. However, beyond ON_2 amount of employment, the aggregate demand curve *AD* lies below aggregate supply curve *AS*, which shows that it is no more profitable to employ extra workers beyond ON_2. We, therefore, conclude that ON_2 is the equilibrium level of employment which is determined by the intersection of aggregate demand curve *AD* and aggregate supply curve *AS*.

Effective Demand : Further Clarification

We are now in a position to explain more clearly what effective demand means and how it is important for determination of employment and output in the economy. We have seen that the magnitude of employment in the economy is determined by the equilibrium between aggregate demand and aggregate supply. There is an aggregate demand function for an economy which shows aggregate demand price at varying levels of employment.

But of these varying levels of employment the *level of employment at which aggregate demand is equal to the aggregate supply is called effective demand.* In other words, effective demand is that aggregate demand price which becomes '*effective*' because it is equal to aggregate supply price and thus represents a position of short-run equilibrium. There are several other points on the aggregate demand curve but what distinguishes effective demand from all these points is that at this point the aggregate demand price is equal to aggregate supply price. On all other points, aggregate demand price is either more or less than aggregate supply price.

It is thus clear that employment in the economy in the short run is determined by effective demand. The higher the level of effective demand, the greater is the amount of employment, and *vice versa. Unemployment is due to the deficiency of effective demand and the basic remedy to remove this unemployment is to raise the level of the effective demand.* The classical economists believed that effective demand was always large enough to ensure full employment. But Keynes proved that it was not so and that is why the phenomenon of involuntary unemployment is common in free-market capitalist economies.

Underemployment Equilibrium : The Problem of Demand Deficiency

It is not necessary that the equilibrium level of employment is always at full employment. Equality between aggregate demand and aggregate supply does not necessarily indicate the full employment level. The economy can be in equilibrium at less than full employment or, in other words, an under-employment equilibrium can exist. The classical economists denied that there could be an equilibrium at less than full employment because they believed that supply would always create its

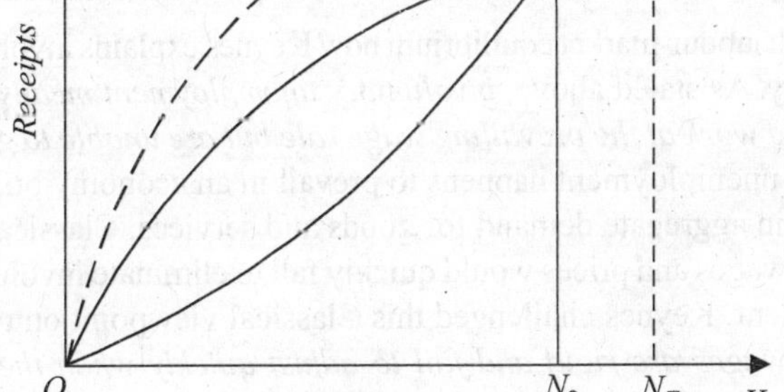

Fig. 5.2. *Raising aggregate demand curve to achieve full employment*

own demand and therefore no problem of deficiency of aggregate effective demand would be experienced. Keynes demolished the classical thesis of full employment both on theoretical grounds and on the basis of illustrations from real life.

It will be seen from Fig. 5.2 that in the situation of equilibrium at the employment level ON_2, the N_2N_F persons remain unemployed. Thus equilibrium at E represents an under-employment equilibrium (or, in other words, less than full-employment equilibrium). It is important to note that N_2N_F persons are *involuntarily unemployed*: they are willing to work at the existing wage rates but are unable to find jobs. It is important to remember that, according to Keynes, this *unemployment is due to deficiency of aggregate demand.*

This unemployment will be removed and full-employment equilibrium will be reached if through increase in investment demand or increase in consumption, or increase in both, aggregate demand curve shifts upward so that it intersects the aggregate supply curve at point R as depicted in Fig. 5.2. It will be seen that with the intersection of aggregate demand and aggregate supply curves at point R, equilibrium is established at full-employment level ON_F.

According to Keynes, *aggregate demand price and aggregate supply price will be equal at full-employment only if investment demand is sufficient to cover the gap between the aggregate supply price corresponding to full-employment level and the consumption expenditure out of income at the full-employment level.* The view of Keynes is that when investment demand falls short of this gap between full-employment income and consumption, recession occurs resulting in the emergence of involuntary unemployment. According to him, when inducement to invest in capitalist countries declines due to the fall in marginal efficiency of capital (*i.e.*, expected rate of profit), aggregate demand falls so that equilibrium is established at less than full-employment level. As a result, output and income of the community also fall.

INVOLUNTARY UNEMPLOYMENT AND MONEY-WAGE RIGIDITY: KEYNES'S VIEW

According to Keynes, due to money wage rigidity, that is, downward inflexibility of money wages results in involuntary unemployment of labour. The workers are rendered unemployed because at a given wage rate supply of labour exceeds demand for labour. Keynes believed that money wage would not change sufficiently in the short run to keep the economy at full employment. Classical economists believed that money wage rate quickly adjusts to bring demand for and supply of labour in equilibrium and keep the economy at full employment level. To understand money-wage rigidity which results in involuntary unemployment we have to examine why labour market does not clear through reduction in money wages, Keynes gave three reasons for the stickiness of money wage rate. It may be noted that stickiness or rigidity of money wage implies that money wage rate will not quickly change, especially in the downward direction to keep equilibrium at full employment level.

Let us explain through labour-market equilibrium how Keynes explains involuntary unemployment with money-wage rigidity. As stated above, *involuntary unemployment means the workers who are seeking work or willing to work at the prevailing wage rate but are unable to get jobs.* According to Keynes, this involuntary unemployment happens to prevail in an economy on a large scale in times of depression due to fall in aggregate demand for goods and services. Classical economists thought that at times of recession wages and prices would quickly fall to eliminate involuntary unemployment and ensure full employment. Keynes challenged this Classical viewpoint on two grounds. First, he pointed out that *money wages are rigid and fail to adjust quickly when there exists involuntary unemployment* as a result of lack of aggregate demand for output during depression. Secondly, even if there is all-round cut in money wages, involuntary unemployment will not be removed. Consider Fig. 5.3 where we have shown labour-market equilibrium. *DD* is the demand curve for labour which is sloping downward to the right. This shows that at lower wage rates more labour is demanded and employed and *vice versa*. *SS* is the supply curve of labour which is sloping upward to the right. This shows that at higher wages more labour is supplied and *vice versa*. These demand and supply curves of labour intersect at point E at which real wage rate $\frac{W}{P}$ and labour employment of ON_0 are determined. At the wage rate $\frac{W}{P}$, all those who are willing to work and supply their labour services are employed. Thus, at this labour market equilibrium, there is full employment of labour and involuntary unemployment does not prevail.

Now suppose aggregate demand for output of goods and services declines, as it happens in times of recession. *Demand for labour is a derived demand.* Decline in aggregate demand for output causes demand curve for labour to shift to the left to $D'D'$. Now, with demand curve $D'D'$ at the given real wage rate $\frac{W}{P}$, the quantity ON_1 labour will be demanded, whereas supply of labour at this real wage rate remains ON_0. Thus, $N_O N_1$, or RE number of workers will be rendered unemployed who are willing to work at the prevailing wage rate but their services are not demanded by the producers in the economy.

According to classical economists, this involuntary unemployment cannot persist for long. The excess supply of labour and competition among unemployed workers will bring down the real wage rate and at lower real wage rate more labour will be demanded and employed. In this way, according to classical economists, due to downward adjustment in wages involuntary unemployment of labour will be eliminated and full employment will be restored.

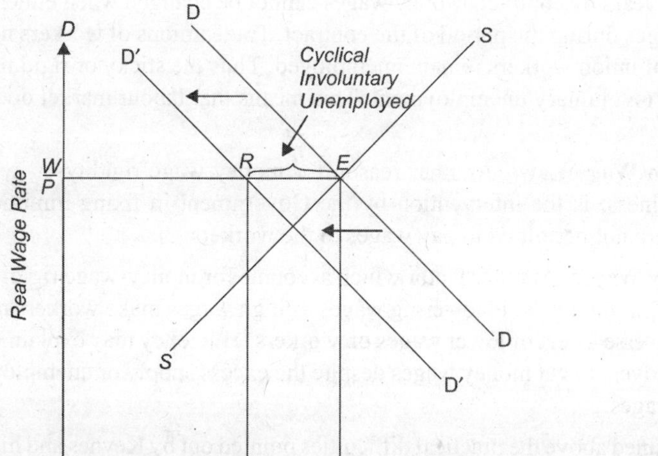

Fig. 5.3. *Labour Market Equilibrium and Involuntary Unemployment with Downward Rigidity of Money Wage Rate*

Rigid Money Wages. However, Keynes contended that *money wages are rigid* and do not fall and as a result involuntary unemployment continues to prevail. There are a number of reasons for rigidity of money wages. First, according to Keynes, workers strongly resist a reduction in money wages whereas they do not resist much the fall in *real* wages which may occur due to rise in price level. For such a behaviour on the part of workers, Keynes laid stress on ***money illusion*** on the part of workers. We explain below this money illusion of workers. There are two reasons for existence of money illusion.

(*i*) First reason for the existence of money illusion is that workers of a firm or industry think that though rise in prices reduces their real wages, but that this rise in prices equally affects workers in other industries so that their relative wages as compared to those employed in other industries remain the same. Therefore, workers who are more concerned with their relative position with other workers will strongly resist the cut in their money wages, while they will not oppose so strongly their cut in real wages through rise in the general price level.

(*ii*) The second reason for strong resistance to cut in money wages is that the workers blame their own employers for this, whereas they think that a cut in real wages through rise in prices in general is the outcome of the working of general economic forces over which strikes in an industry would have little effect. However, it does not necessarily mean that trade unions remain silent spectators if they feel that changes in Government policy adversely affect their economic interests.

From the above two reasons given for money illusion Keynes argued that if additional employment could be created by lowering real wages, it is more practical to do so *through bringing about rise in general price level rather than by cutting money wages*.

After Keynes, his followers have given additional reasons for downward rigidity of money wages. They are:

1. Wage Fixation Through Contracts. In most of the free market economies such as those of USA and Great Britain, wages are fixed by the firms through contracts made with the workers for two years or three. There is little possibility of changing money wages fixed through contracts when the situation of either labour surplus or shortage emerges. For workers organised into trade unions wages are even rigid. Through collective bargaining by trade unions with the employers wage scales are fixed for 3 to 4 years by contract. Money wages cannot be changed when either surplus or shortage of labour emerges during the period of the contract. Trade unions of workers never accept wage cuts even if some of union workers remain unemployed. Thus the sticky or rigid money wages lead to the existence of involuntary unemployment. This means that labour market does not clear in the short run.

2. Minimum Wage Laws. Another reason for money wage rigidity or, what is also called money-wage stickiness, is the intervention by the Government in fixing minimum wages below which employers are not permitted to pay wages to the workers.

3. Efficiency Wages. Another factor which accounts for money-wage rigidity is that employers themselves are not interested in lowering wages as high wages make workers more efficient and productive. The adverse effect of lower wages on workers' efficiency may explain the unwillingness on the part of employers to cut money wages despite the excess supply or unemployment of workers at higher money wages.

We have explained above the practical difficulties pointed out by Keynes and his followers which are faced by firms in reducing wages and which therefore explain money-wage rigidity or stickiness. The sticky or rigid money wages above the equilibrium level cause unemployment of labour.

CUT IN MONEY WAGES AND EMPLOYMENT : KEYNES'S VIEW

During the period 1929-33 when there was a great depression in capitalist economies, eminent classical economist A.C. Pigou suggested a cut in wage rates in order to remove huge and widespread unemployment prevailing at that time. According to him, the cause of depression and unemployment was that the Government and trade unions of workers were preventing the free working of the capitalist economy and were artificially keeping the wage rates at high levels. He expressed the view that if wage rates were cut down, the demand for labour would increase so that all would get employment. Keynes challenged this classical view of increasing employment through cut in wages and thereby fall in prices of goods.

Keynes pointed out a basic flaw in classical argument. The classical economists argued that just as in an individual industry a cut in wages will lead to the increase in employment of labour by the industry, the same applies to the case of the economy as a whole. According to Keynes, there is no justification for applying the principle which is valid for an individual industry to the economy as a whole. Defending Keynes's viewpoint Professors Stonier and Hague write, "*While in particular equilibrium analysis one is justified in taking demand for the product of the industry as given, there is no justification when one considers all industries together.* The demand for the product of one industry depends largely on the wages paid to and amount of money spent by workers in other industries. *A general equilibrium analysis of wage cut is futile unless it pays attention to the problem of whether aggregate demand will rise or fall as wages are reduced*".[1]

Keynes argued that wages are not only cost of production but also incomes of the workers who constitute a majority in a society relative to a few rich people. Since the propensity to consume of workers is high compared to the richer sections of the society, the fall in their incomes as a result of all-round reduction in wages will lead to the fall in aggregate demands for goods which will cause unemployment to increase rather than decrease. To quote Stonier and Hague again, "When there is general unemployment, a general cut in wages in all industries cannot be assumed to leave demand unaltered for a part of the demand results from spending out of wages. It is thus quite likely that a *general cut in wages will merely cause a reduction in demand and will not in itself remove unemployment*".[2]

Pigou Effect. In response to the Keynes's critique of classical view that cut in wages will adversely affect aggregate demand and therefore will lead to the rise in unemployment, Pigou pointed out a beneficial effect of cut in wages on employment of workers. According to Pigou, reduction in money prices of goods resulting from a cut in wages of workers would lead to *increase in 'real' value of money assets* such as cash money, bank deposits, bonds, etc. As a result of the rise in the real value of their money assets, the people will feel themselves to be better off or wealthier and will therefore increase their spending or demand which will raise the level of income and employment. This is called *Pigou effect* or *real balance effect*. Many economists doubt whether this real balance effect will be strong enough to bring the economy back to full employment. Later, a new classical economist, Don Patinkin[3], supported the real balance effect of fall in money prices following the reduction in all-round cut in wages. However, a majority view is that Pigou or real balance effect is quantitatively insignificant. Further, from practical viewpoint, cut in money wages is not possible due to strong resistance by workers (for examples, strike by workers for a very long period.)

Keynes's Effect. Reference here may also be made to Keynes's effect of wage cut and consequent fall in money prices of goods and services. According to Keynes, the decline in money prices as a result of all-round cut in wages will cause decrease in transactions demand for money. With total money supply remaining the same, the decrease in transactions demand for money will lead to the increase in money supply for speculative motive which will cause rate of interest to fall. The decline in interest rate will cause investment demand (and even consumption demand for durable consumer goods) to increase. This implies favourable effect of a wage cut through its effect of lowering interest rate. However, *Keynes pointed out that the decline in interest rate can be easily achieved through increase in money supply by* the Central Bank of the country whereas it is practically not possible to cut money wages due to strong resistance by the workers and their unions.

SUMMARY OF KEYNES'S THEORY OF EMPLOYMENT

After explaining Keynes's theory of employment at some length, we are now in a position to describe it in a summary form bringing out relationship between various elements or factors that go to determine the equilibrium level of employment.

1. Level of output or income of a country depends on the level of employment. Given the capital

---

1. Stonier and Hague, *A Textbook of Economic, Theory,* Orient Longman, 4th edition, p.578. (italics added)
2. Ibid.
3. Don Patinkin, *Money, Interest, and Prices*

stock and technology, greater the employment of labour, the higher the level of aggregate output or national income.

2. *The level of employment depends on the magnitude of effective demand* which is the sum of consumption demand and investment demand at the point where aggregate supply curve intersects the aggregate demand curve.
3. Aggregate supply of an economy depends on physical and technical conditions of production. Since these factors do not change much in the short run, aggregate supply curve remains constant in the short run. Aggregate supply curve slopes upward to the right as level of employment increases. This is because with the increase in labour employment, the greater cost has to be incurred.
4. Aggregate demand in a simple Keynesian model consists of consumption demand and investment demand. Since the consumption demand increases with the increase in labour employment, aggregate demand curve also slopes upward to the right. In Keynes's simple model, *investment demand is regarded as autonomous of changes in income or employment.*
5. Consumption demand depends on the propensity to consume on the one hand and disposable income on the other. Propensity to consume of a community does not change much in the short run. Therefore, consumption function which relates consumption demand with the level of income remains stable in the short run.
6. Investment demand depends on the rate of interest and marginal efficiency of capital. According to Keynes, rate of interest is determined by supply of money and the state of liquidity preference. Marginal efficiency of capital (*i.e.*, expected rate of profit) depends on the expected future yields or *profit expectations* of entrepreneurs on the one hand and *replacement cost of capital* on the other.
7. According to Keynes, while rate of interest is more or less sticky, it is frequent changes in profit expectations of the entrepreneurs, that is, changes in marginal efficiency of capital that cause a great deal of fluctuations in investment by entrepreneurs. Investment demand is thus highly volatile and causes recession or depression when it falls, and boom and prosperity when it increases significantly.

We summarise below the various determinants of employment and income (output) in a tabular form.

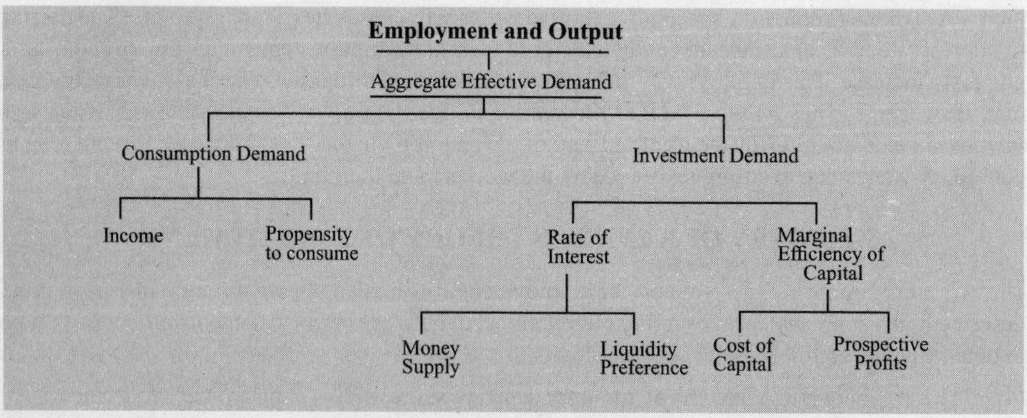

QUESTIONS FOR REVIEW

1. Explain Keynes's theory of employment. How does it differ from classical theory ?
2. In what respects do the Classical and Keynesian theories of employment differ ? Spell out the reasons for under-employment equilibrium in the Keynesian model.
3. Explain how, according to Keynes, *involuntary unemployment* is caused by lack of effective demand. How, according to him, is the money-wage rigidity responsible for the emergence of involuntary unemployment ?
4. The logical starting point of Keynes's theory of employment is the principle of effective demand. Explain.
5. What do you understand by the term '*money illusion*' in the Keynesian theory of employment ? Is money wage-price rigidity a consequence of money illusion ?
6. Define effective demand. How does it determine level of employment in a country ?
7. Explain the classical view about the effect of cut in all-round money wages on employment. Why did Keynes oppose cut in money wages to eliminate unemployment at times of depression ?
8. Explain 'Pigou effect' and 'Keynes's effect' on employment of labour. Why did Keynes oppose cut in money wages when Keynes's effect of wages cut through fall in interest rate on employment is also favourable ?
9. What is meant by real balance effect ? How does it show that a cut in money wages will help in eliminating involuntary unemployment ?

CHAPTER 6

Determination of National Income : Keynes's Simple Two-Sector Model

Keynes's Income-Expenditure Approach

We have explained in the previous chapter how the level of employment is determined in an advanced capitalist economy. We explained there Keynesian theory with special reference to the determination of employment. It is worth noting here that the Keynesian theory is relevant in the context of the short run only since the stock of capital, techniques of production, efficiency of labour, the size of population, forms of business organisation have been assumed to remain constant in this theory. Further in his model of income determination *Keynes assumed that price level in the economy remains unchanged*. Therefore, in the Keynesian theory which deals with the short run, the level of income of the country will change as a result of changes in the level of labour employment. Thus, in free market economy in the short run, when capital stock and technology remain unchanged, income is a function of labour employment. In fact, both income and employment go together. The higher the level of employment, the higher the level of income. As level of employment is determined by aggregate demand and aggregate supply, the level of income is also determined by aggregate demand and aggregate supply. In this chapter, we shall explain how the equilibrium level of national income is determined through *Keynes's income-expenditure analysis*. This analysis explains determination of national income by relating income (output) to aggregate expenditure on goods and services. The aggregate expenditure shows aggregate demand for goods and services. Keynesian theory of income determination can be explained by assuming two sectors in the economy, namely, households and business firms. Keynes focussed on this simple two-sector model of determination of national income and derived conclusions regarding policy formulation from this basic model. Analysis of determination of national income can be extended to incorporate Government and foreign trade. We start with the analysis of determination of national income by *taking a simple two-sector economy with a fixed price level*.

Aggregate Expenditure (with a Fixed Price Level)

Aggregate expenditure is the total expenditure which at given fixed prices all households and business firms want to make on goods and services in a period at various levels of national income. Though J.M. Keynes used the term *aggregate demand*, in modern macroeconomics, the term *aggregate expenditure* is generally used. The terms of aggregate demand and aggregate supply are now generally used in the model with variable price level. In this chapter however we use the term aggregate demand and aggregate expenditure interchangeably but assume that price level remains constant. In a two-sector closed economy, aggregate expenditure or aggregate demand consists of two components: First, there is consumption demand, and secondly, there is a demand for capital goods, which is called investment demand. Thus, by aggregate expenditure we mean how much expenditure the households and the entrepreneurs are willing to make on consumption and investment. Therefore,

Aggregate Demand = Consumption Demand + Investment Demand

$$AE = AD = C + I$$

where *AE* stands for aggregate expenditure, *C* for consumption demand and *I* for investment demand.

Using the term aggregate expenditure instead of aggregate demand we have

Aggregate Expenditure = Consumption expenditure + Investment expenditure

or $$AE = C + I$$

Consumption Demand. As for consumption demand, it depends upon the propensity to consume of the community and the level of national income. Given the propensity to consume, as income increases, consumption demand will also increase. In other words, given the propensity to consume, consumption demand is a function of income. Consumption function can take several forms. The most common form of short-run consumption function is

$$C = a + bY$$

where *a* is the intercept term of the function and represents *autonomous consumption* whereas *b* represents the slope of the consumption function. According to Keynes's theory current consumption expenditure depends primarily on current income. Further, according to Keynes, the chief factor that determines consumption expenditure is disposable income, that is, income available after taxes. Increase in personal taxes reduces personal disposable income and therefore consumption expenditure.

Consider Fig. 6.1 in which national income is measured along the *X*-axis and consumption demand (*C*) is shown on the Y-axis. In this figure, a straight line *OZ* which makes 45° angle with the *X*-axis has been drawn. This straight line *OZ* with 45° angle with the *X*-axis represents the *reference income line* to measure the difference between consumption and level of income. This is also often called *income line*. This 45° line represents national income in money terms. In fact, national product and income are the same things. In this figure a curve *C* has also been drawn which represents consumption function, $C = a + bY$ of the community. This curve of consumption function slopes upward from left to right, which shows that as income increases the amount of consumption demand also increases. As income line *OZ* makes 45° angle with the *X*-axis, the *gap between the consumption function curve C and the income line OZ represents the saving of the community*. The reason for this is that a part of the income is consumed and a part is saved, *i.e.*, National Income = Consumption + Saving. This is also written as $Y = C + S$, where *y* represents income, *C* consumption and *S* saving. It will be seen from Fig. 6.1 that the gap between the consumption function curve *C* and the income line *OZ* goes on increasing as income increases. In other words, the amount of saving or saving gap increases as income increases.

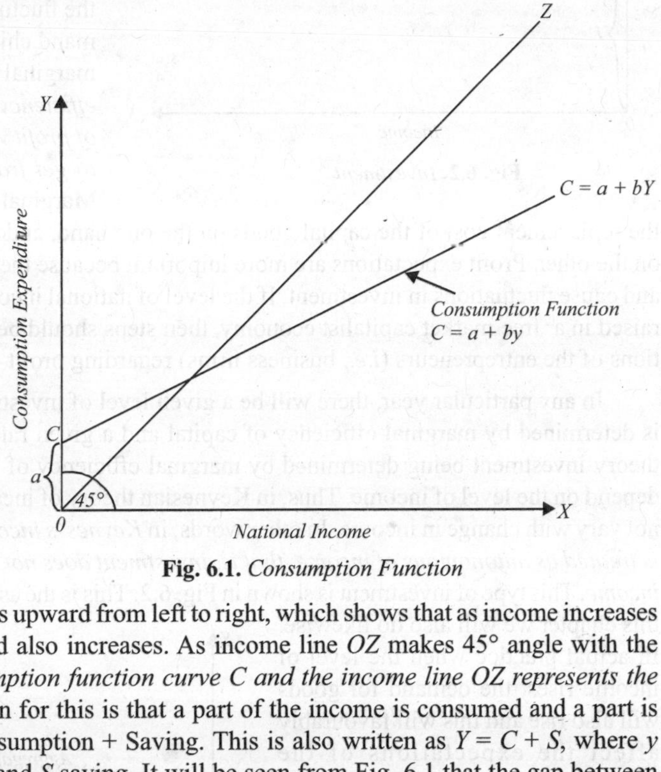

Fig. 6.1. *Consumption Function*

It is worth mentioning that in the short-run consumption function does not change. This is because the propensity to consume, that is, the whole consumption function curve *C* depends upon the tastes, preferences, the income distribution in the society, the population level, wealth of the people, etc., which do not undergo much change in the short run. The implication of the stability of consumption function is that the consumption demand is primarily determined by the level of current national income.

However, through changes in monetary policy and fiscal policy by the Government the consumption function can be shifted. For example, when rate of interest, an instrument of monetary policy, is reduced, the people borrow more for durable consumer goods such as cars, airconditioners, houses and with this at a given level of income consumption demand increases causing upward shift in the consumption function curve. Similarly, when income tax, an instrument of fiscal policy, is reduced disposable income of the households increases and as a result at a given level of national income (GDP), consumption demand increases leading to the upward shift in consumption function.

Investment Demand. The other component of the aggregate demand is investment which is a crucial factor in the determination of equilibrium level of national income. Investment demand depends upon two factors; (1) marginal efficiency of capital and (2) rate of interest. Of these two factors, rate of interest is comparatively stable and does not frequently change in the short run. Therefore, the fluctuations in the level of investment demand chiefly depend upon the changes in the marginal efficiency of capital. *The marginal efficiency of capital means the expected rate of profit which the business community hopes to get from the investment in capital assets.* Marginal efficiency of capital depends upon the replacement cost of the capital goods on the one hand, and profit expectations of entrepreneurs on the other. Profit expectations are more important because they often change even in the short run and cause fluctuations in investment. If the level of national income and employment is desired to be raised in a free market capitalist economy, then steps should be taken which will raise the expectations of the entrepreneurs (*i.e.,* business firms) regarding profit-earning from investment.

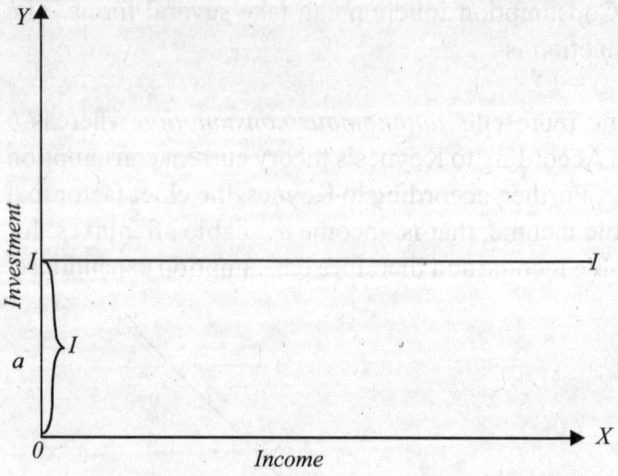

Fig. 6.2. *Investment*

In any particular year, there will be a given level of investment demand which, as seen above, is determined by marginal efficiency of capital and a given rate of interest. However, in Keynes's theory investment being determined by marginal efficiency of capital and rate of interest does not depend on the level of income. Thus, in Keynesian theory of income determination, investment does not vary with change in income. In other words, in *Keynes's income-expenditure analysis investment is treated as autonomous of income, that is, investment does not change with a change in the level of income.* This type of investment is shown in Fig. 6.2. This is the assumption which Keynes made and in this chapter we will also do likewise. In actual practice when the level of income rises, the demand for goods will also rise and this will favourably affect the expectations of the entrepreneurs regarding making of profits. Rise in the profit expectations will raise the marginal efficiency of capital which in turn will increase the level of investment. But it is quite clear that investment demand does not directly depend upon income; it is only affected indirectly by changes in income. Therefore, in our Fig. 6.3 we have taken a given amount of investment demand independent of the level of income and added it to upward sloping consumption function curve to get aggregate expenditure

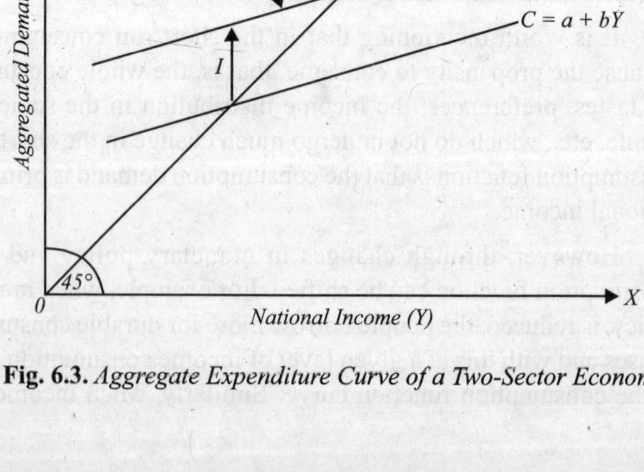

Fig. 6.3. *Aggregate Expenditure Curve of a Two-Sector Economy*

curve $C+I$. The distance between the C curve and the $C+I$ curve is parallel to the C curve throughout which indicates that the level of investment is constant and does not change with the change in income. It may however be noted that with either a change in the rate of interest or in marginal efficiency of capital investment will change. Therefore, in income-expenditure diagram as shown in Fig. 6.3, *a different new amount of investment* of will have to be taken.

Aggregate Output

As mentioned above, in the short run the level of national income and employment in a free-market economy depends upon the equilibrium between aggregate expenditure and aggregate output. We have also explained above the various components of aggregate expenditure on goods and services. We now turn to explain the aggregate supply and factors on which it depends. It is important to note again that Keynes in his analysis assumed that prices and wages remain constant in the short run.

In an economy without any role of Government, national income *means the total money value of goods and services produced in an economy in a year*. There are two important constituents of aggregate output:

1. the supply or output of final consumer goods and services in a year; and
2. the output of capital goods which are also called producer goods because they help in producing further goods.

National income is the same thing as national product as both represent the value of output of final goods and services produced. In fact, aggregate supply or money value of national product of goods and services is distributed among the various factors of production as wages, rent, interest and profits as rewards for their contribution to the national product.

The aggregate output which is also sometimes referred to as aggregate supply of goods of an economy depends upon the stock of capital, the amount of labour used and the state of technology. In the short run, stock of capital remains constant and therefore output can be increased by increasing the amount of labour employed. Like the classical economists Keynes also thought that aggregate output or national income depends on the short-run production function with a given capital stock and constant technology. Thus, we have the following production function in the short run.

$$Y = (N, \bar{K}, \bar{T})$$

where Y is national output, $\bar{K}$ is the constant amount of capital stock, $\bar{T}$ is the constant state of technology and N is the labour employed which is a variable factor.

It may be noted that the amount of production which a given amount of labour can produce depends upon the given stock of capital and state of technology. The higher the level of technology, more can be produced with the help of given resources. Since J.M. Keynes in the nineteen thirties and we at present are concerned with the determination of income and employment *in the short run*, the stock of capital and the state of technology are assumed to be constant. For similar reasons, size of population is also assumed to be constant. However, the amount of labour employed out of this given size of population can vary depending upon the demand for labour.

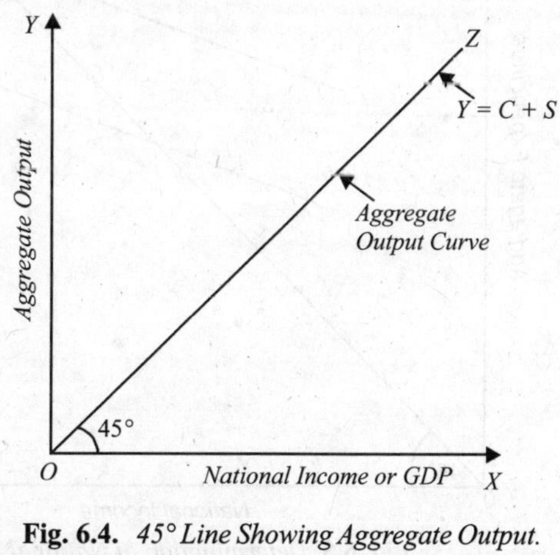

Fig. 6.4. *45° Line Showing Aggregate Output.*

45° Line as Aggregate Output Curve (With Fixed Prices)

In the income-expenditure analysis with which we are presently concerned we need to compare Gross Domestic Product (or National Income) with aggregate expenditure (*AE*), also called aggregate demand (*AD*), which is represented on the vertical axis. For this purpose we draw a 45° line from the origin which helps us to *transfer* Gross Domestic Product or real National Income (*i.e.* gross supply of output at constant prices) from the horizontal axis to the vertical axis for comparing it with total expenditure on goods and services. At every point of this 45° line from the origin, the vertical distance equals horizontal distance which measures real national income or GDP which is generally denoted by *Y*. This 45° line is also called income line along which $Y = C + S$ because income can either be consumed or saved.

The essential feature which emerges from all this is that more output will be produced and supplied at the given price level in response to increase in aggregate demand or expenditure. In other words, whatever the aggregate demand, more output of goods will be produced and supplied at the same price before full-employment of resources is reached. This type of aggregate supply curve has been shown by 45° *OZ* line drawn against the *X* and *Y* axes in Fig. 6.4 where along the *X*-axis real national income (GDP) and along the *Y*-axis aggregate supply of output are measured. However, as noted above, aggregate output and real national income (GDP) are identical.

It follows from above that 45° line shows two things. First, it shows *varying* levels of aggregate production or the supply of goods (both consumer and capital goods) that will be offered for sale at the given price level at various levels of aggregate expenditure. This shows that up to the level of full-employment of resources *any amount* of aggregate supply of output will be forthcoming at the given price level depending on the aggregate demand or expenditures. The greater the aggregate demand or expenditure, the greater the aggregate supply of output at the given price level. Secondly, it represents national income. In fact, as you would have read in national income accounting, national product and national income are the same thing.

Equilibrium Level of National Income

Now, we shall explain how through the intersection of aggregate demand and aggregate supply curves the equilibrium level of national income is determined in Keynes's two-sector model. $C + I$ curve represents the aggregate expenditure and 45° *OZ* line represents aggregate supply of output.

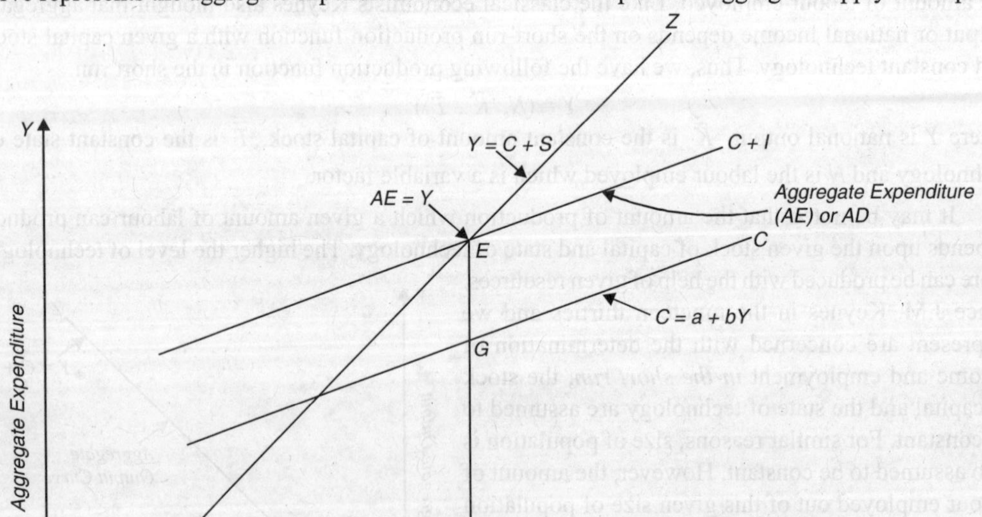

Fig. 6.5. *Determination of National Income : Keynesian Simple Two-Sector Model*

Normally the goods and services are produced by firms when they think they can sell them in the market. There will be equilibrium in the goods market when total output of goods and services produced will be equal to the total demand for output. Aggregate demand for them is represented by aggregate expenditure. In equilbrium aggregate expenditure (which is denoted by *AE*) must equal aggregate output (GDP). Since aggregate output or GDP equals national income (*Y*) we have the following condition for equilibrium.

$$AE = GDP = Y$$

It will be seen in Fig. 6.5 that aggregate expenditure curve (*AE*) or $C + I$ curve intersects 45° line at point *E* which satisfies the equilibrium condition. That is, at point *E* which corresponds to the income level OY_1, aggregate expenditure is equal to aggregate output. Therefore, *E* is the equilibrium point and OY_1 represents the equilibrium level of national income. Now, income cannot be in equilibrium at levels smaller than OY_1, since aggregate expenditure exceeds aggregate supply of output as $C + I$ curve which depicts aggregate expenditure of output lies above 45° line. This excess demand will be met by the firms selling goods from their stocks or inventories of goods kept by them. This leads to the decline in inventories of goods below the desired levels. This unintended fall in inventories will induce the firms to expand their output of goods and services to meet the extra demand for them and keep their inventories of goods at the desired levels. Thus when at a given level of national income, aggregate expenditure (*i.e.*, aggregate demand) exceeds aggregate output, national income will increase. With this increase in national income or output, employment of labour will also rise to produce the increment in output. This process of expansion in output under the pressure of excess demand will continue till national income OY_1 is reached.

On the contrary, the equilibrium level of national income cannot be greater than OY_1 because at any level greater than OY_1 aggregate expenditure or demand $(C + I)$ falls short of aggregate output. This will cause the increase in inventories of goods with the firms beyond the desired levels. To this situation of the unintended increase in inventories of goods, the firms will respond by cutting down production to keep their inventories at the desired levels. Thus, deficiency in aggregate demand relative to the aggregate supply of output will lead to the fall in national income and output until the level OY_1 is reached where aggregate expenditure $(C + I)$ is equal to the value of aggregate output. Thus, OY_1 is the equilibrium level of national income.

Principle of Effective Demand

We have seen above that the equilibrium level of national income is determined by aggregate demand and aggregate supply of output. Consider Fig. 6.5 where it will be seen that the prices remaining constant, aggregate expenditure (*AE*) curve $C + I$ *shows varying levels of aggregate demand at various levels of national income. The particular aggregate demand which is equal to aggregate output and therefore determines the equilibrium national income is called effective demand.* In other words, effective demand is that level of aggregate demand (aggregate expenditure) which becomes effective in determining equilibrium level of income because it is equal to aggregate supply of output. This is called *Keynesian principle of effective demand*. In Fig. 6.5, the effective demand is equal to Y_1E. Note that the level of national income OY_1, which has been determined, equals the effective demand Y_1E $(OY_1 = Y_1E)$.

There are several other points on the aggregate demand (expenditure) curve but what distinguishes effective demand from all these points is that at this point aggregate demand is equal to aggregate output. On all other points aggregate demand is either more or less than aggregate output. Thus, the level of national income is determined by and equal to effective demand. In a two-sector Keynesian model, we can express the principle of effective demand in symbolic terms as under :

$$Y = AE^* \text{ or } AD^*$$

$$AD^* = AE^* = C + I$$

$$Y = AD^* = C + I$$

where Y = National Income
AD^* = Effective demand
C = Consumption demand
I = Investment

Note that *star mark* on *AE* or *AD* shows the aggregate demand which becomes effective.

Importance. It is thus clear that national income and employment in the short run are determined by effective demand (or, in other words, effective aggregate expenditure). The higher the level of effective demand, the greater the levels of national income and employment and *vice versa. Unemployment is due to deficiency of effective demand and the basic remedy to remove this unemployment is to raise the level of effective demand.* Due to their belief in Say's law and in quick adjustment of wages and prices to balance between demand and supply the classical economists believed that effective demand was always large enough to ensure full-employment. But Keynes proved that it was not so and that is why the problem of involuntary unemployment was common in the free-market capitalist economies.

Equilibrium is not Necessarily Established at Full-Employment Level

The most important contention of J.M. Keynes in his now famous work "*General Theory of Employment, Interest and Money*" was that in a capitalist economy it is not necessary that the equilibrium level of income is established at the level of full-employment. This view of Keynes was quite contrary to the views of the classical economists who believed that the economy always tended towards full-employment. Keynes refuted this important idea of the classical economists. To understand the Keynesian viewpoint consider Fig. 6.6. Suppose the full-employment level of labour corresponds to the level of national income equal to OY_F. Thus OY_F represents the level of income at which there is full-employment in the economy. But, as seen above, the equilibrium level of income is not established at OY_F but at OY_1 at which some number of labour will be unemployed. Thus equilibrium at OY_1 is known as ***under-employment equilibrium***. It is worth noting that in the situation depicted in Fig. 6.6 the equilibrium level of national income will be established at full-employment level only when investment demand is sufficiently large to fill the saving gap

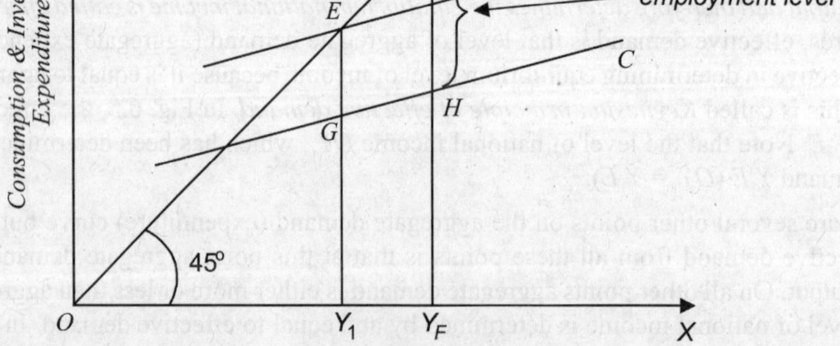

Fig. 6.6. *Under-employment Equilibrium due to Insufficiency of Investment Expenditure*

between income and consumption at the full-employment level of income OY_F. It will be seen from Fig. 6.6, that corresponding to the full-employment level of income OY_F, *RH* is the saving of the community. Therefore, if the equilibrium is to be established at OY_F level, then investment demand must be equal to level of saving *RH* at full employment level of income Y_F. But the prevailing investment demand is only equal to *EG* which is less than *RH*. With *RH* as the level of investment and the *C* curve as the level of propensity to consume, $C + I$ curve intersects the 45° aggregate output curve *OZ* at point *R* and therefore determines equilibrium level of income equal to OY_F at which labour will be fully employed.

But there is no guarantee that the investment demand will be equal to the saving gap corresponding to full-employment level of income. There are various reasons for this. First, the people who save are not necessarily those who make investment; while it is the general public which save but only few people constituting the entrepreneurial class undertake investment. Secondly, the factors which determine saving are quite different from those which determine investment. While the people save for providing for the education, marriages of their children and also for contingency purposes such as diseases and unemployment periods, they also save in order to acquire durable goods such as houses, gold and jewellery. They also save to accumulate sufficient funds for their old age. But the level of investment depends upon marginal efficiency of capital and rate of interest in the short run and on the level of population, technological progress in the long run. Therefore, it is not essential that investment should be equal to the amount of savings by the people at full-employment level. If due to the adverse changes in the profit expectations of the entrepreneurs, level of investment falls, the equilibrium level of national income will also decline.

It is also worth noting that if aggregate expenditure increases beyond the $C + I'$ in Fig. 6.6, it will mean that the economy is spending and demanding more than it can produce. The result of this will be rise in prices of the commodities. In other words, if the investment demand in any year is higher than *HR*, in Fig. 6.6, then the inflationary process will start. In this situation, national income will rise beyond OY_F only in money terms but not in real terms.

DETERMINATION OF EQUILIBRIUM LEVEL OF NATIONAL INCOME: ALGEBRAIC ANALYSIS

A study of how the level of national income is determined will become more clear by using simple mathematics. As has been explained above, the level of national income is in equilibrium at which aggregate demand equals aggregate supply of output. In a simple model of income determination in which we do not consider the impact of Government expenditure and taxation and also exports and imports, the national income is the sum of consumption demand (*C*) and investment demand (*I*), that is,

$$Y = C + I$$

where *Y* stands for the level of national income.

Suppose the consumption function is of the following form :

$$C = a + bY$$

a is the intercept term in the consumption function and therefore represents the autonomous consumption expenditure which does not vary with income. *b* is a constant which represents the marginal propensity to consume (mpc $\Delta C/\Delta Y$). Thus total consumption demand is equal to the sum of autonomous consumption expenditure (*a*) and the induced consumption expenditure (*bY*).

Now suppose that investment demand equals I_a. This investment I_a is autonomous because this does not depend on income. Thus, we get the following three equations for the determination of the equilibrium level of national income.

$$Y = C + I \quad \text{...(i)}$$

$$C = a + bY \quad \text{...(ii)}$$

$$I = I_a \quad \text{...(iii)}$$

Substituting the values of C and I in equation (*i*) we have

$$Y = a + bY + Ia \qquad ...(iv)$$

$$Y - bY = a + Ia$$

$$Y(1 - b) = a + Ia$$

$$Y = \frac{1}{1-b}(a+I_a) \qquad ...(v)$$

The equation (*v*) shows the equilibrium level of national income when aggregated expenditure equals aggregate supply of output. *The equation (v) reveals that autonomous consumption and autonomous investment ($a + I_a$) generates so much expenditure or aggregate demand which is equal to the income generated by the production of goods and services*. From the equation (*v*) it also follows that the equilibrium level of national income can be known from multiplying the elements of autonomous expenditure (that is, $a + I_a$) by the term $\frac{1}{1-b}$ which is equal to the value of multiplier.

Further, it also follows that equilibrium level of income is higher, the greater the marginal propensity to consume (*i.e.*, *b*), autonomous consumption (*a*) and autonomous investment (I_a).

The multiplier tells us how much increase in income occurs when *autonomous investment* (*or consumption*) increases by Re. 1, that is, multiplier is $\frac{\Delta Y}{\Delta I}$ and its value is equal to $\frac{1}{1-b}$ where *b* stands for marginal propensity to consume (MPC). Thus, multiplier $= \frac{\Delta Y}{\Delta I} = \frac{1}{1-b}$. Further, it also follows that equilibrium level of income is higher, the greater the marginal propensity to consume (*i.e.* *b*) and autonomous investment (*I*).

Marginal Propensity to Consume and the Value of Multiplier. The higher the marginal propensity to consume (*b*), the greater the value of multiplier. For example, if marginal propensity to consume (*b*) is 0.8, investment multiplier is

$$\frac{\Delta Y}{\Delta I} = \frac{1}{1-08} = \frac{1}{0.2} = 1 \times \frac{10}{2} = 5$$

If *MPC* or $b = 0.75$, multiplier is

$$= \frac{\Delta Y}{\Delta I} = \frac{1}{1-0.75} = \frac{1}{0.25} = \frac{100}{25} = 4$$

Finding Increase in Income from Increase in Investment. We can find out the increase in income (ΔY) resulting from a certain increase in investment (ΔI) by using this multiplier relationship. Thus

$$\frac{\Delta Y}{\Delta I} = \frac{1}{1-b}$$

$$\therefore \Delta Y = \Delta I . \frac{1}{1-b}$$

If marginal propensity to consume is equal to 0.8, with the increase in investment by ₹ 100 crore the increase in income will be :

$$\frac{\Delta Y}{\Delta I} = \frac{1}{1-b}$$

$$\Delta Y = \Delta I \times \frac{1}{1-b} = 100 \times \frac{1}{1-0.8}$$

$$100 \times \frac{1}{0.2} = 100 \times 5 = 500 \text{ crore}$$

Illustrations of Equilibrium Level of Income with Numerical Examples

A few numerical examples will make it clear how the equilibrium level of national income is determined.

Problem 1. *Suppose in an economy, autonomous investment (I) is ₹ 600 crores and the following consumption function is given :*

$$C = 200 + 0.8Y$$

Given the above, find out the equilibrium level of income.

Solution. The equilibrium level of income is

$$Y = C + I$$

$$C = 200 + 0.8Y \qquad \ldots (i)$$

$$I = 600$$

Putting the values of C and I in the equilibrium (i) we have

$$Y = 200 + 0.8Y + 600$$

$$(Y - 0.8Y) = 200 + 600$$

$$Y(1 - 0.8) = 800$$

or

$$Y = \frac{800}{0.2} = \frac{800}{\frac{2}{10}} = \text{₹ } \mathbf{4000.}$$

Alternative Method. We can directly use equation (*v*) above in our general algebraic analysis using multiplier and autonomous items (*i.e.,* autonomous consumption and investment) to obtain equilibrium national income. The multiplier is given by $\frac{1}{1-b}$ where $b = MPC$ which is equal to 0.8 in the present problem. Autonomous consumption in the present problem is 200 crore and autonomous investment is 600 crore. Thus

$$Y = \frac{1}{1-b}(a + I_a)$$

$$= \frac{1}{1-0.8}(200+600) = 5(800)$$

$$= 4000 \text{ crore}$$

Problem 2. *Suppose the consumption function of an economy is C = 0.8 Y. Planned investment by entrepreneurs for a year is ₹ 500 crores. Find out what will be the equilibrium level of income*

Solution.

$$Y = C + I$$

$$C = 0.8Y$$

$$I = \text{₹ } 500 \text{ crore}$$

Substituting the values of C and I in (i) we have

$$Y = 0.8Y + 500$$

$$Y - 0.8Y = 500$$

$$Y(1 - 0.8) = 500$$

$$0.2 = 500$$

$$y = 500 \times \frac{10}{2} = \text{₹ } 2500 \text{ crore.}$$

Using Alternative Method

$$Y=\frac{1}{1-b}\ (a+I_a) = 5(0 + 500) = ₹\ 2500 \text{ Crore}$$

Problem 3. *Suppose the consumption of an economy is given by*

$$C = 20 + 0.6Y$$

The following investment function is given :

$$I = 10 + 02\ Y$$

What will be the equilibrium level of national income ?

Solution. Note that in this problem, investment varies with income. However, this will not change our method of determining equilibrium level of income.

$$Y = C + I$$

$$C = 20 + 0.6Y \qquad \ldots (i)$$

$$I = 10 + 0.2Y$$

Substituting the values of *C* and *I* in (*i*) we have

$$Y = 20 + 0.6Y + 10 + 0.2Y$$

$$Y = 30 + 0.8Y$$

$$Y - 0.8Y = 30$$

$$Y(1 - 0.8Y) = 30$$

$$0.2Y = 30$$

$$Y=30\times\frac{10}{2}=150$$

Thus, we find that the equilibrium level of income is equal to 150.

National Income and Employment

In the previous chapter we have explained the determination of level of employment and in the present chapter we have discussed the determination of national income. In fact, the levels of national income and employment are determined jointly. It is only for the better understanding of macroeconomic theory that we have presented their analysis separately. It will now be appropriate if we now explain their determination jointly by aggregate demand and supply. It is worth noting that, in Keynesian theory, employment is a function of income. Relation between income and labour employment is given by short-run production function showing diminishing returns to labour. This short-run production function can be stated as under :

$$Y = f(N, \bar{K}, \bar{T})$$

According to above function, given the capital stock and technology, the greater the level of national output (*i.e.* income or *Y*), the greater will be the number of workers (*N*) employed. As explained above in detail that, according to Keynesian theory, levels of national income and employment are determined by aggregate effective demand. In a closed economy with no intervention by the government, aggregate demand consists of consumption demand and investment demand. According to Keynes, consumption function is stable in the short run and it is investment demand which is highly volatile in the short run as it depends on profit expectations of business men. Equilibrium at full employment level of income is determined when investment expenditure fills the saving gap at full employment level of national income. Consider Fig. 6.7 where in panel (*b*) determination of national income is shown through intersection of aggregate demand and aggregate supply curves. According to Keynes, equilibrium at full-employment level of income OY_F will be determined if planned investment expenditure by entrepreneurs is equal to saving *HT* at full-employment level of national income OY_F Total expenditure (*i.e.*, aggregate demand) and output produced are both equal to *OQ* corresponding to equilibrium point *H*, ($OQ = OY_F$). In the left-side panel (*a*) where production function curve *TP* has been drawn , we have measured employment of labour on the *X*-axis and aggregate output on the Y-axis. It will be seen from this left-side panel (*a*) that output OQ is produced by employing ON_F amount of labour. We assume that ON_F represents full employment of labour, that is, all workers who want to work at the prevailing wage rate are getting employment. With this full employment of labour, national income equal to OY_F is being generated ($OY_F = OQ$).

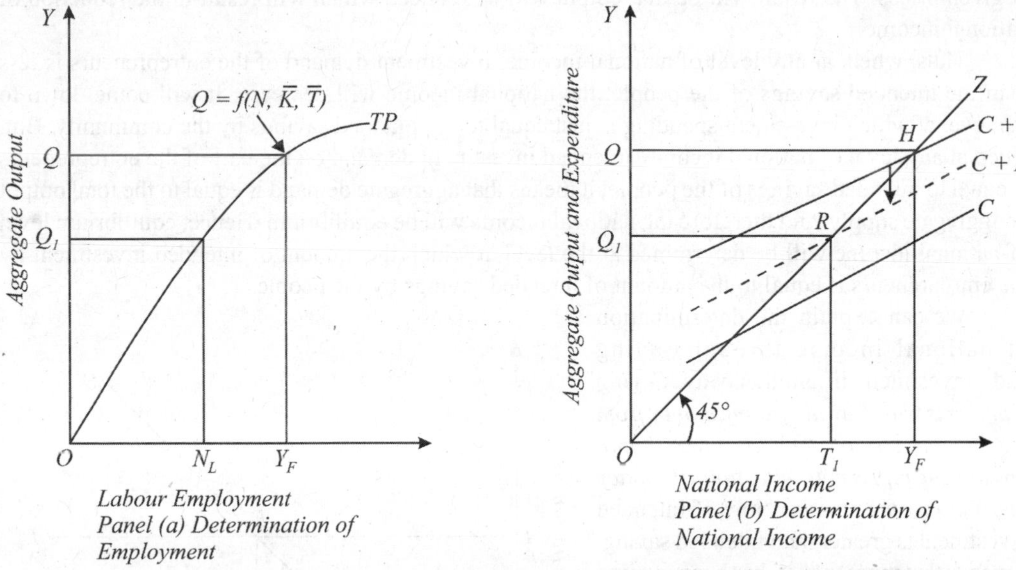

Fig. 6.7. *The Emergence of Involuntary Unemployment.*

Now, Keynes argued that if somehow or the other profit expectations of entrepreneurs become dim, this would cause a fall in the expected rate of return resulting in reduction in investment expenditure. With the fall in investment expenditure, aggregate demand curve shifts downward to the dotted position $C + I'$ which intersects 45° line OZ at point R. As a result, new equilibrium level of national income OY_1 is determined ($OY_1 = OQ_1$).

It will be seen from left-side panel (*a*) that aggregate output (*i.e.,* national product) OQ_1 is produced by employing ON_1 amount of labour. Thus, as a result of fall in aggregate demand, N_1N_F number of workers are rendered unemployed. N_1N_F workers will be involuntarily unemployed. According to Keynes, there is no any mechanism which should ensure that this involuntary unemployment will be automatically eliminated.

DETERMINATION OF NATIONAL INCOME: SAVING-INVESTMENT APPROACH

We have seen how equilibrium level of national income is determined by the interaction of aggregate demand and aggregate supply. The equilibrium level of national income is established at the point where aggregate demand equals aggregate supply. But there is an alternative method for the explanation of the determination of national income. This alternative method explains the determination of national income directly by intended saving and investment.

Look at Fig. 6.5 again. In this figure, at the equilibrium level of national income OY_1, saving and investment are equal to GE. Given the aggregate demand curve $C + I$, the amount of saving at income greater than OY_1 exceeds investment and for income less than OY_1 investment exceeds saving. It is obvious that intended saving and investment are equal only at the equilibrium level of national income and when intended saving and investment are not equal, national income will not be in equilibrium. Let us see why it is so and how national income is determined by intended saving and investment.

When at a certain level of national income, intended investment by the entrepreneurs is more than intended saving by the people, this would mean that aggregate expenditure is greater than aggregate supply of output. This will lead to the decline in inventories below the desired level. This would induce the firms to increase production, raising the level of income and employment. The result will be that national output will be increased on account of which national income will go up. Further, when at any level of income, investment is less than saving, it means that aggregate demand is less than aggregate supply. As a result, the entrepreneurs will not be able to sell their entire output at given prices. The result will be that output will be reduced which will result in the reduction of national income.

Thus, when, at any level of national income, investment demand of the entrepreneurs is less than the intended savings of the people, the national income will decrease. It will come down to the level at which investment spending is just equal to the planned savings by the community. But, when at any level of national income, intended investment demand on the part of the entrepreneurs is equal to intended savings of the people, it means that aggregate demand is equal to the total output or aggregate supply and therefore the national income will be equilibrium. Hence, equilibrium level of national income will be determined at the level at which the amount of intended investment by the entrepreneurs is equal to the amount of intended savings by the people.

We can explain the determination of national income through saving and investment in another way. *Saving represents withdrawal of some money from the income stream. On the other hand, investment represents injection of money into the income stream.* Now, if intended investment is greater than intended saving, it means that more money has been put into the income stream than has been taken out of it. As a result, income stream, *i.e.*, flow of national income would expand. On the contrary, if investment is less than intended saving, it means that less amount of money has been put into the income stream than has been taken out of it. The result would be that national income would decrease. But when investment is just equal to saving, it would mean that as much money has been put into the income stream as has been taken out of it. The result will be that the national income will neither increase nor decrease, *i.e.*, it will be in equilibrium. It is thus clear that the equilibrium level of national income will be determined at the level at which the intended investment is equal to intended saving.

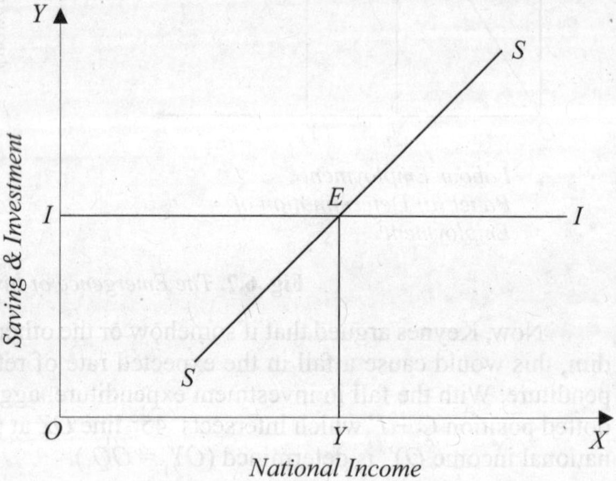

Fig. 6.8. *Determination of National Income : Saving-Investment Approach*

The determination of national income by investment and saving is illustrated in Fig. 6.8. In this figure, national income is shown along the *X*-axis. *SS* is the saving curve which shows intended saving at different levels of income, *II* curve shows investment demand *i.e.*, intended investment. The *II* investment curve has been drawn parallel to the *X*-axis. This is done on the assumption that in any year the entrepreneurs intend to invest a certain amount of money. This implies that we assume that investment is independent of change in income, that is, investment does not change with income.

The saving curve *SS* and the investment curve *II* intersect each other at *E*. That is, the intended investment and intended saving are equal at the *OY* level of income. Hence, *OY* is the equilibrium level of income. It will be seen from Fig. 6.8 that at the level of income less than *OY*, the amount of intended investment is more than intended savings. As a result, income will increase. On the contrary, at a level of income greater than *OY*, the amount of intended investment is less than the intended savings with the result that income will decrease. The decrease in income will continue until it becomes equal to *OY*. At the level of *OY* income, intended investment and intended saving are equal, so that there is neither the tendency for income to increase, nor to decrease. Hence, national income OY is determined. It is thus clear that national income is determined by the investment and saving.

Synthesis between the Two Approaches

The determination of national income has been explained above by two methods. The equilibrium level of national income is determined where two conditions are fulfilled :

(i) *Aggregate Expenditure or Demand = Aggregate Supply of Output*, and

(ii) *Intended Investment = Intended Savings.*

As has been explained above, the equality between aggregate demand (expenditure) and aggregate supply (output) and equality between intended investment and intended saving in reality mean the same thing. This is illustrated in Fig. 6.9. It will be seen in this figure that aggregate demand curve $C + I$ intersects aggregate supply curve OZ at point Q and thereby determines national income equal to OY. In the lower part of this diagram we have drawn intended savings curve SS and intended investment curve II. It is worthwhile to note that saving curve SS has been derived from the consumption function curve C and measures the gap between income and consumption at various levels of income. Further, investment curve II drawn in the lower part of the figure represents the difference between consumption function curve C and aggregate demand curve $C + I$. This difference is the amount of intended investment assumed in this figure. We thus see that both saving and investment curves drawn in the lower part are embedded in the upper part showing aggregate demand and aggregate supply. It is because of this that intended saving and intended investment curves also determine the same level of national income OY which is determined through the equality of aggregate demand ($C + I$) and aggregate supply.

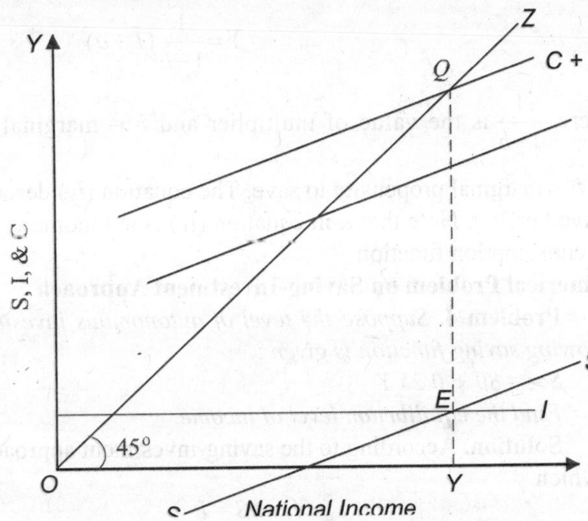

Fig. 6.9. *Synthesis between Aggregate Income-Expenditure Approach and Saving-Investment Approach*

Saving-Investment Approach : Algebraic Analysis

That the level of national income is determined by the equality of planned saving and planned investment can be derived from the equilibrium condition explained above that level of income is equal to effective demand.

That is,

$$Y = AD^* \qquad \ldots (i)$$

where AD^* represents effective aggregate demand or expenditure

Now in our simple economy, effective aggregate demand (AD^*) is equal to the sum of consumption expenditure and investment expenditure. Thus

$$AD^* = C + I$$

or

$$Y = C + I \qquad \ldots (ii)$$

Now

$$C = Y - S$$

Substituting $Y - S$ for C in equation (*ii*) we have

$$Y = Y - S + I$$

$$Y - Y + S = I$$

or

$$S = I \qquad \ldots (iii)$$

Thus, we reach at the alternative condition of equilibrium of national income, namely, planned (intended) saving be equal to planned (intended) investment.

We can further extend saving-investment approach to show the determination of national income as a multiple of autonomous factors. Since investment is treated as autonomous of national income, its amount is taken to be a fixed amount determined *exogenously*. Therefore we have

$$I = \bar{I}$$

Saving function as derived from the consumption function ($C = a + bY$) can be written as**

$$S = -a + (1 - b)\,Y$$

In equilibrium

$$\bar{I} = -a + (1 - b)Y$$

$$(1 - b)Y = \bar{I} + a$$

$$Y = \frac{1}{1-b}(\bar{I} + a) \quad \text{... } (iv)$$

where $\frac{1}{1-b}$ is the value of multiplier and b = marginal propensity to consume and therefore $1 - b$ = marginal propensity to save. The equation (*iv*) describes the same condition which we have derived earlier. Note that a in equation (*iv*) is autonomous consumption which is intercept term in the consumption function.

Numerical Problem on Saving-Investment Approach

Problem 4. *Suppose the level of autonomous investment in an economy is 200 crores. The following saving function is given :*

$S = -80 + 0.25\,Y$

Find the equilibrium level of income.

Solution. According to the saving-investment approach, the level of income is in equilibrium at which

$$S = I \quad \text{... } (i)$$

Given, $S = -80 + 0.25Y$, and

I = Rs. 200 crores

Substituting the values of S and I in the equilibrium equation we have

$$-80 + 0.25Y = 200$$

$$0.25Y = 200 + 80 = 280$$

$$Y = 280 \times \frac{100}{25} = 1120 \text{ crores}$$

Note that we can also use the equation (*iv*) derived above to obtain the equilibrium level of national income. Thus $Y = \frac{1}{1-b} = (I + a)$

Now, $b = 1 - 0.25 = 0.75$, $a = 80$ and $I = 200$

Thus $Y = \frac{1}{1-0.75} = (200 + 80)$

$= \frac{1}{0.25} \times 280 = 1120$ crores.

** This can be derived as follows

Since $C = Y - S$, consumption function can be written as

$Y - S = a + bY$

$S = -a - bY + Y$ or $S = -a + (1 - b)Y$

RELATIONSHIP BETWEEN SAVING AND INVESTMENT

An important controversy in macroeconomics relates to the relationship between saving and investment. Many economists before J.M. Keynes were generally of the view that saving and investment are generally not equal; they are equal only under condition of equilibrium. Besides, they thought that equality between saving and investment is brought about by changes in the rate of interest. Keynes in his famous work "***General Theory of Employment, Interest and Money***" put forward the view that saving and investment are always equal. This gave rise to a severe controversy in economics as to whether saving and investment are always equal or they are generally unequal. This controversy has now been resolved, and there is general agreement among economists about the correct relationship between saving and investment. Modern economists use the concepts of saving and investment in two different senses. In one sense, saving and investment are always equal, equilibrium or no equilibrium. In the second sense, saving and investment are equal only in equilibrium; they are unequal under conditions of disequilibrium. We shall explain below in detail the relationship between saving and investment in these two different senses.

It will be useful to recall here the meaning of saving and investment. In the beginning of this chapter we mentioned that investment is the addition made to the stock of capital during a period. In the stock of capital are included new machines, raw materials, buildings, tools and implements and addition to the inventories of raw materials, goods in process, finished consumer goods. When in a certain year there is net addition to the stock of capital, investment is said to have taken place. It is worth mentioning here that by investment we do not mean the stock of capital but the net addition to the stock of capital, *i.e., investment is a flow concept.* Of course, addition to the stock of capital is made through the flow of investment. In every year stock of capital expands through net investment.

On the other hand, by saving we mean the part of the income which has not been spent on consumer goods and services. In other words, saving is the difference between income and consumption expenditure. It is worth noting that in consumption expenditure all types of expenditure are not included. If an individual spends a part of his income on providing irrigation facilities, for buying tools and machinery, then that expenditure is not the consumption expenditure; it is in fact an investment expenditure. In order to obtain the saving, we have only to deduct the consumption expenditure from income and not the investment expenditure. When an individual makes investment expenditure he is deemed to spend his saved income on investment. For instance, if a farmer's annual income is ₹ 10,000 and he spends ₹ 6,000 on consumer goods and services and spends ₹ 1,000 on the construction of a well for his fields, and another ₹ 1,000 on building a drainage system for his fields and providing fencing, then his saving would be 10,000 – 6,000 = ₹ 4,000. The expenditure of ₹ 2,000 on the well, drainage and fencing will be included in the saving and will not constitute the consumption expenditure. If Y represents the national income of a country and C the total consumption, then the saving of the country will be equal to $Y - C$. Thus,

$$S - Y - C$$

Ex-post Savings and Ex-post Investment are always Equal

Pre-Keynesian economists were of the view that savings and investment are generally not equal. This is firstly because saving and investment are made by two different classes of people. While investment is undertaken by entrepreneurial class of the society, saving is done by the general public. Secondly, saving and investment depend upon different factors and are made for different purposes and motives. Therefore, it is not inevitable that savings and investment of a society must always be equal. Besides, some pre-Keynesian economists pointed out that investment expenditure is also undertaken by borrowing money from the banks which create new credit for this purpose. It was thus pointed out that more amount of investment than savings is possible because excess of investment over savings is financed by new bank credit. But Keynes expressed a totally opposite view that saving and investment are always equal. The sense in which savings and investment are always equal refers to the *actual* savings and *actual* investment made in the economy during a year. They are *also called ex-post saving and ex-post investment*. If we have to calculate that during the year 2004-05, how much actual savings and investment have been made in India, we will have to deduct the total consumption expenditure made by the citizens of India during that year from the national income. Likewise, the real investment during the year 2004-05 of the Indian economy will be obtained by summing up the investments actually made by the Indian people during that year. In fact, in national income accounting, estimates of savings and investment are made in this actual or ex-post sense.

The second sense in which saving and investment terms are used is that in a certain year how much saving or how much investment people of the country *desire or intend* to do. Therefore, saving and investment in this sense are known as *desired, intended or planned savings and investment*. They are also called *ex-ante saving and ex-ante investment*.

Keynes in his book, "***General Theory of Employment, Interest and Money***" showed that in spite of the fact that saving and investment are done by two different classes of people and also for different purposes and motives ex-post (actual) saving and ex-post (actual) investment are always equal. Thus, he used the word saving and investment in the ex-post or actual sense and proved the equality between saving and investment in the following way :

Income of a country is earned in two ways: (1) by producing and selling consumer goods and services, and (2) by producing and selling capital goods. That is, national income of a country is composed of the value of consumer goods and services and the value of capital goods. This can be expressed in the form of the following equation:

$$\text{National Income} = \text{Consumption} + \text{Investment}$$

$$\text{or} \quad Y = C + I \qquad ...(i)$$

where *Y* stands for national income, *C* for consumption and *I* for investment.

The above equation represents the production or earning side of the national income. The second aspect of national income is the expenditure side. The total national income can be fully consumed but generally it does not happen so. In actual practice, a part of the total income is spent on consumption and the remaining part is saved. From this we get the following equation:

$$\text{National Income} = \text{Consumption} + \text{Saving}$$

$$\text{or} \quad Y = C + S \qquad ...(ii)$$

where *Y* stands for national income, *C* for consumption and *S* for saving.

In the above two equations (*i*) and (*ii*) it is clear that national income is equal to the sum of consumption and investment and also equal to the sum of consumption and saving. From this it follows that :

$$\text{Consumption} + \text{Saving} = \text{Consumption} + \text{Investment}$$

$$C + S = C + I \qquad ...(iii)$$

In equation (*iii*) above, since *C* occurs on both sides of the equation, we get:

$$\text{Saving} = \text{Investment}$$

$$\text{or} \quad S = I$$

From the foregoing analysis, it follows that saving and investment are defined in such a way that they are necessarily equal to each other. In equation (*i*), investment is that part of national income which is obtained from the production of goods other than those consumed and in equation (*ii*) saving is that part of national income which is not spent on consumption. Hence in the actual or ex-post sense, saving and investment by definition are equal.

It is worth mentioning that in macroeconomics, saving and investment do not refer to the saving and investment by an individual; they refer to the saving and investment of the whole community or economy. Saving and investment by an individual can differ but *in the ex-post sense, saving of the whole economy must always be equal to investment*.

Now the question arises why ex-post saving and ex-post investment are always equal. For instance, when less investment is planned by the entrepreneurs then how actual (ex-post) investment becomes equal to actual (ex-post) saving. On the other hand, if planned (or intended) investment exceeds intended saving, then how actual (ex-post) investment and saving are made equal. In this connection it is worth mentioning that following Keynes modern economists include inventories of goods in investment. It is changes in these unplanned or unintended inventory investment that make the actual investment and saving equal to each other in any period of time.

For example, when at a level of national income intended (ex-ante) savings exceed planned (ex-ante) investment, aggregate expenditure ($C + I$) will not be sufficient to buy all the goods produced at that level of income. As a result, there will be unplanned or unintended increase in inventories of goods with businessmen. It is unintended because it results from the shortage of aggregate demand to buy the total output of goods produced, prices remaining fixed. Thus *actual (ex-post) investment which equals planned investment plus unplanned or unintended increase in inventory investment becomes equal to actual (ex-post) saving*. Note that since businessmen will not be interested in holding on to these unwanted extra inventories, they will cut back production in the next period.

On the other hand, if in a period planned investment exceeds planned (ex-ante) savings, aggregate expenditure ($C + I$) and therefore sales would exceed planned output of goods. This will lead to the *unintended or unplanned decline in inventories* of goods. As a result, actual (ex-post) investment (that is, planned investment minus unintended decline in inventory investment) will turn out to be equal to actual saving in that period of time. Of course, unintended decline in inventories of goods would induce business men to expand production of goods in the next period and thereby causes increase in level of national income. We thus see that in the ex-post or realised sense, saving and investment are always equal.

Ex-ante Saving and Ex-ante Investment are Equal only in Equilibrium

As said above, in the desired, planned or ex-ante sense, saving and investment can differ. In fact planned or ex-ante saving and investment are generally not equal to each other. This is due to the fact that the persons or classes who save are different from those who invest. Savings are done by general public for various objectives and purposes. On the other hand, investment is made by the entrepreneurial class in the community and is generally governed by marginal efficiency of capital on the one hand and rate of interest on the other. Therefore, savings and investment in planned or ex-ante sense generally differ from each other. But through the mechanism of change in the income level, there is tendency for ex-ante saving and ex-ante investment to become equal. When in a year planned investment is larger than planned saving, the level of income rises. At a higher level of income, more is saved and therefore intended saving becomes equal to intended investment. On the other hand, when planned saving is greater than planned investment in a period, the level of income will fall. At a lower level of income, less will be saved and therefore planned saving will become equal to planned investment. We thus see that *planned or ex-ante saving and planned or ex-ante investment are brought to equality through changes in the level of income.* When ex-ante saving and ex-ante investment are equal, level of income is in equilibrium, *i.e.,* it has no tendency to rise or fall. It is thus clear that whereas realised or ex-post saving is always equal to realised or ex-post investment, intended, planned or ex-ante saving and investment may differ;

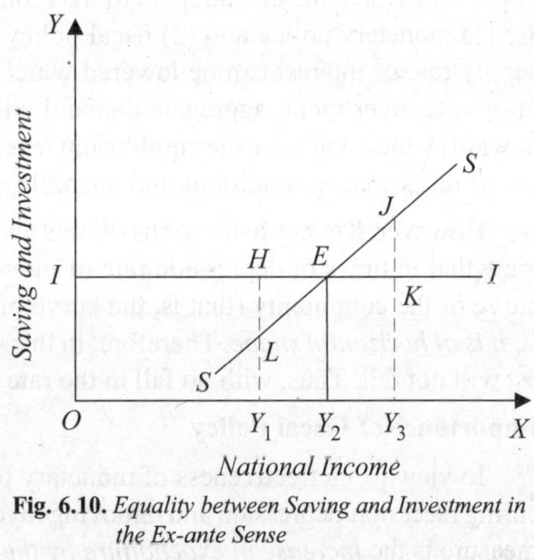

Fig. 6.10. *Equality between Saving and Investment in the Ex-ante Sense*

intended or ex-ante saving and investment have only a tendency to be equal and are equal only at the equilibrium level of income.

That the planned or intended saving is equal to intended investment only at the equilibrium level of income can be easily understood from Fig. 6.10. In this figure, national income is measured along the *X*-axis while saving and investment are measured along the *Y*-axis. *SS* is the saving curve which slopes upward indicating thereby that with the rise in income, saving also increases. *II* is the investment curve. Investment curve *II* is drawn as horizontal straight line because, following Keynes, it has been assumed that investment is independent of the level of income, *i.e.*, it depends upon factors other than the current level of income. It will be seen from Fig. 6.10 that saving and investment curves intersect at point *E*. Therefore, *OY* is the equilibrium level of income. If the level of income is OY_1, the intended investment is Y_1H whereas the intended saving is Y_1L. It is thus clear that at OY_1 level of income, intended investment is greater than intended saving. As a result of this, level of income will rise and at higher levels of income more will be saved. It will be seen that with the rise in income to OY_2, saving rises and becomes equal to investment. On the other hand, if in any period, level of income is OY_3 intended investment is Y_3K and intended saving is Y_3J. As a result of this, level of national income will fall to OY_2 at which ex-ante saving and ex-ante investment are once again equal and thus level of national income is in equilibrium. To sum up, whereas ex-post savings and ex-post investment are always equal, ex-ante saving and ex-ante investment are equal only in equilibrium.

POLICY IMPLICATIONS OF KEYNES'S THEORY OF INCOME AND EMPLOYMENT

Keynes's theory has important policy implications for raising the level of income and employment when the equilibrium of the economy is at less than full-employment level and as a consequence there is depression or recession in the economy with its huge unemployment of labour. There are two types of policies which may be adopted to overcome this situation of recession and unemployment. They are (1) monetary policy and (2) fiscal policy. Under monetary policy, through expansion in money supply rate of interest can be lowered which will encourage private investment. With the increase in private investment, aggregate demand will increase (that is, aggregate demand curve will shift upward) which will raise the equilibrium level of employment. As a result, the economy will be lifted out of recessionary conditions and unemployment will be removed.

However, Keynes had serious doubts about the effectiveness of monetary policy. He was of the view that in times of depression rate of interest is already very low and at this liquidity preference curve of the community (that is, the curve of demand for money to hold) is *absolutely elastic, that is, it is of horizontal shape*. Therefore, in this situation when money supply is increased, rate of interest will not fall. Thus, with no fall in the rate of interest, private investment will not pick up further.

Importance of Fiscal Policy

In view of ineffectiveness of monetary policy, Keynes laid stress on the role of fiscal policy in curing recession/depression and removing involuntary unemployment. Under the fiscal policy, a major measure is the *increase in expenditure by the Government on several types of public works* in times of depression. The increase in Government expenditure will cause an upward shift in the aggregate demand curve. This increase in aggregate demand will bring about increase in employment and output. If the increase in Government expenditure and as a result rise in aggregate demand is sufficient, it will help in achieving equilibrium at full-employment level. As a result, depression and involuntary unemployment will be eliminated. It is worth noting that in this regard Keynes put forward a theory of multiplier which strengthened the case for raising Government expenditure on public works in times of depression or when large-scale unemployment prevailed in the economy. We shall discuss the theory of multiplier at length in later chapter. Briefly, theory of multiplier implies that increase in Government expenditure will raise aggregate demand and therefore output and employment not by the amount of increase in Government expenditure but by a multiple of it.

Another important measure of fiscal policy to raise employment and output is the *reduction in taxes*. When rates of personal taxes such as income tax are reduced, disposable income of the people increases which brings about rise in their demand for consumption. The rise in consumption demand pushes up aggregate demand curve and helps in removing recession and unemployment. It may be noted that on the recommendations of Keynesian economists American President John Kennedy made a drastic cut in income taxes in 1964. This had a great success as output and employment in the USA increased significantly and, as a result, recession and unemployment were removed. Cut in personal taxes to boost aggregate demand has also been applied in later years in the USA as well as in Great Britain. In 2003, the President of the USA George W. Bush had made a 3.5 billion cut in taxes to revive the American economy. .

In the end, it is important to note that modern economists though agree with Keynes's view about the effectiveness of fiscal policy in curing recession, they do not share Keynes's view about the ineffectiveness of monetary policy. It may however be noted that, according to the modern Keynesians and others, liquidity preference curve of the community is fairly elastic even in times of recession which implies that expansion in money supply will cause a decline in interest rate and will therefore stimulate private investment. Further, according to them, investment demand curve is also fairly elastic which implies that fall in interest rate will have significant impact on private investment. Thus, according to modern economists, both monetary and fiscal policies are important instruments whereby aggregate demand of the economy can be changed. We shall discuss in detail the roles of monetary and fiscal policies for attaining economic stabilisation in later chapters.

That the free market system does not guarantee economic stability and full employment has been proved by the recent ***global financial crisis*** (2007-09) which started in the US as a result of collapse of financial system following bursting of housing bubble and spread to other countries (including India) through global linkages of free trade and capital flows and caused global slowdown. The market system which was believed by the classical economists-monetarists, led by Milton Friedman and new classical economists led by Robert Lucas to correct itself automatically and recover from the crisis failed to deliver. As a result, there were loud protests about the failure of the free market system to ensure economic stability and full employment.

Again it were Keynesian policies which came to the rescue of the US, India and other countries which were gripped by severe recession. These countries adopted Keynesian expansionary fiscal and monetary policies to provide stimulus to the economies by raising aggregate demand so as to get out of recessionary conditions. These counter cyclical Keynesian policies worked and in the recession-ridden economies of the US, European countries, Australia, Japan, China and India, economic recovery started and by the early 2010 they seem to have returned to the path growth.

NUMERICAL PROBLEMS

Problem 1. *Given the saving function $S = -10 + 0.2y$ and autonomous investment, $I =$ ₹ 50 crore.*

(*i*) *Find the equilibrium level of income.*

(*ii*) *Find the level of consumption.*

(*iii*) *If investment increases permanently by ₹ 5 crores, what will be the new levels of income and consumption ?*

Solution : (*i*) According to saving-investment approach, equilibrium level of national income is determined by equality between planned saving and investment. Thus,

$$S = I \qquad ...(i)$$

$$-10 + 0.2Y = 50$$

$$0.2\,Y = 50 + 10 = 60$$

$$Y = 60 \times \frac{10}{2} = 300$$

(*ii*) $C = Y - S$ ...(*ii*)

$$S = -10 + 0.2Y$$

$$= -10 + \frac{2}{10} \times 300 = 50$$

Substituting the value of income and saving(*s*) in equation (*ii*), we have

$$C = 300 - 50 = 250$$

(*iii*) With the increase in investment by ₹ 5 crores, the new investment will become equal to ₹ 55 crores.

$$S = I$$

$$-10 + 0.2Y = 55$$

$$0.2Y = 55 + 10 = 65$$

$$Y = 65 \times \frac{10}{2} = 325$$

Thus, new level of income = ₹ 325 crores.

Now, saving $= -10 + 0.2Y$

$$= -10 + \frac{2}{10} \times 325$$

$$= -10 + 65 = 55$$

Consumption $(C) = Y - S$

$$= 325 - 55$$

$$= 270$$

Problem 2. *The following consumption function of an economy is given :*

40 + 0.8Y where Y is national income

If the planned level of investment in a year equals ₹ 75 crores, what will be the equilibrium level of national income and consumption ?

Solution : Equilibrium level of national income is determined where

$$Y = C + I$$

Now, $C = 40 + 0.8\,Y$

$$I = 75$$

$$Y = 40 + 0.8Y + 75$$

$$Y - 0.8Y = 40 + 785 = 115$$

$$0.2Y = 115$$

$$Y = 115 + \frac{10}{2} = 575$$

$$C = Y - I = 575 - 75 = 500$$

Problem 3. *For an economy the following consumption function is given :*

$$C = 60 + 0.75\,Y.$$

(*a*) *If investment in a year is ₹ 35 crores, what will be the equilibrium level of income or output ?*

(*b*) *If full-employment level of income (i.e. level of potential output) is ₹ 460 crores, what investment is required to be undertaken to ensure equilibrium at full-employment ?*

Solution : (*a*) $Y = C + I$

$$Y = 60 + 0.75Y + 35$$

$$Y - 0.75Y = 60 + 35 = 95$$
$$Y(1 - 0.75) = 95$$
$$0.25Y = 95$$
$$Y = 95 \times \frac{100}{25} = 380$$

(*b*) To ensure full-employment equilibrium, investment should be equal to the saving gap at full-employment income. With the given full-employment income equal to ₹ 460,

$$S_F = Y_F - C_F = Y_F - (60 + 0.75Y_F)$$
$$= 460 - 60 - (0.75 \times 460)$$
$$= 400 - 345 = 55$$

Thus, investment required for full-employment equilibrium is 55 crores.

QUESTIONS FOR REVIEW

1. Explain how equilibrium level of national income is determined by level of effective demand in a simple two-sector Keynesian model. Is this equilibrium necessarily established at full-employment level ?

2. Explain the equilibrium of national income by consumption and investment. When will the equilibrium be established at full-employment ?

3. (*i*) Saving and Investment are *always equal.*
(*ii*) Saving and Investment are *equal only in equilibrium.*
How would you reconcile the above two statements ?

4. Explain Keynes's income-expenditure approach to the determination of national income. Why can this equilibrium be reached below full-employment level of output ?

5. Define planned (desired) saving and planned (desired) investment. Explain how equilibrium level of national income is determined by planned saving and planned investment. Why is this equilibrium not always attained at full-employment level ?

6. What do you understand by the equilibrium level of national income ? Explain that both saving–investment approach and aggregate demand-aggregate supply approach yield the same level of equilibrium.

7. In a three-sector economy with firms, households and Government show that aggregate demand will equal aggregate supply only at the level of output and income at which savings and taxes equal Government expenditure and planned investment.

8. Explain the Keynesian concept of aggregate demand. How is the Keynesian aggregate demand function different from the classical demand function ?

9. Explain the concept of deflationary gap. What are the causes and consequences of this gap ?

10. (*a*) What is meant by under-employment equilibrium ? Explain the factors which cause it.

(*b*) Explain the various measures that can be taken to increase the equilibrium level of income and employment. Is it possible to increase the level of income without increasing the level of investment ?

11. Explain the concept of inflationary gap. What are its causes and consequences ?

12. Explain how the Keynesian theory of inflationary gap explains the emergence of inflation in the economy. What steps can be taken to prevent inflation ?

13. What, according to Keynes, is the cause of recession or depression in the economy ? What measures can be adopted to overcome recession in the economy ?

14. The following consumption of an economy is given:

$$C = 75 + 0.8\,Y$$

(*i*) What will be the equilibrium level of national income if investment equals 40 crore ?

(*ii*) Find the equilibrium level of consumption.

(*iii*) How much will national income increase if investment increases to 50 crore ?

(**Hint:** Answer to (*iii*) can be directly found by applying the multiplier principle, that is, $\Delta Y = \Delta I \left(\frac{1}{1 - MPC}\right)$. In the given problem $\Delta I = 50 - 40 = 10$ crore and $MPC = 0.8$).

15. Given the following saving function of the economy; S

$$S = -15 + 0.25\,Y$$

(*i*) If planned investment in a year of the economy equals ₹ 20 crore, what will be the equilibrium level of national income ?

(*ii*) What is the equilibrium level of consumption ?

CHAPTER 7

Determination of National Income in a Three-Sector Economy

We carry our analysis of determination of national income further in this chapter. Having explained the Keynesian two-sector model of determination of national income in the previous chapter, we will explain in this chapter the determination of national income in a three-sector model. The three-sector model incorporates the role of government with its expenditure and taxation in the determination of national income. The government sometimes increases its expenditure and taxes and sometimes reduces them depending on the state of the economy. An important contribution of Keynes was that the government should intervene in the economy to bring about economic stability in the economy. For example, according to him, when an economy goes into recession or depression, the government should increase its expenditure and cut taxes and thereby increase aggregate demand so as to get the economy out of recession and eliminate involuntary unemployment. Besides, at times of inflationary situation, the government cuts its expenditure and imposes more taxes or increases rates of existing taxes so as to reduce aggregate demand and thereby to remove demand-pull inflation. Thus, according to Keynes, through its appropriate fiscal policy it can "***manage aggregate demand***" to bring about stability in the economy. Fiscal policy means the government's policy regarding its expenditure on goods and services, transfer payments, taxation and borrowing. Since demand management to bring about stability in the economy requires deliberate policy decisions by the government, the economists call it ***discretionary fiscal policy***. In what follows we will explain when government plays an active role in working of the economy how the conditions of equilibrium national income change.

DETERMINATION OF NATIONAL INCOME WITH GOVERNMENT : THREE-SECTOR MODEL

Government Expenditure and National Income

In our analysis of two-sector model we have explained how the equilibrium level of national income is determined by the consumption function and autonomous investment demand. In our analysis we did not take into account the role of Government expenditure in the determination of national income. However, in all economies today including the free-market capitalist economies such as those of U.S.A., Britain, and Japan, the Government expenditure on goods and services plays an important role in the determination of national income and therefore it should also be included in the analysis of income determination. It is important to note here that the magnitude of Government expenditure on such things as highways, public parks, education, health services is governed by the consideration of promoting social welfare, employment and growth in the economy and does not depend on the level of income of the economy. Therefore, in the simple Keynesian model of income determination, the Government expenditure is treated as *autonomous expenditure,* that is, it does not vary with change in income. We further assume for the moment that Government spends on goods and services but makes no transfer payment. We denote Government expenditure by G. Thus in the three-sector economy when we take into account the income generating effects of Government expenditure, we get the following equation for aggregate expenditure:

$$AE = C + I + G \qquad \ldots (i)$$

where Y is national income or output and $C + I + G$ represents the level of aggregate demand or expenditure including Government expenditure, G.

Treating government expenditure as a component of aggregate expenditure we turn to explain how taxes imposed by the government to finance its expenditure are treated in our analysis of equilibrium national income in a three-sector economy. We have explained in the previous chapter that aggregate consumption varies with income. As income increases, aggregate consumption usually increases. According to Keynes consumption (C) is a function of *current* income (Y) and is written as:

$$C = a + bY$$

where a is autonomous consumption and is an intercept term in the function, b is marginal propensity to consume.

When we introduce taxes in our equilibrium analysis of income, we modify the consumption function. For simplifying our analysis we assume *lump sum income tax* is imposed which we denote by T. The levying of taxes (T) reduces the disposable income of the people. Disposable income (Y_d) is national income (Y) minus lump sum tax (T). Incorporating this in our consumption function we have

$$C = a + b(Y - T)$$

where $Y - T$ is disposable income (Y_d). As imposition of taxes lowers the level of consumption by reducing disposable income, the consumption curve representing $C = a + b(Y - T)$ will lie at a lower level (that is, its intercept will be smaller than $C = a + bY$.

Condition of Equilibrium National Income: As we know national income (GDP) is in equilibrium when:

$$AE = Y$$

In a three-sector economy

$$AE = C + I + G$$

In equilibrium

$$Y = C + I + G$$

When at a level of national income aggregate expenditure ($C + I + G$) is greater than income or aggregate output, there will be *unintended decline* in inventories of goods with the firms. This will induce firms to increase output and they will go on doing so until national income becomes equal to aggregate expenditure (AE or $C + I + G$). On the other hand, when at a level of national income, aggregate expenditure is less than aggregate output, this means there will be unintended accumulation of inventories of goods with the firm which will induce them to reduce output until it becomes equal to aggregate expenditure. Thus a three-sector economy will be in equilibrium at a level of national income (GDP) at which $Y = C + I + G$.

Graphic Illustration

The impact of Government expenditure on goods and services on the equilibrium level of national income is illustrated in Fig. 7.1. The $C + I + G$ is the aggregate expenditure curve which has been obtained by adding autonomous investment equal to I and the Government expenditure on goods and services (G) to the consumption function curve (C). With this, the equilibrium national income is determined at the level OY at which the aggregate expenditure curve ($C + I + G$) intersects the 45° line, that is, aggregate demand ($C + I + G$) equals aggregate supply of output. The reason for the determination of equilibrium level of income at OY

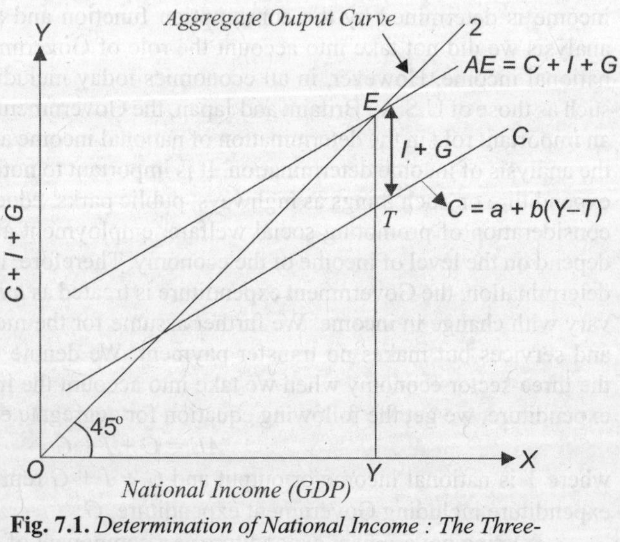

Fig. 7.1. *Determination of National Income : The Three-Sector Model*

when Government expenditure is included in the aggregate demand curve is the same as stated earlier. It will be observed from Fig. 7.1 that at a level of national income *less* than OY, aggregate expenditure $C + I + G$ exceeds aggregate output (GDP). This implies unintended decline in the inventories of goods with the firms which will induce them to expand the level of aggregate output to the level OY. On the contrary, at the level of national income *greater* than OY, the aggregate expenditure is less than aggregate output. This deficiency of aggregate demand for goods will cause unintended accumulation of inventories. The firms would respond to this by cutting back production of goods which will lead to the reduction of national income to OY.

It is important to note that *in the presence of Government expenditure, national income is determined at the level at which the saving gap is equal to the sum of private investment and Government expenditure* $(I + G)$.

This can be shown as under :

In equilibrium, $Y = C + I + G$

or $\quad Y - C = I + G$

Since $\quad Y - C = \text{Saving } (S)$

Therefore, in equilibrium $\quad S = I + G$

Government Expenditure Multiplier

Just as increase in investment, increase in government expenditure has also a multiplier effect on national income. Government expenditure is classified into (*i*) *expenditure on goods and services and* (*ii*) *transfer payments such as expenditure on social security schemes (old-age pensions, unemployment allowance), subsidies on food and fertilizers*, etc. Both types of expenditure have a multiplier effect on national income or aggregate output though the values of their multiplier differ. We will confine ourselves to the multiplier of government expenditure on goods and services.

Suppose the economy goes into recession resulting in involuntary unemployment on a large scale. The government decides to increase its expenditure without raising taxes to get the economy out of recession. In doing so the government will have a budget deficit and to finance this deficit government will have to borrow the money. Suppose the government has been told that due to recession national income (GDP) has declined by ₹ 400 crore from its potential (*i.e.,* full-employment) level. Now, the important thing to understand is that due to multiplier effect government need not increase its expenditure by the amount of ₹ 400 crore to get out of recession and restore equilibrium at potential or full-employment level of output.

When government increases its expenditure on goods, it causes expansion in output of goods and *generate incomes* for those workers who are employed to produce more goods to supply them to the government. With this the incomes of the workers and other persons engaged in production goods will spend a good part of the increase of their incomes on consumption given their propensity to consume and this extra demand for consumer goods will lead to *further increase* in output of consumer goods and generate employment and income for more workers. These newly employed workers will in turn spend a good part of it on consumption, given the marginal propensity to consume and in this way the process of generation of incomes and increase in output will go on. Thus, *increase in government expenditure has same multiplier effect on the equilibrium level of income as the increase in investment and the size of government expenditure multiplier depends on marginal propensity to consume and is given by* $\frac{1}{1-b}$ *where b is marginal propensity to consume*. For example, if marginal propensity to consume (b) is 0.75, government expenditure multiplier is:

$$\frac{\Delta Y}{\Delta G} = \frac{1}{1-b} = \frac{1}{1-0.75} = \frac{1}{0.25} = 4$$

Thus, increase in government expenditure by ₹ 1 will lead to increase in equilibrium level of income by ₹ 4. Now, it is evident that to increase national income (GDP) by ₹ 400 crore to restore equilibrium at potential or full employment level government needs to increase its expenditure by ₹ 100 crore as given 4 as the size of multiplier, increase in government expenditure by ₹ 100 will lead to ₹ 100 × 4 = ₹ 400 crore

Algebraic Derivation of Government Expenditure Multiplier

We can derive government expenditure multiplier algebraically in the same way as in the previous chapter where we derived the value of investment multiplier by using the following consumption function:

$$C = a + b(Y - T)$$

where b is marginal propensity to consume, and T is lump sum tax. The condition for equilibrium level of national income is:

$$Y = C + I + G$$

By substituting $a + b(Y - T)$ for C, we have

$$Y = a + b(Y - T) + I + G$$

$$Y = a + bY - bT + I + G$$

By rearranging we have:

$$Y - bY = a + I + G - bT$$

$$Y(1 - b) = a + I + G - bT$$

Solving for Y we have

$$Y = \frac{1}{1-b}(a + I + G - bT)$$

It follows from the above last equation that if government expenditure (G) increases by one, other determinants such as I, and T remaining constant, the equilibrium national income (Y) will increase by $\frac{1}{1-b}$ where b is marginal propensity to consume (MPC). Similarly, if government expenditure is increased by ΔG, equilibrium national income (Y) will increase by $\Delta G \frac{1}{1-b}$. Thus

$$\Delta Y = \Delta G \frac{1}{1-b}$$

Rearranging we have

$$\frac{\Delta Y}{\Delta G} = \frac{1}{1-b}$$

Thus, the size of government expenditure multiplier as of investment multiplier is equal to $\frac{1}{1-b}$ or $\frac{1}{1-MPC}$. Since $1 - MPC = MPS$, the value of government expenditure multiplier is also equal to $\frac{1}{MPS}$.

Graphic Representation: Graphic representation of government expenditure multiplier is given in Figure 7.2. Initially aggregate expenditure curve is given by the curve $C + I + G$. Since investment and government expenditure are fixed the curve $C + I + G$ rises as with thc increase in national income consumption (C) increases. The slope of the curve $C + I + G$ therefore represents marginal propensity to consume (*i.e.* b) which is given. With the aggregate expenditure curve $C+I+G$, equilibrium level of national income is Y_1. However, if national income Y_2 represents full-employment level of aggregate output, the equilibrium at Y_1 represents less than full-employment equilibrium as is found during recession in the economy. It will be seen from Fig. 7.2 that to get out of recession and to establish equilibrium at full-employment income the government has to increase its expenditure (ΔG) by E_1H. With this increase in government expenditure by E_1H, the aggregate expenditure curve shifts up to $C + I + G + \Delta G$, and the equilibrium is at point E_2 which corresponds to full-employment level of national income Y_2. It should be noted that increase in national income (ΔY) by Y_1Y_2 is much greater than increase in government expenditure (ΔG) which is equal to E_1H. Thus, $\frac{\Delta Y}{\Delta G}$ or $\frac{Y_1Y_2}{E_1H}$ represents government expenditure multiplier which will be equal to $\frac{1}{1-MPC}$ or $\frac{1}{MPS}$ as explained above.

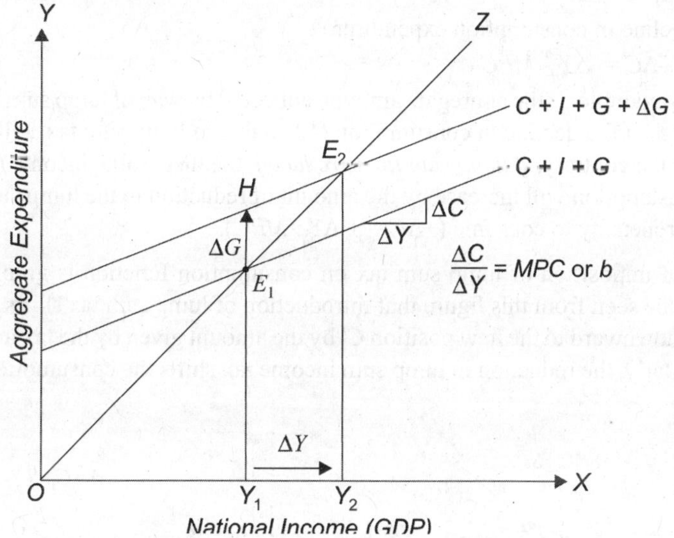

Fig. 7.2. *Government Expenditure Multiplier*

Effect of Lump Sum Tax on National Income and Lump Sum Tax Multiplier

In our above analysis of determination in a three-sector model our focus has been on the impact of government expenditure on equilibrium level of national income and on derivation of government expenditure multiplier though we incorporated in our analysis the lump sum income tax. Now, in the present section we focus our analysis on the impact of lump sum tax on national income and in this context we will derive lump sum tax multiplier. A lump sum tax does not vary with income. In this case if government expenditure equals revenue from lump sum tax, its budget will be in *balance*. On the other hand, if government expenditure exceeds tax revenue, there will be a *budget deficit*. Further, if tax revenue is more than its expenditure, government will have a *surplus budget*. We are thus concerned here with the impact of government expenditure and taxation together on the determination of national income. We assume that there are no *transfer payments* made by the government.

The *lump sum tax* is the simplest kind of a tax in which a given fixed amount of revenue is collected irrespective of the level of income. Suppose government has decided to raise extra ₹ 500 crore by way of imposing lump sum tax on the public. Every one will have to pay the fixed amount out of his income as a lump sum tax. In the aggregate, the disposable income of the economy will be reduced by this fixed amount of lump sum tax (*i.e.*, 500 crore) whatever the level of national income (GNP). Consequently, people will consume less after the levy of lump sum tax. A lump sum tax of ₹ 500 crore imposed by the Government will reduce the disposable income by the same amount, that is, by ₹ 500 crore. As a result, the people will consume less (and also save less) at each level of national income (GNP). However, it is worth mentioning that *consumption will not fall by the full amount of the tax because a part of the reduction in disposable income due to the tax was being consumed and a part of it was being saved prior to taxation*. Therefore, reduction in disposable income due to the lump sum tax will partly cause a decline in consumption and partly a decline in saving. Therefore, the amount by which consumption will fall due to the introduction of lump sum tax will be equal to the amount of tax multiplied by the marginal propensity to consume. If ΔY_d stands for change in disposable income, T for lump sum tax imposed and MPC for marginal propensity to consume, then the decline in consumption ($-\Delta C$) due to the imposition of lump sum tax is given by

$$-\Delta C = T.MPC$$

Since a lump sum tax causes an equal change in disposable income (Y_d), therefore

Lump sum tax, $T = \Delta Y_d$

Therefore, decline in consumption expenditure :

$$-\Delta C = \Delta Y_d .\ MPC$$

Let us take an example. If the aggregate amount collected by way of lump sum tax is ₹ 500 crore and MPC is 0.75, then the decline in consumption ($-\Delta C$) due to lump sum tax will be ₹ 500 × 0.75 = ₹ 375 crore. On the contrary, *if lump sum tax is reduced*, the disposable income (Y_d) will increase and as a result consumption will increase by the amount of reduction in the lump sum tax multiplied by the marginal propensity to consume ($+\Delta C = +\Delta Y_d . MPC$).

The impact of imposition of lump sum tax on consumption function is graphically shown in Figure 7.3. It will be seen from this figure that introduction of lump sum tax shifts the consumption function curve C downward to the new position C' by the amount given by the tax amount multiplied by the MPC. Similarly, the reduction in lump sum income tax shifts the consumption function curve upward to C''.

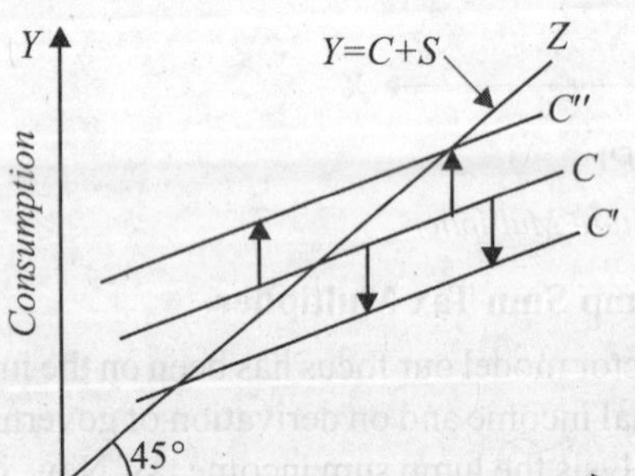

Fig. 7.3. *Effect of Lump Sum Tax on Consumption Function*

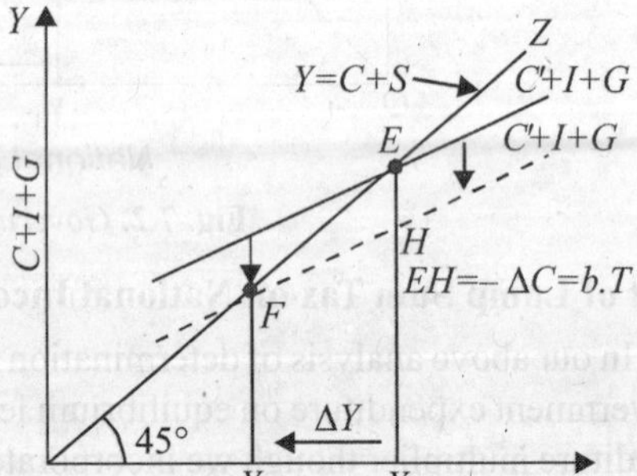

Fig. 7.4. *Effect of Lump Sum Tax on National Income*

Lump Sum Tax Multiplier

Figure 7.4 shows the effect of imposition of lump sum tax on the equilibrium level of national income (GNP). It will be observed from Figure 7.4 that due to lump sum tax equal to T, and consequently downward shift in aggregate expenditure curve to the new dotted position $C'' + I + G$, the equilibrium level of national income falls from OY_0 to OY_1. An important point worth mentioning is that the fall in the level of income ($-\Delta Y$) is not equal to the amount of lump sum tax (T) collected but by a multiple of it, and this tax multiplier is equal to $\frac{-b}{1-b}$ where b stands for marginal propensity to consume. Thus, $\frac{-b}{1-b}$ or $\frac{-MPC}{1-MPC}$ is **tax multiplier of a lump sum tax**. We will derive this expression of lump sum tax multiplier below.

It will also be seen from Figure 7.4 that *if Government **reduces** lump sum income tax*, the consumption function curve shifts upward to the new position C″. From this it follows that *reduction in tax by the government will increase the disposaible income of the society and raise consumption demand. The rise in consumption demand will raise the equilibrium level of income by a multiple amount depending on the marginal propensity to consume.*

Derivation of Lump Sum Tax Multiplier

Three-sector model with the above specifications can be developed as follows :

$$Y = AE = C + \overline{I} + \overline{G}$$

or
$$Y = C + \overline{I} + \overline{G} \qquad ...(i)$$

Now, consumption function can be stated as :

$$C = a + bY_d$$

where a is constant autonomous consumption expenditure, Y_d is disposable income. In this three-sector model with lump sum tax, consumption function can be written as

$$C = a + b(Y - T)$$

where T = lump sum tax

or $C = a + bY - bT$

Substituting the value of C in income equation (i) we have

$$Y = a + bY - bT + \overline{I} + \overline{G}$$

$$Y - bY = a - bT - \overline{I} + \overline{G}$$

$$Y(1-b) = a - bT + \overline{I} + \overline{G}$$

$$Y = \frac{1}{1-b}\left(a - bT + \overline{I} + \overline{G}\right) \qquad ...(ii)$$

The above equation (*ii*) *is the same* as derived above for government expenditure multiplier. From this equation (*ii*), it is evident that increase of lump sum tax (T) by one, other determinants of income such as a, I and G remaining the same, will lead to *decrease* in national income by $\frac{-b}{1-b}$. Similarly, increase in lump sum tax by ΔT will cause decrease in national income (ΔY) by $\frac{1}{1-b} \times -b.\Delta T$ or $\frac{-b}{1-b} \cdot \Delta T$. Thus,

$$\Delta Y = \frac{-b}{1-b} \cdot \Delta T$$

On rearranging we have $\frac{\Delta Y}{\Delta T} = \frac{-b}{1-b}$

$\frac{\Delta Y}{\Delta T}$ is the expression for tax multiplier. It will be seen that tax multiplier of imposition or increase in lump sum tax is *negative*. It will also be seen that increase in tax by ΔT will *reduce* equilibrium income by a multiple. For example, if marginal propensity to consume is 0.75, then the tax multiplier is

$$\frac{\Delta Y}{\Delta T} = \frac{-b}{1-b} = \frac{-0.75}{1-0.75} = \frac{-0.75}{-0.25} = -3$$

This means that increase in lump sum tax by ₹ 1 will cause a decline in equilibrium income by 3. We can similarly prove that a *cut in tax* will *raise* the equilibrium income through the tax multiplier. However, in case of *reduction in lump sum income tax*, the tax multiplier is positive. Thus,

$$\frac{\Delta Y}{\Delta T}=\frac{b}{1-b}$$

With 0.75 as marginal propensity to consume, tax multiplier of cut in tax is,

$$\frac{\Delta Y}{\Delta T}=\frac{0.75}{1-0.75}=\frac{0.75}{0.25}=3.$$

Problem 1. *The following specifications are given for an economy:*
Consumption, $C = 250 + 0.75\ Y_d$ where Y_d is disposable income

Government expenditure $G = 150$

Investment $I = 80$

Taxes $T = 200$

(i) *Find the equilibrium level of income (Y), Consumption (C) and Private Sector Saving (S_p)*

(ii) *Using the value of tax multiplier how much will income increase if taxes are reduced by 30 crore ?* *DU BA (Hons.) 2009*

Ans. *In Equilibrium*

$$Y = C + I + G$$
$$C = 250 + 0.75\ Y_d$$
$$= 250 + 0.75\ (Y - T)$$
$$= 250 + 0.75\ (Y - 200)$$
$$Y = 250 + 0.75\ (Y - 200) + 80 + 150$$
$$= 250 + 0.75Y - 150 + 80 + 150$$
$$(Y - 0.75Y) = 250 - 150 + 80 + 150$$
$$Y(1 - 0.75) = 330$$
$$Y = \frac{330}{1-0.75}=\frac{330}{0.25}=330\times\frac{100}{25}=1320$$

$$\text{Consumption, } C = 250 + 0.75\ (Y - T)$$
$$= 250 + 0.75\ (1320 - 200)$$
$$= 250 + \frac{75}{100}\times 1120$$
$$= 250 + 840$$
$$\text{Therefore, } C = 1090$$
$$\text{Private Sector Saving } (S_p) = \text{Disposable income} - \text{Consumption}$$
$$\text{Disposable Income} = Y - T$$
$$\text{Private Saving } S_p = Y - T - C$$
$$= 1320 - 200 - 1090$$
$$= 30$$

(ii) The *decrease in taxes* well lead to the *increase* in income by raising consumption expenditure through tax multiplier

$$\text{Tax multiplier when taxes are reduced} = \frac{b}{1-b}$$

b stands for marginal propensity to consume.

Decrease in taxes = 30 crore

$$\text{Increase in income} = \Delta T \times \frac{b}{1-b}$$

$$= 30 \times \frac{0.75}{1-0.75}$$

$$= 30 \times \frac{0.75}{0.25} = 90$$

Problem 2. *You are given the following data for an economy:*

Consumption $C = 20 + 0.8\, Y_d$
Investment $I = 50$
Government expenditure $G = 20$
Taxes $T = 10$

Find (a) equilibrium level of income (b) If lump sum taxes increase by 10, (i) what is the equilibrium level of income, and (ii) lump sum tax multiplier ?

(c) If government expenditure decreases by 10, what is (i) equilibrium level of income, (ii) Government expenditure multiplier ?

(d) Can you explain the difference between the answer for (b) and (c)

DU. BA(Hons.) 2006

Ans. (*a*) $Y = C + I + G$

$$C = 20 + 0.8\,Y_d = 20 + 0.8\,(Y - T)$$
$$= 20 + 0.8\,(Y - 10)$$
$$I = 50 \text{ and } G = 20, \text{ and } T = 10$$
$$\therefore \quad Y = 20 + 0.8\,(Y - 10) + 50 + 20$$
$$= 20 + 0.8\,Y - 8 + 50 + 20$$
$$Y - 0.8Y = 82$$
$$Y(1-0.8) = 82$$
$$Y = \frac{82}{1-0.8} = \frac{82}{0.2} = 82 \times \frac{10}{2} = 410$$

(*b*) (*i*) With increase in lump sum tax by 10, the change in equilibrium level of income will be

$$\Delta Y = \Delta T \times \text{Lump Sum Tax Multiplier}$$

$$= 10 \times \frac{-b}{1-b} \quad \text{where } b = MPC = 0.8$$

$$= 10 \times \frac{-0.8}{1-0.8} = 10 \times \frac{-0.8}{0.2} = -40$$

Therefore, new equilibrium level of income is 410 – 40 = 370

(*b*) (*ii*) Lump Sum Tax Multiplier $= \frac{-b}{1-b} = \frac{-0.8}{1-0.8} = \frac{-0.8}{0.2} = -4$

(*c*) (*i*) With decrease in government expenditure by 10 the change in equilibrium level of income will be : $\Delta Y = -\Delta G \times$ Government expenditure multiplier.

$$\text{Government expenditure multiplier} = \frac{1}{1-b} = \frac{1}{1-0.8} = \frac{1}{0.2} = 5$$

Now, $\quad \Delta Y = -\Delta G \times \frac{1}{1-b}$

$$= -10 \times 5 = -50$$

Therefore, new equilbrium level of income = 410 – 50 = 360

(*d*) ***Explaining the Difference of the Impact of Decrease in Government Expenditure and Increase in Lump Sum Tax.***

A decrease in Government expenditure causes a decrease in aggregate expenditure by the same amount and will therefore have a greater negative multiplier effect on income. On the other hand, increase in lump-sum tax which will cause reduction in disposable income by the same amount but reduction in expenditure will be smaller because households will cut their consumption expenditure by the amount of tax multiplied by marginal propensity to consume. Thus, in this case decrease in consumption expenditure ($-\Delta C$) will be equal to $\Delta T \times MPC$, that is, $-\Delta C = \Delta T \times MPC$. Thus, if lump sum tax is increased by ₹ 10, then, given $MPC = 0.8$, the *decrease* in consumption expenditure will be $10 \times 0.8 =$ ₹ 8, that is, less than ₹ 10. Thus, multiplier effect of increase in tax will be relatively less than the decrease in government expenditure.

Proportional Income Tax and Equilibrium Level of National Income

Now, instead of lump sum tax, if Government levies proportional income tax how it will affect the consumption function curve and the equilibrium level of income. With proportional income tax, a *fixed percentage* of income is collected as tax, irrespective of the level of income. If an income tax at the rate of 25 per cent of income is levied regardless of the level of income, it will be an example of a proportional income tax. As in case of lump sum tax, the introduction of proportional income tax will reduce the disposable income. This will bring about decline in the amount of consumption and saving at each level of real national income. However, in case of proportional income tax c onsumption will not fall by the same amount at each level of income but instead it will fall by the *same percentage of the level of income*. Therefore, as a result of proportional income tax, the consumption function curve rotates downward (with point *a* as a pivot) to the right, so that the fall in amount of consumption varies but fall as a percentage of income level remains the same. This is shown in Fig. 7.5 where the vertical distance between the consumption function curve *C* before tax and the consumption function curve *C′* after tax is equal to the fall in consumption due to the proportional income tax. It is however worth noting that in case of proportional income tax at *each level of real national income, consumption falls by the tax revenue multiplied by the marginal propensity to consume.*

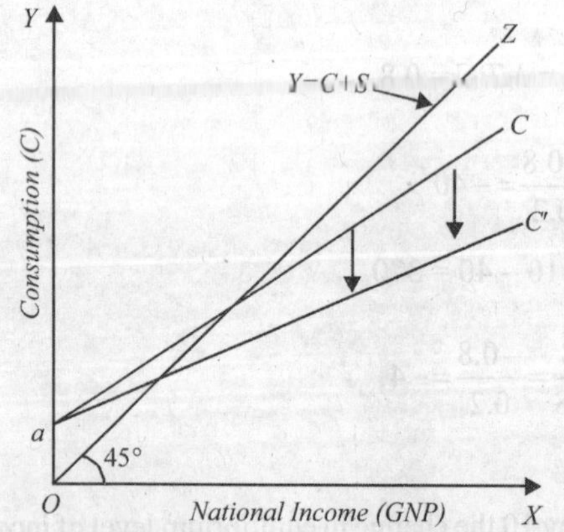

Fig. 7.5. *Effect of Proportional Income Tax on Consumption Function*

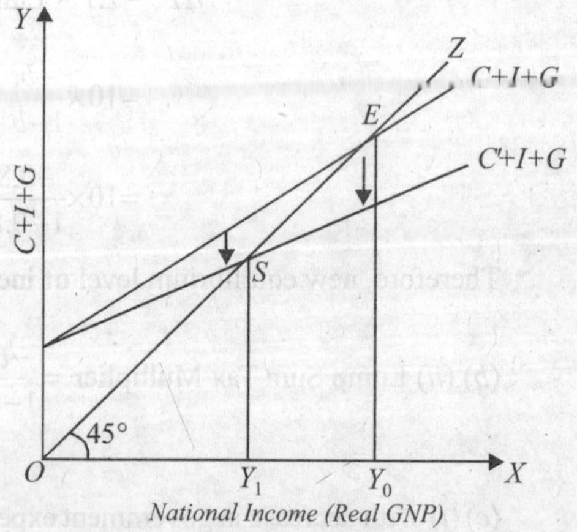

Fig. 7.6. *Effect of Proportional Income Tax on Aggregate Demand and National Income*

In Figure 7.6 we have shown the effect of proportional income tax on the equilibrium level of national income tax. As a result of imposition of proportional income tax, the aggregate demand curve $C + I + G$ rotates downward due to the downward rotation of consumption function curve. It will be seen from Figure 7.6 that due to imposition of proportional income tax, the equilibrium level of national income falls from OY_0 to OY_1. It may be noted that other things remaining the same, the higher the rate of proportional income tax, the greater the fall in consumption and, therefore, the greater the decline in equilibrium level of national income.

BALANCED BUDGET MULTIPLIER

We now analyse the impact of balanced budget of the government. In case of a balanced budget, the government's expenditure is equal to its tax revenue, that is, $G = T$ and therefore when the government increases its expenditure by ΔG, then it also raises taxes to get more tax revenue (ΔT) so that $\Delta T = \Delta G$. The effect of a balanced budget on the equilibrium income is described by the *balanced budget multiplier* which is also called *balanced budget theorem*. According to this, the *balanced budget multiplier is always equal to one.* We prove it below by assuming a lump sum tax.

In order to analyse the effect of a balanced budget multiplier, we reproduce below the equation for equilibrium income for a three-sector economy.

$$Y = \frac{1}{1-b}\left(a - b\overline{T} + I + G\right) \qquad \text{...(1)}$$

where $\overline{T}$ is constant lump sum tax levied by the government.

Let us incorporate increase in government expenditure (ΔG) fully financed by additional lump sum tax (ΔT), that is, $\Delta G = \Delta T$. By doing so we get

$$Y + \Delta Y = \frac{1}{1-b}\left[a - b(\overline{T} + \Delta T) + I + G + \Delta G\right] \qquad \text{...(2)}$$

Subtracting equation (1) from equation (2) we have

$$\Delta Y = \frac{1}{1-b}(-b\Delta T + \Delta G)$$

Since in a balanced budget, $\Delta T = \Delta G$

$$\Delta Y = \frac{1}{1-b}(-b\Delta G + \Delta G)$$

$$\Delta Y(1-b) = \Delta G(1-b)$$

or

$$\Delta Y = \Delta G \qquad \text{...(3)}$$

Dividing both sides of the above equation by ΔG we have

$$\frac{\Delta Y}{\Delta G} = \frac{\Delta G}{\Delta G} = 1$$

where $\frac{\Delta Y}{\Delta G}$ stands for government expenditure multiplier.

Thus, balanced budget multiplier is equal to one. This implies that when $\Delta G = \Delta T$ and budget is therefore balanced, national income increases by the same amount as the increase in government expenditure.

Alternative Proof

That the balanced budget multiplier is equal to one can be proved in an alternative way. Balance budget multiplier is the sum of government expenditure multiplier and lump sum tax multiplier.

Government expenditure multiplier $(G_m) = \frac{1}{1-b}$

where b represents marginal propensity to consume

Lump sum tax multiplier $(T_m) = \frac{-b}{1-b}$

Balanced budget multiplier $= G_m + T_m$

$$= \frac{1}{1-b} + \frac{-b}{1-b}$$

$$= \frac{1-b}{1-b} = 1$$

Thus, the balanced budget multiplier is equal to one.

NUMERICAL EXAMPLES

Problem 1. *Suppose we have an economy characterised by the following functions :*

$$C = 100 + 0.8\,Y_d$$
$$\overline{I} = 100$$
$$\overline{G} = 100$$
$$\overline{T} = 100$$

(Figures are in crores)

(*a*) *Find the equilibrium level of income.*

(*b*) *How much increase in income will take place if government expenditure on goods and services increases by ₹ 60 crore.*

(c) *Find the tax multiplier and balanced budget multiplier*

Solution :

(*a*) Equilibrium $Y = C + \overline{I} + \overline{G}$

$$Y = a + bY_d + \overline{I} + \overline{G}$$

Therefore, $Y = a + b(Y - \overline{T}) + \overline{I} + \overline{G}$

Substituting the values of *a*, *b*, $\overline{T}$, $\overline{I}$ and $\overline{G}$ we have

$$Y = 100 + 0.8\,(Y - 100) + 100 + 100$$
$$= 100 + 0.8Y - 80 + 100 + 100$$
$$Y - 0.8Y = 220$$
$$Y(1 - 0.8) = 220$$
$$0.2Y = 220$$
$$Y = 220 \times \frac{10}{2} = 1100$$

(*b*) Government expenditure multiplier $(G_m) = \frac{1}{1-b} = \frac{1}{1-0.8} = 5$

Increase in national income if government expenditure increases by 60 crore.

$$\Delta Y = G_m . \Delta G$$
$$= 5 \times 60 = 300$$

(*c*) Tax multiplier, $T_m = \frac{-b}{1-b} = \frac{-0.8}{1-0.8} = \frac{-0.8}{0.2}$

$$= -4$$

Balanced Budget Multiplier $= G_m + T_m$

$$= 5 + (-4)$$
$$= 1$$

Problem 2. *The following data characterises the macroeconomic conditions of a hypothetical economy :*

$$C = 50 + 0.8\,Y_d$$
$$I = 100$$
$$G = T = 75$$

where C, I, and Y_d are consumption, investment and disposable income respectively. Calculate equilibrium income of the economy. What is the value of multiplier?

Solution: Note that since $G = T$, budget of the Government is balanced.

$$Y = C + I + G$$
$$C = a + bY_d = a + b(Y - T)$$

Substituting the values of C, I and G we have :

$$Y = 50 + 0.8\,(Y - 75) + 100 + 75$$
$$= 50 + 0.8Y - 60 + 100 + 75$$
$$Y = 165 + 0.8Y$$
$$Y - 0.8Y = 165$$
$$Y(1 - 0.8) = 165$$
$$0.2\,Y = 165$$
$$Y = 165 \times \frac{10}{2} = 825$$

Thus, equilibrium level of income is 825.

Since in the present case $G = T$, there is a balanced budget, therefore

$$\text{value of balanced budget multiplier} = \frac{1}{1-b} + \frac{-b}{1-b}$$

$$= \frac{1}{1-0.8} + \frac{-0.8}{1-0.8} = \frac{1}{0.2} + \frac{-0.8}{0.2} = 5 - 4 = 1$$

Government Expenditure, Budget Deficit and Capital Market

We have explained above how the government expenditure affects the product market by bringing about increase in aggregate demand. Now, an important question is how the Government expenditure is financed. Imposition of taxes is an important way of financing Government expenditure. But taxes reduce aggregate demand in the product market by lowering disposable income of the community and thereby causing a decline in its consumption expenditure. Therefore, if Government expenditure equals tax revenue collected ($G = T$), then Government has a balanced budget and much of the expansionary effect of government expenditure is offset by taxes levied. If Government increases its expenditure without raising taxes, (*i.e.* $G > T$), then it has a *budget deficit* which has a large expansionary effect on the product market and, as seen above, leads to increase in national income (*GDP*). This deficit budget is financed by borrowing from the public. But borrowing by the Government to finance its deficit affects the capital market. This is because borrowing by the Government will compete with private investors for the saving of the public. As a result of borrowing by the Government from the market, less saving is available for private investment. When the Government runs a deficit, private saving has two uses: (1) to finance private investment and (2) to finance Government budget deficit which is met by borrowing from the public. Equilibrium in the capital market occurs when private saving is equal to private investment plus budget deficit, $G - T$, (*i.e.* Government borrowing).

Thus, in equilibrium in the capital market

$$S_p = I + (G - T)$$

where S_p stands for private saving, I for private investment, and $(G - T)$ for budget deficit (*i.e.* Government borrowing). Alternatively, the fiscal deficit of the Government ($G-T<0$, *i.e.*, negative) can be regarded as *government dissaving*. Therefore, in case of fiscal deficit or *negative Government savings*, national saving will decrease and national saving curve will shift to the left. How budget deficit or Government borrowing reduces or crowds out private investment is illustrated through Figure 7.7 where to begin with vertical national saving curve S_0 intersects the downward sloping investment curve *II* at point E_0 and determines real interest rate r_0 at which private investment equal to I_0 takes place. Now as a result of Government borrowing to finance its budget deficit ($G-T$) national saving available for investment falls and the national saving curve shifts to the left[1] to the new position S_1. Thus when Government borrows to finance budget deficit, Government is said to dissave and therefore in this case Government saving is negative ($G - T = - S_g$). Note further that national saving = private saving and Government saving ($S = S_p + S_g$). As a result of fiscal deficit and consequent leftward shift in the national saving curve to S_1, the capital market is now in equilibrium at point E_1 and rate of interest rises to r_1. At this higher interest rate r_1, private investment falls to I_1. Thus, *borrowing by the Government to finance its budget deficit has led to crowding out of private investment*. As mentioned above, a part of private saving is used to finance private investment and a part to finance budget deficit of the Government.

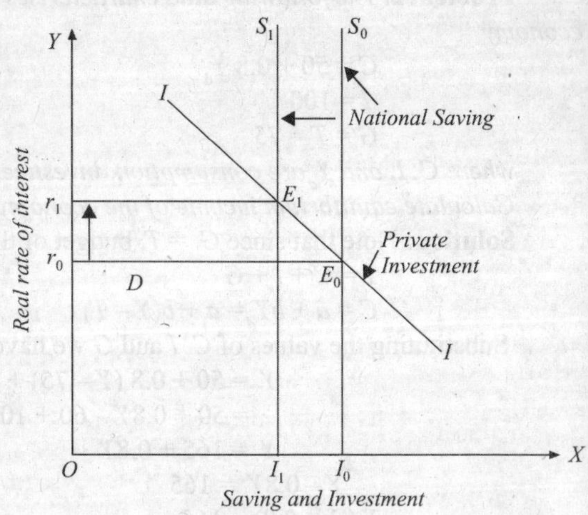

Fig. 7.7. *Effect of Budget Deficit and Government Borrowing on Capital Market*

It is worth noting that when Government expenditure is fully matched by increase in taxes (*i.e.* $G = T$) we have a balanced budget but it will still have an expansionary effect on national income, though, as explained above, the multiplier effect of a balanced budget is equal to one. However, since in case of balanced budget increase in Government expenditure is matched by increase in taxes it reduces disposable income $Y_d = Y - T$, and reduction in disposable income (Y_d) leads to decrease in both consumption and saving ($Y_d = C + S$). This decrease in saving will cause rate of interest to rise and thereby crowds out private investment.

Further, when the Government has a *budget surplus* (i.e. $T > G$), it has a *positive savings* which will lead to the increase in national saving and make more funds available for private sector to borrow. This will cause real rate of interest to fall. As a result, higher private investment will occur in case of surplus budget.

It is worth noting that in our above analysis Government expenditure has been treated as consumption expenditure on goods and services purchased to satisfy collective wants. However, this is strictly true in case of a purely free-market economy such as that of the US where the Government is not a major investor. But in case of India's mixed economy the Government is an important investor and a good part of its borrowing is used for investment purposes, especially for investment in infrastructure projects such as power, transport, highways, roads, ports, etc. Such Government borrowing for investment purposes cannot be considered as consumption expenditure or *dissaving*. Therefore, it has a large expansionary effect on national income with a usual multiplier effect. Viewed as such Government borrowing for investment, especially for infrastructure projects in developing

1. Note that all expenditure by the Government is here treated as consumption expenditure. Besides, borrowing by the Government implies *government dissaving*.

countries, may *crowd in* private investment rather than crowding it out. This is so because lack of adequate infrastructure hinders private investment.

QUESTIONS FOR REVIEW

1. How does Government expenditure on goods and services affect level of national income ? Has it a multiplier effect ? What is the value of government expenditure multiplier ?
2. Show that with Government expenditure in a three-sector economy (households, firms and Government) equilibrium of national income is established at the level where sum of investment and Government expenditure ($I + G$) is equal to the amount of saving.
3. Show how the increase in Government expenditure without raising taxes (*i.e.* incurring budget deficit) affects national income, real rate of interest and private investment. Illustrate diagrammatically.
4. It is often asserted that budget deficit crowds out private investment. Do you agree ? Explain.
5. Show what will be the effect of cut in government expenditure without reduction in taxes (creating budget surplus in this way) affect equilibrium national income, real rate of interest and private investment in the economy.

   [**Hints.** A cut in government expenditure without reducing taxes leads to increase in public saving (*i.e.* $T - G$ increases). This causes a shift in national saving curve to the right and leads to the fall in rate of interest and increase in private investment
6. Show how does a cut in taxes without being balanced by cut in government expenditure affect real interest rate and investment.
7. What is effect of a balanced budget (*i.e.* increasing government expenditure matched by increase in equal amount of taxes) on national income, real interest rate and investment ?
8. Explain how balanced budget has an expansionary effect. What is value of balanced budget multiplier ? Explain.
9. How does cut in direct taxes lead to increase in national income ? What is the size of lump sum tax multiplier ?
10. Assuming full-employment in an economy balanced budget *increase* in taxes and Government expenditure will reduce consumption and investment and raise the real interest rate. Explain.
11. Assuming full-employment prevails in an economy, increased government expenditure matched by taxes crowds out private investment. Explain.
12. When the government runs a budget deficit, how capital market is affected ? Explain.
13. Given the following information about the economy of a country :

    Consumption function, $C = 85 + 0.5\,Y_d$
    Investment function $I = 85$
    Government spending $G = 60$
    Net Taxes, $T = 40 + 0.25\,Y$

    Solve for equilibrium levels of income and consumption
14. For an economy the following data is given:

    Consumption (C) = $100 + 0.8\,Y$
    Investment (I) = 150
    Government Expenditure (G) = 75
    Lump sum income tax (T) = 60

    (*a*) Find the equilibrium level of income.
    (*b*) What is the value of multiplier of (*i*) Government expenditure multiplier and (*ii*) tax multiplier

15. You are given the following information about an economy :

Consumption function, C = 1000 + 0.5 $(Y - T)$

Investment, I = ₹ 2,000 crores.

Government expenditure = ₹ 1,000 crores

Taxes = ₹ 1,000 crores

(*i*) Find the equilibrium level of GDP without taxes.

(*ii*) Find the equilibrium level of GDP with taxes.

(*iii*) Use your answers in (*i*) and (*ii*) above to calculate the tax multiplier.

(*iv*) Explain the working of the tax multiplier. ***DU B.A., (Hons.) 2008***

[**Hints.** Find the equilibrium level of GDP (*i.e.* national income Y), first by laking $T = 0$ and then find the equilibrium GDP *i.e.*, (Y) by taking $T = 1000$. Then tax multiplier is $\frac{\Delta Y}{\Delta T}$.

Note that $\Delta T = 1000$.]

APPENDIX 7A Concepts of Inflationary and Deflationary Gaps

Inflationary Gap

It is useful and important to understand the Keynesian concept of inflationary gap because with it we are able to know the main cause of the rise in general level of prices. The equilibrium of an economy is established at the level of full employment when aggregate demand or total expenditure is equal to the level of income corresponding to full employment. This happens when the amount of investment is equal to the saving gap corresponding to full employment level of income. Consider Fig. 7A.1 where OY_F is national income corresponding to the level of full-employment. Equilibrium at national income OY_F would be established only when aggregate demand or total expenditure $(C+I+G)$ is equal to Y_FE(Note that YF_E is equal to OY_F). Keynes assumed that the aggregate output or real national income cannot increase beyond OY_F because when all means of production including labour are fully employed, there is no possibility of further rise in production or real national income. Thus *when aggregate demand is greater than the aggregate demand YF_E which is required to establish the equilibrium at OY_F level of national income, the equilibrium would not be established at OY_F.*

It would be seen from Fig. 7A.1 that aggregate demand Y_FT is greater than aggregate demand Y_FE which is required to maintain the equilibrium at full-employment GDP level OY_F. Thus with the level of aggregate demand curve $C + I + G'$ (dotted), which is obtained by adding government expenditure ET to the aggregate demand curve $C + I + G$, equilibrium would not be established at OY_F which corresponds to full-employment level of income. The actual aggregate demand being greater than Y_FE by the amount ET the level of national income would be greater than OY_F. Since OY_F is full-employment level of national income, actual production cannot increase beyond that but there would be rise in prices which would raise the *money value of OY_F production. The amount by which the actual aggregate demand exceeds the level of national income corresponding to full employment is known as inflationary gap because this excess of aggregate demand causes inflation or rise in prices in the economy.* In Fig. 7A.1 this excess of aggregate demand or inflationary gap is equal to ET.

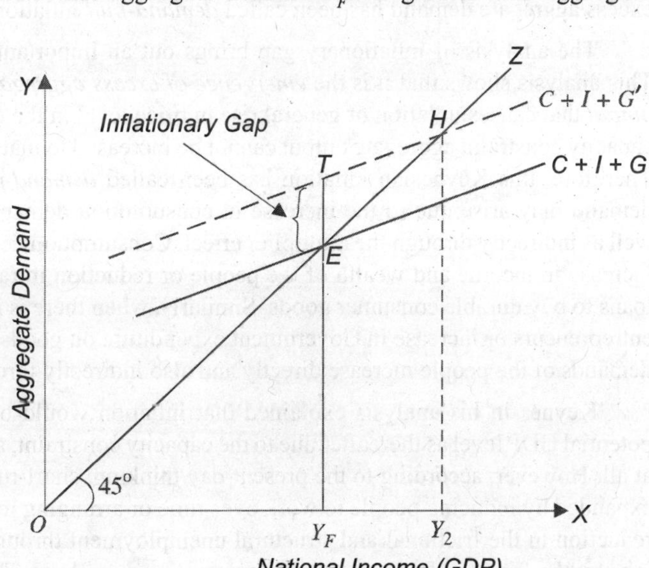

Fig. 7A.1 *Inflationary Gap*

It would be seen from Fig. 7A.1 that the aggregate demand curve $C + I + G'$ (dotted) intersects 45° line (OZ line) at point H so that equilibrium level of national income would be OY_2. It should be carefully understood that there is no difference between OY_F and OY_2 in terms of real income or actual production; only as a result of rise in price level, nominal national income or nominal GDP has increased from OY_F to OY_2 in money terms. Inflationary gap represents excess demand in relation to aggregate production or supply of output which brings about *demand-pull inflation*. J.M. Keynes in his revolutionary book "*General Theory of Employment, Interest and Money*" did not discuss the concept of inflationary gap because he was then preoccupied with the analysis of the state of depression and deflation. During the Second World War when the problem of inflation cropped up, Keynes applied his macroeconomic analysis to explain inflation in terms of excess aggregate demand over aggregate supply and in this connection he put forward the concept of inflationary gap.

It is worthwhile to note that *nominal* national income (GDP) increases not by the size of inflationary gap but by a multiple of it due to the working of multiplier in *money terms* rather than *real terms*. Thus it will be seen that in Figure 7A.1 the inflationary gab ET leads to the increase in nominal national income by Y_FY_2 which is greater than the inflationary gap ET.

We have explained above that inflationary gap arises because of increase in aggregate expenditure as a result of increase in government expenditure (G), aggregate demand can also increase due to any other component of aggregate expenditure such as consumption demand, investment expenditure pushing up aggregate demand. Thus, inflationary gap arises because of excess aggregate demand relative to full-employment level of output. As a result, inflationary gap results in rise in general price level. Thus, inflation emerges because buyers (consumers, business firms and government) are demanding more output than the the economy is capable of producing goods and services at normal operating rate. To put it in terms of famous cliche, '*there is too much demand chasing too little supply*'. Thus, the Keynesian explanation of inflation that it results from inflationary gap or excess aggregate demand has been called *demand-pull* inflation.

The analysis of inflationary gap brings out an important cause of inflation in the economy. This analysis shows that it is the *emergence of excess aggregate demand over aggregate supply of output* that causes inflation or general rise in price level in the economy, especially when due to the capacity constraint aggregate output cannot be increased to match the increase in aggregate demand. Therefore, this Keynesian inflation has been called *demand-pull inflation*. The excess aggregate demand may arise due to the increase in consumption demand or investment demand directly as well as indirectly through the multiplier effect. Consumption demand mainly increases when there is increase in income and wealth of the people or reduction in rate of interest inducing people to get loans to buy durable consumer goods. Similarly, when there is increase in investment by the private entrepreneurs or increase in Government expenditure on goods and services, incomes and therefore demands of the people increase directly and also indirectly through the multiplier effect.

Keynes in his analysis explained that inflation would occur only after full-employment or potential GDP level as thereafter due to the capacity constraint, aggregate supply cannot be increased at all. However, according to the present-day thinking, short-run aggregate supply of output can be expanded by inducing people to work over-time or arranging more shifts in the workplace or by the reduction in the frictional and structural unemployment through easier or more quickly finding of jobs by the frictionally or structurally unemployed workers. Therefore, short-run aggregate supply curve (with flexible price level) slopes upward even after full-employment or potential GDP level. *Before full-employment level* (or what is now generally called level at which only *natural unemployment* exists) short-run aggregate supply curve (with flexible prices) is sloping upward due to rising marginal costs arising from several bottlenecks. Now, given the upward-sloping short-run aggregate supply curve, when due to increase in aggregate demand, aggregate demand curve shifts upward, excess demand at the current price level emerges which leads to the rise in general price level.

We can explain this Keynesian concept of demand-pull inflation in terms of *AD-AS* model with price flexibility. According to Keynes price level remains constant up to the potential or full-employment level of output and therefore aggregate supply (*AS*) curve is horizontal and as beyond full-employment level Y_F, according to Keynes, aggregate supply of output cannot increase, and therefore aggregate supply curve becomes vertical at Y_F as shown in Figure 7A.2.

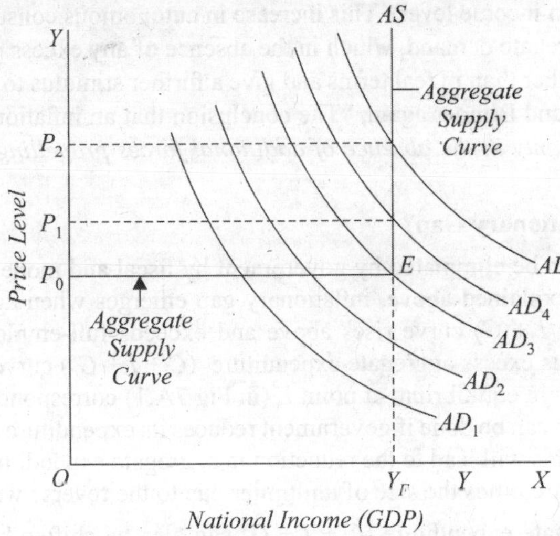

Fig. 7A.2 *Keynes's Demand-pull Inflation*

In Fig. 7A.2 aggregate supply curve *AS* is horizontal straight line P_0E at price level P_0 up to full-employment level Y_F but beyond this it becomes vertical. As aggregate demand increases from AD_1 to AD_2 and then to AD_3 price level remains fixed at P_0 but when aggregate demand curve further shifts upward beyond point *E* (corresponding to full-employment level of output Y_F), price level rises due to excess demand over supply of output, that is, inflationary gap emerges and demand-pull inflation takes place.

Is there a self-correcting mechanism?

Now, an important question is whether there is any self-correcting mechanism to restore equilibrium at full-employment level without any inflationary gap. Some economists, especially classical economists, believe that the inflationary gap destructs itself and equilibrium is reached at full-employment level of output. According to them, *rise in price level or inflation causes fall in purchasing power of wealth or assets* possessed by the people. This decline in purchasing power of wealth or what is called *negative real balance effect* will force people to cut back on consumption. Further, as a result of inflation exports will fall and imports will increase. These will cause lowering of aggregate demand and thereby cure inflation. According to this view, to quote Baunol and Blinder, "Eventually aggregate quantity demanded is scaled down to the economy's capacity to provide those goods; and at this point the self-correcting process stops. That, in essence, is the unhappy process by which the economy cures itself of the problem of excess aggregate demand".[1]

In our view there are two shortcomings of the above self-correcting process leading to the destruction of inflationary gap. First, empirical evidence shows that negative real balance effect that causes consumption demand to fall is too weak to eliminate the inflationary gap and restore equilibrium at full-employment level. Second, when inflationary gap leads to inflation, it gives rise to *wage-price spiral* which causes further rise in prices. In other words, when once demand-pull inflation occurs and

1. William J. Baumol and Allin S. Blinder, *Economics: Principles and Problems*, Harcourt Publishers, New York, Fifth Edition 1991, p. 181.

causes real wage rate to fall, the workers demand higher wages. Wages may be rigid downward but are flexible upward. With higher wages, cost of production of the firms rise adversely affecting supply of goods which causes further rise in price level. In fact, inflation once started feeds on itself so that we find persistent or sustained rise in price level. *Increase in price level also causes an upward shift* in the consumption function because of increase in *autonomous* consumption (that is, consumption independent of change in income level). This increase in autonomous consumption will also have a multiplier effect on aggregate demand, which in the absence of any excess production capacity will work in money terms rather than in real terms and give a further stimulus to the rise in inflation rate. Thus, to quote Baumol and Blinder again, "The conclusion that an inflationary gap sows the seeds of its destruction holds *only in the absence of additional forces propelling the aggregate demand curve outward*".[2]

How to Eliminate Inflationary Gap?

Inflationary gap can be eliminated by government by fiscal and monetary measures to reduce aggregate demand. As explained above, inflationary gap emerges when aggregate expenditure or aggregate demand ($C + I + G$) curve rises above and exceeds full-employment level of output, therefore to eliminate this excess aggregate expenditure, ($C + I + G'$) curve must be shifted below to the level at which it is in equilibrium at point E (in Fig 7A.1) corresponding to full-employment level of output. First, this can be done if government reduces its expenditure (G), especially wasteful non-plan expenditure. This will lead to the reduction in aggregate expenditure equal to the decrease in government expenditure times the size of multiplier due to the reverse working of the multiplier.

Second, the aggregate expenditure ($C + I + G$) can also be shifted below by imposing new taxes or increasing the rates of existing taxes. The increase in taxes will reduce disposable income of the people causing shift in the consumption function curve which is one component of aggregate expenditure curve. It is worth noting that *reductions in government expenditure and increase in taxes lead to the decrease in fiscal deficit* which is an anti-inflationary measure.

Thirdly, tight monetary policy adopted by the Reserve Bank can also work towards removing the inflationary gap. Under the tight monetary policy, the Reserve Bank can raise its bank rate or repo rate which in turn leads to the higher lending interest rates by the banks. These higher interest rates tend to decrease investment demand by business firms and also borrowing for durable consumer goods such as loans for buying cars, colour TVs, airconditionars and houses which is highly interest-sensitive. These cause reduction in investment demand as well as consumption demand and work towards lowering of aggregate expenditure curve ($C + I + G$).

Thus, intervention by government to reduce excess demand through appropriate fiscal and monetary policies is these days an important method to control inflation which emerges due to inflationary gap.

It may however be noted that in developing countries such as ours Keynesian concept of full employment (or the present-day concept of natural unemployment rate) is not relevant as there is no precise full-employment level due to the existence of disguised unemployment. The nature of unemployment in developing countries is different. Moreover, in developing countries like India agricultural output varies a good deal due to uncertain monsoon. When there is fall in agricultural output due to inadequate monsoon, rising aggregate demand outstrips aggregate supply or output resulting in inflation in the economy.

Deflationary Gap

In the theory of income and employment, the concept of deflationary gap occupies an important place, since in a capitalist economy unemployment and depression occur due to this gap. According to Keynesian theory of income and employment, equilibrium at the level of full employment is established when aggregate demand consisting of consumption demand plus investment demand plus

2. *Op.cit*, p.185 (italics in the original).

government demand ($C + I + G$) is equal to the national income at the level of full-employment. This happens when investment and government demand is equal to the saving gap at full-employment level of national income. If aggregate demand is less than the full-employment level of national income, *i.e.,* when investment and government demand is less than the saving gap at full-employment level of income, the deficiency of aggregate demand occurs due to which national income and employment will fall below the full-employment level causing unemployment and depression in the economy. The concept of deflationary gap is illustrated in Fig. 7A.3 in which along the X-axis national income is measured and along the Y-axis level of aggregate demand is measured. Suppose national income at the level of full-employment is equal to OY_F. Now, the equilibrium level of income and employment would be established at OY_F when aggregate demand (consumption demand plus investment demand) plus Government expenditure ($C + I + G$) is equal to Y_FE (which is equal to national income OY_F). But in the real world when recession or depression occurs in the economy, aggregate demand is less than the full-employment level of income OY_F or it is less than Y_FE, then the problem of deficiency of aggregate demand will arise. Therefore, EK in Fig. 7A.3 represents deflationary gap. Hence, *deflationary gap represents the difference between the actual aggregated demand and the aggregate demand which is required to establish the equilibrium at full-employment level of income.*

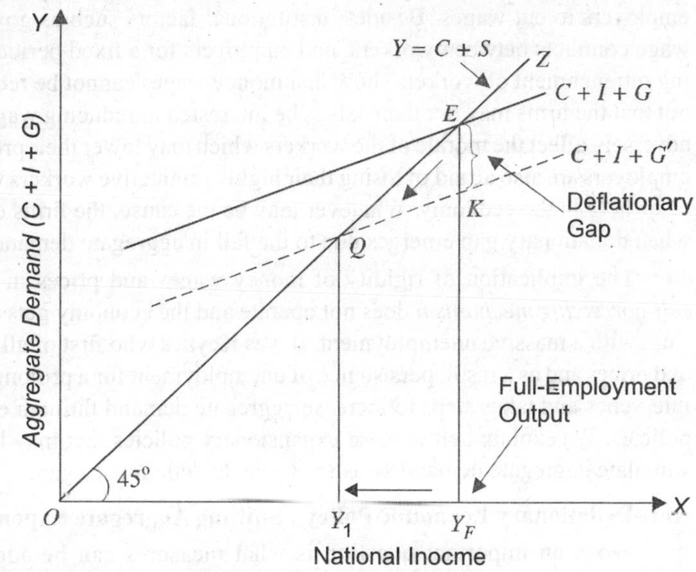

Fig. 7A.3. *Deflationary Gap*

It should be carefully understood that due to the deflationary gap EK, the levels of national income and employment will decline. The decline in national income and employment will not only be equal to the deflationary gap EK but it will be much greater than this. *The decline in national income is determined by deflationary gap times the value of the multiplier*. In Fig. 7A.3 when aggregate demand curve is $C + I + G'$ (dotted) deflationary gap is equal to EK. The aggregate demand curve $C + I + G'$ (dotted) which cuts the 45° line at point Q as a result of which equilibrium is established at OY_1 level of national income. It will be seen from Fig. 7A.3 that OY_1 is less than full-employment level of income OY_F. Deflationary gap represents the situation of deficient demand in the economy. This deficiency in aggregate demand causes fall in national output and level of employment. As a result, involuntary unemployment in the economy emerges. The depression of 1929-33 in capitalist countries was caused by the emergence of deflationary gap or by demand deficiency in these economies.

The classical economists believed that deflationary gap will be automatically removed by self-correcting mechanism through quick reduction in money wages and prices. When aggregate demand is lower than full-employment level of output, recession and unemployment of labour will occur. As a result, wages and prices will fall. The lower wages will lead to reduction in costs of business firms which will cause prices to fall and at lower prices more output will be demanded resulting in increase in national income and employment. Thus, at lower wages the firms will employ more labour and produce more output and in this way deflationary gap will be eliminated and the full-employment equilibrium of the economy will be restored. Keynes challenged this argument and pointed out that wages and prices are rigid in the downward direction. There are several reasons for rigidity of money wages and prices. First, in the modern times workers and their labour unions oppose tooth and nail the reduction in money wages and will go on strike if any attempt is made by employers to cut wages. Besides, institutional factors such as government's minimum wages law, wage contracts between workers, and employers for a fixed period and other legal factors prohibiting retrenchment of workers show that money wages cannot be reduced easily. Further, it is pointed out that the firms may not themselves be interested in reducing wages because of the fear that it may adversely affect the morale of the workers which may lower their productivity. By reducing wages the employers are also afraid of losing their highly productive workers who may have good opportunities elsewhere in the economy. Whatever may be the cause, the firms do not reduce money wages even when deflationary gap emerges due to the fall in aggregate demand.

The implication of rigidity of money wages and prices in the downward reduction is that *self-correcting mechanism* does not operate and the economy gets stuck with a long-lasting equilibrium with a massive unemployment. It was Keynes who first of all pointed out the rigidity of wages and prices and as a result persistence of unemployment for a prolonged period unless the government intervenes and takes steps to increase aggregate demand through expansionary fiscal and monetary policies. We explain below these expansionary policies that may be adopted by the government to stimulate aggregate demand so as to eliminate deflationary gap.

Anti-Deflationary Economic Policy : Shifting Aggregate Expenditure Curve Upward

Now, an important question is what measures can be adopted to overcome recession or involuntary unemployment which comes into existence as a result of deficiency of aggregate demand brought about by a fall in investment.

From our above analysis of determination of income and employment it is clear that increase in equilibrium level of national income can be brought about by increases in any components of aggregate demand, namely, consumption demand (C), private investment demand (I), Government expenditure (G), and net exports (X_n). In order to increase national income through upward shift in the consumption function, *the Government can reduce personal income taxes*. In 1964, the reduction in income tax by John Kennedy Government in USA was quite successful in boosting consumption demand and thereby raising aggregate output. As a result, more income and employment were generated. The rate of unemployment sharply declined and the American economy was lifted out of depression. Recently, in 2002 and again in early 2008, President George W. Bush made a significant cut of 3.5 billion dollars in income tax to revive the American economy. He refunded a good amount of income tax collected from the people in these years. The cut in direct taxes increases the disposable income of the people which tends to raise their consumption demand. However, there is a limitation of cut in direct taxes for raising aggregate demand because a part of the increases in disposable income can be saved rather than being spent on goods and services. This happened in the United States in the year 2008. To boost aggregate demand, indirect tax can also be reduced. In India also in December 2008, to correct the sagging demand for industrial products under the fiscal stimulus package 4 per cent across the board cut in central excise duty was made by the Government. This too has a limitation because benefit of this cut in excise duty may not be fully passed on to the consumers by reducing prices.

Secondly, the equilibrium level of national income (GNP) and employment can be increased by *raising the rate of private investment* (I). Through monetary policy measures businessmen can be induced to invest more by lowering the rate of interest and increasing the availability of credit. We know that the lower the rate of interest, the higher will be the level of private investment. Alternatively, the Government may encourage private investment by reducing tax on profits or corporate income so that post-tax rate of profit will be higher than before. The higher level of investment will shift the aggregate demand or expenditure curve ($C + I + G$) upward and determine a higher level of national income and employment.

Thirdly, the recession can be overcome and national income (GNP) and employment can more efficiently be increased by *increasing Government expenditure* (*G*). It was the increase in Government expenditure on Public Works Programme which was the main recommendation of Keynes to raise the level of national output and income to restore equilibrium at full-employment level. Recently in 1993-94, President Clinton stepped up public expenditure on public works in the USA to overcome recession in the American economy and reduce unemployment. Again, in 2009 President Obama gave a fiscal stimulus of over $ 800 billion the major part of which was the increase in Government expenditure to raise aggregate demand to overcome recession in the American economy. In India also fiscal stimulus packages were announced in 2008-09 under which government expenditure, especially on infrastructure, was increased to revive the slowing Indian economy. It may be noted that increase in Government expenditure not only directly raises national income but also, like the increase in private investment, has the multiplier effect on levels of income and employment.

Lastly, the *expansion in positive net exports* (*NX*) will also cause an increase in equilibrium level of national income and employment. Exports can be promoted through tax concessions on profits earned through exports as well as making credit available at lower interest rate for purpose of exporting goods. Another common measure adopted to promote exports is the depreciation of national currency. Depreciation makes the exports cheaper and imports costlier which raises net exports (*NX*). However, when there is global recession depreciation of its currency by each country will offset the effect of others.

It follows from above that a mix of fiscal and monetary policy measures can be adopted to increase aggregate demand and thereby to lift the economy out of recession.

QUESTIONS FOR REVIEW

1. What is inflationary gap ? What causes it ? What is its consequence ?
2. Is there a self-correcting mechanism to eliminate inflationary gap ? Explain.
3. What is demand-pull, inflation ? Is it the result of inflationary gap ? Show graphically.
4. Explain the measures that can be taken to eliminate inflationary gap.
5. What is deflationary gap ? What can cause deflationary gap ?
6. Classical economists thought that deflationary gap was self-correcting. How did Keynes successfully challenge this viewpoint ?
7. Explain the measures that can be taken to eliminate the deflationary gap and to overcome recession in the economy.

CHAPTER 8 Consumption Function

Introduction

In the previous chapter we have explained how the level of national income is determined. In the present chapter and the succeeding one we shall study the factors that determine consumption demand and investment demand – the two important components of aggregate demand. As we have seen, given the aggregate supply, the level of income or employment is determined by the level of aggregate demand; the greater the aggregate demand, the greater the level of income and employment and *vice versa*. Keynes was not interested in the factors determining the aggregate supply since he was concerned with the short run and the existing productive capacity. We will also not explain in detail the factors which determine the aggregate supply and will confine ourselves to explaining the determinants of aggregate demand. In the present chapter we will explain the consumption demand and the factors on which it depends and how it changes over a period of time. The investment demand will be explained in the next chapter. Consumption demand depends upon the level of income and the propensity to consume.

The Concept of Consumption Function

As the demand for a good depends upon its price, similarly consumption of a community depends on the level of income. In other words, consumption is a function of income. *The consumption function relates the amount of consumption to the level of income.* When the income of a community rises, consumption also rises. How much consumption rises in response to a given increase in income depends upon the marginal propensity to consume. It should be borne in mind that the *consumption function is the whole schedule which describes the amounts of consumption at various levels of income.* We give in Table 8.1 on the next page such a schedule of consumption function.

Consumption function should be carefully distinguished from the *amount of consumption.* By consumption function is meant the whole schedule which shows consumption at various levels of income, whereas *amount of consumption means the amount consumed at a specific level of income.* The schedule given in Table 8.1 reflects the consumption function of a community *i.e.,* it indicates how the amount of consumption changes in response to the changes in income. From the schedule given in Table 8.1 it will be seen that at the level of income equal to ₹ 1200 crore, the amount of consumption is ₹ 1090 crore. As the national income increases to ₹ 1500 crore, the amount of consumption rises to ₹ 1300 crore. Thus, with a given consumption function, amount of consumption is different at different levels of income.

The schedule of consumption function in Table 8.1 reveals an important fact that *when income rises, consumption also rises but not as much as the rise in income.* This fact about consumption function was emphasised by Keynes who first of all evolved the concept of consumption function. The reason why consumption rises less than income is that a part of the increment in income is saved. Therefore, we see that when income increases from ₹ 1000 crore to ₹ 1100 crore, the amount of consumption rises from ₹ 950 crore to 1020 crore. Thus, with the increase in income by ₹ 100 crore, consumption rises by ₹ 70 crore; the remaining ₹ 30 crore are saved. Similarly, when income rises from ₹ 1100 crore to ₹1200 crore, the amount of consumption increases from ₹ 1020 crore to ₹ 1090 crore.

Table 8.1. Linear Consumption Function

Income (₹ in crores) Y	Consumption (₹ in crores) C	Average Propensity to Consume $\left(\frac{C}{Y}\right)$	Marginal Propensity to Consume $\left(\frac{\Delta C}{\Delta Y}\right)$
1000	950	$\frac{950}{1000} = 0.950$	—
1100	1020	$\frac{1020}{1100} = 0.927$	$\frac{70}{100} = .70$
1200	1090	$\frac{1090}{1200} = 0.908$	$\frac{70}{100} = .70$
1300	1160	$\frac{1160}{1300} = 0.892$	$\frac{70}{100} = .70$
1400	1230	$\frac{1230}{1400} = 0.878$	$\frac{70}{100} = .70$
1500	1300	$\frac{1300}{1500} = 0.867$	$\frac{70}{100} = .70$
1600	1370	$\frac{1370}{1600} = 0.856$	$\frac{70}{100} = .70$

Here also, as a result of increase in income by ₹ 100 crore, the amount of consumption has risen by ₹ 70 crore and the remaining ₹ 30 crore have been saved. The same applies to further increases in income and consumption. We shall see later that Keynes based his theory of multiplier on the proposition that consumption increases less than income and this theory of multiplier occupies an important place in macroeconomics.

In the Keynesian Consumption function given in Table 8.1 while marginal propensity to consume $\left(\frac{\Delta C}{\Delta Y}\right)$ remains constant ₹ 0.70, average propensity to consume $\left(\frac{C}{Y}\right)$ is falling with the increase in income. It should be noted that Keynesian consumption function given in Table 8.1 is linear as marginal propensity to consume which measures the slope $\left(\frac{\Delta C}{\Delta Y}\right)$ of the consumption function curve is constant. It is noteworthy that while marginal propensity to consume $\left(\frac{\Delta C}{\Delta Y}\right)$ in the consumption function given in Table 8.1 is constant, average propensity to consume $\left(\frac{C}{Y}\right)$ falls with increase in national income (Y). *The fall in average propensity to consume with the increase in income has an important implication that increase in consumption is not proportional to increase in income*. Besides, as will be seen from Table 8.1 in Keynesian consumption function, $MPC < APC$ at various levels of income. We shall explain the importance of these two features of Keynesian consumption function later.

Consumption demand depends on income and propensity to consume. Propensity to consume depends on various factors such as price level, interest rate, stock of wealth and several subjective factors. *Since Keynes was concerned with short-run consumption function he assumed price level, interest rate, stock of wealth etc. constant in his theory of consumption*. Thus with these factors being assumed constant in the short run, Keynesian consumption function considers consumption as a function of *current* income. Thus

$$C = f(Y)$$

In a specific form, Keynesian linear consumption function can be written as:

$$C = a + bY$$

where *a* and *b* are constants. While *a* is the intercept term of the consumption function, *b* stands for slope of the consumption function and therefore represents marginal propensity to consume and *Y* represents the level of *current income.*

Keynesian consumption function, namely, $C = a + bY$ has been depicted by *CC'* curve in Fig.8.1 in which along the *X*-axis national income and along the *Y*-axis the amount of consumption are measured. In this figure, a line *OZ* making 45° angle with the *X*-axis, has been drawn. Because line *OZ* makes 45° angle with the *X*-axis every point on it is equidistant from both the *X*-axis and *Y*-axis. Therefore, if consumption function curve coincides with 45° line *OZ* it would imply that the amount of consumption is equal to the income at every level of income. In this case, with the increase in income, consumption would also increase by the same amount. As has been said above, in actual practice consumption increases less than the increase in income. Therefore, in actual practice the curve depicting the consumption function will deviate from the 45° line. If we represent the above consumption schedule by a curve, we would get the propensity to consume curve such as *CC'* in Fig. 8.1.

It is evident from Fig. 8.1 that the consumption function curve *CC'* deviates from the 45° line *OZ.* At lower levels of income, the consumption function curve *CC'* lies above the *OZ* line, signifying that at these lower levels of income consumption is greater than the income. It is so because at lower levels of income, a nation may draw upon its accumulated savings to maintain its consumption standard or it may borrow from abroad. As income increases, consumption also increases and at the national income level OY_0, consumption is equal to income. Beyond this, with the increase in income,

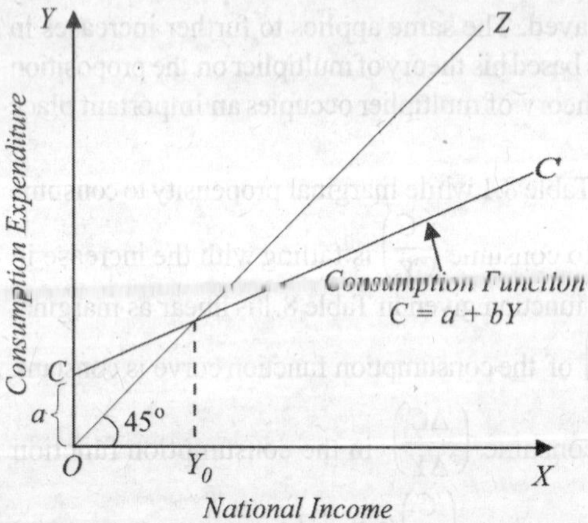

Fig. 8.1. *Keynesian Linear Consumption Function*

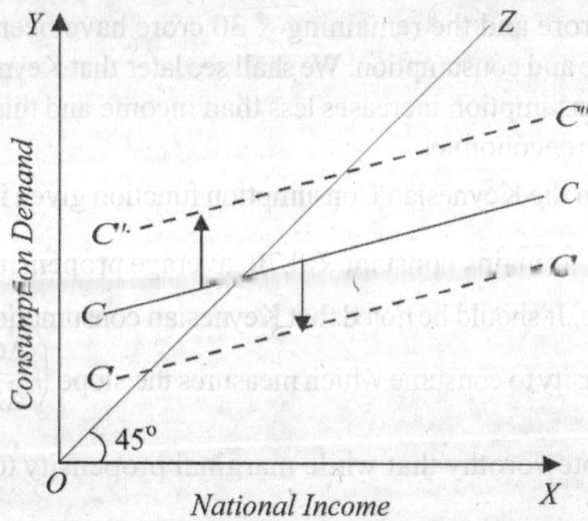

Fig. 8.2. *Shift in Consumption Function*

consumption increases but less than the increase in income and therefore, consumption function curve *CC'* lies below the 45° line *OZ* beyond Y_0. An important point to be noted here is that beyond the level of income OY_0, the gap between consumption and income is widening. The difference between consumption and income represents savings. Therefore, *with the increase in income, saving gap widens* and, as we shall see later, this has a significant implication in macroeconomics.

It is useful to point out here that *when the consumption function of a community changes, the whole consumption function curve changes or shifts.* When propensity to consume increases, it means that at any given level of income more is consumed than before. Therefore, as a result of increase in propensity to consume of the community, the whole consumption function curve shifts upward as has been shown by the upper curve *C''C''* in Fig. 8.2. On the contrary, when the propensity to consume of the community decreases, the whole consumption function curve shifts downward signifying that at any given level of income, less is consumed than before.

Average and Marginal Propensity to Consume

There are two important concepts of propensity to consume, the one being average propensity to consume and the other marginal propensity to consume. They should be carefully distinguished, for they are equal in some cases but different in others. Consider Table 8.1, where we have calculated the average and marginal propensity to consume in columns 3 and 4. As seen above, consumption changes as income changes. Now, how much consumption changes in response to a given change in income depends upon the average and marginal propensity to consume. Thus, propensity to consume of a community can be known by the average and marginal propensity to consume. *Average propensity to consume is the ratio of the amount of consumption to total income*. Therefore, average propensity to consume is calculated by dividing the amount of consumption by the total income. Thus,

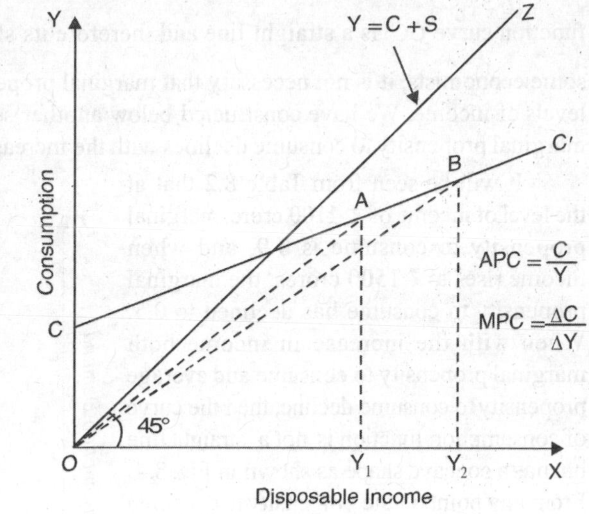

Fig. 8.3. *Consumption Function: Declining Average Propensity to Consume and Constant Marginal Propensity to Consume*

$$APC = \frac{C}{Y}, \text{ where}$$

APC stands for average propensity to consume,
C for amount of consumption, and
Y for the level of income.

In Table 8.1 it will be seen that at the level of income ₹ 1000 crore, consumption expenditure is equal to ₹ 950 crores. Therefore, average propensity to consume is here equal to $\frac{950}{1000} = 0.95$. Likewise, when income rises to ₹ 1200 crore, consumption rises to ₹ 1090 crores. Therefore, the average propensity to consume will be $\frac{1090}{1200} = 0.908$. In this schedule of consumption function, average propensity to consume declines with the increase in income. Keynesian linear consumption function *CC'* is shown in Figures 8.1 and 8.3. Average propensity to consume at a point on the consumption function curve can be obtained by measuring the slope of the ray from the origin to that point. For example, in Fig. 8.3 at income level OY_1, corresponding point on the consumption function curve *CC'* is *A*. Therefore, at OY_1 income level, average propensity to consume (*APC*) is the slope of the ray *OA*. Similarly, at income level OY_2, average propensity to consume is the slope of the ray *OB*. It will be observed from Fig.8.3 that slope of *OB* is less than that of *OA*. Therefore, average propensity to consume at income level OY_2 is less than that at income level OY_1. In other words, average propensity to consume has declined with the increase in national disposable income. However, marginal to consume (*MPC*) which measures the slope $\left(\frac{\Delta C}{\Delta Y}\right)$ of the consumption function curve *CC'* remains constant with the increase in income throughout

Non-Linear Consumption Function : Average and Marginal Propensity to Consume

In the consumption function depicted in Fig. 8.3, though average propensity to consume $\left(\frac{C}{Y}\right)$

declines, marginal propensity to consume which equals $\frac{\Delta C}{\Delta Y}$ remains constant since consumption function curve CC' is a straight line and therefore its slope $\left(\frac{\Delta C}{\Delta Y}\right)$ is constant. But, according to some economists, it is not necessary that marginal propensity to consume should be the same at all levels of income. We have constructed below another schedule of consumption function in which marginal propensity to consume declines with the increase in income.

It will be seen from Table 8.2 that at the level of income of ₹ 1100 crore, marginal propensity to consume is 0.9, and when income rises to ₹ 1500 crores, the marginal propensity to consume has declined to 0.5. When with the increase in income both marginal propensity to consume and average propensity to consume decline, then the curve of consumption function is not a straight line but has a concave shape as shown in Fig. 8.4. From any point on the propensity to consume curve *CC* we can find out average propensity to consume by joining that point with the point of origin by a straight line whose slope will measure the average propensity to consume. In Fig. 8.4, if we have to find out average propensity to consume at point *A* on the consumption function curve *CC*, we connect point *A* with the origin by a straight line. Now, the slope of the line *OA i.e.*, AY_1/OY_1 will measure the average propensity to consume. Similarly, at point *B* of the given consumption function *CC*, the average propensity to consume will be given by the slope of the line *OB* which is equal to BY_2/OY_2.

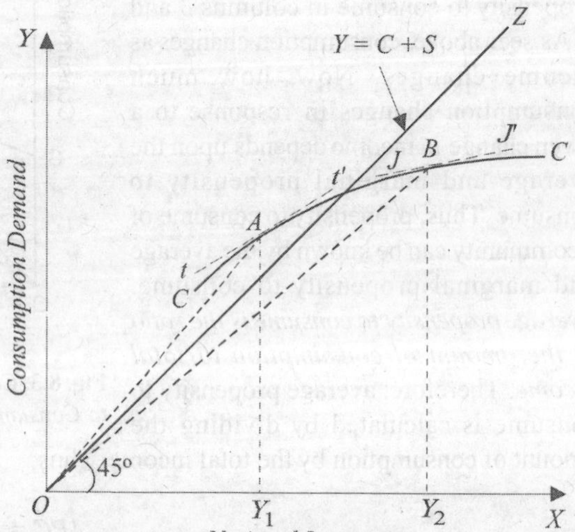

Fig. 8.4. *Non-Linear Consumption Function: Declining both Marginal and Average Propensity to Consume*

Table 8.2

Non-Linear Consumption Function : Average and Marginal Propensity to Consume

Income (₹ *in crores*) Y	*Consumption* (₹ *in crores*) C	*Average Propensity to Consume* $\left(\frac{C}{Y}\right)$	*Marginal Propensity to Consume* $\left(\frac{\Delta C}{\Delta Y}\right)$
1000	950	$\frac{950}{1000} = 0.950$	–
1100	1040	$\frac{1040}{1100} = 0.945$	$\frac{90}{100} = 0.9$
1200	1120	$\frac{1120}{1200} = 0.933$	$\frac{80}{100} = 0.8$
1300	1190	$\frac{1190}{1300} = 0.915$	$\frac{70}{100} = 0.7$
1400	1250	$\frac{1250}{1400} = 0.893$	$\frac{60}{100} = 0.6$
1500	1300	$\frac{1300}{1500} = 0.866$	$\frac{50}{100} = 0.5$

The glance at the figure will show that the slope of the line *OB* is smaller than the slope of the line *OA*. Therefore, average propensity to consume at point *B* or at income level OY_2 is less than at point *A* or income level OY_1.

Marginal Propensity to Consume. The concept of marginal propensity to consume is very important because from it we can know how much part of the increment in income is consumed and how much saved. *Marginal propensity to consume is the ratio of change in consumption to the change in income*. Thus :

$$MPC = \frac{\Delta C}{\Delta Y}$$

where *MPC* stands for marginal propensity to consume,

ΔC for change in consumption, and

ΔY for change in income.

Marginal propensity to consume needs to be carefully distinguished from average propensity to consume. *Whereas average propensity to consume is the ratio of total consumption to total income, i.e.,* $\frac{C}{Y}$, *the marginal propensity to consume is the ratio of* ***change*** *in consumption to the* ***change*** *in income, i.e.* $\frac{\Delta C}{\Delta Y}$.

The concept of marginal propensity to consume can be easily understood with the aid of Table 8.2, in column 4 of which we have calculated the marginal propensity to consume at various levels of income. In this schedule when income rises from ₹ 1000 crore to ₹ 1100 crore, the consumption increases from ₹ 950 crore to ₹ 1040 crore. Here the increment in income is ₹ 100 crore and the increment in consumption is ₹ 90 crore. Therefore, marginal propensity to consume which is $\frac{\Delta C}{\Delta Y}$ is here equal to $\frac{90}{100}$ or 0.9. Similarly, when national income rises to ₹ 1200 crore and as a result consumption increases from ₹ 1040 crore to ₹ 1120 crore, the marginal propensity to consume is now equal to $\frac{80}{100}$ or 0.8. In Table 8.2, it will be seen that *marginal propensity to consume declines as the income* rises. It is worth noting that when with the increase in income average propensity to consume, declines, marginal propensity to consume is less than average propensity to consume, $MPC < APC$. This is in accordance with the usual relationship between the average and marginal quantities.

Marginal propensity to consume can be estimated by drawing the tangent at a point on the consumption function curve. Consider Fig. 8.4 where curve *CC* depicting the consumption function has been drawn. Marginal propensity to consume at point *A* on this will be equal to the slope of the tangent *tt'* drawn at this point. Similarly, marginal propensity to consume at point *B* on it is given by the slope of the tangent *JJ'* drawn at this point. It will be seen that slope of the tangent *JJ'* is less than the slope of the tangent *tt'*. Therefore, marginal propensity to consume at point *B* on the consumption function *CC* in Fig. 8.4 is smaller than the marginal propensity to consume at point *A* on this consumption function. Thus, marginal propensity to consume declines with the increases in income in the non-linear consumption function curve *CC* in Fig. 8.4. Thus *when marginal propensity to consume declines with the increase in income, consumption function is non-linear whose slope declines as income rises*. Non-linear consumption function is shown in Fig. 8.4 where the slope of the propensity to consume curve *CC* declines as income increases. In Fig. 8.1 and Fig. 8.3 propensity to consume curve is a straight line *i.e.,* the slope of the consumption function curve remains constant. Therefore, marginal propensity to consume which is given by the slope of the consumption function curve remains constant in Figures 8.1 and 8.3 though average propoensity to consume declines with the increase in income in these figures.

It is worth noting that marginal propensity to consume is neither zero nor equal to one. It has been found by empirical studies *that marginal propensity to consume varies between zero and unity.* If the marginal propensity to consume was zero, then the whole of the increment in income would have been saved and the consumption function curve would have been a horizontal shape. As we have seen before, this is not so realistic. On the other hand, if the marginal propensity to consume was equal to unity, then the whole of the increment in income would be consumed and in that case consumption function curve would coincide with 45° line.

SAVING FUNCTION

As mentioned above, consumption increases as income increases but less than the rise in income. We will now explain what happens to saving when income increases. *Saving is defined as the part of income which is not consumed* because disposable income is either consumed or saved.

Thus,

$$Y = C + S$$
$$S = Y - C$$

where Y = Disposable income, C = Consumption, S = Saving

Like consumption, saving is also a function of income. Thus, saving function can be written as

$$S = f(Y)$$

Saving function is a counterpart of a consumption function, Therefore, given a particular consumption function, we can derive the corresponding saving function. Let us take the Keynesian consumption, namely, $C = a + bY$. We can derive saving function corresponding to it.

$$\text{Since } Y = C + S$$
$$S = Y - C \qquad \text{... }(i)$$

Now, substituting the Keynesian consumption function for C in (i) we have

$$S = Y - (a + bY)$$
$$= Y - a - bY$$
$$= -a + Y - bY$$
$$= -a + (1 - b)\,Y \qquad \text{... }(ii)$$

Note that $(1 - b)$ in the above saving function in *(ii)* is the value of marginal propensity to save where b is the value of marginal propensity to consume. Let us give a numerical example. Suppose the following consumption function is given.

$$C = 150 + 0.80\,Y$$
$$S = Y - C$$

Substituting the given consumption function for C we have

$$S = Y - 150 - 0.80\,Y$$
$$= -150 + Y - 0.80\,Y$$
$$= 150 + (1 - 0.80)\,Y$$
$$= -150 + 0.20\,Y$$

Note that 0.20 represents marginal propensity to save. It also follows from above that the sum of marginal propensity to consume and marginal propensity to save is equal to one *(MPC + MPS = 1)* as 0.80 + 0.20 = 1. It is important to distinguish between average propensity to save and marginal propensity to save.

Average Propensity to Save (*APS*). An important relationship between income and saving is described by the concept of average propensity to save. *(APS).* Average propensity to save is the proportion of disposable income that is saved *(i.e.* not consumed). Mathematically,

$$APS = \frac{\text{Savings}}{\text{Disposable Income}} = \frac{S}{Y}$$

Like the average propensity to consume *(APC)* average propensity to save also generally varies as income increases. As seen above, average propensity to consume *(APC)* falls as income increases. This implies that average propensity to save will increase as income rises.

Let us derive an important relationship between average propensity to consume and average propensity to save. Restating below the relation that income is either consumed or saved:

$$C + S = Y$$

Dividing both sides by disposable income *Y* we have

$$\frac{C}{Y} + \frac{S}{Y} = \frac{Y}{Y} = 1$$

Since $\frac{C}{Y}$ is average propensity to consume and $\frac{S}{Y}$ is average propensity to save, we have

$$APC + APS = 1$$

or $$APS = 1 - APC$$

This means, for example, that if a society consumes 75 per cent of its disposable income, that is, $APC = 0.75$, then it will save 25 per cent of its disposable income or its average propensity to save *(APS)* will be 0.25 $(1 - 0.75 = 0.25)$.

In Fig. 8.5 we have drawn the saving function curve *SS* in the panel at the bottom. The saving function curve *SS* shows the gap between consumption curve *CC* and the income curve *OZ* in the upper panel of Fig. 8.5. It will be seen that upto income level OY_1, consumption exceeds income, that is, there is dissaving. Beyond income level OY_1, there is positive saving. It is worth mentioning that as average propensity to consume *(APC)* falls with the increase in income in the upper panel, average propensity to save rises as income increases. Thus in Fig. 8.5 with the increase in income not only the absolute amount of saving increases, the average propensity to save also increases.

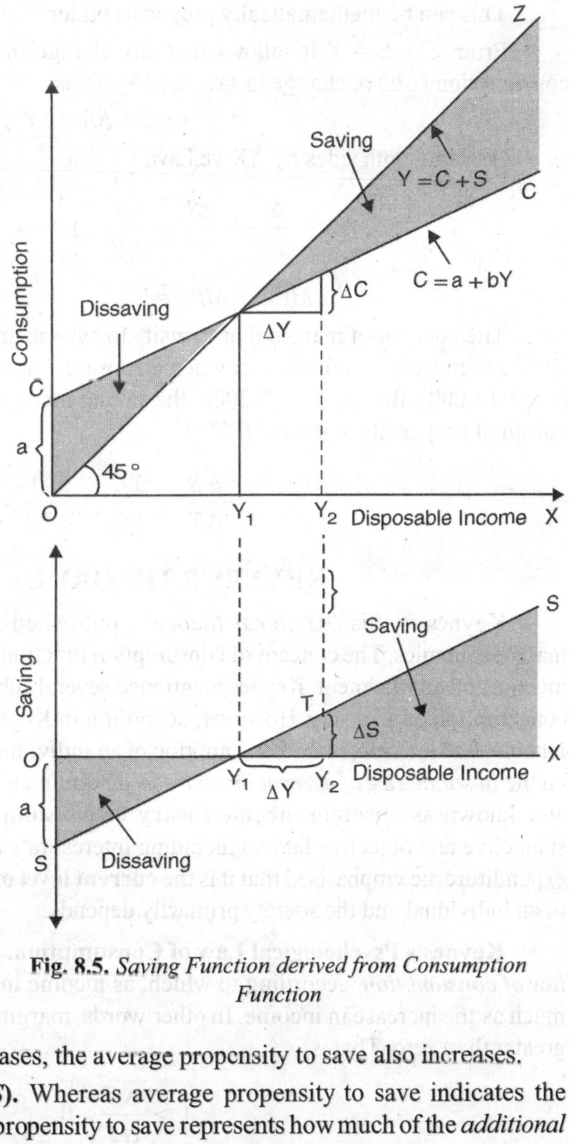

Fig. 8.5. *Saving Function derived from Consumption Function*

Marginal Propensity to Save (*MPS*). Whereas average propensity to save indicates the proportion of income that is saved, marginal propensity to save represents how much of the *additional* disposable income is devoted to saving. The marginal propensity to save is therefore *change* in saving induced by a *change* in the disposable income.

Thus,

$$MPS = \frac{\Delta S}{\Delta Y}$$

For example, if disposable income increases from rupees 10,000 to 12,000 and this causes planned savings to increase by ₹ 500 crores, marginal propensity to save is:

$$MPS = \frac{\Delta S}{\Delta Y} = \frac{500}{2000} = \frac{1}{4} = 0.25$$

Since the additional income is either consumed or saved, *the sum of marginal propensity to consume and marginal propensity to save is equal to one.*

$$MPC + MPS = 1$$

This can be mathematically proved as under :

From $C + S = Y$, it follows that any change in income (ΔY) must induce either change in consumption (ΔC) or change in saving (ΔS). Thus.

$$\Delta C + \Delta S = \Delta Y$$

Dividing both sides by ΔY we have

$$\frac{\Delta C}{\Delta Y} + \frac{\Delta S}{\Delta Y} = \frac{\Delta Y}{\Delta Y} = 1$$

$$MPC + MPS = 1$$

The concept of marginal propensity to save is graphically shown at the bottom of Fig. 8.5. It will be seen from this figure that when disposable income increases from OY_1 (say ₹ 10,000) to OY_2 (say ₹ 12,000), that is, ΔY = ₹ 2000, the saving increases by Y_2T, (₹ 500), that is, ΔS is ₹ 500. Thus marginal propensity to save (*MPS*) is

$$\frac{\Delta S}{\Delta Y} = \frac{Y_2T}{Y_1Y_2} = \frac{500}{2000} = \frac{1}{4} = 0.25$$

KEYNES'S THEORY OF CONSUMPTION

Keynes in his *"General theory"*, published in 1936, laid the foundations of modern macroeconomics. The concept of consumption function plays an important role in Keynes's theory of income and employment. Keynes mentioned several subjective and objective factors which determine consumption of a society. However, according to Keynes, of all the factors it is the *current level of income* that determines the consumption of an individual and also of society. Since Keynes laid stress on the *absolute size of current income* as a determinant of consumption, his theory of consumption is also known as **absolute income theory of consumption.** While Keynes recognized that many subjective and objective factors including interest rate and wealth influenced the level consumption expenditure, he emphasised that it is the **current level of income** on which the consumption spending of an individual and the society primarily depends.

Keynes's Psychological Law of Consumption. Further, Keynes put forward a *psychological law of consumption,* according to which, as income increases consumption increases but not by as much as the increase in income. In other words, marginal propensity to consume is less than one but greater than zero. That is,

$$1 > \frac{\Delta C}{\Delta Y} > 0$$

Thus implies that out of an increment in income a part is consumed and a part saved. To quote Keynes, "*The amount of aggregate consumption depends mainly on the amount of aggregate income. The fundamental psychological law, upon which we are entitled to depend with great confidence both a priori from our knowledge of human nature and from (the detailed facts of experience is that men (and women, too) are disposed, as a rule and on an average to increase their consumption as their income increases, but not by as much as the increase in their income.*"[1]

Keynes's consumption theory has three features. First, he suggests that consumption expenditure depends mainly on absolute income of the current period, that is, consumption is a positive function of the *absolute level of current income*. The more income in a period one has, the more is likely to be his consumption expenditure in that period. In other words, in any period the rich people tend to consume more than the poor people do. Secondly, he propounds a *psychlogical law of consumption, according to which marginal propensity to consume is less than one but greater than zero*. Thirdly, Keynes points out that *consumption expenditure does not have a proportional relationship with income*. According to him, as income increases, a smaller proportion of income is consumed. The proportion of consumption to income is called average propensity to consume (*APC*). Thus, the third property of Keynes's consumption function is that *average propensity to consume (APC) falls as income increases.*

The Keynes' consumption function can be expressed in the following form

$$C = a + bY_d$$

where C is consumption expenditure and Y_d is the real disposable income which equals gross national income minus taxes, a and b are constants, where a is the intercept term, that is, the amount of consumption expenditure at zero level of income. Thus, a is *autonomous consumption.* The parameter b is the marginal propensity to consume (*MPC*) which measures the increase in consumption spending in response to per unit increase in income. Thus, $b = MPC = \frac{\Delta C}{\Delta Y}$

The behaviour of consumption expenditure as perceived by Keynes implies that the marginal propensity to consume is less than average propensity to consume ($MPC < APC$). This is because as income increases consumption does not rise proportionately and as income falls consumption does not fall proportunately. This is because people protect their consumption standards by not reducing their consumption proportionately to the reduction in their income. Implication of the proposition that $MPC < APC$ as income increases is that the ratio of consumption demand to income falls. This can be seen from Figure 8.3 where the slope of consumption function curve is *marginal propensity to consume (MPC) which remains constant* and the slope of the lines such as OA and OB from the origin to points A and B on the consumption function line CC' which measures APC, that is, ratio C/Y at these points is falling showing that consumption demand does not increase proportionately to increase in national income. This Keynesion consumption function is shown in Figures 8.1 and 8.3.

In Fig. 8.3 we have shown a linear consumption function with an intercept term. In this form of linear consumption function, though marginal propensity to consume ($\Delta C/\Delta Y$) is constant, average propensity to consume is declining with the increase in income as indicated by the slopes of the lines OA and OB at levels of income Y_1 and Y_2 respectively. The straight line OB .drawn from the origin indicating average propensity to consume at higher income level Y_2 has a relatively less slope than the straight line OA drawn from the origin to point A at lower income level Y_1. The decline in average propensity to consume as the income increases implies that the *proportion of income that is saved increases with the increase in national income of the country.* This result also follows from the studies of family budgets of various families at different income levels. The fraction of income spent on consumption by the rich families is lower than that of the poor families. In other words, the rich families save a higher proportion of their incomes as compared to the poor families.

The assumption of diminishing average propensity to consume is a significant part of Keynesian theory of income and employment. This implies that as income increases, a progressively larger proportion of national income would be saved. Therefore, to achieve and maintain equilibrium at

1. J.M. Keynes, *The General Theory of Employment, Interest and Money,* (New York : Harcourt), First Edition, 1936, p. 96.

full-employment level of income, increasing proportion of national income is needed to be invested. If sufficient profitable opportunities for investment are not available, the economy would then run into trouble and in that case it would not be possible to maintain full-employment because aggregate demand will fall short of full-employment output. On the basis of this increasing proportion of saving with the increase in income and consequently the emergence of the problem of demand deficiency, some Keynesian economists such as Hanson based the theory of *secular stagnation* on the declining average propensity to consume.

Important Features of Keynes's Consumption Function

In macroeconomics, Keynes's consumption function plays a highly important role. Therefore, it is essential to state its important features. The following are the important features of Keynes's consumption function:

1. First, *absolute level of current income is the important factor that determines consumption* of the community. Increase in national income causes an increase in consumption. On the other hand, classical economists thought that it was rate of interest that primarily determined saving and consumption of the community. A rise in rate of interest induces the people to save more and thus to reduce their level of consumption. According to Keynes, though rate of interest is one of the factors that determine consumption of the community, he did not consider it a very important determinant of it. By considering level of *current income* as the most important factor determining consumption and saving, Keynes made a significant contribution to the macroeconomic theory.
2. The second important feature of Keynes' consumption function is that *marginal propensity to consume is less than one* but greater than zero ($0 < MPC < 1$). As has been explained above, the feature of Keynes's consumption function that marginal propensity to consume is less than one is known as Keynes's psychological law of consumption. According to this law, as income increases, consumption increases but not as much as the increase in income. We will explain in a later chapter that Keynes's theory of multiplier is based on the marginal propensity to consume being less than one but greater than zero.
3. *In Keynes's consumption function, namely, $C = a + by$, as income increases, average propensity to consume (APC) falls.* Keynes was of the view that rich people relatively save a higher proportion of their income so that at higher levels of income average propensity to consume (*APC*), that is, proportion of total consumption to national income falls as national income rises.
4. Another important feature of consumption function as put forward by Keynes is that *it remains stable in the short run.* Consumption function, according to Keynes, depends on various institutional factors such as distribution of income and wealth and psychological factors such as willingness to save. Since there cannot be much changes in these institutional and psychological factors, consumption function remains stable in the short run, that is, it does not shift upward or downward. Therefore, Keynes in his theory explains the determination of income and employment in the short run by considering that the consumption function is stable.

DETERMINANTS OF PROPENSITY TO CONSUME

The important question is on what factors does the consumption demand of a community depend. In other words, what are the factors that determine the level and position of the propensity to consume or the consumption function. Keynes divided the factors determining the propensity to consume into two groups: one group of factors was called by him as objective factors and the second group was named by him as subjective factors. We shall explain below in detail these objective and subjective factors which affect the consumption demand of a community.

Objective Factors

The following six types of objective factors influence the consumption function:

(1) Changes in the General Price Level : Real Balance Effect. The general price level is an important factor which influences the consumption of a community. When the general price level increases or, in other words, when inflation occurs, the consumption function shifts downward. This is because the rise in the general price level, real value (that is, purchasing power) of people's money balances and financial assets with fixed monetary values declines. This causes a downward shift in the consumption function. This is called *real balance effect.* Similarly, when the general price level falls, real value of money balances and financial assets increases. This will induce people to consume relatively more out of their current income. This will cause an upward shift in the consumption function.

(2) Fiscal Policy. Fiscal policy of the Government, especially taxation policy affects the propensity to consume of the country. By levying excise duties, sales tax, the Government can cut down the consumption and thereby increase savings of the community. Likewise, when the Government reduces taxes, consumption of the people increases and this raises the propensity to consume. Rationing and price control by the Government also affects the propensity to consume, as was witnessed during the Second World War. In the modern times, pursuing of the welfare state policy by the Government, under which progressive taxes have been levied on the rich people and the revenue obtained from them have been spent to provide many social security benefits and amenities to the poor people, has tended to raise the consumption function.

(3) Rate of Interest. Rate of interest also affects the propensity to consume and save. It is generally believed that higher rate of interest induces the people to save more and this results in reducing their propensity to consume. But this is not true in the case of all the people. Some individuals are of such a type who want a certain fixed income in the future. And when the rate of interest rises these individuals consume more and save less because with higher rate of interest they can obtain the given fixed income in future with lesser savings. Therefore, when rate of interest rises such individuals save less than before. Thus, it cannot be said with certainty whether with the changes in the rate of interest the propensity to consume of the whole community will change or not.

(4) Stock of Wealth. The stock of wealth owned by the households in the economy is also an important factor that determines propensity to consume. In wealth we include not only *real assets* such as land, houses, automobiles but also *financial assets* such as cash balances, saving and fixed deposits with banks, stocks and bonds possessed by households. The greater the amount of wealth accumulated by households in the economy, the greater is generally the propensity to consume *(i.e.* the greater the amount of consumption out of any level of current income). An important motive of the people to save is to accumulate wealth. Generally speaking, the greater the wealth which people have accumulated, the weaker is the incentive to save further. In other words, the other things remaining the same the increase in wealth generally causes an upward shift in the consumption function and decrease is wealth causes a downward shift in the consumption function.

An important example which is often cited to emphasise the importance of wealth as a determinant of consumption is the stock market crash of 1929 in England (*i.e.* drastic fall in share prices) which substantially reduced the financial wealth of the households overnight resulting in shifting of the consumption function downward.

(5) Monetary Policy, Credit Conditions and Consumer Indebtedness. The availability of easy credit causes an increase in consumption and shifts the consumption function upward. It is now a common experience in India that lowering of lending interest rates by Indian banks on loans for houses, cars, computers and other durable consumer goods greatly increases the consumption of the people and shifts the consumption function upward. On the other hand, tightening of credit produces an opposite effect, that is, causes a downward shift in the consumption function, Furthermore, the recent increase in facilities of Credit Cards by banks and their acceptance buy sellers of consumer goods have also worked to shift the consumption function upward in India.

Similarly, the level of consumer indebtedness also greatly affects the propensity to consume of the people. If the households are heavily indebted, say 25 to 30 per cent of their current income, they are committed to save *(i.e.* consume less) to that extent so that they are able to pay their instalments of previous credit taken. Thus, the greater the degree of indebtedness of households in the economy, the lower will be the consumption function curve and *vice versa.*

(6) Income Distribution. Lastly, distribution of income in a society also determines the level of consumption function. If national income is more unequally distributed, the lower will be the propensity to consume. This is because propensity to consume of the rich is relatively less as compared to that of the poor. Therefore, if inequalities in income distribution increase, this reduces the consumption out of any given level of national income and thus causes a downward shift in the consumption function.

(7) Windfall Gains and Losses. Windfall gains and losses also affect the propensity to consume. When the prices of the shares go up, the shareholders begin to think themselves better off and this raises their consumption. On the other hand, when the prices of the shares go down, the shareholders have to suffer sudden losses and they begin to think themselves relatively poorer than before. This induces them to reduce their consumption. We thus see that the windfall gains and losses affect the propensity to consume.

(8) Change in Expectations. Changes in the expectations of the people also influence the propensity to consume. When people expect that war will break out in the near future and they expect prices to go up, then they will try to spend more on goods so as to meet the needs of the immediate future. This raises the consumption function in the current period. On the other hand, when people expect the prices to fall, they reduce their current consumption so that they should spend more when the prices actually fall.

Subjective Factors

Among the subjective factors are included those factors which induce and prompt people to save some part of their income. First, people save because they want to provide for unforeseen contingencies, such as illness, unemployment, accidents, etc. Secondly, people are induced to save because they want to provide for the expected future needs such as education of the children, marriages of their children, etc. Thirdly, several people wish to save from their current incomes so that they may be able to use accumulated savings for investment which will increase their future income. Investments will bring them more income in the form of more profits and interest. Fourthly, people are motivated to save so that they can accumulate large wealth which will increase their social status. With increased wealth they would think themselves to be economically more independent and they could buy many things with more wealth. Further, many individuals also save so that they can use them for speculative purposes and other business projects. Besides, several people are prompted to save for the sake of leaving a good fortune for their heirs and children. Lastly, many people save because of their miserly instinct and habits. The accumulation of more wealth gives them a great psychic satisfaction.

The above subjective factors increase the propensity to save and therefore reduce the propensity to consume. These subjective factors play a crucial rule in determining the level and shape of the consumption function. However, Keynes pointed out and rightly so that some subjective factors raise the propensity to consume. The *desire for ostentation generally leads to greater consumption expenditure*. People have a natural instint to imitate others' consumption habits. As pointed out by Duesenberry, people in lower and middle income ranges imitate the consumption standards of the higher income groups and this increases their propensity to consume. This has been called ***demonstration effect*** which is a great subjective or psychological force that works to raise the propensity to consume.

Subjective factors also lead the business firms to save much or little from their incomes. Many of the subjective factors which influence the savings of the firms are the following ; (1) *Enterprise*—Many business industrial firms desire to save a part of their current income so that they can make investment in new enterprises and carry out expansion in the future. Business firms generally save a good part of their income for their further expansion. (2) *Liquidity*—Business firms also are induced to save so that they can face contingencies in the future. If they have good amount of liquid wealth in their hands, they would be able to meet the emergent situations more successfully. More cautious and farsighted firms will save more than others on this count. (3) *Successful Management*—Many managers of the business firms are motivated to save more because they want to prove themselves successful managers. With the investment of the saved money, the income of a firm increases and their managers are regarded as successful. (4) *Financial Prudence*—Business firms desire to save for making up the depreciation in plant and machinery. Since after some years business firms have to replace their plant and machinery, if a good part of their current income is not saved, it would not be possible for them to replace plant and machinery. If the firms put aside a greater part of their income for depreciation or replacement purposes, they would pay lower dividends to the shareholders and this will generally lower the propensity to consume of a community. On the other hand, if the firms keep a relatively small amount for depreciation, they will pay larger amounts as dividends to the shareholders and this will generally increase the propensity to consume of the community. Lastly, firms also want to save because they have to repay their debts.

We have explained above various subjective and objective factors which taken together determine the consumption function of a community. It is worth noting that propensity to consume does not generally change in the short run, because it depends more on psychological and institutional factors which change only in the long run. *The institutional factors which determine the distribution of income in the society are important forces determining the consumption function.* And these institutional factors do not change in the short run. Therefore, Keynes was of the view that consumption function remains stable in the short run.

In the appendix to this chapter we shall critically examine post-Keynsian theories of consumption function and compare them with Keynes's theory of consumption function.

Consumption Function Puzzle: Keynes's Consumption Function and Kuznets Findings

Empirical studies of long-term time series data of the US economy for the period 1869-1938 made by the noted American economist Kuznets estimated a consumption function which contradicts Keynes's consumption function which was found to be correct on the basis of cross-section studies of household budget data and short-term time series data. *This contradiction between Kuznets empirical findings and Keynes's consumption function has been called consumption function puzzle.* Efforts have been made by several economists to resolve this puzzle and new theories of consumption function have been put forward to resolve the conflict between Keynes's consumption function and Kuznets's findings. These alternative theories of consumption function will be discussed in the appendix to this chapter.

To compare the Keynes's and Kuznets's consumption functions, it will be useful to write them in algebraic form and graphically represent them. Keynes's consumption function can be algebraically written as below:

$$C = a + bY \qquad ...(1)$$

where a is a positive intercept term which is also called *autonomous consumption* as it does not vary with income. The constant a shows that even when income is zero, a certain consumption is present. This is possible when in any year a community can live either on its past savings or borrow from other communities. Keynes's consumption function is shown in Fig. 8.6

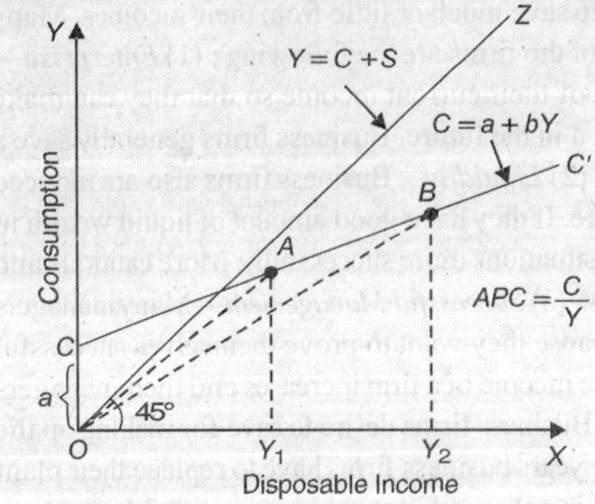

Fig. 8.6. *Keynes's Consumption Function: Falling Average Propensity to Consume*

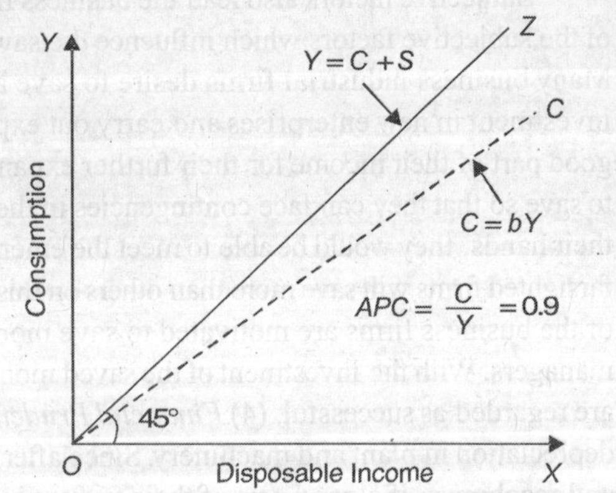

Fig. 8.7. *Kuznets's Consumption Function: Constant APC*

Secondly, b in the above consumption function represents marginal propensity to consume $\left(\frac{\Delta C}{\Delta Y}\right)$. The above mentioned Keynes's consumption function ($C = a + bY$) shows that average propensity to consume $\left(\frac{C}{Y}\right)$ falls as income increases. This can be known by comparing slopes of the rays OA and OB at income levels Y_1 and Y_2 respectively in Fig. 8.6.

Kuznets's Consumption Function

On the other hand, Kuznets found that consumption function is of the following form:

$$C = bY \qquad \ldots (2)$$

In Kuznets's consumption function there is no intercept term (that is, autonomous consumption). This is shown in Fig. 8.7 where it will be seen that Kuznets's consumption function curve starts from the origin and is very near to 45° line depicting that the propensity to consume *(b)* is very high. From his empirical study Kuznets estimated that average propensity to consume was nearly 0.9. Besides, by dividing the entire period (1869-1933) into three overlaping 30 years sub-periods Kuznets found that the proportion of consumption to income (that is, average propensity to consume) was nearly the same and equal to about 0.87 in all the three sub-periods. Thus Kuznets concluded that there was no tendency for the average propensity to consume to decline as disposable income rises. Thus, by rounding off we find Kuznets's estimated propensity to consume is equal to 0.9. His consumption function presented in equation (2) can be rewritten as

$$C = 0.9 \qquad \ldots (3)$$

From the above discussion it follows that implications of Keynes's consumption function ($C = a + bY$) and Kuznets's consumption function ($C = bY$) are different. *Whereas in Keynes's consumption function APC falls as income rises, in Kuznets's function it remains constant over a long period.* Further, the value of marginal propensity to consume which is less than one is much higher in Kuznets's function compared to that of Keynes. The reconciliation between two types of consumption functions has been made by some economists by pointing out that whereas Keynes's function is short-run consumption function, *Kuznets's function is concerned with long run and is referred to as long-run consumption function.* In the long run, short run consumption function curve shifts above and therefore in the long run consumption function, propensity to consume is higher as compared to that in the short run. Further, *Friedman's permanent Income Hypothesis and Modigliani's Life Cycle Hypothesis* have also tried to reconcile the two functions by referring to the short-run and long-run consumption behaviour of the people. We will discuss these consumption hypothesis in the appendix to this chapter.

IMPORTANCE OF CONSUMPTION FUNCTION

The concept of consumption function is greatly important both in theory and actual practice. To remove unemployment and to control economic fluctuations in the economy, it is very essential to adopt a proper macroeconomic policy. In the formation of such a policy, understanding of the concept of propensity of consume is very essential. Therefore. Prof. A.H. Hansen has remarked that "*consumption function is epoch-making contribution of Keynes to economic theory*". We explain below some of the theoretical and practical importance of this consumption function.

(1) **The concept of consumption function helps us to invalidate Say's law of classical economics.** In fact, Keynes relied on his consumption function for proving the invalidity of Say's law. According to Say's law, every supply creates its own demand and therefore there is no problem of deficiency of aggregate demand. Thus, classical economists who based their analysis on Say's law thought that, general overproduction and unemployment in the economy was not possible because adequate amount of aggregate demand would ever be present. Now, according to Keynes's psychological law of consumption, when income increases consumption increases but less than the increase in income (that is, *MPC* is less than one) and therefore saving gap emerges between income and consumption. This saving gap implies that all output produced may not be consumed in a period and the problem of deficiency of demand will arise unless this saving gap is matched by an equal amount of investment demand. There is no guarantee that the saving done will be automatically invested or, in other words, it is not necessary that investment demand will be equal to the saving gap. Thus, the contention of the Say's law that every supply creates its equal demand is not valid. No doubt, every supply or production creates income equal to the output produced. But since all income is not consumed and there is no guarantee that investment will be equal to the saving so emerged, Say's law is proved invalid. When investment is less than the saving gap corresponding to full-employment level of income, the aggregate demand is not sufficient to provide full-employment to the people and other resources. Thus, the problem of deficiency of effective demand and hence general unemployment and overproduction arises in a free-enterprise capitalist economy.

(2) The concept of propensity to consume is also important because **it brings out crucial significance of investment demand** for the determination of the level of income and employment in a capitalist economy. From the concept of propensity to consume we know that consumption increases less than the increase in income and as a result gap emerges between income and consumption. To maintain a certain given level of income and employment, gap between income and consumption at that level must be bridged by investment expenditure otherwise it will not be possible to maintain that level of income and employment because aggregate demand would not be large enough. This indicates the crucial importance of the investment demand in the determination of income and employment. To prevent the establishment of underemployment equilibrium in the economy or, in other words, for achieving full-employment equilibrium, investment demand must be equal to the saving gap at the level of full-employment. Keynes also showed that consumption function remains stable in the short run and therefore economic fluctuations in a capitalist economy are largely due to the fluctuations in investment demand. Thus from the concept of propensity to consume it follows that investment demand is vitally important in determining the level of income and employment. If it were possible to raise the propensity to consume in the short run, then without raising investment, we could have raised the level of income and employment. Since consumption function is stable in the short run, we have to increase investment for achieving full employment in the economy.

(3) Another crucial importance of the Keynesian concept of consumption function is that **we derive the theory of multiplier from it which has a great practical importance in the formulation of macroeconomic policy,** especially of public works in times of depression. As we shall study in the next chapter, the magnitude of multiplier is equal to the reciprocal of one minus marginal propensity to consume $\left(K = \dfrac{1}{1 - MPC}\right)$, where *K* stands for multiplier and *MPC* for marginal propensity to

consume. According to Keynes's psychological law of consumption marginal propensity to consume is less than one. According to his concept of multiplier, when investment increases, income, output and employment increase by a multiple amount, depending upon the size of the multiplier. Income increases manifold than the original investment because of the nature of consumption function. When some investment in certain projects is undertaken, it leads to the increase in income of those employed in the projects but the process does not stop here. The increases in income are further spent on consumption and this leads to further increase in income and so the chain of increases in income and consumption continues and the ultimate increase in income and employment is multiple of the original increment in investment. If the marginal propensity to consume were equal to zero, then all increments in income brought about by additional investment would have been saved and therefore multiplier process would not have worked. Since the marginal propensity to consume is greater than zero, the increase in net investment has a multiplier effect on income, output and employment. Thus, the effect of investment on income depends on the size of the multiplier which depends on the value of the marginal propensity to consume. The greater the marginal propensity to consume, the greater the size of the multiplier.

(4) From the concept of consumption function, we can also explain ***why there is a tendency for the marginal efficiency of capital to decline.*** The declining tendency of the marginal efficiency of capital is due to the nature of the consumption function. Two features of consumption function are important. First, the marginal propensity to consume is less than one which implies that as income increases, consumption increases less than this. Secondly, consumption function is stable in the short run *i.e.,* it does not shift much in the short run. As we know that the level of investment is a crucial factor in the determination of income and employment, fluctuations in the levels of income and employment depend primarily on the fluctuations in investment. The investment demand in the short run is determined by the rate of interest on the one hand and marginal efficiency of capital on the other. Since the rate of interest is relatively sticky, it is the marginal efficiency of capital which greatly affects the level of investment in the short run. Marginal efficiency of capital is nothing but the expected rate of profit on investment in the future. Thus, the marginal efficiency of capital is determined by the expectations of the entrepreneurs regarding the earning of profits from capital assets in the future.

Now, the most important fact that affects the entrepreneurs' expectations regarding profit prospects and thereby the marginal efficiency of capital is the level of future consumption demand for goods and services. Their estimate of future consumption demand depends on, among others, on the growth of population and incomes. If population growth of a country is expected to fall as was estimated in the early thirties when Keynes wrote his book (*General Theory of Employment, Interest and Money*), this would adversely affect future consumption demand which in turn would adversely affect investment in the long run, Besides, according to Keynes, average propensity to consume (*APC*) falls as income of a community increases overtime. This also adversely affects inducement to invest. If there does not occur capital-using technological change, this will result in decline in investment opportunities in the long run, causing secular stagnation. Thus we see that in the Keynesian scheme of things level of investment depends upon the level of consumption demand in the long run.

Since marginal propensity to consume is less than one and also average propensity to consume falls as income increases, consumption does not increase proportionately. As a result, the aggregate demand becomes deficient and the marginal efficiency of capital declines. The decline in the marginal efficiency of .capital adversely affects investment which stops rising. As a result, the growth process stops and economic recession occurs. In this way, Keynes himself and later important Keynesian economist, A.H. Hansen developed the theory of ***secular stagnation*** (i.e., prolonged period of depression of indefinite future) for the mature capitalist economies. This secular stagnation theory is based upon the assertion that investment opportunities in a capitalist economy will be exhausted soon due to the absence of the possibilities of increasing consumption demand. The meagre opportunities of increasing investment in the mature capitalist economies, according to them, are partly due to the stability of consumption function and declining average propensity to consume which cause the marginal efficiency of capital to decline.

(5) As has been explained above, Keynesian concept of propensity to consume also **helps us in explaining the *turning points of a business cycle.*** The economy swings down from the peak it reaches because with marginal propensity to consume being less than one and average propensity to consume falling with increase in income, consumption demand does not increase as much as the increase in income and output. Over time this causes deficiency in aggregate demand causing fall in marginal efficiency of capital which adversely affects investment demand by private business men. Likewise, economy's downward movement stops and it starts recovery because marginal propensity to consume being less than one and average propensity to consume (*APC*) rises as income decreases people do not reduce their consumption as much as the reduction in their income. Even during depression people try to maintain their previous level of consumption. This ultimately induce investment for replacement of capital goods which wear out over a period of business cycle. With the working of Keynesian investment multiplier recovery from recession gathers momentum.

QUESTIONS FOR REVIEW

1. What is consumption function ? Explain the objective and subjective factors which determine consumption expenditure in the economy.
2. What are the two forms of consumption function ? How do *APC* and *MPC* behave in these forms of consumption function ? Which form of the consumption function seems to be realistic ?
3. Explain Keynes' psychological law of consumption. Explain its importance in the determination of income and employment in the economy.
4. Explain and graphically represent Keynesian consumption function $C = a + bY$. How do marginal propensity to consume (*MPC*) and average propensity to consume (*APC*) change with increase in income in this consumption function ?
5. What is consumption function ? Explain the factors that cause shift in the consumption function.
6. Distinguish between Keynes's consumption function and Kuznet's consumption function. How have these two consumption functions been reconciled ?
7. What is consumption function puzzle ? How has it been resolved ?
8. What is consumption function ? Explain its importance in the theory of determination of income and employment
9. (*a*) What is a saving function ? Derive a saving function from the consumption function, $C = a + bY$

   (*b*) Show that the sum of *APC* and *APS* is equal to one .
10. "Consumption function is an epoch-making contribution to the tools of economic analysis analogous to but even more important than Marshall's discovery of the demand function" (Hansen) Discuss.
11. Distinguish between *APC* and *MPC*. What factors other than income are likely to be most important in determining consumption ?
12. Given the data of the disposable income (Y_d) and amount of consumption at the initial level of income (₹ 100). Assuming that marginal propensity consume is 50 per cent. Complete the table and draw the graphs of consumption and saving functions.

Y_d	*C*	*S*	*APC*	*MPC*	*APS*	*MPS*
₹ 100	150					
200						
300						
400						
500						
600						

13. Explain the important features of Keynesian Consumption function.

APPENDIX TO CHAPTER 8

Post-Keynesian Theories of Consumption

Introduction

Since Keynes propounded his theory of consumption there have been significant developments in this field and some alternative theories of consumption have been put forward. However, all these post-Keynesian consumption theories relate consumption to some form of income. First, J.S. Duesenberry expressed the view that consumption expenditure of the individuals depends not on their own absolute incomes but on their incomes relative to the incomes of others. Therefore, his theory is also called '*Relative Income Theory of Consumption*'. Second, Modigliani and Ando put forward a theory known as '*Life Cycle Theory of Consumption*' according to which, individuals plan their consumption profile for their whole lifetime which depends not so much on current income but on their expectations of whole their lifetime income.

Further, a famous American economist, Milton Friedman, advanced an hypothesis regarding consumption behaviour called Permanent Income Hypothesis according to which consumption of individuals depends on their permanent income rather than their current level of income. We discuss below briefly these three post-Keynesian theories of consumption.

LIFE-CYCLE THEORY OF CONSUMPTION

In Keynes's theory of consumption function, consumption expenditure in a period depends mainly on current income. After Keynes some economists such as Franco Modigliani and Milton Friedman pointed out that individuals while making their consumption decisions take into account not only the current income which was emphasised by Keynes but also the income they expect to receive in the future. Therefore, the consumption theories of Franco Modigliani and Milton Friedman, both are Nobel Laureates, have been called *Future-Oriented Consumption Theories* by Joseph Stiglitz.[1]

Consumption theory put forward by Modigliani and Ando is called *Life-Cycle Theory of Consumption*[2] as they lay stress on the fact that in deciding about consumption out of income in the working years of their life individuals attempt to save for the post-retirement period. Their motive for doing so is to smooth out or even their consumption in their entire life span. That is, they save from the income of working period of their life so that they will not have to cut down consumption level after they retire.

The life-cycle theory assumes that an individual in early years of his life earns no income and is maintained by his parents or other relatives. In the middle period of his life he works and earns income. Though in the middle period of his life he spends a good deal on consumption of his own and his family members, on balance he earns more than he consumes and therefore saves a part of his income. **His motive of saving is to accumulate assets or wealth, which yields him enough income so as to maintain satisfactory standard of consumption in later years of his life after he retires.**

According to life-cycle theory, consumption in any period is not the function of current income of that period but of the whole lifetime expected income. Thus, in life cycle hypothesis the individual is assumed to plan a pattern of consumption expenditure based on expected income in his entire lifetime. It is further assumed that individual maintains a more or less constant or slightly increasing level of

1. See J. Stiglitz, *Economics,* 2002, p. 634
2. Ando A. Franco Modigliani, The Life Cycle Hypothesis of Saving : Aggregate Implications and Tests, *American Economic Review*, March 1963, pp. 55-84.

consumption. However, his level of consumption is limited by his expectations of lifetime income. A typical individual in this theory in his early years of life spends on consumption either by borrowing from others or spending the assets bequeathed by his parents. It is in his main working years of his lifetime that he consumes less than the income he earns and therefore makes net positive savings. *He invests these savings in assets, that is, accumulates wealth which he consumes in the future years. He will accumulate enough wealth or assets in his working years* of his life so that he can maintain what he considers satisfactory standard of living even after he retires from work. In his lifetime after retirement he again dissaves, that is, consumes more than his income in these later years of his life but is able to maintain or even slightly increase his consumption in the lifetime after retirement.

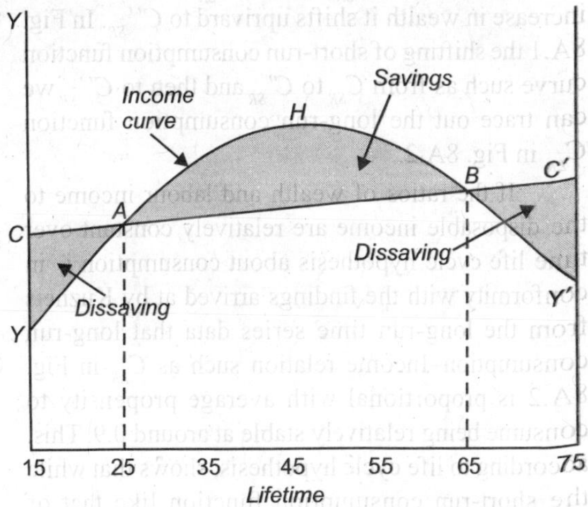

Fig. 8A.1. *Life Cycle Theory of Consumption*

Life cycle hypothesis has been depicted in Fig. 8A.1. It is assumed that a typical individual knows exactly at what age he will die. In Fig. 8A.1 it is taken that the individual would die at the age of 75 years. That is, 75 years is his expected lifetime. If an individual does not want to leave any assets for his children then in the life cycle theory net savings in the entire lifetime will by zero, that is, the savings done by the individual in the working years of his life will be equal to the dissavings made by him in his early years of life before he is able to earn income as well as the dissavings which he makes after retirement. It is also assumed for the sake of simplicity that interest paid on his assets is zero. The curve *YY′* shows income pattern of the whole lifetime of the individual whereas *CC′* is the curve of consumption which is assumed to be slightly increasing as the individual grows old. It is assumed that our individual enters into labour force (i.e., working life) at the age of 15 years. It will be noticed from Fig. 8A.1 that up to the age of 25 years his income, though increasing, is less than his consumption, that is, he will be dissaving during the first 10 years of his working life. To finance his excess consumption over his income, he may be borrowing from others.

In the final stage of his life cycle when the individual has retired from work his earnings from work is very little or nil while he spends a good deal on his consumption. It is income from his past savings or accumulated assets that enables him to maintain satisfactory standard of consumption over his whole life cycle.

Some important conclusions follow from life cycle theory of consumption. The fundamental idea of the life cycle hypothesis is that people make their consumption plans for their entire lifetime and further that they make lifetime consumption plans on the basis of their expectations of lifetime income. *Thus in life cycle model consumption is not a function of current but of expected life-time income. Besides, according to life cycle hypothesis, consumption of an individual also depends on wealth held by him which he accumulates during working years of life by investing his saving.* In fact, wealth is used to balance income streams over his entire life.

The life cycle theory can explain the puzzle that arose from the empirical fundings of consumption function by Kuznets, namely, that APC is constant, that is, increase in consumption is proportional to increase in income. According to life cycle hypothesis, like Keynes's consumption function theory, the relationship between consumption and income is non-proportional, that is, *APC* falls as income rises as will be seen from consumption function curve *CC′* in Figure 8A.1 which has an intercept. The intercept of the consumption function of life cycle consumption hypothesis measures the wealth effect. However, the intercept of such short-run consumption function is not constant. As wealth increases and the intercept rises, the short-run consumption shifts upward as shown in Fig. 8A.2 where as a result of increase in wealth, consumption curve C_{SR} shifts to C'_{SR} and with further increase in wealth it shifts uprivard to C''_{SR}. In Fig. 8A.1 the shifting of short-run consumption function curve such as from C_{SR} to C'_{SR} and then to C''_{SR} we can trace out the long-run consumption function C_{LR} in Fig. 8A.2.

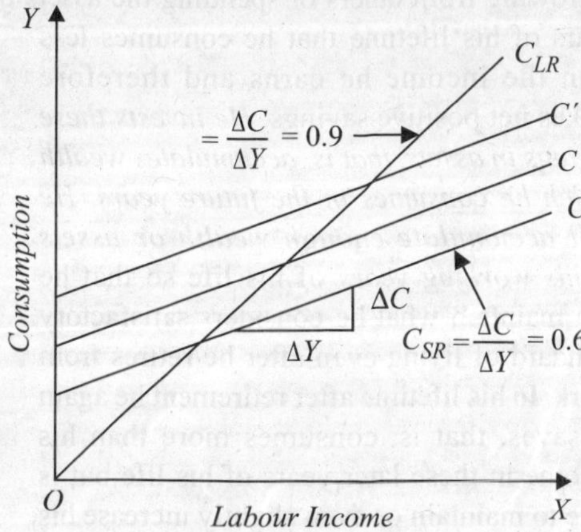

Fig. 8A.2. *Life Cycle Consumption and Income Short Run and Long Run*

If the ratios of wealth and labour income to the disposable income are relatively constant over time life cycle hypothesis about consumption i in conformity with the findings arrived at by Kuznets from the long-run time series data that long-run consumption–Income relation such as C_{LR} in Fig. 8A.2 is proportional with average propensity to consume being relatively stable at around 0.9. This, according to life cycle hypothesis, shows that while the short-run consumption function like that of Keynesian one shows non-proportional relationship between income and consumption (*i.e. APC* falling with increase in income), the long-run consumption function is in accordance with Kuznets's finding that there is proportional relationship between consumption and income in the long run with *APC* as stable. In this way life cycle hypothesis has succeeded in resolving the difference between Keynes's view and Kuznets's findings. While Keynes was concerned with short-run consumption function, Kuznets's findings were about long-run consumption function.

Critique, Although life cycle theory has provided an explanation of various puzzles about consumption function, it is not without critics. Gardner Ackley has criticized the assumption of life cycle hypothesis that in making consumption plans, households have "a definite and conscious vision." According to Ackley, the possession of this long-term vision on the part of households sounds unrealistic. Further, according to him, to assume that a household has complete knowledge of "family's future size, including the life expectancy of each member, entire lifetime profile of income of each member, the extent of credit available in the future, emergencies, opportunities and social pressure which have a bearing on consumption spending" is quite unrealistic.

Life cycle theory has also been criticized that it fails to recognize the importance of liquidity constraints in determining the response of consumption to income. According to critics, even if a household has a concrete vision of future income, the opportunities to borrow from the capital markets for quite a long period on the basis of expected future income, as has been visualised by life cycle hypothesis, are very little. This creates the liquidity constraints for deciding about consumption plans. As a result, the consumption becomes highly responsive to current income which is quite contrary to the life cycle hypothesis.

DUESENBERRY'S RELATIVE INCOME THEORY OF CONSUMPTION

Duesenberry's theory is based on two relative income hypotheses. First, he lays stress on relative incomes of individuals rather than their absolute incomes as determinant of their consumption, that is, *consumption behaviour of individuals is interdependent*. Second, according to him, *consumption of individuals does not depend on their current income but on certain previous reached income levels*. That is, consumption-income relation of individuals is irreversible over time.

Demonstration Effect, Duesenberry's first statement implies that consumption of individuals are not so much concerned with the absolute level of their income as with their relative position in the income distribution in a society, that is, consumption behaviour of an individual is governed not by level of his absolute income but his income relative to the incomes of other individuals in the society. This tendency of an individual arises to keep up with other individuals' consumption standard, or what is called, to "keep up with the Joneses". This is called by Duesenberry as **demonstration effect**.

According to this hypothesis of Duesenberry, if incomes all individuals in society increases by the same percentage, then their relative incomes would remain the same though their absolute incomes would have increased. According to Duesenburry, because relative income of each individual in a society remains the same, every one will be spending the same proportion of his income on consumption as he was doing before the increase in his absolute income. That is, *the average propensity to consume (APC) will remain the same despite the increase in absolute incomes of individuals if the relative incomes of individuals remain the same*. That *APC* remains the same as the community's income increases conforms to the time-series empirical findings such as that of Kuznets. This conclusion of Duesenburry's relative income theory of consumption differs from the Keynesian theory, of consumption, according to which, as seen above, as absolute income of a community increases, it will devote a smaller proportion of its income to consumption expenditure, that is, its *APC* will decline.

Duesenberry's demonstration effect also shows that a person with a given income would devote a larger proportion of his income to consumption if he is living in a community or area where that income is considered relatively low. This is due to the working of demonstration effect. On the other hard, a person will spend a lower proportion of his income if he is living in a community in which that income is considered relatively high. This is because in this later case demonstration effect will not be working.

Ratchet Effect. Duesenberry's second hypothesis of irreversibility of consumption-income relation over time suggests that when incomes of individuals or households falls from a previously attained levels their consumption does not fall to that extent. According to Duesenberry, individuals show resistance to lowering their consumption level once attained. This is called ratchet effect. This is partly due to the demonstration effect explained above. People do not want to show to their neighbour that they do not afford to maintain their previous high standard of living. Further, this is also partly due to the fact that people become accustomed to their previous high level of consumption and it is quite hard and difficult to reduce their consumption expenditure when their income has fallen. They try to maintain their earlier consumption level by reducing their savings. Therefore, the fall in their income, as during the period of recession or depression, does not result in decrease in their consumption expenditure very much as one would conclude from the cross-section family budget studies. Thus, it is because of the ratchet effect that decrease in income of individuals will have less than proportionate effect on consumption. That is, *MPC* is less than *APC*.

It follows from above that through demonstration and ratchet effects Duesenberry's relative income hypothesis provides a convincing explanation for why aggregate short-run consumption function of the community may be flatler than the family budget studies would suggest. It is because, he emphasises, it is relative income rather than absolute income which determines consumption expenditure of the households. Further, *it also follows from Duesenberry's relative income hypothesis that short-run aggregate consumption function of the community is linear rather than curved.* As explained above, if in the short run the level of income increases, the proportion of consumption expenditure does not increase much due to the operation of demonstration effect and with the fall in income the proportion of consumption expenditure to income is not likely to decrease much due to ratchet effect. It is worth mentioning that Duesenberry's theory assumes that income distribution in a society does not change much in the short run which is in conformity with the real world situation.

FRIEDMAN'S PERMANENT CONSUMPTION THEORY

Like Modigliani, Milton Friedman[3] also thinks that expectations about future income affect current consumption in a period. According to Friedman, income of an individual consists of permanent income and temporary or transitory income.

3. Milton Friedman, *A. Theory of Consumption*, Princeton University Press, 1957

$$Y = Y_p + Y_t$$
$$C = C_P + C_t$$

where Y stands for income, Y_p for permanent income, Y_t for temporary or transitory income, C for consumption, C_p for permanent consumption and C_t for temporary or transitory income. It is worth emphasizing that Friedman thinks that *permanent income is viewed to be earned by both human and non-human capital of the individual*. Income from human capital is expected income earned from human labour by individuals and income from non-human capital or wealth is the expected earnings from physical assets held by them.

He points out that people save in good years so that they have not to curtail consumption in bad years. In other words, in Friedman's view consumption of individuals or households depends on permanent income in contrast to current income level as emphasised by Keynes. *By permanent income he means average long-run income*. Therefore, Friedman's theory is known as permanent consumption hypothesis. According to this view, temporary changes in income such as bonus received in a year, or large capital gains received due to rise in prices of shares or real estate would not have much effect on consumption compared to the permanent changes in income, that is, changes in long-run average income. According to Friedman, temporary or transitory changes in income will have little effect on consumption while permanent changes in income will have large effect on consumption. Thus, according to Friedman's permanent consumption theory, if households could predict their future income level, they will adjust their consumption levels according to their permanent or average long-run income.

As mentioned above, Friedman is of the view that both income and consumption of an individual should be divided into two parts—*permanent and transitory*. Permanent income is the part of income that an individual expects to go on receiving over time in future. On the other hand, according to him, there is transitory income which occurs accidently or by chance. These transitory incomes may occur due to bad purchases of commodities or assets which yield him losses which therefore represents negative income or they be the result of favourable chance purchases or winning of lotteries which therefore yield positive income.

Corresponding to the concept of permanent income there is a notion of permanent consumption. **Permanent consumption is the consumption expenditure which an individual expects he will be making over time in future.** The crucial point which Friedman makes is that *permanent consumption of individuals depends on permanent income* rather than current income as believed by J.M. Keynes. Besides, according to Friedman, permanent income is very much a reflection of the capital value or wealth and this wealth consists of capital value of principal assets possessed by an individual and his human capital (*i.e.* his earning ability depending on the knowledge and skills possessed). According to Friedman, *consumption is proportional to permanent income and can be stated as under* :

$$C = kY_p$$

Thus, Friedman's permanent consumption theory is summed up in the following equation:

$$C_p = k\,(i, w, u)Y_p$$

This proportion (k) of permanent income that is consumed depends on rate of interest (i), desire to accumulate wealth (w) and individuals' desire for immediate current consumption (u). Thus, according to Friedman, permanent consumption is function of rate of interest (i), the ratio of non-human (*i.e.*, physical wealth) to income (w) and the preference of individuals for immediate or current consumption as against his willingness to accumulate assets or wealth. According to Friedman, higher rate of interest would induce people to save more and thus reducing his consumption expenditure. Besides, proportion of individuals' consumption to their permanent income depends to a great deal on their assets or wealth, that is, w in the above function. The greater the wealth, or assets of an individual, the higher his consumption expenditure. Lastly, the proportion (k) of consumption expenditure to permanent income depends on individual's desire for immediate or current consumption as against his willingness to add to his wealth or assets and is denoted by u.

Milton Friedman emphasises that consumption of individuals is affected by changes in individuals' wealth which is a stock variable in contrast to the current income which is a flow variable. Friedman's permanent consumption theory suggests that individuals' consumption depends on how well-off they are and that is better measured by their wealth. Individuals' wealth changes when the value of their assets such as prices of stock, shares and real estate change. When their prices rise, people enjoy capital gains which make them wealthier and as a result their consumption out of a given income rises. With this the consumption function curve shifts above. Commenting on the future-oriented theories of consumption and saving of Modigliani and Friedman, Joseph Stiglitz writes, "*Both Modigliani and Friedman stressed that individuals generally try to stabilise their consumption using savings to smooth consumption so that it does not fluctuate dramatically from year to year. They also stressed that individuals will be forward-looking, basing current consumption decisions on their expectations about future income*"[4].

Implications. There are three important implications of the above two future-oriented theories of consumption and saving, namely, life cycle theory of Modigliani and permanent income theory of Friedman. First important implication is that changes in expectations about future income affect the current consumption of individuals even though their current income has not changed. Consider the case when an economy is currently experiening recession, as had been the case in 2008-09 caused by global financial crisis and global meltdown, people become quite pessimistic about their future income prospects which lead them to curtail consumption and save more even though their current income do not change. This causes the consumption function curve to shift downward.

Another implication is that *one-time or transitory changes in income will cause only a small change in consumption.* Suppose a person has a windfall gain of `` 10 lakhs in a year due to his winning a lottery. Given his marginal propensity to consume equal to 0.8, the Keynesian consumption function predicts that his consumption will increase by ₹ 8 lakhs and the remaining ₹ 2 lakhs will be saved by him in that year. On the other hand, the future-oriented theories of both Modigliani and Freidman predict that the consumption of extra income gained by the lottery winner during a year will be spread over his lifetime or over a long period of time. Similarly, a more important case from the viewpoint of economic policy is the temporary reduction in the direct tax at the time of recession by the government to boost consumption demand as had been done by the US government in 2007-08 and 2008-09 to fight recession will have only limited effect on consumption. The above two future-oriented theories, especially that of Friedman, predict that contrary to the prediction of the Keynesian model the **temporary reduction in direct taxes** will be much less effective in boosting consumption demand as due to uncertain economic prospects much of the income gained through temporary tax reduction will be saved. The evidence from the US shows this has in fact been the case.

The third related implication of the future-oriented theories is that since changes in income that individuals expect to be only temporary will have only small effect on consumption spending, marginal propensily to consume will be lower and the multiplier effect of such changes in incomes will be smaller.

To conclude, leaving aside the cases of transitory changes in income and the concern of the forward-looking people to ensure same consumption standard in the future, the Keynesian theory of consumption is right in visualising that individuals' consumption spending is more dependent on current income. To quote Stiglitz, "*The permanent income and life-cycle saving hypotheses contain large elements of truth. Families do save for their retirement and they do smooth their consumption*

4. Stiglitiz, *op. cit.*, p. 634 5.

between good years and bad. Even so, households spending appcar to be more depended on current income than either future-oriented theory would saggest"[5].

QUESTION FOR REVIEW

1. Explain the life cycle hypothesis of consumption, Compare the major differences of this hypothesis with Keynesian theory of consumption. What are its short comings ?
2. Explain relative income hypothesis of consumption behaviour. How does it reconcile long-run (secular) consumption function with the cyclical consumption function ?
3. What is relative income hypothesis ? How does it differ from Keynes's absolute income hypothesis. Explain demonstration effect and rachet effect in the relative income hypothesis of consumption.
4. Explain permanent income hypothesis. How does it differ from Keynes's absolute income hypothesis ? How is permanent income measured ?
5. How does permanent income hypothesis explain that the short-run marginal propensity to consume is lower than the long-run marginal propensity to consume ?

   [*D.U. B.A. (Hons) 2000*]
6. Explain the permanent income hypothesis of consumption. Explain its implications.
7. Both life cycle hypothesis and permanent income hypothesis stress that individuals are forward looking as they base their current decisions on their expectations about future income. Explain ?

5. Stiglitz, *op.cit*, 55 (Italics added)

CHAPTER 9

Investment Demand

Introduction

Levels of national income and employment in the short run depend upon the level of aggregate demand. The aggregate demand in Keynes's simple two-sector model consists of two constituents—consumption demand and investment demand. In the previous chapter we have studied the consumption function and the various factors which determine it. In the present chapter we shall discuss the factors which determine the investment demand or inducement to invest. Since consumption function is more or less stable in the short run, investment demand is of crucial importance in the determination of income and employment. The greater the level of investment, the greater the level of income and employment. According to Keynes, the equilibrium of a capitalist economy is generally not established at the level of full employment, primarily because investment demand is insufficient to fill up the saving gap corresponding to the level of full employment. Therefore, underemployment equilibrium, on which Keynes laid a great stress, is due to the lack of investment demand as compared to the amount of saving at full-employment level of income and as a result there emerges a *deflationary gap* in the economy which brings about the rise in general price level. We thus see that investment demand plays a vital role in the determination of national income, employment and prices in the country.

Meaning of Investment

It is useful to make the meaning of investment clear. When a person buys shares, bonds or debentures of a public limited company from the market, it is generally said that he has made investment. But this is not the real investment which determines income and employment in the country and with which we are here concerned. Buying of *existing* shares and bonds by an individual is merely a financial investment. When one individual purchases the shares or bonds, some other one would sell them. Thus, the purchase and sale of the shares merely represents the change in the ownership of assets which already exists rather than the creation of new capital assets. Investment is the new addition to the stock of physical capital such as plant, machines, trucks, new factories and so on that creates income and employment. Therefore, *by real investment we mean the addition to the stock of physical capital*. Thus, *in economics, investment means the new expenditure incurred on addition to the stock of capital goods such as machines, buildings, equipment, tools, etc*. The addition to the stock of physical capital, i.e., net investment raises the level of aggregate demand which brings about addition to the level of income and employment in the economy. Keynes and many other economists also include the *increase in the inventories of consumer goods* in investment in of the country.

TYPES OF INVESTMENT

Distinction must be drawn between the following three types of investment:

1. Business fixed investment
2. Residential investment
3. Inventory investment

We explain below their meanings and the factors which determine them.

Business Fixed Investment

Business fixed investment means investment in the machines, tools and equipment that businessmen buy for use in further production of goods and services. The stock of these machines or plant equipment etc. represents fixed capital. The term 'fixed' in it implies that expenditure made on the machines, equipment etc. continues to be used for production for a relatively long time. This is in contrast to inventory investment whose components will be either used shortly for production or sold shortly to others for further production.

Business fixed investment is important in two respects. First, business fixed investment is an important component of aggregate demand and therefore plays a significant role in the determination of national income and employment. Business fixed investment is a volatile component of aggregate demand and, as Keynes emphasized, fluctuation in levels of business fixed investment is responsible for business cycles in a free-market economy.

As we shall explain in detail later in this chapter Keynes put forward a theory of investment which states that business fixed investment is determined by *expected rate of profit* (which he calls *marginal efficiency of capital*) and rate of interest. Since rate of interest in the short run is relatively sticky, it is changes in expectations about earning profits in future that cause fluctuations in business fixed investment.

According to the neoclassical theory, business fixed investment is determined by the marginal product of capital the one the hand and user's cost of capital on the other. The user's cost of capital merely depends on the price of capital goods, the interest rate and the depreciation rate. According to the neoclassical model, if marginal product of capital exceeds user's cost of capital, firms will find it profitable to undertake fixed investment. In this model, rate of interest, which is an important component of the user cost of capital, and taxation of profits play an important role in the determination of business fixed investment.

Residential Investment

Residential investment refers to the expenditure which people make on constructing or buying new houses or dwelling apartments for the purpose of living or renting out to others. Residential investment varies from 3 per cent to 5 per cent of GDP in various countries. Two important features of residential investment are worth noting. First, since the average life of a housing unit is 40 to 50 years, the stock of existing housing units at a point of time is very large as compared to the new residential investment in a year (*i.e.*, flow of residential investment). Second, there is well developed resale market for housing units so that people who construct or own them can sell them in this secondary market.

Residential investment depends on price of existing housing units. The higher the price of existing units, the higher will be investment in constructing and buying new housing units. The price of housing units is determined by demand for housing units which slopes downward and the supply of existing units which in the short run is a fixed quantity and its supply curve is therefore a vertical straight line.

In the long run demand for housing is determined by rate of population and formation of new households. The higher rate of population growth will lead to the increase in demand for housing units. The tendency towards two-member households has led to greater demand for housing units. Income is another important factor determining demand for houses and therefore greater residential investment. Since level of income over time fluctuates a good deal, there is strong cyclical pattern of investment in residential construction.

Finally, interest is another important that determines demand for dwelling units. Most houses, especially in cities, are purchased by borrowing funds from banks for a long time, say 20 to 25 years. Generally, the houses purchased are mortgaged with banks or other financial institutions who provide funds for this purpose. The individuals who purchase houses on mortgage borrowing pay monthly instalment of original sum borrowed plus interest. Therefore demand for housing units is highly sensitive to changes in rate of interest. Therefore, monetary policy has a substantial effect on residential investment.

Inventory Investment

Firms hold inventories of raw materials, semi-finished goods to be processed into final goods. The firms also hold inventories of finished goods to be sold shortly. The *change in the inventories or stocks of these goods with the firms is called inventory investment*. Now, why do firms hold inventories? The first motive of holding inventories is *smoothing of the level of production.* The firms experience temporary booms and busts in sales of their output. Instead of adjusting their production each time to match the changes in sales of the product they find cheaper to produce goods *at a steady rate*. With this steady rate of production when sales are low, the firms will be producing more than they are selling and therefore in these periods they will hold the extra goods produced as inventories. On the other hand, when sales are high with a steady rate of production, they will be producing less than they sell. In such periods to meet the market demand for goods, they will take out goods from inventories to meet the demand.

The second reason for holding inventories is that *it is less costly* for a firm to buy inputs such as raw materials *less frequently in large quantities* to produce goods and therefore it is required to hold inventories of raw materials and other intermediate products. Buying small quantities of the materials more frequently to produce goods is a more costly affair.

The third reason for holding inventories by the firms is to avoid '*running out of stock' possibilities* when their sales of goods are high and therefore it is profitable to sell at that time. This requires them to hold inventories of goods.

Autonomous Investment and Induced Investment

After Keynes two types of investments have been distinguished. One is *autonomous investment* and the second is *induced investment*. By autonomous investment we mean the investment which does not change with the changes in the income level and is therefore independent of income. Keynes thought that the level of investment depends upon marginal efficiency of capital and the rate of interest. He thought changes in income level will not affect investment in the short run. Thus, the concept of autonomous investment of Keynes is based upon his preoccupation with short-run problem. He was of the opinion that changes in income level will affect investment only in the long run. Therefore, considering as he was the short-run problem he treated investment as independent of the changes in the income level. In fact the distinction between autonomous investment and induced investment has been made by post-Keynesian economists. *Autonomous investment refers to the investment which does not depend upon changes in the income level.* This autonomous investment generally takes place in houses, roads, public undertakings and in other types of economic infrastructure such as power, transport and communication. This *autonomous investment depends more on population growth and technical progress than on the level of income.* Most of the investment undertaken by Government is of the autonomous nature. The investment undertaken by Government in various development projects to accelerate economic growth of the country is of autonomous type. The autonomous investment is depicted in Fig. 9.1 where it will be seen that whatever the level of national income, investment remains the same at I_a. Therefore, the autonomous investment curve is a horizontal straight line.

On the other hand, induced investment is that investment which is affected by the changes in the level of income. The greater the level of income, the larger will be the consumption of the community. In order to produce more consumer goods, more investment has to be made in capital goods so that greater output of consumer goods becomes possible. Keynes regarded rate of interest as a factor determining induced investment but the empirical evidence gathered so far suggests that induced investment depends more on income than on the rate of interest. Induced investment is shown in

Fig. 9.2 where it will be seen that with the increase in national income, induced investment is increasing. Increase in national income implies that demand for output of goods and services increases. To produce greater output, more capital goods are required to produce them. To have more capital goods more investment has to be undertaken. This induced investment is undertaken both in fixed capital assets and in inventories. The essence of induced investment is that greater income and therefore greater aggregate demand affects the level of investment in the economy. The induced investment underlies the concept of the principle of accelerator, which is highly useful in explaining the occurrence of trade cycles.

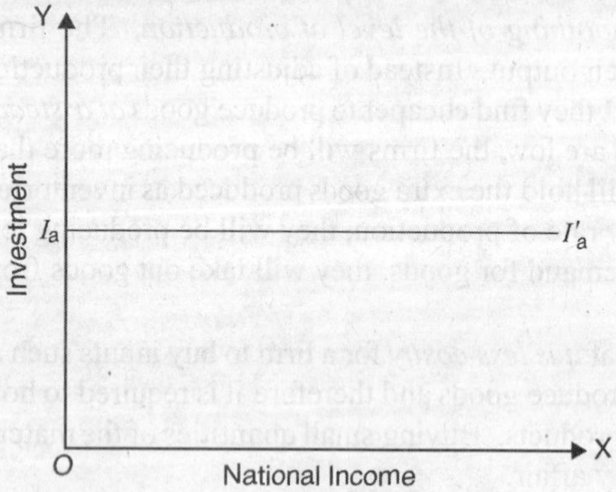

Fig. 9.1. *Autonomous Investment*

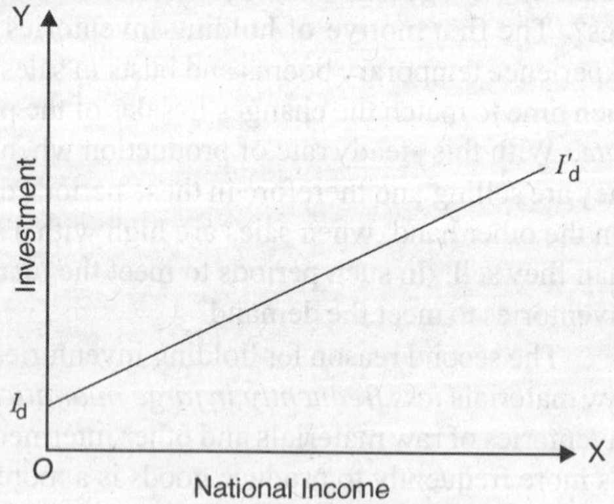

Fig. 9.2. *Induced Investment*

KEYNES'S THEORY OF INVESTMENT

According to Keynes, investment demand depends upon two factors: (1) expected rate of profits to which Keynes gives the name *Marginal Efficiency of Capital,* and. (2) the rate of interest. It can be easily shown that investment is determined by expected rate of profit and the rate of interest. A person having an amount of savings has two alternatives before him. Either he should invest his savings in machines, factories, etc., or he can lend his savings to others at a certain rate of interest. If investment undertaken in machines or factories is expected to fetch 25% rate of profit, while the current rate of interest is only 15%, then it is obvious that the person would invest his savings in machinery or factory.

It follows from above, if investment is to be profitable then the expected rate of profit must not be less than the current market rate of interest. If the expected rate of profit is greater than the market rate of interest, new investment will take place. If an entrepreneur does not invest his own savings but has to borrow from others, then it becomes much clear that the expected rate of profit from investment in any capital asset must not be less than the rate of interest he has to pay. For instance, if an entrepreneur borrows funds from others at 15% rate of interest, then the investment proposed to be undertaken will actually be undertaken only if the expected rate of profit from it is more than 15 per cent. We thus see that investment depends upon marginal efficiency of capital on the one hand and the rate of interest on the other. Investment will be undertaken in any given form of capital asset so long as expected rate of profit or marginal efficiency of capital falls to the level of the current market rate of interest. The equilibrium of the entrepreneur is established at the level of investment where expected rate of profit or marginal efficiency of capital is equal to the current rate of interest. Therefore, the theory of investment is also based upon the assumption that the entrepreneur tries to maximize his profits.

Of the two determinants of inducement to invest, marginal efficiency of capital or expected rate of profit is of comparatively greater importance than the rate of interest. This is because rate of interest does not change much in the short run; it is more or less sticky. But changes in the expectations of profits greatly affect the marginal efficiency of capital and make it very much unstable and volatile. As a result of changes in marginal efficiency of capital, investment demand is greatly affected which causes aggregate demand to fluctuate very much. The changes in aggregate demand bring about economic fluctuations which are generally known as trade cycles. When profit expectations of businessmen are good, large investment is undertaken which causes aggregate demand to rise and bring about conditions of boom and prosperity in the economy. On the other hand, when expectations regarding profits are adverse, the rate of investment falls which causes decline in aggregate demand and brings about depression, unemployment and excess productive capacity in the economy. Thus, the changes in the marginal efficiency of capital play a crucial role in causing changes in investment and economic activity.

According to Keynes, the rate of interest is determined by liquidity preference and the supply of money. The greater the liquidity preference, the greater the rate of interest. Given the liquidity preference curve, the greater the supply of money, the lower will be the rate of interest. We explain below in detail the concept of marginal efficiency of capital and explain the factors on which it depends.

Marginal Efficiency of Capital (MEC)

As has been pointed out above, the concept of marginal efficiency of capital refers to the rate of profit expected to be made from investment in certain capital assets. The rate of profit expected from an extra unit of a capital asset is known as marginal efficiency of capital. Now, the question is how the marginal efficiency of capital is measured. Suppose an entrepreneur invests money in a certain machinery, how will he estimate the expected rate of profit from it. To estimate the marginal efficiency of capital, the entrepreneur will first take into consideration how much price he has to pay for a particular capital asset. The price which he has to pay for the particular capital asset is called its *supply price* or *cost of capital*. The second thing which he will consider is that how much yield he expects to obtain from investment from that particular capital asset. A capital asset continues to produce goods and yield income over a long period of time. Therefore, an entrepreneur has to estimate the prospective yield from a capital asset over his whole life period. Thus, the supply price and the prospective yields of a capital asset determine the marginal efficiency of capital. By deducting the supply price from the prospective yield during whole life of a capital asset the entrepreneur can estimate the expected rate of profit or marginal efficiency of capital. Keynes has defined the marginal efficiency of capital in the following words: "*I define the marginal efficiency of capital as being equal to that rate of discount which would make the present value of the series of annuities given by the returns expected from the capital asset during its life just equal to its supply price.*" Thus, according to Keynes, marginal efficiency of capital is the rate of discount which renders the prospective yields from a capital asset over its whole life period equal to the supply price of that asset. Therefore, we can obtain the marginal efficiency of capital in the following way:

$$\text{Supply Price} = \text{Discounted Prospective Yields}$$

$$C = \frac{R_1}{1+r} + \frac{R_2}{(1+r)^2} + \frac{R_3}{(1+r)^3} \ldots\ldots + \frac{R_n}{(1+r)^n}$$

In the above formula, C stands for Supply Price or Replacement Cost and $R_1, R_2, R_3, .. R_n$ etc., represent the annual prospective yields from the capital asset, r is that rate of discount which renders the annual prospective yields equal to the supply price of the capital asset. Thus, r represents the expected rate of profit or marginal efficiency of capital.

The measurement of marginal efficiency of capital can be illustrated by an arithmatical example. Suppose it costs 3000 rupees to invest in a certain machinery and the life of the machinery is two years, that is, after two years it becomes quite useless, having no value. Suppose further that in the first year the machinery is expected to yield income of ₹ 1100 and in the second year ₹ 2420/-. By substituting these values in the above formula, we can calculate the value of r, that is, the marginal efficiency of capital.

Supply Price = Discounted Prospective Yields

$$C = \frac{R_1}{(1+r)} + \frac{R_2}{(1+r)^2}$$

$$3000 = \frac{1,100}{1+r} + \frac{2,420}{(1+r)^2}$$

On calculating the value of *r* in the above equation it is found to be equal to 10. In other words, marginal efficiency of capital is here equal to 10 per cent. If we put the value of *r*, that is, 0.10 in the above equation, we obtain the following:

$$3,000 = \frac{1,100}{1+0.10} + \frac{2,420}{(1+0.10)^2}$$

$$3,000 = \frac{1,100}{1.10} + \frac{2,420}{(1.10)^2}$$

$$= 1,000 + 2,000 = 3,000$$

Marginal Efficiency of Capital in General. We have explained above the marginal efficiency of a *particular type* of capital asset. But we also require to know the marginal efficiency of capital *in general.* It is the marginal efficiency of capital in general that will indicate the scope for investment opportunities at a particular time in any economy, *At a particular time in an economy the marginal efficiency of that particular capital asset which yields the greatest rate of profit, is called the marginal efficiency of capital in general.* In other words, marginal efficiency of capital in general is the greatest of all the marginal efficiencies of various types of capital assets which could be produced but have not yet been produced. Thus, *marginal efficiency of capital in general represents the highest expected rate of return to the community from an extra unit of a capital asset which yields the maximum profit which could be produced.*

Keeping in view the existing stock of a capital asset, we can always calculate the marginal efficiency of any particular capital asset. The marginal efficiency of capital will vary when more is invested in a given particular capital asset. In any given period of time marginal efficiency of capital from every type of capital asset will decline as more investment is undertaken in it. In other words, marginal efficiency of a particular type of capital asset will be sloping downward as the stock of capital increases. The main reason for the decline in marginal efficiency of capital with the increase in investment in it is that the prospective yields from capital asset fall as more units are installed and used for production of a good. Prospective yields decline because when more quantity of a good is produced with the greater amount of a capital asset, prices of goods decline. The second reason for the decline in the marginal efficiency of capital is that the supply price of the capital asset may rise because the increase in demand for it will bring about increase in its cost of production.

Rate of Interest and Investment Demand Curve

We have explained above how the marginal efficiency of capital is estimated. We can represent diminishing marginal efficiency of capital in general by a curve which will slope downward. This has been done in Fig. 9.3 in which along the X-*axis* investment in capital assets is measured and along the X-axis marginal efficiency of capital in general is shown. It will be seen from this figure that when investment in capital asset is equal to OI_1, marginal efficiency of capital is i_1,. When the investment increases to OI_2, marginal efficiency of capital falls to i_2. Likewise, when investment rises to OI_3, marginal efficiency of capital further diminishes to i_3.

We have seen above that inducement to invest depends upon the marginal efficiency of capital and the rate of interest. With the given particular rate of interest and given the curve of marginal efficiency of capital in general we can show what will be the equilibrium level of investment in the economy. If in Fig. 9.3 along the Y-axis, rate of interest is also shown, then level of investment can be easily determined. The equilibrium level of investment will be established at the point where marginal efficiency of capital becomes equal to the given current rate of interest. Thus, if the rate of interest is i_1, then OI_1 investment will be undertaken. Since at OI_1 level of investment marginal efficiency of capital is equal to the rate of interest i_1. If the rate of interest falls to i_2, investment in the

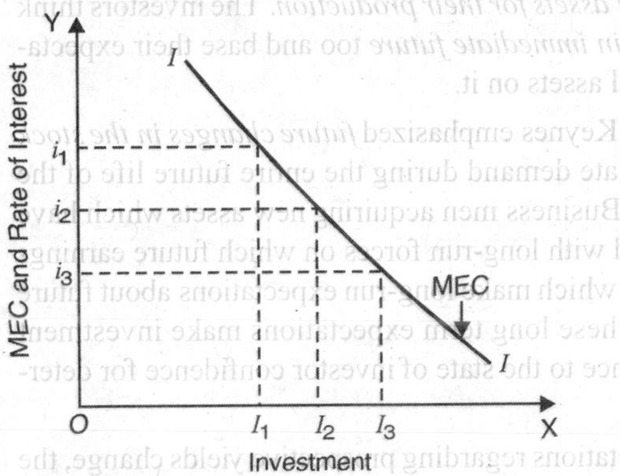

Fig. 9.3. *Investment Demand Curve*

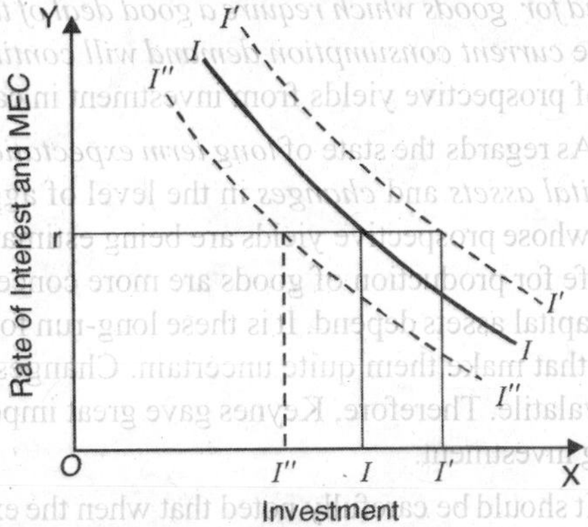

Fig. 9.4. *Shifts in Investment Demand Curve due to Changes Marginal Efficiency of Capital*

capital assets will rise to OI_2 since at OI_2 level of investment the new rate of interest i_2 is equal to the marginal efficiency of capital. Thus, we see that the curve of marginal efficiency of capital in general shows the demand for investment or inducement to invest at various rates of interest. Hence *marginal efficiency of capital curve represents the investment demand curve*. This investment demand curve shows how much investment will be undertaken by the entrepreneurs at various rates of interest. If the investment demand curve is less elastic, then investment demand will not increase much with the fall in the rate of interest. But if the investment demand curve or marginal efficiency of capital curve is very much elastic, then the changes in the rate of interest will bring about large changes in investment demand.

BUSINESS EXPECTATIONS AND INVESTMENT DEMAND

We have studied above that the marginal efficiency of capital depends upon the supply price of capital on the one hand and prospective yields on the other. It is important to note here that the prospective yields are greatly affected by the expectations of the entrepreneurial class regarding profit making. These expectations generally change very frequently. Indeed, it is the profit expectations of the entrepreneur which determine the level of investment. When the expectations of the entrepreneur regarding profit making become dim, the marginal efficiency of capital declines and as a result demand for investment falls. The *occurrence of depression is mainly due to the pessimistic expectations of the entrepreneurial class regarding profit making*. On the contrary, when the expectations of the entrepreneurs regarding profit opportunities increase, their inducement to invest rises. As a result of the increase in investment, aggregate demand in the economy increases and levels of income and employment increase. We thus see that profit expectations of entrepreneurs greatly affect investment demand and consequently the level of income and employment.

Short-run and Long-run Business Expectations. We have explained above that, according to Keynes, marginal efficiency of capital along with rate of interest determines the level of investment and therefore of the levels of income and employment. A significant contribution of Keynes is that he emphasized the important role that business expectations play in determing the prospective yields from assets on which marginal efficiency of capital and therefore the level of investment depends. He drew distinction between *short-term expectations and long-term expectations*. Keynes thought that prospective yields of capital assets depended partly on *existing facts* which we can assume to be known with a fair degree of certainty and partly on *future events* which can be predicted with a degree of uncertainty and involves greater risk. It is the existing facts which are known almost with certainty that determine short-term expectations. *The short-term business expectations about prospective yields from investment depend on (i) the existing stock of capital assets and (ii) the strength of consumer demand for goods which require a good deal of those assets for their production.* The investors think that the *current consumption demand will continue in immediate future* too and base their expectations of prospective yields from investment in capital assets on it.

As regards the state of *long term expectations*, Keynes emphasized *future changes in the stock of capital assets* and *changes* in the level of aggregate demand during the entire future life of the assets whose prospective yields are being estimated. Business men acquiring new assets which have long life for production of goods are more concerned with long-run forces on which future earnings from capital assets depend. It is these long-run forces which make long-run expectations about future yields that make them quite uncertain. Changes in these long term expectations make investment quite valatile. Therefore, Keynes gave great importance to the state of investor confidence for determining investment.

It should be carefully noted that when the expectations regarding prospective yields change, the whole curve of the marginal efficiency of capital will shift. If profit expectations fall, the marginal efficiency of capital curve, that is, investment demand curve will shift downward to left, as shown by the shift of the curve from *II* to *I″I″* in Fig. 9.4. On the other hand, when the profit expectations of the entrepreneurial class become better than before, the marginal efficiency of capital curve will shift upward to the right, as shown by the marginal efficiency of capital curve *I′I′*. Downward shift in the marginal efficiency of capital curve indicates that at the given rate of interest, less investment will be undertaken than before. And upward shift in the marginal efficiency of capital curve indicates that more will be invested at the given rate of interest than before. In Fig. 9.4 when in the beginning, investment demand curve, that is, marginal efficiency of capital curve is represented by *II*, at the rate of interest *r*, demand for investment is *OI*, As a result of downward shift in the marginal efficiency of capital curve to *I″I″*, investment demand at the rate of interest *r* falls to *OI″*. When the marginal efficiency of capital shifts upward to *I′I′*, investment demand at the given rate of interest *r* rises to *OI′*.

It follows, therefore, that the rate of investment depends on marginal efficiency of capital and the rate of interest. If investment demand is interest-elastic, a reduction in rate of interest tends to stimulate investment. But it may fail to do so, if marginal efficiency of investment is already lower than the rate of interest (as may well happen during a depression). Of the two determinants of the rate of investment, marginal efficiency of investment is more volatile than the rate of interest.

The rate of interest is usually 'sticky' in the short run, while marginal efficiency of investment can fluctuate from one extreme to another. If there is a divergence between the two, usually the marginal efficiency of investment will adjust to the rate of interest. If, for example, the marginal efficiency of investment is 20 per cent, while the current rate of interest is 12 per cent, forces will be set in motion so as to bring the former to the level of the latter. In such a situation, there will be more investment because marginal efficiency of investment is greater than the rate of interest, and with the increase in investment, marginal efficiency of investment will fall. At the point where it is just reduced to the level of the current rate of interest, further investment will cease.

Animal Spirits and Expectations

Keynes theory gives importance to profit expectations of business for determining marginal efficiency of capital in the economy. It is worth mentioning here the concept of **animal spirits of Keynes.** Keynes pointed out that it was not possible to make accurate calculations about the future profitability of investment. He believed that the swings of optimism and pessimism of the business class were more important dirving forces in the stock market that determine investment. *It is these* *swings of optimism and pessimism about future profitability of investment which he referred to as animal spirits*. According to Keynes, it is these animal spirits more than the economic fundamentals that determine investment by business firms.

However, marginal efficinecy of capital or investment by a business firm depends to a large extent on the demand it anticipates for its product. For the economy as a whole the marginal efficiency of investment (i.e., expected net return on investment) depends significantly on the consumption expenditure of households on the products produced in the economy. As studied in the previous chapter, apart from income, consumption expenditure on goods and services depends on several factors such as propensity to save of the people, price level, rate of interest, stock of wealth, taxation policy of the government. Changes in these factors would cause a change in consumption of households and demand for the products. As a result, expected rate of return on investment *i.e.*, MEI will change.

Marginal efficiency of capital or investment which depends on prospective yields from investment in capital goods which are used in the production of certain products depends on expected demand for these products. The prospective yields also depend on expected monetary and fiscal policies of the government in the future and stock market situation, etc. Changes in them will change the marginal efficiency of investment and result in shift in investment demand curve.

FACTORS CAUSING SHIFT IN INVESTMENT DEMAND CURVE

Investment is highly volatile and fluctuates greatly. It is fluctuations in investment that is mainly responsible for fluctuations in aggregate demand. We have seen above that investment demand depends on rate of interest and marginal efficiency of capital, that is, expected rate of profit from investment. Now, an important question is what are the factors that determine marginal efficiency of capital which determines investment demand. There are several factors which cause shift in the marginal efficiency of investment curve and brings about change in investment demand. We discuss these factors below :

1. Changes in Marginal Efficiency of Capital due to Changes in Expectations. The Keynesian theory gives importance to profit expectations of businessmen for determining marginal efficiency of capital and therefore investment in the economy. It is worth mentioning here the concept of **animal spirits** of Keynes. Keynes pointed out that it was not possible to make rational calculations about the future profitability of investment. He believed that the swings of optimism and pessimism of the business class were more important driving forces in the stock market that determine investment. It is these swings of optimism and pessimism about future profitability of investment which he referred to as *animal spirits.* According to Keynes, it is these animal spirits rather than economic fundamentals that determine investment by business firms.

We now term to explain **fundamental economic factors** that determine the profitability of investment on which investment demand depends.

2. Expected Demand for Products. Expected net return on investment by a business firm depends to a large extent on the demand for its product it anticipates. For the economy as a whole the marginal efficiency of investment (*i.e.* expected net return on investment) depends significantly on the consumption expenditure of households on the products produced in the economy. As studied in the previous chapter, apart from income, consumption expenditure on goods and services depends on several factors such as propensity to save of the people, price level, rate of interest, stock of wealth, taxation policy of the government. Changes in these factors would cause a change in consumption of households and demand for the products.

3. Technology and Innovations. In the recent years advances in technology and introduction of new products and processes have been important determinants of investment. The introduction new improved technology and new products makes it necessary to build new plants or install new capital equipment. This stimulates investment in new capital goods. An important recent example of this is the introduction of micro-computers for use in various fields of industries and services. This has spurred new investment in computers and other related equipments. Another important recent example is the introduction of mobiie cellular telephones which has boosted investment in telecommunications by business class.

In addition to the above, advances in technology and new inventions *make investment more productive.* Increase in productivity of capital causes the firms to invest more at a given rate of interest. As a result, curve of marginal efficiency of capital shifts to the right.

4. User Cost of Capital. The user cost of capital also greatly influences the rate of return on capital. The user cost of capital depends on the real rate of interest, rate of depreciation, corporate income taxes, investment tax credit, if any. The lower real rate of interest, lower corporate income taxes, higher investment tax credit, the lower will be the user cost of capital which will increase the rate of return on capital and stimulate investment. On the other hand, the higher real rate of interest, the higher corporate income tax will discourage investment and shift the curve of marginal efficiency of capital to the left. It may be noted that *real rate of interest is the nominal rate of interest minus expected rate of inflation.*

5. Availability of Credit. Besides cost of credit, availability of credit also determines investment in the economy. Investment is financed in three ways : (1) Borrowing from the banks and other financial institutions, (2) raising resources through issue of equity capital, that is, selling shares in the stock market and (3) internal savings of the companies (*i.e.* retained earnings of the companies). If the Central Bank of a country follows tight monetary policy [*i.e.,* higher bank rate, the higher cash reserve ratio (CRR)], credit availability for investment will be less which will decourage private investment. If the Central bank adopts expansionary or easy monetary policy credit availability from banks increases which is likely to encourage investment.

6. Fiscal Policy. Fiscal policy of the Government, especially its expenditure and taxation policy can work in two ways. If Government increases investment and finances it by borrowing from the open market, this will raise the rate of interest which will crowd out private investment. However, if expansionary monetary policy is adopted simultaneously rate of interest will not rise and therefore crowding out effect will not occur. But there are beneficial effects of expansionary fiscal policy of the Government as well. Increase in Government expenditure, say on infrastructure such as power, communication, highways, roads will raise the incomes of the people which will through the multiplier effect cause a significant increase in aggregate demand for goods produced by the private sector and raise the profit expectations of business firms. This will encourage private investment. Many Indian economists believe that increase in Government expenditure, especially if it is made on infrastructure projects *crowds in* private investment rather than *crowds it out.*

ACCELERATOR THEORY OF INVESTMENT

We will explain in a later chapter the Keynesian concept of multiplier which states that as the investment increases, income increases by a multiple amount. On the other hand, there is a concept of accelerator which was not taken into account by Keynes but has become popular after Keynes, especially in the discussions of theories of trade cycles and economic growth. The acceleration principle describes the effect quite opposite to that of multiplier. According to this, *when income or consumption increases, investment will increase by a multiple amount.* When income and therefore consumption of the people increases, the greater amount of the commodities will have to be produced. This will require more capital to produce them if the already given stock of capital is fully used. Since in this case, investment is induced by changes in income or consumption, this is known as *induced investment.* The accelerator is the numerical value of the relation between the increase in investment resulting from an increase in income. The net induced investment will be positive if national income increases and induced investment may fall to zero if the national income or output remains constant.

To produce a given amount of output, it requires a certain amount of capital. If Y_t output is required to be produced and v is capital-output ratio, the required amount of capital (K_t) to produce Y_t output will be given by the following equation:

$$K_t = vY_t \quad \text{... (i)}$$

where K_t stands for the stock of capital

Y_t for the level of output or income, and

v for capital-output ratio.

This capital-output ratio v is equal to $\frac{K}{Y}$ and in the theory of accelerator this capital-output ratio is assumed to be constant. Therefore, under the assumption of constant capital-output ratio, changes in output are made possible by changes in the stock of capital. Thus, when output or income is Y_t then required stock of capital K_t to produce it = vY_t, when output or income is equal to Y_{t-1}, then required stock of capital will be $K_{t-1} = vY_{t-1}$.

It is clear from above that when output or income increases from Y_{t-1} in period t–1 to Y_t in period, t, then the stock of capital to produce it will increase from K_{t-1} to K_t. As seen above, K_{t-1} is equal to vY_{t-1} and K_t is equal to vY_t. Hence, the increase in the stock of capital in period t is given by the following equation:

$$K_t - K_{t-1} = vY_t - vY_{t-1} \quad \text{... (ii)}$$

Since increase in the stock of capital in a year ($K_t - K_{t-1}$) represents investment in that year, the above equation (*ii*) can be written as below:

$$I_{t1} = V(y_t - y_{t-1}) \quad \text{... (iii)}$$

Equation (*iii*) reveals that as a result of increase in income in any year t from a previous year $t-1$, investment (I_{t1}) or increase in capital stock will be v times more than the increase in income. Hence, *it is v i.e., capital-output ratio which represents the magnitude of the accelerator.* If the capital-output ratio is equal to 3, then as a result of a certain increase in income, investment will increase three times more *i.e.,* accelerator here will be equal to 3.

It thus follows that *investment is a function of change in income.* If income or output increases over time, that is, when Y_t is greater than Y_{t-1} then investment will be positive. If income declines, that is, Y_t is less Y_{t-1} then disinvestment will take place. And if the income remains constant, that is, $Y_t = Y_{t-1}$ the investment will be equal to zero.

An arithmetical example will make clear the working of the accelerator. This has been represented in the accompanying table. We have made the following assumptions in making this Table 9.1.

Table 9.1. Explanation of the Accelerator

Period	Output (income)	Required Stock of Capital	Investment: Capital Replacement	Investment: Net Investment	Investment: Gross Investment
(1)	(2)	(3)	(4)	(5)	(6)
$t-1$	500	1,500	300	0	300
t	510	1,530	300	30	330
$t+1$	525	1,575	306	45	351
$t+2$	550	1,650	315	75	390
$t+3$	575	1,725	330	75	405
$t+4$	575	1,725	345	0	345
$t+5$	560	1,680	345	−45	300
$t+6$	550	1,650	336	−30	306
$t+7$	500	1,500	330	−150	180
$t+8$	400	1,200	300	−300	0
$t+9$	400	1,200	240	0	240

(*i*) Capital-output ratio remains constant and is equal to 3.

(*ii*) The depreciation that takes place in the stock of capital is equal to one-fifth of the capital stock existing in the *previous year.* Therefore, one-fifth of the stock of capital is to be replaced every year.

In the above table, it is supposed that in period $t-1$ and several periods before it, output or income is equal to ₹ 500. Given that the capital-output ratio is equal to 3, then to produce ₹ 500 worth of output, ₹ 1500 worth of capital will be required. [$K = vY$; 1500 = 3(500)] which is written in column (3). Since depreciation of capital occurred in period $t-1$, will be one-fifth of the stock of capital existing in the previous period (which is also ₹ 1500). Therefore, replacement investment in period $t-1$ will be equal to ₹ 300. Since as compared to the previous period, there is no change in output in period $t-1$, the net investment in period $t-1$ will be equal to zero. As a result, the gross investment in period $t-1$ will be equal to ₹ 300.

Now suppose that production in the period t rises to ₹ 510 crores as a result of increase in Government expenditure or autonomous investment. To produce output worth ₹ 510 crores, total capital worth ₹ 1530 is required [$K_t = vY_t$; 1530 = 3(510)] which is written in column (3). Thus, as a result of increase in output (income) by ₹ 10, net investment has increased by ₹ 30, that is, 1530 – 1500 = 30 which means that accelerator is here equal to 3. In period t the depreciation equation equal to l/5th of the capital stock of period $t-1$ will occur, that is, capital depreciation of ₹ 300, (1/5 × 1500 = 300) will occur in period t. Therefore, capital replacement investment in period t will be equal to ₹ 300. Thus, gross investment in period t will be equal to 30 + 300 = 330. In this way, if output (or income) increases by ₹ 15 in period $t+1$, ₹ 25 in period $t+2$, and also ₹ 25 in period $t+3$, the net investment will increase by three times the increment in output (or income), that is, net investment will increase by ₹45 in period $t+1$, ₹ 75 in period $t+2$ and also ₹ 75 in period $t+3$. It will be further observed from Table 9.1 that when output falls in period $t+5$ by ₹ 15, the net, investment will decline by 3 times of it, that is, equal to ₹ 45. Likewise, from changes in output in different periods we can find out net investment that will take place in any period and with the capital replacement investment we can obtain the gross investment that will occur in any period.

A glance at columns 2, 5 and 6 of Table 9.1 will show that *with a change in output, investment will increase by a multiple of it*. This shows that acceleration principle is a powerful destabilising force working in the economy. If the accelerator is the only force at work, then we shall have too much of instability in the economy—more than is actually found. In real life, we find that there are limits to instability, both in the upward as well as the downward direction, so that fluctuations in economic activity or what are called business cycles must have a peak as well as a bottom.

Criticism of the Accelerator Theory

The principle of acceleration has come in for a good deal of criticism in recent years. For example, it has been pointed out by Kaldor that we cannot assume a constant value of the accelerator throughout the trade cycle, that is, it is not true that an increase in output or income by an amount must always give rise to the same multiple increase in investment. This is because, if already, some machines are lying idle, we shall try to use them before rushing in for new equipment. Also, if expectations of entrepreneurs are that the rise in demand brought about by increase in income or output is only a temporary one, they well try to meet it by overworking the existing machinery rather than installing a new plant. Thus, *in the theory of accelerator it has been assumed that there is no excess capacity existing in consumer goods industries.* In other words, it has been assumed that no machines are lying idle and no extra shift working is possible. If there had been excess capacity and extra shift working was possible, the supply of goods could be increased with the existing equipment and the accelerator would not come into play.

Further, in the principle of acceleration principle it *has also been assumed that in the capital goods industries, there exists surplus productive capacity.* If there is no excess capacity in the machine-making industries, increased demand for machines caused by the requirement for additional output would not lead to increase in the supply of machines. In the absence of supply of machines, investment cannot increase in the short run. It is thus assumed in the accelerator theory that the machine-making industry is capable of increasing its output for the time being at least. The supply can be increased by reducing stocks of finished machines, by working extra shifts, and so on. But stocks cannot be reduced below zero and working double shifts or adoption of other methods to expand the supply of capital goods or machines is found to be expensive. Thus, only when the demand has increased permanently, the entrepreneurs will find it worthwhile to increase investment in machine-making industries.

The size of the accelerator does not remain constant over time. Its value will be affected by the businessmen's calculation regarding the profitability of installing new plants to make more machines on the basis of their probable working life. It is also assumed that the demand for machines will remain stable in future, although the increase in demand has suddenly cropped up. However, in spite of the above limitations acceleration principle points out an important factor which causes fluctuations in the economy. Economists like Samuelson, J.R. Hicks have shown how accelerator combined with multiplier provides a satisfactory explaination of trade cycles.

MONETARY AND FISCAL POLICY MEASURES AND INVESTMENT

Both monetary and fiscal policy measures affect investment. In what follows we first analyse the effect of discretionary monetary policy and then of discretionary fiscal policy.

Monetary Policy and Investment

As explained above, interest rate measures the cost of capital and along with marginal efficiency of capital (*i.e*. expected rate of return on investment) determines the level of investment. It is primarily through its *effect on interest rate* that monetary policy affects investment decisions. Besides interest rate, investment also depends on the *availability of funds or credit*, especially from the banks. The easy monetary policy which aims at lowering interest rate and increasing the availability of credit will lead to more investment. It may be noted that under easy monetary policy the Central Bank lowers the bank rate and other rates of interest such as ***repo rate***. It can also lower the cash reserve ratio. The lowering of bank rate and other rates of interest sends a signal to the banks to reduce their lending rates. The lowering of cash-reserve ratio (CRR) leads to the more liquidity or extra cash reserves with banks. This not only increases the availability of more credit for investment by businessmen but also puts downward pressure on lending interest rates as a result of increase in the supply of lendable funds with the banks. In India, Reserve Bank of India often lowers a *repo rate* (*which is a interest rate charged by RBI for borrowing by commercial banks at times of need for a very short period, even for a day*) to ensure lowering of lending rates by banks and thereby to stimulate private investment. At a lower interest rate, given the schedule of marginal efficiency of capital, more investment will be undertaken by business firms. The Central Bank can also undertake open market operations to increase availability of bank credit for investment. For thus purpose it buys government securities from the banks and pays rupee funds to them. This raises money supply in the economy which not only make more funds available for lending to businessmen but also tends to lower interest rates.

Keynes and his early followers believed that monetary policy is not very effective for increasing private investment. This view was based on the assumption that during the period of depression the rate of interest was already very low and at this low interest rate there is *liquidity rap* in the demand curve for money. Under these conditions, they thought the expansion in money supply by the banks will not lower interest rate. Besides, they believed that investment demand is relatively inelastic so that even lowering of interest rate will not cause much increase in investment. However, later empirical evidence shows that at relevant rates of interest demand for money in normal times is quite elastic (that is , liquidity trap does not exist at the generally prevailing interest rates). As a result, expansionary monetary policy lowers interest rate and thereby stimulates private investment. Besides, later empirical evidence also shows that investment demand schedule is quite elastic and therefore lowering of interest rate and more availability of funds lead to more investment. Therefore, the modern economists have veered round to the view that discretionary monetary policy can be effective in raising private investment to get rid of recession in the economy and to promote economic growth.

One modification in our above analysis of the impact of monetary policy on investment that is required is the incorporation of distinction between *nominal interest rate and real interest rate*. As explained earlier, it is the real interest rate that is relevant for investment decisions. Therefore, monetary policy must affect the real interest rate if it has to stimulate private investment. However, it is worth noting that in both the Keynesian and monetarist theories *expected inflation depends primarily on the inflation prevailing in the recent past* and further that it changes slowly over time. Under these conditions changes in monetary rate of interest will mean changes in real interest rate for all practical purposes. In view of this, our above analysis of the effect of monetary policy on investment remains unchanged.

Fiscal Policy and Investment

We now turn to explain the effect of fiscal policy on investment. It is generally believed that there is *adverse effect* of expansionary fiscal policy on private investment. According to this view, though increase in government spending financed by borrowing would bring about increases in aggregate demand for goods and services, it would raise interest rate. Borrowing by the government would raise the demand for funds or money in the market which, given the supply of money, would cause interest rate to rise. The higher interest rate would lower private investment. Thus, it is asserted that expansionary fiscal policy *crowds out private investment*. Another route through which adverse effect of expansionary fiscal policy is brought out is that the increase in aggregate demand as a result of expansionary fiscal policy in terms of either increase in government expenditure or cut in taxes would raise aggregate demand and lead to increase in national income. The increase in national income would bring about increase in transactions demand for money which, given the supply of money, would cause interest rate to rise and lower private investment. The reduction or crowding out of private investment would offset a part of the initial expansionary effect on aggregate demand brought about by increase in government expenditure or reduction in taxation. If investment demand is highly elastic , the decrease in private investment resulting from the rise in interest rate will be quite substantial.

However, in view of the present author even if there is significant crowding-out effect on private investment of expansionary fiscal policy, it can be avoided if as a part of expansionary fiscal policy the tax policy of providing adequate *investment tax credit* to the business firms is adopted. Under investment tax credit policy, a deduction from business income or profits equal to a certain percentage of investment made in machinery and equipment is allowed. As this lowers the tax liability of the firm and reduces the cost of capital, *policy of investment tax credit stimulates investment and will offset adverse effect on private investment of expansionary fiscal policy*. Thus, our Finance Minister Mr. P. Chitambaram in 2013-14 budget has announced investment tax credit at the rate of 15 per cent on investment in capital equipment for the corporate firms which make investment of ₹ 100 crore or more in plant and equipment in a year. This is in addition to the annual depreciation allowance on capital already enjoyed by these firms.

Further, in our view, the crowding-out effect of expansionary fiscal policy has been exaggerated by the critics of Keynes. As a matter of fact when government raises its expenditure or cuts personal income tax, aggregate demand for goods and services increases which raises expectations of increased sales and revenue of the business firms. This improves profitability or marginal efficiency of investment. This is more valid at times of depression when private investment declines due to lack of demand for goods and services. Thus when expected profitability or marginal efficiency of capital rises due to increase in aggregate demand resulting from expansionary fiscal policy, investment demand curve shifts to the right and businessmen invest more at any given rate of interest. This can more than offset any adverse effect on private investment due to rise in interest.

Further, according to *investment theory based on acceleration principle* investment depends on expected changes in output or national income. Thus, even in the absence of investment tax credit expansionary fiscal policy that increases national output or national income through its beneficial effect on aggregate demand will stimulate private investment through accelerator principle.

In the context of developing country like India the expansionary fiscal policy even when increased government expenditure is financed by borrowing can have beneficial effect on private investment, especially when the economy is experiencing recession or slowdown in economic growth. If in such a situation the government increases its expenditure and spends money on infrastructure projects such as power, roads, ports telecommunication, highways, it will have a favourable effect on private investment as the latter is often constrained by lack of adequate infrastructure facilities. Besides, when manufacturing industries in developing countries experience recessionary conditions due to sluggish demand, as happened in India during the period 1997 to 2002 and again in 2008-09, increase in public expenditure will lead to increase in aggregate demand through its multiplier effect and thereby improve the demand conditions for increase in private investment.

It follows from above that it is not necessarily true that expansionary fiscal policy crowds out private investment. The expansion in public expenditure can have a beneficial effect on private investment.

NUMERICAL PROBLEM

Problem : *Given the saving function $S = -10 + 0.2Y$ and autonomous investment $I =$ ₹ 50 cores*

(*i*) *Find the level of consumption*

(*ii*) *If investment decreases permanently by ₹ 5 crore, what is the new level of consumption.*

Solution : (*i*)

$$C = Y - S$$

Given $S = -10 + 0.2Y \ldots$

$$C = Y - (-10 + 0.2Y)$$
$$= Y + 10 - 0.2Y \qquad \ldots(i)$$

Now, in equilibrium $S = I$

$$I = 50$$
$$-10 + 0.2Y = 50$$
$$0.2Y = 60$$
$$Y = 60 \times \frac{10}{2} = 300$$

Now substituting the value of Y in (*i*) we have

$$C = 300 + 10 - 0.2 \times 300 = 310 - 60 = 250$$

(*ii*) Decrease in investment by ₹ 5 core will cause national income to decline by a multiple of decrease in investment. Thus $\Delta Y = \Delta I \times$ multiplier. Further note that $mpc = 1 - mps$. From the saving function, it is found that $mps = 0.2$. Therefore, $mps = 1 - 0.2 = 0.8$.

Now, multiplier $= \frac{1}{1-mpc} = \frac{1}{1-0.8} = 5$ Therefore, $\Delta Y = -5 \times 5 = -25$ crores

New, income = 300 – 25 = 275 crore

The new level of consumption

$= 275 \times mpc$

$= 275 \times 0.8 = 220$

QUESTIONS FOR REVIEW

1. What do you understand by investment function ? Explain the factors that influence the level of investment in the economy.
2. Distinguish between autonomous investment and induced investment. Explain the factors that determine the level of investment in the economy.
3. What is meant by marginal efficiency of capital ? How is it calculated ? What are the factors that determine marginal efficiency of capital in the economy ?
4. What is marginal efficiency of investment ? What role do expectations of entrepreneurs play in determining marginal efficiency of investment or capital ?
5. How do changes in the rate of interest influence the decision to invest ? Is investment interest elastic ?
6. What is the accelerator theory of investment ? Is it a good representation of investment behaviour ?
7. Critically examine the view that investment spending depends on the changes in the level of output.
8. "Consumption and investment are complementary during deflation, but competitive at full employment." Discuss.
9. The accelerator principle becomes inoperative during periods of excess capacity. Explain.
10. Discuss the view that investment spending depends on change in the level of income.
11. Define marginal efficiency of capital. How does it determine the volume of investment ?
12. Explain role of cheap monetary policy in promoting private investment. Is it effective in stimulating private investment ?
13. Critically examine the role of expansionary fiscal policy in boosting private investment. How can its adverse effect on private investment be offset ?

CHAPTER 10

Theory of Investment Multiplier

THE CONCEPT OF MULTIPLIER

The theory of multiplier occupies an important place in the modern theory of income and employment. The concept of multiplier was first of all developed by F.A. Kahn in the early 1930s. But Keynes later further refined it. F.A. Kahn developed the concept of multiplier with reference to the increase in employment, direct as well as indirect, as a result of initial increase in investment and employment. Keynes, however, propounded the concept of multiplier with reference to the increase in total income, direct as well as indirect, as a result of initial increase in investment and income. Therefore, whereas Kahn's multiplier is known as *'employment multiplier'*, Keynes's multiplier is known as *investment* or *income multiplier.* The essence of multiplier is that total increase in income, output or employment is manifold the original increase in investment. For example, if investment equal to ₹ 100 crore is made, then the income will not rise by ₹ 100 crore only but by a multiple of it. If as a result of investment of ₹ 100 crore, the national income increases by ₹ 300 crore, multiplier is equal to 3. If as a result of investment of ₹ 100 crore, total national income increases by ₹ 400 crore, multiplier is 4. *The multiplier is, therefore, the ratio of increment in income to the increment in investment*. If ΔI stands for increment in investment and ΔY stands for the resultant increase in income, then multiplier is equal to the ratio of increment in income (ΔY) to the increment in investment (ΔI).

Thus, $k = \dfrac{\Delta Y}{\Delta I}$ where k stands for multiplier.

Now, the question is why the increase in income is many times more than the initial increase in investment. It is easy to explain this. Suppose Government undertakes investment expenditure equal to ₹ 100 crore on some public works, say the construction of rural roads. For this Government will pay wages to the labourers engaged, prices for the materials to the suppliers and remunerations to other factors who make contribution to the work of road-building. The total cost will amount to ₹ 100 crore. This will increase incomes of the people equal to ₹ 100 crore. But this is not all. The people who receive ₹ 100 crore will spend a good part of them on consumer goods. Suppose marginal propensity to consume of the people is 4/5 or 80%. Then out of ₹ 100 crore they will spend ₹ 80 crore on consumer goods, which would increase incomes of those people who supply consumer goods equal to ₹ 80 crore. But those who receive these ₹ 80 crore will also in turn spend these incomes, depending upon their marginal propensity to consume. If their marginal propensity to consume is also 4/5, then they will spend ₹ 64 crore on consumer goods. Thus, this will further increase incomes of some other people equal to ₹ 64 crore. In this way, the chain of consumption expenditure would continue and the income of the people will go on increasing. But every additional increase in income will be progressively less since a part of the income received will be saved. Thus, we see that the income will not increase by only ₹ 100 crore, which was initially invested in the construction of roads, but by many time more.

Derivation of Investment Multiplier

How much increase in national income will take place as a result of an initial increase in investment can be expressed in the following mathematical form:

Increase in income or

$$\Delta Y = 100 + 100 \times 4/5 + 100(4/5)^2 + 100(4/5)^3 + 100(4/5)^4 \ldots$$
$$= 100[1 + (4/5) + (4/5)^2 + (4/5)^3 + (4/5)^4 \ldots]$$

But the above series is one of geometric progression. Therefore, increase in income (ΔY)

$$= 100 \frac{1}{1-4/5} \qquad \ldots (i)$$

$$= 100 \frac{1}{1/5}$$
$$= 100 \times 5$$
$$= 500$$

It is thus clear that if marginal propensity to consume is 4/5, the investment of ₹100 crore leads to the increase in the national income by ₹ 500 crore. Therefore, multiplier is here equal to 5. We can express this in a general formula. If ΔY stands for increase in income, ΔI stands for increase in investment and *MPC* for marginal propensity to consume, we can write the equation (*i*) above as follows:

$$\Delta Y = \Delta I \frac{1}{1 - MPC}$$

$$\frac{\Delta Y}{\Delta I} = \frac{1}{1 - MPC}$$

$\frac{\Delta Y}{\Delta I}$ measures the size of the multiplier. Therefore,

$$\text{Size of multiplier or } k = \frac{1}{1 - MPC} \qquad \ldots (ii)$$

It is clear from above that the size of multiplier depends upon the marginal propensity to consume of the community. The multiplier is the reciprocal of one minus marginal propensity to consume. However, we can express multiplier in a simpler form. As we know that saving is equal to income minus consumption, one minus marginal propensity to consume will be equal to marginal propensity to save, that is, $1 - MPC = MPS$. Therefore, multiplier is equal to $\frac{1}{1 - MPC} = \frac{1}{MPS}$.

Algebraic Derivation of Multiplier

The multiplier can be derived algebraically as follows:

Writing the equation for the equilibrium level of income in a two-sector economy we have

$$Y = C + I \qquad \ldots (1)$$

As in the multiplier analysis we are concerned *with changes in income induced by changes in investment*, rewriting the equation (1) in terms of changes in the variables we have

$$\Delta Y = \Delta C + \Delta I \qquad \ldots (2)$$

In the simple Keynesian model of income determination, change in investment is considered to be autonomous or independent of changes in income while changes in consumption are function of changes in income.

In the Keynesian consumption function,

$$C = a + bY$$

where a is a constant term, b is marginal propensity to consume which is also assumed to remain constant. Therefore, change in consumption can occur only if there is change in income. Thus

$$\Delta C = b\Delta Y \qquad \ldots (3)$$

Substituting (3) into (2) we have

$$\Delta Y = b\Delta Y + \Delta I$$
$$\Delta Y - b\Delta Y = \Delta I$$
$$\Delta Y(1-b) = \Delta I$$
$$\Delta Y = \frac{1}{1-b}\Delta I$$
$$\frac{\Delta Y}{\Delta I} = \frac{1}{1-b}$$

As b stands for marginal propensity to consume

$$\frac{\Delta Y}{\Delta I} = \frac{1}{1-MPC} = \frac{1}{MPS}$$

This is the same formula of multiplier as obtained earlier. Note that the value of multiplier $\frac{\Delta Y}{\Delta I}$ will remain constant as long as marginal propensity to consume remains the same.

Calculating the Size or Value of Multiplier

The multiplier tells us how much increase in income occurs when *autonomous investment* increases by ₹ 1, that is, investment multiplier is $\frac{\Delta Y}{\Delta I}$ and its value is equal to $\frac{1}{1-b}$ where b stands for marginal propensity to consume (*MPC*). Thus, multiplier $= \frac{\Delta Y}{\Delta I} = \frac{1}{1-b}$. Further, since $1-b$ equals marginal propensity to save (*MPS*), the value of investment multiplier is equal to $\frac{1}{1-b} = \frac{1}{s}$ where s stands for marginal propensity to save. In other words, the size of multiplier is equal to $\frac{1}{1-MPC} = \frac{1}{MPS}$. Thus, the value of multiplier can be obtained if we know either the value of *MPC* or *MPS*.

Now, the higher the marginal propensity to consume (b) (or the lower the value of marginal propensity to save (s), the greater the value of multiplier. For example, if marginal propensity to consume (b) is 0.8, investment multiplier is

$$\frac{\Delta Y}{\Delta I} = \frac{1}{1-08} = \frac{1}{0.2} = 1 \times \frac{10}{2} = 5$$

If *MPC* or $b = 0.75$, multiplier is

$$= \frac{\Delta Y}{\Delta I} = \frac{1}{1-0.75} = \frac{1}{0.25} = \frac{100}{25} = 4$$

As mentioned above, the size or value of multiplier can be calculated using either the value of marginal propensity to consume (*MPC*) or the value of marginal propensity to save (*MPS* or s). In fact, the value of multiplier is the reciprocal of marginal propensity to save $\left(\frac{\Delta Y}{\Delta I} = \frac{1}{MPS} \text{ or } \frac{1}{s}\right)$. When marginal propensity to consume is 0.8, marginal propensity to save will be $1 - 0.8 = 0.2$. The multiplier will be $\frac{1}{0.2}$ or $\frac{1}{2/10} = 5$. Likewise if marginal propensity to consume (b) is 0.75, marginal propensity to save will be $1 - 0.75 = 0.25$ and multiplier will be $\frac{1}{0.25} = \frac{1}{25/100} = 4$.

Given the size of multiplier, we can find out the increase in income (ΔY) resulting from a certain increase in investment (ΔI) by using the multiplier relationship. Thus

$$\frac{\Delta Y}{\Delta I} = \frac{1}{1-b}$$

$$\Delta Y = \Delta I . \frac{1}{1-b}$$

If marginal propensity to consume is equal to 0.8, with the increase in investment by ₹ 100 crore, the increase in income will be :

$$\Delta Y = \Delta I \times \frac{1}{1-b} = 100 \times \frac{1}{1-0.8}$$

$$100 \times \frac{1}{0.2} = 100 \times 5 = 500 \text{ crore}$$

Two Limiting Cases of the Value of Multiplier. There are two limiting cases of the multiplier. One limiting case occurs when the marginal propensity to consume is equal to one, that is, when whole of the increment in income is consumed and nothing is saved. In this case, the size of multiplier will be equal to infinity, that is, a small increase in investment will bring about a very large increase in income and employment so that full employment is reached and even the process goes beyond that. "In such circumstances, the Government would need to employ only one road builder to raise income indefinitely, causing first full employment and then a limitless spiral of inflation."[1] However, this is unlikely to occur since marginal propensity to consume in the real world is less than one. The other limiting case occurs when marginal propensity to consume is equal to zero, that is, when nothing out of the increment in income is consumed, and the whole increment in income is saved. In this case, the value of the multiplier will be equal to one. That is, in this case, the increment in income will be equal to the original increase in investment and not a multiple of it. But in actual practice the marginal propensity to consume is less than one but more than zero $\left(1 > \frac{\Delta C}{\Delta Y} > 0\right)$. Therefore, *the value of the multiplier is greater than one but less than infinity.*

Assumptions of Multiplier Theory

In our above explanation of multiplier, we have made many simplifying assumptions. First, we have assumed that the *marginal propensity to consume remains constant throughout* as the income increases in various rounds of consumption expenditure. However, the marginal propensity to consume may differ in various rounds of consumption expenditure. But this constancy of marginal propensity to consume is a realistic assumption, since all available empirical evidence shows that marginal propensity to consume is very stable in the short run. Secondly, we have assumed that there is a net increase in investment in a period and no further indirect effects on investment in that period occur or if they occur they have been taken into account so that there is a given net increase in investment. Further, we have assumed that *there is no any time-lag* between the increase in investment and the resultant increment in income. That is, increment in income takes place instantaneously as a result of increment in investment. J.M. Keynes ignored the time-lag in the process of income generation and therefore his multiplier is also called ***instantaneous multiplier***. In recent years, the importance of time lag has been recognised and concept of dynamic multiplier has been developed on that basis. But in an elementary study as the present one the time lags will be ignored as was done by Keynes.

Another important assumption in the theory of multiplier is that *excess capacity exists in the consumer goods industries* so that when the demand for them increases, more amounts of consumer

1. Stonier and Hague, *A Textbook of Economic Theory,* 4th edition, 1972.

goods can be produced to meet this demand. If there is no excess capacity in consumer goods industries, the increase in demand as a result of some original increase in investment will bring about rise in prices rather than increases in real income, output and employment. As we shall see later, Keynes's multiplier was evolved in the context of advanced capitalist economies which were in grip of depression and in times of depression there does exist excess capacity in the consumer goods industries due to lack of aggregate demand. The Keynesian multiplier effect is small in developing countries like India where there is not much excess capacity in consumer goods industries.

In our above analysis of the multiplier process we have taken a closed economy, that is, we have not taken into account imports and exports. If ours were an open economy, then a part of the increment in consumption expenditure would have been made on imports of goods from abroad. This would have caused increment in income in foreign countries rather than within the domestic economy. This will reduce the value of the multiplier. *Imports are important leakage from the multiplier process* and we have ignored them in our above analysis for the purpose of simplicity.

It is worth noting that *multiplier not only works in money terms but also in real terms*. In other words, multiple increment in income as a result of a given net increase in investment does not take place only in money terms but also in terms of real output, that is, in terms of goods and services. When incomes increase as a result of investment and these increments in income are spent on consumer goods, the output of consumer goods is increased to meet the extra demand brought about by increased incomes. Therefore, real income or output increases by the same amount as the increment in money incomes, since *the prices of goods have been assumed to be constant.* Of course, we have assumed, as has been mentioned above, that there exists excess productive capacity in the consumer goods industries so that when the demand for consumer goods increases, their production can be easily increased to meet this demand. However, if due to some bottlenecks output of goods cannot be increased in response to increase in demand, prices will rise and as result the real multiplier effect will be small.

Diagrammatic Representation of Multiplier

We have already explained that the level of national income is determined by the equilibrium between aggregate demand and aggregate supply. In other words, the level of national income is determined at the level where $C + I$ curve intersects the 45° income curve. With such a diagram we can explain the multiplier. The multiplier is illustrated in Fig. 10.1. In this figure the curve C represents consumption function. Marginal propensity to consume has been here assumed to be equal to $\frac{1}{2}$ *i.e.*, 0.5. Therefore, the slope of the consumption function curve C has been taken to be equal to 0.5. $C + I$ represents aggregate demand or expenditure curve. It will be seen from Fig. 10.1 that the aggregate demand curve $C + I$ intersects the 45° line at point E so that the equilibrium level of income equal to OY_1 is determined. If investment increases by the amount EH we can then find out how much increment in income occurs as a result of this. As a consequence of increase in investment by EH, the aggregate expenditure curve shifts upward to the new position $C + I'$. This new aggregate demand curve $C + I'$ intersects 45° income line at point F so that the equilibrium level of income increases to

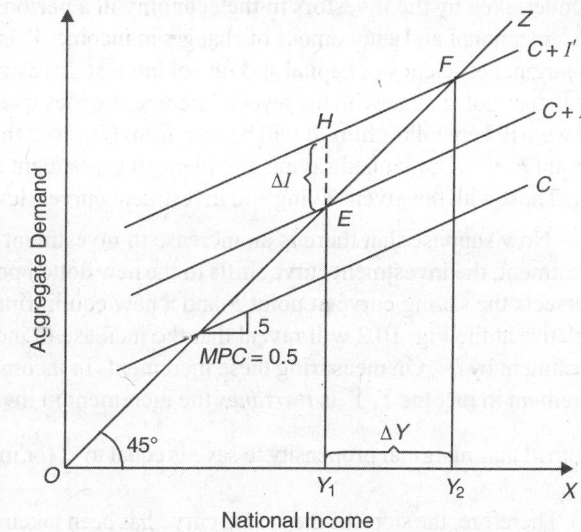

Fig. 10.1. *Keynes's Investment Multiplier*

OY_2. Thus, as a result of increase in investment equal to *EH*, income has increased by Y_1Y_2. It will be seen from the Fig.10.1 that Y_1Y_2 is greater than *EH*. On measuring it will be found that Y_1Y_2 is *twice* the length of *EH*. This is as it is expected because the marginal propensity to consume is here equal to $\frac{1}{2}$ and therefore the size of multiplier will be equal to 2.

Multiplier Explained with Saving-Invstment Approach

The multiplier can be illustrated through saving-investment diagram also. In a previous chapter we explained the determination of national income also through saving and investment. Therefore, the multiplier can also be explained with the help of saving-investment diagram, as has been shown in Fig. 10.2. In this figure *SS* is the saving curve indicating that as the level of income increases, the community plans to save more. *II* is the investment curve showing the level of investment planned to

Fig. 10.2. *Multiplier Explained with the Aid of Savings-Investment Diagram*

be undertaken by the investors in the economy in a period. The investment has been taken to be a constant amount and autonomous of changes in income. This investment level *OI* has been determined by marginal efficiency of capital and rate of interest. Investment being autonomous of income means that it does not change with the level of income. Keynes treated investment as autonomous of income and we will here follow him. It will be seen from Fig. 10.2 that saving and investment curves intersect at point *E*, that is, planned saving and planned investment are in equilibrium at the level of income OY_1. Thus, with the given saving and investment curves, level of income equal to OY_1 is determined.

Now suppose that there is an increase in investment by the amount *II'*. With this increase in investment, the investment curve shifts to the new dotted position *I'I'*. This new investment curve *I'I* intersects the saving curve at point *F* and a new equilibrium is reached at the level of income OY_2. A glance at the Fig. 10.2 will reveal that the increase in income Y_1Y_2 is greater than the increase in investment by *II'*. On measuring these increments in income and investment it will be found that the increment in income $Y_1 Y_2$ is *two times* the increment in investment *II'*. This is because we have here assumed that marginal propensity to save is equal to $\frac{1}{2}$ (or marginal propensity of consume is equal to 0.5). Therefore, the slope of the saving curve has been taken to be equal to $\frac{1}{2}$ or 0.5. Thus, in this case multiplier is equal to 2.

$$\text{Multiplier} = \frac{\Delta Y}{\Delta I} = \frac{Y_1 Y_2}{II'} = \frac{1}{MPS} = 2$$

LEAKAGES IN THE MULTIPLIER PROCESS

We have seen above that as a result of increase in investment, the level of income increases by a multiple of it. In our above analysis, saving is a leakage in the multiplier process. Had there been no saving and as a result marginal propensity to consume were equal to 1, the multiplier would have been equal to infinity. In that case as a result of some initial increase in investment, income would go on rising indefinitely. Since marginal propensity to consume is actually less than one, some saving does take place. Therefore, multiplier in actual practice is less than infinity. But besides saving, there are other leakages in the process of income generation which reduces the size of the multiplier. Therefore, the increase in income as a result of some increase in investment will be less than warranted by the size of the multiplier measured by the given marginal propensity to consumer. We explain below the various leakages that occur in the income stream and reduce the size of multiplier in the real world.

Paying off debts. The first leakage in the multiplier process occurs in the form of payment of debts by the people, especially by businessmen. In the real world, all income received by the people as a result of some increase in investment is not consumed. A part of the increment in income is used for paying back the debts which the people have taken from money-lenders, banks or other financial institutions. The incomes used for paying back the debts do not get spent on consumer goods and services and therefore leak away from the income stream. This reduces the size of the multiplier. Of course, when incomes received by the moneylenders, banks or institutions are again lent back to the people, they come back to the income stream and enhance the size of multiplier. But this may or may not happen.

Holding of idle cash balances. If the people hold a part of their increment in income as idle cash balances and do not use it for consumption, they also constitute leakage in the multiplier process. As we have seen, people keep a part of their income for satisfying their precautionary and speculative motives, money kept for such purposes is not consumed and therefore does not appear in the successive rounds of consumption expenditure and therefore reduces the increments in total income and output.

Imports. In our above analysis of working of the multiplier process we have taken the example of a closed economy, that is, an economy with no foreign trade. If it is an open economy as is usually the case, then a part of increment in income will also be spent on the imports of consumer goods. The proportion of increments in income spent on the imports of consumer goods will generate income in other countries and will not help in raising income and output in the domestic economy. Therefore, imports constitute another important leakage in the multiplier process. Suppose marginal propensity to save of an open economy is 0.25, *i.e.,* marginal propensity to consume is 0.75. Suppose further that marginal propensity to import is 0.25 the size of the multiplier without imports will be equal to 4 but the size of the multiplier with the marginal propensity to import equal to 0.25 and the marginal propensity to consume equal to 0.75 will be smaller.

$$\text{Multiplier in an Open Economy} = \frac{1}{1-(MPC-MPI)} = \frac{1}{1-MPC+MPI}$$

where *MPC* stands for marginal propensity to consumed and *MPI* for marginal propensity to import.

In our example quoted above, where marginal propensity to consume is equal to 0.75 or $\frac{3}{4}$ and marginal propensity to import is equal to 0.25 or $\frac{1}{4}$, the multiplier is:

$$K = \frac{1}{1-\left(\frac{3}{4}-\frac{1}{4}\right)} = \frac{1}{\frac{1}{2}} = 2$$

We, therefore, see that the size of multiplier instead of being equal to 4, as it would have been in the case of a closed economy, is equal to 2 in the open economy with 0.25 or $\frac{1}{4}$ as the marginal propensity to import.

Taxation. Taxation is another important leakage in the multiplier process. The increments in income which the people receive as a result of increase in investment are also in part used for payment of taxes. Therefore, the money used for payment of taxes does not appear in the successive rounds of consumption expenditure in the multiplier process, and the multiplier is reduced to that extent. However, if the money raised through taxation is spent by the Government, the leakage through taxation will be offset by the increase in Government expenditure. But it is not necessary that all the money raised through taxation is spent by the Government as it happens when Government makes a surplus budget. No doubt, if the Government expenditure increases by an amount equal to the taxation, it would not have any adverse effect on the increases in income and investment and in this way there would be no leakage in the multiplier process.

Increase in Prices. Price inflation constitutes another important leakage in the working of the multiplier process in real terms. As we have noted above, the multiplier works in real terms only when as a result of increase in money income and aggregate demand, output of consumer goods is also increased. When output of consumer goods cannot be easily increased, a part of the increases in the money income and aggregate demand raises prices of the goods rather than their output. Therefore, the multiplier is reduced to the extent of price inflation. In developing countries like India the extra incomes and demand are mostly spent on foodgrains whose output cannot be increased so easily. Therefore, the increments in demand raise the prices of goods to a greater extent than the increase in their output. Besides, in developing countries like India, there is not much excess capacity in many consumer goods industries, especially in agriculture and other wage-goods industries. Therefore, when income and demand increase as a result of increase in investment, it generally raises the prices of these goods rather than their output and therefore weakens the working of the multiplier in real terms. Thus, in 1950s and 1960s it was often asserted, especially by Dr. V.K.R.V. Rao and Dr. A.K. Das Gupta that Keynesian theory of multiplier was not very much relevant to the conditions of developing countries like India.[2] However, we shall discuss later in this chapter that this old view of the working of Keynesian multiplier in the present-day developing countries is not fully correct.

The above various leakages reduce the multiplier effect of the investment undertaken. If these leakages are plugged, the effect of change in investment on income and employment would be greater.

Importance of the Concept of Multiplier

Multiplier is one of the most important concepts developed by J.M. Keynes to explain the determination of income and employment in an economy. The theory of multiplier has been used to explain the cumulative upward and downward swings of the trade cycles that occur in a free-enterprise capitalist economy. When investment in an economy rises, it has a multiple and cumulative effect on national income, output and employment. As a result, economy experiences rapid upward movement. On the other hand, when due to some reasons, especially due to the adverse change in the expectations of the business class, investment falls, then backward working of the multiplier causes a multiple and cumulative fall in income, output and employment and as a result the economy rapidly moves on downswing of the trade cycle. Thus, Keynesian theory of multiplier helps a good deal in explaining the movements of trade cycles or fluctuations in the economy. Paul Samuelson and J.R. Hicks have put forward models of business cycles that involve *interaction of multipher and accelerator*. These models adequately explain why business cycles occur in free-enterprise capitalist economies.

The theory of multiplier has also a great practical importance in the field of fiscal policy to be

2. See, V.K.R.V. Rao, Investment, Income and the Multiplier in an Underdeveloped Economy printed in A.N. Agarwala and S.P. Singh (edited). *The Economics of Underdevelopment,* Oxford, 1958.

pursued by the Government to get out of the depression and achieve the state of full employment. To get rid of depression and remove unemployment, Government investment in public works was recommended even before Keynes. But it was thought that the increase in income will be limited to the amount of investment undertaken in these public works. But the importance of public works is enhanced when it is realised that the total effect on income, output and employment as a result of some initial increase in investment has a multiplier effect. Thus, Keynes recommended Government investment in public works to solve the problem of depression and unemployment. The public investment in public works such as road building, construction of hospitals, schools, irrigation facilities will raise aggregate demand by a multiple amount. The multiple increase in income and demand will also encourage the increase in private investment. Thus, the deficiency in private investment which leads to the state of depression and underemployment equilibrium will now be made up and a state of full employment will be restored. If the multiplier had not worked, the income and demand would have risen as a result of some public investment but not as much as they rise with the multiplier effect. Inspired by the Keynesian theory of multiplier, expansionary fiscal policy of increase in Government expenditure and reduction in income tax was adopted by President John Kenedy and president George W. Bush in the United State of America to remove involuntary unemployment and depression. This had a great success in removing unemployment and, depression and, therefore, Keynesian theory of multiplier was vindicated and as a result people's belief in it increased.

The theory of multiplier also brings out the importance of *foreign direct investment* (FDI) for accelerating economic growth in developing countries. Like the domestic investment foreign direct investment also causes increase in income and employment in developing countries not only *directly* but also *indirectily* through the working of multiplier.

A Numerical Problem on Multiplier

Problem 1. *Suppose the level of autonomous investment in an economy is ₹ 200 crores and consumption function of the economy is :*

$$C = 80 + 0.75Y$$

(*a*) *What will be the equilibrium level of income?*

(*b*) *What will be the increase in national income if investment increases by ₹ 25 crores.*

Solution. (*a*) For equilibrium level of income,

$$Y = C + I \quad ...(i)$$

where

$$C = 80 + 0.75\,Y$$

$$I = 200 \text{ crore}$$

Substituting the values of C and I in (1) we have

$$Y = 80 + 0.75Y + 200$$

$$(Y - 0.75Y) = 80 + 200 = 280$$

$$0.25\,Y = 280$$

$$Y = 280 \times \frac{100}{25} = 1120$$

Equilibrium level of income is therefore equal to 1120 crore.

(*b*) How much increase in income will occur as a result of increase in investment by ₹ 25 crores depends on the size of multiplier. The size of multiple is determined by the value of marginal propensely to consume. In the given consumption function ($C = 80 + 0.75Y$) marginal propensity to consume is equal to 0.75 or $\frac{3}{4}$. Thus,

$$\text{multiplier} = \frac{1}{1-MPC} = \frac{1}{1-\frac{3}{4}} = 4$$

Thus, with increase in investment by ₹ 25 crore, national income will rise by 25 × 4 = 100 crore.

Problem 2. *Suppose in a country investment increases by ₹ 100 and consumption is given by C = 10 + 0.6Y (where C = consumption and Y = income). How much increase will there take place in income ?*

Solution.

Multiplier, $k = \frac{\Delta Y}{\Delta I}$

or $\Delta Y = k.\, \Delta I$ . . . (i)

Now, multiplier, $k = \frac{1}{1-MPC}$

In the given consumption function, $MPC = 0.6$

Therefore, $k = \frac{1}{1-0.6} = \frac{1}{0.4} = 2.5$

$\Delta I =$ ₹ 100

Substituting $\Delta I = 100$ and $k = 2.5$ in (*i*) above, we have

$$\Delta Y = 2.5 \times 100 = 250$$

Problem 3. *What increase in investment is needed to raise income by ₹ 4,000 crore, if MPC is 0.75 ? How much will there be increase in consumption and saving due to this increase in income ?*

Solution. How much increase in investment is required to raise income by ₹ 4,000 crore depends on the value of multiplier and the size of multiplier (*k*) depends on the marginal propensity to consume (*MPC*). Thus,

Multiplier $(k) = \frac{1}{1-MPC} = \frac{1}{1-0.75} = \frac{1}{0.25} = 4$

Now, $k = \frac{\Delta Y}{\Delta I}$

or $\Delta I = \frac{\Delta Y}{k}$ . . . (*i*)

Substituting the value of ΔY and k in (*i*), we have

$$\Delta I = \frac{4000}{4} = 1000 \text{ crore}$$

Thus, investment should be increased by ₹ 1,000 to achieve ₹ 4,000 crore increase in income.

Given $MPC = 0.75$, the increase in consumption will be 4,000 × 0.75 = ₹ 3,000 crore and increase in saving will be 4000 × 0.25 = 1,000 crore.

THE PARADOX OF THRIFT

An interesting paradox arises when all people in a society try to save more but in fact they are unable to do so. The multiplier theory of Keynes helps a good deal in explaining this paradox. According to this paradox of thrift, the attempt by the people as a whole to save more for hard times such as impending period of recession or unemployment may not materialise and in their bid to save more the society in fact may not only end up with the same savings but also in the process cause their consumption or standard of living to decline. Thrift (*i.e.,* the desire to save more) is considered to be a virtue in most of the societies and it is regarded as an act of prudence on the part of individuals to save for a rainy day. According to a proverb, "a penny saved is a penny earned". Further, according to classical economists, savings determine investment which plays a crucial role in accelerating the rate of economic growth. However, the paradox of thrift shows that the efforts to save more, especially in times of

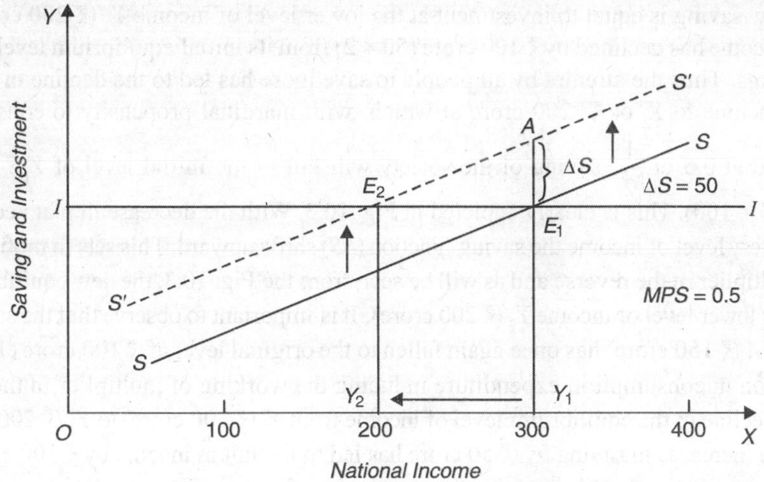

Fig. 10.3. *The Paradox of Thrift*

depression, may actually deepen the economic crisis and cause output to fall and unemployment to increase. It goes to the credit of Keynes that with his multiplier theory he was able to resolve the paradox of thrift. Keynesian explanation of paradox of thrift has been shown in Fig. 10.3. According to the Keynesian theory, the saying "penny saved is penny earned" is quite inappropriate for the economy as a whole when it is working at underemployment equilibrium, that is, when there prevails recession or depression in the economy. Keynes has showed that if *all* people in a society decide to save more, they may actually fail to do so but nevertheless reduce their consumption. This is because, according to Keynes, the effort to save more by all in a society will lower the aggregate demand for goods and services resulting in a drop in the level of national income. At the lower level of national income, the saving fall to the original level but consumption will be less than before which implies that the people would become worse off.

Consider Fig. 10.3, where *SS* is the saving curve with a slope equal to 0.5, and *II* is the planned investment curve. It will be seen that saving and investment curves intersect at point E_1 and determines level of income equal to Y_1 or ₹ 300 crore. Now suppose that expecting hard times ahead all people try to save more by the amount of ₹ 50 crore which would cause an autonomous downward shift in the consumption function. This downward shift in the consumption function brings about an upward shift by ₹ 50 crore or E_1A in the saving function curve to *S′S′*. This new saving function curve *S′S′* cuts the planned investment curve *II* at point E_2 according to which new equilibrium level of income falls to Y_2 or ₹ 200 crore. It is important to note that level of income does not drop only by the amount (E_1A or ₹ 50 crore), that is, by the extent of reduction in consumption due to more saving but by a multiple of it. With marginal propensity to save (*MPS*) being equal to 0.5 or $\frac{1}{2}$, the value of multiplier would be $1/MPS = \frac{1}{\frac{1}{2}} = 2$. Further, the decline in consumption due to more saving would cause the multiplier to work in reverse, that is, the multiplier would operate to reduce the level of consumption and income by a magnified amount. The decline in consumption expenditure of the people by ₹ 50 crore in the first instance due to more saving by them implies that the producers and sellers of goods and services will find their income to fall by ₹ 50 crore. But the reverse process will not stop here. Given the marginal propensity to consume being equal to 0.5 or $\frac{1}{2}$, the producers/sellers of goods and services in turn would spend ₹ 25 crore less when they find their income has fallen by ₹ 50 crore. It will be observed from Fig. 10.3 that this process of reduction in the level of income will continue till the new saving is equal to investment at the lower level of income Y_2 (₹ 200 crore), that is, the level of income has declined by ₹ 100 crore (50 × 2) from its initial equilibrium level of income Y_1 of ₹ 300 crores. Thus the attempt by all people to save more has led to the decline in the equilibrium level of income to Y_2 or ₹ 200 crore at which, with marginal propensity to consume remaining unchanged at 0.5 or $\frac{1}{2}$, saving of the society will fall to the initial level of Y_1E or ₹ 100 crore (200 × 0.5 = 100). This is clearly depicted in Fig. 10.3. With the decrease in planned saving by ₹ 50 crore at every level of income the saving function (*SS*) shifts upward. This sets in motion the operation of the multiplier in the reverse and as will be seen from the Fig. 10.3, the new equilibrium is reached at the new lower level of income Y_2 (₹ 200 crore). It is important to observe that the saving which had risen to Y_1A (₹ 150 crore) has once again fallen to the original level of ₹ 100 crore ($Y_2E_2 = Y_1E_1$) due to reduction in consumption expenditure inducing the working of multiplier in the reverse which causes a decline in the equilibrium level of income from Y_1 (₹ 300 crore) to Y_2 (₹ 200 crore). In other words, the increases in saving by ₹ 50 crore has led to the fall in income by ₹ 100 crore because the multiplier is equal to 2. This explains the paradoxical feature of an economy gripped by recession. *This is paradoxical because in their attempt to save more the people have caused a decline in their income and consumption with no increase in the saving of the society at all.*

In our analysis we have assumed that the planned investment is fixed, that is, determined outside the model. In other words, the investment has been assumed to be *autonomous of income,* that is, it does not vary with income.

Can We Avert the Paradox of Thrift?

Paradox of thrift holds good when a free market economy is in the grip of recession or depression and investment demand is inadequate due to lack of profit opportunities. However, it has been pointed out by some economists that paradox of thrift can be averted if the extra savings that the people do for a rainy day are somehow channeled into additional investment through financial markets. Indeed, the classical economists argued that the increase in the supply of savings would lead to the fall in the rate of interest which would induce increase in planned investment. If this happens, then in our saving-investment diagram the investment curve *II* would shift up to *I′I′* in Fig. 10.4 and as will be seen from this figure the new equilibrium level of income may not fall and therefore the paradox of thrift is averted. In Fig. 10.4, initially the saving curve (*SS*) and investment curve *II* intersect at point E_1

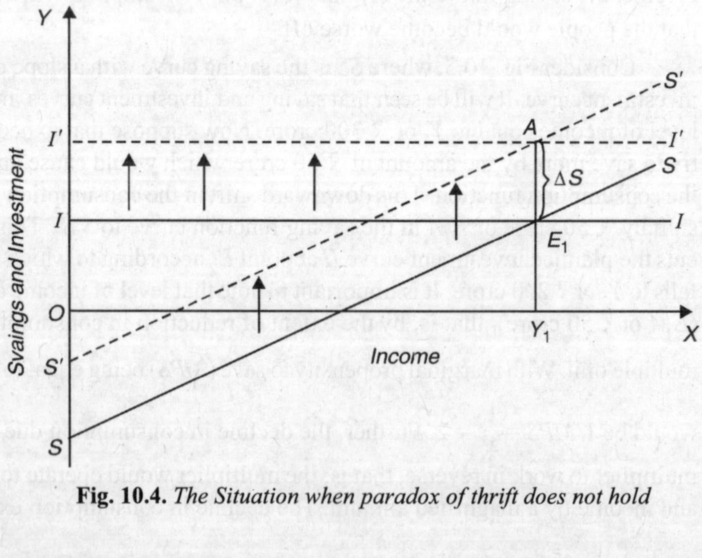

Fig. 10.4. *The Situation when paradox of thrift does not hold*

and determine OY_1 level of income. Now, if the people of the society expecting difficult times ahead, desire to save E_1A more. If these extra savings, for reasons mentioned above, result in more investment, the investment curve will also shift to $I'I'$, so that the new equilibrium will be at point A corresponding to the original level of income Y_1. In this way the paradox of thrift has been averted.

However, according to the modern economists, especially the followers of Keynes, the empirical evidence does not support the above argument of averting the paradox of thrift. This is because at times of recession or depression, the prospective yields from investment are so small that no possible reduction in the rate of interest will induce sufficient increase in investment. Thus, according to them, in a free-market economy without Government intervention the paradox of thrift cannot be averted. Of course, if the Government intervenes as it does even in the present-day predominantly private enterprise economies of the USA and Great Britain, it can mobilise the extra savings of the people and invest them in some worthwhile projects and thus prevent aggregate demand and income from falling. This can happen because undertaking of investment by the Government is not motivated by profit motive but by the considerations of promoting social interest and economic growth. It is because of this that the role of the Government has greatly increased for overcoming recession in the capitalist countries.

LIMITATIONS AND APPLICABILITY OF THE KEYNESIAN MULTIPLIER FOR THE DEVELOPING COUNTRIES

The Old View

In the early fifties an eminent Indian economist Dr. V.K. R.V. Rao and some others explained that in developing countries like India Keynesian multiplier did not work in real terms, that is, did not operate to increase income and employment by a multiple of the initial increase in investment.[3] He claimed that the concept of investment multiplier was valid in the context of the situation of depression in the industrialised developed economies of the UK and the USA where there existed a lot of access productive capacity and a large number of open involuntary unemployment. He argued that in such a situation of a depressed economy there was a high elasticity of supply of output to changes in demand for them. Therefore, in the developed capitalist economies ridden with depression increase in investment leading to successive rounds of consumption expenditure raises aggregate demand. Due to the existence of large excess capacity and involuntary unemployment under conditions of depression aggregate supply of output is highly elastic, increase in aggregate demand brings about increase in real income, output and employment which is a multiple of original increase in investment.

On the other hand, they claimed that in underdeveloped countries there was little excess capacity in consumer goods industries and therefore supply of output was inelastic. Therefore, when there is injection of investment, and as a result through successive rounds of the operation of multiplier, aggregate demand for consumer goods increases, it results mainly in rise in money income brought about through rise in prices and not an increase in real national income.

The second condition, according to Dr. Rao and his followers for the working of multiplier in raising national income and employment was that the supply of raw materials, financial capital must be sufficiently elastic so that when aggregate demand increases as a result of multiplier effect of increase in investment the supply of output could be increased adequately to meet this higher demand for goods and services. They argued that in underdeveloped countries like India due to underdeveloped nature of their economies, there was acute scarcity of raw materials, other intermediate goods such as steel, cement and financial capital which put great obstacles for the working of multiplier in real terms.

3. Dr. V.K.R.V. Rao, Investment, Income and Multiplier in an Underdeveloped Economy, *Indian Economic Review,* February 1952.

The third condition required for the working of multiplier in real terms was that there should be involuntary open unemployment so that when aggregate demand for goods increases as a consequence of new investment, the adequate supply of workers must be forthcoming to be employed in the production processes of various industries. They argued this condition too was not fulfilled in case of underdeveloped countries where there existed disguised unemployment, especially in the agricultural sector. The disguisedly unemployed workers who are supported by joint family system could not be easily shifted to be employed in the industries for expansion of output to achieve the multiplier effect.

Lastly, it was pointed out that the underdeveloped countries like India had predominantly agricultural economies and income elasticity of demand for foodgrains was very high in these economies. In view of this when increase in investment leads to the rise in money incomes of the people, a large part of it is spent on foodgrains. But the supply of agricultural products is inelastic because their production is subject to uncertain natural factors like monsoon and climate and further there was lack of irrigation facilities, improved seeds, fertilizers etc. Hence it was difficult to increase agricultural production in response to the increase in demand through the multiplier effect of increase in investment.

It follows from above that the Keynesian assumptions for the working of multiplier in real terms, namely (*a*) the supply of output of goods is elastic due to the existence of large excess capacity, (*b*) the supply of raw materials and others intermediate goods can be adequately increased, (c) there exists involuntarily unemployed workers searching for work and, (d) sufficiently elastic agricultural output. In view of the earlier economists these assumptions for realising the multiplier effect in terms of rise in real income and employment were not valid in case of underdeveloped countries. Therefore, according to them, Keynesian multiplier did not operate in real terms in underdeveloped countries and actually leads to the rise in prices or inflationary conditions in them.

The Relevance of Multiplier for Developing Countries : The Modern View

We have explained above the views of some eminent Indian economists, such as Dr. V.K.R.V. Rao, Dr. A.K. Dass Gupta expressed during the early fifties regarding non-operation of the Keynesian multiplier in the underdeveloped countries. But the situation in the present-day developing countries has substantially changed in the last 60 years. There has been a lot of economic growth and structural transformation in the Indian economy during the last half a centuary so that supply conditions today have become significantly elastic. So in the present state of the Indian economy and also of some other developing economies, it cannot be said that Keynesian multiplier is not applicable in real terms in them. However, it may be noted that even in the fifties and early sixties the view that Keynesian multiplier did not work in the under-developed countries did not go entirely unchallanged. Thus commenting on Dr. Rao's article Dr. K.N. Raj remarked that "*Discarding the Keynesian thesis as altogether inoperative in under-developed countries is really throwing the baby away with the bath water*".[4] Similarly Dr. D.R. Khatkhate wrote, "In conclusion we may state that the multiplier can operate in an under-developed economy when it is associated with a carefully designed pattern of investment. The theory that the multiplier works in a backward economy only with reference to the money income is based on static assumptions and is, therefore, not correct"[5]. Likewise, Dr. Ashok Mathur writes. "Our main objection against the view that Keynesian multiplier does not operate in the under-developed countries is that it views the operation of multiplier process in a completly static setting and as a purely short-period concept, whereas the very rationale of economic development is long run dynamic change. Once we relax these two restrictive assumptions, the essential content of the Keynesian multiplier that the increase of investment results in an increase in output which is much in excess of the original outlay on investment holds true in case of the developing as much as in the

4. Dr. K.N. Raj, "Dr. Rao on Investment, Income and the Multiplier in an Under-developed Economy -a comment" *Indian Economic Review,* p. 1952.-
5. D.R. Khatkhate "The Multiplier Process in Developing Economies" *Indian Economic Journal,* Oct. 1954.

developed economies"[6]

At present, in the beginning of the new millenium as a result of economic growth both in the industrial and agricultural sectors the Indian economy has a widely diversified structure and supply of output has become quite elastic, at least in the industrial sector. Besides, at times there is a lot of excess or unutilised capacity in several industries in India due to the deficieny of aggregate demand. The potential for increasing raw materials and intermediate products such as cement, steel and fertilizers has significantly increased to meet the rising demand for them.

If there is injection of investment, it will result in manifold increase in output or real income and employment through the working of the multiplier. If the injection of new investment package is quite diversified and balanced, as is generally planned in our Five Years Plans, the investment and growth in several industries simultaneously will create not only additional demand for each other as was visualised by Nurkse[7] but will also create productive capacities in them which will ultimately over a period of time will result in multiple increase in output and employment.

It is worth noting that in India today there is not only a lot of pre-existing excess production capacity in the Indian industries but new investment every year also creates additional production capacity which with some time lag will result in increase in real income or output, if adequate aggregate demand is forthcoming for its utilisation. Harrod-Domar in their famous dynamic growth models emphasised that investment not only creates demand but also new productive capacity[8]. Thus, if we look at increment in investment from the viewpoint of dynamics of development and take a longer time horizon, multiplier effect of new investment in the developing countries can become a reality. It is true that increase in money incomes and demand may tend to occur ahead of the increase in real income but subject to some time lag between investment and consequent increase in production capacity, the latter would tend to catch up with the former. The significant point to note is that investment not only creates demand but it also creates production capacity. Ultimately there is no reason as to why multiplier effect of new investment on real income or output may not materialise, though the actual period required for realisation of the multiplier effect depends on various time lags in the process of income generation and capacity creation. The wider the range of industries over which initial investment is undertaken the greater will be the multiplier effect. This is because monetary demand or expenditure generated by investment in any one industry would be easily met by the increase in production capacity in a variety of industries. In this way increase in demand resulting from investment would not lead to rise in prices but will cause real output to rise.

Agriculture and Multiplier. As mentioned above, the argument for non-operation of multiplier in underdeveloped countries was also partly based on the inelastic nature of supply of agricultural output, especially foodgrains, as it was pointed out that a large part of monetary demand or money incomes generated by investment would be spent on foodgrains. Inability to meet the rise in demand for foodgrains would cause rise in price level or inflation in the economy rather than increase in real output. It may be pointed out that thanks to the spread of green revolution technology expansion in irrigation facilities in various states of India, foodgrains production can be adequately increased in response to rising demand for foodgrains.

Furthermore, it was asserted by Dr. Rao, the existence of disguised unemployment in underdeveloped countries instead of Keynesian type involuntary open unemployment also prevented the working of multiplier in real terms. In the Indian economy today there are a large number of involuntarily unemployed workers crying out for employment. So this argument for failure of multiplier to work in real terms no longer holds good in the present economic situation.

6. Ashok Mathur, On Throwing the Baby away with the Bath Water, *Indian Economic Journal,* April-June; 1965
7. Ragnar Nurkse, *Problems of Capital Formation in Underdeveloped Countries,*
8. See E. Domar, Capital Expansion, Rate of Growth and Employment, *Economica*, Vol. 14, 1946 and R.E. Harrod, *Towards Dynamic Economics*, Macmillan & Co. London, 1948.

To conclude, in the present economic situation of the Indian economy with a lot of excess production capacity in several consumer goods industries and a large potential for expanding agricultural production, increase in investment would produce a real multiplier effect on increasing real income and output without causing inflationary pressures in the economy. Multiplier effect of new investment can be further increased, if investment package is quite diversified covering a large number of industries (including agriculture) so that monetary demand and income generated by any one industry can be adequately met by increase in output capacity in other industries. Further, even when their is no pre-existing excess capacity in the industries, increase in investment leads to the increase is demand for consumption goods which in turn cause further rise in investment to meet that consumption demand. The effect of increase in consumption demand on expansion in investment is generally referred to as *accelerator.* Indeed, the combined working of multiplier and acceleration, which is called *super-multiplier,* leading to manifold increase in output can take place in the growth process in the developing countries like India[9].

QUESTIONS FOR REVIEW

1. What is investment multiplier ? How is it related to marginal propensity to consume ?
2. Wht is income multiplier ? Find out the value of multiplier given the following :
   (a) MPC = 0.80, *(b) MPC* = 0.75, *(c) MPS* = 0.20, *(d) MPS* = 0.50.
   [**Hints :** Keynes' investment multiplier is also called Income multiplier.]
3. Explain the concept of investment multiplier. If marginal propensity to save is 0.1, what is the value of multiplier.
4. Explain the Keynesian theory of investment multiplier. What are possible leakages in the multiplier mechanism ?
5. Keynesian investment multiplier does not operate in the developing countries like India." Do you agree ? Discuss.
6. "Multiplier does not work in real terms in developing countries" *(Dr. V.K.R.V Rao)*. What prevents the multiplier to work in real terms in India ?
7. Even though marginal propensity to consume is quite high in LDCs, an increase in government expenditure may have little expansionary effect. Discuss
   D.U., B.A. (Hons) 1995.
8. (*a*) Explain the concept of multiplier. How does it work ?
9. What is paradox of thrift ? How would you explain it.
10. "If all people in a society decide to save more, they may actually fail to do so, but nevertheless reduce their consumption.". Expalin.
11. Explain and illustrated diagrammatically the concept of multiplier. Discuss the leakages that may occur in the operation of multiplier in an economy.
12. Explain how Keynes showed that *if all people* in a society decide to save more, they may actually fail to do so. Under what circumstances is it true ?
13. Explain the significance of multiplier in the Keynes's explanation of depression in the economy.
14. Does Keynesion multiplier work in developing countries ? Discuss.
15. In developing countries Keynesian multiplier works in money terms and not in real terms of increase in output and employment. Discuss.

9. See V.N. Pandit, Macroeconomic Characteristics of the Indian Economy, in Prabhat Patnaik, ed., *Macroeconomics,* Oxford University Press, p. 205.

APPENDIX TO CHAPTER 10

Explanation of Depression or Recession and Global Financial Crisis (2007-2009)

In this appendix we will explain in detail what causes recession or depression in the economy. We will explain both Keynesian and Friedman's monetarist view about this. Besides, we will explain in detail what led to global financial crisis of 2007-09 resulting in global meltdown.

What Causes Depression or Recession : Keynes's View

During 1929-33, capitalist economies of the world found themselves in the grip of depression. Such was the severity of this depression that in the United States, the rate of unemployment rose from 3.2 per cent in 1929 to 25% of the labour force in 1933. Besides, there was a drastic decline in Gross National Product (GNP) which fell from 315 billion dollars in 1929 to 222 billion dollars in 1933, that is, national income declined by about 30 per cent during this four-year period. This reflects a dismal picture of the American economy during the period of Great Depression. In England as well as in other European countries also such a grave situation of severe recession and huge unemployment prevailed during this period. Before 1929-33 and even after it, recessions have occurred in these capitalist economies but they have not been as severe as that took place during 1929-33.

Classical economists had no valid explanation of such a severe depression and large-scale cyclical unemployment of labour. A.C. Pigou and other economists of his view attributed this situation to the high wage rates kept by trade unions and Government. Pigou, therefore, suggested all-round cut in wages to increase employment and to remove depression and unemployment. However, this solution of the problem was neither logically sound nor practical to be implemented. Keynes challenged this view of the classical economists and put forward a different explanation of depression and cyclical unemployment which was accepted by many as logical and correct. He explained his viewpoint in his now noted work, '*General Theory of Employment, Interest, and Money*'. He not only gave a sound and valid explanation of depression and its associated problem of cyclical unemployment but also suggested effective policy measures to cure them.

According to Keynes, the cause of depression and cyclical unemployment in the industrialised capitalist countries was a sharp decline in private investment due to the adverse business expectations about profit making. There was a wave of pessimism prevailing among investors. The decline in private investment due to fall in marginal efficiency of capital (that is, expected rate of return) caused a fall in aggregate demand and resulted in less than full-employment equilibrium. Consequently, level of output and employment fell drastically and involuntary unemployment came to prevail on a large scale. The involuntary unemployment that prevails in times of recession/depression is called cyclical unemployment and, according to Keynes, it is due to deficiency of aggregate demand.

Large fluctuations in investment, according to Keynes, is due to the uncertain basis of profit expectations on which investment decisions are made. To quote him, "*We have to admit that our basis of knowledge for estimating the yield ten years hence of a Railway, a copper mine, a textile factory, the goodwill of a patent medicine ... amounts to little and sometimes to nothing.*" In view of this uncertainty of future. Keynes stressed that investment decisions were greatly influenced by how

1. J.M. Keynes, *op. cit.* pp., 149-150

optimistic or pessimistic investors feel about making of profits from their investments. He used the term ***animal spirits*** to describe the pessimistic or optimistic expectations of the investors about profit earning from investment projects. The term animal spirits implies that there may be no good or intelligent basis for expectations on which investors base their decisions. Thus the cause of depression or cyclical involuntary unemployment is the deficiency of aggregate demand due to fall in private investment that results from adverse business expectations and loss of confidence of the investors in a market economy.

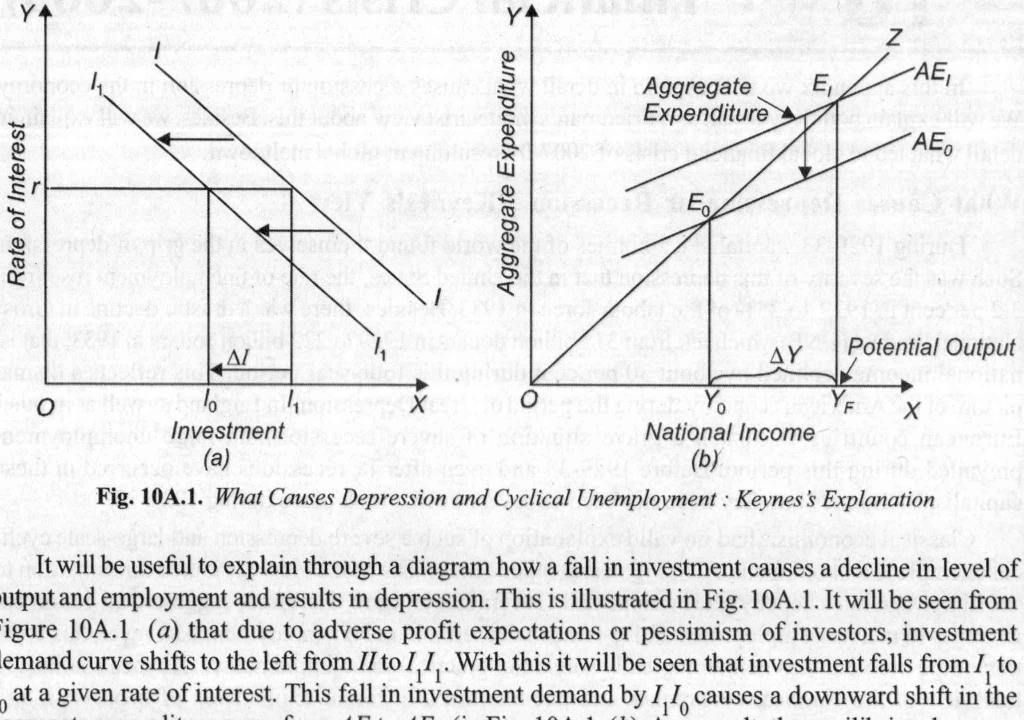

Fig. 10A.1. *What Causes Depression and Cyclical Unemployment : Keynes's Explanation*

It will be useful to explain through a diagram how a fall in investment causes a decline in level of output and employment and results in depression. This is illustrated in Fig. 10A.1. It will be seen from Figure 10A.1 (*a*) that due to adverse profit expectations or pessimism of investors, investment demand curve shifts to the left from *II* to I_1I_1. With this it will be seen that investment falls from I_1 to I_0 at a given rate of interest. This fall in investment demand by I_1I_0 causes a downward shift in the aggregate expenditure curve from *AE* to AE_0 (in Fig. 10A.1 (*b*). As a result, the equilibrium between aggregate expenditure and aggregate output which was initially at full-employment level Y_F (which corresponds to point E_1 where the aggregate expenditure curve AE_1 intersects 45° line) falls to the new equilibrium level of income OY_0. Therefore, the *cause of depression or recession is deficiency of aggregate demand*. It should also be noted, that the decline in the level of GNP or national income following the fall in investment and aggregate demand will also result in decrease in level of employment in the economy and causes the emergence of large-scale cyclical unemployment.

The huge decline in national income and the emergence of unemployment in the USA, UK and other industrialised capitalist countries during the period of depression is graphically shown in Fig. 10A.2. It is assumed that, to begin with, say in 1929, the aggregate demand curve $C + I_2$ intersects 45° line at point *H* and determines equilibrium level of income at full-employment or potential output level OY_F. The sharp decline in investment by the amount *HT* due to the fall in profitability of investment following a crash in stock markets in 1929 and other unfavourable events caused a downward shift in the aggregate demand curve to $C + I_1$ (where $I_1 < I_2$). This new aggregate demand curve $C + I_1$ intersects the 45° line at point *E* and accordingly determines equilibrium level of income OY_1 which is much lower than full-employment level OY_F and thus represents a state of depression with a large unemployment of workers. *The important point made by Keynes was that income would not fall merely equal to the decline in investment but by a multiple of it.* In fact, during the depression period of 1930s, it actually happened so and is evident from the Table 10A.1. It will be seen from the Figure 10A.2 that the decline in national income Y_FY_1 is not equal to the fall in investment by *HT* but by a multiple of it. Y_FY_1 is twice that of HT. As explained above, this is due to the working of multiplier in the reverse. Further note that after taking into all leakages in the multiplier process it has been assumed that marginal propensity to consume is equal to 0.5 which yields the value of multiplier 1/1-MPC = 1/1-1/2 = 2, That is why fall in income by Y_FY_1 is twice the decline in investment by HT.

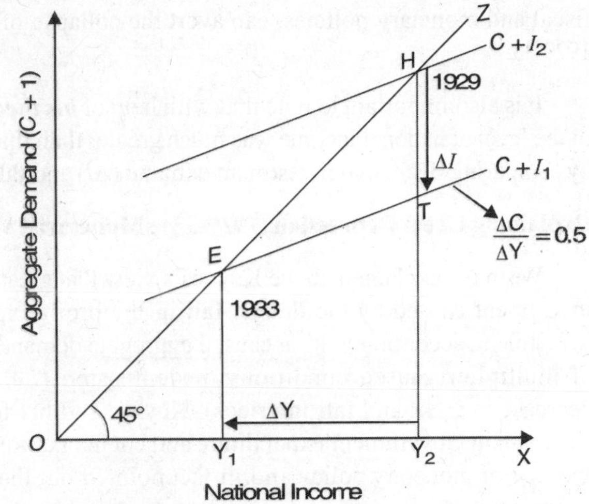

Fig. 10A.2. *Depression of 1930s Caused by a Decline in Investment and Working of Multiplier in Reverse*

Now, the historical record of this period about the various components of aggregate demand of the US economy shows that changes in net exports and Government expenditure were quite small and they mostly offset each other during the period 1929-33. The drastic drop in private investment appears to be the basic reason for the huge fall in aggregate demand or spending. The private investment which was \$ 56 billion in 1920 fell to only \$8.5 billion in 1933 in the USA, the decline of \$ 47.5 billion in four years. But, as has been explained by Keynes,

Table 10A.1

	1929	1933	(in billion US \$) Change
Investment	56	8.5	47.5
National Income	315	222	93
Unemployment (% of labour force)	3.2	25	21.8

the decrease in national income was not merely equal to \$ 47.5 billion, but by a multiple amount due to the operation of the multiplier in the reverse. It has been estimated that taking into account all leakages in the multiplier process, the value of the multiplier was around 2 during the period. Therefore, as a result of sharp decline in investment by \$ 47.5 billion and consequently operation of the multiplier in the reverse there was a fall in the induced consumption expenditure. Thus, as a result of the sharp drop in private investment and resultant fall in induced consumption due to working of multiplier caused much bigger decrease (\$ 93 billion) in the level of aggregate effective demand, income and output. This is in accordance with the value of multiplier being equal to around 2. Multiplier is here equal to

$$\frac{\Delta Y}{\Delta I} = \frac{93}{47.5} = 1.96$$

Thus, the Keynesian theory of income determination provides a fairly accurate explanation of the first four years of the great depression. This looks rather simple but during the early 1930s it was not understood at all. Only after when the Keynesian policy prescription to ward off depression and involuntary unemployment, namely, launching by the Government public works programme financed by the deficit budgets to raise aggregate demand, such as adopted under New Deal Policy in the U.S.A. proved to be a great success that economists and intellectuals were convined about the validity of the Keynes's explanation of depression. An important result of the success of the Keynesian model was that fiscal policy as an instrument for controlling business cycles came into prominence. Further, it now becomes clear that the Government intervention, through the adoption of appropriate fiscal and monetary policies, can avert the collapse of the economy such as that happened during 1929-33.

It is also important to note that with help of ***his theory of multiplier*** Keynes showed that the fall in the level of national income was much greater than that of decline in investment. This can be known by comparing decline in investment demand (ΔI) and fall in national income. (ΔY) in Figure 10A.2.

Explaining Great Depression (1929-33) : Monetarist View

We have explained above Keynes's view that great depression of 1929-33 was caused by fall in investment caused by the drastic fall in the profit expectations of business class. The decline in investment, according to him, caused aggregate demand to fall which along with the reverse working of multiplier caused conditions of depression (*i.e.* high rate of unemployment, substantial decrease in GNP and fall in prices). Keynes and his followers emphasise the role of fiscal policy (increase in Government expenditure and cut in taxation) to stimulate investment. They downplayed the role of monetary policy and in fact pointed out that monetary policy in the thirties during the depression period proved to be unimportant and ineffective. As a matter of fact, they asserted that monetary policy was tried during the depression period to revive the economy but miserably failed. At times of depression, according to them, businessmen are in the grip of pessimism about future profitability of investment and more money made available through easy and liberal monetary policy would not be effective in reviving the economy. It was in this context that some Keynesian economists remarked that '***money does not matter***' and also referred to the failure of policy of making more credit available for stimulating investment by businesses at times of depression as '*you can bring horse to water but cannot make it drink*'. Thus Keynesian view prevailed during the forties and fifties almost unchallenged.

Keynes's view was attacked by Milton Friedman, a Nobel Laureate in economics, in the middle of fifties. Friedman and Schwartz in their important work '*A Monetary History of the United States*' written in 1963 quoted statistical evidence from the United States, and argued that "*a re-examination of the Great Depression of the 1930s demonstrated that, contrary to general belief, it had been a tragic testament to the great power of monetary policy, not to its impotence*'[2] They pointed out drastic decline in the quantity of money was made by Federal Reserve System (the Central Banks of the USA) from 1929 to 1933 which was responsible for severe depression in the American economy. They argued that the failure of the Federal Reserve to prevent bank failures and the drastic decrease in money supply during 1930-1933 increased the intensity of depression. To quote them, "The US Federal Reserve System, could have prevented the *decline of one-third* in the quantity of money that occurred from 1929 to 1933. Had it done so, the evidence indicated, the depression would have been far milder and briefer".

We thus see that Freidman and other monetarists emphasise monetary policy in causing depression. In fact, they go to the other extreme view of '***money alone matters***'. However, in our view, in recent recession during 2000-2003.the Fed Reserve System made successive cuts in rate of interest more than 7 times to revive the American economy without any success. For stimulating investment and growth, it cut the rate of interest even below 1 per cent, the lowest in the last 50 years but failed in its objective to overcome recession. Even in India Reserve Bank also lowered the bank rate, several times during 1998 – 2003 and reduced it to 6 per cent - the lowest in forty years to bring about industrial recovery but it had also not much effect. In case of the USA, the signs of recovery in the first quarter of 2003-04 seems to have been the result of drastic reduction in taxation to the extent of 3.5 billion

2. M.Friedman and Schwartz, *A Monetary History of the United States*.

dollars and huge increase in defence expenditure for war in Iraq. Both of these are fiscal policies suggested by Keynesians that seems to have worked to start a recovery in the American economy.

To conclude, in the view of present author the truth lies in between the two extreme views of Keynes and Friedman. Therefore, a majority of modern economists give importance to both fiscal and monetary policies for influencing investment and growth in GNP. Both can be complements to each other. Furthermore, profit expectations of entrepreneurs and cost and availability of credit play a significant role in determining investment national income and employment in the economy.

GLOBAL FINANCIAL CRISIS 2007-09

Burst of Sub-prime Housing Bubble : The Origin of Crisis

From the second half of 2007 in the United States a financial crisis started with a burst of housing bubble which led to widespread mortgage defaults and hence large losses to banks and other financial institutions. This crisis occurred due to sub-prime housing loans given on a large scale by the American banks in the past several years. Why did this crisis occur ? But the foundations of this crisis were laid earlier. Housing prices in the US rose higher and higher during the early 2000s. Many people found themselves incapable of buying a house because monthly mortgage payments were too high relative to their monthly incomes. However, since housing prices were rising rapidly, the borrowers thought that they would sell their houses and make profits and would again get mortgage loans. On the other hand, money lenders i.e. banks and financial institutions) in order to make profits started giving mortgage loans to the people who did not have adequate incomes to make monthly mortgage payments. Therefore, these housing loans have been called **'sub-prime housing loans'**.

These sub-prime housing loans grew rapidly in the early 2000s in the US. To cover the risks money-lending banks and other financial institutions charged higher interest rate on them. The question is why mortgage lenders gave such risky loans to sub-prime borrowers. In the words of Abel, Bernanke and Croushore, "To a large degree the answer is that they expected house prices to continue to rise rapidly for the foreseeable future. As long as house prices kept rising substantially, a borrower who might otherwise have a trouble making mortgage payments in the future could either sell the house for a profit and pay off the mortgage or could borrow against the house's equity value which would be higher as house prices increase further. So both the borrowers and lenders thought they were insulated from risk."[3]

The IT bubble burst in 2000 throwing the American economy into recession. To get the economy out of recession the US Federal Reserve cut interest rates bringing about large increase in liquidity or money supply with the banks. With cheap availability of credit, the households even with poor credit-worthiness borrowed funds from the banks to buy cars and houses. Americans went on a home buying spree. Prices of houses and real estate were rising rapidly. This rise in housing prices made both households and banks believe that their prices would continue rising. In view of low interest rates and excess liquidity with them lending for houses by banks was found to be quite attractive. As a results, banks provided housing finance even to sub-prime households, that is, households that had no capacity to pay back the loans on time.[4]

One imprudent and irresponsible financial behaviour on the parts of banks was to provide loans to households or persons who had no income and no assets. All this went on well as long as housing prices were rising. In the US in 2005 mortgage interest rates across the country began to rise that caused increase in prices of houses to slow down. Besides, the building of houses in excess

3. Andrew B. Abel, Ben Bernanke, Dean Croushore, *Macroeconomics*, 7th edition, Pearson, 2011, p. 249.
4. Niranjan Rajadhaksha, Meltdown reconstructed, *Hindustan Times*, Delhi, Oct. 2008

during the boom period led to their oversupply in the market which caused house prices to decline in 2006. But, like the IT bubble, housing bubble burst in the second half of 2007. With the fall in prices of houses which were held as mortgage the sub-prime households started defaulting on a large scale in making their installments. This caused heavy losses to the banks. With this the sub-prime housing market which had expanded on a large scale when there were soft interest rates and huge amount of liquidity with the banks tumbled. The size of this sub-prime housing market can be judged from the fact that as large as $ 1.4 trillion worth of sub-prime loans were given by the banks earlier.

Securitisation of Sub-prime Mortgage Housing Loans

But the above was not the end of the story of crisis. The banks that sold the sub-prime mortgage loans did not keep them with themselves. They sold them to other banks and investors through a financial innovation generally called CDO (collateralised debt obligations) securities which were backed by a host of mortgage assets. Therefore, CDO are also called '**Mortgage Based Securities** (MBS). Investment banks associated with Wall Street in the US repackaged the sub-prime housing mortgage loans into synthetic securities CDO that they were quite complex. To make them quite safe for investment and thereby increase their marketability they were given AAA, BBB rating by credit agencies. "*A complex financial security that has been created by mixing hundreds of thousands of independent loans can fox even the smartest investor. Specialist agencies tell investors how safe a security really is. But these credit rating agencies did not do their job well enough. All sorts of rubbish were sold as good stuff.*"[5]

The American and European intermediaries such as banks, hedge funds, pension funds, mutual funds invested heavily in these complex securities (CDO) based on sub-prime mortgage loans being unaware of the risks involved. Further problem arose from leverage. Those who bought these mortgage-backed securities *borrowed heavily* from banks and other financial institutions to make investment in them. It has been reported that some Wall Street Investment Banks had borrowed 40 times more than they were worth. This was quite dangerous and risky adventure.

Huge Losses by American Investment Banks and Liquidity Crunch

The sub-prime mortgage loans burst in 2007 when housing prices fell at the fastest rates leading to defaults in payment schedules by borrowers. As a result, the value of underlying sub-prime housing securities declined along with the prices of special complex securities, CDOs based on them. As a result, the banks and investment funds that had bought billions of dollars worth of these complex securities based on sub-prime mortgages suffered heavy losses leading to the liquidity crunch. Many securities held by them could not the valued at all inflicting heavy losses on banks. As a result of huge losses a number of banks and investment institutions including Lehman Brothers went bankrupt. The other banks and financial intermediataries such as Citi Bank came to the brink of bankruptcy and lacked liquidity. They therefore stopped giving credit to consumers and corporate companies. This led to credit crunch which adversely affected consumption demand and investment and therefore caused slowdown in economic growth. In fact in the second and third quarters of 2008 in the United States there was drop in GDP and therefore the US economy slipped into recession. Paul Krugman the winner of 2008, Novel Prize for economics writes "*The current crisis started with a burst of housing bubble which led to widespread mortgage defaults and hence to large losses at many financial institutions. The initial shock was compounded by secondary effects as lack of capital forced banks to pull back leading to further decline in the prices of assets leading to more*

5. Paul Krugman, Moment of Truth, *New York Times*, Oct. 2008

losses and soon a vicious circle of "de-leveraging". Pervasive loss of trust in banks including on the part of other banks reinforced the vicious circle"[6].

Thus, top five US investment banks which had significantly increased their financial leverage during the 2004-2007 time period increased their vulnerability to the CDO related losses. As these institutions registered mounting sub-prime losses, the financial markets panicked and liquidity was sucked out of the market, so much so that these institutions found it very difficult to raise capital to provide for the losses. The month of September 2008 eventually saw the "Top 5" of Wall Street succumbing to Sub-prime losses, with Lehman Brothers filing for chapter 11 bankruptcy, Merill Lynch being merged with Bank of America and Goldman Sachs and Morgan Stanley coverting into commercial banks, subjecting themselves to much tighter regulations. Bear Sterns had already been acquired by JP Morgan Chase in March 2008.

After the demise of the "Top 5", several other financial institutions who had large exposure to CDO faced closures or opted for hasty mergers to shore up capital. Investor confidence shrank significantly, and the credit markets around the world virtually dried up. The Federal Reserve and other central banks since then have injected substantial liquidity in the markets, either by means of lowering of interest rates or by bailing out distressed financial institutions, thus leading to nationalization of financial institutions on a large scale.

When in Aug. 2008, a very important American investment bank **Lehman Brothers** which had world-wide financial dealings and investment was allowed to go bankrupt by the US Treasury Department, it caused the world financial crisis, already severe, to get much more worse. This affected not only the confidence in the financial system of the US but also in the whole world financial structure. The redemption pressure on securities added to the liquidity problem of banks not only in the US but it spread to the banks and financial institutions of Europe, Brazil, Japan, China, India and others. The banks of other countries felt the pinch of the liquidity crisis and being risk-averse stopped providing credit to the companies which adversely affected economic growth in Europe, China and others. Recession emerged in Europe, Japan and growth in GDP in India and Japan slowed down. In September 2008, when the financial crisis gripped not only the US but also the whole world, Bush Government realised that rescue measures were needed to prevent the collapse of the financial system. It got $700 billion rescue plan passed by the American Congress to bail out the banks and other financial institutions to restore the confidence of the public. Delivering a note of warning Paul Krugman, Novel Laureate in economics wrote in early Sept. 2, 2008, "The consequences of Lehman's fall were apparent within days, yet the policy makers have largely wasted the past four weeks. *Now they have reached the moment of truth*. They would do better to do some thing soon – in fact they would better a coordinated rescue plan this weekend or the world economy may well experience its worst slump since the Great Depression".[7] In fact, the US Government delayed its rescue operations to salvage the US economy from slipping into recession by the end of 2008, GDP in the US had declined by 6.3 per cent. Not only the US but Europe and Japan also went into recession in the second and third quarters of the year 2008.

Rescue Measures Adopted in the US to Fight Crisis

It is evident from above that when there were defaults on payment of housing loans the prices of complex securities started falling. The erosion of the values of these securities dented banks' investment portfolio and led to the decline in the capital base of the banks. Many American banks

6. Paul Krugman, *op. cit.*
7. Paul Krugman "Don't cry for me, America" *New York Times*, Jan., 2008

lost heavily and called for rescue by the Government. Getting $700 billion rescue plan passed by the US Congress the US government purchased the complex and so called 'toxic' securities called CDO from the banks. This helped some banks from going bankrupt. Later the US Government also purchased the shares of some banks and financial institutions to bail them out.

Besides, *the US Government cut direct taxes* and sent refunds to the people to boost aggregate spending. However, it has been found that due to great uncertainty about future economic conditions a good part of increase in disposable income as a result of tax cut was saved by the American people and therefore tax reduction did not have the desired effect on stimulating expenditure and demand. Further, a fiscal stimulus package of $783 billion was provided by newly elected US President Barack Obama. This new package contains *increase in Government expenditure* as well as cut in taxes to boost consumption demand and investment by businesses. With the various fiscal measures of increase in public expenditure and tax cuts, fiscal deficit in the US was estimated to rise to 12.5% of GDP for the year 2009.

To overcome recession the US Federal Reserve (which is the Central Bank of the US) cut overnight interest rate to near zero so that credit becomes cheaper and more loans are provided by the US banks to businesses for investment and to consumers for buying durable consumer goods including houses. The Federal Reserve also took measures to increase money supply in the US economy so as to increase the availability of credit. However, these monetary measures did not seem to work. Due to uncertain economic environment risk-averse banks were reluctant to give loans due to the risk of defaults by the borrowers. As a result, recession in the US further depepened in the last quarter of 2008 and the earlier months of the year 2009. Therefore, in the fourth week of March 2009, a new plan of investing $ 1 trillion for buying *toxic assets* from banks that were blocking lending by banks. This plan involved public-private partnership to clean up the US banking sector to get credit flowing again. It is thought that it would clean up the banking of bad debts and restore provision of credit by them. Therefore, to end the crisis in the US, under this programme the government were provided the lion's share of the funding to purchase toxic assets to encourage private investors to participate.

Failure of Free Market System

It is evident from above that free-market economy of the United States did not work well to automatically correct the crisis that *gripped* it following burst of housing loan bubble and therefore the intervention of the Government was called for to rescue the *sagging* financial system. In this regard it is worth noting that the role played by the Federal Reserve of America and policy of unregulated free market pursued by it earlier, especially under the Chairmanship of Greenspan. Since the seventies when Reagan was the president of the United States, a policy of *complete deregulation* of market economy including its financial architecture had been followed. It is this lack of proper regulation of financial institutions, banks and stock market that led to the creation of complex and non-transparent securities (CDO).

Expressing his views about the cause of American financial crisis, Paul Krugman writes, "The real sin both of the Fed and Bush administration was the failure to exercise adult supervision over markets running wild. It was not just Alan Greenspan's unwillingness to admit that there was anything more than a lot of "froth" in housing markets or his refusal to do anything about sub-prime abuses. The fact is that as America's financial system has grown ever more complex *it has also outgrown the framework of banking regulation that used to protect us*–yet instead of an update that framework all we got were paeans to the wonders of free market."

Crash in Stock Market

The problems of liquidity and credit crunch as a result of financial crisis led to the stock market crash in the United States and Europe. Share prices of many companies tumbled which caused heavy decline in the capital value of the companies and inflicted huge losses on the investors leading to the crisis of confidence for making more investment. The crash in Wall Street hit financial firms the hardest. Even cash-rich banks were scared of lending money to other banks and to the corporate companies following failure of Lahman Brothers. Some European banks suddenly went bust leading to severe credit crunch.

Adverse Effect on Flow of Credit, Investment and Growth

As a result of erosion of capital base of banks and other financial institutions, the liquidity problem faced by them adversely affected the flow of credit to the companies for financing working capital and fixed investment and to the consumers for buying durable goods such as cars, houses etc. This affected the real economy and adversely affected economic growth in the United States and Europe. As lines of credit to corporate firms dried up in the US and Europe even for meeting their needs of working capital, it affected payments to employees and suppliers. Lack of liquidity and credit crunch also stalled the ongoing investment projects. Fears of several banks and corporate companies going bankrupt arose as several companies and banks started laying off workers. As industrial output started falling the recessionery conditions *reminiscent* of Great Depression came to prevail in the developed economies of the US and Europe. As a result of these, Japan and Asian economies could not remain unaffected.

The loss of asset value of consuming households made them poorer and along with the credit crunch led to the decrease in demand for consumer durables such as cars, houses and a host of other goods. When a few years ago there was a boom in stock market, high stock prices made them wealthier and the **wealth effect** brought about increase in consumption demand leading to consumption–led growth in the United States. Now, from the second half of 2007, when there was a drastic slide-down in share prices, the *negative wealth effect* worked to lower the demand for consumer goods and through the working of accelerator dampened investment in the economies of the US and European Countries. This caused *first slowdown in their economies and ultimately recession in the second and third quarters of 2008.*

As mentioned above, the downward spiral accelerated after the failure of Lehman Brothers in September 2008. Money markets already badly affected stopped giving credit to consumers and corporate companies. The people and the banks in the United States and Europe started investing only in Government's treasury bills which were considered as quite safe.

As mentioned above, the financial crisis spilled over to the real economy. The failure of companies to get adequate credit for working capital and fixed investment brought the growth engine to a halt in the United States. The US economy went into recession in December 2007 and this downturn continued in 2008. It is estimated that GDP of the US declined by 6.3 per cent in the last quarter of 2008, the worst in the last 28 years (that is, since 1982). For a large number of industries, the growth rate year-on-year basis fell. Many companies cut jobs and started laying off workers. As a result of recession, unemployment rate in the US rose to a high rate of 6.7 per cent in Nov. 2008 and further to 8.1 per cent in February 2009. Rate of unemployment in the US went on increasing further and cuts in jobs of several lakh persons in March to June 2009 drove the US unemployment rate to 26 years high level of 9.5 per cent in June 2009. Though in the last two quarters of 2009 the US economy recovered and registered a growth of around 3 per cent, unemployment rate still further rose to 10 per cent of labour force in Dec. 2009 worst after the depression of 1929-33. The US economy seemed to recover as it grew at 3.2 per cent year-on-year basis in the first quarter of the year

2010, while in the first quarter of the year 2009, the US economy shrank at a rate of 6.4%. In the whole year 2010, the growth of US economy had been estimated at 2.6 per cent. However, despite the recovery of the US economy in terms of GDP growth, the rate of unemployment still remained high at 9.6% of labour force in Dec. 2010.

However, the US recovery was short-lived. The rate of economic growth again slipped to 1.7 per cent in the first two quarters of the year 2011. This is despite the fact that the Federal Reserve went in for Quantity Easing 2 (QE2) under which it purchased bonds of the US Government to the extent of $600 billion in 2010-11 (upto June 2011). Besides, due to lower growth rate unemployment had stuck at 9.6 per cent of labour force. Further, in July 2011 due to **excessive *sovereign debt*** of the US S&P rating agency downgraded the US rating from AAA to AA+. This made the matters worse. Along with extremely low economic growth rate and high unemployment, this downgrading of the US rating due to excessive public debt of the US Government, gave rise to the fears of ***double-dip recession*** of the US economy which many economists predicted earlier. The emergence of the recession again, like the previous one in 2008, in the US economy had adverse effects on the global economy.

Crisis Spread to Europe and Other Countries

It is often said that "*when America sneezes, the whole world catches cold*" This has been found true in case of financial crisis too. Therefore, when all powerful US economy experienced severe financial crisis, the rest of the world could not escape from its fall-out. Due to the globalisation with its free flow of capital and goods between the US and other countries, especially the European countries which were closely integrated with the US economy, suffered a lot. In fact the surplus funds in the European countries and Japan were invested in the United States. Directly or indirectly capital flowing into America from global investors ended up financing the housing credit bubble that ultimately burst with painful consequences. Thus investors and banks of European countries and Japan suffered heavy losses and called for their being bailed out by their Governments or Central Banks. Following the cues from the crash in stock prices in Wall Street share prices in stock markets in European countries (and Asian countries including India) also crashed leading to heavy losses to the investors.

Besides, recession in the US economy affected exports of the European countries as well as of Japan and others Asian Countries (including India) to the United States leading to the decline in output of export goods in these countries with heavy job losses. This caused recessionary conditions in these countries as well.

Summing up. In 2009, the global economy not only experienced a 'great contraction', but there was also significant uncertainty about the impact of the financial crisis in the advanced economies on their real economy. The successive and large revisions in the IMF's growth outlook for 2009 indicated the extent of uncertainty that resulted from the sub-prime financial crisis. In the first quarter of 2010, stronger evidence of recovery in the global economy started to emerge, though the speed of the recovery turned increasingly divergent as the emerging market economies remained ahead of the advanced economies in terms of both pace and strength of the recovery. The global recovery turned out to be fragile subsequently, following the concerns relating to sovereign debt in the Eurozone.

Persistence of high growth in India and China largely moderated the depth of the global recession in 2009, even though these countries also experienced slowdown in growth in relation to their high growth before the onset of global crisis. World trade contracted much sharper than the contraction in GDP in 2009, and was projected to stage a recovery in 2010. Reflecting the impact of weak global demand conditions as also the protectionist measures adopted by many countries, the decline in world merchandise trade volume was as high as 11.8 per cent in 2009. According to WTO, world exports of commercial services also declined for the first time after 1983 by 13.0 per cent during 2009. The impact of recession in the advanced economies was particularly strong on the employment situation in the USA and European countries.

As a result of the crisis, net capital flows to the emerging market economies declined. Unprecedented use of policy stimulus by countries around the world helped in averting another 'Great Depression' but the fiscal conditions of the advanced economies weakened significantly in that process. In managing the financial crisis, the costs of financial excesses in the private sector shifted to the public sector creating in turn the risk of potential sovereign debt crisis.

CHAPTER 11

AD–AS Model (With Price Flexibility)

Introduction to AD-AS Model

Keynes in his theory of income and employment assumed that price level remained constant. As explained in the previous chapters, Keynes in his macroeconomic analysis used these concepts which related aggregate demand and supply to the levels of national income. Concerned as he was with the problem of an economy under the grip of depression characterised by demand deficiency and excess capacity in the economy he assumed price level to remain constant.

On the other hand, classical economists thought national output or income was determined by real factors such as capital stock, state of technology, labour supply and in no way was affected by the general price level which was determined by the quantity of money. This classical doctrine is generally referred to as **classical dichotomy**. Thus *AD-AS* model of determination of national income and employment with flexible price level highlights the breakdown of **classical dichotomy**. The aggregate demand and aggregates supply model, which is generally referred to as *AD-AS* model, is used to explain fluctuations in aggregate output, price level and rate of inflation in the economy.

In what follows we explain the concepts of aggregate demand and aggregate supply with flexible price level and analyse how the interaction between the two determines jointly the aggregate output (*i.e.* real GDP) and the general price level.

Aggregate Demand (AD)

Let us first explain aggregate demand. ***Aggregate demand** is the total desired quantity of goods and services that are bought by consumer households, private investors, government and foreigners at each possible price level, other things being held constant.* Thus aggregate demand is not any quantity demanded at a particular price level but is a whole schedule of total output demanded at various price levels and is represented by a curve. The aggregate demand has four components: consumption demand, private investment demand, Government purchases of goods and services and net exports. *Thus, aggregate demand curve depicts the total output of goods and services which households, firms, and Government are willing to buy at each possible price level.* Thus aggregate demand curve represents aggregate expenditure $C + I + G + NX$ at various price levels.

Thus aggregate demand curve shows the relationship between the total quantity demanded of goods and services and general price level. It is worth noting that aggregate demand curve (*AD*) differs from the ordinary demand curve of an individual commodity with which we are concerned in microeconomics though both slope downward to the light. In case of a demand curve of an individual commodity when price of a commodity rises, it will tend to be substituted by other commodities which are its close substitutes resulting in fall in the quantity demanded of the commodity at a higher price. Thus, the slope of demand curve of an individual commodity depends mainly on the possibility of substitution between the commodities. On the other hand, as we shall see below, the slope of aggregate demand curve depends on factors totally different from those that cause demand curve of an individual commodity to slope downward. We have drawn an *AD* curve in Figure 11.1 where on the horizontal axis we measure level of aggregate output and on the vertical axis we measure the general price level. As will be seen from Figure 11.1 aggregate demand curve *AD* slopes downward to the right.

It is important to note that the *AD-AS* model is unlike that of market demand-supply model of microeconomic theory. When we consider demand and supply in a particular market, say for cotton cloth, rise in its price will cause increase in its quantity supplied but in doing so resources will be withdrawn from other goods. Such reallocation of resources between products and consequently rise in output of one product and fall in that of the other is not considered in macroeconomics where we are concerned with determination of aggregate output, total employment of resources in the economy as a whole. Similarly, in macroecnomic model of aggregate demand and aggregate supply we study the determination of general price level and does not explain the relative prices of various products.

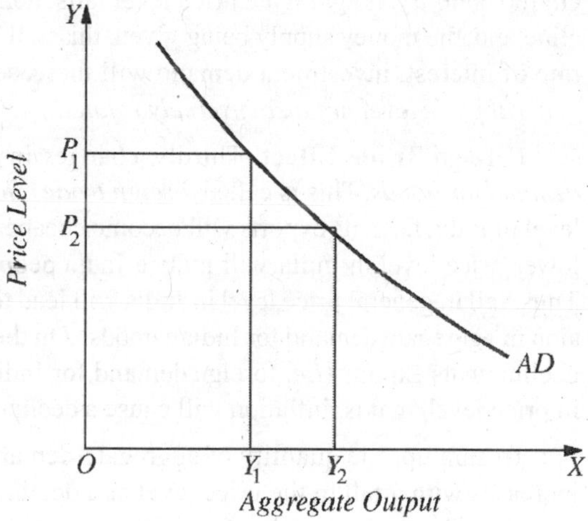

Fig. 11.1. *Aggregate Demand Curve with Varying Price Level*

In what follows we will explain in detail the concepts of aggregate demand (*AD*) and aggregate supply (*AS*) curves and their likely shape and factors determining them. We will also explain some important controversial issues of macroeconomics with this *AD-AS* model.

Why does Aggregate Demand Curve Slope Downward ?

Like the demand curve of an individual commodity, aggregate demand curve showing graphically the relationship between total spending and price levels slopes downward to the right. This means that at higher price levels, the total spending or quantity of aggregate output purchased or demanded is less and at lower price level the total spending or total purchases of aggregate output of goods is higher.

This is depicted in Figure 11.1. Aggregate output demanded per period of time is measured along the *X*-axis, and the general price level along the *Y*-axis. It should be carefully understood why aggregate demand for output or total spending falls at higher aggregate price level and increases at lower price levels, or, in other words, why aggregate demand (*AD*) curve slopes downward. The following factors are responsible for this.

Real Balance Effect. First, the changes in the general price level affect the real value or *purchasing power of money balances and monetary assets* with fixed nominal values (such as bank deposits, bonds, etc.) held by the people. With the rise in the general price level, the real value of these monetary assets will fall making people feel poorer than before. This induces them to consume less and therefore leads to the decline in quantity of output purchased by them. Conversely, if the price level falls, the real value of their monetary assets increases inducing them to buy more. This is called *real balance effect* of the change in the price level.

Rate of Interest Effect. Secondly, another important reason for the downward-sloping nature of aggregate demand curve is *the effect of change in general price level on the rate of interest and through it on investment demand.* At a higher price level, the people will require more money for conducting a given amount of transactions. This will lead to the increase in the demand for money for making transactions. Given the money supply, the increase in demand for money will cause the rate of interest to go up. *At a higher rate of interest, demand for investment in new capital goods (i.e. plant, machinery and equipment) which is a component of aggregate demand will decrease.* On the contrary, if aggregate price level falls, demand for money for transaction purposes will decline and, the money supply being given, this will lead to the fall in the rate of interest. At the lower rate of interest, investment demand will increase. To conclude, *the investment demand and the general price level are also inversely related.*

Foreign Trade Effect. Thirdly, changes in the price level also causes a change in *foreign demand for goods*. This is called *foreign trade effect of the change in price level*. If a general price level in India falls, its exports will become cheaper leading to their increase. On the other hand, the lower price level in India will induce India people to buy India goods instead of imported ones. Thus, fall in general price level in India will lead to more exports and lesser imports causing expansion in aggregate demand for Indian goods. On the contrary, a rise in price level in India will lead to decline in its exports (*i.e.* foreign demand for Indian goods) and increase in its imports. Thus, rise in price level, that is, inflation will cause a decline in net exports.

To sum up, the quantity of aggregate demand for consumption, investment and net exports increases with a fall in the price level and declines with a rise in the price level. This means that aggregate demand curve showing relationship between aggregate output demanded and the general price level slopes downward to the right as is shown in Figure 11.1.

Shift in Aggregate Demand Curve and Multiplier Effect

As in microeconomic analysis of demand, it is important to know the factors that cause a shift in aggregate demand curve. As seen above, an aggregate demand curve depicts relation between aggregate expenditure ($C + I + G + NX$) and changes in price level. Now, *when some factors other than the price level change which cause changes in aggregate expenditure*, they will cause a shift in aggregate demand curve, that is, there will be increase or decrease in aggregate output demanded *at every price level*. In our analysis of aggregate demand curve, we explained the changes in aggregate expenditure and hence aggregate output demanded resulting from changes in price level. In our above analysis of aggregate demand curve *we considered Government expenditure (G), taxation (I), investment (I) and money supply (M) constant as they were treated as autonomous of changes in price level* (and induced changes in the rate of interest). *When these non-price factors change, aggregate demand curve will shift*. These factors are changes in expectations regarding future income by consumers or changes in expectations of future profits by investors leading to the increase in consumption demand (C) or investment demand (I) respectively. These will cause *increase in aggregate output demanded at any given price level* shifting aggregate demand curve to the right. Similarly, if government adopts expansionary fiscal policy and increases its expenditure (G), it will also cause more quantity of goods and services demanded at any given price level shifting the aggregate demand curve to the right as shown in Figure 11.2. For example, suppose Government expenditure increases by ΔG, this will raise aggregate expenditure curve upward. As a result, equilibrium level of aggregate output will increase at the given price level. This means rightward shift in aggregate demand curve at the given price level.

Similarly, *increase in money supply* (M) will cause a rightward shift in aggregate demand curve. In the derivation of a given aggregate demand curve, money supply in the economy is held constant. If, at a given price level, money supply is increased, the interest rate will fall. The fall in interest rate will cause investment demand to increase. Aggregate output demanded will thus be greater at any given price level. Thus, expansion in money supply brings about shift in aggregate demand curve to the right.

Likewise, changes in foreign demand for our goods and our demand curve for imported goods, which we have so far not included in our analysis, also influence aggregate demand of the economy. For example, if foreign exchange rate of rupee falls, that is, if rupee depreciates against US dollar, this will encourage our export and discourage our imports and will lead to the increase in net exports (*NX*) and will therefore lead to the shift in aggregate demand curve to the right.

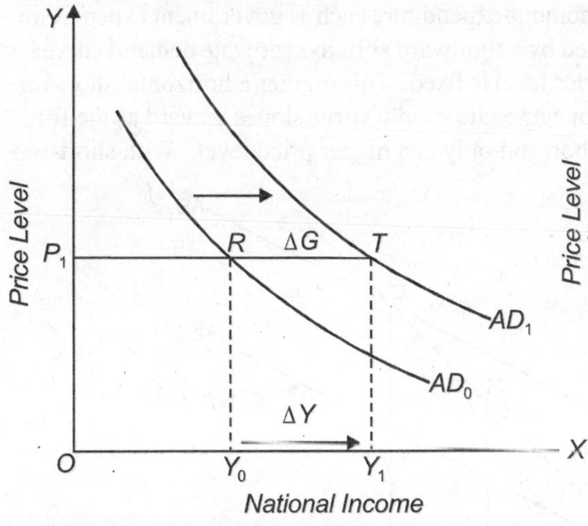

Fig. 11.2. *Shift in Aggregate Demand Curve*

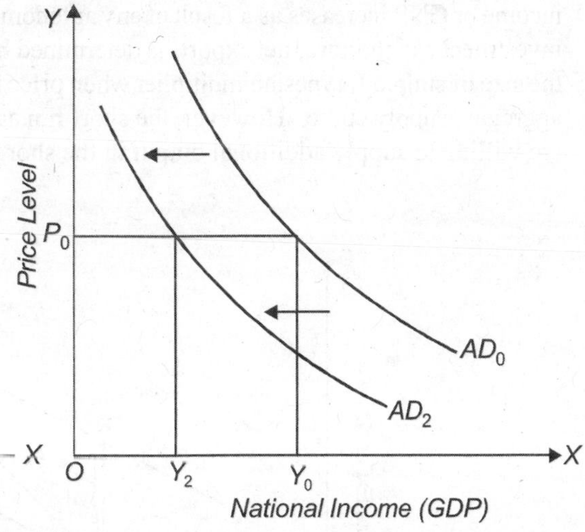

Fig. 11.3. *Shift in AD curve to the Left to the right*

In Figure 11.2 we have depicted the shift in aggregate demand curve to the right from AD_0 to AD_1 which might have taken place as a result of any of the non-price factors determining aggregate demand. It will be seen from Figure 11.2 that with rightward shift in aggregate demand curve from AD_0 to AD_1, aggregate quantity demanded of goods and services at the given price P_0, increases from Y_0 to Y_1.

Leftward Shift in Aggregate Demand. On the other hand, when expectations of investors and consumers regarding their future profits or income decline as they have become more pessimistic or if government contractionary fiscal policy to control inflation reduces its expenditure on goods and services and transfer payments aggregate demand curve will shift to the left so that at any given price level less aggregate quantity of goods and services will be demanded. Likewise, if Reserve Bank adopts tight monetary policy to check inflation and therefore contracts money supply or raises its interest rate, it will also cause shift in aggregate demand curve to the left. This is shown in Figure 11.3 where as a result of autonomous decrease in investment or consumption or decrease in government expenditure by government or reduction in money supply and increase in interest rate causes a leftward shift in aggregate demand curve from AD_0 to AD_2 so that at any given price, say P_0, smaller aggregate quantity of goods and services is demanded

Keynesian Multiplier effect

It will be recalled, as explained by Keynes, that increase in Government expenditure or investment has a multiplier effect on aggregate output depending on the size of multiplier. In our Figure 11.2 increase in Government expenditure by ΔG equal to RT has caused aggregate output to increase by Y_0Y_1. Thus the increase of Y_0Y_1 in *GNP* or increase in aggregate output demanded *RT* is given by

$$\Delta Y = Y_0Y_1 = \Delta G \frac{1}{1-mpc}$$

where *mpc* is the marginal propensity to consume and $\frac{1}{1-mpc}$ is the value of Keynesian multiplier. As in case of increase in Government expenditure, *reduction in taxes* will also increase aggregate output demanded at each price level and will therefore cause a rightward shift in aggregate demand curve.

Multiplier Effect with Changes in Price Level

In our above analysis of multiplier with aggregate demand curve, it is assumed that price level remains constant and the firms are willing to supply more output at a given price. How much national income or GNP increases as a result of any autonomous expenditure such as government expenditure, investment expenditure, net exports is determined by a rightward shift in aggregate demand curve by the size of simple Keynesian multiplier when price level is fixed. This implies a horizontal short-run aggregate supply curve. However, the short-run aggregate supply curve slopes upward as the firms are willing to supply additional output in the short run only at a higher price level. With short-run

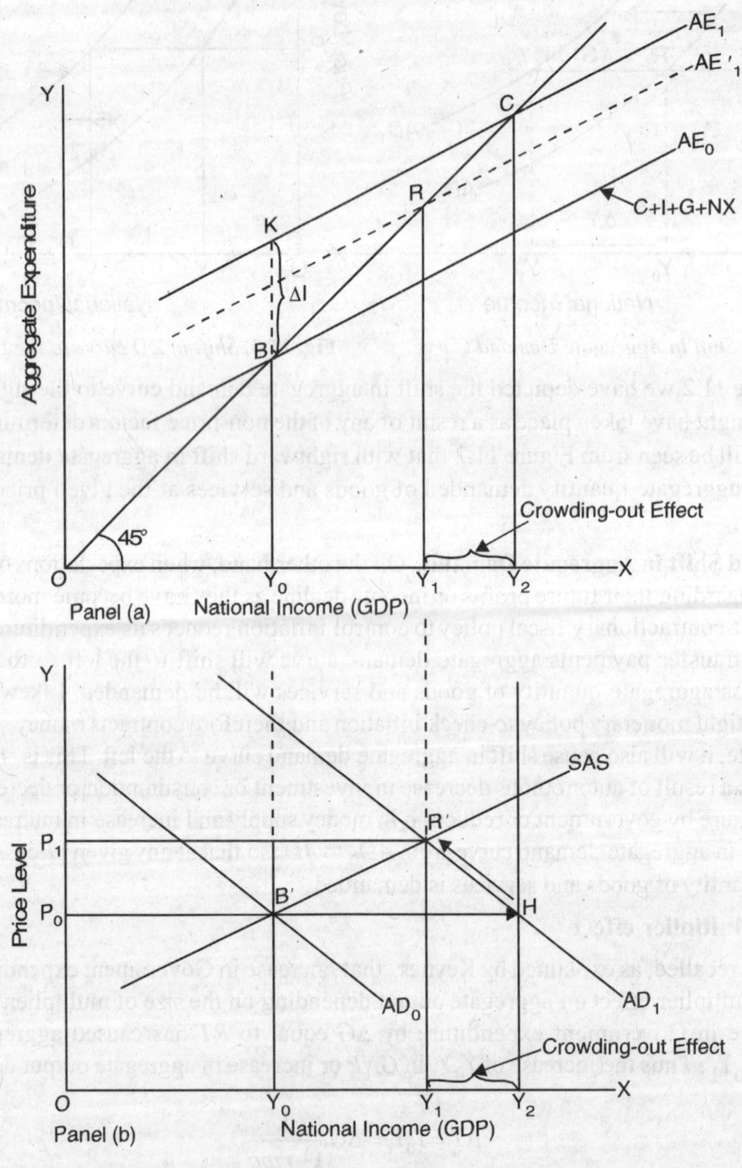

Fig. 11.4. *Multiplier Effect with Changes in Price Level*

aggregate supply curve sloping upward, a rightward shift in aggregate demand curve raises new equilibrium GNP level not equal to the horizontal shift in the aggregate demand curve but less than this. Consequently, the size of multiplier is smaller than that of simple Keynesian multiplier with a given fixed price level. This is because a part of expansionary effect of GNP of the increase in autonomous government expenditure is offset by rise in the price level.

The multiplier effect in case of upward-sloping short-run aggregate supply curve is shown in Fig. 11.4. To begin with, in the top panel of Fig. 11.4 aggregate expenditure curve AE_0 intersects 45° line at point B and determines Y_0 equilibrium level of GNP. In the panel at the bottom of Fig. 11.4 the corresponding aggregate demand curve AD_0 and the short-run aggregate supply curve SAS intersect at B' at the above determined GNP level Y_0. Now, suppose *autonomous investment expenditure* (which is independent of changes in income level) increases by ΔI. As a result, in the upper panel (a) of Fig. 121.4, aggregate expenditure curve AE shifts upward to AE_1 and determines new equilibrium GNP level equal to Y_2. In the lower panel (*b*), due to the upward shift in aggregate expenditure curve, aggregate demand curve shifts rightward from AD_0 to AD_1. The *horizontal shift* in the aggregate demand curve *at a given price level* is determined by the investment in aggregate expenditure multiplied by the simple Keynesian multiplier at the given fixed price level ($B'H$ or $\Delta Y = \Delta I \dfrac{1}{1-MPC}$)

But given the upward-sloping short-un aggregate supply curve SAS with new aggregate demand curve AD_1, price level does not remain fixed. As will be seen from the lower panel (*b*) of Fig. 11.4, the aggregate demand curve AD_1 intersects the short-run aggregate supply curve SAS at point R' and as a result price level rises to P_1.

Now, with this rise in price level to P_1, aggregate expenditure curve in the upper panel (*a*) will not remain unaffected but will shift downward. This fall in aggregate expenditure curve is due to the adverse effects of rise in price level on wealth or real balances, interest rate and net exports. Much of wealth is held in the form of bank deposits, bonds and shares of companies and other assets. With the rise in price level, *real value or purchasing power* of wealth possessed by the people declines. This induces them to spend less. As a result, consumption expenditure declines due to this wealth effect. Secondly, the rise in price level *reduces the supply of real money balances* (M^s / P) that causes a shift in money supply curve to the left. Given the demand function for money (M^d), the decline in the real money supply will cause rate of interest to rise. Now, the rise in interest rate will induce private investment expenditure to decline. Lastly, rise in price level in the domestic economy will adversely affect exports of a country causing net exports to fall,

Thus, as a result of negative effects of rise in price level on real wealth, private investment and net exports, in the upper panel (*a*) of Fig. 11.4 aggregate expenditure curve shifts downward to AE_1' (dotted) so that it determines GDP level Y_1 corresponding to the intersection of aggregate demand curve AD_1 and short-run aggregate supply curve SAS point R' in the lower panel (*b*) of this Fig. 11.4.

Thus with the upward-sloping short-run-aggregate supply curve SAS, the effect of increase in autonomous investment expenditure (or for that matter increase in any other autonomous expenditure such as Government expenditure, net exports, autonomous consumption) on the GDP level can be visualised to occur in two stages. First, increase in investment expenditure shifts aggregate expenditure curve AE upward in the upper panel (*a*) of Fig. 11.4 and correspondingly aggregate demand curve in the lower panel (*b*) shifts to the right to AD_1 and brings about increase in GDP level from Y_0 to Y_2 with the given fixed price level P_0. In the second stage due to the upward sloping short-run aggregate supply curve SAS, the rightward shift in the aggregate demand curve causes price level to rise from P_0 to P_1 and causes decrease in GDP from Y_2 to Y_1.

However, as shall be seen from Fig. 11.4, when price level effect is taken into account, the increase in autonomous investment expenditure has still a multiplier effect on real GDP but this effect is smaller than it would be if price level remained fixed. It may *be further noted that steeper the slope of the short-run supply curve, the greater is the increase in the price level and smaller is the multiplier effect of increase in autonomous investment on real GDP*.

AGGREGATE SUPPLY

We will now explain the concept of aggregate supply with flexible price level. Aggregate supply is the total output of goods and services that firms want to produce at each possible price level. Thus, like aggregate demand, aggregate supply is the whole schedule of total quantities of aggregate output that firms in the economy are willing to produce at each possible price level and is represented by an aggregate supply curve. It is worth noting that aggregate supply is the outcome of the decisions of all producers in the economy to hire workers and buy other inputs for production of goods and services for selling them to consumers, other producers, government as well as for exporting them to other countries. It may be noted that while drawing aggregate supply curve that depicts the quantities of aggregate output that are produced for sale in the market by all firms in the economy at various price levels, all other factors that affect aggregate supply are held constant.

Aggregate Supply Curve

In the model of determination of general price level, the concept of aggregate supply curve which relates aggregate supply of output with price level is used. In this sense, *aggregate supply curve shows the various amounts of aggregate output which the producers in the economy are willing to produce and sell in the market at various price levels*. There is a lot of disagreement among economists about the shape of aggregate supply curve. The classical economists assumed that normally there prevailed full-employment of resources in the economy. According to them, if at any time there is deviation from this full-employment level, the wages, interest and prices quickly and automatically adjust or change to restore equilibrium at the full-employment level. Thus, in the classical theory, the aggregate supply curve of output is perfectly inelastic (*i.e.* a vertical straight line) at the output level corresponding to full-employment level of resources. This aggregate supply curve relating aggregate supply with price level of the classical theory of income and employment is shown in Figure 11.5. by *AS* curve.

As mentioned above, Keynes considered the situation of economic depression when the economy was operating below the level of full-employment of resources. He further believed that in such a situation money wage rates were sticky *i.e.* remain constant. He further assumed that average and margined products of labour remain constant when more of it is employed following the increase in aggregate demand. *With these assumptions, in Keynes's theory more aggregate output is produced and supplied at the given price level in response to increase in aggregate demand.* But when full employment of labour and capital stock is attained and aggregate demand further increases, aggregate supply of output being unable to increase any more, it is the price level that will rise in response to the increase in aggregate demand. The Keynes's aggregate supply curve depicting the relationship between price level and the aggregate production (supply) *during the period of depression and involuntary unemployment* when there is a lot of excess capacity in the economy is shown in Figure 11.6 where it will be seen that aggregate supply is a horizontal straight line (*i.e.* perfectly elastic) up to the level of full employment showing thereby that in response to increase in aggregate demand more is produced and supplied at the same price level *OP*. Since output of goods and services cannot be increased beyond the full-employment level, Keynes's aggregate supply curve becomes vertical at the aggregate output level Y_F which represents full-employment level of output.

It may however be noted that Keynes recoganised that as aggregate supply approaches close to the full-employment level the cost of output per unit tends to rise due to the rise in wage rate and also due to diminishing returns to extra factors employed. But, according to Keynes, the rise in price level before full employment or less than capacity output (*i.e.*, potential GDP) will not be much.

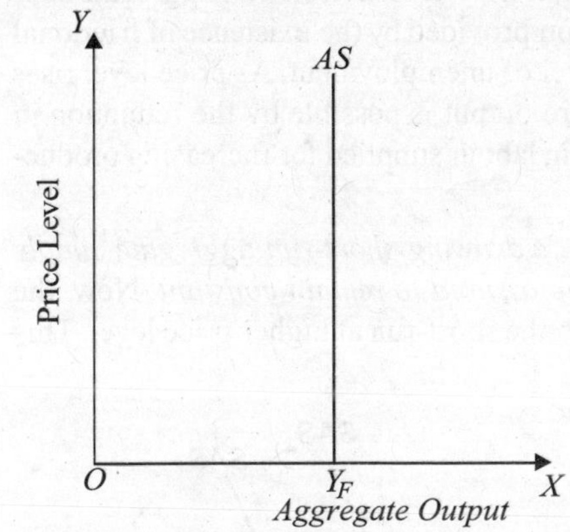

Fig. 11.5. *Aggregate Supply Curve : Classical View*

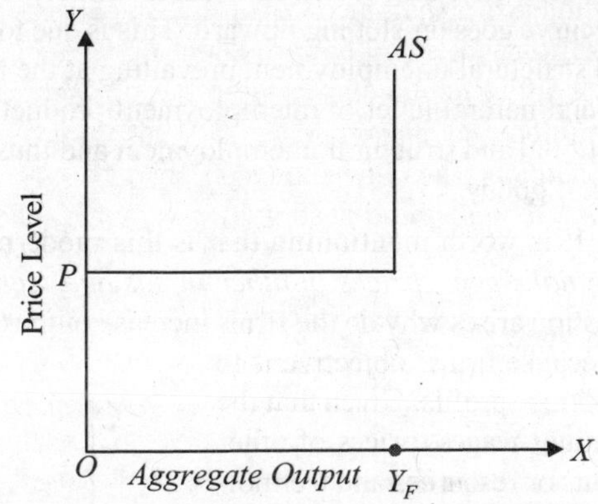

Fig. 11.6. *Keynes's Original Aggregate Supply Curve*

It is evident from above that shape of aggregate supply curve is a highly controversial issue. As mentioned above, aggregate supply curve indicates the total output which the producers are willing and able to sell at different price levels. It is important to note that as the average price level rises above the current marginal cost of production, producers find it profitable to expand output. When the economy is working substantially below capacity, that is, at times of depression or severe recession, the more can be produced without much rise in marginal cost of production and therefore the short-run aggregate supply curve is nearly flat. With the given stock of capital (*i.e.* plant and equipment) when output is expanded the diminishing returns and rising marginal costs occur which ultimately cause the short-run aggregate supply curve to slope upward gently. But as the firms in the economy approach near their capacity output their marginal costs sharply rise which causes sharply rising aggregate supply curve . Keynes however thought that at *the level of capacity output*, that is, when the given resources of the economy are fully employed, aggregate supply curve (*AS*) becomes a vertical straight line as classical economists assumed.

Short-Aggregate Supply Curve (SAS) : Modern View

The modern economists distinguish between aggregate short-run aggregate supply curve and long-run aggregate supply curve. Long-run aggregate supply curve (LAS) is vertical drawn at the level of *potential GDP* at which there prevails natural rate of unemployment, (consisting of only frictional and structural unemployment). The natural rate of unemployment represents full-employment level of employment as at it cyclical or demand-deficiency unemployment does not exist. We will explain long-run aggregate supply curve in detail later. At present we confine ourselves to explain the short-run aggregate supply curve. *The short-run aggregate supply curve depicts how much output business firms are willing to produce at different price levels* in the short run. Short-run aggregate supply curve can have different possible shapes. As seen above, Keynes who considered the short-run aggregate supply at times when the economy was in recession or depression assumed that due to the existence of excess productive capacity and large-scale unemployment of labour as firms expand output in response to increase in aggregate demand the price remained fixed. Therefore, as explained above, Keynes's aggregate supply curve is a horizontal straight line up to the level of full-employment level of output. He assumed that beyond full-employment level output cannot be increased and, therefore, at full-employment level aggregate supply curve becomes vertical straight line as shown in Figure 11.6.

However, the view of modern economists about short-run aggregate supply is different from that of Keynes. According to them, short aggregate supply curve slopes upward showing that business firms produce more as price level rises. An important thing to note is that, according to the modern concept of short-run aggregate supply curve (*SAS*), even after natural level of unemployment (which is also called full-employment level or potential GDP level), short-run aggregate supply curve goes on sloping upward. This is due to the cushion provided by the existence of frictional and structural unemployment prevailing at the natural level of unemployment. As price level rises beyond natural level of unemployment production of more output is possible by the reduction in frictional and structural unemployment and thus increase in labour supplied for increasing production of goods.

It is worth mentioning that is this modern view, *while drawing short-run aggregate supply nominal wages, prices of other inputs and technology are assured to remain constant*. Now, the question arises why do the firms increase output of goods in the short-run at higher price level. This is because firms' objective is to maximise profits. Given that the nominal wages, prices of other inputs or resources and technology remain constant, higher price level will yield more profits to them. This motivates them to produce more in the short at higher price level. The short-run aggregate supply is drawn in Figure 11.7. Suppose Y_F is natural level of unemployment at which only frictional and structural unemployments exist. To the left of Y_F, the economy will be in recession. At price level P_1, aggregate output Y_1 is being produced, Now suppose price level rises to P_2, nominal wages, prices of other inputs, state of technology remaining unchanged (which implies cost per unit of output remain the same), firms in order to increase their profits employ more labour and other resources to produce more output. Thus, at a higher price level P_2 aggregate output will increase to Y_F by employing more labour and other resources. At aggregate output level Y_F cyclical or demand-deficiency unemployment will be removed and only frictional and structural unemployment will exist. Now, if price level further rises to P_3, the firms will produce more output Y_2, nominal wage rate and prices of other resources remaining constant, it will be profitable to do so. Contrary to the Keynes' view, according to present thinking of the economists, aggregate output can be increased even beyond the natural level of unemployment by employing more labour made possible by reduction in frictional and structural unemployments. *By joining points A, B and C we get and upward-sloping short-run aggregate supply curve* SAS_1 in Figure 11.7.

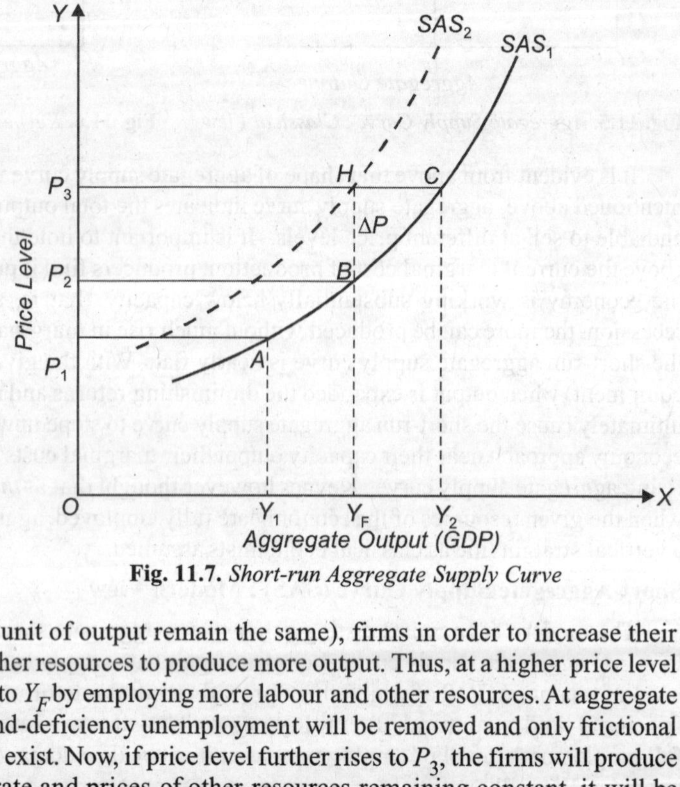

Fig. 11.7. *Short-run Aggregate Supply Curve*

It is worth noting that as we move along the short-run aggregate supply curve (SAS_1) *though nominal* (*money*) *wage* rate remains constant, *real* wage rate falls as price level rises. Note that real wage rate (which represents purchasing power of money) is nominal wage rate (W) divided by the price level (P), that is, $\frac{W}{P}$. Thus, at natural unemployment level Y_F, real wage rate is $\frac{W}{P_2}$ and when aggregate output increases to Y_2, real wage rate falls to $\frac{W}{P_3}$ as price level P_3 is higher than P_2 by $P_2 P_3$. Money wage rate may remain constant for some time but after this workers will realise that their real wage rate has fallen. They would therefore demand higher wages to restore their real wages at the previous level. As starting from natural unemployment level Y_F to the aggregate output level Y_2, price has risen by P_2P_3, to restore their real wages, money wage rate must be increased by $P_2 P_3$ (= *BH*). As a result, short-run aggregate supply shifts upward to the left to new position SAS_2. We will explain below in detail the factors that cause shift is the short-run supply curve.

Shifts in Short-run Aggregate Supply Curve

In explaining the upward-sloping nature of short-run aggregate supply we stated that aggregate supply curve depicts the relationship between price level and aggregate output (i.e. real GDP), *other factors* such as money wages, input prices, technology and indirect taxes that determine aggregate supply being held constant. Now, it is the *changes in these other determining factors* that cause a *shift* in the aggregate supply curve. We explain below the various factors that cause a shift in aggregate supply curve.

Changes in Nominal Wage Rate. As explained above, change in nominal wage rate of workers is an important factor that causes a shift in short-run aggregate supply curve. For example, when wage rate of workers increases, they cause a leftward shift in short-run aggregate supply curve. This is because increase in money wages raises cost per unit of output. With a given price of output, higher money wage rate means profit per unit of output will decline. As production becomes less profitable, it is likely that the firms will cut back on production and supply less output. Thus, when money wage rate of workers increases, it causes a leftward shift in short-run aggregate supply curve as shown in Fig. 11.8.

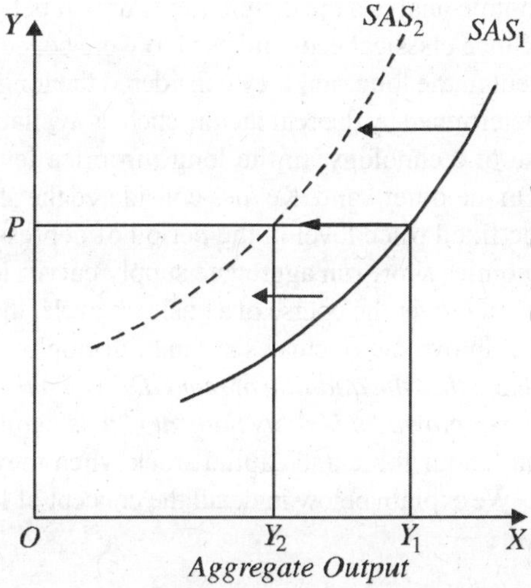

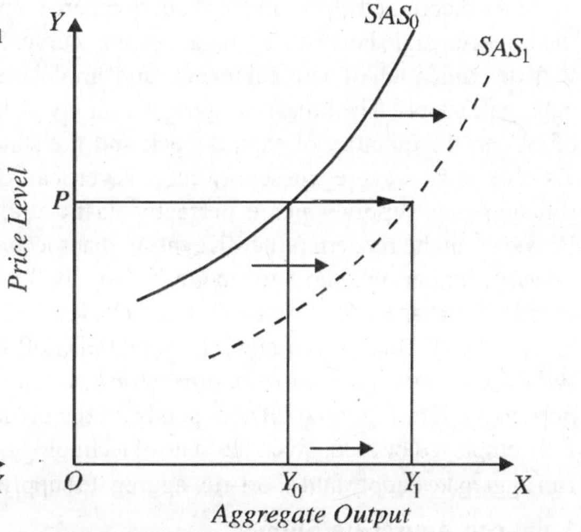

Fig. 11.8. *Leftward Shift in Aggregate Supply Curve* **Fig. 11.9.** *Rightward Shift in Aggregate Supply Curve*

Prices of Inputs. Changes in prices of other inputs such as energy (for example, crude oil) and raw materials also bring about a shift in short-run aggregate supply curve. It is well known that increase in price of crude oil by OPEC in 1973 and again in 1979 affected aggregate supply by raising cost per unit of production. This causes a leftward shift in short-run aggregate supply curve as shown in Fig. 11.8. This *leftward shift* in the aggregate supply curve implies that at any given price level less output is supplied than before.

On the other hand, when price of crude oil falls as has happened at several occasions in the past, aggregate supply curve shifts to the right as is shown Fig. 11.9 indicating that at any given price level more output will be produced and supplied than before.

Change in Technology. The change in technology is another important factor that causes a shift in aggregate supply curve. When there is improvement in technology, productivity of factors rises causing a fall in the unit cost of production. This brings about a rightward shift in aggregate supply curve (as depicted in Fig. 11.9) showing that at any given price level more will be produced and supplied than before.

Business Taxes and Subsidies. Increase in rates of business taxes such as excise duty, sales tax, customs duties raises per unit cost of production just as rise in wage rate. (Note that an indirect tax is considered as cost of production as it raises the supply price of output). Thus, by levying business taxes or increasing their rates causes a leftward shift in the aggregate supply curve. On the other hand, lowering of indirect taxes such as excise duty as happened during the recent global slowdown (2008-09), caused by bursting of sub-prime housing loans bubble in the United States, causes a shift in the aggregate supply curve to the right. Provision of subsidies on products of various industries also causes a shift in the aggregate supply curve to the right.

Available Supply of Resources. Lastly, a very important factor determining the position of aggregate supply curve is the available quantity of resources. When the available supplies of resources such as labour and capital increase, the short-run aggregate supply curve will shift to the right. As labour force grows and supply of capital is increased through investment, the short-run short-run aggregate supply curve will shift to the right implying that more output will be produced for sale at any given price level. Similarly, expansion in infrastructure facilities leads to the increase in supply of output and causes a rightward shift in aggregate supply curve.

LONG-RUN AGGREGATE SUPPLY CURVE

As mentioned above in the modern macroeconomic analysis the distinction is drawn between the long-run and short-run aggregate supply curve. Since classical economists who were concerned with determination of national income and employment in the long run, they considered the long-run aggregate supply. The long-run aggregate supply is determined by the real factors such as availability of labour, the quantity of capital stock and the state of technology. In the long run price level is variable and the aggregate supply curve is vertical. On the other hand, Keynes considered the short-run aggregate supply which is perfectly elastic at the fixed price level in the period of depression. However, in the modern or new Keynsian macroeconomics short-run aggregate supply curve slopes upward. Further, this short-run aggregate supply fluctuates over the course of a business cycle, that is, in different phases of the business cycle. The level of employment fluctuates around full employment level and GDP fluctuates around the potential GDP. Note *that the quantity of real GDP when there is full employment of labour or in other words, when unemployment is at its natural rate is known as* ***potential GDP***. Potential GDP depends on the given labour force and capital stock when they are fully employed or used, given the state of technology. We explain below in detail the concept of long-run aggregate supply and short-run aggregate supply.

Long-run Aggregate Supply

The long-run aggregate supply of output or real GDP depends on three important factors : (1) the quantity of available labour, (2) the stock of capital, and (3) the state of technology. The aggregate production function which describes the influence of these three factors is written as :

$$Y = F(L, K, T)$$

Where Y is the quantity of aggregate output or real GDP, L is the quantity of labour, K is the stock of capital and T is the state of technology. At any given time, the stock of capital and state of technology are given and fixed. Though at any time population of a country is fixed but the quantity of labour is variable; it depends on the preferences between work and leisure of the people on the one hand and the decisions of the firms about the demand for labour on the other. People supply labour only if wage rate which is reward for their work effort is sufficient to overcome their preference for leisure. The higher the wage rate, the greater is the quantity of labour supplied. On the other hand, the firms demand labour if it is profitable to use it for production. The lower the wage rate, which is the cost of labour, the greater is the quantity of labour used. The equilibrium wage rate and the quantity of labour employed are determined by labour market equilibrium. The labour market is in equilibrium at the wage rate at which the quantity of labour demanded equals the quantity of labour supplied. *At this equilibrium wage rate, all those who are willing to supply their labour are in fact demanded and employed. Therefore, at this equilibrium wage rate, full employment of labour is said to prevail.*

However, even at full employment, there are always some workers searching for jobs and some firms are looking for workers to offer them employment. This is because of two factors, frictional and structural. Every week some workers leave their old jobs and search for new better jobs more suited to their skills and ability. But due to lack of information, it takes time to find the new jobs even though they are available. This represents what is called *frictional unemployment*. Second, every week or month some industries are declining due to changes in technology or preferences of the people for goods while others are expanding. In this case while some people are laid off from the declining industries but sometime is required before they acquire new skills and training needed for employment in the expanding industries. Therefore, for some time they remain unemployed though job vacancies for them exist. This second type of unemployment is called *structural unemployment.*

Thus, at any time some frictional and structural unemployment inevitably exist in a free-market economy. Therefore, in modern macroeconomics, the amount of frictional and structural unemployment is called the *natural rate of unemployment.* Around 4 to 5 per cent of labour force in the developed free-market economies represents the natural rate of unemployment. And full employment is said to exist despite the existence of frictional and structural unemployment. As mentioned above, the *quantity of real GDP produced and supplied when there is full employment (that is, when there exists only natural rate of unemployment) is called potential GDP*. It may be noted again that potential GDP depends on full employment of labour, the full use of the existing stock of capital and the available technology.

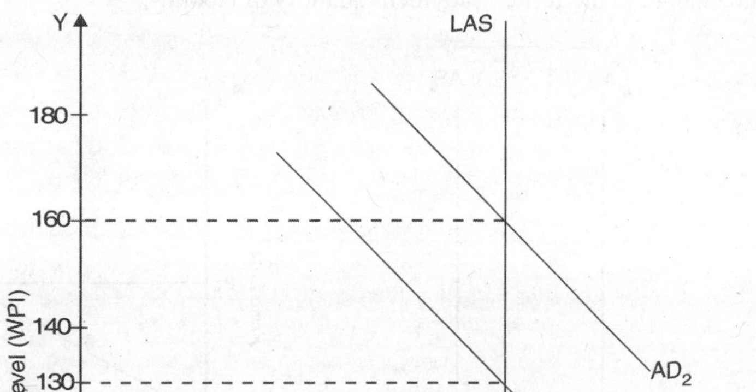

Figure 11.10. *Long-Run Aggregate Supply Curve*

The long-run aggregate supply describes the relationship between the quantity of real GDP and the price level in the long run when real GDP equals potential GDP. The long-run aggregate supply curve is a vertical line (at potential GDP level) as shown by *LAS* in Figure 11.10. *The long-run aggregate supply is vertical because potential GDP does not vary with price level, that is, it is independent of the price level.* For example, when aggregate demand curve is AD_2, price level (WPI) is at 160 and when aggregate demand falls and aggregate demand curve shifts to the left to AD_1 and determines price level (WPI) equal to 130, aggregate output remains unchanged at potential GDP equal to $\overline{Y}$. *The reason for the independence of potential GDP from the price level is that the movement along the long-run aggregate supply curve involves not only the change in price level of goods but also prices of factor inputs such as wages of labour etc.* For example, when there is 5 per cent decrease in the prices of goods and services, this is matched by the same (*i.e.* 5 per cent) decline in wage rate and other factor prices so that relative prices and real wage rate remain unchanged. This explains why it is profitable to produce the same quantity of real GDP at lower price level of goods and services. When price level of goods and services falls, the cost also falls as wage rate and other factor prices fall by the same percentage. Therefore, aggregate supply of output (*i.e.* real GDP) in the long run also remains constant at potential GDP level.

It is evident from above that long-run aggregate supply curve is the same as the classical aggregate supply curve.

Changes or Shifts in Long-run Aggregate Supply Curve

We have seen above that long-run aggregate supply curve is a vertical straight line at the level of potential GDP. Changes in price level bring about a movement along the long-run aggregate supply but the quantity of aggregate supply remains fixed at the level of potential GDP. *It is changes in potential GDP that causes a shift in the long-run aggregate supply curve.* The following factors cause a change in potential GDP resulting in a shift in the long-run aggregate supply curve :

1. The change in the full-employment quantity of labour.

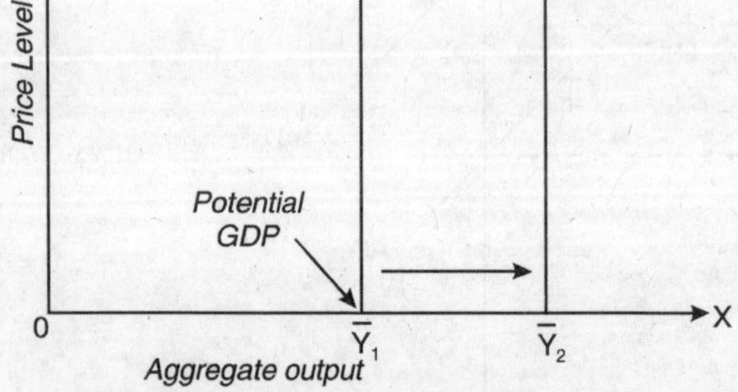

Fig. 11.11. *Increase in Labour Force, Capital Stock and Progress in Technology increase potential GDP and shifts LAS curve to the right.*

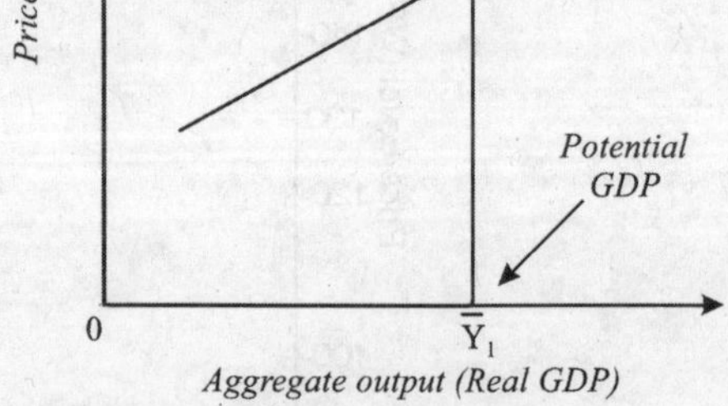

Figure 11.12. *Short-run Aggregate Supply Curve along with Long-run Aggregate Supply Curve*

2. Change in the stock of capital.
3. Progress in technology.

Increase in Labour Force. Labour is an important resource of production. Over time, given the capital stock and the state of technology, potential GDP will increase as full-employment quantity of labour force increases. Therefore, the increase in the full-employment quantity of labour force causes a shift in the long-run aggregate supply curve to the right as shown in Figure 11.11. It may be noted that changes in labour employment over the business cycle cause fluctuations in real GDP. But these changes in real GDP that take place over the business cycle are not changes in potential GDP. As mentioned above, changes in potential GDP occur due to changes in labour force and stock of capital, and improvement in technology.

Growth in the Stock of Capital The stock of capital in an economy determines the productive capacity of the economy. The larger the stock of capital in the economy, the more productive is the labour force of the economy and the greater is its potential GDP. The higher per capita output and potential GDP of the American economy as compared to those of the Indian economy are mainly due to the greater stock of capital in the United States. Note that in the capital stock the modern economists include not only physical capital but also human capital. Human capital means the acquired skills, education and training of the workers. Like the increase in labour force, growth in capital stock also brings about increase in potential GDP and causes a shift in the long-run aggregate supply curve (*LAS*) to the right.

Progress in Technology. Progress in technology enables firms to produce more from the given resources. Empirical research studies have shown that technological progress is by far the most important source of increase in GDP over the past two centuries. It is due to advances in technology that a modern worker, both in industry and agriculture, produces many times more output than the worker in the olden times. Thus, even with the fixed quantities of labour and capital, progress in technology raises potential GDP and causes in shift in the long-run aggregate supply curve to the right.

Change in Money Wages and Other Resource Prices. It is worthwhile to note that changes in money wages and other factor prices such as *the price of oil affect the short-run aggregates supply curve but do not affect the long-run aggregate supply curve*. This is because along the long-run aggregate supply curve any change in the money wage rate or other resource prices bring about an equal percentage change in the price level so that *relative prices* and *real* wage rate remain constant. Since the relative prices remain the same, the firms do not have any incentive to increase or reduce their production and therefore potential GDP and long-run aggregate supply curve remains constant. However, *changes in money wage rate and other resource prices affect firms' cost of production and therefore cause a shift in short-run aggregate supply curve*. For example, when money wage rate and other resource prices rise, firms' costs go up and therefore they will be willing to supply smaller quantity of output at each price level. As a result, short-run aggregate supply curve shifts to the left.

Relation of Short-Run Aggregate Supply Curve with Long-Run Aggregate Supply Curve

In macroeconomics short run is defined as the period during which aggregate output has fallen either below potential GDP or has risen above potential GDP. Accordingly, in the short run, the rate of unemployment either increases above the natural rate of unemployment or falls below the natural rate of unemployment. Thus, short-run aggregate supply curve describes the relationship between the aggregate output (*i.e.* real GDP) produced and the price level in the short run when money wage rate and other factor prices remain constant. The *short-run aggregate supply curve (SAS) slopes upward to the right and intersects the long-run aggregate supply curve at the current and expected price level*. Consider Figure 11.12. If the current and expected price level is P_1, then on this basis the contracts about wage rate and other resource prices would have been made. Therefore, the short-run aggregate supply curve will intersect the vertical long-run aggregate supply curve (LAS) at the current and expected price level. Now, if the actual price level rises, wages and other factor prices remaining constant, it will become profitable for the firms to expand production resulting in the increase in short-run aggregate supply of output. With this, the real GDP will increase beyond potential GDP and the economy will move rightward along the short-run aggregate supply curve *SAS* in Fig. 11.12. On the other hand, with the current long-run price equal to P_1, if price level falls, wages **and** other resource prices remaining the same, the firms will not be able to cover the higher marginal costs of producing a larger output $\bar{Y}_1$ and will therefore cut back on production. As a result, the economy will move leftward along the short-run aggregate supply curve *SAS*. With this, real GDP falls below the potential GDP level.

It is evident from above why short-run aggregate supply curve (*SAS*) slopes upward. The firms produce the output that maximises profits and if the price level of goods and services rises while the wage rate and other resource costs per unit remain the same, it pays the firms to expand production. Thus more real GDP is produced and supplied at a higher price level.

Let us briefly distinguish between the movement along the short-run aggregate supply curve (*SAS*) and the movement along the long-run aggregate supply curve (*LAS*). When price level rises, with money wage rate and other resource prices remaining the same, it is profitable to produce more goods and services which bring about increase in the quantity of real GDP produced and supplied. As a result, there is a movement along the short-run aggregate supply curve (*SAS*) as shown in Figure 11.12 by the upward-sloping arrow. On the other hand, when the price level rises and *also there is the same percentage rise in wage rate and other resource prices*, relative prices of goods and services remaining unchanged it is not profitable to produce more output of goods and services. As a result, real GDP remains equal to the potential GDP and there is a movement along the long-run aggregate supply curve (*LAS*) as shown by vertical arrow mark in Fig. 11.12.

MACROECONOMIC EQUILIBRIUM : AD-AS MODEL WITH PRICE FLEXIBILITY

Having explained the concepts of aggregate demand and aggregate supply with variable price level. Now we shall explain how macroeconomic equilibrium is reached between the aggregate supply and aggregate demand to determine the amount of real GDP and the price level. As there is difference between the long-run and the short run aggregate supply curves, the long-run equilibrium differs from the short-run macroeconomic equilibrium. while long-run equilibrium is the state towards which the economy is moving, short-run equilibrium is the actual state of the economy in the short run as it fluctuates around potential GDP. The purpose of AS-AD model is to explain how the various events, fiscal and monetary policies bring about changes in both real GDP and price level. We explain below both the short-run and long-run macroeconomic equilibrium.

Short-run Macroeconomic Equilibrium

Short-run macroeconomic equilibrium occurs at the price level at which aggregate output demanded equals aggregate supply of output. That is, short-run equilibrium is reached at the price level at which aggregate demand curve *AD* intersects the short-run aggregate supply curve *SAS*. This is shown in Fig. 11.13 where *AD* is the aggregate demand curve and *SAS* is the aggregate supply curve. It will be seen that the short-run macroeconomic equilibrium occurs at point *E* at which the price level is P_0 and the real GDP is Y_0. If price level is different from P_0, the economy will not be in equilibrium. Suppose, for example, price level is P_2, the quantity P_2A of the real GDP demanded at P_2 is less than the quantity P_2B of real GDP supplied. This means the firms will not be able to sell

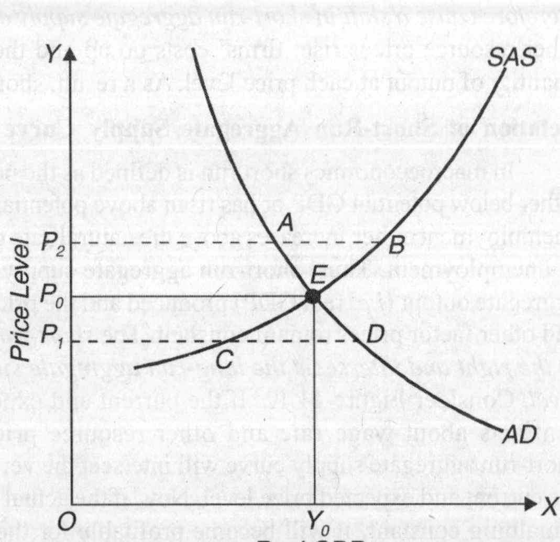

Fig. 11.13. *Short-run Macroeconomic Equilibrium : Joint Determination of GDP and Price Level*

all their output. As a result ,unintended inventories will pile up and firms will cut both production and prices. The process of cutting production and prices will continue until the equilibrium price level P_0 is reached and real GDP produced and sold is Y_0.

Now suppose that price level is P_1. It will be seen from Fig. 11.13 that at price level P_1 the quantity of aggregate output demanded (P_1D) exceeds the aggregate quantity supplied (P_1C). Thus at the price level P_1, the people will not be able to get all the goods and srevices they want to buy. As a result, inventories of goods with the firms will decrease below the desired level to meet the higher demand. This will induce firms to increase production and raise prices. The production and price level will rise until price level P_0 is reached and real GDP produced is Y_0 which meets the demands of the people fully at the price level P_0. Thus, the price level P_0 and real GDP equal to Y_0 represents the short-run macroeconomic equilibrium.

It is worthwhile to note that in the short run the money wage rate is fixed. *It does not adjust to bring macro equilibrium at full-employment level of real GDP.* Thus, in the short run macro equilibrium can be attained with real GDP less than or greater than potential GDP (*i.e.* the level of GDP at which there is full employment of labour) depending on the level of aggregate demand. It is only in the long run when money wage rate adjusts that equilibrium is restored at potential GDP.

Further, it may be noted that fluctuations in the economy occur due to changes in the factors that cause changes in either aggregate demand or aggregate supply. For example, changes in money supply, the government expenditure, taxes, investment demand by business firms or consumption demand of households will bring about changes in aggregate demand and cause shift in the short-run macroeconomic equilibrium. On the other hand, changes in money wage rate and other resource prices such as oil price stock will cause a shift in aggregate supply curve and bring about a change in the short-run macroeconomic equilibrium

It is important to note that, according to Keynes, this equilibrium at less than full-employment level when there prevails recession in the economy comes into existence in the short run due to deficiency of aggregate demand caused by a fall in private investment by the business class. He argued that unless the Government intervenes in the economy through adoption of expansionary fiscal policy (that is, increasing its expenditure and cutting taxes) and finance its budget deficit through deficit financing, a free-market economy cannot be brought into equilibrium at full employment. (*i.e.* potential GDP) level. He emphasized that a *free-market economy was not self correcting through any quick adjustment in wages and prices to restore equilibrium at full employment level.* According to him, without intervention by the Government, under-employment equilibrium with recession prevailing in the economy will persist in the long run. Keynes therefore did not discuss how through adjustment of wages and prices the long-run equilibrium of a free market economy is reached. On the other hand, classical economists, monetarists and New Classical economists believe in the establishment of long-run equilibrium at full employment level through automatic adjustments in wages and prices . We explain below their viewpoint.

Long-Run Macroeconomic Equilibrium

The long-run macroeconomic equilibrium occurs at the price level where the aggregate demand curve intersects the long run aggregate supply curve which is vertical at the potential GDP level. Thus, long-run equilibrium occurs *when real* GDP *equals potential* GDP. *But this long-run equilibrium of price level and real* GDP *is reached when money wage rate adjusts so that the short-run aggregate supply curve shifts to intersect the long-run aggregate supply curve (LAS) at the point at which aggregate demand curve intersects the latter.* The long-run macro equilibrium and how it is reached is illustrated in Figures 11.14 & 11.15. From Fig. 11.14 it will be seen that the short-run aggregate supply curve SAS_0 intersects the given aggregate demand curve AD at point E and determines the price level equal to P_0 and real GDP equal to Y_0 in the short run. Thus, in this short-run macroeconomic equilbrium, real GDP which is equal to Y_0 is less than the potential GDP (remember that the potential GDP corresponds to full employment of labour, with the given stock of capital and the given state of technology). *The difference* $Y_0\overline{Y}$ *between the short-run equilibrium GDP and the potential GDP is called* **recessionary gap** *which exists because at the short-run equilibrium price level* P_0 *aggregate demand is not sufficient for the purchase of potential GDP. Besides, the production of less than potential GDP implies that in the short-run equilibrium, there will exist cyclical unemployment, that is, the rate of unemployment will exceed the natural rate of unemployment.*

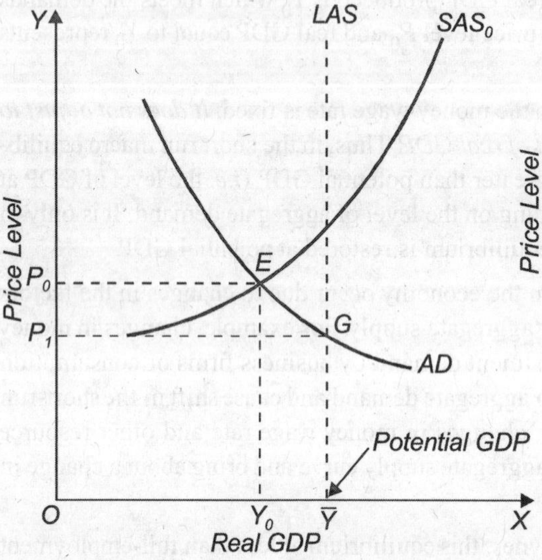

Fig. 11.14. *Short-run Equilibrium at Less Than Full-employment (or Potential GDP).*

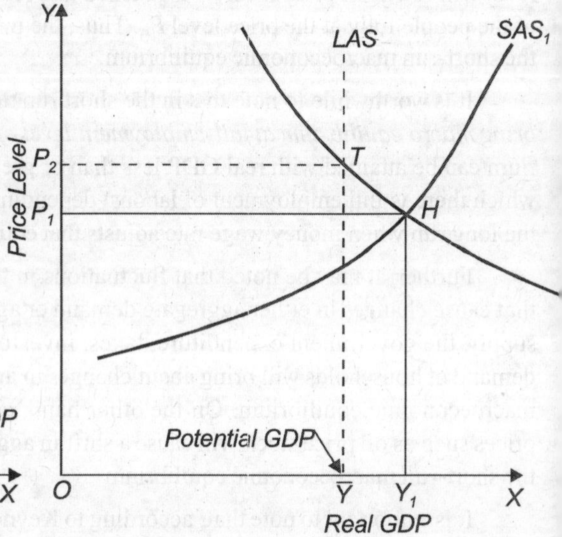

Fig. 11.15. *Short run Equilibrium at more than Full-Employment Level with Inflation.*

If money wage rate is flexible as classical economists, monetarists and new classical economists think they are, then in the short run equilibrium at point *E* with more than natural rate of unemployment, money wage rate will fall. As a result, short-run aggregate supply curve (*SAS*) will shift to the right. This rightward shift in the short-run aggregate supply curve will continue until it intersects the long-run aggregate supply curve (*LAS*) at point *G* (see Figure 11.14) where the given aggregate demand cuts the latter. At the new equilibrium point *G* price level has fallen to P_1 and aggregate quantity of output demanded has increased to the potential GDP. Point *G* in the Figure 11.14 represents the long-run equilibrium at full-employment level, that is, the level at which only natural rate of unemployment prevails.

Let us consider the opposite case when the short-run equilibrium is initially at more than potential GDP, that is, above full employment level. Suppose in Fig. 11.15, initially with aggregate demand curve *AD* and the short-run aggregate supply curve SAS_1, the short-run equilibrium is at point *H* at which the price level is P_1 and real GDP is Y_1 which is greater than potential GDP equal to $\overline{Y}$.

Now, the question may be asked how real GDP has risen to the level which is more than the potential GDP. The answer is that even beyond potential GDP, real GDP rises as labour-employment increases by reduction in rate of unemployment more than the natural rate and the given capital stock is utilised more intensively. The amount $\overline{Y}Y_1$ by which real GDP which is equal to Y_1 exceeds potential GDP ($\overline{Y}$) represents the ***inflationary gap*** as this gap creates inflationary pressures in the economy

When equilibrium of the economy is established at more than full-employment or potential GDP level, unemployment falls below the natural rate of unemployment, shortage of labour will emerge which will push up wages. With the rise in money wages short-run aggregate supply curve will shift to the left and this process of rise in wages and leftward shift in short run aggregate supply curve *SAS* will continue until it intersects the long-run aggregate supply *LAS* at point *T* (in Fig. 11.15) at which long-run equilibrium is establiesheed.

Again, it may be noted that, according to Keynes, equilibrium at more than full employment when inflation prevails in the economy comes into existence due to the excess of aggregate demand over aggregate supply cannot be automatically corrected through adjustment in wages and prices. He rightly argued that inflation in the economy can be overcome by *demand management policy*, that is, by reducing aggregate demand through contractionary fiscal policy (*i.e.*, reducing Government expenditure and imposing taxes) and tightening of monetary policy (*i.e.* raising interest rates) by the central Bank of the country. It is only classical, monetarist and new classical economists who believe in automatic adjustment of wages and prices to achieve long-run equilibrium at full-employment.

It follows from above that equilibrium between aggregate and aggregate supply can be there at less than full-employment level (*i.e.* at less than potential GDP), at more than full-employment level (*i.e.* at more than potential GDP or at full employment level of potential GDP.

AD-AS MODEL : EXPLAINING ECONOMIC FLUCTATIONS

The propose of AD-AS model is to explain fluctuation in output and price level which occur due to changes in either aggregate demand or aggregate supply. As menioned before, Keynes in his original model assumed price level and money wages to remain fixed in the downward direction and explained fluctuations in economic activity or what are called business cycles through changes in aggregate demand alone and did not consider changes in aggregate supply. However, *AD-AS* model consider fluctuations in price level, wages and output through changes in both aggregate demand and aggregate supply but, *unlike classical model, money wages and price level do not adjust quickly enough to maintain equilibrium at full-employment or potential GDP level*. As a result, the economy remains for sometime either at less than potential GDP or for some time at more than full-employment level. But it is worth noting that aggregate demand curve with variable price level is derived from Keynesian income-expenditure approach. We explain below how changes in aggregate demand bring about fluctuations in GDP and price level.

Decrease in Aggregate Demand

Let us fist show how decrease in aggregate demand brings about changes in real GDP and price level. Aggregate demand consists of consumption demand (*C*), investment demand (*I*), government

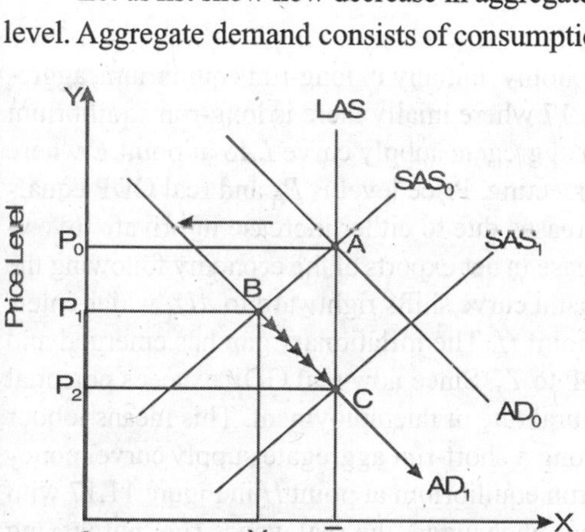

Fig. 11.16. *Impact of Decrease in Aggregate Demand on Real GDP and Price Level.*

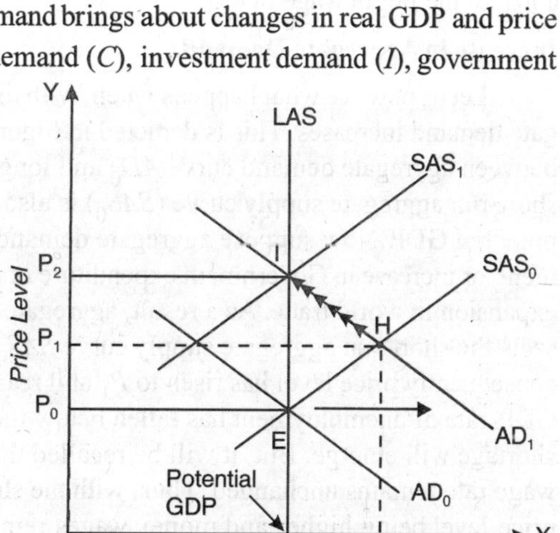

Fig. 11.17. *Impact of Increase in Aggregate Demand on Real GDP and Price Level.*

expenditure (*G*) and net exports (*NX*). Decrease in any of these components of demand will shift the aggregate demand curve to the left. Keynes emphasised that private investment is very volatile. When profit expectations of business men in future become dim, they reduce investment which through the working of the multiplier adversely affects consumption demand too. In developing countries like India where agriculture is also still a relatively important sector failure of monsoon resulting in loss of output can cause reduction in consumption demand of the farmers and bring about a shift in aggregate demand curve to the left. Thirdly, when government reduces its investment expenditure, it will also cause a leftward shift in aggregated demand curve if it is not matched by the increase in private investment. Lastly, the world trade also affects the aggregate demand of an economy. Suppose the world trade declines in a year and, as a result, the demand for Indian exports decreases, it will also reduce aggregate demand in India.

If there is adverse change in any of the above components of *aggregate demand, aggregate* demand curve shifts to the left, say from AD_0 to AD_1 (see Figure 11.16). In Figure 11.16 initially the long-run equilibrium between aggregate demand curve AD_0 and short-run aggregate supply curve SAS_0 is at point *A*. Price level is OP_0 and real GDP is $\overline{Y}$. With the leftward shift in aggregate demand curve from AD_0 to AD_1, the new short-run equilibrium is at *B* at which price level has fallen to P_1 and real GDP has declined to Y_1. The recessionary gap $\overline{Y}Y_1$ has emerged and therefore there are recessionary conditions in the economy. Not being able to sell their total output, the firms will reduce prices of their output. The money wage rate remaining sticky, the lower price level will increase the real wage rate. As a result, the firms' costs will increase relative to the prices of their outputs. Since real GDP has declined below potential GDP, unemployment in the economy will increase more than the natural rate of unemployment. The existence of a large amount of unemployment will put downward pressure on wages. Thus, eventually recessionary conditions will lead to fall in money wage rates if they are flexible. With the fall in wage rate, short-run aggregate supply curve will shift rightward and real GDP will tend to rise. However, *according to modern economists, wage rate falls gradually*, therefore the real GDP will increase slowly to potential GDP equal to $\overline{Y}$. (Note that a large number of arrow marks indicates that there is slow and gradual adjustment). As a result price level will fall to P_2. Thus long-run equilibrium in Fig. 11.16 is established at point *C* of the long-run aggregate supply curve *LAS*. As mentioned in an earlier section, the fall in price level equal to P_0P_2 will be relatively equal to the fall in wage rate.

Increase in Aggregate Demand.

Let us now see what happens when, with the economy initially in long-run equilibrium, aggregate demand increases. This is depicted in Figure 11.17 where inially there is long-run equilibrium between aggregate demand curve AD_0 and long-run aggregate supply curve *LAS* at point *E* where short-run aggregate supply curve (SAS_0) is also intersecting. Price level is P_0 and real GDP equals potential GDP. Now suppose aggregate demand increases due to either increase in private investment, or increase in Government expenditure or increase in net exports of the economy following the expansion in world trade. As a result, aggregate demand curve shifts rightward to AD_1 which intersects the short-run aggregate supply curve SAS_0 at point *H*. The inflationary gap has emerged and consequently price level has risen to P_1 and real GDP to Y_2. Since now real GDP exceeds potential GDP, rate of unemployment has fallen below the natural rate of unemployment. This means lobour shortage will emerge. But, it will be recalled that along a short-run aggregate supply curve money wage rate remains unchanged. Thus, with the short-run equilibrium at point *H* in Figure 11.17 with price level being higher and money wages remaining unchanged, the real wages (*i.e.* purchasing power of wages) of the workers will fall. The economy cannot therefore remains stable at point *H* because the workers will demand higher wages to maintain their real income. In view of the fact that labour-shortages have arisen because rate of unemployment has fallen below the natural rate of unemployment and being anxious to maintain their labour employment and output levels the firms will concede to the demand for higher wages.

As wage rates rise the short-run aggregate supply curve (*SAS*) will begin to shift to the left. Since the wage rates gradually adjust, the short-run aggregate supply curve will slowly move along the higher aggregate demand curve AD_1 towards SAS_1. The new equilibrium will be eventually reached at point *T* on the long-run aggregate supply curve *LAS* where the short-run aggregate supply curve SAS_1 intersects the aggregate demand curve AD_1. With equilibrium at point *T*, real GDP returns to the level of the potential GDP and price level has risen to P_2. Note that the rise in long-run price level from P_0 to P_2 (which is equal to *ET*) will be equal to the ultimate percentage rise in wage rate.

It is evident from above that fluctuations in aggregate demand can cause short-run fluctuations in output, employment and price level. This is how AS-AD model explain business cycles in the economy. But the second important cause of fluctuations in real GDP, employment and price level is the changes in aggregate supply. This is explained below.

Role of Fiscal and Monetary Policies in Keynesian, Monetarist and Classical Models

With this aggregate demand-aggregate supply model, popularly known as *AD-AS* model, we can explain the effects of fiscal and monetary policies on aggregate output (*i.e., GNP*) and price level in the economy. For example, if Government steps up its expenditure without increasing taxes, this will cause aggregate demand curve *AD* to shift to the right and thereby will lead to the increase in Gross-National Product (*i.e.*, National Income) and the price level as is illustrated in Figure 11.18. Likewise, expansion in money supply, increase in private investment, or reduction in taxes without reducing Government expenditure will also result in shift in the aggregate demand curve to the right causing price level and national output to increase

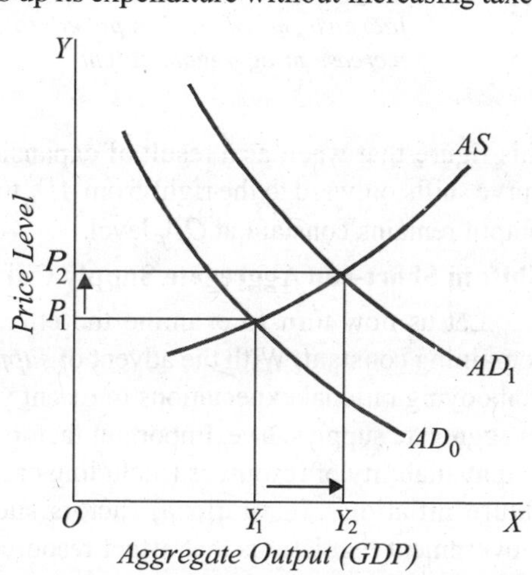

Fig. 11.18. ***Keynesian View :*** *Expansionary Fiscal and Monetary Policies in times of recession lead to more increase in GNP and less rise in Price Level.*

An important result follows from this *AD*–AS model with flexible prices when under the influence of expansionary policies aggregate demand curve shifts to the right. *To what extent it will affect the national output and the price level depends on the elasticity of aggregate supply curve.* Keynesian economists (*i.e.* followers of Keynes) are of the view that the aggregate supply curve is relatively elastic (*i.e.* flat), especially in times of recession, and therefore most of the response to expansion in aggregate demand will be the increase in output rather than rise in the price level as is shown in Figure 11.18. On the other hand, if the supply curve is *steep as is shown* in Fig. 11.19, the expansionary fiscal and monetary policies causing outward shift in *AD* curve will bring about rise in price more than the increase in output. In the extreme case of *perfectly elastic aggregate supply curve* which Keynes assumed in his analysis of depression increase in aggregate demand will not affect the price level and its full effect will be to raise the level of GDP.

Lastly, when the economy is operating at the level of capacity output (*i.e.* full-employment level), as the classical economists assumed, increase in aggregate demand in this case will lead only to higher price level or inflation in the economy without affecting aggregate output (national income). The view of classical economists is illustrated in Figure 11.20 where aggregate supply curve *AS* is a vertical straight line at the full-employment level of output OY_F. It will be seen from

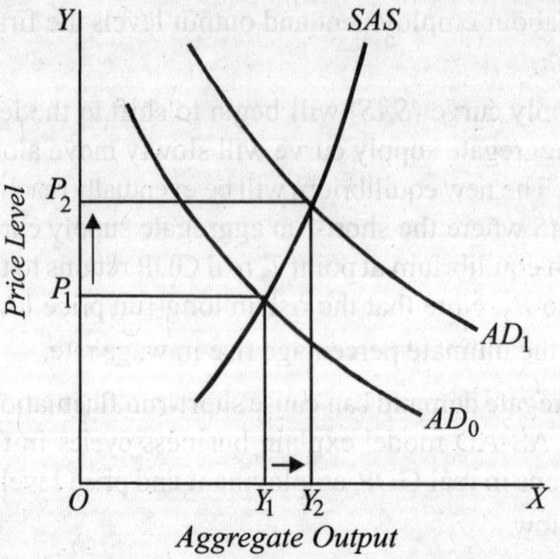

Fig. 11.19. *When aggregate supply curve is steep, expansionary fiscal and monetary policies cause price level to increase more as compared to increase in aggregate output*

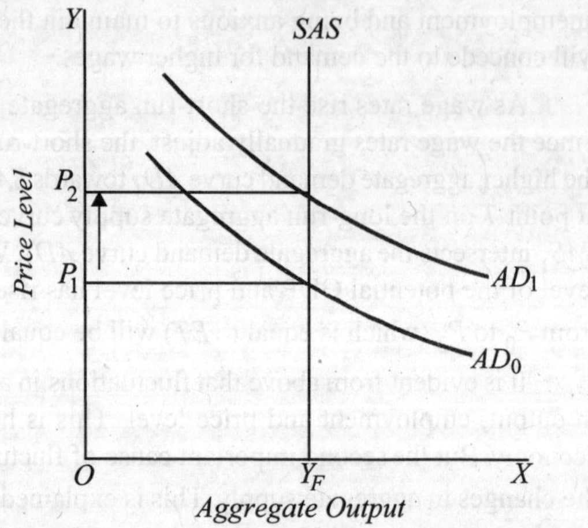

Fig. 11.20. *Classical View : With full-employment of resources aggregate supply curve is* ***vertical straight*** *line and an increase in aggregate demand will cause price level to rise without change in aggregate output.*

this figure that when as a result of expansionary fiscal and monetary policies aggregate demand curve shifts outward to the right from AD_0 to AD_1, price level rises from P_1 to P_2 whereas aggregate output remains constant at OY_F level.

Shift in Short-run Aggregate Supply Curve and Stagflation

Let us now turn to examine the effect of changes in aggregate supply, aggregate demand remaining constant. With the advent of *supply-side economics and new classical macroeconomics* embodying rational expectations in recent years economists are increasingly concerned with shifts in aggregate supply curve. Important factors that cause a shift in supply are changes in factor-prices and availability of resources (including crude oil), change in productivity and expectations about future inflation. Institutional factors such as Government regulations that affect resource use efficiency also cause shift in aggregate supply curve.

An important cause of shift in aggregate supply curve is the *rise in prices of resources such as large increase in oil price by OPEC* in 1973-74 and again in 1979-80. The rise in oil prices causes the aggregate supply curve to shift to the left as shown in Figure 11.21 where due to the higher per unit resource cost aggregate supply curve has shifted leftward from SAS_0 to SAS_1. The aggregate demand curve *AD* remaining constant, with the leftward shift in aggregate supply curve from SAS_0 to SAS_1, leads to the new macro-economic equilibrium being established at *T*, at which price level is higher and aggregate output smaller than before.

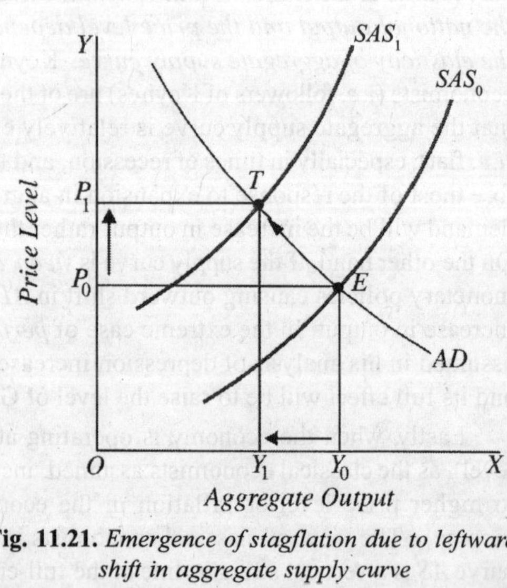

Fig. 11.21. *Emergence of stagflation due to leftward shift in aggregate supply curve*

The emergence of rise in price level or inflation due to the leftward shift in aggregate supply curve is called *cost-push inflation*. There is important differences between demand-pull inflation cost-push inflation. *Whereas in case of demand-pull inflation, price rises along with rise in GDP, in case of cost-push inflation price level rises but GDP declines.* Thus, in Fig. 11.21 leftward shift in the *SAS* curve leads to rise in the price level from P_0 to P_1, while national output falls from Y_0 to Y_1. ***When both inflation and recession occur simultaneously, economists call this situation as stagflation.*** We thus see that increase in costs or rise in resource prices are both inflationary and recessionary.

It may be noted that in the context of developing countries such as India stagflation is even said to occur when instead of absolute fall in aggregate output there is ***slowdown in economic growth rate*** **along with inflation rate remaining steadly high.**

It is evident from above that stagflation occurs as a result of supply shock, that is, rise in price of essential inputs such as crude oil which causes a shift in the short-run aggregate supply curve to the left. Given the aggregate demand curve, the new equilibrium is reached at a higher price level (*i.e.* inflation) and at the same time aggregate output (*i.e.* GDP) falls which generates unemployment in the economy.

We have explained above stagflation as a result of sharp rise in price of crude oil effected by restriction of oil output by callusive agreement of OPEC. In India stagflation can arise when there is decline in agricultural output due to failure of monsoon. The decline in agricultural output causes *food inflation* which in turn leads to rise in wages of workers which cause a shift in the short-run aggregate supply curve to the left. Besides, drastic decline in agricultural output also leads to the rise in prices of raw materials provided by agricultural sector to industries. The rise in raw material prices for industries shifts aggregate supply curve to the left causing both inflation and reduction in output.

Solution. To solve the problem of stagflation is a difficult task. In the seventies when the problem of stagflation was first faced efforts were made to solve it through demand management policies. However, when to control inflation, steps were taken to reduce aggregate demand by cutting expenditure, the result was decline in aggregate output which further worsened the unemployment problem. On the other hand, when to reduce unemployment attempt was made to increase aggregate expenditure through expansionary fiscal and monetary policies the result was acceleration in inflation.

The proper solution of stagflation is to shift the short-run aggregate supply curve to the right by reducing cost through raising productivity levels. The productivity in both industry and agriculture can be raised through technological improvements and more capital accumulation. Besides, rightward shift in short-run aggregate supply can be made by reducing indirect taxes such as excise duties, sales tax, customs duties not only on final products but also on essential inputs used in the production of commodities.

QUESTIONS FOR REVIEW

1. Briefly explain AS–AD model of determination of national product. With this model explain the impact of (1) increase in aggregate demand and (2) decrease in aggregate supply on price level and aggregate output.
2. Explain the components of aggregate demand. Draw an aggregate demand curve (with varying price level). Why does it slope downward? Show the effect of an increase in nominal money stock on aggregate demand curve.

3. Compare the Keynesian and Classical aggregate supply curves. Briefly explain their policy implications.
4. With AS–AD model explain the multiplier effect of increase in Government expenditure on aggregate output when (1) price level remains constant and (2) when price level rises.
5. What is stagflation? Explain with AS–AD model what can cause stagflation.
6. Distinguish between short-run aggregate supply and long-run aggregate supply. What are the factors that cause shift in them?
7. Draw a short-run aggregate supply curve with the given nominal wages. Why does it slope upward ? When will it shift upward to the left ?
8. With AS–AD model explain economic fluctuations in the economy. Explain the impact of increase and decrease in aggregate demand on GDP and price level in the economy.

CHAPTER

12

Unemployment and Full Employment

Introduction

In the last few chapters we have explained how the equilibrium level of income and employment is determined. When the economy is in equilibrium at less than full-employment level of output, unemployment comes into existence. There are several types of unemployment depending upon the different factors which cause it. Further, the nature and causes of unemployment in developing countries like India are different from those of developed countries. One of the frequent causes of labour unrest in moderns societies, both developed and developing, is unemployment among workers and the insecurity of employment. The specter of unemployment constantly haunts the working classes. Full employment has therefore become the goal of all countries. In what follows we will explain the various types of unemployment and their causes. We shall also explain the concept of full employment and what policies should be pursued to eliminate unemployment and achieve full employment.

Meaning of Unemployment. Technically speaking, *unemployment is defined as a state of affairs when in a country there are a large number of able-bodied persons of working age who are willing to work but cannot find work at the current wage levels*. People who are either unfit for work for physical or mental reasons, or don't want to work, *e.g., sadhus*, are excluded from the category of the unemployed.

Mere engagement in some productive occupation does not necessarily mean absence of unemployment. People, who are only partially employed or are engaged in inferior jobs, though they can do better jobs, are not adequately employed. It is called a state of *underemployment* which is equally bad for the prosperity of a country. Under capitalism, it seems some amount of unemployment is inevitable. The best that can be done is to keep the number of unemployed as low as possible.

TYPES OF UNEMPLOYMENT

There are three main types of unemployment: (1) frictional unemployment, (2) structural unemployment; and (3) cyclical unemployment. In order to understand the concept of full employment the difference between these types of unemployment needs to be grasped.

Frictional Unemployment

There is always some minimum amount of unemployment that prevails in the economy among workers who have voluntarily quit their previous jobs and are searching for new better jobs or looking for employment for the first time. They are said to be *between jobs*. They are not able to get jobs immediately because of frictions such as lack of market information about availability of jobs and lack of perfect mobility on the part of workers. The distinguishing feature of frictionally unemployed persons is that the number of job vacancies equal to them are available in the economy. They remain unemployed for a relatively short period of time before they are able to get new jobs. This is because some time is required for job searchers to have information about the availability of jobs. When presently fractionally unemployed persons get jobs, the new frictionally unemployed persons come into existence and thus there is always some frictional unemployment prevailing in the economy due to imperfections or lack of market information about the availability of jobs. Since frictionally unemployed are those who have either quit their old jobs voluntarily and are looking for better jobs or those who have entered into the labour force *for the first time* and searching for jobs according to their acquired skills or those who had re-entered the labour force for some time, for example, after having children, the frictional unemployment is considered as voluntary unemployment.

Structural Unemployment

Structural unemployment is another type of unemployment which always exists to some extent in a growing economy. Structural unemployment refers to the mismatch between the unemployment persons and the demand for specific types of workers for employment occurs because whereas demand for one kind of labour is expanding, the demand for another kind of labour is declining either due to the changes in the structure (*i.e.*, composition) of demand for the industrial products or due to the changes in technology that take place in an economy. *The distinguishing feature of structural unemployment is that the unemployed workers lack skills required by the expanding industries*. Structural unemployment also occurs because of the mismatch between the location of job-vacancies of the expanding industries and the present location of the unemployed workers.

Let us give an example of structural unemployment. In a growing economy techniques of production are constantly changing with the result that people are likely to lose their jobs when these are replaced by newer and more efficient techniques. The unemployment created in this way is structural unemployment and is inevitable consequence of technological progress. These structurally unemployed persons will need to acquire new skills and training before they will be absorbed in the new technologically superior jobs. Take another example, when computerisation of banks, offices occurred in India recently some workers were rendered unemployed. But computerisation created new job opportunities. On being given training in computer operations some of them again got jobs. But for some time they remain unemployed. Further, due to changes in demand for some goods, the output of industries producing them declines rendering some people unemployed. On the other hand, those industries the demand for whose products are increasing, new jobs are created and unemployed workers are absorbed in them but before getting jobs in the expanding industries they remain unemployed.

Structural unemployment tends to last much longer than frictional unemployment because more time is required for people to get new training or acquire new skills or to move to new locations of expanding industries. Structural unemployment is more serious than frictional unemployment. This is because frictionally unemployed are likely to get jobs in a relatively short period of time as job vacancies exist for them. On the other hand, structurally unemployed have no immediate job prospects as they have to get training or acquire new skills required for the jobs available. The structurally unemployed persons can be expected to get only low paying unskilled types of jobs in the immediate future. Some accept such jobs while others prefer to remain unemployed and go on searching for better jobs which match their skills.

It may be noted that frictional and structural types of unemployment together constitute what is called **natural rate of unemployment** which may be of the order of 4 to 5 per cent of labour force in free-market economies. Thus, natural rate of unemployment arises due to labour market frictions and structural changes in a free market economy. Note that *when unemployment is equal to the natural rate of unemployment, full employment is said to exist*. In the late nineties, natural rate of unemployment was estimated to be 5.2 per cent of labour force in the United States. In 2010 actual unemployment rate rose to 10 percent in the United States. The higher than natural rate of unemployment is due to recessionary conditions prevailing in the American economy. Thus, *full employment is said to prevail despite the existence of natural rate of unemployment which is unavoidable in a changing economy.*

Cyclical Unemployment

This unemployment is due to deficiency of effective demand. It is also called cyclical '*Keynesian unemployment*'. Advanced capitalist countries have been suffering from time to time from this type of unemployment. This type of unemployment greatly increases during periods of recession or depression. Since recession or depression is one phase of the business cycles that generally occur in the industrialised developed economies this type of unemployment is called cyclical unemployment. This type of unemployment is due to the fact that the total effective demand of the community is not sufficient to absorb the entire production of goods that can be produced with the available stock of capital. In a private enterprise economy, production takes place in response to the profit motive. When businessmen cannot sell their entire output, their profit expectations are not fulfilled so that their reaction in the next period is to reduce their output. The factors of production earn their incomes because of their participation in the process of production and when entrepreneurs decide to reduce their production, some factors of production become unemployed. Since employment is the major source of income for a great majority of the people, a fall in employment signifies a fall in their incomes also.

The deficiency of aggregate demand as an explanation of involuntary unemployment in the industrially advanced countries is associated with the name of J.M. Keynes. Classical and neo-classicial economists often denied the very existence of the problem. In the view of classical economists, symbolised in *Say's Law of Markets*, a freely competitive capitalist economy could never suffer from a deficiency of aggregate effective demand. The argument advanced by Say (a French economist) and accepted implicity by many others in support of this contention was that there could never be a problem of general over-production and that if there was any unemployment it was because of hindrances placed in the working of the freely competitive price system by artificial monopolistic action on the part of trade unions or the government.

Now, it is true that supply does create a demand for goods and services because various factors of production earn their incomes in the process of production by helping to create additional supply of output. When factors of production are employed to produce a good they get their reward in the form of wages, rents, interest and profit. But from this it does not follow that the entire supply of national output will always be demanded by them. The incomes of the factors of production are necessarily equal to the value added in the productive process but it does not mean that the entire income will be automatically spent on goods and services created in a given time period. A part of income will be saved so that this part of income is not available to create demand for goods and services. Unless investors are willing to invest to an equivalent extent of intended savings, the total effective demand which consists of demand for consumers' goods and producers' good $(C + I)$ will not be sufficient to absorb the entire available supply of output. And if it happens like this, producers will not be able to sell their entire output, their profits will fall and they will reduce their production and this will create unemployment.

In a given period, consumers are planning to spend a given part of their income and save the rest. Similarly, entrepreneurs are planning to invest in factories, machines, etc., to a given extent. The total effective demand is the sum of the consumption and the investment demand. Savers are saving for different reasons than the investors whose investment is determined by different factors and in a private enterprise economy there is no mechanism to ensure that what savers are planning to save is just equal to what investors are planning to invest. If there is any discrepancy between planned saving and investment, output, income and employment will change to correct this discrepancy. If planned investment is greater than planned saving, the current output will not be sufficient to meet the emerging demand and hence income, output and employment will increase and vice versa. Thus, we see that the *basic weakness of Say's law arises because of lack of any agency to ensure that intended savings are just equal to intended investment* and that since savings and investment are undertaken by different persons and for different reasons a discrepancy between the two is bound to arise and when it arises the necessary mechanism to correct it is through changes in the volume of employment and income.

Cyclical Unemployment and Labour Market Equilibrium

Let us explain through labour market equilibrium how Keynes explain the emergence of cyclical involuntary unemployment. As stated above, *involuntary unemployment refers to those workers who are seeking work or willing to work at the prevailing wage rate but are unable to get jobs.* According to Keynes, this involuntary unemployment happens to prevail in an economy on a large scale in times of depression due to fall in aggregate demand for goods and services. Classical economists thought that at times of recession wages and prices would fall to eliminate involuntary unemployment and ensure full employment. Keynes challenged this classical viewpoint on two grounds. First, he pointed out that *money wages are rigid and fail to adjust even when there exists involuntary unemployment due to lack of aggregate demand for output*. Secondly, even if money wages are flexible downward or there is all-round cut in money wages, involuntary unemployment will not be removed. Consider Figure 12.1 where we have shown labour market equilibrium. *DD* is the demand curve of labour which is sloping downward to the light.

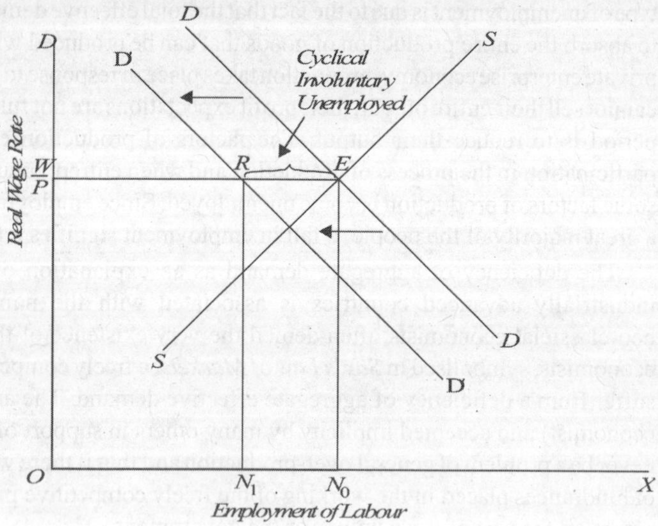

Fig. 12.1: *Labour Market Equilibrium and Involuntary Unemployment*

This shows that at lower wage rates more labour is demanded and employed and vice versa. *SS* is the supply curve of labour which is sloping upward to the right. This shows that at higher wages more labour is supplied and vice versa. These demand and supply curves of labour intersect at point *E* at which real wage rate $\frac{W}{P}$ and labour employment of ON_0 are determined. At the wage rate $\frac{W}{P}$, all those who are willing to work and supply their labour services are employed. Thus, at this labour market equilibrium, there is full employment of labour and involuntary unemployment does not prevail.

Now, suppose aggregate demand for output of goods and services declines, as it happens in times of recession. *Demand for labour is a derived demand.* Decline in aggregate demand for output causes demand curve of labour to shift to the left to *D′D′*. Now, at the given real wage rate, $\frac{W}{P}$ the quantity ON_1 labour will be demanded, whereas supply of labour at this real wage rate remains ON_0. Thus, N_0N_1 or *RE* number of workers will be rendered unemployed who are willing to work at the prevailing wage rate but their services are not demanded by the economy.

According to classical economists, this involuntary unemployment cannot persist for long. The excess supply of labour and competition among unemployed workers will bring down the real wage rate and at lower real wage rate more labour will be demanded and employed. In this way, according to classical economists, due to downward adjustment in wages as well as prices of goods involuntary unemployment of labour will be eliminated and full employment will be restored.

Rigid Money Wages. However, Keynes contended that *money wages are rigid* and do not fall and as a result involuntary unemployment continue to prevail. There are a number of reasons for rigidity of money wages. First, workers strongly resist a reduction in money wages. Second, there is usually a wage contract between workers (or their trade unions) with the employers for a period of two to three years during which wage rates cannot be changed. Thirdly, there are minimum wages fixed by the government below which employers are not permitted to pay wages to the workers.

Lastly, employers themselves may not be interested in reducing wages, as lower wages are likely to reduce efficiency or productivity of labour. Thus, if in Figure 12.1, wages remained rigid at $\frac{W}{P}$ despite the leftward shift in the demand curve of labour to $D'D'$, involuntary unemployment would continue to exist.

All-round Cut in Wages and Employment. However, Keynes argued that even if money wages are cut all round during the period of recession caused by lack of effective demand, even this will not ensure elimination of involuntary unemployment. This is because *wages are not only costs of production for firms and industries but are also incomes of workers.* In case of all-round cut in wages, incomes of the working class, which constitutes a majority in a society, will fall which will work to reduce aggregate demand for output. Reduction in aggregate demand will further deepen the depression and result in more involuntary unemployment rather than removing it.

The Concept of Full Employment

The above analysis of the types of unemployment requires us to make the concept of full employment clear. *Full employment may be defined as the situation wherein all those who are willing and able to work at prevailing wage rates are in fact employed for the work in which they are trained.* Two things must be noted in regard to this definition. First, full employment does not mean that every one is employed. Some people like children, old men and physically or mentally handicapped people are not able to work. There can be no question of their being employed. In fact these people are not included in the labour force of the country. Full employment will exist in spite of their not working. Secondly, some people called 'idle rich' though able to work are not willing to work because they get enough unearned incomes to live. These people are also not included in the labour force of the country.

From above it follows that *the unemployed people are those who are involuntarily idle. They are able and willing to work but the economy does not provide them jobs.*

Another important qualification to the above definition is worth noting. It is that, at any given time, there is bound to be some frictional and structural unemployment owing to labour-saving technological improvements or a change in consumer tastes for the product of some individual industries, some workers are in the process of voluntarily changing jobs. Some time may elapse before they get a new job after leaving the old one and, therefore, they remain temporally unemployed. Similarly, some amount of seasonal unemployment is also in inevitable. Experience indicates that the total amount of frictional and structural unemployment may amount to 4 to 5 per cent of the labour force.

Thus, *full employment is said to exist in the economy even if there is prevailing some amount of frictional and structural unemployment in the economy.* If the number of unemployed is greater than frictional and structural unemployment, only then we shall say that full employment does not prevail.

Keynesian full employment is, by definition, the maximum level of employment that private enterprise countries can attain without experiencing strong inflationary pressure. But for purposes of practical policy it is necessary to reduce the concept to quantitative terms. It should be possible to say precisely when employment is less than full so that remedial action is called for. The concept, as defined above, raises two quantitative problems, namely, how to determine (1) the amount of employment sought by those who at the ruling wage-rates wish to be employed, and (2) the inevitable minimum amount of frictional and structural unemployment? The first, in turn, depends upon (a) the number of people able and willing to work for wages, and (b) the average number of hours of work which each of them wants to be employed.

The number of wage-employment seekers depends upon the following: the size of the population of working age, the number who, having sufficient unearned incomes, choose to remain idle; the number who, being in command of the requisite means of production, are self-employed; and the prevailing wage-rates and other incentives provided. Normally, apart from the size of the population of working age, these factors are likely to be more or less stable over short periods. For instance, the span of life regarded as falling within the working age, while subject to variation as a result of changes in the period of schooling or in the normal age for retirement consequent on changes in health standards and longevity, is likely to remain unchanged in the short period.

Again, since most workers have no large unearned incomes or accumulated savings, they are compelled to try to remain continuously in employment. They cannot, therefore, throw their labour power in the market or withhold it therefrom in some unpredictable manner. Accordingly, the number who choose to remain idle is unlikely to vary much in any short period. Moreover, even when some of these factors change somewhat, the net quantitative effect may not be important. *Higher wages, for instance, may induce some of the older workers to postpone their retirement while these may impel some of the married women workers, now that their husbands are better off, to relinquish their jobs and withdraw themselves from labour force. The net effect of a rise in a wages will not, therefore, be quantitatively important.*[1] *The same applies to other of factors.* The size of the population of working age too, though not invariant, is measurable as it changes according to definite trends. It follows that in the developed countries with a wide network of employment exchanges the number of wage-seeking population can be determined with a great measure of accuracy. And since the average number of hours of work which each wage-employment seeker wants to put in is likely to be more or less stable in any short period, the total amount of wage-employment sought is quite precisely measurable.

Similar observations may be made regarding the permissible allowance for structural and frictional unemployment. It varies from year to year, in accordance with the magnitude of the structural shifts in demand and production that together with immobility of labour and lack of adequate information about the availability and locations of new jobs cause structural and frictional unemployment. It may, therefore, be better defined as a range rather than as a precise figure. Since normally structural changes in demand and production are unlikely to be large and therefore in industrialised countries the incidence of frictional, unemployment is bound to be quite low, the allowance for frictional and structural unemployment needs to be very small. A US study has suggested that this allowance need not be beyond a range of 4 to 5.5 per cent of the available labour force.

The possibility of measuring the size of the available labour force and the inevitable minimum of frictional and structural unemployment makes full employment a determinate quantity. As suggested by a UN study, as a necessary step in the effective implementation of full-employment policies, each country should fix a full-employment target expressed in terms of the permissible range of frictional and structural unemployment. Unemployment in excess of the fixed target would indicate a lapse from full employment calling for a remedial action. The fixation of such a target would help to reduce the chances of government inaction and vacillation in the face of growing unemployment. It may also help to maintain confidence among businessmen whose pessimism ordinarily plays a notable part in magnifying the downswing. There is, of course, the danger of the government not acting in time when unemployment may exceed the level of frictional and structural unemployment due to insufficient demand.

WAGE CUT AND EMPLOYMENT

The relationship between wages and employment has been a highly controversial issue between Keynes and classical economists. As seen earlier, classical economists believed that a cut in money wages would increase employment and help in removing unemployment. Keynes pointed out that workers would strongly resist any attempt to cut *money wages*, though they might be prepared for cuts in *real wages* caused by rise in prices. Therefore, according to him, money wages remain rigid and any cut in money wages for the purpose of promoting employment was not a practical policy proposal. However, though wage cuts may not be practically possible, it is important to know whether it is a theoretically valid proposition that wage cuts or downward wage-flexibility will promote employment and help in removing unemployment. In fact, Keynes made two-pronged attack on the classical view of cutting wages to remove unemployment. First, he challenged the classical view that

1. Pigou, A.C., *Lapses from Full Employment,* 1945, p. 45.

wage cuts would promote employment at times of depression on grounds of practical feasibility. Second, he showed that even theoretically cut in money wages would not promote employment and attain full employment of labour. We discuss below both classical and Keynesian viewpoints about the relationship between wage-cut and employment.

Wage Cut and Unemployment : Classical View

The analysis of wage reduction on employment is important because, according to classical economists, wage flexibility provides the economy with a self-adjusting mechanism that worked to restore full-employment equilibrium when there is recession and involuntary unemployment. Wage rigidity, according to them, was to blame for any prevailing unemployment. The classical view was simple; if there was an excess supply of labour (*i.e.* involuntary unemployment), wage rate must be too high and if unemployment was to be eliminated, wage rate must fall.

For analysing the effect of wage cut on employment the classical economists applied partial or microeconomic analysis to the macro level. They argued that if wages fell, the prices of products made by labour would also fall. The price of products will fall because reduction in wages causes reduction in marginal costs of production. Since they used partial equilibrium analysis they assumed that the demand for the output of an industry would remain unaffected when cut in wages was made. They argued that with a fall in price of the product of the industry consequent to the cut in wages, the amount of product produced would increase and the new price-output equilibrium will be established at a lower price and larger quantity of the product. The expansion in output of the products will lead to the increase in employment of labour and other inputs. The extent of expansion in output (and therefore increase in employment) following the cut in wages and consequent fall in the price of the product depends on the elasticity of demand for output made by labour. On the basis of this partial equilibrium analysis of the impact of wage cut on price, output and employment in an industry the classical economists applied this result to the impact of *all-round cut in money wages* on the increase in output and employment in the economy.

Keynes's Critique of the Classical View

Keynes challenged the classical viewpoint regarding the impact of all-round cut in money wages on output and employment of labour. According to him, while in case of the analysis of price and output determination in an individual industry, it is justified to assume that a cut in wages by the industry would not significantly affect the demand for the product of that industry because most of the demand for the product of that industry comes from the workers and persons employed in other industries. However, to assume that *demand for output of all industries* will remain unchanged when *cut in wages in all industries together* is made is not valid. In other words, to apply the result of partial equilibrium analysis of the determination of price, output and employment to the economy as a whole is quit misleading and invalid. This is because wages are not only costs from the viewpoint of individual industries, they also constitute incomes of the workers and these incomes determine the demand for the products of various industries. When all-round cut in wages is made in all industries, it will reduce the aggregate demand for the products because workers would have now less incomes and therefore would spend less on goods and services. With reduced demand for the products of industries smaller output will be produced and, therefore, smaller amount of labour will be demanded and employed. To quote Stonner and Hague, *"When there is general unemployment, a general cut in wages in all industries cannot be assumed to leave demand unchanged, for part of that demand results from spending out of wages. It is thus quite clear that a general cut in wages will merely cause a reduction and will not in itself remove unemployment"*.[2] Thus, we see that classical economists neglected the adverse effect of all-around cut in wages on the level of aggregate demand. Instead, Keynes argued that unemployment had come into existence due to fall in aggregate demand.

2. Stonier and Hague, *A Textbook of Economic Theory*, Fourth Edition, 1977, p. 397.

The effect of all-around reduction in wages on aggregate output and employment is illustrated through *AS-AD* in Fig. 12.2 where short-run aggregate curve supply curves SAS_0 and aggregate demand curve AD_0 intersect at point *E* and determine aggregate output Y_0 which is less than full-employment level of output Y_F. Thus, in macro equilibrium at point *E* there is recession in the economy and involuntary unemployment will prevail. According to classical viewpoint, cut in wages will cause a downward shift in aggregate supply curve, say to the new position SAS_1 (dotted) with the result that new equilibrium is established at full-employment output Y_F. But, according to Keynes, all-round cut in wages will reduce incomes of the workers and therefore expenditure made by them which will cause a leftward shift in the aggregate demand curve *AD*, say to the new position AD_1. If the decrease in aggregate demand is proportional to the increase in aggregate supply, then equilibrium might be reached at the original level of output Y_0. Besides, if fall in the price level is in proportion to the cut in wages, the real wage rate will remain the same. Consequently, level of employment will remain below the full-employment level.

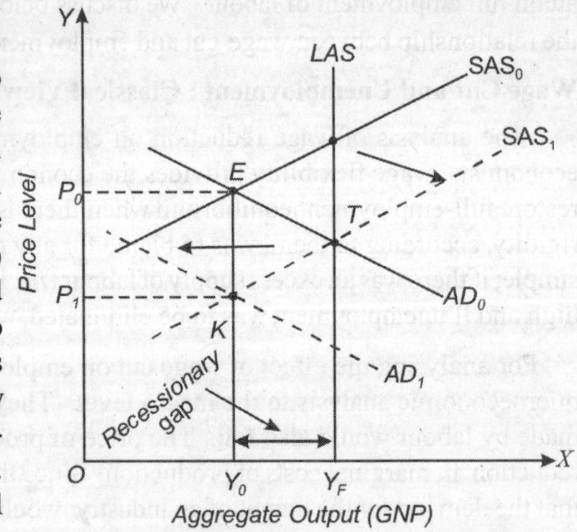

Fig. 12.2. *Impact of All-round Cut in Wages on Aggregate Output and Employment*

It may be noted that the classical view was based on the two fundamental theoretical foundations, namely, (1) The Law of Diminishing Returns, and (2) The Theory of Marginal Productivity of Distribution. According to the law of diminishing returns, as more workers are employed, given a fixed amount of capital equipment and given the state of technology, the less would each additional worker produce and the marginal productivity theory says the wage rate of the workers employed would be equal to the value of the product produced by the last worker employed. Taken both these principles together, the classical economists put forth the view that if more men are to employed, the wage rate must be lower. Therefore, the classical economists said '*cut wages and employment will rise*'.

The interesting thing about Keynes's view is that he accepted both of the above classical premises. He agreed that as employment and output increase in the short run, marginal product per man will diminish. And he also agreed that it was true that the men employed will be paid the wage rate equal to the value of the marginal product of the last man employed. How did then Keynes refute the conclusion of the classical economists that for increasing employment one must reduce real wages ? In fact, *Keynes turned the classical theory upside down*. He showed that we need not reduce real wages to get more employment, but we should raise employment to get a reduction in real wages.

This brings us to distinguish between money wages and real wages. Real wages represent the amount of goods a man can buy with his money wage, that is, real wages mean the purchasing power of the money wages. Real wages increase if a person can buy more with his given money wages. If *W* stands for money wage and *P* stands for the price level, then $\frac{W}{P}$ measures the level of real wages. Keynes believed, as did the classicial economists, that real wages and employment are inversely related. This follows from the principle of diminishing marginal productivity of labour. The classical economists argued that money wages (*W*) should be reduced to reduce real wages $\left(\frac{W}{P}\right)$. Keynes opposed the reduction of money wages as he thought it would reduce aggregate demand and therefore adversely affect employment. Instead, Keynes argued that, keeping *money wage* rate constant, one should increase the level of employment by raising aggregate demand. Given the downward-sloping marginal product curve of labour, the increase in employment of labour under increasing marginal cost conditions cause higher price of output and therefore will result in lower real wage rate $\left(\frac{W}{P}\right)$.

If money wage (W) remains constant and price level (P) rises, real wages will fall. Thus, Keynes put forward the view that the cut in money wage rate is not an effective way to increase employment. The increase in aggregate demand is a far more effective policy to raise employment. Thus, explaining Keynes's view A.H Hansen writes, "*With substantially stable money wage rates employment could thereby be raised and as a result, real wage rate (under conditions of increasing marginal cost) would fall to a level consistent with the increased volume of employment. Thus employment is not raised by cutting real wages. Rather it is the other way round real wage rates fall because employment has been increased via an increase in demand.*"[3]

Keynes emphasized that if real wages remain unchanged, then there can be no reason to expect that the consumption expenditure by households or investments expenditure by businessmen will change. In fact, with no change in expenditure or aggregate demand, no change in output and employment can occur. To further clarify this point, consider that money wages of workers are reduced by 15 per cent and prices of all goods produced by them also fall by 15 per cent, then real wages $\left(\frac{W}{P}\right)$ will remain constant. As a result, output and employment will remain unaffected. Consider Figure 12.2 again where as a result of reduction in money wages, the short-run aggregate supply curve shifts from SAS_0 to SAS_1. But with the reduction of money incomes of workers, aggregate demand curve also shifts downward from AD_0 to AD_1. The shifts in aggregate supply curve and aggregate demand curve together cause a fall in the price level from P_0 to P_1. It is assumed that fall in price level is proportionately equal to the fall in money wages so that real wages remain constant. It will be seen from the Figure 12.2 that at the new equilibrium point K, the aggregate output (GNP) remains unchanged at Y_0, the recessionary level of output and hence the amount of unemployment remains the same.

Though the assumption in our above analysis that reduction in money wages will cause equal proportionate fall in the price level is not strictly true, but it clearly brings out a fundamental flaw in the classical theory that downward flexibility in money wages and prices will secure reduction in real wages and moves the economy back to full employment. The classical view ignores the effect of cut in money wages on aggregate demand for goods and services. In short, while on the basis of marginal productivity theory the classical economists indicated that a cut in real wages was needed to secure increase of labour employment, in practice it was not possible to achieve it through cut in money wages as it would adversely affect aggregate demand.

However, it may be noted that a cut in money wages will not generally lead to proportionate reduction in prices. This is because wages account for only a part of the sale proceeds of goods produced, the other elements in the sale proceeds such as incomes of profits, rent and interest would not fall, at least immediately. Therefore, a general reduction in money wages by 15 per cent might lead to 10 per cent fall in prices. Real wages would therefore fall only by 10 per cent. However, as explained below, Keynes stressed that the favourable effect on employment of the reduction in real wages would not be large enough to offset the adverse effect on employment of the fall in consumption demand of the workers whose money incomes have been reduced.

Wage Cut, Aggregate Demand and Employment

As illustrated in Figure 12.2 that wage-price flexibility with real wages remaining unchanged does not guarantee the restoration of full-employment when the economy is in the grip of recession. Even

3. A.H. Hansen, *A Guide to Keynes,* McGraw-Hill, New York, 1953, p. 23.

when, as is likely the case, real wages fall to some extent as a result of cut in money wages, this would not lead to increase in employment because of the adverse effect of cut in money wages on aggregate demand. This is because consumption demand of workers who constitute majority in a society would fall as their incomes have been reduced. Consumption demand, it will be recalled, depends on income. Besides, a fall in consumption will lead via the working of the multiplier to a further fall in output and employment.

Keynes recognised that income of entrepreneurs, that is, profits, incomes of rentiers, that is, interest, dividends, rent may increase at least for some time following the reduction in money wages. But he rightly thought that the higher consumption demand of the recipients of higher incomes in the form of profits, interest, rent, etc. would not be large enough to offset lower consumption demand of wage earners and that the net effect of the general cut in money wages would still be to depress output and employment.[4]

A General Equilibrium Analysis of the Effect of Wage Cut on Employment

It may however be noted that the impact of a wage cut on aggregate demand is more complicated than described above. As a matter of fact, as a result of all-round cut in wages the extent to which aggregate demand will decline depends on several factors such as its effect on propensity to consume, rate of interest, marginal efficiency of capital etc. But the classical analysis that there is a direct link between wage cuts and rising employment through reduction in cost of production is also not valid because it neglects the role of aggregate effective demand when all-round cut in money wages is made. Professors Stoner and Hague rightly write, "*A general equilibrium analysis of wage cuts is futile unless it pays attention to the problem of whether aggregate demand will rise or fall as wages are reduced.*"[5]

Whether employment will rise or fall when wages are cut depends on whether aggregate demand in terms of money will remain constant, will it fall less than in proposition to the cut in money wages or will it fall more than in proportion to cut in money wages. In Keynesain macroeconomic analysis, the impact of cut in money wages is explained through its effect on the three main determinants of aggregate demand, namely, (1) propensity to consume, (2) rate of interest and (3) marginal efficiency of capital.

We have seen above that classical economists' suggestion of cutting money wages can be rarely put into practice, although workers might accept cut in real wages through rise prices. We have explained in an earlier chapter the various reasons for money wage-rigidity or sticky wages which explain the persistence of involuntary unemployment despite the fact that labour market is in disequilibrium. However, Keynes opposed cut in money wages to promote employment during depression not only on practical grounds of rigidity of money wages but also on theoretical grounds. He argued that even if wages and prices were flexible downward, they were not likely to lead to the increase in employment in a free-market economy.

However, Keynes argued that while in partial equilibrium analysis, it was theoretically right to take the demand for the product of an individual industry as given when cut in money wages is made by it, to extend this conclusion to the macro level or general equilibrium framework was not justified. Thus, according to Keynes, we need to analyse whether aggregate demand or aggregate monetary expenditure will rise or fall as wages are reduced all-round in the economy (that is, in all industries together). Keynes examined the effect of reduction in wages on employment by considering its effect on the following determinants of aggregate demand:

1. Propensity to consume
2. The rate of internest
3. The marginal efficiency of capital

4. See Michael Stewart, *Keynes and After,* Penguin Books, 1967, p. 134.
5. Stonier and Hague, *op. cit.* p.575

After having examined the effect of cut in money wages on the above determinants of aggregate demand he reached the conclusion that when all things are considered, cut in money wages is likely to affect aggregate effective demand adversely and will therefore be unable to remove unemployment in the economy. In any case, according to him, *favourable effect of wage-price flexibility on aggregate demand and employment occurs through reduction in rate of interest which gives a boost to investment demand.* But reduction in rate of interest can be easily achieved through expansion in money supply in the economy and therefore for that purpose it is not a sound policy to adopt the policy of cutting money wages of workers. We examine below the effect of wage cuts on three determinants of aggregate demand.

Propensity to Consume. The effect of reduction in money wages is likely to reduce consumption demand by adversly affecting proensity to consume. All-round cut in money wages will reduce prices of products since wages are an important element of cost. The greater the ratio of wage costs to total production costs, the greater the fall in prices of products. The *reduction in money wages and fall in prices of products are likely to lead to the redistribution of real income from wage earners to those sections of the society whose money incomes have not been reduced.* Since propensity to consume of wage earners is higher than the non-wage earners who happen to be relatively richer sections of a society, this redistribution of income is likely to reduce propensity to consume causing a decline in aggregate consumption demand.

Another type of redistributive effect of fall in prices is that redistribution of income from debtors to creditors occurs which also reduces consumption expenditure. The debit repayments are usually fixed in money terms so that fall in prices due to all-round reduction in wages which was not expected when debts were incurred causes an increase in the real value of mortgage and instalment payments by debtors to creditors which usually happen to be individual savers and banks. Even banks receive funds from individuals and companies who save and deposit their savings. This redistribution of income also reduces aggregate consumption demand, because creditors spend a relatively small part of the addition to their incomes due to fall in prices whereas debtors have to reduce their consumption greatly to meet their higher real interest payments caused by fall in prices.

It follows from above that cut in money wages will have an adverse effect on propensity to consume and will therefore reduce aggregate demand.

Marginal Efficiency of Capital. The effect of cut in money wages on marginal efficiency of capital is quite uncertain. This effect depends on what has been called *expectation effect*. If entrepreneurs expect that although money wages have been reduced in the present, they will rise again in the future, this will have a favourable effect on marginal efficiency of capital in the present. This is because higher money wages in the future will ensure better prospects of future demand for goods which will raise marginal efficiency of capital. Further, the fact that entrepreneurs expect money wages and therefore prices to rise in future, the people will prefer to buy goods in the present rather than in the future. This will improve prospects of making profits temporarily in the present and will therefore raise marginal efficiency of capital. However, this favourable effect of wage cut on marginal efficiency of capital is unlikely to be significant.

But the expectation effect of fall in wages and prices is likely to have more adverse affect on marginal efficiency of capital. If fall in wages and prices lead people to expect that they will fall even further in the future, it will reduce consumption demand. This will make entrepreneurs to become pessimistic about future economic prospects. As a result, marginal efficiency of capital will fall which will cause a reduction in investment demand.

It follows from above that the effect of a wage cut and fall in price on the marginal efficiency of capital is uncertain because much depends in expectations of entrepreneurs. However, cut in money wages is likely to reduce consumption demand which ultimately determines the future prospective yields from investment. It is believed by Keynesians that cut in wages and falling prices make future prospects of selling consumer goods less rosy and therefore adversely affect marginal efficiency of capital.

KEYNES'S EFFECT, PIGOU EFFECT AND EMPLOYMENT

Rate of Interest : Keynes's Effect

The cut in money wages and consequent fall in prices is likely to reduce the rate of interest which will favourably affect investment demand. This is generally referred to as Keynes's effect as compared to Pigou effect which traces out the favourable effect of money wage cuts on consumption demand through the increase in real value of money balances. According to Keynes, when cut in money wages is made and consequently prices fall, transactions demand for money will decline which will cause increase in the money supply for speculative motive. This increase in money supply for speculative motive will cause a reduction in the rate of interest. At a lower rate of interest, more investment will be forthcoming which will raise the level of aggregate demand and employment. It is important to notice here that in Keynesian analysis the hope of stimulus to investment following the cut in money wages and resultant fall in prices lies in the *lowering of rate of interest.* However, Keynes asserted that rate of interest can be easily lowered through expansion in money supply. Therefore, according to Keynes, theoretically "*We can produce the same effect on the rate of interest by increasing the quantity of money while keeping the level of wages unchanged*".[6] Further, according to him, expansionary monetary policy to reduce rate of interest is preferable to the policy of reducing money wages since the latter will not only be strongly resisted by workers but also an all-round wage cut will reduce consumption demand for goods and will therefore adversely affect employment. Keynes scarstically remarks that while the flexible wage policy and monetary policy produce the same effect on investment demand through lowering rate of interest but there is a "world of difference between them in practice, only a foolish person would prefer a flexible wage policy to a flexible monetary policy"[7]

However, Keynes emphasised that expansionary monetary policy (and for that matter flexible wage policy so far its effect on rate of interest is concerned) will not necessarily ensure full employment. To *what extent increase in money supply will succeed in lowering rate of interest and boost investment demand depends first on interest-elasticity of the liquidity preference curve and secondly on interest-elasticity of investment demand curve*. If the liquidity preference curve is highly elastic, (or in the extreme case, the economy is in the region of *liquidity trap*), the increase in quantity of money would not bring about much fall in the rate of interest. Again, if the investment demand curve is relatively inelastic, then even the fall in rate of interest as a consequence of expansion in money supply would not be able to achieve much increase in investment.

Thus, Keynes was not hopeful of securing adequate increase in employment through either flexible wage policy or flexible monetary policy at times of depression.

Real Balance Effect or Pigou Effect

All-round cut in wages and consequent fall in prices produces a favourable effect on aggregate demand and employment in another way which was first pointed out by Pigou and is, therefore, known after his name as Pigou effect. According to Pigou effect, when wage cut causes a fall in prices, *real value of money balances increases* making people richer which induces them to increase their consumption expenditure and raises aggregate demand and employment. Though Keynes and his followers admitted that real balance effect operated but they expressed doubts about its *quantitative significance*. Of course, Pigou effect or real balance effect is theoretically possible but empirical evidence shows that it is not strong enough to raise aggregate demand sufficiently to ensure full employment.

---

6. J.M. Keynes, *The General Theory of Employment, Interest and Money*. P. 267.
7. Ibid, pp. 267-268
8. Don Patinkin, *Money, Interest and Prices,* Evanston, 1956

It may be noted that 'Pigou effect' has been subsequently developed by Don Patinkin under the title of *real balance effect*. Don Patinkin[8] tried to revive the classical economics and tried to show that Keynes was wrong for advancing the view that the free market economy did not have a mechanism to restore full employment equilibrium after an initial disturbance. Like the Pigou effect, real balance effect means that when the economy goes into recession or depression, wages and prices fall and as result *real value or purchasing power of money balances increases*. This enables people to buy more than they could before. At lower prices they will actually purchase more than they did before. This increase in demand will lead to rise in output and employment. Thus, the operation of real balance effect, according to Patinkin, will bring the economy back automatically to full employment.

Of course, there may be some increase in output and employment as a result of the working of the real balance effect. But the crucial question, is whether it is quantitatively strong enough to get the economy out of depression and restore full employment. As mentioned above, the real balance effect is not very significant to ensure the return to full employment. Thus Steward writes, "*The process of falling prices was limited in its extent, it was not possible for the expansionary effect of its purchasing power to be more than a minor effect to the contractionary effect of falling incomes, consumption and investment, particularly when account was taken of the multiplier.*"[9]

Insider-Outsider Model

A recent approach about wage-employment relation known as insider-outsider model is worth mentioning[10]. According to this approach, those who become unemployed as a result of fall in aggregate demand resulting in recession in the economy lose their influence on the wage-setting process and do not participate in wage negotiations with the employers. This is because the unemployed often lose their status as union members and therefore neither the employers nor the labour union care about them. As a result, while the unemployed workers would want firms to cut wages so as to create more jobs which would enable them to get back employment but the firms ignore them and negotiate with the workers who have jobs and are members of unions. It may be noted that it is quite expensive for the firms to often turnover the workers as costs have to be incurred for hiring new workers, training them and when not required retrenching them. Therefore, insiders have advantage over the outsiders who are seeking employment. Therefore, it is difficult for the firms to cut wages of the insiders *(i.e.*, their employed labour force), especially if their labour-union is strong. Even threats by the firms to the workers that they will be fired and rendered jobless if they do not accept wage cuts may not succeed.

Even if the workers yield to these threats and accept cut in wages to retain their employment it may not be in the interest of the firms themselves to lower wages as it is likely to adversely affect the morale, effort and productivity of workers. The firms will therefore think it better for them to deal with the insiders and pay them good wages even if there are unemployed workers outside who are eagerly seeking employment even at lower wages. Thus, "*The insider-outsider model predicts that wages will not respond substantially to unemployment and thus another reason why we do not quickly return to full employment once the economy experiences recession.*"[11]

Some economists believe that the insider-outsider model provides an important explanation of the persistent high unemployment in the European countries for the last about three decades starting in early 1980s. This is because labour unions in the European countries are quite strong and force the firms to bargain with the insiders and ignore the outsiders, the unemployed. This keeps the wages at high levels despite the existence of large unemployment in the European countries. However, if the labour union were not strong, the firms might like to hire the outsiders (*i.e.*, unemployed) at lower

9. Michael Stewart, *Keynes and After,* 2nd edition 1972 Penguin Books, pp. 139 – 40.
10. See Assar Lindech and Dennis Snower, *The Insider-Outsider Theory of Employment and Unemployment* (Cambridge, M.A: MIT Press 1988).
11. Dornbusch, Fischer and Startz, *Macroeconomics,* Tata McGraw-Hill, 8th edition, 2002. p.116

wages and thereby reduce unemployment and the new firms might be set up to take advantage of cheap labour and provide employment. This would reduce European unemployment but the strong unions would resist lowering of wages. As a result there is persistent high unemployment in European countries.

Summing up. Let us now sum up the debate between Keynes and the classical economists on pursuing a flexible wage policy to ensure full employment. In the recent years the quantitative importance of Keynes's effect and real balance effect has been hotly debated. Many modern economists doubt the importance of real balance effect though its theoretical possibility is not denised. Again, as regards the choice between flexible wage policy and flexible monetary policy for increasing investment demand through lowering the rate of interest is concerned one is likely to achieve much less success by reducing the level of money wages than by increasing the supply of money. Besides, there are strong practical objections to following a flexible wage policy as an alternative to monetary policy. First, as has been mentioned above, workers and their trade unions will strongly oppose all-round cut in money wages for every section of workers. It is much easier to lower interest rate through expansionary monetary policy than by cuts in money wages. Secondly, it is inequitable and unreasonable to expect that workers alone should accept cut in their money wages while other sections of the society continue enjoying higher money incomes. Thus, to increase the supply of money to reduce unemployment during depression is preferable to cutting wages. Thirdly, reduction in money wages and consequent fall in prices would increase the real burden of debt whereas expansionary monetary policy would reduce it.

Thus, there is wide agreement among modern economists that, in practice, cut in money wages is unlikely to be brought about to make them a practical policy of achieving full employment. Further, what can be achieved by cuts in money wages can be easily achieved through increase in money supply to raise aggregate demand and employment.

ANTI-RECESSIONARY POLICY TO REMOVE CYCLICAL UNEMPLOYMENT

As explained in a previous chapter, when aggregate demand falls short of aggregate supply at full-employment level of resources, a deflationary or recessionary gap emerges in the economy. This gap or demand deficiency arises due to the fact that investment demand is not large enough to be equal to the amount of saving at full-employment level of income. Investment demand depends upon expected rate of profit. When businessmen have adverse expectations about future profits, the expected rate of return on capital falls causing decline in investment demand. The decline in investment demand leads to a multiple fall in overall aggregate demand resulting in unemployment of resources, especially unemployment of labour. This is recession (*if it is very severe, it is called depression*). To pull the economy out of recession or depression, the adoption of measures to raise aggregate demand is called for. We spell out below the various measures for raising aggregate demand so as to correct demand deficiency.

1. Deficit Budgeting : Expanding Aggregate Demand

An important fiscal measure to correct demand deficiency is to plan for deficit budgets. Deficit budgets can be attained in two ways. First, government should increase its expenditure on goods and services without being matched by imposition of fresh taxes or without raising the rates of old taxes. In 1930's when all capitalist economies of the world suffered from severe depression Keynes recommended the increase in government expenditure on *public works programmes* such as constructions of roads, railways, canals, school buildings, irrigation works, electrification of villages etc., to tackle the problem of demand deficiency. It should be noted that increase in public expenditure will have a multiplier effect on raising income and employment, that is, income and employment will not rise to the extent of increase in government expenditure but by much more than that depending upon the magnitude of multiplier. The magnitude of the multiplier which is generally denoted by the letter k in turn depends upon the marginal propensity to consume. Thus, $k = \frac{1}{1-mpc}$. The greater the marginal propensity to consume, the higher the multiplier and therefore the greater the effect of public expenditure on income employment.

If government increases its expenditure by ₹ 5,000 crores and multiplier is 3, then national income and output will expand by ₹ 15,000 crores. Corresponding to this expansion in national output there will be three-fold increase in employment of labour, given the labour-output ratio.

It is important to note that for maximum effect on income and employment, deficit budget should be financed not by *borrowing* from the general public but by creating *new money* (*i.e.*, issuing of new notes) by Reserve Bank of India. Thus deficit budget should be financed by what is called *monetisation of budget deficit* which would lead to the expansion in money supply in the economy.

2. Reduction in Taxes : Increasing Disposable Income

Another fiscal measure to raise aggregate demand is cutting down taxes. With reduction in taxes, people's disposable income will rise and consequent to this, their spending on goods and services will rise. If corporate taxes are reduced, this will increase the profitability of investment due to which business class will be induced to invest more. Thus, with reduction in taxation the two components of aggregate demand, namely, consumption demand and investment demand will increase. This would help in taking the economy out of depression. In 1964 on the advice of the Keynesian economists government in US made significant cut in income tax. And this did a miracle in reviving the American economy and soon output and employment increased substantially. The recession was thus overcome with the help of fiscal policy. In June 2008, the President of the United States announced a tax cut of 3.5 billion dollars to revive the American economy which was experiencing recession as a result of global financial crisis started from the US.

3. Monetary Policy : Expanding Credit

Monetary policy can also be used to overcome depression by removing demand deficiency. The following three types of monetary measures may be taken under monetary policy to raise aggregate demand. Whereas the first measure works to raise the *cost of credit*, the other two increase the *availability of credit*. When there is a depression in the economy, the central bank tries to overcome it by lowering the bank rate. As a result of the fall in the bank rate, the market rates of interest also fall. With the fall in the market rates of interest borrowing costs decline and therefore investment by business class is stimulated which brings about the increase in aggregate demand and helps to remove depression.

Another method to stimulate expansion in credit supply is lowering of *Cash Reserve Ratio* (CRR). With lower cash reserve ratio banks will have more available funds with them which they will be willing to lend to business firms for investment purposes. This will raise investment and aggregate demand in the economy leading to the expansion in income and employment. Likewise, statutory liquidity ratio (SLR) can also be lowered which will also increase the availability of credit by banks.

4. Export Promotion to Raise Aggregate Demand

Deficiency in aggregate demand can also be corrected through promotion of exports of goods. When domestic demand or market for goods is limited or has shrinked due to the operation of some adverse factors, the goods can be sold abroad. But growth of expors of a country depends on several factors. The first important factor is the prices of the goods to be exported. We can export those goods which can be produced comparatively at lower costs and therefore can be sold abroad at competitive prices. That is, expansion in exports of those products can be achieved in which the country has a comparative advantage. We can also lower the cost of production by modernisation and upgradation of technology in export industries. Industrial licensing policy may also be suitably modified so that export industries are able to enjoy the economies of scale.

To achieve growth in exports we should also pay attention in the *quality* of exports. If the quality of our goods to be exported is superior, they can favourably compete with the goods of other countries. Besides, we should enter into bilateral agreements with other countries to ensure that our exports do not suffer from heavy tariff duties. The developed countries have taken several steps chief among which are heavy import duties to protect their industries. Efforts should be made through bilateral talks as well as through international forums to convice and pressure them to remove thee tariff barriers on the exports from the developing countries.

To expand exports substantially we have to diversify our exports. Not only the exports of products of agro-based industries such as tea, cotton textiles, hides and skins, jute manufactures, tobacco and iron-ore, which are our traditional exports, have to be promoted but also exports of new manufactured goods such as engineering goods, chemicals, leather and leather products and handicrafts. India now exports a wide range of light manufactured goods such as typewriters, plastic goods, sewing machines, electric fans, cycles, transistors, some types of machinery. Exports of all these need to be encouraged by providing suitable incentives.

QUESTIONS FOR REVIEW

1. What is meant by involuntary unemployment ? Explain Keynes's theory of involuntary unemployment.

2. Explain the following types of the unemployment. What factors are responsible for their existence ?

1. Frictional Unemploymnt
2. Structural Unemployment
3. Cyclical Unemployment.

3. Explain the concept of full employment. Is it consistent with the existence of natural rate of unemployment ? Explain the measures that can be adopted to achieve it.

4. What is natural rate of unemployment ? How do the unemployment benefits affect it ?

5. What is full employment ? Discuss with the help of a diagram the different ways of attaining full employment ?

6. Distinguish between fiscal policy and monetary policy. How is monetary policy helpful in generation of employment opportunities in the economy ?

7. What is meant by disguised unemployment ? How can the problem of disguised unemployment in developing countries be solved ?

8. Discuss the nature of unemployment in developing countries like India. Explain the limitations of Keynesian policy prescription, namely, deficit financing to increase aggregate demand to solve the problem of unemployment.

9. Discuss the causes of unemployment and underemployment in developing countries like India. What policy measures would you suggest to solve the unemployment problem in these countries?

10. Explain Insider-Outsider Model. How does it explain the persistent high unemployment rate in Western European Countries ?

11. What is *Pigou effect* (or real balance effect) ? How has it been used to support wage cut at times of a recession or depression ? Why did Keynes oppose it ?

12. What is '*Keynes's effect*' regarding impact of wage cut on employment ? Why did Keynes oppose it when Keynes's effect has a favourable effect on employment ?

13. What are the causes of rigidity of money wages ? How is it responsible for involuntary unemployment during recession or depression ?

14. Explain the classical viewpoint regarding cut in wages at times of depression to restore full-employment. On what grounds Keynes opposed it ?

APPENDIX TO CHAPTER 12

Unemployment in Developing Countries with Special Reference to India

Basic Explanation of Unemployment in Developing Countries : Lack of Capital and other Productive Assets

As stated above, Keynesian theory is mainly concerned with cyclical unemployment which emerges in the developed capitalist countries, especially in times of depression due to the fall in aggregate demand. During the period 1929-33, the developed capitalist economies suffered from seververe depression which caused huge magnitude of unemployment. Keynes analysed this cyclical type of unemployment and asserted that it was caused by deficiency of aggregate demand. *The nature of unemployment in developing countries such as India is however quite different; rather than being cyclical it is of chronic and long-term nature.* Caused by the operation of structural factors, namely, the rate of capital formation has not been large enough to absorb increase in labour force in productive employment. It is now almost universally recognised that the chronic unemployment and underemployment in India are not due to the lack of aggregate effective demand which, according to J.M. Keynes, was responsible for unemployment in developed countries in times of depression. *Rather it is stated to be due to the lack of land, capital and other complementary resources in relation to the total population and labour force.* Besides, extreme unequal distribution of land resulting in lack of access of land to a vast majority of rural population and use of capital-intensive technology in industries has accentuated the problem of unemployment and underemployment in developing countries. In the phenomenon examined by Keynes, not only labour force but also capital equipment was unemployed due to the deficiency of aggregate effective demand. In other words, in the Keynesian scheme, both the labour force and capital equipment was crying out for full employment which could be achieved by raising the level of aggregate monetary expenditure. Thus, according to Joan Robinson: "*Keynes's theory has little to say, directly, to the underdeveloped countries, for it was framed entirely in the context of an advanced industrial economy, with highly developed financial institutions and a sophisticated business class. The unemployment that concerned Keynes was accompanied by underutilisation of capacity already in existence. It had resulted from a fall in effective demand. The unemployment of underdeveloped economies arises because capacity and effective demand never have been great enough*"[1].

The existence of unemployment due to lack of capital or other cooperating factors was an important question which was discussed by Marx in the context of advanced industrialised countries. Therefore, such unemployment has often been called *Marxian unemployment*[2] as distinguished from Keynesian unemployment which is caused by the deficiency of aggregate demand. According to Marx, the number of workers employed by the capitalists depends upon the amount of capital in existence, and there is, what he called, "reserve army of unemployed labour" because there is inadequate capital to employ all the available labour. If A stands for the total amount of available labour, N for the amount of labour-employment which is necessary to work with the existing stock of capital at its normal capacity, then $A–N$ is the reserve army of unemployed labour.[3]

1. Joan Robinson, *Economic Philosphy*, p. 119.
2. See Joan Robinson, *An Essay on Marxian Economics*.
3. It may also be noted that, according to Marx, accumulation of industrial capital, that is, establishment of

Thus, the standard explanation for the existence of labour surplus or unemployment and under-employment in less developing countries like India is that as compared with the magnitude of population and labour force there is limited availability of capital or complementary resources which include land, factories, machines, tools and implements–the means with which labour produces. Now, if the population grows faster than the stock of capital of a country, the entire addition to the labour force cannot be absorbed in productive employment because not enough instruments of production would be there to employ them. Since in less developed countries, the stock of capital has not been growing at a rate fast enough to keep pace with the growth of population, the ability to offer productive employment is not adequate. This has resulted in surplus labour which is manifested in the existence of huge magnitude of open unemployment, underemployment and disguised unemployment in both the rural and urban areas.

Capital as the major bottleneck to growth of employment was made popular by Harrod-Domar model of economic growth in which capital accumulation plays a pivotal role and according to which rate of growth of output depends upon the proportion of national income saved, divided by the capital-output ratio ($g = s/v$, where g stands for growth rate, s for the proportion of income saved and v for the capital-output ratio). This model assumes capital coefficients (*i.e.,* capital-output ratio and capital-labour ratio) to remain constant. With constant capital-output and capital-labour ratios, the more the capital, the more will be both output and employment. Therefore, when adapted to the less developed countries, this model suggests that the *rate of growth of output and therefore of employment is determined by the growth of capital stock.*

Wage Goods Constraint and Unemployment in Developing Countries

It is worth mentioning a dissenting view regarding the cause of unemployment and under-employment in developing countries. This dissenting view has heen put forward by Prof. P.R. Brahmananda and C.N. Vakil of Bombay University. According to them, the basic cause of unemployment in developing countries is the deficiency of the availability of essential consumer goods, often called *wage goods.* They point out that when the unemployed people or disguisedly unemployed people who are withdrawn from agriculture are engaged in some public works, they will have to be supplied with wage-goods so that employed labourers can subsist. If the wage-goods are not sufficiently available, their employment in capital-creation works cannot be sustained. Given the real wage rate, a particular number of people can be employed in the economy, depending upon the supply of wage-goods in the economy. Now, the total quantity of wage-goods required to employ all the disguisedly unemployed workers in agriculture, according to them, would exceed the actual available supply of wage-goods even when the release of wage-goods by the withdrawal of disguised unemployed is taken into account. Thus, according to Prof. Brahmananda and Vakil, there exists a *wage-goods* gap which is the fundamental cause of unemployment in labour-surplus developing countries.[4]

A prominent Indian economist, Prof. Amartya Sen, has also emphasised the supply of wage-goods in determining employment in developing countries. According to Prof. Sen, the quantum of wage employment in the economy depends on the total supply of wage-goods on the one hand and the real wage rate on the other. If E represents the quantum of employment, M represents the supply of wage-goods and W, the real wage-rate, then the employment which can be provided will be given by the following equation :[5]

---

large-scale factories and machines displaces labour engaged in handicrafts or artisan activities because the latter would not be able to withstand the competiton from the former. *Marx believed that the accumulation of industrial capital could never proceed fast enough to create employment for all who were displaced by the new machines.* Therefore, Marxian unemployment in our view is of the nature of "*technological unemployment*".

4. Amartya Sen, *Technology and Employment,* Oxford University Press.
5. Ibid.

$$E = \frac{M}{W}$$

It is thus evident from Sen's above equation that if the supply of wage-goods (M) is less than their required supply to provide them to all labour force, then all workers cannot be fully employed, which will result in the emergence of unemployment. Thus, to generate enough employment and solve the problem of unemployment and underemployment, the wage-goods industries, especially agriculture, must be accorded a high priority in the strategy of economic development.

Most of the unemployment in developing countries is therefore of a different nature from that in advanced developed countries. A major part of unemployment in present-day developed countries is of cyclical nature which is due to *deficiency of aggregate effective demand.* But most of the unemployment in developing countries is not cyclical. Thus, in developing countries, there is not much Keynesion type short-term unemployment. Instead, it is a chronic problem.

Causes of Unemployment in the Indian Economy

We have explained above the two **basic** explanations of unemployment and underemployment prevailing in the developing countries. We now explain below in some detail the various causes which account for unemployment and underemployment that prevails in the developing countries.

1. Lack of the Stock of Physical Capital. The major cause of unemployment and underemployment in developing countries like India is *the deficiency of the stock of capital* in relation to the needs of the growing labour force. In the modern world, man by himself can hardly produce anything. Even the primitive man needed some elementary tools like the bow and arrow to engage in hunting for the earning of his livelihood. With the growth of technology and specialisation, he needs much more capital with which to engage in the productive activity. If he is an agriculturist, he needs a piece of land and also a plough, a pair of oxen, fertilizers, means of irrigation to produce agricultural products. In the industrial sector, he needs factories to work in and machines to work with. All these aids to production belong to the community's stock to capital. Now, if the working force grows faster than the stock of capital of a country, the entire addition of labour force cannot be absorbed in productive employment because not enough instruments of production would be there to employ them. The resulting unemployment is known as the *long-term* or *chronic unemployment.*

A nation's stock of capital can be enlarged by increased investment which, in the absence of any unutilised resources, requires additional saving on the part of the community. The concern of the classical economists was to ensure that the rate of capital formation be kept sufficiently high so that employment opportunities were successively enlarged to absorb the additions to the working force of a country as a result of population growth. This is also the problem that the developing countries like India are facing today. In recent times, the labour force in India has been growing at more than 2 per cent per year, yet our rate of investment *expressed as a percentage of our stock of capital* has not been growing at a fast enough rate so as to keep pace with the growth of population. As a result, the country's ability to offer productive employment to the new entrants in the labour force has been severely limited. This manifests itself in two things: first, the prevalence of large-scale open unemployment in the urban areas, and second, it manifests itself in the form of open unemployment and underemployment in the rural areas as well as disguised unemployment in agriculture.

2. Use of Capital-Intensive Techniques. An important factor responsible for slow growth of employment has been the use of capital-intensive techniques of production, even in consumer goods industries where alternative labour-intensive techniques are available. Even before 1991, under the Industrial Policy Resolution 1956, the development of consumer goods industries was left open for the private sector. However, private sector prefers to invest in highly capital-intensive plants and equipment on the basis of technology developed in labour-scarce western countries. It is argued by them that the alternative labour-intensive techniques have low productivity and low surplus-generating capacity.

However, the important reason for the use of capital-intensive techniques has been the availability of cheap capital. Even firms in modern small industry sector which were expected to generate large employment opportunities have also tended to use capital-intensive techniques of production. Thus, Prof. J.C. Sandesara states, "*The availability of cheap capital has tended to encourage the modern small-scale industries sector to over-capitalise and use more capital-intensive methods of production and thus reduce employment potential*".[6]

In agriculture, reckless mechanisation of various agricultural operations despite the existence of surplus labour has reduced the employment-augmenting effect of new high-yielding technology involving the use of HYV seeds, fertilisers and pesticides. This has prevented the generation of enough employment opportunities in rural areas.

Now, a pertinent question is why capital-intensive techniques are used in industries despite the condition of labour abundance in the economy. First reason, as mentioned above, is the *relatively low price of capital*. Relatively low price of capital has been caused by (*a*) lower rate of interest, (*b*) liberal depreciation allowance on capital investment permitted in the taxation system of the country, (*c*) relatively cheap capital equipment imported from abroad. Second, higher wages of labour in the organised sector relative to their productivity under pressure from trade unions. Thirdly, *rigid labour* laws also discourage the employment of labour. It is difficult to retrench labour even when it is not required in case an industrial unit becomes sick and proposes to close down or exit. Fourthly, Research and Development (R & D) activity has not been adequately directed to discover and identify *labour-intensive appropriate techniques* to be used in industries which, though labour-intensive, have also reasonably good productivity.

3. Inequitable Distribution of Land. Another cause of unemployment prevailing in the developing countries like India is inequitable distribution of land so that many agricultural households have *no adequate access to land* which is an important asset for agricultural production and employment. Sub-division of land holdings under the pressure of rapid population growth since 1951 has further reduced access to land for several agricultural households. As a result, many persons who were self-employed in agriculture have become landless agricultural labourers who suffer from acute unemployment and underemployment.

4. Rigid Protective Labour Legislation. Another reason for the slow growth of employment in the organised sector has been the existence of unduly rigid protective labour legislation which makes it very difficult to retrench a worker who has been employed for 240 days. Labour legislation is so much rigid that it is even difficult to close down the unit and quit the industry. Thus, this excessively protective labour legislation induces private entrepreneurs to prefer the maximum use of capital in place of labour.

5. Neglect of the Role of Agriculture in Employment Generation. An important factor responsible for slow growth of employment opportunities is the neglect of agriculture for generating employment opportunities. The general perception, as existed in the first three five year plans in India (1951-65) as well as in the theoretical models of growth for dualistic economies such as Lewis' "*Economic Development with Unlimited Supplies of Labour*" was that agriculture already contained surplus labour and it was required to withdraw this surplus labour from agriculture and employ them in the modern industrial sector. By the mid-sixties it was realised that not to speak of employing new entrants to the labour force year after year, the modern industrial sector could not absorb productivity even a fraction of the then existing unemployed persons in the foreseeable feature.

Agriculture though containing surplus labour can generate employment opportunities if proper strategy for its development is adopted. For instance, the empirical evidence shows that on an irrigated

---

6. J.C. Sandesara, *Small-scale Enterprises in Industrial Development. The Indian Experience* (1998), Sage Publications, Delhi.

hectare of land the number of manhours employed is almost twice that on the unirrigated hectare. Irrigation requires more labour input for watering the fields, and also since output per hectare on irrigated land is much higher, more labour is used for harvesting and threshing the crop. Besides, irrigation makes the *adoption of double cropping* possible which greatly raises the employment potential of agriculture.

It is worth noting that new agricultural technology, commonly called green revolution technology, involving the use of HYV (High Yielding Varieties) seeds, greater use of fertilisers and pesticides along with water is highty labour absorptive. What is equally important, this new green revolution technology is **size-neutal**, that is, it can be equally well adopted by small farmers. Further, HYV seeds are of short-duration type, that is, they mature in a short time making multiple cropping more feasible. The use of double or multiple cropping greatly enhances the opportunities of employment generation in agriculture. The experience of Punjab, Haryana and Western U.P. is a shining example of large employment generation in agriculture through green revolution technology. What is needed for the generation of large employment opportunities in agriculture is that the new green revolution technology should be widely diffused and adopted in the backward and lagging agricultural regions in India.

6. Lack of Infrastructure. We have explained above lack of physical capital with which labour is equipped for productive employment as the cause of unemployment prevailing in the developing countries like India. By capital we generally mean machines, plant and equipment, factory buildings etc. But a similar factor responsible for huge unemployment prevailing in these countries is lack of infrastructure such as roads, power, telecommunications, highways, irrigation facilities in agriculture. Inadequate availability of infrastructure is a great obstacle for the generation of opportunities for productive employment. Expansion in infrastructure facilities generate employment *directly as well as indirectly* in the production of industrial products and services as they have a large *forward linkages*.

It follows from above that unemployment and underemployment prevailing in India and other developing countries is *not cyclical Keynesian type of unemployment caused by decline in aggregate demand. Unemployment and underemployment in India are caused by more basic structural factors such as lack of capital, use of capital-intensive technologies, lack of access to land for agricultural households, lack of infrastructure, rapial growth of population resulting in large annual increments in labour force year after year*.

MEASUREMENT OF UNEMPLOYMENT IN THE INDIAN ECONOMY

The surplus labour in a developing economy such as ours manifests itself in (*a*) open unemployment, (*b*) underemployment and (*c*) disguised unemployment. Therefore, a realistic assessment of the magnitude of surplus labour that exists in the Indian economy should contain information about all these three forms of unemployment. However, the measurement of unemployment in an economy such as ours where self-employment is predominant and the bulk of productive activity is carried on within household enterprises is a different task. A slight difference in the definitions and criteria adopted to measure unemployment often makes enormous change in its magnitude. For example, late Professor Raj Krishna suggested the following four criteria to measure unemployment :

(*a*) *Time Criterion*: This refers to identifying those persons as unemployed who have no gainful work for less than some normal standard of hours in a week or less than a certain normal standard days in a month or a year.

(*b*) *Willingness Criterion*: This calls a person unemployed when he is either seeking or is available for work at the prevailing wage rate.

(*c*) *Income Criterion*: This considers those persons unemployed or underemployed who have income (or expenditure) less than a certain '*poverty norm*' generally fixed on the basis of minimum calories required for subsistence.

(*d*) *Productivity Criterion*: This considers those persons as unemployed or underemployed who may be working but they have less than some normal standard of productivity.

Thus, a change from time and willingness criteria to productivity criterion changes the estimate of rural unemployment for the year 1972-73 from 8.21 per cent of rural labour force (on daily status basis) to 33.7 per cent.[7]

Note that both willingness and time criteria have been used in India in the various rounds of National Sample Survey to measure unemployment in the economy. Productivity criterion has been used by Ashok Mathur, Shakuntala Mehra, Ashok Rudra and Amartya Sen to measure the extent of disguised unemployment in the Indian agriculture. Further, using household expenditure data from earlier rounds of NSS, Dandekar-Rath in their study of "*Poverty in India*" adopted income criterion to measure the magnitude of unemployment in the Indian economy.

Measurement of Unemployment in India : Dantwala Committee Approach

Let us now discuss the actual approaches that have been adopted in India to measure open unemployment and underemployment in India. On the basis of time and willingness criteria open unemployment and underemployment have been estimated using the following three approaches which were recommended by an expert committee headed by Prof. M.L. Dantwala:

(*i*) **Usual Status Approach.** This approach records only those persons as unemployed who had no gainful work for a *major time* during the 365 days preceding the date of survey and are seeking or are available for work. Thus, the estimates of unemployment obtained on the basis of usual status approach are expected to capture long-term open unemployment.

(*ii*) **Weekly Status Approach.** In this approach current activity status relating to the week preceding the date of survey is recorded and those persons are classified as unemployed who did not *have gainful work even for an hour on any day in the preceding week and were seeking or were available for work.* The persons who may be employed on usual status approach may however become intermittently unemployed during some seasons or parts of the year. Thus, unlike the usual status approach, *weekly status approach would capture not only open chronic unemployment but also seasonal unemployment*. This approach provides us a weekly average rate of unemployment.

(*iii*) **Daily Status Approach.** As noted above, the weekly status approach records a person employed *even if he works only for an hour on any day of the whole week*. It is thus clear that the weekly status approach would tend to underestimate unemployment in the economy because it does not appear to be proper to treat all those who have been unemployed for the whole week except an hour as employed. Indeed, the demand for labour in farming and non-farming households often fluctuates over a small period within a week. Hence the need for the use of daily status approach to measure the magnitude of unemployment and underemployment in India.In the daily status approach current activity status of a person with regard to whether employed or unemployed or outside labour force is recorded *for each day in reference week.* Further, for estimating employment and unemployment, *half-day has been adopted as a unit of measurement*. A person who works for 4 hours or more up to 8 hours in a day is recorded as employed for the full day and one who works for an hour or more but less than 4 hours on a day is recorded as employed for half-day. Accordingly, persons having no gainful work even for one hour on a day are described as unemployed for full day provided that they are either seeking or are available for work.

7. 33.7 per cent of labour force was Sen's estimate of rural unemployment for the year 1972-73 on the basis of his productivity criterion.

Thus, the daily status approach would capture not only the unemployed days of those persons who are usually unemployed but also the unemployed days of those who are recorded as employed on weekly status basis. Hence daily status concept of unemployment is more inclusive than those of usual status and weekly status approaches and would yield an average number of unemployed person-days per day in the year indicating the magnitude of both open unemployment and underemployment. They are also referred to as *person-years unemployed* so as to distinguish them from persons unemployed.[8]

The estimates of unemployment on the basis of above three approaches are presented in Table 12.1. It may be observed from this table that according to NSS 1999-2000 round, 2.8 per cent of labour force were unemployed on usual status basis and 4.4 per cent of labour force were unemployed on weekly status basis and 7.3 per cent of labour force on current daily status (CDS) basis. In 2004-05 (60th Round) unemployment rate further increased. On current weekly status basis, unemployment rate was estimated at 4.4 per cent in 2004-05 for India as a whole. On current daily status basis, in 2004-05 rate of unemployment rose to 8.3 per cent in case of All India. In absolute numbers, Planning Commission estimated unemployment to be of the order of 35 million persons on current daily status basis in April 2002 in the beginning of the 10th Plan. On the basis of 60th round, number of persons unemployed on the current daily status basis rose to 34.7 millions in 2004-05. However, according to 66th round of National Sample Survey (NSS) for the year 2009-2010, current daily status (CDS) unemployment rate as per cent of labour declined to 6.8 in rural areas and to 5.8 in urban areas giving us unemployment rate as 6.6% of labour force for whole India. However, in our view, this is the result of special employment guarantee scheme, MGNREGA, started in 2007-08 under which people are employed in construction activities for a short period of time and does not represent the *stable growth* of employment opportunities.

Table 12.1. Magnitude of Unemployment in the Indian Economy (% of Labour Force)

Approach	1972-73	1977-78	1983	1987-88	1993-94	1999-2000	2004-05	2009-10	2011-12
Usual Principal Status	1.61	4.23	2.77	3.77	2.58	2.8	3.1	2.5	2.7
Current Weekly Status	4.32	4.48	4.51	4.80	3.6	4.4	4.4	3.6	–
Current Daily Status	8.35	8.18	8.28	6.09	6.0	7.3	8.3	6.6	5.6

Source: Planning Commission, *Eighth Five Year Plan* 1992-97, Vol. I, p. 134 and *Tenth Five Year Plan.*

As compared to 1993-94, *all rates of unemployment* (*usual status, weekly status and daily status*) increased in 2004-05. This clearly shows that economic reforms initiated since 1991 led to the worsening of unemployment situation in the Indian economy.

Note that, contrary to what could be expected, weekly status unemployment is not much greater than that of the usual status approach. This is for two reasons. First, a person to be identified as unemployed on weekly status approach has to pass through a severe test, namely, he did not work even for only an hour in the whole reference week. Now, in an economy where there is predominance of self-employed households engaged in family-based enterprises, it is quite easy for a person to have worked for an hour in a week even during the lean periods of the year and therefore get registered himself as employed rather than unemployed. Secondly, during the slack seasons of the year some persons, mainly women, withdraw themselves from the workforce. Therefore, instead of being counted as unemployed, they are treated as 'outside labour force', for they generally report as 'not available for work'. As a result, whereas weekly status employment estimates are relatively greater than that of usual status, their unemployment estimates are not much higher.

Further, it is noteworthy that both the usual and weekly status approaches reveal a rather small magnitude of surplus labour. This is because, as mentioned above, *both these approaches measure open unemployment in the country*. However, in India with predominance of self-employed households and

8. See CSO, *National Sample Survey,* 32nd round (1977-78), Report No. 298, p. 20

absence of social security system to support the people, they can hardly afford to remain absolutely unemployed. The new hands that are added to the labour force every year as a result of increasing population do not remain openly unemployed; they share employment and work with others so that there is more of underemployment and disguised unemployment rather than open unemployment.

Thus, quite expectedly, the daily status approach which seeks to capture both open unemployment and underemployment reveals that quite a large magnitude of surplus labour exists in India. It will be seen from Table 12.1 that 8.3 per cent of labour force was found unemployed in 2004-05 on daily status basis. It has been estimated that the absolute magnitude of daily status unemployment increased to 36.7 million person-years in 2006-07.

However, in our view, even the daily status approach does not fully measure the magnitude of surplus labour in the Indian economy. Evidently, this also would have a tendency to under-record unemployment as it considered a person working for only 4 hours (1/2 of the standard day) as fully employed and a person who worked for an hour (1/8th of the standard day) as employed for half-day. In fact, as an alternative, hourly status approach measuring employment and unemployment in terms of manhours would be probably more appropriate.

Further, the daily status approach (or even the alternative hourly approach), like the usual and weekly status approach, cannot fully capture disguised unemployment of those persons whose intensity of work and consequently productivity is very low even though they are employed for a long time. In India, as in other labour-surplus developing countries, people are generally found to be working longer hours and larger number of days than one is really required to do the given work by **stretching or spreading the work.** Therefore, *for the proper assessment of the magnitude of surplus labour that currently exists in the Indian economy, unemployment on the basis of daily/hourly status ought to be supplemented by a measure of disguised unemployment based on a norm of productivity or work intensity.*

Despite the above limitations it is clear that daily status unemployment is a relatively better measure of the magnitude of surplus labour as it covers open unemployment as well as a good amount of underemployment.

Disguised Unemployment

A good number of unemployment in a labour-surplus country such as India manifests itself in the form of disguised unemployment, especially in the agricultural sector. It is a common knowledge that with minor changes in organisation and with the existing techniques, our agriculture can be looked after by a much smaller number of workers and they can be withdrawn from agriculture without reduction of agricultural output if alternative employment opportunities are available. Since employment opportunities in the non-agricultural sector have not been increasing large enough to absorb the new entrants of the labour force a good number of additional workers are compelled to remain in agriculture and related activities and this perpetuates the phenomenon of disguised unemployment. To be precise *disguised unemployment is said to prevail when so many workers are employed in agriculture that the marginal productivity of workers or labourers is zero*. Therefore, if they are withdrawn from agriculture, techniques of cultivation remaining the same, agricultural output will not fall. Thus, Prof. Ragnar Nurkse defines disguised unemployment in underdeveloped countries in the following way. "*These countries suffer from large-scale unemployment in the sense that even with the unchanged techniques of agriculture a large part of population engaged in agriculture could be removed without reducing agricultural output. The same farm output could be obtained with a smaller labour force. In technical terms, the marginal productivity of labour is zero*"[9]

It is worth noting that the concept of disguised unemployment is applicable to self-employed labourers of extended family system in agriculture and does not apply to wage employment which usually takes place on the large-sized capitalist farms. Thus the significance of the "term" 'disguisedly'

9. R. Nurkse, *Problems of Capital Formation in Underdeveloped Countries*, p.32

is that it is applied only to persons who are not normally engaged in wage employment but are self employed.

The measurement of disguised unemployment is very difficult. However, it is generally believed that around 25 per cent of labour force in labour-surplus developing countries such as India is disguisedly unemployed.

Prof. Amartya Sen's Analysis of Disguised Unemployment

Though the concept of disguised unemployment visualises production aspect of unemployment, it mainly manifests itself in idleness, that is, time not worked. In other words, disguised unemployment appears in the form of reduction in the hours worked in a day or a week and days in a week, or a month or year. As long as more work opportunities are available on the family farms, the additional labour is employed for that and as a result total output increases, though at a diminishing rate. When all the work opportunities on the farm are exhausted, no more addition to labour input will bring about increase in output. When the size of the families continues to increase due to the rapid growth of population and when alternative employment opportunities outside their families are not available, the additional members have to be absorbed on the family farms. Since on the family farms a point reaches beyond which no increase in labour input leads to the rise in total output, additional workers are absorbed by sharing of the work among more workers rather than by increasing the quantum of labour input employed on the farms. In other words, *the same quantity of labour is now applied by more workers. As a result, the number of working hours performed by all labourers in a day, or week and days in a month or year are reduced.*[10]

Distinction between marginal productivity of labourers and marginal productivity of labour. In explaining the concept of disguised unemployment, Amartya Sen has drawn the distinction between ***marginal product of labourers*** and ***marginal product of labour***. He explain that it is the marginal productivity of labourers over a wide range which is zero and not the marginal productivity of labour (i.e., labour input) over a wide range of labour used. In fact, marginal productivity of labour is just equal to zero at the margin. Therefore, the distinction drawn between labour and labourers by Prof. Amartya Sen is significant since it helps in understanding the nature of disguised unemployment and the form in which it appears as well as in removing the apparent contradiction between the disguised unemployment and rational behaviour. Thus, Prof. Amartya Sen writes :

"This confusion arises because of not distinguishing between labour and labourer. It is not that too much labour is being spent in the production process, but that too many labourers are spending it. Disguised unemployment thus normally takes the form of a smaller number of working hours per head per year; for example, each of three brothers shepherding the sheep every third day. It is thus, the marginal productivity of the labourer, so to say that is nil over a wide range and the productivity of labour may be just equal to zero at the margin. *It may also take the form of lower intensity of work with people 'taking it easy'*, e.g. the peasant having time to watch the birds while working. If a number of labourers went away, the others would be able to produce about the same output working longer and harder. There is not contradiction between disguised unemployment will naturally put on this disguise. A piece of land that can be cultivated fully by two, may actually be looked after by four, if a family of four working men having no other employment opportunity happens to own it."[11]

It is evident from Professor Sen's quotations given above, the disguised unemployment appears not only in the form of the idle man hours (that is, all workers work for lesser hours of work than those considered standard or normal and remain idle for the rest) but also in the reduced intensity of work-hours performed. In other words, the disguised unemployment also creeps into work hours performed by labourers. This happens through what has been called work-spreading or work-stretching devices.

10. Amartya Sen, *Choice of Techniques*, Basil Blakwell, 1957
11. *Op. cit.*, p.3

It is worth noting that not all sizes of farms suffer from disguised unemployment. As mentioned above, large-sized farms generally use hired labour (or are cultivated through tenancy system) and granting that landlords of those farms operate on the principle of profit maximisation, no disguised unemployment will exist on those farms. As the size of the farms goes on declining, man-land ratio on them will be increasing. As the man-land ratio rises with the decrease in the size of farms, the average and marginal products of the labourers will diminish due to the operation of diminishing returns. Since a certain minimum ratio of land to labour is required even in the most labour-intensive agricultural processes, a point will reach when the further reduction in the size of the farm and consequently further increase in the man-land ratio will result in zero marginal product of labour.

Graphic Illustration of Sen's Concept of Disguised Unemployment. Let us graphically explain the concept of disguised unemployments as has been clarified by Prof. Amartya Sen. Consider Fig. 12A.1 where along the *Y*-axis total output is measured and along the *X*-axis, labour (say labour hours) is measured. *TP* represents total product curve which in the beginning rises and after a point it becomes horizontal indicating thereby that total output remains constant after OL_1 amount of labour is spent. Now, according to Amartya Sen, it will be irrational on the part of the family to put in more labour on the farm beyond OL_1 since extra labour spent beyond OL_1 does not add to total output. Thus if the family goes beyond OL_1 and devotes OL_2 labour, then L_1L_2 labour input has been unnecessarily spent, for it has not brought any increment in output. Marginal product of labour is zero when OL_1 amount of labour is put in. Therefore, a rational family will put in OL_1 amount of labour.

But, according to Prof. Amartya Sen, the disguised unemployment occurs due to the fact that a given amount of labour is spent by too many labourers. Consider Fig. 12A.1. again. Along the south, number of labourers are measured. Suppose in the beginning OL_1 amount of labour is being put in by ON_1 labourers who are working normal hours in a week. If now the size of the family expands and the number of labourers increases from ON_1 to ON_2, the amount of land, other factors and technique of production remaining the same. As stated above, it will be futile and irrational to put in more labour beyond OL_1 even though the number of labourers in the family has increased. If the additional labourers do not get employment outside the family farm, the reaction of the family will be that the same amount of labour input OL_1 be shared by ON_2 labourers. As a result, the number of work hours devoted by each labourer will be reduced. The total output will not increase since the same amount of labour input OL_1 is being put in. It follows therefore that the increase in the number of labourers from ON_1 to ON_2 has not resulted in any increment in total output: only the same amount of labour is being shared by ON_2 labourers instead of ON_1. Thus number of labouers N_1N_2 represents disguised unemployment since marginal productivity of laboureres over this range is zero. Now if N_1N labourers are withdrawn from the agricultural family, total output will not decline. With the withdrawal of N_1N_2 workers, the remaining workers will put in OL_1 labour so that each of them will work for normal hours.

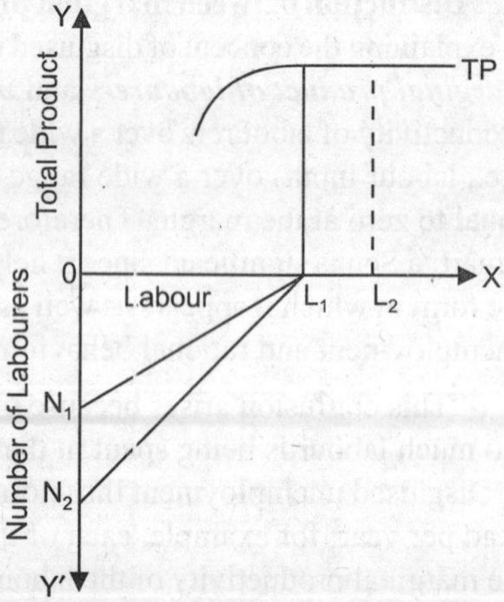

Fig. 12A.1. *The Emergence of Disguised Unemployment*

The magnitude of disguised unemployment has been increasing in underdeveloped countries since the rate of capital accumulation has not kept pace with the rapid growth of population. It has been estimated that 15 to 30 per cent of agricultural labour force is disguisedly unemployed in various labour-surplus underdeveloped countries. This type of unemployment can be relieved by the development of non-agricultural sectors and by increasing the rate of capital formation that will open new avenues of employment. But the economies of such over-populated agricultural countries are generally stagnant and economic development has been slow to generate sufficient employment opportunities to absorb surplus farm labour. All this leads to the emergence of the phenomenon of continuously mounting pressure of disguised unemployment. The increasing pressure of population leads to subdivision and fragmentation of holdings with all their attendant evils. The farm income goes down with every generation. Low consumption of the unemployed presses down level of economic activity. Surplus available for investment is meagre. Thus mass disguised unemployment is a drag on economic progress. The problem can be solved only by stepping up the rate of investment above the rate of population growth. The central problem of economic growth in such countries is thus to create conditions under which rate of investment can be increased above that of growth of population.

Solution. The basic solution to the problem of disguised unemployment is faster rate of capital formation and economic growth that creates a large number of employment opportunities. For this purpose rate of saving must be raised for increasing the rate of investment. In the developing countries investment incentives for the private sector are very low and the Government can assist in the process of capital formation directly as well as indirectly. Through a fiscal policy which encourages savings and investment and an easy monetary policy it can do much to encourage investors. The Government itself can participate in the process of capital formation by building infrastructure such as roads, power, ports, airports as undertaking of such development activities do not attract the private investors. Therefore, the Government has got to assume a special role in speeding up the rate of economic development and employment generation.

The other line of attack has got to be on the rate of population growth. If population grows at a rapid rate, then to maintain the people even at their existing levels, large amounts of capital are needed which could otherwise have been used to raise the amount of capital available per man and hence to raise the living standards at a faster rate. Apart from accumulation of capital (i.e., machines, factory buildings, tools and equipment), we should increase investment in agriculture and expand irrigation facilities to generate opportunities for productive employment. Besides, we should give incentives to *small and medium enterprises* which being labour-intensive will generate a lot of employment. Further, by adopting suitable fiscal and monetary policies we should discourage the use of capital-intensive techniques. Lastly, land reforms initiated in the earlier periods of planning should be effectively implemented to ensure access to land for agricultural households. We explain below in general what measures should be taken as a part of employment strategy to create employment opportunities.

Employment Strategy to Reduce Unemployment

The following measures should be adopted if unemployment problem is to be solved

Use of Labour-Intensive Technology. Both the organised and unorganised sectors must adopt *labour-intensive technology* if sufficient employment opportunities are to be generated in both the rural and urban sectors of the economy. The decline in employment elasticity of output growth[12] in recent years in India is primarily due to the *increasing trend in capital intensity* in the organised industrial sector as well as in agriculture. Increasing mechanisation of agriculture in various states has lowered the employment elasticity of growth of agricultural output. Therefore, for raising labour intensity, suitable monetary and fiscal measures need to be adopted to discourage the use of capital-intensive techniques. Of course, the use of labour-intensive techniques with lower productivity of workers in the industry and agriculture may lower the growth of output. Thus, there might be some *trade off between employment and growth of output.* In our view due to the seriousness of unemployment problem some output growth should be sacrificed for the sake of more employment.

Accelerating Investment in Agriculture. Second, an important reason for slow growth of employment in agriculture and rural sector has also been a *shortfall in investment or capital formation in agriculture*. Both the public and private sector investment in agriculture has declined since the

12. Note that employment elasticity with respect to output growth means percentage growth in employment resulting from one per cent growth in output.

early nineties. Of special importance from the viewpoint of employment generation is investment in irrigation, rural roads, flood control projects, power generation and other infrastructure. It is worth noting that investment not only generates employment directly but also has a multipier effect which operates through backward and forward linkages. Therefore, stepping up of investment in agriculture and rural infrastructures will greatly help in employment generation. The announcement by the government *to furnish more credit to farmers at lower than market rates of interest* from commercial banks will also ensure that the small and medium farmers will be able to buy fertilizers, other high-yielding inputs, and arrange for their irrigation. This will raise their productivity and tend to reduce under-employment and disguised unemployment. Despite more than six decades of planned development in India, agriculture continues to be principal source of employment in the Indian economy. Though the share of GDP from agriculture has come down to around 14 per cent, still about 50 per cent of labour force continues to be employed in agriculture. In fact, agriculture continues to be the parking lot of the unemployed in the country. But a good number of persons engaged in agriculture and related activities are not productively employed. In fact there is widespread under-employment and disguised unemployed. Economic reforms initiated in 1991 has by and large neglected agriculture which even now does not get enough credit from commercial banks.

No wonder that there has been a fall in investment or capital formation in agriculture both by the private and public sectors. This is an important reason why employment opportunities in agriculture have not risen much causing increase in rural unemployment. What is needed is the substantial investment in agriculture so as to generate enough employment opportunities in this sector.

Diversification of Agriculture. Besides there is urgent need for diversification of agriculture. For example, there is an urgent need for a relative shift from growing of crops to horticulture, vegetable production, floriculture, animal husbandry, fisheries etc. which are more labour absorbing and higher income-yielding. In addition to this, promotion of agro-processing industries for export purposes has a large employment potential.

For the rapid growth of employment opportunities in agriculture and related sectors and agro-processing industries, investment in infrastructure including irrigation, rural reads, power supply, and development of agricultural markets are required.

Labour-Intensive Industrial Growth. For solving unemployment problem in the urban areas, the organised industrial sector must also absorb a sufficient number of workers. The failure of the organised industrial sector to generate enough employment opportunities is due to the use of capital-intensive technologies imported from abroad. The tendency to use the higher capital-intensive technology by the Indian industries in the post reform period has been intensified because they are trying *to improve competitiveness to face competition from imported commodities*. The other factor responsible for the use of higher capital intensive technologies is the **factor-price distortions** such as cheap capital and relatively higher wages of workers who have strong labour unions. Capital has become relatively cheap due to various fiscal concessions such as liberal depreciation and investment allowance and low interest rates on borrowed funds for investment. Consequent to the use of high capital-intensive technologies in our industries the labour productivity has been increasing while employment has been growing at a snail pace. Therefore, to encourage the use of relatively more labour-intensive technologies and thereby to generate more employment opportunities, fiscal and monetary concessions mentioned above on use of capital must be withdrawn. In this case there is bound to be some loss of workers' productivity. Therefore, this will involve some trade-off between employment and output. In our view, because unemployment problem is very serious and greatly hurts people's welfare, some growth of output is worth sacrificing for more employment opportunities.

Services and Employment Growth. The growth of services in India has a large employment potential. In 1993-94 to 1999-2000, next to the construction sector the employment elasticity of output growth in services was higher and was estimated at about 0.50. Of special mention are software services and BPO (Business Processing Outsourcing) which have a lot of employment potential, especially for the educated youth of the country. The other services such as finance, insurance, trade, hotels, and restaurants have also a lot of employment potential. But an important thing to note is that growth of these services is dependent on industrial and agricultural growth in the economy.

Education, Health and Employment Generation. Lastly, the expansion of education and health care not only promotes accumulation of human capital and thereby contributes to growth of output, it will also generate a good deal of employment opportunities. More schools, hospitals, health care clinics in the rural and urban areas will not only create employment during their construction but also, and more important, when they start working to provide education and health services. Their working provides employment to both the educated and unskilled persons. Therefore, a higher allocation of resources is required to be made for them in government budgets and in our future plans.

PART – II

IS-LM MODEL, INFLATION-UNEMPOYMENT TRADE-OFF : PHILLIPS CURVE

- The IS-LM Curve Model : The Integration of Commodity and Monetary Markets
- Inflation-Unemployment Trade-off : Phillips Curve

CHAPTER 13

The IS-LM Curve Model

THE GOODS MARKET AND MONEY MARKET : LINKS BETWEEN THEM

Keynes in his analysis of national income explains that national income is determined at the level where aggregate demand (i.e., aggregate expenditure) for consumption and investment goods (C + I) equals aggregate output. In other words, in Keynes' simple model the level of national income is shown to be determined by the *goods market equilibrium.* In this simple analysis of equlibirum in the goods market Keynes considers investment to be determined by the rate of interest along with the marginal efficiency of capital and is shown to be independent of the level of national income. The rate of interest, according to Keynes, is determined by money market equilibrium by the demand for and supply of money. In this Keynes' model, changes in rate of interest either due to change in money supply or change in demand for money will affect the determination of national income and output in the goods market through causing changes in the level of investment. In this way changes in money market equilibrium influence the determination of national income and output in the goods market. Thus, an important contribution of Keynes has been that he integrated money market with goods market. Thus, an important contribution of Keynes has been that he integrated money market with goods market.

It has been shown by J.R. Hicks and others that with greater insights into the Keynesian theory one finds that the changes in income caused by changes in investment or propensity to consume in the goods market also influence the determination of interest in the money market. According to him, the level of income which depends on the investment and consumption demand determines the transactions demand for money which affects the rate of interest. Hicks, Hansen, Lerner and Johnson have put forward a complete and integrated model based on the Keynesian framework wherein the variables such as investment, national income, rate of interest, demand for and supply of money are interrelated and mutually interdependent and can be represented by the two curves called the *IS* and *LM* curves. This extended Keynesian model is therefore known as *IS-LM* curve model which explains integration of goods and money markets. In this model they have shown how the level of national income and rate of interest are jointly determined by the simultaneous equilibrium in the two interdependent goods and money markets. Now, this *IS-LM* curve model has become a standard tool of macroeconomics and the effects of monetary and fiscal policies are discussed using this *IS* and *LM* curves model.

GOODS MARKET EQUILIBRIUM : THE DERIVATION OF THE *IS* CURVE

The *IS-LM* curve model emphasises the interaction between the goods and money markets. The goods market is in equilibrium when aggregate demand is equal to income. The aggregate demand is determined by consumption demand and investment demand. In the Keynesian model of goods market equilibrium we also now introduce the rate of interest as an important determinant of investment. With this introduction of interest as a determinant of investment, the latter now becomes an endogenous variable in the model. When the rate of interest falls the level of investment increases and *vice versa*. Thus, changes in the rate of interest affect aggregate demand or aggregate expenditure by causing changes in the investment demand. When the rate of interest falls, it lowers the cost of investment projects and thereby raises the profitability of investment. The businessmen will therefore undertake greater investment at a lower rate of interest. The increase in investment demand will bring about increase in aggregate demand which in turn will raise the equilibrium level of income. *In the derivation of the IS curve we seek to find out the equilibrium level of national income as determined by the equilibrium in goods market by a level of investment determined by a given rate of interest.* ***Thus IS curve relates different equilibrium levels of national income with various rates of interest.*** As explained above, with a fall in the rate of interest, the planned investment will increase which will cause an upward shift in aggregate demand function ($C + I$) resulting in goods market equilibrium at a higher level of national income.

The lower the rate of interest, the higher will be the equilibrium level of national income. Thus, the *IS* curve is the locus of those combinations of rate of interest and the level of national income at

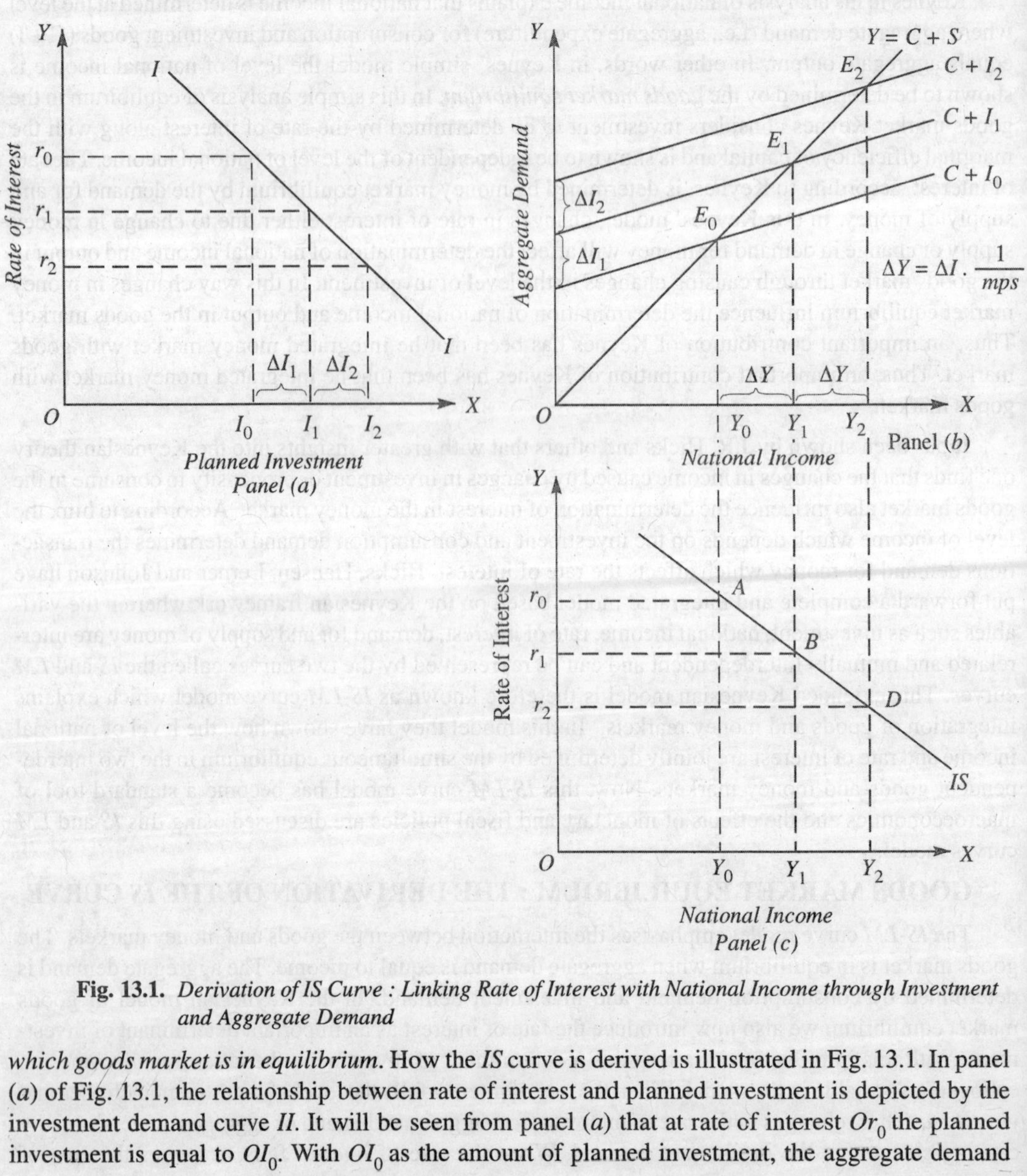

Fig. 13.1. *Derivation of IS Curve : Linking Rate of Interest with National Income through Investment and Aggregate Demand*

which goods market is in equilibrium. How the *IS* curve is derived is illustrated in Fig. 13.1. In panel (*a*) of Fig. 13.1, the relationship between rate of interest and planned investment is depicted by the investment demand curve *II*. It will be seen from panel (*a*) that at rate of interest Or_0 the planned investment is equal to OI_0. With OI_0 as the amount of planned investment, the aggregate demand curve is $C + I_0$ which, as will be seen in (*b*) of Fig. 13.1 equals aggregate output at OY_0 level of national income. Therefore, in the panel (*c*) at the bottom of Fig. 13.1, against rate of interest Or_0, level of income equal to OY_0 has been plotted. Now, if the rate of interest falls to Or_1, the planned investment by businessmen increases from OI_0 to OI_1 [see panel (*a*)]. With this increase in planned investment, the aggregate demand curve shifts upward to the new position $C + I1$ in panel (*b*), and the goods market is in equilibrium at OY_1 level of national income. Thus, in panel (*c*) at the bottom of Fig. 13.1 the level of national income OY_1 is plotted against the rate of interest, Or_1. With further lowering of the rate of interest to Or_2, the planned investment increases to OI_2 (see panel *a*). With this further rise in planned investment the aggregate demand curve in panel (*b*) shifts upward to the new position $C + I_2$ corresponding to which goods market is in equilibrium at OY_2 level of income. Therefore, in panel (*c*) the equilibrium income OY_2 is shown against the interest rate Or_2. By joining points A, B, D representing various interest-income combinations at which goods market is in equilibrium we obtain the *IS* curve. It will be observed from Fig. 13.1 that the *IS* curve is downward sloping (*i.e.*, has a negative slope) which implies that when rate of interest declines, the equilibrium level of national income increases.

Why does *IS* Curve Slope Downward?

What accounts for the downward-sloping nature of the *IS* curve ? As seen above, the decline in the rate of interest brings about an increase in the planned investment expenditure. The increase in investment spending causes the aggregate demand curve (*i.e*, $C + I$ curve) to shift upward and therefore leads to the increase in the equilibrium level of national income. Thus, a lower rate of interest is associated with a higher level of national income and *vice versa*. This makes the *IS* curve, which relates the level of income with the rate of interest, to slope downward.

Steepness of the IS curve depends on (1) the elasticity of the investment demand curve, and (2) the size of the multiplier. The elasticity of investment demand signifies the degree of responsiveness of investment spending to the changes in the rate of interest. Suppose the investment demand is highly elastic or responsive to the changes in the rate of interest, then a given fall in the rate of interest will cause a large increase in investment demand which in turn will produce a large upward shift in the aggregate demand curve. A large upward shift in the aggregate demand curve will bring about a large expansion in the level of national income. Thus when investment demand is more elastic to the changes in the rate of interest, the investment demand curve will be relatively flat (or less steep). Similarly, when investment demand is not much sensitive or is less elastic to the changes in the rate of interest, the *IS* curve will be relatively more steep.

The steepness of the IS curve also depends on the magnitude of the multiplier. As has been explained in a previous chapter, the value of multiplier depends on the marginal propensity to consume (*mpc*). It may be noted that the higher the marginal propensity to consume, the aggregate demand $(C + I)$ curve will be more steep and the magnitude of multiplier will therefore be large. In case of a higher marginal propensity to consume (*mpc*) and therefore a higher value of multiplier, a given increment in investment demand caused by a given fall in the rate of interest will help to bring about a greater increase in equilibrium level of income. Thus, the higher the value of multiplier, the greater will be the rise in equilibrium income produced by a given fall in the rate of interest and this makes the *IS* curve flatter. On the other hand, the smaller the value of multiplier due to lower marginal propensity to consume, the smaller will be the increase in equilibrium level of income following a given increment in investment caused by a given fall in the rate of interest. Thus, in case of smaller size of multiplier the *IS* curve will be more steep.

Shift in *IS* Curve

It is important to understand what determines the position of the *IS* curve and what causes shifts in it. *It is the level of autonomous expenditure which determines the position of the IS curve and changes in the autonomous expenditure cause a shift in it. By autonomous expenditure we mean the expenditure, be it autononous investment expenditure, the Government spending or autonomous consumption expenditure which does not depend on the level of income*. The government expenditure is an important type of autonomous expenditure. Note that the Government expenditure, which is determined by several factors as well as by the policies of the Government, does not depend on the level of income and the rate of interest. Similarly, some consumption expenditure has to be made by individuals if they have to survive even by borrowing from others or by spending their savings made in the past years. Such consumption expenditure is a sort of autonomous expenditure and changes in it do not depend on the changes in income and rate of interest.

Further, autonomous changes in investment can also occur. In the goods market equilibrium of the simple Keynesian model the investment expenditure is treated as autonomous or independent of the level of income and therefore does not vary as the level of income increases. However, in the complete Keynesian model, the investment spending is thought to be determined by the rate of interest along with marginal efficiency of investment. Following this complete Keynesian model, in the derivation of the *IS* curve we consider the level of investment and changes in it as determined by the rate of interest along with marginal efficiency of capital. However, there can be changes in investment spending autonomous or independent of the changes in rate of interest and the level of income. For instance, growing population requires more investment in house construction, school buildings, roads, etc., which does not depend on changes in level of income or rate of interest. Further, autonomous changes in investment spending can also take place when new innovations come about, that is, when there is progress in technology and new machines, equipment, tools etc., have to be built embodying the new technology. Besides, Government expenditure is also of autonomous type as it does not depend on level of income and rate of interest in the economy. As is well known, government increases its expenditure for the purpose of promoting social welfare and accelerating economic growth. Increase in Government expenditure or autonomous increase in investment and consumption will cause a rightward shift in the *IS* curve.

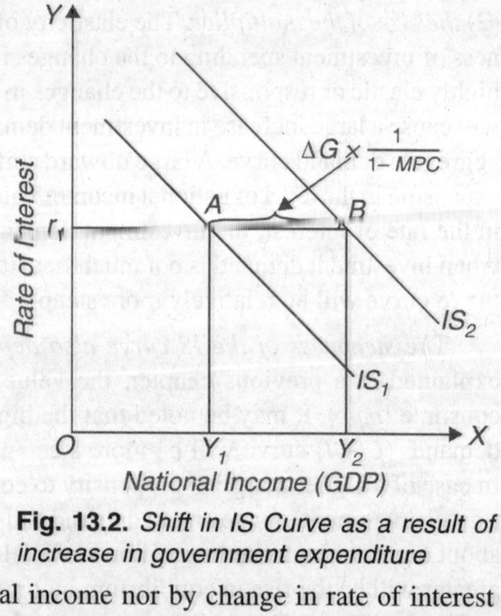

Fig. 13.2. *Shift in IS Curve as a result of increase in government expenditure*

Let us illustrate how *IS* curve shifts as a result of increase in government expenditure. Consider Figure 13.2. Suppose government increases its expenditure by ΔG. According to Keynes, *given the rate of interest* r_1, national income will increase by *ΔG times the size of multiplier, that is, by* $\Delta G \times \frac{1}{1-MPC}$ and, according to this, there is a horizontal shift from point *A* on IS_1 curve to point *B* on IS_2 curve equal to $\Delta G \times \frac{1}{1-MPC}$. Likewise, at any other given rate of interest, as a result of increase in government expenditure national income will increase by ΔG times the size of Keynsian multiplier. Similarly, if autonomous investment that is neither induced by change in national income nor by change in rate of interest increases, there will be horizontal shift in the *IS* curve equal to the increase in investment (ΔI) times the value of multiplier, that is, by $\Delta I \times \frac{1}{1-MPC}$. Likewise, *IS* curve will shift to the right when consumption increases due to the reduction in personal income tax. In the case of increase in consumption as a result of reduction in personal tax, rightward shift in the *IS* curve will be determined by $\Delta T \times \frac{MPC}{1-MPC}$ where $\frac{MPC}{1-MPC}$ is tax multiplier and ΔT is the reduction in personal taxes that leads to increase in disposable income that causes increase in consumption.

If instead of increase in government expenditure (G), or autonomous investment (I), *there is decrease* in government expenditure or autonomous investment or increase in taxes causing *decrease* in consumption, *IS* curve will shift to the left determined by change in a variable times the size of multiplier.

MONEY MARKET EQUILIBRIUM : DERIVATION OF *LM* CURVE

Derivation of the *LM* Curve

The *LM* curve can be derived from the Keynesian theory from its analysis of money market equilibrium. According to Keynes, demand for money to hold depends upon transactions motive and speculative motive. It is the money held for transactions motive which is a function of income. The greater the level of income, the greater the amount of money held for transactions motive and therefore higher the level of money demand curve.

The demand for money depends on the level of income because they have to finance their expenditure, that is, their transactions of buying goods and services. The demand for money also depends on the rate of interest which is the cost of holding money. This is because by holding money rather than lending it and buying other financial assets, one has to forgo interest.

Thus demand for money (M^d) can be expressed as:

$$M^d = L(Y, r)$$

where M^d stands for demand for money, Y for real income and r for rate of interest. Thus, we can draw a family of money demand curves at various levels of income. Now, the intersection of these various money demand curves corresponding to different income levels with the supply curve of money fixed by the monetary authority would give us the *LM* curve. The *LM* curve relates the level of income with the rate of interest which is determined by money market equilibrium corresponding to different levels of demand for money. The *LM* curve tells what the various rates of interest will be (given the quantity of money and the family of demand curves for money) at different levels of income. But the money demand curve or what Keynes calls the liquidity preference curve alone cannot tell us what exactly the rate of interest will be. In Fig. 13.3 (*a*) and (*b*) we have derived the *LM* curve from a family of demand curves for money. As income increases, money demand curve shifts outward and therefore the rate of interest which equates supply of money with demand for money rises. In Fig. 13.3(*b*) we

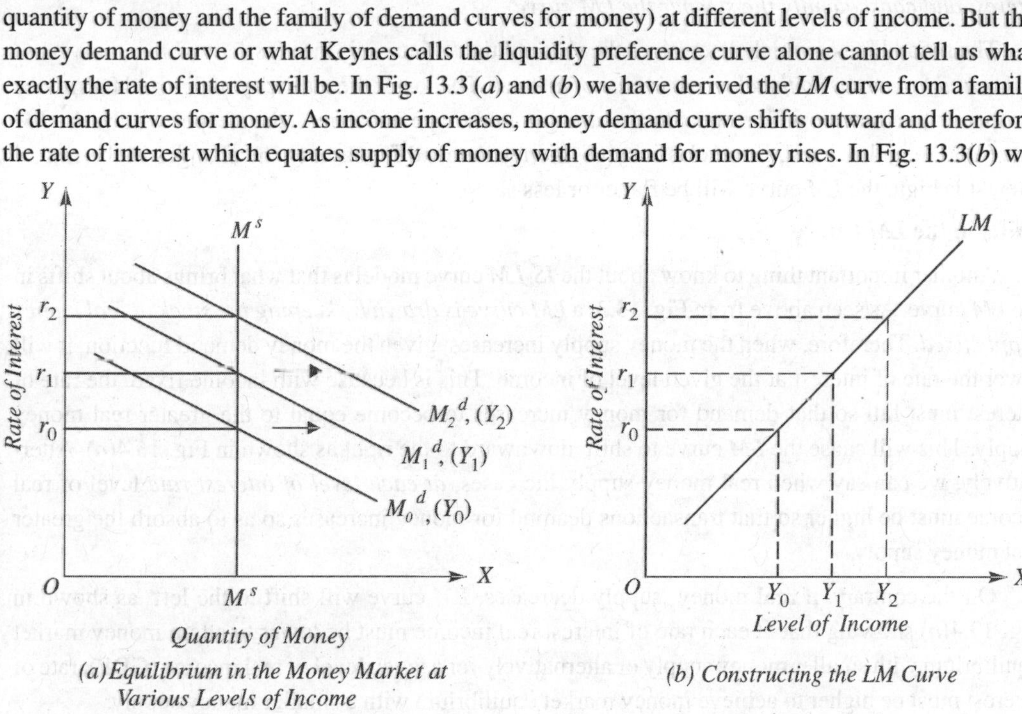

(*a*) *Equilibrium in the Money Market at Various Levels of Income*

(*b*) *Constructing the LM Curve*

Fig. 13.3. *Derivation of LM Curve*

measure income on the *X*-axis and plot the income levels corresponding to the various interest rates determined at those income levels through money market equilibrium by the equality of demand for and the supply of money in Fig. 13.3 (*a*).

It is important to note that *LM* curve by itself does not determine either national income or the interest rate that will prevail in the economy. *LM* curve represents only the relationship between levels of national income and interest rates at which money market is in equilibrium. As we will explain below, *LM* and *IS* curves together determine equilibrium national income and rate of interest.

Slope of *LM* Curve

It will be noticed from Fig. 13.3 (*b*) that the *LM* curve slopes upward to the right. This is because with higher levels of income, demand curve for money (M^d) is higher and consequently the money market equilibrium, that is, the equality of the given money supply with money demand curve occurs at a higher rate of interest. This implies that rate of interest varies directly with income. It is important to know the factors on which the slope of the *LM* curve depends. There are two factors on which the slope of the *LM* curve depends. First, *the responsiveness of demand for money (i.e., liquidity preference) to the changes in income*. As the income increases, say from Y_0 to Y_1, the demand curve for money shifts from $M_0{}^d$ to $M_1{}^d$, that is, with an increase in income, demand for money would increase for being held for transactions motive, $M_t{}^d$ or $L_1 = f(Y)$. This extra demand for money would disturb the money market equilibrium and for the equilibrium to be restored the rate of interest will rise to the level where the given money supply curve intersects the new demand curve corresponding to the higher income level. It is worth noting that in the new equilibrium position, with the given stock of money supply, money held under the transactions motive will increase whereas the money held for speculative motive will decline. *The greater the extent to which demand for money for transactions motive increases with the increase in income, the higher the rise in the rate of interest and consequently the steeper the LM curve.*

The second factor which determines the slope of the *LM* curve is the *elasticity or responsiveness of demand for money to the changes in rate of interest*. The lower the elasticity of demand for money for speculative motive with respect to the changes in the rate of interest, the steeper will be the *LM* curve. On the other hand, if the elasticity of money demand function to the changes in the rate of interest is high, the *LM* curve will be flatter or less steep.

Shifts in the *LM* Curve

Another important thing to know about the *IS-LM* curve model is that what brings about shifts in the *LM* curve. As seen above from Fig. 13.3, a *LM curve is drawn by keeping the stock of real money supply fixed.* Therefore, when the money supply increases, given the money demand function, it will lower the rate of interest at the given level of income. This is because with income fixed, the rate of interest must fall so that demand for money increases to become equal to the greater real money supply. This will cause the *LM* curve to shift downward to the right as shown in Fig. 13.4(*a*). Alternatively, we can say when real money supply increases, *at each level of interest rate* level of real income must be higher so that transactions deamnd for money increases so as to absorb the greater real money supply.

On the contrary, if real money supply decreases, *LM* curve will shift to the left as shown in Fig. 13.4(*b*) showing that at each rate of interest real income must be lower to attain money market equilibrium with smaller money supply or alternatively for a given level of real income (GDP), rate of interest must be higher to achieve money market equilibrium with a smaller money supply.

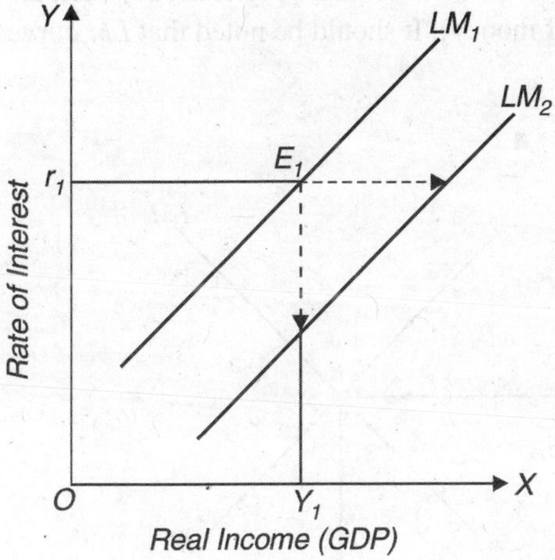

Fig. 13.4(a). *Increase in Real Money Supply (M/P) Causes a Rightward Shift in LM Curve. (shown by horizontal arrow mark)*

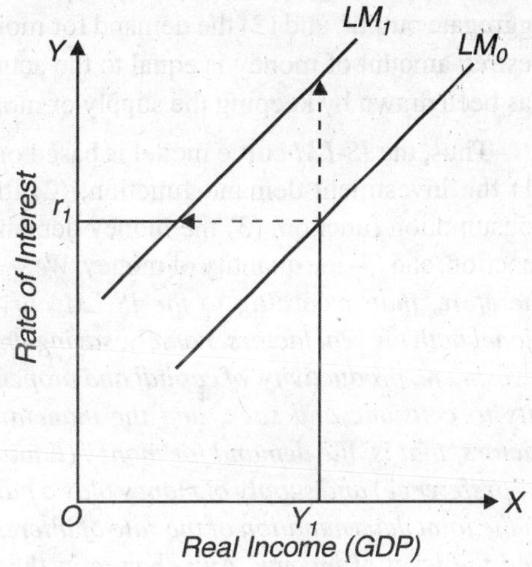

Fig. 13.4(b). *Decrease in Real Money Supply Causes a Shift in LM Curve Upward (or to the Left).*

The other factor which causes a shift in the LM curve is the change in liquidity preference (i.e., money demand function) for a given level of income. If money demand function increases, this, given the stock of money, will lead to the rise in the rate of interest for a given level of income and will therefore will bring about a shift in the *LM* curve up and to the left as shown in Fig. 13.4(*b*). It therefore follows from above that *increase in the money demand function causes the LM curve to shfit to the left*. Similarly, on the contrary, if money demand function decreases, with a given stock of money, it will lower the rate of interest for a given level of income and will therefore shift the *LM* curve down and to the right as shown in Fig. 13.4(*a*).

The *LM* Curve : The Essential Features

From our analysis of the *LM* curve, we arrive at its following essential features:

1. The *LM* curve is a schedule that describes the combinations of rate of interest and level of income *at which money market is in equilibrium*.
2. The *LM* curve slopes upward to the right.
3. The *LM* curve is flatter if the interest elasticity of demand for money is high. On the contrary, the *LM* curve is steep if the interest elasticity demand for money is low.
4. The *LM* curve shifts to the right when the stock of money supply is increased and it shifts to the left if the stock of money supply is reduced.
5. The *LM* curve shifts to the left if there is an increase in the money demand function which will raise interest rate at a given level of income. On the other hand, the *LM* curve shifts to the right if there is a decrease in the money demand function which lowers the interest rate at a given level of and income.

SIMULTANEOUS EQUILIBRIUM OF THE GOODS MARKET AND MONEY MARKET

The *IS* and the *LM* curves relate the two variables: (*a*) income and (*b*) the rate of interest. Income and the rate of interest are therefore determined together at the point of intersection of these two curves, *i.e.*, *E* in Fig. 13.5. The equilibrium rate of interest thus determined is Or_2 and the level of income determined is OY_2. At this point income and the rate of interest stand in relation to each other such that (1) the goods market is in equilibrium, that is, the aggregate demand equals the level of aggregate output, and (2) the demand for money is in equilibrium with the supply of money (*i.e.*, the desired amount of money is equal to the actual supply of money). It should be noted that *LM* curve has been drawn by keeping the supply of money fixed.

Thus, the *IS-LM* curve model is based on: (1) the investment-demand function, (2) the consumption function, (3) the money demand function, and (4) the quantity of money. *We see, therefore, that according to the IS-LM curve model both the real factors, namely, saving and investment, productivity of capital and propensity to consume and save, and the monetary factors, that is, the demand for money (liquidity preference) and supply of money play a part in the joint determination of the rate of interest and the level of income. Any change in these factors will cause a shift in IS or LM curve and will therefore change the equilibrium levels of the rate of interest and income.*

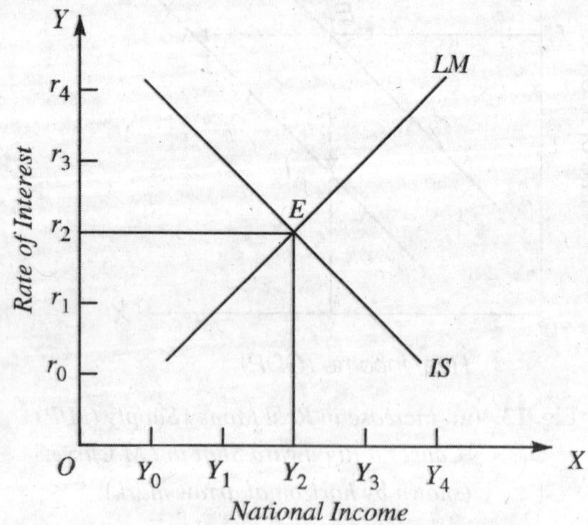

Fig. 13.5. *The IS and LM Curves Combined: The Joint Determination of the Interest Rate and the Income Level*

The *IS-LM* curve model explained above has succeeded in integrating the theory of money with the theory of income determination. And by doing so, as we shall see below, it has succeeded in synthesising the monerary and fiscal policies. Further, with the *IS-LM* curve analysis, we are better able to explain the effect of changes in certain important economic variables such as desire to save, the supply of money, investment, demand for money on the rate of interest and level of income.

Effect of Changes in Supply of Money on the Rate of Interest and Income Level

Let us first consider what will happen if the supply of money is increased by the action of the Central Bank. Given the liquidity preference schedule, with the increase in the supply of money, more money will be available for speculative motive at a given level of income which will cause the interest rate to fall. As a result, the *LM* curve will shift to the right. With this rightward shift in the *LM* curve,

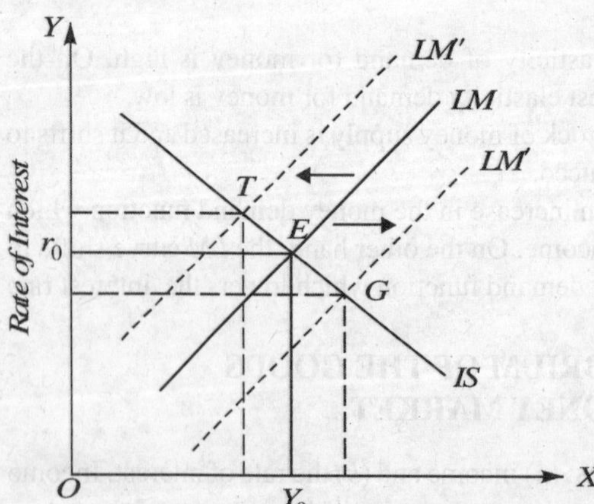

Fig. 13.6. *Impact of Change in Supply of Money*

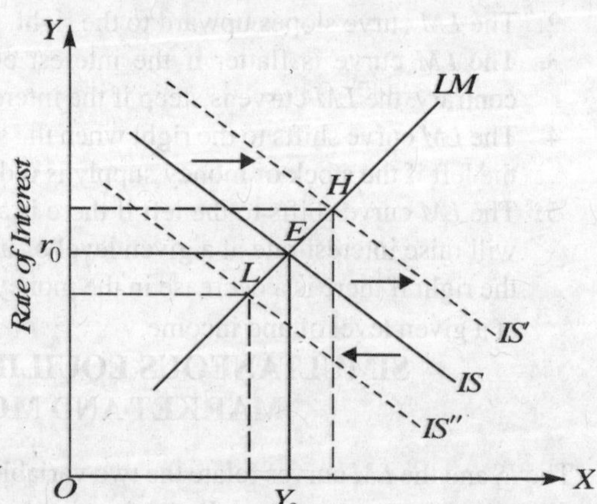

Fig. 13.7. *Impact of Changes in Government Expenditure or Autonomous Investment*

in the new equilibrium position, rate of interest will be lower and the level of income greater than before. This is shown in Fig. 13.6 where with a given supply of money, *LM* and *IS* curves intersect at point *E*. With the increase in the supply of money, *LM* curve shifts to the right to the position *LM′*, and with *IS* schedule remaining unchanged, new equilibrium is at point *G* corresponding to which rate of interest is lower and level of income greater than at *E*. Now, suppose that instead of increasing the supply of money, Central Bank of the country takes steps to reduce the supply of money. With the reduction in the supply of money, less money will be available for speculative motive at each level of income and, as a result, the *LM* curve will shift to the left of *E*, and the *IS* curve remaining unchanged, in the new equilibrium position (as shown by point *T* in Fig. 13.6) the rate of interest will be higher and the level of income smaller than before.

Changes in Autonomous Investment and Government Expenditure

Changes in autonomous investment and Government expenditure will also shift the *IS* curve. If either there is increase in autonomous private investment or Government steps up its expenditure, aggregate demand for goods will increase and this will bring about increase in national income through the multiplier process. As is seen from Figure 13.7, this will shift *IS* curve to the right from *IS* curve to *IS′* curve (dotted), , and given the *LM* curve, the rate of interest as well as the level of income will increase. On the contrary, if somehow private investment expenditure falls or the Government reduces its expenditure, the *IS* curve will shift to the left to *IS″* and, given the *LM* curve, both the rate of interest and the level of income will fall.

Changes in the Desire to Save or Propensity to Consume

Let us consider what happens to the rate of interest when desire to save or, in other words, propensity to consume changes. When people's desire to save falls, that is, when propensity to consume rises, the aggregate demand curve will shift upward and, therefore, level of national income will rise at each rate of interest. As a result, the *IS* curve will shift outward to the right. In Fig. 13.7 suppose with a certain given fall in the desire to save (or increase in the propensity to consume), the *IS* curve shifts rightward to the dotted position *IS′*. With *LM* curve remaining unchanged, the new equilibrium position will be established at *H* corresponding to which rate of interest as well as level of income will be greater than at *E*. Thus, *a fall in the desire to save has led to the increase in both rate of interest and level of income*. On the other hand, if the desire to save rises, that is, if the propensity to consume falls, aggregate demand curve will shift downward which will cause the level of national income to fall for each rate of interest and as a result the *IS* curve will shift to the left. With this, and *LM* curve remaining unchanged, the new equilibrium position will be reached to the left of *E*, say at point *L* (as shown in Fig. 13.7) corresponding to which both rate of interest and level of national income will be smaller than at *E*.

Changes in Demand for Money or Liquidity Preference

Changes in liquidity preference will bring about changes in the *LM* curve. If the liquidity preference or demand for money of the people rises, the *LM* curve will shift to the left. This is because greater demand for money, given the supply of money, will raise the rate of interest corresponding to each level of national income. With the leftward shift in the *LM* curve, given the *IS* curve, the equilibrium rate of interest will rise and the level of national income will fall.

On the contrary, if the demand for money or liquidity preference of the people falls, the *LM* curve will shift to the right. This is because, given the supply of money, the rightward shift in the money demand curve means that corresponding to each level of income there will be lower rate of interest. With rightward shift in the *LM* curve, given the *IS* curve, the equilibrium rate of interest will fall and the equilibrium level of national income will increase.

Conclusion

We thus see that changes in propensity to consume (or desire to save), autonomous investment or

Government expenditure, the supply of money and the demand for money will cause shifts in either *IS* or *LM* curve and will thereby bring about changes in the rate of interest as well as in national income. *The integration of goods market and money market in the IS-LM curve model clearly shows that Government can influence the economic activity or the level of national income through monetary and fiscal measures*. Through adopting an appropriate monetary policy (*i.e.*, changing the supply of money) the Government can shift the *LM* curve and through pursuing an appropriate fiscal policy (expenditure and taxation policy) the Government can shift the *IS* curve. Thus both monetary and fiscal policies can play a useful role in regulating the level of economic activity in the country.

The Critique of the *IS-LM* Model

The *IS-LM* model makes a significant advance in explaining the simultaneous determination of the rate of interest and the level of national income. It represents a more general, inclusive and realistic approach to the determination of interest rate and level of income. Further, the *IS-LM model succeeds in integrating and synthesising fiscal with monetary policies, and theory of income determination with the theory of money*. But the *IS-LM* model is not without limitations. Firstly, it is based on the assumption that the rate of interest is quite flexible, that is, free to vary and not rigidly fixed by the Central Bank of a country. If the rate of interest is quite inflexible, then the appropriate adjustment explained above will not take place.

Secondly, the model is also based upon the *assumption that investment is interest-elastic*, that is, investment varies with the rate of interest. If investment is interest-inelastic, then the *IS-LM* model breaks down since the required adjustments do not occur. Thirdly, Don Patinkin[1] and Milton Friedman have criticised the *IS-LM* model as being too artificial and over-simplified. In their view, division of the economy into two sectors – monetary and real – is artificial and unrealistic. According to them, monetary and real sectors are quite interwoven and act and react on each other. Further, Patinkin has pointed out that the *IS-LM* model has ignored the possibility of changes in the price level of commodities and inflation. According to him, the various economic variables such as supply of money, propensity to consume or save, investment and the demand for money not only influence the rate of interest and the level of national income but also the prices of commodities and services. Like Keynes's income-expenditure approach, *IS-LM* curve model also assumes *fixed price level*. When price level is variable aggregate demand and aggregate supply also vary with changes in price level and thereby affects equilibrium of national income in the economy. In fact modern economists derive aggregate demand curve with varying price level from *IS-LM* curve model and this *AD* curve with varying price level together with *AS* curve with varying price level together determine equilibrium national inocme and price level. Thus with the assumption of fixed price level *IS-LM curve model ignores the problem of inflation* which is facing many economies of the world including India. Patinkin has suggested a more integrated and general equilibrium approach which involves the simultaneous determination of not only the rate of interest and the level of income but also of the prices of commodities and services.

IS-LM CURVE MODEL : EXPLAINING ROLES OF FISCAL AND MONETARY POLICIES

With the help of *IS-LM* curve model we can explain how the *intervention by the Government* with proper fiscal and monetary policies can influence the level of economic activity, that is, inocme and employment level. We explain below the impact of changes in fiscal and monetary policy on the economy in the *IS-LM* model.

Impact of Fiscal Policy

Increase in Government Expenditure. Let us first explain how *IS-LM* model shows the effect of increase in Government expenditure on level of income. This is illustrated in Fig. 13.8.

1. Don Patinkin, *Money, Interest and Prices*, Harper and Row, 1965.

As explained above, increase in Government expenditure which is of autonomous nature raises aggregate demand for goods and services and thereby causes an outward shift in *IS* curve, as is shown in Fig. 13.8 where increase in Government expenditure leads to the shift in *IS* curve from IS_1 to IS_2.

Note that the horizontal distance between the two *IS* curves is equal to $\Delta G \times \frac{1}{1-MPC}$ which shows the increase in national income equal to the horizontal distance *EK* that occurs in Keynes's multiplier model. However, in the *IS-LM* model actual increase in national income is not equal to *EK* caused by the working of Keynes's multiplier. This is because with the rightward shift in the *IS* curve rate of interest also rises which causes reduction in private investment. It will be seen from Fig. 13.8 that with the *LM* curve remaining unchanged, the new IS_2 curve intersects *LM* curve at point *B*. Thus, in *IS-LM* model with the increase in Government expenditure (ΔG), the equilibrium moves from point *E* to *B* and with this the rate of interest rises from r_1 to r_2 and income level rises from Y_1 to Y_2. Income equal to *CK* has been wiped out because of rise in interest rate causing a decline in private investment. Thus *CK* represents *crowding-out effect* of increase in government expenditure. Thus, *IS-LM* model shows that expanoinary fiscal policy of increase in Government expenditure raises both the level of income and rate of interest.

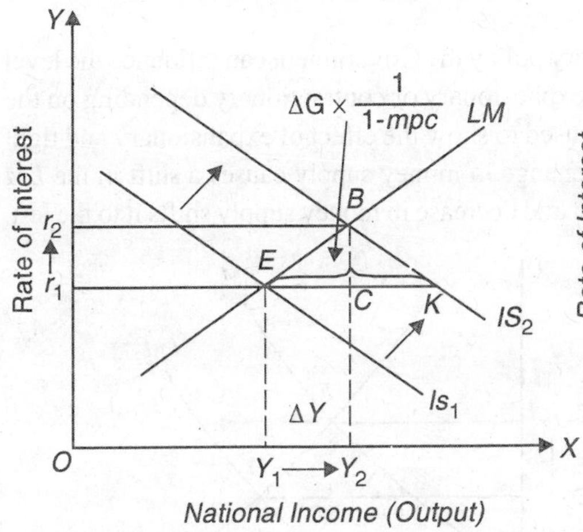

Fig. 13.8. *Fiscal Policy: Impact of Increase in Government Expenditure on Interest Rate and Income*

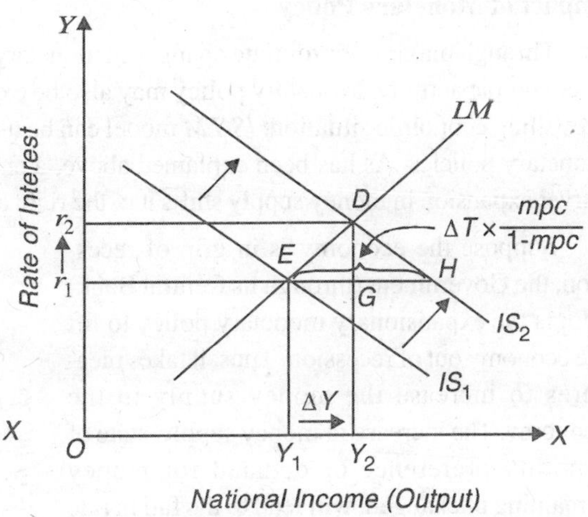

Fig. 13.9. *Fiscal Policy: Effect of Cut in Taxes on Income and Interest Rate*

It is worth noting that in the *IS-LM* model increase in national income by Y_1Y_2 in Fig. 13.8 is less than *EK* which would occur in Keynes's model. This is because Keynes in his simple multiplier model (popularly called Keynesian cross model) assumes that investment is fixed and autonomous, whereas *IS-LM* model takes into account the fall in private investment due to the rise in interest rate that takes place with the increase in Government expenditure. That is, increase in Government expenditure crowds out some private investment. Therefore, in *IS-LM* model increase in national inocme is less than that under the simple Keynesian model.

Likewise, it can be illustrated that the reduction in Government expenditure will cause a leftward shift in the *IS* curve, and given the *LM* curve unchanged, will lead to the fall in both rate of interest and level of income. It should be noted that Government often cuts expenditure to control inflation in the economy.

Expansionary Fiscal Policy : Reduction in Taxes. An alternative measure of *expansionary fiscal policy* which may be adopted is the reduction in taxes which through increase in disposable income of the people raises consumption demand of the people. As a result, cut in taxes causes a shift in the *IS* curve to the right as is shown in Fig. 13.9, from IS_1 to IS_2. It may however be noted that in the Keynesian multiplier model, the horizontal shift in the *IS* curve is determined by the the *cut in taxes* (ΔT) times value of *tax multiplier* which is equal to $\Delta T \times \frac{MPC}{1-MPC}$ and causes level of income to increase by *EH*. However, in the *IS-LM* model, with the shift of the *IS* curve from IS_1 to IS_2 following the reduction in taxes, the economy moves from equilibrium point *E* to *D* and, as is evident from Fig. 13.9, rate of interest rises from r_1 to r_2 and level of income increases from Y_1 to Y_2. Due to the rise in rate of interest increase in national income as a result of reduction in tax is less than *EH* $\left(=\Delta T \frac{MPC}{1-MPC}\right)$ that would occur in the simple Keynesian model. Income equal to *GH* has been wiped out because of crowding-out effect on private investment as a result of rise in interest rate.

On the other hand, if the Government intervenes in the economy to *reduce inflationary pressures, it will raise the rates of personal taxes to reduce disposable income of the people. Rise in personal taxes will lead to the decrease in aggregate demand.* Decrease in aggregate demand will help in controlling inflation. This case can also be shown by *IS-LM* curve model.

Impact of Monetary Policy

Through making appropriate changes in monetary policy the Government can influence the level of economic activity. Monetary policy may also be expansionary or contractionary depending on the prevailing economic situation. *IS-LM* model can be used to show the effect of expansionary and tight monetary policies. As has been explained above, a change in money supply causes a shift in the *LM* curve; expansion in money supply shifts it to the right and decrease in money supply shifts it to the left.

Suppose the economy is in grip of recession, the Government (through its Central Bank) adopts the expansionary monetary policy to lift the economy out of recession. Thus, it takes measures to increase the money supply in the economy. The increase in money supply, state of liquidity preference or demand for money remaining unchanged, will lead to the fall in rate of interest. At a lower interest there will be more investment by businessmen. More investment will cause aggregate demand and income to rise. This implies that with expansion in money supply *LM* curve will shift to the right as is shown in Fig. 13.10. As a result, the economy will move from equilibrium point *E* to *D* and with this the rate of interest will fall from r_1 to r_2 and national income will increase from Y_1 to Y_2. Thus, *IS-LM* model shows the expansion in money supply lowers interest rate and raises income. We have also indicated what is called **monetary transmission mechanism,** that is, *IS-LM* curve model shows how the expansion in money supply leads to the increase in aggregate demand for goods and services. We have thus seen that increase in money supply lowers the rate of interest which then stimulates more investment demand. Increase in investment demand through multiplier process leads to a greater increase in aggregate demand and national inocme.

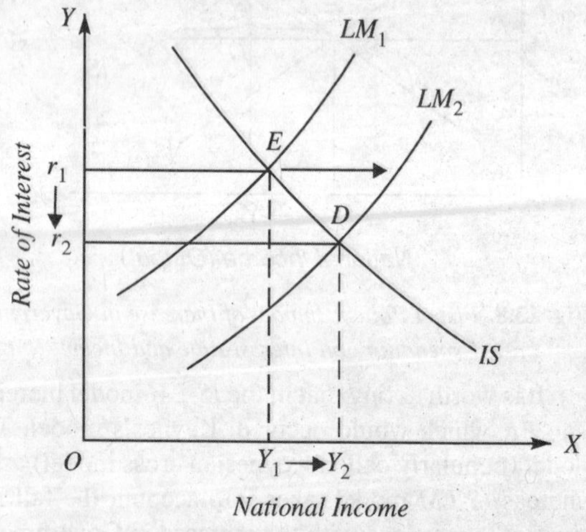

Fig. 13.10. *Effect of Expansion in Money Supply on Interest Rate and Income*

If the economy suffers from inflation, the Government will like to check it. Then its Central Bank should adopt tight or contractionary monetary policy. To control inflation the Central Bank of a country can reduce money supply through open market operations by selling bonds or government securities in the open market and in return gets currency funds from those who buy the bonds. In this way liquidity in the banking system can be reduced. To reduce money supply for fighting inflation, the Central Bank can also raise cash reserve ratio of the banks. The higher cash reserve ratio implies that the banks have to keep more cash reserve with the Central Bank. As a result, the cash reserves with the banks fall which force them to contract credit. With this money supply in the economy declines. *IS-LM* model can be used to show that reduction in money supply will cause a lefward shift in *LM* curve and will lead to the rise in interest rate and fall in the level of income. This is shown in Fig. 13.11.

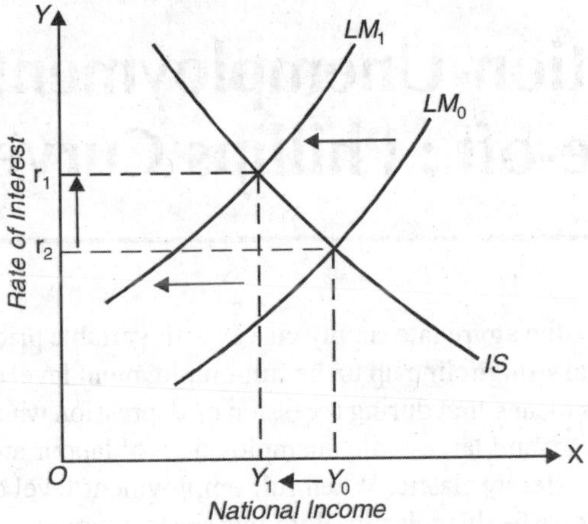

Fig. 13.11. *Contractionary Monetary Policy to Fight Inflation*

QUESTIONS FOR REVIEW

1. What is *IS* curve ? How is it derived from goods market equilibrium ?
2. Define *IS* curve. What are the factors that cause shift in the *IS* curve ?
3. What is *LM* curve ? How is it derived from money market equilibrium ? On which factors does its slope and position depend ?
4. How do the product and money markets interact to determine the short-run equilibrium level of national income and the rate of interest ?
5. Using *IS-LM* model analyse the impact of an increase in money supply on the equilibrium level of income and rate of interest.
6. Using *IS-LM* curve model analyse the impact of an increase in the money supply on the equilibrium level of national income and the rate of interest.
7. What is crowding-out effect of Government's fiscal policy ? Is it very significant ? What role does interest elasticity of investment play in determining the slope of *IS* curve ?
8. Explain and show graphically how product market is in equilibrium along *IS* curve.
9. Explain *IS* and *LM* curves. What is the role of these two curves in simultaneous determination of equilibrium rate of interest and level of income ?
10. (*a*) Derive *IS* curve for an economy. What are the factors which determine slope of the *IS* curve ?
    (*b*) Show how *IS* curve will change as a result of increase in Government expenditure.
11. Why does *IS* curve slope downward ? How is *IS* curve related to investment multiplier in the Keynesian income theory ? What are the factors which cause a shift in *IS* curve ?
12. How is *LM* curve derived from money market equilibrium ? Why does *LM* curve slope upward ? How will *LM* curve shfit with increase in money supply in the economy ?
13. Explain with the aid of *IS-LM* curves role of monetary policy for stabilisation of the economy.
14. Explain with the help of *IS-LM* curve model role of fiscal policy in overcoming recession in the economy.
15. Show with *IS-LM* curve model how Keynes succeeded in integrating money market with goods market.

CHAPTER 14

Inflation-Unemployment Trade-off : Phillips Curve

Introduction

In the simple Keynesian model of an economy, the aggregate supply curve (with variable price level) is of inverse L-shape, that is, it is a horizontal straight line up to the full-employment level of output and beyond that it becomes horizontal. This means that during recession or depression when the economy is having a good deal of excess capacity and large-scale unemployment of labour and idle capital stock, the aggregate supply curve is perfectly elastic. When full-employment level of output is reached, aggregate supply curve becomes perfectly inelastic. With this shape of aggregate supply curve assumed in the simple Keynesian model, increase in aggregate demand before the level of full employment causes increase in the level of real national output and employment with price level remaining unchanged. That is, no cost has to be incurred in the form of rise in the price level (i.e., inflation rate) for raising the level of output and reducing unemployment. In the Keynesian model, once the full-employment level of output is reached and aggregate supply curve becomes vertical, further increase in aggregate demand caused by the expansionary fiscal and monetary policies will only raise the price level in the economy. That is, in this simple Keynesian model, inflation occurs in the economy only after full-employment level of output has been attained. Thus, *in the simple Keynesian model with inverse* L-*shaped aggregate supply curve there is no trade-off or clash between inflation and unemployment*.

INFLATION-UNEMPLOYMENT TRADE-OFF: PHILLIPS CURVE

However, the actual empirical evidence did not fit well in the above simple Keynesian macro model. A noted British economist, A.W. Phillips[1], published an article in 1958 based on his good deal of research using historical data from the U.K. for about 100 years in which he arrived at the conclusion that *there in fact existed an inverse relationship between rate of unemployment and rate of inflation*. This inverse relation implies a trade-off, that is, for reducing unemployment, price in the form of a higher rate of inflation has to be paid, and for reducing the rate of inflation, price in terms of a higher rate of unemployment has to be borne. On graphically fitting a curve to the historical data Phillips obtained a downward sloping curve exhibiting the inverse relation between rate of inflation and the rate of unemployment and this curve is now named after his name as *Phillips Curve*. This Phillips curve is shown in Fig. 14.1 where along the horizontal axis the rate of unemployment and along the vertical axis the rate of inflation is measured. It will be seen that when rate of inflation is 10 per cent, the unemployment rate is 3 per cent, and when rate of inflation is reduced to 5 per cent per annum, say by pursuing contractionary fiscal policy and thereby reducing aggregate demand, the rate of unemployment increases to 8 per cent of labour force. The actual Phillips curve drawn from the data of sixties (1961-69) for the United States also shows the inverse relation between unemployment rate and rate of inflation (see Fig. 14.2). Such empirical data

1. A.W. Phillips, "Relation between Unemployment and Rate of Change in Money Wages in the United Kingdom, 1861-1957." *Economica,* 25 (Nov. 1958), pp. 283-299.

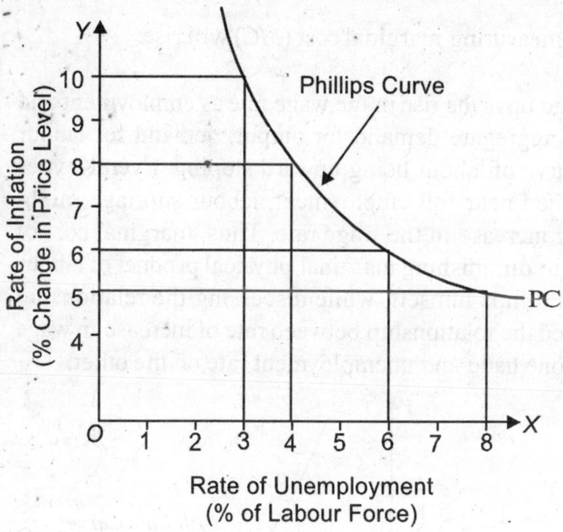

Fig. 14.1. *Phillips Curve Showing Negative Relationship between Rates of Inflation and Unemployment.*

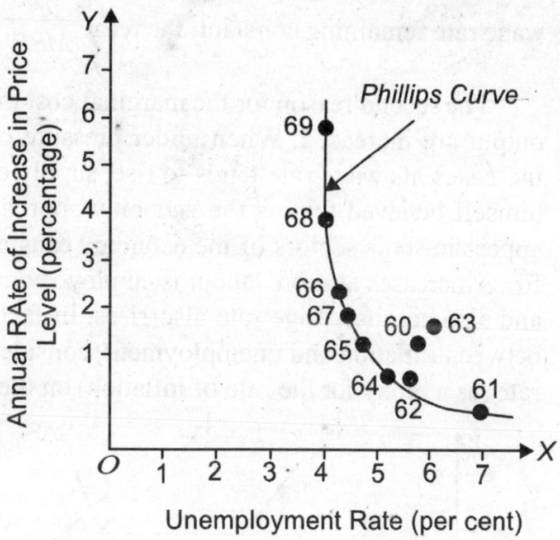

Fig. 14.2. *Phillips Curve of the United States in the Sixties*

pertaining to the fifties and sixties for other developed countries seemed to confirm the Phillips curve concept. On the basis of this, many economists came to believe that there existed a *stable Phillips curve* which depicted a predicatable inverse relation between inflation and unemployment. Further, on the basis of a *stable Phillips curve* for a country, they emphasised the trade-off that confronts the economic policy makers. This trade-off presents a dilemma for the policy makers; should they choose a higher rate of inflation with lower unemployment or a higher rate of unemployment with a low inflation rate. In what follows we first explain the rationale underlying the Phillips curve, that is, how the inverse relationship between inflation and unemployment can be theoretically explained. We will further explain why this concept of stable Phillips curve depicting inverse relation between inflation and unemployment broke down during seventies and early eighties. During seventies a strange phenomenon was witnessed in the USA and Britain when there existed *a high rate of inflation side by side with high unemployment rate*. This was contrary to both Phillips curve concept and the simple Keynesian model. This simultaneous existence of both high rate of inflation and high unemployment rate (or low level of real national product) during the seventies and early eighties has been described as *stagflation* which has been explained in the previous chapter.

Keynesian Explanation of Phillips Curve

Let us first provide an explanation for the Phillips curve. Both Keynesians and Monetarists agreed to the existence of the Phillips curve. The explanation of Phillips curve by the Keynesian economists is quite simple and is graphically illustrated in Fig. 14.3. It may be noted that Keynesian economists assume the upward-sloping short-run aggregate supply curve. In fact, Keynes himself recognised that the curve *SAS* is upward sloping in intermediate range, that is, as the economy approaches near full employment level, the aggregate supply curve slopes upward. According to Keynesian economists, short-run aggregate supply curve is upward sloping for two reasons. First, as output is increased by the firms in the economy, diminishing returns to variable factors, especially to labour, occur resulting in fall in marginal physical product (MPP_L) of labour. With money wage rate (W) as given and fixed, the fall in the marginal physical product of labour causes the rise in the marginal cost (MC) of production $\left(\text{Note that } MC = \dfrac{W}{MPP_L}\right)$. With the fall in the *MPP* of labour, wage rate remaining constant, the term $\frac{W}{MPP_L}$ measuring marginal cost (*MC*) will rise.

The second reason for the marginal cost to go up is the rise in the wage rate as employment and output are increased. When under pressure of aggregate demand for output, demand for labour increases, its wage rate tends to rise, supply curve of labour being upward sloping. Even Keynes himself believed that as the economy approached near full employment, labour shortage might appear in some sectors of the economy causing increase in the wage rate. Thus, marginal cost of firms increases as more labour is employed due to diminishing marginal physical product of labour and also because wage rate also rises. In fact Phillips himself, while discussing the relationship between inflation and unemployment, considered the relationship between rate of increase in wage rate (as a proxy for the rate of inflation) on the one hand and unemployment rate on the other.

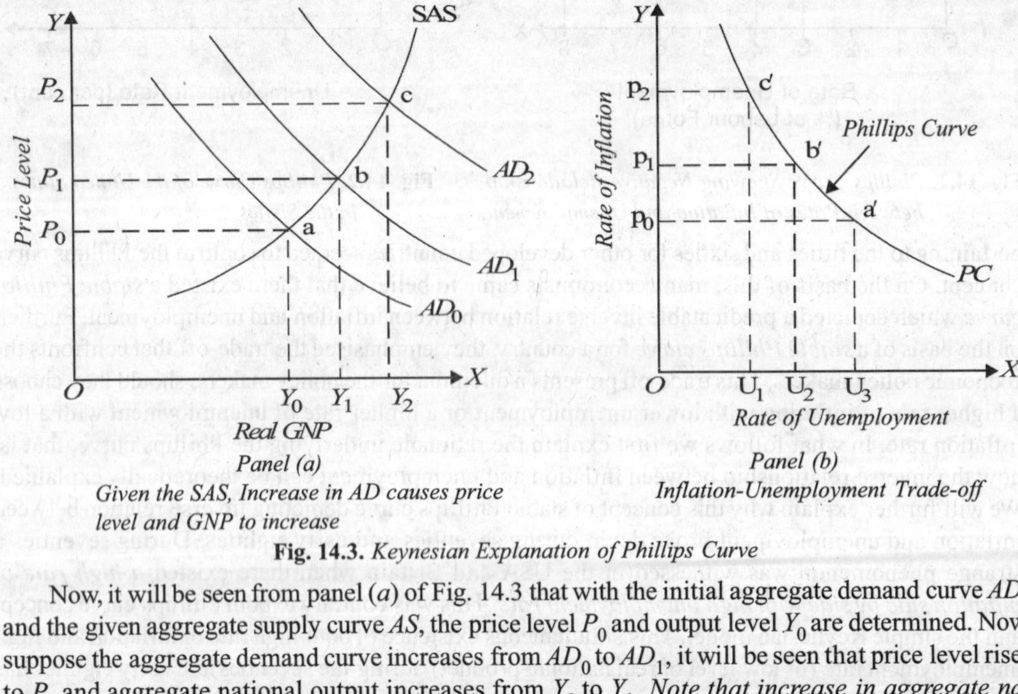

Fig. 14.3. *Keynesian Explanation of Phillips Curve*

Now, it will be seen from panel (*a*) of Fig. 14.3 that with the initial aggregate demand curve AD_0 and the given aggregate supply curve *AS*, the price level P_0 and output level Y_0 are determined. Now, suppose the aggregate demand curve increases from AD_0 to AD_1, it will be seen that price level rises to P_1 and aggregate national output increases from Y_0 to Y_1. *Note that increase in aggregate national product means increase in employment of labour and therefore reduction in unemployment rate.* Thus the rise in the price level from P_0 to P_1 (*i.e.*, occurrence of inflation) results in lowering of unemployment rate showing inverse relation between the two. Further, if aggregate demand increases to AD_2, the price level further rises to P_2 and national output increases to Y_2 which will further lower the rate of unemployment. The greater the rate at which aggregate demand increases, the higher will be the rate of inflation which will cause greater increase in aggregate output and employment resulting in much lower rate of unemployment. Thus, *a higher rate of increase in aggregate demand and consequently a higher rate of rise in price level is associated with the lower rate of unemployment and vice versa.* This is what is represented by Phillips curve.

Consider panel (*b*) of Fig. 14.3 where point *a'* on the downward sloping Phillips curve *PC* corresponds to point *a* of panel (*a*) of Fig. 14.3. In panel (*b*) of Fig. 14.3 we have shown the rate of unemployment equal to U_3 corresponding to the price level P_0 of panel (*a*). When the aggregate demand shifts to AD_1, there is a certain rate of inflation and price level rises to P_1 and aggregate output increases to Y_1. As seen above, this increase in aggregate output leads to the increase in employment of labour bringing about decline in unemployment rate. Suppose the rate of rise in the price level (*i.e.*, the rate of inflation) when it increases from P_0 to P_1 in panel (*a*) following the increase in aggregate demand is greater than the rate of rise in the price level of the previous period, we obtain a lower rate of unemployment U_2 than before corresponding to a higher inflation rate p_1 in the Phillips curve *PC* in panel (*b*). With a still higher rate of inflation, say p_2, when price level rises from P_1 to P_2 in panel (*a*) following the increase in aggregate demand to AD_2, we have a further lower rate of unemployment equal to U_1 in panel (*b*) corresponding to point *c′* on the Phillips curve *PC*. This gives us a downward-sloping Phillips curve *PC*.

It is clear from the above that through increase in aggregate demand and upward-sloping aggregate supply curve, Keynesians were able to explain the downward-sloping Phillips curve showing the negative relation (i.e., trade-off) between rates of inflation and unemployment.

Collapse of Phillips Curve in the USA (1971-91)

During the sixties Phillips curve became an important concept of macro-economic analysis. The stable relationship described by it suggested that policy makers could have a lower rate of unemployment if they could bear with a higher rate of inflation. On the contrary, they could achieve a low rate of inflation only if they were prepared to reconcile with a higher rate of unemployment. But a stable Phillips curve could not hold good during the seventies and eighties, especially in the United States. Therefore, experience in the two decades (1971-91), has prompted some economists to say that the stable Phillips curve has disappeared. Figure 14.4 shows that data regarding the behaviour of inflation and unemployment during the seventies and eighties in the United States do not conform to a stable Phillips curve. *In these two decades we have periods when rates of both inflation and unemployment increased (that is, a high rate of inflation was associated with a high unemployment rate, which shows the absence of trade off.* We have shown the data of inflation rate and unemployment in case of the United States in Fig. 14.4. From the data it appears that instead of remaining stable, the Phillip curve shifted to the right in the seventies and early eighties and to the left during the late eighties. (see Fig. 14.4).

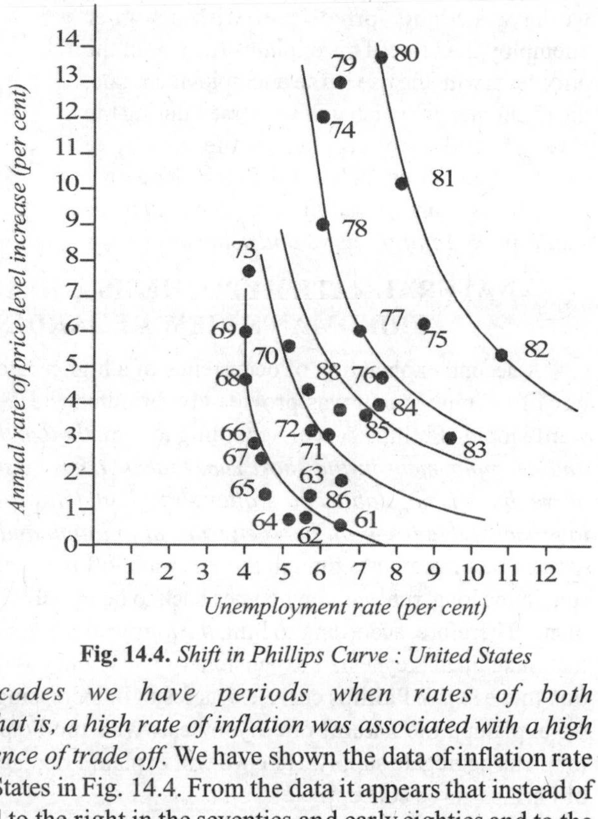

Fig. 14.4. *Shift in Phillips Curve : United States*

Causes of Shift in Phillips Curve

Now, what could be the cause of shift in the Phillips curve. There are two explanations for this. First, according to Keynesians, the occurrence of higher inflation rate along with the increase in unemployment rate witnessed during the seventies and early eighties was due to the *adverse supply shocks* in the form of fourfold increase in the prices of oil and petroleum products delivered to the American economy first in 1973-74 and then again in 1979-80. Consider Fig. 14.5 where AD_0 and AS_0 are in equilibrium at point *E* and determine price level OP_0 and aggregate national output OY_0. The hike in price of oil by *OPEC*, the cartel of oil producing Middle East countries brought about a rise in the cost of production of several commodities for the production of which oil was used as an energy input. Further, the oil price hike also raised the transportation costs of all commodities. The increase in cost of production and transportation of commodities caused a shift in the aggregate supply curve upward to the left. This is generally described as adverse supply shock which raised the unit cost at each level of output. It will be seen from Fig. 14.5 that due to this adverse supply shock aggregate supply curve has shifted to the left to the new position AS_1 which intersects the given aggregate demand curve AD_0 at point H. At the new equilibrium point H, price level has risen to P_1 and output has fallen to OY_1 which will cause unemployment rate to rise. Thus, we have a higher price level with a higher unemployment rate. This explains the rise in the price level with the rise in the unemployment rate, the phenomenon which was witnessed during the seventies and early eighties in the developed capatalist countries such as the U.S.A. Note that *this has been interpreted by some economists as a shift in the Phillips curve and some as demise or collapse of the Phillips curve.*

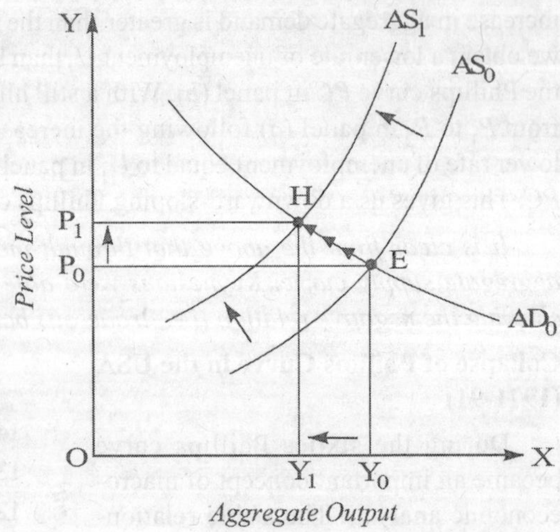

Fig. 14.5. *Adverse Supply Shock Giving Rise to Stagflation and Breakdown of Phillips Curve*

NATURAL RATE HYPOTHESIS AND ADAPTIVE EXPECTATIONS: FRIEDMAN'S VIEW REGARDING PHILLIPS CURVE

A second explanation of occurrence of a higher rate of inflation simultaneously with a higher rate of unemployment was provided by Friedman.[2] He challenged the concept of a *stable* downward-sloping Phillips curve. According to him, *though there is a trade-off between rate of inflation and unemployment in the short run, that is, there exists a short-run downward sloping Phillips curve, but it is not stable and it often shifts both leftward and rightward. He argued that there is no long-run stable trade-off between rates of inflation and unemployment.* According to Friedman's natural rate hypothesis though there is trade-off between inflation and unemployment in the short run, in the long run economy comes back to be in stable equilibrium at the natural rate of unemployment. Therefore, according to him, *the long-run Phillips curve is a vertical straight line*. He argues that misguided Keynesian expansionary fiscal and monetary policies based on the wrong assumption that a *stable* Phillips curve exists result in increasing the rate of inflation. In a previous chapter we explained the natural rate hypothesis with the help of short-run aggregate supply curve and long-run aggregate supply. Here we will explain Friedman's natural rate hypothesis with his version of Phillips curve concept.

Natural Rate of Unemployment

It is necessary to explain first the concept of natural rate of unemployment on which the concept of long-run Phillips curve is based. *The natural rate of unemployment is the rate at which in the labour market the current number of unemployed is equal to the number of jobs available. These unemployed workers are not employed for the frictional and structural reasons, though the equivalent number of jobs are available for them.* For instance, due to lack of information or lack of mobility the fresh entrants to the labour force may spend a good deal of time in searching for the jobs before they are able to find work. This is called *frictional unemployment*. Besides, some indus-

2. Milton Friedman, "Inflation and Unemployment", *Journal of Political Economy*, 1977.

tries may be registering a decline in their production rendering some workers unemployed, while others may be growing and therefore creating new jobs for workers. But the unemployed workers may have to be provided new training and skills before they are employed in the newly created jobs in the growing industries. These are *structurally unemployed* workers. Thus, it is these frictional and structural unemployments that constitute the natural rate of unemployment. Since the equivalent number of jobs are available for them, full employment is said to prevail even in the presence of this natural rate of unemployment. It is presently believed that 4 to 5 per cent rate of unemployment represents a natural rate of unemployment in the developed countries. However, this natural rate of unemployment is not constant but varies over time due to changes in mobility and availability of information. If mobility of workers increases and quick information about new jobs are available *frictional unemployment* falls. Similarly, if facilities for training unemployed workers and equipping them with new skills required for jobs increase, structural unemployment will decline.

Phillips Curve, Adaptive Expectations and Natural Rate Hypothesis

Another important thing to understand from Friedman's explanation of shift in the short-run Phillips curve is that *expectations about the future rate of inflation play an important role in it. Friedman put forward a theory of adaptive expectations according to which people form their expectations on the basis of previous period rate of inflation, and change or adapt their expectations only when the actual inflation turns out to be different from their expected rate.* According to this Friedman's theory of adaptive expectations, there may be a trade-off between rates of inflation and unemployment in the short run, but there is no such trade-off in the long run.

The view point of Friedman and his follower monetarists is illustrated in Figure 14.6. To begin with, SPC_1 is the short-run Phillips curve and the economy is at point A_0, on it corresponding to the natural rate of unemployment equal to 5 per cent of labour force. The location of this point A_0 on the short-run Phillips curve depends on the level of aggregate demand. Further, we assume that the economy has been experiencing a rate of inflation equal to 5%. The other assumption we make is that nominal wages have been set on the expectations that 5 per cent rate of inflation will continue in the future.

Now, suppose for some reasons the government adopts expansionary fiscal and monetary policies to raise aggregate demand. The consequent increase in aggregate demand will cause the rate of inflation to rise, say to seven per cent. Given the level of money wage rate which was fixed on the basis that the 5 per cent rate of inflation would continue to occur, the higher price level than expected would raise the profits of the firms which will induce the firms to increase their output and employ more labour. As a result of the increase in aggregate demand resulting in a higher rate of inflation and more output and employment, the economy will move to point A_1 on the short-run Phillips curve SPC_1 in Figure 14.6, where unemployment has decreased to 3.5 per cent while inflation rate has risen to 7%. It may be noted from Figure 14.6 that in

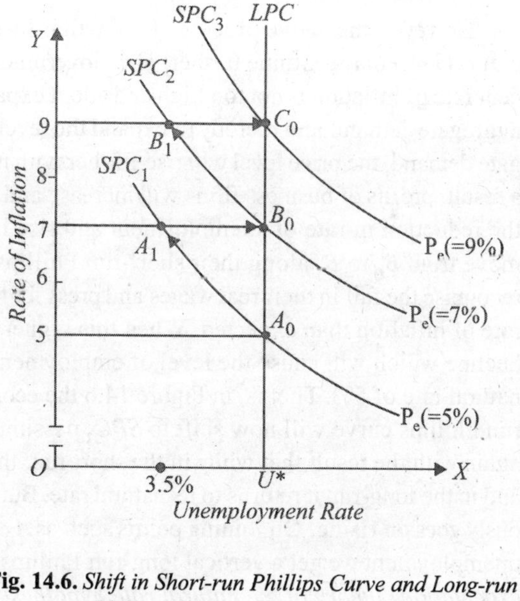

Fig. 14.6. *Shift in Short-run Phillips Curve and Long-run Phillips Curve.*

moving from point A_0 to A_1, on SPC_1 the economy accepts a higher rate of inflation as the cost of achieving a lower rate of unemployment. Thus, this is in conformity with the concept of Phillips curve explained earlier. However, the advocates of natural unemployment rate hypothesis interpret it in a slightly different way. They think that lower rate of unemployment achieved is only a temporary phenomenon. They think *when the actual rate of inflation exceeds the one that is expected, unemployment rate will fall below the natural rate only in the short run. In the long run, the natural rate of unemployment will be restored.*

Long-Run Phillips Curve and Adaptive Expectations. This brings us to the concept of long-run Phillips curve, which Friedman and other natural rate theorists have put forward. According to them, the economy will not remain in a stable equilibrium position at A_1. This is because the workers will realise that due to the higher rate of inflation than the expected one, their real wages and incomes have fallen. The workers will therefore demand higher nominal wages to restore their real income. But as nominal wages rise to compensate for the higher rate of inflation than expected, profits of business firms will fall to their earlier levels. This reduction in their profit implies that the original motivation that prompted them to expand output and increase employment resulting in lower unemployment rate will no longer be there. Consequently, they will reduce employment till the unemployment rate rises to the natural level of 5%. That is, with the increase in nominal wages in Figure 14.6 the economy will move from A_1 to B_0, at a higher inflation rate of 7%. It may be noted that the higher level of aggregate demand which generated inflation rate of 7% and caused the economy to shift from A_0 to A_1 still persists.

Further, at point B_0, and with the actual rate of inflation equal to 7 per cent, the workers will now expect this 7 per cent inflation rate to conitnue in future. As a result, the short-run Phillips curve *SPC* shifts upward from SPC_1 to SPC_2. It therefore follows, according to Friedman and other natural rate theorists, the movement along a short-run Phillips curve *SPC* is only a temporary or short-run phenomenon. In the long run when nominal wages are fully adjusted to the changes in the inflation rate and consequently unemployment rate comes back to its natural level, a new short-run Phillips curve is formed at the higher expected rate of inflation.

However, the above process of reduction in unemployment rate and then its returning to the natural level may continue further. The Government may misjudge the situation and think that 7 per cent rate of inflation is not too high and adopt expansionary fiscal and monetary policies to increase aggregate demand and thereby to expand the level of employment. With the new increase in aggregate demand, the price level will rise further with nominal wages lagging behind in the short run. As a result, profits of business firms will increase and they will expand output and employment causing the reduction in rate of unemployment and rise in the inflation rate. With this, the economy will move from B_0 to B_1 along their short-run Phillips curve SPC_2. After some time, the workers will recognise the fall in their real wages and press for higher normal wages to compensate for the higher rate of inflation than expected. When this higher nominal wages are granted, the business profits decline which will cause the level of employment to fall and unemployment rate to return to the natural rate of 5%. That is, in Figure 14.6 the economy moves from point B_1 to C_0. The new short-run Phillips curve will now shift to SPC_3 passing through point C_0. The process may be repeated again with the result that while in the short run, the unemployment rate falls below the natural rate and in the long-run it returns to its natural rate. But throughout this process the inflation rate continuously goes on rising. On joining points such as A_0, B_0, C_0 corresponding to the given natural rate of unemployment we get a vertical long-run Phillips curve *LPC* in Figure 14.6. Thus, *in the adaptive expectations theory of the natural rate hypothesis while the short-run Phillips curve is downward sloping indicating that trade-off between inflation and unemployment rate in the short run, the long-run Phillips curve is a vertical straight line showing that no trade-off exists between inflation and unemployment in the long run.*

It is important to remember that adaptive expectations theory has also been applied to explain the *reverse process of disinflation*, that is, fall in the rate of inflation as well as inflation itself. Suppose in Figure 14.6 the economy is originally at point C_0 with 9% rate of inflation. Now, if a decline in aggregate demand occurs, say as a result of contraction of money supply by the Central Bank of a country, this will reduce inflation rate below the 9 per cent expected rate. As a result, profits of business firms will decline because the prices will be falling more rapidly than wages. The decline in profits will cause the firms to reduce employment and consequently unemployment rate will rise. Eventually, firms and workers will adjust their expectations and the unemployment rate will return to the natural rate. The process will be repeated and the economy in the long run will slide down along the vertical long-run Phillips curve showing falling rate of inflation at the given natural rate of unemployment.

It follows from above that, *according to adaptive expectations theory, any rate of inflation can occur in the long run with the natural rate of unemployment.*

LONG-RUN PHILLIPS CURVE : RATIONAL EXPECTATIONS

In the end we explain the viewpoint about inflation and unemployment put forward by Rational Expectations Theory which is the cornerstone of recently developed macroeconomic theory, popularly called *new classical macroeconomics*. As explained above, Friedman's adaptive expectations theory assumes that nominal wages lag behind changes in the price level. This lag in the adjustment of nominal wages to the price level brings about rise in business profits which induces the firms to expand output and employment in the short run and leads to the reduction in unemployment rate below the natural rate. But, according to the rational expectations theory, which is another version of natural unemployment rate theory, there is no lag in the adjustment of nominal wages consequent to the rise in price level. The advocates of this theory further argue that nominal wages are *quickly adjusted* to any expected changes in the price level so that there does not exist the type of Phillips curve that shows trade-off between rates of inflation and unemployment. According to them, as a result of increase in aggregate demand, there is no reduction in unemployment rate. The rate of inflation resulting from increase in aggregate demand is *fully and correctly anticipated* by workers and business firms and get completely and quickly incorporated into the wage agreements resulting in higher prices of products. Thus, it is the price level that rises, the level of real output and employment remaining unchanged at the natural level. Hence, aggregate supply curve according to the rational expectations theory is a vertical straight line at the potential GNP level, that is, at the natural rate of unemployment, given the resources and technology. Long-run Phillips curve, according to rational expectations theory, corresponds to this long-run aggregate supply curve and is a vertical straight line at the natural unemployment rate as shown in Fig. 14.7.

Rational expectations theory rests on two basic elements. First, according to it, workers and producers being quite rational have a correct understanding of the economy and therefore correctly anticipate the effects of the Government's economic policies *using all the available relevant information.* On the basis of these anticipations of the effects of economic events and Government's policies they take correct decisions to promote their own interests.

The second premise of rational expectations theory is that, like the classical economists, *it assumes that all product and factor markets are highly competitive*. As a result, wages and product prices are highly flexible and therefore can quickly change upward and downward. Indeed, the rational expectations theory considers that new information is quickly assimilated (*i.e.*, taken into account) in the demand and supply curves of markets so that new equilibrium prices immediately adjust to the new economic events and policies, be it a new technological change or a supply shock such as a drought or act of OPEC oil cartel or change in Government's monetary and fiscal policies.

Figure 14.7 illustrates the standpoint of rational expectations theory about the relation between inflation and unemployment. In this, OY_F is the level of potential national output corresponding to the full employment of labour (with a given natural rate of unemployment). *AS* is aggregate supply curve at Y_F level of real national output. To begin with, AD_1 is the aggregate demand curve which intersects the aggregate supply curve *AS* at point *A* and determines price level equal to P_1. Suppose Government adopts an expansionary monetary policy to increase output and employment. As a consequence, aggregate demand curve shifts upward to the new position AD_2. According to rational expectations theory, people (*i.e.*, workers, businessmen, consumers, lenders) will correctly anticipate that this expansionary policy will cause inflation in the economy and they would take prompt measures to protect themselves against this inflation. Accordingly, workers would press for higher wages and get it granted, businessmen would raise the prices of their products, lenders would hike their rates of interest. All these increases would take place immediately. It is thus clear that the increase in aggregate demand (*i.e.*, aggregate expenditure) brought about by expansionary monetary policy will cause the price level to rise to P_2. Thus, the increase in aggregate demand or expenditure will be fully reflected in higher wages, higher interest rates and higher product prices, all of which will rise in proportion to the anticipated rate of inflation. Consequently, the levels of real national product and employment, wage rate, interest rate, levels of investment and consumption would remain unchanged.

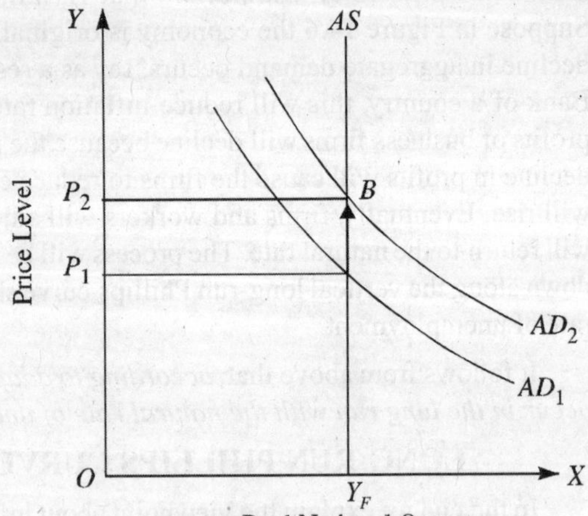

Fig. 14.7. *Inflation and Output : Rational Expectations Theory*

This can be easily understood with the help of monetarist equation of exchange $P = \frac{MV}{Q}$. Expansionary monetary policy leads to the increase in money supply *M*. As a result, aggregate expenditure, which in quantity theory is equal to *MV*, increases. (Note that *V* is the velocity of circulation of money which remains stable). But people's anticipations or expectations of inflation causes an increase in *P* in equal proportion to the expansion in *MV*. This means that despite the increase in *MV*, real output *Q* and the level of employment will remain unchanged.

It is clear from above that people's anticipations or expectations of inflation and acting upon them in their decision making when expansionary monetary policy is adopted frustrate or nullify the intended effect (that is, increase in real output and employment) of Government's monetary policy. In other words, according to the rational expectations theory, the intended effect of expansionary monetary policy on investment, real output and employment does not materialise. As seen above, in Fig. 14.7 it is due to the anticipation of inflation by the people and quick upward adjustments made in wages, interest, etc., by them that the price level instantly rises from P_1 to P_2, the level of output *Q* remaining constant. That is why, according to the rational expectations theory, aggregate supply curve is a vertical straight line. The vertical aggregate supply curve means that there is no trade-off between inflation and unemployment, that is, downward-sloping Phillips curve does not exist. Thus, according to rational expectations theory, the increase in aggregate demand or expenditure as a consequence of easy monetary policy of the Government will fail to reduce unemployment and instead will only cause inflation in the economy.

QUESTIONS FOR REVIEW

1. What is Phillips curve ? What kind of trade-off between unemployment rate and inflation rate does it imply ?
2. What is Phillips curve ? What are its policy implications ?
3. Explain the factors causing downward-sloping Phillips curve. What is the policy significance of its downward sloping ?
4. What is meant by trade-off between the rate of inflation and unemployment ? Explain the Keynesian explanation of this trade-off.
5. What is meant by adaptive expectations ? Explain how with their help Friedman proves that short-run Phillips curve is downward-sloping while the long-run Phillips curve is vertical.
6. What is *natural rate hypothesis.* How does Friedman explain it with his concepts of Phillips curve and adaptative expectations.
7. While there is trade-off between inflation and unemployment in the short run, there is no such trade-off between them in the long run. Explain how Friedman explains with his concepts of short-run and long-run Phillips curves.
8. What effect do expectations regarding rate of inflation have on the short-run Phillips curve ? Can this help to explain stagflation ?
9. What is meant by rational expectations ? How does rational expectations theory show that aggregate supply curve is a vertical straight line and that there is no trade-off between rate of inflation and rate of unemployment ?
10. Distinguish between short-run and long-run Phillips curve. Explain why long-run Phillips curve is vertical, while the short-run Phillips curve is negatively sloping.

PART – III
MONETARY DEMAND AND SUPPLY

- Money : Nature and Functions
- Credit and Commercial Banking
- Central Banking
- Objectives and Instruments of Monetary Policy
- Supply of Money
- Demand for Money

CHAPTER 15

Money : Nature and Functions

Barter System and Invention of Money

Money was not used in the early history of man. Exchanges were few since each family was self-sufficient. Whatever exchanges there were, they took the form of barter, that is, exchange of goods for the other goods. Various difficulties were faced by the people in the barter economy. There was no acceptable means of payment for the direct purchase of goods and services in the barter economy. In other words, in a purely barter system, there was no generally acceptable medium of exchange in the form of a particular good or asset which could be used to buy goods and services and do other types of transactions. Many difficulties were found under the barter system. They are explained below.

Owing to lack of generally acceptable medium of exchange, a difficult **problem of double coincidence of wants** was faced by the persons who wanted to sell and buy goods. For exchange of goods persons desiring to exchange goods must specifically want those goods what others offer in exchange. Thus, an individual who wanted to have a good he must locate another person who offers to give up the good wanted by him and also was willing to accept in exchange the good offered by him. Thus, under barter system only when wants for buying and selling goods of different persons coincided the exchange of goods was possible. A good deal of time was spent by a person in searching for a man with whom his wants coincided. Halm rightly says, "*It is next to impossible that all wishes of bartering individuals should coincide as to the kind, quality and quantity and value of things which are mutually desired, especially in a modern economy in which on a single day millions of persons may exchange millions of goods and services.*"[1]

A barter economy lacked not only a common medium of exchange but also **a standard unit of account** in which prices could be measured and quoted. In the absence of a common unit of account, the number of exchange ratios (that is, prices of goods expressed in terms of each other) between goods would be very large. For example, two cows for one horse, one cow for two quintals of wheat, one pen for three pencils and so on. Thus, lack of a standard unit of account with which to measure values of different goods and services made exchange or trade difficult.

Another problem faced under the barter system for exchange of goods was **impossibility of subdivision of goods** without loss of their value. For instance, if a person has a cow and wants to have 5 kg of wheat, obviously, it is too costly to give one cow for 5 kg of wheat he requires. Then, to do this transaction cow has to be divided. But cow cannot be divided or cut into pieces because cow will lose much of its value if it is divided. Thus, impossibility of division of goods for the purpose of exchange posed a great difficulty and obstructed the growth of trade.

A good deal of time and resources were needed to obtain information for exchange of goods under the barter system. If there existed a medium of exchange, it would solve half the problem. However, a person will still have to determine the value of a good he wants to sell in terms of the medium of exchange. Thus, if there exists a medium of exchange, with well-known characteristics, it will reduce the information costs of trading. Without the medium of exchange information costs will indeed be very large.

1. G.N. Halm, *Monetary Theory*, 1946, p. 1.

Another problem of a barter economy relates to the **production of costly goods.** Suppose an individual who has technical skill and equipment to manufacture a car will not have much incentive to manufacture it in the barter economy. This is because he can exchange a car with a person who has enough goods having a value equal to a car so that their exchange with a car can take place. The car maker must obtain food, clothing and several other commodities of day-to-day consumption in exchange for a car. It will be very difficult, almost impossible, to find a prospective buyer who has enough of these goods and services to give in return for a car. This makes the production of goods on a large scale costly and not feasible.

It is evident from above that barter system could work in a primitive economy where life was simple and man was self-sufficient. As man made some economic progress, division of labour or specialisation and large-scale production came to exist, barter system could not fulfil the increasing needs for exchange of goods. Due to the difficulties of exchange barter economy would have no large-scale production, no advantage of the use of capital-intensive specialised machinery and no easy and cheap means in which wealth could be stored. *The range of goods produced must be much smaller than those produced in the modern developed economies. To meet the needs for a common unit of account and also as a generally accepted medium of exchange and thereby to overcome the difficulties faced under the barter system, money was invented. Money is any thing that is generally acceptable as a medium of exchange and that also acts as a measure and store of value.*

Evolution of Money

Today when in India we think of money, it is generally in terms of rupee notes, in the USA it is in terms of dollar notes and in Great Britain it is in terms of Pound Sterling, and all of these are mostly made of paper. However, in the beginning money was commodities which was selected as a medium of exchange and thus came to be used as money. Bows, sea shells, beads, arrows, furs and skin, etc. were adopted as money at different times in the early stages of development, especially in the hunting stage of human development. With further development and in the pastoral stage, animals such as sheep and cattle (goats and cows) were started being used as money, that is, as a medium of exchange of goods. The use of cattle and other animals as money suffered from certain disadvantages. Since all cows and goats were not identical, they could not serve as a standard unit of measurement. Secondly, the supply of animals such as cows, sheep and goats was subject to large and abrupt fluctuations. Thirdly, ordinary commodities and animals cannot serve as a satisfactory store of value.

In view of the above limitations of ordinary commodities and animals for being used as money and with further progress of human civilisation, ordinary commodities and animals were replaced by precious metals such as gold and silver for being used as money. Crowther thus sums up the superiority of precious metals like gold and silver for monetary use : *"They are easily handled and stored, they do not deteriorate, they have just the right degree of scarcity and they can be relied upon neither to increase nor to diminish in quantity except gradually."*[2] But with invention of coinage, it was coins made of gold and silver which began to be widely used as money rather than simple and plain bits of gold and silver whose value was difficult to be ascertained. It is important to note that precious metals were used as money not because they were valuable but because they were scarce. *For a thing to serve as money scarcity is more important than value*. These days, *it is the scarcity of paper money which is responsible for its efficiency as money*; its lack of value is no hindrance for it to serve as money.

Use of Paper Money. As it came to be firmly realised for a sound money, **scarcity is more important than value,** precious metals were replaced by *paper money*. In the beginning paper money, that is, paper notes were simple claims to and substitutes for metallic money. But in the course of time paper money came to be regarded as money itself. Paper money took the form of bank notes which

2. G. Crowther, *An Outline of Money*.

were not mere substitutes but were considered as an addition to the supply of money. At first, notes could be issued by all commercial banks but with the passage of time when paper money became inconvertible into metallic money issuing of notes became the monopoly of the Central Bank of a country. Central Bank of India is named as Reserve Bank of India.

In early times when notes were introduced they were backed by an exactly equal amount in gold or silver kept in reserve by the issuing authority. Such notes could be exchanged for gold or silver coins when demanded and did nothing more than representing metallic coins. Such paper money or notes were therefore called *representative paper money*. Since paper money now-a-days is not convertible into gold or silver, representative paper money is now not found anywhere in the world.

For a long time, paper money remained a convertible paper money. Under this, money was convertible into standard coins made of gold or silver. Under it the paper currency issued by the Central Bank was fully backed by the reserves of gold and silver of equal value kept by it. Therefore, this paper currency system was called "***Full Reserve System***".

But with the passage of time it was thought that a cent per cent reserve of gold against paper currency issued was not needed and instead only proportion of 30 to 50 per cent was enough to convert the notes presented for conversion into gold. Therefore, ***proportional reserve system*** was adopted. According to this, the issuing authority was called upon to keep a 30 to 50% of the total amount of notes issued as gold reserves. A percentage of 30 to 50 was considered enough to honour the notes when they were presented for exchange into gold. It was based upon the fact that people found notes very convenient and they seldom thought of presenting them to the issuing authority. Therefore, full backing of gold was not required. In India, this proportional reserve system was adopted in 1927 and continued till 1957.

Thus, ***now-a-days paper money is of inconvertible type.*** Under the inconvertible paper money system, money is not convertible into gold or other precious metals. Thus, when paper money is inconvertible, the issuing authority is not responsible to convert the paper notes into gold or gold coins. The currency notes that are issued by Reserve Bank of India are **'fiat' paper money**, that is, they are issued by the fiat *i.e.* order, of the Government. As they are legal tender, they are generally acceptable in exchange for goods and services and for payment of debt. It may be noted that '*promises to pay*' written on the currency notes are not 'promises to pay' something else. For these notes, only other paper notes can be given whose value would be equal to the face value of the note you present for payment.

But as time passed even proportional reserve system was thought to be inadequate for the monetary needs of a growing economy. Therefore, it was abandoned in India in 1957 and was replaced by the **minimum reserve system**. According to this, Reserve Bank was required to keep only a minimum amount of gold and other approved securities (such as dollar and Pound Sterling) of the value of ₹ 200 crores. Out of these reserves it was required that gold must not be less than the value of ₹ 115 crores. *On the basis of these minimum reserves, Reserve Bank of India could issue any number of notes or currency subject to the economic condition of the country.*

However, one important disadvantage of inconvertible paper currency is that government is tempted to over-issue the currency to meet its ever increasing expenditure. This causes serious inflationary pressures in the economy. However, for this paper currency system should not be blamed. Desired benefits from inconvertible paper currency can be obtained if the government properly manages it. If the adoption of paper currency system causes instability in the economy, the Government is responsible for it and not the paper currency system. The paper currency system is very elastic and its main advantage is that the quantity of money can be increased or decreased according to the requirements of the economy. But if improper use of its elastic nature is made by the Government by creating excessive quantity of money, the Government should be blamed and not the standard.

Emergence of Bank Deposits as Money. Finally, there was further development in the form of money. In the developed countries the main type of money is not paper notes issued by the central bank but the *bank deposits* (especially, *demand deposits*) which people hold with the commercial banks and against which cheques can be drawn. In India too *bank money* (*i.e., bank deposits*) or which is also called *credit money* has become a significant part of the total money supply. It is worth mentioning that chequeable bank deposits held by the public in the banks serve as money because through drawing cheques on them we can use them for making payments for purchase of goods and services and assets.

It is worthwhile to note that it is not only the currency deposited by the people that constitutes a part of money supply in the economy, but as will be explained later, *banking system as a whole itself creates deposits depending on the reserve requirements and they also form a part of money supply in the economy.*

It is also worth noting that *deposits in the banks are money* and *not the cheques drawn on them.* Through a cheque a person instructs the bank to transfer some specified amount of money from his deposit account to another person or institution. On receipt of the cheque bank debits the specified amount from the account of the drawer and credits the amount in the deposit account of the drawee. It is therefore the person's deposits that are used as a medium of exchange and therefore serve as money.

Similarly, credit card is not money. Presenting your credit card to pay for something, the credit card company gives you loan at the moment you buy a thing. Later the credit card company sends you the bill and you have to pay the credit card company either paper currency or drawing a cheque on your bank and also generally pays interest on the loan taken for a certain period. Unless you have currency or bank deposits in the bank you cannot make the necessary payments to the credit card company. Thus, it is the currency or bank deposits that serve as money and not the credit card. In fact, credit card is just like an identity card for providing you loan by the credit card company.

An essential prerequisite of money which needs to be emphasised is that it should be generally acceptable in a society as a medium of exchange.

Definition of Money

To give a precise definition of money is a difficult task. Various authors have given different definitions of money. Professor D.H. Robertson defines money as *"anything which is widely accepted in payment for goods or in discharge of other kinds of business obligations". According to Crowther, "Money can be defined as anything that is generally acceptable as a means of exchange and that at the same time acts as a measure and a store of value".*

Two important things about money emerge from the above two definitions of money. Firstly, money has been defined in terms of the functions it performs. That is why some economists have said that money is what money does. That is, money is anything which performs the functions of money. Secondly, *an essential requirement of any kind of money is that it must be generally acceptable to every member of the society* as a medium of exchange and settlement of debt. You accept paper notes in payment for goods or services you sell because you are confident that others will accept them from whom you wish to buy goods or services. If people lose confidence in any money, they will not accept it in payment for goods and services. Thus, when people lose confidence in any money as, for instance, when its value is fast depreciating, the money ceases to be generally acceptable. Indeed, in that case it ceases to be money. In the early twenties this happened to 'Mark' in Germany and it also happened to 'Rouble' of Soviet Russia in late eighties as its value was fast depreciating. But the general acceptability is not the physical quality possessed by a good. General acceptability is a social phenomenon and is conferred upon a good when the society by law or convention adopts it as a medium of exchange.

It is worthwhile to note that in the modern times in almost all countries of the world paper money (that is, notes) are inconvertible into precious metals such as gold and silver. This inconvertible paper money is accepted in transactions as a medium of exchange and settlement of debt because it is backed by the authority of the government which has declared it a legal tender. Though paper notes are just pieces of paper and inconvertible to gold or silver, they are valuable because others will accept it in transactions of goods and services. Thus, paper money (for example, rupee notes, US dollar notes) are valuable because it enables its bearer to buy some quantities of food, drink, clothing and other goods and services. However, money loses its value sharply due to rapid inflation, people lose confidence in it and they start using some other substitutes as money. Thus, Milton Friedman, a noted economist, writes, "When great changes occur in the quantity of these pieces of paper . . . as they have during and after war . . . they seem to be, after all, no more than pieces of paper. People will then seek substitutes like the cigarettes, which for a time became the medium of exchange in Germany after world war"[3] Such a situation occurs because the value of a currency in terms of what it can buy is falling rapidly due to runaway inflation. And this inflation generally occurs because governments increase the quantity of money (*i.e.,* paper notes) to meet its large increases in expenditures, for example in war periods. The governments can print or issue a very large quantity of money because, as mentioned above, against it the government is not required to keep gold or any other precious metal. Gold standard or paper money that is convertible into gold has been given up long ago.

Functions of Money

There are four main functions of money which are summed up in the following couplet:

"*Money is a matter of functions four,*
A medium, a measure, a standard, a store"

We explain below these four functions of money in some detail.

1. **Medium of Exchange.** The most important function of money is that it serves as a medium of exchange. In the barter economy a great difficulty was experienced in the exchange of goods as the exchange in the barter system required double coincidence of wants. Money has removed this difficulty. Now a person *A* can sell his goods to *B* for money and then he can use that money to buy the goods he wants from others who have these goods. As long as money is generally acceptable, there will be no difficulty in the process of exchange. The function of medium of exchange that money performs has become possible because *money has enabled us to separate the act of buying from the act of selling and thus avoids double coincidence of wants.* We saw above that under the barter system because of this double coincidence of wants exchange of goods and services was difficult and inconvenient to occur. The use of money which is generally accepted as a medium of exchange has made it possible to sell anything to anyone who wants to buy it and accept in return some amount of money as a price. He then uses the money to buy the good he wants from someone who has it. In this way separation of the acts of selling and buying through the use of money helps us to avoid double coincidence of wants. By serving as a very convenient medium of exchange money has made possible the complex division of labour or specialisation in the modern economic organisation.

2. **Measure of Value or a Unit of Account.** Another important function of money is that it serves as a common measure of value or a unit of account. Under barter economy there was no common measure of value in which the values of different goods could be measured and compared with each other. Money has also solved this difficulty. Under barter values of different goods were expressed and measured in terms of quantities of each other such as so many bushels of wheat, so many litres of milk, so many number of cigarettes and this makes the comparison of values of different goods difficult. For example, rupee is the basic unit of account in India for measuring economic values. Almost all prices of goods, rent of land, wages of labour, interest on capital, prices of gold and silver

3. Milton Friedman, "Money', *Encyclopaedia Britannica.*

and real estate are expressed and measured in rupees. Measuring values of all goods and services in a single uniform account simplifies the comparison of values of different goods and services. Money serves as a yardstick for measuring the value of goods and services. When the value of all goods and services is measured in a standard unit of money, say rupee, their relative values can be easily compared to achieve optimum of one's budget expenditure among different goods for consumption.

3. **Standard of Deferred Payments.** Another function of money is that it serves as a standard for deferred payments. Deferred payments mean those payments which are to be made in the future. If a loan is taken today, it would be paid back after a period of time. The amount of loan is measured in terms of money and it is paid back in money. A large number of credit transactions involving huge future payments are made daily. Money performs this function of standard for deferred payments because its value remains more or less stable.

If the prices are falling, *i.e.*, the value of money is rising, the creditors will gain in real terms and the debtors will lose. Conversely, if the prices are rising (or value of money is falling) creditors will be the losers. Thus, if the money is to serve as a fair and correct standard for deferred payments, its value must remain stable. In case the value of money is changing very much, the creditors or debtors will be put to much loss and sufferings. Thus, when there is severe inflation or deflation, money ceases to serve as a standard for deferred payments.

4. **Store of Value.** Lastly, money acts as store of value. Money being the most liquid of all assets is a convenient form in which to store wealth, that is, *money can be held as an asset*. Thus, store of value function is also called *asset function of money*. It is, therefore, essential that the good chosen as money should be such as can be easily stored without deterioration or wastage. That is why gold was popular in the past as money material. Gold could be kept safely without deterioration. But in the modern times even paper money can be kept as deposits in banks to serve as asset. Of course, there are other assets like houses, factories, bonds, shares, etc., in which wealth can be stored. But money performs the store of value function with a difference. Money being the most liquid of all assets has the advantage that an individual or a firm can buy with it anything at any time. But this is not the case with other assets. Other assets like houses and shares have to be sold first and converted into money and only then they can be used to buy other things. *Money would perform the store of value function properly if it remains stable in value.* For example, if there is a high rate of inflation in the economy, real value or purchasing power of money goes on falling. This adversely affects the store of value function of money. Since a high rate of inflation erodes the real value of money, it discourages people to save. Besides, a high rate of inflation induces people to invest whatever savings they do in unproductive assets such as gold and jewellery, real estate etc. rather than storing their savings in cash money or deposits in banks with a fixed rate of interest or in bonds and shares of corporate companies and mutual funds from which real return is uncertain.

It may however be noted that while only money performs function of medium of exchange or a unit of account but *any other asset* such as bonds, shares, gold or real estate can serve as a store of value. These other assets generally provide the holder of these assets a higher return compared to that of money. The question arises as to why people usually use money as a store of value though return from it is relatively low. Cash money yields no return at all and money in the form of *savings bank deposits* yields a very low return of 4% per annum in India.

From above it is clear that money has removed the difficulties of barter system. It has facilitated trade and has made possible the complex division of labour and specialisation of the modern economic system. Without the use of money, modern economy will not run smoothly and the production will get a serious setback. For these reasons, monetary economy is preferred to barter economy.

FORMS OF MONEY

Money of Account. Money of account is the monetary unit in terms of which the accounts of a country are kept and transactions settled, i.e., in which general purchasing power, debts and prices are expressed. The rupee is, for instance, our money of account, sterling is the money of account of Great Britain and mark that of Germany. Money of account need not however be actually circulating in the country. During 1922-24 the mark in Germany depreciated to such an extent that it ceased to be money of account. The paisa in India is not in circulation and yet it is money of account.

Limited and Unlimited Legal Tender : Coins may be limited legal tender or unlimited legal tender. A legal tender currency is one in terms of which debts can be legally paid. It is an offence to refuse to accept payment in legal tender money. A currency is unlimited legal tender when debts up to any amount can be paid through it. It is limited legal tender when payments only up to a given limit can be made by means of it. For instance, rupee coins and rupee notes are unlimited legal tender in India. And so is the half-rupee coin. But coins of lower denominations are only limited legal tender. They are legal tender only up to ten rupees.

When a coin is worn out and becomes light beyond a certain limit, then it ceases to be a legal tender. When one rupee and half-rupee coins are more than 20% below the standard weight, they are no longer legal tender. A Government may take away the legal tender quality of a currency. For instance, the old rupee coins of one hundred and eighty grains 11/12 fine are no longer legal tender in India. In 1978 the Government declared currency notes of rupees one thousand denomination and above as no longer legal tender. it is usually done to bring such currency out of the hoards. However, recently notes of ₹ 1000 have again been issued by Reserve Bank of India and have unlimited legal tender status.

Standard Money. Standard money is that in which the value of goods as well as all other forms of money are measured. Thus, in India all prices of goods are measured in terms of rupees. Moreover, the other forms of money such as two-rupee notes, ten-rupee notes, hundred-rupee notes and one-half rupee coins are expressed in terms of rupees. Thus rupee is the standard money of India. Standard money is always made the unlimited legal tender money. In old days the standard money was a *full-bodied money*, i.e., its face value was equal to the real or intrinsic worth of the metal it contained. But now-a-days in almost all countries of the world, even the standard money is only a *token money*, i.e., the material contained in it is very much less than the face value written on it. Thus, the rupee in India is available in the form of paper notes which have no intrinsic worth. Even the rupee coin has a metallic value much less than its face value. Rupee coin has been called a '*note printed on nickel*' (Rupee coin these days is made of nickel).

Fiat Money. When money was in the form of commodity money such as gold, silver, cigarettes, it had an intrinsic value as it had an alternative use apart from serving as money. But this commodity money is no longer in use and has become a thing of the past. The paper money such as currency notes is just a token money as it has no intrinsic value being worthless scraps of paper. The paper money is also not backed by gold or silver and is generally acceptable by the public as a medium of exchange and for settlement of debts because of the *fiat* (i.e., *legal order or sanction*) of the government. The government declared the paper money issued by it or by its authorised bank called as the Central Bank of the country as *legal tender* by passing a law to this effect. Therefore, it is the legal order of the government that the paper money must be accepted as a medium of exchange and in settlement of debts. It is also worth noting that even one-rupee, two-rupee, 5-rupee, 10-rupee coins are fiat or token money as their intrinsic metalic value is very much less than their face value.

It may be further noted that *chequeable bank deposits* are also these days treated as money though they are not fiat money because activities of banks are regulated by the government or Reserve Bank of India so that people are confident that the cheques on these bank deposits will be honoured by the banks.

Bank Money. Demand deposits of banks are usually called bank money. Bank deposits are created when somebody deposits money with them. Banks also create deposits when they advance loans to the businessmen and traders. Today these demand deposits are the important constituent of the money supply in the country.

It is important to note that bank deposits are generally divided in two categories : demand deposits and time deposits. Demand deposits are those deposits which are payable on demand through cheques and without any serving prior notice to the banks. On the other hand, time deposits are those deposits which have a fixed term of maturity and are not withdrawable on demand and also cheques cannot be drawn on them. Clearly, it is only the demand deposits which serve as a medium of exchange, for they can be transferred from one person to another through drawing a cheque on them as and when deired by them. However, since even time or fixed deposits can be withdrawn by foregoing some interest and can be used for making payments, they are included in the concept of broad money, generally called M_3. It may be noted that latest addition to the forms of money are credit cards issued by the banks which are these days extensively used for making purchases.

MODERN MONETARY SYSTEM OR MANAGED CURRENCY STANDARD

Paper money has come to occupy a very important place in the modern monetary system of almost all the countries of the world. The term paper money only applies to Government notes and the notes issued by the Central Bank of the country. In early times when notes were introduced they were backed by an exactly equal amount in gold or silver kept in reserve by the issuing authority. Such notes could be exchanged for gold or silver coins when demanded and did nothing more than representing metallic coins. Such paper money or notes are therefore called representative paper money. Paper money now-a-days is not wholly backed by gold or silver. Representative paper money is now not found anywhere in the world.

Convertible Paper Money. For a long time, paper money remained a convertible paper money. Under this, money is convertible into standard coins made of gold or silver. Under it the paper currency issued by the Central Bank was fully backed by the reserves of gold and silver of equal value kept by it. Therefore, this paper currency system was called "*Full Reserve System*". But with the passage of time it was thought that a cent per cent reserve against paper currency issued was not needed and instead only proportion of 30 to 50 per cent was enough to convert the notes presented for conversion into gold. Therefore, *proportional reserve system* was adopted. According to this, the issuing authority was called upon to keep a 30 to 50% of the total amount of notes issued as gold reserves. A percentage of 30 to 50 was considered enough to honour the notes when they were presented for exchange into gold. It was based upon the fact that people found notes very convenient and they seldom thought of presenting them to the issuing authority. Therefore, full backing of gold was not required. In India, this proportional reserve system was adopted in 1927 and continued till 1957.

Inconvertible Paper Money. Thus, now-a-days paper money is of *inconvertible type*. Under the inconvertible paper money system, money is not convertible into gold or other precious metals. Thus, when paper money is inconvertible, the issuing authority is not responsible to convert the paper notes into gold or gold coins. The currency notes that are issued by Reserve Bank of India are '***fiat' paper money***, that is, they are issued by the fiat *i.e.* order) of the Government. As they are legal tender, they are generally acceptable in exchange for goods and services and for payment of debt. It may be noted that 'promises to pay' written on the currency notes are not 'promises to pay' something else. For these notes, only other paper notes can be given whose value would be equal to the face value of the note you present for payment

Minimum Reserve System. But as time passed even proportional reserve system was thought to be inadequate for the monetary needs of a growing economy. Therefore, it was abandoned in India in 1957 and was replaced by the minimum reserve system. According to this, Reserve Bank was required to keep only a minimum amount of gold and other approved securities (such as dollar and Pound Sterling) of the value of ₹ 200 crores. Out of these reserves it was required that gold must not be less than the value of ₹ 115 crores. On the basis of these minimum reserves, Reserve Bank of India could issue any number of notes or currency subject to the economic condition of the country.

Managed Paper Currency Standard : Its Advantages

Paper currency standard or managed currency system which prevails in the modern economy has several advantages and disadvantages. Its main advantage is that under it the quantity of money can be easily increased according to economic needs of the country. When any country is under gold standard, it cannot increase the quantity of money unless the quantity of gold with it increases, despite the fact that the country needs expansion in money supply badly for purpose of promoting economic growth. Therefore, paper or fiat currency standard, which delinks the creation of money from gold, facilitates expansion in the quantity of money for promoting economic growth. The process of economic growth brings about an increase in output of goods and services in agriculture, industry, transport and communication. As a result, there is need for financing these activities so that transactions involving a larger amount of goods and services take place easily. But this requires the availability of sufficient amount of money. If the required amount of money is not forthcoming, as is the case under gold and silver standards, then the process of economic growth will be retarded.

In times of depression there is need to increase the aggregate demand in the economy so that the state of full employment is reached. The best way to increase aggregate demand is the creation of new money by the Government and spending it on various public works. Following the increase in aggregate demand, production will expand and employment for workers will increase causing their incomes to rise. But, as we have seen above, only under paper currency standard, the quantity of money can be increased easily, whereas under gold standard, without the increase in the quantity of gold, money supply cannot be increased. In this way we see that paper currency standard is helpful to overcome depression and to achieve the objective of full employment.

On the other hand, when inflation occurs in the economy-the Government can make a surplus budget and in this way it can withdraw the extra money from the public. This will lower the aggregate demand which will help in controlling inflation. With the appropriate monetary and fiscal policies price stability can be achieved. But these appropriate monetary and fiscal policies are possible only under paper currency standard. J.M. Keynes also supported the managed currency standard on the ground that, as compared to gold standard or any other monetary standard, this is very elastic and under it the quantity of money can be varied according to the needs of the economy.

Unlike the gold and silver standard, paper currency is not a fair-weather friend. This standard is very helpful to the Government in situations of crisis such as war, drought, etc. when it needs extra quantity of money. By creating new paper money the Government can conduct the war successfully. With the newly created money the Government can buy real resources and goods when sufficient quantity of money cannot be procured through taxes. Under gold and silver standards, money cannot be increased unless the quantity of gold or silver increases. This is true that under paper currency standard Governments are tempted to issue excessive notes which results in inflation. But if proper controls are applied and production of goods expands, the issue of more money within reasonable limits to match the extra output does not result in inflation.

Besides, paper currency standard is very economical. As compared to the prices of metals, the price of paper is very low. Even those countries can adopt this standard which have no or few resources of gold and silver. Besides this, with the adoption of paper currency standard the gold and silver are saved which can be used for industrial and productive purposes. Lastly, under the paper currency standard, rate of foreign exchange automatically changes according to the conditions of demand and supply and therefore disequilibrium in the balance of trade is automatically removed. According to a foreign exchange specialist, Agnas, "the beauty of paper system is that as soon as any disequilibrium between demand and supply occurs, sharp fluctuation in the price of foreign exchange immediately takes place which by its immediate action on both exports and imports rapidly restores equilibrium."

Disadvantages of Paper or Managed Currency Standard

But paper currency standard has several disadvantages too. First, it creates foreign exchange instability. Due to excessive changes in the foreign exchange rate, the prices of exports and imports of a country go on changing rapidly which affects foreign exchange earnings of the country. As a result of this, the country has to continually face foreign exchange instability and this instability is very dangerous for those countries which predominantly depend on foreign trade. These days when most of the countries of the world have floated their currencies (*i.e.*, foreign exchange rate is left to be determined by demand and supply), foreign exchange instability has assumed serious proportions. Therefore, many suggestions have been put forward to reform the international monetary system so that the problem of foreign exchange instability is avoided. Secondly, it is also asserted that even internal economic stability cannot be achieved with paper currency standard. The over-issue of paper currency can lead to inflation in the economy. This has been actually so in India where too much new paper money has been created to finance ever increasing Government expenditure. This has caused serious inflationary pressures in the Indian economy. Thus, the paper currency standard can give rise to both internal and foreign exchange instability. However, for this paper currency system should not be blamed. Desired benefits from paper currency system can be obtained if the Government properly manages it. If the adoption of paper currency system causes instability in the economy, the Government is responsible for it and not the paper currency system. The paper currency system is very elastic and its main advantage is that the quantity of money can be increased or decreased according to the requirements of the economy. But if improper use of its elastic nature is made by the Government by creating excessive quantity of money, the Government should be blamed and not the standard.

IMPORTANCE OR ROLE OF MONEY

Classical economists thought that money is a just veil and does not affect the real volume of goods and services in the economy, that is, the level of national product. According to them, money only affects the price level in the economy with no effect on the levels of real income and employment. They contended that what we really want was goods and services which satisfy the wants of the people and promote their welfare. Therefore, according to them, we must go behind the veil of money to see changes in the total output of goods and services or in real income. It is true that what we really want is not money but the goods and services which money can buy. It is the goods and services which satisfy the wants of the people and not money as such. But it must not be concluded from this that money is of no real importance. Modern economic life based on the complex division of labour or specialization which has added so greatly to the productivity of the economy will not be possible without money. The following are some of the advantages of money which show that money plays a vital and significant role in the modern economy.

1. Moeny has Facilitated Exchange and Promoted Trade. In the first place by serving as a medium of exchange and a common measure of value, money has removed the difficulties of the barter system and promoted trade in the economy. The difficulties of the barter system, namely, lack of double coincidence of wants, lack of division and lack of common measure of value are well known. By removing these difficulties, money has greatly facilitated the process of exchange. In the absence of money, trade and exchanges must have been few and far between and entailed a great waste of time and energy.

2. Money Promotes Division of Labour and Productivity. Money is of great importance as it promotes division of labour and productivity in the modern economies. Since under the barter system, exchange was difficult, a man had to be self-sufficient, that is, produced most of the goods for himself. In the absence of money there were great difficulties in exchanging goods and services. This worked as an obstacle to the division of labour and specialisation among various individuals and nations. Long ago Adam Smith clearly brought out in his now well-known book "Wealth of

Nations" how the division of labour and specialisation enhance productivity and efficiency of labour force. It is this division of labour and specialisation that has made the use of more efficient machines and advanced technology possible for production of goods. Indeed, it is because of the output-augmenting effect of division of labour that *Adam Smith regarded increase in the division of labour as progress in technology*. By opening up the opportunities of effecting division of labour, and through facilitating exchange and trade of goods and services money contributes to the expansion of production. Therefore, money enables the increase in the amount of production and variety of goods and services produced. *"If a modern economy were somehow deprived of the monetary mechanism and were driven back to a system of barter, the level of output would be much lower and the variety of goods and services much smaller than is enjoyed with a money system."*[4] In fact money serves as a 'factor of production' which enables us to increase and diversify output

3. Money helps in Maximising Satisfaction by Consumers or Profits by Producers. Money is of immense advantage both to the consumers and producers. To the consumers money represents a general purchasing power. They can buy anything with money they have and at any time convenient to them. Since the values of goods are expressed in terms of common measure i.e. money, the consumer can easily compare the relative money prices of the goods and expected utilities from them. A consumer can easily spend his given money income on various goods in such a way that marginal utilities goods are proportional to their prices. With this he will be maximising his satisfaction from his given income. Thus the existence of money helps the consumer to maximise his satisfaction by acting on the principle of equi-marginal utility.

4. Money Helps the Producer Too. The producer can easily compare the money cost and money income of the different levels of output. He can thus easily decide about the level of output which maximises his profits by equating marginal cost with marginal revenue (MC = MR). He can also easily decide about the units of a factor to be employed by comparing its marginal revenue product with the money payment he has to make to it. To maximise profits he can easily equate marginal revenue product (MRP) of a factor with the marginal factor cost (MFC) on that factor. Moreover, the workers engaged by a producer want goods and services to satisfy their wants. They want food, clothing, shelter and so many other things. The producer cannot supply them all these things easily. But what be can do is to pay them in money with which they buy the commodities they like at their own convenience and when they need them.

5. Money can Help in Reviving the Economy from Recession or Depression. According to modern economists, money may play an important role in bringing about real changes. They point out that at times of recession or depression when there exist a lot of idle productive capacity and unemployment of labour, expansion of money supply, say through Government's deficit budget financed by the creation of new money, will cause aggregate expenditure or demand to shift upward. This increase in aggregate expenditure or demand will cause output and employment in the economy to rise and thus will help the economy to recover from recession or depression.

Beneficial effect on output and employment of expansion in money supply can be obtained even if Central Bank of a country takes steps to expand money supply in the economy, say through reduction in Cash Reserve Ratio (CRR) and through buying securities in the open market. These steps by the central bank aim at expansion in credit availability for the businessmen. The greater credit availability will lead to more private investment which through multiplier process will cause income, output and employment to rise. It is important to note that for the last three years (2010-2013) Federal Reserve (which is the Central Bank of the US) under the governorship of Ben Beruanke has adopted unusual monetary policy of what is called ***Quantitative Easing (QE)*** under which it is purchasing bonds, both government bonds and private bonds, from the market and paying for them

4. A.A. Walters, *Money and Banking*, Pengiun Readings, pp. 8-9.

by printing new money, keeping interest rate at zero. The pumping of new billions of dolars in the US economy in this way has been done to spur growth of investment and employment to revive the US economy from recession. It has now been found (August 2013) that this policy of *quantitative easing* (*QE*) has in fact succeeded to overcome recession in the US economy. The economic growth rate has risen to 2.5 per cent per annum and unemployment, was reported to have fallen to 7.6 per cent from its recent peak of 10 per cent in December 2010. Therefore, it has been decided to tapering of quantitative easing in the first quarter of 2014. It, therefore follows that ***money is not neutral in its effect on real income and employment. In fact, as seen just above, it plays an important role in the determination of the level of real economic activity***.

It is evident from above that ***money helps us to avoid double coincidence of wants***. It enables the complex system of a large of number of prices of goods and services in terms of each other that prevail under barter system which makes it difficult to compare various prices and take optimal decisions. For example, if I sell my services as an economist, I need to know only money price of that service and money prices of the goods and services that I will buy; I do not require a complete list of various offers of goods as price of my service. In view of this significant role of money in the modern complex production system and transactions of goods and services that enhances productive capacity of the economy that **it is not proper to call money as a mere 'veil'** and intrinsically unimportant and serves as *a mere* medium of exchange. Of course, money is a veil in the sense that what matters most is the amount of goods and services that one can purchase with money. Thus, while considering the amount of money one should keep in mind money's purchasing power of goods and services. Therefore, in order to stress the importance of purchasing power of money, economists have evolved the concept of ***real money balances***. *By real money balances we mean the value of money balances in terms of goods and services that we can buy*. Real money balances are measured by dividing the money balances divided by the price level as measured by price index. Thus, real money balances are equal to $\frac{M}{P}$ where M is the magnitude of money balances and P is the price level.

6. Money Promotes Saving and Investment. A great significance of money is that it contributes a great deal to the increase in saving of the economy. Money has made saving easier than in the barter system. Increase in saving leads to the increase in investment which determines economic growth of a country. Further, money has made easier the acts of borrowing and lending and has given birth to various financial institutions which promote saving. Investment which is made possible by saving raises the rate of capital formation in the economy. The higher level of output in the modern economy is mainly due to the extensive use of capital in the production process.

From the viewpoint of development, another important *role of money lies in making the magnitude of investment independent of the current level of savings*. In a barter system, the goods not consumed constitute the savings as well as investment. That is, investment is not different from current savings. The greater the current savings, the greater the investment. However, in a modern economy, this is not so. Whereas it is households which save in the form of money, it is the firms which invest money in capital goods. Therefore, investment can differ from saving because investment activity is separated from the act of saving. More importantly, investment in a monetary economy can exceed the current level of savings. This excess of investment over savings is possible because new money can be created by the Government in the form of currency or by banks in the form of bank deposits. And this is what is important for the purpose of economic growth.

In the developed countries in times of depression when idle productive capacity exists, the increase in investment made possible by creation of new money by the Government or banks would lead to the increase in aggregate demand for goods and services. In such times the supply of goods and services is elastic due to the existence of excess capacity. Therefore, increase in aggregate demand generated by the investment financed by created money brings about expansion in output of goods and services and thereby causes an increase in the level of employment.

In developing countries, the created money can play a useful role in promoting economic development. Rapid economic development can be achieved by stepping up the rate of investment or capital formation. But additional resources are required to increase the rate of investment. But in a country where a majority of the people are living at the bare subsistence level, voluntary savings, taxation, Government borrowing cannot by themselves provide sufficient investible resources for development. The government therefore attempts to increase the volume of investible resources beyond what is possible on the basis of current level of savings through creating new money. The newly created money can be spent on investment projects both in the industrial and agricultural fields which would lead to the increase in output, income and employment. However, it is important to note that creation of new money or what is these days called *monetisation of fiscal deficit* must be within *safe limits*. If excessive amount of new money is created, it will cause inflation in the economy that would hinder growth rather than promoting it.

Money and Investment in Quick-Yielding Projects. It is widely believed that any increase in the supply of money in developing countries would lead to the rise in prices or to the emergence of inflationary pressures. However, this is not always true. A reasonable amount of newly created money helps the development of the economy by raising the level of investment. In the developing economies a lot of natural and human resources lie unutilised and underutilised which can be employed for productive purposes. If the newly created money is used for investment in those projects such as small irrigation works, land reclamation schemes, flood control and anti-soil erosion measures, cottage industries which yield quick returns, then the danger of inflation will not be there. These quick-yielding projects will increase the production of essential consumer goods in the short run and will therefore prevent the rise in prices. Further, if development strategy is such that a higher priority is assigned to agriculture and other wage goods industries and further that organisational and institutional reforms are undertaken to provide all farmers with irrigation facilities, fertilizers and high-yielding varieties, agricultural output can be raised in the short period. In this framework, new money can be created to increase the level of investment without much adverse effect on prices.

Whether economic growth should be financed through such inflationary method is however a very controversial issue. Critics have pointed out several adverse effects of inflation on saving propensity of the people and the pattern of investment, but we shall not go into this controversy here. Suffice it to say here that *newly created money can be used for development purposes to some extent without causing a rise in prices if it is used for specific quick-yielding projects and in the framework of a development strategy which assigns a high priority to agriculture and other wage goods industries.*

QUESTIONS FOR REVIEW

1. What is money ? Show how it has removed the difficulties of barter system.
2. Define money. Describe its functions in a modern economy.
3. What is the necessary condition which makes something money ? How is the store of value function of money derived from its function as a medium of exchange ?
4. Money is what money does. Discuss
5. Define money. Explain tis important functions.
6. Explain the following forms of money.

   (*a*) Demand deposits
   (*b*) Paper money
   (*c*) Legal tender money
   (*d*) Convertible and inconvertible money.
   (*e*) Fiat money.

7. What is money ? Would you include time deposits in money supply ? Are cheques and credit card money ?

   [**Hints.** At present there are various measures of money supply such as M_1, M_2, M_3. Time deposits are not included in M_1 measure of money supply but they are an important part of M_3 measure of money supply. It may also be noted that these days measure M_3 of money supply is extensively used. For details see Chapter 19.]

8. Discuss the various functions of money. What would happen to an economy if money supply suddenly disappeared ?

9. Explain the paper monetary system as it prevails today in the modern economies. For issuing new money whether Government or Reserve Bank of India needs to keep proportionate amount of gold as reserve ? Explain the advantages and disadvantages of paper currency system.

10. Explain the role of money in the economy for promoting (*a*) division of labour, (*b*) saving, (*c*) income and employment.

11. Explain the importance of money for economic growth of a developing country.

12. "Money which is a source of so many blessings to mankind becomes, unless we control it, a source of peril and confusion". Discuss.

13. Under what circumstances money does not perform well as a store of value function ? What are its consequences ?

14. Is it proper to call money as a mere 'veil' ? Discuss. In this connection explain why economists distinguish between 'money balances' and 'real money balances' ?

15. What is meant by 'double confidence of wants'? How does money enable us to avoid this problem ?

16. "If a modern economy were somehow deprived of monetary mechanism and were driven back to a system of barter, the level of output would be much lower and the variety of goods and services much smaller than is enjoyed with a money system" (A.A. Walters), Discuss.

17. What is quantitative easing ? Has it been successful in reviving the US economy ?

CHAPTER 16

Credit and Commercial Banking

Credit : Meaning and Functions

With the introduction and use of money credit also came into existence. Credit is created when one party (a person, a firm or an institution) lends money to another party, the borrower. Thus, credit is generally understood to mean the finance provided to others at a certain rate of interest. The act of lending and borrowing creates both credit and debt. Whereas debt means the obligation to pay the finance borrowed, the credit means the claim to receive this money payments from the other party. Every credit involves debt, that is, obligation to pay money and therefore creates claim.

The act of borrowing and lending and thereby the creation of credit is a special type of exchange transaction which involves future payment of the principal sum borrowed as well as the rate of interest on it. The lending and borrowing of money and the institution of money lending came into vogue ever since money was invented by man. In the modern times there are a variety of institutions which specialise in borrowing and lending of money. The bank credit is only one form of credit. Money lenders, indigenous bankers, credit cooperative societies, commercial and cooperative banks, industrial financial institutions, LIC, export finance houses etc. are all credit institutions and do the business of borrowing and lending money. *Different credit institutions lend money for different purposes and are collectively called the financial system*. Thus commercial banks are only one segment, though an important one, of the financial or credit system of an economy.

Credit institutions can be differentiated according to the type and purpose of credit they offer. There are credit institutions which lend money only for agriculture. There are others which provide credit only to industries and still others to finance exports only. Credit institutions also differ in respect of the duration of period for which they lend money to their clients. Some provide short-term credit, some medium-term credit and others only long-term credit. We shall study only one type of credit institution, namely, the commercial banks.

Functions of Credit

The main function of credit is to relieve the constraint imposed by balanced budgets on economic agents, that is, to meet the financial requirements of investors who have to spend more on trade and investment than their own savings. Accordingly, it is through the means of credit that the surplus funds with some individuals and institutions are made available to the deficit spenders, that is, those who are required to spend more than their resources, for instance, traders, companies, investors. It is the performance of this function, that is, the transferring of surplus funds of some to meet the spending by the businessmen and investors, that the banking and other segments of the financial system are able to promote savings and investment, to ensure better allocation of financial resources and thereby to encourage economic growth in the economy.

But, for the credit system to perform these functions, it needs to be efficiently managed and controlled. If credit is not efficiently managed, it can cause inflation or deflation, recession and unemployment in the economy. Besides, the mismanagement of credit can lead to misallocation of invisible resources and thereby hinder economic growth. It can also cause concentration of economic power in a few hands and exploitation of weaker sections and thus work against the achievement of social justice.

Purpose or End-Uses of Credit

Credit is required for different purposes and by all sectors of the economy. Therefore, there is need for the proper allocation of credit between different uses and sectors if the society is to achieve its objectives. When credit is demanded and used for productive purposes, it may be used to finance the needs of working capital or for fixed investment (*i.e.* capital equipment, machinery etc.). The broad categories of economic activity for which credit for productive purposes is demanded are (*a*) agriculture, (*b*) industry, (*c*) construction, and (*d*) trade, both domestic and foreign. Further, in each of these categories, the allocation of credit between different users is of crucial importance from the viewpoint of economic growth and social justice. Thus, in agriculture allocation of credit between large landowners and small farmers has been a matter of serious debate. Likewise, the allocation of credit between the large-scale industries and small-scale industries has been a major concern in India's credit policy. Credit policy in India in recent years has emphasised certain priority sectors such as agriculture, small-scale industries, export and weaker sections of society such as small and marginal farmers, young entrepreneurs for whom greater amount of credit is to be made available.

Origin and Evolution of Commercial Banking

A commercial bank is a business organisation which deals in money; it borrows and lends money. In this borrowing and lending of money, it makes profit. The distinction between a money lender and a commercial bank may be noted. Whereas money lender only lends money to others and that too from his own sources, a commercial bank does both the lending and borrowing businesses. A commercial bank raises its resources through borrowing from the public in the form of deposits and lends them to the businessmen. Its lending rate of interest is greater than that it pays to its depositors. It is because of this difference in lending and borrowing rates of interest that it is able to make profits.

Now, a curious student will ask the question as to how the institution of banking originated and evolved. The banking owes its origin to the activities of goldsmiths in England. In the Seventeenth Century, goldsmiths in England possessed strongest safe vaults where valuable goods such as gold, silver, diamonds could be kept safely. Therefore, the rich people in England at that time used to keep their valuable things such as gold and silver with the goldsmiths and obtained receipts from them for their deposits of gold and silver. At a later stage it was found that these deposits with goldsmiths could serve as money, that is, a medium of exchange. The person who had deposits of gold and silver with a goldsmith could pay off his debt simply by endorsing the deposit receipt in favour of the person to whom he has to pay back the loan. In this way gold and silver got automatically transferred to another person even though they remained in the safe custody of the goldsmiths. It was soon discovered that there was no need for endorsing the whole deposit receipt in favour of the other person. With deposits of gold and silver a person could issue a letter to his goldsmith instructing him to transfer a certain amount of gold or silver to another person. Obviously from this practice emerged the present-day system of payment through cheques.

Another important development took place when goldsmiths realised that a good amount of gold deposited with them remained idle for long as only the ownership of them changed through transfer. From this they concluded that they could issue more deposit receipts than the actual deposits of gold and silver with them to meet the financial needs of some persons and started charging some interest on them. In this practice one can see the beginning of the creation of deposits or credit by the modern banks which will be described in detail later in this chapter.

BALANCE SHEET OF A BANK: LIABILITIES AND ASSETS STRUCTURE

Balance sheet of a bank is of great importance for understanding the sources of funds it possesses and the uses to which these funds are put. As is well known, a balance sheet of an institution indicates its liabilities and assets. The liabilities of a bank show the sources of its funds and assets show its uses by it. The balance sheet of Bank of Baroda as on 31st March 1997 is given below :

(₹ *in crores*)

Liabilities		*Assets*	
Capital	254.3	Cash and Balances with RBI	3,048.2
Reserves and Surplus	1,733.4	Balances with other banks and money at call and short notice	4,683.4
Deposits	32,156.7	Investment in Govt. and other securities	10,927.2
Borrowings	339.9	Advances	16,531.6
Other Liabilities and Provisions	3,155.4	Fixed Assets	570.1
		Other Assets	1,872.2
Total	37,639.7	Total	37,639.7

Liabilities

It will be observed from the balance sheet of a bank given above that deposits constitute a very large proportion of the total funds available with a bank. It should be borne in mind that these deposits are bank's liabilities as they are depositors' claim against the bank. Deposits are mainly of two types: (1) demand deposits, (2) time deposits. Demand deposits are payable on demand and therefore can be withdrawn by the public through cheques. On the other hand, the time deposits are repayable by the bank only after a certain fixed period of time. In addition to these, in India there is another type of deposits called Savings Bank Deposits. Though money in such deposits can be withdrawn through cheques, there are limits to the amount withdrawable in a week or a month.

Banks also borrow from the Central Bank of the country and these borrowings also constitute its liabilities and source of funds. In the balance sheet, these borrowings from the Reserve Bank of India (*i.e.,* Central Bank of India) are included in other items of the liabilities. When supply of money is very tight, the borrowings from Central Bank is of immense help to the banks.

Assets Structure : Liquidity Vs. Profitability

The asset side of the balance sheet of a bank shows for what purposes it has used the funds obtained from the depositors. As pointed out above, a viable bank has to operate so as to make reasonable profits. On the other hand, in order to meet the demands for withdrawals by the public and thus to retain faith and creditibility, it has to keep some ready cash with it, that is, it has to ensure some liquidity. Profitability and liquidity are the two major considerations that weigh with the commercial banks in deciding about the composition of its assets. If all of its deposits are kept by the bank in the form of cash, it will have perfect liquidity in this case but will make no profits at all. But if the bank advances all its deposits as long-term loans to the industries it will lose liquidity and will be unable to honour the demands of withdrawals by the depositors. Therefore, a bank has to keep such an asset structure (that is, a combination of different types of assets) that strikes a balance between liquidity and profitability.

A glance at the balance sheet of a commercial bank given above shows that *cash in hand* and with other banks, which is a liquid asset, constitutes about 8 per cent of the total assets of a bank. There is another quite a good liquid asset, namely, *money at call and short notice,* which is about 12 per cent of the total assets. Another important liquid asset is the *investment in government and other securities.* Investment in government securities and other securities by the bank are also liquid as they can be sold in a short time and cash realised therefrom. It may be noted that in India the banks are by law required to invest a given percentage of their deposits in government securities. But legal requirements apart, the investment in government securities by the banks ensures their liquidity position such as these can be readily converted into cash. It will be seen from the balance sheet of the bank that investment in Government and other securities by the bank constitutes about 29 per cent of its assets.

Loans and advances by the banks to industries and traders are the most profitable item of asset. It is against these profitable assets that liquid assets, mentioned above, have to be balanced. It will be noticed that loans and advances account for about 44 per cent in the asset structure of the banks.

It is worthwhile to note that asset structure of different banks will vary depending upon the composition of their deposits. A bank that has relatively more demand deposits will have to keep a greater proportion of its assets in liquid form. On the other hand, if a bank possesses more time deposits, it will need to hold a relatively smaller proportion of its assets in liquid form.

FUNCTIONS OF COMMERCIAL BANKS

The main functions of the commercial banks can be summed up in one sentence : *the banks borrow to lend.* To receive deposits and to advance loans are thus the two main functions of all commercial banks. They borrow in the form of deposits and lend in various types of advances. Besides, there are other miscellaneous functions of commercial banks which have developed according to the needs of the society.

(a) Accepting Deposits

The banks borrow in the form of deposits. This function is important because banks mainly depend on the funds deposited with them by the public. The deposits received by the banks may be of the following types.

(*i*) **Demand Deposits or Current Account Deposits.** If a depositor deposits money in the bank in the current account (*i.e.,* demand deposits), he can withdraw it in part or in full at any time he likes without notice. These accounts are generally kept by businessmen whose requirements of making business payments are quite uncertain. Usually no interest is paid on them, because the bank cannot utilise these short-term deposits for lending purposes and must keep almost cent per cent reserve against them. But in return for these current account deposits, the banks offer some facilities or concessions to the account holders. The most important is the cheque facility made available to them, that is, the account holders make payment to the parties through cheques on these accounts. Further, on behalf of the holders of current account deposits, banks collect cheques, drafts, dividend warrants, postal orders, etc.

(*ii*) **Fixed Deposits or Time Deposits.** These deposits are made for a fixed period of time, which varies from fifteen days to a few years. These deposits cannot, therefore, be withdrawn before the expiry of that period. However, a loan can be taken from the bank against the security of these deposits within that period. A higher rate of interest is paid on the fixed deposits. As the fixed deposits carry a good rate of interest, they are a good source of investment by the people who are in a position to save. In India, the increase in the rates of interest on fixed deposits of various durations has attracted a good deal of savings in the banks. Since June, 1998, the interest on these deposits for 6 months and above but less than 1 year is 8 per cent, on deposits for one year and above is not regulated by RBI but varies from 9 per cent to 12 per cent depending on the period.

(*iii*) **Savings Bank Deposits.** In this case the depositor can generally withdraw money usually once a week. Sometimes there are also restrictions as to the total amount that can be withdrawn at one time and the total amount that can be placed in one deposit. These deposits are generally made by the people of small means, usually people with fixed salaries, for holding their short-term savings. Like the current account deposits, the saving bank deposits are payable on demand and also they can be drawn upon through cheques. But in order to discourage people to use the savings bank deposits very frequently, there are some restrictions on the number of times of withdrawals (through cheque or otherwise) that can be made from these accounts. The saving deposits carry lower rate of interest than the fixed deposits. Since March 1, 1996, the interest on savings bank deposits in India is 4.5 per cent per annum.

(*b*) Advancing Loans

Another function of the bank is to give loans to others. If the bank does not lend the deposited money to others, how can it pay the interest on the deposits to depositors? Banks give loans to businessmen and firms usually for short periods only. This is so because the bank must keep itself ready to meet the demands of the people who have deposited money for short period only. In advancing loans, the bank has to shoulder a heavy responsibility. The bank makes profit by advancing loans. But the bank deals in other people's money and it has to keep some ready cash to meet the depositors' demands. Hence a great care has to be exercised in the matter of lending and keeping resources. The bank must strike a fine balance between liquidity and profitability. If it keeps its assets in too liquid a form, it loses profit and if it tries to make too much profit, it may not be able to meet the depositor's demand. It must aim at both liquidity and profitability. Banks advance loans in the following ways.

1. By allowing an overdraft. Those people who keep current account with the banks are sometimes given the right to overdraw their accounts. In other words, people make arrangements with the banks that if a cheque has been drawn by them which is not covered by the deposit, then the bank should grant the overdraft and honour the cheque. Thus under overdraft arrangements, people can get more than they have deposited but they have to pay interest on the extra amount which has to be paid back within a short period. Overdraft facilities are generally granted to businessmen who can pay off the money after the sale of the goods.

2. Cash-Credit Loan. Under the cash-credit system, borrower is sanctioned a credit limit up to which he can borrow from the bank. But before granting a credit limit the bank satisfies itself about the credit-worthiness of the borrower. However, the actual utilisation of the credit limit by the borrower depends on his withdrawing power. Withdrawing power of a borrower is determined by his current assets which consists of stocks of goods, that is, stocks of raw materials, semi-finished goods and payments receivable from others. The borrower has to submit periodically a list of his assets showing his borrowing power. The interest payable by the borrower is calculated on the amount of the credit limit actually drawn.

3. Demand Loans. Demand loans granted by a bank are those loans which can *be recalled on demand by the bank any time.* The entire sum of demand loan granted to a borrower is paid in lump sum by crediting it to his account. Therefore, the interest is payable on the entire sum of demand loan granted. Usually demand loans are granted to stock-brokers whose need for credit fluctuates from day to day.

4. Short-Term Loan. Short-term loans are given as personal loans against security. Car loans, computer loans, housing loans are some examples of short-term loans. Short-term loans are also given to finance needs for working capital of businessmen. In case of short-term loans also the whole amount of loan granted is paid in lump sum by crediting it to the loan account of the borrower. The interest is payable on the entire sum of loan granted.

(c) Discounting Bills of Exchange or Hundies

A very important function of a modern bank is to discount bills or hundies of businessmen. It is like this: a businessman buys goods and is granted credit, say, for a month. The seller of the goods draws a bill of exchange which the purchaser is asked to sign. The bill orders the purchaser to pay a certain sum after the expiry of one month. If the seller goes on selling goods on this basis, he will soon find that all his stock is gone and he has got only these hundies in his cash box. Unless these hundies are changed into cash, his business will come to a standstill. He, therefore, does not keep these hundies with him till they mature for payment. But he takes them to the bank and gets the present worth of the hundies, leaving the bank to realise them when the date of payment comes. This is called discounting a bill. It is obvious that the bank has advanced money to the businessman for the period of the currency of the bill.

Bill discounting is considered a very suitable investment for a bank. The bills are certain to be paid on maturity. They can be rediscounted with the central bank, if necessary. They set up a regular flow of incomings and outgoings of cash. Being negotiable instruments, the bills do not create any difficulty at the time of payment and do not involve the bank in any litigation. It represents a short-term investment, which suits the bank very well because most of its deposits are also of short term. For all these reasons this form of advance represents the most suitable investment from the bank's point of view. That is why it is sometimes remarked that a good banker knows the difference between a bill and a mortgage.

(*d*) Transfer of Money

Banks transfer money from one place to another for their customers. Banks remit the funds of the people by means of a bank draft or a cheque. This is a cheap as well as safe method of transferring money from one place to another.

(*e*) Miscellaneous Functions

A bank now-a-days serves its customers in various other ways. It has lockers or 'safe deposit vaults'. They are meant to keep the valuables of customers in safe custody. Further, a bank collects interest on behalf of its customers as well as pays dividends on behalf of joint-stock companies. It purchases and sells stocks and shares of companies for its clients. It pays insurance premium on behalf of their customers from their deposits. It executes the wills of deceased customers and acts for them as a trustee.

From the above discussion it follows that these days the functions of banks are many and varied. Banks are not merely the *traders of money* but they are also the *manufacturers of money.* In other words, they not only deal in money, *i.e.,* borrow and lend money but also manufacture or make money. They create money through credit creation. Bank deposits these days are as much money as any other form of money.

ROLE OF COMMERCIAL BANKS IN ECONOMIC DEVELOPMENT

As is well known, the rate of economic development depends to a large measure on the rate of capital formation. The rate of capital formation in turn depends on the rate of savings and investment and the proper allocation of investible funds among different sectors and users. The banking system helps economic growth in all these ways, that is, by (*a*) promoting savings, *(b)* mobilizing savings, and (*c*) allocating savings among alternative uses and users. Let us explain how commercial banking, which is an important part of the financial system of the country, performs these functions.

(*a*) Promotion of Savings

People save for various reasons. Thus people save to provide for future needs such as periods of unemployment, old age, sickness, to provide for education and marriage of their children, to own property such as real estate, houses etc. in future, and to purchase durable consumer goods. But they require assets in the form of which they should keep their savings in safe custody and earn a rate of return as well. Commercial banks promote savings by providing a wide range of deposits with varying combinations of liquidity and rate of interest to suit the needs and preferences of different savers. It has been found that with the growth of commercial banking in unbanked and under-banked regions, the household savings go up. As a store of value, bank deposits enjoy certain advantages over tangible assets (physical capital, inventories of commodities) and other financial assets. The bank deposits are convenient to hold as store of value and are more safe and more liquid, *i.e.,* they can be converted into cash easily. They are also greatly divisible and less risky. With all these advantages, they earn varying rates of interest depending upon the type of deposits into which the savers put their savings. These advantages of bank deposits induce households to save more and encourage the habit of thrift.

Despite a low level of per capita income compared to most of the large economies Indians are known to be big savers. Even in 2011-12, when India achieved a very low GDP growth rate of 6.2 per cent, saving rate was 30.8 per cent of GDP which is considered to be quite high compared to international standards. But a good proportion of these savings go into non-financial assets such as gold, silver or real estate. However, the proportion of financial saving to GDP has shown a declining trend. What is needed is to reverse this trend. This can be achieved only if banks provide a reasonable positive real rate of interest on fixed deposits and RBI and SEBI should ensure *safe real returns* on other financial assets such as bonds, shares and mutual funds.

It is worth noting that the commercial banks would perform well this function of promoting savings in the framework of price stability. If the prices of goods are rising, that is, inflation grips the economy, then the savers would prefer to use their savings to buy gold and silver, other commodities, and real estate whose prices are also rising. This is because the real rate of interest on bank deposits goes down to the extent of rise in prices. This underlines the importance of keeping prices stable, if savings by households are to be promoted.

(*b*) Mobilisation of Savings

Not only do the banks encourage savings but they also mobilise savings done by several households and make them available for the purposes of production and investment to the entrepreneurs in various sectors of the economy. This function of mobilizing savings is of crucial importance because in the modern monetary economy, the act of saving has been separated from the act of real investment. Savings are done by millions of households and firms, whose individual savings may be very small, savings of some may be of short-term and of others of long-term nature. Banks and other financial intermediaries collect or mobilise these savings before these can be made available to the producers or investors. Without the banks (and other financial intermediaries), these savings would have remained scattered and also idle, that is, would not have been utilised for productive and investment purposes. As pointed out above, banks mobilise savings of households and firms through offering variety of deposits to suit the needs and preference of different households possessing surplus funds.

It follows from above that the *commercial banks, like other financial institutions, provide a link between those who have savings (i.e. surplus funds) and those who are in need of such funds to use them for production and investment purposes.* If commercial banks and other financial intermediaries were not there, those with surplus funds would have to search for appropriate borrowers and strike individual bargains with them and bear risks of lending them. The existence of commercial banks makes the tasks of lenders easy and with the control over commercial banks by the Government or central bank of the country, the risks of depositors have almost been eliminated. This enables the banks to mobilise more resources for production and investment purposes.

The acceleration of economic growth requires an increasing proportion of savings getting channelized into financial assets such as bank deposits, bonds, shares, mutual funds to facilitate their deployment in their most productive uses. It is a matter of concern that at present in India financial savings as a percentage of GDP have shown a declining trend as people prefer to *investment in physical assets like gold, silver or real estate*. This is because real rate of interest (interest rate minus inflation rate) on bank deposits has been negative in the past some years due to the high rate of inflation and failure of banks offer high interest on bank deposits. Besides, due to a lot of uncertainty and macroeconomic instability, investors often doubt the *likely real returns on financial assets* such as shares and debentures in the corporate companies and mutual funds. It is imperative that RBI and SEBI of India should adopt such policies and measures to regulate the financial institutions in such a way that real positive returns are assured to the people on investment in financial assets.

It is evident from above that banks act as a financial intermediary between lender and borrower. The financial assets can be classified into two categories: (1) primary securities, (2) secondary securities. Equity shares, debentures, and company deposits of corporate firms represent primary securities. When households buy these securities they directly invest or lend money to the investor and bear risk of such investment. On the other hand, bank deposits represent secondary securities and when households go in for them, they provide their savings to banks who allocate them among competing borrowers—traders, producers and investors. In this way it is the banks who bear risks of lending, whereas the depositors' money and interest are safe and certain. Those savers who are risk averters find the secondary securities (bank deposits) more acceptable than the primary securities.

(*c*) Allocation of Funds

Allocation of funds or economic surplus among different sectors, users and producers so as to make maximum social return and thus to ensure optimum utilisation of savings is another important function performed by the banks. Whereas the corporate firms can raise resources through sale of equity shares and debentures, the non-corporate firms and borrowers depend greatly on banks for financing the needs of both working capital and fixed capital. Through the lending rates of interest determined by market mechanism or fixed by the central bank of the country credit advanced by the banks get rationed among various potential borrowers and sectors. Further, before lending banks take into account the credit-worthiness or capacity to pay back the loans. Thus the banks are in a better position to judge the returns or productivity from the uses for which the funds are lent out. This helps in maximisation of returns from scarce financial resources.

However, it may be mentioned that commercial banks do not always work and allocate resources in the way that maximises production or social welfare. For instance, before nationalisation in 1969 the commercial banks in India in their allocation of funds neglected socially highly desirable sectors such as agriculture, small-scale industries and the weaker sections of the society such as small and marginal farmers, the young entrepreneurs seeking self-employment. On the contrary, they preferred to invest funds collected from the public in the business concerns of the big business houses which controlled these banks. Therefore, it was thought necessary to nationalise them so that they should allocate resources in socially desirable directions.

(*d*) Promotion of Trade, Production and Investment

By encouraging inducement to save and also mobilising savings from the public, banks help to increase the aggregate rate of investment in the economy. It may also be noted that banks not only mobilise the saved funds from the public, but also themselves create deposits or credit which serve as money. The new deposits are created by the banks when they lend money to the investors or other users. These deposits are by the banks in excess of the cash reserves they obtain through deposits by the public. These days, the bank deposits, especially demand deposits, are as much good money as the currency issued by the Government or Reserve Bank of India. This creation of credit, if it is used for productive purposes, greatly enhances production and investment and thus promotes economic growth.

CREDIT CREATION BY BANKS

Creation of credit is one of the most outstanding functions of a modern bank. A bank has sometimes been called a factory for the manufacture of credit. How credit is created? It is an open secret that the banks do not keep cent per cent reserves against deposits in order to meet the demands of depositors. The bank is not a cloakroom where you can keep your currency notes or coins and claim those very notes or coins back when you desire. It is generally understood that money received by the bank is meant to be advanced to others. A depositor has to be content simply with the bank's promise or undertaking to pay him whenever he makes a demand. Thus the banks are able to do with a very small reserve, because all the depositors do not come to withdraw money simultaneously; some withdraw, while others deposit at the same time. The bank is thus enabled to create much more credit on the basis of a small cash reserve. The bank is able to lend money and charge interest without parting with cash, as the bank loan creates simply a deposit or it creates a credit for the borrower. This is what is meant by creation of credit.

In the previous chapter we have explained that chequable bank deposits are treated as money as by drawing a cheque on his bank a person transfers some amount of funds to another person or institution. In developed countries most money is in the form of bank deposits. However, its may be noted that deposits are created not only by the public depositing their currency funds with the banks. The banks themselves create deposits when they give loans to the businessmen. *The creation of bank deposits themselves by the banks while giving loans to businessmen is called credit creation* by banks. The banks create credit or bank deposits much more than the currency funds deposited by the public with them. Banks also create deposits or money when they buy securities of the government or the private corporate sector.

The creation of bank deposits in excess of the currency reserves with them has become possible because of the **fractional reserve system.** The fraction of banks' total deposits that are held in currency reserves is called *reserve ratio*. Suppose 10 per cent is currency reserve ratio against its deposits that a bank maintains. Then, if a person deposits currency notes of ₹ 1000 with the bank, then the bank will keep 10% of ₹ 1000, that is, ₹ 100 as reserves and give loans of the remaining amount of ₹ 900 to businessmen. When the bank gives loans to the businessman of ₹ 900, it generally credits this amount in chequable deposits of his customer businessman. Before it is withdrawn the chequable deposits of the bank rise to ₹ 1900. The extra ₹ 900 of the deposits which the bank itself creates will also be treated as money. Thus bank has created extra money of ₹ 900 as if out of thin air. But the process of creation of credit or bank deposits does not stop here. As will be explained later in detail, when ₹ 900 will be transferred by the bank's customer to another person by issuing a cheque to him, this may be deposited in another bank whose reserves will increase by ₹ 900. With 10 % as reserve ratio, the other bank will keep 10% of ₹ 900 (that is, ₹ 90) as reserves and the remaining ₹ 810 will be given as loan to his customer by crediting ₹ 800 to his chequable deposits. This process will go on and creation of bank deposits will go on increasing until they rise by $\frac{1}{r}$ where r is reserve ratio. $\frac{1}{r}$ represents deposit multiplier. If reserve ratio is 10 per cent, then the deposit multiplier will be equal to $\frac{1}{0.10} = 10$. Thus, with the original currency deposit of ₹ 1000 will cause total deposits to rise by 10 × 1000 = ₹ 10,000. If the cash reserve is 5 per cent then the deposit multiplier will be equal to $\frac{1}{0.05} = \frac{1}{\frac{5}{100}} = 20$. Thus, with 5% as cash reserve ratio banks will create with ₹ 1000 deposits total deposits equal to 20 × 1000 = ₹ 20,000. Thus, the fractional reserve system enables the banking system as a whole to create much more demand deposits than the amount of the original deposit of currency.

Similarly, the bank buys securities and pays the seller with its own cheque which again is no cash; it is just a promise to pay cash. The cheque is deposited in some bank and a deposit is created or credit is created for the seller of the securities. This is credit creation. The term 'credit creation' implies a situation, to use Benham's words, when "a bank may receive interest simply by permitting a customer to overdraw their accounts or by purchasing securities and paying for them with its own cheques, thus increasing the total bank deposits."

The bank also creates credit when it purchases securities. The bank can purchase securities without paying any cash. It issues its own cheque to pay the purchase price. The cheque is deposited in this bank or some other bank and the small cash reserve which the bank keeps is sufficient to meet an obligation arising from this transaction too. It is thus that on a small cash foundation, a vast superstructure of credit is built up.

Credit Creation by the Banking System as a Whole : Balance Sheet Approach

Let us now understand the process of credit creation when there are *several* banks in the country, as they are in the real world. In the case of several commercial banks in the country, one individual bank cannot create all the credit as described above. But what no single bank can do individually, the banking system as a whole can do, *i.e.,* create credit. We shall explain the process of credit creation or the expansion of money supply in the country by the banking system collectively with the help of *balance sheets* of the banks. We shall illustrate how deposit of ₹ 1,00,000 of currency in a commercial bank enables the banking system as a whole to expand deposits by another ₹ 4,00,000, that is, deposits of ₹ 1,00,000 in currency leads to the total deposits of ₹ 5,00,000 in the banking system.

Banks, as other business firms, show their financial condition on a balance sheet. A simple balance sheet has two columns, its left column represents all the *assets* of a bank and its right column represents all the *liabilities* of a bank. Assets are all the things or claims a bank owns, liabilities, on the other hand, are claims against those assets; some of the claims are of creditors and some of them are of owners of the banks themselves. Because assets show everything that a bank owns and because liabilities represent claims against those assets, the two sides of the balance sheet, that is, assets and liabilities must equal each other.

Let us suppose that an individual or a firm deposits ₹ 1,00,000 in cash with a bank *A*. Ignoring everything else in the balance sheet, let us know how the balance sheet of bank *A* will look like with this fresh deposit of ₹ 1,00,000 in currency with it. The cash of ₹ 1,00,000 which the bank *A* will receive will become its assets, and at the same time individual's deposits of ₹ 1,00,000 will be its liabilities, the assets and liabilities of bank A will therefore be equal to each other.

BANK A

Balance Sheet

Assets		*Liabilities*	
Cash	₹ 1,00,000	Deposits	₹ 1,00,000

Let us assume that cash reserve ratio is 20%. Now the bank does not require all the ₹ 1,00,000 in cash against the deposits of ₹ 1,00,000. The bank *A* requires only 20% of it, that is, ₹ 20,000 cash against its deposits of ₹ 1,00,000. The bank can lend or invest in securities the remaining amount of ₹ 80,000. Actually if the bank does not lend or invest it will suffer a loss, since it will pay the interest to the depositor with no profit from the cash it possesses. Therefore, the bank *A* will lend ₹ 80,000 to the business firms or individuals whom it finds creditworthy. Now, when a bank lends to a person or firm it does not give him cash immediately. The bank makes deposits in the name of the person whom he lends the money and gives him the right to draw cheques against it when required. It is a new deposit, one that did not exist before. The person or firm getting loans from the bank will, however, after some time completely withdraw the money through cheques from his deposits. When the loan of ₹ 80,000 has been sanctioned to a person, but before that person starts withdrawing his money, the balance sheet of bank *A* will look like as follows:

BANK A

Balance Sheet

(When the bank sanctions loan of ₹ 80,000 but before loan is cashed)

Assets		*Liabilities*	
Cash	₹ 1,00,000	Deposits	₹ 1,00,000
Loan	₹ 80,000	New Deposits (Created)	₹ 80,000
	₹ 1,80,000		₹ 1,80,000

In this balance sheet, loan of ₹ 80,000 becomes asset of the bank, while the new deposits created constitute the liability of the bank, since the person getting the loan has the right to draw upon these deposits.

Now, when the person wholly withdraws his deposits through cheques and the recipients of these cheques deposit them in some other bank, say bank *B*, then the bank *A* will have to surrender to bank *B* cash money equal to ₹ 80,000. After the whole newly created deposits of ₹ 80,000 have been thus withdrawn, the balance sheet of bank A will now look like as follows:

BANK A

Balance Sheet

Assets		*Liabilities*	
Cash	₹ 20,000	Original Deposits	₹ 1,00,000
Loan	₹ 80,000	New Deposits	0
Total	₹ 1,00,000	Total	₹ 1,00,000

As said above, cheques worth ₹ 80,000 against bank *A* are deposited in bank *B*, for the bank *B* these will constitute new cash money and will therefore become the assets of bank *B*. But ₹ 80,000 will also be the liability of the bank *B* in the form of deposits in the name of those persons who have deposited the cheques with it. Ignoring other assets and liabilities of bank *B* and taking into account only this above transaction, the balance sheet of bank *B* will be as follows:

BANK B

Balance Sheet

Assets		*Liabilities*	
Cash	₹ 80,000	Deposits	₹ 80,000

Now against the deposits of ₹ 80,000 bank *B* requires to keep its 20%, that is, ₹ 16,000 and it can lend or invest the remaining amount of ₹ 64,000. When bank *B* lends ₹ 64,000 to a firm, it will create deposits for that firm. Before the firm draws upon that deposits, the balance sheet of bank *B* will took like:

BANK B

Balance Sheet

Assets		*Liabilities*	
Cash	₹ 80,000	Deposits	₹ 80,000
Loan	₹ 64,000	New Deposits Created	₹ 64,000
Total	₹ 1,44,000	Total	₹ 1,44,000

Now, when the firm which has got loan from bank *B* completely withdraws ₹ 64,000 through cheques, the balance sheet of bank *B* will be as follows. As a result of the firm spending the loan money of ₹ 64,000, the bank *B* will transfer cash of ₹ 64,000 to another bank, say *C*, in which the cheques drawn by the firm are deposited. As a result of this, the cash with bank *B* will fall to ₹ 16,000 (₹ 80,000 – ₹ 64,000 = ₹ 16,000).

BANK B
Balance Sheet

Assets		*Liabilities*	
Cash	₹ 16,000	Deposits	₹ 80,000
Loan	₹ 64,000	New Deposits	0
Total	₹ 80,000	Total	₹ 80,000

Now when the bank C will get ₹ 64,000, it will also require to keep 20% of it *(i.e.,* ₹ 12,800) and the remaining amount of ₹ 51,200 will be lent out or invested by it.

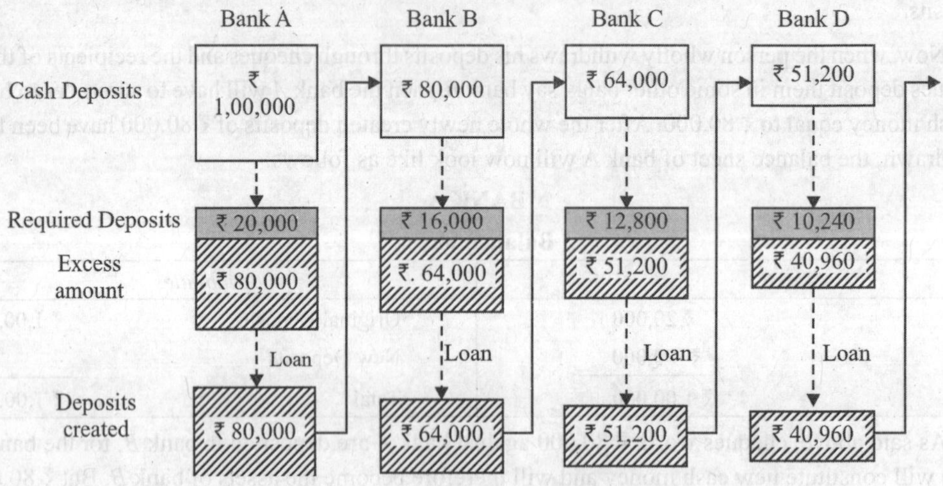

Fig. 16.1. *Credit Creation by Banks*

From the foregoing analysis it is clear that the currency deposits of ₹ 1,00,000 led to the creation of deposits of ₹ 80,000 by bank *A*, ₹ 64,000 by bank *B*, ₹ 51,200 by bank *C*. But the process of expansion of deposits will not stop here, it will go on as the money lent out by one bank is spent through cheques and these cheques are deposited in other banks, till the total deposits of ₹ 5,00,000 in all the banks (including original deposits of ₹ 1,00,000) are created. But it should be remembered that at each stage the new deposits created by a bank goes on declining. This is because at each stage a bank is required to keep 20% of the money it receives as cash reserves and therefore lends and creates deposits equal only to the remaining amount. Thus bank *A* created deposits of ₹ 80,000, bank *B* created deposits of ₹ 64,000, bank *C* created deposits of ₹ 51,200 and so on.

We are now in a position to state how much deposits have been created by the banking system out of the currency deposits of ₹ 1,00,000.

Total Deposits = ₹ 1,00,000 + 80,000 + 64,000 + 51,200 + ... = ₹ 5,00,000

Out of the total deposits of ₹ 5,00,000, the deposits of ₹ 1,00,000 in cash were made in the banking system, the remaining deposits have been created by the banking system itself, as if out of thin air.

Deposits created by the banking system = ₹ 5,00,000 – 1,00,000

= ₹ 4,00,000

It should be further noted that the *total expansion of deposits by the banking system depends upon the cash reserve ratio* (CRR). The smaller the cash reserve ratio, the larger the expansion of deposits or credit. Thus, in the above case, we noted that, given the cash reserve ratio of 20%, the total deposits expansion from the cash deposits of ₹ 1,00,000 was equal to ₹ 5,00,000. Thus the total deposits expanded to was five times the original cash deposits. Therefore the deposits of cash in the banking system leads to multiple expansion in the total deposits. This is known as *deposits* or *credit multiplier.* In our above case, the deposits or credit multiplier is 5. It should be remembered that the *magnitude of deposits multiplier depends on the cash reserve ratio.*

$$\text{Deposit multiplier } d_m = \frac{\Delta D}{\Delta R} = \frac{1}{r}$$

where r stands for cash reserve ratio.

Thus deposit multiplier is the reciprocal of cash reserve ratio (CRR) which we have denoted by r in the measure of deposit multiplier.

Thus, when the cash reserve ratio is 20%, that is, 0.20 or 1/5, the deposit multiplier.

$$= \frac{1}{\frac{1}{5}} = 5$$

Now, if the cash reserve ratio is raised by Reserve Bank to 25 per cent, that is, 0.25, the deposit multiplier,

$$d_m = \frac{1}{0.25} = \frac{1}{1/4} = 4$$

Thus, *the greater the cash reserve ratio, the lower will be the value of deposit multiplier. In other words, increase in the cash reserve ratio (CRR or r) will lead to the contraction of credit created by the banks, and vice versa*

Similarly, if the cash reserve ratio is 10%, *i.e.*, 1/10, then the deposits multiplier = 1/1/10 = 10. In this case initial deposits of some cash amount in the banking system will lead to ten times expansion in the total deposits. Figure 16.1 makes clear the process of deposits expansion by the banking system.

Limitations on the Credit Creating Power of the Banks

From the foregoing account of credit or deposit creation by the banks, it would seem that the banks reap where they have not sown. They advance loans or buy securities without actually paying cash. But they earn interest on the loans they give or earn dividends on the securities they purchase all the same. This is very tempting. They make profits without investing cash. They would, of course, like to make as much profit like this as they can. But they cannot go on expanding credit indefinitely. In their own interest, they have to apply the brake, and they do actually apply it, for it is well known that the profits made by the banks are not very high. The overriding limitation arises from the obligation of the banks to meet the demands of their depositors.

Benham has mentioned three limitations on the powers of the banks to create credit:

(*i*) The amount of cash in the country;

(*ii*) The amount of cash which the public wishes to hold; and

(*iii*) The minimum percentage of cash to deposits, called cash revenue ratio which the banks have to maintain.

(*iv*) The amount of money which the public wants to hold as deposits in the banks.

As for (*i*), it may be said that credit can be created on the basis of cash. *The larger the cash (i.e., legal tender money), the larger the amount of credit that can be created.* But the amount of cash that a bank may have is subject to the control of the central bank. The central bank has the monopoly of issue of cash. It may increase it or decrease it, and credit will expand or contract accordingly. The power of the central bank to control currency helps it to control the extent of credit that the banks have the power to create.

The second limitation arises from *the habit of the people regarding the use of cash i.e. currency.* If people are in the habit of using cash and not cheques, as in India, then as soon as credit is granted by the bank to a borrower, he will draw the cheque and get cash. When the bank's cash reserves are thus reduced, its power to create credit is correspondingly reduced. On the other hand, if people use cash only for very small and odd transactions, then the cash reserve of the banks is not much drawn upon and their power of creating credit remains unimpaired. This is the case in advanced countries like the USA, England and other European countries. There the banks hardly keep 10 per cent cash reserve.

The third limitation is the most important. It arises from the *cash reserve ratio cash, which the banks must maintain* to ensure the safety of the bank and to retain the degree of liquidity that is considered desirable. It is clear that when a bank creates a credit or grants a loan, it undertakes a liability. There is an increase in its liabilities and there is correspondingly a fall in cash reserve ratio. The bank will not let the cash reserve ratio fall below a certain minimum. When that minimum is reached, the power of the bank to create credit comes to an end. To grant any further credit will be risky unless the bank's experience is reassuring enough to permit the adoption of a lower percentage. Then that would be the limit.

The other important limitation on the credit creating power of banks is *the amount of money which the public choose to hold as deposits in banks.* The more money which the public deposits with the banks, the more reserves banks would have and therefore more credit they will be able to create and *vice versa*. It may be noted that public can use their saved money in more than one way. The public can buy shares or debentures of the companies, it can invest in mutual funds of both public and privates sectors. But the credit creation by the banks depends on the money the public deposits with them. It is important to note than rate of interest paid by the banks on deposits determines to a good extent the amount of money deposits with them by the public. Other things being equal, the higher the rate of interest, the greater the amount of money the public will deposit money with the banks.

To these may be added the fourth limitation that *the bank cannot create credit without acquiring some asset.* An asset is a form of wealth. Thus the bank only turns immobile wealth into mobile wealth. Hence, as Crowther observes, "the bank does not create money out of thin air, it transmutes other forms of wealth into money." However, banking system today has become quite advanced. These days banks give credit on the basis of personal goodwill rather than on the basis of any form of wealth.

QUESTIONS FOR REVIEW

1. Explain credit creation. Describe the factors which determine the volume of credit which can be created.
2. Explain the process of credit creation through the 'Balance Sheet Approach'. What factors limit credit creation ?
3. What are the functions of a commercial bank ?
4. Explain the role of commercial bank in the economic development of India.
5. Explain the process of creation of credit by commercial banks. What are the limitations on the credit creating power of banks ?
6. Explain how commercial banks create credit. Are there any limit to credit creation by them? If cash deposits ratio changes from 0.1 to 0.2, will there be any change in the credit creating power of banks ?
7. Explain the functions of commercial banks. How is a commercial bank different from the Central Bank ?
   (*a*) Explain why commercial banks should be concerned about liquidity.
   (*b*) Is there a conflict between the profit motive of a bank and the need for liquidity ?
   (*c*) Which assets are a bank's principal sources of profitability ?

CHAPTER 17

Central Banking

In the monetary system of all countries, the central bank occupies an important place. The central bank is an apex institution of the monetary system which seeks to regulate the functioning of the commercial banks of a country. The central bank of India is called the Reserve Bank of India which was set up in 1935. As explained in the previous chapter, the commercial banks keep only a fraction of their deposits in cash and the rest they lend out to the traders and investors. Therefore, the commercial banking is often known as *fractional reserve system.* In view of the fact that commercial banks keep only a fraction of their deposits in cash, they will run into difficulties if at a time there is rush of depositors to withdraw their money. This indicates the need for an institution which should come to the rescue of the commercial banks and provide them the money required to meet the excessive demand of the depositors. The central bank fulfils this need. However, in the modern times, the central bank not only provides monetary aid to the commercial banks in time of crisis but also performs many other functions. Indeed, the control over cost and availability of credit in the economy and regulation of the growth of money supply are special responsibilities of the central bank.

The Principles of Central Banking

The central bank of a country enjoys a special status in the banking structure of the country. The principles on which a central bank is run differ from the ordinary banking principles. An ordinary bank is run for profits. A central bank, on the other hand, is primarily meant to promote the financial and economic stability of the country. "The guiding principle of a central bank", says DeKock, "is that it should act only in the public interest and for welfare of the country and without regard to profit as primary consideration". Earning of profit for a central bank is thus a secondary consideration.

The central bank is thus not a profit hunting institution. It does not act as rival of other banks. In fact, it is a monetary authority of the country and has to function in a manner so as to promote economic stability and development. The functions of the central bank, especially the Reserve Bank of India, have increased enormously in recent years. Not only does the Reserve Bank of India regulate credit and money supply in the country, but it also promotes economic development and price stability. Guiding principles of the Reserve Bank are to operate its most instruments in a way that serves the objectives of economic policy laid down by the Government and Planning Commission.

FUNCTIONS OF CENTRAL BANK

The following are the main functions of a central bank :

1. It acts as a note issuing agency.
2. It acts as the banker to the state.
3. It acts as the bankers' bank.
4. It controls credit.
5. It acts as the lender of the last resort.
6. It manages exchange rate.

Note Issuing Agency

The central bank of the country has the monopoly of issuing notes or paper currency to the public. Therefore, the central bank of the country exercises control over the supply of currency in the country. In India with the exception of one rupee notes which are issued by the Ministry of Finance of the Government of India, the entire note issue is done by the Reserve Bank of India. In the past the central bank of various countries used to keep as reserves some gold and foreign exchange securities against the notes issued. The percentage of the reserves to be kept against the total amount of notes issued was fixed by law and is subject to change by the Government. Theoretically, there is no need of the backing of gold reserves against the notes issued. It may be pointed out that paper notes these days cannot be converted into gold or some other precious metals; they are inconvertible. This is called ***proportional reserve system***. Before 1956 in India also, there was proportional reserve system of issuing currency or notes. According to this, the Reserve Bank was required to keep as reserves 40 per cent of the total notes issued in the form of gold and foreign exchange securities.

Since 1956 proportional reserve system in India system has been given up and instead ***minimum reserve system*** has been adopted according to which the Reserve Bank is required to keep only a *minimum amount of reserves* in the form of gold and foreign exchange securities and given this minimum reserve it can issue notes as much as it thinks desirable in view of the needs and conditions of the economy. There is even no need for backing of gold for the currency issued by the Government or the central bank. From the economic point of view what matters is the production of real goods and services and not the amount of gold supporting a currency. The real value of a currency depends on how much it can buy goods and services and not how much gold or silver is kept as reserve against it.

Thus, ultimately the credibility of the currency of a country depends not upon whether it is convertible into gold or silver but upon to what extent it is possible to maintain the stability of its value by suitable monetary control.

Banker to the Government

Another important function of the central bank is to act as the banker to the Government. All the balances of the Government are kept with the central bank. On these balances the central bank pays no interest. The central bank receives and makes all payments on behalf of the Government. Further, the central bank has to manage the public debt and also to arrange for the issue of new loans on behalf of the Government. The central bank also provides short-term loans to the Government. This is usually done through the central bank discounting the Government treasury bills either directly or when presented by other banks. Thus the central bank performs a number of services to the Government. In fact, the central bank is the fiscal agent of the Government and advises the latter in matters relating to currency and exchange as well as finance.

Bakers' Bank

Broadly speaking, the central bank acts as a bankers' bank in three capacities: (*i*) as the custodian of the cash reserves of the commercial banks; (*ii*) as the lender of the last resort; and (*iii*) as bank of central clearance, settlement and transfers. All other banks in the country are bound by law to keep a fixed portion of their total deposits as reserves with the central bank. These reserves help the central bank to control the issue of credit by commercial banks. They in return can depend upon the central bank for support at the time of emergency. This help may be in the form of a loan on the strength of approved securities or through rediscounting of bills of exchange. Thus the central bank is the lender of the last resort for other banks in difficult times because on such occasions there is no hope of getting help from any competing institution.

In India, scheduled banks have to keep deposits with the Reserve Bank not less than 5% of their current demand deposits and 2% of their fixed deposits as reserves. In return they enjoy the privilege of rediscounting their bills with the Reserve Bank as well as securing loans against approved securities when in need.

Clearing function is also performed by the central bank for the banks. Since banks keep cash reserves with the central bank, settlement between them may be easily effected by means of debits and credits in the books of the central bank. If clearings go heavily against some bank, its cash reserves with the central bank will fall below the prescribed limit and therefore the bank concerned will have to make up the deficiency.

Control of Credit

The chief objective of the central bank is to maintain price and economic stability. Price instability—both inflation and deflation—has harmful effects. Moreover, fluctuations in overall economic activity, that is, trade cycles, entail a lot of human sufferings. Main reason for the fluctuations in prices as well as in overall economic activity is the changes in aggregate demand. Aggregate demand, especially the investment demand, depends upon the supply of money. And credit these days is the important constituent of the money supply. Thus the supply of credit greatly affects the prices, national income and employment through changes in investment demand.

Now it is the responsibility of the central bank of a country to guide the money market, *i.e.,* the commercial banks, regarding supply of credit so as to maintain stability in prices as well as in overall economic activity. To overcome inflation it has to restrict the supply of credit and to prevent or get rid of depression and deflation it has to expand the credit. There are various methods by which the central bank can control the supply of credit in the economy. These methods are: *(a)* varying the bank rate; (*b*) engaging in open market operations; (*c*) changing the reserve ratio, and *(d)* exercising selective credit controls. We shall explain these methods of credit in detail in later sections of this chapter.

It is through controlling the supply of credit and cost of credit *(i.e.,* rate of interest on it) that the central bank of a country tries to bring about stability in prices as well as in overall level of economic activity. The central bank is the monetary authority of the country and monetary policy is one of the important measures which are taken to avoid and cure both depression and inflation. To remedy inflation the central bank tries to restrict the supply of credit by raising the bank rate and using other weapons of credit control. To overcome depression it tries to expand credit by lowering the bank rate and cash reserve ratio and also by buying securities from the open market.

In India Reserve Bank which is the central bank of the country has been making important contribution to the achievement of the objective of price stability. To achieve price stability Reserve Bank has been setting forgets of expansion in money supply which are consistent with the growth of output. Control of inflation by checking excessive expansion in credit supply has been the major concern of monetary policy imposed by Reserve Bank of India.

Lender of the Last Resort

As mentioned above, the commercial banks operate on the basis of fractional reserve system. Therefore, even a well-managed commercial bank can run into difficulty if there is a great rush of demand for cash by the depositors, because with a fraction of its deposits in cash, it will not be able to meet a sudden and large demand for cash. The central bank must therefore come to their rescue at such times. Thus, central bank is the last source of supply of credit. It is the duty of the central bank to meet demand.for cash by a bank at the time of emergency when panic prevails among the public and people's confidence has been shaken and when other banks have refused to supply credit. The central bank boldly steps forward to supply cash and allay panic. The central bank must meet situation of high liquidity preference.

To Promote Economic Growth

A very important function of central bank these days in developing countries like India is to promote economic growth. It can help in both agricultural and industrial growth in the country. The central bank can promote agricultural and industrial growth by providing finance or credit to agriculture and industry. Central bank adopts such a monetary policy as is conducive to economic growth. In order to accelerate the rate of investment or capital formation, the central bank takes steps to make more credit available for investment at lower lending rates of interest. In the developing countries, the role of central bank as promoter of economic development is very important.

Thus, in India apart from regulatory function, Reserve Bank of India has been playing a promotional role. RBI has been making important contribution for building up appropriate financial institutions such as Industrial Finance Corporation of India, State Finance Corporations to promote saving and investment. By ensuring adequate supply of agricultural credit, term finance to industries, credit for exports, RBI has performed a useful promotional role in encouraging economic growth.

Managing Exchange Rate of the National Currency

Another important function of a central bank is to maintain the exchange rate of the national currency For example, the Reserve Bank of India has the responsibility of maintaining the exchange value of the rupee. When a country has adopted flexible exchange rate system under which value of a currency is determined by demand for and supply of a currency, the value of a currency, that is, its exchange rate with other currencies, is subject to large fluctuations which are harmful for the economy. Under these circumstances, it is the duty of the central bank to prevent large depreciation or appreciation of the national currency. Since 1991 when the rupee has been floated, the value of Indian rupee, that is, its exchange rate with US dollar and other foreign currencies, has been left to be determined by market forces, RBI has been taking several steps from time to time to stabilise the exchange rate of rupee, especially in terms of US dollar.

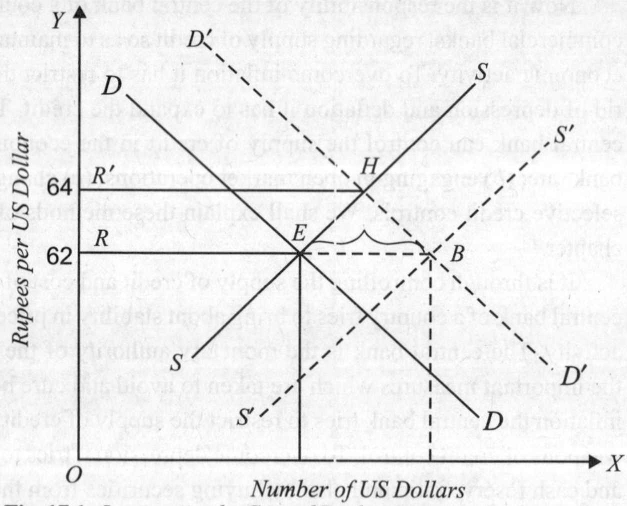

Fig. 17.1. *Intervention by Central Bank to Maintain Exchange Rate*

There are several ways by which RBI can manage or maintain the exchange rate of the rupee. First, if due to speculative activities of foreign exchange operators, the rupee starts depreciating rapidly, RBI can intervene in the market. It can use its reserves of dollars and supply dollars in the market from its own reserves. With the increase in supply of dollars, the rupee will be prevented from depreciation. It may however be noted that the success of this step depends on the amounts of dollar reserves with Reserve Bank of India. This is illustrated in Fig. 17.1 where we have depicted demand and supply curves of US dollars which intersect at point *E* and determine exchange value of rupee equal to ₹ 62 to a US dollar. Now suppose that demand for dollars by Indian traders and companies importing goods from abroad and market operators increases so that demand curve for dollar shifts to the right to *D′ D′* position. It will be seen that the intersection of this new demand curve for the US dollars *D′D′* intersects the supply curve *SS* of dollars at point *H* and determines the exchange rate of rupee for the US dollars equal to ₹ 64 per dollar. Thus with increase in demand for dollars rupee has depreciated (and the US dollar appreciated). Now, if RBI intervenes and from its foreign exchange reserves, it supplies extra dollars equal to *EB,* the supply curve of dollars in the foreign exchange market will shift to the right to the position *S′S′* which intersects the higher demand curve *D′D′* of dollars at point *B* so that again ₹ 62 to a US dollar becomes the equilibrium exchange rate of rupees for the US dollar. In this way by its intervention and supplying extra dollars from its foreign exchange reserves, RBI can succeed in maintaining the exchange rate of rupee at ₹ 62 to a US dollar. In actual practice in Aug.-Sept. 1998 and July–October 2013, when rupee was depreciating RBI intervened and succeeded in preventing the rapid depreciating rupee against US dollar.

Another method by which RBI can manage the exchange rate of rupee is adopting measures which will reduce the demand for dollars. Some importers, foreign investors, foreign exchange operators try to avail of cheap credit facilities of banks and borrow rupee funds from the banks and try to convert them into dollars. This raises the demand for dollars and leads to the depreciation of the Indian rupee. Such a situation occurred in July-September 1998. RBI intervened and raised the Cash Reserve Ratio (CRR) and increased its repo rate. This succeeded in mopping up the excess liquidity with the banks and reduced their lending capacity. This led to the reduction in the demand for dollars and helped in preventing the rupee from depreciating.

On the contrary, if rupee is appreciating against the US dollar and it is thought desirable to check undue appreciation of the Indian rupee, RBI can intervene to check its further appreciation. For this purpose, it can buy dollars from the market. This will raise the demand for dollars in the foreign exchange market and appreciation of Indian rupee will be checked.

Methods of Credit Control

The central bank of a country has the responsibility of controlling the volume and direction of credit in the country. Bank credit has become these days an important constituent of the money supply in the country. The volume and direction of bank credit has, therefore, an important bearing on the level of economic activity. Excessive credit will tend to generate inflationary pressures in the economy, while deficiency of credit supply may tend to cause depression or deflation. Lack of the availability of cheap credit may also hinder economic development of a country. At times of depression, there is a need to expand credit and at times of boom there is need to contract credit. For promoting economic development, expansion of cheap credit (credit at low rates of interest) is desirable. In order to prevent booms and depressions *(i.e.,* to maintain economic stability) and to promote economic growth, central bank seeks to control credit in accordance with the needs of the situation.

Broadly speaking, there are two types of methods of controlling credit.

1. **Quantitative or General Methods.** These methods seek to change the total quantity of credit in general. These are three in number: (*i*) changing the bank rate; (*ii*) open market operations; (*iii*) changing the cash reserve ratio.

2. **Qualitative or Selective Control Methods.** These methods aim at changing the volume of a specific type of credit. In other words, the selective control method affects the use of credit for particular purposes.

We will discuss these methods in detail, in the next chapter

QUESTIONS FOR REVIEW

1. What are the main functions of a Central Bank ? How does a Central Bank control the *direction of credit* ?
2. How are the main functions of a Central Bank different from the functions of a commercial bank ?
3. Explain the quantitative methods of credit control. Do you think these methods are adequate for effective control of credit supply ?
4. Why does a Central Bank seek to control bank credit in the economy ? What are the various methods of credit control by it ?

5. Discuss the functions of a Central Bank. Between bank rate and open market operations which is more effective as an instrument of credit control ?
6. Explain the proportional reserve system and minimum reserve system of issuig notes. Which system of issuing rupee notes is presently adopted in India by the RBI. Is 100 per cent backing of gold against issue of notes required by it ?
7. Central Bank is the lender of the last resort. Explain?
8. Central Bank is said to be bankers' bank. Explain how it helps commercial banks.

CHAPTER 18 Objectives and Instruments of Monetary Policy

Introduction

Monetary policy is concerned with the measures taken to regulate the supply of money, the cost and availability of credit in the economy. Further, it also deals with the distribution of credit between uses and users and also with both the lending and borrowing rates of interest of the banks. In developed countries the monetary policy has been usefully used for overcoming depression and inflation as an anti-cyclical policy. However, in developing countries it has to play a significant role in promoting economic growth. As Prof. R. Prebisch writes, "The time has come to formulate a monetary policy which meets the requirements of economic development, which fits into its framework perfectly." Further, along with encouraging economic growth, the monetary policy has also to ensure price stability, because the excessive inflation not only adversely affects distribution of income but also hinders economic growth.

It is important to understand the distinction between *objectives* or *goals*, *targets* and *instruments* of monetary policy. Whereas **goals** of monetary policy refer to its objectives which, as mentioned above, may be price stability, full employment, exchange rate stability or economic growth, ***targets*** *refer to the variables such as supply of money or bank credit, interest rates which are sought to be changed through the tools or instruments of monetary policy so as to attain these objectives.* The various tools of monetary policy are changes in the supply of currency, variations in bank rate and other interest rates, open market operations, selective credit controls, and variations in reserve requirements.

Objectives of Monetary Policy

Before explaining in detail the monetary tools undertaken by the Central Bank to regulate credit and growth of money supply, it is important to explain the objectives of monetary policy pursued by RBI which is India's central bank in formulation of its policy. Since monetary policy is one instrument of economic policy, its objectives cannot be different from those of overall economic policy. The three important objectives of monetary policy are:

1. ensuring *price stability,* that is, containing inflation.
2. to encourage *economic* growth.
3. to ensure *stability of exchange rate of the rupee,* that is, exchange rate of rupee with the US dollar, pound sterling and other foreign currencies.

Let us explain below these objectives in some detail.

Price Stability or Control of Inflation. It may be noted that each instrument of economic policy is better suited to achieve a particular objective. Monetary policy is better suited to the achievement of price stability, that is, containing inflation. To quote C. Rangarajan, a former Governor of Reserve Bank of India, "Faced with multiple objectives that are equally relevant and desirable, there is always the problem of assigning to each instrument the most appropriate target or objective. Of the various objectives, *price stability is perhaps the one that can be pursued most effectively by monetary policy.* In a developing country like ours, acceleration of investment activity in the context of supply shocks in the agricultural sector tends to be accompanied by pressures on prices and, therefore, monetary policy has much to contribute in the short-run management."[1]

Thus, achieving price stability has remained the dominant objective of monetary policy of Reserve Bank of India. It may however be noted that price stability does not mean absolutely no change in price at all. In a developing economy like ours where structural changes take place during the process of economic growth, some changes in relative prices do occur that generally put upward pressure on prices. Therefore, some changes in price level or, in other words, a certain rate of inflation is inevitable in a developing economy. Thus, *price stability means reasonable rate of inflation.* A high degree of inflation has adverse effects on the economy. Firstly, inflation raises the cost of living of the people and hurts the poor most. Therefore, inflation has been described as enemy No. 1 of the poor. Inflation sends many people below the poverty line. Secondly, inflation makes exports costlier and, therefore, discourages them. On the other hand, due to higher prices at home people are induced to import goods to a large extent. Thus, inflation has an adverse effect on the balance of payments. Thirdly, when due to a higher rate of inflation value of money is rapidly falling, people do not have much incentives to save. This lowers the rate of saving on which investment and economic growth depend. Fourthly, a high rate of inflation encourages businessmen to invest in the unproductive assets such as gold, jewellery, real estate, etc.

An expert committee on monetary reforms headed by Late Prof. S. Chakravarty suggested 4 per cent rate of inflation as a reasonable rate of inflation and recommended that monetary policy by RBI should be so formulated that ensures that rate of inflation does not exceed 4 per cent per annum.

Economic Growth. Promoting economic growth is another important objective of the monetary policy. In the past Reserve Bank has been criticised that it pursued the objective of achieving price stability and neglected the objective of promoting economic growth. Monetary policy can promote economic growth through ensuring adequate availability of credit and lower cost of credit. There are two types of credit requirements of businesses. Firstly, they have to finance their requirements of working capital and for importing needed raw materials and machines from abroad. Secondly, they need credit for financing investment in projects for building fixed capital. Easy availability of credit at low interest rate stimulates investment and thereby quickens economic growth.

However, during the seventies, eighties and the first half of nineties, Reserve Bank followed a tight monetary policy under which Cash Reserve Ratio (CRR) and Statutory Liquidity Ratio (SLR) were continually raised to restrict the availability of credit for private sector. Besides, lending rates of interest were kept at high levels which discouraged private investment. This tight monetary policy worked against promoting growth. However, in the opinion of Prof. Rangarajan, there is no conflict between the objectives of price stability and growth. Price stability, according to him, is a means to ensure economic growth. To quote him, "*It is price stability which provides the appropriate environment under which growth can occur and social justice can be ensured.*"[2] In our opinion, this may be true in the long run but *in the short* run *there* exists *trade-off between growth and inflation.* To ensure higher economic growth the adequate expansion of money supply and greater availability of credit at a lower rate of interest is needed. But large expansion in money supply and bank credit leads to the increase in aggregate demand which tends to cause a higher rate of inflation. This raises the issue of what is *acceptable trade-off* between growth and inflation, that is, what rate of inflation is acceptable to promote growth through appropriate monetary policy. Expert Committee on monetary policy headed by Late Prof. Chakravarty suggested a target of 4 per cent as "the acceptable rise in prices". According to it, the growth of money supply and availability of credit should be so regulated

1. C. Rangarajan, "Issues in Monetary Management" printed in *Indian Economy : Essays on Money and Finance,* 1998, p. 6.
2. C. Rangarajan, "*The Changing Context of Monetary Policy*", Address to 31st Convocation of the Indian Statistical Institute, March 31, 1997.

that rate of inflation does not exceed 4 per cent per annum. However, C. Rangarajan, former Governor of Reserve Bank, fixed a higher target, namely, 5 to 6 per cent rate of inflation in the context of objective of achieving 6 to 7 per cent rate of economic growth.[3]

It may be noted that in the context of the openness of the economy and floating exchange rate system, as is the case of the Indian economy today, the objective of achieving higher rate of economic growth through monetary measures may also conflict with objective of exchange rate stability, that is, value of rupee in terms of the U.S dollar and other foreign currencies. Whereas prevention of the depreciation of rupee requires tightening of monetary policy, that is, raising of interest rate and reducing liquidity of the banking system so that banks restrict their credit supply, the promotion of growth objective requires lower lending rates of interest and greater availability of credit for encouraging private investment. It is this dilemma of conflicting objectives of achieving higher economic growth rate or price stability which is being presently faced in India (2013-14).

Exchange Rate Stability

Until 1991, India followed fixed exchange rate system and only occasionally devalued the rupee with the permission of IMF. The policies of floating exchange rate and increasing openness and globalisation of the Indian economy, adopted since 1991, have made the exchange rate of rupee quite volatile. The changes in capital inflows and capital outflows and changes in demand for and supply of foreign exchange, particularly US dollar, arising from the imports and exports cause great fluctuations in the foreign exchange rate of rupee. In order to prevent large depreciation and appreciation of foreign exchange rate Reserve Bank has to take suitable monetary measures to ensure foreign exchange rate stability. Owing to the fixed exchange rate system prior to 1991 the concern about foreign exchange rate had not played a significant role in the formulation of monetary policy.

Today, the exchange rate of rupee is determined by demand for and supply of foreign exchange (say, U.S dollar). When there is mismatch between demand for and supply of foreign exchange, external value of rupee changes. For instance, from August 2011 to December 2011 depreciation of rupee as against U.S dollar had been caused by the increase in demand for dollars from (1) the corporate sector for financing their imports, (2) Foreign Institutional Investors (FII) who wanted to take out their dollars from India (*i.e.,* capital outflow) to the U.S risen and (3) increase in demand for U.S dollar by the Indian banks on the instructions of the public sector undertakings for financing necessary imports from abroad. Since export earnings and capital inflows which determine the supply of dollars had not risen adequately, mismatch between dollars and supply of dollars had arisen causing the depreciation of rupee as against the U.S dollar.

Thus when there is large current account deficit (CAD) that exceeds comfortable level (which in Indian situation is estimated at 2.5 per cent of GDP as it can be financed by normal capital inflows), it tends to depreciate the Indian rupee. In 2011-12 there was current account deficit (CAD) of 4.2 per cent and for 2012-13 it is expected that current account deficit (CAD) will be around 5 per cent of GDP. This is too high current account deficit which is putting downward pressure on the exchange rate of rupee. The depreciation of rupee raises the costs of imports which adds to the inflationary pressures in the Indian economy. Therefore, reducing current account deficit (CAD) to the comfortable level is not only essential for exchange rate stability but also for controlling inflation and achieving price stability. According to D. Subbarao, the present Governor of RBI, the widening of current account deficit in India during the last two years (2011-12 and 2012-13) has emerged as a major constraint on easing of monetary policy as causing lower lending interest rates and large availability of funds with banks will lead to more imports which will add to the current account deficit.

To arrest the fall in value of rupee Reserve Bank raises the bank rate and repo rate and thus

3. *Op. cit,*

sending signals to the banks to raise their lending rates. It also raises cash reserve ratio (CRR) to reduce the liquidity in the banking system and thus reducing lendable resources of the banks. Thus, through rise in the cost of credit and reduction in the availability of credit, borrowings from the banks are discouraged which is expected to reduce the demand for dollars. The higher interest rates in India would also discourage foreign institutional investors and Indian corporates to invest abroad. This will also work to reduce the demand for dollars which will prevent the fall in the value of the rupee.

Alternatively, to prevent the depreciation of the rupee, Reserve Bank can release more dollars from its foreign exchange reserves. The release of more dollars by Reserve Bank will increase the supply of U.S dollars in the foreign exchange market and will therefore tend to correct the mismatch between demand for and supply of the U.S dollars. This will help in stabilising the exchange rate of the rupee.

It is clear from above that in the context of flexible exchange rate system, Reserve Bank has to intervene frequently to achieve stability of exchange rate at a reasonable level.

INSTRUMENTS OF MONETARY POLICY

The central bank of a country has the responsibility of controlling the volume and direction of credit in the country. Bank credit has become these days an important constituent of the money supply in the country. The volume and direction of bank credit has, therefore, an important bearing on the level of economic activity. Excessive credit will tend to generate inflationary pressures in the economy, while deficiency of credit supply may tend to cause depression or deflation. Lack of the availability of cheap credit may also hinder economic development of a country. At times of depression, there is a need to expand credit and at a time of inflation there is need to contract credit. For promoting economic development, expansion of cheap credit (credit at low rates of interest) is desirable. In order to prevent booms and depressions (*i.e.,* to maintain economic stability) and to promote economic growth, central bank seeks to control credit in accordance with the needs of the situation.

Broadly speaking, there are two types of tools or instruments of monetary policy of controlling credit :

(1) Quantitative or General Tools. These tools seek to change the total quantity of credit in general. These are three in number: (*i*) changing the bank rate and repo rate; (*ii*) open market operations; and (*iii*) changing the cash reserve ratio.

(2) Qualitative or Selective Control Tools. These tools aim at changing the volume of a specific type of credit. In other words, the selective credit control tools affect the use of credit for particular purposes.

We discuss below these tools in detail.

Bank Rate Policy

Bank rate is the minimum rate at which the central bank of a country provides loans to the commercial banks of the country. Bank rate is also called *discount rate* because in the earlier days central bank used to provide finance to the commercial banks by rediscounting bills of exchange. Through changes in the bank rate, the central bank can influence the creation of credit by the commercial banks. Bank credit these days is an important component of the supply of money in the economy. Changes in money supply affect aggregate demand and thereby output and prices. For instance, when the central bank raises the bank rate, the cost of borrowings by the commercial banks from the central bank would rise. This would discourage the commercial banks to borrow from the central bank. Further, when the bank rate is raised, the commercial banks also raise their lending rates. When the lending rates of interest charged by the commercial banks are higher, businessmen and industrialists would feel discouraged to borrow from commercial banks. This would tend to contract bank credit and hence would result in the reduction of money supply in the economy. The reduction in the supply of money would reduce aggregate demand or money expenditure. This would reduce prices and check inflation in the economy. Thus when the economy is gripped by inflation or rising prices, the bank rate is generally raised to contract credit creation by the banks.

On the other hand, when there is recession or depression in the economy, the bank rate is lowered to overcome it. A fall in the bank rate will cause the reduction in lending interest rates of the commercial banks. With credit or loans from banks becoming cheaper, businessmen would borrow more from the commercial banks for investment and other purposes. This would lead to the increase in aggregate demand for goods and services and help in overcoming recession and bringing about recovery of the economy.

If a country permits the free flow of funds in and out of the country, then the changes in the bank rate will also have an effect on the external capital flows. For instance, as said above, when the bank rate is raised all interest rates in the market would also generally rise. With the rise in the deposit rates of interest of the banks, capital flows from outside would be attracted to the banks of the country for investment in debt and equity markets. Further, with the rise in deposit rates, outflow of funds from the banks to the other countries would be prevented. Therefore, these effects on the capital flows of the rise in bank rate will have a favourable effect on the balance of payments of the country as it will help to meet the current account deficit of the country. At present in India we are facing a huge current account deficit in our balance of payments as our import bill of crude oil, petroleum products and gold has gone up while our exports have slowed down.

Capital outflows create a lot of problems. When foreign capital is withdrawn from our debt and equity markets, not only our stock market crashes but also they raise the demand for U.S dollars to send abroad. As a result of increase in demand for dollars, the exchange rate of rupee per U.S dollar falls, that is, Indian rupee depreciates. Though depreciation of a currency is generally considered as desirable as it tends to raise exports and reduce imports. However, because our demand for imports is inelastic, their prices rise as a result of depreciation, but the volume of imports remains unaffected. The rise in prices of imports therefore contributes to inflation in the economy and worsens it further. To prevent this, rate of interest must be kept high.

It is important to note that the *changes in bank rate affect the credit creation by banks through altering the cost of credit.* Changes in the cost of credit affect borrowings by the commercial banks from the central bank and also affect the demand for credit by businessmen from the commercial banks.

Repo Rate in India

However, changes in bank rate as a tool of monetary policy in India has been quite limited. Before 1991, bank rate remained unchanged at 10 per cent in the whole decade of 1981-1991. This was because prior to 1991, interest rates charged by banks were administered by the Reserve Bank and therefore could not be used as a reference rate by the banks for the purpose of fixing their lending rates. In the post-reform period from July 1991, to control inflationary pressures in the Indian economy bank rate was raised from 10 per cent to 11 per cent. However, since then bank rate has been rarely used. This is for two reasons. First, the bank rate is meant **for a longer intermediate period for regulating interest rates charged by the banks** from their customers and thereby influences the cost of credit. However, in the Indian context what is needed is to regulate liquidity of the banks for a very short period, even on daily basis. Secondly, even now when lending rates of interest have been freed from control by RBI, **there is not much refinance** being made available at the bank rate and therefore the banks can ignore this as a reference in setting their own lending rates.

However, the need for influencing the lending rates of banks and liquidity of the Indian banks is very much needed. Therefore, for this purpose in 1997 RBI introduced under its **liquidity adjustment facility (LAF),** a rate of interest called **repo rate.** Under *repo rate system* banks could get overnight short-term loans from the RBI to meet their needs of liquidity if they arise. Through repo system RBI buys securities from the banks and thereby provides loans to them. *The rate of interest at which the RBI lends overnight funds to the banks against securities is called repo ratio.* Repo rate is short-run interest rate and bank rate is the long-term interest rate at which banks could borrow from the RBI. The introduction of repo rate helps the Reserve Bank to increase the liquidity of the banks by purchasing from them Government securities and meeting their needs for liquidity when they arise. There is also ***reverse repo*** mechanism in which the banks park their surplus funds with the RBI on which they earn interest. The interest rate which RBI pays to the banks for the funds they keep with it for the short term under this scheme is called *reverse repo rate.* Through reverse repo system, the RBI mops up liquidity from the banking system.

Repo refers to agreement for a transaction between RBI and banks through which RBI supplies funds immediately against Government securities and simultaneously banks agree to repurchase the same or similar securities after a specified time which may be one day to 14 days. Through *reverse repo,* RBI mops up liquidity from the banking system by selling them securities when it finds that there is excess liquidity in the system which may create inflationary pressures. Under the repo agreement banks can get short-term loans from RBI against the securities to meet the needs of liquidity when they arise. Thus, *Repo and Reverse Repo operations are useful tools of short-run liquidity management by RBI*. Repo and Reverse Repo operations should not be confused with open market operations as the latter involve sale and purchase of Government securities in the market for a longer intermediate period and not for one day or few days. Besides, on Repo and Reverse Repo rates of interest are fixed by RBI while in open market operations rate of interest varies and depends on demand and supply conditions of funds.

As a tool of monetary policy when Reserve Bank of India wants to check inflation, **it raises the repo rate.** When the commercial banks find that borrowing from the RBI has become costly and if they have not much excess reserves with them they will raise their lending rates. At higher lending rates businessmen will be discouraged for taking loans from the banks to finance their investment projects. Likewise, persons who want loans for building or purchasing houses and cars will also be discouraged to get loans from the banks. This will result in contraction of credit which will tend to lower aggregate demand and thereby help in controlling inflation.

On the other hand, when there are recessionary conditions in the economy, the RBI lowers the repo rate. With fall in the repo rate the banks can borrow from the banks at lower short-term rate of interest. In turn they lower their lending rates to businessmen for investment and to the consumers who seek home loans and car loans. This raises investment and consumption demand which through the operation of multiplier helps to raise the level of income and employment. As a result, the economy is lifted out of recession. Such a situation prevailed in India in 2007-09 when following the global financial crisis there was decline of our exports landing the Indian economy into industrial slowdown. Then RBI lowered its repo rate from 9 per cent to 4.5 per cent during the period from Oct. 2008 to March 2009. This helped to raise investment and consumption demand which led to recovery of the Indian economy in 2009-10 and 2010-11.

Limitations of Bank Rate and Repo Rate Policy

Both bank rate and repo rate are interest rate policy of RBI and therefore both have common limitations. Bank rate or repo rate policy does not have always the desired effect on investment, output and prices. There are certain conditions which must be met for the successful working of the bank rate or repo rate policy. These conditions are:

(1) All other rates should follow the bank/repo rate in its movement so that bank credit should expand or contract as desired. This will not happen if the commercial banks have considerable reserves of their own at their disposal and, therefore, their dependence on borrowed funds from the central bank may be very less. Further, for the changes in the bank rate to cause changes in

all other interest rates in the market, a well-organised money market is needed. If well-organised money market does not exist as is the case in India where indigenous bankers contribute a good part of the money market, changes in the bank rate or repo rate would not be followed by the appropriate changes in all rates.

(2) The second important condition for the successful working of the bank/repo rate policy is the responsiveness of businessmen to the changes in the lending rates of interest. If businessmen and investors reduce their borrowings when the bank rate/repo rate and hence the lending rates of commercial bank are raised, and increase their borrowings for investment when the bank rate and lending rates of the banks are reduced, the changes in the bank/repo rate will have the desired effect, predicted in the bank rate theory. However, empirical studies conducted recently have shown that rate of interest does not exercise a strong influence on borrowings for investment and other purposes. When there is inflationary situation in the economy, the rate of interest will have to be raised very high in order to have desired effects. Similarly, the response of investment to the fall in the rate of interest is never vigorous. Demand by businessmen for loans for investment purposes from the banks depends on the economic situation prevailing in the economy. When the economy is gripped by severe depression and consequently prospects for making profits are bleak, businessmen would be reluctant to borrow for investment even though the lending rates of interest have been lowered considerably to induce them to borrow. It has been aptly remarked that '*you can bring the horse to water but you cannot make it drink*'.

The present belief is that interest rate policy will play only a subsidiary role in the monetary control. The bank rate or repo rate at the best could check a boom and inflation but could not bring about a recovery if the country was suffering from recession or depression. Thus it has much greater potential effectiveness if it is desired to arrest credit expansion than when it is sought to stimulate credit. But used in conjunction with other methods, it can still play a useful role. The bank rate and repo rate have the value as a signal. If the traditions are that a signal must be obeyed, the bank rate or repo rate policy can fulfil its purpose since it will be in keeping with respectable conduct.

Open Market Operations

Open market operations are another important tool of monetary control, especially in the developed countries. The term open market operations means the purchase and sale of securities by the central bank of the country. The theory of open market operations is like this: The sale of securities by the central bank leads to the contraction of credit and the purchase thereof to credit expansion. When the central bank sells securities in the open market, it receives payment in the form of a cheque on one of commercial banks. If the purchaser is a bank, the cheque is drawn against the purchasing bank itself. In both cases the result is the same. The cash reserves of the bank in question, which it keeps with the central bank, is to that extent reduced. With the reduction of its cash reserves, the commercial bank has to reduce its lending. Thus, credit contracts. On the other hand, when the central bank purchases securities, it pays through cheques drawn on itself. This increases the cash balance of the commercial banks and enables them to expand credit. "Take care of the legal tender money and credit will take care of itself" is the maxim.

The open market operations method is sometimes adopted to make the bank/repo rate policy effective. If the member-banks do not raise lending rates following the rise in the bank or repo rate due to surplus funds available with them, the central bank can withdraw such surplus funds by the sale of securities and thus compel the member-banks to raise their rates. Scarcity of funds in the market compels the banks directly or indirectly to borrow from the central bank through rediscounting of bills or through repo rate system of liquidity. If the bank rate or repo rate is high, the market rate of interest cannot remain low.

It may be noted that to check inflation the RBI sells government securities to the banks through open market operations and receives in return cash from them. This reduces the cash reserves with the banks and thus reducing their liquidity. This causes contraction of credit which helps in fighting inflation.

On the other hand, when RBI faces recessionary problem in the economy, it will seek to expand credit or money supply in the economy. This can be done through open market operations by buying securities from the open market. With this purchase of securities from the market the RBI pays cash funds to the banks and thus raising their cash reserves or liquidity. Against this increase in cash reserves, banks are able to create credit or bank deposits through providing loans by a multiple of the increase in their cash reserves depending on the value of deposit multiplier.

Limitations of the Open Market Operations. It is obvious that this method will succeed only if certain conditions are satisfied. The limitations are discussed below:

(1) According to the theory of open market operations, when the central bank purchases securities, the cash reserves of the member-banks will be increased and, conversely, the cash reserves will be decreased when the central bank sells securities. This, however, may not happen. The sale of securities may be offset by return of notes from circulation and hoards. The purchase of securities, on the other hand, may be accompanied by a withdrawal of notes for increased currency requirements or for hoarding by the public. In both the cases, therefore, the cash reserves of the member-banks may remain unaffected.

(2) But even if the cash reserves of the member-banks are increased or decreased, the banks may not expand or contract credit accordingly. The percentage of cash to credit is not rigidly fixed and can vary within quite wide limits. The banks will expand and contract credit according to the prevailing economic and political circumstances and not merely with reference to their cash reserves.

(3) The third condition is that when the commercial bank's cash reserves increase, the demand for loans and advances should increase too and *vice versa*. This may not happen. Owing to economic or political uncertainty, even cheap money rate may not attract borrowers. Conversely, when there is boom in the economy and prospects of profits bright, entrepreneurs would borrow even at high rates of interest.

(4) Finally, the circulation of bank credit should have a constant velocity. But the velocity of bank deposits is rarely constant. It increases in periods of rising business activity and decreases in periods of depression. Thus, a policy of contracting credit may be neutralised by increased velocity of circulation, and *vice versa*.

Open market operations as an instrument of credit control have proved to be quite successful in regulating the availability of credit in developed countries. This is for two reasons. First, when the central bank purchases or buys securities, the reserves of the commercial banks automatically expand or contract. The changes in the reserves of the banks directly affect their capacity to lend. Unlike in the case of instrument of bank rate, the success of the market operations does not depend on the attitude or responsiveness of the commercial banks; their capacity to provide credit is affected automatically. Secondly, the open market operations can be managed in a way that the cash reserves of the banks increase or decrease to the desired extent.

Since for the success of market operations it is necessary that there should be broad and active market in short and long-term government securities, and such markets exist only in the U.S.A. and Great Britain and other developed countries, this method of credit control has been most effectively used in these countries.

Open market operations which did not play a significant role as an instrument of credit control in India in the past have now become important tool and are being used extensively by RBI. This is because market for Government securities in India has now become quite wide and there is often excess liquidity in the banking system. General public do not buy more than a fraction of government securities. It is banks and other financial institutions that buy or sell government securities. When there is excess liquidity in the banking system, banks willingly invest in Government securities more than the statutory limits.

Changing the Cash Reserve Ratio (CRR)

Another monetary tool to vary the quantity of credit is to change the required cash reserve ratio. By law, banks have to keep a certain amount of cash reserves with RBI as reserves against the demand and time deposits. If the legal minimum cash reserve ratio, for example, is 10%, the bank will have to keep ₹ 2,000 as reserves with RBI against its deposits of ₹ 20,000. Now the central bank of a country has the authority to vary the cash reserve ratio. If now the central bank increases the cash reserve ratio from 10% to 20%, then the reserves of ₹ 2,000 could support only deposits of ₹ 10,000 and therefore the banks having reserves of ₹ 2,000 will have to reduce their deposits form ₹ 20,000 to ₹ 10,000. This will cause the contraction of credit.

On the other hand, if the central bank reduces the cash reserve ratio from 20% to 10% then the reserves of ₹ 2,000 could support the deposit of ₹ 20,000. Therefore the bank having reserves of ₹ 2,000 can increase their deposits, *i.e.,* expand credit to ₹ 20,000. To sum up, increase in the legal cash reserve ratio leads to the contraction of credit and decrease in the legal cash reserve ratio leads to the expansion of credit. *An increase in the legal cash reserve ratio will succeed in contracting credit only when banks have no excess reserves.* If banks are holding excess reserves, the increase in the legal reserve ratio will not bring about the contraction of credit. On the other hand, the reduction in the cash reserve ratio will have the desired effect of expanding credit only if the borrowers respond favourably. As a result of reduction in the cash reserve ratio, the availability to lend by the banks increases and the banks tend to make more credit available to borrowers, or to make it available at lower rates. Now, if the borrowers for one reason or another do not respond favourably, *i.e.,* are not prepared to borrow, credit will not be expanded.

Reserve Bank of India has often used this monetary tool to influence the availability of bank credit depending on the conditions prevailing in the Indian economy. For example, when there were recessionary conditions in the Indian economy following the global financial crisis in 2007-09, RBI over several stages sharply reduced the cash reserve ratio (CRR) to overcome economic slowdown and bring about recovery. With the reduction in cash reserve ratio, a lot of cash reserves were released for the banks which was used by the banks to provide more loans to businessmen for investment purposes and to individuals for buying houses, cars and scooters. This led to the increase in aggregate demand in the economy which helped in recovery of the Indian economy.

On the other hand, when during 2011-12 and 2012-13, a serious problem of inflation (*i.e.,* rise in general price level) prevailed in the Indian economy, Reserve Bank of India raised the cash reserve ratio (CRR). As a result, banks had to keep more cash reserves with the RBI resulting in decline in the credit availability of the banks. This helped to curtail consumption and investment demand in the economy due to lack of credit. This increase in cash reserve ratio for the banks helped a lot in reducing aggregate demand in the economy and bringing about fall in the WPI inflation rate to around 5 per cent in April 2013.

SELECTIVE CREDIT CONTROLS

The methods of credit control described above are known as quantitative or general methods as they are meant to control the availability of credit in general. Thus, bank rate policy, open market operations and variations in cash reserves ratio expand or contract the availability of credit for all purposes. On the other hand, selective credit controls are meant to regulate the flow of credit for particular or specific purposes. Whereas, the general credit controls seek to regulate the total available quantity of credit (through changes in the high powered money) and the cost of credit, the selective credit control seeks to change the distribution or allocation of credit between its various uses. The selective credit controls have both the positive and negative aspects. In its positive aspect, measures are taken to stimulate the greater flow of credit to some particular sectors considered as important. Thus in India, agriculture, small and marginal farmers, small artisans, small-scale industries are the priority sectors to which greater flow of bank credit has been sought to be encouraged by the Reserve Bank of India. In its negative aspect, several measures are taken to restrict the credit flowing into some specific activities or sectors which are regarded as undesirable or harmful from the social point of view. The selective credit controls generally used are:

(1) Changes in the minimum margin for lending by banks against the stocks of specific goods kept or against other types of securities.

(2) The fixation of maximum limit or ceiling on advances to individual borrowers against stocks of particular sensitive commodities.

(3) The fixation of minimum discriminatory rates of interest chargeable on credit for particular purposes.

(4) Prohibition of the discounting of bills of exchange involving sale of sensitive commodities.

The selective credit controls originated in U.S.A. to regulate the flow of bank credit to the stock market *(i.e.,* the market for shares). They were also used to restrict the volume of credit available for purchasing durable consumer goods during the period of the Second War. However, in India, the selective credit controls are being used by the Reserve Bank to prevent speculative hoarding of commodities so as to check the rise in prices of these commodities. The selective credit controls in India are being used in the case of foodgrains, oilseeds, vegetable oils, cotton, sugar, gur and khandsari.

Though all the above techniques of selective credit control are used, in India it is the first technique, namely, the changes in the minimum margin against stocks of commodities or other securities, that has been mostly used. It may be noted that the central bank of a country has the power to vary the minimum margin requirements against the security of stocks of commodities. While lending advances to businessmen, the commercial banks leave a margin of the value of stock kept as security to be financed by the businessmen from their own sources and lend funds to them equal to the remaining amount of the value of the stock. This minimum requirement of the value of the stock left to be financed by the borrowers themselves is known as margin. Suppose the margin fixed for a stock of particular commodity is 60 per cent. In this case the businessmen can borrow up to the value of 40 per cent of the stock of that commodity while the 60 per cent of the value of stock will be financed by the businessmen themselves. Now, if the bank raises the margin to 70 per cent, then businessmen can borrow from the bank to the extent of 30 per cent of the value of the stock of that commodity. This will lead to the contraction of credit for holding the stock of the commodity by the businessmen. If the businessmen are not able to finance the holding of 10 per cent extra stock of the commodity, they will be forced to sell that in the market and thus raising market supply of the commodity. This will lower the prices of the commodity, other things remaining the same.

In developed countries, the selective credit controls are generally used to prevent excessive speculation in share market. In the share market, the buyers purchase a good amount of shares by making a small payment and the remaining value of shares are paid by brokers through borrowing from the banks against the shares thus purchased. When the central bank raises the margin, the buyers of shares have to pay a larger sum of money for the shares purchased and as a result bank credit contracts and the speculative activity in the stock market is discouraged.

Conditions Necessary for Success of Selective Credit Controls

Some conditions are necessary for the successful operations of selective credit controls of commodities. However, the clever businessmen can obtain credit from the banks by offering other securities and use the funds so obtained to finance the speculative holdings of the stocks of sensitive commodities. Therefore, if the selective credit controls are to succeed in preventing the rise in prices of sensitive commodities, they have to be accompanied by general credit controls aimed at reducing the capacity of banks to lend money. It also follows from above that end-use or purpose of all credit ought to be taken into account by the banks and credit advanced accordingly if selective credit controls are to be effective.

In India the selective credit controls have been in operation since 1956 to check the rise in prices of sensitive commodities. However, the success of selective credit controls in achieving its objective of restraining the rise in commodity prices depends upon certain conditions explained below:

1. The Use of Quantitative Credit Controls. Selective credit controls are effective only when they are accompanied by the general quantitative credit controls such as variation in bank rate and cash reserve ratio. This is because the selective credit controls operate through regulating credit against particular securities or stocks.

2. The Availability of Non-Bank Finance. The success of the selective credit control also depends upon the exent to which the funds from non-bank sources (*i.e.,* from their own funds and also from the unregulated credit market) is available to the businessmen. When the bank credit for a particular purpose is reduced, the businessmen can use their own funds or borrow from non-regulated markets to indulge in speculative holding of inventories. In India today the businessmen have large quantities of black money with them which they generally use for speculative holding of inventories of sensitive commodities and in this way succeed in defeating the purpose of selective credit controls.

QUESTIONS FOR REVIEW

1. What are the objectives of monetary policy, especially of Reserve Bank of India? Is there a trade-off between the objectives of controlling inflation and promoting economic growth? Discuss.
2. What are the instruments of monetary policy? Which tools of monetary policy are mostly used by the Reserve Bank of India?
3. What are repo and reverse repo rates? How are they used by RBI to regulate liquidity in the Indian banking system?
4. What is Bank Rate? What is the effect of increase in bank rate? What is the effect of reducing the bank rate? What are the limitations of using the tool of changes in bank rate to influence the level of economic activity ?
5. What are open market operations? If Reserve Bank of India wants to promote economic growth, how will it use the tool of open market operations ?
6. If Reserve Bank of India seeks to control inflation, how will it conduct its open market operations ? Trace the events that follow from the sale of securities by the Reserve Bank of India in this context.
7. What is cash reserve ratio? How has a reduction in cash reserve ratio by Reserve Bank of India a multiplier effect on the aggregate demand?
8. How does increase in cash reserve ratio help to check inflation in the economy ?
9. How does the open market purchase of government securities by the Reserve Bank of India help to overcome recession in the economy ? What are its limitations ?
10. Prior to 1991, what monetary policy tools were used by Reserve Bank of India to neutralise the inflationary impact of expansionary fiscal policy ? Explain.

APPENDIX TO CHAPTER 18

Role of Monetary Policy in Economic Growth

Economic growth implies the expansion in productive capacity or capital stock in the economy so that increases in real national output or income are attained. As is well known, economic growth can be speeded up by accelerating the rate of savings and investment in the economy. This requires the following steps:

(*a*) Increase in the aggregate rate of savings in the economy ;

(*b*) Mobilisation of these savings so that they are made available for the purpose of investment and production ;

(*c*) Increase in the rate of investment; and

(*d*) Allocation of investment funds for productive purposes and priority sectors of the economy.

Proper monetary policy can help in producing favourable effects on the above requirements of economic growth. We explain below the appropriate monetary policy to promote growth in developing countries.

1. Monetary Policy and Savings

Several monetary measures can be adopted to raise the aggregate rate of saving. First, a high interest rate policy can promote savings. In the fifties and sixties of the 20th Century, it was widely believed that interest rate reflected the price of capital and since capital was scarce in developing countries, the real interest rates should be kept at higher levels to promote saving so that capital accumulation is speeded up. However, this argument in favour of higher real interest rates in developing countries was based upon the belief or assumption that *savings were positively elastic or sensitive to the interest rate.*

It is worthwhile to mention an opposite viewpoint regarding interest rate policy which has gained large support in recent years. According to this view (emphasised by Keynes in his monetary theory), rate of interest represents the cost of investment, and lower the rate of interest, the greater will be inducement to invest. However, Keynes was of the view that investment was not much sensitive or elastic to lower rate of interest Dr. K.N.Raj argued that *since investment is an important factor determining economic growth in developing countries, it should be promoted by lowering the interest rates*. However, this is not fully correct. This is because whereas inducement to invest may be promoted by lowering the interest rates, the adequate amount of savings or resources needed to finance larger investment may not be forthcoming at lower interest rates. Further, a low interest rate policy in developing countries like India is likely to promote more investment in inventories and luxury consumer goods such as cars, airconditioners, luxury houses rather than that in fixed capital goods.

In our view therefore in a developing economy *a reasonably positive real interest rate policy* should be pursued to provide incentives for more savings so that large sources are made available for investment in fixed capital stock. If monetary policy in a developing country is to promote economic growth it must aim at raising the rate of saving. It may be recalled that *real rate of interest is nominal rate of interest minus rate of inflation*. In our view real rate of interest should be positive and preferably should not be allowed to fall below 5 per cent per annum, if it is to provide reasonable rate of return on savings. Therefore, with the rise in rate of inflation nominal rate of interest should also be raised to keep incentives for saving intact. It may be noted that in recent years (2011-12 and 2012-13) in India low deposit rates offered to the public by banks have prompted the people to invest their savings in unproductive assets such as gold, jewellery and real estate. *This led to the fall in financial saving* required for productive investment. This led the Finance Minister, Mr. Chidambaram, in his budget for 2013-14 to announce issuing of **inflation-indexed bonds** on which nominal interest rate will automatically rise with the increase in inflation rate.

Besides, the monetary policy can play a strategic role in increasing national savings by promoting the expansion of banking facilities and other financial intermediaries in the developing countries, especially in their rural areas. With more bank branches in under-banked and underdeveloped regions, the people who consume away their surplus incomes will be induced to save them in the form of bank deposits which are quite safe as a store of value. The commercial banking encourages thrift or propensity to save by offering a return on savings in the form of interest rate on bank deposits. It also induces more savings by providing outlets for mutual funds which can be equity linked and other saving schemes for fruitful investment of the savings by the people who would have otherwise put them to unproductive or wasteful uses such as buying land, real estate, gold and jewellery. But to tap and raise savings sufficiently and to prevent its unproductive use, banks and other financial institutions need to be numerous and dispersed throughout the economy in both the urban and rural areas. Speaking from the development experience of various countries, Prof. Lewis, a development economist, has emphasised that the volume of savings depends partly upon how widespread banking and other financial institutions are. To quote him, "*if the saving institutions are placed under the individual's nose, people save more than if the nearest saving institutions is some distance away*."[1]

Thus growth in saving in the form of bank deposits will be greater, if a reasonable real rate of interest policy is pursued. Similarly, with the expansion of other financial institutions, the people will feel induced to save more for buying financial assets. It is generally agreed that the rapid expansion of banking facilities after the nationalisation of major commercial banks in 1969 promoted by the Reserve Bank of India has contributed considerably to the growth of aggregate savings. While the aggregate saving rate has gone up from 16.5 per cent in 1969-70 to 22.7 per cent in 1982-83, bank deposits, which accounted for 8.7 per cent of total domestic savings in 1969-70, accounted for 22.5 per cent of these savings in 1982-83. The number of commercial banks offices increased from 8,262 in July 1969 to 44,521 in 1984 and to 62,350 in 1995. Although it is difficult to establish a precise quantitative relationship between expansion of bank branches and savings in the form of bank deposits, its significant contribution to the promotion of savings cannot be denied. Therefore, the future branch expansion policy must fully take into account the untapped saving potential of under-banked and underdeveloped regions.

It may be noted that in order to facilitate mobilisation of an increasing proportion of savings by the banking system, it is essential to maintain a reasonable price stability. Dr. Manmohan Singh, when he was Governor of Reserve Bank of India, pointed out, "*It is only under conditions of reasonable price stability that people will have less attraction for savings in the form of physical assets such as gold, real estate and excessive accumulation of inventories*." Further, if banks are to mobilise adequate amount of savings in the form of bank deposits, interest rates on bank deposits must remain positive in real terms. That is, the rate of interest be maintained at a higher level than the rate of inflation. If through excessive rise in prices, real rate of interest becomes negative, people will be discouraged to save.

2. Monetary Policy and Investment

Monetary policy has an important role to play in boosting up the level of investment by making available savings or resources mobilised by banks for purposes of investment and production. The banks fulfil this task by offering bank credit for investment to business and industry.

1. Arthur Lewis, *Theory of Economic Growth*, George Allen and Unwin, 1960.

Cost of Credit. It may be noted that Keynesian theory of monetary policy emphasises that the effect of a change in the supply of money on the level of production and investment operates through the changes in the rate of interest. The increase in the supply of money by the monetary authority will cause the market rate of interest to fall. At lower rate of interest, the entrepreneurs will be induced to invest more. Accordingly, Keynesian monetary theory has been described as "*cost of credit*" theory. However, Keynes himself and several economists after him believed that this effect of changes in money supply on investment which operates through rate of interest is not very vigorous. It has been asserted that investment in fixed capital is interest inelastic. That is why Keynes did not have much faith in the effectiveness of monetary policy and instead emphasised the role of fiscal policy in influencing the level of economic activity. However, it is now generally believed by the economists that since interest is an important cost of investment, *investment demand is fairly interest elastic*. Therefore, to promote investment, the easy monetary policy should be adopted.

It may be noted that in the post-economic reforms period from 1996 to 2003 easy or low interest rate policy was adopted to promote private investment so as to revive the industrial sector whose growth slowed down from 1996-97 to 2002-03. Following the soft-interest rate policy of Reserve Bank of India prime lending rates of interest of commercial banks, which varied between 15 and 16 per cent prior to 1996, were reduced over a period of time to 9 to 10 per cent in 2003. Again when in September 2008 global financial crisis occurred as a result of bust of housing bubble in the U.S, there was worldwide (including India) economic slowdown, Reserve Bank of India in October 2008 reduced its repo interest rate from 9 per cent in July 2008 to 7 per cent in October 2008 and further to 4.75 per cent on March 4, 2009, to promote private investment so as to prevent sharp economic slowdown in India.

However, the soft interest rate policy does not always, especially during recession, achieve much success in stimulating private investment. This is because when there are sluggish demand conditions, the existing fixed capital is underutilised, it is not profitable to make more investment for expanding fixed capital stock, private enterprises are therefore not willing to make further investment despite lower interest rates. It is for such economic conditions that it has been said that '*you can bring the horse to water but you cannot make it drink*'. However, in normal circumstances cheap interest rate policy promotes private investment and therefore helps to achieve higher economic growth.

Availability of Credit. It is noteworthy that in the recent times monetary theory emphasises the **credit-availability effect on investment** of the changes in the supply of money. According to this, an increase in the supply of money causing expansion in the reserve money with the banks directly enlarges the availability of bank credit for investment purposes and thereby raises the level of investment in the economy. On the contrary, contraction in money supply will directly reduce the availability of credit and hence tend to decrease investment in the economy.

Further, in this context it is noteworthy that in developing countries, Government or public investment plays a crucial role in the development of their economies. Therefore, monetary policy requires to promote not only private investment but also public investment by making available adequate amount of credit for it.

Monetary Policy and Private Investment. If the private sector plays an important role in the development process, as it does in India after economic reforms undertaken since 1991, monetary policy has also to ensure that the needs for bank credit for investment and production in the private sector are fully met. The banks must provide adequate bank credit to meet at least essential working capital requirements of industry and agriculture. Both large-scale and medium industries require funds for investment in fixed capital, working capital and for maintaining inventories. Subject to appropriate norms fixed for inventory holdings, the credit needs of the private sector should be met if existing capacities in the private sector are to be fully used and also more productive capacity is to be built up. In India banks have been asked by the Reserve Bank of India to give specific percentage of loans at concessional rates of interest to some priority sectors such as agriculture and small and medium enterprises.

Monetary Policy and Public Investment. Let us first explain the promotion of the public investment through monetary policy. Monetary policy has to ensure that the banking system contributes to the financing of the planned public investment. For this a good part of bank deposits mobilised by the banks should be invested in Government and other approved securities so that the government should be able to finance its planned investment, especially in infrastructure. At present in India, there is lack of infrastructure such as power, roads, highways, ports, irrigation facilities which is obstructing economic growth. Besides, when industry faces demand recession, public investment is an ideal tool to develop infrastructure and to increase the demand for industrial products through the operation of multiplier. This will stimulate private investment. Therefore, in our view, policy of raising public investment will *crowd in* private investment rather than *crowding it out*. In India a new technique of monetary policy has been designed to secure larger resources from the banking system for financing public investment. This technique has been described as *Statutory Liquidity Ratio* (SLR). According to this, *in addition to cash reserve requirements* banks in India are required to keep a minimum proportion of their total demand and time deposits in the form of specified liquid assets. And the most important specified liquid asset for this purpose is the investment in Government and other securities. To raise the lendable resources of the banks, cash reserve ratio of the banks must be kept at low level.

3. Allocation of Investment Funds

Mobilisation of savings alone would not do. Proper canalisation of these into suitable directions of investment is or perhaps more important than mobilisation itself. The monetary policy should restrict the growth of wasteful lines of investment which are inimical to economic growth. It should be able to direct investment in productive channels. In this regard, the monetary policy has to play a selective or qualitative role in so far as it is possible through its operations to *discriminate between productive and unproductive outlays. It should give a fillip to the former and stint* the growth of the latter. Further, it has to be so designed as to influence the specific sectors and industries which are most significant to affect the growth of the economy. In fact, the particularised application of credit can greatly activise the process of economic growth. Therefore, it is necessary to operate the *selective credit rationing with a view to influence the pattern of investment*. However, in the gamut of monetary policy, there are selective credit control measures of both general and specific nature. In the general category are included measures such as voluntary credit restriction and moral suasion. In the category of specific measures there exist measures to control credit institutions.

For the purpose of regulating the individual credit institutions, the method of varying the reserve requirements is quite effective. On the other hand, in order to divert the financial resources into desired channels, the method of **credit rationing** should be used by the Central Bank. This may be done by fixation of a ceiling on the aggregate portfolio of the commercial banks, thereby making it incumbent that loans and advances do not exceed the fixed ceiling. Alternatively, it may be done by directly allocating funds that can be granted and used. Besides, policies such as the selective rediscount policy, prior deposit requirement policy and the fixation of deposit requirement policy can also be adopted to achieve similar goals. However, it may be pointed out that the potency of credit planning depends upon the extent of the area over which it operates. The developing economies must strive for an extension of credit planning over wider areas.

Credit control measures such as noted above promote growth by directing the stream of domestic savings into the desired lines of investment. Measures such as lengthening the periods of repayment, lowering of margin requirements, providing rediscounting facilities at rates below the bank rate, provision of special loans by commercial banks to be used for specific purposes or the setting up of special Investment institutions such as Industrial Development Bank can provide the required inducement to channelise savings in the desired directions. In the indirect sense, these measures may prove conducive to growth in two ways. Firstly, the qualitative credit control measures prevent the savings from being wasted in unproductive channels. Through their application it becomes possible to deny or discourage certain lines of investment that are inimical to the growth of the economy. However, the extent to which such measures can help providing resources for investment in the desired directions depends on the extent to which the flow of credit towards the undesirable channels can be prevented.

Secondly, such measures may go a long way in galvanising the process of growth by restraining inflation and its adverse effects. When inflationary tendencies set in, generally the bank advances to businessmen tend to rise. In this way certain undesirable and unproductive enterprises may grow and flourish. For instance, activities such as speculative demand for building up inventories, accumulation of precious metals for purchase of foreign exchange and real estate get a fillip. Growth of these and such other unproductive activities can be held in check by raising the margin requirements for the blackballed collaterals. Further, the monetary authority can fix a ceiling by holding the loans and advances of the value of the collateral. Thus, it *serves the dual purpose of curbing inflation and protecting certain essential productive forms of investment from being restricted.*

In the context of the planned development of the underdeveloped countries, the use of methods of selective credit controls and credit rationing is not only necessary but also essential. They greatly widen the horizons of development along predetermined and desired directions. They are not only helpful in preventing inflation but also *act as a positive means of directing the process of economic development on the desired lines*. Furthermore, the policy of selective credit controls is especially suited to the needs of underdeveloped countries where the orthodox monetary techniques have limited applicability. As it is, the structure of these economies is not very conducive to the general methods of credit control.

The huge investment expenditure made by the government in the public sector in its endeavour to accelerate the process of growth is not amenable to control by the monetary authority. The monetary authority is, in fact, subversive to the wishes of the government in the matter of providing resources for development. Further, in order to help government borrowings, the bank rate policy of the Reserve Bank tends to become more or less inflexible. Besides, for the sake of supporting government loans, the institutions such as SEBI (Stock Exchange Board of India) is also required to stabilise the securities market.

QUESTIONS FOR REVIEW

1. Economic growth depends on saving and investment. Explain the role of monetary policy in promoting saving and investment in a developing country such as India.
2. Explain the dilemma faced by Reserve Bank of India to achieve its to objectives of price stability and economic growth.
3. Role of monetary policy in India is to achieve economic growth with stability. Discuss
4. Explain the role of monetary policy to ensure proper allocation of funds among uses and sectors to ensure *inclusive economic growth.*

CHAPTER 19

Supply of Money and its Determinants

Money supply plays a crucial role in the determination of price level and interest rate. In the present chapter we shall explain what determines the money supply in an economy. In economic analysis it is generally presumed that money supply is determined by the policy of Central Bank of a country and the Government. However, this is not fully correct as in the determination of money supply, besides Central Bank and Government, the public and commercial banks also play an important role. There are various measures of money supply depending upon which types of deposits of banks and other financial institutions are included in it. We will explain various measures of money supply later in this chapter.

Importance of Money Supply

Growth of money supply is an important factor not only for acceleration of the process of economic development but also for the achievement of price stability in the economy. What constitutes the money supply and what factors cause variation and growth in money supply will be explained in the present chapter. There must be controlled expansion of money supply if the objective of development with stability is to be achieved. A healthy growth of an economy requires that there should be neither inflation nor deflation. Inflation is the greatest headache of a developing economy. A mild inflation arising out of the creation of money by deficit financing may stimulate investment by raising profit expectations and extracting forced savings. But a runaway inflation is highly detrimental to economic growth. The developing economies have to face the problem of inadequacy of resources in initial stages of development and it can make up this deficiency by deficit financing. But it has to be kept strictly within safe limits. Thus, increase in money supply affects vitally the rate of economic growth. In fact, it is now regarded as a legitimate instrument of economic growth. Kept within proper limits it can accelerate economic growth but exceeding of the limits will retard it. Thus, management of money supply is essential in the interest of steady economic growth.

THE CONCEPT OF MONEY SUPPLY AND ITS MEASUREMENT

By money supply we mean the total stock of monetary media of exchange available to a society for use in connection with the economic activity of the country. According to the standard concept of money supply, it is composed of the following two elements :

1. Currency with the public,
2. Demand deposits with the public.

Before explaining these two components of money supply two things must be noted with regard to the money supply in the economy. First, the money supply refers to the total sum of money available to the public in the economy *at a point of time*. That is, money supply is a *stock concept* in sharp contrast to the national income which is a flow representing the value of goods and services produced *per unit of time*, usually taken as a year. Secondly, money supply always refers to the amount of money *held by the public*. In the term public are included households, firms and institutions other than banks and the government. The rationale behind considering money supply as held by the public is to separate the producers of money from those who use money to fulfil their various types of demand for money. Since the Government and the banks produce or create money for the use by the public, the money (cash reserves) held by them are not used for transaction and speculative purposes and are excluded from the standard measures of money supply. This *separation of producers of money from the users of money is important from the viewpoint of both monetary theory and policy.*[1]

Let us explain the two components of money supply at some length.

Currency with the Public

In order to arrive at the total currency with the public in India we add the following items:

1. Currency notes in circulation issued by the Reserve Bank of India.
2. The number of rupee notes and coins in circulation.
3. Small coins in circulation.

It is worth noting that *cash reserves* with the banks has to be deducted from the value of the above three items of currency in order to arrive at the total currency with the public. This is because cash reserves with the banks must remain with them and cannot therefore be used for making payments for goods or by any commercial bank's transactions. It may further be noted that these days paper currency issued by Reserve Bank of India (RBI) are not fully backed by the reserves of gold and silver, nor it is considered necessary to do so. Full backing of paper currency by reserves of gold prevailed in the past when gold standard or silver standard type of monetary system existed. According to the modern economic thinking the magnitude of currency issued should be determined by the monetary needs of the economy and not by the available reserves of gold and silver. As mentioned in the last chapter, as in other developed countries, since 1957 Reserve Bank of India follows Minimum Reserve System of issuing currency. Under this system, minimum reserves of ₹ 200 crores of gold and other approved securities (such as dollars, pound sterling, etc.) have to be kept and against this any amount of currency can be issued depending on the monetary requirements of the economy.

As stated earlier, RBI is not bound to convert notes into equal value of gold or silver. In the present times currency is inconvertible. The words written on the note, say 100 rupee notes and signed by the governor of RBI that '*I promise to pay the bearer a sum of 100 rupees*' are only a legacy of the past and do not imply its convertibility into gold or silver. Another important thing to note is that paper currency or coins are *fiat money*, which means that currency notes and metallic coins serve as money on the basis of the *fiat* (*i.e.* order) of the Government. In other words, on the authority of the Government no one can refuse to accept them in payment for the transaction made. That is why they are called *legal tender*.

Demand Deposits with the Public

The other important component of money supply are demand deposits of the public with the banks. These demand deposits held by the public are also called *bank money* or *deposit money*. Deposits with the banks are broadly divided into two types: demand deposits and time deposits. Demand deposits in the banks are those deposits which can be withdrawn by drawing cheques on them. Through cheques these deposits can be transferred to others for making payments from whom goods and services have been purchased. Thus, cheques make these demand deposits as a medium of exchange and therefore make them to serve as money. It may be noted that demand deposits are *fiduciary money proper*. Fiduciary money is one which functions as money on the basis of *trust* of the persons who make payment rather than on the basis of the authority of Government. Thus, despite the fact that demand deposits and cheques through which they are operated are not legal tender, they function as money on the basis of the trust commanded by those who draw cheques on them. They are money as they are generally acceptable as medium of payment.

Bank deposits are created when people deposit currency with them. But far more important is that banks themselves create deposits when they give advances to businessmen and others. On the

1. S. B. Gupta, *Monetary Economics : Institutions, Theory and Policy*, S. Chand & Co., New Delhi, 3rd Edition, 1997, p. 272.

basis of small cash reserves of currency, they are able to create a much larger amount of demand deposits through a system called *fractional reserve system* which will be explained later in detail.

In the developed countries such as USA and Great Britain deposit money accounted for over 80 per cent of the total money supply, currency being a relatively small part of it. This is because banking system has greatly developed there and also people have developed banking habits. On the other hand, in the developing countries banking has not developed sufficiently and also people have not acquired banking habits and they prefer to make transactions in currency. However in India after 50 years of independence and economic development the proportion of bank deposits in the money supply has risen to about 50 per cent.

FOUR MEASURES OF MONEY SUPPLY

Several definitions of money supply have been given and therefore various measures of money supply based on them have been estimated. First, different components of money supply have been distinguished on the basis of the different functions that money performs. For example, demand deposits, credit card and currency are used by the people primarily as a medium of exchange for buying goods and services and making other transactions. Obviously, they are money because they are used as a medium of exchange and are generally referred to as $M1$. Another measure of money supply is $M3$ which includes both $M1$ and time deposits held by the public in the banks. Time deposits are money that people hold as store of value.

The main reason why money supply is classified into various measures on the basis of its functions is that effective predictions can be made about the likely effects on the economy of changes in the different components of money supply. For example, if $M1$ is increasing fastly it can be reasonably expected that pepole are planning to make a large number of transactions. On the other hand, if time deposits component of money supply measure $M3$ which serves as a store of value is increasing rapidly, it can be validly concluded that people are planning to save more and accordingly consume less. Therefore, it is believed that for monetary analysis and policy formulation, a single measure of money supply is not only inadequate but may be misleading too. Hence various measures of money supply are prepared to meet the needs of monetary analysis and policy formulation.

Recently in India as well as in some developed countries, four concepts of money supply have been distinguished. The definition of money supply given above represents a narrow measure of money supply and is generally described as $M1$. From April 1977, the Reserve Bank of India has adopted four concepts of money supply in its analysis of the quantum of and variations in money supply. These four concepts of measures of money supply are explained below.

1. Money Supply M1 or Narrow Money. This is the narrow measure of money supply and is composed of the following items:

$$M1 = C + DD + OD$$

where C = Currency with the public

DD = Demand deposits with the public in the commercial and cooperative banks.

OD = Other deposits held by the public with Reserve Bank of India.

The money supply is the most liquid measure of money supply as the money included in it can be easily used as a medium of exchange, that is, as a means of making payments for transactions.

Currency with the public (C) in the above measure of money supply consists of the following:

(*i*) Notes in circulation.

(*ii*) Circulation of rupee coins as well as small coins

(*iii*) Cash reserves on hand with all banks.

Note that in measuring demand deposits with the public in the banks (*i.e., DD*), inter-bank deposits, that is, deposits held by a bank in other banks are excluded from this measure.

In the other deposits with Reserve Bank of India (*i.e., OD*) deposits held by the Central and State Governments and a few others such as RBI Employees Pension and Provident Funds are excluded. However, these other deposits of Reserve Bank of India include the following items :

(*i*) Deposits of Institutions such UTI, IDBI, IFCI, NABARD etc.

(*ii*) Demand deposits of foreign Central Banks and foreign Governments.

(*iii*) Demand deposits of IMF and World Bank.

It may be noted that other deposits of Reserve Bank of India constitute a very small proportion (less than one per cent).

Money Supply *M2*

M2 is a broader concept of money supply in India than *M*1. In addition to the three items of *M*1, the concept of money supply M2 includes savings deposits with the post office savings banks. Thus,

M2 = M1 + Savings deposits with the post office savings banks.

The reason why money supply M2 has been distinguished from *M*1 is that saving deposits with post office savings banks are not as liquid as demand deposits with commercial and co-operative banks as they are not chequable accounts. However, saving deposits with post offices are more liquid than time deposits with the banks.

Money Supply *M3* or Broad Money

M3 is a broad concept of money supply. In addition to the items of money supply included in measure *M*1, in money supply M_3 time deposits with the banks are also included. Thus

M3 = *M*1 + Time Deposits with the banks.

It is generally thought that time deposits serve as store of value and represent savings of the people and are not liquid as they cannot be withdrawn through drawing cheque on them. However, since loans from the banks can be easily obtained against these time deposits, they can be used if found necessary for transaction purposes in this way. Further, they can be withdrawn at any time by forgoing some interest earned on them.

It may be noted that recently *M3* has become a popular measure of money supply. The working group on monetary reforms under the chairmanship of Late Prof. Sukhamoy Chakravarty recommended its use for monetary planning of the economy and setting target of the growth of money supply in terms of *M3*. Therefore, recently RBI in its analysis of growth of money supply and its effects on the economy has shifted to the use of M_3 measure of money supply. In the terminology of money supply employed by the Reserve Bank of India till April 1977, this M3 was called *Aggregate Monetary Resources* (AMR).

Money Supply M4

The measure *M4* of money supply includes not only all the items of M3 described above but also the total deposits with the post office savings organisation. However, this excludes contributions made by the public to the national saving certificates. Thus, *M4* = *M3* + *Total Deposits* with *Post Office Savings Organisation.*

Let us summarise the four concepts of money supply as used by Reserve Bank of India in the following tabular form:

Money Supply

M1	*M2*	*M3*	*M4*
=	=	=	=
Currency (*C*)	*M1*	*M1*	*M3*
+	+	+	+
Demand Deposits (*D*)	Savings Deposits with Post Office Savings Banks	Time Deposits with the Banks	Total Deposits of Post Office Savings Organisation (excluding NSC)
+			
Other Deposits of RBI (*OD*)			

DETERMINANTS OF MONEY SUPPLY : MONEY MULTIPLIER THEORY

In order to explain the determinants of money supply in an economy we shall use M_1 concept of money supply which is the most fundamental concept of money supply. We shall denote it simply by *M* rather than M1. As seen above, this concept of money supply is composed of currency held by the public (C_p) and demand deposits with the banks (D). Thus

$$M = C_p + D \qquad \ldots(1)$$

where
M = Total money supply with the public
C_p = Currency with the public
D = Demand deposits held by the public

The two important determinants of money supply as described in equation (1) are (*a*) the amounts of high-powered money which is also called *Reserve Money* by the Reserve Bank of India and (*b*) the size of money multiplier. We explain below the role of these two factors in the determination of money supply in the economy.

1. **High-Powered Money (*H*).** The high-powered money which we denote by *H* consists of the currency (notes and coins) issued by the Government and the Reserve Bank of India. A part of the currency issued is held by the public, which we designate as C_p and a part is held by the banks as reserves which we designate as *R*. A part of these currency reserves of the banks is held by them in their own cash vaults and a part is deposited in the Reserve Bank of India in the Reserve Accounts which banks hold with RBI. Accordingly, the high-powered money can be obtained as sum of currency held by the public and the part held by the banks as reserves. Thus

$$H = C_p + R \qquad \ldots(2)$$

where
H = the amount of high-powered money
C_p = Currency held by the public
R = Cash Reserves of currency with the banks.

It is worth noting that Reserve Bank of India and Government are *producers of the high-powered money* and the commercial banks do not have any role in producing this high-powered money (*H*). However, commercial banks are *producers of demand deposits* which are also used as money like currency. But for producing demand deposits or credit, banks have to keep with themselves cash *reserves of currency* which have been denoted by *R* in equation (2) above. Since these cash reserves with the banks serve as a basis for the multiple creation of demand deposits which constitute an important part of total money supply in the economy, it provides high-poweredness to the currency issued by Reserve Bank and Government. A glance at equations (1) and (2) above will reveal that the difference in the two equations, one describing the total money supply and the other high-powered money, is that whereas in the former, demand deposits (*D*) are added to the currency held by the public, in the latter it is cash reserves (*R*) of the banks that are added to the currency held by the public. In fact, it is against these cash reserves (*R*) that banks are able to create a multiple expansion of credit or demand deposits due to which there is large expansion in money supply in the economy.

The theory of determination of money supply is based on the supply of and demand for high-powered money. Some economists therefore call it *the 'H Theory of Money Supply*[2]. However, it is more popularly called '*Money-Multiplier Theory of Money Supply*' because it explains the determination of money supply as a certain multiple of the high-powered money. How the high-powered money (H) is related to the total money supply is graphically depicted in Fig. 19.1. T*he base of this figure shows the supply of high-powered money (H), while the top of the figure shows the total stock of money* supply. It will be seen that the total stock of money supply (that is, the top) is determined by a multiple of the high-powered money (H). It will be further seen that whereas currency held by the public (C_p) uses the same amount of high-powered money, that is, there is one-to-one relationship between currency held by the public and the money supply. In sharp contrast to this, bank deposits (D) are a multiple of the cash reserves (R) of the banks which are part of the supply of high-powered money. That is, one rupee of high-powered money kept as bank reserves gives rise to much more amount of demand deposits. Thus, the relationship between money supply and the high-powered money is determined by the money multiplier. The money multiplier which we denote by m is the ratio of total money supply (M) to the stock of high-powered money, that is, $m = \frac{M}{H}$. The size of money multiplier depends on the preference of the public to hold currency relative to deposits, (that is, ratio of currency to deposits which we denote by K) and banks' desired cash reserves ratio to deposits which we call r. We explain below the precise multiplier relationship between high-powered money and the total stock of money supply.

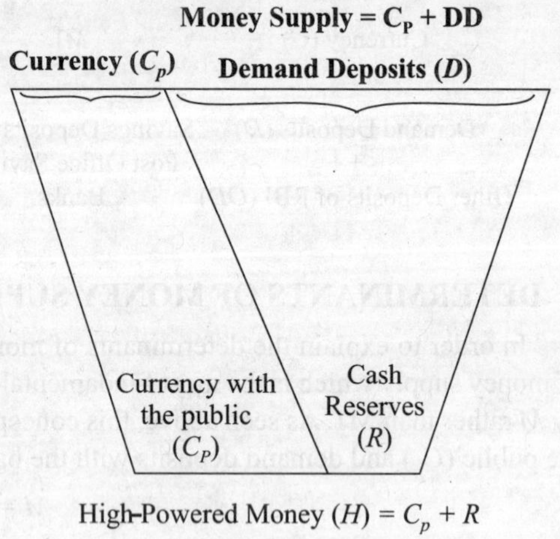

Fig. 19.1. *The High-Powered Money and the Stock of Total Money Supply*

It follows from above that if there is increase in currency held by the public which is a part of the high-powered money with demand deposits remaining unchanged, there will be a direct increase in the money supply in the economy because this constitutes a part of the money supply. If instead currency reserves held by the banks increase, this will not change the money supply immediately but will set in motion a process of multiple creation of demand deposits of the public in the banks. Although banks use these currency reserves held by the public which constitutes a part of the high-powered money to give more loans to the businessmen and thus create demand deposits, they do not affect either the amount of currency or the composition of high-powered money. The *amount of high-powered money is fixed by RBI by its past actions. Thus, changes in high-powered money are the result of decisions of Reserve Bank of India or the Government which owns and controls it.*

2. **Money Multiplier.** As stated above, money multiplier is the degree to which money supply is expanded as a result of the increase in high-powered money. Thus

$$m = \frac{M}{H}$$

Rearranging we have, $$M = H.m \qquad ...(3)$$

2. See S.B. Gupta, *Monetary Economics: Institutions, Theory and Policy*, 3rd Edition, 1992, S. Chand & Co., New Delhi.

Thus money supply is determined by the size of money multiplier (m) and the amount of high-powered money (H). If we know the value of money multiplier we can predict how much money will change when there is a change in the amount of high-powered money. As mentioned above, change in the high-powered money is decided and controlled by Reserve Bank of India, the money multiplier determines the extent to which decision by RBI regarding the change in high-powered money will bring about change in the total money supply in the economy.

Size of Money Multiplier

Now, an important question is: what determines the size of money multiplier ? It is the cash or currency reserve ratio r of the banks (which determines deposit multiplier) and currency-deposit ratio of the public (which we denote by k) which together determines size of money multiplier. We derive below the expression for the size of multiplier.

From equation (1) above, we know that total money supply (M) consists of currency with the public (C_p) and demand deposits with the banks. Thus

$$M = C_p + D \quad \ldots (1)$$

The public hold the amount of currency in a certain ratio of demand deposits with the banks. Let this currency-deposit ratio be devoted by k,

$$C_p = kD$$

Substituting kD for C_p in equation (1) we have

$$M = kD + D = (k + 1)D \quad \ldots (2)$$

Now take equation which defines high-powered money (H) as

$$H = C_p + R \quad \ldots (3)$$

where R represents cash or currency reserves which banks keep as a certain ratio of their deposits and is called cash-reserve ratio and is denoted by r. Thus

$$R = rD$$

Now substituting rD for R and kD for C_p in equation (3) we have

$$H = kD + rD$$

$$H = (k + r) D \quad \ldots (4)$$

Now money multiplier is ratio of total money supply to the high-powered money, therefore we divide equation (1) by equation (4), to get the value of multiplier, which we denote by m. Thus

$$m = \frac{M}{H} = \frac{(k+1)D}{(k+r)D} = \frac{k+1}{k+r}$$

or, Money multiplier $(m) = \frac{M}{H} = \frac{1+k}{r+k}$

or

$$M = H\frac{1+k}{r+k} \quad \ldots (5)$$

where r = Reserve ratio of the *banks*

k = Currency-deposit ratio of the *public*.

From above it follows that money supply is determined by the high-powered money (which is also called reserve money) times the *money multiplier which is equal to* $\frac{1+k}{r+k}$. Thus the following factors determine money supply in the economy:

1. H, that is, the amount of high-powered money.
2. r, that is, *cash reserve ratio* of banks (*i.e.*, ratio of currency reserves to deposits in the banks). This cash reserve ratio of banks determines the magnitude of money multiplier. The smaller the cash reserve ratio of the banks, the larger is the money multiplier.
3. k, that is, *currency-deposit ratio of the public*. The smaller the currency-deposit ratio of the public, the larger is the size of money multiplier.

From equation (4) expressing the determinants of money supply, it follows that *money supply will increase* :

1. When the supply of high-powered money (*i.e.*, reserve money) H increases;
2. When the currency-deposit ratio (k) of the public decreases[3]; and
3. When the ratio of currency reserves to deposits of the banks (*i.e.*, cash reserve ratio) of the banks (r) falls.

The Reserve Ratio and the Deposit Multiplier

In a later chapter we will see that because of *fractional reserve system*, with a small increase in cash reserves with the banks, they are able to create a multiple increase in total demand deposits which are an important part of money supply. The ratio of change in total deposits to a change in reserves is called the *deposit multiplier* which depends on cash reserve ratio. The value of deposit multiplier is the reciprocal of cash reserve ratio, $\left(d_m = \frac{1}{r}\right)$ where d_m stands for deposit multiplier. If cash reserve ratio is 10 per cent of deposits, then $d_m = \frac{1}{0.10} = 10$. Thus deposit multiplier of 10 shows that for every ₹ 100 increase in cash reserves with the banks, there will be expansion in demand deposits of the banks by ₹ 1000 assuming that no leakage of cash to the public occurs during the process of deposit expansion by the banks. In India, this currency-reserve ratio of banks is called Cash Reserve Ratio (CRR) and is regulated by RBI.

Currency-Deposit Ratio of the Public and Multiplier

However, in the real world, with the increase in reserves of the banks, demand deposits and money supply do not increase to the full extent of deposit multiplier. This is for two reasons. First, the public does not hold all its money balances in the form of demand deposits with the banks. When as a result of increase in cash reserves banks start increasing demand deposits, the people may also like to have some more currency with them as money balances. This means during the process of creation of demand deposits by banks, some currency is leaked out from the banks to the people. This drainage of currency to the people in the real world reduces the magnitude of expansion of demand deposit and therefore the size of money multiplier. Suppose the cash reserve ratio is 10 per cent and cash or currency of ₹ 100 is deposited in a bank *A*. The bank *A* will lend out ₹ 90 and therefore create demand deposit of ₹ 90 and so the process will continue as the borrowers use these deposits for payment through cheques to others who deposit them in another bank *B*. However, if borrower of bank *A* withdraws ₹ 10 in cash from the bank and issues cheques of the

---

3. It will be noticed that in the equation $M = H\frac{1+k}{r+k}$ k appears both in the numerator and denominator. *While in the numerator k is added to unity, in the denominator it is added to fraction*. Mathematically, it means that a fall in k will affect the denominator relatively more than the numerator. Therefore, with fall in k, the value of multiplier term $\frac{1+k}{r+k}$, will increase. Thus, with decrease in k, the money supply will increase and *vice versa*.

remaining borrowed amount of ₹ 80, then bank *B* will have only ₹ 80 as new deposits instead of ₹ 90 which it would have if cash of ₹ 10 was not withdrawn by the borrower. With these new deposits of ₹ 80, bank *B* will create demand deposits of ₹ 72, that is, it will lend out ₹ 72 and keep ₹ 8 as reserves with it $\left(80 \times \frac{10}{100} = 8\right)$. The drainage of currency may occur during all the subsequent stages of deposit expansion in the banking system. The greater the leakage of currency, the lower will be the money multiplier. We thus see the currency-deposit ratio, which we denote by *k*, is an important determinant of the actual value of money multiplier.

It is important to note that deposit multiplier works both ways, positively when cash reserves with banks increase, and negatively when the cash reserves with the banks decline. That is, when there is a decrease in currency reserves with the banks, there will be multiple contraction in demand deposits with the banks.

Excess Reserves

In the explanation of the expansion of demand deposits or deposit multiplier we assumed that banks do not keep currency reserves in excess of the *required* cash reserve ratio. The ratio *r* in the deposit multiplier is the *required cash reserve ratio* fixed by Reserve Bank of India. However, banks like to keep with themselves some excess reserves, the amount of which depends on the extent of liquidity (*i.e.* availability of cash with them) and profitability of making investment and rate of interest on loans advanced to business firms. Therefore, the *desired reserve ratio* is greater than the statutory minimum required reserve ratio. Obviously, the holding of excess reserves by the banks also reduces the value of deposit multiplier.

Conclusion

Theory of determination of money supply explains how a given supply of high-powered money (which is also called *monetary base or reserve money*) leads to multiple expansion in money supply through the working of money multiplier. We have seen above how a small increase in reserves of currency with the banks leads to a multiple expansion in demand deposits by the banks through the process of deposit multiplier and thus causes growth of money supply in the economy. Deposit multiplier measures how much increase in demand deposits (or money supply) occurs as a result of a given increase in cash or currency, reserves with the banks depending on the required cash reserve ratio (*r*) if there are no cash drainage from the banking system. But in the real world drainage of currency does take place which reduces the extent of expansion of money supply following the increase in cash reserves with the banks. Therefore, *the deposit multiplier exaggerates the actual increase in money supply from a given increase in cash reserves with the banks*. In contrast, money multiplier takes into account these leakages of currency from the banking system and therefore measures actual increase in money supply when the cash reserves with the banks increase. *The money multiplier can be defined as increase in money supply for every rupee increase in cash reserves (or high-powered money), drainage of currency having been taken into account. Therefore, money multiplier is less than the deposit multiplier.*

It is worth noting that rapid growth in money supply in India has been due to the increase in high-powered money *H*, or what is also called Reserve Money by Reserve Bank of India, the money multiplier remaining almost constant.

The money supply in a country can be changed by Reserve Bank of India by undertaking open market operations, changing minimum required currency reserve-deposit ratio, and by varying the bank rate. The main source of growth in money supply in India is creation of credit by RBI for Government for financing its budget deficit and thus creating high-powered money. Further, though the required currency reserve-deposit ratio of banks can be easily varied by RBI, the actual currency reserve-deposit ratio cannot be so easily varied as reserves maintained by banks not only depend on minimum required cash reserve ratio but also on their willingness to hold excess reserves.

Lastly[4], an important noteworthy point is that though money multiplier does not show much variation in the long run, it can change significantly in the short run causing large variations in money supply. This unpredictable variation in money multiplier in the short run affecting money supply in the economy prevents the Central Bank of a country from controlling exactly and precisely the money supply in the economy.

FACTORS DETERMINING MONEY SUPPLY : RBI'S APPROACH

In its analysis of factors determining money supply in India and sources of variation in it, Reserve Bank of India does not follow any explicit theory of money supply such as money multiplier theory explained above. It provides only purely *accounting or ex-post analysis* of variations in money supply and the factors or sources causing these variations. Although Reserve Bank provides figures of the high powered money in its analysis, it virtually clubs high-powered money with the ordinary money to calculate the total money supply in the country and therefore does not give due importance to the high-powered money as an important factor causing variation in money supply in the economy. Further, *Reserve Bank also does not lay emphasis on the two behavioural ratios, namely, desired currency-deposit ratio (k) of the public and desired cash reserve ratio* (r) of the banks as determinants of money supply, though it provides *ex-post* or realised figures of these ratios. We explain below Reserve Bank's analysis of sources of variation in money supply.

Reserve Bank of India classifies factors determining money supply into the following categories:

(a) Government borrowing from the banking system;

(b) Borrowing of the private or commercial sector from the banking system;

(c) Changes in net foreign assets held by the Reserve Bank of India caused by changes in balance of payments position; and

(d) Government's currency liabilities to the public.

Bank Credit to the Government. When the Government expenditure exceeds government revenue and there is deficit in government's budget, then *it may* resort to borrowing from Reserve Bank of India which creates new currency notes for the purpose. This creation of new currency for financing the deficit of the Central Government Budget is known as *monetistion of deficit*. It was previously called *deficit financing*. Monetisation of deficit is an important source of change in money supply in the economy. It may be noted here that since 1995 when Fiscal Responsibility and Budget Management (FRBM) Act was passed Central Government fiscal deficit is financed by borrowing through selling Government bonds to the banks. This has caused a stoppage of RBI's credit to the Government through monetisation of fiscal deficit. However, for the years 2008-09 and 2009-10 the Government is thinking of *directly borrowing from RBI* by selling its bonds to it and thus monetising a part of its fiscal deficit which has greatly risen due to large increase in Government expenditure incurred to prevent slowdown in economic growth. Thus in recent years budget deficit of the Central Government has been largely financed by borrowing from the commercial banks and other financial institutions who buy government securities or bonds.

The commercial banks also lend money to the Government for purchase of foodgrains by the Food Corporation of India. The creation of credit by the banks when they lend to the Government leads to the increase in money supply in the economy. When the Government uses this bank credit for meeting its expenditure, money supply with the public increases.

Bank Credit to the Commercial or Private Sector. The private sector also borrows from the banking system when its own resources are less than its total expenditure. This also adds to the money supply with the public because when the banks lend they create credit or deposits. Bank deposits, as we have seen above, is a part of money supply in the economy. This also affects the money supply

4. Note that Reserve Bank of India calls the high-powered money as *Reserve Money* (RM).

in the same manner as the Government borrowing from the banking system. There is, however, an important difference. However, the Central Bank can influence the credit supply by the banks to the private sector by changing liquidity with the banks through making changes in cash reserve ratio.

Changes in Net Foreign Exchange Assets. Changes in the foreign exchange assets held by the Reserve Bank can also bring about a change in the money supply. The change in the net foreign assets may be caused by balance of payment situation. Suppose there is deficit in balance of payments and therefore available foreign exchange is less than the country needs to pay for its imports, both visible and invisible. In order to meet this deficit in balance of payments the country will have to dispose of some of its foreign exchange assets. If there is a net deficit in balance of payments, rupees would flow into the Reserve Bank which pays out foreign exchange reserves in return for the rupee currency. This would have the effect of reducing the *Reserve Money* (*i.e.* the high-powered money) in India and the contraction of money supply with the public. Opposite result would follow when there is a net surplus in balance of payments of a country.

It follows from above that a deficit in the balance of payments decreases the supply of rupee currency (that is, high-powered or reserve money) in the economy and thereby causes contraction in money supply with the public. On the contrary, a surplus in the balance of payments will increase the foreign exchange assets and thereby will lead to the expansion in reserve money and money supply in the economy.

It may also be noted that apart from surplus in balance of payments foreign exchange reserves or assets may also come through *capital inflows* by either foreign aid or deposits in Indian banks by NRI or foreign direct investment made by foreign companies in India or by portfolio investment by foreign institutional investors (FII). For example, in years 2005 to 2008 there had been a large-scale inflow of foreign exchange through investment made by foreign companies in India. As a result, our foreign exchange reserves substantially went up which resulted in the issue and expansion of rupee currency in circulation. But RBI neutralised its monetary impact to a large extent by mopping up liquidity of the banks through open market operations by selling them Government bonds.

The plenty of foreign exchange received posed a problem of its optimal use during 2005-2008. One proposal was to use foreign exchange reserves to finance the infrastructure projects which are crucial for accelerating economic growth. But argument against this was that the use of foreign exchange reserves will lead to expansion in money supply which would cause higher rate of inflation. The other proposal was that these foreign exchange reserves should be used to import goods in short supply which help in lowering inflation rate. But since September 2008, the opposite problem of *capital outflows* arose due to foreign institutional investors selling shares in Indian stock market and repatriating dollars abroad following the global financial crisis. These capital outflows increased the demand for dollars and caused depreciation of Indian rupee. In order to prevent the rapid depreciation of rupee, RBI sold dollars from its reserves and in return got rupees resulting in decline in the number of rupees in circulation, that is, decrease in money supply.

(*d*) **Government's Currency Liabilities to the Public.** Changes in money supply in the economy are also brought about by Government's currency liabilities to the public. Coins and one-rupee notes represent Government's currency liabilities to the public. On January 28, 2005, there were ₹ 7374 crores of coins and one-rupee notes as compared to ₹ 7296 crores on March 31, 2004. If Government's currency liabilities increase, the money supply also increases.

FISCAL DEFICITS AND MONEY SUPPLY

A budget deficit is also an important source of expansion of money supply in the economy. There are two possible links between budget deficit and growth in money supply. First, when following an expansionary fiscal policy the government raises its expenditure without financed by extra taxation and thereby causing a budget deficit, it will tend to raise interest rate. This happens when budget deficit is financed through borrowing from the market. As a result, demand for money or loanable funds increases which, given the supply of money, causes interest rate to rise. Rise in interest rate tends to reduce or crowd out private investment. If the Central Bank is following the policy of a fixed interest rate target, when the government resorts to borrowing to finance the budget deficit, then to prevent the rise in interest rate the Central Bank will take steps to increase the money supply in the economy.

The second link between budget deficit and expansion in money supply is direct. This occurs when the Central Bank itself purchases government securities when the government resorts to borrowing.[5] The Central Bank is said to *monetise* budget deficit when it purchases government securities as it prints new notes for the purpose and gives it to the government for meeting public expenditure. In some countries such as the U.S, Federal Reserve (which is the Central Bank of the USA) enjoys a good deal of independence from the Treasury (*i.e.,* the Government) and voluntarily decides when and how much to purchase government securities to finance its budget deficit.

Central Bank's Dilemma

The Central Bank of a country faces a dilemma in deciding whether or not to monetise budget deficit. If the Central Bank does not monetise budget deficit to meet its increased expenditure, the government will borrow from the market and in the absence of any accommodating monetary policy this will tend to raise interest rate and thereby *reduce or crowd out private investment.* Referring to the policy of Federal Reserve of the United States, Dornbusch, Fischer and Startz write, " There is accordingly a temptation for the Federal Reserve to prevent crowding out by buying government securities thereby increasing the money supply and hence allows an expansion in income without a rise in interest rates".[6]

But the policy of monetisation of budget deficit by the Central Bank involves a risk. If the economy is working near full-employment level, that is, at near full-production capacity, monetisation of budget deficit will cause inflation in the economy. However, if the economy is in the grip of a severe depression, the risk of causing inflation through monetisation of budget deficit and consequent growth in money supply is not much there.

It follows from above that in any particular case the Central Bank, if it enjoys freedom from the Government, has to judge whether it should adopt accommodatory monetary policy to achieve its goal of interest-targeting or allow fiscal expansion through monetisation of budget deficit accompanied by the tight monetary policy to check inflation. It is the latter course of action that was adopted by Reserve Bank of India before 1995 when government's fiscal deficit was high and a good part of it was monetised by it.

MONEY SUPPLY AND THE OPEN ECONOMY

The transactions of an open economy also affect the growth of money supply in it. In the open economy there is free flow of goods and services through trade with foreign countries. Besides, in the open economy there are flows of capital between countries. The impact of transactions of an open economy on the money supply can be better understood from national income identity of an open economy. National income of the open economy is written as

$$Y = C + I + G + NX \qquad \ldots (1)$$

or

$$NX = Y - (C + I + G) \qquad \ldots (2)$$

where NX stands for net exports or trade balance. In the trade balance if we also include exports and imports of services (*i.e.,* invisibles), then NX can be taken as current account balance.

The current account balance (NX) can be either positive or negative. If in equation (2) above

5. It is important to note that when government borrows from the market, it does so through sale of its securities (*i.e.* bonds)
6. Dornbusch, Fischer, and Startz, *op.cit.* 9th edition, 2004, p.275.

aggregate expenditure ($C + I + G$) exceeds national output (Y), current account balance or NX will be negative, that is, imports will be greater than exports. In other words, there will be deficit in current account of the balance of payments. On the other hand, if aggregate expenditure is less than national income [$(C + I + G) < NX$], there will be surplus in current account balance of payments. This implies that our exports will be greater than imports.

Now, if in a year there is deficit in current account, that is, NX is negative, it means our demand for foreign exchange, say the US dollars, for imports of goods and services will exceed the supply of foreign exchange. This situation is depicted in Fig. 19.2 where the curve DD represents demand curve for foreign exchange (US \$) and SS is the su ply curve of foreign exchange (US \$) at exchange rate (₹ per US dollar) *i.e.*, OR and LK represents deficit in current account.

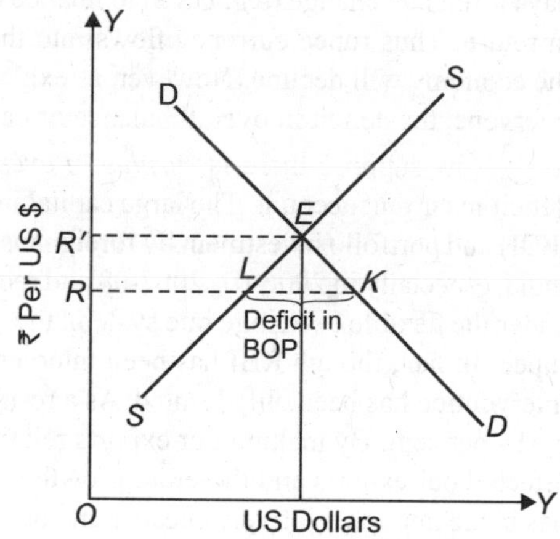

Fig. 19.2. *Deficit in Balance of Payments and Foreign Exchange Market*

If the economy is under flexible exchange rate regime and the Central Bank of the country does not intervene at all, the exchange rate will change to OR' and as a result deficit in current account balance will be eliminated and equilibrium restored at the new exchange rate. If there is such a situation, there is no impact on the money supply. However, if the Central Bank wants to maintain the exchange rate at OR, then current account deficit equal to LK has to be met. If there are no capital inflows, then to maintain the exchange rate at OR, the Central Bank of the country has to supply foreign exchange equal to LK out of the reserves held by it. But when the Central Bank (RBI in case of India) pays out foreign exchange from its reserves, *it will receive money (i.e., rupees in India)* from *importers of goods and services in return for foreign exchange paid to them to meet the deficit*. Thus some money (say Indian rupees) will flow into the Central Bank and thus withdrawn from circulation. As a result of Central Bank intervention to meet the current account deficit and to maintain the exchange rate money supply in the economy decreases. It is important to note that the Central Bank of the country cannot go on supplying foreign exchange reserves, year after year, for a long time because foreign exchange assets with the Central Bank are available in limited amcunt.

The above analysis of expansion in money supply as a result of use of foreign exchange reserves to meet the current account deficit is based on the two assumptions. First, it is assumed that there are no capital flows to meet the deficit in current account balance. Second, it is assumed the exchange rate is not allowed to change as a result of imbalance between demand and supply of foreign exchange due to current account deficit.

Capital inflows. However, if there are sufficient net capital inflows accruing from the capital account of balance of payments, then deficit in current account (*i.e.*, negative NX) can be met by these capital inflows. In this case there will be no impact of deficit in current account balance of payments on money supply in the economy.

Now take the opposite case of surplus in current account balance (*i.e.*, when NX is positive). This implies that the supply of foreign exchange exceeds demand for it. In the absence of capital outflows this excess supply of foreign exchange will have to be purchased by the Central Bank if exchange rate is to be maintained. The Central Bank (RBI) will print new notes to pay for the purchase of foreign exchange. This will lead to the increase in money supply in the economy. However, if exchange rate is allowed to change, as is the case under flexible exchange rate system, the exchange rate will adjust to bring supply and demand for foreign exchange in equilibrium.

Overall Balance of Payments and Capital Inflows

When in an open economy with flexible exchange rate regime there is *deficit in overall balance of payments* (*i.e.,* on both current and capital accounts), it means that capital inflows are insufficient to bridge the gap in the balance of payments, then, in case of India, this has to be met with use of foreign exchange reserves by the Reserve Bank of India. When Reserve Bank of India pays foreign exchange (*e.g.* US $) to finance the deficit in overall balance of payments, it gets rupees in return. Thus rupee currency flows into the RBI. As a result, money supply (rupee currency) in the economy will decline. However, as explained above, under flexible rate system, if RBI does not intervene, the deficit in overall balance of payments will cause rupee to depreciate.

Now suppose there is *surplus in overall balance of payment* as capital inflows exceed the deficit in current account. The large capital inflows can occur due to heavy foreign direct investment (FDI) and portfolio investment by foreign institutional investors (FII) as it happened in some years in India, especially in 2006-07, 2007-08 and recently in 2010-11. In the absence of intervention by RBI under the flexible exchange rate system, these large capital inflows will cause appreciation of Indian rupee. In fact, though RBI has been intervening in foreign exchange market from time to time, its intervention has been only limited. As a result, between Oct. 2006 and Oct. 2007, rupee appreciated by 15 per cent. By making our exports relatively expensive the appreciation of rupee has adversely affected our exports and therefore growth in GNP and employment. Besides, appreciation of rupee has made imports relatively cheaper and has led to large imports of goods and materials and thereby harming our domestic manufacturing industries.

To prevent the high appreciation of the Indian rupee RBI has been purchasing US dollars from the foreign exchange market from time to time. When RBI purchases dollars from the foreign exchange market, it pays rupees to the sellers of foreign exchange. To do so more rupee currency is printed by RBI to pay for US dollars purchased by it. In this way more rupee currency (*i.e.,* high–powered money) comes into existence in the economy. Thus intervention by RBI to prevent appreciation of rupee results in increase in money supply in the economy.

On the other hand, in 2011 and again in 2013 the RBI faced the opposite problem of depreciation. When, after August 2011, there was net *large capital outflow* from India due to uncertainty caused by European debt crisis and economic slowdown in the U.S, the FIIs started selling Indian equity and bonds and converting rupees into US dollars. This led to the increase in demand for dollars resulting in appreciation of US dollar and *depreciation of Indian rupee*. The value of rupee which was around ₹ 45 to a US dollar in the first week of September 2011 depreciated to around ₹ 53 in the second week of November 2011 and further to ₹ 54 in mid-December 2011. This depreciation of rupee will make our imports constlier which will tend to raise inflation if not matched by fall in international commodity prices. To prevent sharp depreciation of rupee the RBI intervened in the foreign exchange market by selling dollars in the market. As a result in the first week of January 2012 it moved in the range of ₹ 51 to ₹ 52 to a US dollar. Again its intervention was only limited. In fact, the RBI has no fixed target for maintaining exchange rate of rupee at any level and instead its policy is to *allow exchange rate of rupee to fluctuate within a band. In fact, RBI faces a dilemma which we discuss below.*

RBI Dilemma : External Balance and Internal Balance

RBI faces a dilemma because if it does not intervene in the face of large capital inflows, rupee will appreciate much which will adversely affect our exports and therefore growth of GNP and employment in our economy. On the other hand, if it intervenes and purchases enough US dollars from the market to prevent any appreciation of rupee, it will cause large increase in money supply that would cause higher rate of inflation. A major objective of RBI is to control inflation. Therefore, RBI has to strike a balance between the two alternatives. It has been intervening in the foreign exchange market to prevent large appreciation of rupee. But it cannot buy inflows of foreign exchange indiscriminately as it leads to higher inflation. RBI has also resorted to *sterilization* of increase in money supply by selling government securities to the banks and thereby getting back the money issued by it. But there is a limit to this sterilization operation as it has not unlimited amount of government securities to sell them to the banks. Hence the dilemma faced by it. We explain the sterilization operations by RBI later.

It follows from above that the two objectives of external balance and internal balance clash with each other. External balance occurs when balance of payments is in equilibrium or close to it. When external balance does not exist the Central Bank will either go on losing foreign exchange reserves which it cannot do so for long or it will be gaining foreign exchange reserves which also poses a problem as it leads to increase in money supply and causes inflationary pressures in the economy.

On the other hand, internal balance exists when the economy is in equilibrium at full employment or full productive capacity level without any inflationary pressures. Thus, to ensure internal balance requires that money supply should not be allowed to increase much. Since the two require different types of policy measure by the Central Bank, they clash with each other. Hence, the dilemma faced by the Central Bank.

Sterilization by the Central Bank

Sterilization provides a way out of the problem of clash between the goals of external balance and internal balance. *Sterilization refers to the action by the Central Bank of a country to offset or cancel the impact of its foreign exchange market intervention on the money supply through open market operations.* The sterilization measures can be used both to offset the reduction in money supply when in case of current account deficit the Central Bank of the country sells foreign exchange in the market and also when the Central Bank offsets the effect of increase in money supply when it buys foreign exchange from the market in case of surplus in balance of payments or when large capital inflows are coming into the economy.

Let us first explain sterilization operation by the Central Bank in case of deficit in current account of the balance of payments. As seen above, the deficit in current account balance requires the Central Bank to sell foreign exchange from its reserves to prevent the depreciation of domestic currency (that is, to maintain the exchange rate constant). The sale of foreign exchange in foreign exchange market by the Central Bank causes money supply in the economy to decrease that has deflationary effect on the economy. To avoid this adverse effect, the Central Bank buys government securities (*i.e.,* bonds) through open market operations. When it does so the Central Bank prints domestic currency to pay for the bonds it purchases. In this way money supply in the economy increases which offsets the decrease in money supply brought about by the Central Bank when it sells foreign exchange to prevent the depreciation of the domestic currency. Thus, provided it has enough foreign exchange assets, with sterilization operations by the Central Bank *persistent* deficit in balance of payments is possible because it *insulates* the money supply changes in the domestic economy from the Central Bank intervention in the foreign exchange market.

Sterilization Operations in Case of Surplus in Balance of Payments or Large Capital Inflows

Now, we take up the opposite case when there is surplus in balance of payments or when large capital inflows are taking place. This situation requires that Central Bank intervenes in the foreign exchange market and buys foreign exchange inflows from the market to maintain the foreign exchange rate or to prevent the appreciation of domestic currency. As mentioned above, in the two years (2006 - 08) due to large net capital inflows in the Indian economy there has been a quite large appreciation of the Indian rupee against US dollar that has produced undesirable effects. Therefore Reserve Bank has intervened in the foreign exchange market by buying US dollars to prevent too much appreciation of the Indian rupee. The purchase of foreign exchange (US dollars) from the foreign exchange market by the Reserve Bank has led to the increase in money supply in the Indian economy that has caused inflationary pressures. To sterilize the effect of this increase in money supply RBI has undertaken open market operations by *selling* government securities to the banks which have paid rupees to it. In this way through the sale of government securities some rupee currency has been withdrawn from the economy. In this way inflationary pressures created by the original increase in money supply through intervention in foreign exchange market have been offset.

QUESTIONS FOR REVIEW

1. Explain the concept of money supply. What are the factors responsible for the rapid increase in money supply ?
2. Explain how supply of money depends upon the high-powered money, the currency deposit ratio and cash reserve ratio.
3. Explain the impact of budget deficit on the supply of money in the economy. Explain the Central Bank's dilemma in this connection.
4. Explain the impact of (1) deficit in balance of payments, and (2) large capital inflows on the money supply in the open economy. Explain sterilization operations by the Central Bank of the country in each case.
5. Explain the Reserve Bank's dilemma in the face of large capital inflows in the Indian economy.

CHAPTER 20 Demand for Money and Keynes's Liquidity Preference Theory of Interest

Introduction

Why people have demand for money to hold is an important issue in macroeconomics. The level of demand for money not only determines the rate of interest but also prices and national income of the economy. *Classical economists considered money as simply a means of payment or medium of exchange*. In the classical model, people therefore demand money in order to make payments for their purchase of goods and services. In other words, they want to keep money for transactions purposes. *On the other hand, J.M. Keynes laid stress on the store of value function of money*. According to him, money is an asset and people want to hold it so as to take advantage of changes in the price of this asset, that is, the rate of interest. Therefore, Keynes emphasised another motive for holding money which he called speculative motive. As will be explained in detail below, under speculative motive people demand to hold money balances to take advantages from the future changes in the rate of interest, or what means the same thing, from the future changes in bond prices.

An essential point to be noted about people's demand for money is that what people want is not *nominal* money holdings but *real money balances* (This is also referred to as simply *real balances*). This means that people are interested in the purchasing power of their money holdings, that is, the value of money balances in terms of goods and services which they could buy. Thus, people would not be interested in merely nominal money holdings irrespective of the price level, that is, the number of rupee notes and bank deposits. If with the doubling of price level, nominal money holdings are also doubled, their *real money balances* would remain the same. If people are merely concerned with nominal money holdings irrespective of the price level, they are said to suffer from *money illusion*.

The demand for money has been a subject of lively debate in economics. Interest in the study of demand for money has been due to the important role that monetary demand plays in the determination of the price level, interest and income. Till recently there were three approaches to demand for money, namely, transactions approach of Fisher, Cash-balance approach of Cambridge economists, Marshall and Pigou, and Keynes theory of demand for money. However, in recent years Baumol, Tobin and Friedman have put forward new theories of demand for money. We critically examine below all these theories of demand for money.

FISHER'S TRANSACTIONS APPROACH TO DEMAND FOR MONEY

In his theory of demand for money Fisher[1] and other classical economists laid stress on the medium of exchange function of money, that is, money as a means of buying goods and services. All transactions involving purchase of goods, services, raw materials, assets require payment of money as value of the transaction made. If accounting identity, namely value paid must equal value received is to occur, value of goods, services and assets sold must be equal to the value of money paid for them. Thus, in any given period, the value of all goods, services or assets sold must equal to the number of transactions T made multiplied by the average price of these transactions. Thus, the total value of

1. Irving Fisher, *Purchasing Power of Money,* Macmillan, 1911.

transactions made is equal to *PT*.

On the other hand, because value paid is identically equal to the value of money flow used for buying goods, services and assets, the value of money flow is equal to the nominal quantity of money supply *M* multiplied by the average number of times the quantity of money in circulation is used or exchanged for transactions purposes. The average number of times a unit of money is used for transactions of goods, services or assets is called *transactions velocity of circulation* and is denoted by *V*.

Symbolically, Fisher's equation of exchange is written as under :

$$MV = PT \qquad \ldots (1)$$

where M = the quantity of money in circulation

V = transactions velocity of circulation

P = Average price

T = the total number of transactions.

The above equation (1) is an identity, that is true by definition. However by taking some assumptions about the variables *V* and *T*, Fisher transformed the above identity into a theory of demand for money.

According to Fisher, the nominal quantity of money *M* is fixed by the Central Bank of a country (note that Reserve Bank of India is the Central Bank of India) and is therefore treated as an exogenous variable which is assumed to be a given quantity in a particular period of time. Further, the number of transactions in a period is a function of national income; the greater the national income, the larger the number of transactions required to be made. Further, *since Fisher assumed that full employment of resources prevailed in the economy, the level of national income is determined by the amount of the fully employed resources*. Thus, with the assumption of full employment of resources, the volume of transactions *T* is fixed in the short run.

But most important assumption which makes Fisher's equation of exchange as a theory of demand for money is that velocity of circulation (*V*) remains constant and is independent of *M*, *P* and *T*. This is because he thought that *velocity of circulation of money (V) is determined by institutional and technological factors involved in the transactions process*. Since these institutional and technological factors do not vary much in the short run, the transactions velocity of circulation of money (*V*) was assumed to be constant.

With the above assumptions, Fisher's equation of exchange can be rewritten as

$$M^d = \frac{PT}{V}$$

or

$$M^d = \frac{1}{V}.PT \qquad \ldots (2)$$

Thus, according to Fisher's transactions approach, demand for money depends on the following three factors:

(1) the number of transactions (*T*)

(2) the average price of transactions (*P*)

(3) the transaction velocity of circulation of money

It has been pointed out that Fisher's transactions approach represents some kind of a mechanica relation between demand for money (M^d) and the total value of transactions (*PT*). Thus Prof. Sura Bhan Gupta says that in Fisher's approach the relation between demand for money M^d and the valu of transactions (*PT*) "betrays some kind of a mechanical relation between it (*i.e. PT*) and M^d as *P* represents the total amount of *work to be done* by money as a medium of exchange. This makes demand for money (M^d) a technical requirement and not a behavioural function"[2].

In Fisher's transactions approach to demand for money some serious problems are faced when it is used for empirical research. First, in Fisher's transactions approach, not only transactions involving current production of goods and services are included but also those which arise in sales and purchase of capital assets such as securities, shares, land etc. Due to frequent changes in the values of these capital assets, it is not appropriate to assume that T will remain constant even if Y is taken to be constant due to full-employment assumption.

The second problem which is faced in Fisher's approach is that it is difficult to define and determine a general price level that covers not only goods and services currently produced but also capital assets just mentioned above.

The Cambridge Cash-Balance Theory of Demand for Money

Cambridge Cash-Balance theory of demand for money was put forward by Cambridge economists Marshall and Pigou[3]. This Cash-Balance theory of demand for money differs from Fisher's transaction approach in that it *places emphasis on the function of money as a store of value or wealth* instead of Fisher's emphasis on the use of money as a medium of exchange. It is worth noting that the exchange function of money eliminates the need to barter and solves the problem of double coincidence of wants faced in the barter system. On the other hand, the function of money as a store of value lays stress on holding money as a general purchasing power by individuals over a period of time between the sale of a good or service and subsequent purchase of a good or service at a later date. Marshall and Pigou focussed their analysis on the factors that determine individual demand for holding cash balances. Although they recognised that current interest rate, wealth owned by the individuals, expectations of future prices and future rate of interest determine the demand for money, they however believed that changes in these factors remain constant or they are proportional to changes in individual's income. Thus, they put forward a view that individual's demand for cash-balances (*i.e.* nominal money balances) is proportional to the nominal income (*i.e.* money income). Thus, according to their approach, aggregate demand for money can be expressed as

$$M^d = kPY$$

where Y = real national income

P = average price level of currently produced goods and services

PY = nominal income

k = proportion of nominal income (PY) that people want to hold as cash balances

Cambridge cash-balance approach to demand for money is illustrated in Fig. 20.1 where on the X-axis we measure nominal national income (PY) and on the Y-axis the demand for money (M^d). It will be seen from Fig. 20.1 that *demand for money (M^d) in this Cambridge cash-balance approach is a linear function of nominal income*. The slope of the function is equal to k, that is, $k = \frac{M^d}{P_y}$. Thus important feature of cash-balance approach is that *it makes the demand for money as function of money income alone*. A merit of this formulation is that it makes the relation between demand for money and income as behavioural in sharp contrast to Fisher's approach in which demand for money was related to total transactions in a mechanical manner.

---

2. S.B. Gupta, *Monetary Economics, Theory, Policy and Institutions*, 4th edition, S. Chand & Co. 1997, p. 183.
3. A.C. Pigou, "Value of Money", *Quarterly Journal of Economics*, Vol. 32, 1917, pp. 38-65.

Although, as mentioned above, Cambridge economists recognised the role of other factors such as rate of interest, wealth as the factors which play a part in the determination of demand for money but these factors were not systematically and formally incorporated into their analysis of demand for money. In their approach, these other factors determine the proportionality factor k, that is, the proportion of money income that people want to hold in the form of money, *i.e.* cash balances. It was J.M. Keynes who later emphasised the role of these other factors such as rate of interest, expectations regarding future interest rate and prices and formally incorporated them explicitly in his analysis of demand for money. Thus, Glahe rightly writes, "*Cambridge approach is conceptually richer than the transactions approach, the former is incomplete because it does not formally incorporate the influence of economic variables just mentioned in the demand for cash balances... John Maynard Keynes first attempted to eliminate this shortcoming.*"[4]

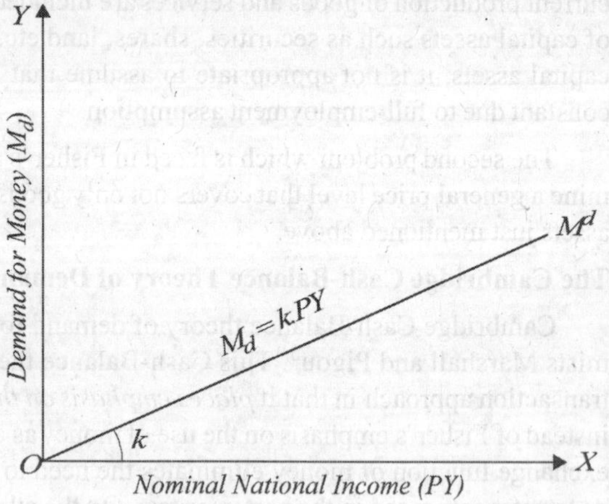

Fig. 20.1 : *Demand for Money : Cambridge Cash Balance Approach*

Another *important feature of Cambridge demand for money function is that the demand for money is proportional function of nominal income* ($M^d = kPY$). Thus, it is proportional function of both price level (P) and real income (Y). This implies two things. First, income elasticity of demand for money is unity and, secondly, price elasticity of demand for money is also equal to unity so that any change in the price level causes equal proportionate change in the demand for money.

Criticism. It has been pointed out by critics that other influences such as rate of interest, wealth, expectations regarding future prices and rate of interest have not been formally introduced into the Cambridge theory of the demand for cash-balances. These other influences remain in the background of the theory. "It was left to Keynes, another Cambridge economist, to highlight the influence of the rate of interest on the demand for money and change the course of monetary theory."[5]

Another criticism levelled against this theory is that income elasticity of demand for money may well be different from unity. Cambridge economists did not provide any theoretical reason for its being equal to unity. Nor is there any empirical evidence supporting unitary income elasticity of demand for money. Besides, price elasticity of demand is also not necessarily equal to unity. In fact, changes in the price level may cause non-proportional changes in the demand for money. However, these criticisms are against the mathematical formulation of cash-balance approach, namely, $M^d = kPY$. They do not deny the important relation between demand for money and the level of income. Empirical studies conducted so far point to a strong evidence that there is a significant and firm relation between demand for money and level of income.

KEYNES'S THEORY OF DEMAND FOR MONEY

In his well-known book[6], Keynes propounded a theory of demand for money which occupies an important place in his monetary theory. It is also worth noting that for demand for money to hold Keynes used the term *liquidity preference*. How much of his income or resources will a person hold in the form of ready money (cash or non-interest-paying bank deposits) and how much will he part

4. Fred R. Glahe, *Macroeconomics: Theory and Policy*, 2nd Edition, 1977, Harcourt, p. 164.
5. S.B. Gupta, *op. cit.*, p. 184.
6. J.M. Keynes, *General Theory of Employment, Interest and Money*, Macmillan, 1936.

with or lend depends upon what Keynes calls his "*liquidity preference*." Liquidity preference means the *demand for money to hold* or the desire of the public to hold cash.

Liquidity preference or demand for money of a particular individual depends upon several considerations. The question is: Why should the people hold their resources liquid or in the form of ready money when they can get interest by lending money or buying bonds? The desire for liquidity arises because of three motives : (*i*) the transactions motive, (*ii*) the precautionary motive, and (*iii*) the speculative motive.

The Transactions Demand for Money. The transactions motive relates to the demand for money or the need for money balances for the current transactions of individuals and business firms. Individuals hold cash in order "to bridge the interval between the receipt of income and its expenditure". In other words, people hold money or cash balances for transactions purposes, because receipt of money and payments do not coincide. Most of the people receive their incomes weekly or monthly while the expenditure goes on day by day. A certain amount of ready money, therefore, is kept in hand to make current payments. This amount will depend upon the size of the individual's income, the interval at which the income is received and the methods of payments prevailing in the society.

The businessmen and the entrepreneurs also have to keep a proportion of their resources in money form in order to meet daily needs of various kinds. They need money all the time in order to pay for raw materials and transport, to pay wages and salaries and to meet all other current expenses incurred by any business firm. It is clear that the amount of money held under this business motive will depend to a very large extent on the turnover (*i.e.*, the volume of trade of the firm in question). The larger the turnover, the larger, in general, will be the amount of money needed to cover current expenses. It is worth noting that money demand for transactions motive arises primarily because of the use of money as a medium of exchange (*i.e.* means of payment).

Since the transactions demand for money arises because individuals have to incur expenditure on goods and services during the receipt of income and its use for payment of goods and services, money held for this motive depends upon the level of income of an individual. A poor man will hold less money for transactions motive as he spends less because of his small income. On the other hand, a rich man will tend to hold more money for transactions motive as his expenditure will be relatively greater.

The demand for money is a demand for *real* cash balances because people hold money for the purpose of buying goods and services. The higher the price level, the more money balances a person has to hold in order to purchase a given quantity of goods. If the price level doubles, then the individual has to keep twice the amount of money balances in order to be able to buy the same quantity of goods. Thus the demand for money balances is demand for *real* rather than *nominal* balances.

According to Keynes, the transactions demand for money depends only on the real income and is not influenced by the rate of interest. However, in recent years, it has been observed empirically and also according to the theories of Tobin and Baumol transactions demand for money also depends on the rate of interest. This can be explained in terms of *opportunity cost* of money holdings. Holding one's asset in the form of money balances has an opportunity cost. The cost of holding money balances is the interest that is foregone by holding money balances rather than other assets. The higher the interest rate, the greater the opportunity cost of holding money rather than non-money assets. Individuals and business firms economise on their holding of money balances by carefully managing their money balances through transfer of money into bonds or short-term income yielding non-money assets. Thus, at higher interest rates, individuals and business firms will keep less money holdings at each level of income.

Precautionary Demand for Money. Precautionary motive for holding money refers to the desire of the people to hold cash balances for unforeseen contingencies. People hold a certain amount of money to provide for the danger of unemployment, sickness, accidents, and the other uncertain perils. The amount of money demanded for this motive will depend on the psychology of the individual and the conditions in which he lives.

Speculative Demand for Money. The speculative motive of the people relates to the desire to hold one's resources in liquid form in order to take advantage of market movements regarding the future changes in the rate of interest (or bond prices). The notion of holding money for speculative motive was a new and revolutionary Keynesian idea. Money held under the speculative motive serves as a store of value as money held under the precautionary motive does. But it is a store of money meant for a different purpose. The cash held under this motive is used to make speculative gains by dealing in bonds[7] whose prices fluctuate. If bond prices are expected to rise which, in other words, means that the rate of interest is expected to fall, businessmen will buy bonds to sell when their prices actually rise. If, however, bond prices are expected to fall, *i.e.*, the rate of interest is expected to rise, businessmen will sell bonds to avoid capital losses. Nothing is certain in the dynamic world, where guesses about the future course of events are made on precarious basis, businessmen keep cash to speculate on the probable future changes in bond prices (or the rate of interest) with a view to making profits.

Given the expectations about the changes in the rate of interest in future, less money will be held under the speculative motive at a *higher current* rate of interest and more money will be held under this motive at a *lower current* rate of interest. The reason for this inverse correlation between money held for speculative motive and the prevailing rate of interest is that at a lower rate of interest less is lost by not lending money or investing it, that is, by holding on to money, while at a higher current rate of interest holders of cash balance would lose more by not lending or investing.

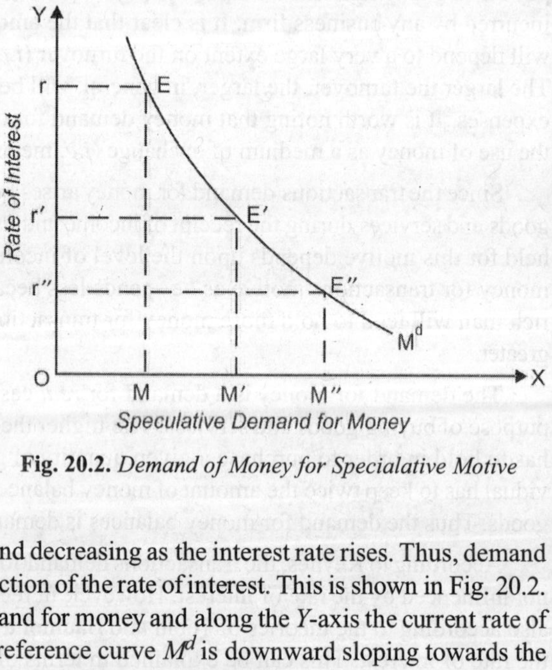

Fig. 20.2. *Demand of Money for Specialative Motive*

Thus the demand for money under speculative motive is a function of the current rate of interest, increasing as the interest rate falls and decreasing as the interest rate rises. Thus, demand for money under this motive is a decreasing function of the rate of interest. This is shown in Fig. 20.2. Along *X*-axis we represent the speculative demand for money and along the *Y*-axis the current rate of interest The demand for money or liquidity preference curve M^d is downward sloping towards the right signifying that the higher the rate of interest, the lower the demand for money for speculative motive, and *vice versa*. Thus at the high current rate of interest *Or*, a very small amount *OM* is held for speculative motive. This is because at a high current rate of interest more money would have been lent out or used for buying bonds and therefore less money would be kept as inactive balances. If the rate of interest falls to *Or*′, then a greater amount of money *OM*′ is held under speculative motive. With the further fall in the rate of interest to *Or*″, money held under speculative motive increases to *OM*″.

Liquidity Trap. It will be seen from Fig. 20.3 that the demand for money or liquidity preference curve M^d or *LP* becomes quite flat *i.e.*, perfectly elastic at a very low rate of interest; it is horizontal

7. All securities and other such papers that yield a fixed and known rate of interest over a period of time are known as bonds.

line beyond point E'' towards the right. This perfectly elastic portion of liquidity preference curve indicates the position of *absolute liquidity* preference of the people. That is, at a very low rate of interest people will hold with them as inactive balances any amount of money they come to have. This portion of liquidity preference curve with absolute liquidity preference is called *liquidity trap* by the economists because expansion in money supply gets trapped in the range of liquidity trap and therefore cannot affect rate of interest and therefore the level of investment. According to Keynes, it is because of the existence of liquidity trap that monetary policy becomes ineffective to tide over economic depression.

But the demand for money to satisfy the speculative motive does not depend so much upon what the current rate of interest is, *as on expectations about changes in the rate of interest*. If there is a change in the expectations regarding the future rate of interest, the whole curve of demand for money or liquidity preference for speculative motive will change accordingly. Thus, if the public on balance expect the rate of interest to be higher (*i.e.*, bond prices to be lower) in the future than had been previously supposed, the speculative demand for money will increase and the whole liquidity preference curve for speculative motive will shift upward.

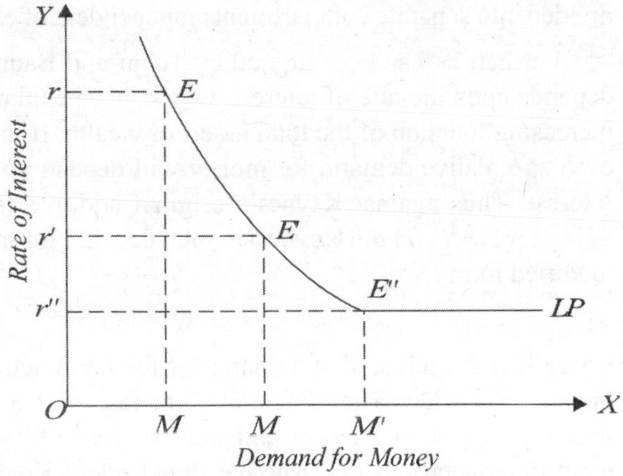

Fig. 20.3. *Liquidity Preference Curve and Liquidity Trop*

Aggregate Demand for Money : Keynes's View

If the total demand for money is represented by M_d we may refer to that part of M held for transactions and precautionary motive as M_1 and to that part held for the speculative motive as M_2. Thus $M_d = M_1 + M_2$. According to Keynes, the money held under the transactions and precautionary motives, *i.e.*, M_1, is completely interest-inelastic unless the interest rate is very high. The amount of money held as M_1, that is, for transactions and precautionary motives, is mainly a function of the size of income and business transactions together with the contingencies growing out of the conduct of personal and business affairs. We can write this in a functional form as follows:

$$M_1 = L_1(Y) \quad \ldots (i)$$

where Y stands for income, L_1 for demand function, and M_1 for money demanded or held under the transactions and precautionary motives. The above function implies that money held under the transactions and precautionary motives is a function of income.

On the other hand, according to Keynes, money demanded for speculative motive, *i.e.*, M_2, as explained above, is primarily a function of the rate of interest. This can be written as:

$$M_2 = L_2(r) \quad \ldots (ii)$$

where r stands for the rate of interest, L_2 for money demand function for speculative motive.

Since total demand for money $M_d = M_1 + M_2$, we get from (*i*) and (*ii*) above

$$M_d = L_1(Y) + L_2(r)$$

Thus, according to Keynes's theory, total demand for money is an *additive demand function* with two separate components. The one component, $L_1(Y)$, representing the transactions demand for money arising out of transactions and precautionary motives is an increasing function of the level of money income. The second component of the demand for money, that is, $L_2(r)$ representing the speculative demand for money, which depends upon rate of interest, is a decreasing function of the rate of interest.

Critique of Keynes's Theory. By introducing speculative demand for money, Keynes made a significant departure from the classical theory of money demand which emphasized only the transactions demand for money. However, Keynes' theory of speculative demand for money has been challenged. Keynes's Theory of demand for money has been criticized on the ground that money represents a single asset and not the several ones there may be more than one motive to hold it and the same unit of money can serve several motives. Therefore, the demand for money cannot be divided into separate compartments independent of each other.

Further, as has been argued by Tobin and Baumol, the transactions demand for money also depends upon the rate of interest. Others have explained that speculative demand for money is an increasing function of the total assets or wealth. If income is taken as a proxy for total wealth then even speculative demand for money will depend upon the size of income, apart from the rate of interest. Thus against Keynes's original additive form of demand for money function, namely $M^d = L_1(Y) + L_2(r)$ the Keynesian total demand for money function is now written in the following modified form :

$$M^d = L(Y, r)$$

where it is conceived that demand for money function (M^d) is increasing function of the level of income, it is a decreasing function of the rate of interest. The presentation of the demand for money function in the above revised and modified form, $M^d = L(Y, r)$ has been a highly significant development in monetary theory. Another drawback of Keynes's speculative demand for money is that *it visualises that people hold their assets in either all money or all bonds*. This seems quite unrealistic as individuals hold their financial wealth in some combination of both money and bonds. This gave rise to *portfolio approach to demand for money* put forward by Tobin, Baumol and Freidman. The portfolio of wealth consists of money, interest-bearing bonds, shares, physical assets etc. Further, while according to Keynes's theory, demand for money for transaction purposes is insensitive tc interest rate, the modern theories of money demand put forward by Baumol and Tobin show that money held for transaction purposes is also interest elastic.

KEYNES'S LIQUIDITY PREFERENCE THEORY OF RATE OF INTEREST

In his epoch-making book *"The General Theory of Employment, Interest and Money"*, J.M. Keynes gave a new view of interest. According to him, the rate of interest is a purely monetary phenomenon and is determined by demand for money and supply of money. According to him, *"interest is a reward for parting with liquidity for a specified period."* Since people prefer liquidity or want to hold money to meet their various motives, they need to be paid some reward for surrendering liquidity or money. And this reward is the rate of interest that must be paid to them in order to induce them to part with liquidity or money. Further, according to Keynes, rate of interest is determined by liquidity preference or demand for money to hold and the supply of money known as *Liqudity Preference Theory.*

The Demand for Money in a Two-Asset Economy. In order to explain the demand for money and interest-rate determination. Kenyes assumed a simplified economy where there are two assets which people can keep in their portfolio balance. These two assets are : (1) money in the form of currency and demand deposits in the banks which earn no interest and (2) long term bonds. It is important to note that rate of interest and bond prices are inversely related. When bond prices go up, rate of interest rises and *vice versa.* The demand for money by the people depends upon how they decide to balance their portfolios between money and bonds. This decision about the portfolio balance can be influenced by two factors.

First, the higher the level of nominal income in a two-asset economy people would want to hold more money in their portfolio balance. This is because of transactions motive according to which at the higher level of nominal income, the purchases by the people of goods and services in their daily life will be relatively larger which require more money to be kept for transactions purposes.

Second, the higher the nominal rate of interest, the lower the demand for money for speculative motive. This is, firstly, because a higher nominal rate of interest implies a higher opportunity cost for holding money. At higher rate of interest holders of money can earn more incomes by holding bonds instead of money. Secondly, if the current rate of interest is higher than what is expected in the future, the people would like to hold more bonds and less money in their portfolio. On the other hand, if the current rate of interest is low (in other words, if the bond prices are currently high), the people will be reluctant to hold larger quantity of bonds (and instead they could hold more money in their portfolio) for the fear that bond prices would fall in the future causing capital losses to them.

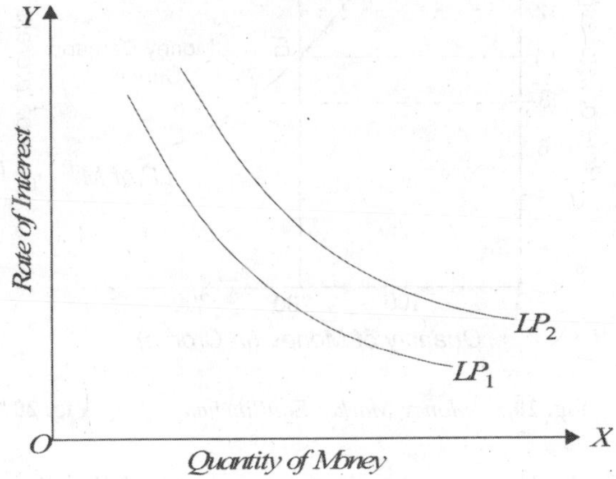

Fig. 20.4. *Demand for Money (Liquidity Preference) depends on Rate of Interest and Level of Income*

Money Demand Curve. It follows from above that quantity of money demanded increases with the fall in the rate of interest or with the increase in level of nominal income. At a given level of nominal income, we can draw a money demand curve showing the quantity of money demanded at various rates of interest. As demand for money is inversely related to the rate of interest, the money demand curve at a given level of income, say Y_1, will be downward-sloping as is shown by the curve LP_1 in Figure 20.4. When the level of money income increases, suppose from Y_1 to Y_2, the curve of demand for money shifts upward to the right the new position LP_2.

Determination of Rate of Interest : Equilibrium in the Money Market

The rate of interest, according to J.M. Keynes, is determined by demand for money (Liquidity Preference) and supply of money. The factors which determine demand for money have been explained above. The supply of money, at a given time, is fixed by the monetary authority of the country. In Figure 20.5 LP or M^d is the demand curve for money at a given level of nominal income. MS is the money supply curve which is a vertical straight line showing that 200 crores of rupees is the money supply fixed by the monetary authority. It will be seen that quantity demanded of money equals the given money supply at 10 per cent rate of interest. So the money market is in equilibrium at 10 per cent rate of interest. There will be disequilibrium if rate of interest is either higher or lower than 10 per cent.

Suppose the rate of interest is 12 per cent. It will be seen from Figure 20.5 that at 12 per cent rate of interest, supply of money exceeds the demand for money. The excess supply of money reflects the fact that people do not want to hold as much money in their portfolio as the monetary authority has made it available to them. The people holding assets in the present two-asset economy would react to this excess money supply with them by buying bonds and thus replace some of money in their portfolios with bonds. Since the *total money supply* at a given moment remains fixed, it cannot be reduced by buying bonds by individuals. The bonds-buying spree would lead to the rise in prices of

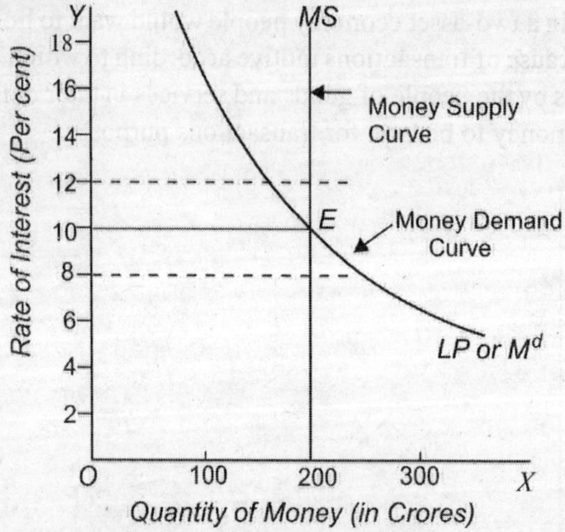

Fig. 20.5. *Money Market Equilibrium*

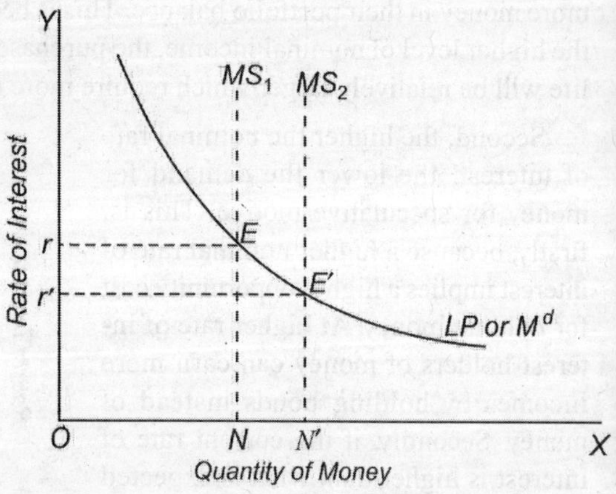

Fig. 20.6. *Effect of Increase in Money Supply on the Rate of Interest*

bonds. The rise in bond prices means the fall in the rate of interest. As will be seen from the Fig. 20.5, with the fall in the interest rate from 12 per cent to 10 per cent, quantity demand of money has increased to be once again equal to the given supply of money and the excess supply of money is entirely eliminated and money market is in equilibrium.

On the other hand, if the rate of interest is lower than the equilibrium rate of 10 per cent, say it is 8 per cent, then as will be seen from Figure 20.5, there will emerge *excess demand for money*. As a reaction to this excess demand for money, people would like to sell bonds in order to obtain a greater quantity of money for holding at lower rate of interest. The stock of money remaining fixed, the attempt by the people to hold more money balances at a rate of interest lower than the equilibrium level through sale of bonds will only cause the bond prices to fall. The fall in bond prices implies the rise in the rate of interest. Thus, the process started as a reaction to the excess demand for money at an interest rate below the equilibrium will end up with the rise in the interest rate of the equilibrium level.

Effect of an Increase in Money Supply

Let us now examine the effect of increase in money supply on the rate of interest. In Fig. 20.6, M^d is the demand for money for satisfying various motives. To begin with, *ON* is the quantity of money available. Rate of interest will be determined where the demand for money is in balance or equal to the fixed supply of money *ON*. It is clear from Fig. 20.6 that demand for money is equal to *ON* quantity of money at *Or* rate of interest. Hence *Or* is the equilibrium rate of interest. Assuming no change in expectations and nominal income, an increase in the quantity of money (through buying securities by the Central Bank of the country from the open market), will lower the rate of interest. In Fig. 20.6, when the quantity of money increases from *ON* to *ON′*, the rate of interest falls from *Or* to *Or′* because the new quantity of money *ON′* is in balance with the demand for money at *Or′* rate of interest. In this case we move down on the curve. Thus, given the money demand curve or curve of liquidity preference, an increase in the quantity of money brings down the rate of interest.

Let us see how increase in money supply leads to the fall in the rate of interest. With initial equilibrium at *Or*, when the money supply is expanded from *ON* to *ON′*, there emerges excess supply of money at the initial *Or* rate of interest. The people would react to this excess quantity of money supplied by buying bonds. As a result, the bond prices will go up which implies that the rate of interest will decline. This is how the increase in money supply leads to the fall in rate of interest.

Shifts in Money Demand or Liquidity Preference Curve

The position of money demand curve depends upon two factors: (1) the level of nominal income, (2) the expectations about the changes in bond prices in the future which implies changes in rate of interest in future. As has been explained above, a money demand curve is drawn by assuming a certain level of nominal income. With the increase in nominal income, money demand for transactions and precautionary motives increase causing an upward shift in the money demand curve.

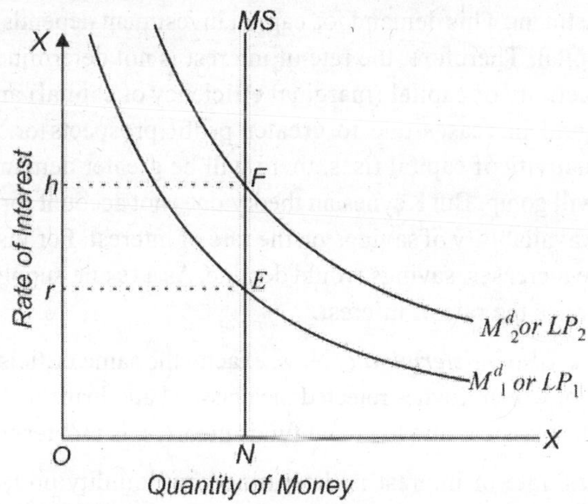

Fig. 20.7. *Effect of Increase in Demand for Money (Liquidity Preference) on the Rate of Interest*

Shift in money demand curve (or what Keynes called liquidity preference curve) can also be caused by changes in the expectations of the people regarding changes in bond prices or movements in the rate of interest in the future. If some changes in events lead the people on balance to expect a higher rate of interest in the future than they had previously supposed, the money demand or liquidity preference for speculative motive will increase which will bring about an upward shift in the money demand curve or liquidity preference curve and this will raise the rate of interest.

In Fig 20.7 assuming that the quantity of money remains unchanged at *ON*, the rise in the money demand or liquidity preference curve from $M_1{}^d$ or LP_1 to $M_2{}^d$ or LP_2, the rate of interest rises from *Or* to *Oh* because *at Oh*, the new speculative demand for money is in equilibrium with the supply of money *ON*. It is worth noting that when the demand for money curve rises from LP_1 to LP_2, the amount of money held does not increase; it remains at *ON* as before. Only the rate of interest rises from *Or* to *Oh* to equilibrate the new liquidity preference or money demand with the available quantity of money *ON*.

Thus we see that Keynes explained interest in terms of purely monetary forces and not in terms of real forces like productivity of capital and thrift which formed the foundation-stones of both classical and loanable fund theories. According to him, demand for money for speculative motive together with the supply of money determines the rate of interest. He agreed that the marginal revenue product of capital tends to become equal to the rate of interest but the rate of interest is not determined by marginal revenue productivity of capital. Moreover, according to him, interest is not a reward for saving or thriftiness or waiting but for parting with liquidity. Keynes asserted that it is not the rate of interest which equalises saving an investment. But this equality is brought about through changes in the level of income.

Critical Appraisal of Keynes's Liquidity Preference Theory of Interest

1. *Keynes ignored the role of real factors in the determination of interest.* Firstly, it has been pointed out that rate of interest is not purely a monetary phenomenon. Real forces like productivity of capital and thriftiness or saving also play an important role in the determination of the rate of interest. Keynes makes the rate of interest independent of the demand for investment funds. In fact, it is not so independent. The cash balances of the businessmen are largely influenced by their demand for capital investment. This demand for capital investment depends upon the marginal revenue productivity of capital. Therefore, the rate of interest is not determined independently of the marginal revenue productivity of capital (marginal efficiency of capital) and investment demand. When investment demand increases due to greater profit prospects or, in other words, when marginal revenue productivity of capital rises, there will be greater demand for investment funds and the rate of interest will go up. But Keynesian theory does not account for this. Similarly, Keynes ignored the effect of the availability of savings on the rate of interest. For instance, if the propensity to consume of the people increases, savings would decline. As a result, supply of funds in the market will decline which will raise the rate of interest.

2. *Keynesian theory is also indeterminate*. Now, exactly the same criticism applies to Keynesian theory itself on the basis of which Keynes rejected the classical and loanable funds theories. Keynes's theory of interest, like the classical and loanable funds theories, is indeterminate.

According to Keynes, rate of interest is determined by liquidity preference (*i.e.* demand for money) and supply of money. However, as we have seen, liquidity preference, especially demand for money for transactions motive, depends on level of income. Now, when income increases, liquidity preference curve (that is, money demand curve) will shift to the right and, given the supply of money, new equilibrium rate of interest will be obtained. Thus at different levels of income there will be different liquidity preference curve or money demand curve. As a result, at different levels of income, there will be different equilibrium rates of interest. Thus, we cannot know the rate of interest unless we know the liquidity preference curve, and also we cannot know the liquidity preference curve unless we know the level of income. However, we cannot know the level of income unless we first know the rate of interest. This is because rate of interest influences investment which in turn determines the level of income. Thus, Keynes's theory is indeterminate, that is, we are not able to arrive at a single determinate rate of interest; rate of interest varies as income varies.

Thus, Keynes's analysis at the most helps us to obtain *LM* curve which shows what will be the rate of interest at different levels of income and not any unique or particular rate of interest. Thus, the Keynesian theory, like the classical theory, is indeterminate. "In the Keynesian case the supply and demand for money curves cannot give the rate of interest unless we already know the income level, in the classical case the demand and supply schedules for saving offer no solution until the income is known. Precisely the same is true of loanable funds theory. Keynes's criticism of the classical and lonable funds theories applies equally to his now theory"[8].

3. *No liquidity without savings*. According to Keynes, interest is a reward for parting with liquidity and in no way a compensation and inducement for saving or waiting. But without saving how can the funds be available to be kept as liquid and how can there be the question of surrendering liquidity if one has not already saved money ? Jacob Viner rightly maintains, "*Without saving there can be no liquidity to surrender.*" Therefore, the rate of interest is vitally connected with saving which is neglected by Keynes in the determination of interest.

8. A. H. Hansen, *Guide to Keynes*. p. 141.

It follows from above that Keynesian theory of interest is also not without flaws. But the importance Keynes gave to liquidity preference as a determinant of interest is correct. A valid and an adequate explanation of interest must incorporate this important factor of demand for money to hold.

QUESTIONS FOR REVIEW

1. Explain Fisher's transactions approach to demand for money. Classical economists such as Fisher considered money as simply a medium of exchange. Examine critically.
2. Critically examine the Cambridge Cash-Balance Theory of Demand for Money. How does it differ from Fisher's transactions approach to demand for money ?
3. What, according to Keynes, are the motives for holding money ? What are the factors that determine the money held under these motives ?
4. Why do people hold money when they can earn interest by lending it to others or by buying interest yielding bonds of the companies ?
5. In what ways is the Keynesian theory of demand for money a departure from the classical theory ? Discuss. *[D.U. B.Com. (Hons) 2001]*
6. Explain the speculative motive for holding money. Why is it interest elastic ?
7. What is meant by liquidity preference ? Explain various motives of liquidity preference. What role does it play in determining rate of interest ?
8. Explain why demand for money is considered to be declining function of rate of interest. *[D.U. B.Com. (Hons), 1995]*
9. Why does an increase in interest rate causes a decline in bond prices ? What is its effect on demand for money ?
10. Explain the Keynesian theory of interest. How is the Keynesian theory of interest different from the classical theory ? *[D.U. B.Com (Hons) 1999]*
11. Explain Keynes' liquidity preference theory of interest. Why is it considered to be indeterminate ? Show that at best we can get *LM* curve from it. *[D.U. B.Com (Hons), 1998]*
12. What is meant by liquidity trap ? How does its existence make the expansionary monetary policy ineffective at times of depression ?
13. Keynes's criticism that classical theory of interest is indeterminate "applies equally to his own theory" (A.H. Hansen). Discuss.
14. "It was left to Keynes to highlight the influence of rate of interest on the demand for money and change the course of monetary theory". Discuss.

APPENDIX TO CHAPTER 20

Post-Keynesian Theories of Demand for Money

By introducing speculative demand for money, Keynes made a significant departure from the classical theory of money demand which emphasized only the transactions demand for money. However, as seen above, Keynes' theory of speculative demand for money has been challenged. The main drawback of Keynes' speculative demand for money is that *it visualises that people hold their assets in either all money or all bonds*. This seems quite unrealistic as individuals hold their financial wealth in some combination of both money and bonds. This gave rise to portfolio approach to demand for money put forward by Tobin, Baumol and Friedman. The portfolio of wealth consists of money, interest-bearing bonds, shares, physical assets, etc. Further, while according to Keynes' theory, demand for money for transaction purposes is insensitive to interest rate, the modern theories of money demand put forward by Baumol and Tobin show that money held for transaction purposes is interest elastic. We discuss below the post-Keynesian theories of demand for money put forward by Tobin, Baumol and Friedman.

TOBIN'S PORTFOLIO APPROACH TO DEMAND FOR MONEY

An American economist, James Tobin[1], in his important contribution explained that rational behaviour on the part of the individuals is that they should keep a portfolio of assets which consists of both bonds and money. In his analysis he makes a valid assumption that people prefer more wealth to less. According to him, an investor is faced with a problem of what proportion of his portfolio of financial assets he should keep in the form of money (which earns no interest) and interest-bearing bonds. The portfolio of individuals may also consist of more risky assets such as shares. *According to Tobin, faced with various safe and risky assets, individuals diversify their portfolio by holding a balanced combination of safe and risky assets*. According to Tobin, individual's behaviour shows *risk aversion*. That is, they prefer less risk to more risk at a given rate of return. In Keynes's analysis an individual holds his wealth in either all money or all bonds depending upon his estimate of the future rate of interest. But, according to Tobin, individuals are uncertain about future rate of interest. If a wealth holder chooses to hold a greater proportion of risky assets such as bonds in his portfolio, he will be earning a high average return but will bear a higher degree of risk. Tobin argues that a risk averter will not opt for such a portfolio with all risky bonds or a greater proportion of them.

On the other hand, a person who, in his portfolio of wealth, holds only safe and riskless assets such as money (in the form of currency and demand deposits in banks) he will be taking almost zero risk but will also be having no return and as a result there will be no growth of his wealth. *Therefore, people generally prefer a mixed diversified portfolio of money, bonds and shares, with each person opting for a little different balance between riskiness and return.*

It is important to note that a person will be unwilling to hold all risky assets such as equity shares and bonds unless he obtains a higher average return on them. In view of the desire of individuals to have both safety and reasonable return, they strike a balance between them and hold a mixed and balanced portfolio consisting of money (which is a safe and riskless asset) and risky assets such as

1. James Tobin, "Liquidity Preference as Behaviour Towards Risk," *Review of Economic Studies,* Vol. 25 (1958)

bonds and shares though this balance or mix varies between various individuals depending on their attitude towards risk and hence their trade-off between risk and return.

Tobin's Liquidity Preference Function

Tobin considers money as an asset which is free from risk but yields no return or interest. Tobin derived his liquidity preference function depicting relationship between rate of interest and demand for money (that is, preference for holding wealth in money form which is a safe and "riskless" asset[2]. He argues that with the increase in the rate of interest (*i.e.* rate of return on bonds), wealth holders will be generally attracted to hold a greater fraction of their wealth in bonds and thus reduce their holding of money. That is, at a higher rate of interest, their demand for holding money (*i.e.*, liquidity) will be less and therefore they will hold more bonds in their portfolio. On the other hand, at a lower rate of interest they will hold more money and less bonds in their portfolio. This means, like the Keynes' speculative demand for money, in Tobin's portfolio approach demand function for money as an asset (*i.e.*, his liquidity preference function curve) slopes downwards as is shown in Fig. 20A.1, where on the horizontal axis asset demand for money is shown. This downward-sloping liquidity preference function curve shows that the asset demand for money in the portfolio increases as the rate of interest on bonds falls. Tobin's liquidity preference theory has been found to be true by the empirical studies conducted to measure interest elasticity of the demand for money. As shown by Tobin through his portfolio approach, these empirical studies reveal that aggregate demand for money as an asset curve is negatively sloped. This means that most of the people in the economy have demand for money function similar to the one shown by curve M_d in Fig. 20A.1.

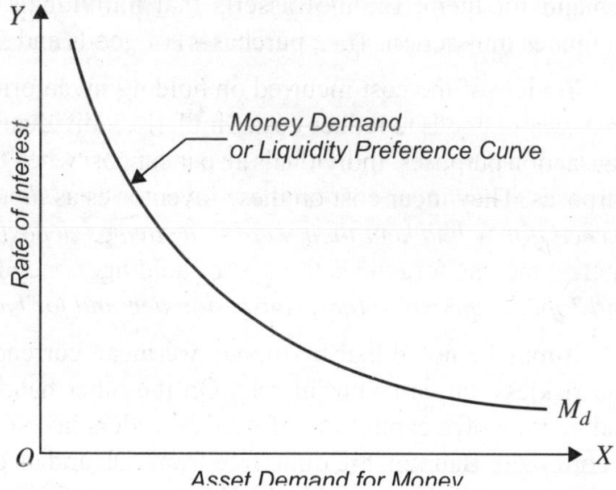

Fig. 22.1. *Tobin's Money Demand as an Asset*

Evaluation

Tobin's approach has done away with the limitation of Keynes' theory of liquidity preference for speculative motive, namely, individuals hold their wealth in *either all money or all bonds*. Thus, Tobin's approach, according to which individuals simultaneously hold both money and bonds but in different proportion at different rates of interest, yields a *continuous* liquidity preference curve. Further, Tobin's analysis of simultaneous holding of money and bonds is not based on the erroneous Keynes' assumption that interest rate will move only in one direction but on a simple fact that individuals do not know with certainty which way the interest rate will change. It is worth mentioning that Tobin's portfolio approach, according to which liquidity preference (*i.e.*, demand for money) is determined by the individuals's attitude towards risk, can be extended to the problem of asset choice when there are several alternative assets, not just two, of money and bonds.

2. Note that riskless is written in quotes because strictly speaking even money defined as currency and demand deposits is also not completely riskless in view of the frequent changes in prices of commodities. If inflation occurs, it reduces the value of money and thus inflicts a capital loss on its holders.

BAUMOL'S INVENTORY APPROACH TO TRANSACTIONS DEMAND FOR MONEY

Instead of Keynes's speculative demand for money, Baumol concentrated on transactions demand for money and put forward a new approach to explain it. Baumol explains the transaction demand for money from the viewpoint of the inventory control or inventory management similar to the inventory management of goods and materials by business firms. As businessmen keep inventories of goods and materials to facilitate transactions or exchange in the context of changes in demand for them, Baumol asserts that individuals also hold *inventory of money* because this facilitates transactions (*i.e.*, purchases) of goods and services.[3]

In view of the cost incurred on holding inventories of goods there is need for keeping *optimal inventory* of goods to reduce cost. Similarly, individuals have to keep *optimum inventory of money* for transaction purposes. Individuals also incur cost when they hold inventories of money for transactions purposes. They incur cost on these inventories as *they have to forgo interest which they could have earned if they had kept their wealth in savings deposits or fixed deposits or invested in bonds*. This interest income forgone is the cost of holding money for transactions purposes. In this way *Baumol and Tobin emphasised that transaction demand for money is not independent of the rate of interest.*

It may be noted that by money we mean currency and demand deposits which are quite safe and riskless but carry no interest. On the other hand, bonds yield interest or return but are risky and may involve capital loss if wealth holders invest in them. However, savings deposits in banks, according to Baumol, are quite free from risk and also yield some interest. Therefore, Baumol asks the question why an individual holds money (*i.e.*, currency and demand deposits) instead of keeping his wealth in savings deposits which are quite safe and earn some interest as well. According to him, it is for convenience and capability of it being easily used for transactions of goods that people hold money with them in preference to the savings deposits. Unlike Keynes both *Baumol and Tobin argue that transactions demand for money depends on the rate of interest.* People hold money for transaction purposes "*to bridge the gap between the receipt of income and its spending.*"[4] As interest rate on savings deposits goes up people will tend to shift a part of their money holdings to the interest-bearing savings deposits, or buy bonds.

According to Baumol, an individual compares the costs and benefits of holding money instead of interest-bearing savings deposits. As explained above, cost of holding money is interest forgone on savings deposits which an individual could earn. The main benefit of holding money instead of savings deposits is *avoidance of time and transaction costs* that have to be made by making trips to the bank for withdrawing money. The larger the number of trips an individual makes to the banks for with drawing money the greater the time and transactions costs. Therefore, *a rational individual will try to optimise his case management by deciding how much money he withdraws in a single trip to hold money with him for transactions and how much he keeps his salary in interest-learning savings deposits.*

Thus, individuals compare the costs and benefits of funds in the form of money with the interest-bearing savings deposits. According to Baumol, the cost which people incur when they hold funds in money is the *opportunity cost of these funds*, that is, interest income forgone by not putting them in savings deposits.

Transactions Demand for Money

Baumol analyses the transactions demand for money of an individual who receives income at a specified interval, say every month, and spends it gradually at a steady rate. This is illustrated in

3. See James Tobin, "The Interest Elasticity of Transactions Demand for Cash," *Review of Economics and Statistics*, Vol. 38 (1956).
4. W.J. Baumol, "The Transactions Demand for Cash: an Inventory Theoretic Approach", *Quarterly Journal of Economics*, Vol. 66 (Nov. 1952).

Fig. 20A.2. It is assumed that individual is paid ₹ 12000 salary cheque on the first day of each month. Suppose he gets it cashed (*i.e.* converted into money) on the very first day and gradually spends it daily throughout the month (₹ 400 per day) so that at the end of the month he is left with no money. It can be easily seen that his average money holding in the month will be ₹ $m = \frac{M}{H}$ ₹ 6,000 (before 15th of a month he will be having more than ₹ 6,000 and after 15th day he will have less than ₹ 6,000). Average holding of money is equal to ₹ 6,000 which has been shown by the dotted line in Fig. 20A.2.

Now, the question arises whether it is the optimal strategy of managing money or what is called *optimal cash management*. The simple answer is no. This is because the individual is losing interest which he could have earned if he had deposited some funds in interest-bearing savings deposits instead of withdrawing all his salary in cash on the first day of the month. He can manage his money balances so as to earn some interest income as well. Suppose, instead of withdrawing his entire salary on the first day of a month, he withdraws only half of it *i.e.*, ₹ 6,000 in cash and deposits the remaining amount of ₹ 6,000 in saving account which gives him interest of 5 per cent, his expenditure per day remaining constant at ₹ 400. This is illustrated in Fig. 20A.3. It will be seen that his money holdings of ₹ 6,000 will be reduced to zero at the end of the 15th day of each month. Now, he can

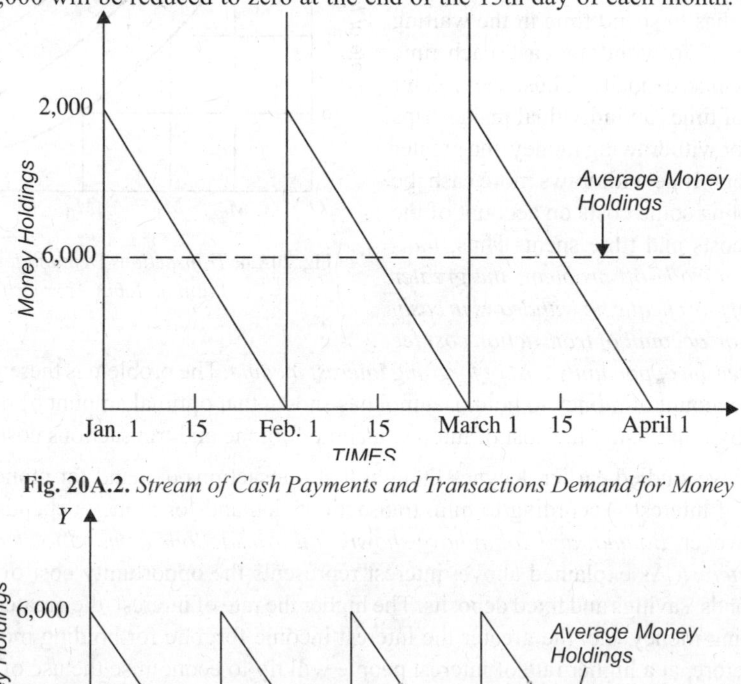

Fig. 20A.2. *Stream of Cash Payments and Transactions Demand for Money*

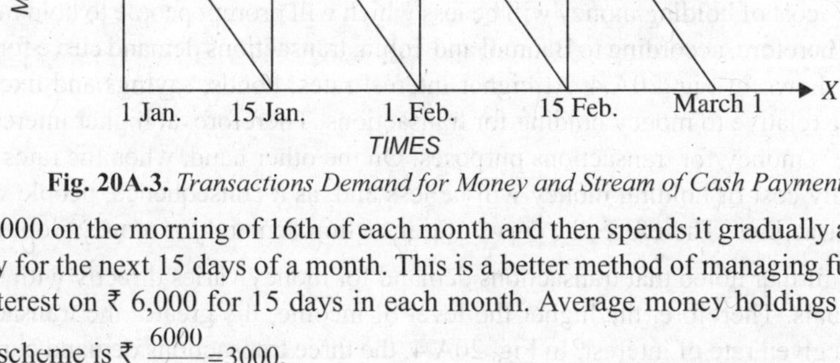

Fig. 20A.3. *Transactions Demand for Money and Stream of Cash Payments*

withdraw ₹ 6,000 on the morning of 16th of each month and then spends it gradually at a steady rate of 400 per day for the next 15 days of a month. This is a better method of managing funds as he will be earning interest on ₹ 6,000 for 15 days in each month. Average money holdings in this money management scheme is ₹ $\frac{6000}{2}$=3000.

Likewise, the individual may decide to withdraw ₹ 4,000 (*i.e.*, 1/3rd of his salary) on the first day of each month and deposits ₹ 8,000 in the saving deposits. His ₹ 4,000 will be reduced to zero, as he spends his money on transactions, (that is, buying of goods and services) at the end of the 10th day and on the morning of 11th of each month he again withdraws ₹ 4,000 to spend on goods and services till the end of the 20th day and on 21st day of the month he again withdraws ₹ 4,000 to spend steadily till the end of the month. In this scheme on an average he will be holding ₹ = $\frac{4000}{2}$ 2000 and will be investing remaining funds in savings deposits and earn interest on them. Thus, in this scheme he will be earning more interest income.

Now, which scheme will he decide to adopt? It may be noted that investing in savings deposits and then withdrawing cash from it to meet the transactions demand involves cost also. *Transactions costs* are incurred when one invests in interest-bearing bonds and sells them. Even in case of savings deposits, the asset which we are taking for illustration, one has to spend on transportation costs for making extra trips to the bank for withdrawing money from the Savings Account. Besides, one has to spend time in the waiting line in the bank to withdraw cash each time from the savings deposits. Thus, the greater the number of times an individual makes trips to the bank for withdrawing money, the greater costs will incur. If he withdraws more cash, he will be avoiding some costs on account of the transaction costs and time spent. Thus, *individual faces a trade-off problem; the greater the amount of pay cheque he withdraws in cash, less the cost on account of transaction cost fee but the greater the opportunity cost of forgoing interest income*. The problem is therefore to determine an optimum amount of money to hold. Baumol has shown that optimal amount of money holding is determined by minimising the cost of interest income forgone and transactions cost.

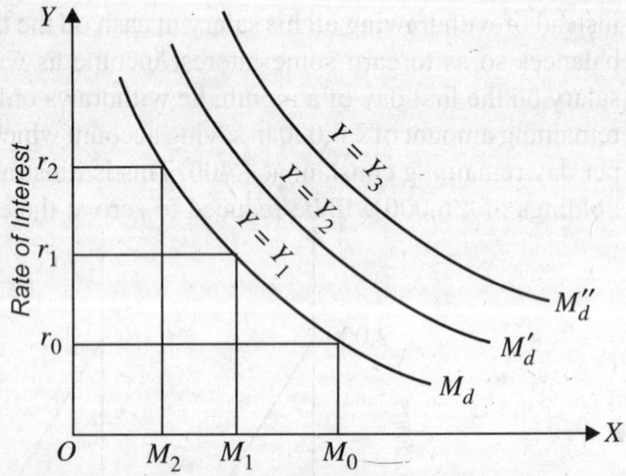

Fig. 20A.4. *Transactions Demand for Money : Baumol-Tobin Approach*

As we have studied earlier, Keynes thought that transactions demand for money was independent of rate of interest. According to him, transactions demand for money depends on the level of income. However, *Baumol and Tobin have shown that transactions demand for money is sensitive to rate of interest*. As explained above, interest represents the opportunity cost of holding money instead of bonds, savings and fixed deposits. The higher the rate of interest, the greater the opportunity cost of holding money (i.e. the greater the interest income forgone for holding money for transactions). Therefore, at a higher rate of interest people will try to economise the use of money and will demand less money for transactions. At a lower interest rate on bonds, savings and fixed deposits, the opportunity cost of holding money will be less which will prompt people to hold more money for transactions. Therefore, according to Baumol and Tobin, transactions demand curve for money slopes downward as shown in Fig. 20A.4. At higher interest rates, bonds, savings and fixed deposits are more attractive relative to money holding for transactions. Therefore, at higher interest rates people tend to hold less money for transactions purposes. On the other hand, when the rates of interest are low, opportunity cost of holding money will be less and, as a consequence, people will hold more money for transactions. Therefore, the curve of transaction demand for money slopes downward.

It may be further noted that transactions demand for money varies directly with the income (Y) of the individuals. Therefore, the higher the level of income, the greater the transactions demand for money at a given rate of interest. In Fig. 20A.4. the three transactions demand curves for money

M_d, M'_d and M_d'', for three different income levels, Y_1, Y_2, Y_3 are shown. Thus, transactions demand for money, according to Baumol and Tobin, is function of both rate of interest and the level of income.

$$M_{td} = f(r, Y)$$

where M_{td} stands for transactions demand for money, r for rate of interest and Y for the level of income.

FRIEDMAN'S THEORY OF DEMAND FOR MONEY

A noted monetarist economist, Friedman put forward demand for money function which plays an important role in his restatement of the quantity theory of money and prices. In this section we shall be concerned with Friedman's money demand function and will explain in a later chapter money which shows how the changes in money supply affect the price level in the economy. *Friedman believes that money demand function is most important stable function of macroeconomics. He treats money as one type of asset in which wealth holders can keep a part of their wealth.* Business firms view money as a capital good or a factor of production which they combine with the services of other productive assets or labour to produce goods and services. Thus, according to Friedman, individuals hold money for the services it provides to them. It may be noted that the service rendered by money is that it serves as a general purchasing power so that it can be conveniently used for buying goods and services. *His approach to demand for money does not consider any motives for holding money*, nor does it distinguish between speculative and transactions demand for money. Friedman considers the demand for money merely as an application of a general theory of demand for capital assets.

Like other capital assets, money also yields return and provides services. He analyses the various factors that determine the demand for money and from this analysis derives demand for money function. Note that the value of goods and services which money can buy represents the real yield on money. Obviously, this real yield of money in terms of goods and services which it can purchase will depend on the price level of goods and services. Besides money, *bonds* are another type of asset in which people can hold their wealth. Bonds are securities which yield a stream of interest income, fixed in nominal terms. Yield on bond is the *coupen rate of interest* and also anticipated capital gain or loss due to expected changes in the market rate of interest.

Equities or Shares are another form of asset in which wealth can be held. The yield from equity is determined by the dividend rate, expected capital gain or loss and expected changes in the price level. The fourth form in which people can hold their wealth is the *stock of producer and durable consumer commodities*. These commodities also yield a stream of income but in kind rather than in money. Thus, the basic yield from commodities is implicit one. However, Friedman also considers an explicit yield from commodities in the form of expected rate of change in their price per unit of time.

Friedman's nominal demand function (M_d) for money can be written as

$$M_d = f(W, r_m, r_b, r_e, P, \frac{\Delta P}{P}, U)$$

Note that *real money balances is nominal demand for money divided by the price level. Thus*

$$\frac{M_d}{P} = f\left(W, r_m, r_b, r_e, \frac{\Delta P}{P}, U\right)$$

where M_d stands for *nominal demand for money* and $\frac{M_d}{P}$ for demand for *real money balances*. W stands for wealth of the individuals, including human wealth held by the individuals, r_m for rate of return or interest on money, r_b for rate of interest on bonds, r_e for rate of return on equities, P for the price level, $\frac{\Delta P}{P}$ for the change in price level (*i.e.* rate of inflation), and U for the institutional factors.

We explain below the above factors in some detail.

1. Wealth (*W*): The major factor determining the demand for money is the wealth of the individual (*W*). In wealth Friedman includes not only *non-human wealth* such as bonds, shares, money which yield various rates of return but also *human wealth* or *human capital.* By human wealth Friedman means the value of an individual's present and future earnings.

Individual's demand for money directly depends on his total wealth. Indeed, *the total wealth of an individual represents an upper limit of holding money by an individual and is similar to the budget constraint of the consumer in the theory of demand. The greater the wealth of an individual, the more money he will demand for transactions and other purposes.* As a country becomes richer, its demand for money for transaction and other purposes will increase.

2. Rates of Interest or Return (r_m, r_b, r_e). Friedman considers three rates of interest, namely, r_m, r_b and r_e which determine the demand for money. r_m is the own rate of interest on money. Note that money kept in the form of currency and demand deposits does not earn any interest. But money held as savings deposits and fixed deposits earns certain rates of interest and it is this rate of interest which is designated by r_m in money demand function. Given the other rates of interest or return, the higher the own rate of interest, the greater the demand for money.

In deciding how large a part of his wealth to hold in the form of money the individual will compare the rate of interest on money with rates of interest (or return) on bonds and other assets. As mentioned earlier, *the opportunity cost of holding money is the interest or return given up by not holding these other forms of assets.* As rates of return on bond (r_b) and equities (r_e) rise, the opportunity cost of holding money will increase which will reduce the demand for money holdings. Thus, the *demand for money is negatively related to the rate of interest (or return) on bonds, equities and other such non-money assets.*

3. Price Level (*P*). *Price level also determines the demand for money balances.* A higher price level means people will require a larger *nominal money balances* in order to do the same amount of transactions, that is, to purchase the same amount of goods and services. *If income (Y) is used as proxy for wealth (W) which, as stated above, is the most important determinant of demand for money, then nominal income which is given by Y.P* becomes a crucial determinant of demand for money. Here *Y* stands for real income (*i.e.* in terms of goods and services) and *P* for price level. As the price level goes up, the demand for money will rise and, on the other hand, if price level falls, the demand for money will decline. As a matter of fact, people adjust the nominal money balances (*M*) when price level changes to achieve their desired level of real money balances $\left(\frac{M}{P}\right)$.

4. The Expected Rate of Inflation $\left(\frac{\Delta P}{P}\right)$. If people expect a higher rate of inflation, they will reduce their demand for money holdings. This is because inflation reduces the value of their money balances in terms of its power to purchase goods and services. If the rate of inflation exceeds the nominal rate of interest, there will be negative rate of return on money. Therefore, when people expect a higher rate of inflation they will tend to convert their money holdings into goods or other assets which are not affected by inflation. On the other hand, if people expect a fall in the price level, their demand for money holdings will increase.

5. Institutional Factors (U). Institutional factors such as mode of wage payments and bill payments also affect the demand for money. Several other factors which influence the overall economic environment affect the demand for money. For example, if recession or war is anticipated, the demand for money balances will increase. Besides, instability in capital markets, which erodes the confidence of the people in making profits from investment in bonds and equity shares, will also raise the demand for money. Even political instability in the country influences the demand for money. To account for these institutional factors Friedman includes the variable U in his demand for money function.

Simplifying Friedman's Demand for Money Function

A major problem faced in using Friedman's demand for money function has been that due to the non-existence of reliable data about the value of wealth (W), it is difficult to estimate the demand for money. To overcome this difficulty Friedman suggested that since the present value of wealth or $W = \frac{Y_p}{r}$ (where Y_p is the permanent income and r is the rate of interest on money.), permanent income Y_p can be used as a proxy variable for wealth. Incorporating this in Friedman's real demand for money function we have

$$M_d = \left(Y_p, r_m, r_b, r_e \frac{\Delta P}{P}, U\right)$$

QUESTIONS FOR REVIEW

1. Explain Tobin's Portfolio Approach to demand for money. Why, according to Tobin, asset demand for money increases as the rate of interest on bonds falls ?
2. How does Tobin's approach to liquidity preference or asset demand for money differ from Keynes's liquidity preference function ?
3. How does Baumol-Tobin model explain that the transaction demand for money is a function of interest rate and level of income.
4. Explain why the transactions demand for money depends not only on the level of income but also on the rate of interest.
5. Explain Friedman's theory of demand for money. How does it differ from Keynes's theory of demand for money ?
6. What, according to Friedman, are the main factors that determine demand for money ? How do the stock of wealth and rate of interest influence the demand for money ?

PART – IV
MONEY, PRICES AND INFLATION

- Money and Prices : Quantity Theory of Money
- Keynesian Theory of Money and Prices
- Friedman's Restatement of Quantity Theory of Money and Monetarism
- Inflation and Hyperinflation : Nature, Causes and Effects

CHAPTER 21

Money and Prices : Quantity Theory of Money

Value of Money and the Price Level

Value in economics means value-in-exchange. The value of a commodity means what it can be exchanged for or what it can buy. It means the purchasing power of a commodity. Similarly, the value of money means its purchasing power in terms of goods and services in general. The purchasing power of money obviously depends on the prevalent price level. If the prices are high, money will buy less and its value will be low. Conversely, if the price level is low, the value of money is high. The value of money is thus inversely proportional to the price level, or the value of money is the reciprocal of price level.

QUANTITY THEORY OF MONEY: FISHER'S TRANSACTIONS APPROACH

We are now in a position to explain how the general level of prices is determined, that is, why sometimes the general level of prices rises and sometimes it declines. Some time back it was believed by the economists that the quantity of money in the economy is the prime cause of fluctuations in the price level. The theory that increase in the quantity of money leads to the rise in the general price was effectively put forward by Irving Fisher.[1] They believed that the greater the quantity of money, the higher the level of prices and *vice versa*. Therefore, the theory which linked prices with the quantity of money came to be known as quantity theory of money. In the following analysis we shall first critically examine the quantity theory of money and then explain the modern view about the relationship between money and prices and also the determination of general level of prices.

The quantity theory of money seeks to explain the value of money in terms of changes in its quantity. Stated in its simplest form, the quantity theory of money says that the level of prices varies directly with quantity of money. "Double the quantity of money, and other things being equal, prices will be twice as high as before, and the value of money one-half. Halve the quantity of money and, other things being equal, prices will be one-half of what they were before and the value of money double." The theory can also be stated in these words: *The price level rises proportionately with a given increase in the quantity of money. Conversely, the price level falls proportionately with a given decrease in the quantity of money, other things remaining the same.*

There are several forces that determine the value of money and the general price level. The general price level in a community is influenced by the following factors:

(*a*) the volume of trade or transactions;

(*b*) the quantity of money; and

(*c*) velocity of circulation of money.

The first factor, the volume of trade or transactions, depends upon the supply or amount of goods and services to be exchanged. The greater the amount or supply of goods in an economy, the larger the number of transactions and trade, and *vice versa*. But the classical and neoclassical economists who

1. Irving Fisher, *Purchasing Power of Money*, Macmillan, 1911.

believed in the quantity theory of money assumed that *full employment* of all resources (including labour) prevailed in the economy. Resources being fully employed, the total output or supply of goods (and therefore the total trade or transactions) cannot increase. Therefore, those who believed in the quantity theory of money assumed that the total volume of trade or transactions remained the same.

The second factor in the determination of general level of prices is the quantity of money. It should be noted that the quantity of money in the economy consists of not only the notes and currency issued by the Government but also the amount of credit or deposits created by the banks.

The third factor influencing the price level is the velocity of circulation. A unit of money is used for exchange and transaction purposes not once but several times in a year. During several exchanges of goods and services, a unit of money passes from one hand to another. Thus, if a single rupee is used five times in a year for exchange of goods and services, the velocity of circulation is 5. Hence, the velocity of money is the *number of times* a unit of money changes hands during exchanges in a year. The work done by one rupee which is circulated five times in a year is equal to that done by the five rupees which change hands only once each.

Let us illustrate the quantity theory of money. Suppose in a country there is only one good, wheat, which is to be exchanged. The total output of wheat is 2,000 quintals in a year. Further, suppose that the government has issued money equal to ₹ 25,000 and no credit is issued by the banks. We further assume that one rupee is used four times in a year for exchange of wheat. That is, velocity of circulation of money is four. Under these circumstances, 2,000 quintals of wheat are to be exchanged for ₹ 1,00,000, (25,000 × 4 = 1,00,000). The price of wheat will be $\frac{1,00,000}{2,000}$ = ₹ 50 per quintal. Sup- pose the quantity of money is doubled to ₹ 50,000, while the output of wheat remains at 2,000 quintals. As a result of this increase in the quantity of money, the price of wheat will rise to $\frac{2,00,000}{2,000}$ = ₹ 100 per quintal. Thus with doubling of the quantity of money, the price has doubled. If the quantity of money is further increased to ₹ 75,000, the amount of wheat remaining constant, the price level will rise to $\frac{3,00,000}{2,000}$ = ₹ 150 per quintal. It is thus clear that if the volume of transactions, *i.e.*, output to be exchanged remains constant, the price level rises with the increase in the quantity of money.

Fisher's Equation of Exchange

An American economist, Irving Fisher, expressed the relationship between the quantity of money and the price level in the form of an equation, which is called 'the equation of exchange'. This is:

$$PT = MV \qquad \ldots (1)$$

or

$$P = \frac{MV}{T} \qquad \ldots (2)$$

where P stands for the average price level:

T stands for total amount of transactions (or total trade of amount of goods and services, raw materials, old goods etc.);

M stands for the quantity of money; and

V stands for the transactions velocity of circulation of money.

The equation (1) or (2) is an accounting identity and true by definition. This is, because MV which represents money spent on transactions must be equal to PT which represents money received from transactions.

However, the equation of exchange as given in equations (1) and (2) has been converted into a theory of determination of general level of prices by the classical economists by making some assumptions. First, it has been assumed that *the physical volume of transactions is constant* because it is determined by a given amount of real resources, the given level of technology and the efficiency with which the given available resources are used. These real factors determine a level of aggregate output which necessitates various types of transactions. Another crucial assumption is that *transactions velocity of circulation (V) is also constant*. The quantity theorists accordingly believed that velocity of circulation (V) depends on the methods and practices of factor payments such as frequency of wage payments to the workers, and habits of the people regarding spending their money incomes after they receive them. Further, velocity of circulation of money also depends on the development of banking and credit system, that is, the ways and speed with which cheques are cleared, loans are granted and repaid. According to them, these practices do not change in the short run. This assumption is very crucial for the quantity theory of money because when the quantity of money is increased this may cause a decline in velocity of circulation of money, then MV may not change if the decline in V offsets the increase in M. As a result, increase in M will not affect PY.

The quantity theorists believed that the volume of transactions (T) and the changes in it were largely independent of the quantity of money. Further, according to them, changes in velocity of circulation (V) and price level (P) do not cause any change in volume of transactions except temporarily. Thus classical economists who put forward the quantity theory of money believed that the number of transactions (which ultimately depends on aggregate real output) does not depend on other variables (M, V and P) in the equation of exchange. Thus we see that **the assumption of constant V and T converts the equation of exchange ($MV = PT$), which is an accounting identity, into a theory of the determination of general price level.**

The quantity of money is fixed by the Government and the Central Bank of a country. Further, it is assumed that quantity of money in the economy depends upon the monetary system and policy of the central bank and the Government and is assumed to be autonomous of the real forces which determine the volume of transactions or national output.

Now, with the assumptions that M and V remain constant, the price level P depends upon the quantity of money M; the greater the quantity of M, the higher the level of prices. Let us give a numerical example. Suppose the quantity of money is ₹ 5,00,000 in an economy, the velocity of circulation of money (V) is 5; and the total output to be transacted (T) is 2,50,000 units, the average price level (P) will be:

$$P - \frac{MV}{T}$$

$$= \frac{5,00,000 \times 5}{2,50,000} = \frac{2,500,000}{2,50,000}$$

$$= ₹\ 10 \text{ per unit.}$$

If now, other things remaining the same, the quantity of money is doubled, *i.e.*, increased to ₹ 10,00,000, then:

$$P = \frac{10,00,000 \times 5}{2,50,000} = ₹\ 20 \text{ per unit}$$

We thus see that *according to the quantity theory of money, price level varies in direct proportion to the quantity of money*. A doubling of the quantity of money (M) will lead to the doubling of the price level. Further, since changes in the quantity of money are assumed to be independent or autonomous of the price level, the changes in the quantity of money become the cause of the changes in the price level.

Quantity Theory of Money: Income Version

Fisher's transactions approach to quantity theory of money described in equations (1) and (2) above considers such variables as total volume of transaction (T) and average price level of these transactions are conceptually vague and difficult to measure. Therefore, in *later years quantity theory was formulated in income form which considers real income or national output (i.e., transactions of final goods only) rather than all transactions.* As the data regarding national income or output is readily available, the income version of the quantity theory is being increasingly used. Moreover, the average price level of output is a more meaningful and useful concept. Indeed, in actual practice, the general price level in a country is measured taking into account only the prices of final goods and services which constitute national product. It may be noted that even in this income version of the quantity theory of money, the function of money is considered to be a means of exchange as in the transactions approach of Fisher. In this approach, the concept of *income velocity of money* has been used instead of transactions velocity of circulation. *By income velocity we mean the average number of times per period a unit of money is used in making payments involving final goods and services, that is, national product or national income.* In fact, income velocity of money is measured by $\frac{Y}{M}$ where Y stands for real national income and M for the quantity of money.

In view of the above, the income version of quantity theory of money is written as under:

$$MV = PY \quad \ldots (3)$$

$$P = \frac{MV}{Y} \quad \ldots (4)$$

where

M = Quantity of money
V = Income velocity of money
P = Average price level of final goods and services
Y = Real national income (or aggregate output)

Like that in the transactions approach, in this new income version of the quantity theory also the different variables are assumed to be independent of each other. Further, income velocity of money (V) and real income or aggregate output (Y) are assumed to be given and constant during a short period. More specifically, they do not vary in response to the changes in M. In fact, *real income or output (Y) is assumed to be determined by the real sector forces such as capital stock, the amount and skills of labour, technology etc.* But as these factors are taken to be given and constant in the short run, and further that full-employment of the

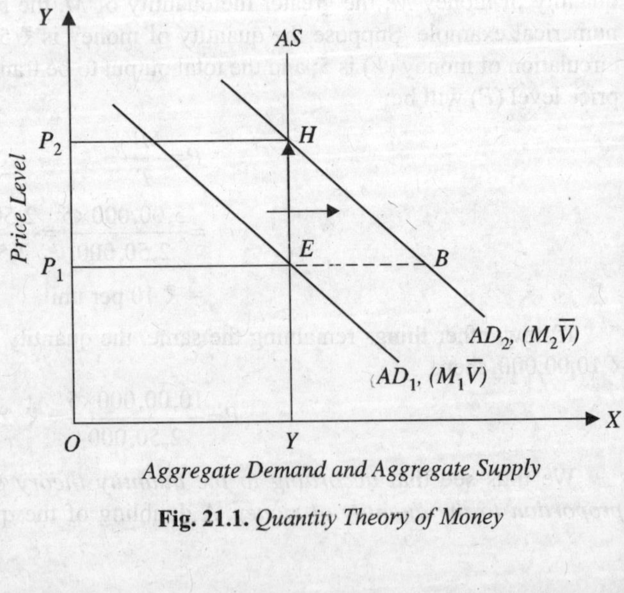

Fig. 21.1. *Quantity Theory of Money*

given resources is assumed to be prevailing due to the operation of Say's law and wage-price flexibility, supply of output is taken to be inelastic and constant for purposes of determination of price level.

It follows from equations (3) and (4) above that with income velocity (V) and national output (Y) remaining constant, price level (P) is determined by the quantity of money (M).

Classical quantity theory of money is illustrated in Fig. 21.1 through aggregate demand and aggregate supply model. It is worth noting that the quantity of money (M) multiplied by the income velocity of circulation (V), that is, MV gives us aggregate expenditure in the quantity theory of money. Now, with a given quantity of money, say M_1 and constant velocity of money $\bar{V}$, we have a given amount of monetary expenditure ($M_1 \bar{V}$). Given this aggregate expenditure, at a lower price level more quantities of goods can be purchased and at a higher price level, less quantities of goods can be purchased. Therefore, in accordance with classical quantity theory of money aggregate demand representing $M_1 \bar{V}$ slopes downward as shown by the aggregate demand curve AD_1 in Fig. 21.1. If now the quantity of money is increased, say to M_2, aggregate demand curve representing new aggregate monetary expenditure $M_2 \bar{V}$ will shift to the right.

As regards aggregate supply curve, due to the assumption of wage-price flexibility, it is perfectly inelastic at full-employment level of output as is shown by the vertical aggregate supply curve AS in Fig. 21.1. Now, with a given quantity of money equal to M_1, aggregate demand curve AD_1 cuts the aggregate supply curve AS at point E and determines price level OP_1. Now, if the quantity of money is increased to M_2, the aggregate demand curve shifts upward to AD_2. It will be seen from Fig. 21.1 that with the increase in aggregate demand to AD_2 consequent to the expansion in money supply to M_2, excess demand equal to EB emerges at the current price level OP_1. This excess demand for goods and services will lead to the rise in price level to OP_2 at which again aggregate quantity demanded equals the aggregate supply which remains unchanged at OY due to the existence of full employment in the economy.

QUANTITY THEORY OF MONEY: THE CAMBRIDGE CASH BALANCE APPROACH

The equation of exchange has been stated by Cambridge economists, Marshall and Pigou, in a form different from Irving Fisher. Cambridge economists explained the determination of value of money in line with the determination of value in general. Value of a commodity is determined by demand for and supply of it and likewise, according to them, the value of money (*i.e.*, its purchasing power) is determined by the demand for and supply of money. *In cash balance approach to demand for money Cambridge economists laid stress on the store of value function of money in sharp contrast to the medium of exchange function of money emphasised in Fisher's transactions approach to demand for money.* According to cash balance approach, the public likes to hold a proportion of nominal income in the form of money (*i.e.*, cash balances). Let us call this proportion of nominal income that people want to hold in money as k. Then cash balance approach can be written as:

$$M^d = kPY \quad \ldots (1)$$

where

Y = *real* national income (*i.e.*, aggregate output)

P = the price level

PY = *nominal* national income

k = the proportion of nominal income that people want to hold in money

M^d = the amount of money which public wants to hold

Now, *for the achievement of money-market equilibrium, demand for money must equal with the supply of money which we denote by M.* It is important to note that the supply of money M is exogenously given and is determined by the monetary policies of the central bank of a country. Thus, for equilibrium in the money market,

$$M = M^d$$

As $$M^d = kPY$$

Therefore, $$M = kPY \qquad \ldots (2)$$

It is worth mentioning that k in the equations (1) and (2) is related to velocity of circulation of money V in Fisher's transactions approach. Thus, when a greater proportion of nominal income is held in the form of money (*i.e.*, when k is higher), V falls. On the other hand, when less proportion of nominal income is held in money, V rises. In the words of Crowther, "*The higher the proportion of their real incomes that people decide to keep in money, the lower will be the velocity of circulation, and vice versa.*"[2]

It follows from above that $k=\frac{1}{V}$. Now, rearranging equation (2) we have cash balance approach in which P appears as dependent variable. Thus, on rearranging equation (2) we have

$$P=\frac{1}{k}.\frac{M}{Y} \qquad \ldots (3)$$

Like Fisher's equation, cash balance equation is also an accounting identity because k is defined as:

$$\frac{\text{Quantity of Money Supply}}{\text{National Income}}, \text{ this is, } \frac{M}{PY}$$

Now, Cambridge economists also assumed that k remains constant. Further, due to their belief that wage-price flexibility ensures full employment of resources, the level of real national income was also fixed corresponding to the level of aggregate output produced by full employment of resources.

Thus, from equation (3) it follows that with k and Y remaining constant, price level (P) is determined by the quantity of money (M); changes in the quantity of money will cause proportionate changes in the price level.

Some economists have pointed out similarity between Cambridge cash balance approach and Fisher's transactions approach. According to them, k is reciprocal of V $\left(k=\frac{1}{V} \text{ or } V=\frac{1}{k}\right)$. Thus in equation (2) if we replace k by $\frac{1}{V}$, we have

$$M=\frac{1}{V}PY$$

or $$MV = PY$$

which is income version of Fisher's quantity theory of money. However, despite the formal similarity between the cash balance and transactions approaches, there are important conceptual differences between the two which makes cash balance approach superior to the transactions approach. First, as mentioned above, Fisher's transactions approach lays stress on the medium of exchange function of money, that is, according to it, people want money to use it as a means of payment for buying goods and services. On the other hand, cash-balance approach emphasises the store-of-value function of money. The people hold money so that some value is stored for spending on goods and services after some lapse of time.

2. Crowther, *Outline of Money*, p. 150.

Further, in explaining the factors which determine velocity of circulation, transactions approach points to the mechanical aspects of payment methods and practices such as frequency of wages and other factor payments, the speed with which funds can be sent from one place to another, the extent to which bank deposits and cheques are used in dealing with others and so on. On the other hand, k in the cash balance approach is *behavioural in nature*. Thus, according to Prof. S.B. Gupta, "*Cash balance approach is behavioural in nature: it is built around the demand for money, however simple. Unlike Fisher's V, k is a behavioural ratio. As such it can easily lead to stress being placed on the relative usefulness of money as an asset.*"[3]

Thirdly, cash-balance approach explains determination of value of money in a framework of general demand-supply analysis of value. Thus, according to this approach, value of money (that is, its purchasing power) is determined by the demand for and supply of money.

To sum up, cash balance approach has made some improvements over Fisher's transactions approach in explaining the relation between money and prices. However, it is essentially the same as the Fisher's transactions approach. Like Fisher's approach it considers substitution between money and commodities. That is, if they decide to hold less money, they spend more on commodities rather than on other assets such as bonds, shares, real property, durable consumer goods. Further, like Fisher's transactions approach it visualises that changes in the quantity of money cause proportional changes in the price level. Like Fisher's approach, cash balance approach also assumes that full-employment of resources will prevail due to the wage-price flexibility. Hence, it also believes the aggregate supply curve as perfectly inelastic at full-employment level of output.

An important limitation of cash balance approach is that it also assumes that the proportion of income that people want to hold in money, that is, k, remains constant. Note that in practice it has been found that proportionality factor k or velocity of circulation has not remained constant but has been fluctuating, especially in the short run.

Besides, **cash-balance approach falls short of considering *demand for money as an asset*.** If demand for money as an asset were considered, it would have a determining influence on the rate of interest on which amount of investment in the economy depends. Investment plays an important role in the determination of level of real income in the economy. It was left to J.M. Keynes who later emphasised the role of demand for money as an asset which was one of the alternative assets in which individuals can keep their income or wealth. Finally, it may be mentioned that other criticisms of Fisher's transactions approach to quantity theory of money discussed above equally apply to the Cambridge cash balance approach.

Keynes's Critique of the Quantity Theory of Money

The quantity theory of money has been widely criticised. The following criticisms have been levelled against the quantity theory of money held by Keynes and his followers.[4]

1. **Useless truism.** With the qualification that velocity of money (V) and the total output (Y) remain the same, the equation of exchange ($MV = PY$) is a *useless truism*, that is, true by definition. The real trouble is that these things do not remain the same as the quantity of money is increased or decreased. They change not only in the long run but also in a short period. Fisher's equation of exchange simply tells us that expenditure made on goods (MV) is equal to the value of output of goods and services sold (PY). However, in our view this criticism of the quantity theory is not valid. While Fisher's equation of exchange ($MV = PY$) is true by definition, it is converted into theory by assuming (i) the velocity of circutation remains unaffected by the change in quantity of money and

3. S.B. Gupta, *op. cit.*, p. 206.
4. For detailed analysis of Keynes's theory of money and prices, see Chapter 22.

(2) national income (GDP or Y) remains constant when the quantity of money is increased. Given these assumptions, quantity theory of money tells us a change in the quantity of money will cause an equal proportionate change in the price level. In the equation of exchange $\left(P=\frac{MV}{Y}\right)$, with V and Y remaining constant, increase in quantity of money (M) will cause proportionate increase in price level (P). In fact, every theory makes some assumptions, therefore, it cannot be said that the quantity theory is a mere truism. Of course, this theory can be validly criticized that the assumptions it makes are not realistic. For example, when the quantity of money increases, velocity of circulation usually falls.

2. **Velocity of money is not stable.** *Keynesian economists have challenged the assumption of the quantity theory of money that velocity of money remains stable.* According to them, velocity of money changes inversely with the change in money supply. They argue that increase in money supply, demand for money remaining constant, leads to the fall in the rate of interest. At a lower rate of interest, people will be induced to hold more money as idle cash balances (under speculative motive). This means velocity of circulation of money will be reduced. Thus, *if a decline in interest rate reduces velocity, then increase in the money supply will be offset by reduction in velocity*, with the result that price level need not rise when money supply is increased.

3. **Price level rises as a result of imbalances between aggregate expenditure or aggregate demand and aggregate supply.** Increase in quantity of money may not always lead to the increase in aggregate expenditure. According to the Keynesian economists, the quantity theory of money to be true, the following two assumptions must hold:

(*i*) An increase is money supply must lead to an increase in aggregate expenditure, that is, aggregate demand, *i.e.*, no part of additional money created should be kept in idle hoards.

(*ii*) The resulting increase in spending or aggregate demand must face a totally inelastic output.

Both the assumptions, according to Keynes, lack generality and, therefore, if either of them does not hold, the quantity theory cannot be accepted as a valid explanation of the changes in price level.

Let us take the first assumption. Under this assumption, the entire increase in the quantity of money must express itself in the form of increased expenditure. If expenditure does not increase, there is no question of a change in prices or output. But, is it valid to make such an assumption? Obviously, *there is no such direct link* between the increase in the quantity of money and the increase in the volume of aggregate spending or aggregate demand. No one is going to increase his expenditure simply because the government is printing more notes or the banks are more liberal in their lending policies.

Besides, *if the demand for money is highly interest-elastic, the increase in money supply will not lead to any appreciable fall in the rate of interest.* With no significant fall in rate of interest, the investment expenditure and expenditure on durable consumer goods will not increase much. As a result, increase in money supply may not lead to increase in aggregate expenditure or aggregate demand and therefore price level may remain unaffected. Further, suppose Reserve Bank of India increases money supply through open market operations and reduces cash reserve (CRR) of banks. As a result, banks are flush with the funds and are ready to give loans or credit to investors. *Recall this credit its money.* However, the investors being pessimistic about profit making may not be willing to take loans even at lower rate of interest. As a result, investment expenditure will not increase. Likewise, consumers may also not be confident about their future earnings and will not borrow for financing their purchases of houses, cars, colour TVs etc and as a result their consumption expenditure may not rise.

This is not to say, however, that changes in the quantity of money have no influence whatsoever on the volume of aggregate expenditure. Changes in the quantity of money are often capable of inducing changes in the volume of aggregate spending. When investors are ready to take loans from banks for increasing their investment and consumers take loans from banks to purchase durable consumer goods such as houses, cars, air conditioners etc., the expansion in money supply or credit leads to the increase in aggregate expenditure and influences price level. What Keynes and his followers deny is the assertion that there exists a direct, simple, and more or less a proportional relation between variation in money supply and variation in the level of total expenditure.

4. **Assumption of constant level of aggregate output is not valid.** Keynes asserted that the assumption of constant aggregate output is valid only under conditions of full employment. It is only then that we can assume a totally inelastic supply of output, as all the available resources being already fully utilised aggregate output cannot be increased further. In conditions of less than full employment, the supply curve of output will be elastic. Thus, if we assume that aggregate spending or demand increases with an increase in the quantity of money, it does not follow that prices must necessarily rise. If the supply curve of output is fairly elastic, the effect of an increase in spending will be more to raise production rather than prices. At full-employment level every further increase in spending or aggregate demand must lead to the rise in the price level as supply of output is inelastic at full-employment level. Since full-employment cannot be assumed to be a normal affair, we cannot accept the quantity theory of money as a valid explanation of changes in the price level in the short run.

Consider Fig. 21.2. As mentioned above, according to Keynes, aggregate supply curve *AS* is perfectly elastic up to full-employment or potential GDP level Y_F (that is, horizonal segment PE_3 of the *AS* curve in Fig. 21.2 at the fixed price level *OP*) depicting the situation of depression or recession in the economy with unemployment of labour and the existence of underutilised capital stock or excess productive capacity. Initially, the economy is in equilibrium at point E_1 where aggregate demand curve AD_1 intersects aggregate supply curve *AS*. Suppose now to pull out the economy from recession government *increases its expenditure by printing new money.* As a result, aggregate demand curve shifts to the right to AD_2 and still intersects the horizontal segment of the aggregate supply curve at point E_2 and therefore price level remains the same at *OP*. This is due to unemployment of labour and existence of excess capacity in the economy. More is produced and supplied at the given wage rate as due to unemployment of labour and the existence of excess capacity wage rate and other costs per unit of output docs not rise. Similarly, further increase in money supply shifts the aggregate demand curve to the right to AD_3, the equilibrium is at point E_3 with price level remaining the same as even now unemployed labour and excess capacity are utilized to increase aggregate supply of output.

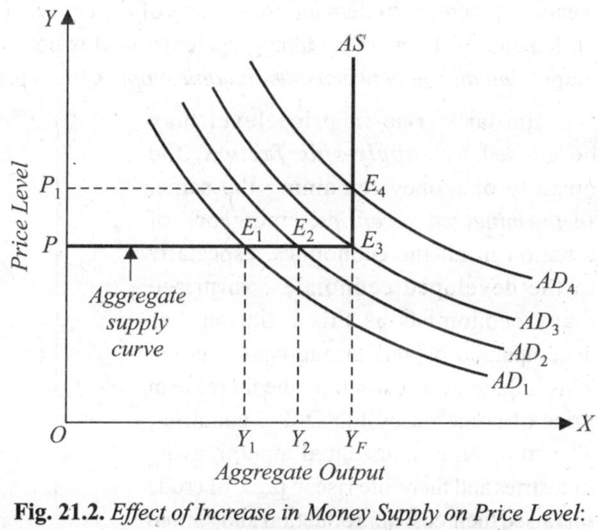

Fig. 21.2. *Effect of Increase in Money Supply on Price Level: Original Keynesian Model*

However, from point E_3 corresponding to full-employment or potential GDP level Y_F, if government further increases its expenditure by printing more money, aggregate demand curve shifts further to the right but as it now intersects the vertical segment of the aggregate supply curve *AS* at point E_4, price level rises to OP_1. Thus, according to Keynes, it is only when the economy is operating at full-employment or potential GDP level that increase in money supply leads to the proportionate rise in price level. However, full-employment cannot be assumed to be normal affair in a free-market economy.

Keynes put forward the view that increase in money supply does not affect price level *directly* but through its effect on rate of interest. The increase in money supply, the demand for money remaining the same, lowers rate of interest. The lower interest rate causes increase in investment expenditure which through the working of multiplier will raise aggregate demand for goods and services. In case of increase in aggregate demand for goods and services what will be its effect on change in price level depends on the elasticity of aggregate supply curve. If aggregate supply curve is fairly elastic as is the case during depression or recession, the increase in aggregate demand will not cause rise in price level. Keynes laid stress on the fact *there was no any direct and precise* effect of increase in the quantity of money on the price level. Much depends on the interest elasticity of money demand function, (*i.e.,* liquidity preference curve, the sensitivity of investment demand to changes in interest rate and finally elasticity of aggregate supply curve).

Factors Other than Quantity of Money also Affects the Price Level

The quantity theory with its *sole emphasis on quantity of money* as a determinant of price level does not consider other factors that can cause changes in aggregate demand and influence changes in price level. For example, increase in government expenditure (with quantity of money remaining unchanged), increase in investment by investors when they are optimistic about profit making, increase in consumers' demand (for example, as a result of increase in stock prices which make them wealthier, increase in demand for exports of a country lead to the increase in aggregate expenditure or demand. If the increase in aggregate demand is not matched by sufficient increase in supply of output, *imbalance between demand and supply* causes price level to rise.

Similarly, rise in price level may be caused by ***supply-side factors***, the quantity of money remaining the same. *In the nineteen seventies*, emergence of inflation in all the economies, especially in the developed economies, surprised many economists as this inflation was accompanied by fall in aggregate output. This inflation was caused by the increase in price of crude oil by the OPEC countries. The crude oil is an essential input in many industries and therefore rise in price of crude oil raised their cost of production and shifted the short-run aggregate supply curve to the left as shown in Figure 21.3. Initially, the equilibrium is at point E_0 which represents simultaneously long-run and short-run equilibrium. With the increase in crude oil price short-run aggregate supply curve shifts to the left to SAS_1. Price level rises from P_0 to P_1 but at the same tune GDP falls from Y_F to Y_1. *Rise in price level* occurs along with the fall in GDP level. This is therefore called ***stagflation***.

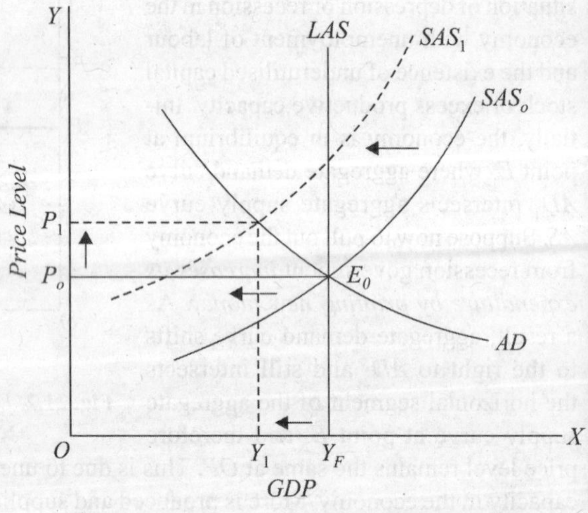

Fig. 21.3. *Inflation Caused by Supply-Side Factor*

Empirical Evidence

If interpreted in terms of growth of the quantity of money and inflation, *i.e.,* rate of change in price level, *the quantity theory predicts that, given its assumptions of constant velocity of money* (V) and *constant level of output i.e., GDP, the inflation rate will be equal to the rate of growth of money supply*. However, this is not supported by historical evidence from the US, UK, India in the short run (*i.e.,* ranging from 1 to 5 years period). These empirical studies reveal that though changes in money supply and inflation are correlated but *this relation is quite weak in the short period.* Changes in inflation rate have been found to be less than the growth in money supply. It is only in a long period of a decade or more that average fluctuations in money growth and inflation show a stronger correlation. The weak correlation between money growth and inflation in the short period that is contrary to the quantity theory of money, has been validly explained by the growth in GDP and change in velocity of money (V) which, as had been pointed out by Keynes and others, do not remain the same. Roger E. Farmer rightly writes,. "*The connection between money growth and inflation is not particularly strong because real GDP and changes in propensity to hold money (which determines velocity of money) have almost as important as the rate of money creation in determining of inflation*".[3] He further adds: "The connection between money growth and inflation is strong in countries with very high inflation because movements in the propensity to hold money and movements in real GDP are very small relative to large movements in the stock of money."[4]

It follows from above that changes in price level or inflation depends not only on the increase in money supply but also changes in velocity of money growth in GDP.

QUESTIONS FOR REVIEW

1. Explain the Quantity Theory of Money. Will a doubling of money supply always lead to a doubling of general price level ?
2. Does increase in money supply always lead to a proportional increase in prices ? Give reasons in support of your answer.
3. Critically examine the Quantity Theory of Money. Does an increase in money supply always lead to a proportionate increase in prices ?
4. Explain Keynes's criticism of the Quantity Theory of Money.
5. Discuss Fisher's and Keynes's approaches to the relationship between the quantity of money and price level.
6. Explain Fisher's equation of exchange. It is asserted by some that Fisher's equation of exchange is a '*useless truism.*' Do you agree ? Discuss.
7. Explain Cambridge Cash-Balance Approach of the Quantity Theory of Money. How does it differ from Fisher's transactions approach ?
8. Cash-Balance Approach of the Quantity Theory of Money is behavioural in nature and is built around the demand for money. Discuss.
9. On what grounds the Quantity Theory of Money has been criticised? Explain.

3. Roger E.A. Farmer, *Macroeconomics,* 2nd Edition Thomson, 2002, p. 130.
4. *Op.cit.,* pp.131–132.

CHAPTER 22

Keynes's Theory of Money and Prices

Introduction

The main thrust of Keynes's criticism of classical quantity theory of money was directed at its conclusion that (*i*) velocity of circulation is constant, and (*ii*) full employment of resources is the natural state of a free-market economy. Keynes believed that velocity of circulation was volatile and there often existed underemployment of resources due to recessionary conditions in the economy. As seen in the previous chapters, classical economists believed that people demanded money only for transactions purposes and money balances held for transactions purposes were proportional to nominal income. Keynes challenged this viewpoint and held that people could hold income-earning assets such as bonds instead of holding money balances. To the transactions motive for holding money, Keynes added precautionary motive and speculative motive (that is, demand for money as an asset) for holding money. Income or interest earned on assets such as bonds is the opportunity cost of holding money. The higher the rate of interest on these assets, the less money will be held by the public. It is worth noting that people adjust their money holdings until the amount of money they demand equals what they actually have. If people have more money than what they demand, they will spend either on consumer goods and services or invest more. On the other hand, if their demand for money to hold is greater than what they presently have, they will try to acquire more money either by reducing expenditure on goods and services or selling some of their assets such as bonds and shares. Keynes laid stress on financial investment in bonds as a major way to reduce one's money holdings.

The task of a monetary theory is to explain the influence of changes in money supply on the level of economic activity (*i.e.*, levels of real income, output and employment) and the price level. *Keynes's monetary theory explains the effect of variation in money supply on the level of economic activity and price level through its effect on the rate of interest which determines investment in the economy*. In what follows we first explain the impact of expansion in money supply on the levels of real income and employment. In the second stage of our analysis of Keynes's monetary theory we show how changes in money supply affect the price level in the economy.

KEYNES'S THEORY OF MONEY AND PRICES

We now explain Keynes's monetary theory with regard to the relationship between the supply of money and the price level. Keynes believed that changes in money supply could bring about changes in the price level but, contrary to the classical economists' view, he explained that there was no direct and proportionate relationship between the quantity of money and the price level. He showed that changes in money supply indirectly affect the price level through its effect on the rate of interest. When money supply is increased, given the demand for money holding curve, it leads to the fall in the rate of interest depending upon how far money demand curve is sensitive to the rate of interest. A change in the rate of interest affects investment which through multiplier process affects aggregate expenditure or demand. It is then the magnitude of aggregate demand relative to aggregate supply of output that causes price level to change. Thus, relation between money and the price level far from direct and proportionate is only indirect.

The Keynesian theory emphasises that the price level is in fact a consequence of aggregate demand or expenditure relative to aggregate supply rather than of quantity of money. The real cause of fluctuations in price level is to be found in fluctuations in the level of aggregate expenditure. Therefore, changes in the quantity of money can bring about changes in the level of prices only if they change aggregate demand in relation to the supply of output. Unless aggregate expenditure increases, there can be no increase in demand for goods. And if demand for goods does not increase, the question of rise in price level does not arise. However, even if aggregate demand or expenditure does increase, prices may still not rise if the supply curve of output is fairly elastic. Therefore, the effect of a change in quantity of money on the price level depends on the following factors:

(i) effect of changes in money supply on the level of aggregate demand or spending;

(ii) relation between aggregate spending and the volume of production.

As regards the volume of aggregate expenditure or aggregate demand, in the Keynesian theory it depends on the following:

(a) rate of interest which is determined by the demand for money and the supply of money;

(b) the investment demand curve which determines the increase in investment demand following a fall in the rate of interest; and

(c) the propensity to consume which determines the magnitude of the multiplier effect of increase in investment.

(d) supply of money.

Transmission Mechanism. According to Keynes, there is no any *direct* relationship between changes in money supply and the change in price level. *Increase in money supply affects the price level through change in rate of interest.* The mechanism through which increase in money supply can lead to the rise in aggregate demand and price level can be represented by the following scheme:

$$M^S\uparrow \longrightarrow r\downarrow \longrightarrow I\uparrow \longrightarrow AD\uparrow \longrightarrow Y\uparrow \text{ and } P\uparrow$$

where M^S = supply of money

r = rate of interest

I = amount of investment

AD = aggregate demand

Y = level of real national income, that is, aggregate output (GDP)

P = price level

The above scheme represents the chief proposition of Keynesian monetary theory. According to this, expansion in money supply *(M^S)* causes the rate of interest to fall. Then, given the investment demand function, at a lower rate of interest, there is more demand for investment. This higher rate of investment boosts up the level of aggregate demand or expenditure through the multiplier process. However, as we will see below, *whether or not this increase in aggregate demand or expenditure will cause the rise in the price level depends upon the nature of aggregate supply curve.*

It is evident from above that in the Keynesian theory the general price level is determined by the same forces that determine the level of national income and employment, that is, the level of aggregate demand and aggregate supply. It needs to be emphasised that price level and national income *(i.e.,* aggregate output) are determined jointly by aggregate demand and aggregate supply. However, in the analysis of determination of real national income in the *income-expenditure approach diagram,* we have used the concept of aggregate demand *with a given fixed price level and have therefore also called it as aggregate expenditure.*

But to explain the Keynesian theory of money and prices, we need to use the concept of *aggregate demand with varying price level.* Aggregate demand (with varying price level) is the sum of total expenditure which consumers, businessmen, Government and foreigners are willing to make on aggregate output of goods and services at different price levels during a given period. That is, aggregate demand (with flexible prices) shows how much output the consumers, businesses, Government and foreigners are willing to buy at various price levels. Thus aggregate demand curve in Keynesian theory is $C + I + G + NX$ at various price levels.[1] At higher price levels, aggregate output demanded or purchased is less at a higher price level and it increases at a lower price level. In other words, aggregate demand ($C + I + G + NX$) curve with variable price level slopes downward as shown in Fig. 22.1. Three factors account for the downward sloping nature of the aggregate demand curve. These three factors are *real balance effect, interest effect* and *foreign trade effect* of the change in the price level which have been explained in an earlier chapter concerning *AD-AS* model (with flexible prices). As explained in an earlier chapter concerning *AD-AS* model (with flexible prices), the sum of aggregate demand for consumption, investment and net exports increases with a fall in the price level and declines with a rise in the price level. This means that aggregate demand curve showing relationship between aggregate output demanded and the general price level slopes downward to the right as shown in Fig. 22.1

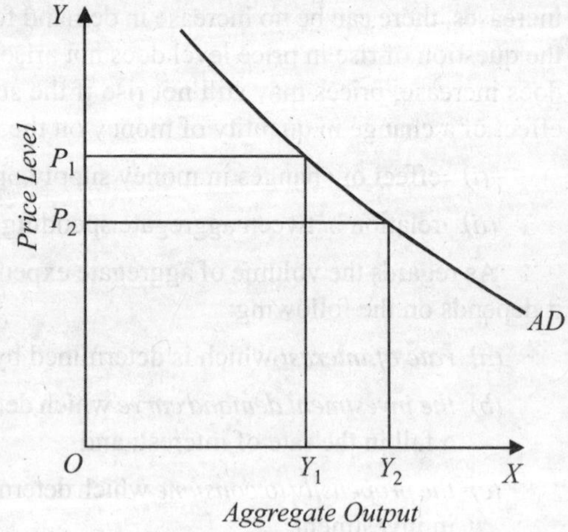

Fig. 22.1. *Aggregate Demand Curve and Varying Price Level*

Aggregate demand curve is derived from changes in aggregate expenditure caused by changes in the price level. If there is a change in the *non-price factors such as money supply, investment demand, Government expenditure, taxation,* the aggregate demand curve will shift. Thus, when money supply is increased by the central bank of a country, it will lower the rate of interest. As seen above, at a lower rate of interest more investment is undertaken depending on the elasticity of investment demand curve. Further, with more autonomous investment expenditure the entire aggregate demand curve (with variable price level) depicting $C + I + G + NX$ will shift to the right implying thereby that at each price level, the aggregate quantity demanded will increase.

Money Supply, Aggregate Demand and Price Level

But what happens to the equilibrium price level and real national product as a result of change in money supply, we must consider aggregate supply as well. Thus, even if aggregate demand or expenditure increases it does not follow that prices must necessarily rise. Whether or not the increase in aggregate demand will cause a rise in price level depends upon the nature of aggregate supply curve. If the supply curve of output is fairly elastic, it is more likely that the effect of increase in aggregate demand or spending will be more to raise production or real income than prices. In the model of determination of general price level, the concept of aggregate supply curve with variable price level is used. Precisely speaking, in this sense, *aggregate supply curve shows the various amounts of aggregate supply which the producers in the economy are willing to produce and sell in*

---

1 Note that in sharp contrast to Keynes's theory, in the quantity theory of money aggregate demand at various price levels is determined by *MV*, that is, quantity of money (*M*) times the velocity of money (*V*) which is assumed to remain constant.

the market at various price levels. The classical economists assumed that there normally prevailed full employment of resources in the economy. According to them, if at any time there is deviation from this full-employment level, the *wages, interest and prices quickly and automatically adjust or change to restore equilibrium at the full-employment level.* Thus, in the classical theory, the aggregate supply curve of output is perfectly inelastic (*i.e.,* a vertical straight line) at the output level corresponding to the full-employment level of resources.

As mentioned above, Keynes considered the situation of economic depression when the economy was operating at less than full-employment level of resources. *He further believed that in such a situation money wage rates were sticky, i.e., remained stable.* He further assumed that average and margined products of labour remained constant when more of it was employed following the increase in aggregate demand. With these assumptions, more aggregate output is produced and supplied at the given price level in response to increase in aggregate demand. But when full-employment of labour and capital stock is attained and aggregate demand further increases, aggregate supply curve being unable to increase any more, it is the price level that will rise in response to the increase in aggregate demand. Keynes's aggregate supply curve depicting the relationship between price level and the aggregate production (supply) is shown in Fig. 22.2 where it will be seen that up to the level of aggregate output OY_F aggregate supply curve is a horizontal straight line (*i.e.,* perfectly elastic) showing thereby that more is produced and supplied at the same price level *OP*. OY_F is the full-employment level of aggregate production (*i.e.,* potential GNP) and therefore beyond that aggregate supply curve becomes vertical (*i.e.,* perfectly inelastic). It may however be noted that Keynes recognised that as the aggregate supply approaches close to the full-employment level cost of output per unit tends to rise due to the rise in wage rate and also due to diminishing returns to extra units of factors employed. But, according to Keynes, the rise in price level before full employment or less than capacity output will not be much.

Suppose the economy is in a state of depression so that a lot of resources including labour are lying idle. Initially, the aggregate demand curve is AD_1 which cuts the aggregate supply curve *AS* at point E_1 and as a result price level *OP* is determined (see Fig. 22.2). Now, suppose that expansion in money supply succeeds in raising aggregate demand curve to AD_2. It will be seen from Fig. 22.2 that the new aggregate demand curve still cuts the aggregate supply curve in its horizontal range at point E_2. Thus increase in aggregate demand to AD_2 caused by expansionary monetary policy has led to the increase in aggregate output (*i.e.,* real national income) from Y_1 to Y_2 without any rise in general price level. If money supply is further increased and as a result aggregate demand curve shifts upward to AD_3, and cuts aggregate supply curve *AS* at point E_3, even then only aggregate output rises to its full-employment level Y_F, price level remaining unchanged. Thus, with aggregate demand curve AD_3 economy is operating at full-employment level of output Y_F. Now, if there is further expansion in money supply causing aggregate demand curve to rise above AD_3, say to AD_4, in Fig. 22.2, resources being already fully utilised, supply of output will not respond to the increased demand and will cause the price level to rise to P_1. This happens when firms try to hire more workers and other resources for expanding output to meet the increased demand. In case full

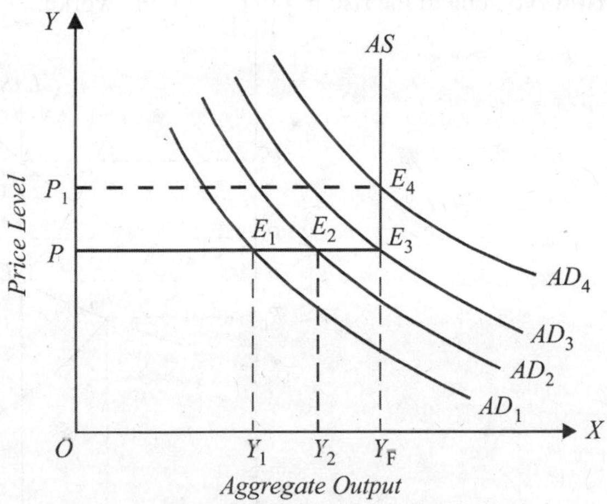

Fig. 22.2. *Effect of Increase in Money Supply on Price Level: Keynes's Model*

employment of resources have been already achieved, they will only bid up wages and their cost of production. Hence the price level will rise. Thus when full employment is prevailing, increase in aggregate demand for goods brought about by increase in money supply leads only to higher price level and not to higher output.

It is clear from above that *it is not necessary that even if expansion in money supply succeeds in raising aggregate demand, price level must rise.* The effect of increase in aggregate demand depends on whether the economy is operating at less than full-employment level when there are recessionary conditions in the economy or the economy is working at full-employment level at which aggregate supply curve is perfectly inelastic.

Money Supply, Price Level and National Income in the Short Run and Long Run

In modern macroeconomics, the distinction is drawn between short-run aggregate supply curve (*SAS*) and long-run aggregate supply curve (*LAS*). Long-run aggregate supply curve is vertical at the potential GDP or full-employment level whereas short-run aggregate supply curve slopes upward as shown in Figure 22.3. It is worth noting that short-run aggregate curve is drawn with a given money wage rate.

Now, suppose there is recession in the economy and due to this aggregate demand curve AD_0 lies at a lower level and intersects the short-run aggregate supply curve *SAS* at point E_0 to the left of the long-run aggregate supply curvy *LAS* in Fig. 22.3. Thus, the equilibrium at point E_0 represents less than full employment equilibrium. Now, suppose, money supply is increased which causes rate of interest to fall. The lower interest rate leads to the increase in investment expenditure causing aggregate demand curve to shift to AD_1. With this, as will be seen from Figure 22.3, the equilibrium is at full-employment level Y_F and price level rises to P_1. If aggregate demand further shifts to the right to AD_2 due to the expansion in money supply, the level of GDP increases to Y_1 as a result of employment falling below the natural rate of unemployment but price level further rises to P_2. However, due to the rise in price level, the workers will soon realise that their real wage has fallen

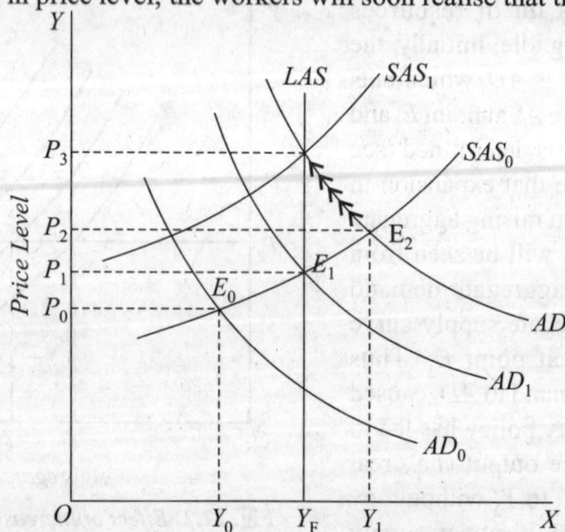

Fig. 22.3. *Effect of Increase in Money Supply on the Price Level and National Income in the Short Run and Long Run*

and when their wage contracts with the employers mature, they will demand higher wages. However, unlike classical economists and Friedman's view that wage rate will rise quickly and short-run aggregate supply curve (*SAS*) will shift above to SAS_1, according to Keynesian economists, money wage rate and therefore price level will not rise quickly but only slowly as shown by various arrows in Figure 22.3.

Ineffectiveness of Monetary Policy: Keynes's View

It may however be noted that Keynes and early Keynesians were not very optimistic about the success of expansionary monetary policy in lifting the economy out of depression. They point out various weak links in the chain of causation in the process of increase in money supply leading to the rise in aggregate demand. The first weak link occurs at the stage of increase in money supply causing lowering of the rate of interest. Keynes was considering an economy which was in the grip of depression and rate of interest prevailing then was already at a low level and therefore they did not expect any further fall. According to him, whatever expansion in money supply is made at that time, all of it would be held by them rather than investing it in bonds. In other words, according to Keynes and his earlier followers, the demand for money (*i.e.,* liquidity preference curve) was perfectly elastic at a very low rate of interest as shown in Fig. 22.4 where at rate of interest r_3 demand for money becomes perfectly elastic. It is said that at a very low rate of interest economy gets caught up in the **liquidity trap** in times of depression.

Thus. if the rate of interest is already very low, as is usually the case in times of depression. the expansion in the quantity of money will not be able to reduce it still further. As shown in Fig. 22.4, when the rate of interest is already at a low level so that people demand any amount of money (*i.e.,* the economy is caught in the liquidity trap) at it, the rate of interest will not fall further

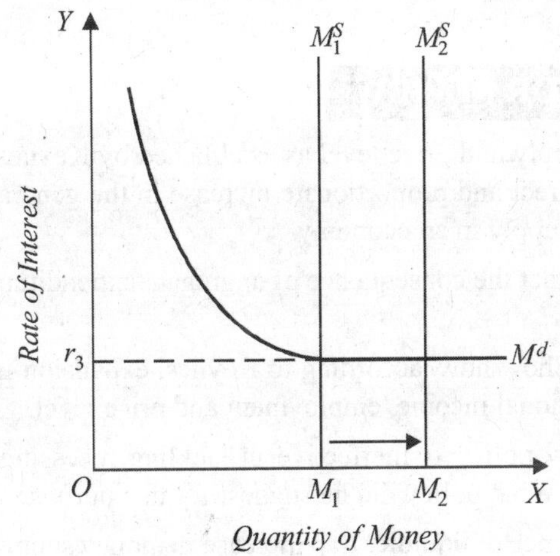

Fig. 22.4. *In liquidity-trap Situation Increase in Money Supply does not Cause Fall in Interest Rate.*

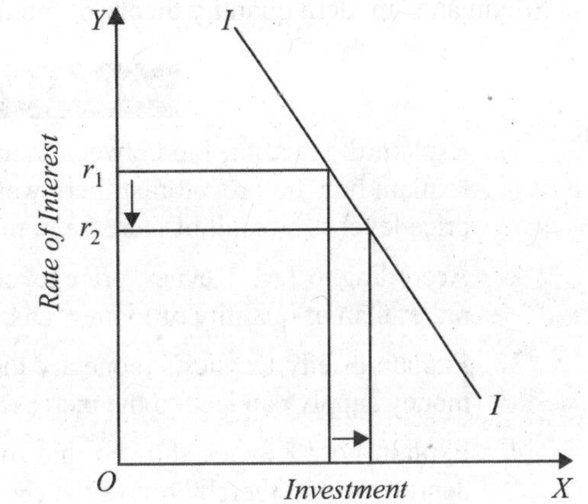

Fig. 22.5. *Interest-elasticity of Investment is very low.*

even when the supply of money is increased. The curve M^d is the money demand curve with a horizontal segment (*i.e.,* liquidy trap) on the right side. Suppose the quantity of money is initially M_1. With the given money demand curve M^d and the money supply M_1 the rate of interest Or_3 is determined which is very low. Now. if the money supply is increased to M_2. the rate of interest does not fall; all the additional money is held by the people with themselves and not lent out or used for buying bonds or debentures. Thus, when we are operating along the perfectly elastic part of the liquidity preference or money demand curve, the rate of interest cannot be reduced by the increase in money supply. With no fall in the rate of interest, investment demand curve remaining the same, the rate of investment will not increase and if investment does not increase, aggregate demand and expenditure will not increase.

Another weak link in the transmission mechanism occurs in the effect of change in the rate of interest on the investment. Keynes and early Keynesians believed that investment demand curve is not much sensitive to the rate of interest, that is, interest-elasticity of investment demand is very low. If this is so, then even if there is a large fall in the rate of interest brought about by increase in money supply by the central bank, investment will not increase much. This is illustrated in Fig. 22.5 where we have drawn an inelastic investment demand curve *II*. It will be seen from Fig. 22.5 that when rate of interest falls from r_1 to r_2, there is only small increase in investment because investment demand curve is not sensitive to the rate of interest. Therefore, when investment does not increase much even when there is a large fall in rate of interest as a result of expansion in money supply, aggregate demand or expenditure will not increase much.

Thus, there are circumstances, especially when recessionary conditions prevail in the economy with large-scale unemployment and excess capacity in the economy, expansionary monetary policy may fail to increase the level of aggregate demand or expenditure. With no increase in aggregate demand, real national income, that is, GNP will not increase. Besides, in this Keynesian system, when due to either highly interest-elastic nature of the money demand curve *(i.e.,* due to liquidity trap) or due to the interest-inelastic nature of the investment demand curve, increase in money supply fails to raise aggregate demand, it will not cause rise in the level of national income.

It is thus clear from above that the *Keynesian theory traces the effect of the increase in money supply on the level of economic activity (i.e., income, output and employment) via its effect on the rate of interest.* Thus, in the Keynesian monetary theory the relationship between money supply and national income is not direct but it is thought to be much more indirect and uncertain than is assumed in Friedman's' modern quantity theory of money.

QUESTIONS FOR REVIEW

1. Explain the relationship between money supply and price level as established by Keynes. Explain how he proved that there was no direct and proportionate increase in the general price level as a result of increase in money supply in an economy.
2. According to J.M. Keynes, price level is in fact the consequence of aggregate expenditure rather than of quantity of money. Discuss.
3. Explain briefly Keynes's monetary theory. Show how, according to Keynes, expansion in money supply can lead to the increase in national income, employment and price level.
4. Explain how Keynes showed that monetary policy is ineffective in tackling recession/ depression and thereby revive the economy. What policy did he suggest for this purpose ?
5. What is liquidity trap ? Why does in the presence of liquidity trap increase in money supply does not affect the level of economic activity?

CHAPTER 23

Friedman's Restatement of Quantity Theory of Money

Monetarism : An Introduction

The quantity theory of money as put forward by classical economists emphasised that increase in the quantity of money would bring about an equal proportionate rise in the price level. The quantity theory of money had come into disrepute, together with the rest of classical economics as a result of the Great Depression of the 1930s. J.M. Keynes criticised quantity theory of money and brought out that expansion in money supply did not always cause the price level to rise.

However, in the fifties and sixties, the new thinking emerged under the influence of Milton Friedman, an eminent American economist and a Nobel Laureate in economics, who laid stress on the importance of money not only in determining the general price level but more importantly in influencing the level of economic activity. Friedman asserted that events of 1930s had been wrongly assessed and did not in fact offer evidence against the quantity theory of money. He however realised that there was a need to *restate* or *reformulate the quantity theory of money* which should re-establish the importance of money for determining the level of economic activity and the price level. However, in his restatement of the quantity theory of money he took account of Keynes's contribution to monetary theory, especially his emphasis on the demand for money as an asset. While restating the quantity theory of money Friedman put forward a new macroeconomic theory known as monetarism. We describe the following five propositions of Friedman's monetarism.

1. The level of economic activity in current rupee terms, that is, the level of *nominal income* is determined *primarily* by the stock of money.

   However, unlike the old quantity theory of money, Friedman lays stress on the *demand or desire for money to hold.* When increase in money supply causes excess of money supply over demand for it, people spend the excess money on goods and services leading to the rise in price level.
2. In the long run, the effect of expansion in money supply is *primarily* on the price level and other *nominal* variables. In the long run, the level of economic activity in real terms, that is, level of real output (GDP) and employment are determined by the real factors such as stock of capital goods, the state of technology, the size and quality of labour force. Therefore, long-run aggregate supply curve of output (LAS) is a vertical straight line.
3. In the short run price level as well as the level of real national income (*i.e.*, real output) and employment are determined by the supply of money and demand for money. In the short run, changes in the quantity of money are the dominant factor causing cyclical fluctuations in income and employment.
4. In the short run, the effect of expansion in money supply is divided between the rise in price level and increase in real national income depending on the elasticity of short-run aggregate supply curve. However, according to Friedman, in the long run wages and prices are perfectly flexible and lead to the establishment of equilibrium at full-employment (*i.e.* potential GDP) level.
5. Unlike Keynes's monetary theory, in Friedman's monetarist theory increase in money supply affects prices *directly* and not indirectly through its effect on rate of interest.

The above propositions derived by Friedman depends on the restatement of the quantity theory of money. It is important to note that Friedman's modern quantity theory of money is in fact based on his theory of demand for money. Therefore, in our analysis below we start from Friedman's theory of demand for money. We then explain how his theory of money demand explains the determination of the level of economic activity and the price level, both in the short run and long run.

FRIEDMAN'S RESTATEMENT OF QUANTITY THEORY OF MONEY

Friedman's modern quantity theory of money is very close to Cambridge's cash balance approach. Friedman and other modern monetarists have emphasised that k in Cambridge approach should be *interpreted as proportion of nominal income that people desire* or *demand to hold in the form of money balances*. Interpreting k in this *desired or ex-ante* sense helps to convert the Cambridge equation of exchange into a *theory of nominal income*. Thus, rewriting Cambridge equation as demand for money (M^d) we have:

$$M^d = kPY \quad \ldots (1)$$

where k is assumed to be constant. PY is the nominal income obtained by multiplying the real income (Y) with the price level (P). Like Cambridge economists, Friedman regards the quantity of money being fixed exogenously by the central bank of the country. If M represents the quantity of money set exogenously by the central bank, we have the equation which describes the Cambridge theory of determination of *nominal income*.

$$M^s = M^d = \bar{k}PY \quad \ldots (2)$$

or

$$M.\frac{1}{k} = PY \quad \ldots (3)$$

According to Cambridge equation (3), nominal income (*i.e.* PY) is determined by the supply of money (M^s) multiplied by the reciprocal of constant k.

Now, Friedman *introduced changes in the above Cambridge theory of money demand* incorporating important aspects of Keynes's theory of demand for money. Keynes emphasised the *role of money as an asset* apart from its role in meeting transactions demand. In studying the factors that determine demand for money as an asset relative to other assets, Keynes simplified his analysis by lumping together all non-monetary assets under a single category '*bonds*'. He then examined what determined people's allocation of their wealth between money and bonds. According to him, the level of income and rate of interest determined the allocation of wealth between money and bonds. According to Keynes, rate of interest was the most important determinant of k in the Cambridge cash-balance approach. It may be recalled that k in Cambridge theory indicates how much proportion of income people actually hold as money. However, Keynes regarded k as the proportion of income that people *want to hold in money as an asset*. *Friedman accepted Keynes's emphasis on the role of money as an asset* and presented his own theory of demand for money. In his analysis of determinants of money demand, Friedman included not only level of income and rate of interest on bonds but also rates of return on other assets such as equity shares, durable goods including real property. Thus, Friedman's theory of demand for money can be written as follows:

$$M^d = F(P, Y, r_B, r_E, r_D)$$

where

P = price level

Y = level of real income

r_B = rate of interest on bonds

r_E = rate of return on equity shares

r_D = rate of return on durable goods

It will be seen from Friedman's money demand function that the product of the first two variables, namely, P and Y, gives us the level of *nominal income*. It therefore follows that, in Friedman's function, demand for money depends on nominal income. The higher the level of nominal income, the greater the demand for money. It is worth mentioning that for a given level of nominal income, in Friedman's money demand function as in that of Keynes, demand for money depends on the rates of return on non-monetary alternative assets. But, unlike Keynes, *Friedman regards money demand function as stable.* Stability of money demand function implies that it will not shift erratically and that variables in the function will determine the quantity of money that will be demanded. Friedman's theory of demand for money can be used to restate the Cambridge money demand equation so as to bring out the important role of money demand function in the determination of the nominal national income which is the product of real national income and price level. Thus, Friedman's money demand function can be restated as follows:

$$M^d = k\,(r_B, r_E, r_D)\,PY \qquad ...(4)$$

It is worth noting that whereas in Cambridge cash-balance equation, k, that is, the proportion of income that is held in money, is mainly dependent on the transactions demand for money, *in Friedman's theory, it has been taken to be a function of rates of return on alternative non-monetary assets such as bonds, equity shares, durable goods*. Any rise in the rates of return on these alternative assets will cause k to fall showing the increased desirability of alternative non-monetary assets. "*In these terms Friedman can be seen to have restated the quantity theory, providing a systematic explanation of k, an explanation that takes account of the Keynesian analysis of money's role as an asset.*"[1]

Money Market Equilibrium: Friedman's Analysis of Determination of Nominal Income

In terms of Friedman's money demand function, the condition for equilibrium in the money market can be stated as under:

$$M^s = M^d = k\,(r_B, r_E, r_D)PY$$

where M^s stands for the supply of money which is determined by the central bank policies. k is the proportion of nominal national income (PY) that is held in the form of money and is determined by the rates of return (r_B, r_E, r_D) on alternative non-monetary assets such as bond, equity shares, durable goods respectively. Friedman assumes that money demand function is stable. *Given the stable money demand function, any increase in money supply by the central bank will cause either increase in nominal income (PY) or decline in rates of return so that k rises or alternatively some increase in nominal income (PY) and some rise in k*. Friedman believes that much of the effect of exogenous increase in money supply will be to bring about increase in nominal income (PY) rather than k. Thus Friedman concludes that *quantity of money is an important determinant of the level of economic activity, that is, output, employment and prices.* Here, according to Friedman, the short-run and long-run effects of exogenous increase in money supply must be distinguished. In the short run, the increase in money supply will lead to a change partly in real income (*i.e.*, real aggregate output or Y) and partly in the price level (P). That is, in the short run the effect of increase in money supply will be distributed between change in real income (Y) and change in price level (P) depending upon the elasticity of the aggregate supply curve. Friedman recognised that at times of depression, aggregate supply curve was fairly elastic so that the effect of the increase in money will be more in the form of expansion in real output and less in the form of rise in the price level. But, in the long run, the aggregate supply curve is perfectly inelastic at full-employment level and, therefore, the exogenous increase in money supply will be reflected in the rise in price level.

Let us show how in Friedman's modern quantity theory nominal income is determined. To show this Friedman makes some strong assumptions about the behaviour of k. Friedman converts his money demand function into a theory of nominal income by assuming that variables in his money demand function other than nominal income (PY), that is, r_B, r_E, r_D have little effect on k. With this assump-

1. Richard Froyen, *Macroeconomics: Theories and Policies*, 3rd edition, Macmillan, New York, p. 278.

tion, money held as a proportion of income will be nearly constant. It may be noted by taking this assumption Friedman's theory comes very close to Cambridge theory of determination of nominal income. With this assumption Friedman's theory of nominal income can be derived as follows:

$$M^d = k\ (r_B, r_E, r_D)\ PY$$

With variables r_B, r_E, r_D having little or no effect on k, k can be assumed to be constant. Therefore,

$$M^d = kPY$$

In equilibrium demand for money (M^d) equals money supply (M) which is *exogenously* given, we have

$$kPY = M^s$$

or

$$PY = \frac{1}{k} M^s$$

The last condition shows that *nominal national income is determined by the supply of money, k remaining constant*. The determination of nominal income in the short run is graphically shown in Fig. 23.1 where we measure nominal income (PY) on the Y-axis, and the supply and demand for money on the X-axis. Suppose the Central Bank sets money supply equal to OM^s. With OM^s as the supply of money, supply curve of money is a vertical straight line M^S. It will be seen that at the level of nominal income P_0Y_0, money market is in equilibrium as at it demand for money (M^d) equals the supply of money (M^s). If the nominal national income is more or less than P_0Y_0, demand for money (M^d) is not equal to the supply of money (M^s) and therefore there will be tendency for the market to move towards point E at which $M^d = M^s$.

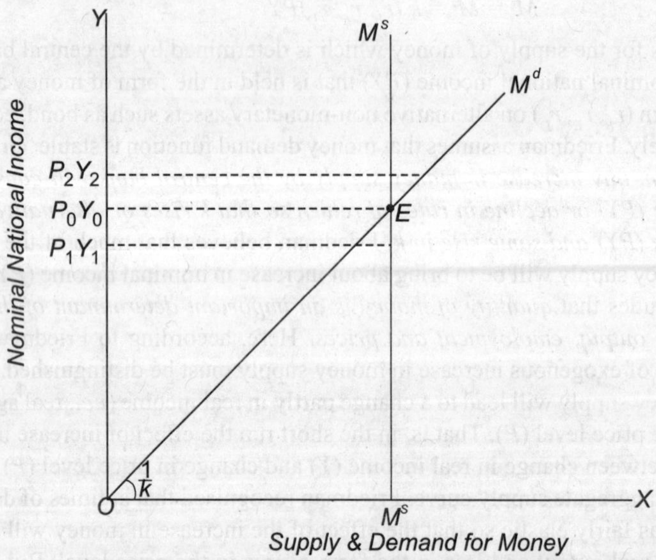

Fig. 23.1. *Determination of Nominal National Income : Monetarist Theory*

As seen above, **according to Friedman's view, the impact of increase in the money supply on prices and real income is direct**. The expansion in money supply is seen as putting more money in the hands of both consumers and investors. Since monetarists believe that demand for money to hold (M^d) is a stable function of nominal income, expansion in money supply leads to the excess money supply or, *in other words, excess cash balances with the people relative to their demand for money holdings. The excess money balances are soon spent leading to the increase in aggregate demand for goods and services*. Unlike the transmission mechanism of Keynesian analysis wherein increase in money supply first reduces the rate of interest and thereby raises investment and aggregate demand and then affects prices, in the analysis of Friedman and other modern monetarists, the expansion in *money supply has a direct impact on prices and income through increase in aggregate demand.* Liquidity trap and inelastic nature of investment demand are not involved in this adjustment process which in Keynesian analysis could prevent or curtail the effect of monetary expansion on prices and national income.

Increase in Money Supply and the Price Level

Let us now explain in more detail how in Friedman's quantity theory the increase in money supply will affect the price level and national income. We will also spell out the transmission mechanism through which increase in money supply operates to bring about rise in the price level and income. Consider again the equation for money equilibrium,

$$kPY = M^S$$

$$PY = \frac{1}{k} M^S \qquad \ldots (5)$$

Now, if k and Y are constant, then it follows from equation (5) above that price is directly proportional to money supply. This was the viewpoint of the old quantity theory of money which thought velocity of money (V) or, in other words, k [which equals $\frac{1}{v}$] as well as real national income or output remained constant. *Friedman and his followers, in their restatement of quantity theory of money, assume k to be stable, the effect of expansion in money supply will be distributed between the increase in real income (i.e., Y) and increase in price level (P) in the short run.*

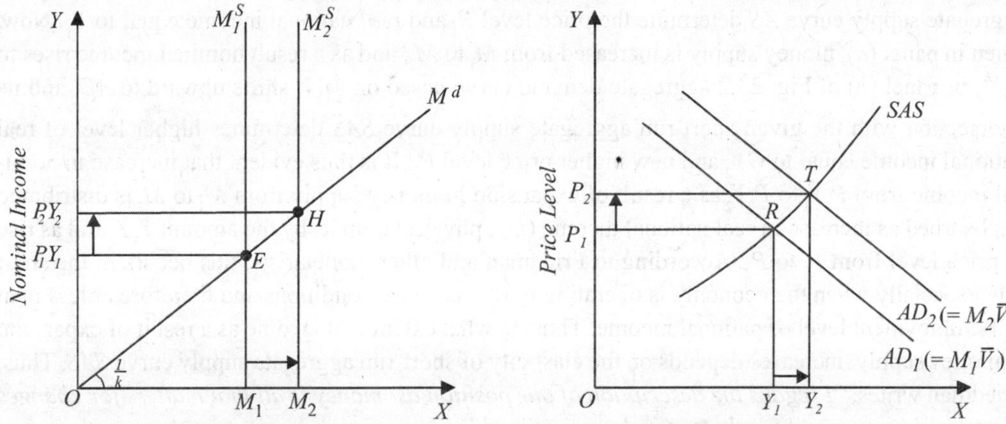

Fig. 23.2. *Friedman's Modern Quantity Theory of Money*

To consider fully Friedman's restatement of quantity theory, look at Panel (a) in Fig. 23.2. Let us suppose the supply of money is raised from M_1 to M_2. As will be seen from the figure, the expansion in money supply causes the nominal income to rise. In panel (a) of Fig. 23.2 with M_1 as the supply of money and M^d as the curve of demand for money, money market is initially in equilibrium at point E with P_1Y_1 as the equilibrium level of nominal income. When the supply of money is increased from M_1 to M_2 and as a result money supply curve shifts to the left to M_2^S, then at nominal income P_1Y_1, money supply becomes excessive relative to the demand for money to hold at it. As a result, people will be induced to spend the excess money supply and thereby increase the aggregate demand for goods and services. This increase in aggregate demand for or expenditure on goods and services leads to the increase in nominal income. With this increase in nominal income demand for money increases and the new money market equilibrium is reached at point H at the new nominal income level P_2Y_2.

How much increase in nominal income will occur in terms of increase in real income (*i.e.*, physical output) and how much in terms of rise in price level can be explained in the framework of aggregate demand (AD) and aggregate supply (AS) curves with flexible prices. This is shown in panel (*b*) of Fig. 23.2 where on the X-axis we measure aggregate demand and aggregate supply and on the Y-axis price level is measured. The concept of aggregate demand curve in this framework needs to be spelled out. In the monetarist view aggregate demand curve is determined by the quantity of money supply (M) and the velocity of circulation (V). That is, aggregate demand or aggregate expenditure in this approach is obtained from multiplying a given quantity of money supply by the velocity of circulation (V) which is assumed to remain constant. Note that velocity of circulation (V) is equal to $\frac{1}{k}$. Thus, if ₹4,000 crores is the quantity of money supply and velocity of circulation is 5, the aggregate expenditure or aggregate demand or expenditure (MV) will be equal to ₹ 20,000 crores. Now, if money supply is raised to ₹ 5,000 crores, aggregate demand or expenditure will increase to ₹ 25,000 crores, velocity of circulation remaining constant at 5. Now, *with a given aggregate expenditure (MV), aggregate demand curve slopes downward because at a lower price level, with the given quantity of money, more quantity of goods and services can be purchased, velocity of circulation remaining constant.*

Now, a glance at panel (*b*) of Fig. 23.2 reveals that with money supply equal to M_1, the aggregate demand curve is AD_1 with the constant velocity V. Aggregate demand curve AD_1 and aggregate supply curve AS determine the price level P_1 and *real* national income equal to Y_1. Now, when in panel (*a*), money supply is increased from M_1 to M_2, and as a result nominal income rises to P_2Y_2, in panel (*b*) of Fig. 23.2 aggregate demand curve based on $M_2\overline{V}$ shifts upward to AD_2 and its intersection with the given short-run aggregate supply curve SAS determines higher level of real national income equal to OY_2 and new higher price level P_2. It is thus evident that increase in nominal income from P_1Y_1 to P_2Y_2 as a result of expansion in money supply from M_1 to M_2 is distributed or absorbed as increase in real national income (*i.e.*, physical output) by the amount Y_1Y_2 and as rise in price level from P_1 to P_2. According to Friedman and other monetarists, this occurs in the short run, especially when the economy is operating in recessionary conditions and therefore at less than full-employment level of national income. Thus, to what extent real income as a result of expansion in money supply increases depends on the elasticity of short-run aggregate supply curve SAS. Thus, Friedman writes, "*I regard the description of our position as 'money is all that matters for changes in nominal income and for short-run changes in real income as an exaggregation but one that gives the right flavour to our conclusion.*"[2]

Short-run and Long-run Impact of Expansion in Money Supply on Price Level and Real National Income

If in the short run the economy is working below the full-employment level of output, that is, if there is depression or recession in the economy, the increase in money supply will cause increase in real income (*i.e.*, output) much more than the rise in price level. Thus, according to them, *if in the short run the economy is in recession, then the effect of increase in money supply, with k or V remaining constant, is likely to lead to the increase in output or real income* (*i.e.*, *Y*) *more than rise in the price level* (*P*). However, Friedman and his followers, as shall be explained in detail later, think that since

2. Milton Friedman, "A Theoretical Framework for Monetary Analysis" in Robert Gordon, ed., *Milton Friedman's Monetary Framework*, University of Chicago Press, 1974, p. 27

in the long run the aggregate supply curve is a vertical straight line at the full-employment level of output and Y and k remain constant, the increase in money supply will raise the price level or cause inflation in the economy, real GDP remaining constant.

Friedman draws distinction between short run and long run in his analysis of impact of increase in money supply on price level and national income (GDP). In this regard it is important to know whether the economy in the short run is working when there prevails depression or recession. According to the monetarists, though short-run aggregate supply curve of output at times of recession is fairly elastic, the long-run aggregate supply curve of output is perfectly inelastic, that is, it is a vertical straight line. As mentioned above, the position of vertical long-run aggregate supply curve is determined by the amounts of real resources such as labour force, capital stock, availability of infrastructure, state of technology. Besides, *according to Friedman, in the long run wages and prices are perfectly flexible.* Therefore, in the long run with a given vertical aggregate supply curve any increase in aggregate demand brought about by increase in money supply will cause price level to rise, (that is, will cause inflation), real national income (GDP) remaining the same. However, according to him, in the short run wages are temporarily fixed and short-run aggregate supply curve (*SAS*) is sloping upward as shown in Figures 23.3 and 23.4. Consider Figure 23.3. Let us assume that the economy is in the state of depression and the aggregate demand curve is at *AD* corresponding to the available money supply equal to ₹ 4000 crore, and a given velocity of circulation (V), cuts the short-run aggregate supply curve *SAS* at point T and thus determines the price level equal to P_1 and the income level Y_1 which is less than full-employment level of output Y_F. In such an equuilibrium situation idle or unutilized productive capacity would prevail causing unemployment of labour. Thus, in equilibrium at point T, the economy will find itself in the grip of recession. However, according to Friedman and his followers, this only represents a short-run situation. They argue that if in such a situation the money supply and aggregate demand curve were held constant, then in view of the prevailing unutilized capacity and unemployment, prices and wages would **eventually** fall so that equilibrium at point R is reached in the long run. The point R represents full-employment equilibrium though at a lower price level and lower wages.

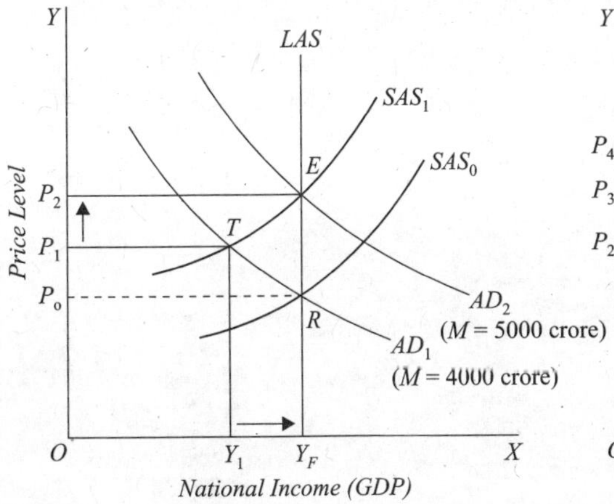

Fig. 23.3. *Short-run Impact of Monetary Expansion During Depression*

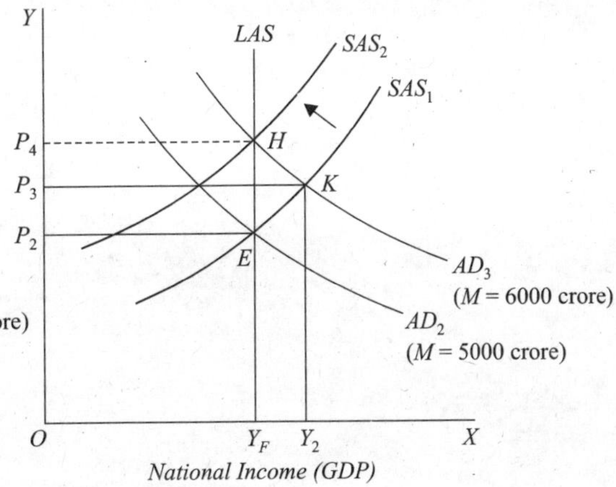

Fig. 23.4. *Short-run and Long-run Impact of Monetary Expansion on National Income and Price*

However, Friedman and other modern monetarists accept that if instead of waiting for the downward adjustment in prices and wages, money supply is increased, say from ₹ 4,000 crore to ₹ 5,000 crore, raising the aggregate demand curve from AD_1 to AD_2, the new equilibrium is attained at point E where the effect of increase in money supply has been divided into rise in price level from P_1 to P_2 and increase in real national income (GDP) from Y_1 to Y_F. The extent to which price level will rise and output will increase depends on the elasticity of short-run aggregate supply curve.

Now, consider Figure 23.4 where initially the aggregate demand curve is AD_2 with money supply equal to 5,000 crore and the economy is in state of full-employment at which, according to monetarists, only natural rate of unemployment prevails. Friedman and his followers argue that, if money supply is increased further to ₹ 6,000 crore so that aggregate demand curve rises to AD_3, the price level will rise to P_3 and output will increase to Y_2 in the short run. However, with some time lag wages would rise causing a shift in the short-run aggregate supply to shift upward the to SAS_2 which cuts the long-run aggregate supply curve *LAS* at point *H*. Thus, it will be seen from Fig. 23.4 that in the long run only price level will rise to P_4, GDP (*i.e.*, real national income) remaining unchanged, at Y_F.

QUESTIONS FOR REVIEW

1. What is monetarism ? Explain its main features and propositions.
2. Explain Friedman's restatement of quantity theory of money. How does it differ from old quantity theory of money?
3. Friedman restates the quantity theory of money on the basis of his concept of demand for money function. Explain.
4. According to Friedman, growth of money supply is prime determinant of nominal national income. How does Keynesian view differ from it?
5. According to monetarists, in the long run wages and prices change so that equilibrium is determined at full-employment level. Explain.

CHAPTER 24 Inflation and Hyperinflation, Causes, Social Costs and Effects

Meaning of Inflation

Having discussed the relationship between quantity of money and price level in the previous chapter, we are now in a position to explain the nature and causes of inflation. By inflation we mean *a general rise in prices*. To be more correct, *inflation is a persistent rise in the general price level rather than a once-for-all rise in it*. On the other hand, *deflation represents persistently falling prices*. Inflation or persistently rising prices is a major problem in India today. When price level rises due to inflation, the value of money falls. When there is a persistent rise in price level, the people need more and more money to buy goods and services. To enable the people to meet their daily needs of consumption of goods and services when their prices are rising, their incomes must rise if they have to maintain their standard of living. For government employees, their dearners allowance is increased. Wages and salaries employed in the organised private sector are also raised, though after some time lag. But people with fixed incomes and those who are self-employed are unable to raise their prices suffer a lot due to inflation. The poor suffer the most from persistent rise in prices, especially of foodgrains and other essential items. Rate of inflation during the seventies and eighties was very high as compared to the rates of inflation experienced earlier during previous periods. In India, in recent years, 2010-11, 2011-12 and 2012-13, rate of inflation as measured by consumer price index (CPI) has been in double digit figures. Prior to Jan. 2013, even WPI inflation was quite high which compelled Reserve Bank of India to adopt tight monetary policy.

Causes and Theories of Inflation

Let us understand how the inflation originates or what causes it. Depending upon the specific causes, three types of inflation have been distinguished: (1) *Demand-pull inflation,* (2) *Cost-push inflation,* and (3) *Structuralist inflation*. An important cause of demand-pull inflation is the excessive growth of money supply in the economy. We will explain this cause of inflation in the *Monetarist Theory of Inflation*. We will explain and discuss below these three theories of inflation.

DEMAND-PULL INFLATION

This represents a situation where the basic factor at work is the increase in aggregate demand for output either from the households or the entrepreneurs or government organised. The result is that the pressure of demand is such that it cannot be met by the currently available supply of output. If, for example, in a situation of full employment, the government expenditure or private investment goes up, this is bound to generate inflationary pressures in the economy. Keynes explained that inflation arises when there occurs an *inflationary gap* in the economy which comes to exist when aggregate demand for goods and services exceeds aggregate supply at full employment level of output. Basically, inflation is caused by a situation whereby the pressure of aggregate demand for goods and services exceeds the available supply of output (both being counted at the prices ruling at the beginning of a period). In such a situation, the rise in price level is the natural consequence.

Now, this imbalance between aggregate demand and supply may be the result of more than one force at work. As we know aggregate demand is the sum of consumers' spending on consumer goods and services, government spending on goods and services and net investment being contemplated by the entrepreneurs. *When aggregate demand for all purposes—consumption, investment and government expenditure—exceeds the supply of goods at current prices, there is a rise in price level. Since inflation is a continuous increase in the price level, not a one time rise in it, sustained inflation requires continuous increase in aggregate demand.* In the modern macroeconomics, inflation is explained with AD-AS model. Inflation can be explained by increase in aggregate demand (called "***demand shock***") or decrease in aggregate supply or rise in cost of production generally called "***supply shock***". Demand-pull inflation occurs when there is upward shift in aggregate demand when supply shocks are absent.

As stated above, demand-pull inflation occurs when there is increase in any component of aggregate demand, namely, consumption demand by households, investment by business firms, increase in government expenditure unmatched by increase in taxes (that is, deficit spending by the government financed by either creation of new money by the central bank or borrowing by the government from the market). To illustrate the cause of demand-pull inflation, let us assume the government adopts expansionary fiscal policy under which it increases its expenditure without levying extra taxes to finance its increased expenditure by borrowing from the Reserve Bank of India.

To illustrate the above point, let us assume that the government adopts expansionary fiscal policy under which it increases its expenditure on education, health, defence and finances this extra expenditure by borrowing from Reserve Bank of India which prints new notes for this purpose. This will lead to increase in aggregate demand ($C + I + G$). If aggregate supply of output does not increase or increases by a relatively less amount in the short run, this will cause demand-supply imbalances which will lead to demand-pull inflation in the economy, that is, general rise in price level.

Similarly, an inflationary process will be initiated if business firms anticipating the opportunities of making profits decide to invest more and to finance the new investment projects by borrowing from the banks being unable to get sufficient funds throught savings out of profits and savings invested by the public in them. This new investment by the firms leads to the increase in aggregate demand for goods and services. However, inflation will occur by this new investment if aggregate supply of output does not increase adequately in the short run to match the increase in aggregate demand. Therefore, *demand-pull inflation generally occurs when the economy is already working at full-employment level of resources or what is now generally called when there is natural rate of unemployment.* This is because if aggregate demand increases beyond the full-employment level of output, output of goods cannot be increased adequately without much increase in cost. Note that in developing countries such as India, there are difficulties of measuring employment, unemployment and full employment. Therefore in the Indian context, instead of full-employment level of output, we use ***full capacity output of the economy beyond which supply of output cannot be increased.***

It is important to note that Keynes in his booklet, *How to Pay for the War,* published during the Second World War explained inflation in terms of excess demand for goods relative to the aggregate supply of their output. His notion of the *inflationary gap* which he put forward in his booklet represented excess of aggregate demand over full-employment output. This inflationary gap, according to him, leads to the rise in prices. Thus, Keynes explained inflation in terms of demand-pull forces. Therefore, the theory of demand-pull inflation is associated with the name of Keynes. Since beyond full-employment level aggregate supply of output cannot increase in response to increase in demand, this results in rise in prices under the pressure of excess demand. Aggregate supply curve, according to him, is vertical at full-employment level.

Demand pull inflation is shown in Figure 24.1. In the modern macoreconomics distinction is drawn between *long-run aggregate supply cure (LAS) and short-run aggregate supply curve (SAS).* The long-run aggregate supply curve (*LAS*) is a *vertical line drawn at the full-employment level* (*i.e.* at natural rate of unemployment) or in the Indian context *full-capacity output level.* This full-employment level or full-capacity output is also called ***potential output.*** The short-run aggregate supply curve SAS_0 slopes upward to the right which shows more supply of output is forthcoming at a higher price and *is drawn with a constant wage rate*. This short-run aggregate supply curve (*SAS*) slopes upward because with the increase in employment of labour, diminishing returns to labour occur which raises marginal cost of production. This short-run aggregate supply curve slopes upward to the right even beyond full-employment or potential level of output. This is because, as explained earlier, even at full-employment level, some unemployment occurs due to frictional and structural factors and therefore beyond full-employment level, employment of labour can increase with reduction in natural unemployment under the pressure of aggregate demand. It will be seen from Figure 24.1 that short-run aggregate supply curve SAS_0 cuts long-run aggregate supply curve *LAS* at point E_0. To begin with, aggregate demand curve AD_0 intersects both short-run aggregate supply curve SAS_0 and long-run aggregate supply curve (*LAS*) at point E_0 and this shows that at point E_0 there is long-run equilibrium at potential or full-employment GDP level $\bar{Y}$ and at price level P_0.

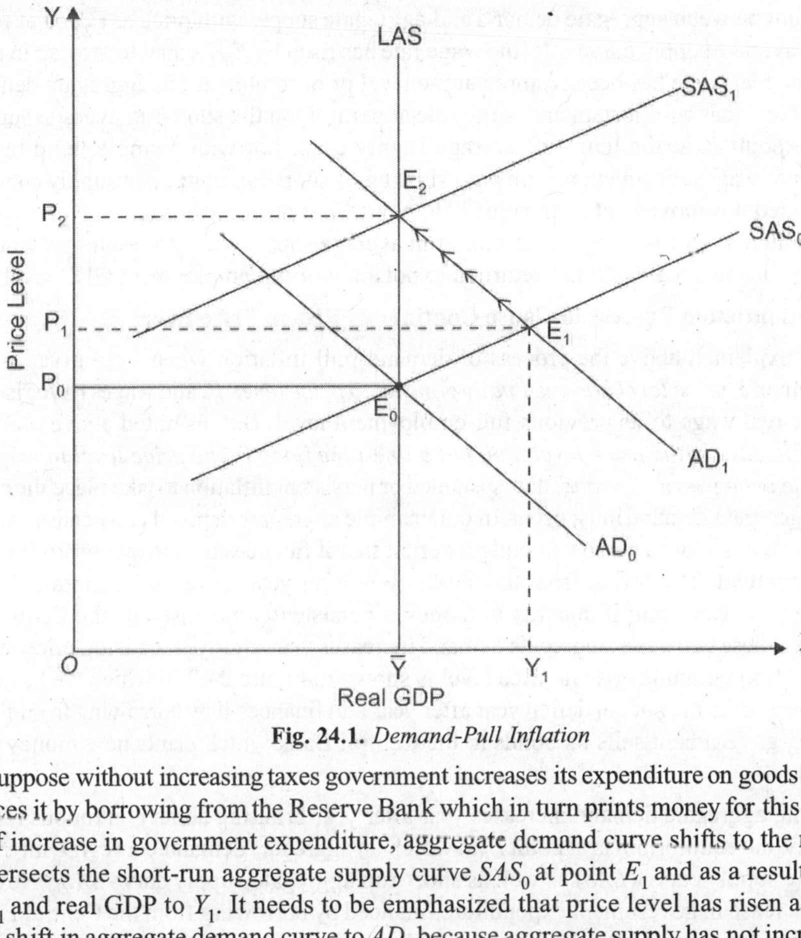

Fig. 24.1. *Demand-Pull Inflation*

Now suppose without increasing taxes government increases its expenditure on goods and services and finances it by borrowing from the Reserve Bank which in turn prints money for this purpose. As a reuslt of increase in government expenditure, aggregate demand curve shifts to the right to AD_1 which intersects the short-run aggregate supply curve SAS_0 at point E_1 and as a result price level rises to P_1 and real GDP to Y_1. It needs to be emphasized that price level has risen as a result of rightward shift in aggregate demand curve to AD_1 because aggregate supply has not increased to the extent of increase in aggregate demand and thereby creating demand-supply imbalances. If short-run aggregate curve had been horizontal line through point E_0, the aggregate supply would have increased by an equal amount to the increase in aggregate demand when aggregate demand curve shifts to right to AD_1. Thus, *the price level has risen because aggregate demand has increased relatively more than the aggregate supply, that is, due to demand-supply imbalances.*

However, the response to the initial increase in aggregate demand to AD_1 does not stop at point E_1. It may be recalled that in drawing short-run aggregate supply curve wage rate of labour is kept constant. Now, the rightward shift in aggregate demand curve to AD_1 has caused the price level to rise from P_0 to P_1 and real gross domestic output (GDP) has risen to Y_1. This rise in price level, the wage rate remaining constant, would cause decline in workers' real wage rate, $\frac{W}{P_1} < \frac{W}{P_0}$ where $P_1 > P_0$. When workers realise that their real wage has fallen as a result of increase in aggregate demand causing rise in price level, they will demand higher wages in their negotiations with their employers which are likely to be conceded to. Further, as pointed out above, equilibrium to the right of potential GDP level $\bar{Y}$ implies that unemployment has fallen below the natural rate of unemployment and will cause shortage of labour which implies wage rate will rise. When wages are raised by the firms short-run aggregate supply curve will shift upward and this process of shifting short-run aggregate supply curve upward will continue until it reaches SAS_1 which cuts the new aggregate demand curve AD_1 at point E_2 that lies at the long run supply curve LAS and as a result pri ce level further rises to P_2. Equilibrium between aggregate demand and aggregate supply with price as P_2 and at point E_2 on the long-run average supply curve LAC the wage rate has risen by E_0E_2 equal to the rise in price level by P_0P_2. Thus, real wage has been restored at the level prior to increase in aggregate demand from AD_0 to AD_1. Note that equilibrium and wage rate at point E_1 on the short-run average supply curve will move to point E_2 at the long-run average supply curve not with a single jump but through various steps of wage adjustment and upward shifting of short-run aggregate supply curve. That is why we depicted this movement from point E_1 to point E_2 on the LAS through *various* arrows. Note that not only there is shifting upward of short-run average supply curve to resotre previous level of real wage rate but also real GDP has returned to potential or full employment GDP level $\bar{Y}$.

Demand-Pull inflation Process to Cause Continuous Rise in Price Level

We have explained above the process of demand-pull inflation when for a given increase in aggregate demand, *price level has eventually gone up to price level* P_2 and wages have risen enough to restore the real wage to its previous full-employment level. But, as noted above, *inflation is a continuous increase in the price level and not a one-time jump in the price level in response to a given increase in aggregate demand.* For sustained or persistent inflation to take place the continuous increase in aggregate demand must occur. In our example aggregate demand can persistently increase if a government has a large persistent budget deficit that it finances by borrowing from the Central Bank or alternatively borrowing from the market year after year. Besides, continuous increase in aggregate demand can occur if quantity of money is persistently increased by the Central Bank of the country. In these two cases aggregate demand increases year after year causing price level to rise persistently. This continuous rise in price level is shown in Figure 24.2 in which we have assumed that government runs the budget deficit year after year and finances it by borrowing from the Central Bank (that is, government sells its bonds to the Central Bank which prints new money to pay for these bonds).

As a result, aggregate demand increases year after year bringing about continuous rise in price level. Initially, the equilibrium is at point E_0 at which an aggregate demand curve AD_0 intersects long run aggregate supply curve (*LAS*) as well as short-run aggregate supply curve SAS_0. Now suppose that due to increase in government expenditure financed by borrowing from the Central Bank shifts aggregate demand curve to AD_1 which intersects the short-run aggregate supply curve SAS_0 at point E_1 raising the price level to P_1. As explained above, with rise in price level to P_1 real wages of labour will fall and they will demand higher wages. As a result of rise in wage rate over a number of stages or steps short-run aggregate supply curve (*SAS*) shifts to the left till it intersects the new aggregate demand curve AD_1 at point E_2 that lies at the long-run aggregate supply curve (*LAS*). With this equal rise in price level and wage rate, real wage rate of workers is restored.

Now suppose next year the government again incurs a budget deficit and finances its further increase in expenditure by borrowing more from the Central Bank. With this aggregate demand curve shifts to the right to AD_2 and cuts the short-run aggregate supply curve SAS_1 at E_3 and causes price level to rise further to P_3 as shown in Fig. 24.2. The rise in price level will cause the fall in real wage rate of workers who will demand increase in their money wage rate further. When higher money wage rate is conceded to, short-run aggregate supply curve will start shifting to the left and the process will eventually end when short-run aggregate supply curve has shifted to the position SAS_2 which intersects aggregate demand curve AD_2 at point E_4 at which price level has risen to P_4 and with that real wage rate of workers is restored at full-employment level with potential GDP equal to $\bar{Y}$. If government further increases its expenditure next year and finances it by borrowing from the Central Bank, price level will further rise. In this way there is continuous inflation triggered by increase in government expenditure and the operation of wage price spiral under the pressure of increase in aggregate demand. In Figure 24.2 we *have traced the rise in price level through arrows as aggregate demand increases and short-run aggregate supply curve shifts to the right as a result of increase in money wage rate.*

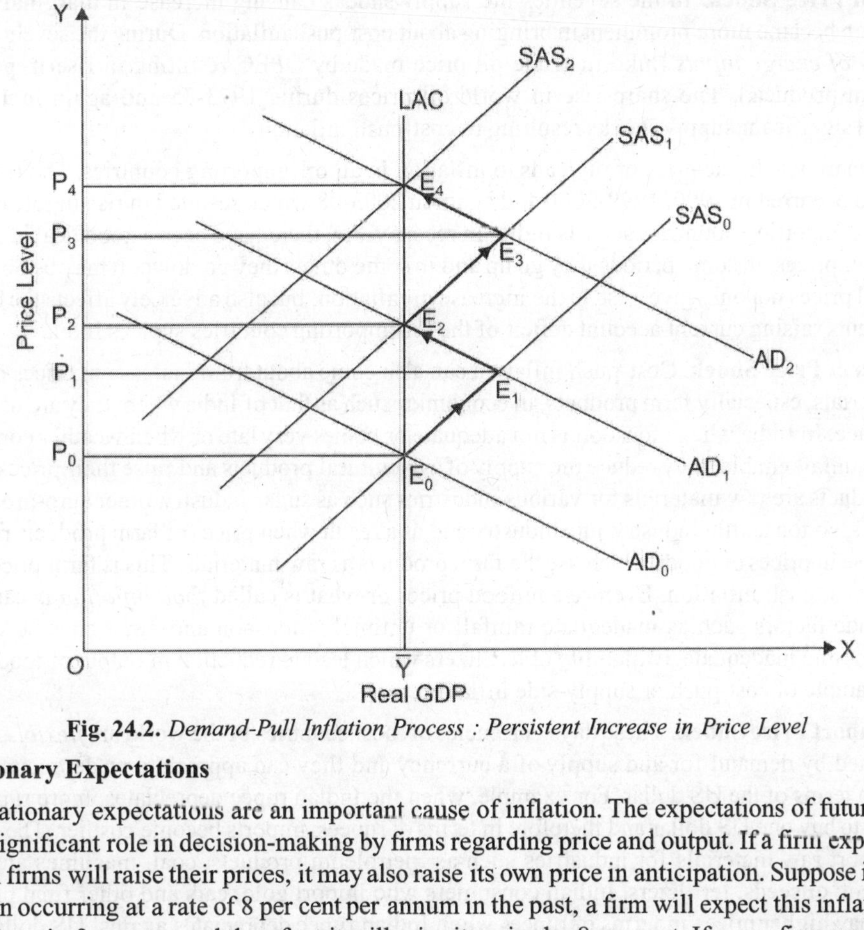

Fig. 24.2. *Demand-Pull Inflation Process : Persistent Increase in Price Level*

Inflationary Expectations

Inflationary expectations are an important cause of inflation. The expectations of future prices play a significant role in decision-making by firms regarding price and output. If a firm expects that its rival firms will raise their prices, it may also raise its own price in anticipation. Suppose inflation has been occurring at a rate of 8 per cent per annum in the past, a firm will expect this inflation rate to continue in future too and therefore it will raise its price by 8 per cent. If every firm expects that other firms will raise their prices by 8 per cent, every one will raise its prices by 8 per cent. As a result, inflation rate of about 8 per cent will occur. This is how inflationary expectations cause inflation. Elaborating on this, Case and Fair write, "*Expectations can lead to an inertia that makes it difficult to stop an inflationary spiral. If prices have been rising and if people's expectations are adaptive, that is, if they form their expectations on the basis of past pricing behaviour – that firms may continue raising prices even if demand is slowing.*"[1] Therefore, to check inflation, steps should be taken to break the inflationary expectations.

1. Karl E. Case and Race C. Fair, *Principles of Economics*, Pearson Education, 6th Edition, 2002,

COST-PUSH INFLATION

We can visualise situations where even though there is no increase in aggregate demand, prices may still rise. This may happen if there is initial increase in costs *independent of any increase in aggregate demand.* The four main autonomous increases in costs which generate cost-push inflation have been suggested :

1. *Oil Price Shock*
2. *Farm Price Shock*
3. *Import Price Shock*
4. *Wage-push inflation*

Cost-push inflation is also called *supply-side inflation*.

1. Oil Price Shock. In the seventies the supply shocks causing increase in marginal cost of production became more prominent in bringing about cost-push inflation. During the seventies, *rise in prices of energy inputs* (hike in crude oil price made by OPEC resulting in rise in prices of petroleum products). The sharp rise in world oil prices during 1973-75 and again in 1979-80 produced significant supply shocks resulting in cost-push inflation.

The sharp rise in the price of oil leads to inflation in all oil-importing countries. The rise in oil price also occurred in 1990, 1999-2000 and again in 2003-08 which resulted in rise in rate of inflation in oil-importing countries such as India. In recent years, there have been a good deal of fluctuations in oil prices; in some periods they go up and in some others they go down. It may be noted that rise in oil prices not only gives rise to the increase in inflation, but also adversely affects the balance of payments raising current account deficit of the oil-importing countries such as India.

2. Farm Price Shock. Cost-push inflation can also come about from increase in prices of other raw materials, especially farm products, in economies such as that of India where they are of greater importance. In India when monsoon is not adequate or comes very late or when weather conditions are quite unfavourable, they reduce the supply of agricultural products and raise their prices. These farm products are raw materials for various industries such as sugar industry, other agro-processing industries, cotton textile industry, jute industry and as a result when prices of farm products rise they lead to rise in prices of goods which use the farm products as raw materials. This is farm price shock causing cost-push inflation. Even rise in food prices or what is called *food inflation* is caused by supply-side factors such as inadequate rainfall or untimely monsoon and other adverse weather conditions and inadequate availability of fertilizers which lead to reduction in output of foodsgrains is the example of cost-push or supply-side inflation.

3. Import Price Shock. These days currencies of most countries of the world are *flexible*, that is, determined by demand for and supply of a currency and they can appreciate or depreciate every month in terms of the US dollar. For example, when the Indian rupee depreciates, more rupees are required to buy one US dollar and therefore in terms of rupees, imports become costlier. The Indians who import raw materials for industries such as petroleum products, coal, machines and other equipment, oilseeds, fertilizers, Indian consumers who import gold, cars and other final products have to pay higher prices in terms of rupees when Indian rupee depreciates against US dollar. This raises the cost of production of the producers who in turn raise the prices of final products produced by them. *This inflation is the result of import price shock.* Thus depreciation of rupee causes cost-push inflation. For example, in the month of June 2013, there was sharp depreciation of the Indian rupee. The value of rupee fell by about 9.5 per cent in this single month from about ₹ 56 to a US dollar in the first week of June 2013 to around ₹ 61 to a dollar in the last week of June 2013.

4. Wage-Push Inflation. It has been suggested that the growth of powerful trade unions is responsible for the spread of inflation, especially in the industrialized countries. When trade unions push for higher wages which are not justifiable either on grounds of a prior rise in productivity or of cost of living they produce a cost-push effect. The employers in a situation of high demand and employment are more agreeable to concede to these wage claims because they hope to pass on these rises in costs to the consumers in the form of hike in prices. If this happens we have cost-push inflation. It may be noted that as a result of cost-push effect of higher wages, short-run aggregate supply curve of output shifts to the left and, given the aggregate demand curve, results in higher price of output.

Cost-Push Inflation Spiral

Let us consider Figure 24.3 where to begin with aggregate demand curve AD_0 and short-run aggregate supply curve SAS_0 intersect at point E_0 and determine price level P_0 and output level Y_0. Further suppose that Y_0 is the full-capacity (*i.e.*, full-employment) level of output and therefore long-run aggregate supply curve *LAS* is vertical at Y_0 level of output. Suppose there is increase in oil prices which causes shifts in short-run aggregate supply curve to the left from SAS_0 to SAS_1. As a result, price level rises to P_1 but output falls from Y_0 to Y_1. With decline in output unemployment will also increase. *Thus cost-push inflation not only causes rise in price level (or inflation) but also brings about fall in GDP level. The rise in price level or inflation and simultaneously fall in GDP level is called* ***stagflation****. Thus cost-push inflation* ***results in stagflation***.

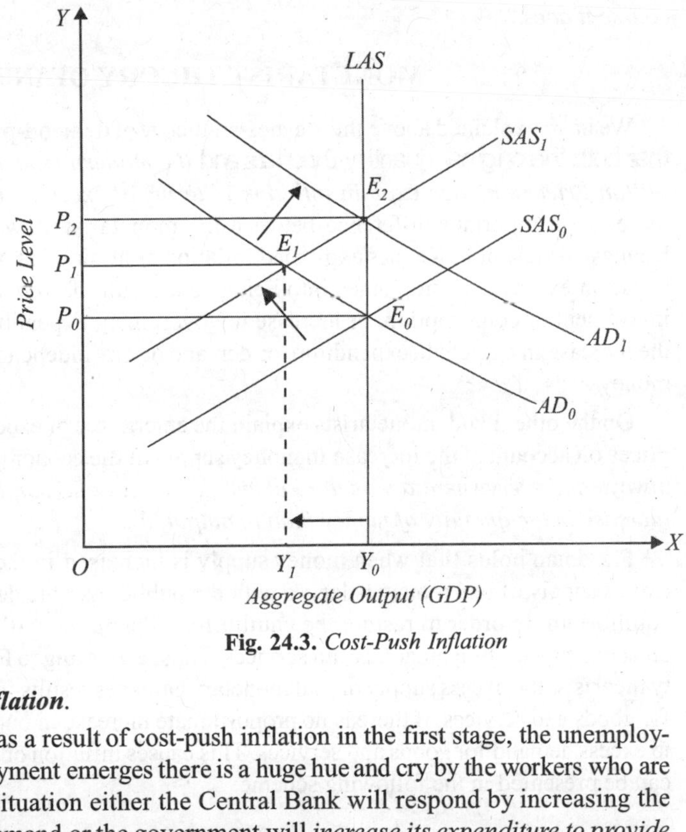

Fig. 24.3. *Cost-Push Inflation*

When the real GDP decreases as a result of cost-push inflation in the first stage, the unemployment will also rise. When unemployment emerges there is a huge hue and cry by the workers who are rendered unemployed. In such a situation either the Central Bank will respond by increasing the money supply to raise aggregate demand or the government will *increase its expenditure to provide fiscal stimulus to aggregate demand.* As a result of either of these responses, aggregate demand curve shifts to the right from AD_0 to AD_1. With this, the economy moves from equilibrium position E_1 to the equilibrium position E_2. As will be seen from Fig. 24.3, as a result of this increase in aggregate demand while real GDP has returned to the potential GDP level Y_0, price level has further risen to P_2 (that is, more inflation will occur). But the inflationary process of cost-push inflation will not stop at equilibrium point E_2. If there is further rise in any of the cost-push factors such as rise in oil price, increase in price of farm output, import price shock or wage rate increase takes place short-run aggregate supply curve *SAS* will shift further to the left of SAS_1 and intersects the aggregate demand curve AD_1 to the left of the long-run aggregate supply curve *LAS* causing further rise in price level or inflation above P_2 and fall in GDP from the potential level Y_0 *resulting again in unemployment of workers*. To restore full employment and raise GDP to the potential level Y_0, the Central Bank will further increase the money supply or the government will further increase its expenditure. As a result, aggregate demand curve will again shift to the right of AD_1. With this, *GDP* level will be back at the potential level Y_0 and full employment of workers will be restored but price level or inflation will further rise. In this way cost-push inflation spiral will work to cause sustained or persistent inflation.

Many economists think inflation in the economy is generally caused by the interaction of the demand-pull and cost-push factors. The inflation may be started in the first instance either by cost-push factors or by demand-pull factors-both work and interact to cause sustained inflation over time. Thus, according to Machlup, "there cannot be a thing as cost-push inflation because without an increase in purchasing power and demand, cost increases will lead to unemployment and depression, not to inflation"[2] Likewise, Cairncross writes, "*there is no need to pretend that demand and cost inflation do not interact or that excess demand does not aggrevate wage inflation, of course it does.*"[3]

MONETARIST THEORY OF INFLATION

We have explained above the Keynesian theory of demand-pull inflation. It is important to note that both the original quantity theorists and *the modern monetarists, prominent among whom is Milton Friedman, also explain inflation in terms of excess demand for goods and services.* But there is an important difference between the monetarist view of demand-pull inflation and the Keynesian view of it. Keynes explained inflation as arising out of real sector forces. In his model of inflation excess demand comes into being as a result of *autonomous* increase in expenditure on investment or consumption, or increase in government expenditure on goods and services, that is, the increase in aggregate expenditure or demand occurs independent of any increase in the supply of money.

On the other hand, monetarists explain the emergence of excess demand and the resultant rise in prices on account of the increase in money supply in the economy. To quote Friedman, *"Inflation is always and everywhere a monetary phenomenon . . . and can be produced only by a more rapid increase in the quantity of money than in output"*.[4]

Friedman holds that when money supply is increased in the economy, then there emerges an excess supply of real money balances with the public over the demand for money. This disturbs the equilibrium. In order to restore the equilibrium, the public will reduce the money balances by increasing expenditure on goods and services. Thus, according to Friedman and other modern quantity theorists, the excess supply of real monetary balances results in the increase in aggregate demand for goods and services. If there is no proportionate increase in output, then extra money supply leads to excess demand for goods and services. This causes inflation or rise in prices. The whole argument can be presented in the following scheme:

$$M^S > kPY \rightarrow AD\uparrow \rightarrow P\uparrow \qquad \ldots (1)$$

where M^S stands for quantity of money and P for the price level. Therefore, $\frac{M^S}{P}$ represents real cash balances. Y stands for national income and k for the ratio of income which people want to keep in cash balances. Hence kPY represents demand for cash balances (*i.e.*, demand for money). AD represents aggregate demand for or aggregate expenditure on goods and services which is composed of consumption demand (C) and investment demand (I).

In the above scheme it will be seen that when the supply of money (M^S) is increased, it creates

2. Fritz Machlup, "Another View of Cost-Push and Demand-Pull Inflation" in *Review of Economics and Statistics*, Vol. 42. 1960.
3. Alec Cairncross, *Inflation, Growth and International Trade*, George Allen and Unwin, 1975.
4. See N.G. Mankiw, *Principles of Economics*, Second Edition, p. 641

excess supply of real cash balances. This is expressed by $M^S > kPY$. This excess supply of real money balances leads to (→) the rise (↑) in aggregate demand (*AD*). Then increase (↑) in aggregate demand (*AD*) leads to (→) the rise (↑) in prices (*P*).

Friedman's monetarist theory of inflation can be better explained with quantity equation $\left(P=\frac{MV}{Y}=\frac{M}{Y}\cdot\frac{1}{k}\right)$ written in percentage form which is written as below taking *V* or *k* as constant

$$\frac{\Delta P}{P}=\frac{\Delta M^S}{M^S}-\frac{\Delta Y}{Y} \quad \ldots (2)$$

where $\frac{\Delta P}{P}$ is the rate of inflation, $\frac{\Delta M^S}{M^S}$ is the rate of growth of money supply and $\frac{\Delta Y}{Y}$ is the rate of growth of output. Thus, according to equation (2), rate of inflation $\left(\frac{\Delta P}{P}\right)$ is determined by growth of money supply $\left(\frac{\Delta M^S}{M}\right)$ and rate of growth of output $\left(\frac{\Delta Y}{Y}\right)$, with velocity of circulation (*V*) or *k* remaining constant. Friedman and other monetarists claim that *inflation* is predominantly a monetary phenomenon which implies that changes in velocity and output are small.

It thus follows that when money supply increases, it causes disturbance in the equilibrium, that is, $M^S > kPY$. According to Friedman and other monetarists, the reaction of the people would be to spend the excess money supply on goods and services so as to bring money supply in equilibrium with the demand for money. This leads to the increase in aggregate demand or expenditure on goods and services which, *k* remaining constant, will lead to the increase in *nominal* national income (*PY*). They further argue that the real national income or aggregate output (*i.e.*, *Y* in the demand for money function stated above) remains stable at full-employment level in the long run due to the flexibility of wages. Therefore, according to Friedman and his followers (modern monetarists), in the long run, the increase in nominal national income (*PY*) brought about by the expansion in money supply and resultant increase in aggregate demand will cause a proportional increase in the price level.

However, in the short run, like Keynesians, they believe that the economy may be working at less than full employment, that is, in the short run there may prevail excess capacity and unemployment of labour so that expansion in money supply and consequent increase in nominal income partly induces expansion in real income (*Y*) and partly results in rise in the price level as shown in Fig. 24.4. To what extent price level increases depends upon the elasticity of supply or aggregate output in the short run. It will be seen from Fig. 24.4 that effect of increase in money supply from M_0 to M_1 and resultant increase in aggregate demand curve for goods and services from AD_0 to AD_1 is split up into the rise in price level (from P_0 to P_1) and the increase in real income or aggregate output (from Y_0 to Y_1).

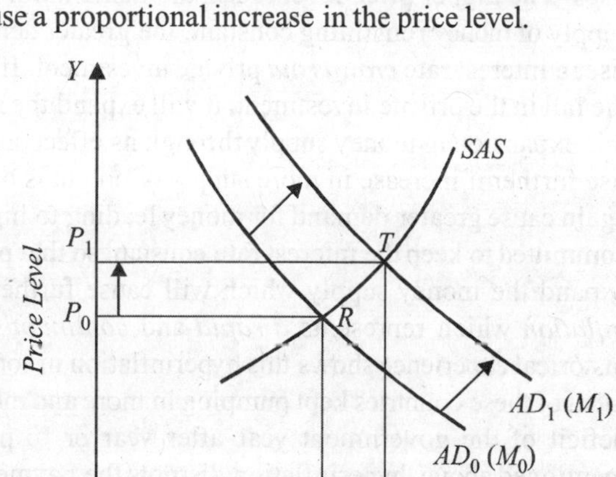

Fig. 24.4. *The effect of Expansion in Money Supply in the Short-run is Split up into price rise and Increase in Real National Income: Friedman's Monetarist Approach.*

It should be noted that Friedman and other modern quantity theorists believe that in the short-run full employment of labour and other resources may not prevail due to recessionary conditions and, therefore, they admit the possibilities of increase in output. But they emphasise that in the short run when the growth in money supply is greater than the growth in output, the result is excess demand for goods and services which causes rise in prices or demand-pull inflation.

It follows from above that both Friedman and Keynesians explain inflation in terms of excess demand for goods and services. Whereas Keynesians explain the emergence of excess demand due to the increase in *autonomous expenditure,* independent of any increase in money supply. Friedman explains that inflation is caused by *proportionately greater increase in money supply than the increase in aggregate output.* In both views inflation is of demand-pull variety.

Money and Sustained Inflation

Many economists believe in the monetarist view of inflation. Increase in money shifts the aggregate demand curve to the right and if the economy is operating at full capacity (*i.e.*, along the vertical part of the aggregate supply curve), the upward shift in aggregate demand curve will cause price level to rise. A big drawback of this approach is that it assumes that supply of output does not increase sufficiently to counter this effect of expansion in money supply on aggregate demand. In this context there is a need to distinguish between a *one-time increase* in the price level and *sustained inflation* which occurs when the general price level continues to rise over a long period of time. It is generally believed by most of the economists that whatever be the initial cause of inflation (demand-pull, cost-push or inflationary expectations), for the price level to continue rising, period after period, it must be *accommodated* by expansion in money supply. *Sustained inflation is therefore considered as a purely monetary phenomenon*. It is not possible for the price level to continue rising if the money supply remains constant. The increase in money supply continues shifting the aggregate demand curve to the right; if aggregate supply does not increase sufficiently to match the increase in aggregate demand, price level will continue rising.

Sustained inflation can be better understood when Government increases its expenditure without raising taxes. This leads to the increase in aggregate demand which, *aggregate supply remaining constant*, will cause a rise in price level. It is important to know what happens when the price level rises. The higher price level raises the demand for money to rise for transactions purposes. With supply of money remaining constant, the greater demand for money causes interest rate to rise. The rise in interest rate *crowds out* private investment. If the Central Bank of a country wants to prevent the fall in the private investment, it will expand the money supply to keep the interest constant. But this expansion in money supply through its effect on aggregate demand will cause the price level to rise further if increase in more supply of output is not possible. This further rise in price level will again cause greater demand for money leading to higher interest rate. And the Central Bank, if it is committed to keep the interest rate constant so that private investment does not decline, will further expand the money supply which will cause further inflation. This process could lead to *hyperinflation* which represents *a rapid* and *continuous rise in price level*, period after period. The historical experience shows this hyperinflation in some countries when the Central Bank or Government of these countries kept pumping in more and more money either to finance its persistent budget deficit of the government year after year or to prevent the interest rate to rise. However, as mentioned above, hyperinflation disrupts the payment system and people's loss of credibility of the currency. This leads to a deep crisis in the economy. If hyperinflation is to be avoided, then the process of rapid expansion in money supply must be halted.

THE SOCIAL COSTS OF INFLATION

Having discussed the so called inflation fallacy we proceed to explain in detail the social cost of monopoly. Apart from reducing the purchasing power of people's incomes, inflation inflicts some other costs on the society. To explain such costs of inflation it is necessary to distinguish between anticipated inflation and unanticipated (*i.e.*, unexpected) inflation. As noted above, in case of anticipated inflation, the expected rise in price level is taken into account while making economic transactions, for example, in negotiating wage rate of labour etc.

Costs of Anticipated Inflation

Suppose in an economy there has been annual inflation rate of 5 per cent for a long time in the past and everybody expects that this 5 per cent rate of inflation will continue in the future too. In such a case all contracts made by the people such as loan agreements with borrowers, wage contracts with labour, property lease contracts will provide for 5 per cent annual rise in rates of interest, wages, rent to compensate for inflation of that order. That is, in any contract in which passage of time is involved 5 per cent rate of inflation will be taken into account and rates will be agreed to rise per period equal to the anticipated rate of inflation. If rates of interest, wages, rent etc are agreed to rise at the anticipated rate of inflation, then there will be no cost of inflation except the following two types of costs – shoe-leather costs and menu costs which are not very high. We explain below both these types of costs.

1. **Shoe-leather Costs.** This type of cost occurs because on account of inflation cost of holding money in the form of currency *i.e.*, (notes and coins) rises with the increase in inflation rate. Such cost arises because no interest is paid on holding currency, while money kept in deposits with the bank or used for keeping bonds earns interest. When inflation rate rises, the nominal interest rate on bank deposits rises, the interest lost by holding currency by the people therefore increases. In order to reduce the cost of holding currency people will tend to reduce their holdings of currency for transaction purposes. Accordingly, at a time people will hold less currency with them and keep as long as possible greater amount of money in bank deposits that yield interest. Therefore, rather than withdrawing a large amount of currency from banks at a time, they will withdraw less money which is sufficient for meeting daily expenses for a few days, say for a week. But for doing so the people will make more trips to withdraw cash. More trips to a bank in a month involves greater cost to the people. These costs have to be incurred on spending on petrol if car is used for making trips, more wear and tear of car, the time spent for making a trip. These costs of making more trips to the bank for withdrawing currency is metaphorically called *shoe-leather costs* of inflation, as walking to banks more often, one's shoes wear out more rapidly and one has to spend money on new shoes more often.

2. **Menu Costs.** The second type of anticipated inflation is menu costs, a term derived from a restaurant's cost of printing a new menu. Menu costs arise because high inflation requires them to change their listed prices more often. Changing prices is somewhat more expensive because the firms have to print new catalogues listing new prices and distribute them among their customers. They have even to incur expenditure on advertisements to inform the public about their new prices.

3. **Macroeconomic Inefficiency in Resource Allocation.** A third cost of inflation arises because firms having menu costs change their prices quite infrequently. Given the reluctance to change prices frequently, the higher the rate of inflation, the greater the variability in relative prices of a firm. Suppose a firm issues a new catalogue listing prices of its products once in a year, say in the month of January of every year. If during the year inflation occurs, there will be change in the relative prices of a firm to the general price level. If inflation rate of one per cent per month lakes place in a year the firm's relative prices to the general price level will *fall* by 12 per cent by the end of the year. As a result, his sales will tend to be lower in the early part of the year (when its prices are relatively high) and higher in the later part of the year (when its prices are relatively low). Thus when due to inflation relative prices of a firm vary during a year as compared to the overall price level, it causes destortion in production and therefore leads microeconomic inefficiencies in resource allocation.[5]

5. Mankiw, *op. cit.*, p. 98.

4. Inconvenience of Living. Lastly, another social cost of inflation is the *inconvenience of living* in a world with a changing price level. Money is the yardstick with which we measure the value of transactions. When inflation is taking place the value of money changes and as a result it becomes difficult to correctly estimate the value of transactions in real terms every time a transaction is made during a year. The rising price level makes it difficult to make optimal decisions about saving and investment and thus do the rational financial planning covering a long period of time. To quote Mankiw, "A dollar saved today and invested at a fixed nominal interest rate will yield a fixed dollar amount in the future. Yet the real value of that dollar amount – which will determine the retiree's living standard – depends on the future price level. *Deciding how much to save would be much simpler* if people could count on the price level in 30 years being similar to its level today."[6]

Conclusion. Taking account of all costs of anticipated inflation one finds that the costs of anticipated inflation are quite small or trivial and if these alone are considered, it is then surprising why inflation is a matter of serious concern for the policy makers and politicians. In our opinion the above view of costs of inflation does not consider the true cost of inflation which, as mentioned above, refers to the reduction in purchasing power or real incomes of the people which lowers their standard of living. Besides, there is ample cross-country evidence that *high rates of inflation lead to low rate of sustanced economic growth*[7].

It may be further noted that in the above analysis of cost of inflation it is assumed that there is only small to moderate inflation rate, say a single digit rate of inflation occurs so that it does not disrupt the payment system. With such a low to moderate inflation, costs of inflation are small. The hyperinflation has more harmful effect as it disrupts the payment system which leads to the collapse of the economy.

Cost of Unanticipated Inflation

Unanticipated inflation has a more substantial and harmful effect as compared to the cost of anticipated infllation rate. The significant effect of unanticipated inflation is that it *arbitrarily redistributes wealth* among individuals. Consider the value of assets fixed in nominal terms. Between 1995 and 2006, price level in India rose by about 100 per cent. This implies that those who held *claims on assets fixed in nominal terms in 1996*, their real value in terms of purchasing power would have declined significantly. Thus, a person who bought government bond of 10 years maturity with a face value of ₹ 1000 bearing 8 per cent nominal interest rate in 1996 will find that ₹ 1000 he gets bank in 2006 has far less value than when he purchased the bond in 1996.

Similarly, unanticipated inflation harms the individuals, who retire on pensions fixed in rupee terms. After some years of inflation, the real value or purchasing power of the fixed nominal pension will greatly decline and will therefore reduce his standard of living in his old age. Thus inflation hurts individuals with fixed pensions. Workers and the private firms often agree on fixed nominal pension payable to the workers after retirement. Workers are greatly harmed when inflation is higher than anticipated. Likewise, higher than anticipated inflation rate hurts the creditors who give loans to the others and get back the principal amount after the stipulated period. Thus *inflation redistributes wealth in favour of debtors*.

Bad Effects of Inflation on Long-Term Economic Growth : An Important Social Cost of Inflation

An important social cost of inflation, especially in developing countries, is its bad effect on long-run economic growth. Some economists have argued that inflation of a creeping or mild variety has a tonic effect on the long-run economic growth. In their support they give the example of today's

6. Stanley Fischer, Macroeconomic Factors in Economic Growth, *Journal of Monetary Economics*, Dec. 1993.
7. See D. Felix, "Profit Inflation and Industrial Growth, "*Quarterly Journal of Economics, August* 1956, pp. 441-63 and E.J. Hamilton, "Prices as a Factor in Business Growth", *Journal of Economic History*, December 1952, pp. 325-49.

industralised countries in the eighteenth and nineteenth centuries when the rate of growth of output had been more rapid during long periods of inflation witnessed in these countries. The driving force in the process of economic growth, according to them, has been *high profit margins* created by inflation. They argue that wages lag behind the rise in general price level and thus creating higher profit margins for businessmen and industrialists. This tends to increase the profit share in national income. The businessmen and industrialists who receive profits as income belong to the upper income brackets whose propensity to save is higher as compared to the workers. As a result, savings go up which ensures higher rate of investment. With greater rate of investment more accumulation of capital is made possible. More rapid capital accumulation generates a higher rate of long-run economic growth.

Looking at the problem from an alternative angle, with wages lagging behind rise in prices, inflation causes a large shift of resources away from the production of consumer goods for the wage earners to the production of capital goods. The higher rate of expansion in capital stock raises the growth of productive capacity of the economy and productivity of labour. This generates rapid economic growth.

However, it is now widely recognised that, far from encouraging savings and generating higher rate of economic growth, inflation slows down the rate of capital accumulation. There are several reasons responsible for this. First, as seen above, when due to rapid inflation value of money is declining, people will not like to keep money with themselves and will, therefore, be eager to spend it before its value goes down heavily. This raises their consumption demand and therefore lowers their saving. Besides, people find that the rapid inflation will erode the real value of their savings. This discourages them to save. Thus, *inflation or rapid rise in prices serves as a disincentive to save*. Further, as a consequence of the rise in prices, a relatively greater part of the income of the people is spent on consumption to maintain their level of living and therefore little is left to be saved. Thus, not only does inflation reduce the willingness to save, it also slashes their ability to save.

Secondly, *inflation or rising prices lead to unproductive form of investment* in gold, jewellery, real estate, construction of houses etc. These unproductive forms of wealth do not add to the productive capacity of the economy and are quite useless from the viewpoint of economic growth. Thus, inflation may lead to more investment but much of this is of unproductive type. In this way economic surplus is frittered away in unproductive investment.

Thirdly, a highly undesirable consequence of inflation, especially in developing countries, is that *it accentuates the problem of poverty in these countries*. It is often said inflation is enemy number one of the poor people. Due to rising prices poor people are not able to meet their basic needs and maintain minimum subsistence level of consumption. Thus inflation sends many people to live below the poverty line with the result that the number of people living below the poverty line increases. Besides, due to inflation, consumption of a large number of poor people is reduced much below what may be regarded as *productive consumption*, that is, essential consumption required to maintain health and productive efficiency. In India, rapid inflation in recent years is as much responsible for the mounting number of people below the poverty line as the lack of employment opportunities.

Fourthly, *inflation adversely affects balance of payments* and thereby hampers economic growth, especially in the developing countries. When prices of domestic goods rise due to inflation, they cannot compete abroad and as a consequence exports of a country are discouraged. On the other hand, when domestic prices rise relative to prices of foreign goods, imports of foreign goods increase. Thus, falling exports and rising imports create disequilibrium in the balance of payments which may, in the long run, result in a foreign exchange crisis. The shortage of foreign exchange prevents the country to import even essential materials and capital goods needed for industrial growth of the economy. The Indian experience during 1988-92 when foreign exchange reserves declined to abysmally low level and created an economic crisis in the country, shows the validity of this argument.

There is no agreement among economists whether or not moderate or mild inflation encourages saving and therefore ensures higher rate of capital accumulation and economic growth. However, there is complete unanimity that a rapid inflation discourages saving and hinders economic growth. However, barring the special case of hyperinflation, whether or not saving is encouraged by inflation depends on whether there exists *wage lag*. While there is sufficient evidence in the industrialised countries such as the U.S.A., Great Britain, France etc., about the existence of wage lag in the period before *World War II*, in the period after this there is no solid evidence of it. In the present wages quickly catch up with the rising prices. Indeed, there is evidence in some developed countries that the share of profits in national income has declined and that of wages has gone up during the post- World War II period. Therefore, "To the extent that rate of long-run economic growth depends on the rate of capital accumulation, *a major basis for the conclusion that inflation promotes rapid economic growth is undermined given that wages no longer lag during inflation as they apparently did in time of past.*"[8]

However, it may be noted that in the developing countries like India where labour is mostly unorganised and trade unions of labour are not strong and further there is a lack of information which causes wages lagging behind prices during periods of inflation. This itself will cause greater proportion of national income going to profits and other business incomes which should ensure higher saving rate. However, in India, businessmen are prone to make unproductive investment in speculative activities, gold, jewellery, real estate and palatial houses whose prices rise rapidly during periods of inflation. Such kind of investment is not only counter-productive and anti-growth but is repugnant to social justice as it further accentuates inequalities in the distribution of income and wealth.

It follows from above that rising prices as a goal of monetary policy are full of disastrous consequences for the economy and the people and therefore cannot be recommended as a desirable goal for the economic policy. Rising prices often get out of hand and hyperinflation might set in which will shake the confidence of the people in the monetary and fiscal system of the country.

FURTHER BAD EFFECTS OF INFLATION

Inflation is a very unpopular happening in an economy. Opinion surveys conducted in India, the U.S.A. and other countries reveal that inflation is the most important concern of the people as it badly affects their standard of living. The political fortunes of many political leaders (Prime Ministers and Presidents) and Governments in India and abroad have been determined by how far they have succeeded in tackling the problem of inflation. So much so that some American presidental candidates called '*inflation as enemy number one*'. Same is the case in India where inflation is the most hotly debated issue during the general elections for the Parliament and Assemblies. A high rate of inflation makes the life of the poor very miserable. It is, therefore, described as anti-poor. It redistributes income and wealth in favour of some and greatly harms others. By making the rich richer and the poor poorer, it militates against social justice. Besides, inflation lowers national output and employment and impedes long-run economic growth, especially in developing countries like India. We shall discuss below all these effects of inflation.

Anticipated and Unanticipated Inflation

The difference between anticipated inflation and unanticipated inflation is of crucial importance as the effects of inflation, especially its redistributive effect, depend on whether it is anticipated or not. If rate of inflation is anticipated, then people take steps to make suitable adjustments in their contracts to avoid the adverse effects which inflation could bring to them. For example, if a worker correctly anticipates the rate of inflation in a particular year to be equal to 10 per cent and if his

8. E. Shapiro, *Macroeconomic Analysis,* Harcourt, Fourth Edition, 1978, p. 443 (*Italics added*)

present wage rate is ₹ 5,000 per month, he can enter into contract with the employer that to compensate for the 10 per cent rise in prices his money wage per month next year be raised by 10 per cent so that next year he gets ₹ 5,500 per month. In this way he has been able to prevent the erosion of his real income with the automatic revision of his money wage depending on the anticipated rate of inflation.

Take another example. You lend ₹ 10,000 to a person at a rate of 10 per cent per annum. After a year you will receive ₹ 11,000. But if it is anticipated that during the year there will be 8 per cent rate of inflation, then 8 per cent of your income will be offset by the rise in prices that would occur so that you will get only 2 *per cent real rate of interest*. Therefore, in order to receive 10 per cent real rate of interest, in view of 8 per cent anticipated inflation rate you must demand 18 per cent nominal rate of interest.

On the other hand, effects of unanticipated inflation are unavoidable because in this case you do not know what would be the rise in the price level. That is, unanticipated inflation catches you by surprise. In what follows we shall examine the *effects of unanticipated inflation*. The effects of inflation can be divided into three categories:

Inflation Erodes Real Incomes of the People

To examine the effect of inflation it is important to note the difference between money income and real income. It is the change in the general price level that creates the crucial difference between the two. Money income or what is also called nominal income means the income such as wages, interest, rent *received in terms of rupees*. On the other hand, *real income* implies the amount of goods and services which you can buy. In other words, real income means the purchasing power of your income. If your money or nominal income increases at a lower rate than the rate of rise in the general price level (*i.e.*, the rate of inflation), you will be able to buy less goods and services, that is, your real income will decline. Real income will rise only if nominal income rises faster than the rate of inflation. For illustration, take the case of workers who enter into contract with their employer at an agreed wage rate of ₹ 5,000 per month for the period, say 5 years. Now, suppose the rate of inflation is 10 per cent per annum. This means after a year, with money wage rate of ₹ 5,000 workers will be able to buy less goods and services. That is, their real income will decrease and therefore their standard of living will fall.

Take another example. Suppose you deposit your saving of ₹100 in a savings account which carries 5 per cent rate of interest. After a year you will receive ₹ 105. However, if during that year rate of inflation has been 12 per cent, you will be a loser in real terms. In fact your real interest-income will be negative as, with 12 per cent rate of inflation, ₹ 105 after a year will buy less goods and services than what you can purchase with ₹ 100 today.

The above two examples clearly show that inflation reduces the purchasing power of money and thereby adversely affects real income of the people.

Effect on Distribution of Income and Wealth

An important effect of inflation is that it redistributes income and wealth in favour of some at the cost of others. Inflation adversely affects those who receive relatively fixed incomes and benefits such as businessmen, producers, traders and others who enjoy flexible incomes. Inflation brings windfall profits for the producers and traders. Thus, all do not lose as a result of inflation, rather some gain from it. We examine below how inflation redistributes income and wealth and thereby harms some people and benefits others.

Creditors and Debtors. Unanticipated inflation harms creditors and benefits debtors and in this way redistributes income in favour of the latter. As explained above, value of money declines due to inflation. For creditors (including financial institutions such as banks and insurance companies) who enter into agreement with the borrowers to provide loans at fixed nominal rate of interest, the real value of money in terms of goods and services which they will receive at the end of the period would be much less if during the period prices rise sharply. Thus, the debtors or borrowers gain because they would return the loan-money when its real value has declined greatly due to the unexpected rapid rate of inflation.

Fixed Income Groups. Those who get fixed incomes and pensioners stand to lose from inflation. Workers and salaried people who earn fixed wages and salaries are hit hard by unanticipated inflation. These people often enter into contract with the employers regarding wages or salaries fixed in nominal terms. When inflation occurs, the purchasing power of their nominal incomes falls greatly causing a decline in their levels of living. Thus, when inflation persists for some years there are demands for revision of wages and salaries. It may be mentioned that now-a-days workers and other salaried people get dearness allowances to compensate them for the rise in cost of living due to inflation. However, these dearness allowances do not fully neutralise the rise in price level and therefore they also demand revision of wages and pay scales.

Businessmen : Producers and Traders. Businessmen, that is, entrepreneurs and traders, stand to gain by inflation. During periods of inflation, the prices of goods produced by entrepreneurs rise relatively faster than the cost of production because wages lag behind the rise in prices of goods. Consequently, *inflation increases the profits of businessmen*. The value of the inventories or stocks of goods and materials kept by the entrepreneurs and traders increases due to rise in prices of goods which brings about an increase in their profits.

Wealth Holders of Cash, Bonds and Debentures. Inflation also adversely affects wealth holders who hold their wealth in the form of cash money, demand deposits, savings and fixed deposits and interest-bearing bonds and debentures. These wealth holders are severely hurt by inflation as inflation reduces the real value of their wealth. Savings and demand deposits, bonds and debentures represent assets whose value is fixed in terms of money. The rise in prices reduces the purchasing power of these fixed-value money assets such as savings and time deposits, bonds and debentures which bear a fixed nominal rate of interest.

Inflation, therefore ,reduces the real rate of interest earned by them. Consequently, it has been observed that during periods of rapid inflation people try to convert their holdings of money and near money into goods and physical property so as to avoid the loss due to inflation. It may also be noted that if inflation is anticipated and all expect equal rates of inflation the nominal rates of interest are adjusted upward so as to obtain targeted real rate of interest. Thus, if creditors want real rate of interest equal to 10 per cent and anticipate rate of inflation equal to 8 per cent, they will try to have nominal rate of interest fixed at 18 per cent. This is known as **Fisher effect** which states that *market or nominal rate of interest is equal to the real rate of interest (based on productivity of capital and rate of time preference) plus the anticipated rate of inflation*. Thus nominal rate of inflation includes what is called *inflation premium* to prevent the erosion of purchasing power due to inflation.

HYPERINFLATION AND ECONOMIC CRISIS

When inflation is extremely rapid, it is called hyperinflation. *A hyperinflation is generally defined as inflation at the rate of 50 per cent or more per month*. Some economists, prominent among them is R. Dornbusch, have defined *hyperinflation as rise in price level at the rate of 1000 per cent in a year*.[9] There are several examples of hyperinflation that occurred in European countries after World Wars I and II. The most important episode of hyperinflation took place in Germany between Aug. 1922 and Nov. 1923. German inflation occurred at the rate of 322 per cent per month during this period and in the final months rate of inflation in Germany reached the highly extreme rate of 32000 per cent per month.[10] It may be noted that German hyperinflation was caused by deficit financing by the government (*i.e.*, creation of new money to finance the budget deficit during World War I when

9. See R. Dornbusch, et. al; "Extreme Inflation, Dynamics and Stabilisation", *Brookings Paper on Economic Activity*, 1977.
10. Robert J. Gordon, *Macroeconomics*, 12th edition, 2012, p. 14

it had to pay massive reparations to Britain and France. Argentina, Brazil, Peru and Poland all suffered from inflation rate of 1000 per cent per year for one or more years in late 1980 or 1990. The effect of hyperinfilation on national output and employment turns out to be devastating. *Thus hyperinflation is generally caused when Government issues too much currency which greatly adds to the money supply in the economy.*

However, some economists are of the view that even mild or moderate inflation may ultimately lead to hyperinflation. They argue that when prices go on creeping upward for some time, people start expecting that prices will rise further and value of money will depreciate. In order to protect themselves from the fall in the purchasing power of money in the future, they try to spend money now. That is, they try to beat the anticipated price increases. This raises the aggregate demand for goods in the present. Businessmen too increase their purchases of capital goods and build up larger than normal inventories if they anticipate rise in prices. Thus, inflationary expectations raise the pressure on prices and in this way inflation feeds on itself. Further, the rise in prices and the cost of living under the influence of rising aggregate demand prompts the workers and their unions to demand higher wages to compensate them for the rise in the prices. During the periods of boom these demands of the workers for hike in wages are generally conceded. But rise in labour costs due to higher wages are recovered by business firms from the consumers by raising the prices of their products. This increase in prices gives rise to demand for further increases in wages resulting in still higher costs. Thus, *cumulative wage-price inflationary spiral starts operating which may culminate in hyperinflation.*

The major reason for hyperinflation is rapid growth of money supply as a result of financing budget deficits through creation of new money. During wars government expenditure increases more than the revenue. But hyperinflation does not occur during the war period as controls are imposed on prices during the war period and therefore inflation remains suppressed. When controls are lifted after the war, hyperinflation takes places as a consequence of excessive deficit financing and monetary growth duirng the war period.

Some economists attribute hyperinflation to the *accommodation of adverse supply shocks* that may take place as a result of rise in wage rates or rise in oil prices as these supply shocks cause inflation on the one hand and unemployment or fall in GDP on the other. To increase employment opportunities to get rid of unemployment, the government or its Central Bank increases the supply of money to raise aggregates demand. This higher aggregate demand succeeds in eliminating unemployment but generates still higher inflation. This gives rise to *wage-price spiral* under which every time when the price level rises, money wages are raised to restore real wages. This process goes on and ultimately ends in hyperinflation.

The Costs of Hyperinflation

The costs of hyperinflation are much greater than the costs of moderate inflation. For example, when prices are rising at an extremely high rate, the incentives to minimise holding of currency become quite strong that result in enormous *shoe-leather costs*. In the situation of hyperinflation workers are paid much more frequently, even on daily basis and people rush out to spend their wages on goods (or to convert their currency in some other form such as a foreign currency or into gold and silver) before the prices rise even more. Greater time and energy are spent in getting rid of currency as soon as possible. Thus hyperinflation involves lot of wastes of resources and leads to disruption of production.

Hyperinflation not only has disruptive redistributive effect, it also brings about economic crisis and may even cause collapse of the economic system. Hyperinflation encourages speculative activity on the part of people and businessmen who shy away from productive activities, as they find it highly profitable to hoard both finished goods and materials on the basis of expectations of further rise in prices. But such hoardings of goods and materials restrict the supply and availability of goods and tend to intensify the inflationary pressures in the economy. Instead of making productive investment, people and businesses tend to invest in unproductive assets such as gold and jewellery, real estate, houses etc., as a means of protecting themselves from inflation.

In the extreme when as a result of issuing too much money supply to finance government deficit or working of wage-price spiral, inflation becomes extremely rapid or what economists called hyper-inflation, normal working of the economy collapses. In this situation, "prices are so rapidly rising and consequently purchasing power of money is so much dwindling that businessmen do not know what to charge for their products and consumers do not know what to pay. Resource suppliers will want to be paid with actual output rather than with rapidly depreciating money. Creditors will avoid debtors to escape the rapayment of debts with cheap money. Money becomes virtually worthless and ceases to do its job as a measure of value and a medium of exchange. The economy may be literally thrown into a state of barter. Production and exchange grind towards a halt and the net result is economic, social and political chaos." [11]

Such grim and gloomy situation created by hyperinflation did occur in Germany during 1920s and in Hungary and Japan in the forties. At that time, money depreciated so much that for some time barter system came to prevail and after some time, the new currency had to be issued. It is therefore desirable that appropriate anti-inflationary measures be taken so that inflation should not go out of control and get transformed into hyperinflation.

Measures to End Hyperinflation

It is important to note that all hyperinflation episodes lasted for one to 2 years. The governments succeeded in controlling them through the adoption of proper *stabilisation policy*. The stabilisation measures adopted were the following:

1. The most important measure was to reduce sharply budget deficit *by cutting down government expenditure and subsidies and raising more resources through taxes*. This resulted in slowdown in growth of money and helped in controlling infaltion.

2. The Central Bank made creditable announcement that it would not automatically monetise the budget deficits of the government. The government on its part also assured it would finance its expenditure through taxes and would not resort to deficit financing. Once the people were convinced about the commitments by the Central Bank and the government they did not rush to spend the money income they earned and kept it with them to spend when needed. This helped to curb inflationary expectations.

As suggested by some economists, to control hyperinflation some type of control on wages often called **incomes policy** was needed. This visualised reducing the frequency of wages-indexation or agreement among firms and labour unions not to raise wages until hyperinflation was brought under control. Besides, this also involved commitments by the firms not to raise their profit margins. However, the experience of several countries which succeeded in ending hyperinflation suggests that, "stopping hyperinflation is a complex and difficult task. Much depends on the credibility of the government, that is, public belief that budget deficit and monetary growth are really going to stop. It may take several dramatic actions all at once to achieve credibility."

MEASURES TO CONTROL DEMAND-PULL INFLATION

As has been explained above, inflation occurs due to the emergence of excess demand for goods and services relative to their supply of output at the prevailing prices. Inflation of this type is called *demand-pull inflation*. Various fiscal and monetary measures can be adopted to check this inflation. We discuss below the efficacy of the various policy measures to check demand-pull inflation which is caused by excess aggregate demand.

11. Robert J. Gordon, *op. cit.*, p.337.

1. Fiscal Policy: Reducing Fiscal Deficit

The budget deals with how a Government raises its revenue and spends it. If the total revenue raised by the Government through taxation, fees, surpluses from public undertakings is less than the expenditure it incurs on buying goods and services to meet its requirements of defence, civil administration and various welfare and developmental activities, there emerges a fiscal deficit. It may be noted here that the budget of the government has two parts: (1) *Revenue Budget*, (2) *Capital Budget*. In the revenue budget on the receipts side revenue raised through taxes, interests, fees, surpluses from public undertakings are given and on the expenditure side consumption expenditure by the government on goods and services required to meet the needs of defence, civil administration, education and health services, subsidies on food, fertilizers and exports, and interest payments on the loans taken by it in the previous years are important items. In the capital budget, the main items of receipts are market borrowings by the government from the banks and other financial institutions, foreign aid, small savings (*i.e.*, Provident Fund, National Savings Schemes etc.). The important items of expenditure in the capital budget are defence, funding of public enterprises for developmental purposes, especially those relating to infrastructure projects and loans to States and Union territories.

Fiscal deficit can be financed in two ways. First, borrowing by the government from the central bank (RBI in case of India) against its own securities. This leads to the creation of more money supply and therefore gives rise to inflationary pressures in the economy. Some years ago, this was called *deficit financing* which was held to be the main cause of demand-pull inflation in India. Now, we call it *monetisation of fiscal deficit*. However, in recent years *fiscal deficit in India is financed mainly through borrowing by the Government through sale of its bonds which are generally purchased by banks, insurance companies, mutual funds and corporate firms*. The increase in government expenditure made possible by borrowing without being matched by extra taxation causes aggregate demand to increase. The net increase in Government expenditure leads to multiple increase in aggregate demand through *Government expenditure* multiplier.

In the opinion of many economists, the expansion in aggregate expenditure caused by fiscal deficit leads to the excess aggregate demand and inflationary pressures in the economy, especially when aggregate supply of output is inelastic. To some extent increase in aggregate demand may not generate demand-pull inflation because if the aggregate output increases, especially of essential consumer goods such as foodgrains, cloth, the extra demand arising out of increase in expenditure would be matched by extra supply of output.

But when increase in expenditure occurs and the economy is already utilising its production capacity fully or working near to it, this leads to demand-pull inflation. Therefore, to tackle the problem of demand-pull inflation fiscal deficit should be reduced. In its recommendation for India, IMF has suggested that fiscal deficit must be reduced to 3 per cent of GDP if inflation has to be kept under check.

To reduce fiscal deficit the Government can mobilise more resources through taxes, both direct and indirect. In India there is a lot of scope for raising resources through taxation. In both personal and corporate income taxes, there are a large number of unnecessary exemptions which lower the effective rate of income tax. Thus it has been found that though there is 33 per cent tax on corporate income but because of several exemptions which have outlived their utility, effective rate of corporate income tax in India is only about 24 per cent. Thus with withdrawal of these exemptions can lead to significant increase in revenue of the Government. Besides, improving efficiency of tax-collecting administration tax evasion which occurs on a large scale in India and generates a lot of black money can *yield* large revenue for the Government. On the other hand, it can reduce fiscal deficit by curtailing its wasteful and inessential expenditure, especially subsidies to the non-poor people. In India, it is often argued that there is a large scope for pruning down non-plan expenditure on defence, police and general administration and on subsidies being provided on food, fertilizers and fuel oil. Though it is easy to suggest cutting down of Government expenditure, it is difficult to implement it in practice. However, in our view, there is a large-scale inefficiency in resource use and also a lot of corruption involved in spending by the Government which can be curtailed to a good extent. Thus, both by greater resource mobilisation on the one hand and pruning down of wasteful and inessential Government expenditure on the other, the fiscal deficit can be reduced. This will help in controlling inflation.

2. Monetary Policy to Control Inflation : Monetary Tightening

Monetary policy refers to the adoption of suitable policy regarding *interest rate* and the *availability of credit*. Monetary policy is an important measure for reducing aggregate demand to control inflation. As an instrument of demand management, monetary policy can work in two ways. First, it can affect the *cost of credit* and second, it can influence the *credit availability* for private business firms. Let us first consider the cost of credit. The higher the rate of interest, the greater the cost of borrowing from the banks by the business firms. As anti-inflationary measure, the rate of interest has to be raised to discourage businessmen to borrow more so that less bank credit is created. The cheap credit policy (*i.e.*, lower interest rates) is recommended on the ground that lower rate of interest will promote more private investment which is an important factor determining economic growth. Keeping in view this consideration, cheap money policy was adopted in India up to 1972 and accordingly bank rate was kept low.

The dear money policy (that is, *higher interest rate policy*) has often been used in India to curb the inflationary pressures in the Indian economy. In India, bank rate has not been generally used to check inflation. Instruments like *repo rate* and *reverse repo* rate have often been used to manage aggregate demand. Repo rate is the interest rate at which Reserve Bank of India lends funds to the commercial banks *for a short period*. To curb inflation *repo rate* is raised. Hike in repo rate raises the cost of funds for the banks which will, if they do not have excess reserves, raise their *lending rates*. The higher lending rates will lower the demand for bank credit for investment and for purchases of cars (auto loans) and housing (housing loans). Under these circumstances to mobilise funds banks raise their deposit rates. The higher rate of interest on savings and fixed deposits will induce more savings by the households and help in cutting down aggregate consumption expenditure. Besides, higher rates of interest will discourage more investment in inventories and consumer durables and will help in reducing aggregate demand.

However, rise in repo rate will lead to the decline in credit growth if *monetary transmission mechanism* works. This will happen only if banks are short of liquid funds. If the banks have excess liquid reserves with them they would not raise their lending rates when the RBI raises repo rate. Therefore, for monetary transmission mechanism to work liquidity with the banks must be curtailed. This can be done by the RBI by raising cash reserve ratio (CRR) and by *open market operation* through sale of Government securities.

It is noteworthy that a recent monetary theory emphasizes that it is the changes in the ***credit availability*** rather than ***cost of credit*** (*i.e.*, rate of interest) that is a more effective instrument of regulating aggregate demand. There are several methods by which credit availability can be reduced. Firstly, it is through *open market operations* that the central bank of a country can reduce the availability of credit in the economy. Under open market operations, the Reserve Bank sells Government securities. Those, especially banks, who buy these securities will make payment for them in terms of cash reserves. With their reduced cash reserves, their capacity to lend money to the business firms will be curtailed. This will tend to reduce the supply of credit or loanable funds by the banks which in turn would tend to reduce aggregate demand.

However, in the past in India open market operations did not play a significant role as an instrument of credit control to fight against inflationary situation. This was because market for Government securities was narrow as well as captive. However, with financial reforms this is no more the situation. At present RBI often uses open market operations to influence liquidity of the banking system. General public do not buy more than a fraction of Government securities. It is the institutions such as commercial banks, LIC, GIC and Provident Funds which are required by law to invest a certain proportion of their funds in buying Government securities. The RBI can reduce the liquidity with the banks by selling Government securities to them through open market operations.

In India, it is the ***Cash Reserve Ratio (CRR)*** which can be effectively used to curb inflation. By law banks have to keep a certain proportion of cash money as reserves against their demand and time deposits. This is called cash reserve ratio. To reduce liquidity with the banks and thereby to contract credit availability Reserve Bank can raise this ratio. In recent years to squeeze credit for checking inflation, cash reserve ratio in India has been raised from time to time.

Statutory Liquidity Ratio (SLR). Another instrument with Reserve Bank of India for affecting credit availability is the statutory liquidity ratio. In addition to *CRR*, banks have to keep a certain minimum proportion of their deposits in the form of specified liquid assets. And the most important specified liquid asset for this purpose is the Government securities. To mop up extra liquid assets with banks which may lead to undue expansion in credit availability for the business class, the Reserve Bank has often raised statutory liquidity ratio.

Limitations of Tight Monetary Policy

However, tight monetary policy for controlling inflation is not without its limitations. First, monetary transmission mechanism may be weak and raising of short-term interest rates by the RBI may not actually lead to the restriction of bank credit. First, the banks may have surplus liquidity (*i.e.*, cash reserves) with them and therefore they may not follow tight monetary policy and raise their lending rates. As a result, supply of credit by banks will not be restricted. Secondly, if the economic environment is such that boom conditions prevail in the economy and aggregate demand for products is quite high, demand for credit may not be much affected by higher lending rates. As emphasized by J.M. Keynes, investment is determined more by marginal efficiency of capital (that is, expected rate of return) rather than rate of interest. Thirdly, at present in India corporate firms are more easily able to borrow from foreign capital markets (*i.e.*, external commercial borrowing, ECB) especially when rates of interest in the US, European zone and Japan are extremely low. Therefore, unless this debt-capital inflow (*i.e.* ECB) is checked RBI's monetary policy may not be effective to check the supply of credit to control inflation in the economy.

Thirdly, when the stock market prices are rising and aggregate demand is quite high, the corporate sector is able to raise funds itself more easily from the capital market. This will also offset the impact of tight monetary policy of the RBI to control inflation. Fourthly, if adequate internal funds are available with the corporate firms as a result of *retained profit earnings* by the companies they can use them to finance their expansion plans and thereby add to the aggregate expenditure or demand. This will also nullify the tight monetary policy of the RBI to curb inflation.

It may be noted that in recent years to control inflation the Reserve Bank of India raised its *repo rate* 13 times from March 2010 to Nov. 2011 (from 4.75% in March 2010 to 8.50% in Nov. 2011) but inflation as measured by the WPI remained at an elevated level. It was estimated at 10 per cent (YoY) in September 2011, 9.73% in Oct. 2011 and 9.11 per cent in Nov. 2011. After Nov. 2011, WPI inflation declined because of dip in food inflation due partly to the base effect and partly to easing of supply position of some food articles. Thus tight monetary policy failed to check inflation despite 3.75 per centage points increase in repo rate. The RBI explained failure of its tight monetary policy to curb inflation by blaming the *large fiscal deficit* of the Government in 2011-12. Due to large fiscal deficit, aggregate demand was increasing which was feeding inflation in the Indian economy. According to the RBI, unless fiscal deficit is brought down by the Government, tight monetary policy alone will not succeed in checking inflation. Besides, the RBI *blamed supply-side factors* responsible for food inflation which has contributed to overall rise in WPI inflation.

Lastly, if inflation in the economy has originated from the **supply-side factors**, for example, if production of foodgrains and other essential food articles such as milk, vegetables, fruits etc. in a year declines or does not increase adequately to meet the growing demand for them due to certain supply-side bottlenecks, this will cause the demand-supply imbalances leading to the rise in inflation. Such supply-side inflation cannot be checked by raising interest rates under the tight monetary policy. This happened in 2009-10 when due to the shortage of monsoon rainfall, drop in agricultural production was expected, inflationary pressures emerged in the Indian economy raising food inflation to around 20 per cent in December 2009. This food inflation continued to prevail at double digit level till November 2010. Tight monetary policy which is aimed at management of aggregate demand rather than augmentation of supply is ineffective in tackling this supply-side inflation as in case of food inflation in 2010. Likewise, in 2010-11 and 2011-12 *shortage of protein-based food* products such as pulses, milk, fruits and vegetables, eggs, meat and fish, contributed a good deal to the persistence of food inflation. It is only after Oct. 2011 when there was a drop in food inflation, that headline WPI inflation also declined. Similarly, supply-side inflation arises when prices of petroleum products rise which is passed on to the domestic consumers and cannot be tackled with use of tight monetary policy. In addition to fuel, if output growth in *core industries* such as steel, cement, coal declined as they did during 2011-12 in India, they create supply-side bottlenecks in various industries leading to supply-side inflation.

Now to control food inflation what is required is to take long-term measures to augment supply of foodgrains and other food articles by raising agricultural productivity and undertaking appropriate technological changes and land-reform measures. In the short, run to control food inflation what is needed is to release food stocks through public distribution system (PDS) which should be properly monitorad to check black market. Besides, to control rise in food prices in the short run release of food stocks for sale in the open market should be made. However, this presupposes enough food stocks with the Government. Further, to check foodinflation, foodgrains, pulses, oilseeds and other food articles in short-supply can be imported.

It may however be noted that when inflationary expectations arise as a result of emergence of shortage of supply of some essential commodities, there is tendency on the part of traders to hoard stocks of goods in short supply for speculative purposes. To discourage such speculative hoarding of goods in short supply monetary policy of high interest rates can be helpful. Besides, as explained above, selective credit controls of monetary policy can also be used to check excessive hoarding.

OTHER MEASURES TO CONTROL INFLATION

Supply Management through Imports

To correct excess demand relative to aggregate supply, the latter can also be raised by importing goods in short supply. In India, to check the rise in prices of foodgrains, edible oils, sugar etc., the Government has often taken steps to increase imports of goods in short supply to enlarge their available supplies. When inflation is of the type of *supply-side inflation*, imports are increased to augment the domestic supplies of goods. To increase imports of goods in short supply the Government can reduce customs duties on them so that their imports become cheaper and therefore their imports help in containing inflation. For example, in 2008-09 the Indian Government removed customs duties on imports of wheat and rice and reduced them on oilseeds, steel etc. to increase their supplies in India. Besides, to increase the domestic supplies the government can ban the exports of some commodities for some time. Thus, in 2010 the Indian Government banned the exports of onions and pulses.

At times of inflationary expectations, there is a tendency on the part of businessmen to hoard goods for speculative purposes. The attempt by the Government to import goods in short supply would compel the hoarders to release their hoarded stocks. This will have a favourable impact on prices of these goods. However, when international prices of commodities are high, their imports cannot be very helpful for tackling domestic inflation. This was the case in 2009-10 and 2010-11 in India when commodities such as sugar, wheat, oil seeds could not be imported sufficiently to augment domestic supplies because of their high world prices.

Incomes Policy: Freezing Wages

Another anti-inflationary measure which has often been suggested is the avoidance of wage increases which are unrelated to improvements in productivity. This requires exercising control over wage-income. As seen in the previous chapter, it is through wage-price spiral that inflation gets momentum. When cost of living rises due to the initial rise in prices, workers demand higher wages to compensate for the rise in cost of living. When their wage demands are conceded to, it gives rise to cost-push inflation. And this generates inflationary expectations which add fuel to the fire. To check this vicious circle of wages-chasing prices, an important measure will be to exercise control over wages. However, if wages are raised equal to the increase in the productivity of labour, then it will have no inflationary effect. Therefore, the proposal has been to *freeze wages* in the short run and wages should be linked with the changes in the level of productivity over a long period of time. According to this, wage increases should be allowed to the extent of rise in labour productivity only. This will check the net growth in aggregate demand relative to aggregate supply of output.

However, freezing wages and linking it with productivity only irrespective of what happens to the cost of living has been strongly opposed by trade unions. It has been validly pointed out why freeze wages only; to ensure social justice, the other kinds of income such as rent, interest and profits should also be freezed similarly. Indeed, an effective way to control inflation will be to adopt a broad-based incomes policy which should cover not only wages but also profits, interest and rental incomes.

It is thus clear that with the adoption of various monetary, fiscal and other policy measures, the aggregate demand can be reduced on the one hand and the aggregate supply of output can be increased on the other. This would help in bridging the gap between aggregate demand and aggregate supply which would enable us to contain the inflationary pressures in the economy.

QUESTIONS FOR REVIEW

1. Define demand-pull inflation. How is it caused by the Central Bank insistence of keeping the market rate of interest low so as to stimulate investment ?
2. What are the main factors that cause cost-push inflation ? Suggest measures to control cost-push inflation.
3. Distinguish between demand-pull inflation and cost-push inflation. How are they often intertwined ?
4. Inflation may originate because of cost-push but it cannot be sustained for long unless it is supported by demand-pull inflation.
5. Critically examme monetarist theory of inflation.
6. What is stagflation ? Explain how cost-push inflation leads to stagflation.

7. An inflationary process may begin on the supply side but it will not continue for long unless there is increase in demand. Discuss.
8. Distinguish between demand-pull and cost-push inflation. How can demand-pull inflation be controlled ?
9. Inflation is always and everywhere a purely monetary phenomenon. Critically examine.
10. Define inflation. Explain its effects on (*a*) creditors and debtors and (*b*) persons of fixed income group.
11. Explain the effects of inflation on economic growth and distribution of income.
12. How does inflation distort the pattern of production and distribution in an economy?
13. Define inflation. What measures would you suggest to control it?
14. What are the main causes of inflation in India? Which policies of government have helped to check rise in prices ?
15. What is *inflation fallacy* with regard to cost of inflation ? How far is it valid ? Discuss.
16. Explain the social cost of (*a*) anticipated inflation and (*b*) unanticipated inflation.
17. How does inflation adversely affect long-term economic growth of a country?
18. What is hyperinflation ? How does it lead to economic crisis ?

APPENDIX TO CHAPTER 24

Measurement of Inflation And Price Indices: WPI and CPI

We have explained above that inflation has been one of the important problems facing the economies of the world. Precisely stated, *inflation is the rate of change of general price level during a period of time*. And the general price level in a period is the result of inflation in the past. Through rate of inflation economists measure the *cost of living* in an economy. Let us explain how rate of inflation is measured. Suppose P_{t-1} represents the price level on 31st March 2012 and P_t represents the price level on 31st Mach 2013. Then the rate of inflation in year 2012-13 will be equal to

$$\pi = \frac{P_t - P_{t-1}}{P_{t-1}}$$

where *p* represents rate of inflation. Suppose Consumer Price Index (CPI) on March 31, 2012 which was 250, rose to 275 on March 31, 2013, rate of inflation in 2012-13 will be

$$\pi = \frac{275-250}{250} \times 100 = \frac{25}{250} \times 100 = 10\%$$

Thus rate of inflation during 2012-13 will be 10 per cent. This is called *point-to-point inflation rate*. There are 52 weeks in a year, average of price indexes of 52 weeks of a year (say 2011-12) can be calculated to compare the average of price indexes of 52 weeks of year 2012-13 and find the inflation rate on the basis of average weekly price levels of a year. In both these ways rate of inflation in different years is measured and compared. We now explain in detail how inflation is measured with the help of various price indices.

Measuring Inflation with Price Indices

Having explained the meaning of inflation we will now explain how inflation rate is measured. As inflation means rate of change in average or general price level over a period time we need to explain how the prices of various individual goods are aggregated to obtain the measure of general price level. This is done through construction of price index numbers. There are a number of price indices that are prepared to assess the changes in price level (*i.e.*, inflation). The following types of price indices are generally used :

1. The Consumer Price Index Number (CPI)
2. The Wholesale Price Index (WPI)
3. GDP Deflator

In India, inflation is generally measured by changes in wholesale price index (WPI), while in the developed countries such as U.S it is consumer price index (CPI) that is used for this purpose. We explain below all these three price indices.

Consumer Price Index (CPI)

The Consumer Price Index (CPI) is used to measure *cost of living* of the people and is based on *retail prices* of the selected goods constituting the consumption basket of a particular group of consumers. For instance, in India CPI is prepared for (1) industrial workers (CPI-IW) and for its preparation retail prices of those goods are selected which generally form the consumption basket of industrial workers. Second, consumer price index for agricultural labour (CPI-AL) is prepared and this includes the retail prices of consumer goods that constitutes the consumption basket of agricultural labour. Third, CPI for urban non-manual employees (CPI-UNME) is constructed to measure retail prices of those consumer goods and services purchased by urban non-manual employees.

Method of Constructing Consumer Price Index (CPI)

We now proceed to explain the method used for constructing consumer price index (CPI). The first step is to *choose the basket of consumer goods and services* that is generally purchased by a specific group of consumers, for example, industrial workers.

The second step in the construction of CPI is to select the base year. In India at present the year 2001 is selected as the base year for the construction CPI for industrial workers. It is the retail prices in the base year with which retail prices of the current year are compared that enable us to obtain the relative price.

The third step is collecting the retail prices for the current year of various goods included in the consumption basket of the specific group of consumers. The price data from different centres or locations in the country is gathered for this purpose. The fourth step involves choosing weights to be given to the prices of different items in the consumption basket of the specific group of consumers. If simple average prices of various items of consumption are used, it would mean treating all items equally for the specific group. However, this is not realistic as consumers spend different amounts on various items. Therefore, different weights are assigned to different items in consumers' basket of goods. The weight assigned to an item is the proportion of expenditure on an item to the consumers' total expenditure on the consumption basket. It is calculated as follows :

Expenditure on an item in the base year = $P_i^0 Q_i^0$

Superscript '0' in the above expression stands for the base year. P_i stands for price of an item and Q_i for the quantity of the item. The total expenditure of all items in the consumption basket in the base year is given by :

$$\text{Total expenditure} = \sum_{i=1}^{n} P_i^0 Q_i^0$$

Thus weight assigned to an item is given by

$$W_i = \frac{P_i^0 Q_i^0}{\sum_{i=1}^{n} P_i^0 Q_i^0} \qquad \ldots (1)$$

Suppose expenditure on a commodity of a household, say rice, in a week is ₹ 500 (i.e., $P_i^0 Q_i^0$ = ₹ 500) and total expenditure on all items in its consumption basket is ₹ 1,500 (i.e. $\sum_{i=1}^{n} P_i^0 Q_i^0$ = ₹ 1,500), then weight to be assigned to the item 'rice' will be 500 ÷ 1500 = 0.33).

As said above, a consumer price index expresses the current price relative to its price in the base period. Thus the consumer price index for a period *t* is given by

$$\text{CPI}_t = \frac{P^t}{P^0} \times 100 \qquad \ldots (2)$$

Thus, if price of rice in the base year is ₹ 5 per kg and the price in the current period t is ₹ 9 per kg, then

$$CPI_t = \frac{9}{5} \times 100 = 180$$

This means the price of rice in the current period has risen by 80 per cent.

But the expression $\frac{P_t}{P_0}$ is price index of an individual item. A general consumer price index is *weighted average* of various items in the consumption basket. Therefore, general consumer price index is written as

$$\text{CPI} = \sum W_i \left(\frac{P_i^t}{P_i^0}\right) \times 100 \qquad \ldots (3)$$

Substituting the value of W_i in (3), we have

$$CPI_i = \sum \left(\frac{P_i^0 Q_i^0}{\Sigma P_i^0 Q_i^0}\right)\left(\frac{P_i^t}{P_i^0}\right) \times 100$$

Simplifying

$$CPI = \frac{\sum Q_i^0 . P_i^t}{\sum Q_i^0 . P_i^0} \times 100 \qquad \ldots (4)$$

The expression (4) of consumer price index is known as *Laspeyre's index* as in it takes base year's quantity while finding weighted average of the relative prices of different items.

An example will make clear the process of calculating CPI . This is done in the following table.

Table 24A.1. Calculating CPI

Item	Quantity Q_i^0	Price in 2001 P_i^0	Expenditure in 2001, $P_i^0 Q_i^0$	Price in the Current Period (2012)	Expenditure in the current period $P_i^t . Q_i^t$
Rice	25 kg	₹ 5/kg	₹ 125	₹ 10/kg	250
Pulses	5 kg	₹ 10/kg	₹ 50	₹ 25/kg	125
Clothing	5 m	₹ 20/m	₹ 100	₹ 50/m	250
Housing1 (room set)		₹ 500 per one room set	₹ 500	₹ 800	800
			$\sum P_i^0 Q_i^0 = 775$		$\sum P_i^t . Q_i^0 = 1425$

This implies that price in 2012 is 84 per cent higher compared to the base year 2001.

$$\text{CPI} = \frac{\sum P_i^t Q_i^0}{\sum P_i^0 Q_i^0} \times 100 = \frac{1425}{775} \times 100 = 184$$

Wholesale Price Index (WPI)

While consumer price index is based on retail prices of a few consumer goods making up the consumption basket of a specific group of consumers, wholesale price (WPI) is constructed to measure the *average wholesale prices of all commodities* produced and/or transacted in the economy. Two things must be noted in this regard. First, wholesale price index (WPI) measures wholesale prices of commodities, and not their retail prices. Second, it is based on all commodities produced and/or transacted in the economy. Thus it includes not only consumer goods but also raw materials used in industrial production such as coal, cotton, steel and capital goods such as machines, tractors, pump sets and other equipment. However, WPI does not cover the prices of services such as health, education, transport, communication.

The commodities included in the construction of WPI are classified into the following three categories :

1. Primary articles such as food, non-food and minerals
2. Manufactured goods
3. Fuel, power, light and lubricants

In India at present wholesale price index is prepared with 2004-05 as the base year. Movements in WPI over a period of time is used to measure inflation rate. Since WPI is based on changes in prices of all commodities, from change in inflation rate it can be ascertained which particular group of commodities, for example, whether changes in prices of food products or manufactured goods or of fuel and power, are responsible for rise in general price level.

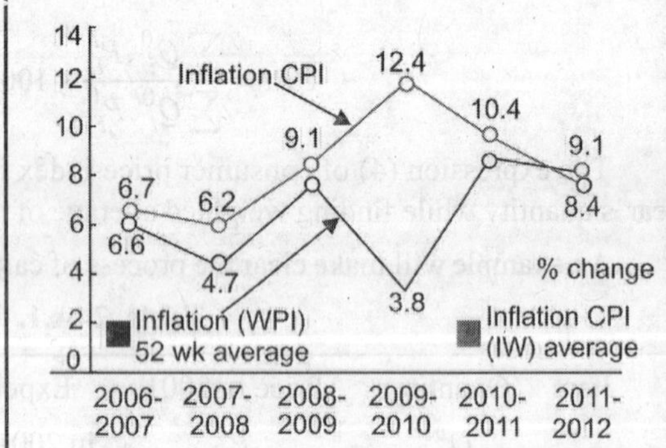

Fig. 24A.1. India's Inflation rate based on CPI (IW) and WPI

The method of constructing WPI is the same as used in case of CPI. *The WPI is the weighted average of wholesale prices of all commodities*. The weights to various commodities are assigned on the basis of relative values of different commodities to the total value of commodities produced and/or transacted in the economy. For preparing WPI, price data is collected from all important wholesale markets or centres in the country like that of construction of CPI, Laspeyre's formula is used to construct WPI, namely, base year's values of commodities produced or transacted are used as weights in its preparation. Thus $\text{WPI} = \dfrac{\sum P_i^t Q_i^0}{\sum P_i^0 Q_i^0} \times 100$

The above formula indicates the percentage change in the price level of commodities in period *t* compared to the base year. If wholesale price index for the year 2011 is 198 with base year 2004-05, then it implies that in 2011 general wholesale price level is 98 per cent higher than in 2004-05. We have depicted in Fig. 24A.1 inflation rate in India since 2006-07 both in terms of CPI and WPI.

GDP Deflator

As a measure of changes in price level or inflation rate GDP deflator is important because besides all goods it also includes *all services* that go to make up the Gross Domestic Product (GDP). It shows the relation between nominal GDP and real GDP as the two differ because of the changes in prices of commodities and services over a period of time. It may be noted that nominal GDP is the value of GDP at *current prices*, while real GDP is the value of GDP at constant prices (*i.e.* prices of a certain year taken as the base year).

$$\text{Thus, GDP Deflator} = \frac{\text{Nominal GDP}}{\text{Real GDP}} \times 100$$

Since GDP of a country consists of market value of all *final* goods and services produced in a year, GDP deflator does not include value of *intermediate goods* to avoid double counting. Besides, since the quantities of goods and services in both the nominal GDP and real GDP refer to the current year, weights computed for the construction of WPI will not be fixed but will vary from year to year.

It needs to be emphasized that since GDP deflator measures the changes in prices of goods and services produced domestically, it does not capture the changes in prices of goods imported from abroad, such as petrol and petroleum products.

The calculation of GDP deflator in India is illustrated in the following table where we have calculated it from India's GDP at current prices and GDP at constant prices with 2004-05 as the base year. The last column in this table shows GDP deflator.

Table. 24A.2. GDP Deflator

Year	*GDP at current prices (in lakh crore)*	*GDP at constant prices (2004-05 = 100) (in lakh crore)*	*GDP Deflator* = $\frac{\textit{GDP at current prices}}{\textit{GDP at 2004 - 05 prices}} \times 100$
2004-05	29.5	29.5	$\frac{29.5}{29.5} \times 100 = 100$
2005-06	33.6	32.3	$\frac{33.6}{32.3} \times 100 = 104.0$
2006-07	39.2	35.4	$\frac{39.2}{35.4} \times 100 = 110.7$
2007-08	45.6	36.8	$\frac{45.6}{36.8} \times 100 = 123.9$
2008-09	52.5	41.4	$\frac{52.5}{41.4} \times 100 = 126.8$
2009-10	61.0	44.6	$\frac{61.0}{44.6} \times 100 = 136.7$

In India the wholesale price Index (WPI) of all commodities with base year 1993-94 price level at the end of fiscal year is used to measure rate of inflation and is widely reported in the media. Since the wholesale price index does not truly indicate the cost of living, separate consumer price index (CPI) for agricultural labourers and consumer price index (CPI) for industrial workers (with base 1982 = 100) at the end of fiscal year are constructed to measure rate of inflation. In constructing the consumer price index (CPI) the prices of a *basket* of goods which a typical consumer, industrial worker or agricultural labourer uses, as the case may be, are taken into account. We will explain the nature and causes of inflation in a separate chapter.

Table 14.2 GDP Deflator

Year	GDP at current prices (₹ lakh crore)	GDP at constant prices (2004-05 prices) (₹ lakh crore)	GDP Deflator = GDP at current prices / GDP at constant prices × 100
2004-05	[illegible]	[illegible]	[illegible] × 100 = 100
2005-06	[illegible]	[illegible]	[illegible]
2006-07	[illegible]	[illegible]	[illegible]
2007-08	[illegible]	[illegible]	[illegible]
[illegible]	[illegible]	[illegible]	[illegible]

In India the wholesale price index (WPI) [illegible] is used to measure [illegible] inflation [illegible] reported in the media [illegible] wholesale price index [illegible] consumer price index [illegible] consumer price index [illegible] for industrial workers (with base 1982 = 100) [illegible] are constructed [illegible] inflation. [illegible] consumer price index [illegible] of a basket of goods which a typical consumer [illegible] industrial workers [illegible] We will explain [illegible] measuring inflation [illegible]

PART – V

BUSINESS CYCLES AND MACROECONOMIC POLICY

- Analysis of Business Cycles
- Economic Stabilisation : Role of Fiscal Policy
- Economic Stabilisation : Monetary Policy

CHAPTER 25

Analysis of Business Cycles

Introduction

Many free enterprise capitalist countries such as USA and Great Britain have registered rapid economic growth during the last two centuries. But economic growth in these countries has not followed steady and smooth upward trend. There has been a long-run upward trend in Gross National Product (GNP), but periodically there have been large short-run fluctuations in economic activity, that is, changes in output, income, employment and prices around this long-term trend. The period of high income, output and employment has been called the period of *expansion, upswing* or *prosperity,* and the period of low income, output and employment has been described as *contraction, recession, downswing* or *depression.* The economic history of the free market capitalist countries have shown that the period of economic prosperity or expansion alternates with the period of contraction or recession. *These alternating periods of expansion and contraction in economic activity have been* called business cycles. They are also known as *trade cycles.* J.M. Keynes writes, "A trade cycle is composed of periods of good trade characterised by rising prices and low unemployment percentages with periods of bad trade characterised by falling prices and high unemployment percentages."[1]

A noteworthy feature about these fluctuations in economic activity is that they are recurrent and have been occurring periodically in a more or less regular fashion. Therefore, these fluctuations have been called business cycles. It may be noted that calling these fluctuations as 'cycles' means they are periodic and occur regularly, though perfect regularity has not been observed. The duration of a business cycle has not been of the same length; it has varied from a minimum of two years to a maximum of ten to twelve years, though in the past it was often assumed that fluctuations of output and other economic indicators around the trend showed repetitive and regular pattern of alternating periods of expansion and contraction. However, actually there has been no clear evidence of very regular cycles of the same definite duration. Some business cycles have been very short lasting for only two to three years, while others have lasted for several years. Further, in some cycles there have been large swings away from trend and in others these swings have been of moderate nature.

A significant point worth noting about business cycles is that they have been very costly in the economic sense of the word. During a period of recession or depression many workers lose their jobs and as a result large-scale unemployment, which causes loss of output that could have been produced with full employment of resources, come to prevail in the economy. Besides, during depression many businessmen go bankrupt and suffer huge losses. Depression causes a lot of human sufferings and lowers the levels of living of the people. Fluctuations in economic activity create a lot of uncertainty in the economy which causes anxiety to the individuals about their future income and employment opportunities and involve a great risk for long-run investment in projects. Who does not remember the great havoc caused by the great depression of the early thirties of the present century? Even boom when it is accompanied by inflation has its social costs. Inflation erodes the real incomes of the people and makes life miserable for the poor people. Inflation distorts allocation of resources by drawing away scarce resources from productive uses to unproductive ones. Inflation redistributes income in favour of the richer sections and also when inflation rate is high, it impedes economic growth. About the harmful effects of the business cycles Crowther writes, "On the one hand, there is

1. J.M. Keynes, *The General Theory of Employment, Interest and Money,* 1936.

the misery and shame of unemployment with all the individual poverty and social disturbances that it may create. On the other hand, there is the loss of wealth represented by so much wasted and idle labour and capital."[2]

Phases of Business Cycles

Business cycles have shown distinct phases the study of which is useful to understand their underlying causes. These phases have been called by different names by different economists. Generally, the following phases of business cycles have been distinguished :

1. Expansion (Boom, Upswing or Prosperity)
2. Peak (upper turning point)
3. Contraction (Downswing, Recession or Depression)
4. Trough (lower turning point)

The four phases of business cycles have been shown in Fig. 25.1 where we start from trough or depression when the level of economic activity *i.e.,* level of production and employment is at the

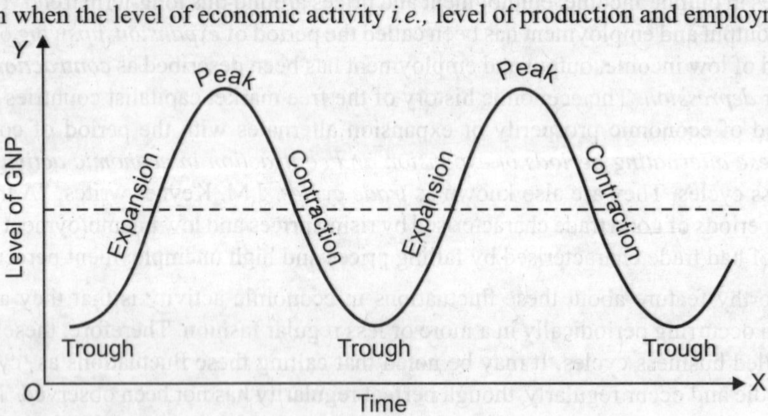

Fig. 25.1. *Four Phases of Business Cycles without Growth Trend*

lowest level. With the revival of economic activity the economy moves into the expansion phase, but due to the causes explained below, the expansion cannot continue indefinitely, and after reaching peak, contraction or downswing starts. When the contraction gathers momentum, we have a depression. The downswing continues till the lowest turning point which is also called trough is reached. In this way

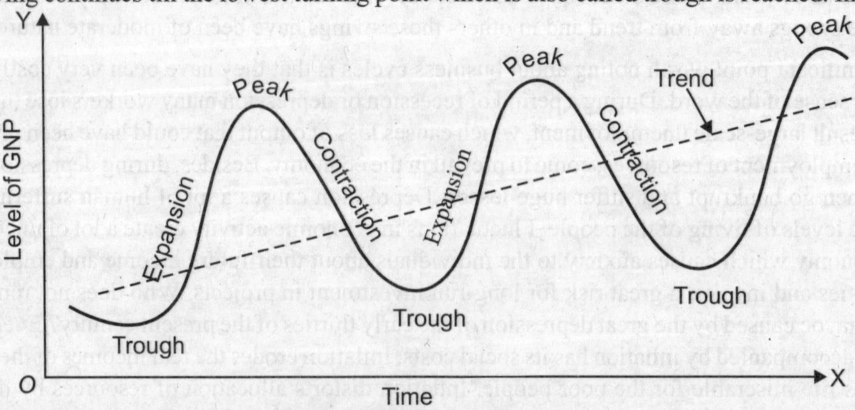

Fig. 25.2. *Cycles with Trend (i.e., Growth)*

2. G. Crowther, *An Outline of Money* (London 1962), p. 192.

cycle is complete. However, after remaining at the trough for some time the economy revives and again the new cycle starts. Haberler in his important work[3] on business cycles has named the four phases of business cycles as (1) Upswing, (2) Upper turning point, (3) Downswing, and (4) Lower turning point.

There are two types of patterns of cyclic changes. One pattern is shown in Fig. 25.1 where fluctuations occur around a stable equilibrium position as shown by the horizontal line. It is a case of dynamic stability which depicts change but without growth or trend. The second pattern of cyclical fluctuations is shown in Fig. 25.2 where cyclical changes in economic activity take place around a growth path *(i.e.,* rising trend). J.R. Hicks in his model of business cycles explains such a pattern of fluctuations with long-run rising trend in economic activity by imposing factors such as autonomous investment due to population growth and technological progress causing economic growth on the otherwise stationary state. We briefly explain below various phases of business cycles.

Expansion and Prosperity. In its expansion phase, both output and employment increase till we have full employment of resources and production is at the highest possible level with the given productive resources. There is no involuntary unemployment and whatever unemployment prevails is only of frictional and structural types. Thus, when expansion gathers momentum and we have prosperity, the gap between potential GNP and actual GNP is zero, that is, the level of production is at the maximum production level. A good amount of net investment is occurring and demand for durable consumer goods is also high. Prices also generally rise during the expansion phase but due to high level of economic activity people enjoy a high standard of living.

Then something may occur, whether banks start reducing credit or profit expectations change adversely and businessmen become pessimistic about future state of the economy that bring an end to the expansion or prosperity phase. As shall be explained below, economists differ regarding the possible causes of the end of prosperity and start of downswing in economic activity. Monetarists have argued that contraction in bank credit may cause downswing. Keynes has argued that sudden collapse of expected rate of profit (which he calls marginal efficiency of capital, MEC) caused by adverse changes in expectations of entrepreneurs lowers investment in the economy. This fall in investment, according to him, causes downswing in economic activity.

Contraction and Depression. As stated above, expansion or prosperity is followed by contraction or depression. During contraction, not only there is a fall in GNP but also level of employment is reduced. As a result, involuntary unemployment appears on a large scale. Investment also decreases causing further fall in consumption of goods and services. At times of contraction or depression prices also generally fall due to fall in aggregate demand. A significant feature of depression phase is the fall in rate of interest. With lower rate of interest people's demand for money holdings increases. There is a lot of excess capacity as industries start producing capital goods and consumer goods work much below their capacity due to lack of demand. Capital goods and durable consumer goods industries are especially hit hard during depression. Depression, it may be noted, occurs when there is a severe contraction or recession of economic activities. The depression of 1929-33 is still remembered because of its great intensity which caused a lot of human suffering.

Trough and Revival. There is a limit to which level of economic activity can fall. The lowest level of economic activity, generally called trough, lasts for some time. Capital stock is allowed to depreciate without replacement. The progress in technology makes the existing capital stock obsolete. If the banking system starts expanding credit or there is a spurt in investment activity due to the emergence of scarcity of capital as a result of non-replacement of depreciated capital and also because of new technology coming into existence requiring new types of machines and other capital goods.

3. See G. Haberler, *Prosperity and Depression, A Theoretical Analysis of Cyclical Movements,* Harvard University Press, 1960.

The stimulation of investment brings about the revival or recovery of the economy. The recovery is the turning point from depression into expansion. As investment rises, this causes induced increase in consumption. As a result industries start producing more and excess capacity is now put into full use due to the revival of aggregate demand. Employment of labour increases and rate of unemployment falls. With this the cycle is complete.

Features of Business Cycles

Though different business cycles differ in duration and intensity, they have some common features which we explain below:

1. Business cycles occur *periodically.* Though they do not show same regularity, they have some distinct phases such as expansion, peak, contraction or depression and trough. Further the duration of cycles varies a good deal from minimum of two years to a maximum of ten to twelve years.
2. Secondly, business cycles are *synchronic.* That is, they do not cause changes in any single industry or sector but are of all-embracing character. For example, depression or contraction occur simultaneously in all industries or sectors of the economy. Recession passes from one industry to another and chain reaction continues till the whole economy is in the grip of recession. Similar process is at work in the expansion phase, prosperity spreads through various linkages of input-output relations or demand relations between various industries, and sectors.
3. Thirdly, it has been observed that fluctuations occur not only in level of production but also simultaneously in other variables such as employment, investment, consumption, rate of interest and price level.
4. Another important feature of business cycles is that investment and consumption of durable consumer goods such as cars, houses, refrigerators are affected most by the cyclical fluctuations. As stressed by J.M. Keynes, investment is greatly volatile and unstable as it depends on profit expectations of private entrepreneurs. These expectations of entrepreneurs change quite often making investment quite unstable. Since *consumption of durable consumer goods* can be deferred, it also fluctuates greatly during the course of business cycles.
5. An important feature of business cycles is that consumption of *non-durable goods and services* does not vary much during different phases of business cycles. Past data of business cycles reveal that households maintain a great stability in consumption of non-durable goods.
6. The immediate impact of depression and expansion is on the *inventories of goods.* When depression sets in, the inventories start accumulating beyond the desired level. This leads to cut in production of goods. On the contrary, when recovery starts, the inventories go below the desired level. This encourages businessmen to place more orders for goods whose production picks up and stimulates investment in capital goods.
7. Another important feature of business cycles is that *profits fluctuate more than any other type of income.* The occurrence of business cycles causes a lot of uncertainty for businessmen and makes it difficult to forecast the economic conditions. During the depression period profits may even become negative and many businesses go bankrupt. In a free market economy profits are justified on the ground that they are necessary payments if the entrepreneurs are to be induced to bear uncertainty.
8. Lastly, business cycles are *international in character.* That is, once started in one country they spread to other countries through trade relations between them. For example, if there is a recession in the USA, which is a large importer of goods from other countries, it will cause a fall in demand for imports from other countries whose exports would be adversely

affected causing recession in them too. Depression of 1930s in USA and Great Britain engulfed the entire capital world.

THEORIES OF BUSINESS CYCLES

We have explained above the various phases and common features of business cycles. Now, an important question is what causes business cycles. Several theories of business cycles have been propounded from time to time. Each of these theories spells out the factors which cause business cycles. Before explaining the modern theories of business cycles we first explain below the *earlier* theories of business cycles as they too contain important elements whose study is essential for proper understanding of the causes of business cycles.

Sun-Spot Theory

This is perhaps the oldest theory of business cycles. Sun-spot theory was developed in 1875 by Stanley Jevons. Sun-spots are storms on the surface of the sun caused by violent nuclear explosions there. Jevons argued that sun-spots affected weather on the earth. Since economies in the olden world were heavily dependent on agriculture, changes in climatic conditions due to sun-spots produced fluctuations in agricultural output. Changes in agricultural output through its demand and input-output relations affect industry. Thus, swings in agricultural output spread throughout the economy.

Other earlier economists also focused on changes in climatic or weather conditions in addition to those caused by sun-spots. According to them, weather cycles cause fluctuations in agricultural output which in turn cause instability in the whole economy. Even today weather is considered important in a country like India where agriculture is still important. In the years when due to lack of monsoon there are drought in the Indian agriculture, it affects the income of farmers and therefore reduces demand for the products of industries. This causes industrial recession. Even in USA in the year 1988 a severe drought in the farm belt drove up the food prices around the world. It may be further noted that higher food prices reduce income available to be spent on industrial goods.

Critical Appraisal. Though the theories of business cycles which emphasise climatic conditions for business cycles contain an element of truth about fluctuations in economic activity, especially in the developing counties like India where agriculture still remains important, they do not offer an adequate explanation of business cycles. Therefore, much reliance is not placed on these theories by modern economists. Nobody can say with certainty about the nature of these sun-spots and the degree to which they affect rain. There is no doubt that climate affects agricultural production. But the climate theory does not adequately explain periodicity of the trade cycle. If there was truth in the climatic theories, the trade cycles may be pronounced in agricultural countries and almost disappear when the country becomes completely industrialised. But this is not the case. Highly industrialised countries are much more subject to business cycles than agricultural countries which are affected more by famines rather than business cycles. Hence variations in climate do not offer complete explanation of business cycles.

Hawtrey's Monetary Theory of Business Cycles

An old monetary theory of business cycles was put forward by Hawtrey.[4] His monetary theory of business cycles relates to the economy which is under gold standard. It will be remembered that economy is said to be under gold standard when either money in circulation consists of gold coins or when paper notes are fully backed by gold reserves in the banking system. According to Hawtrey, increases in the quantity of money raises the availability of bank credit for investment. Thus, by increasing the supply of credit expansion in money supply causes rate of interest to fall. The lower rate of interest induces businessmen to borrow more for investment in capital goods and also for investment in keeping more inventories of goods. Thus, Hawtrey argues that lower rate of interest

4. R.G. Hawtrey, *Good and Bad Trade,* Constable and Co., London, 1913.

will lead to the expansion of goods and services as a result of more investment in capital goods and inventories. Higher output, income and employment caused by more investment induces more spending on consumer goods. Thus, as a result of more investment made possible by increased supply of bank credit, economy moves into the expansion phase. The process of expansion continues for some time. Increases in agregate demand brought about by more investment also cause prices to rise. Rising prices lead to the increase in output in two ways. First, when prices begin to rise businessmen think they would rise further which induces them to invest more and produce more because prospects of making profits increase with the rise in prices. Secondly, the rising prices reduce the real value of idle money balances with the people which induces them to spend more on goods and services. In this way rising prices sustain expansion for some time.

However, according to Hawtrey, the expansion process must end. He argued that rise in incomes during the expansion phase induces more expenditure on domestically produced goods as well as more on imports of foreign goods. He further assumes that domestic output and income expand faster than foreign output. As a result, imports of a country increase more than its exports causing *trade deficit* with other countries. If exchange rate remains fixed, trade deficit means there will be *outflow of gold* to settle its balance of payments deficit. Since the country is on gold standard, outflow for gold will cause reduction in money supply in the economy. The decrease in money supply will reduce the availability of bank credit. Reduction in the supply of bank credit will cause the rate of interest to rise. Rising interest rate will reduce investment in physical capital goods. Reduction in investment will cause the process of contraction to set in. As a result of reduced order for inventories, producers will cut production which will lower income and consumption of goods and services. In this state of reduced demand for goods and services, prices of goods will fall. Once the prices begin to fall businessmen begin to expect that they will fall further. In response to it traders will cut order of goods still causing further fall in output. The fall in prices also causes real value of money balances to rise which induce people to hold larger money holdings with them. In this way contraction process gathers momentum as demand for goods starts declining faster and with this economy plunges into depression.

But after a lapse of some time depression will also come to an end and the economy will start to recover. This happens because in the contraction process imports fall drastically due to decrease in income and consumption of households, whereas exports do not fall much. As a result, *trade surplus* emerges which causes *inflow of gold.* The inflow of gold would lead to the expansion of money supply and consequently availability of bank credit for investment will increase. With this, the economy will recover from depression and move into the expansion phase. Thus, the cycle is complete. The process, according to Hawtrey, will go on being repeated regularly.

Critical Appraisal. Hawtrey maintains that the economy under gold standard and fixed exchange rate system makes his model of business cycles self-generating as there is built-in tendency for the money supply to change with the emergence of trade deficit and trade surplus which cause movements of gold between countries and affect money supply in them. Changes in money supply influence economic activity in a cyclical fashion. However, Hawtrey's monetary theory does not apply to the present-day economies which have abandoned gold standard in 1930s. However, Hawtrey's theory still retains its importance because it shows how changes in money supply affects economic activity through changes in price level and rate of interest. In modern monetary theories of trade cycles this relation between money supply and rate of interest plays an important role in determining the level of economic activity.

Under-Consumption Theory

Under-consumption theory of business cycles is a very old one which dates back to the 1930s. Malthus and Sismodi criticised Say's Law which states '*supply creates its own demand*' and argued that consumption of goods and services could be too small to generate sufficient demand for goods and services produced. They attribute over-production of goods due to lack of consumption demand for them. This over-production causes piling up of inventories of goods which results in recession.

Under-consumption theory as propounded by Sismodi and Hobson was not a theory of recurring business cycles. They made an attempt to explain how a free enterprise economy could enter a long-run economic slowdown. A crucial aspect of Sismodi and Hobson's under-consumption theory is the distinction they made between the rich and the poor. According to them, the rich sections in the society receive a large part of their income from returns on financial assets and real property owned by them. Further, they assume that the rich have a large propensity to save, that is, they save a relatively large proportion of their income and, therefore, consume a relatively smaller proportion of their income. On the other hand, less well-off people in a society obtain most of their income from work, that is, wages from labour and have a lower propensity to save. Therefore, these less well-off people spend a relatively less proportion of their income on consumer goods and services. In their theory, they further assume that during the expansion process, the incomes of the rich people increase relatively more than the wage-income. Thus, during the expansion phase, income distribution changes in favour of the rich with the result that average propensity to save falls, that is, in the expansion process saving increases and therefore consumption demand declines.[5]

According to Sismodi and Hobson, increase in saving during the expansion phase leads to more investment expenditure on capital goods and after some time lag, the greater stock of capital goods enables the economy to produce more consumer goods and services. But since society's propensity to consume continues to fall, consumption demand is not enough to absorb the increased production of consumer goods. In this way, lack of demand for consumer goods or what is called under-consumption emerges in the economy which halts the expansion of the economy. Further, since supply or production of goods increases relatively more as compared to the consumption demand for them, the prices fall. Prices continue falling and go even below the average cost of production bringing losses to the business firms. Thus, when under-consumption appears, production of goods becomes unprofitable. Firms cut their production resulting in recession or contraction in economic activity.

Karl Marx and Under-Consumption. It is worth mentioning that Karl Marx, the philosopher of scientific socialism, had also predicted the collapse of the capitalist system due to the emergence of under-consumption. He predicted that capitalism would move periodically through expansion and contraction with each peak higher than its previous peak and each crash *(i.e.,* depression) deeper than the last. Ultimately, according to Marx, in a state of acute depression when the cup of misery of working class is full, they will overthrow the capitalist class which exploits them and in this way the new era of socialism or communism would come into existence.

Like other under-consumption theorists, Marx argues that driving force behind business cycles is ever increasing income inequalities and concentration of wealth and economic power in the hands of the few capitalists who own the means of production. As a result, the poor workers lack income to purchase goods produced by the capitalist class resulting in under-consumption or over-production. With the capitalist producers lacking market for their goods, capitalist economy plunges into depression. Then the search for ways of opening of new markets is started. Even wars between capitalist countries take place to capture other countries to find new markets for their products. With the discovery of new methods of production of finding new markets, the economy recovers from depression and the new upswing starts.

Critical Appraisal. The view that income inequalities increase with growth or expansion of the economy and further that this causes recession or stagnation is widely accepted. Therefore, even many modern economies suggest that if growth is to be sustained (that is, if recession or stagnation is to be avoided), then consumption demand must be increasing sufficiently to absorb the increasing

5. J.A. Hobson, *The Economics of Unemployment,* London: Allen & Unwin Ltd., 1922.

production of goods. For this deliberate efforts should be made to reduce inequalities in income distribution. Further, under-consumption theory rightly states that income redistribution schemes will reduce the amplitude of business cycles.

Besides, the suggested behaviour of average propensity to save and consume of the property owners and wage earners in this theory have been found to be consistent with the observed phenomena. Even in the theory of economic development the difference in average propensity to save (APS) of the property owners and workers has been widely used.

It is clear from above that under-consumption theory contains some important elements, especially the emergence of the lack of consumption demand as the cause of recession but it is regarded as too simple. There are many features other than growing income inequalities which are responsible for causing recession or trade cycles. Although under-consumption theory concentrates on a significant variable, it leaves too much unexplained.

Over-Investment Theory

It has been observed that over time investment varies more than that of total output of final goods and services and consumption. This has led economists to investigate the causes of variation in investment and how it is responsible for business cycles. Two versions of over-investment theory have been put forward. One theory offered by Hayek emphasises monetary forces in causing fluctuations in investment. The second version of over-investment theory has been developed by Knut Wickshell which emphasises spurts of investment brought about by innovation. We explain below both these versions of over-investment theory. It is worth noting that in both the versions of this theory distinction between natural rate of interest and money rate of interest plays an important role. Natural rate of interest is defined as the rate at which saving equals investment and this equilibrium interest rate reflects marginal revenue product of capital or rate of return on capital. On the other hand, money rate of interest is the rate at which banks give loans to the businessmen.

Hayek's Monetary Version of Over-investment Theory. Hayek[6] suggests that it is monetary forces which cause fluctuations in investment which are prime cause of business cycles. In this respect Hayek's theory is similar to Hawtrey's monetary theory except that it does not involve inflow and outflow of gold causing changes in money supply in the economy.

To begin with, let us assume that the economy is in recession and businessmen's demand for bank credit is therefore very low. Thus, lower demand for bank credit in times of recession pushes down the money rate of interest below the natural rate. This means that businessmen will be able to borrow funds, that is, bank credit at a rate of interest which is below the expected rate of return in investment projects. This induces them to invest more by undertaking new investment projects. In this way, investment expenditure on new capital goods increases. This causes investment to exceed saving by the amount of newly created bank credit. With the spurt in investment expenditure, the expansion of the economy begins. Increase in investment causes income and employment to rise which induces more consumption expenditure. As a result, production of consumer goods increases. According to Hawtrey, the competition between capital goods and consumer goods industries for scarce resources causes their prices to rise which in turn push up the prices of goods and services.

But this process of expansion cannot go on indefinitely because the excess reserves with the banks come to an end which force the banks not to give further loans for investment, while demand for bank credit goes on increasing. Thus, the inelastic supply of credit from the banks and mounting demand for it cause the money rate of interest to go above the natural rate of interest. This makes further investment unprofitable. But at this point of time there has been over-investment in the sense that savings fall short of what is required to finance the desired investment. When no more bank

6. F.A. Hayek, *Monetary Theory and Trade Cycle,* New York, Harcourt Brace, 1933 and also *Profits, Interest and Investment,* London, Routledge, 1935.

credit is available for investment, there is decline in investment which causes both income and consumption to fall and in this way expansion comes to an end and the economy experiences downswing in economic activity.

However, after a lapse of some time the fall in demand for bank credit lowers the money rate of interest which goes below the natural rate of interest. This again gives boost to investment activity and as a result recession ends. In this way alternating periods of expansion and contraction occur periodically.

Wicksell's Over-investment Theory. Over-investment theory developed by Wicksell[7] is of non-monetary type. Instead of focusing on monetary factors, it attributes cyclical fluctuations to spurts of investment caused by new innovations introduced by entrepreneurs themselves. The introduction of new innovations or opening of new markets makes some investment projects profitable by either reducing cost or raising demand for the products. The expansion in investment is made possible because of the availability of bank credit at a lower money rate of interest. The expansion in economic activity ceases when investment exceeds saving. Again it may be noted that there is over-investment because the level of saving is insufficient to finance the desired level of investment. The end of investment expenditure causes the economy to go into recession. However, another set of innovations occurs or more new markets are found which stimulates investment. Thus, when investment picks up as a result of new innovations, the economy revives and moves into the expansion phase once again.

Appraisal. Though the over-investment theory does not offer an adequate explanation of business cycles, it contains an important element that fluctuations in investment are the prime cause of business cycles. However, it does not offer a valid explanation as to why changes in investment take place quite often. Many exponents of this theory point to the behaviour of banking system that causes diverges between money rate of interest and natural rate of interest. However, as Keynes later on emphasised, investment fluctuates quite often because of changes in profit expectations of entrepreneurs which depends on several economic and political factors operating in the economy. Thus, the theory fails to offer adequate explanation of business cycles.

KEYNES'S THEORY OF BUSINESS CYCLES

J.M. Keynes in his seminal work, *General Theory of Employment, Interest and Money*, made an important contribution to the analysis of the causes of business cycles. According to Keynes's theory, in the short run, the level of income, output or employment is determined by the level of aggregate effective demand. In a free private enterprise, the entrepreneurs will produce that much of goods as can be sold profitably. Now, if the aggregate demand is large, that is, if the expenditure on goods and services is large, the entrepreneurs will be able to sell profitably a large quantity of goods and therefore they will produce more. In order to produce more they will employ a larger amount of resources, both men and materials. In short, a higher level of aggregate demand will result in greater output, income and employment. On the other hand, if the level of aggregate demand is low, smaller amount of goods and services can be sold profitably. This means, that the total quantity of national output produced will be small. And a small output can be produced with a small amount of resources. As a result, there will be unemployment of resources, both labour and capital. Hence, the *changes in the level of aggregate effective demand will bring about fluctuations in the level of income, output and employment.* Thus, according to Keynes, the fluctuations in economic activity are due to the fluctuations in aggregate effective demand. Fall in aggregate effective demand will create the conditions of recession or depression. If the aggregate demand is increasing, economic expansion will take place.

Now the question arises : What causes fluctuations in aggregate demand? The aggregate demand is composed of demand for consumption goods and demand for investment goods. Thus aggregate

7. Knut Wicksell, *Interest and Prices,* London: Macmillan, 1936.

demand depends on the total expenditure of the consumers on consumption goods and entrepreneurs on investment goods. Propensity to consume being more or less stable in the short run, fluctuations in aggregate demand depend primarily upon the fluctuations in investment demand. Keynes shows that the fundamental cause of fluctuations in aggregate demand and hence in fluctuations in economic activity is the fluctuations in investment demand. *Investment demand is very unstable and volatile and brings about business cycles in the economy.*

Let us start from the phase of economic expansion to explain Keynes's theory of business cycles. We first explain how in Keynesian theory expansion comes to end and recession or depression sets in. During an economic expansion two factors eventually work to cause investment to fall. First, during the expansion phase increase in demand for capital goods due to large-scale investment activity leads to the rise in prices of capital goods due to rising marginal cost of their production. Higher prices of capital goods raise the cost of investment projects and thereby reduce marginal efficiency of capital (that is, expected rate of return). Secondly, as income rises during expansion phase, the demand for money increases which raises interest rate. Higher interest rate makes some potential projects unprofitable. Thus, fall in marginal efficiency of capital on the one hand and rise in interest rate on the other cause decline in investment demand. Declining trend of investment, according to Keynes, raises doubts about the *prospective yield on capital goods* which is more important factor determining marginal efficiency of capital than cost of investment projects and rate of interest. When among businessmen pessimism sets in about future profitability of investment projects, stock prices tumble. The crash in stock prices worsens the situation and causes investment to fall even more. Besides, fall in prices of shares reduces wealth of households. Wealth, according to Keynes, is an important factor determining consumption. Thus, the decline in stock prices reduces autonomous consumption demand of households. With the fall in both investment and consumption demand aggregate demand declines which results in accumulation of unintended inventories with the firms. This induces the firms to cut production of goods.

It follows from above that besides the rise in cost of capital goods and rise in rate of interest towards the end of the expansion phase, it is the fall in expected prospective yield that reduces the marginal efficiency of capital and causes investment demand to fall. This induces a wave of pessimistic expectations among businessmen and speculators. These pessimistic expectations cause stock prices to tumble which work like adding fuel to the fire. They cause a further fall in the marginal efficiency of capital. *The turning point from expansion to contraction is thus caused by a sudden collapse in marginal efficiency of capital.* In terms of graph, a sudden fall in the marginal efficiency of capital causes a leftward shift in the investment demand curve, for example from I_0I_0 to I_1I_1 in Figure 25.3 resulting in decline in investment from I_0^* to I^*_1 at the given rate of interest. Note that decrease in investment does not automatically decrease in rate of

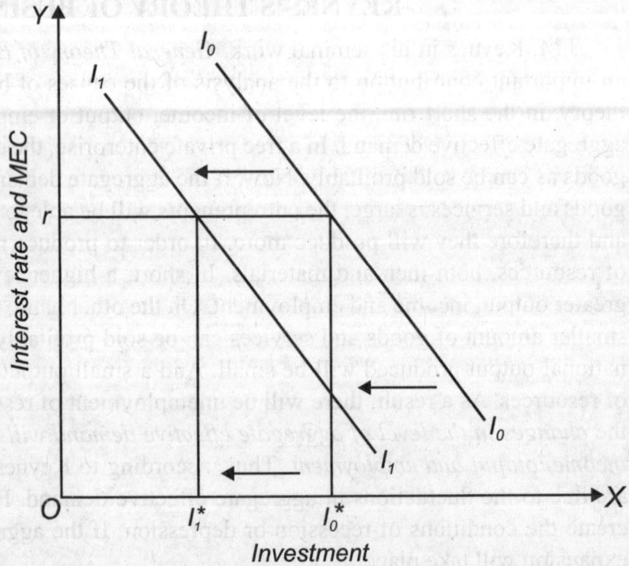

Fig. 25.3. *A Decline in Investment Expenditure due to Fall in Marginal Efficiency of Capital*

interest to offset the fall in the marginal efficiency of capital.

However, additional factor that makes Keynes's business cycle theory potent is the working of multiplier which was an important discovery of J.M. Keynes. According to Keynes, a decrease in investment expenditure causes a decline in income which in turn reduces consumption expenditure. The reduction in consumption expenditure further reduces income and this process of reduction in income continues further. The total fall in income (ΔY) due to an initial decline in investment (Δ*I*) will be equal to $m=\frac{M}{H}$ where $\frac{1}{1-MPC}$ is the value of multiplier. If marginal propensity to consume is 0.75, the multiplier will be equal to 4. Thus, a decline in investment by 100 crores will lead to the decline in income by 400 crores. Note that multiplier here works in reverse. Thus, the multiplier process magnifies the effect of decline in investment expenditure on aggregate demand and income and further deepens the depression. As income and output are falling rapidly under the multiplier effect, the employment also goes tumbling down. Thus, the Keynes's theory of income multiplier plays a significant role in causing magnified changes in income, output and employment following a reduction in investment.

It is important to note that, in Keynes's views, wages and prices are not flexible enough to offset the decline in investment expenditure and thereby restore full employment. This is in sharp contrast to the classical theory where changes in wages and prices ensure continuous full employment. In Keynes's model wages and prices are "sticky" downward which implies that though wages and prices do not remain constant but when demand falls wages and prices will fall but not sufficient to restore full employment in the economy.

Since wage and price flexibility does not ensure the recovery of the economy out of the state of depression, Keynes thinks that marginal efficiency of capital must rise to stimulate investment. During depression investment falls to a very low level, capital stock begins to wear out and requires replacement. Further, some existing capital equipment becomes technologically obsolete and has to be abandoned. This generates demand for replacement investment. A long period of time is necessary for existing capital to depreciate because most capital goods are durable as well as irreversible. By durability of capital goods we mean that they last for a long time and by irreversibility we mean that they cannot be used for purposes other than those for which they are meant.

Thus, just as the collapse of marginal efficiency of capital is the main cause of the upper turning point, similarly the lower turning point, *i.e.,* change from recession to recovery is due to the revival of the marginal efficiency of capital, that is, expected rate of profit. Restoration of business confidence is the most important, yet the most difficult factor to achieve. Even if the rate of interest is reduced, the investment will not increase. This is because of the fact that in the absence of confidence the profitability of investment may remain so low that no practicable reduction in the rate of interest will stimulate investment. The interval which will elapse between the upper turning point and the start of recovery is conditioned by two factors: (*i*) the time necessary for wearing out of durable capital assets, and (*ii*) the time required to absorb the excess stocks of goods left over from the boom. Just as the expected rate of profit was pushed down by the growing abundance of capital during the period of boom, similarly as the stocks of capital goods are depleted and there grows a scarcity of capital goods, then the expected rate of profit rises thereby inducing the businessmen to invest more. When the level of investment increases, income increases by a magnified amount due to the multiplier effect. So the cumulative process starts upward.

Thus, over time as depreciation of capital stock occurs without replacement and also some existing capital equipment becomes technologically obsolete, the size of capital stock declines. New investment must be undertaken even to produce reduced depression level of output. Thus with the emergence of scarcity of capital, marginal efficiency of capital rises which boosts investment. Once investment increases, it induces further rise in income and consumption demand through the multiplier process. Now, the multiplier works to magnify the effect of increase in investment on raising aggregate demand. The mood of businessmen changes from pessimism to optimism which drives up stock prices. All these factors work to lift the economy out of depression and put it on the road to prosperity.

However, it is noteworthy that the recovery process from depression takes a very long time. Keynes argued that Government should not wait for long for the natural recovery to occur. This is because persistence of depression creates a lot of human sufferings. He, therefore, advocated for the active intervention by the Government to raise aggregate through fiscal policy, that is, stepping up its expenditure or reducing taxes. Thus, he argued for the adoption of policy of deficit budget to boost aggregate demand so that economy is lifted out of depression.

It may be noted that Keynes's business cycle theory is self-generating. In it the economy passes through a long phase of expansion. But eventually some forces automatically work, for example, the growing abundance of capital stock, which reduces marginal efficiency of capital. Pessimisin overtakes businessmen. This causes reduction in investment which is responsible for bringing about downswing in the economy. The idea that it is the fluctuations in investment that bring about the fluctuations in the level of economic activity is an important contribution made by Keynes. Of course, even before Keynes, it was believed that the fluctuations in the investment demand have something to do with the business cycles, but a systematic exposition was lacking. Keynes propounded a definite relationship between a change in investment and the resulting change in income and employment. This relationship is embodied in his famous theory of multiplier.

The Critical Appraisal of Keynes's Theory

J.M. Keynes has made three important contributions to the business cycle theory. First, it is fluctuations in investment that cause changes in aggregate demand which bring about changes in economic activity (*i.e.,* income, output, and employment). Secondly, fluctuations in investment demand are caused by changes in expectations of businessmen regarding making of profits (that is, marginal efficiency of capital). Thirdly, Keynes put forward an important theory of multiplier which tells us how changes in investment bring about magnified changes in the level of income and employment.

But the Keynesian theory of multiplier alone does not offer a full and satisfactory explanation of the trade cycles. A basic feature of the trade cycle is its cumulative character both on the upswing as well as on the downswing, *i.e.,* once economic activity starts rising or falling, it gathers momentum and for a time feeds on itself. Thus, what we have to explain is the cumulative character of economic fluctuations. The theory of multiplier alone does not prove adequate for this task. For example, suppose that investment rises by 100 rupees and that the magnitude of multiplier is 4. From the theory of multiplier we know that national income will rise by 400 and if multiplier is the only force at work, that will be the end of the matter, with the economy reaching a new stable equilibrium at a higher level of national income. But in real life this is not likely to be so, for a rise in income produced by a given rise in investment will have further repercussions in the economy. This reaction is described in the *principle of the accelerator.* According to the principle of acceleration, a change in national income will tend to induce changes in the rate of investment. *While multiplier refers to the change in income as a result of change in investment, the acceleration principle describes the relationship between a change in investment as a result of change in income.*

In the above example, when income has risen by 400 rupees, people's spending power has risen by an equivalent amount. This will induce them to spend more on goods and services. When the demand for goods rises, initially this will be met by overworking the existing plant and machinery. All this leads to an increase in profits with the result that businessmen will be induced to expand their productive capacity and will instal new plants, *i.e.,* they will invest more than before. Thus, *a rise in income leads to a further induced increase in investment.* The accelerator describes this relation between an increase in income and the resulting increase in investment. Thus, Samuelson combined the accelerator principle with the multiplier and showed that the interaction between the two can bring about cyclical fluctuations in economic activity.

SAMUELSON'S MODEL OF BUSINESS CYCLES : INTERACTION BETWEEN MULTIPLIER AND ACCELERATOR

We have briefly explained above that Keynes made an important contribution to the understanding of the cyclical fluctuations by pointing out that it is the ups and downs in investment demand, depending as it is on the profit expectations of the entrepreneurs, that causes changes in aggregate demand which affect the levels of income, output and employment. Further, by putting forward the theory of multiplier, Keynes has shown how the effect of increase and decrease in investment on output and employment get magnified when multiplier is working during either the upswing or downswing of a business cycle. However, Keynes did not explain the cyclical and cumulative nature of the fluctuations in economic activity. This is because Keynes did not give any importance to the accelerator in his explanation of business cycles. Samuelson in his seminal paper[8] convincingly showed that it is the interaction between the multiplier and accelerator that gives rise to cyclical fluctuations in economic activity. The multiplier alone cannot adequately explain the cyclical and cumulative nature of the economic fluctuations. An autonomous increase in the level of investment raises income by a magnified amount depending upon the value of the multiplier. This increase in income further induces the increases in investment through the acceleration effect. The increase in income brings about increase in aggregate demand for goods and services. To produce more goods we require more capital goods for which extra investment is undertaken. Thus the relationship between investment and income is one of mutual interaction; investment affects income which in turn affects investment demand and in this process income and employment fluctuate in a cyclical manner.

We have shown below in Fig. 25.4 how income and output will increase by even larger amount when accelerator is combined with the Keynesian multiplier,

where ΔI_a = Increase in Autonomous Investment

ΔY = Increase in Income.

$\frac{1}{1-MPC}$ = Size of Multiplier where MPC = Marginal Propensity to Consume.

ΔI_d = Increase in Induced Investment

v = Size of accelerator.

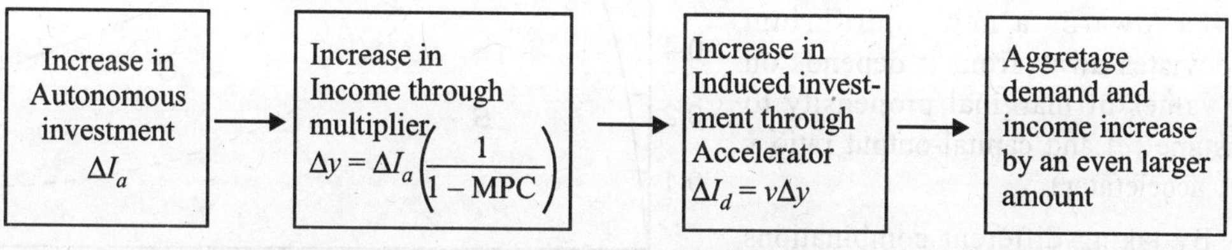

Fig. 25.4. *Combining Accelerator with Keynesian Multiplier*

Fluctuations in investment are the main cause of instability in a free private-enterprise economy. This instability further increases due to the interaction of the multiplier and accelerator. The changes in any component of aggregate demand produce a multiplier effect whose magnitude depends upon the marginal propensity to consume. When consumption, income and output increase under the influence of multiplier effect, they induce further changes in investment and the extent of this induced investment in capital goods industries depends on the capital-output ratio, that is, the interaction between the multiplier and accelerator without any external shocks can give rise to the business cycles whose pattern differs depending upon the magnitudes of the marginal propensity to consume and capital-

8. Samuelson, P.A; "Interaction Between the Multiplier Analysis and the Principle of Acceleration" in *Review of Economic Statistics,* May 1939, p. 751.

output ratio. The model of interaction between multiplier and accelerator can be mathematically represented as under:

$$Y_t = C_t + I_t \qquad ...(i)$$

$$C_t = C_a + c\,(Y_{t-1}) \qquad ...(ii)$$

$$I_t = I_a + v\,(Y_{t-1} - Y_{t-2}) \qquad ...(iii)$$

where Y_t, C_t, I_t stand for income, consumption and investment respectively for a period t, C_a stands for autonomous consumption, I_a for autonomous investment, c for marginal propensity to consume and v for the capital-output ratio or accelerator.

From the above equations it is evident that consumption in a period t is a function of income of the previous period Y_{t-1}. That is, one period lag has been assumed for income to determine the consumption of a period. As regards induced investment in period t, it is taken to be the function of the change in income in the previous period. This means that there is two periods gap for changes in income to determine induced investment. In equation (*iii*) above, induced investment equals $v(Y_{t-i} - Y_{t-2})$ or $v(\Delta Y_{t-1})$. Substituting equations (*ii*) and (*iii*) in equation (*i*) we have the following income equation which states how changes in income are dependent on the values of marginal propensity to consume (c) and capital-output ratio v (*i.e.*, accelerator).

$$Y_1 = C_a + c(Y_{t-1}) + I_a + v\,(Y_{t-1} - Y_{t-2}) \qquad ...(iv)$$

In static equilibrium, the level of income determined will be:

$$Y = C_a + cY + I$$

This is due to the fact that in static equilibrium, given the data of the determining factors, the equilibrium level of income remains uncharged, that is, in this case, $Y_t = Y_{t-1} = Y_{t-2} = Y_{t-n}$ so that period lags have no influence at all and accelerator is reduced to zero. Thus, in a dynamic state when autonomous investment changes, equation (*iv*) describes the path which a disequilibrium system follows to reach either a final equilibrium state or moves away from it. But whether the economy moves towards a new equilibrium or deviates away from it depends on the values of marginal propensity to consume (c) and capital-output ratio v (*i.e.*, accelerator).

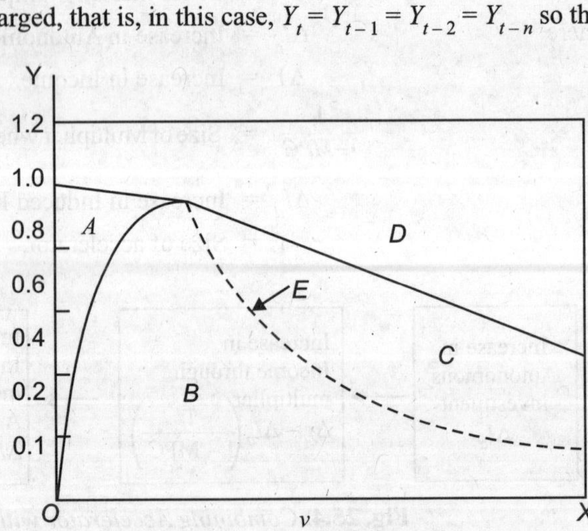

Fig. 25.5. *Combinations of c and v*

By taking different combinations of the values of marginal propensity to consume (c) and capital-output ratio (v), Samuelson has described different paths which the economy will follow. The various combinations of the values of marginal propensity to consume and capital-output ratio (which respectively determine the magnitudes of multiplier and accelerator) are shown in Fig. 25.5. The four paths or patterns of movements which the economic activity (as measured by gross national product or income) can have depending upon various combinations of the values of marginal propensity to consume (c) and capital-output ratio (v) are depicted in Fig. 25.6. When the combinations of the value of marginal propensity to consume (c) and capital-output ratio (v) lie within the region marked A, with a change in autonomous investment, the gross national product or income moves upward or downward at a decreasing rate and finally reaches a new equilibrium as is shown in panel (*a*) of Fig. 25.6. If the values of c and v are such that they lie within the region B, the change in autonomous investment or autonomous consumption will generate fluctuations in income which follow the pattern of a series of *damped cycles* whose amplitudes go on declining until the cycles disappear as is shown in panel (*b*) of Fig. 25.6.

The region C in Fig. 25.6 represents the combinations of c and v which are relatively high as compared to the region B and determine such values of multiplier and accelerator that bring about explosive cycles, that is, the fluctuations of income with successively greater and greater amplitude. The situation is depicted in panel (*c*) of Fig. 25.6 which shows that the system tends to explode and diverges greatly from the equilibrium level. The region D provides the combinations of c and v which cause income to move upward or downward at an increasing rate which has somehow to be restrained if the cyclical movements are to occur. This is depicted in panel (*d*) of Fig. 25.6. Like the values of multiplier and accelerator of region C, their values in region D cause the system to *explode* and diverge from the equilibrium state by an increasing amount.

In a special case when values of c and v (and therefore the magnitudes of multiplier and accelerator) lie in region E, they produce fluctuations in income of *constant amplitude* as is shown in panel (*e*) of Fig. 25.6.

It follows from above that regions A and B are alike, they after a disturbance caused by a change in autonomous investment or consumption finally bring about stable equilibrium in the system. On the other hand, the values of c and v and therefore the magnitudes of multiplier and accelerator of region C and D resemble each other but are such that they cause great instability in the system as both of these values cause successively greater divergence from the equilibrium level and the system tends to explode. The case of region E lies in between the two as the combinations of values of c and v in it are such that cause cyclical movements of income which neither move toward nor away from the equilibrium.

It is worth noting that all the above five cases do not give rise to cyclical fluctuations or business cycles. *It is only combinations of c and v lying in regions B, C and E that produce business cycles.* The values of accelerator and multiplier in the

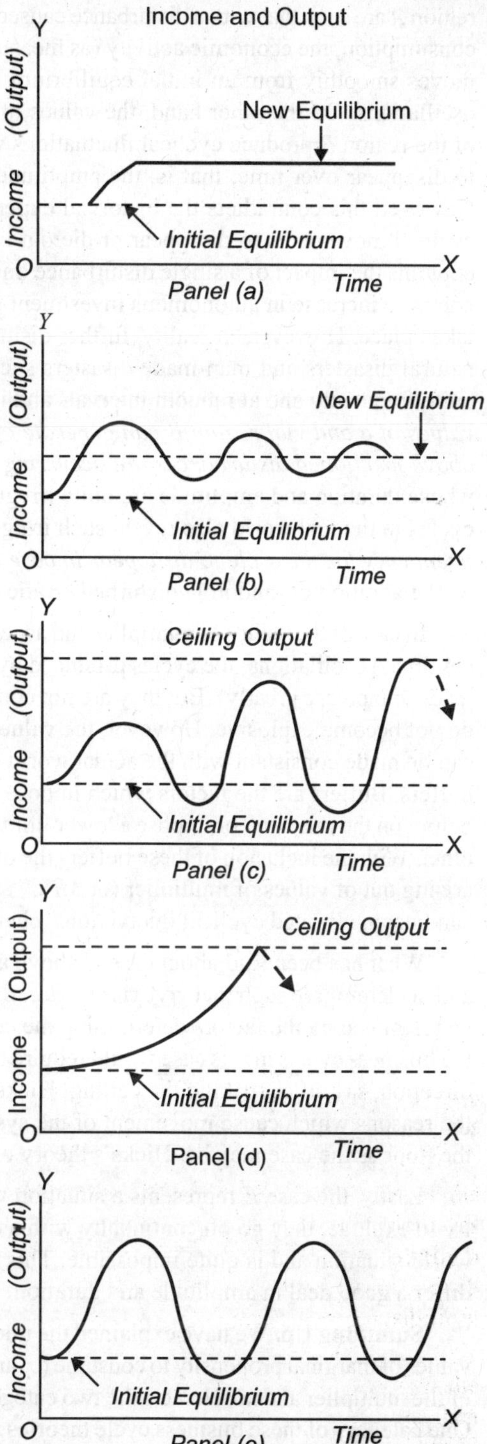

Fig. 25.6. *Interaction between Multiplier and Accelerator: Different Patterns of Income (output) movements for various values of c and v*

region *A* are such that with a disturbance caused by a change in autonomous investment or autonomous consumption, the economic activity (as measured by the level of income or Gross National Product) moves smoothly from an initial equilibrium to a new equilibrium with no cyclical fluctuations or oscillations. On the other hand, the values of *c* and *v* (and therefore of multiplier and accelerator) of the region *B* produce cyclical fluctuations which are of the type of *damped oscillations* that tend to disappear over time, that is, the amplitude of the cycles shrinks to zero over a period of time. However, this contradicts the historical experience which reveals that there is no tendency for the cyclical movements to disappear or die out over time. However, it is worth noting that the case *B* explains the impact of a single disturbance on income and employment. For example, the effect of a one time increase in autonomous investment goes on diminishing over time if no other disturbance takes place. However, in reality, further disturbances such as technological advances, innovations, natural disasters and man-made disasters such as security scam in India in 1991-92 do take place quite frequently and at random intervals and in a way they provide shocks to the system.[9] Thus, *the values of c and v of region B can generate cyclical fluctuations over time without dying out if the above-mentioned disturbances are occurring frequently at random.* This results in business cycles whose duration and amplitude are quite irregular and not uniform. As a matter of fact, the business cycles in the real world also reveal such irregular pattern. To sum up, "*what otherwise shows up as a tendency for the cycle to disappear in case B may be converted into unending sequence* of cycles by the addition of randomly disturbed erratic shock system."[10]

In case of the values of multiplier and accelerator falling within the region *C*, though they generate continued oscillations, the cycles produced by them tend to become 'explosive' (*i.e.* their amplitude tends to increase greatly). But they are not consistent with the real world situation where oscillations do not become explosive. However, the values of multiplier and accelerator falling within region *C* can be made consistant with the actual world situation by incorporating in the analysis the so called buffers. Buffers are the factors which impose upper limit or ceiling on the expansion of income and output on the one hand or impose a lower limit or floor on the contraction of output and income on the other. With the inclusion of these buffers the otherwise explosive upward and downward fluctuations arising out of values of multiplier (or *MPC*) and accelerator (or capital-output ratio) of the region *C* can become limited cyclical fluctuations, characteristic of the real world situation.

What has been said about case *C* above also applies to region *D* where the values of multiplier and acclerator are such that give rise to *directly explosive upward or downward movement* which can be restrained by the factors determining the ceiling and floor. However, the adequate explanation of the business cycles in this case would require the reasons why the system starts moving in the reverse direction, say, after striking the ceiling. Hicks in his famous theory of the business cycles provides the reasons which cause movement of the system in the reverse direction after it hits the ceiling or the floor as the case may be. Hicks's theory of business cycles will be explained below at length.

Lastly, the case *E* represents a situation where the business cycles neither try to disappear, nor try to explode, they go on continually with a *constant amplitude.* This however contradicts the real world situation and is quite impossible. This is because in the real world situation, business cycles differ a good deal in amplitude and duration.

Summing Up. We have explained the interaction of multiplier and accelerator in case of various values of marginal propensity to consume (*c*) and capital-output ratio (*v*). On the basis of the interaction of the multiplier and accelerator the two categories of business cycle theories have been put forward. One category of these business cycle theories assumes the values of multiplier and accelerator which

9. The concept of erratic shocks has been put forward by a Nobel Prize winner in economics. *R.* Frisch, "Propagation Problems and Impulse Problems in Dynamic Economics" in *Economic Essays in Honour of Gustav Cassel.* Allen and Unwin, 1993, pp. 171-205.
10. Shapiro Edward, *Macroeconomic Analysis,* Fourth Edition, 1978, p. 378.

generate explosive cycles. For example, Hicks' theory of business cycles falls in this category. On the other hand, Hansen has propounded a business cycle theory based on the interaction of multiplier with a *weak* accelerator which produces only damped oscillations. Further, as indicated above, the interaction theories have been modified either by incorporating in the analysis erratic shocks or random disturbances or by including so called buffers which check the upward movement of income and output by imposing ceiling of expansion and checking a downward movement by imposing a floor on the contraction of output. One of the famous theories of business cycles based on the interaction of multiplier and accelerator which also incorporate buffers in his analysis of fluctuations is that put forward by the noted English economist, J.R. Hicks. We discuss below his theory of business cycles in detail.

Table 25.1. A Multiplier-Acceleration Interaction Model

Period	*Autonomous Investment*	*Induced Consumption* ($c = 2/3$)	*Induced Investment* ($v = 2$)	*Change in Income from the base period t*
1	2	3	4	5
	₹ in Crores	₹ in Crores	₹ in Crores	₹ in Crores
t	0	0	0	0
$t+1$	10	0	0	10
$t+2$	10	6.7	13.4	30.1
$t+3$	10	20.0	26.6	56.6
$t+4$	10	37.8	35.6	83.4
$t+5$	10	55.6	35.6	101.2
$t+6$	10	67.6	23.8	101.2
$t+7$	10	67.6	0.2	67.8
$t+8$	10	51.8	−10.0	51.8
$t+9$	10	34.6	−10.0	33.8
$t+10$	10	23.0	−10.0	23.0
$t+11$	10	15.4	−10.0	15.4
$t+12$	10	10.2	−10.0	10.2
$t+13$	10	6.8	− 6.8	10.0
$t+14$	10	6.6	+ 0.2	16.8

A Numerical Example of the Interaction of the Multiplier and Accelerator

How the interaction between the multiplier and accelerator gives rise to the cyclical movements in economic activity (as measured by income or output) will become clear from Table 25.1. In formulating this table we have assumed that marginal propensity to consume (c) being equal to 2/3 or 0.66 and capital-output ratio (v) or accelerator being equal to 2. Further, one period time lag has been assumed which implies that an increase in income in a period induces the increase in consumption in the next period. It is assumed that initially in period $t + 1$, autonomous investment is of ₹ 10 crores. In period $t + 3$, with autonomous investment being maintained constant at ₹ 10 crores, the deviation of total income in the period $t + 3$ as compared to the base period will be equal to 10 + 20 + 26.6 = ₹ 56.6 crores. Similarly, the changes in induced consumption and induced investment and hence in income brought about by the initial increase in autonomous investment of ₹ 10 crores, which is maintained throughout, can be found out. It will be seen from column 5 of the Table 25.1 that there are large fluctuations in income. Under the influence of the interaction between the multiplier and accelelrator, the income increases up to the period $t + 6$. In other words, period up to $t + 6$ represents the expansion phase or upswing of the business cycle. Therefore, the period $t + 6$ is the upper turning point of the business cycle beyond which the contraction phase or downswing of the business cycle begins. It will be further observed that beyond the period $t + 13$, income again starts rising, that is, *recovery from the depression begins*. Thus, $t + 13$ represents the lower turning point of the business cycle. In this way we see that the interaction between the multiplier and accelerator can give rise to the cyclical movements of the economic activity and its various phases. It is worth mentioning that we have taken particular values of marginal propensity to consume (which determine the size of the multiplier) and capital-output ratio (which determines the size of the accelerator). The other values of multiplier and accelerator that have been explained above would give rise to the different patterns of fluctuations.

HICKS' THEORY OF BUSINESS CYCLES

Hicks[11] put forward a complete theory of business cycles based on the interaction between the multiplier and accelerator by choosing certain values of marginal propensity to consume (c) and capital-output ratio (v) which he thinks are representative of the real world situation. According to Hicks, the values of marginal propensity to consume and capital-output ratio fall in either region C or D of Fig. 25.1. As seen above, in case values of these parameters lie in the region C, they produce *cyclical movements (i.e.,* oscillations) whose amplitude increases over time and if they fall in region D they produce an *explosive upward movement* of income or output without oscillations. To explain business cycles of the real world which do not tend to explode, Hicks has incorporated in his analysis the role of buffers. On the one hand, *he introduces output ceiling* when all the given resources are fully employed and prevent income and output to go beyond it, and, on the other hand, he visualises a *floor or the lower* limit below which income and output cannot go because some autonomous investment is always taking place.

Another important feature of Hicks' theory is that business cycles in the economy occur in the background of economic growth (*i.e.,* the rising trend of real income of output over time). In other words, cyclical fluctuations in real output of goods and services take place *above and below this rising line of trend* or growth of income and output. Thus in his theory he explains business cycles along with an equilibrium rate of growth. In Hicks' theory of long-run equilibrium growth that is determined by rate of increase of autonomous investment over time and, therefore, long-run equilibrium growth of income is determined by the autonomous investment and the magnitudes of multiplier and accelerator. Hicks assumes that autonomous investment, depending as it is on technological progress, innovations and population growth, grows at a constant rate. With further assumptions of stable multiplier and accelerator, equilibrium income will grow at the same rate as autonomous investment. It follows therefore that the failure of actual output to increase along the equilibrium growth path, sometimes to move above it and sometimes to move below it, determines the business cycles.

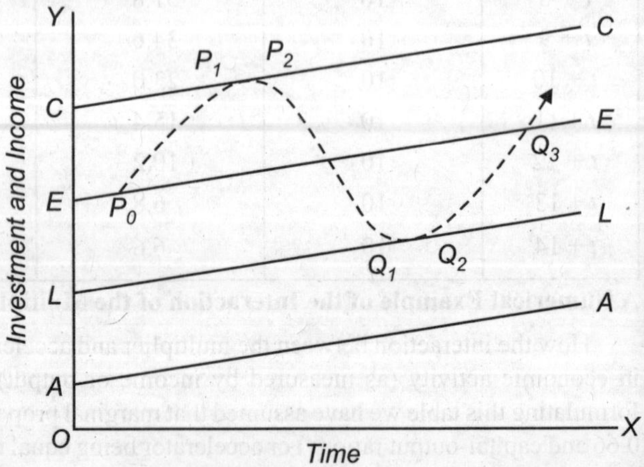

Fig. 25.7. *Hicks' Model of Business Cycles*

11. Hicks, J.R., A *Contribution to the Theory of Trade Cycles,* Oxford University Press, p. 50.

Hicks' Theory of business cycles has been explained with the help of Fig. 25.7. In this figure, *AA* line represents autonomous investment. Autonomous investment is that investment which is not induced by changes in income and is made by entrepreneur as a result of technological progress or innovations or population growth. Hicks assumes that autonomous investment grows annually at a constant rate given by the slope of the line *AA*. Given the marginal propensity to consume, the simple multiplier is determined. Then the magnitude of multiplier and autonomous investment together determine the equilibrium path of income shown by the line *LL*. Hicks calls this the floor line as this sets the lower limits below which income (output) cannot fall because of a given rate of growth of autonomous investment and the given size of the multiplier. But induced investment has not yet been taken into account. If national income grows from one year to the next, as it would move along the line *LL*, there is some amount of induced investment via accelerator. The line *EE* shows the equilibrium growth path of national income determined by autonomous investment and the combined effect of the multiplier and accelerator. *FF* is the full employment ceiling. It is a line that shows the maximum national output at any period of time when all the available resources of the economy are fully employed. Given the constant growth of autonomous investment, the magnitude of multiplier and the induced investment determined by the accelerator, the economy will be moving along the *equilibrium growth* path line *EE*. Thus starting from point *E*, the economy will be in equilibrium moving along the path *EE* determined by the combined effect of multiplier and accelerator and the growing level of the autonomous investment.

Suppose when the economy reaches point P_0 along the path *EE*, there is an *external shock*—say an outburst of investment due to certain innovation or jump in governmental investment. When the economy experiences such an outburst of autonomous investment it pushes the economy above the equilibrium growth path *EE* after point P_0. The rise in autonomous investment due to external shock *causes national income to increase at a greater rate than that shown* by the slope of *EE*. This greater increase in national income will cause further increase in induced investment through acceleration effect. This increase in induced investment causes national income to increase by a magnified amount through multiplier. So under the combined effect of multiplier and accelerator, national income or output will rapidly expand along the path from P_0 to P_1. Movement from P_0 to P_1 represents the upswing or expansion phase of the business cycle. But this expansion must stop at P_1 because this is the full employment output ceiling. The limited human and material resources of the economy do not permit a greater expansion of national income than shown by the ceiling line *CC*. Therefore, when point P_1 is reached the rapid growth of national income must come to an end. Prof. Hicks assumes that the full employment ceiling grows at the same rate as autonomous investment. Therefore, *CC* slopes gently unlike the very steep slope of the line from P_0 to P_1. When point P_1 is reached the economy must grow at the same rate as the usual growth in autonomous investment.

For a short time the economy may crawl along the full employment ceiling *CC*. But because national income has ceased to increase at the rapid rate, the induced investment via accelerator falls off to the level consistent with the modest rate of growth determined by the constant rate of growth of autonomous investment. But the economy cannot crawl along its full employment ceiling for a long time. The sharp decline in growth of income and consumption when the economy strikes the ceiling causes a sharp decline in induced investment. Thus with the sharp decline in induced investment when national income and hence consumption ceases to increase rapidly, the contraction in the level of the income and business actually must begin. Once the downswing starts, the accelerator works in the reverse direction. That is, since the change in income is now negative the inducement to invest must begin to decrease. Thus there is slackening off at point P_2 and national income starts moving toward equilibrium growth path *EE*. This movement from P_2 downward therefore represents the downswing or contraction phase of the business cycle. In this downswing investment falls off rapidly and therefore multiplier works in the reverse direction. The fall in national income and output resulting from the sharp fall in induced investment will not stop on touching the level *EE* but will go further down. The economy must consequently move all the way down from point P_2 to point Q_1. But at point Q_1 the floor has been reached.

Whereas the upswing was limited by the output ceiling set by the full employment of available resources, in the downswing the national income cannot fall below the level of output represented by the floor. This is because the floor level is determined by simple multiplier and autonomous investment growing at constant rate, while during the downswing after a point accelerator ceases to operate. It may be noted that during downswing the limit to negative investment (disinvestment) and therefore the limit to the contraction of output is set by the depreciation of capital stock. There is no way for the businessmen to make disinvestment at a desired rate higher than the depreciation. When during downswing such conditions arise, accelerator becomes inoperative. After hitting the floor the economy may for some time crawl along the floor through the path Q_1 to Q_2. In doing so, there is some growth in the level of national income. This rate of growth as before induces investment and both the multiplier and accelerator come into operation and the economy will move towards Q_3 and the full employment ceiling *CC*. This is how the upswing of cyclical movement again starts.

Critical Appraisal

But Hicks' theory of trade cycles is not without critics. A major weakness of Hicks' theory, according to Kaldor, is that it is based on the principle of acceleration in its rigid form.[12] If the rigid form of acceleration principle is not valid, then the interaction of the multiplier and accelerator which is the crucial concept of the Hicksian theory of trade cycles is not valid. Thus Duesenberry writes, "the basic concept of multiplier-accelerator interaction is important one but we cannot really accept to explain observed cycles by a mechanical application of that concept"[13] and, according to him, Hicks in his business cycle theory actually tries to do so.

It may be noted that Kaldor puts forward a theory of business cycles which does not make use of the rigid or strict form of the acceleration principle. In his trade cycle theory Kaldor provides for investment being *directly related* to the level of income and *inversely related* to the stock of capital. Thus Kaldor's approach which is also supported by Goodwin abandons the rigid and inflexible relation of investment to changes in income (output) as implied by the rigid acceleration principle [*i.e.*, $I_t = I_a + v(Y_{t-1} - Y_{t-2})$] and instead has used the following form of the investment function

$$I_t = I_a + gY_{t-1} - jK_t$$

where I_t stands for investment in period *t*, I_a for autonomous investment, Y_{t-1} for income in the previous period, K_t for the stock of capital, and *g* and *j* are constants.

A look at the above investment function used by Kaldor will reveal that investment is directly related to the income and inversely related to the stock of capital. Thus in Kaldor-Goodwin investment function, the increase in income, the capital stock remaining constant, will cause an increase in investment which will enlarge the stock of capital. On the other hand, according to this new investment function, if capital stock increases, output or income remaining constant, investment will fall due to its being negatively related to capital stock. Thus, Kaldor-Goodwin approach to investment while gives up the rigid acceleration principle but still retains the basic idea of investment related to income because in this approach investment will cause the capital stock to expand towards the stock of capital as desired for the production of output of the preceding year.

However, despite the shortcomings of Hicks' theory of business cycles, this is a valuable contribution to the theory of business cycles. Even its critics such as Kaldor though indicating some of its weaknesses acknowledge its merit. Thus Kaldor writes that Hicks' theory of trade cycles provides us "many brilliant and original pieces of analysis". Duesenberry considers it as an "ingenious piece of work".

12. See Kaldor N., "Hicks on the Trade Cycles" in *Economic Journal,* Dec. 1951, pp. 433-478.
13. Duesenberry, J.S., "Hicks on the Trend and Cycles" in *Quarterly Journal of Economics,* August 1950, pp. 464-76.

QUESTIONS FOR REVIEW

1. Explain briefly characteristics of a trade cycle.
2. Explain briefly the different phases of business cycle.
3. Explain Hawtrey's Monetary Theory of Business Cycles. Show that his model of business cycles is self-generating.
4. What is meant by under-consumption? What factors, according to Karl Marx, are responsible for it ? How does under-consumption cause trade cycles in the economy ?
5. Critically examine Hayek's over-investment theory of business cycles. Compare it with Wicksell's over-investment theory of business cycles.
6. Explain Keynes's contribution to business cycle theory. Is his theory a sufficient explanation of business cycles ?
7. What is accelerator? What role does it play in explaining business cycles in the economy?
8. Explain how the interaction of multiplier and accelerator explain cyclical fluctuations in the economy.
9. Critically examine Hicks' model of trade cycles. What determines floor and ceiling in his model ?

CHAPTER 26

Economic Stabilisation : Fiscal Policy

Introduction: Macroeconomic Policy and Stabilisation

The economy does not always work smoothly. There often occur fluctuations in the level of economic activity. At times the economy finds itself in the grip of recession when levels of national income, output and employment are far below their full potential levels. During recession, there is a lot of idle or unutilised productive capacity, that is, available machines and factories are not working to their full capacity. As a result, unemployment of labour increases along with the existence of excess capital stock. On the other hand, at times the economy is '*overheated*' which means inflation (*i.e.* rising prices) occurs in the economy. Thus, in a free market economy there is a lot of economic instability. The classical economists believed that an automatic mechanism works to restore stability in the economy; recession would cure itself and inflation will be automatically controlled. However, the empirical evidence during the 1930s when severe depression took place in the Western capitalist economies and also the evidence of Post-World War period amply shows that no such automatic mechanism works to bring about stability in the economy. That is why Keynes argued for intervention by the Government to cure depression and inflation by adopting appropriate tools of macroeconomic policy. *The two important tools of macroeconomic policy are fiscal policy and monetary policy.* According to Keynes, monetary policy was ineffective to lift the economy out of depression. He emphasized the role of fiscal policy as an effective tool of stabilising the economy. However, in view of the modern economists both fiscal and monetary policies play a useful role in stabilising the economy. In the present chapter we shall dwell upon the role of fiscal policy for stabilising the economy and will discuss the role of monetary policy in bringing about stabilisation in the next chapter.

Goals of Macroeconomic Policy

Stabilising the economy at a higher level of employment and national output is not the only goal of macroeconomic policy. Ensuring price stability is its another goal. Both inflation (that is, rising prices) and deflation (that is, falling prices) have bad economic consequences. It is therefore desirable to achieve price stability. Similarly, every nation wants to raise the level of living of its people which can be attained through bringing about economic growth which in turn depends on raising the rates of saving and investment and accumulating capital. Macroeconomic policies can play a useful role in raising the rate of saving and investment and therefore ensure rapid economic growth. Thus, three important goals or objectives of macroeconomic policy (both fiscal and monetary) are as follows :

1. Economic stability at a high level of output and employment.
2. Price stability.
3. Economic growth.

In the present chapter we shall confine ourselves to the discussion of the role of fiscal policy in achieving economic stability at full employment level and in controlling inflation and deflation and thus attaining price stability. The role of monetary policy for encouraging economic growth will be discussed at length in a later chapter.

DISCRETIONARY FISCAL POLICY FOR STABILISATION

Fiscal policy is an important instrument to stabilise the economy, that is, to overcome recession and control inflation in the economy. Fiscal policy is of two kinds : *Discretionary fiscal policy and Non-discretionary fiscal policy of automatic stabilisers.* By discretionary policy we mean deliberate change in the Government expenditure and taxes to influence the level of national output and prices. Fiscal policy generally aims at managing aggregate demand for goods and services. On the other hand, non-discretionary fiscal policy of automatic stabilisers is a built-in tax or expenditure mechanism that automatically increases aggregate demand when recession occurs and reduces aggregate demand when there is inflation in the economy without any special deliberate actions on the part of the Government. In this section we shall confine ourselves to the discussion of discretionary fiscal policy.

At the time of recession the Government increases its expenditure or cuts down taxes or adopts a combination of both. On the other hand, to control inflation the Government cuts down its expenditure or raises taxes. In other words, *to cure recession expansionary fiscal policy and to control inflation contractionary fiscal policy is adopted.* It is worth mentioning that fiscal policy aims at changing aggregate demand by suitable changes in Government spending and taxes. Thus, *fiscal policy is mainly a policy of demand management.* It should be further noted that when the Government adopts expansionary fiscal policy to cure recession, it raises its expenditure without raising taxes or cuts down taxes without changing expenditure or increases expenditure and cuts down taxes as well. With the adoption of any of these types of expansionary fiscal policy Government's budget will have a deficit. Thus expansionary fiscal policy to cure recession and unemployment is a deficit budget policy. If, on the other hand, to control inflation, Government reduces its expenditure or increases taxes or adopts a combination of the two, it will be planning for a budget surplus. *Thus policy of budget surplus, or at least reducing budget deficit is adopted to remedy inflation.* In what follows we will discuss fiscal policy first to cure recession and then to control inflation.

Fiscal Policy to Cure Recession

As we know, the recession in an economy occurs when aggregate demand decreases due to a fall in private investment. Private investment may fall when businessmen become highly pessimistic about making profits in future, resulting in decline in marginal efficiency of investment. As a result of fall in private investment expenditure, aggregate demand curve shifts down creating a *deflationary or recessionary gap.* It is the task of fiscal policy to close this gap by increasing Government expenditure, or reducing taxes. Thus there are two fiscal methods to get the economy out of recession :

(*a*) Increase in Government expenditure

(*b*) Reduction of taxes.

We discuss below both these methods.

(*a*) **Increase in Government Expenditure to Cure Recession.** For a discretionary fiscal policy to cure depression, the increase in Government expenditure is an important tool. Government may increase expenditure by starting public works, such as building roads, dams, ports, telecommunication links, irrigation works, electrification of new areas etc. For undertaking all these public works, Government buys various types of goods and materials and employs workers. The effect of this increase in expenditure is both direct and indirect. The direct effect is the increase in incomes of those who sell materials and supply labour for these projects. The output of these public works also goes up together with the increase in incomes. Not only that, Keynes showed that increase in Government expenditure also has an *indirect effect* in the form of the working of a multiplier. Those who get more incomes spend them further on consumer goods depending on their marginal propensity to consume. As during the period of recession there exists *excess capacity* in the consumer goods industries, the increase in demand for them brings about expansion in their output which further generates employment and incomes for the unemployed workers and so the new incomes are spent and respent further and the process of multiplier goes on working till it exhausts itself.

How large should be the increase in expenditure so that equilibrium is established at full employment or potential level of output ? This depends on the magnitude of GNP gap caused by deflationary gap on the one hand and the size of multiplier on the other. It may be recalled that the size of the multiplier depends on the marginal propensity to consume. The impact of increase in Government expenditure in a recessionary condition is illustrated in Fig. 26.1. Suppose to begin with the economy is operating at full-employment or potential level of output Y_F with aggregate demand curve $C + I_2 + G_2$ intersecting 45° line at point E_2. Now, due to some adverse happening (say due to the crash in the stock market), investor's expectations of making profits from investment projects become dim causing a decline in investment. With the decline in investment, say equal to E_2B, aggregate demand curve will shift down to the new position $C + I_1 + G_1$ which will bring the economy to the new equilibrium position at point E_1 and thereby determine Y_1 level of output or income. The fall in output will create involuntary unemployment of labour and also excess capacity *(i.e.* idle capital stock) will come to exist in the economy. Thus emergence of deflationary gap equal to E_2B and the reverse working of the multiplier has brought about conditions of recession in the economy. It will be observed from Fig. 26.1 that, to overcome recession if the Government increases its expenditure by E_1H, the aggregate demand curve will shift upward to original position $C + I_2 + G_2$ and as a result the equilibrium level of income will increase to the full-employment or potential level of output Y_F and in this way the economy would be lifted out of depression. Note that the increase (ΔY) in national income or output by Y_1Y_F is not only equal to the increase in Government expenditure by ΔG or E_1H but a multiple of it depending on the marginal propensity to consume. Thus, increase in national income is equal to $\Delta G \times \frac{1}{1-MPC}$ where $\frac{1}{1-MPC}$ the value of multiplier.

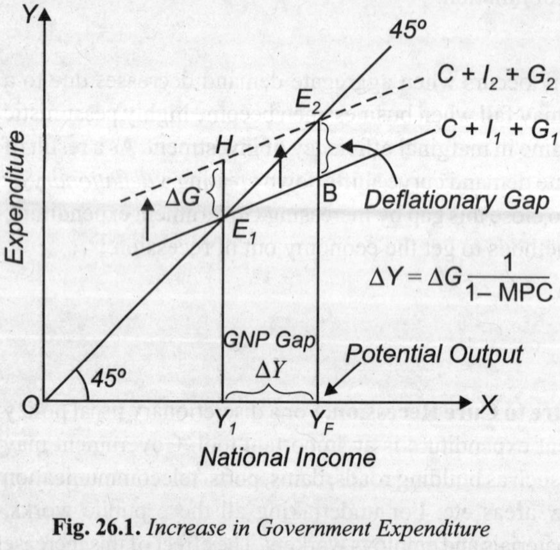

Fig. 26.1. *Increase in Government Expenditure to Cure Recession*

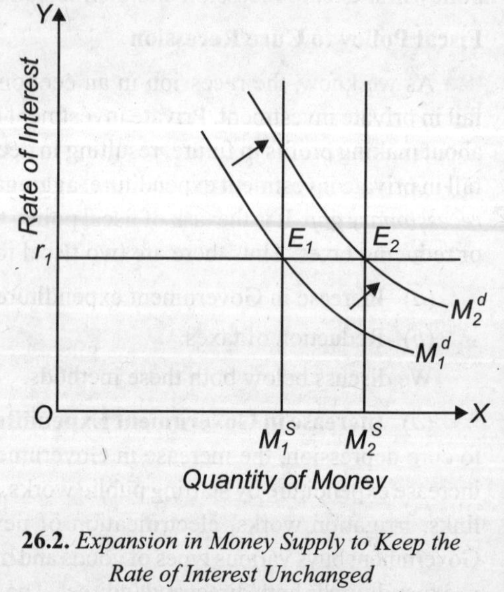

26.2. *Expansion in Money Supply to Keep the Rate of Interest Unchanged*

It may also be further noted that increase in Government expenditure without raising taxes (and therefore the policy of deficit budgeting) will fully succeed in curing recession if rate of interest remains unchanged. With the increase in Government expenditure and resultant increase in output and employment demand for money of transactions purposes is likely to increase as is shown in Fig. 26.2 where demand for money curve shifts to right from M_1^d to M_2^d as a result of increase in transactions demand for money. Money supply remaining constant, with increase in demand for money rate of interest is likely to rise which will adversely affect the private investment. The decline in private investment will tend to offset the expansionary effect of rise in Government expenditure. Therefore, if fiscal policy of increase in Government expenditure (or of deficit budgeting) is to succeed in overcoming recession, the Central Bank of the country should also pursue expansionary monetary policy and take steps to increase the money supply so that increase in Government expenditure does not lead to the rise in rate of interest. It will be noticed from Fig. 26.2 that if money supply is increased from M_1^S to M_2^S, the rate of interest does not rise despite the increase in demand for money. With rate of interest remaining unchanged, private investment will not be adversely affected and increase in Government expenditure will have full effect on raising national income and employment.

Financing Increase in Government Expenditures and Budget Deficit

An important question is how to finance the increase in Government expenditure which is undertaken to cure recession. This increase in Government expenditure must not be financed by raising taxes because rise in taxes would reduce disposable incomes and consumers' demand for goods. As a matter of fact, rise in taxes would offset the expansionary effect of rise in Government spending. Therefore, proper discretionary fiscal policy at times of recession is to have the budget deficit if expansionary effect is to be realised.

Borrowing. A way to finance budget deficit is to borrow from the public by selling interest-bearing bonds to them. However, there is a problem in adopting borrowing as a method of financing budget deficit. When the Government borrows from the public in the money market, it will be competing with businessmen who also borrow for private investment. The Government borrowing will raise the demand for loanable funds which in a free market economy, if rate of interest is not administered by the Central Bank, will drive up the rate of interest. We know the rise in rate of interest will reduce or crowd out some private investment expenditure and interest-sensitive consumer spending for durable goods.

Creation of New Money. The more effective way of financing budget deficit is the creation of new money. By creating new money to finance the deficit, the crowding out of private investment can be avoided and full expansionary effect of rise in Government expenditure can be realised. Thus, creation of new money for financing budget deficit or what is called *monetisation of budget deficit* has a greater expansionary effect than that of borrowing by the Government.

(*b*) **Reduction in Taxes to Overcome Recession.** Alternative fiscal policy measure to overcome recession and to achieve expansion in output and employment is reduction of taxes. The reduction in taxes increases the disposable income of the society and causes the increase in consumption spending by the people. If tax reduction of ₹ 200 crores is made by the Finance Minister, it will lead to ₹ 150 crores in consumption, assuming marginal propensity to consume is 0.75 or 3/4. Thus reduction in taxes will cause an upward shift in the consumption function. If along with the reduction in taxes, the Government expenditure is kept unchanged, aggregate demand curve $C + I + G$ will shift upward due to rise in consumption function curve. This will have an expansionary effect and the economy will be lifted out of recession, and national income and employment will increase and as a result unemployment will be reduced. Note that reduction in taxes, with Government expenditure remaining constant, will also result in budget deficit which will have to be financed either by borrowing or creation of new money.

It is worth noting that *reduction in taxes has only an indirect effect on expansion and output* through causing a rise in consumption function. But, like the increase in government expenditure, the increase in consumption achieved through reduction in taxes will have a multiplier effect on increasing income, output and employment. As we have shown in a previous chapter, the value of *tax multiplier,* as it is called, is given by

$$\Delta T \times \frac{MPC}{1-MPC} \text{ or } \Delta C \times \frac{MPC}{1-MPC}$$

The effect of reduction in taxes in curing recession and in causing expansion in income and output can be graphically shown by a figure such as Fig. 26.1. In case of reduction in taxes, instead of increase in Government expenditure *G*, it is increase in consumption *C* which will cause upward shift in the aggregate demand curve *(C + I + G)* and will result in, through the working of multiplier, a higher level of equilibrium national income.

There are some instances in the history of the capitalist world, especially U.S.A, when taxes were reduced to stimulate the economy. In 1964, President Kennedy reduced personal and business taxes by about $12 billion to give a boost to the American economy when there was high unemployment and lower capacity utilisation in the American economy. This tax cut was quite successful in reducing unemployment substantially and expanding national income through full utilisation of excess capacity. Again, over the period 1981-84, President Reagan made a very large tax reduction to get out of recession and to achieve expansion in national income to reduce unemployment. There is some debate whether President Reagan's tax cut alone had positive effect on national income as some economists attribute the recovery in that period to the monetary expansion that took place. However, tax reduction by President Reagan did play a significant role for bringing about the recovery.

Fiscal Policy Option: Increase in Government Expenditure or Reduction in Taxes

Is it better to use Government expenditure or changes in taxes to stabilise the economy at full employment and potential level of output. The answer depends to a great extent upon one's view regarding the role of public sector. Those who think that public sector should play a significant role in the economy to meet various failures of a free market system will recommend the increase in Government expenditure during recession on public works to achieve expansion in output and employment. On the other hand, those economists who think that public sector is inefficient and involves waste of scarce resources would advocate for reduction in taxes to stimulate the economy.

The choice between tax reduction and increase in Government expenditure depends on the basis of another factor, namely, the magnitude of the effect of expenditure multiplier and tax multiplier. The value of tax multiplier is less than the Government expenditure multiplier. Ignoring the signs of the multipliers, it should be noted that whereas expenditure multiplier is equal to $\frac{1}{1-MPC}$, the tax multiplier equals $\frac{MPC}{1-MPC}$ or $MPC \times \frac{1}{1-MPC}$ which is less than $\frac{1}{1-MPC}$. Suppose marginal propensity to consume is 0.75 or 3/4 so that value of expenditure multiplier is 4. Increase in Government expenditure by ₹ 100 crores will raise national output by ₹ 400 crores. On the other hand, reduction in taxes by ₹ 100 crores will increase income and output by $100 \times \frac{MPC}{1-MPC} = 100 \times \frac{3/4}{1-3/4}$ = ₹ 300 crores. Thus, the effect of reduction in taxes by an equal amount as the increase in Government expenditure has a smaller impact on national income than that of increase in Government expenditure. This difference in the effects of the two methods of expanding output has implications for the size of the Government deficit. If we want to achieve expansion in income by the same amount, we need to cut taxes by more than we would need to increase Government expenditure because the size of the tax multiplier is less than that of expenditure multiplier. In other words, in case we adopt the policy of tax reduction, to achieve expansion by a given amount the budget deficit planned will have to be much greater.

However, the size of expenditure multiplier relative to the size of the tax multiplier is not the sole deciding factor for the choice of a policy option. For example, reduction in taxes is greatly welcomed by the people as it directly increases their disposable incomes. Further, it is individual or households who themselves decide how to spend their extra disposable income made possible by a tax cut, while in case of increase in expenditure the Government decides how to spend it.

Fiscal Policy to Control Inflation

When due to large increases in consumption demand by the households or investment expenditure by the entrepreneurs, or bigger budget deficit caused by too large an increase in Government expenditure, aggregate demand increases beyond what the economy can potentially produce by fully employing its given resources, it gives rise to the situation of *excess demand* which results in inflationary pressures in the economy. This inflationary situation can also arise if too large an increase in money supply in the economy occurs. In these circumstances *inflationary gap* occurs which tends to bring about rise in prices. If successful steps to check the emergence of excess demand or close the inflationary gap are not taken, the economy will experience a period of inflation or rising prices. For the last some decades, problem of demand-pull inflation has been faced by both the developed and developing countries of the world[1]. An alternative way of looking at inflation is to view it from the angle of business cycles. After recovery from recession, when during upswing an economy finds itself in conditions of boom and becomes overheated, prices start rising rapidly. Under such circumstances *anticyclical fiscal policy* calls for reduction in aggregate demand. Thus, *fiscal policy measures to control inflation are* (1) *reducing Government expenditure and* (2) *increasing taxes.* If in the beginning the *Government is having balanced budget,* then increasing taxes while keeping Government expenditure constant will yield budget surplus. The creation of budget surplus will cause downward shift in the aggregate demand curve and will therefore help in easing pressure on prices. If there is a balanced budget to begin with and the Government reduces its expenditure, say on defence, subsidies, transfer payments, while keeping taxes constant, this will also create budget surplus and result in removing excess demand in the economy.

It is important to mention that in the developing countries like India, the main factor responsible for inflationary pressures is *heavy budget deficit* of the Government for the last several years resulting in excess demand conditions. Rate of inflation can be reduced not necessarily by planning for budget surplus which is in fact impracticable but by *trying to take steps to reduce budget deficits.* It has been estimated that the aim should be to reduce fiscal deficit[2] to 3 per cent of GNP to achieve price stability in the Indian economy.

How the reduction in Government expenditure will help in checking inflation is shown in Fig. 26.3. It will be seen from this figure that an aggregate demand curve $C + I + G_1$ intersects 45° line at point E and determines

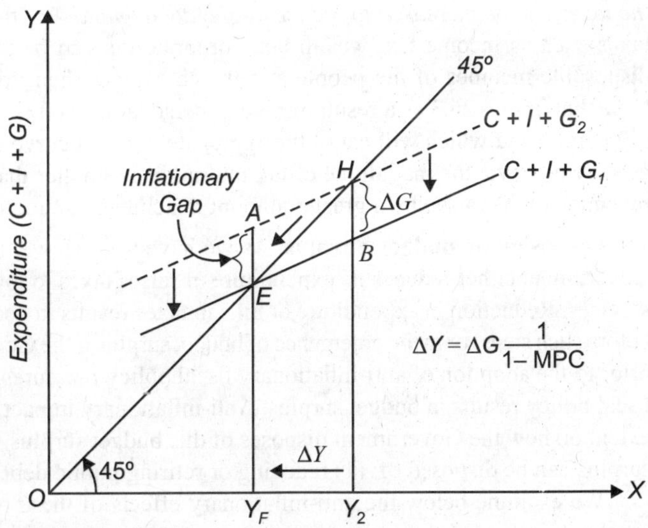

Fig. 26.3. *Reducing Expenditure to Check Inflation*

1. It is worth noting that in the mid-nineties in the developed countries inflation had become very moderate which is currently at the rate of about 4 per cent per annum.
2. There is some difference in the meaning of *budget deficit* and *fiscal deficit*. However, we shall not go into this issue and will be treating them to be of the same meaning.

equilibrium national income at full-employment level of income Y_F. However, if due to excessive Government expenditure and a large budget deficit, the aggregate demand curve shifts upward to $C + I + G_2$, this will determine Y_2 level of income which is greater than full employment or potential output level Y_F. Since output cannot increase beyond Y_F income will rise only in money terms through rise in prices, real income or output remaining unchanged. To put it in other words, while the economy does not have labour, capital and other resources sufficient to produce Y_2 level of income or output, the households, businessmen and Government are demanding Y_2 level of output. This excess demand pushes up the price level so that level of only *nominal income* increases, real income or output remaining constant.

It is thus clear that with the increase in aggregate demand beyond the full-employment level of output to $C + I + G_2$ causes excess demand equal to *EA* to emerge in the economy. It is this excess demand *EA* relative to full-employment output Y_F which causes the price level to rise and thus creates inflationary situation in the economy. This excess demand *EA* at full-employment level has therefore been called inflationary gap. *The task of fiscal policy is to close this inflationary gap by reducing Government expenditure or raising taxes.* With equilibrium at point *H* and nominal income equal to Y_2, if Government expenditure equal to *HB* (which is equal to inflationary gap *AE)* is reduced, aggregate demand curve will shift downward to $C + I + G_1$ which will restore the equilibrium at the full-employment level Y_F. The reduction in Government expenditure equal to *HB* through the operation of multiplier will result in a multiple decline in the level of national income or output. It will be seen from Fig. 26.3 that the decrease in Government expenditure by *HB* has led to a much bigger decline in output by Y_2Y_F. Ideally Government should cut down its expenditure on non-developmental or unproductive heads such as defence, unnecessary subsidies. It may however be noted that in India to control inflation the Government has been reducing *capital expenditure* which is mainly of development nature and has therefore been validly criticised.

Raising Taxes to Control Inflation. *As an alternative to reduction in Government expenditure, the taxes can be increased to reduce aggregate demand.* Fcr this purpose especially personal direct taxes such as income tax, wealth tax, corporate tax can be raised. The hike in taxes reduces the disposable incomes of the people and thereby forces them to reduce their consumption demand. Note that in Fig. 26.3 as a result of hike in personal taxes it is the decrease in consumption-demand (*C*) component which will cause the aggregate demand curve $C + I + G_2$ to shift downward. Since, as shown above, the magnitude of tax multiplier is smaller than the expenditure multiplier, the tax revenue will be raised by a greater amount to achieve contraction in national income by Y_2Y_F.

Disposing of Budget Surplus. As we have seen above, to control demand-pull inflation, the Government either reduces its expenditure or raises taxes to lower aggregate demand for goods and services. Reduction in expenditure or hike in taxes results in decrease in budget deficits (if occurring before such steps) or in the emergence of budget surplus if the Government was having balanced budget prior to the adoption of anti-inflationary fiscal policy measures. Let us assume that anti-inflationary fiscal policy results in budget surplus. Anti-inflationary impact of budget surplus depends to a good extent on how the Government disposes of this budget surplus. There are two ways in which budget surplus can be disposed of: (1) reducing or retiring public debt and (2) impounding public debt.

We examine below the anti-inflationary effects of these two ways of disposing of the budget surplus.

1. **Retiring Public Debt.** The budget surplus created by anti-inflationary policy can be used by the Government to pay back the outstanding debt. However, using budget surplus for retiring public debt will weaken its anti-inflationary effect. In paying off the debt held by the public, the Government will be returning the money to the public which it has collected through taxes. Further, this will also add to the money supply with the public. The general public will spend a part of the money so received which will raise consumption demand. Besides, retiring of public debt will result in the expansion of money supply in the money

market which will tend to lower the rate of interest. The lower rate of interest will stimulate consumption and investment demand while anti-inflationary policy requires that they should be reduced.

2. **Impounding of Public Debt.** To realise a large anti-inflationary effect of budget surplus it is desirable to impound the surplus fund. Impounding surplus funds means that they should be kept idle. Thus by impounding the budget surplus, the Government shall be withdrawing some income or purchasing power from the income-expenditure stream and thus will not create any inflationary pressures to offset the deflationary impact of the budget surplus. To conclude, the impounding of budget surplus is a better method of disposing of budget surplus than of paying off public debt.

NON-DISCRETIONARY FISCAL POLICY: AUTOMATIC STABILISERS

There is an alternative to the use of discretionary fiscal policy which generally involves problems of lags in recognising the problem of recession or inflation and lag of taking appropriate action to tackle the problem. In this non-discretionary fiscal policy, *the tax structure and expenditure pattern are so designed that taxes and Government spending vary automatically in appropriate direction with the changes in national income.* That is, these taxes and expenditure pattern *without any special deliberate action* by the Government and Parliament automatically raise aggregate demand in times of recession and reduce aggregate demand in times of boom and inflation and thereby help in ensuring economic stability. These fiscal measures are therefore called *automatic stabilisers* or *built-in stabilisers.* Since these automatic stabilizers do not require any fresh deliberate policy action or legislation by the Government, they represent non-discretionary fiscal policy. Built-instability of tax revenue and Government expenditure of transfer payments and subsidies is created because they vary with national income. These taxes and expenditure automatically bring about appropriate changes in aggregate demand and reduce the impact of recession and inflation that might occur in an economy at some times. This means that because of the existence of these automatic or built-in stabilisers recession and inflation will be shorter and less intense than otherwise be the case. Important automatic fiscal stabilisers are personal income taxes, corporate income taxes, transfer payments such as unemployment compensation, welfare benefits, corporate dividends.

We discuss below these taxes, revenue from which varies directly with the change in national income.

Personal Income Taxes. The tax rate structure is so designed that revenue from these taxes directly varies with income. Moreover, personal income taxes have progressive rates; the higher rates are charged from the upper income brackets. As a result, when national income increases during expansion and inflation, increasing percentage of the people's income are paid to the Government. Thus, through causing a decline in their disposable income these taxes automatically reduce people's consumption and therefore aggregate demand. This decline in aggregate demand because of imposition of progressive personal income taxes tends to check inflation from becoming more severe. On the other hand, when national income declines at times of recession, the tax revenue declines as well which prevents aggregate demand from falling by the same proportion as the decline in income.

Corporate Income Taxes. Companies, or corporations as they are called now, also pay a percentage of their profits as tax to the Government. Like personal income taxes, corporate income tax rate is also generally higher at higher levels of corporate profits. As recession and inflation affect corporate taxes greatly, they have a powerful stabilising effect on aggregate demand; the revenue from them rises greatly during inflation and boom which tends to reduce aggregate demand, and revenue from them falls greatly during recession which tends to offset the decline in aggregate demand.

Transfer Payments: Unemployment Compensation and Welfare Benefits. When there is recession and as a result unemployment increases, the Government has to spend more on compensation for unemployment and other welfare programmes such as food stamps, rent subsidies, subsidies to farmers. This hike in Government expenditure tends to make recession short-lived and less intense.

On the other hand, when at times of boom and inflation national income increases and therefore unemployment falls, the Government curtails its programme of social benefits which results in lowering Government expenditure. The smaller spending by the Government helps to control inflation.

Corporate Dividend Policy. With economic fluctuations, corporate profits also rise and fall. However, corporations do not so quickly increase or reduce dividends in tune with fluctuations in profits and follow a *fairly stable dividend policy.* This permits the individuals to spend more during recession and spend less than would have the case if dividends were lowered in time of recession and raised in conditions of boom and inflation. Thus, fairly stable dividends tend to cushion a recession and curb inflation by stabilising consumption expenditure.

Conclusion

It follows from above that automatic stabilisers reduce the intensity of business fluctuations, that is, both recession and inflation. However, the automatic or built-in stabilisers cannot alone correct the recession and inflation significantly. According to an estimate made for the U.S.A., automatic stabilisers have been able to reduce fluctuations in national income only by one-third. Therefore, the role of discretionary fiscal policy, namely, deliberate and explicit changes in tax rates and amount of Government expenditure are required to cure recession and curb inflation.

CROWDING-OUT EFFECT AND EFFECTIVENESS OF FISCAL POLICY

The critics of Keynesian theory have pointed out that expansionary effect of fiscal policy is not as much large as Keynesian economists suggest. In the Keynesian theory it is asserted that when Government increases its expenditure without raising taxes or when it reduces taxes without changing expenditure, it will have a large expansionary effect on national income. In other words, deficit budget would lead to the large increase in aggregate demand and thereby help to expand national output and income. However, it has been pointed that the above analysis of effect of expansionary fiscal policy of budget deficit ignores the effect of increase in Government expenditure or budget deficit on private investment. It has been argued that increase in Government expenditure or creation of budget deficit adversely affects private investment which offsets to a good extent the expansionary effect of budget deficit. This adverse effect comes about as increase in Government expenditure or reduction in taxes causes rate of interest to go up. There are two ways in which rise in rate of interest is explained. First, within the framework of Keynesian theory increase in Government expenditure leads to the rise in national output which raises the transactions demand for money. Given the supply of money in the economy, the increase in transactions demand for money will cause the rate of interest to go up. Secondly, in order to finance its budget deficit the Government will borrow funds from the market. This will raise the demand for loanable funds which will bring about rise in the rate of interest.

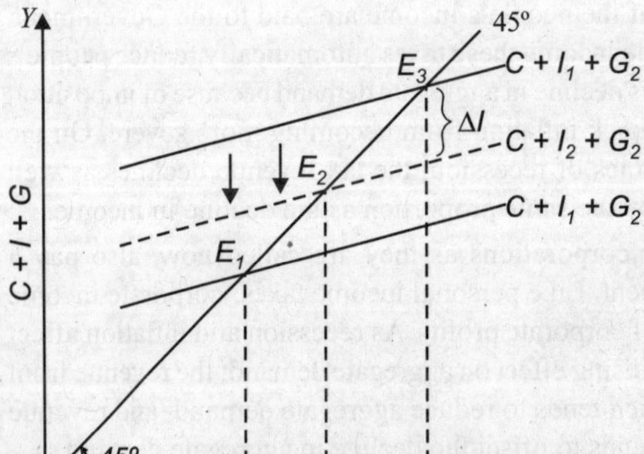

Fig. 26.4. *Effect of Crowding Out on National Output or Income*

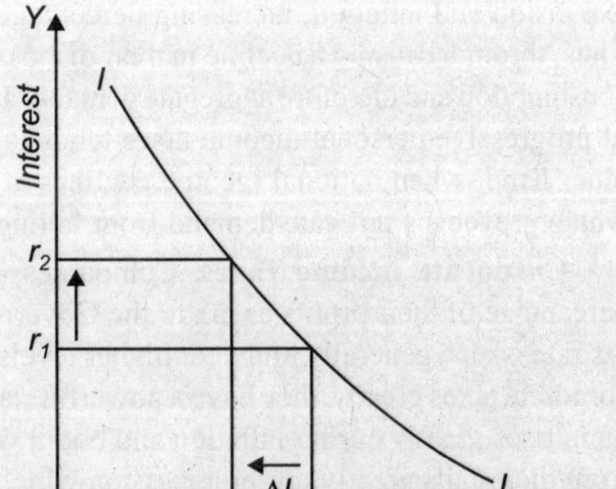

Fig. 26.5. *Crowding Out of Private Investment*

Whatever the mechanism the budget deficit or increase in Government expenditure to achieve expansion in national income and output will cause the rate of interest to go up. The rise in the rate of interest will discourage private investment. As we know from the theory of investment, at a higher rate of interest, private investment declines. Thus, *increase in Government expenditure or fiscal policy of budget deficit crowds out private investment.* This fall in private investment as a result of the rise in rate of interest will offset or cancel out a part of the expansionary effect of increase in Government expenditure. The magnitude of this crowding out effect depends on the elasticity of the investment demand. If investment demand is more elastic, the decrease in private investment consequent to the rise in rate of interest will be quite substantial and will greatly offset the expansionary effect of the increase in Government expenditure. On the contrary, if investment demand is relatively inelastic, the rise in rate of interest will lead to only a small decline in private investment and therefore crowding out effect will be relatively small.

It, therefore, follows that the magnitude of crowding out weakens the effectiveness of fiscal policy. The crowding out effect of expansionary fiscal policy and its effect on national output and employment is graphically shown in Fig. 26.4 and 26.5. To begin with, the economy is in equilibrium at Y_1 level of income where aggregate demand curve $C + I_1 + G_1$ intersects the 45° line and determines Y_1 level of income. Let us assume that this is much below the potential or full-employment level of output. Suppose in order to raise the level of national income and output, the Government raises its expenditure from G_1 to G_2 so that the aggregate demand curve shifts upward to the new position $C + I_1 + G_2$ which intersects the 45° line at point E_3. With increase in Government expenditure national income will rise by $\Delta G \times$ multiplier, that is, by $\Delta G \times \left(\frac{1}{1-MPC}\right)$. In the absence of crowding out effect, national income will rise to Y_3. This change in national income, ΔY or by Y_1Y_3 is equal to the increase in Government expenditure (G) times the value of multiplier $\frac{1}{1-MPC}$. However, as explained above, the increase in Government expenditure or the creation of budget deficit causes the rate of interest to rise, say from r_1 to r_2 (See Figure 26.5). It will be seen from Fig. 26.5 that with the rise in interest from r_1 to r_2, private investment decreases from I_1 to I_2. Now, with the decline in private investment expenditure, aggregate expenditure curve in Fig. 26.4 shifts below to the new lower position $C + I_2 + G_2$ (dotted) and as a result new equilibrium is reached at Y_2 level of income. Thus, net result of increase in Government expenditure (ΔG) and crowding out of private investment equal to I_1I_2 or ΔI is the expansion in national income equal to only Y_1Y_2 which is relatively very small as compared to the rise in income by Y_1Y_3 in the absence of crowding out effect. Thus, the crowding out effect has weakened the expansionary effect of fiscal policy.

However, in view of this author crowding out effect has been blown out of all proportions by the critics of Keynes. As a matter of fact, when Government raises its expenditure, it leads to a large increase in aggregate demand for several goods and services through working of the multiplier. This rising aggregate demand improves investment climate by raising expectations of making profits by the private sector. As a result, the investment demand curve *II* shown in Fig. 26.5 will shift outward to the right showing that at each rate of interest more private investment will be forthcoming. Thus, while negative crowding out effect takes place as a result of moving upward along the given investment demand curve, there is positive effect of increase in aggregate demand on private investment which occurs as a result of rightward shift in the investment demand curve, Thus, we see that crowding out effect is a highly controversial issue of macroeconomics.

QUESTIONS FOR REVIEW

1. What is meant by fiscal policy? Why did Keynes argue for the adoption of proper fiscal policy as an instrument of demand management to get out of depression ?
2. Explain the various objectives of fiscal policy in the advanced developed economies.
3. Explain the role of fiscal policy in overcoming recession and in achieving economic stability at full-employment level.
4. What is meant by discretionary fiscal policy? How does it differ from the fiscal policy of automatic stabilisers? Explain the effectiveness of discretionary fiscal policy in curing recession and attaining equilibrium at full employment level.
5. Expansionary fiscal policy and expansionary monetary policy are complementary with each other.
6. What is effective demand ? How will it change if the Government covers its entire expenditure by *(a)* raising tax or *(b)* printing more currency ?
7. Explain fiscal policy measures to control inflation. How far do you think they can be effective?
8. In an inflationary situation, the task of fiscal policy is to close the inflationary gap by reducing government expenditure or raising taxes. Discuss.
9. What is balanced budget multiplier ? Explain that even balanced budget multiplier has an expansionary effect.
10. Derive mathematically to show that the balanced budget multiplier is equal to one.
11. What is meant by crowding out effect ? Show how the expansionary effect of fiscal policy is reduced by the crowding out effect.
12. Increase in government expenditure, especially financed by borrowing from the open market, crowds out private investment. Discuss.
13. How does mechanism of crowding out of private investment work? Does it always occur ?
14. How is private investment affected if increase in Government spending is financed by sale of Government bonds ? Do you think borrowing from the Central Bank to finance budget deficit is preferable if desired expansionary effect is to be realised ?

CHAPTER 27

Economic Stabilisation : Mnetary Policy

Introduction

Monetary policy is another important instrument with which objectives of macroeconomic policy can be achieved. It is worth noting that it is the Central Bank of a country which formulates and implements the monetary policy in a country. In some countries such as India the Central Bank (the Reserve Bank is the Central Bank of India) works on behalf of the Government and acts according to its directions and broad guidelines. However, in some countries such as the USA, the Central Bank (*i.e.*, Federal Reserve Bank System) enjoys an independent status and pursues its independent policy. Like the fiscal policy, the broad objectives of monetary policy are to establish equilibrium at full-employment level of output, to ensure price stability and to promote economic growth of the economy. Monetary policy is concerned with changing the supply of money stock and rate of interest for the purpose of stabilising the economy at full-employment or potential output level by influencing the level of aggregate demand. More specifically, at times of recession monetary policy involves the adoption of some monetary tools which tend to increase the money supply and lower interest rates so as to stimulate aggregate demand in the economy. On the other hand, at times of inflation, monetary policy seeks to contract the aggregate spending by tightening the money supply or raising the rate of interest.

It may however be noted that in a developing country such as India, in addition to achieving equilibrium at full-employment or potential output level, monetary policy has also to promote and encourage economic growth both in the industrial and agricultural sectors of the economy. Thus, in the context of developing countries the following three are the important goals or objectives of monetary policy:

(1) to ensure economic stability at full-employment or potential level of output;
(2) to achieve price stability by controlling inflation and deflation; and
(3) to promote and encourage economic growth in the economy.

In line with the above goals of monetary policy it has often been asserted by Governors of Reserve Bank of India that *growth with price stability is the goal of monetary policy of the Reserve Bank of India*. The role of monetary policy in achieving economic stability at a higher level of output and employment will be discussed below and its role in promoting economic growth in developing countries with special reference to India will be explained and critically examined at length in a later chapter.

Tools of Monetary Policy

There are four major tools or instruments of monetary policy which can be used to achieve economic and price stability by influencing aggregate demand or spending in the economy. They are:

1. Open market operations;
2. Changing the bank rate;
3. Changing the cash reserve ratio; and
4. Undertaking selective credit controls.

How these tools of monetary policy work to influence aggregate spending and economic activity has been explained in a previous chapter. We shall explain how these various tools can be used for formulating a proper monetary policy to influence levels of aggregate output, employment and prices in the economy. In times of recession or depression, *expansionary monetary policy* or what is also called *easy money policy* is adopted which raises aggregate demand and thus stimulates the economy. On the other hand, in times of inflation and excessive expansion, *contractionary monetary policy* or what is also called *tight money policy* is adopted to control inflation and achieve price stability through reducing aggregate demand in the economy. We discuss below both these policies.

EXPANSIONARY MONETARY POLICY TO CURE RECESSION OR DEPRESSION

When the economy is faced with recession or involuntary cyclical unemployment, which comes about due to fall in aggregate demand, the central bank intervenes to cure such a situation. Central Bank takes steps to expand the money supply in the economy and/or lower the rate of interest with a view to increase the aggregate demand which will help in stimulating the economy. The following three monetary policy measures are adopted as a part of an expansionary monetary policy to cure recession and to establish the equilibrium of national income at full-employment level of output.

1. The central bank undertakes open market operations and *buys securities in the open market.* Buying of securities by the central bank from the public, chiefly from commercial banks, will lead to the increase in reserves of the banks or amount of currency with the general public. With greater reserves, commercial banks can issue more credit to the investors and businessmen for undertaking more investment. More private investment will cause aggregate demand curve to shift upward. Thus buying of securities will have an expansionary effect.

2. The Central Bank *may lower the bank rate or what is also called discount rate*, which is the rate of interest charged by the central bank of a country on its loans to commercial banks. At a lower bank rate, the commercial banks will be induced to borrow more from the central bank and will be able to issue more credit at the lower rate of interest to businessmen and investors. This will not only make credit cheaper but also increase the availability of credit or money supply in the economy. The expansion in credit or money supply will increase the investment demand which will tend to raise aggregate output and income.

3. Thirdly, the *central bank may reduce the Cash Reserve Ratio (CRR) to be kept by the commercial banks.* In countries like India, this is a more effective and direct way of expanding credit and increasing money supply in the economy by the central bank. With lower reserve requirements, a large amount of funds is released for providing loans to businessmen and investors. As a result, credit expands and investment increases in the economy which has an expansionary effect on output and employment. In April 1996, when *Reserve Bank* lowered the CRR from 14 per cent to 13 per cent, it was estimated that this would release funds equal to ₹ 5,000 crores for the banks and thereby would significantly increase their lending capacity.

Similar to the Cash Reserve Ratio (CRR), in India there is another monetary instrument, namely *Statutory Liquidity Ratio* (SLR) used by the Reserve Bank to change the lending capacity and therefore credit availability in the economy. As explained in a previous chapter, according to Statutory Liquidity Ratio, in addition to the Cash Reserve Ratio (CRR) banks have to keep a certain minimum proportion of their deposits in the form of some specified liquid assets such as Government securities. To increase the lendable resources of the banks, Reserve Bank can lower this Statutory Liquidity Ratio (SLR). Thus, when Reserve Bank of India lowers statutory liquidity ratio (SLR), the credit availability for the private sector will increase.

It may be noted that the use of all the above tools of monetary policy leads to an increase in reserves or liquid resources with the banks. Such reserves are the basis on which banks expand their credit by lending, the increase in reserves raises the money supply in the economy, Thus, *appropriate monetary policy at times of recession or depression can increase the availability of credit and also lower the cost of credit.* This leads to more private investment spending which has an expansionary effect on the economy.

How Expansionary Monetary Policy Works : Keynesian Transmission Mechanism

Now, it is important to understand how expansionary monetary policy works to cause increase in output and employment and thus help the economy to recover from recession. In Keynes's theory, rate of interest is determined by the demand for and supply of money. According to Keynesian theory, expansion in money supply causes the rate of interest to fall. An this fall in the rate of interest will encourage businessmen to borrow more for investment spending. As is well known, *rate of interest is the opportunity cost of funds invested for purchasing capital goods.* As rate of interest falls, it becomes profitable to invest more in producing or buying capital goods. Thus, fall in the rate of interest rate raises the investment expenditure which is an important component of aggregate demand. The increase in aggregate demand causes expansion in aggregate output, national income and employment. How, according to Keynesian view, expansion in money supply can help to cure recession is illustrated in Fig. 27.1. In panel (*a*) of Fig. 27.1 it will be seen that when as a result of some measures taken by the central bank, the money supply increases from M_1 to M_2, the rate of interest falls from r_1 to r_2. It will be seen from panel (*b*) that with this fall in rate of interest, investment increases from I_1 to I_2. Now, in panel (*c*), it is shown how the increase in investment expenditure from I_1 to I_2 shifts the aggregate demand curve $(C + I_1 + G)$ upward so that the new aggregate demand curve $C + I_2 + G$ intersects the 40° line at point E_2 and thus establishes equilibrium at full-employment output level Y_F. It may be noted that with the given increase in investment how much aggregate output or national income will increase depends on the size of income multiplier which is determined by marginal propensity to consume. The greater the size of multiplier, the greater the impact of increment in investment on expansion of output and income.

From above, it is clear that monetary policy can play an important role in stimulating the economy and ensuring stability at full-employment level. But it is worth mentioning that there are several weak links in the full chain of increase in money supply achieving a significant expansion in economic activity. In fact, *Keynes himself was of the view that in times of depression, monetary policy will be ineffective in reviving the economy and therefore he laid stress on the adoption of fiscal policy to overcome depression.*

The first weak link in the above argument of expansionary monetary policy relates to the elasticity of money demand (*i.e.*, liquidity preference) curve M^d in panel (*a*) of Fig. 27.1. As shall be explained at length below, if demand for money curve M^d is nearly flat (*i.e.*, highly elastic), the increase in money supply by the central bank will not greatly affect the rate of interest and consequently further steps of significant expansion in investment and aggregate demand will not be realized. Besides, even if money demand curve is elastic and, therefore, expansion of money supply lowers the rate of interest significantly, the investment may not rise much. This is because if the investment demand curve is steep or inelastic, that is, investment is not sensitive to the changes in rate of interest, the fall in the rate of interest will fail to cause any significant increase in investment. As a result, aggregate demand curve will not change much and expansionary effect on output and employment will not be realised.

Further, the effect of increase in investment on output and employment depends on the size of multiplier. If there are several leakages in the multiplier process, even increase in investment may not bring about much change in output and employment. Thus, because of several weak links in the process or chain of expansion in money supply bringing about expansion, Keynes remarked that *there are many a slip between the cup and the lip.* Therefore, for all these reasons (especially because of the liquidity trap in the demand for money curve at lower rates of interest), Keynes was of the view that monetary policy is not an effective instrument in bringing about revival of the economy from the depressed state.

It may however be noted that modern Keynesians do not share the pessimistic view of the effectiveness of monetary policy. They think that liquidity preference curve is not flat and further that investment demand is fairly sensitive to the changes in the rates of interest. Therefore,

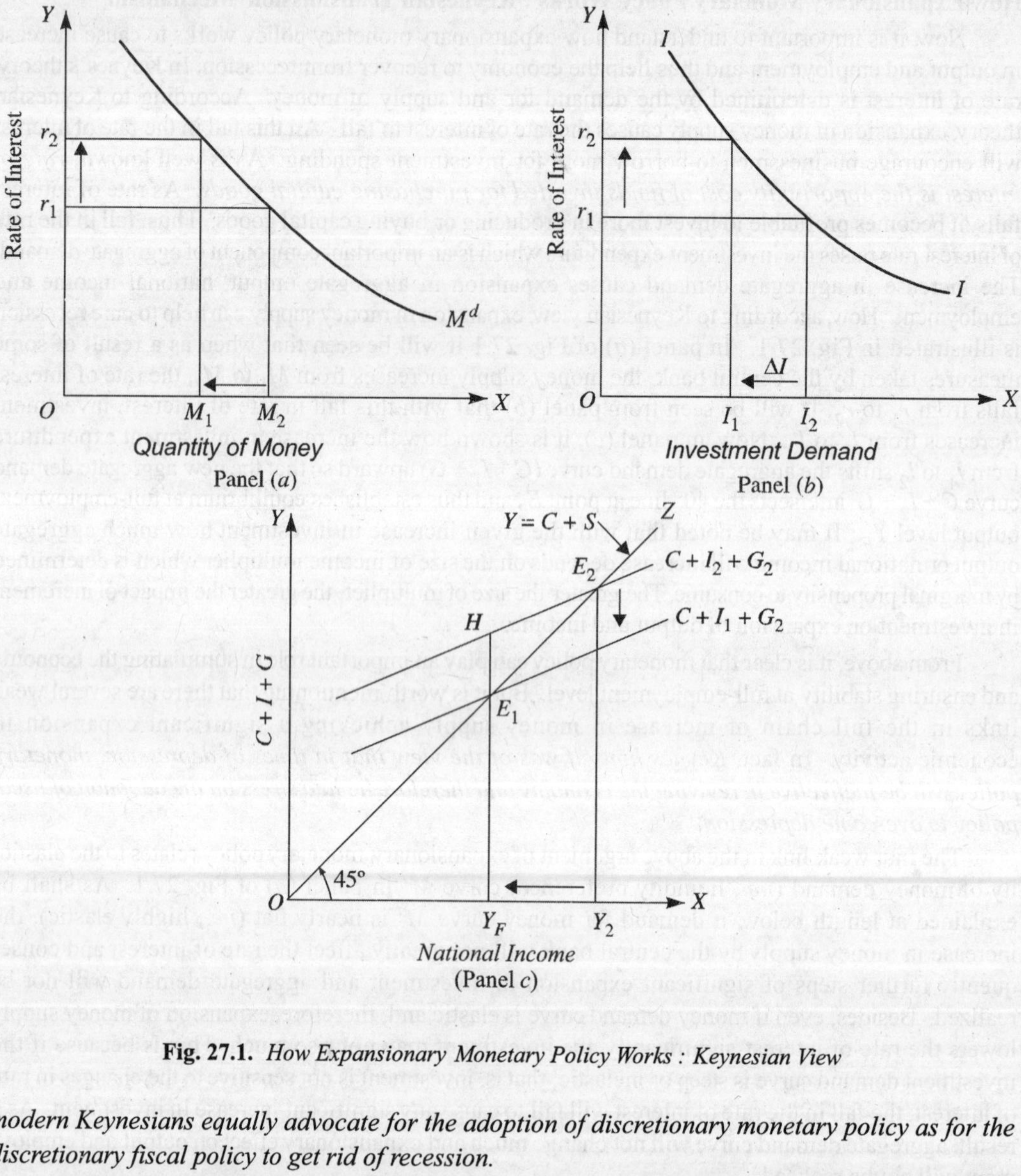

Fig. 27.1. *How Expansionary Monetary Policy Works : Keynesian View*

modern Keynesians equally advocate for the adoption of discretionary monetary policy as for the discretionary fiscal policy to get rid of recession.

TIGHT MONETARY POLICY TO CONTROL INFLATION

When aggregate demand rises sharply due to large consumption and investment expenditure or more imprantly, due to the large increase in Government expenditure relative to its revenue resulting in huge budget deficits, a demand-pull inflation occurs in the economy. Besides, when there is too much creation of money for one reason or the other, it generates inflationary pressures in the economy. To check the demand-pull inflation which has been major problem in India and several other countries in recent years the adoption of *contractionary* monetary policy which is popularly called tight monetary policy is called for. Note that tight or restrictive money policy is one which reduces the availability of credit and also raises its cost. The following monetary measures which constitute tight money policy are gen-erally adopted to control inflation:

1. *The Central Bank sells the Government securities to the banks, other depository institutions and the general public through open market operations.* This action will reduce the reserves with the banks and liquid funds with the general public. With less reserves with the banks, their lending capacity will be reduced. Therefore, they will have to reduce their demand deposits by refraning from giving new loans as old loans as old loans are paid back. As a result, money supply in the economy will shrink.

2. *The bank rate may also be raised which will discourage the banks to take loans from the central bank.* This will tend to reduce their liquidity and also induce them to raise their own lending rates. Thus this will reduce the availability of credit and also raise its cost. This will lead to the reduction in investment spending and help in reducing inflationary pressures.

It may be noted that in India changes in bank rate have not been generally used to bring stability in the economy. It is the instruments of **repo rate and reverse repo rate changes** that have often been used to fight inflation and recessionary situation. *Repo rate is the interest rate at which Reserve Bank of India lends funds to the commercial banks for a short period of time.* To control inflation repo rate is raised. Hike in repo rate raises the cost of funds for the banks which, if they do not have excess reserves or enough liquidity, would raise their lending rates. The rise in lending rates of banks which will raise the borrowing costs for businessmen will lead to the reduction in demand for bank credit and thus lower investment and consumpiton demand. The opposite happens when to fight recession the RBI lowers repo rate and thus reducing lending rate for the banks.

3. The most important anti-inflationary measure is *raising of statutory Cash Reserve Ratio (CRR).* Rise in cash reserve ratio (CRR) reduces cash reserves of banks. To meet the new higher reserve requirements, banks will reduce their lending, that is, credit availability. This will have a direct effect on the contraction of money supply in the economy and help in controlling demand-pull inflation. Besides Cash Reserve Ratio (CRR), the Statutory Liquidity Ratio (SLR) can also be increased through which excess reserves of the banks are mopped up resulting in contraction in credit.

4. Fourthly, an important anti-inflationary measure is the use of qualitative credit control, namely, *raising of minimum margins for obtaining loans from banks against the stocks of sensitive commodities* such as foodgrains, oilseeds, cotton, sugar, vegetable oil. As a result of this measure, businessmen themselves will have to finance to a greater extent the holding of inventories of goods and will be able to get less credit from banks. This selective credit control has been extensively used in India to control inflationary pressures.

How the Tight Monetary Policy Works : Keynesian Transmission Mechanism

It is important to understand how tight monetary policy works to check inflation. As explained above, tight monetary policy seeks to reduce the money supply through contraction of credit in the economy and also raising the cost of credit, that is lending rates of interest. The reduction in money supply itself raises the rate of interest. The higher interest rate reduces investment spending which results in lowering of aggregate demand curve ($C+I+G$). The decrease in aggregate demand tends to restrain demand-pull inflation. How tight money policy helps in checking inflation is graphically shown in Fig. 27.2. Let us assume that full-employment level of national income is Y_F as depicted in panel (*c*) of Fig. 27.2. Now, if due to a large budget deficit and excessive creation of money supply, aggregate demand curve shifts to $C+I_2+G_2$; inflationary gap of E_1H comes to exist at full-employment level. That is, the sum of consumption expenditure, private investment spending and Government expenditure exceeds the full-employment level of output by E_1H. This creates a demand-pull inflation causing rise in prices. Though with aggregate demand curve $C+I_2+G_2$ equilibrium reaches at point E_2 and as a result national income increases but only in money terms ; real income or output level remaining constant at OY_F.

Now, it will be seen from panel (*a*) that if tight money policy succeeds in reducing money supply from M_2 to M_1, the rate of interest will rise from r_1 to r_2. Panel (*b*) of Fig. 27.2 shows that at a higher interest rate r_2, private investment falls from I_2 to I_1. This reduction in investment expenditure shifts aggregate demand curve $C + I_2 + G_2$ downward to $C + I_1 + G_2$ and in this way inflationary gap is closed and equilibrium at full-employment output level Y_F is once again established. In our figure it

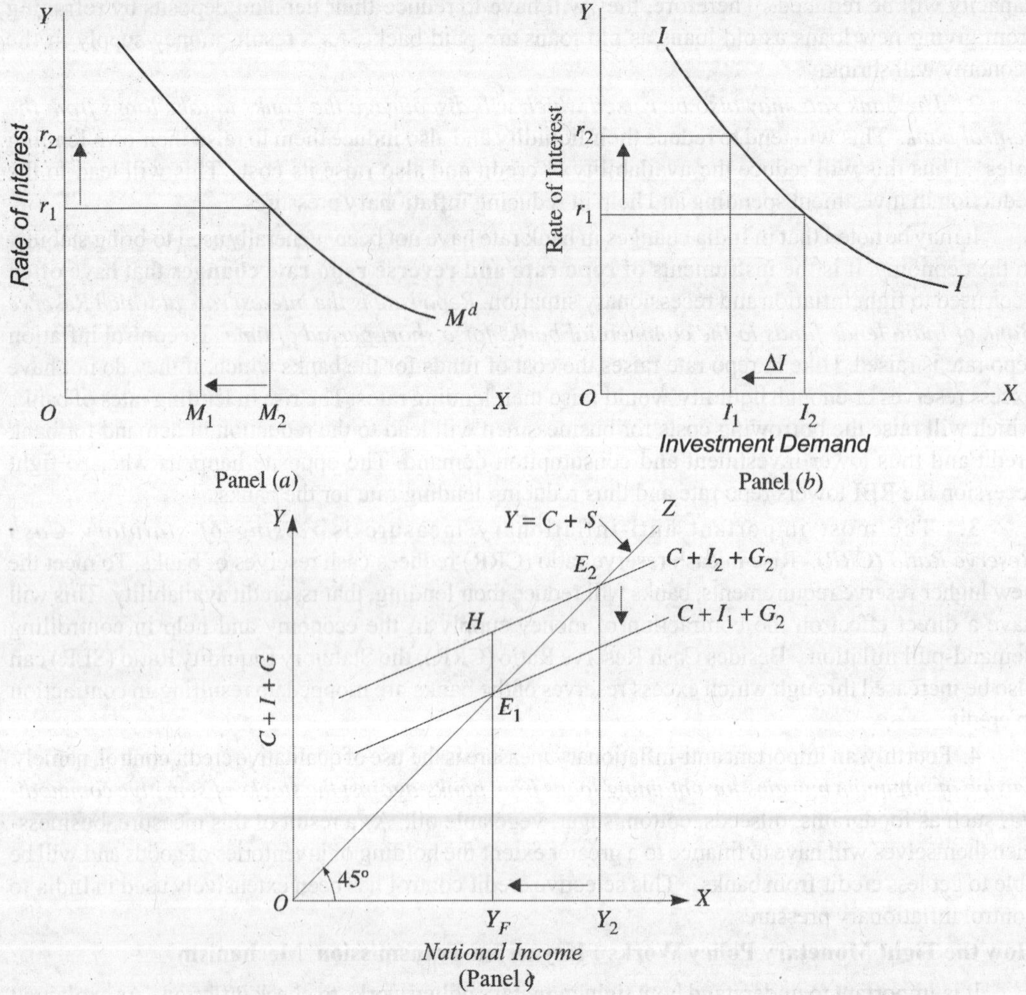

Fig. 27.2. *How Anti-Inflationary Monetary Policy Works : Keynesian View*

has been assumed that there is contraction of money supply from M_2 to M_1 and as a result rise in rate of interest from r_1 to r_2 is sufficient to reduce investment expenditure equal to $I_2 - I_1$ which is equal to inflationary gap and in this way macroeconomic equilibrium without any inflationary pressure is established at output level Y_F.

It should be further remembered that in our analysis of the successful working of the tight monetary policy it is assumed that demand for money curve (*i.e.*, liquidity preference curve) is fairly steep so as to push up the rate of interest from r_1 to r_2 and further that investment demand curve *II* in panel (*b*) of Fig. 27.2 is fairly elastic so that rise in rate of interest from r_1 to r_2 is sufficient to reduce investment by $I_2 - I_1$ or ΔI. If these conditions regarding the slopes of the money demand curve and investment demand curve represent the real world situation, then tight monetary policy will succeed in controlling inflation and ensuring price stability.

To sum up, Keynesian view of how expansionary and contractionary (tight) monetary policies work to achieve the twin goals of price stability and equilibrium at full-employment level of output is shown in the accompanying box.

Monetary Policy : Keynesian Transmission Mechanism

Expansionary Monetary Policy	Tight Monetary Policy
Problem : Recession and Unemployment	***Problem*** : Inflation
Measures: (1) Central Bank buys securities through open market operations	***Measures***: (1) Central Bank sells securities through open market operations
(2) It reduces cash reserve ratio (CRR)	(2) It raises Cash Reserve Ratio (CRR) and Statutory Liquidity Ratio (SLR)
(3) It lowers bank rate	(3) It raises Bank Rate
	(4) It raises maximum margin against holding of stocks of goods.
↓ Money supply increases	↓ Money supply decreases
↓ Interest rate falls	↓ Interest rate rises
↓ Investment increases	↓ Investment expenditure declines
↓ Aggregate demand increases	↓ Aggregate demand declines
↓ Aggregate output increases by a multiple of the increase in investment	↓ Price level or inflation rate falls

Liquidity Trap and Ineffectiveness of Monetary Policy

Keynes and his early followers doubted the effectiveness of monetary policy in pulling the economy out of depression. They therefore emphasized the role of fiscal policy for fighting severe recession. According to Keynes and his followers, during severe recession people have a high elastic demand for money at low rates of interest. At low rates of interest banks hold on to whatever money

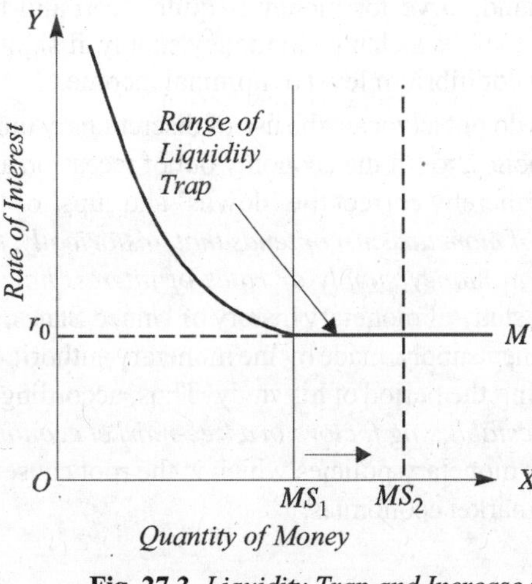

Fig. 27.3. *Liquidity Trap and Increase in Money Supply*

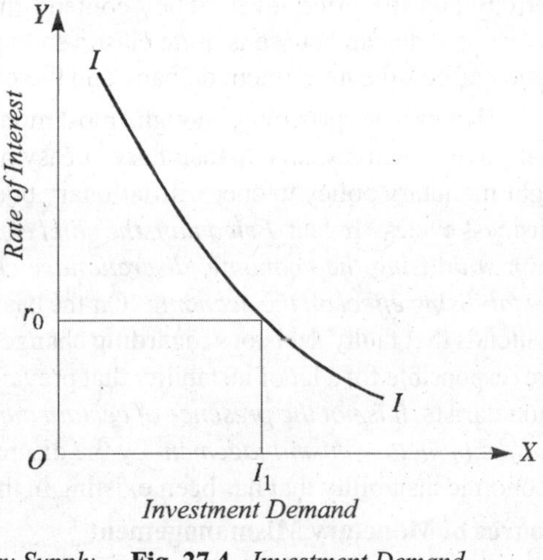

Fig. 27.4. *Investment Demand*

reserves they happen to get and the people in general also hold on to whatever money they spare. According to Keynes, demand for money or what he calls liquidity preference is determined mainly by transactions and speculative motives. Whereas transactions demand for money is determined by the level of national income, the speculative demand for money depends on the expectations regarding future rates of interest. During depression, current rate of interest may fall so low that most of the people expect the interest rate to rise in future and therefore they hold on to their money for the present. This makes the demand for money absolutely elastic at a low rate of interest as is shown in Fig. 27.3. It will be seen from Fig. 27.3 that at a low rate of interest r_0 demand curve for money M^d is absolutely elastic showing people demand or hold on to all the increases in money supply beyond MS_1 for speculative purposes and not invest in bonds. Under these circumstances the economy is said to have fallen in a liquidity trap. A liquidity trap occurs when under conditions of depression the economy finds itself in a situation where people hold all the increments in the stock of money and money demand curve M^d takes a horizontal shape.

Suppose during a recession, stock of money is equal to MS_1 and money demand curve is given by M^d. The interaction between these two determines r_0 rate of interest. Suppose now, to pull the economy out of recession, the stock of money supply is expanded to MS_2. A glance at Fig. 27.3 reveals that expansion in money supply from MS_1 to MS_2 does not lower the rate of interest as the economy is operating in the range of liquidity trap. Now, Fig. 27.4 shows that with the rate of interest remaining unchanged at r_0, the level of investment does not rise. With level of investment remaining the same, there is no increase in aggregate demand and the economy remains in a state of depression. Thus, under these circumstances Keynes and his early followers contended that expansionary monetary policy did not help the economy in staging a recovery from recession.

It may, however, he noted that the concept of liquidity trap is not supported by empirical studies. The empirical studies show that demand for money (liquidity preference) never becomes flat and instead it falls throughout. Therefore, modern Keynesians and other economists now believe that monetary policy can play a useful role in stabilising the economy at full-employment level. However, as shall be discussed below, it is the *monetarists* led by Friedman who do not favour discretionary monetary policy to check cyclical instability.

MONETARY POLICY : MONETARIST VIEW

Though most of the modern economists regard both fiscal and monetary policies as important tools for stabilising the economy, there is a group of economists known as *monetarists* led by Friedman who think that changes in money supply are the key determinants in the level of economic activity and the price level. They contend that demand curve for money is quite steep and the investment demand curve is quite elastic so that when there is a change in money supply, it significantly affects the investment demand and therefore the equilibrium level of nominal income.

However, surprisingly, enough, most monetarists do not advocate the use of discretionary monetary policy, namely, an expansionary or easy money policy, to lift the economy out of recession and tight monetary policy to check inflationary boom and thereby correct the `downs' and `ups' of the business cycles. In fact, *Friedman, the chief exponent of monetarism, contends that, historically, far from stabilising the economy, discretionary changes in money supply or rates of interest have a destabilising effect on the economy.* On the basis of his study of monetary history of United States, he contends that faulty decisions regarding changes in money supply, made by the monetary authorities, are responsible for a lot of instability that prevailed during the period of his study. Thus, according to monetarists, *it is not the presence of certain inherent destabilising factors in a free-market economy but the monetary mismanagement* by the discretionary monetary policies which is the root cause of economic instability that has been existing in the free-market economies.

Source of Monetary Mismanagement

According to monetarists, there are two important sources of monetary mismanagement : (1) *variable time lags* concerning the effect of money supply on the nominal income and (2) *treating interest rate as the target of monetary policy* for influencing investment demand for stabilising the economy. We examine below both these sources of monetary mismanagement.

1. Variable Time Lags. First, there is a problem of variable long time lags that occur for changes in money supply to bring about desirable effect on nominal income. From his empirical studies Friedman concludes that it takes six months to two years for the changes in money supply to produce a significant effect on nominal income. Monetarists argue that since it is extremely difficult to know the time lag involved in a specific monetary policy measure adopted to tackle the problem, it is impossible to determine *when* a particular policy measure should be taken and *which policy measure*, expansionary or tight, is suitable under the given situation. In fact, according to the monetarists, in view of the uncertainty about the exact duration of time lags involved, the use of discretionary monetary policy to stabilise the economy may backfire and further intesify the cyclical instability. For example, if expansionary monetary policy is adopted because the various economic indicators show the situation of mild recession, then, due to the time lags involved, say six to eight months, for the policy to yield results, the economic situation might change and becomes reverse during that period and becomes one of mild inflationary situation. Expansionary monetary policy which produces the effect after 6 to 8 months may, therefore, acutally intensify the inflationary situation.

2. Interest Rate as a Wrong Target Variable. The second source of money mismanagement is the wrong target variable chosen by the monetary authorities. Monetarists have asserted that monetary authorities have tried to control the interest rates to stabilise the economy. It has been argued that Central Bank cannot simultaneously stabilise both the interest rate and money supply. By controlling the interest rate it has actually destabilised the economy. For example, if the economy is recovering from recession and is presently approaching full employment with aggregate demand, output, employment and prices all registering a rise, the transactions demand for money will increase. This increase in transactions demand for money will cause the rate of interest to rise. But if the monetary authorities have chosen to stabilise the interest rate, they would adopt tight monetary policy to prevent the interest rate from going up. This will have a recessionary effect and make the economy unstable. Similarly, when the economy is going into recession, it will result in lowering aggregate output and prices. This fall in aggregate output and prices will cause a decline in the transactions demand for money. And the decrease in transactions demand will lead to the fall in interest rate. To prevent this fall in interest rate, if money supply is increased, it will generate instability in the economy rather than removing it.

Monetary Rule : Monetary Policy Prescription

From the above analysis it follows that monetarists are not in favour of stabilising the interest rate, they advocate for the *adoption of a rule rather than pursuing discretionary monetary policy* to stabilise the economy. They prescribe a *rule for the growth of the money supply* to achieve economic grow with stability. According to the monetary rule suggested by Friedman, *money supply should be allowed to grow at the rate equal to the rate of growth of output*. If the economy is expected to grow annually at the rate of 3, 4 or 5 per cent, money supply should also grow at this rate. The grow of output of an economy will absorb the extra money supply created as per this rule, without generating inflationary or recessionary conditions, and will thus ensure stability in the economy. To quote Ritter and Silber, "such a rule would eliminate the major cause of instability in the economy—the capricious and unpredictable impact of counter cyclical monetary policy. As long as the money supply grows at a constant rate each year, be it 3, 4 or 5 per cent, any decline into recession will be temporary. The liquidity provided by a constantly growing money supply will cause the aggregate demand to expand. Similarly, if the supply of money does not rise at a more than average rate, any inflationary increase in spending will burn itself out for lack of fuel.

Monetary rule has been criticised by the Keynesian economists. They have argued that monetary rule will have a destabilising effect. Given that the velocity of money (V) is unstable or variable, increase in money supply (*M*), according to this rule, may not ensure growth of aggregate demand (which, according to monetarist theory, is equal to *MV*) equal to the rate of growth of output in a year which is difficult to predict. Thus, money supply increase may sometimes exceed the growth of output and sometimes fall short of it and as a result may cause sometimes demand-pull inflation and sometimes necessary conditions. Thus, according to Keynesian economists, policy of monetary rule does not guarantee economic stability and it may itself create economic instability.

QUESTIONS FOR REVIEW

1. What is meant by monetary policy ? Briefly explain the instruments of monetary policy.
2. Expaling the objectives of monetary policy.
3. Explain monetary policy measures that should be adopted for curing recession (or depression) and reviving the economy. How does expansionary monetary policy work ? How does Keynesian view in this regard differ from the monetarist view ?
4. What are the factors that determine the effectiveness of monetary policy in reviving the economy from recession ? Why Keynes thought that monetary policy was ineffective in reviving the economy from depression ?
5. What is liquidity trap ? How does it make the expansionary monetary policy ineffective in reviving the economy from recession ?
6. Explain the main instruments of monetary policy that can be adopted to control inflation in the economy.
7. Explain the mechanism through which tight monetary policy works to check inflation. Illustrate diagrammatically.
8. Discretionary monetary policy can play an important role in stabilising the economy at full employment. Discuss.
9. Explain the views of Friedman and his follower modern monetarists regarding monetary policy as a tool of economic stabilisation. In this connection also comment on the monetarist view that interest rate is a wrong target variable of proper monetary policy.
10. What is meant by 'time lags' ? How do they affect the efficiency of monetary policy to stabilise the economy?
11. What are the instruments of monetary policy ? Explain the role of changes in bank rate and open market operations in controlling trade cycles.
12. "Monetary policy for its success depends on fiscal policy." Explain and critically examine this statement.

PART – VII
OPEN ECONOMY MACROECONOMICS

- Determination on National Income in an Open Economy and Foreign Trade Multiplier
- Balance of Payments
- Foreign Exchange Rate

CHAPTER 28

Determination of National Income in an Open Economy and Foreign Trade Multiplier

Introduction

In modern times economies of different countries are integrated with each other though some are more integrated than others. *An open economy is one which has not only trade relations with other countries but has also financial capital flows between it and other economies of the world.* It is because of such openness and integration of the economies of the world that recent financial crisis that occurred in the United States in 2007-09 significantly affected other economies of the world (including that of India) causing global meltdown through its effect on trade and capital flows. Under capital flows, funds flow from one country to another. Foreign trade of goods and services affects product minus and influences the determination of national income of a country as net exports (*i.e.*, exports–imports) is a part of aggregate demand for output produced by an economy. On the other hand, capital flows in an open economy provide funds for financing domestic investment or for financing government budget deficits. If the demand for funds in an economy exceeds domestic national saving, the private sector and Government of an open economy can get them from abroad either through borrowing or direct and portfolio investment by foreign investors. We start with the analysis of impact of inclusion of foreign trade on the determination of national income of a country.

Foreign Trade and National Income in an Open Economy

In the four-sector model of determination of national income, we add the foreign trade sector to the three sectors, namely, households, firms, and Government. Foreign trade, that is, volume of exports and imports of a country also affects the level of national income of a country. We now extend the Keynesian model of determination of national income by including the effect of exports and imports of a country on the generation of income. For example, the exports of India represent the foreign demand and generate income for the Indian people. On the other hand, imports represent the demand for foreign goods by the Indians and generate incomes for the people of other countries. Therefore, imports tend to reduce the domestic aggregate expenditure. It therefore follows that national income will depend on the net exports, that is, exports minus imports ($X - M$) where X stands for exports and M for imports. The exports and imports of a country depend to a great extent on the level of economic activity (that is, the level of output and income of the country). Thus, when the growth of industrial output in India is rapid, it will generate greater demand for imported materials. On the other hand, the higher industrial growth would also cause our exports to rise provided there is demand for our goods abroad. However, in the simple Keynesian model of income determination, exports and imports are considered as autonomous, that is, independent of income, being determined outside the model. Further, as mentioned above, the increase or decrease in aggregate expenditure or demand due to exports and imports depends on the *net exports*, that is, $X-M$ which we may write as NX. If the net exports are positive, there will be addition to the aggregate demand or expenditure of a country. On the other hand, if the net exports are negative, there will be decrease in aggregate expenditure.

When we include net exports (NX) in our analysis we get the following equation for the equilibrium level of income:

$$Y = C + I + G + (X - M) \quad ...(i)$$

where $C = a + b\,(Y - T) = a + bY - bT$

$X - M = NX$

Replacing these values of C and $X–M$ in equation (*i*) above we have

$$Y = a + bY - bT + I + G + NX$$

or $Y(1 - b) = a - bT + I + G + NX$

$$Y = \frac{1}{1-b}\,(a - bT + I + G + NX) \quad ...(ii)$$

Thus, the equilibrium level of income is the sum of all fixed autonomous expenditures (*i.e.*, $a - bT + I + G + NX$) times the value of multiplier $[1/1 - b]$. It is worth noting that in the four-sector model, national income is determined at the level at which saving gap between consumption and income is equal to the sum of investment, Government expenditure and net exports (that is, $I + G + NX$).

Graphic Illustration. In Fig. 28.1, we have depicted the determination of national income when there are positive net exports (that is, when exports exceed imports, NX or $(X - M) > 0$. To obtain the aggregate expenditure curve incorporating the positive net exports (NX) we add the $I + G + NX$ to the consumption function curve C to get the higher aggregate expenditure curve $C + I + G + NX$ which intersects the 45° line at point R and determines a level of income OY. If the net exports NX were negative, that is, imports exceed exports, NX or $(X - M) < 0$, the aggregate demand curve incorporating net exports would lie at a lower level than $C + I + G$ curve and determine a lower level of income.

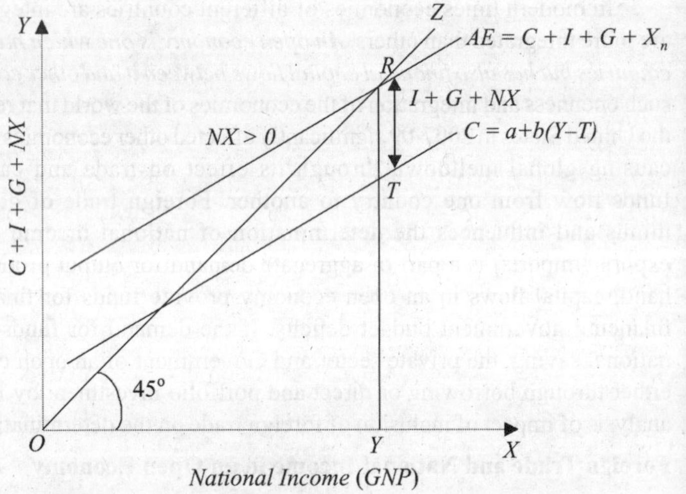

Fig. 28.1. *Determination of National Income in an Open Economy: Four-Sector Model*

The Import Function

So far in our analysis of four-sector model of income determination we have assumed that both exports and imports are constant autonomous items, that is, independent of income. In next two chapters concerning the external sector we shall explain in detail what are the factors that determine exports and imports of a country. In the model of income determination while exports are regarded as constant autonomous factor *determined exogenously* (that is, $X = \overline{X}$), imports are treated as function of two variables, namely, (1) autonomous imports (*i.e.*, independent of income), and (2) level of income.

In an open economy consumers of a country also spend some income on imported goods. The imports of a country depend on its level of income. The higher the level of income, the prices of imported goods and tastes of consumers remaining the same, the greater will be its imports. *The relationship between imports and level of income of a country is called the import function* $M = f(Y)$ where M stands for imports and Y for income of a country.

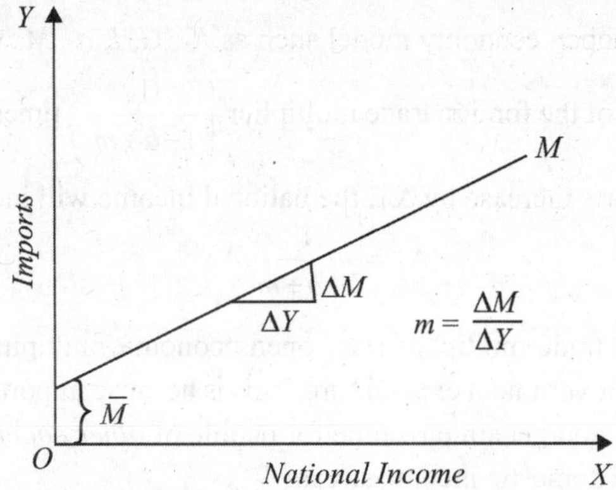

Fig. 28.2. *The Import Function.*

We have shown the import function in Fig. 28.2 where on the *X*-axis the level of national income and on the *Y*-axis imports of a country are measured. It will be seen that even at zero level of national income some imports are undertaken by exporting some capital accumulated in the past or by borrowing from abroad. There are two concepts of propensity to import which should be understood. First, *average propensity to import* is defined as the *proportion or percentage of national income spent on imports*, that is, it is rupee value of imports divided by national income or $\frac{M}{Y}$. Large countries such as the U.S.A., Russia and India have low average propensity to import and small countries such as Great Britain and Holland have high average propensity to import. The average propensity to import in India is between 0.02 and 0.03.

With a part of imports as autonomous, import function can be written as $M = \overline{M} + mY$ where $\overline{M}$ represents autonomous imports, mY represents imports dependent on level of income (Y) and m is marginal propensity to import. Given the marginal propensity to import (m), as income increases, imports (mY) will increase.

Determination of National Income in an Open Economy and Foreign Trade Multiplier

By incorporating the above import function we can derive the complete four-sector model of income determination as follows

$$Y = C + I + G + (X - M) \qquad \ldots(i)$$

Assuming taxes equal to zero, then, $C = a + bY$

and $\quad M = \overline{M} + mY$

Substituting the consumption function and import function in the income equation (*i*) we have

$$Y = a + bY + I + G + \left[X - \left(\overline{M} + mY\right)\right]$$

$$= a + bY + I + G + X - \overline{M} - mY$$

$$Y - bY + mY = a + I + G + X - \overline{M}$$

$$Y(1 - b + m) = a + I + G + X - \overline{M}$$

$$Y = \frac{1}{1 - b + m}(a + I + G + X - \overline{M})$$

where the term $\frac{1}{1-b+m}$ is known as **foreign trade multiplier** whose value is determined by marginal propensity to consume (b) and marginal propensity to import (m). Note that change in any autonomous factor of this open economy model such as X, G, I, a, $\overline{M}$ will cause a change in national income by the value of the foreign trade multiplier $\left(\frac{1}{1-b+m}\right)$ times the change in the amount of the factor. Thus, if exports increase by ΔX, the national income will increase by

$$\Delta Y = \frac{1}{1-b+m} \cdot \Delta X$$

The value of foreign trade multiplier (*i.e.,* open economy multiplier) is less than the closed economy's investment or Government expenditure. This is because imports represent the demand for foreign goods and services and generate income for people of *other countries*. Like saving, imports represent leakage from the domestic income stream.

Graphic Representation of Equilibrium National Income Foreign Trade Multiplier in an Open Economy when Imports Vary with Income

Given that import function is of the form, $M = \overline{M} + mY$ where $\overline{M}$ are autonomous imports and m is marginal propensity to import and therefore mY part of the import function varies with income. To simplify graphic representation of equilibrium national income we assume that autonomous imports $(\overline{M})$ are zero. In Figure 28.3, the solid line OZ is 45° line. To begin with, we draw a line $C + I + G + X$ representing aggregate expenditure curve $(C + I + G + X)$ by adding constant amounts of autonomous fixed amounts of investment (I), government expenditure (G) and exports (X) to the upward-sloping consumption function curve C with a constant term a. However, this aggregate expenditure curve $C + I + G + X$ includes expenditure by consumers, business firms and government on imported goods they use and therefore it does *not represent aggregate planned expenditure on domestically produced goods and services*. To obtain planned aggregate expenditure on domestically imported goods we must subtract the amount of output that is imported at each level of national income (GDP). As stated above, with autonomous imports $(\overline{M})$ assumed to be equal to zero, our

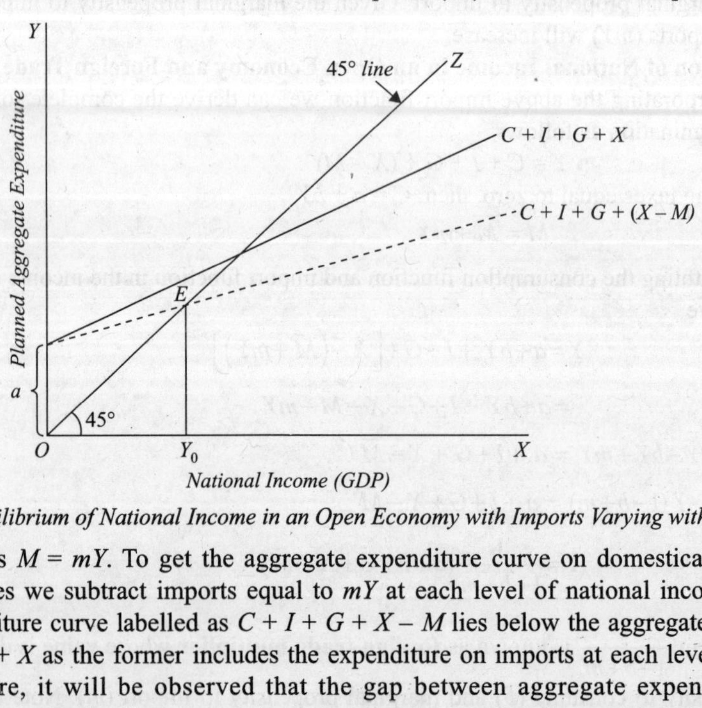

Fig. 28.3 *Equilibrium of National Income in an Open Economy with Imports Varying with Income*

import function is $M = mY$. To get the aggregate expenditure curve on domestically produced goods and services we subtract imports equal to mY at each level of national income. Such an aggregate expenditure curve labelled as $C + I + G + X - M$ lies below the aggregate expenditure curve $C + I + G + X$ as the former includes the expenditure on imports at each level of national income. Therefore, it will be observed that the gap between aggregate expenditure curve

$C+I+G+(X-M)$, and aggregate expenditure curve $C+I+G+X$ goes on widening because, given the propensity to import (m), as national income increases imports which are given by mY go on increasing. Equilibrium national income (GDP) occurs at the level Y_0 because at this curve of aggregate expenditure $C+I+G+(X-M)$ intersects the 45° line OZ.

If now there is increase in exports (X), the curve of aggregate expenditure on domestically produced goods will shift upward as shown in Fig. 28.4 and causes increase in national income to Y_1 by a multiplier that equals $\frac{1}{1-b+m}$ where b stands for MPC and m for marginal propensity to import. Thus, in Figure. 28.4 as a result of increase in exports by ΔX, national income increases by ΔY. It will be found that foreign trade multiplier, $\frac{\Delta Y}{\Delta X}=\frac{1}{1-b+m}$.

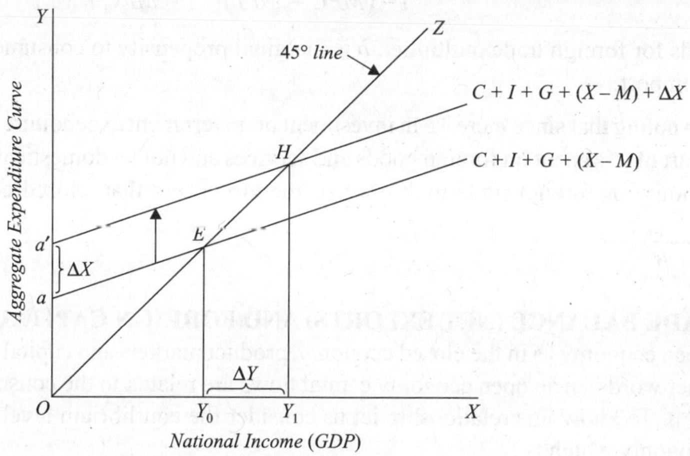

Fig. 28.4. *Depicting Foreign Trade Multiplier*

How the Foreign Trade Multiplier Works ?

The foreign trade multiplier works in the same way as Keynes's investment multiplier. When there is increase in exports, it will cause the increase in income of the exporters and those employed in the export industries. They will save some of the increase in their incomes and will spend a good part of the increases in their incomes on consumer goods, both domestic and imported ones. While savings do not generate further income and represent leakage from the income stream, expenditure on imports leads to the increase in the incomes of the foreign countries from which goods are imported. Thus expenditure on imports also represents a leakage from the income stream as far as domestic economy is concerned. But the increased expenditure on domestic goods as a result of increase in exports will go on increasing incomes in the domestic economy in various successive rounds of spending till the multiplier fully works itself out.

It may be noted that increase in exports of a country can occur due to several reasons. There may be change in tastes or demand of the people of foreign countries for goods of a country. To begin with, the exporters may meet the demand for exported goods by selling their inventories and enjoy higher incomes. But in the next periods, they will make efforts to increase the production of exported goods and employ more workers. This will generate new income and employment in the export industries. But the working of multiplier does not stop here. Those employed in export industries will spend a good part of their increased incomes on goods produced by other industries and in this way increases in income, production and employment will spread in the whole of the domestic economy.

In an open economy when increase in domestic investment or government expenditure takes place, it causes increase in national income, some part of it is spent on imports of goods from foreign countries which therefore causes increase in incomes of foreign countries. Imports are leakage from domestic income stream. Therefore, to determine the foreign trade multiplier we require to know how much increase in income as a result of increase in domestic investment or government expenditure is spent on domestically produced goods. This depends on marginal propensity to import (*MPI* or *m*) and marginal propensity to consume (*MPC* or *b*). The marginal propensity to consume in the open economy on domestically produced goods is given by the difference between marginal propensity to consume (*MPC*) and marginal propensity to import (*MPI*) (that is, *MPC – MPI* or *b – m*). Therefore, in the open economy multiplier which is also called foreign trade multiplier as derived above:

$$K_f = \frac{1}{1-(MPC-MPI)} = \frac{1}{1-MPC+MPI} = \frac{1}{1-b+m}$$

where K_f stands for foreign trade multiplier, *b* is marginal propensity to consume and *m* is marginal propensity to import.

It is worth noting that since increase in investment or government expenditure that causes increase in income, a part of it is spent on foreign goods and services and not on domestically produced goods, the open economy or foreign trade multiplier is, therefore, less than closed economy multiplier, $\frac{1}{1-b+m} < \frac{1}{1-b}$.

TRADE BALANCE (NET EXPORTS) AND FOREIGN CAPITAL FLOWS

In an open economy as in the closed economy, product markets and capital markets are closely related. In other words, in an open economy capital flows are related to the consumption, saving and investment in it. To know this relationship let us consider the equilibrium level of national income in an open economy which is :

$$Y = C + I + G + (X - M) \qquad \ldots (1)$$

where $X - M$ are net exports (*NX*)

Therefore, rearranging the above equation and writing *NX* for $X - M$ we have

$$Y - C - G = I + NX \qquad \ldots (2)$$

Now $Y–C–G$ represents national saving[1] which we represent by *S*.

Writting *S* for national saving ($Y–C–G$) in equation (2) we have

$$S = I + NX \qquad \ldots (2)$$

or $$S - I = NX \qquad \ldots (3)$$

or $$S - I = X–M \qquad \ldots (4)$$

From equation (3) it is evident that difference between domestic saving and domestic investment ($S – I$) equals net exports (*NX*). *When there is difference between domestic saving and investment, it represents mismatch between exports and imports* (that is, net exports (*NX*) will be either positive or negative). This difference between exports and imports of goods and services, that is, positive or negative net exports, must be met by capital flows into or out of the economy. Equation (3) reveals that capital flows between an economy and the foreign ones are related to net exports (*NX*) which are also called *trade balance*. If for a country domestic saving exceeds domestic investment ($S > I$), then the country would have *positive* net exports (*NX*) and equation (3) to hold there will be *capital outflows* which means residents of the country would be lending or investing abroad more than the foreigners would be lending or investing in the country concerned. The equation (3) above shows that these *positive net capital outflows* imply that they will be equal to *positive net exports* (*NX*), that

1. Note that national saving $Y – C – G$ is the sum of private saving ($Y – T – C$) and Government saving ($T – G$). Thus $Y– T – C + T – G = Y – C – G$

is, the country will be exporting more than it will be importing. Foreigners will need financial loans from the domestic firms to buy that country's more goods and services than they are exporting to it. This has been the relationship between Japan and the US. Japan has a trade surplus (*i.e.,* positive net exports) with the US and to enable the US to buy more Japanese goods than Japan is importing from it, it has been lending to the US which has been running a trade deficit, that is, there has been net capital outflows from Japan to the US.

Now, when domestic saving of a country is less than the domestic investment ($S < I$ or $S - I$ is negative), the equation (3) above reveals that the net exports (NX) will be negative (*i.e.,* the country has a trade deficit for its imports of goods and services exceed its exports of them. To enable it meet this trade deficit the country must get capital funds from abroad, that is, there will be *net capital-inflow*. Thus the net capital inflow implies that the country will be borrowing from abroad or receiving foreign investment. The country having negative net exports or deficit trade balance requires foreign capital funds either through borrowing from foreigners or foreign investment so as to enable it to import more goods and services than it is exporting them. For example, in India we have a *deficit in the current account of balance of payments* (which has the same meaning as the concept of trade balance involving both goods and services) for several years now so that foreign saving or capital inflows have contributed to the increase in investment in India, though the share of capital inflows (foreign savings) as a per cent of its GDP in India has been relatively very small.

It follows from above that *international flow of capital to finance investment and international flow of goods and services are two sides of the same coin.*[2]

NUMERICAL PROBLEMS

Problem 1. *An economy is characterised by the following equations:*

$$\begin{aligned} C\ (Consumption) &= 60 + 0.9Y_d \\ I\ (Investment) &= 10 \\ G\ (Government\ expenditure) &= 10 \\ T\ (Tax) &= 0 \\ X\ (Exports) &= 20 \\ M\ (Imports) &= 10 + 0.05\,Y \end{aligned}$$

(a) *What is the equilibrium income?*

(b) *Calculate trade balance.*

(c) *What is the value of foreign trade multiplier ?*

Solution : (*a*) *National Income*

$$\begin{aligned} Y &= C + I + G + NX \\ &= (60 + 0.9\,Y_d) + 10 + 10 + 20 - (10 + 0.05Y) \\ &= 60 + 0.9\,(Y - T) + 10 + 10 + 20 - 10 - 0.05Y \\ &= 60 + 0.9Y - 0 + 30 - 0.05Y \\ Y &= 90 + .85Y \\ Y - 0.85Y &= 90 \\ (1\text{–}0.85)Y &= 90 \\ 0.15Y &= 90 \\ Y &= 90 \times \frac{100}{15} = 600 \end{aligned}$$

2. See N. Gregory Mankiw, *Macroeconomics*, Worth Publishers, New York, 5th edition, 2003, p. 118

(b) *Trade Balance* $= X - M$

$= 20 - (10 + 0.05Y)$

Substituting the value of Y we have

$$\text{Trade balance} = 20 - \left(10 + \frac{5}{100} \times 600\right)$$

$$= 20 - 10 - 30 = -20$$

Therefore, trade balance is in deficit.

(c) *Value of foreign trade multiplier* $= \dfrac{1}{1-b+m}$

where b is marginal propensity to consume, and m is marginal propensity to import.

$$\text{Foreign trade multiplier} = \frac{1}{1-0.9+0.05}$$

$$= \frac{1}{1-0.85} = \frac{1}{0.15}$$

$$= \frac{100}{15} = 6.66$$

Problem 2. *Behavioural and structural equations of an economy are given below :*

$C = 40 + bY$

$I = 50$ crore

$G = 40$ crore

$X = 11$ crore

$M = 5 + 0.2Y$

The marginal propensity to consume (b) is equal to 0.8

(a) *Find the equilibrium national income*

(b) *Find foreign trade multiplier*

(c) *Find equilibrium value of imports*

(d) *If equilibrium national income falls short of full-employment income by Rs. 50, how much government should increase its expenditure to attain full-employment?*

Solution : (a) *Income*

$Y = C + I + G + (X - M)$

Substituting the values of various variables and parameters we have

$$Y = 40 + 0.8Y + 50 + 40 + 11 - (5 + 02Y)$$

$$= 40 + 0.8Y + 50 + 40 + 11 - 5 - 0.2Y$$

$$Y - 0.8Y + 0.2Y = 136$$

$$Y(1 - 0.8 + 0.2) = 136$$

$$Y(0.4) = 136$$

$$\therefore Y = \frac{136}{0.4} = \frac{136}{4/10} = 136 \times \frac{10}{4}$$

$$= 340$$

(b) *Foreign Trade Multiplier* $= \dfrac{1}{1 - b + m}$

$$= \frac{1}{1 - 0.8 + 0.2} = \frac{1}{0.4}$$

$$= \frac{1}{4/10} = \frac{10}{4} = 2.5$$

(c) Equilibrium value of imports can be obtained by substituting equilibrium income (340) in the import function. Thus

$$\begin{aligned} \text{Imports } (M) &= 5 + 0.2Y \\ &= 5 + 0.2 \times 340 \\ &= 5 + \frac{2}{10} \times 340 \\ &= 5 + \frac{1}{5} \times 340 = 5 + 68 \\ &= 73 \end{aligned}$$

(d) Required increase in government expenditure to attain ₹ 50 increase in income to achieve full-employment can be obtained as under:

$$\Delta Y = K_f \times \Delta G$$

where K_f is foreign trade multiplier which has been found to the equal to 2.5.

$$\begin{aligned} \Delta Y &= 2.5 \times \Delta G \\ 50 &= 2.5 \times \Delta G \\ \Delta G &= \frac{50}{2.5} = 50 \times \frac{10}{25} = 20 \text{ crore} \end{aligned}$$

QUESTIONS FOR REVIEW

1. How is national income determined in an open economy? Suppose both exports and imports are treated as autonomous and net exports are positive. Graphically show the determination of national income.
2. What is import function? Derive the equation for equilibrium level of national income with given import function of the form, $M = \overline{M} + mY$. Graphically represent the determination of national income with import function of the form $M = mY$.
3. What is foreign trade multiplier? How does it work? Graphically show the foreign trade multiplier. Why is foreign trade multiplier less than the investment multiplier in a closed economy ?
4. What is meant by *trade balance?* How is it related to saving and investment in the economy?
5. What is current account balance of payments? How is it related to capital flows in the economy ?
6. If investment in the economy exceeds domestic saving, how will it affect capital flows?
7. "International flow of capital to finance investment and international flows of goods and resources are the two sides of the same coin". Explain.
8. You are given the following features of an open economy:
   1. Consumption function: $C = 100 + 0.8\, Y_d$
   2. Planned investment $= I = 38$ crore
   3. Government spending : $G = 75$ crore
   4. Exports : $X = 75$ crore
   5. Imports : $M = 0.05Y$
   6. Taxes : $T = 40$ crore

   (Note that disposable income : $Y_d = Y - T$)

   (*i*) What will be equilibrium national income ?

   (*ii*) Calculate foreign trade multiplier

   (*iii*) What is the current account balance ?

CHAPTER 29

Balance of Payments

Balance of Payments: Meaning

In the modern world, there is hardly any country which is self-sufficient in the sense that it produces all the goods and services it needs. Every country imports from other countries the goods that cannot be produced at all in the country or can be produced only at an unduly high cost as compared to the foreign supplies. Similarly, a country exports to other countries the commodities which those countries prefer to buy from abroad rather than produce at home.

"*The balance of payments is a systematic record of economic transactions of the residents of a country with the rest of the world during a given period of time.*" The record is so prepared as to provide meaning and measure to the various components of a country's external economic transactions. Thus, the aim is to present an account of all receipts and payments on account of goods exported, services rendered and capital received by residents of a country, and goods imported, services received and capital transferred by residents of the country. The main purpose of keeping these records is to know the international economic position of the country and to help the Government in reaching decisions on monetary and fiscal policies on the one hand, and trade and payments questions on the other.

Balance of Trade and Balance of Payments

Balance of trade and balance of payments are two related terms but they should be carefully distinguished from each other because they do not have exactly the same meaning. *Balance of trade refers to the difference in value of imports and exports of commodities only, i.e., visible items only.* Movement of goods between countries is known as visible trade because the movement is open and can be verified by the customs officials.

During a given period of time, the exports and imports may be exactly equal, in which case, the balance of payments of trade is said to be balanced. But this is not necessary, for those who export and import are not necessarily the same persons. If the value of exports exceeds the value of imports, the country is said to experience an *export surplus* or a favourable balance of trade. If the value of its imports exceeds the value of its exports, the country is said to have a *deficit or an adverse balance of trade*.

Distinction between Current Account and Capital Account

The distinction between the current account and capital account may be noted. The current account deals with payment for *currently produced goods and services*; it includes also interest earned or paid on claims and also gifts and donations. *The capital account, on the other hand, deals with payments of debts and claims*. The current account of the balance of payments affects the level of national income directly. For instance, when India sells its currently produced goods and services to foreign countries, the producers of those goods get income. In other words, current account receipts have the effect of increasing the flow of income in the country. On the other hand, when India imports goods and services from foreign countries and pays for them, money which would have been used to demand goods and services within the country flows out to foreign countries; current account payments to foreigners involve reduction of the flow of income within the country and constitute a leakage. Thus, the current account or trade account of the balance of payments has a direct effect on the level of income in a country. The capital account, however, does not have such a direct effect on the level of income; it influences the volume of assets which a country holds.

Determinants of Balance of Payments

The main cause of disequilibrium in the balance of payments arises from imbalance between exports and imports of goods and services, that is, deficit or surplus in balance of trade. When for one reason or another value of exports of goods and services of a country are smaller than the value of its imports, the disequilibrium in balance of payments is likely to occur. The value of exports may be small due to the lack of exportable surplus which in turn results from the low production of goods to be exported or the exports may be small because of the high cost and prices of exportable goods and severe competition in the world markets. The important causes of lower exports are inflation or rising prices in the country or over-valued exchange rate. When there is higher rate of inflation in a country resulting in higher prices of exportable goods, its exports are discouraged and imports encouraged . If it is not matched by other items in the balance of payments, disequilibrium will occur.

There are several factors which determine exports and imports and therefore balance of payments position of a country. They are (1) national income at home and abroad, (2) exchange rate of national currency, (3) the domestic prices of goods and factors, (4) international oil and commodity prices and (4) demand for and supply of foreign currency. At the back of these variables lie the supply factors, production function, the state of technology, tastes, distribution of income, economic conditions, the state of expectations, etc. If there is a change in any of these variables and there are no appropriate changes in other variables, disequilibrium in balance of payments will occur.

Balance of Payments on Current Account

Balance of payments on the other hand is more comprehensive in scope than balance of trade. It includes not only imports and exports of goods which are visible items but also such invisible items as shipping, banking, insurance, tourism, interest on investments, gifts, etc.

A country, say India, has to make payments to the other countries not only for its imports of merchandise but also for banking, insurance and shipping services rendered by other countries; it has to pay further the royalties for foreign firms, expenditure of Indians in foreign countries, interest on foreign investments in India, or on loans obtained by India from other countries and such international organizations as the I.M.F., I.B.R.D., etc. These are debit items for India, since these transactions involve payments abroad. In the same way, foreign countries import goods from India, make use of Indian films and so on, for all of which they make payments to India. These are the credit items for India as the latter receives payments. Balance of payments thus gives a comprehensive picture of all such transactions including imports and exports of goods and services.

In Table 29.1 we give the position of India's balance of payments on current account for the years 2005-06 to 2012-13. In this table of balance of payments are given the visible as well as invisible items of trade. The *visible items* are export-import trade and the *invisible items of balance of payments on current account are travel, transportation and insurance, interest on loans given and other investment income and private transfers such as remittances from Indians living abroad.* Both visible and invisible items together make up the *current account*. Invisible items such as interest on loans, tourist expenditure, banking and insurance charges, etc., are similar to visible trade since receipts from selling such services to the foreigners are very similar in their effects on receipts from sales of goods; they provide income to the people who produce the goods or services.

Table 29.1. India's Balance of Payments on Current Account *(in Billion US $)*

S.No. Items	2005-06	2006-07	2007-08	2008-09	2009-10	2010-11	11-12	12-13
1. Exports	105.1	128.9	166.2	189.0	182.2	256.2	309.8	305.6
2. Imports	157.1	190.7	257.6	307.6	300.6	383.5	499.5	502-2
3. **Trade Balance**	–52.0	–61.8	–91.5	–118.6	–118.4	–127.3	–189.9	–195.7
	(–6.2)	(–6.5)	(–7.4)	(–9.8)	(–8.6)	(–7.8)	(–10.1)	(–10.6)
4. **Invisibles (Net)**	42.0	52.2	75.7	89.9	79.9	79.3	111.6	–
(*i*). Non-Factor Services	23.2	29.5	38.9	49.6	35.7	44.1	64.1	–
(*ii*). Investment Income	–5.9	–7.2	–5.1	–4.0	–8.0	–17.9	–16.0	–
(*iii*). Private Transfers	24.5	29.8	41.7	44.6	52.3	53.1	63.5	–
5. **Goods and Services Balance**	–28.7	–32.3	–52.6	–69.0	–83.0	–83.2	–125.7	–130.7
6. **Current Account Balance (Net)**	**–10.0**	**– 9.6**	**–15.7**	**–28.7**	**–38.4**	**–48.1**	**–78.2**	**–87.8**
	(–1.2)	**(–1.0)**	**(–1.3)**	**(–2.4)**	**(–2.8)**	**(–2.7)**	**(–4.2)**	**(–4.8)**

Source : RBI

Note : *Figures in brackets show per cent of GDP at market prices.*

It will be noted from Table 29.1 above that the most important item in the balance of payments on current account is balance of trade which refers to imports and exports of goods. In Table 29.1 balance of trade does not balance and shows a deficit in all the seven years. In the years 2011-12 and 2012-13 trade deficit has substantially increased. Trade deficit was over 10 per cent of GDP in both these years. In fact, it is huge trade deficit in these two years that has caused huge current account deficit of over 4% of GDP in these two years Economic slowdown in advanced countries and its spillover effects on Emerging Market Economies coupled with high crude oil and gold prices were responsible for sharp increase in trade deficit. Due to *surplus in invisibles account*, there was a surplus on current account for three years, 2001-2002, 2002-03 and 2003-04. In India's balance of payments on current account for three years, 2004-05 onwards there has been a deficit. Contrary to popular perception, deficit on current account is not always bad provided it is within reasonable limits (which in case of India is estimated to be 2.5% of GDP) and can be easily met by non-debt capital receipts. In fact, *deficit on current account represents the extent of absorption of capital inflows in India during a year*.

It may be noted that when there is deficit on the current account, it is financed either by using *foreign exchange reserves* held by Reserve Bank of India or by *capital flows* that come into the country in the form of foreign direct investment (FDI) and portfolio investment by FIIs, external commercial borrowing (ECB) from abraod and by NRI deposits in foreign exchange account in our banks. However, due to global financial crisis in 2008-09, there was first slowdown and then decrease in exports. As a result, there was a large deficit of 2.4 of per cent of GDP on current account which could not be met by capital inflows as they were quite meagre ($ 8.6 billion) as a result of global financial crisis. Therefore, to finance the deficit on current account in 2008-09 we had to withdraw US $ 20 billion from our foreign exchange reserves. Again in the last two years 2011-12 and 2012-13 the current account deficit (CAD) has been quite high.

It may be noted that high current deficit tends to weaken the rupee by raising the demand for US dollars. In 2011-12, current account deficit tended to weaken the rupee by raising the demand for US dollars. In 2011-12, the current account deficit was 4.2 per cent of GDP. Since capital inflows in this year were not adequate to finance the current account deficit, RBI had to withdraw 12.8 billion US dollars from its foreign exchange reserves to meet the demand for US dollars (see Table 29.2) . In the year 2012-13 the current account deficit was estimated to be even higher at 4.8 per cent of GDP, capital inflows through portfolio investment by FIIs picked up in the latter half of 2012-13 but capital inflows through FDI had fallen. However, in 2012-13 we were able to finance the current account deficit with capital inflows without withdrawing from our foreign exchange reserves.

In 2013-14 current account deficit situation has worsened as FIIs have pulled out both from debt and equity markets since June 2013. This has led to the sharp depreciation of rupee by increasing demand for dollars. Thus current account deficit poses a serious challenge to macroeconomic management of the economy. The dependence on volatile capital inflows through FIIs to meet the current account deficit is unsustainable as these capital flows go back when economic situation in their home countries improve and thereby causes sharp depreciation in exchange rate of rupee and crash in stock market prices.

Since in the recent years, 2011-12, 2012-13 and 2013-14 current account deficit has widened, which has increased the balance of payments vulnerability to sudden reversal of capital flows, especially when sizable flows are comprised of debt and volatile portfolio investment by FIIs, the priority has therefore been to reduce current account deficit (CAD) through improving trade balance. Efforts have been made to promote exports by diversifying the export commodity basket and export destinations. One way to limit imports is to bring prices up to the international level so that users bear the full cost. Accordingly, petrol has been decontrolled and diesel prices have been revised upward in Jan. 2013 to curtail subsidy on it. To discourage the imports of gold which has played a significant role in causing trade deficit, customs duty on its import was first raised from 6% to 8% and then to 10 per cent.

Further, to improve the current account deficit emphasis has been on facilitating remittances and encouraging software exports that have been responsible for surplus on the invisible account. In recent years this surplus has lowered the impact of widening trade deficit on current account deficit (CAD) significantly. The two components together constituted nearly two-thirds of the trade deficit that was more than 10 per cent of GDP in 2011-12 and 2012-13. Remittances particularly are known to exhibit resistance when the country is hit by external shock as was evident during the global crisis of 2008. Besides, several incentives have been given to NRIs to deposit their foreign exchange savings in Indian banks.

Balance of Payments on Capital Account

In the balance of payments on capital account given in Table 29.2 important items are borrowings from foreign countries and lending funds to other countries. This takes two forms: (*i*) *External assistance* which means borrowing from foreign countries under concessional rate of interest; (*ii*) *Commercial borrowing* under which the Indian Government and the Private sector borrow funds from world money market at higher market rate of interest. Besides, *non-resident deposits* are another important item in capital account. These are the deposits made by non-resident Indians (NRI) who keep their surplus funds with Indian banks. Another important item in balance of payments on capital account is *foreign investment* by foreign companies in India. There are two types of foreign investment. First is *portfolio investment* under which foreign institutional investors (FII) *purchase shares (equity) and bonds* of Indian companies and Government. The second is *foreign direct investment* (FDI) under which foreign companies set up plants and factories on their own or in collaboration with the Indian companies. Still another item in capital account is other capital flows in which the important source of funds is remittances from abroad sent by the Indian citizens working in foreign countries. Table 29.2 gives the position of India's capital account for the years 2004-05 to 2011-12.

Table 29.2. India's Balance of Payments on Capital Account *(in Billion US $)*

	2005-06	2006-07	2007-08	2008-09	2009-10	2010-11	2011-12
External Assistance (Net)	1.7	1.8	2.1	2.6	2.9	4.94	2.3
Commercial Borrowing (Net)	2.5	16.1	22.6	7.0	2.8	12.16	10.3
Non-Resident Deposits (Net)	2.8	4.3	0.2	– 4.3	2.9	3.14	11.9
Foreign Investment (Net)	15.5	14.8	43.3	3.5	50.4	42.13	39.2
of which							
(i) FDI net	3.0	7.7	15.9	17.5	18.0	11.83	22.1
(ii) Portfolio Investment (Net)	12.5	7.1	27.4	–15.0	32.4	30.3	17.2
(iii) Other capital flows (Net)	2.4	9.2	39.7	–9.7	–13.1	–10.48	–7.0
Capital Account Balance (Net)	**24.9**	**46.1**	**107.9**	**8.6**	**51.6**	**63.74**	67.8
Use of Exchange Reserves*	–15.0	–36.6	–92.2	+20.1*	–13.4*	(–13.1)*	(+12.8)*

* *Also includes errors and omissions*

Source: RBI Annual Report 2012-13. Use of foreign exchange reserves (–indicates increase of reserves, and + indicates decrease of reserves on BOP basis.

Capital inflows in the capital account can be classified into ***debt creating*** and ***non-debt creating.*** Foreign investment (both direct and portfolio) represents non-debt creating capital inflows, whereas external assistance (*i.e.* concessional loans taken from abroad), external commercial borrowing (ECB) and non-resident deposits are debt-creating capital inflows.

It will be seen from Table 29.2 that during 2007-08, there was net capital inflow of 43.3 billion US dollars on account of *foreign investment (both direct and portfolio)*. Table 29.2 gives the position of India's balance of payments on capital account for seven years, 2005-06, 2006-07, 2007-08, 2008-09 and 2009-10, 2010-11 and 2011-12. When all items of balance of payments on capital account are taken into account we had *a surplus* of 107.9 billion US dollars in 2007-08. Taking into account current account deficit of $ 15.7 billion in year 2007-08 there was accretion to our foreign exchange reserves by $ 92.2 billion in 2007-08. Global financial crisis affected our capital account balance as there was ***reversal of capital flows after Sept. 2008*** with the result that ***we used*** $ 20.1 billion of our foreign exchange reserves in 2008-09 resulting in *decrease* of our foreign exchange reserves. That is, because we used our foreign exchange reserves equal to $ 20.1 billion, there was decline in our foreign exchange reserves by $ 20 billion in 2008-09. The situation improved in 2009-10 as foreign direct investment (FDI) and portfolio investment by FIIs picked up. As a result there was net capital account surplus of $ 51.6 billion in 2009-10 and after meeting the current account deficit of $ 38 billion there was addition to our foreign exchange reserves by $ 13.4 billion in 2009-10. In 2010-11 also there was surplus on capital account of $ 63.74 billion and after meeting current deficit we added $ 13.1 billion in our foreign exchange reserves in 2010-11.

However, in 2011-2012 and 2012-13 the situation regarding capital flows changed significantly and capital flows were not sufficient to meet the large current account deficit (CAD). Consequently, in 2011-12 withdrawal from foreign exchange reserves of 12.8 billion US dollars was made. However, in 2012-13 we were able to finance large deficit on current account by capital inflows and therefore without withdrawal from our foreign exchange reserves.

Capital flows are driven by pull factors such as economic fundamentals of recipient countries and push factors such as policy stance of source countries. The capital flows have implications for exchange rate management, overall macroeconomic and financial stability including liquidity conditions. Capital account management therefore needs to emphasize promoting foreign direct investment (FDI) and reducing dependence on volatile portfolio capital. This would ensure that to the extent current account defect is bridged through capital surplus it would be better if it is done through stable and growth enhancing foreign direct investment flows. In the present international financial situation, reserves are the first line of defence against the volatile capital flows. However, the decline in reserves as a percentage of GDP is a source of concern.

EQUILIBRIUM AND DISEQUILIBRIUM IN THE BALANCE OF PAYMENTS

Before we analyse the causes of disequilibrium in the balance of payments, we would like to explain what is meant by equilibrium in the balance of payments. We have noted above that when we add up all the demand for foreign currency and all the sources from which it comes, these two amounts are *necessarily equal* and thus the overall account of the balance of payments necessarily balance or must always be in *equilibrium*.

What then do we mean by when we say that the balance of payments of a country is 'in equilibrium or disequilibrium'. As a matter of fact, when we speak of equilibrium or disequilibrium in the balance of payments we refer to the balance on those parts of the account which do not include the accommodating items such as borrowing from the IMF, use of SDRs, drawing from the reserves of foreign currencies held by the Central Bank, etc. *When excluding these accommodating items there is neither deficit nor surplus in the overall balance of payments, it is said to be in equilibrium. When in this sense, there is either deficit or surplus, the balance of payments is said to be in disequilibrium.* The deficit in balance of payments can be financed by drawings from the IMF, use of SDRs, drawings from the reserves of foreign currencies and loan and aid received from abroad. For example in 2001-02, we added to our foreign exchange reserves to the tune of 11,757 million US dollars. However for previous several years India's balance of payment on current account was in deficit. To finance the deficits India borrowed from IMF or from other countries or even resorted to commercial borrowing from abroad. But India's balance of payments for the year 2001-02 was favourable.

Basic Balance of Payments, Autonomous Items and Accommodating Items

However, a more important and popular concept of balance of payments equilibrium has been of *basic balance*. The concept of basic balance is based upon the idea of *autonomous items* in the balance of payments. The autonomous items in the balance of payments are those items which cannot be influenced or changed so easily or quickly by the Government and they are determined by some long-term factors. In this concept of basic balance, besides the items in the current account *the long-term capital movements* both on private or Government account contained in the capital account balance of payments are regarded as autonomous. On the other hand, in the capital account *short-term capital movements* such as borrowing from IMF or Central Banks of other countries, drawings from SDR, change in foreign exchange reserves are transitory and of *accommodating nature* and are therefore excluded from the concept of *basic balance of payments* or *equlibrium in the balance of payments*. The recourse has to be made to these accommodating items (also called *compensatory items*) so as to ensure equality between payments and receipts of foreign exchange. Changes in the compensatory items are made so as to offset the surplus or deficit in the autonomous items. Thus, "*when autonomous movements cancel out over some appropriate time period and there is no need for compensatory movements, the balance of payments is in equilibrium.*[1] *Note that the equilibrium is a state of balance which can be sustained without intervention by the Government.*

The concept of balance of payments in the sense of *basic balance or equilibrium in the balance of payments can* be represented by the following equation:

1. C.P. Kindleberger, *op. cit.*, p. 311.

$$(X - M) + LTC = 0$$

where X stands for exports including invisible items.

M stands for imports including invisible items.

LTC stands for long-term capital movements.

If $(X - M)$ is positive (*i.e.*, $X > M$), then for balance of payments to be in equilibrium, LTC will be negative and equal to $(X - M)$. This implies that there will be *net capital outflow*. On the other hand, if $M > X$, then for the balance of payments to be in equilibrium LTC must be positive (that is, there will be *net capital inflow* to offset the deficit in the current account).

When the balance of payments of a country is in equilibrium, the demand for the domestic currency is equal to its supply. The demand and supply situation is thus neither favourable nor unfavourable. If the balance of payments moves against a country, adjustments must be made by encouraging exports of goods, services or other forms of exports, or by discouraging imports of all kinds. No country can have a permanently unfavourable balance of payments. Total liabilities and total assets of nations, as of individuals, must balance in the long run.

This does not mean that the balance of payments of a country should be in equilibrium individually with every other country with which she has trade relations. This is not necessary, nor is it the case in the real world. Trade relations are multilateral. India, for instance, may have balance of payments deficit with the United States and surplus with the United Kingdom and/or other countries, but each country, in the long run, cannot receive more value than she has exported to other countries taken together.

Equilibrium in the balance of payments, therefore, is a sign of the soundness of a country's economy. But disequilibrium may arise either for short or for long periods. A continued disequilibrium indicates that the country is heading towards economic and financial bankruptcy. Every country, therefore, must try to maintain balance of payments in equilibrium. To know how this can be done involves the study of the causes of disequilibrium.

CAUSES OF DISEQUILIBRIUM IN THE BALANCE OF PAYMENTS

There are several variables which join together to constitute equilibrium in the balance of payments position of a country, *viz.*, national income at home and abroad, the prices of goods and factors, the supply of money, the rate of interest, etc., all of which determine the exports, imports and demand and supply of foreign currency. At the back of these variables lie the supply factors, production functions, the state of technology, tastes, the distribution of income, the state of anticipations, etc. If there is a change in any of these variables and there are no appropriate changes in other variables, disequilibrium will be the result.

The main cause of the disequilibrium in the balance of payments arises from imbalance between exports and imports of goods and services. When for one reason or another exports of goods and services of a country are smaller than their imports, disequilibrium in the balance of payments is the likely result. Exports may be small due to the lack of exportable surplus which in turn result from low production or the exports may be small because of the high costs and prices of exportable goods and severe competition in the world markets. An important cause of small exports is the inflation or rising prices in the country. When the prices of goods are high in the country, its exports are discouraged and imports encouraged. If it is not matched by other items in the balance of payments, disequilibrium emerges.

Cyclical Disequilibrium

Cyclical disequilibrium is caused by the fluctuations in the economic activity or what are known as trade cycles. During the periods of prosperity, prices of goods fall and incomes of the people go down. These changes in incomes of the people and prices of goods affect exports and imports of goods and thereby influence the balance of payments."If prices rise in prosperity and decline in depression, a country with a price elasticity for imports greater than unity will experience a tendency for a decline in the value of imports in prosperity, while those for which imports price elasticity is less than one will experience a tendency for increase. These tendencies may be overshadowed by the effects of income changes, of course. Conversely, as prices decline in depression, the elastic demand will bring about an increase in imports, the inelastic demand a decrease."[2]

Secular or Long-Run Disequilibrium

Secular (long-run) disequilibrium in balance of payments occurs because of long-run and deep-seated changes in an economy as it develops from one stage of growth to another. The current account in the balance of payments follows a varying pattern from one stage to another. In the initial stages of development, domestic investment exceeds domestic savings and imports exceed exports. Disequilibrium arises due to lack of sufficient funds available to finance the import surplus, or the import surplus is not covered by available capital from abroad. Then comes a stage of growth when domestic savings tend to exceed domestic investment and exports outrun imports. Disequilibrium may result because the long-term capital outflow falls short of the surplus savings or because surplus savings exceed the amount of investment opportunities abroad. At a still later stage of growth domestic savings tend to equal domestic investment and long-term capital movements are, on balance, zero.

Thus we see that a secular disequilibrium will occur when either the long-term capital movements get out of adjustment with deep-seated factors affecting savings and investment, or planned savings and investment change without an offsetting change in the movement of long-term capital. If investment adjusted itself readily to the amount of domestic savings plus foreign capital there could be no tendency for secular disequilibrium.

The balance of payments position will be in equilibrium if the international capital flow falls into line with the requirements of domestic investment minus domestic savings. There is a tendency to secular disequilibrium because of domestic savings and domestic investments are independent of the foreign capital flow and are of different magnitudes. There is a strong tendency for underdeveloped countries to over-invest and/or under-save. The underdeveloped countries are investing larger than their domestic savings and exports allow them because they are eager to acclerate the rate of economic growth. This tendency to over-invest causes a secular disequilibrium in the balance of payments.

Technological Disequilibrium

Technological disequilibrium in the balance of payments is caused by various technological changes. Technological changes involve inventions or innovations of new goods or new techniques of production. These technological changes affect the demand for goods and productive factors which in turn influence the various items in the balance of payments. Each technological change implies a new comparative advantage to which a country adjusts. The innovation leads to increased exports if it is a new good and export-biased innovation. The innovation may lead to decline in imports if it is import-biased. This will create a disequilibrium. A new equilibrium will require either increased imports or reduced exports.

Structural Disequilibrium

Let us see how the structural type of disequilibrium is caused."*Structural disequilibrium at the goods level* occurs when a change in demand or supply of exports alters a previously existing equilibrium, or when a change occurs in the basic circumstances under which income is earned or spent abroad, in both cases without the requisite parallel changes elsewhere in the economy."[3]

2. C.P. Kindleberger, *op. cit.*, p. 526.
3. *Ibid.*, p. 526.

Suppose demand in foreign countries for Indian handicrafts falls. The resources engaged in the production of these handicrafts must shift to some other line or the country must restrict imports, otherwise the country will experience a structural disequilibrium. A change in supply may also cause a structural disequilibrium. Suppose Indian jute crop falls because of the change in the shift in the crop-pattern, Indian jute exports will fall and a disequilibrium will be created. Apart from goods, a loss of service income may also upset the balance of payments position on current account. Besides, the loss of income may arise because foreign investment has proved a failure or it has been confiscated or nationalised, *e.g.,* nationalisation of Anglo-Iranian Company in Iran. A war also produces structural changes which may affect not only goods but also factors of production.

A deficit arising from a structural change can be filled by increased production or decreased expenditure, which in turn affect international transactions in increased exports or decreased imports. Actually, it is not so easy because the resources are relatively immobile and expenditure not readily compressible. Under such circumstances, more drastic steps are called for to correct a serious disequilibrium.

"Structural disequilibrium *at the factor level* results from factor prices which fail to reflect accurately factor endowments . . . *i.e.*, when factor prices are out of line with factor endowments, distort the structure of production from the allocation of resources which appropriate factor prices would have indicated."[4] If, for instance, the price of labour is too high, it will be used more sparingly and the country will import highly capital-intensive equipment and machinerry. This will lead to disequilibrium in the balance of payments on the one hand and unemployment of labour on the other.

Conclusion

We have explained above four types of disequilibria–cyclical, secular and two kinds of structural disequilibria–and how they are caused. In each case, the causes manifest themselves through changes in export of goods and services, making one exceed the other.

We have already detailed the various items that enter into the balance of payments. Any cause that leads to a persistently one-sided movement in those items may cause a disequilibrium. For instance, certain causes may lead to falling off in the export of merchandise, imports remaining unaffected or moving in the opposite direction. Falling off in exports may be due to all sorts of causes. Take, for example, the case of exports and imports of goods. Our exports may fall because of decreased production due to seasonal factors or other causes. The demand for our goods in the international market may fall off because of a fall in the purchasing power of consumers of such goods or because of a comparatively high cost of production in India which reduces our competitive strength in the international market. Our exports may become dear to foreigners because of an appreciation of our exchange rate, that is, a rise in the value of the rupee, say from ₹ 42.50 per US dollar to ₹ 40 per US dollar. If we persist in artificially keeping the value of the rupee at a higher level than justified by economic forces, unfavourable balance of trade and payments will tend to persist.

In the same way, disequilibrium may arise due to excessive imports or services neither balanced by exports nor import of capital, etc. Compulsory exports in the form of reparations or indemnities also cause international disequilibrium and obstruct the harmonious trade relations between the countries concerned.

HOW DISEQUILIBRIUM CAN BE CORRECTED

When serious disequilibrium arises in a country's balance of payments, steps must be taken to correct it, if the country's economy is to be kept in a sound condition. Obviously, the causes which are responsible for such a state of affairs must be removed. The 'classical' view of the adjustment

4. C.P. Kindleberger, *International Economics*, 1978.

mechanism is: "An active or passive balance, accompanied by an inflow or outflow of gold, was formally supposed to result in an expansion or contraction of the domestic money supply; and this expansion or contraction was expected to bring about a rise or fall in the level of domestic costs and prices tending, in the former case, to stimulate imports and discourage exports or, in the latter to discourage imports and stimulate exports. Gold flows, changes in the quantity of money and changes in relative levels thus appeared as the principal factors in the mechanism of adjustments"[5]

But gold standard has been abandoned long ago. These days different countries of the world are under managed currency standard. Therefore gold flows no longer occur to bring the balance of payments into equilibrium. Recent currency experience has, however, led to certain modifications in the classical theory. It is now thought that changes in the flow of income induced by balance of payments serve as an equilibrating factor."The main point is that any active or passive balance of current transaction....tends directly to expand or contract the total flow of money income within a given country... The changes induced by the balance of payments in the flows of income and expenditure affect, in turn, the demand for imported as well as home-produced goods and so react on the balance of payments to bring it into equilibrium".[6]

However, these automatic adjustments or corrections in the balance of payments through either changes in prices of goods and factors or through changes in the incomes do not always work due to the presence of various rigidities and immobilities in the system. When the causes of disequilibrium in the balance of payments arc deeper and serious, then the automatic correction via price and income changes does not work at all. Under such circumstance, some concrete measures arc required to be taken to restore the equilibrium in the balance of payments. Disequilibrium in the balance of payments may be corrected by the following methods by the Government.

There are four well-known methods of correcting adverse balance of payments:

1. Trade Policy Measures : Expanding Exports and Restraining Imports

Trade policy measures to improve the balance of payments refer to the measures adopted to promote exports and reduce imports. Exports may be encouraged by reducing or abolishing export duties and lowering the interest rate on credit used for financing exports. Exports are also encouraged by granting subsidies to manufacturers and exporters. Besides, on export earnings lower income tax can be levied to provide incentives to the exporters to produce and export more goods and services. By imposing lower excise duties, prices of exports can be reduced to make them competitive in the world markets.

On the other hand, imports may be reduced by imposing or raising tariffs (*i.e.*, import duties) on imports of goods. Imports may also be restricted through imposing import quotas, introducing licences for imports. Imports of some inessential items may be totally prohibited.

Before the economic reforms carried out since 1991 India had been following all the above policy measures to promotc cxports and restrict imports so as to improve its balance of payments position. But they had not achieved nuch success in their aim to correct balance of payments disequilibrium. Therefore, India had to face great difficulties with regard to balance of payments. At several occasions it approached IMF to bail it out of the foreign exchange crisis that emerged as a result of huge deficits in the balance of payments. At long last, economic crisis caused by persistent deficits in balance of payments forced India to introduce structural reforms to achieve a long-lasting solution of balance of payments problem.

2. Expenditure-Reducing Policies

The important way to reduce imports and thereby reduce deficit in balance of payments is *to adopt monetary and fiscal policies that aim at reducing aggregate expenditure* in the economy. The

5. See C.P. Kindleberger, *International Economics,* 1978.
6. *Ibid.*

fall in aggregate expenditure or aggregate demand in the economy works to reduce imports and helps in solving the balance of payments problem. The two important tools of reducing aggregate expenditure are the use of (1) tight monetary policy and (2) contractionary fiscal policy. We explain them below.

Tight Monetary Policy. Tight monetary is often used to check aggregate expenditure or demand by raising the cost of bank credit and restricting the availability of credit. For this bank rate is raised by the Central Bank of the coutnry which leads to higher lending rates charged by the commercial banks. This discourages businessmen to borrow for investment and consumers to borrow for buying durable cosnumer goods. This therefore leads to the reduction in investment and consumption expenditure. Besides, availability of credit to lend for investment and consumption purposes is reduced by raising the cash reserve ratio (CRR) of the banks and also undertaking of open market operations (selling Government securities in the open market) by the Central Bank of the country. This also tends to lower aggregate expenditure or demand which helps in reducing imports. But there are limitations of the successful use of monetary policy to check imports, especially in a developing country like India.This is because tight monetary policy adversely affects investment increase in which is necessary for accelerating economic grwoth. If a developing country is experiencing inflation, tight monetary policy is quite effective in curbing inflation by reducing aggregate demand. This will help in reducing aggregate expenditure and, depending on the income propensity to import, will curtail imports. Besides, tight monetary policy helps to reduce prices or lower the rate of inflation. Lower price level or lower inflation rate will curb the tendency to import, both on the part of businessmen and consumers.

But when a developing country like India is experiencing recession or slowdown in economic growth along with deficits in balance of payments, use of tight monetary policy that reduces aggregate expenditure or demand will not help much as it will adversely affect economic growth and deepen economic recession. Therefore, in a developing country, monetary policy has to be used along with other policies such as an appropriate fiscal policy and trade policy to tackle the problem of disequilibrium in the balance of payments.

Contractionary Fiscal Policy. Appropriate fiscal policy is also an important means of reducing aggregate expenditure. An increase in direct taxes such as income tax will reduce aggregate expenditure. A part of reduction in expenditure may lead to decrease in imports. Increase in indirect taxes such as excise duties and sales tax will also cause reduction in expenditure. The other fiscal policy measure is to reduce Government expenditure, especially unproductive or non-developmental expenditure. The cut in Government expenditure will not only reduce expenditure directly but also indirectly through the operation of multiplier.

It may be noted that if tight monetary and contractionary fiscal policies succeed in lowering aggregate expenditure which causes reduction in prices or lowering the rate of inflation, they will work in two ways to improve the balance of payments. First, fall in domestic prices or lower rate of inflation will induce people to buy domestic products rather than imported goods. Second, lower domestic prices or lower rate of inflation will stimulate exports. Fall in imports and rise in exports will help in reducing deficit in balance of payments.

However, it may be emphasised again that the method of reducing expenditure through contractionary monetary and fiscal policies is not without limitations. If reduction in aggregate demand lowers investment, this will adversely affect economic growth. Thus, correction in balance of payments may be achieved at the expense of economic growth. Further, it is not easy to reduce substantially government expenditure and impose heavy taxes as they are likely to affect incentives to work and invest and invite public protest and opposition. We thus see that correcting the balance of payments through contractionary fiscal policy is not an easy matter.

3. Expenditure-Switching Policies : Devaluation

A significant method which is quite often used to correct fundamental disequilibrium in balance of payments is the use of expenditure-switching policies. Expenditure switching policies work through changes in relative prices. Prices of imports are increased by making domestically produced goods relatively cheaper. Expenditure-switching policies may lower the prices of exports which will encourage exports of a country. In this way by changing relative prices, expenditure-switching policies help in correcting disequilibrium in balance of payments.

The important form of expenditure-switching policy is the reduction in foreign exchange rate of the national currency, namely, devaluation. By devaluation we mean reducing the value or exchange rate of a national currency with respect to other foreign currencies. It should be remembered that devaluation is made when a country is under fixed exchange rate system and occasionally decides to lower the exchange rate of its currency to improve its balance of payments.

Under the Bretton-Woods System adopted in 1946, fixed exchange rate system was adopted, but to correct fundamental disequilibrium in the balance of payments, the countries were allowed to make devaluation of their currencies with the permission of IMF. Now, Bretton-Woods System has been abandoned and most of the countries of the world have floated their currencies and have thus adopted flexible exchange rate as determined by market forces of demand for and supply of them. However, even in the present flexible exchange rate system, the value of a currency or its exchange rate as determined by demand for and supply of it can fall. Fall in the value of a currency with respect to foreign currencies is described as depreciation. If a country permits its currency to *depreciate* without taking effective steps to check it, it will have the same effects as devaluation. Thus, in our analysis we will discuss effects of fall in value of a currency whether it is brought about through devaluation or depreciation. In July 1991, when India was under Bretton-Woods fixed exchange rate system, it devalued its rupee to the extent of about 20% (from ₹ 20 per dollar to ₹ 25 per dollar) to correct disequilibrium in the balance of payments.

Now the question is, how devaluation of a currency works to improve balance of payments. As a result of reduction in the exchange rate of a currency with respect to foreign currencies, the prices of goods to be exported fall, whereas prices of imports go up. This encourages exports and discourages imports. With exports so stimulated and imports discouraged, the deficit in the balance of payments will tend to be reduced. Thus policy of devaluation is also referred to as *expenditure–switching policy* since as a result of reduction of imports, people of a country switche their expenditure on imports to the domestically produced goods. It may be noted that as a result of the lowering of prices of exports, export earnings will increase if the demand for a country's exports is price elastic (*i.e.*, ep > 1). And also with the rise in prices of imports the value of imports will fall if a country's demand for imports is elastic. If demand of a country for imports is inelastic, its expenditure on imports will rise instead of falling due to higher prices of imports.

Devaluation: Marshall-Lerner Condition. It is clear from above that whether devaluation or depreciation will lead to the rise in export earnings and reduction in import expenditure depends on the price elasticity of foreign demand for exports and domestic demand for imports. Marshall and Lerner have developed a condition which states that devaluation will succeed in improving the balance of payments if sum of price elasticity of exports and price elasticity of imports is greater than one. Thus, according to Marshall-Lerner Condition, devaluation improves balance of payments if

$$e_x + e_m > 1$$

where e_x stands for price elasticity of exports

e_m stands for price elasticity of imports

If in case of a country $e_x + e_m < 1$, the devaluation will adversely affect balance of payments position instead of improving it. If $e_x + e_m' = 1$, devaluation will leave the disequilibrium in the balance of payments unchanged.

Income Absorption Approach to Devaluation. Further, for devaluation to be successful in correcting disequilibrium in the balance of payments, a country should have sufficient exportable surplus. If a country does not have adequate amount of goods and services to be exported, fall in their prices due to devaluation or depreciation will be of no avail. This can be explained through income-absorption approach put forward by Sidney S Alexander[7]. According to this approach, trade balance is the difference between the total output of goods and services produced in a country and its absorption by it. By absorption of output of goods and services we mean how much of them is used up for consumption and investment in that country. That is, absorption means the sum of consumption and investment expenditure on domestically produced goods and services. Expressing algebraically we have

$$B = Y - A$$

where B = trade balance or exportable surplus

Y = national income or value of output of goods and services produced

A = Absorption or sum of consumption and investment expenditure

It follows from above that if expenditure or absorption is less than national product, it will have positive trade balance or exportable surplus. To create this exportable surplus, expenditure on domestically produced consumer and investment goods should be reduced or national product must be raised sufficiently.

To sum up, it follows from above that *for devaluation or depreciation to be successful in correcting disequilibrium in the balance of payments, the sum of price elasticities of demand for a country's exports and imports should be high (that is, greater than one) and secondly it should have sufficient exportable surplus*. The devaluation will also not be successful in the achievement of its aim if other countries retaliate and make similar devaluation in their currencies and thus competitive devaluation of the exchange rate may start.

After Independence India devalued its currency three times, first in 1949, the second in June 1966 and third in July 1991, to correct the disequilibrium in the balance of payments. The devaluation of June 1966 was not successful for some time to reduce deficit in the balance of payments. This is because the demand for bulk of our traditional exports was not very elastic and also we could not reduce our imports despite their higher prices. However devaluation of July 1991 proved quite successful as after it our exports grew at a rapid rate for some years and growth of imports remained within safe limits.

4. Exchange Control

Finally, there is the method of exchange control. We know that deflation is dangerous; devaluation has a temporary effect and may provoke others also to devalue. Devaluation also hits the prestige of a country. These methods are, therefore, avoided and instead foreign exchange is controlled by the government. Under it, all the exporters are ordered to surrender their foreign exchange to the Central Bank of a country and it is then rationed out among the licensed importers. None else is allowed to import goods without a licence. The balance of payments is thus rectified by keeping the imports within limits.

After the Second World War a new international institution, **'International Monetary Fund (IMF)'** was set up for maintaining equilibrium in the balance of payments of member countries for a short term. Member countries borrow from it for a short period to maintain equilibrium in the balance of payments. IMF also advises member countries how to correct fundamental disequilib-

---

7. Sidney S. Alexander, "Effects of Devaluation on Trade Balance", *IMF Staff Papers*, Vol. 11 (April, 1952).

rium in the balance of payments when it does arise. It may, however, be mentioned here that no country now needs to be forced into deflation (and so depression) to root out the causes underlying disequilibrium as had to be done under the gold standard. On the contrary, the IMF provides a mechanism by which changes in the rates of foreign exchange can be made in an orderly fashion.

Conclusion. In short, correction of disequilibrium calls for a judicious combination of the following methods:

(*i*) Monetary and fiscal changes affecting income and prices in the country;
(*ii*) Exchange rate adjustment, *i.e.*, depreciation or appreciation of the home currency;
(*iii*) Trade restrictions, *i.e.*, tariffs, quotas, etc.;
(*iv*) Capital movement, *i.e.*, borrowing or lending abroad; and
(*v*) Exchange control.

No reliance can be placed on any single tool. There is room for more than one approach and for more than one device. But the application of the tools depends on the nature of the disequilibrium. There are, as we have said, three types of disequilibrium: (1) cyclical disequilibrium, (2) secular disequilibrium, and (3) structural disequilibrium (at the goods and the factor level). It is more appropriate that fiscal measures should be used to correct cyclical disequilibrium in the balance of payments. To correct structural disequilibrium adjustment in exchange rate should be avoided. Capital movements are needed to offset deep-seated forces in secular disequilibrium.

The main methods of desirable adjustment are, therefore, monetary and fiscal policies which directly affect income, and exchange depreciation (that is, devaluation) which affects prices in the first instance. Devaluation or depreciation of exchange rate can also have income effect through price effects. Monetary and fiscal policies affect relative prices also.

GLOBALISATION, CAPITAL FLOWS AND BALANCE OF PAYMENTS

Let us first explain what is meant by globalisation. Globalisation refers to the increased openness of an economy to the international trade, capital flows (both portfolio and foreign direct investment, FDI), transfer of technology and free movement of labour or people. Thus **globalisation means the integration of economies of the world resulting from free flows of trade, capital, labour (or people) and technology between countries.** The term globalisation signifies new international economic order which envisages the following :

(*a*) free flow of trade of goods and services between different countires of the world.
(*b*) free flow of capital among countries.
(*c*) free flow of technology among different countries of the world.
(*d*) free movement of labour or people internationally.

The growing interaction between different countries of the world has made the idea of globalisation increasingly popular in recent years.

The globalisation of the economy has an important consequence with regard to capital flows into the economy. Suppose India faces given prices of its imports and a given demand for its exports of goods and services. Under these circumstances, if domestic rate of interest (or rate of return on investment) is higher as compared to what exists abroad, then, given the mobility of capital, foreign capital will flow into the Indian economy to a very large extent. This principle can be expressed as follows :

$$BP = NX(Y_d, Y_f, R) + CF(i_f - i_d)$$

where BP = balance of payments, NX is net exports (*i.e.* exports-imports which is also called trade balance), Y_d stands for level of domestic income, Y_f for level of income of foreign countries, and R for foreign exchange rate CF stands for surplus in the capital account of the balance of payments, that is, capital flows. i_f represents rate of interest in foreign market and i_d represents rate of interest in the domestic economy.

The above equation reveals that trade balance (*NX*) is a function of level of domestic income (Y_d) and foreign income (Y_f) and real rate of exchange (*R*). An increase in the domestic income due to higher industrial growth or fall in real exchange rate of rupee will adversely affect the trade balance (*NX*) by increasing imports. $i_f - i_d$ in the above equation measures interest rate differential between the foreign country and domestic economy on which *i.e.* net capital flows depend. Further, the above equation shows that higher interest rate or rate of return in India as compared to that in the foreign country such as the United States will cause large capital inflows into India. Such capital inflows have actually taken place in India since 2003. Due to large capital inflows into the Indian economy our foreign exchange reserves crossed 100 billions US dollars in December 2003, reached 170 billion US $ in December 2006 and further increased to 247 billion US $ dollars in September 2007, and to 300 billion US $ in Sept. 2008. Due to reversal of capital flows, there was decline in our foreign exchange reserves in 2008-09 and in March 2009, they stood at US $252 billion. In December 2013 our foreign exchange reserves were $ 295 billion.

Globalisation has both advantages and disadvantages. It is through globalisation and openness of an economy that foreign trade of a country increases which promotes economic growth. Trade between countries help them to specialise in the production of goods and services according to their factor endowments and comparative efficiency. Besides, globalisation helps in the transfer of technology from the developed countries to the developing countries. Globalisation also promotes capital flows between countries which in general are welcome. Capital inflow in the form of foreign direct investment (FDI) adds to the productive capacity of a country by increasing capital accumulation. Capital inflows in the form of portfolio investment by FIIs (Foreign Institutional Investors), which are invested in buying equity shares and corporate and Government bonds lead to the development of financial markets. Besides, capital flows provide foreign exchange which can be used to meet the current account deficit which generally emerges in a developing country such as India due to large imports of fuel, machines and industrial raw materials required for industrial growth of the economy.

However, the global financial crisis of 2007-09 which originated in the sub-prime housing loan market in the US and enveloped the entire world has clearly brought out the adverse impact of globalisation. It adversely affected growth of exports of developing countries such as India which brought about large current account deficit. It also caused capital outflows from them which led to the stock market crash. When capital flows are large and volatile they hurt macroeconomic stability. Large capital inflows as they occurred in India in 2010 lead to appreciation of exchange rate of the national currency (Rupee in case of India) which adversely affects growth of our exports and encourage imports. As a result they widen current account deficit.

Owing to these adverse effects of globalisation each country decides about the extent of openness of its economy with which it is quite comfortable by imposing some restrictions on their foreign trade, especially in financial services. Besides, because of the adverse effects of large capital outflows India is trying to woo foreign investors and NRIs to make investment in India so that there are adequate capital inflows into India to meet our widening current account deficit (CAD).

Since current account deficit of India in 2008-09 was financed by withdrawing from foreign exchange reserves in 2008-09 but in the years 2009-10 and 2010-11 it was financed by capital inflows, and thus there was gainful absorption of foreign capital inflows. Therefore, if India wants to continue to grow at a high rate of 8% to 9% there will be deficit in current account of BOP since growth in our exports cannot keep face with our higher growth in imports due to rapid increase in our industrial activity. Current account deficit is a matter of concern only if growth is not high or if stable capital inflows represented by foreign direct investment (FDI) are not adequate to finance the current account deficit. It will be seen from Table 29.1 and 29.2 that from 2004-05 to 2010-11capital surplus [*i.e.* capital account (net)] exceeded our current account deficit, except for the years

2008-09 and 2011-12 with the result that *there was addition to our foreign exchange reserves* (see last row of Table 29.2). Note that minus (–) sign in the use of reserves for various years implies that instead of using foreign exchange reserves in these years we added to our foreign exchange reserves. In the year 2008-09 when there was global financial crisis which caused not only negative growth in our exports but also large capital outflows from the Indian economy with the result that capital surplus in 2008-09 was quite small and fell short of our current account deficit. Similarly, in 2011-12 our current account deficit could not be financed by capital inflows. As a result we withdrew $20 billion and $ 12.8 billion from our foreign exchange reserve to meet the current account deficit in 2008-09 and 2011-12 respectively. Hence the plus sign before US $ 20 billion in 2008-09 and $ 12.8 billion in 2011-12. However, in 2009-10 and 2010-11 there was revival of large capital inflows with capital account (net) equal to US $ 53.6 billion in 2009-10. With $ 38.4 billion deficit in current account we instead of withdrawing from our foreign exchange reserves we added to them in 2009-10. This means India successfully tackled global financial crisis and its consequences. However, it may be noted that in 2010-11 capital inflows into India through foreign direct investment declined and our current account deficit which was estimated to be 2.8 of our GDP had been financed mostly by *volatile capital flows by FIIs which is not desirable*. This is because these volatile capital flows affect our foreign exchange rate stability, stock market prices, price stability, and thus create macroeconomic instability.

QUESTIONS FOR REVIEW

1. Distinguish between balance of trade and balance of payments.
2. What is meant by balance of payments on current account? Explain the visible and invisible items on the current account.
3. Distinguish between current account and capital account of the balance of payments. Mention the various items on both these accounts of the balance of payments.
4. When is a country's balance of payments said to be in equilibrium ? Explain the factors that cause disequilibrium in the balance of payments.
5. Balance of payments must always balance. Is it true? Explain.
6. What is devaluation ? Is it an effective way of correcting disequilibrium in the balance of payments ?
7. Explain the various measures that can be adopted to correct disequilibrium.
8. What is expenditure-reducing fiscal policy ? How does it help to maintain the current account of the balance of payments in equilibrium?
9. What is meant by devaluation ? Under what conditions is it expected to improve the balance of payments position of an economy ?
10. Discuss the absorption approach to devaluation as a measure of correcting balance of payments deficit.
11. Distinguish between Expenditure-Reducing and Expenditure-Switching policies to correct the balance of payments disequilibrium.
12. What is globalisation ? Explain its advantages and disadvantages with special reference to India.

CHAPTER 30

Foreign Exchange Rate

In the last chapter we have discussed the balance of payments which describes the transactions of goods and services and movements of financial capital between countries. The value of these transactions depends upon the prices of the currencies of various countries. For example, in India the value of transactions involving balance of payments is measured either in rupee terms or in terms of US dollars. Given the volume of these transactions, their value in rupees or dollars would depend on the rate of exchange of rupee with US dollar.

Foreign Exchange Rate and Foreign Exchange Market

It may be noted that the *foreign exchange is the name given to any foreign currency. Thus US dollars* or *British pounds* are *foreign exchange for India*. Further, the exchange rate is the *price of a country's currency in terms* of another country's currency. Thus, on Aug. 30, 2013 one US dollar was exchanged for about 65.70 rupees of India (the spot exchange rate). Thus 65.70 Indian rupees for one US dollar on Aug. 30, 2013 was the exchange rate of a dollar in terms of rupees.

Table 30.1. Foreign Exchange Rates of Indian Rupee

(Market Rate in ₹ Per Unit of Foreign Currency)

Foreign Currency	*Exchange rate (on Nov. 27, 2008)*	*Dec. 29, 2011*	*March 5 2013*	*August 30 2013*
US Dollar	49.44	52.71	54.9	65.70
British Pound	75.96	82.41	83.26	101.82
Canadian Dollar	40.35	51.75	53.56	62.36
Euro*	64.24	68.91	71.5	86.87
UAE (*Dirham*)	13.57	14.35	14.39	17.88
Swedish Kroner		7.57	8.21	9.93
Swiss Francs	–	56.10	57.8	70.69
Japanese 100 Yen	52.89	67.63	58.5	66.92
Australian Dollar	32.09	53.57	56.2	58.48
Singapore Dollar	32.81	40.78	44.0	51.53
New Zealand Dollar	–	40.62	44.6	50.79

*Euro is the Common Currency of European Union consisting of a number of European countries.

In the above table we give the exchange rates of Indian rupee in terms of currencies of some important countries of the world. It will be seen from the above table that there has been a lot of volatility in the exchange rate of rupee. There had been 15 per cent appreciation of Indian rupee vis-a-vis US Dollar between Oct. 2006 and Dec. 2007. Beyond Jan.2008, rupee started depreciating under pressure of capital outflows by FIIs and it fell to ₹ 49.44 to a US dollar on Nov. 27, 2008. From later half of 2009-10 to Aug. 2011, as a result of return of capital flows to India, rupee started appreciating and its value rose to around ₹ 45 to a US dollar at end-Aug. 2011. However, again from

Sept. 2011 due to Eurozone sovereign debt crisis there had been large capital outflows by FIIs from India (and other emerging economies) resulting in drastic depreciation of Indian rupee which fell to even ₹ 54 to a US dollar on Dec. 15, 2011. But due to intervention of RBI by way of selling dollars in the foreign exchange market from its foreign exchange reserves, the value of rupee fluctuated within range of ₹ 52 to ₹ 53 to a US dollar between December 16, 2011 and January 13, 2012. It will be seen that Indian rupee depreciated against currencies of all countries in March 5, 2013 except Japan. On March 5, 2013, value of rupee was 54.9 rupees per US dollar.

However, a very large depreciation of rupee has occurred since May 22, 2013. In the month of June 2013, the rupee fell from around ₹ 56 to a US dollar in the first week of June 2013 to ₹ 60 to a US dollar in the end of June 2013 and hit a high level of ₹ 61.21 to a US dollar on July 8, 2013. The RBI intervened by selling US dollars from its foreign exchange reserves and took steps to discourage the import of gold so as to reduce the demand for dollars. The Finance Minister also raised the duty on gold, first from 6% to 8% and then to 10% to restrict the imports of gold to check further depreciation of rupee. However, despite these measures, depreciation of rupee continued and the value of rupee hit a record of ₹ 68.83 to a US dollar on Aug. 28, 2013. Then with aggressive intervention by the RBI through sale of dollars from its foreign exchange reserves and as a result the value of rupee rose to ₹ 65.70 to a US dollar on Aug. 30, 2013. That is, about 18% fall in the value of rupee from early June 2013.

Both domestic and external factors are responsible for this sharp depreciation of rupee since May 2013. The domestic factor responsible for this steep slide of rupee has been the emergence of large current account deficit (CAD) which was estimated at $ 88 billion in 2012-13 (4.8% of GDP of the year) due to sluggish exports and rise in imports causing a net increase in demand for US dollars over their supply. The external factor which triggered the sharp depreciation of rupee was the announcement by the governor of the US Reserve System in May 2013 that since the US economy had recovered, he would start the unwinding of the policy of *quantitative easing* (QE) under which it was purchasing bonds worth $ 85 billion per month from the market to revive the US economy. This triggered capital outflows by FIIs from the emerging economies including India. These capital outflows on a large scale from India contributed to the sharp slide in the exchange rate of rupee.

Floating (Flexible) and Fixed Exchange Rate System

Since exchange rate is a price, its determination can be explained through demand for and supply of currencies. Suppose we consider the transactions between two countries, India and USA. In this case therefore the demand for and supply of dollar is the demand for and supply of foreign exchange from the Indian perspective and the price of a US dollar in terms of Indian rupees or a number of dollars per Indian rupee is the exchange rate. *The system of exchange rate in which the value of a currency is allowed to adjust freely or to float as determined by demand for and supply of foreign exchange is called a flexible exchange system which is also known as floating exchange system.*

On the other hand, if the exchange rate instead of *being determined by demand for and supply of foreign exchange is fixed by the Government, it is called the fixed exchange rate system* which prevailed in the world under an agreement reached at Bretton Woods in New Hampshire in July 1944. It may be noted that under the fixed exchange rate system, exchange rate is not determined by demand for and supply of foreign exchange but is pegged at a certain rate. At the fixed exchange rate, if there is disequilibrium in the balance of payments giving rise to either excess demand or excess supply of foreign exchange, the Central Bank of the country has to buy and sell the required quantities of foreign exchange to eliminate the excess demand or supply.

In 1977 USA decided to float its dollar and switched over to the flexible exchange system resulting in the collapse of Bretton-Woods System of fixed exchange rate. Both the floating (flexible) and fixed exchange rate system have their merits and demerits which will be discussed in a later section.

Appreciation and Depreciation of Currencies

It is important to explain the meanings of the terms 'appreciation and depreciation', of currencies which are often mentioned in the discussion of foreign exchange rate. Let us consider the exchange rate of rupee for dollar. Appreciation of a currency is the increase in its value in terms of another foreign currency. Thus, if the value of a rupee in terms of U S dollar increases from ₹ 45.50 to ₹ 44 to a dollar, Indian rupee is said to appreciate. This indicates strengthening of the Indian rupee. Note that when Indian rupee in dollar terms appreciates, the dollar would depreciate. On the other hand, if the value of Indian rupee in terms of US dollars falls, say from ₹ 45.5 to ₹ 46 to a dollar, the Indian rupee is said to depreciate which shows the weakening of Indian rupee. Thus, under a flexible exchange system, the exchange value of a currency frequently appreciates or depreciates depending upon the demand for and supply of a currency.

In a fixed exchange rate system the government has to buy or sell foreign exchange in order to maintain the rate at the controlled level. However, even under the fixed exchange rate system, the value of one's currency can be changed only occasionally. For instance, in June 1966, the value of rupee in terms of US dollar and U.K.'s pound sterling was lowered. Again in July 1991 India reduced its value of rupee in terms of dollar by about 20 per cent. Such a one-time lowering of value of its currency in terms of foreign exchange occasionally by a country is called *devaluation* as distinguished from depreciation which can often take place under the influence of changes in demand for and supply of a currency. On the other hand, with a fixed rate exchange system if a country raises the value of its currency in terms of foreign currency, it is called *revaluation*. It should be noted that since March 1993 India has also now made its rupee convertible into a foreign currency and allowed its value to adjust freely depending upon demand and supply forces.

DETERMINATION OF EXCHANGE RATE

We are now in a position to explain how in a flexible exchange rate system the exchange of a currency is determined by demand for and supply of foreign exchange. We assume that there are two countries, India and USA, the exchange rate of their currencies (namely, rupee and dollar) is to be determined. Thus, we explain below how the value of a dollar in terms of rupees (which will conversely indicate the value of a rupee in terms of dollars) is determined.

At present in both USA and India there is floating or flexible exchange regime. Therefore, the value of currency of each country in terms of the other depends upon the demand for and supply of their currencies.

It is in the foreign exchange market that the exchange rate among different currencies is determined. The foreign exchange market is the market in which the currencies of various countries are converted into each other or exchanged for each other. In our case of the determination of exchange rate between US dollar and Indian rupee, the Indians sell rupees to buy US dollars (which is a foreign currency) and the Americans or others holding US dollars will sell dollars in exchange for rupees. It is the demand for and supply of a foreign currency or exchange that will determine the exchange rate between the two.

Demand for Foreign Exchange (US Dollars)

The demand for US dollars comes from the Indian people and firms who need US dollars to pay for the goods and services they want to import from the USA. The greater the imports of goods and services from the USA, the greater the demand for the US dollars by the Indians. Further, the demand for dollars also arises from Indian individuals and firms wanting to purchase assets in the

USA, that is, desire to invest in US bonds and equity shares of the American companies or build factories, sales facilities or houses in the USA. The demand for dollars also arises from those who want to give loans or send gifts to some people in the USA. Thus, for whatever reasons the Indian residents need dollars they have to buy them in the foreign exchange market and pay for them with the Indian currency, the rupees. All of these constitute demand for dollars, the foreign exchange.

To sum up, the demand for dollars by the Indians arises due to the following factors:

1. The Indian individuals, firms or Government who import goods from the USA into India.

2. The Indians travelling and studying in the USA would require dollars to meet their travelling and education expenses.

3. The Indians who want to invest in equity shares and bonds of the US companies and other financial instruments.

4. The Indian firms who want to invest directly in building factories, sales facilities, shops in the USA.

An important thing to understand is how the demand curve for a foreign exchange would look like. *When there is a fall in the price of dollar in terms of rupees, that is, when the dollar depreciates, fewer rupees than before would be required to get a dollar.* With this, therefore, a dollar's worth of US goods could be purchased with fewer rupees, that is, the US goods would become cheaper in terms of rupees for Indians. This will induce the Indian individuals and firms to import more from the USA resulting in the increase in quantity demanded of dollars by the Indians. On the other hand, *if the price of US dollar rises, (that is US dollar appreciates) a dollar's worth of US goods would now cost more in terms of rupees making American goods relatively expensive than before*. This will discourage the imports of US goods to India causing a decrease in quantity demanded of dollars for imports.

It therefore follows from above that at a lower price of dollars, the greater quantity of dollars is demanded for imports from the USA and at a higher price of dollar, the smaller quantity of dollars is demanded for imports from the USA by the Indians. This makes the demand curve for dollars downward sloping as shown by the *DD* curve in Fig. 30.1.

Supply of US Dollars (i.e., Foreign Exchange)

What determines the supply of dollars in the foreign exchange market ? The individual firms and Government *which export Indian goods to the USA will earn dollars from the American residents who would buy the Indian goods imported into the USA and pay their price in dollars.* Further, the Americans who travel in India and use the services of Indian transport, hotels etc., will also supply dollars to be converted into rupees for meeting these expenses.

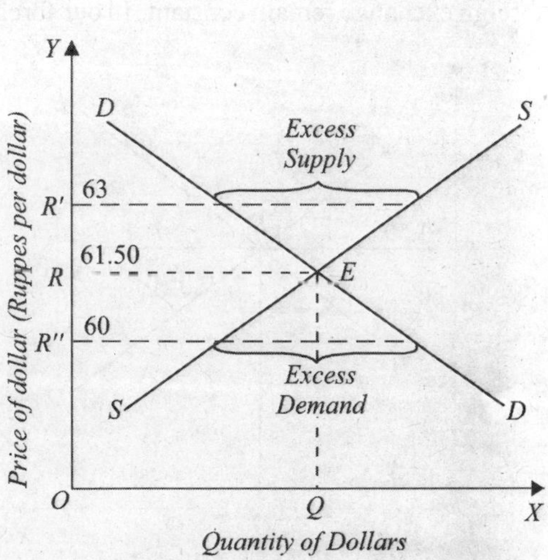

Fig. 30.1. *Determination of Exchange Rate of a Dollar in Terms of Rupees*

Besides, the *American firms and individuals who want to buy assets in India, such as bonds and equity shares of Indian companies or wish to make loans to the Indian individuals and firms will also supply dollars*. There are Indians who are working in the USA and send their earnings in dollars to their relatives and friends.

The supply of these dollars by the Indians working in the USA, popularly called *remittances from the USA,* also add to the supply of dollars. Those holding dollars who have earned them from exports to the USA and the foreign firms and individuals who want to invest in India or those who want to make loans to Indians or the American tourists travelling in India, and remittances from USA by the Indians working there will supply dollars in the foreign exchange market.

The supply curve of dollars plotted against the price of dollar in terms of rupees is positively sloping as shown in Fig. 30.1. What accounts for the upward sloping nature of the supply curve of the dollars ? At a higher price of dollar in terms of rupees (or, in other words, lower value of the Indian rupee in terms of dollar), 100 rupees worth of Indian goods would be relatively cheaper in terms of dollars. This will tend to boost exports of the Indian goods to the USA at a higher price of dollar and thus ensure more supply of dollars in the foreign exchange markets. On the other hand, if the price of US dollar in terms of rupees falls (*i.e.* its exchange rate for Indian rupee declines) the 100 rupees worth of Indian goods would become relatively expensive in terms of dollars. This will discourage the exports of Indian goods to the USA and reduce the quantity supplied of dollars in the foreign exchange market.

The Equilibrium Exchange Rate

It will be seen from Figure 30.1 that the equilibrium exchange rate, that is, the equilibrium price of dollar in terms of rupees, is equal to *OR* or ₹. 61.50 per dollar at which demand for and supply curve of dollars intersect and therefore the market for dollars is cleared at this rate. At a higher price of dollars *OR′* or ₹ 63, the quantity supplied of dollars exceeds the quantity demanded. With the emergence of excess supply of dollars, its price, that is, the exchange rate will again fall to *OR* or ₹ 61.50. On the other hand, if the rate of exchange is lower than *OR*, say it is *OR″* or ₹ 60 to a dollar, there will emerge the excess demand for dollars. This excess demand of dollars would push up the price of dollars to the level of *OR* or ₹ 61.50 per dollar.

CHANGES IN EXCHANGE RATE

In our analysis of determination of exchange rate through demand for and supply of foreign exchange we have assumed that the underlying forces which determine demand for and supply of foreign exchange remain constant. In our foregoing analysis it is only changes in the exchange rate

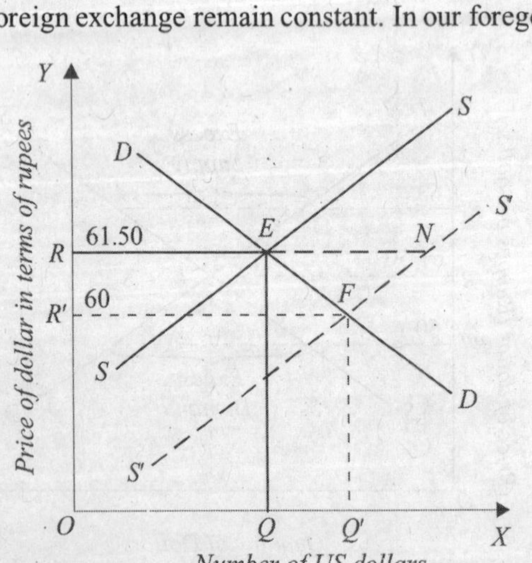

Fig. 30.2. *Increase in Incomes of US People Leading to More Exports from India will lower the Price of Dollar.*

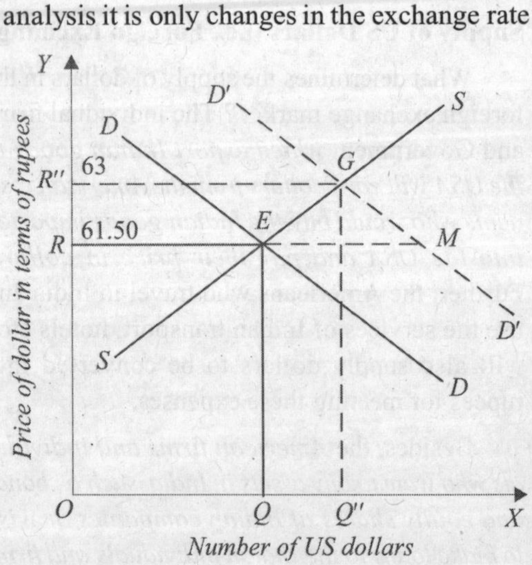

Fig. 30.3. *Increase in the Imports from USA by the Indians Causes Increase in Demand for Dollars and Lowers the Price of Rupee or Raises the Price of US dollar.*

that cause the quantity supplied and demanded of foreign exchange to change and bring about the equilibrium between demand for and supply of foreign exchange.

The equilibrium in the foreign exchange market will be disturbed if some changes occur in the underlying factors that determine the demand for and supply of foreign exchange. For example, if there is increase in incomes of the American people due to the boom conditions in the US economy, it will affect the equilibrium rate of exchange. The increase in incomes of the people of USA will lead to the increase in demand for imported goods including those of India. Now, with this increase in demand for imported Indian goods, they will spend more dollars on the Indian goods. This will increase the supply of dollars to buy Indian goods in the foreign exchange market causing a rightward shift in the supply curve from *SS* to *S'S'*, as shown in Fig. 30.2. This increase in the supply of dollars in foreign exchange market will lower the price of dollar in terms of rupees from *OR* (₹ 61.50 to a dollar) to *OR'* (₹ 60 to a dollar). This implies that increase in imports by USA from India leading to more exports from India will cause the dollar to depreciate and the Indian rupee to appreciate. It will be seen from Figure 30.2 that with the increase in India's exports to the USA and as a result increase in supply of dollars, supply curve of US dollars shifts to the right to *S'S'* position. With this, at the original price *OR* (or ₹ 61.50 to a dollar) there is excess supply of dollars by *EN* amount which will result in lowering the price of dollar to the level of *OR'* or ₹ 60 to a dollar. This means increase in supply of dollars has led to *the appreciation of rupee* from ₹ 61.50 to a dollar to ₹ 60 to a dollar and depreciation of US dollar.

On the other hand, if due to the increase in incomes of the Indian people causing a rise in demand for American consumer goods or there is pick up of industrial activity in India requiring more imports of materials, machines, equipments and other capital goods from the USA, the Indian imports from USA will increase. The increase in imports from USA by India will have to be paid in dollars causing the demand for dollars to increase and as a result demand curve for dollar shifts to the right from *DD* curve to *D'D'* curve (see Fig. 30.3). This will upset the initial equilibrium at price *OR* (₹ 61.50 to a dollar) as with the increase in demand for dollars following the increase in imports from USA there will emerge excess demand for dollars which will push up the price of dollar to *OR''* (₹ 63 to a dollar) so as to bring balance between demand for and supply of dollars (*i.e.*, foreign exchange). Note that rise in price of dollar in terms of rupees implies depreciation of the value of rupee from ₹ 61.50 to ₹ 63 to a dollar.

It will be observed in Fig. 30.3 that as a result of adjustments following the increase in demand for dollars, the price of dollar has risen to *OR''* (₹ 63 to a dollar) and the amount of dollars spent by Indians on imports from the USA increases to *Q''*.

FACTORS AFFECTING EXCHANGE RATE

Having now explained how the exchange rate between different currencies of various countries is determined, we can now explain the factors that are likely to affect the exchange rate between currencies. Changes in all those factors mentioned above which determine the demand for and supply of currencies can influence the exchange rate which will adjust according to the changes that have occurred.

Purchasing Power Parity: The Relative Price Levels

If there are no restrictions imposed on trade by the countries the exchange rate between two national currencies is allowed to adjust freely and with the further assumption that costs of transport of goods between the countries is nil, then the exchange rate between the two currencies will reflect the differences in the price levels in the two countries. This is because with the above-mentioned assumptions if the price of the same good, BPL TV set, is lower in Britain than in India, then it will pay traders to buy the BPL TV sets in Britain and sell them in India. This will reduce the supply of

TV set, in Britain pushing up its price there and increase the supply of TV sets in India and thus causing a decline in its price in India. This process would continue till the price differential of the same quality of TV sets is eliminated and the same price of TV set prevails in the two countries. Thus, if law of same price holds and each country consumes the same market basket of goods, the exchange rate between the two currencies would be determined by the relative price levels in the two countries. For example, if prices in Britain and India are such that a pair of same quality of shoes costs 5 pounds in England and 350 rupees in India, then the exchange rate between rupees and pound would be 1 pound for 70 rupees. If the exchange rate between the two is different from this, it will be possible for the businessmen to make profits in sending pairs of shoes from one country to the other depending on the price levels in the two countries. We therefore conclude that price levels of commodities in the different countries influence the exchange rate between their currencies.

It may however be noted that it is only in the long run and with no restrictions on the trade between the two countries that relative price level in the two countries will be reflected in the exchanges rate.

Rate of Inflation and Exchange Rate

Having shown the effect of relative price levels in the countires on the exchange rate between their currencies, we can now explain how a relatively higher rate of inflation in a country can affect the exchange rate of its currency. Suppose in India a relatively higher rate of inflation prevails than in the USA, how will it affect the exchange rate between the rupee and dollar?

A relatively higher rate of inflation causing rise in prices of the goods in India as compared to those in the USA will make US goods relatively cheapter and the Indian goods expensive. This will serve as incentive for the Indian individuals and firms to increase their imports of goods from USA.

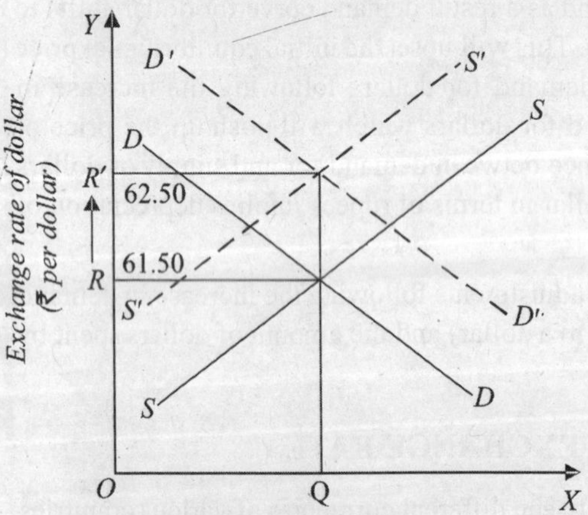

Fig. 30.4. *Effect of a Relatively Higher rate of Inflation in the Domestic Economy on the Exchange Rate of a Country : Rupee Depreciates and US dollar Appreciates*

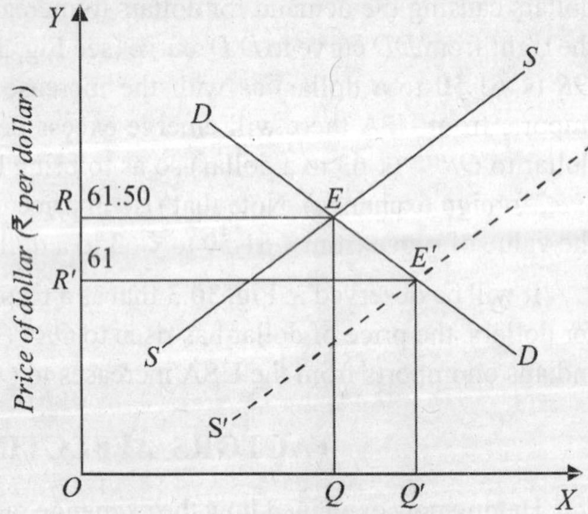

Fig. 30.5. *Effect of a Relatively Higher rate of Interest in India on the Exchange Rate : Indian Rupee Appreciates*

This will raise the demand for US dollars shifting the demand curve for dollars in the foreign exchange market to the right, as shown in Fig. 30.4 where the demand curve of US dolars is shown to have shifted from *DD* to *D'D'* under the influence of higher rate of inflation in India leading to greater imports by India.

However, at the same time due to higher price level American people will find Indian goods more expensive and as a result will reduce their imports of Indian goods. This will cause a decline in exports of goods from India to the USA, shifting the supply curve of dollars to the left to *S'S'*. Both these effects of a higher price level due to higher rate of inflation in a country, namely, rise in imports of US goods into India and the reduction in Indian exports to the USA will cause the foreign exchange rate of dollar in terms of rupees to rise and the price of Indian rupee in terms of dollar will fall. *Thus, as a result of higher rate of inflation in India, the US dollar will appreciate and the Indian rupee will depreciate* (See Figure 30.4).

Interest Rates and Exchange Rate

Another important factor influencing the exchange rate is the interest rate in a country relative to interest rate of other countries with which it trades its goods. Suppose there are no restrictions imposed by the Governments on the flow of capital funds between the countries. Assume that interest on securities or bonds in USA is 5 per cent whereas it is 8 per cent in India. Thus businessmen, firms, banks etc., with funds to invest would obviously have incentive to buy securities and bonds of Indian companies. That is, there will be *flight of capital* from the USA or capital inflows into India as the American business corporations, firms, banks etc. will use their funds to purchase high-yielding Indian securities. In order to buy the Indian securities, they will have to convert dollars into rupees, and thus increasing the supply of dollars. Consequently, the supply curve of dollar will shift to the right. This will pull down the foreign exchange rate of dollar in terms of rupees (Conversely, the exchange rate of rupee in terms of dollar will appreciate). Thus, *a relatively higher interest rate in India as compared to the USA would lead to the depreciation of dollar and appreciation of rupee.* This is what actually happened in India in the fiscal years 2003-04, 2004-05 and 2005-06 .

Figure 30.5 illustrates the effect of higher interest rates in India on the dollar-rupee exchange rate. Initially, the demand for and the supply of US dollar are given by the curves *DD* and *SS* respectively. The balance between the two determines *OR* (or ₹ 61.50 to a dollar) as the exchange rate between the two. With the flow of United States funds into India to buy the Indian securities and stocks, the supply curve of dollars shifts to the right to the new position *S′S′* (dotted) and lowers the equilibrium exchange rate to *OR′* (₹ 61 to a dollar).

It may be noted that during the early eighties, the Federal Reserve Bank of USA adopted a tight monetary policy to fight inflation which caused very high interest rates in USA. These high interest rates attracted a lot of foreign capital, particularly from Japanese firms which due to high saving rate in Japan had a large amount of funds to make investment in American bonds. To purchase American bonds Japanese had to convert Yens into dollars. This caused increase in demand for dollars and caused a sharp rise in the price of dollar. It is thus clear that *like the relative price levels, relative interest rates can also have a significant effect on the exchange rate.*

Capital Flows and Exchange Rate

We have explained above that relative interest rate affects exchange rate through changes in capital flows. But capital flows are not determined by relative interest rate alone. For example, in India and China capital inflows in the form of foreign direct investment (FDI) are occurring due to higher rate of return that foreign investors (*i.e.*, multinational corporations) expect to earn in these countries than in their domestic economies. Besides, capital inflows in India occur when foreign institutional investors (FII) and Non-Resident Indians buy in the equity (*i.e.*, share capital) of Indian companies in Indian stock market. On the other band, when Indian business class invests abroad, capital outflows from India occur. It may be noted that these capital inflows and capital outflows are recorded in the capital account of the balance of payments. On the other hand, trade of goods and services are recorded in the current account of the balance of payments.

We are interested here to show how capital flows affect exchange rate of the currency of a country. This is shown in Figure 30.5 (a) and 30.5 (b) where determination of exchange rate between rupee and US dollar is shown. To begin with in Fig. 30.5 (a), we have drawn demand curve *DD* and supply curves *SS* of US dollar as determined by flows of trade of goods (that is, imports and exports) between the two countries, without any capital flows taking place between the two countries. These demand and supply curves, *DD* and *SS*, determine equilibrium exchange rate *OR* (or ₹ 61 to a US dollar). Note that at this equilibrium exchange rate, there is equilibrium in the current account balance of payments since we are so far assuming that no capital flows occur.

Now suppose foreign institutional investors (FII) and Non-Resident Indians buy shares of the Indian companies. They will therefore bring dollars and convert them into rupees for buying shares of the Indian companies. These capital inflows will increase the supply of US dollars causing a shift in the supply curve to the right, say to the new position S_1S_1. The new supply curve of dollars S_1S_1

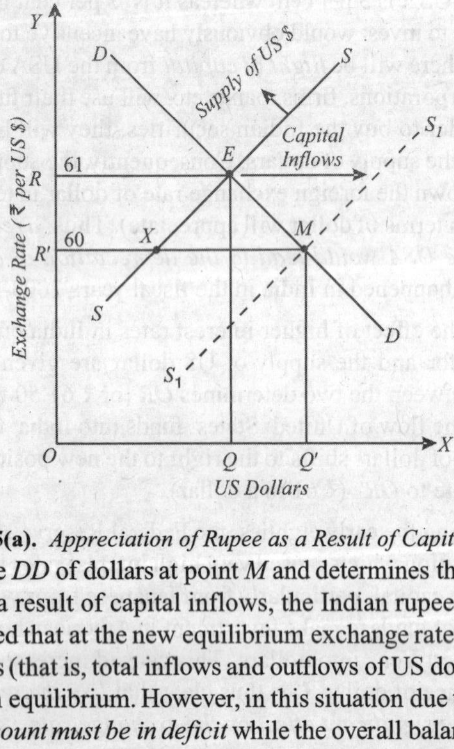

Fig. 30.5(a). *Appreciation of Rupee as a Result of Capital Inflows*

intersects the demand curve *DD* of dollars at point *M* and determines the new exchange rate *OR*' (or ₹ 60 to a dollar). Thus, as a result of capital inflows, the Indian rupee has appreciated (and dollar depreciated). It may be noted that at the new equilibrium exchange rate *OR*' (or ₹ 60 to a dollar), the overall balance of payments (that is, total inflows and outflows of US dollars on account of both trade and capital flows) will be in equilibrium. However, in this situation due to capital inflows as depicted in Fig. 30.5 (*a*), *current account must be in deficit* while the overall balance of payments is in equilibrium. Since as a result of capital inflows the exchange rate of rupee has appreciated, this will cause the total Indian exports of goods and services to decline. Total exports of goods and services at the new exchange rate *OR*' (or ₹ 60 to a dollar) is given by the point *X* on the *original* supply curve of dollars *SS* corresponding to this new exchange rate *OR*'. From Figure 30.5(*a*), it is clear that total exports of goods and services *R'X* are less than the imports of goods and services *R'M*. Thus there is deficit of *XM* on current account. This deficit on current account is met by surplus in capital inflows of capital account since overall balance of payments balances at the new equilibrium exchange rate. We thus reach an important conclusion that the *deficit in current account implies capital inflows (i.e., foreign investment) of that order occur in the economy in that year, if there are no withdrawals from foreign exchange reserves.*

Capital Outflows. Let us take the opposite case when instead of net capital inflows, there are net capital outflows. For example, the rate of return on investment rises in the USA or interest rate falls in India as compared to that in USA. This will cause capital outflows from India and result in shifting the demand curve of US dollars to the right in foreign exchange market. This is illustrated in Figure 30.5 (b). where demand curve of US dollars *DD* and supply curve *SS* of US dollars determine equilibrium exchange rate *OR* (or ₹ 61 to a dollar) when there are no capital flows. Now suppose that net capital outflows occur due to the factors mentioned above. Capital outflows require that those who want to invest abroad will convert Indian rupees into US dollars to invest in the USA. This will cause an increase in demand for US dollars resulting in a shift of the demand curve for US dollars to the right, say to D_1D_1. The new demand curve for US dollars intersects the given supply curve *SS* of dollars at the new point *T* and determines the exchange rate *OR*" (or ₹ 62 to a dollar), that is, US dollar appreciates and the Indian rupee depreciates. Since the Indian rupee depreciates, the Indian exports of goods and services will increase because depreciation of Indian rupee will make the Indian goods

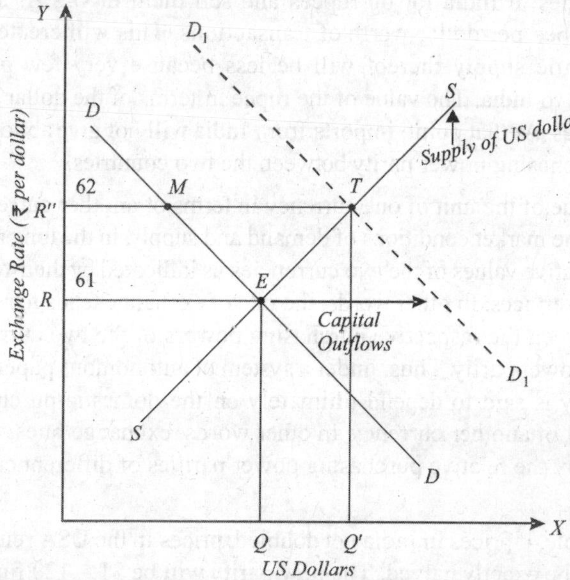

Fig. 30.5(b). *Depreciation of Rupee as a Result of Capital Outflows*

PURCHASING POWER PARITY THEORY

and services cheaper. In Figure 30.5 (*b*), at the new exchange rate *OR*" (₹ 62 to a dollar) exports of Indian goods and services increase to *R"T*. On the other hand, depreciation of Indian rupee will make the Indian imports costlier than before and will therefore lead to the decrease in imports to *R"M* at the new exchange rate *OR*". With this Indian exports of goods and services exceed its imports by the amount *MT*. Thus, there will be surplus in balance of payments on current account of India which will be equal to the capital outflows. We thus reach an important conclusion that *surplus on current account of the balance of payments implies that there will be capital outflows of that order.*

No country today is rich enough to have a free gold standard, not even the USA. All countries have now paper currencies and these paper currencies of the various countries are not convertible into gold or other valuable things. Therefore, these days various countries have paper currency standards. The exchange situation is difficult in such cases. In such circumstances the ratio of exchange between the two currencies is determined by their respective purchasing powers.

The purchasing power parity theory was propounded by Professor Gustav Cassel of Sweden. According to this theory, rate of exchange between two countries depends upon the relative purchasing power of their respective currencies. Such will be the rate which equates the two purchasing powers. For example, if a certain assortment of goods can be had for £1 in Britain and a similar assortment with ₹ 80 in India, then it is clear that the purchasing power of £1 in Britain is equal to the purchasing power of ₹ 80 in India. Thus, the rate of exchange, according to purchasing power parity theory, will be £1 = ₹ 80.

Let us take another example. Suppose in the USA one $ purchases a given collection of commodities. In India, same collection of goods cost 60 rupees. Then rate of exchange will tend to be

$1 = 60 rupees.

Now, suppose the price levels in the two countries remain the same but somehow exchange rate moves to $1 = 61 rupees. This means that one US $ can purchase commodities worth more than 60 rupees. It will pay people to convert dollars into rupees at this rate ($1 = ₹ 61), purchase the given collection of commodities in India for 60 rupees and sell them in U.S.A. for one dollar again, making a profit of 1 rupee per dollar worth of transactions. This will create a large demand for rupees in the USA while supply thereof will be less because very few people would export commodities from USA to India. The value of the rupee in terms of the dollar will move up until it will reach $1 = 60 rupees. At that point, imports from India will not give abnormal profits. $1 = 60 rupees is called the purchasing power parity between the two countries.

Thus while the value of the unit of one currency in terms of another currency is determined at any particular time by the market conditions of demand and supply, in the long run the exchange rate is determined by the relative values of the two currencies as indicated by their respective purchasing powers over goods and services. In other words, the rate of exchange tends to rest at the point which expresses equality between the respective purchasing powers of the two currencies. This point is called the purchasing power parity. Thus, under a system of autonomous paper standards the external value of a currency is said to depend ultimately on the domestic purchasing power of that currency relative to that of another currency. In other words, exchange rates, under such a system, tend to be determined by the relative purchasing power parities of different currencies in different countries.

In the above example, if prices in India get doubled, prices in the USA remaining the same, the value of the rupee will be exactly halved. The new parity will be $1 = 120 rupees. This is because now 120 rupees will buy the same collection of commodities in India which 60 rupees did before. We suppose that prices in the USA remain as before. But if prices in both countries get doubled, there will be no change in the parity.

In actual practice, however, the parity will be modified by the cost of transporting goods (including duties etc.) from one country to another.

A Critique of Purchasing Power Parity Theory

The purchasing power parity theory has been subject to the following criticisms:

The actual rates of exchange between the two countries very seldom reflect the relative purchasing powers of the two currencies. This may be due to the fact that governments have either controlled prices or controlled exchange rates or imposed restrictions on import and export of goods. Moreover, the theory is true if we consider the purchasing power of the respective currencies in terms of goods which enter into international trade and not the purchasing power of goods in general. But we know that all articles produced in a country do not figure in international trade. Therefore, the rate of exchange cannot reflect the purchasing power of goods in general. For example, in India we may be able to get a dozen shirts washed with ₹ 40, but only 2 shirts with one dollar in the USA. Obviously, the purchasing power of one dollar in the USA is much less than the purchasing power of ₹ 40 in India. This is due to the fact that *dhobis* do not form an article of international trade. If *dhobis* entered into international trade and freely moved into the U.S.A., then in terms of clothes washed, the purchasing power of ₹ 40 may be equalised with the purchasing power of a dollar.

Further, it is very difficult to measure purchasing power of a currency. It is usually done with the help of index numbers. But we know that the index numbers are not infallible. Among the difficulties connected with index numbers are the following important ones: (*i*) Different types of goods that enter into the calculation of index numbers; (*ii*) Many goods which may enter into domestic trade may not figure in international trade; (*iii*) Internationally traded goods also may not have the same prices in all the markets because of differences in transport costs.

Besides, the theory of purchasing power applies to a stationary world. Actually the world is not static but dynamic. Conditions relating to money and prices, tariffs, etc., constantly go on changing and prevent us from arriving at any stable conclusion about the rates of exchange. The internal prices and the cost of production are constantly changing. Therefore, a new equilibrium between the two currencies is almost daily called for. As Cassel observes, "differences in two countries' economic situation, particularly in regard to transport and customs, may cause the normal exchange rate to deviate to a certain extent from the quotient of the currencies intrinsic purchasing powers." If a country raises its tariffs, the exchange value of its currency will rise but its price level will remain the same.

Besides, many items of balance of payments like insurance and banking transactions and capital movements are very little affected by changes in general price levels. But these items do influence exchange rates by acting upon the supply of and the demand for foreign currencies. The Purchasing Power Parity Theory ignores these influences altogether. Further, the theory, as propounded by Cassel, says that changes in price level bring about changes in exchange rates but changes in exchange rates do not cause any change in prices. This latter part is not true, for exchange movements do exercise some influence on internal prices.

The purchasing power parity theory compares the general price levels in two countries without making any provision for distinction being drawn between the price level of domestic goods and that of the internationally traded goods. The prices of internationally-traded goods will tend to be the same in all countries (transport costs are, of course, omitted). Domestic prices, on the other hand, will be different in the two countries, even between two areas of the same country.

The purchasing power parity theory assumes that there is a direct link between the purchasing power of currencies and the rate of exchange. But in fact there is no direct relation between the two. Exchange rate can be influenced by many other considerations such as tariffs, speculation and capital movements.

Keynes' Critique. According to Keynes, there are two basic defects in the purchasing power parity theory, namely, (*i*) it does not take into consideration the elasticities of reciprocal demand, and (*ii*) it ignores the influences of capital movements. In Keynes' view, foreign exchange rates are determined not only by the price movements but also by capital movements, the elasticities of reciprocal demand and many other forces affecting the demand for and supply of foreign exchange. "By elasticity of reciprocal demand is meant the responsiveness of one country's demand for another country's exports with respect to price or income." As for price elasticity, generally speaking, greater the proportion of luxuries and semi-luxuries in the exports demanded, the more elastic will be the country's demand for another country's exports. It will also be more elastic, when there is a greater number of alternative markets in which to buy and greater the capacity to produce the effective substitutes for goods imported. As for the income elasticity of demand for imports, changes in demand for goods and services and in the derived demand for foreign exchange is functionally related to the changes in national income. How far is a country's demand for another's exports responsive to a change in national income, will influence the rate of exchange. In other words, it is the character of the propensity to import out of a given income that is supposed to affect the exchange rate independently of international price movements. Technological improvement adding to the productivity of the country and making its goods cheaper and better, tariff changes and exports subsidies affect exchange rates via their influence upon reciprocal demand quite independently of international price movements.

Capital movements, both short-term and long-term, are the other important influences. There is hot money flying from a country so as to make profits or avoid losses on exchange rate fluctuations and there is a 'refugee capital' seeking safety and security abroad. An actual or expected change in the domestic price of a foreign currency may lead to inflow or outflow of 'hot money' causing a further change in the exchange rate without there being price changes in either country. The inflows tend to raise the exchange value of the currency of the capital receiving country and outflows will lower it. Long-term movements of capital also has a similar effect.

In view of the defects pointed out above, the purchasing power parity theory does not offer an adequate or satisfactory explanation of fluctuations in the rates of exchange. The determination of the exchange rate depends not only on international price relations but also on many other factors as mentioned above. This leads to a more adequate explanation of the determination of foreign exchange rates through demand for and supply of foreign exchange viz. balance of payments theory. This theory has been explained above.

EFFECTS OF CHANGES IN EXCHANGE RATE (DEPRECIATION OR DEVALUATION)

Under the recent economic reforms in India, not only have we liberalised the industrial sector but have also opened up the economy, made our currency convertible and allowed exchange rate to adjust freely. It is important to understand the full implications of opening up the economy and allowing our currency to 'float'. It is worthwhile to note that under a fixed exchange rate system when citizens of a country spend some of their income on imports, it reduces the value of multiplier because imports, like savings and taxes, serve as a leakage from the circular flow of income. On the other hand, exports, like investment and Government expenditure, raise the aggregate demand for domestically produced goods and services and thereby cause an expansion in output through a multiplier process.

However, under a variable or floating exchange rate system, the effect of imports and exports on real output is highly complicated. First, the volume of imports and exports depends not only on income, price level, interest rate but also on the exchange rates themselves. Thus when due to some factors, foreign exchange rate changes, it will have an effect on the level of GNP and the price level. Further, exchange rates themselves will adjust to the changes in the economy. We discuss below the effects of changes in the exchange rate, especially of depreciation and devaluation of the exchange rate, on exports, imports, national income, balance of payments and the price level in the economy.

Effects of Depreciation (or Devaluation) on Imports, Exports and Real National Income

From our foregoing discussion of determination of exchange rate through demand and supply curves of foreign exchange, it follows that when a currency of a country, say Indian rupee, depreciates as a result of demand and supply conditions or is devalued by the Government, the prices of Indian exports in terms of foreign currency (say dollar) will fall. This will cause the increase in quantity demanded of Indian exports. As a result, Indian exports will increase. On the other hand, depreciation or devaluation of Indian rupee will make the imports from foreign countries more expensive in terms of rupees (for example, a dollar's worth of US goods will cost more in terms of the Indian rupee) when the Indian rupee depreciates or is devalued. Thus, higher prices of imports will induce individuals and firms in India to import less and they will make an attempt to substitute domestically produced goods for imports from abroad. Thus, *as a result of depreciation or devaluation and consequently increase in exports and decline in imports, the net aggregate demand for domestically produced goods will increase*. And if level of output, especially industrial output, is lower because of demand recession, the increase in net aggregate demand or increase in expenditure on domestic output will cause expansion in output and is therefore likely to increase GNP or real national income. This is illustrated in Fig. 30.6 where as a result of increase in net exports aggregate demand curve shifts to the right. As a result, given the short-run aggregate supply curve the levels of GDP (National income) and price level increases. Thus a *devaluation or depreciation can therefore serve as a stimulus to the economy*.

It will be recalled that in the Keynesian model of determination of real national income (GNP), the effect of net exports, that is, X–M, where X denotes value of exports and M denotes value of imports, is similar to investment in its effect on national income. Both raise national income through a multiplier process. It may be noted here that because of the favourable effect of depreciation or devaluation of currency on exports, imports and real GNP, the countries are tempted at times to intervene in the foreign exchange market, devalue their currency to provide stimulus to their economies. However, if one country devalues its currency to stimulate its economy, the other countries can also do so. Now, when all countries attempt to devalue their currencies, there will be no gain in real income for any of them. Such a situation actually occurred during the early years of Great Depression (1929-33). In their attempt to maintain their exports and protect their level of income and employment, many countries devalued their currencies without bothering about its adverse effects on the economies of the other countries. Such policies of competitive devaluation are generally called "**beggar-thy-neighbour**" policies. Since all followed this beggar-thy-neighbour policy, no one could maintain their export sales and protect domestic employment and level of economic activity which were badly hurt by the severe depression that gripped their economies.

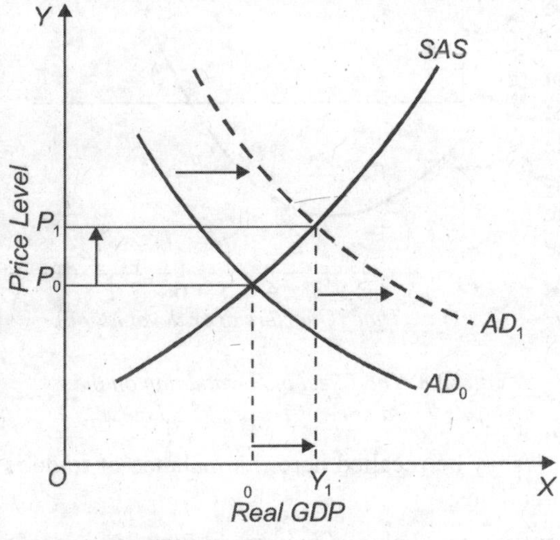

Fig. 30.6. *Depreciation Causes net Exports to rise which Leads to the Increase in Both GDP and Price Level.*

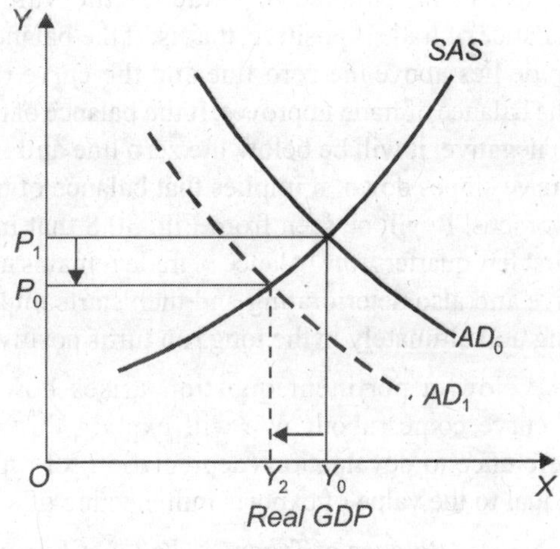

Fig. 30.7. *Appreciation of National Currency Causes fall in net Exports and Leads to Decline in both GDP and Price Level.*

On the contrary, the appreciation of a national currency will have opposite effect. When the currency of a country appreciates, its exports will become costlier causing a decline in them, whereas its imports will become cheaper resulting in increase in them. As a result net exports of the country will decline leading to the decrease in net exports and will therefore cause leftward shift in the aggregate demand curve *AD* as is shown in Fig. 30.7. This will cause fall in both real GDP and price level.

Devaluation and the Balance of Trade: The J Curve

As explained above, lowering of the value of a currency of a country tends to raise its exports by making its goods cheaper for foreigners. On the other hand, devaluation or depreciation makes the imports from abroad expensive in terms of domestic currency (rupees in case of India) and therefore the imports tend to fall. *With exports increasing and imports declining, it is expected that devaluation (depreciation) will reduce a country's trade deficit*. As a matter of fact, in recent years when a country experienced a severe disequilibrium in the balance of trade or balance of payments, it devaluated its currency to raise exports and reduce imports and thus to restore equilibrium in the balance of payments. However, it may be noted that the effect of devaluation or depreciation on balance of trade is ambiguous and quite uncertain because a good deal depends on the price elasticity of exports and imports of a country. For example, if the *price-elasticity of exports* in terms of a foreign currency of a country is less than unity, the value of exports in terms of a foreign currency will fall as increase in physical volume of exports will be more than offset by the depreciation of the currency. On the other hand, if the demand for imports is inelastic, they will not decrease despite devaluation.

Many economists are of the view that devaluation is likely to worsen the balance of trade for the few quarters (probably three to six) after the initial devaluation. However, they think after a time lag, the balance of trade may improve. In fact, a concept called *J. Curve effect* has been put forward. According to this, after the initial depreciation the balance of trade moves according to the shape of the letter *J*. This means that in the first few quarters following devaluation the balance of trade becomes worse and after that it becomes positive and starts improving. This *J*-curve effect is shown in Fig. 30.8 where along the *X*-axis we measure time, that is, quarters after devaluation and on the *Y*-axis we measure the balance of trade. If the value of balance of trade is positive, that is, if the balance of trade lies above the zero line and the curve rises, the balance of trade improves. If the balance of trade is negative, it will be below the zero line and if the curve slopes down, it implies that balance of trade worsens. It will be seen from Fig. 30.8 that in the first few quarters, the balance of trade remains negative and also deteriorating and then starts improving and ultimately in the long run turns positive.

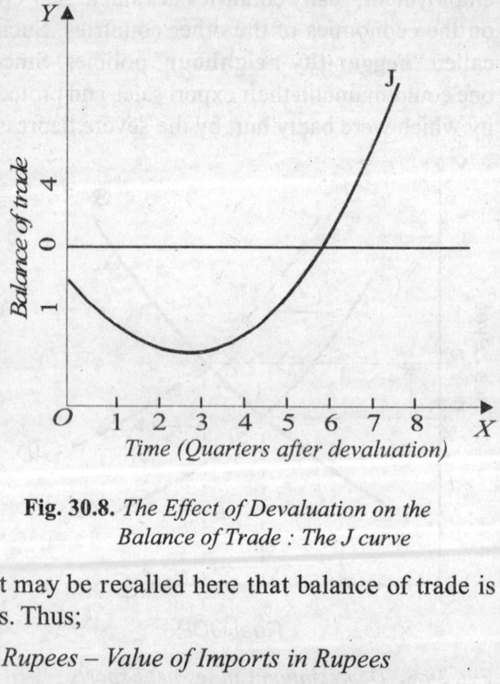

Fig. 30.8. *The Effect of Devaluation on the Balance of Trade : The J curve*

Now, a pertinent question arises how the *J*-curve comes about. We will explain this with reference to devaluation (depreciation) of rupee. It may be recalled here that balance of trade is equal to the value of exports minus value of imports. Thus;

Balance of Trade = Value of Exports in Rupees – Value of Imports in Rupees

It may be noted that value of both exports and imports is equal to the volume of exports or imports multiplied by the rupee price of exports and imports respectively. The depreciation (devaluation) of the currency affects both the volume and rupee price of exports and imports. First, depreciation (devaluation) of currency increases the volume of exports and reduces the volume of imports, both of which have a favourable effect on the balance of trade, that is, they will lower the trade deficit or increase the trade surplus. This has been explained above. Secondly, as a result of devaluation, rupee-price of exports is not likely to change much in the short run. The rupee-price of exports depends on the domestic price level and, in the short run, the devaluation (depreciation) of rupee will have only a very small effect on the domestic price level. On the other hand, the rupee-price of imports increases immediately after devaluation. Imports into India from abroad would be more costly because as a result of devaluation a hundred rupee note will buy fewer US dollars and pound sterlings than before. Thus, *a rise in the rupee-price of imports has a negative effect on the balance of trade*, that is, it will tend to increase the trade deficit or reduce the trade surplus.

Price effect and quantity effect of devaluation. An example will make clear the negative effect of depreciation or devaluation on the balance of trade as a result of devaluation or depreciation. Suppose the rupee cost of a particular US machine goes up from ₹ 50,000 to ₹ 60,000 following the devaluation of rupee from ₹ 46 per dollar to ₹ 44 per dollar. Thus with the rise in price of a US machine, Indians *will spend more* on a US machine than before. This is a *price effect*. But increase in the price of the US machine will lead to *the decrease in the quantity demanded* of US machines by the Indians. This is the *quantity effect*. Now, the net effect of devaluation on the *value of imports* depends on whether quantity effect is larger than price effect or *vice versa*. And this depends on the price elasticity of imports. It therefore follows that net effect of devaluation (depreciation) on the balance of trade could go either way. The historical experience shows that initially the negative effect predominates. This is because whereas the effect of devaluation/depreciation on the price of imports is quite fast, it takes some time for quantity of imports to decline in response to the rise in rupee-price of imports and the value of exports to increase in response to the fall in price of exports in terms of foreign currency. According to the *J-Curve Effect*, the initial effect of devaluation/depreciation on the balance of trade is negative and when in the long run imports and exports adjust to the changes in prices, the net effect on the balance of trade becomes positive. The more price elastic is the demand for exports and imports, the greater the improvement in the balance of trade in the long run.

Devaluation and Inflation

The devaluation or depreciation of currency tends to raise the price level in the country and thus increases the rate of inflation. This happens because of two reasons. As a result of depreciation/devaluation, prices of imported goods rise. In case of imports of consumer goods rise in their prices directly leads to the increase in the rate of inflation. In case of imports of capital goods and raw materials, the rise in their import prices will not only directly raise the price level but as they are used as inputs in the production of other goods, rise in their imports prices will also push up the cost of production of these other goods and thus will bring about cost-push inflation.

Second, as explained above, depreciation makes the exports cheaper and therefore more competitive in the world markets. This causes the exports of goods to increase and reduces the supply and availability of goods in the domestic market which tends to raise the domestic price level. Besides, due to higher prices of imported goods, people of a country tend to substitute domestically produced goods for the now more expensive imports. As a result, the aggregate demand or expenditure on domestically produced goods and services will increase causing either expansion in output of goods or rise in their prices or both. However, if the economy is working close to the capacity output, the effect will be more on raising prices of goods.

FIXED EXCHANGE RATE AND THE BRETTON-WOODS SYSTEM

Until a few years ago, there was fixed exchange rate system introduced during the last year of the Second World War. This fixed exchange rate system under Bretton-Woods System of foreign exchange is known as the Bretton-Woods System as a group of economists from the United States and Europe met at the Bretton-Woods, a town in New Hampshire, to devise this system. According to the agreement made there, an international organisation, called *International Monetary Fund* (IMF), was set up to administer the new fixed exchange rate system. According to the rules framed under the agreement, the USA was to fix a parity or par value for its dollar *in terms of gold*, whereas other countries were required to fix parities for their currencies *in terms of dollars*. Since US dollar was tied to gold, the currencies of other countries with fixed exchange rate with US dollar automatically got pegged (that is, fixed) with a certain gold value. The Government of the USA made a commitment to maintain the convertibility between dollar and gold at a fixed rate, whereas other countries agreed to maintain the convertibility of their currencies with US dollar. The USA fixed $35 per ounce of gold as the convertible rate. The change in these fixed exchange rates (devaluation or revaluation) was to be made with the consent of IMF in case of *fundamental disequilibrium* in the balance of payments. The Bretton- Woods agreement did not define the fundamental disequilibrium but in practice it came to mean *chronic and large* deficit in the balance of payments. Therefore, when a country was experiencing a *large and persistent* deficit in balance of payments, it was allowed by IMF to devalue its currency to the extent required to improve the balance of payments position. Thus, faced with the serious problem of balance of payments India devalued its rupee by 36.5 per cent in 1966. Again in July 1991, India devalued its rupee by about 20 per cent to tide over the serious foreign exchange crisis which arose due to deficits in balance of payments.

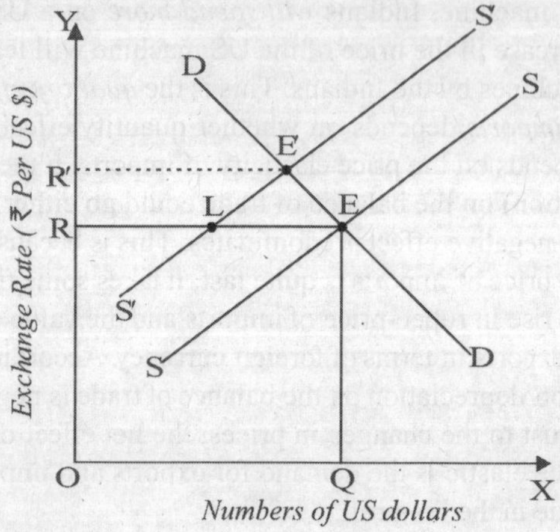

Fig. 30.9. *Government Intervention to Maintain the Exchange Rate at a Fixed Level*

IMF maintains funds or reserves with itself which are contributed by member countries. IMF was given power to give loans to the member countries when they had short-term or temporary deficit in the balance of payments from its reserves. In case of fundamental disequilibrium its function was to advise the countries to devalue their currency to tide over the problem of deficit in balance of payments. The purpose was to achieve a relatively fixed or stable exchange rate system which was required for promotion of world trade.

It may be noted that, under Bretton-Woods System, *to maintain the exchange rate at the specified level, the Governments (or their Central Banks) were to keep with themselves reserves of internationally accepted foreign currencies.* Thus gold, which in the previous years served as an international currency, was substituted by reserves of foreign currencies that were widely used in international dealings. The US dollar became the important currency in which the reserves were to be kept by the other countries to maintain the exchange rate of their currency. Pound Sterlings, German Marks, Japanese Yen were also kept for this purpose.

To maintain the fixed exchange rate Bretton-Woods System required the intervention by the Governments or their Central Banks. How they maintained the exchange value of their currency by using the reserves of foreign currencies is illustrated in Fig. 30.9 where the *demand and supply curves DD and SS of US dollars* are drawn. Along the *X*-axis the quantity of US dollars and on the *Y*-axis, the exchange rate of rupee in terms of US dollar is measured.

Suppose the Government of India is committed to maintain the exchange rate of its currency at *OR* level which is also assumed to be the equilibrium rate as determined by demand for and supply of rupees. Now, suppose due to the recessionary conditions the demand of the USA for Indian exports greatly declines. This will reduce the supply of US dollars causing a shift to the left of the supply curve of dollars to *S′S′*. Now, given the demand curve *DD* of dollars remaining unchanged, at fixed exchange rate *OR*, the quantity supplied of dollars falls to *RL* whereas quantity demanded of dollars continues to be *RE*. As a result, the excess demand for dollars emerges at the fixed exchange rate *OR* and, if left free to the market forces, the equilibrium exchange rate *will rise to OR′ level.* That is, price of US dollar in terms of rupees will appreciate or in other words, the Indian rupee will depreciate. *In order to maintain the exchange rate of rupee in terms of dollar, and to prevent it from depreciating, the Government or Reserve Bank of India must sell dollars from its foreign exchange reserves.* With the sufficient sale of dollars in the market, the supply curve of dollars will shift to the right to the original position *SS* which will restore the exchange rate *OR*. This is how the exchange rates of different countries remained fixed under Bretton-Woods System despite the frequent changes in demand for and supply of their currencies.

Collapse of the Bretton-Woods System

Fixed exchange rate system under the Bretton-Woods arrangement came under heavy pressure during the sixties and it ultimately collapsed in the early seventies. As seen above, under the Bretton Woods System the US dollar became internationally accepted currency in which reserves of the countries were kept for international transactions. Before the Bretton-Woods System gold was accepted as international medium of exchange. Under the Bretton-Woods System, the US dollar also assumed the role of international currency for three reasons. First, after World War II, the United States emerged as the strongest economy. Secondly, the United States had accumulated a large stock of gold. Thirdly, during 1934 and 1971, the United States had been following the policy of selling and buying gold to other countries at a fixed exchange rate of $35 per ounce. As under the Bretton-Woods System, the dollar was converted into gold at a fixed rate (that is, $35 per ounce), it was considered '*as good as gold*'.

Since the world's supply of gold did not increase adequately to meet the requirements of rapidly expanding international trade and finance, the dollar increasingly became the world currency in which international reserves were kept by various countries. But a serious problem arose which caused the demise of Bretton-Woods System. The United States had a large and persistent deficit in balance of payments during the fifties and sixties. To meet these deficits, the US used its gold reserves for making payments to other countries, especially Germany and Japan. Obviously, this could not go on for ever because its gold reserves would have eventually run out. In fact, this was the big flaw in the fixed exchange rate system adopted under the Bretton-Woods arrangement. Further, as a result of surplus balance of payments with the United States, other countries, especially Germany and Japan, acquired not only gold but also a large quantity of the dollars from the US which were kept as reserves.

With the passage of time reserves of dollars and gold held by other countries increased very much while the reserves of gold with USA declined a great deal, the doubts arose about the ability of the USA to fulfil its commitments of converting dollars into gold at the agreed exchange rate of $35 per ounce. Widespread fears emerged that there would be run on the dollar, that is, countries holding dollars would *en masse* try to exchange dollars for gold. If it had actually happened it would have greatly hurt the international trade and finance. Therefore, in view of the large and persistent deficit in balance of payments, it was decided by the US Government to withdraw convertibility of dollar into gold at the rate of $35 per ounce on August 15, 1971. This brought about the collapse of the Bretton-Woods System which was supported by the US commitment to convert dollar into gold at a fixed rate. With this the link between gold and international value of the dollar ended and consequently the *dollar was floated*, that is, permitted its exchange rate with other currencies to be determined by market forces.

FIXED AND FLEXIBLE EXCHANGE RATES

A study of economic history shows that three different exchange rate systems have been prevailing in the world economy. The first exchange rate system, popularly called *Gold Standard,* prevailed over 1879-1934 period with the exception of World War I years. Under the gold standard, currencies of different countries were tied to gold (that is, the value of currency of each country was fixed in terms of a certain quantity of gold). With this the exchange rate between different countries got automatically fixed. Thus, the gold standard represented fixed exchange rate system. As explained above, from the end of World War II to 1971, another fixed exchange rate system, generally known as Bretton-Woods, System prevailed. Under this the US dollar was tied to a certain quantity of gold and the currencies of other countries were tied to dollar or in some countries directly to gold. However, as seen above, in 1971 due to large and persistent deficit in balance of payments of the United States, Bretton-Woods system also broke down. Since then, the *flexible* or what is also called *floating exchange rate system* has been existing. But even in this flexible or floating exchange rates the Government (or the Central Bank) of the countries intervenes to keep the international value of their currencies (*i.e.*, exchanges rate) within certain limits. Therefore, even in the post–1971 period, the exchange rate system is not *purely* flexible and has therefore been called **Managed Float System**. We discuss below the merits and demerits of the fixed and flexible exchange rate system.

Merits of Fixed Exchange Rate System

Exchange rate stability. In defence of fixed exchange rate system, it has been pointed out that it ensures stability in exchange rate. Exchange rate stability, it is said, is necessary for orderly development of the international economy and rapid growth of world trade. If the exchange rate is unstable or variable, the exporters will not be certain about the price they would receive for the goods to be exported by them; the importers will not be certain about the price and the payments they have to make for their imports. These uncertainties involve risks for exporters and importers. This greatly harms the growth of world trade. Thus, the chief merit of fixed exchange rate system is that it eliminates the possibilities of such uncertainties and associated risks and thereby promotes foreign trade.

It is important to note that for the developing countries a stable or fixed exchange rate system has a special advantage. This is because the developing countries have a large and persistent balance of payment deficit. As a consequence, if the exchange rate is flexible and not fixed, due to these large persistent deficits, the exchange rate or international value of their currencies will be continuously falling. Thus fixed exchange rate system prevents this continuous tendency for the depreciation of their currencies.

Promotes capital movements. Another advantage of fixed exchange rate is that it facilitates capital movement by private firms. A stable currency does not involve any uncertainties about capital loss on account of changes in exchange rate. Therefore, fixed exchange rate system would attract foreign capital investments. Foreign private firms would not be interested in making investment in those countries whose currency is not stable. Since foreign investment is an important source of economic growth, the fixed exchange rate system would promote rapid economic growth of the developing countries.

Prevents capital outflow. Further, flexible and unstable exchange rates may at times of difficult economic situation encourage *flight of capital*, as happened in case of Mexico a few years ago causing a serious balance of payments problem. On the other hand, a stable exchange rate ensures that such capital outflow would not occur.

Prevents Speculation in foreign exchange market. Another important merit of fixed exchange rate system is that it does away with speculation in foreign exchange markets. The advocates of fixed exchange rate system point out that the flexible and unstable exchange rate encourages speculation in foreign exchange market. The operators in foreign exchange market try to take advantage of the fluctuations in exchange rate as freely determined by demand and supply forces. They try to manipulate the exchange rate through their actions of buying and selling foreign exchange and try to obtain speculative gain in this way. Ragnar Nurkse in his study of *International Currency Experience* which he conducted for the period of twenties found that because of speculative activities, flexible exchange rate had a destabilising influence. It caused greater fluctuations than would have been the case otherwise. By eliminating speculation fixed exchange rate system ensures stability in the exchange rate.

Serves as an anchor against inflation. Another important advantage of fixed exchange rate system is that it prevents the Government of the countries from adopting inflationary policies. Generally, Governments have often been tempted to pursue undue expansionary fiscal and monetary policies to lower unemployment and create boom conditions. However, inflation has several bad effects for the economies. It increases inequalities of income and wealth and hurts the poor most. Further, inflation hampers economic growth in the long run. Fixed exchange rate system forces the Governments to achieve price stability by taking effective anti-inflationary measures. This is because in the case of fixed exchange rate, inflation will cause balance of payments deficits and result in loss of international reserves. Therefore, this forces the Government to adopt measures to check inflationary pressures in the economy. To quote B. Soderston, "Fixed exchange rates can serve as an anchor. Inflation will cause balance of payments deficits and losses in reserves. Hence the authorities will have to take counter measures to stop inflation. Fixed exchange rates should therefore impose a discipline on governments and stop them from pursuing inflationary policies which are out of tune with the rest of the world."[1]

Promotes economic integration of the world. It has also been argued in favour of fixed exchange rate system that it is necessary for achieving economic integration of the world community. This is similar to a single common currency in a country which promotes economic integration of a nation in the sense that it facilitates communication, trade and free movement of finance between different regions of a country. It ensures free competition among all producers and consumers of various countries. Similarly, a common currency would promote economic integration of the world. Fixed exchange rate between the currencies of the various countries approximately serves the purpose of a single currency between different countries. Thus, fixed exchange rates among different currencies is a necessary condition for the purpose of *forming economic union* between various countries, that is, forming a regional grouping. To enjoy the advantages of economic unity in recent years, there is a proposal for issuing a single currency for European countries to strengthen the economic integration of European countries.

Promotes growth of internal money and capital markets. Another big advantage of the fixed exchange rate system is that it promotes growth of internal money and capital markets. Since flexible exchange rates cause uncertainties about the future exchange rates, individuals, companies and institutions are reluctant to lend to and borrow from the internal money and capital markets.

In view of the above advantages, a fixed exchange rate system prevailed for a long time from 1944 to 1971. As we have seen above that the Bretton-Woods aggreement adopted a fixed exchange rate system because of the above mentioned merits, IMF permitted a change in the exchange rate only in case of fundamental disequlibrium in the balance of payments.

Demerits and Problems of Fixed Exchange Rate System

Fixed exchange rate had however a great flaw in that the countries with a large and persistent balance of payments deficit were losing gold and other foreign assets. This could not go on forever as evidently stock of gold and foreign currencies would have run out. That is why the USA abandoned Bretton-Woods System which represented fixed exchange rate system. The other countries facing problem of balance of payment deficit found their international reserves dwindling which forced them to devalue their currency. The devaluation has an inflationary potential.

1. B.Soderston, *International Economics*, 2nd edition, Macmillan, 1980, p. 402.

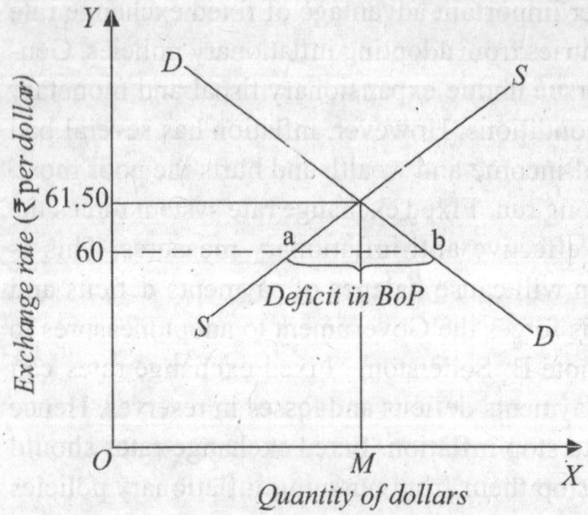

Fig. 30.10. *Overvaluation of a Currency Causing Deficit in BoP.*

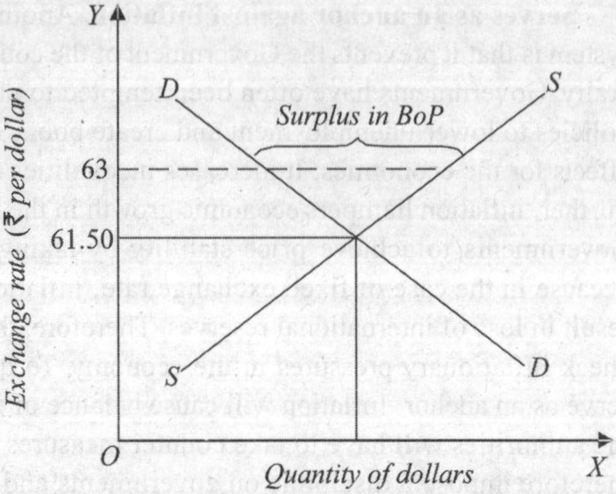

Fig. 30.11. *Undervaluation of a Currency Leading to the Problem of Surplus in BoP.*

On the other hand, under the fixed exchange rates, the countries with a balance of payments surplus will be providing its national currency and in return it will receive foreign currencies and assets such as US dollar, pounds, gold. The increase in foreign assets would lead to the expansion in money supply which is likely to create inflationary pressures in the economy. But remember an important difference between the countries with balance of payments deficits and the countries having balance of payment surplus. Whereas due to depletion of reserves of gold and foreign currencies, the countries with deficit balance of payments are forced to *devalue* their currency to overcome the deficit, the countries with a balance of payments surplus generally do not *revalue* their currency for the fear that it would discourage exports. Instead, the countries with surplus BoP face the problem of inflation and try to tackle it with other policies.

Another problem with the fixed exchange rate system is that *at what level exchange rate should be fixed*. If the exchange rate of a foreign currency with a national currency is fixed or pegged at the equilibrium level, that is, at the rate at which its quantity demanded equals quantity supplied, no problem arises. However, for the Government it is difficult to find such an equilibrium exchange rate of a foreign currency in terms of the national currency. Further, as underlying conditions change as they do so frequently, the equilibrium exchange rate will also change giving rise to the problems. If the exchange rate of a national currency in terms of the foreign currency, say US dollar, is fixed at a higher level, there will be deficit in the balance of payments (BoP). On the other hand, if the exchange rate of a national currency in terms of US dollar is fixed at a lower than the equilibrium level, there will be surplus in balance of payments (BoP). Consider Fig. 30.10, where demand and supply curves of dollars respectively for India are drawn. ₹ 61.50 to a US dollar is the equilibrium exchange rate. If the Government or Reserve Bank of India fixes the exchange rate at a higher rate, say ₹ 60 to a US dollar as the exchange rate, the quantity demanded of dollars by Indians would exceed the quantity supplied so that there would be deficit in India's balance of payments. This means that at ₹ 60 to a dollar *Indian rupee is overvalued*. As a result, India's stock of foreign exchange (*i.e.*, dollars) and other foreign assets will decline. Sooner or later India will be forced to take policy measures to correct this deficit in BoP. India will have to adopt contractionary fiscal and monetary policies to reduce aggregate expenditure in the economy so that imports decrease or it will impose various restrictions on imports to reduce them. With the reduction in imports through these policy measures demand curve of dollars in Fig. 30.10 will shift to the left and may intersect the supply curve *SS* at point *a* to be in equilibrium at the exchange rate of ₹ 60 to a dollar. To reduce persistent deficit in BoP, it may even resort to devaluation if it has a fixed exchange rate system.

Now, consider Fig. 30.11. If the Government fixes the exchange rate of rupee at a lower rate, say ₹ 63 to a US dollar, the quantity supplied of dollars by other countries would exceed the quantity demanded by the Indians. As ₹ 63 to a US dollar, the *Indian rupee is undervalued* (or, which is the same thing, *dollar is overvalued* in terms of rupees). Historical experience shows that countries with surplus in BoP have been reluctant to *revalue* their currency (that is, to raise the international value of their currency). Thus, a *surplus in balance of payments also gives rise to a problem*. As a result of this surplus due to undervaluation of the rupee, India will accumulate dollars (*i.e.*, foreign exchange) for which it would pay rupees, the national currency. The new rupee notes would be printed to pay for dollars. Thus, surplus in BoP leads to the expansion in money supply generating inflationary pressures in the Indian economy. To check inflation, the Indian Government might therefore take steps to eliminate the surplus in BoP by encouraging imports or restricting exports. Further, it may try to take steps to neutralise the impact of surplus in BoP on expansion in money supply. For this purpose, it might encourage *capital outflows* (*i.e.*, investment abroad) by private firms or provide concessional financial assistance to other countries.

In view of the above drawbacks and problems, the fixed exchange rate system has been given up despite its various advantages as explained above.

Merits of Flexible Exchange Rates System

Under the flexible exchange rate system, exchange rates between different currencies, like the prices of commodities, are freely determined by market forces, that is, by demand and supply forces. With the change in economic conditions underlying demand and supply, the exchange rate will automatically change without any intervention by the Government. That is why, it is called flexible or variable exchange rate system. It has the following merits :

Problems of undervaluation and overvaluation are avoided. The advocates of flexible exchange rates contend that under it the problems of undervaluation and overvaluation of currencies which are found in the fixed exchange rate system are avoided. Whenever there is deficit in balance of payments implying overvaluation of the national currency under the flexible exchange rates, it will depreciate (that is, its value will fall) which on the one hand will make exports cheaper and thereby encourage them and on the other will make the imports costlier than before which will tend to discourage them. Thus, increase in exports and decline in imports as a result of depreciation will lead to the automatic correction in the balance of payments.

On the other hand, whenever there is surplus in the balance of payments, the exchange rate will appreciate which will tend to reduce exports and raise imports. This again will tend to automatically restore the balance of payments equilibrium. This is how the flexible exchange rate system works to ensure the equilibrium in the balance of payments. To quote Prof. Soderston, "The same factors which under the fixed rates give rise to deficits and surpluses in the balance of payments would under floating rates make the exchange rate depreciate or appreciate. Thereby equilibrium would be preserved and the Government could be freed from consideration regarding external balance".

Promotes growth of multilateral trade. The advocates of flexible exchange rate system are strongly of the view that as unlike fixed exchange rate system, this does not create serious and difficult problems, it will ensure rapid growth of multilateral world trade. Further, they point out that promotion of world trade under the flexible exchange rates would not interfere in any way the adoption of policies to achieve domestic economic stability.[3]

2. Milton Friedman, 'The Case for Flexible Exchange Rate', AEA, *Readings in International Economics*, Vol. XI.
3. *Ibid.*

Flexible exchange rate system does not necessarily show large fluctuations. It has been pointed out in defence of the flexible exchange rate system that the problems of undervalued or overvalued currency found under the fixed exchange rate regime are not found in the flexible exchange rate system. Further, it is contended that exchange rates being flexible do not necessarily mean there will be large fluctuations in them. Even under flexible exchange system there need not be large fluctuations in exchange rates. According to them, changes in exchange rates will occur only when economic conditions underlying demand for and supply of foreign currencies change. Further, according to them, random fluctuations around the normal exchange rates would be smoothened out through operations by private speculators. Thus, according to Soderston, "if the currency appreciated above its equilibrium value, if its price fell in terms of foreign currency, speculators would buy the currency; and if it depreciated, speculators would sell the currency. Thereby they would smooth out fluctuations and help to keep the exchange rate stable. If the underlying conditions changed, however, the price of foreign exchange would also change."

It ensures individual freedom. The system of floating exchange rate is advocated on the basis of philosophy that Government should intervene in the economy as little as possible and the individuals should be left free to pursue their economic interests. It has been noted above that the alternative to floating exchange rates system is the fixed exchange rates which require controls and restrictions which are implemented by experts who generally do not work under effective democratic controls. Generally, they fix the exchange rate out of consideration for other than economic objectives, for example, for the purpose of retaining a certain market structure or influencing income distribution.

It frees the Government from problems of balance of payments. A great merit of flexible exchange rates is that it frees the Government from problems of balance of payments. As has been seen above, the fixed exchange rates system leads either to deficit or surplus in balance of payments. Under this system the Government remains preoccupied with the questions of devaluation or revaluation of their currencies. Since floating exchange rates work automatically to restore balance of payments equilibrium, the Government need not pay any attention to the balance of payments. Instead, the Governments can concentrate on solving their domestic problems of economic stability, inflation and unemployment. "Flexible exchange rates should therefore give an increased freedom both to individuals and countries to pursue whatever aims they have for their economic policies."[4]

Demerits of Flexible Exchange Rate System

Flexible exchange rate system is also not without shortcomings. It has been opposed on some important grounds. We briefly explain below some important arguments given against flexible exchange rates.

1. Flexible Exchange Rates Create a Situation of Instability and Uncertainty. An important argument against flexible exchange rates is that too frequent fluctuations in exchange rate under it create uncertainty about the exact amount of receipts and payments in foreign exchange transactions. *This instability hampers foreign trade and capital movements between the countries.* However, Friedman does not accept this charge against flexible exchange rates. He argues that flexible exchange rate is not necessarily an unstable exchange rate. According to him, it is the underlying economic conditions determining foreign trade that often change causing changes in the foreign exchange rate and for this the flexible exchange rates should not be blamed.

2. Dampening Effect on Foreign Trade. Under the flexible exchange rates, the price of foreign exchange or international value of the national currency is quite uncertain. As a result, they are unable to take proper decisions regarding exports and imports of goods. Obviously, this has a dampening effect on the volume and growth of foreign trade. However, Friedman does not agree with this and points out that traders can always protect themselves against risks arising out of the

4. B. Soderston, *op. cit.*

changes in the exchange rate by hedging in the future market.[5] However, Soderston has challenged this view of Friedman and points out that no markets exist today that can protect traders against risks arising out of flexible exchange rates.[6]

It may however be noted that from the empirical evidence since 1971 when exchange rates have been flexible, it does not appear that flexible exchange rates have a dampening effect on the growth of foreign trade. In fact, the growth of world trade since 1971 has been fairly good.

3. Widespread Speculation with a Destabilising Effect. The system of flexible exchange rates has been opposed on the ground that under it there is widespread speculation regarding exchange rates of currencies which has a large destabilising effect on these rates. Friedman, on the other hand, contends that *speculation has a stabilising influence on exchange rates*. However, whether or not speculation has a destabilising or stabilising effect is a highly controversial issue in economics which has so far remained unresolved.

4. Provides an inflationary Bias to an Economy. Another shortcoming of the flexible exchange rates is that they have an inflationary impact on the economy. It has been pointed out that whenever due to deficit in balance of payments the currency depreciates, the prices of imports go up. The higher prices of imported materials raise the prices of industrial products and thus generate cost-push inflation. However, in defence of flexible exchange rates, it has been pointed out that when demand for imports declines due to appreciation of national currency, the *foreign suppliers are compelled to reduce their prices* to protect markets. Though this reduction in prices in the face of declining demand is theoretically possible, it may not happen in actual practice.

To sum up, there are merits and demerits of flexible exchange rate system. Whether a flexible exchange rate system suits an economy depends on circumstances. It depends on characteristics of the economy which adopts flexible exchange rate system. Further, it may be noted that since 1971 when Bretton-Woods System representing the fixed exchange rate system was abandoned, it is not perfectly free flexible exchange rate system that has been adopted. Instead, it is what is called *Managed Float System* that has been prevailing. Under the managed float system, the exchange rates are flexible, that is, they change as a result of changes in demand and supply of currencies, but the Government or Central Bank intervenes through demand and supply to keep the variations in exchange rate within certain limits so as to ensure stability and certainty of the foreign exchange rates.

Managed Float System in India

It is important to note that in India as in most of other countries including USA, Great Britain, France, there is at present flexible or floating exchange rate system. Besides, like other countries India has not adopted a perfectly flexible or floating exchange rate system. The changes in exports and imports, capital outflows and capital inflows bring about large fluctuations in foreign exchange rate of rupee. It may be noted that large depreciation or appreciation of exchange rate adversely affects the economy, especially its exports and imports. In order to prevent large appreciation and depreciation of Indian rupee, Reserve Bank of India often invervenes to ensure that exchange rate should remain within reasonable limits. When the rupee is depreciating too much, Reserve Bank of India intervenes and sells dollars from its reserves of foreign exchange. This increases the supply of dollars in the market and prevents the depreciation of the rupee.

On the other hand, when rupee is appreciating too much, Reserve Bank of India intervenes and buys dollars from the market. This reduces the supply of dollars in foreign exchange market which prevents the appreciation of exchange rate of rupee. Therefore, through the intervention by Reserve Bank of India, exchange rate of rupee is not allowed to change beyond certain limits. Therefore, such a system that has been adopted by India is not completely flexible or floating exchange rate system. Therefore, it is called *managed float system*.

5. Milton Friedman, *op. cit*
6. B. Soderston, *op. cit.*, p. 303.

ANALYSIS OF SOME EXCHANGE RATE CONCEPTS

As the Indian economy gets more integrated with the world economy (that is, has extensive trade and capital flows with the rest of the world), exchange rate of rupee with foreign currencies will play a very important role as it will determine competitiveness of Indian goods and services in the international markets. The rupee has different exchange rates with foreign currencies of its various trade partners. A bilateral exchange rate with a foreign currency, say the US dollar, in nominal terms is not a good exchange rate with which to measure the competitiveness of the rupee. Further, the exchange rate of rupee with a single currency in nominal terms would not measure the differences in changes in prices and costs in the domestic economy as compared to the changes in prices in all the trade partners. To deal with this issue, the effective exchange rate (EER) concept is used.

Nominal Exchange Rate (NER). Foreign exchange rate is generally quoted as the number of units of a domestic currency required to purchase one unit of a foreign currency. For example, ₹ 40 per US dollar refers to foreign exchange rate of the Indian rupee in terms of US dollar and means that ₹ 40 can buy one US dollar in foreign exchange market. Likewise, there is foreign exchange rate between rupee and the pound sterling, between rupee and the Yen, between rupee and Mark and so on. This exchange rate of rupees per US dollar, or per pound sterling is called *nominal exchange rate* (NER).

Nominal Effective Exchange Rate (NEER). In addition to the nominal exchange rate, the economists often use the concept of nominal effective exchange rate. The *nominal effective exchange rate is the weighted average of nominal exchange rates* where the weights used are the shares of the trading partners in the foreign trade of a country. Suppose the US accounts for 60 per cent of total trade with India, and the United Kingdom accounts for 40 per cent of trade with India, then the nominal effective exchange rate is given by

Nominal Effective Exchange Rate (NEER) = $(NER_{US}\ W_{US}) + (NER_{UK} \times W_{UK})$

where NER_{US} and NER_{UK} are the nominal exchange rates of the US and UK respectively for the Indian rupee and W_{US} and W_{UK} are trade shares of the US and UK respectively with India. Suppose the US accounts for 60 per cent in India's trade and NER of the Indian rupee with the US dollar is ₹ 44 while UK accounts for 40 per cent in India's trade and nominal exchange rate of rupee with pound sterling is ₹ 85, the nominal effective exchange rate is

$$\begin{aligned} NEER &= 44 \times 0.6 + 85 \times 0.4 \\ &= 26.4 + 34.0 = 60.4 \end{aligned}$$

Real Exchange Rate. Real exchange rate measures the relative price of the two currencies after adjusting for price levels prevailing within two countries. For example, *real exchange rate between rupee and US dollar is defined as the rupee price of a basket of goods in India relative to a dollar price of the same basket of goods in the USA.* Thus real exchange rate is given by

$$RER = NER\left(\frac{P_{US}}{P_{in}}\right)$$

where NER is the nominal exchange rate between the two currencies and P_{us} is the price level in the USA and P_{In} is the price level in India. While the nominal exchange rate measures the rate at which currencies of the two countries are exchanged, real exchange rate measures the rate at which domestic goods can be exchanged for foreign goods. An example will clarify the meaning of real exchange rate. Suppose ₹ 44 are required to buy one US dollar, that is ₹ 44 per US dollar is the nominal exchange rate (NER) between the Indian rupee and the US dollar. If a basket of goods costs ₹ 200 in India and the same basket of goods costs 20 dollars, then real exchange rate (RER) will be

$$RER = (NER)\frac{P_{US}}{P_{In}} = 44 \times \frac{20}{200} = 4.4$$

Thus 4.4 is the real exchange rate of the Indian rupee. This means 4.4 units of Indian goods are needed to buy one unit of US goods. Real exchange rate is used as a measure of *international competitiveness*. A rise in real exchange rate indicates foreign goods (in our example the US goods) have become more expensive relative to domestic goods of a country. This means competitiveness of our goods has increased relative to that of the USA.

Real Effective Exchange Rate (REER). *Real effective exchange rate is the weighted average of real exchange rates with all its trade partners, the shares of different countries in its total trade are used as weights*. Thus, in India 5 countries' real effective exchange rate (REER) is prepared and the shares of major trade partners such as the USA, UK, other European countries, Japan with India are used as weights for calculating real effective exchange rate.

Changes in India's Nominal Effective Exchange Rate (NEER) and Real Effective Exchange Rate (REER)

India's NEER (base 2000 = 100) which is composed of 5 foreign currencies, namely, US dollar, Euro, Pound sterling and Japanese Yen. This India's NEER depreciated on a yearly basis till 2004-05 to reach a level of 90.75. With a bout of appreciation during April-June 2005, it depreciated thereafter but it again rose during Jan. to Feb. 2006 to 94.06. In 2006-07 it depreciated steadily till Aug. 2006 when it reached a low of 88.05. It once again rose to 91.31 in Nov. 2006. This shows there have been quite a large changes in NEER causing uncertainty about what exchange rate will prevail in future.

As regards the real effective exchange rate (REER), it appreciated to 106.79 in 2005-06. After depreciating to 100.6 in Aug. 2006, it rose to 109.0 in Nov. 2006.

Devaluation and Depreciation of Exchange Rate

An important issue in regard to foreign exchange rate has been at what level it should be fixed or stabilised. Even under Bretton-Woods system 1 per cent change in fixed exchange rate on either side the parity value was allowed to be varied. For more than one per cent change in the exchange rate the permission of IMF was necessary to restore equilibrium in the balance of payments. A proposal was mooted to increase this *permissible band* for variation or adjustment to be raised to 10 per cent from the parity value to correct disequilibrium in the balance of payments. However, in 1973 Bretton-Woods System of fixed exchange rate collapsed. The US dollar and Pound Sterling were floated, that is allowed to be determined freely by demand for and supply of these currencies. However, India continued with the fixed exchange rate system. But instead of based on parity value in terms of gold or the US dollar it fixed the exchange rate of rupee on the basis of exchange rate movements of a basket of foreign currencies, namely, the Pound Sterling, US dollar, Yen and Mark.

In 1991 India faced a serious balance of payments crisis with stagnant exports and rising imports, especially of petroleum oil. On the advice of IMF India devalued its rupee in July 1991 to solve the balance of payments problem. It was about 25 per cent devaluation against the currencies of our major trading partners. As a result of this devaluation India's exports increased substantially and also black market in foreign exchange that prevailed before came to an end.

In addition to devaluation, ***a dual exchange rate system*** was introduced in 1992. Under the dual exchange rate system there were two rates: (1) the official exchange rate that was controlled and (2) the market rate of exchange which was free to change according to demand and supply conditions. Under this dual exchange rate system 40 per cent of earnings from the exports of goods and services were to be surrendered to RBI through authorised dealers at officially fixed exchange rate. The foreign exchange reserves received in this way was used by RBI for financing preferred imports. The remaining 60 per cent of export earnings in foreign exchange were converted into rupees by the exporters at the market determined exchange rate.

However, in the year 1993-94 the policy of dual exchange rates was dropped and rupee was allowed to float. With this a *unified market determined exchange* rate came to prevail which can change as a result of changes in demand and supply of foreign currencies.

Managed Float System and Implications of RBI Intervention

It is important to note that even with the present flexible exchange rate system in India there is a managed float system because RBI intervenes in foreign exchange market to influence the exchange rate of rupee and keep fluctuations in it within reasonable limits. Thus when rupee in the free market depreciates much and RBI does not want much depreciation, it will sell foreign exchange from its reserves in the foreign exchange market to prevent it from depreciating. On the other hand, when rupee appreciates much against foreign currencies RBI intervenes and buys foreign exchange. This move of RBI prevents rupee from appreciating.

Note that appreciation of rupee as compared to other currencies makes the Indian exports expensive and therefore discourages them. Although RBI does not follow any fixed exchange rate target through sale and purchase of foreign exchange, it aims at preventing large volatility in foreign exchange rate of rupee.

However through sale and purchase of foreign exchange by RBI has implications for maintaining price stability. This is because when RBI buys foreign exchange from the market it issues new money (*i.e.*, rupee currency) to pay for it. This new money comes into circulation in the Indian economy and thus leads to the expansion in money supply. If aggregate supply of goods remains the same or does not increase much, this expansion in money will cause rise in general price level (*i.e.*, inflation) in the economy. To check inflation, RBI can *sterilise* the impact of increase in foreign exchange inflows by selling government securities to the banks. The banks will give cash to RBI against the purchase of these securities. In this way RBI mops up excess liquidity (*i.e.*, cash reserves) of the banks caused by the inflows of foreign exchange. The proceeds of the government securities sold to the banks can be kept by RBI in a separate account which cannot be used by the Government and therefore cannot affect prices. However, there is limit to which the sterilisation can take place.

As noted above, from Aug. 2006 the Indian rupee started appreciating and its exchange rate with US dollar rose to eight-year high of ₹ 43 to a US $ on March 27, 2007 and further to ₹ 41.57 on April 23, 2007. In the last four months (Jan-April 2007) RBI did not intervene much to buy foreign exchange from the market and as a result continued inflows of dollars in India resulted in the exchange rate of rupee to appreciate. On Nov. 12, 2007, the exchange rate of rupee per US $ rose to ₹ 39.4. The RBI did not intervene to a large extent in the foreign exchange market and let the rupee appreciate in order to check inflation in the Indian economy. If RBI intervenes in the foreign exchange market to mop up excess US dollars from the market, it, as explained above, leads to the increase in money supply in the economy and this causes inflation. Further, appreciation of rupee makes imports cheaper which encourages imports. The increase in imports leads to the rise in aggregate supply of goods which helps in checking inflation.

Changes and Volatility in Foreign Exchange Rate of Rupee

As a result of the above developments, rupee depreciated a good deal from 1991-92 to 2000-03. From ₹ 21 per US dollar in 1990-91 average annual exchange rate was reduced to ₹ 27 in 1991-92 (*i.e.*, about 25 per cent fall in value as a result of devaluation made in July 1991), and it then gradually fell to ₹ 36 in 1997-98 and to ₹ 48 in 2001-02. With effect from 2002-03 under pressure of capital inflows, rupee started appreciating and rose to ₹ 47 to a US dollar in 2002-03, to ₹ 44.27 in 2005-06. In 2006-07 and 2007-08, there was a large inflow of capital through portfolio investment which led to further appreciation of rupee which rose to 39.4 to a dollar on Nov. 12, 2007 which was ten years high level. In the year 2007 alone there was net capital inflow of 17 billion US dollars through FII which pushed up the value of rupee to a dollar. Then there was a sub-prime housing loan crisis in the United States which created liquidity crisis in America. To meet the requirements of liquidity at home, FIIs started selling shares in the Indian market and as a result capital outflows occurred during 2008 which gathered momentum in the months of September and October 2008 when rupee depreciated rapidly and its value fell to ₹ 48.53 to a US dollar on Oct. 10, 2008 and to ₹ 49.5 for a US dollar in Nov. 2008 (For some days it fell to ₹ 50 for a US dollar). The capital outflows by FIIs not only caused depreciation of rupee but also stock market crash in Oct. 2008 and Nov. 2008 and liquidity crunch in the Indian banking system. To ensure credit needs of industries for investment the RBI intervened in the economy by reducing cash reserve ratio (CRR) from 9 per cent to 6.5% and thereby infused liquidity in the economy to the extent of ₹ 1,40,000 crores and promised to do more if needed.

In the later half of 2011 from September to December 2011, due to uncertainty caused by Eurozone Crisis there has been capital outflow by FIIs from India which caused a sharp depreciation of rupee. Despite some limited intervention by RBI, the value of rupee fell to ₹ 53 to US $ in mid-December 2011 against ₹ 44 in August 2011, that is, ₹ 18 per cent fall in the value of rupee in four months. This is a matter of serious concern as it has raised the costs of imports of crude oil and other commodities and therefore will not only raise inflation in the economy but will also adversely affect our balance of payments. Besides, the weak rupee will discourage foreign investment in India as investors will suffer losses due to the fall in exchange value of the Indian rupee.

DEPRECIATION OF RUPEE IN 2013: CAUSES

From May 22, 2013 the value of Indian rupee was ₹ 55.48 to a US dollar and within fifteen days it fell to ₹ 57.07 to a US dollar and its slide went on as a result of surge in dollar demand from imports and capital outflows by FIIs pulling out the debt market that resulted in fall in value of rupee to ₹ 60.72 on June 26, 2013, that is, around 6 per cent in single month of June. Though RBI had a foreign exchange reserve of $ 291 billion, it tried to stem the slide of rupee through sale of some US dollars from its foreign exchange reserves but failed to stabilise the exchange rate of rupee because capital outflows gathered momentum.

The RBI was selling dollars at ₹ 59.90 to a US dollar but such was the pressure on the rupee by FIIs pulling out capital from the debt and equity markets and demand for dollars by the corporates, oil firms that rupee slipped below ₹ 60 to ₹60.73 to a dollar on June 20, 2013. This made imperative for the RBI to take more tough measures to check the fall in the value of rupee.

Capital Outflows from India and Unwinding of Quantitative Easing. It is worth noting that capital outflows by FIIs were triggered by the announcement by Ben Bernanke, the governor of the US Reserve System, that since the US economy had shown the signs of recovery from recession as shown by the decline in unemployment rate to 7.6 per cent in April 2013, as against its peak level of 10 per cent in December 2010, it would soon start unwinding of the stimulus in the form of *quantitative easing* (*QE*) that was being pursued by it. At present under the Quantitative Easing Policy (*QE*) the US Reserve System was pumping in 85 billion dollars per month by ***purchasing government and other bonds*** to provide stimulus to the US economy and now it will soon unwind this stimulus in a phased manner and to begin with it will reduce buying of bonds to 65 billion dollars per month. Ben Bernanke's statement immediately prompted FIIs to pull out swiftly from first debt market and then equity market to send dollars to safe haven of the US where they expected to earn higher returns as a result of revival of the US economy. These large capital outflows coupled with the increased demand for dollars by the Indian importers such as oil firms, corporate companies and banks increased pressure on dollars resulting in rupee depreciation despite efforts made by the RBI to stabilise the value of rupee by selling US dollars from its foreign exchange reserves through public sector banks. However, the RBI could not sell sufficient dollars to stem the downward slide of the rupee as it also needed dollars to meet the current account deficit that had reached 6.7 per cent of GDP in December quarter of the year 2012-13 and 4.8 per cent of GDP for the whole year 2012-13.

The vicious circle came into operation. The weakening of rupee further hit the debt and equity markets as the worried foreign investors saw their returns from investment in India being eroded who had already pulled out away around $ 6 billion in June 2013 continued this process in July 2013 as well. These outflows of dollars were bound to weaken the rupee further and on July 8, 2013, the rupee fell to a very low level of ₹ 61.21 to a dollar. The RBI which was initially slower in response to fast depreciation of rupee started taking tough measures to stem further slide of rupee. These measures will be explained later. However, the process of depreciation continued despite raising customs duty on imports of gold and imposing various restrictions on outflows of foreign exchange. The value of rupee depreciated to a record low level of ₹ 68.83 on Aug. 28, 2013.

Widening of Current Account Deficit. Besides capital outflows, widening current account deficit (CAD) is a basic factor that is responsible for large depreciation of rupee. Two factors have been blamed for widening of current account deficit (CAD). *One important factor is the import of gold.* India is one of the largest consumers of gold. The gold is demanded for making of jewellery, for sale to the public for consumption. The second reason for import of gold is investment in it by the people as a hedge against inflation and for investment purposes was more in 2012-13 and 2013-14 because of high rate of inflation that prevailed in these years. For imports of gold the importers of gold have to buy dollars from the market. *The crude oil is other major import which causes a large increase in demand for dollars.* India imports crude oil for more than 75 per cent of its requirements. The current account deficit rose to 6.7 per of GDP in December 2012-13 quarter which was above the RBI comfort level of 2.5%. In the fourth quarter of 2012-13, CAD fell to 3.6 per cent but for the whole year it was quite high at 4.8 per cent. This shattered the confidence of foreign investors about capability of India to finance its current account deficit. This also caused slowdown in capital inflows and therefore contributed to further weakening of rupee. At a time when the currency of a country is depreciating and economic growth is sluggish (the rate of economic growth was 5% in 2012-13, the lowest in a decade), foreign investors were wary of investing in India since every dollar they would bring in India for investment their earnings from it will be eroded by further depreciation of rupee against US dollar when they repatriate their earnings out of India. Thus a sort of vicious circle was set in as the value of rupee falls. FIIs tried to pull out their money and that in turn made the rupee dip further. This can be offset only by stable capital inflows through FDI or longer-term overseas borrowing.

QUESTIONS FOR REVIEW

1. What is meant by foreign exchange rate ? How is it determined ?
2. Distinguish between floating exchange rate and fixed exchange rate. What type of exchange rate system has been currently adopted by India ?
3. Explain the factors that cause changes in the exchange rate of a currency. How the exchange rate of rupee in terms of US dollar will be affected if India has a deficit on current account of the balance of payments ?
4. Explain the factors which determine demand for foreign exchange, say US dollars.
5. Explain the factors which determine supply of foreign exchange, say US dollar, for India.
6. Explain the fixed exchange rate system adopted under the Bretton-Woods System. Why did it collapse?
7. Explain how a foreign exchange rate is determined. How will the following factors affect foreign exchange rate of rupee ?
   (*a*) Higher rate of inflation in India (*b*) Higher rates of interest in India
8. Critically examine purchasing power parity theory of foreign exchange. What shortcomings of this theory was pointed out by Keynes ?
9. What is meant by depreciation of Indian rupee? How will it affect the Indian economy.
10. Distinguish betwen depreciation and devaluation. How will devaluation or depreciation affect balance of trade and the national economy ? Explain in this connection the concept of *J-Curve*.
11. What is meant by appreciation of a currency ? What will be the effect of appreciation of rupee against dollar on our balance of trade, foreign exchange reserves and price level in the Indian economy ?
12. How is exchange rate determined in open market ? What factors make exchange rate fluctuate?
13. Explain the merits of a flexible exchange rate system. Discuss why Bretton-Woods System had favoured relatively fixed exchange rates.
14. A real depreciation will worsen the trade balance in the short run, but will gradually improve in the long run. Discuss.
15. How do exchange rate changes help in the trade adjustment process ? Discuss the role of monetary or domestic credit factors.
16. How far under flexible exchange rates can countries pursue their own national monetary and fiscal policies without having to worry about the balance of payments ? Is there a need for policy synchronization ?

PART – VII

GOVERNMENT AND THE MACROECONOMY : PUBLIC FINANCE AND FISCAL POLICY

- Public Finance : Public Expenditure
- Public Revenue : Taxation and Budget
- Incidence of Taxation
- Fiscal Policy and Economic Growth in a Developing Country

CHAPTER 31

Public Finance : Public Expenditure

What is Public Finance?

In public finance we study the finances of the Government. Thus, public finance deals with the question how the Government raises its resources to meet its ever-rising expenditure. As Dalton puts it, *public finance is "concerned with the income and expenditure of public authorities and with the adjustment of one to the other."*[1] Accordingly, effects of taxation, Government expenditure, public borrowing and deficit financing on the economy constitutes the subject matter of public finance. Thus, Prof. Otto Eckstein writes "*Public Finance is the study of the effects of budgets on the economy, particularly the effect on the achievement of the major economic objects—growth, stability, equity and efficiency*"[2] Further, it also deals with fiscal policies which ought to be adopted to achieve certain objectives such as price stability, economic growth, more equal distribution of income.

The Importance of Public Finance

Economic thinking about the role that public finance is expected to play has changed from time to time according to the changes in economic situation. Before the Great Depression that gripped the Western industrialised countries during the thirties, the role of public finance was considered to be raising sufficient resources for carrying out the Government functions of civil administration and defence from foreign countries. During this period, the classical economists considered it prudent to keep expenditure to the minimum so that taxing of the people is avoided as far as possible. Further, it was thought that Government budget must be balanced. Public borrowing was recommended mainly for production purposes. During a war, of course, public borrowing was considered legitimate but it was thought that the Government should repay or reduce the debt as soon as possible.

But under the impact of the Great Depression of thirties and the Keynesian explanation of it, the thinking about and role of public finance underwent a sea change. The classical view of public finance could not meet the requirements of the then prevailing situation. In order to increase aggregate effective demand and thereby raise the level of income and employment in the country, public finance was called upon to play an active role. Thus, according to Keynesian economists, to get the economy out of depression the government should increase its expenditure and cut taxes to raise aggregate demand. During the Second World War and after, the Western economies suffered from serious inflationary pressures which was attributed to the excessive aggregate demand. So, in such inflationary conditions, the public finance was expected to check prices through reducing aggregate demand. Thus the budget which was previously meant to raise resources for limited activities of the Government assumed a *functional role* to serve as an instrument of *economic stabilisation*.

It came to be realised that government's taxing and spending policies could go a long way in mitigating economic fluctuations. Balanced budgets are no longer considered sacrosanct and the governments can spend beyond their resources without offending canons of sound finance to restore the health of the economy. Public borrowing and consequent increase in public debt at the time of depression raises aggregate demand and thereby helps in raising the level of income

1. Dalton, *Public Finance,*
2. O. Eckstein, *Public Finance,* Prentice Hall of India Private Ltd., 3rd Edition, p. 53.

and employment. Therefore, deficit budget and increase in public debt at such times is a thing to be welcomed. It was further demonstrated by Keynes that deficit spending by the Government could activise a depressed economy by creating income and employment much more than the original amount of deficit financing through the process of multiplier. Thus, after Keynesian revolution public finance assumed a functional role of *maintaining economic stability at full employment level.* Therefore, the present view of public finance is not one of mere resource-raising for the Government but one of serving as an instrument for maintaining stability through management of demand. Therefore, this present view of public finance has been described by A.P. Lerner as one of "*Functional Finance*".

In developing countries, public finance has to perform another important role. Whereas in the developed industrialised countries, the basic problem in the short run is to ensure stability at full employment level and in the long run to ensure steady rate of economic growth, that is, growth without fluctuations, the developing countries confront a more difficult problem of how to generate and sustain a higher rate of economic growth so as to tackle the problems of proverty and unemployment. Therefore, public finance has to play a special role of promoting economic growth in the developing countries besides maintaining price stability. Further, for developing countries mere economic growth is not enough; the composition of growing output and distribution of additional incomes ought to be such as will ensure removal of poverty and unemployment in the developing countries. Therefore, public finance has not only to augment resources for development and to achieve optimum allocation of resources, but also to promote fair distribution of income and expansion in employment opportunities. This is the functional view of public finance in the context of the developing countries.

PUBLIC FINANCE VS. PRIVATE FINANCE

Before we explain in detail how the Government raises it revenue to meet its ever increasing expenditure, it will be useful to study the difference between Public Finance and Private Finance. It may be noted that there are also some similarities between Public Finance and Private Finance. They are: (*i*) Both the Government and an individual have to balance their budgets either by cutting the expenditure or by raising the resources including borrowing of funds. (*ii*) Both may borrow from others to fill up the gap between their current revenue and current expenditure. (*iii*) According to the basic law of rational choice both the Government and individual try to maximise their benefit with the minimum use of resources. An individual tries to maximise his satisfaction or profit, the Government tries to maximise social benefit. Despite these, there are important differences between the two. They are :

1. Objectives of the two are different. Whereas an individual tries to maximise his satisfaction or profit from the given resources, *the objective of the Government is to maximise social advantage*. According to the law of equi-marginal utility, every individual tries to spread his expenditure on different goods in such a way that he gets the same marginal utility from the last rupee spent on all goods purchased by him. For this purpose he weigh the marginal utilities of various goods he purchases. But, when a Government spends money weighing of social utility or benefit is not possible because it involves interpersonal comparison of utility.

Besides, the Government has to achieve other social objectives. Through its expenditure and taxation policies the Government has to ensure price stability, achieve full employment of resources and above all to promote economic growth of the country as a whole. Achievement of such objectives is out of question for an individual.

2. Budgeting period. For the Government the unit of time for preparing estimates of its revenue and expenditure, that is, a Government budget is for one year. But individual attaches no special sanctity to one-year period for preparing his budget. Further, he need not balance his budget during a given period or by a paritcular date.

3. There can be internal borrowing by the Government but not in case of an individual. To raise resources for financing its mounting expenditure, the Government can borrow not only from abroad *but also from within its own* (*i.e., internally*). On the other hand, an individual can borrow only from others than his own, that is, externally only.

4. Adjustment of Income and Expenditure. A prudent rule followed by an individual is "cut your coat according to your cloth." In other words, an individual adjusts is expenditure to his income, that is, he lives within his given means. But the Government first estimates the expenditure it has to incur and then devises ways and means to raise the required resources to meet that expenditure. In other words, unlike an individual, the Government adjusts its income to the expenditure.

This, however, is not always the case. The individual too some times fixes expenditure to be made, then takes steps to raise his income to be required extent. The Government also sometimes acts like the individual to adjust its expenditure to income.

5. Deficit financing (i.e., printing new money) is a unique privilege of the Government. As explained in a previous chapter, deficit financing means the creation of new money. Financing its expenditure through printing new money is only available to the Government but not to the private individual. When the Government is unable to raise sufficient revenue through taxes, borrowing, raising the prices of its products or services, it takes recourse to deficit financing to balance its budget. But the private individual cannot print new money to balance its budget. If he does so he will be put behind the bars.

6. Provision for the future. In the matter of providing for the future, a government is much more liberal and far-sighted. The Government spends large amounts of money on schemes of development, public works and social security schemes from which either there may be no monetary return or the return may be delayed for generations. The individual, on the other hand, is anxious to reap quick returns. Human life is so uncertain that some individuals discount the future at a very heavy rate. But the community outlasts the individual. It exists in perpetuity. Hence, the Government is bound to make a suitable provision for the future.

7. Surplus budgeting is a virtue for an individual but need not be so for the State. A prudent individual must spent less than he earns. He must have a surplus budget, that is, he should save from his current income. For an individual this is considered a virtue. But for a Government it need not be so. Deficit budgeting during times of a depression to stimulate effective demand has become increasingly acceptable as a means to revive the economy and achieve full employment.

PUBLIC EXPENDITURE

Of the two main branches of public finance, namely, public revenue and public expenditure, we shall first study the public expenditure. The classical economists did not analyse in depth the effects of public expenditure as public expenditure throughout the nineteenth century was very small owing to the very restricted Government activities. The Governments followed *laissez faire* economic policies and their functions were only confined to defend the country from foreign aggression and to maintain law and order within their territories. But now, the expenditure of Government all the world over have greatly increased. Therefore, the modern economists have started analysing the effects of public expenditure on production, distribution and the levels of income and employment in the economy.

Importance of Public Expenditure

Thanks to the macroeconomic theory advanced by J.M. Keynes, the role of public expenditure in the determination of level of income and its distribution is now well recognised. Keynesian macroeconomics provides a theoretical basis for recent developments in public expenditure programmes in the developed countries. The public expenditure can be used as a lever to raise aggregate demand and thereby to get the economy out of recession. On the other hand, through variation in public expenditure, aggregate demand can be managed to check inflation in the economy. Public expenditure can also be used to improve income distribution, to direct the allocation of resources in the desired lines and to influence the composition of national product. In the developing countries also, the role of public expenditure is highly significant.

In the developing countries, the variation in public expenditure is not only to ensure economic stability but also to generate and accelerate economic growth and to promote employment opportunities. The public expenditure policy in developing countries also plays a useful role in alleviating mass poverty existing in them and to reduce inequalities in income distribution. In what follows, we shall study the types of public expenditure, the causes of growth of public expenditure and its effects on production, distribution and economic growth in both the developed and the developing countries.

Classification of Public Expenditure

Revenue Expenditure and Capital Expenditure. Public expenditure has been classified into various categories. Firstly, Government expenditure has been classified into *revenue expenditure* and *capital expenditure.* Revenue expenditure is a current or consumption expenditure incurred on civil administration (*i.e.,* police, jails and judiciary), defence forces, public health and education. This revenue expenditure is of recurrent type which is incurred year after year. On the other hand, capital expenditure is incurred on building durable assets. It is a non-recurring type of expenditure. Expenditure incurred on building multipurpose river projects, power plants, ports, highways, steel plants etc., and buying machinery and equipment is regarded as capital expenditure.

Transfer Payments and Expenditure on Goods and Services. Another useful classification of public expenditure divides it into transfer payments and non-transfer payments. *Transfer payments refer to those kinds of expenditure against which there is no corresponding transfer of real resources (i.e., goods and services) to the Government.* Expenditure incurred on old-age pensions, unemployment allowance, sickness benefits, interest on public debt during a year etc., are examples of transfer payments because the Government does not get any service or goods against them in the particular year. On the other hand, *expenditure incurred on buying or using goods and services is a non-transfer payment as against such an expenditure, the Government receives goods or services.* It is therefore called expenditure on goods and services. It may be noted that expenditure on defence, education, health etc., are non-transfer expenditure as in return for these, Government obtains the services of army personnel, teachers, doctors etc., as well as some goods or equipments used in these activities. Investment expenditure is undoubtedly a non-transfer expenditure as through it Government obtains capital goods. It is worthwhile to mention that whereas in case of transfer payments, it is the beneficiaries who decide about the use of resources, in the case of non-transferable type of expenditure, the Government itself decides about the use of real resources, especially whether they are to be used for consumption or investment purposes.

Developmental and Non-Development Expenditure. Another useful classification of public expenditure rests on whether a particular expenditure by the Government promotes development. All those expenditures of Government which promote economic growth are called developmental expenditure. Expenditure on irrigation projects, flood control measures, transport and communication, capital formation in agricultural and industrial sectors are described as developmental. On the other hand, expenditure on defence, civil administration *(i.e.,* police, jails and judiciary), interest on public debt etc., are put into the category of non-development expenditure. It may be noted that, till recently, expenditure on education and health were regarded as non-developmental type. It has now been realised that the expenditure on education and public health promotes the growth of what is called *human capital* which promotes economic growth as much as physical capital, if not more. Therefore, these days, expenditure on education, research and health are generally regarded as developmental expenditure.

In Indian budgets government expenditure is often classified into *plan expenditure and non-plan expenditure*. Plan expenditure is government expenditure that is made on the schemes and projects included in Five Year Plans and is considered as development expenditure. On the other hand, non-plan expenditure is incurred on civil administration (police, law and order, judiciary), defence and is generally considered as non-developmental expenditure.

It is worth noting that division of Government expenditure into developmental or non-developmental is the modern counterpart of the distinction drawn by classical economists between *productive* and *unproductive public expenditure,* which has been a subject of great controversy. For instance, it has been pointed out that even Government expenditure on defence and civil administration helps to maintain conditions in which productive activity can be carried out. It is, therefore, claimed by some that, indirectly, expenditure on defence and civil administration is also productive. Thus, we see that what Government expenditure is developmental or productive and what non-developmental or unproductive is not based on any objective or fool-proof criteria and is therefore somewhat arbitrary.

CAUSES OF INCREASE IN PUBLIC EXPENDITURE

Public expenditure has phenomenally increased all the world over. A pertinent question is what are the causes of this phenomenal growth in public expenditure. It will be useful to discuss this with reference to India. This is because the factors responsible for a large increase in public expenditure over time in India are generally applicable to other countries too. It will be interesting to mention here two laws about the growth of public expenditure.

Wagner's Law of Increasing State Activity

First, there is *Wagner's Law of Increasing State Activity.* According to Wagner, a German economist, there are inherent tendencies for the activities of the Government to increase both extensively and intensively. In other words, according to this law, as an economy develops over time, the activities or functions of the Government increase. With the development of the economy, new functions and activities are undertaken by the Government and old functions are performed more thoroughly. The expansion in the Government functions and activities leads to the increase in public expenditure. Though Wanger based his law on the historical evidence drawn from economic growth of Germany, this applies equally to other countries, both developed and developing ones.

Wiseman-Peacock Hypothesis

The second hypothesis about the growth of public expenditure has been put forward by Wiseman and Peacock in their study of public expenditure of U.K. According to this *Wiseman-Peacock hypothesis,* Government expenditure does not increase at a steady rate continuously but in jerks and step-like manner. However, in the view of the present author, both these factors, one making for a continuous increase in Government activity and consequently public expenditure as emphasised by Wagner and others like war and depression causing the public expenditure to rise by jerks as emphasised by Wiseman and Peacock have been responsible for the enormous increase in public expenditure. In what follows, we shall explain the factors responsible for the increase in public expenditure with special reference to the Indian economy.

1. Defence. An important factor responsible for public expenditure is the mounting defence expenditure incurred by countries all the world over. It is not only during actual wars that defence expenditure has been rising but even during peace time, the countries have to remain in the state of military preparedness demanding large defence expenditure. There is arms race going on between countries. A poor country like India has to safeguard its hard earned freedom and this involves a lot of expenditure on building up efficient and adequate armed forces. India is wedged in between two enemies, namely, expansionist China and aggressive Pakistan, which have been strengthening their armed forces. India had to fight three wars since independence. India has thus to remain in a state of military preparedness. Internally also in view of clash of linguistic, territorial and political interests, lot of expenditure has to be incurred on maintaining internal security.

2. Population Growth and Urbanisation. Another factor responsible for the increase in public expenditure is the growth in population and urbanisation of the economies. Population has been increasing in almost all countries of the world, though at varying rates. In India the population has been increasing at an alarming rate since independence. The population of India which was 36 crores in 1951 has now gone upto about 121crores in 2011. The scale of government activities such as providing education, public health, roads and transport facilities has to increase in harmony with the growth of population. Further, when population increases, more has to be spent on administrative services (police, jails, judiciary etc.) to maintain law and order in the country.

With the progress of the economy and the growth of population, the extent of urbanisation increases. In India, the proportion of urban population to the total population has risen from 11.3 per cent in 1921 to 25.5 per cent in 1991 and to 27.8 per cent in 2001. As a result of the increasing urbanisation, the existing towns expand and the new ones come up. Urbanisation calls for greater per capita expenditure on social and administrative services. Therefore, the increase in urbanisation in India has tended to increase the government expenditure.

3. Activities of a Welfare State. The Government activities and functions have been increasing due to the change in the nature of State. The modern States are no longer Police States concerned mainly with the maintenance of law and order. They have now become Welfare States. *A Welfare State is one which provides for social insurance of its citizens against old age, sickness, unemployment etc.* The modern Governments have therefore to incur a lot of expenditure on social security measures such as old age pensions, unemployment allowances, sickness benefits.

4. Maintaining Economic Stability. As pointed out by Wagner, state functions increase with the advancement and progress of the economy. In the nineteenth and early twentieth century, the Government followed *laissez-fair* policy. Now, need for active intervention of the Government has been increasingly felt. Thanks to J.M. Keynes whose macroeconomic theory has clearly brought out that the working of free-market mechanism does not ensure economic stability at full employment level. According to his theory, lapses from full employment or depressions are caused by deficiency of aggregate demand due to the slackened private investment activity. In order to compensate for this shortfall in private investment, the Government has to step up its expenditure on public works. The increase in Government expenditure raises aggregate demand manifold through the working of what Keynes has been called income multiplier. This helps to push the economy out of depression and to raise levels of income and employment. Now, this compensatory fiscal policy is being followed by all the world over, since achievement of full employment and maintenance of economic stability has become an important objective of the Government.

It is in line with the objective of employment that, in India, the Government has taken over several *private sick mills* and incurs a lot of expenditure on them so that workers employed in them are not rendered unemployed. Further, the Indian Governments, both of Centre and States, incur a lot of expenditure on relief public works in rural areas when drought and other natural calamities occurs. Besides, a lot of public expenditure is being incurred on *special employment and anti-poverty* schemes to promote the growth of employment in the economy.

5. Economic Growth and Development. The most important factor in developing countries such as ours that has led to a phenomenal increase in public expenditure is the expansion in developmental activities of the Government. In developing countries like India which have socialistic tendencies the public sector plays an important role in promoting economic growth and development. Not only public utility services such as water supply, electricity, post and petroleum and transport services are being provided by the public sector, but also the Government has invested a huge sum of resources in industrial and agricultural development of the economy. Several steel plants, multipurpose irrigation projects, fertilizer factories, coal mining, exploration and production of oil and petroleum, different kinds of machine-making industries and chemical plants have been started and are being operated in the public sector. On these a huge amount of expenditure is being incurred by the

Government in India. Owing to these developmental activities of the Government in India, the proportion of developmental expenditure to the total Government expenditure has greately increased and is greater than that of non-developmental expenditure. In 2003-04, Central Governments plan expenditure, which is mainly development expenditure, was 122.3 thousand crores which rose to 137.4 thousand crores in 2004-05.

6. Mounting Debt Service Charges. The Governments in all developing countries (including India) has been borrowing heavily in recent years to finance their increasing activities. Not only the debt money has to be paid back when it matures, interest payments have also to be made annually to the creditors. These debt service charges have resulted in enormous increase in public expenditure. It should be noted that the Government in India has not only been borrowing from within the country but also from abroad through foreign aid or commerical loans from private capital markets to finance its development plans. It has been estimated that for the year 1998-99, ₹ 75,000 crore were spent on the interest payments which went up to ₹ 125,900 crore in 2004-05 and to 3,80,000 crore in 2013-14 by the Central Government.

7. Mounting Expenditure on Subsidies. Governments, both in the developed and developing countries, incur a lot of expenditure on subsidies to the various sections of population. In India, the Government has been providing subsidies on food, fertilizers, and oil expenditure on them has been increasing at a rapid rate which is the main cause of large fiscal deficit in India. For example while in 2004-2005, the Central Government expenditure on subsidies on these three items was of the order of ₹ 46.5 thousand crore and for the year 2013-14 it was estimated to go up to ₹ 244 thousand crores (RE). The expenditure of Central Government's expenditure on subsidies on food, fertilizers, oil now account for about 12 per cent of total budget expenditure of the Central Government. While the aim of giving food subsidy is to help the people below the poverty line, the aim of fertilizer subsidy is to promote the growth of agriculture and help small farmers.

8. Anti-Poverty Schemes. Another important cause of increasing public expenditure in India is huge expenditure which the Government is incurring on employment generating anti-poverty schemes. It has now been realised that economic growth alone will not eradicate poverty, at least in the short run. Therefore, various employment schemes have been started by the Government for the people living below the poverty line. Prominent among these anti-poverty schemes in India are Mahatma Gandhi National Rural Employment Gurantee Scheme (MGNREGS) and subsidies on food (food secunity) etc. Expenditure on these schemes has greatly risen in recent years.

Conclusion

We have seen above that several factors have been working to cause increase in public expenditure in all the economies of the world. Though most of the factors are common operating all the world over, there are some additional factors in developing countries like India in which public sector plays an important role in the process of socio-economic development. This calls for more rapid growth of public expenditure.

EFFECTS OF PUBLIC EXPENDITURE ON PRODUCTION AND DISTRIBUTION

Having studied the causes of large increase in public expenditure, it will be useful to explain the effects of public expenditure on the production and distribution in the economy. Public expenditure, if properly allocated and efficiently used, can have a wholesome effect on the economy. Public expenditure can augment productive capacity of the economy and improve productivity of its working class. It can also reduce inequalities in income distribution, if properly designed. In the following we shall spell out in detail the impact of public expenditure on production and income distribution in the economy.

Effect of Public Expenditure on Production

It is generally pointed out that all kinds of expenditure by Government is not productive. For instance, Government expenditure on defence and civil administration (police, jail and judiciary) is said to be non-development expenditure for it does not apparently add to the volume of production of the economy. It is true that public expenditure on defence and civil administration are unproductive *directly,* but even they can *under certain circumstances* in an indirect way promote production and employment. This will be made clear a bit later. Further, the effects of public expenditure on production may be different in the case of a developed economy from that of a developing economy, for the circumstances in them differ a good deal. Let us first take the case of a developed economy,

Effect of Public Expenditure on National Output at Times of Depression

Developed economies often find themseleves in the grip of a depression or recession caused by lack of aggregate effective demand. At certain times in the developed countries effective demand falls due to the decline in private investment. At times of depression in an industrialised developed economy, there is idle productive capacity on the one hand and unemployed manpower on the other. Under these circumstances, the increase in Government expenditure on public works or any other type of investment or even expenditure on defence and civil administration will lead to the manifold increase in income and employment through the process of multiplier, as has been explained by J.M. Keynes. The increase in aggregate demand will cause fuller utilization of the existing productive capacity and unemployed manpower resulting in expansion of volume of production, employment and national income. This will become clear from Fig. 31.1 where along the *X*-axis we measure national product or income and on the *Y*-axis aggregate demand which comprises consumption demand (*C*) and investment demand (*I*). It will be seen from Fig. 31.1 that prior to the Government expenditure the aggregate demand curve cuts the 45° line representing aggregate supply curve at point *E*. Thus OY_1 is the equilibrium level of national product or income determined by aggregate demand and supply.

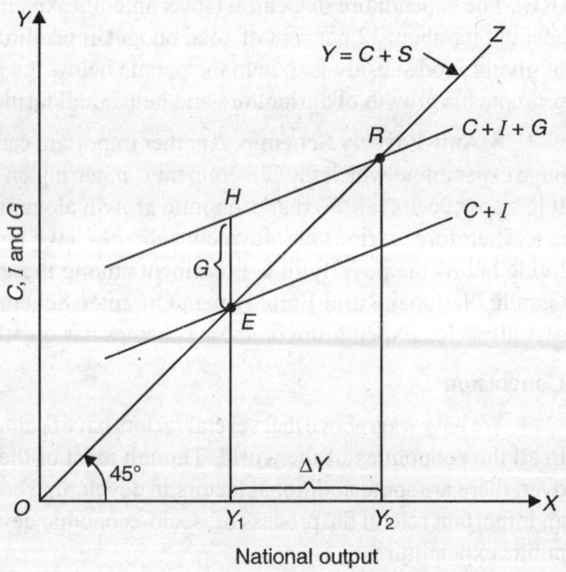

Fig. 31.1. *Effect of Government Expenditure on National Output and Income*

Now, as has been explained in the chapters relating to macroeconomic theory that this equilibrium level may not be established at full-employment level. Suppose full employment of labour and other resources corresponds to OY_2 level of national product. This implies that in equilibrium at OY_1, level of income aggregate demand is not sufficient to ensure full employment. If under these circumstances the Government undertakes extra expenditure, say equal to *EH* or G, then the aggregate demand curve shifts upward to $C + I + G$ position (dotted). As will be seen from Fig. 31.1, the increase in Government expenditure by *EH* will cause the equilibrium level to shift to OY_2 level of national product resulting in higher level of employment. It will be further noticed that the increase in national output (*i.e.,* income) equal to Y_1Y_2 (*i.e.,* ΔY) will be greater than the Government expenditure (*G*) depending upon the magnitude of multiplier. It may be noted that the magnitude of Government expenditure multiplier depends upon the marginal propensity to consume of the people. The size of this multiplier is also equal to $\frac{1}{1-mpc}$ where *mpc* stands for marginal propensity to consume.

From the foregoing analysis we conclude that the increase in Government expenditure preferably financed by borrowings from the banks or printing new notes at times of depression will raise aggregate demand and thereby lead to the multiple increase in national output and employment. But once the level of full employment is attained the increase in Government expenditure cannot raise production through raising aggregate demand. Instead, prices will rise.

Public Expenditure and Economic Growth in Developing Countries. However, even in the developing countries such as India there there are ways in which government expenditure, if judiciously planned, can promote production. First, if the Government expenditure is incurred on *investment projects for capital formation,* for instance on building of canals, power, fertilizer, roads and highways, railways, and other infrastructural facilities, it will expand productive capacity and generate long-term economic growth. Secondly, if public expenditure is directed to *scientific research and development (R & D)*, it will ensure progress in technology and raise productivity or power to produce of workers. Thirdly, it has now been found that Government expenditure on education and public health helps in building "*human capital*" which also greatly enhances productivity or power to produce of the people.

It may however be pointed out that certain types of Government expenditure have been said to adversely affect production. Government expenditure on social insurance like health insurance, unemployment insurance, and old age pensions is said to be of such a type. By insuring against their future and uncertain contingencies like sickness, unemployment and old age, they blunt the edge of the desire to work and save more. The social security expenditure by the Government makes the people indifferent towards the future and makes them neglect savings. This is bound to affect adversely productive efforts in the present. Because of the future security, people will work less and save less. However, *in our view, if such social security expenditure is kept within proper limits and if it is used to help the really needy and helpless, the adverse effects of social security expenditure on production efforts and savings may be negligible*. Further, Government expenditure on social security makes the working people contented and create healthy social environment and industrial peace which is conducive to production. It may be further noted that the higher social security expenditure is an essential element of a *welfare state*. The need for a welfare state was felt because growth under capitalism did not cater to the needs of the poor working class and common man.

Apart from augmenting total production, the Government expenditure also affect *allocation of resources* as between different industries and can divert resources to socially desirable channels. Through subsidies and grants and also through its purchase policy, the Government may succeed in diverting resources to hitherto neglected industries. Thus, besides raising the level of production, the Government expenditure can influence *the pattern of production or composition of output.* Likewise, by diverting resources through subsidies and bounties to the backward regions it can promote growth of output in backward regions. We thus see that public expenditure, if wisely planned, can promote production by raising the levels of productivity or powers to produce and save. It can also cause reallocation of resources between industries and regions and exert wholesome influence on the pattern of production work by the Government undertaken through public enterprises.

Effects of Public Expenditure on Distribution

In the modern times the Government modifies the free working of market mechanism in respect of income distribution not only through devising proper tax structure but also through various forms of public expenditure. Through public expenditure the Government redistributes income in favour of the poor. Too large inequalities in income distribution as produced by the free working of market system is not only socially unjust, but also not conducive to the maximisation of social welfare. Not all types of public expenditure reduce inequalities in income distribution. The following forms of public expenditure redistribute income in favour of the poor and thus reduce inequalities.

1. Social Security Measures. Expenditure on unemployment insurance, sickness benefits, old age pensions are some of the social security measures which help the people at times of contingencies. In India only in recent years some State Governments such as those of Haryana, Punjab, Delhi have introduced old age pension scheme. In capitalist countries such as U.S.A., Great Britain the social security system to help the people emerged with the idea of a Welfare State and in these countries Governments spend a large sum of money on the social security system.

2. Expenditure on Subsidies. Expenditure on various types of subsidies have also a redistributive effect. In India subsidies on food, cooking gas, sugar, kerosene oil, handloom cloth, fertilizers are provided to the people and Government spend a good part of its budget on these subsidies. Food, sugar, kerosene oil are sold through ration shops (*i.e.,* public distribution system) at prices below the market prices and the difference is borne by the Government as a subsidy. It may be noted that at present benefits of these subsidies are enjoyed not only by the poor but all those who are relatively well off. *If the public expenditure on subsidies is to have a real redistributive effect, these subsidies should be targeted at the poor.*

3. Expenditure on Social Infrastrucure. Public expenditure by the Government on social infrastructure such as education, health care of the people, housing for the poor also tend to reduce income inequalities. With free or subsidised education, free or highly subsidised health-care facilities the poor people's real income go up. The modern government spend a lot of money on schools, colleges, etc., to promote education. In most states in India education upto the middle class is free and for higher levels wards of the poor people are either given free education or charged only low fees. However, expenditure on education by the Central Government is relatively very low. In 2013-14, the Central Government's expenditure on education is 74,600 crore which is only 1.29% of GDP.

Similarly, the Governments spend a lot on public hospitals and dispensaries to provide health care to the poor people. In 2013-14 Central Government expenditure on health was 29,360 crore which is only 0.51% of GDP. Likewise, in many countries poor people are given financial aid by the Government to build houses : In India under Indira Awas Yojna, poor people are being given aid to build their low cost houses.

4. Expenditure on Anti-Poverty Programmes. An important step for increasing incomes of the poor people is starting of several employment generating anti-poverty schemes. Prominent among these anti-poverty schemes in India are Mahatma Gandhi National Rural Unemployment Gurantee Scheme (MGNREGS), Integrated Rural Development Programme (IRDP), Indira Awas Yojna, food security.

5. Encouragement to Labour-intensive Industries. The Indian Government gives various types of subsidies to the cottage and small-scale Industries which adopt labour-intensive techniques. Being labour-intensive, the growth of these industries generate a large number of employment opportunities which improve income distribution.

6. Negative Income Tax to Achieve More Equal Distribution of Income. Last but not the least, to achieve more equal distribution of income and make a big dent into the poverty problem, a proposal which has been recently put forward by some economists in the USA and Great Britain is introduction of negative Income Tax. Though the name shows it is a tax, but in fact it is a form of expenditure, called *transfer expenditure.* In this negative income tax scheme, payments are made by the Government to the poor to raise their incomes. Under this system, the Government has first to define *poverty income standard* for families of different sizes. Then it makes payment in the form of direct money transfers to bring the incomes of all families upto that standard or at least to close a large part of the gap between their income and poverty income standard.

However, some economists think that the use of public expenditure to reduce inequalities in income distribution has certain bad effects also. They think it *adversely affects incentives to work and save of the people.* Thus, when people know that in times of difficulties such as unemployment, old age, sickness, the Government will come to their help they will be less willing to work hard. The poor would not work more when they know whatever their income, the gap between the minimum income and theirs will be filled by the Government. Likewise, many people save to live comfortably in old age, and in periods of sickness. But when all these difficult periods are taken care of by the Government their willingness to work more and save more will be badly hurt. Thus, *expenditure to reduce income inequalities, according to this view, will tend to affect adversely incentives to work, save and invest more. All these discourage production and growth.* However, in our view, these adverse effects of the use of public expenditure for reducing income inequalities are exagerated. *Most of the income inequalities are non-functional.* In fact, the public expenditure on employment schemes for the poor and for their health and education will help to build their productive capabilities which, as has been pointed out by Prof. Amartya Sen, will contribute to the growth of the economy.

It is important to note that *redistributive effects of public expenditure must be considered in the light of how it is financed.* For example, if redistributive public expenditure is financed through taxation and if the tax system of the country is regressive, it will work against the desirable distributive effects of public expenditure. For example, if public expenditure is financed through deficit financing, as has been the case in India for several years, it causes inflation in the economy. This inflation hurts the poor most and will therefore cancel out the desired redistributive effects of public expenditure. Thus, if reduction in income inequalities has to be achieved not only the pattern of public expenditure, but also method of financing it and the system of taxation has to be suitably designed and adjusted.

QUESTIONS FOR REVIEW

1. Explain Wagner's Law and Wiseman-Peacock Hypothesis of growth in public expenditure. How do they explain rising expenditure in the developing countries ?
2. Explain the main causes of rapid growth of public expenditure in India. Is this growth justifiable ?
3. Explain the effects of public expenditure on production and distribution in an economy.
4. How does public expenditure reduce inequality in income distribution. ?
5. What are the principles of public expenditure ? What are the effects of public expenditure on production and distribution of income?

CHAPTER 32

Public Revenue : Taxation and Budget

Government Budget Constraint

Having studied the increasing importance of public expenditure in both the developed and developing countries and its effects on production and distribution, we now turn to study of financing Government expenditure. The Government has to finance its expenditure including interest payments on accumulated public debt by using taxation, borrowing from the market (i.e. sale of new bonds) and use of printed money. Increase in rates of income and other taxes not only adversely affects incentives to work more, save and invest more but also causes tax evasion. Further, as Laffer curve concept shows that increase in rate of income tax beyond a point causes revenue from taxes to decline. Thus there are limits to increasing revenue from taxes to finance its increased expenditure fully through normal taxes. This means the government faces a resource constraint resulting in budget deficit which is called these days as *fiscal deficit*. The fiscal deficit is financed either through borrowing from the market or getting new money printed by the Reserve Bank of India. Both borrowing from the market and printing new money to finance increased government expenditure, as shall be explained later, have limitations. It is therefore said that government faces a *budget constraint*. **The government budget constraint refers to the limit to which it can raise resources through taxation, borrowing from the market (i.e., through sale of its bonds) and getting new money printed to meet its expenditure**. The government has to make a choice between the magnitudes of taxation, borrowing from the market and using new printed money to finance its expenditure. Government's budget constraint equation can be written as

$$G = T + \Delta B + \Delta M \quad \ldots (i)$$

where G stands for Government expenditure, T for tax revenue, ΔB for new borrowing (i.e. issue of new bonds) and ΔM for new money created.

Rearranging government budget constraint (*i*) we have

$$G - T = \Delta B + \Delta M \quad \ldots (ii)$$

When G exceeds T, we have a budget deficit. Budget constraint equation (*ii*) says, that budget deficit must be financed either by new borrowing by the Government (ΔB) or by using printed money (ΔM). In this chapter we will explain taxation as a mean of financing Government expenditure and use of borrowing (*i.e.* debt financing) and printed money (*i.e.* money financing) will be explained in the next few chapters.

What is Tax?

A tax is a *compulsory payment* levied on the persons or companies to meet the expenditure incurred on conferring *common benefits* upon the people of a country. Two aspects of taxes follow from this definition : (1) A tax is a compulsory payment and no one can refuse to pay it. (2) Proceeds from taxes are used for *common benefits* or *general purposes* of the State. In other words, there is no direct *quid pro quo* involved in the payment of a tax. This implies that an individual cannot expect or demand that the Government should render him a specific service in return for the tax paid by him. However, this does not imply that Government does nothing for the people from whom it receives taxes. In fact. Government spends the tax money for the general or common benefits of all the people rather than conferring any special benefit on a particular tax payer. To quote Taussig. "The essence of a tax, as distinguished from the other charges by Government is the absence of any direct *quid pro quo* between the tax payer and the public authority."[1]

Tax should be carefully distinguished from a *fee*. Fee is also compulsory payment made by a person who receives in return a particular benefit or service from the Government. For paying fee on a television or radio, a person gets the benefits of programmes relayed by the Government on television or radio. Likewise, students who pay the education fee in schools and colleges, obtain the benefits of teaching arranged by the Government. The amount of fee is always less than the cost of service rendered by the Government in return and therefore covers only a part of the cost of service rendered. Thus, even in case of fee, there is a general public interest or common benefit of the service rendered by the Government. In this case, the Government undertakes a service for the common benefits of the citizens and obtains a fee from those who avail of that service to cover a part of the cost of service rendered.

CLASSIFICATION OF TAXES

The taxes have been variously classified. Taxes can be direct or indirect, they can be progressive, proportional or regressive, and indirect taxes can be *specific* or *ad-valorem*. We spell out below the meanings of these different types of taxes.

Direct and Indirect Taxes. The distinction between direct and indirect taxes is based on whether or not the burden of a tax can be shifted wholly or partly to others. If a tax is such that its burden cannot be shifted to others and the person who pays it to the Government has also to bear it, it is called a direct tax. Income tax, annual wealth tax, capital gains tax are examples of direct taxes. In case of a direct tax there is a direct contact between the tax payer and tax levying public authority.

On the other hand, indirect taxes are those whose burden can be shifted to others so that those who pay these taxes to the Government do not bear the whole burden but pass it on wholly or partly to others. For instance, excise duty on the production of sugar is an indirect tax because the manufactures of sugar include the excise duty in the price and pass it on to buyers. Ultimately, it is the consumers on whom the incidence of excise duty on sugar falls as they will pay higher price for sugar than before the imposition of the tax. Thus, though excise duties are on the production of commodities but they can be shifted to the consumers. Likewise, sales tax on commodities can also be passed on to buyers or consumers in the form of higher prices charged for the commodities. Therefore, excise duties and sales taxes on commodities are examples of indirect tax. They are also known as *commodity taxes.* In the case of indirect taxes, there is an indirect relation between the Government and those who ultimately bear the burden of the taxes.

Specific and Ad-Valorem Taxes. Indirect taxes can be either *specific* or *ad-valorem.* A specific tax on a commodity is a tax *per unit* of the commodity, whatever its price. Thus the amount of total specific tax will vary in accordance with the changes in total output or sales of the commodity and not with the total value of output or sales. On the other hand, an ad valorem type of an indirect tax is levied according to the value of the commodity. For instance, sales tax in India is an ad-valorem tax as the rate of sales tax in case of several commodities is 10 per cent of the value of sales of the commodities. Ad-valorem taxes are progressive in their burden on consumers whereas specific taxes are regressive.

Progressive, Proportional and Regressive Taxes. According to another classification, taxes can be progressive, proportional or regressive. In case of proportional tax, the *same rate* of the tax is charged, whatever be the magnitude of the base on which it is levied. For instance, if rate of income tax is 25 per cent whatever the size of income of a person, it will then be a proportional income tax. Likewise, if rate of wealth tax is 5 per cent, it will be porportional wealth tax. Thus, in case of

1. Taussig, *Principles of Economics*.

proportional tax it is the *rate* which is fixed and not the *absolute* amount of the tax. Thus with the rate of 25 per cent proportional income tax, a person with income of ₹ 25,000 will pay ₹ 6,250 as the tax, and a person with income of 50,000 will pay ₹ 12,500 as the tax. Thus, even under proportional income tax, a richer person has to pay a greater amount of tax though rate of the tax is the same.

On the other hand, *in case of a progressive tax, rate of the tax increases as the amount of the tax base (income, wealth or any other object) increases*. The principle underlying a progressive tax is that greater the tax base, the higher the tax rate. In India income tax, an important direct tax levied by the Central Government, is progressive. Its rate at present (2013-14) varies from 10 per cent in the slab of ₹ 2,00,000 to 5,00,000 to 30 per cent in the slab of income above ₹ 10,00,000. Under progressive income tax, the richer person pays not only absolutely more tax but also a higher rate of the tax. Thus, the burden of progressive tax falls more heavily on the richer persons as compared to proportional income tax.

A regressive tax is the opposite of a progressive tax. In case of a regressive income tax, the rate is lowered as the income rises. Thus, under regressive tax system, the burden of the tax is relatively more on the poor than on the rich. A regressive tax is therefore inequitable and no civilised Government in the world today will levy such a tax.

PRINCIPLES OR CANONS OF A GOOD TAX SYSTEM

A good tax system must fulfil certain principles if it is to raise adequate revenue and fulfil certain social objectives. Adam Smith had explained four canons of taxation which he thought a good tax must fulfil. These four canons are: of (1) *Equality,* (2) *Certainty,* (3) *Convenience,* and (4) *Economy.* These are still regarded as characteristics of a good tax system. However, there has been significant developments in economic theory and policy since Adam Smith wrote his book *"The Wealth of Nations"*. Activities and functions of Government have enormously increased. Now, the Governments are expected to maintain economic stability at full employment level, to reduce inequalities in income distribution, and to perform the functions of a Welfare State. Above all, they are expected to promote economic growth and development, especially in the developing countries, not only through encouraging private enterprise but to undertake themselves the task of production in some strategic industries. Thus, in order to devise a good tax system, these objectives and functions of Government's economic policy must be kept in view.

It may be noted that Adam Smith was basically concerned with how the wealth of nations or, in other words, production capacity of the economy can be increased and he thought that private enterprise working on the basis of free market mechanism would ensure efficient use of resources and, if left unfettered, would bring about rapid economic growth. His ideas about public finance were influenced by his economic philosophy of virtues of free private enterprise. In proposing the above mentioned canons of taxation, he was guided only by the sole objective that Government should be able to raise sufficient revenue to discharge its limited functions of providing for defence, maintaining law and order, and, public utility services. However, as mentioned above, both the objectives and functions of modern Governments have increased necessitating large resources. Therefore, the modern economists have added other principles or characteristics which taxation system of a country must satisfy if the objectives of modern Governments are to be achieved. In what follows we shall spell out in detail the principles and characteristics of a good tax system starting with the explanation of Smith ian canons of taxation.

1. Principle or Canon of Equality

The first canon or principle of a good tax system emphasised by Adam Smith is of equality. According to the canon of equality, every person should pay to the Government according to his ability to pay, that is, in proportion of the income he earns under the protection of the State. Thus under the tax system based on equality principle the richer persons in the society will pay more than the poor. On the basis of this canon of equality or ability to pay Adam Smith argued that taxes should be proportional to income, that is, everybody should pay the same rate or percentage of his income as tax. However, modem economists interpret equality or ability to pay differently from Adam Smith. Based on the assumption of diminishing marginal utility of money income, they argue that ability to pay principle calls for progressive income tax, that is, the rate of tax increases as income rises. Now, in most of the countries, progressive system of income and other direct taxes have been adopted to ensure equality in the tax system.

We shall discuss at length later in this chapter the principle of ability to pay. It may, however, be mentioned here that there are two aspects of ability to pay principle. First is the concept of ***horizontal equity***. According to the concept of horizontal equity, those who are equal, that is, similarly situated persons ought to be treated equally. This implies that those who have same income should pay the same amount of tax and there should be no discrimination between them. Second is the concept of ***vertical equity***. The concept of vertical equity is concerned with how people with different abilities to pay should be treated for the purposes of division of tax burden. In other words, what various tax rates should be levied on people with different levels of income, A good tax system must be such as will ensure the horizontal as well as vertical equity.

2. Canon of Certainty

Another important principle of a good tax system on which Adam Smith laid a good deal of stress is the canon of certainty. To quote Adam Smith, '*The tax which each individual is bound to pay ought to be certain and not arbitrary. The time of payment, the manner of payment, the quantity to be paid ought all. to be clear and plain to the contributor and to every other person.*"[2] A successful function of an economy requires that the people, especially business class, must be certain about the sum of tax that they have to pay on their income from work or investment. The tax system should be such that sum of tax should not be arbitararily fixed by the income tax authorities. While taking a decision about the amount of work effort that a person should put in or how much investment should he undertake under risky circumstances, he must know with certainty the definite amount of the tax payable by him on his income. If the sum of tax payable by him is subject to much discretion and arbitrariness of the tax assessment authority, this will weaken his incentive to work and invest more. Moreover, lack of certainty in the tax system, as pointed out by Smith, encourages corruption'in the tax administration. Therefore in a good tax system, "individuals should be secure against unpredictable taxes levied on their wages or other incomes. The law should be clear and specific; tax collectors should have little discretion about how much to assess tax payers, for this is a very great power and subject to abuse."[3] In the opinion of the present author the Indian tax system violates this canon of certainty as under the Indian income tax law a lot of discretionary powers have been given to the income tax officers, which have been absued with impunity. As a result, there is a lot of harassment of the tax payers and corruption is rampant in the income tax department.

3. Canon of Convenience

According to the third canon of Adam Smith, the amount, time and manner of payment of a tax should not only be certain but the time and manner of its payment should also be convenient to the contributor. If a land revenue is collected at the time of harvest, it will be convenient since at this time farmers reap their crop and obtain income. In recent years efforts have made to make the Indian income tax convenient to the tax payers by providing for its payments in instalments as advance payments at various times during the year. Further, income tax in India is levied on the basis of *income received* rather than *income accrued* during a year. This also makes the income tax system convenient, However, there is a lot of harassment of the tax payers as they are asked to come to the income tax office several times during a year for clarifications of their income tax returns.

2. Adam Smith, *The Wealth of Nations,* Vol. *11,* p. 327.
3. Otto Eckestein, *Public Finance.* Prentice Hall of India Private Ltd., 3rd Edition, p. 53.

4. Canon of Economy

The Government has to spend money on collecting taxes levied by it. Since collection costs of taxes add nothing to the national product, they should be minimised as far as possible. If the collection costs of a tax is more than the total revenue yielded by it, it is not worthwhile to levy it. More complicated a tax system, more elaborate administrative machinary will be employed to collect it and consequently collection costs will be relatively larger. Therefore, even for achieving economy in the tax collection, the taxes should be as simple as possible and tax laws should not be subject to different interpretations.

Other Principles of a Good Tax System For Developing Countries

We have explained above the Smithian canons of a good tax system. Adam Smith viewed the problem of devising a good tax system chiefly from the *viewpoint of tax payers*. Taxation system should also be such that it meets the requirements of increasing state activity and achieves the objectives the society has placed before it. We explain below the characteristics and principles of a good tax system, especially in the context of the developing countries.

1. Productivity or Fiscal Adequacy: An important principle of a good tax system for a developing country is that it should yield adequate amount of resources for the Government so that it should be able to perform its increasing welfare and developmental activities. If the tax system fails to yield enough resources, the Government will resort to money financing, that is, printing new money. An excessive dose of deficit financing is bound to raise prices which are harmful for the society. To make the tax system sufficiently productive it should be broad-based and both direct and indirect taxes find place in it. Moreover, taxes should be progressive so that the revenue from them rises with the increase in income of the people.

2. Elasticity of Taxation : Another principle of taxation suitable for the developing countries is the principle of elasticity of taxation. According to the concept of elasticity of the taxation system, as national income increases as a result of economic growth, the Government revenue from taxes should also increase. In developing countries, the share of tax revenue as a proportion of national income is low as compared to the developed countries. This share of tax revenue will rise as national income increases if the tax system is sufficiently elastic. Progressive taxation of income and wealth provides this elasticity to the tax system. Imopositions of higher indirect taxes on luxury goods having a high income elasticity of demand also makes the tax system elastic.

3. Diversity : A good tax system should follow the principle of diversity. This implies that there should not be a single or a few taxes from which Government seeks to raise large revenue. This is because if a Government tries to get large revenue from a single tax or few taxes, it will have to raise the rates of taxation too high which will not only adversely affect the incentives to work, save and invest but also encourage evasion of taxes. Therefore, the tax system should be a multiple tax system with a large variety of taxes so that all those who can contribute to the public revenue should be made to do so. This calls for a mix of various direct and indirect taxes. With the diverse tax system, the principles of fiscal adequacy and equity will also be better satisfied. Commending a diversity in the tax system Arthur Young writes, "*If I were to define a good system of taxation, it should be that of bearing lightly on an infinite nurpber of points, heavily on none*". Similarly, another expert of public finance writes, "*Excessive reliance on any one base may produce adverse economic effects because the rates may become too high. Therefore, a tax system may do less economic damage if it raises moderate amounts from several bases rather than large amounts from one or two.*"[4]

4. Role of Taxation in Promoting Economic Growth. In a developing economy such as ours, taxation should serve as an instrument of economic growth. Economic growth is primarily a function of rate of capital formation. If in the development strategy public sector has been assigned an eminent place, then capital formation in the public sector must occur at a relatively higher rate. This

4. Otto Eckestein, op.cit.

calls for mobilisation of resources by the Government so as to finance capital formation in public sector. Therefore, a good tax system for a developing country will be such as will enable the Government to mobilise adequate resources for capital formation or economic growth. This it can do in the following two ways.

(*a*) ***Mobilisation of Economic Surplus.*** An important principle for a developing country is that it should mobilise economic surplus found in the economy. Economic surplus is the "surplus of national income over *essential consumption*". It is the task of taxation system that it should restrain non-essential or unproductive consumption through appropriate system of progressive direct and indirect taxes and thereby mobilise economic surplus. "In an underdeveloped economy, there are particular economic sectors and classes of people where the economic surplus is generally found and which therefore should receive the special attention of tax authorities in such countries."[5]

(*b*) ***Increase in the Intermental Saving Ratio.*** A good tax system not only tries to mobilise the existing economic surplus but also seeks to raise it with a view to mop up relatively greatei amount of increase in national income for the purpose of capital formation. Thus taxation in a developing economy has not only to restrain current unproductive consumption but also to check the large increases in consumption when with the increase in national income, economic surplus goes up. This will ensure rise in the incremental or marginal saving ratio which is a prime determinant of continuous economic growth. In other words, through the means of taxation consumption should not be allowed to increase in proportion to increase in incomes. Expansion in economic surplus accruing to the individuals should be mobilised and invested in the public sector for further growth. Progressive income tax and indirect taxes on goods with higher income elasticity will ensure this,

5. Taxation as sn Instrument for Improving Income Distribution. A good tax system for a developing economy should also serve as an instrument for reducing economic inequalities. The purpose of a good tax system for a developing economy is not merely to raise revenue for the Government but also to ensure that burden of taxes falls more on the rich. This requires that the rates of progressive direct taxes on income, wealth, expenditure, capital gains etc., must be sufficiently high. This objective of reducing income inequalities will be better served if a good part of the tax revenue is used for proverty alleviation programmes.

6. Taxation for Ensuring Economic Stability. A tax system must also ensure economic stability. Economic fluctuations have been a big problem in the developed countries and for reducing these fluctuations taxation can play a useful role. For this purpose, tax system must have built-in-flexibility. To have built-in-flexibility, the taxation system must be progressive in relation in the changes in national income. This will ensure that when national income rises, an increasing part of the rise in income should automatically accrue to the Government. On the other hand, when national income falls, as in a recession or depression, the revenue obtained from progressive taxes will fall more rapidly than the decline in national income. Built-in-flexibility attained through progressive taxation ensures that when incomes are increasing during the period of boom or inflation, the relatively greater amount of tax revenue accruing to Government will moderate the increase in purchasing power with the people and thus help in keeping prices under check. Likewise, under progressive taxation at times of depression or recession, tax revenue will fall faster than the income so that purchasing power of the people does not fall as fast as their pre-tax income. This will serve to check decline in economic activity.

However, in developing countries, the problem is more of restraining inflation so as to achieve price stability. By discouraging or restraining consumption, especially of non-essential or unproductive type, taxation can pay a useful role in controlling inflation in the developing countries.

5. T. Mathew, *Tax Policy: Some Aspects of Theory and Indian Experience,* p. 31.

Conclusion

From the foregoing analysis, we conclude that in the world today taxation is called upon to achieve several socio-economic objectives. It is not just a means of raising revenue for the limited functions of the State. ***Neutrality principle*** of taxation, that is, leave them as you find them, no longer finds favour with the modern economists. Tax system today has to play a more positive role. It is intended to bring about rapid economic growth, reduce inequalities of incomes, promote stability and to achieve other socio-economic objectives.

PRINCIPLES OF EQUITY IN TAXATION

An important question widely discussed in public finance is what kind of tax system is fair, just or equitable. As seen above, equity in taxation was the first canon of taxation on which Adam Smith laid a good deal of stress. A fair tax system is not merely an issue in pure economic analysis but also in social philosophy. There are two prominent theories put forward to devise a fair or equitable tax system. They are (1) Benefits Received Theory and (2) Ability to pay Theory. We discuss below these two theories of equity in taxation.

Benefits Received Theory

According to this theory of taxation, citizens should be asked to pay taxes in proportion to the benefits they receive from the services rendered by the Government. This theory is based upon the assumption that there is an exchange relationship or *quid pro quo* between the tax payer and Government. The Government confers some benefits on the tax payers by performing various services or providing them what are called social goods. In exchange for these benefits individuals pay taxes to the Government. Further, according to this theory, equity or fairness in taxation demands that an individual should be asked to pay a tax in proportion to the benefits he receives from the services rendered by the Government.

However, there are some difficulties in application of this theory. The most crucial problem faced by benefits received approach is that it is *difficult to measure the benefits* received by an individual from the services rendered by the Government. For instance, how much benefit an individual tax payer derives from providing for national defence and education, and maintaining law and order by the Government cannot be measured with any objective criterion. Secondly, most of the Government expenditure is incurred on common indivisible benefits so that the division of benefits of Government expenditure is not possible.

Further, benefits received theory miltilates against the very notion of a tax. A tax is defined as a payment for general purposes of the State and not in return for a specific service. The benefit theory can have meaning if the benefits of the Government services to the community as a whole is considered. But this will only indicate how much total tax revenue the community should pay to the Government. This will not help us in dividing the tax liability among various individuals comprising the community. It may be noted that most important common benefits are peaceful enjoyment of life, liberty and property. So far as life and liberty are concerned, Government's protection is the same for all. This will indicate levying of a toll tax. But toll tax has long been discarded as it was found to be highly regressive and also a small yielder of revenue.

The benefit principle is applicable only in cases where the beneficiaries can be clearly identified. Thus benefit principle is applied to the collection of road tax from vehicle owners. This is also applied when local bodies collect special levies for the services such as construction of sewers and roads they render to the people of their locality. The benefit principle is also applied to social security programmes for workers. Social security contributions, or what are called payroll taxes, are collected from workers and are kept in reserves out of which benefit payments are made to them. To conclude, therefore, "at best the benefit principle can provide a partial solution to the problem of fairness in taxation."[6]

6. Otto Kckstein, *op*. cit, p.54

Ability to Pay Theory

The ability to pay is another criterion of equity or fairness in taxation. This theory requires that individuals should be asked to pay taxes according to their ability to pay. The rich have greater ability to pay, therefore they should pay more tax to the Government than the poor. Essentially, the ability to pay approach to fairness in taxation requires that *burden of tax* falling on the various persons should be the same. In the discussion of various characteristics of a good tax system, we mentioned about the two concepts of equity, namely, horizontal equity and vertical equity based on the principle of ability to pay. According to the concept of horizontal equity, equals should be treated equally, that is, persons with the same ability to pay should be made to bear the same amount of tax burden. According to the vertical equity, unequals should be treated unequally, that is, the tax burden among poeple with different abilities to pay be so divided that those who have greater ability to pay should be asked to pay more. In both these cencepts of equity, what excatly do we mean by ability to pay and what are the objective measures of ability to pay are crucial. Some have explained the ability to pay treating it as a subjective concept. Others have treated the ability to pay in terms of some objective bases such as income, wealth, consumption expenditure etc. We shall explain below both these approaches to the measurement of ability to pay.

Ability to Pay : Subjective Approach

In the subjective approach to tax paying ability, the concept of *sacrifice* undergone by a person in paying a tax occupies a crucial place. In paying a tax, a person feels a pinch or suffers from some disutility. This pinch or disutility felt by a tax payer is the sacrifice made by him. In this subjective approach to ability to pay, tax burden is measured in terms of sacrifice of utility made by the tax payers. The following three principles of sacrifice have been put forward by various authors:

1. The Principle of Equal Absolute Sacrifice;
2. The Principle of Equal Proportional Sacrifice; and
3. The Principle of Equal Marginal Sacrifice (or Minimum Aggregate Sacrifice).

Equal Absolute Sacrifice

The principle of equal absolute sacrifice implies that the *tax burden in terms of utility sacrificed* should be the same for all tax payers. If U stands for total utility, Y stands for income and T for the amount of tax paid, then the principle of equal absolute sacrifice requires that $U(Y) - U(Y - T)$ should be the same for all individuals. The term $U(Y)$ implies that total utility of a given income Y and $U(Y - T)$ implies the total utility of the post-tax income $(Y - T)$. If the *equal absolute sacrifice principle* is applied, none will be exempted from taxation and every body will pay same amount of the tax. Now, the pertient question is what type of tax, proportional or progressive, follows from this principle. If marginal utility of money income falls, as is generally believed, and if this fall in marginal utility of money income equals the rate of increase in income, then this principle suggests proportional income tax. However, if the fall in marginal utility of income is greater than the rate of increase in income, then equal absolute sacrifice principle will suggest progressive income tax.

Equal Proportional Sacrifice. This principle requires that every person should be made to pay so much tax that the sacrifice of utility as a proportion of his income is the same for all tax payers. In terms of the notation used above, this implies that $\frac{U(Y) - U(Y - T)}{U(Y)}$ of all tax payers should be equal. If a person enjoying higher income is to bear same proportion of sacrifice, then given the falling marginal utility of income, he will have to pay income tax at a higher rate. This means progressive income tax.

Equal Marginal Sacrifice. According to this principle, tax burden should be so apportioned among various individuals that marginal sacrifice of utility of each person paying the tax should be the same. *This approach seeks to minimize the aggregate sacrifice of the society as a whole.* When all persons pay so much tax that their marginal sacrifice of utility is the same, the loss of total utility by the society will be minimum. Thus, the principle of equal marginal sacrifice looks at the problem of dividing the tax burden from the point of view of welfare of the whole society. The social philosophy underlying this principle is that the total sacrifice imposed by taxation on the community ought to be minimum. Assuming that marginal utility of income falls, the principle of equality of marginal sacrifice implies very high marginal rates of taxation. Indeed, in the extreme this principle can be used to recommend 100 per cent rate of tax on the people in highest income bracket in the society. Thus this principle recommends a highly progressive tax structure. This principle of taxation has been recommended among others by Edgeworth, Pigou and Musgrave who consider this as the ultimate principle of taxation. It is worthwhile to quote Edgeworth, a chief exponent of this principle. "The minimum sacrifice is the sovereign principle of taxation. If one is utilitarian and believes not only in the measurability of utility but also in the view that the law of diminishing utility is applicable to money also, then this principle would involve a high level of minimum exemption and a very steep progression as income increases .... The less the aggregate sacrifice, the better the distribution of tax burden in the community. The State exists to maximize human welfare. This it will be able to do by minimizing the sacrifices involved."

Comments. The whole subjective approach to ability to pay based on the sacrifice of utility has been termed as invalid because utility being a subjective entity cannot be measured in cardinal sense. Further, it is alleged there is no definite evidence that marginal utility of money income falls as income increases. Interpersonal comparison of utility which the sacrifice approach requires is held to be unscientific. However, in the view of the present author, these objections against ability to pay or sacrifice principle are not valid. We may not be able to measure utility of money income in exact absolute terms but a sufficiently good measure of utility of income can be obtained and this is enough for the application of this principle of ability to pay in terms of sacrifice. Observations in the world clearly indicate that people in the lower income brackets spend most of their incomes on buying necessaries, while people in the higher income groups spend a relatively greater proportion of their incomes on luxuries and non-essential goods. In view of this it is quite valid to assume diminishing marginal utility of money for purpose of taxation.

Ability to Pay : Objective Approach

The objective approach to the ability to pay principle considers what should be objective base of taxation which measures ability to pay correctly. There is even no agreement on this question also. However, income is generally considered to be the best measure of ability to pay. This is because a person's income determines a person's command over resources during a period to consume or to add to his wealth. However, it may be noted that ability to pay does not increase in direct proportion to money income. Ability to pay increases more than proportionately to the amount of income. Justification of progressive income tax is based on this. Further, in order to ensure equity in taxing income distinction ought to be made between earned income and unearned income, and considerations should also be given for a number of dependents on the person paying the tax.

Wealth of a person is another objective measure of ability to pay that has been suggested as a tax base. The ownership of the property or wealth of an individual determines how much resources he has accumulated. Saving from every year's income adds to his wealth. The wealth or property is therefore said to be a better index of taxable capacity.

It may however be noted that wealth alone is not considered to be adequate measure of taxable capacity and instead a combination of income and wealth taxes is regarded as a better measure from the viewpoint of ability to pay. Thus, according to Prof. Kaldor, *"Only a combination of income and property taxes can give approximation to taxation in accordance with ability to pay"*.[7] Arguing the case for levying annual wealth tax in India, he writes "income taken by itself is an inadequate yardstick

7. See Nicholas Kaldor, *An Expenditure Tax,* Allen and Unwin, 1955.

of taxable capacity as between income from work and income from property, and also as between different property owners". He further writes, "the ownership of property in the form of disposable assets endows the property-owner with a taxable capacity as such quite apart from the money income which that property yields."

It follows form above that a combination of income tax and wealth tax will be a better measure of ability to pay.

Prof. Kaldor has also advocated another base for taxation. He has been a strong advocate of *levying of expenditure tax* in both the developed and developing countries.[8] It should be noted that his expenditure tax is in fact a tax on consumption, that is, income minus saving. He claims that *it is consumption that is a fair or equitable base of taxation.* According to him, it is consumption that measures the resources that a person actually withdraws from the economy for his personal use. The part of his income not consumed, that is, savings lead to the increase in the capital stock and thus add to society's productive capacity. If a person consumes more than his income, he should the made to pay a higher tax because he reduces the capital stock of the country.[9] *The imposition of expenditure tax, according to Kaldor, is particularly relevant for developing countries where high consumption expenditure of richer classes reduces the rate of capital accumulation.* Imposition of expenditure tax will discourage consumption by taxing it heavily and promote savings by exempting it. In 1958 on the recommendation of Kaldor expenditure tax was levied in India. But after some years it was withdrawn on the ground that it was difficult to administer it and also that the revenue from it was very small.

Conclusion. In conclusion it may be said that it is *better to levy taxes on various bases instead of a single base.* As explained in the section of characteristics of a good tax system, *diversity of tax bases is preferable not only from the viewpoint of a measure of ability to pay but also because it will have less adverse economic effects.* Eckstein rightly points out, "Excessive reliance on any one base may produce adverse economic effects because the rates may become *too high. Therefore, a tax system may do less economic damage if it raises moderate amounts from several bases rather than larger amounts from one or two.*"[10] Perhaps it is because of these reasons that in actual practice, a good variety of taxes are levied. In India, income tax, corporation tax, wealth tax and union excise duties are the most important taxes levied by the central Government, while sales tax, land revenue, and certain excise duties are the important taxes at the state level.

DIRECT TAXES VS. INDIRECT TAXES

We have explained above the characteristics of a good tax system. A controversial issue in public finance is concerned with whether in tax structure of an economy direct or indirect taxes should be preferred. Indeed, both direct taxes and indirect taxes have their merits and demerits and therefore a good tax system should contain a proper mix of these two types of taxes. Direct taxes, it may be recalled, are those which are levied directly on the individuals and firms and their burden is borne by those on whom they are levied. Personal income tax, corporate income tax, wealth tax, expenditure tax, gift tax are some examples of direct taxes. On the other hand, indirect taxes are levied on production and sale of commodities and services. A small or a large part of the burden of an indirect tax is passed on to the consumers. Excise duties on the production of commodities, sales tax, service tax, tax on railway or bus fare are some examples of the indirect tax. The Indian tax system contains a combination of both direct and indirect taxes. We discuss below the merits and demerits of both direct and indirect taxes. It should be noted that tax has to be judged especially from the following viewpoints:

8. *Ibid.*
9. Nicholas Kaldor, *Indian Tax Reforms.*
10. Otto, Eckstein, *op. cit.,* p. 56.

1. Equity;

2. Efficiency in allocation of resources;

3. Economic growth, that is, whether it promotes or discourages supply of work effort (labour), saving and investment on which economic growth depends;

4. Buoyancy, that is, to what extent revenue from tax increases with the increase in income; and

5. Economic stability.

Merits of Direct Taxes

1. An important merit of direct taxes is their rate structure be *so designed which is closely related to the ability jo pay principle.* The direct taxes can be made progressive and the degree of progression among different income brackets can be determined so as to satisfy the principle of ability to pay. The larger burden of these progressive taxes fall on the rich people who have capacity to bear them and the poor people with less ability to pay have to bear less burden.

2. Direct taxes are *important instrument of reducing inequalities of income and wealth.* A progressive income tax, imposition of progressive wealth tax and estate duties have been used in different countries to reduce inequalities in income distribution. Large inequalities are harmful for maximization of social welfare. They are even bad from the viewpoint of achieving economic stability.

3. Another important merit of direct taxes is that unlike indirect taxes *they do not cause distortion in the allocation of resources.* As a result, they leave the consumers better off as compared to indirect taxes. Direct taxes such as general income and wealth taxes do not affect relative prices of goods and services and therefore leave the relative profitability of different industries unchanged. As a result, resource allocation among them remain unaffected. Therefore, from the viewpoint of efficiency in resource allocation direct taxes are preferred to indirect taxes.

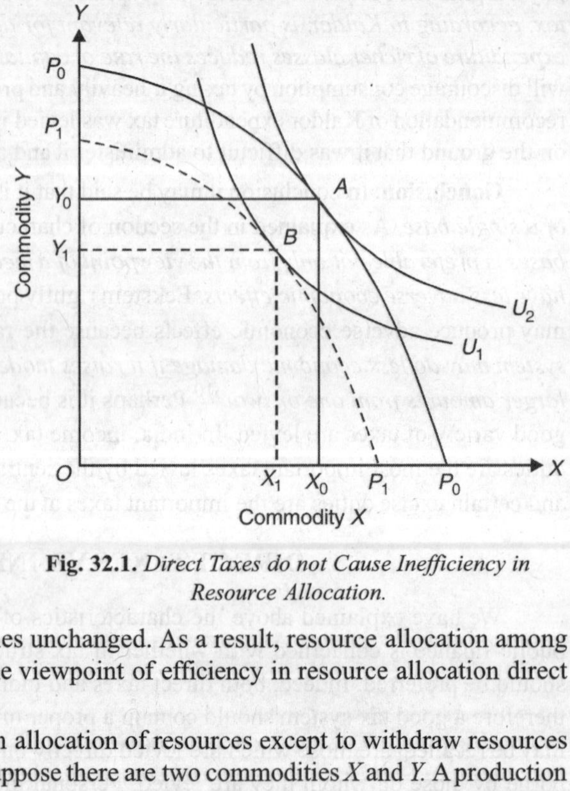

Fig. 32.1. *Direct Taxes do not Cause Inefficiency in Resource Allocation.*

That the direct taxes have no effect on allocation of resources except to withdraw resources from private use is illustrated in Fig. 32.1. Suppose there are two commodities X and Y. A production possibility curve P_0P_0 of a community is drawn. U_1, U_2 are the indifference curves of the community showing successively higher levels of welfare. In equilibrium and without a direct tax, the economy is producing X_0 of commodity X and Y_0 of commodity Y. Allocation of resources is efficient as by producing X_0 of good X and Y_0 of good Y, the community is reaching the highest possible indifference curve U_2. *With this social welfare is maximum because marginal rate of transformation (MRT_{xy})in production is equal to marginal rate of substitution (MRS_{xy})of the community between the two commodities.*

Now suppose a certain amount of revenue is collected by leying a direct tax, say personal income tax. Since through this tax private purchasing power has been reduced, some resources will be freed for Government use. The new production possibility curve for the private economy shifts downward to P_1P_1. Now, the private economy is in equilibrium at point B, where P_1P_1 is tangent to the community indifference curve U_1 and X_1 of good X and Y_1 of good Y are being produced. At point B, marginal rate of substitution between X and Y of the community (MRS_{xy}) equals marginal rate of transformation (MRT_{xy}) in production between the two goods. Thus, resource allocation between the two goods remains efficient. Of course, resources for the use of private sector have been reduced.

4. Fourthly, *revenue elasticity of direct taxes, especially if they are of progressive type is quite high.* As the national income increases, the revenue from these taxes also rises a great deal. It is due to this fact that progressive direct taxes serve as *automatic stabilizers.* When during upswing the economy gains momentum and boom conditions emerge, a relatively larger fraction of increasing income are siphoned of through the progressive direct taxes. This acts as a brake on the economy getting into serious inflationary situation. Similarly, when during downswing the income and employment of the community is falling, due to the progressive nature of the direct taxes a relatively smaller part of income is taken away by way of these taxes. Therefore, the consumption demand does not fall to the same extent as the decrease in income. This prevents further slowdown of the economy which turns around and thereby recovery of the economy starts.

Demerits of Direct Taxes

We have seen from above that the viewpoints of achieving equity, efficiency, economic stability direct taxes are desirable. However, there are some demerits of direct taxes which we discuss below:

1. Direct Taxes may Reduce Supply of Work Effort. An important harmful effect of direct taxes, especially if their marginal rates are quite high, is that they *reduce people's willingness to put forth larger productive effort, that is, as a result of, say income tax, They supply less labour for productive work.* With lesser productive effort or smaller labour supply economic performance of the economy is undermined and economic growth is adversely affected. There are two alternatives before an individual: either enjoy more leisure or do more work. When income tax is imposed, after-tax wage rate, that is, return from work diminishes or, in other words, opportunity cost of leisure falls. This induces the individual to substitute leisure for work effort. As a result, supply of work effort is reduced. To quote Eckstein, "*If a worker has to pay taxes, say one half of his income from extra work, perhaps a lawyer working week-ends, a doctor taking on additional patients or a sales-person making evening calls—his incentives will certainly be reduced.*" He further writes about direct taxes, "*if their high rates diminish work effort substantially throughout the economy, we are giving up a lot of economic performance for the sake of equity.*"[10]

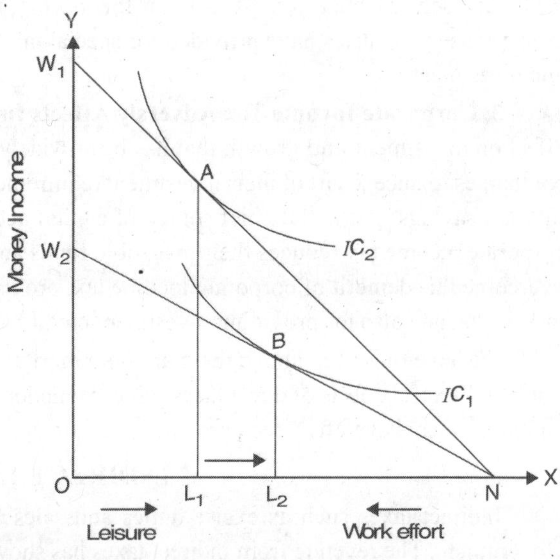

Fig. 32.2. *Effect of Income Tax on Supply of Work Effort*

Let us illustrate the harmful effect of a direct tax, say income tax, on supply of work effort (*i.e.,* labour). In Fig. 32.2 we have drawn the indifference curves of an individual between income and leisure. Suppose before taxation, the wage rate is depicted by the slope of the wage line NW_1. The individual is in equilibrium at point A on indifference curve IC_2 where he is enjoying OL_1 leisure and

10. Otto, Eckstein, *Public Finance,* Prentice Hall.

working NL_1 hours.

Suppose a proportional income tax at the rate of 50% is levied. As a result, after-tax wage rate is reduced and after-tax wage line shifts below to NW_2. The individual moves to equilibrium point B on indifference curve IC_1. In this equilibrium situation B the individual has increased his leisure to OL_2 and reduced his work effort to NL_2. Thus, as a result of levying of income tax and consequently lowering of the wage rate the individual has substituted leisure for work, resulting in the decrease of labour supply (*i.e.,* work effort). This is a normal behaviour. Of course, there are some exceptions to this normal behaviour.

2. Direct Taxes Reduce Incentives to Save and Invest. A significant adverse effect of direct taxes is that *they reduce incentives to save and invest.* People save and invest their savings by sacrificing present consumption. Investment of savings yields a return. Here the *choice is between present consumption and saving for investment.* A direct tax, say income tax, reduces the rate of return on investment since a part of the return is taken away through tax. Thus, with the imposition of income tax, rate of return on investment is reduced which induces the individuals to substitute present consumption for saving and investment. As a consquence, *levying of income tax induces more consumption and discourages saving and investment.* The lower saving and investment retards economic growth. Empirical studies made in India and USA have shown that high rates of direct taxes have adversely affected savings. It is for this reason, that in recent years budgets in India and the industrialised countries have provided for special tax treatment of some particular forms of saving and investment.

3. Corporate Income Tax Adversly Affects Investment. It is corporate income tax and its effect on investment and growth that has been widely discussed. Corporations, that is, joint stock companies finance a part of their investment requirements by using their internal savings. It is these internal savings that is the chief source of capital accumulation by the companies. Imposition of corporate income tax reduces their investible funds and thereby ratards investment and growth. To overcome this demerit of corporate income tax, provisions for exempting depreciation funds from income tax and also for providing investment credit have been generally made in the budgets.

We have thus seen above there are both merits and demerits of direct taxes. In order to have minimal harmful effects of direct taxes some exemptions, special tax treatment of depreciation, saving and investment have often been provided in income tax and wealth tax laws.

INDIRECT TAXES

Indirect taxes such as excise duties and sales tax are important source of revenue for the Government. The revenue from indirect taxes has shown a great deal of buoyancy. In India revenue from indirect taxes has been continuously increasing. In Table 32.1 given below we give the tax revenue raised from direct and indirect taxes as percentage of gross tax revenue of the Central Government. It will be seen from the table that in 1995-96 indirect taxes, (customs and union excise duties) accounted for about 70 per cent of tax revenue of the Central Government while personal income tax and corporation tax accounted for about 28 per cent of total tax revenue. However, as a result of reduction in customs duties and excise duties by the Central Government in recent years, the proportion of indirect taxes to the total Central revenue has fallen to about 44 per cent and correspondingly the proportion of direct taxes has risen to about 55 per cent in the fiscal year 2011-12. The rise in proportion of direct taxes implies that tax structure has become more progressive. Let us now explain the merits and demerits of indirect taxes.

Table 32.1. Tax Revenue as Percentage of Gross Tax Revenue of Central Government in India

	1994-95	1995-96		2007-08		2011-12	
Personal Income Tax	13.0	13.0	28.0	17.5	49.9	18.6	54.9
Corporation	15.0	15.0		32.3		36.3	
Customs	29.0	32.0	69.2	17.6		16.8	
Excise Duties	40.5	37.2		20.8	47.0	16.3	44.1
Service tax	–	–		8.6		11.0	

Source : GOI, *Economic Survey,* 2007-08, 2011-12 and 2012-13

Merits of Indirect Taxes

1. Convenient to Pay and Less Cumbersome. A significant merit of indirect taxes is *that they are convenient to pay and less cumbersome as compared to direct taxes.* In case of indirect taxes such as an excise duty or a costum duty people have to pay these taxes *bit by bit* when they produce, sell and buy these commodities. This piecemeal payment of an indirect tax makes it easier for the tax payers who do not feel its pinch in contrast to direct taxes. Indirect taxes are also not difficult to collect as they are collected from the firms and traders who pass them on to the buyers in the form of higher prices of goods.

2. Large Revenue Potential. Another important merit of indirect taxes is that *they have a large revenue potential* for the Government. Through indirect taxes even the poor and low-income people can be brought in the tax net. Whoever, rich or poor, buys commodities ultimately bears the burden of indirect taxes. But direct taxes such as income tax cannot be levied on the poor as cost of collection from them will be much higher and also there is need for some exemption limit. For example in India with a population of over 121 crore only about 12 million people pay income tax. On the other hand, a much large number of people pay indirect taxes such as excise duties, sales tax, tax on railway and bus fare. Thus through indirect taxes, *a large amount of resources can be raised* for meeting increasing requirements of the Government.

A large revenue potential of indirect taxes has a special importance for the developing countries like India where resources are needed by the Government not only to run the general administration and provide for defence but also for *investment and economic growth.* For accelerating capital formation and economic growth, the developing countries cannot rely on revenue from direct taxes alone. Revenue from indirect taxes can be increased substantially by bringing more commodities under their purview and increasing their rates. It has been found that revenue from indirect taxes show a great deal of *buoyancy,* that is, revenue from them increases very much with the growth of national income.

3. Important Instrument for Influencing Pattern of Production and Investment Another merit of indirect taxes is that it serves as an important tool for influencing pattern of production and investment in an economy. The working of market mechanism, left to itself, does not always ensure desirable or optimum pattern of productions and investment allocation. For example, left to itself market mechanism may lead to greater investment in producing harmful goods such as alcohol, cigarettes, luxury goods such as airconditioners, washing machines, luxury cars. By imposing heavy excise and sales taxes, the production and investment in these industries can be discouraged. Similarly, indirect tax structure can be so designed as to encourage employment generation and the use of appropriate technology. For example, in India heavy excise duties have been levied on mill-made cloth while handloom cloth has been exempted from them. This has been done to promote the production of handloom cloth, a labour-intensive product, to promote employment generation. The point which is being emphasised is that *indirect faxes can be selective commodity-wise and ratewise* so as to affect the prices of different commodities to promote higher priority industries and discourage low priority ones.

Demerits of Indirect Taxes

Indirect taxes have been criticized for some of their shortcomings which we explain below :

1. Indirect Taxes are Regressive. An important criticism of indirect taxes is that they are *regressive,* that is, people with lower incomes bear a higher burden as compared to the rich people. Rich or poor has to pay the same rate of excise duty or sales tax levied on commodities irrespective of their ability to pay. Thus, the fact that same rate of an excise duty on sugar, mill-made cloth etc., has to be paid both by the poor and rich, violates the principle of equity as poor people have lower ability to pay than the rich. However, the regressive nature of indirect taxes has been sought to be removed by levying higher taxes on luxuries which only rich people buy.

2. Indirect Taxes are Inflationary. Another important ground on which indirect taxes have been opposed is that they are *inflationary,* that is, they cause a rise in prices of commodities. In India before 1991 in order to raise more revenue rates of indirect taxes were often raised by Finance ministers. Even essential commodities such as sugar, cloth, petroleum products were subjected to heavy excise duties and sales taxes. These taxes were wholly or partly added to the prices of goods which caused *cost-push inflation.*

In this connection it is to important to mention the *cascading effect* of indirect taxes which add to their inflationary potential. Cascading effect refers to the effect of indirect taxes on the prices of inputs of the industrial commodities. Higher prices of inputs as a result of levying indirect taxes on them lead to the rise in prices of industrial products in whose production they are used as inputs. In this way through cascading effect much higher rise in price of industrial goods occur when *their several inputs* are subjected to indirect taxes.

3. Excess Burden of Indirect Taxes or Inefficiency in Resource Allocation. The most important harmful effect of indirect taxes is that they make the allocation of resources inefficient and cause *excess burden* on the consumers. As explained above, resource allocation is efficient when resources are so allocated to the production of goods as maximises social welfare. This is achieved when the pattern of production of goods is such that marginal rate of transformation (MRT_{xy}) between goods in production equals marginal rate of substitution between them of consumers (MRS_{xy}). Indirect taxes distort the pattern of production or resource allocation from this ideal one and thereby cause inefficiency and loss of consumer welfare. The prices of commodities on which indirect taxes are levied rise causing reduction in their quantities demanded and as a result less resources are devoted to their production. Resources so released are used for the production of those goods which are not covered by indirect taxes. Thus indirect taxes cause distortion in the prices of goods and thereby reallocate resources away from the efficient or optimum state. As a result, consumer welfare decreases more as a result of indirect taxes than in case of direct taxes.

Graphic Illustration of Inefficient Resource Allocation of Indirect Taxes

Consider Fig. 32.3 where *AB* is the production possibility curve between two commodities *X* and *Y* before taxation. IC_1, IC_2, IC_3 are social indifference curves. Equilibrium is reached at point *H* where production possibility curve is tangent to social indifference curve IC_3 and the quantities of the two goods produced are indicated by the point *H.* At point *H,* the community is at the highest possible indifference curve and therefore social welfare is maximum. It should be noted that at the tangency point *H,* MRT_{xy} in production equals MRS_{xy} of consumers.

Now, suppose excise duty is levied on commodity *X,* while commodity *Y* remains untaxed. As a result, price of *X* rises, while price of *Y* remains unchanged. With this, the price line shifts to PL_2. Further, as a result of withdrawal of resources by the Government through indirect tax on *X,* the production possibility curve for private use shifts to the left to *CD*. Now, the equilibrium of the private economy will be at point *K* of the production possibility curve *CD* where the new price line PL_2 is tangent to the indifference curve IC_1. Thus, consumers suffer a loss of welfare as they have been shifted from a higher indifference IC_3 to the lower indifference curve IC_1 as a result of imposition of indirect tax on commodity *X*. Resource allocation at *K* is inefficient because slope of the price PL_2 (which is tangent to indifference curve IC_1) showing MRS_{xy} is greater than MRT_{xy} as measured by the slope of the tangent *tt'*. If a direct tax (say income tax) of *equal yield* is levied by the Government shifting the private production possibility curve to *CD*, the society will reach at point *R* on indifference curve IC_2. The social indifference curve IC_2 is higher than IC_1 which was reached by levying indirect tax on *X*. Thus indirect tax causes inefficient allocation of resources and reduces social welfare more than a direct tax. That is, an indirect tax causes an *excess burden* on consumers by distorting prices.

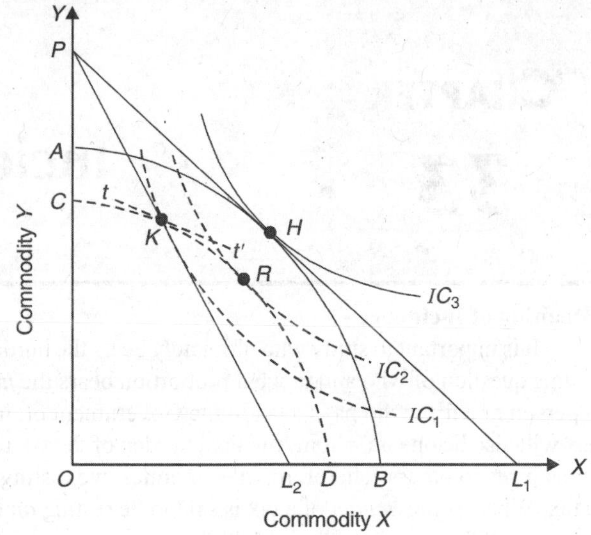

Fig. 32.3. *An Indirect Tax Causes Inefficiency in Resource Allocation.*

QUESTIONS FOR REVIEW

1. Describe the characteristics of a good tax system. How do you rate the Indian tax system in this context ?
2. Discuss the merits and demerits of direct and indirect taxes. Do you think indirect taxes are regressive ?
3. Distinguish between direct tax and indirect tax. Explain the role of indirect tax in the Indian economy.
4. Distinguish between progressive and proportional taxation. What are the effects of a progressive tax system ?
5. Explain the various canons of taxation. Discuss the principle of equity in taxation in a country like India.
6. Discuss the various objectives of taxation policy in India.
7. Explain the objectives and role of fiscal policy in a developing economy.
8. Discuss the role of fiscal policy in an economy. Do you think its role is expanding in the real world ?
9. Explain the main features of the Indian tax structure and examine the role of indirect taxes in a developing economy like India.

CHAPTER 33

Incidence of Taxation

Meaning of Incidence

It is important to study who ultimately bears the burden of a tax. The incidence of taxation refers to this question of who and in what proportion bears the *final* burden of a tax. It is not necessary that a person or a firm who pays a tax to the Government or, in other words, bears the initial burden of a tax will also be one on whom 'the final burden of the tax rests. This is because a tax can be shifted or transferred to others. Therefore, in economics, we distinguish between the ***impact*** and ***incidence*** of a tax. Whereas the *impact* of a tax is said to be resting *on* the person or firm who pays the amount of the tax and thus receives the *initial burden,* the *incidence* of the tax rests on the person or firms who *ultimately bears the money burden* of the tax. If a person or a firm who pays the tax to the Government is also one who ultimately bears it, then the impact and incidence of the tax rests on the same person or firm. In such a case, there is no shift.

Shifting the Burden of a Tax

The burden of the tax can be transferred to others through a process of shifting. It may be noted that the whole burden of the tax may not be shifted to others. It may be that a part of the tax may be shifted to others and a part be borne by the one who initially pays the tax. As a matter of fact, a part of the tax burden rests on all the persons to a larger or smaller degree in the chain of transferring the burden so that at the ultimate end only a small burden rests. The process of shifting the burden of a tax goes on so long as different persons who come in the chain are able to pass on the burden to others till it ultimately rests on a person or a group of persons who cannot shift this unwelcome baby further. Theory of incidence of tax studies in what proportion the burden or incidence of a tax is shared among different persons. It may be noted that a tax can be shifted through a *process of exchange* or, in other words, an individual or a firm can shift the burden of the tax if there occurs exchange relations which are conducted on the basis of prices of goods and factors. The person who initially pays the tax can pass it on to the other either in the form of higher prices of goods he sells or in the form of lower prices of factors he buys.

Whether shifting can take place or if it does so how much tax burden can be shifted depends on a number of factors. They are briefly explained below:

1. The Nature of a Tax. The nature of a tax as to whether it is a tax on, the production or sale of some commodities or it is a personal income or property tax. Tax shifting can easily take place in the case of taxes on the production and sale of commodities. The taxes on production or sale of commodities are called indirect taxes. The important examples of indirect taxes are excise duties and sales tax. On the other hand, the burden of direct taxes such as income and wealth taxes cannot be shifted.

2. Market Conditions. Whether commodity is being produced under conditions of perfect competition, monopolistic competition or monopoly goes to determine the extent to which the burden of a tax can be shifted. A monopolist who has a full control over the supply of a commodity is in a better position to shift the burden of a tax on the commodity produced. Likewise, a producer working under monopolistic competition who produced a product somewhat different from others exercises a good deal of influence over the price of its product and therefore can pass on a part of the burden of the tax to the buyers. Even the firms working under perfect competition can shift the tax burden as the tax levied on a commodity raises its supply price for all of them. The difference in the three market forms lies in the extent to which the burden of the tax can be shifted.

3. Physical Conditions of Production. The shifting of the tax burden on a commodity also depends upon whether the commodity is being produced under increasing, constant or diminishing returns. This will be explained in detail a little later.

Factors Determining Incidence of Indirect (Commodity) Taxes

The questions of tax shifting especially arises in the case of indirect taxes, that is, taxes on the production and sale of goods such as excise duties and sales tax. In this regard, *whether and to what extent a tax on commodity can be shifted depends on the price elasticity of demand for and supply of a commodity.*

It is these elasticities of demand and supply that determine the bargaining strengths of the sellers and buyers of the taxed commodity. Sellers can shift the tax burden to the buyers if they are able to reduce the supply of the commodity and thereby raise its price. Thus, the power to shift the tax depends on the elasticity of supply of the taxed commodity. The elasticity of reducing supply of a commodity will be relatively smaller if there is excess capacity in the industry producing it. Further, the elasticity of supply of a commodity will be larger in the long run than in the short run.

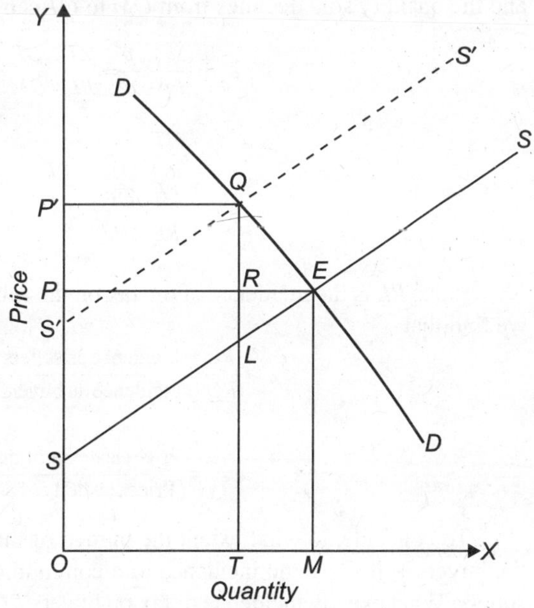

Fig. 33.1. *Incidence of an Indirect Tax*

Apart from the elasticity of supply, power to transfer the tax burden depends on the elasticity of demand for a commodity. The greater the elasticity of demand of the buyers, the smaller the extent to which the tax will be shifted to them. As shall be shown below, under conditions of perfect competition the incidence of a commodity tax is shared between the sellers and buyers in the ratio of the elasticity of demand and supply. Figure 33.1 illustrates the incidence of an indirect tax under conditions of perfect competition.

DD is the demand curve for a commodity and *SS* is its supply curve before the imposition of tax on it. Interaction of these demand and supply curves determines price *OP* of the commodity and *OM* is the quantity sold and purchased. Suppose a unit sales tax, that is, sales tax per unit of the commodity equal to *SS'* or *LQ* is levied by the Government on the commodity in question. This will raise the supply price of the commodity by the sellers as the unit tax *SS'* will now be included by the sellers in their supply price. As a result, the supply curve of the commodity will shift to the left by the magnitude of the tax *SS'*. The new supply curve *S'S'* intersects the demand curve *DD* at point *Q* and determines the new price *OP'* and quantity exchanged *OT*. It will be seen from Fig.33.1 that price for the buyers has risen by *PP'* or *RQ* whereas the tax per unit is *SS'* or *LQ* which the buyers will bear. It may be noted that the buyers will bear the burden of a tax to the extent that they have to pay the higher price than before. Thus the incidence of the tax borne by the buyers will be equal to *RQ*. The remaining part of the tax *RL* will be borne by the sellers. Thus, of the tax *SS'* or *LQ* per unit, *RQ* is incidence of the tax on the buyers and *RL* is the incidence on the sellers. Now, we can show that the incidence of the tax *RL* and *RQ* on the sellers and buyers respectively is equal to the ratio of the elasticity of demand and the elasticity of supply.

$$\frac{RL}{RQ} = \frac{\text{Incidence of tax on the sellers}}{\text{Incidence of tax on the buyers}}$$

$$\text{Price elasticity of demand} = \frac{\Delta q}{\Delta p} \cdot \frac{p}{q}$$

By referring to Fig. 33.1, elasticity of demand when the price rises from OP to OP' for the buyers will be

$$e_d = \frac{\Delta q_d}{\Delta p} \cdot \frac{p}{q} = \frac{MT}{RQ} \cdot \frac{OP}{OM} \qquad \ldots (i)$$

Likewise, elasticity of supply when the price received by the sellers falls from OP or ME to TL and the quantity sold declines from OM to OT can be found out. Thus :

$$e_s = \frac{\Delta q_S}{\Delta p} \cdot \frac{p}{q} = \frac{MT}{RL} \cdot \frac{OP}{OM} \qquad \ldots (ii)$$

$$\frac{e_d}{e_s} = \frac{\frac{MT}{RQ} \cdot \frac{OP}{OM}}{\frac{MT}{RL} \cdot \frac{OP}{OM}} = \frac{RL}{RQ}$$

Since RL is the incidence of the tax on the sellers and RQ is the incidence of tax on the buyers, we find that

$$\frac{RL}{RQ} = \frac{\text{Incidence on sellers}}{\text{Incidence on buyers}}$$

$$= \frac{\text{Price elasticity of demand}}{\text{Price elasticity of supply}} \qquad \ldots (iii)$$

To conclude, to what extent the burden of the tax will be shifted and the proportion in which the buyers will share the incidence of a commodity tax depends on the elasticities of demand and supply. What exactly incidence of tax on buyers RQ and incidence of tax on sellers RL will be equal to is given below:

$$\frac{e_d}{e_s} = \frac{RL}{RQ} = \frac{\text{Incidence of tax on sellers}}{\text{Incidence of tax on buyers}} \qquad \ldots (iv)$$

If elasticity of demand for a commodity is zero, then from *(iv)* it follows that the incidence of tax on the sellers RL will be zero and therefore the incidence of tax RQ on buyers will be equal to whole tax t per unit. On the other hand, if the elasticity of supply is zero, then it follows from *(iv)* above that the incidence of tax on sellers RL will be equal to the whole amount of the tax t and as a result the incidence of tax on the buyers in this case will be zero in this case.

If elasticity of demand is infinity ($e_d = \infty$) then it also follows from above that $RL = t$, that is, the whole burden of the tax will fall on the sellers. On the other hand, if elasticity of supply is infinity, then it follows from above that $RQ = t$. that is, the whole burden of the tax will fall on the buyers. Let us graphically explain these cases of incidents of tax.

Incidence of Indirect Taxation and Elasticity of Demand

If demand for a commodity on which a unit tax has been imposed is elastic, then as a result of the rise in price caused by the imposition of a tax, the people will buy substitute goods and the quantity demanded of the good will fall greatly. In such a case, the incidence of the tax on the buyers will be relatively less. This is illustrated in Fig. 33.2. Take first, the demand curve DD which is

relatively more elastic as compared with the demand curve $D'D'$ (dotted). SS is the supply curve which with the intersection of demand curve DD determin the price OP and quantity exchanged OM. With the imposition of a unit tax, the supply curve shifts to the left and intersects the demand curve DD at point Q determining new price OP' and the equilibrium amount ON. The distance between the two supply curves measures the tax per unit which is equal to LQ. It will be seen from the figure that with the more elastic demand curve DD price has risen by PP' or RQ. The remaining tax LR will be borne by the sellers. It will be seen that in this case of elastic demand the incidence of the tax RQ fallen on the buyers is smaller than that on the sellers RL.

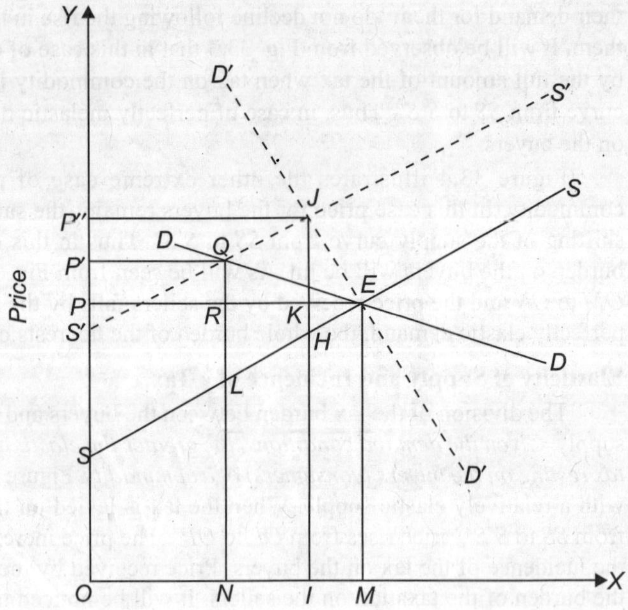

Fig. 33.2. *Elasticity of Demand and the Incidence of the Tax*

Now take the case of less elastic demand curve $D'D'$ (dotted). It will be seen from Fig. 33.2 that the supply curve $S'S'$ obtained after the imposition of the tax per unit intersects the less demand curve $D'D'$ at point J. In this case of less elastic demand curve, price has risen by a greater magnitude PP'' or KJ which will be the incidence of the tax on the buyers, whereas the sellers will receive HK less than before the imposition of tax. It will be thus noticed that in this case of less elastic demand curve, the incidence of the tax on the buyers *(KJ)* is much greater than the incidence on the sellers *(HK)*. It follows from above, *the less the elasticity of demand, the greater the incidence of tax on the buyers, and in the extreme case when the elasticity of demand is zero, the whole tax will be passed on to buyers. On the other extreme, when demand for a commodity is perfectly elastic, the whole tax will be borne by the sellers of the commodity*. These are illustrated in Figs. 33.3 and 33.4. Take Fig. 33.3 which illustrates the case where demand curve is completely inelastic (*i.e.*, $ed = 0$) as actually happens in the case of necessities which cannot be substituted by some other goods and therefore

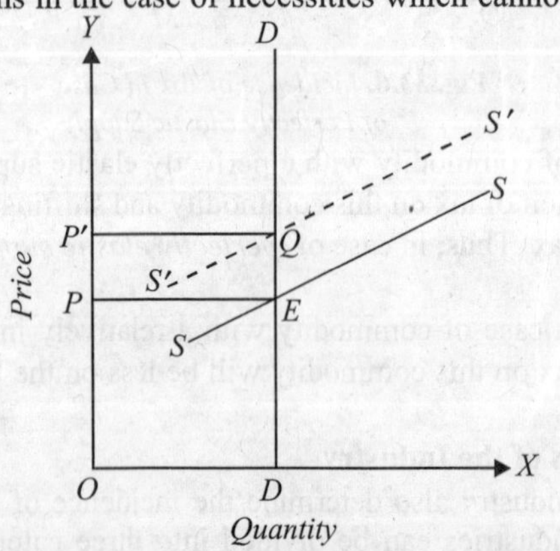

Fig. 33.3. *Incidence of a Tax in Case of Perfectly Inelastic Demand*

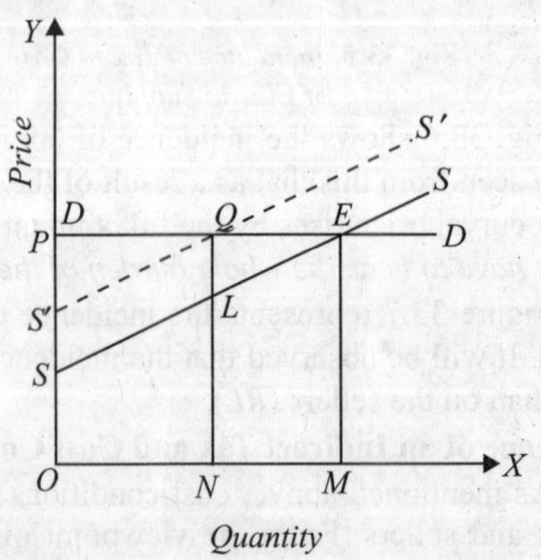

Fig. 33.4. *Incidence of a Tax in Case of Perfectly Inelastic Demand*

their demand for them 'do not decline following the rise in the price after the imposition of a tax on them, It will be observed from Fig. 33.3 that in this case of completely inelastic demand price rises by the full amount of the tax when tax on the commodity is levied resulting in shift in the supply curve from *SS* to *S′S′*. Thus, in case of perfectly inelastic demand the whole incidence of tax rests on the buyers.

Figure 33.4 illustrates the other extreme case of perfectly elastic demand curve for a commodity. In this case price for the buyers remains the same following the imposition of tax and shifting of the supply curve from *SS* to *S′S′*. Thus in this case of perfectly inelastic demand, tax burden on the buyers will be nil. As will be seen from Fig. 33.4, the quantity demanded falls from *OM* to *ON* and the price received by the sellers falls by the full amount of the *QL*. Thus, in case of perfectly elastic demand, the whole burden of the tax rests on the sellers.

Elasticity of Supply and Incidence of a Tax

The division of the tax burden between the buyers and sellers also depends on the elasticity of supply. *Given the demand conditions, the greater the elasticity of supply, the greater the incidence of tax resting on the buyers (consumers) of a commodity.* Figure 33.5 represents the case of a commodity with a relatively elastic supply. When the tax is levied on this commodity and supply curve shifts from *SS* to *S'S'*, price rises from *OP* to *OP'*. The price increase is equal to *PP'* or *RQ* which will be the incidence of the tax on the buyers. Price received by the sellers is lower by *RL* and this will be the burden of the taxation on the sellers. It will be noticed that in this case of elastic supply curve, the incidence of tax on the buyers is greater than that on the sellers.

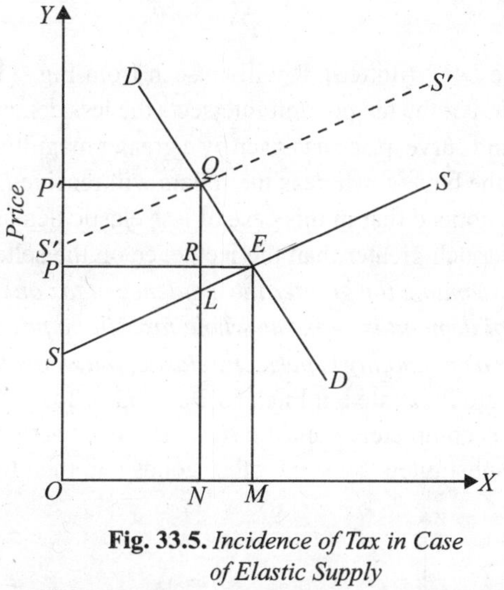

Fig. 33.5. *Incidence of Tax in Case of Elastic Supply*

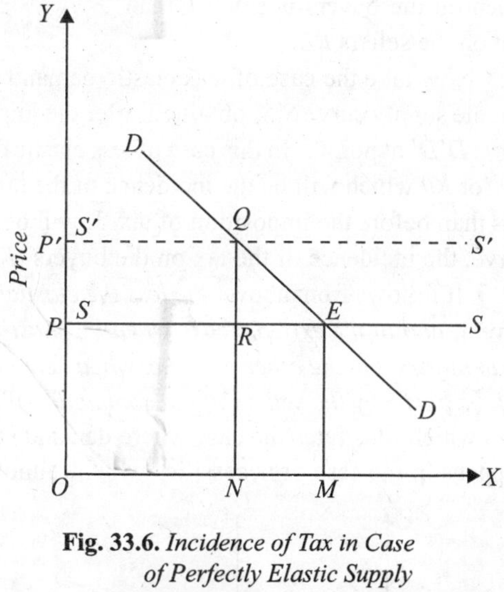

Fig. 33.6. *Incidence of Tax in Case of Perfectly Elastic Supply*

Fig. 33.6 shows the incidence of tax in case of commodity with a perfectly elastic supply. It will be seen from this that as a result of the imposition of tax on this commodity and shifting of the supply curve, price rises by the full amount of the tax. Thus, in case of *perfectly elastic supply the buyers have to bear the whole burden of the tax.*

Figure 33.7 represents the incidence of tax in case of commodity with a relatively inelastic supply. It will be observed that the incidence of a tax on this commodity will be less on the buyers (*RQ*) than on the sellers (*RL*).

Incidence of an Indirect Tax and Cost Conditions of the Industry

As mentioned above, cost conditions of the industry also determine the incidence of tax on buyers and sellers. From the viewpoint of cost, industries can be divided into three categories: (1) Increasing Cost Industries, (2) Constant Cost Industry, (3) Decreasing Cost Industry.[1]

1. Since there is inverse relation between cost and physical returns, these industries can also be classed as (1) Diminishing Returns Industry, (2) Constant Returns Industry (3) Increasing Returns Industry.

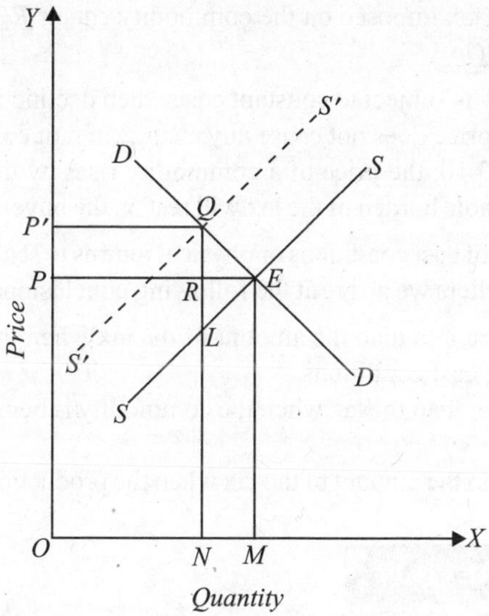

Fig. 33.7. *Incidence of a Tax in Case of a Relatively In elastic Supply*

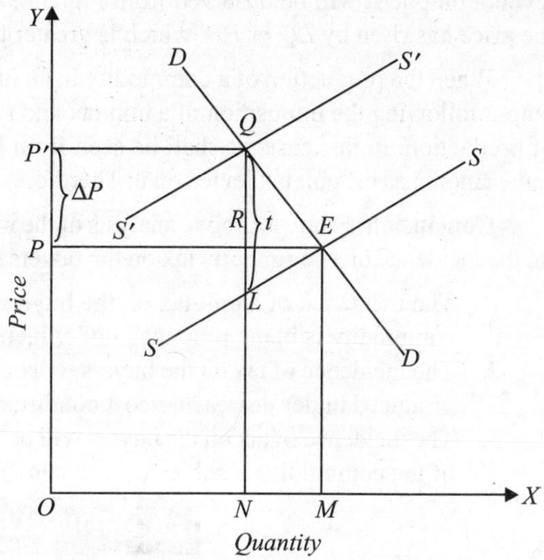

Fig. 33.8. *Incidence of a Unit or Specific Tax in Case of Increasing Costs*

Following the imposition of a tax on a commodity, its price rises and, given the demand curve, at a higher equilibrium price less is demanded and produced. If a commodity is being produced under increasing cost conditions, then at a lower level of output cost per unit of output will fall. And due to this reduction in cost per unit as a result of imposition of a tax on that commodity, the price of the commodity will rise by less than the amount of the unit tax levied. Thus, in this case which is illustrated in Fig. 33.8 the burden of the tax on the buyers will be less than the amount of the unit tax. It will be seen from Fig. 33.8 that while the burden of a unit tax on the consumers is *RQ* which is less than the tax per unit *LQ*.

On the contrary, when a commodity is being produced by an industry subject to decreasing costs, the decline in demand and output as a result of the imposition of a unit tax and rise in its price, will cause cost per unit to rise. In this case, as shall be seen from Fig. 33.9, the *price will rise more than unit tax* on account of (1) imposition of tax on the commodity, and (2) rise in unit cost at a lower

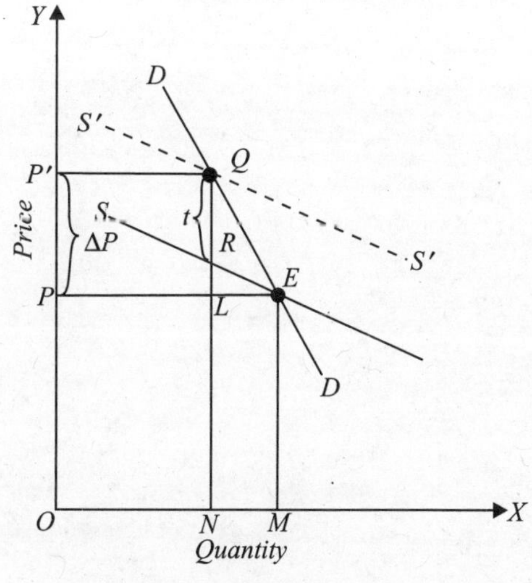

Fig. 33.9. *Incidence of a Unit Tax in Case of Decreasing Costs*

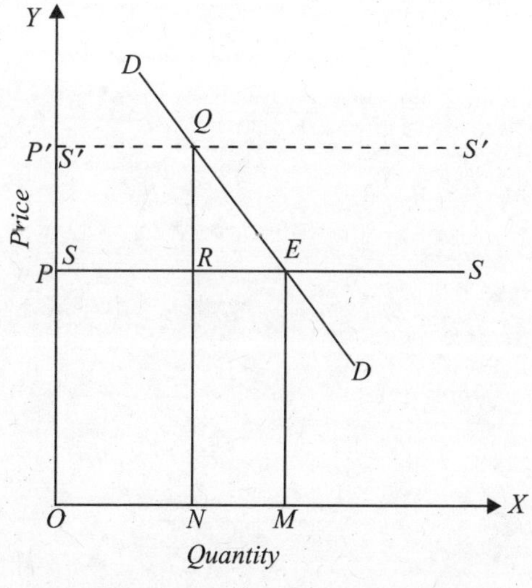

Fig. 33.10. *Incidence of a Unit Tax in Case of Constant Costs*

level of output. It will be observed from Fig. 33.9 while tax imposed on the commodity equals *RQ*, the price has risen by *LQ* or *PP′* which is greater than *RQ*.

When the production of a commodity in an industry is subject to constant costs, then decline in output following the imposition of a unit tax and rise in price does not cause any change in unit cost of production. In this case, as shall be seen from Fig. 33.10, the price of a commodity rises by the same amount as the unit tax levied on it. Therefore, the whole burden of the tax will rest on the buyers.

Conclusion: From our above analysis of the impact of cost conditions or physical returns to scale on the incidence of a commodity tax on the buyers and sellers we arrive at the following conclusions:

1. The incidence of a unit tax on the buyers will be less than the amount of the tax when the commodity is being produced under increasing cost conditions.
2. The incidence of tax on the buyers will be greater than the tax when the commodity is being produced under decreasing cost conditions.
3. The incidence of tax on the buyers will be equal to the amount of the tax when the production of the commodity is subject to constant costs.

QUESTIONS FOR REVIEW

4. Distinguish between incidence and impact of a tax. How is the burden of a unit tax on a commodity shared between producer and consumer under perfect competition.
5. Suppose a commodity is being produced under conditions of monopoly. Explain and illustrate how the burden of a unit tax on that commodity will be borne by the consumers and producer. Compare it with that under perfect competition
6. Define the incidence of taxation. Analyse the incidence of a (*i*) unit tax, and (*ii*) lump-sum tax under conditions of perfect competition.
7. What do you mean by incidence of a tax. Explain the circumstances under which the incidence of a unit tax imposed under competitive conditions is passed on wholly on the consumers.
8. Explain that the incidence of a unit tax on a commodity on the buyers is more, the greater the elasticity of supply.
9. Show that the less the elasticity of demand, the greater the incidence of a unit tax on the buyers.

CHAPTER 34 Fiscal Policy and Economic Growth in a Developing Country

Introduction

The most important instrument of government intervention in the economy today is that of fiscal or budgetary policy. Fiscal policy refers to the taxation, expenditure and borrowing by the Government. The economists now hold that government intervention through fiscal policy is essential in the matter of overcoming recession and inflation as well as of promoting and accelerating economic growth. Monetary policy alone will not do. There is no doubt that the Government budgetary or fiscal policy must be sound, keeping in view the needs and requirements of a developing economy.

Objectives of Fiscal Policy in Developing Countries

In developing countries, taxation, Government expenditure and borrowing have to play a very important role in accelerating economic development. In fact, fiscal policy is a powerful instrument in the hands of the Government by means of which it can achieve the objectives of development. There are several peculiar characteristics of a developing country which necessitate the adoption of a special fiscal policy which ensures a rapid economic growth. There are vast and diverse resources, human and material, which are lying underutilised. Such countries have weak infrastructure, *i.e*, they lack adequate means of transport and communications, roads, ports, highways, irrigation and power. They also lack technical know-how. Their population is increasing at an explosive rate which necessitates rapid economic development to meet the requirements of the rapidly growing population. Above all, these countries suffer from deficiency of capital. They are caught up in a vicious circle of poverty. In order to overcome these handicaps, a suitable fiscal and taxation policy is called for.

The principal objectives of fiscal policy in a developing economy are:

1. to mobilise resources for economic growth, especially for the public sector;
2. to promote economic growth in the private sector by providing incentives to save and invest;
3. to restrain inflationary forces in the economy in order to ensure price stability; and
4. to ensure equitable distribution of income and wealth so that fruits of economic growth are fairly distributed.

ROLE OF FISCAL POLICY FOR MOBILISATION OF RESOURCES IN DEVELOPING COUNTRIES

In developing economies, the Government has to play a very active role in promoting economic development and fiscal policy is the instrument that the state must use. Hence the great importance of public finance in developing countries desirous of rapid economic development. In a democratic society, there is an inherent dislike for direct (physical) controls and regulation by the state. The entrepreneurs would not like to be orderd about to produce this or that, how much to produce or where to produce. Fiscal incentives in the form of tax concessions, rebates or subsidies are, therefore, preferable. Similarly, the consumers would not like to be told directly to curtail their consumption or to consume this and not to consume that. Taxation of goods whose consumption is to be discouraged is therefore preferable. Hence, a democratic state must rely on indirect methods of control and regulation and this is done through fiscal and monetary policies. Thus, in democratic countries, fiscal policy is a powerful and least undesirable weapon on which the states can rely for promoting economic development.

Capital formation is of strategic importance in the matter of rapid economic development and the developing economies suffer from capital deficiency. It is, therefore, necessary to achieve a higher ratio of savings to national income. In early days of capitalism, payment of low wages and the existence of inequalities of income helped capital formation in the present-day developed countries. But no democratic country can adopt this method in modern times; the effort rather is to raise wages and reduce inequalities of income and wealth. Under a regime of socialist dictatorship, capital formation was brought about by ruthlessly curtailing consumption and keeping down the standards of living. But in modern democracies with every adult person having a right to cast vote very low levels of living for a long time is not feasible. *Hence the state must rely on instruments of fical policy to mobilise resources for economic development*. Taxation can be used to to raise collective savings for public investment and also at the same time to promote private investment. A well-conceived scheme of taxation is an important way of raising ratio of savings to national income which is one of the crucial determinants of the rate of economic growth. As Nurkse says, "*public finance assumes a new significance in the face of the problem of capital formation in underdeveloped countries.*"[1]

On the expenditure side, there is positive need for public investment, especially in those branches of economic activity where the private investments are not easily attracted, for example, the development of infrastructure such as power resources, means of transport and communications, basic heavy industries, education and research. Such investments are very often the very foundations of rapid economic advance. Thus, fiscal policy is of crucial importance in accelerating the pace of development in developing countries.

We explain below in detail how fiscal policy measures can be used to achieve the objectives of economic growth, more equal distribution of income and price stability in the developing countries.

Promoting Private Saving

As mentioned above, capital formation is an imoportant determinant of economic growth. For accelerating the rate of capital formation, saving and investment rate in the economy has to be stepped up. For this purpose savings have to be mobilised and channelled into productive investment. The alternative means other than fiscal policy available to promote savings and investment in the developing countries are not very effective in mobilising enough resources for investment and capital formation. The propensity to consume is very high in these countries. There exist large inequalities of income in these countries and this should ensure a large voluntary savings by the richer sections of the society. But the richer sections in them indulge in conspicious consumption such as building of luxury houses, indulging in five star culture, buying air-conditioners and such other things and, therefore, the volume of their voluntary savings is meagre. This propensity to indulge in conspicuous consumption is reinforced by demonstration effect which is operating strongly these days due to the development of electronic media and superior means of advertisement. Further, rich people tend to invest their rising incomes on unproductive investment such as gold and jewellery, real estate etc., which yield high profits due to their appreciation. In view of these, sufficient voluntary savings cannot be made available for raising significantly the rate of capital formation.

---

1. Ragnar Nurkse, *Problems of Capital Formation in Underdeveloped Countries.*

The alternative to taxation and Government borrowing to finance capital formation is to obtain *forced savings through creation of excessive creation of new money, often called money financing (i.e. monetisation of budget deficit) that results in price inflation.* But this is not a desirable, equitable and efficient way of obtaining the needed funds for development. First, the inflation tends to direct private investment into unproductive types of investment such as inventory holdings, purchase of real estates, gold and jewellery etc. Secondly, inflation raises the cost of public sector investment projects which lowers the rate of real investment. Thirdly, inflation reduces the voluntary savings of the people. This is because inflation reduces the real value of money which adversely affects willingness to save money. Fourthly, since inflation raises the incomes of the industrialists and traders on the one hand and reduces the real incomes of the general public on the other, it increases disparities of income in a society which runs counter to the objective of social justice. Therefore, most economists do not favour financing development through forced savings generated by deliberate inflation caused by excessive money financing.

Due to the severe limitations of alternative ways of mobilising resources for capital formation, the role of fiscal policy in performing this task assumes greater importance. Fiscal policy, if properly designed, is an efficient and equitable way of mobilising resources for augmenting public investment. Through it not only collective public savings can be raised for financing public investment but also at the same time private savings and investment can be encouraged. "In fact" *taxation is one of the effective means of increasing the total volume of saving and investment in an economy where the propensity to consume is normally high.*" Further, the fiscal policy can be so devised that not only the objective of rapid capital accumulation or growth, but also other objectives of economic policy such as equitable distribution of income and wealth, price stability and promotion of employment opportunities can be achieved.

In what follows we shall explain how the various instruments of fiscal policy such as taxation and Government borrowing can be used to mobilise resources for economic development.

TAXATION AND MOBILISATION OF RESOURCES FOR ECONOMIC GROWTH

Taxation is an important instrument for fiscal policy which can be used for mobilising resources for capital formation in the public sector. To raise ratio of savings to national income and thereby raise resources for development, it is necessary that marginal saving rate be kept higher than the average saving rate. By imposition of direct progressive taxes on income and profits and higher rates of indirect taxes such as excise duties and sales tax on luxury goods for which income elasticity of demand is higher, the marginal saving rate can be made higher than the average saving rate. This will cause a continuous increase in the saving rate of the economy. An important merit of taxation is that it is not only a good instrument of resource moblisation for development but it also cuts down consumption of goods and thereby helps in checking inflation. Whereas direct taxes on income, profits and wealth reduce the disposable incomes of the people and thereby tend to reduce aggregate demand in the economy, indirect taxes directly discourages the consumption of the goods on which they are levied by raising their prices.

Taxation policy should be used to prevent this potential economic surplus from being wasted in conspicuous consumption and unproductive investment. It may be noted that this potential economic surplus is not a given amount but it increases in the very process of economic development. Firstly, economic development raises the incomes of the people, especially of the business class and agriculturists, and this augments the economic surplus. Secondly, some inflation is inherent in the process of development and this greatly benefits the traders, farmers and businessmen whose incomes rise much faster than others. The prices rise more than the costs and they get a good deal of profits. Further, due to the inflationary pressures market values of their investment in real

1. Baran, *Political Economy of Development.*

estate, gold, shares, etc., go up and enormous capital gains accrue to them. All these enlarge economic surplus and therefore the taxation potential of the economy.

Direct Taxes and Mobilisation of Resources

Now the question arises what should be the taxation structure of a developing economy which will mobilise the potential economic surplus to the maximum, that is, what kinds of taxes be levied, how much progressive should be their rates and what should be the exemptions and concessions in various taxes. This is, however, a highly controversial issue. It has been suggested that an appropriate tax which would mobilise resources or mop up economic surplus is the progressive income tax. In India and the other developing countries income has been regarded as a good base for direct taxation. And the imposition of highly progressive income tax not only mops up relatively greater amount of resources but also tend to reduce inequalities of income. However, a progressive income tax with high marginal rates of taxes adversely affects private saving and investment and also raises the propensity to evade the tax. In view of this, two proposels have been put forward to make the income tax both as an effective instrument of resource mobilisation for the public sector and of providing incentives to save and invest. First, Prof. Kaldor of Cambridge University, who in 1956 was invited by Government of India to suggest reforms in the Indian tax system for mobilising resources for development, suggested that whereas the marginal rate of income tax be reduced to, say, 45 to 50 per cent, expenditure tax be levied to discourage the people belonging to upper income brackets from dissipating their income in conspicuous consumption. According to him, this will also reduce the tendency to evade income tax on the one hand and promote private savings on the other. The second proposal to reform the income tax put forward by others is that whereas marginal rates of income tax be kept high but *some exemptions for approved forms of saving and investment* be allowed to the individuals. This will channel individual savings along desired lines and at the same time mobilise resources for development.

Apart from the income tax on individuals and companies, the imposition of other direct taxes such as wealth tax, gift tax, and estate duty are also needed to mobilise sufficient resources for capital formation. Unlike income tax, these capital taxes do not have any adverse effects on incentives to save and invest.[2] They are also important instruments of reducing inequalities of income and wealth. Because of these advantages, Professor Kaldor in his report of taxation reforms in India recommended the imposition of these capital taxes and this recommendation was accepted and the annual wealth tax and gift tax were levied in 1957 with estate duty having been already introduced in 1954.

Agricultural Taxation and Resource Mobilisation. A major part of national income in India and other developing countries originates in the agricultural sector which has substantial economic surplus which can be tapped for capital formation. This economic surplus mainly goes to rich farmers, landlords, merchants and other intermediaries and, in the absence of suitable taxation on agriculture, this is used for conspicuous consumption and for investing in unproductive activities such as buying gold, jewellery, real estate. Thus, according to Professor Kaldor, "*the taxation of agriculture by one means or another has a critical role to play in the acceleration of economic development.*"[3] Further, owing to economic growth in general and agricultural development in particular income of the agricultural class and therefore economic surplus enormously increases and therefore need to be mopped up for further development. Besides, the agricultural sector has to be taxed not only because it has a potential surplus but also to achieve maximium utilisation of land through devising a system of land taxation which would penalise poor use of good land. In this regard, a progressive land tax "the effective rates of taxation of which vary with the total value of landholdings of the family unit" may be suitable one. Besides this, progressive agricultural income tax with

2. See, S. Gulati, *Capital Taxation in India*, Orient Longman, 1957.
3. N. Kaldor, The Role of Taxation in Economic Development, in E.A.G. Robinson (ed.), *Problems in Economic Development*, 1965, p. 177.

appropriate exemption may be levied to tap resources from affluent sections of the agricultural sector.

It may be noted that as compared to the non-agricultural sector, agricultural sector in India and other developing countries is quite under-taxed. Land revenue which was at one time the greatest source of revenue for government has now become an insignificant yielder of revenue. In the context of India, Agricultural Taxation Committee under the Chairmanship of Dr. K.N. Raj recommended Agricultural Holdings Tax (AHT) which was to be imposed at a progressive rate on the rateable value of an agricultural holdings of ₹ 5000 and above. It was expected to yield annually ₹ 200 crores. However, Agricultural Holdings Tax was found to be difficult to assess and administer. In our view, a *graded surcharge on the existing land revenue* will be far easier to assess and administer and make land revenue a more elastic source of revenue. However, it may be noted that in India agricultural taxation is a state subject and there is lack of political will on the part of the State Governments to raise the level of land taxation in a country. But if sufficient resources are to be mobilised for development, the level of agricultural taxation has to be raised.

Merits and Demerits of Direct Taxes for Resource Mobilisation

As seen above, as an instrument of resource mobilisation for development direct taxes enjoy several advantages. (1) They raise resources in a non-inflationary way. Indeed, they tend to check inflation by curtailing consumption demand. (2) They help to reduce inequalities of income and wealth, and (3) They discourage conspicuous and non-essential consumption and thereby enlarge economic surplus. But the direct taxation of agricultural and non-agricultural sectors has its own limits. The coverage of direct taxes is quite narrow and difficult to expand. For instance, in India not more than two per cent of the population comes within the purview of income tax as incomes of the majority of the people fall below the exemption limit which has now been raised to the annual income of ₹ 2,00,000. Moreover, there is a considerable evasion of income tax. Yield from other direct taxes such as wealth tax, gift tax is quite meagre due to very small coverage, low rates and considerable evasion of them.

Role of Indirect Taxes in Resource Mobilisation

As a result of limitations of direct taxes, developing countries have resorted to extensive use of indirect taxes. *In India, almost all commodities have been brought within the net of indirect taxes such as excise duties and sales tax. Besides, there are custom duties (i.e., taxes on imports).* Indirect taxation is an important source of development funds in a developing country. In the last six decades of planned development, revenue from several indirect taxes has been rising as a percentage of total revenue as well as of national income. It has been found that indirect taxes are better suited to the conditions obtaining in developing countries for reducing current consumption and mobilising resources for development. This is because in such countries quite a large proportion of national income tends to be diverted to current consumption instead of being productively invested. The average propensity to consume in such countries is much higher than is the case in advanced countries. Indirect taxes which reduce consumption must thus play a more important part. They will raise the rate of savings which are so essential for economic growth.

"High rates of taxes on commodities with a high income elasticity of demand are quite effective in siphoning a substantial proportion of increase in output into the resources of the public sector needed for development financing and a stiff rate of commodity taxes on luxury articles tends to introduce an element of progressiveness in an otherwise predominantly regressive tax structure in developing countries."[4] But in order to make sure that the resources raised through commodity taxes are adequate, it will be necessary to extend their coverage to include some articles of mass consumption. In the poor countries, it is not possible to exempt entirely goods of general and neces-

4. R.N. Tripathy, *Public Finance in Developing Countries*, 1966, p. 200.

sary consumption, because they are the only goods that provide a base broad enough to assure an adequate amount of resources. It may be noted that it is revenue from indirect takes that has substantially increased during the last six decades of planned development. From a small sum of ₹ 227 crores in 1950-51, the revenue raised from indirect taxes rose to about 81,000 crores in 1998-98. Moreover the share of indirect takes to total tax revenue (direct plus indirect taxes) has gone down from about 69% in 1995-96 to about 44 per cent in 2012-13. It is thus clear that for mobilisation of resources for growth and capital formation indirect taxes have made an important contribution. It is worth mentioning that despite reduction in rates of customs duties under economic reforms in India, revenue from *custom duties* (*i.e.*, taxes on imports) has increased. Whereas in 1980-81, revenue of ₹ 3,400 crores was raised through custom duties, this rose to 48,000 crores in 1998-99 and further to 1,75,000 crore in 2013-14. Revenue raised through union excise duties has also been quite substantial; +revenue from them increased from ₹ 6,500 crores in 1980-81 to about ₹ 57,000 crores in 1998-99 further and further to 1,79,500 crores in 2013-14.

Limitations. But there are some limitations of raising resources through indirect taxes. First, they lead to *cost-push inflation*. The burden of indirect taxes are passed on to the consumers in the form of higher prices charged from them. In India excise duties on sugar, cloth, kerosene oil, petrol etc., has raised the prices and have contributed a good deal to cost-push inflation witnessed in last several years. Secondly, levying of customs duties on imports of capital goods, raw materials used for industrial production have accelerated cost-push inflation in the Indian economy. Thirdly, imposition of customs duties on imports of goods also protect inefficiency in domestic industries. This also contributes to high-cost production and promotes inefficiency. Lastly, indirect taxes are *regressive* in nature; both the rich and poor have to pay the same rate on the taxed commodities. The regressive character of indirect taxes have been attempted to be reduced by imposing higher rates of excise and custom duties on luxury items and smaller rates of duties on goods of mass consumption. However, the need for mobilising greater resources have forced the finance ministers to levy higher indirect taxes even on articles of mass consumption.

Role of Taxation in Promoting Private Saving and Investment

It is worth mentioning that in a mixed economy such as ours, there is need to raise not only the public savings and investment but also to promote private saving and investment so that the overall rate of saving and investment in the economy is stepped up. This implies that taxation measures should not impair incentives to save and invest of the people. Therefore, a developing economy encounters a crucial dilemma in augmenting larger resources for public investment on the one hand and to promote private savings and investment on the other. Thus, according to Prof. Heller, "Tax Policy faces a basic dilemma in its role as a an instrument of capital formation for economic development. On the one hand, high levels of taxes are necessary to finance that part of the development which falls in the government share and to mobilise for investment the private resources that might otherwise be dissipated. On the other hand, the lower the taxes the greater will be the inducement to private investment... The dilemma is worsened by the fact that those taxes which are most effective in capturing a large share of the gains from economic development for further capital formation are the ones most likely to affect the returns from private investment. *Only way of the dilemma may be to combine high rates of taxation in general, with preferential treatment for categories of desired development activity.*"

Thus, while the policy of high rates of taxation on income and profit may be adopted but even with this private saving and investment can be promoted through preferential treatment of them. Rather than lowering the rate of income tax, private savings can be promoted in several other ways. First, interest on several types of private savings such as bank deposits, investment in units of Unit Trust of India and National Savings Certificates, and other approved forms of saving be totally or substantially exempted from taxation. This will encourage private savings through raising the rate of return on savings as the savers would earn interest income free of income tax. Secondly, voluntary savings in certain selective lines such as voluntary contributions to provident fund, life insurance premium, certain specific schemes of UTI and National Savings Certificates be substantially exempted from income tax. This will also stimulate private savings by raising the rate of return on these savings. For, people will not only earn rate of interest or dividend but will save a good amount of income tax on these approved forms of savings. Thirdly, some economists have suggested that if progressivity in tax rates is avoided (that is, if rates of income taxes do not increase much with the increase in income) private saving and investment will be boosted up. However, this is based upon a questionable assumption that richer people in countries like India have high propensity to save. In view of the present author, the lower marginal rates of taxes will place more disposable income in the hands of higher income brackets which will tend to raise their conspicuous consumption, especially when goods catering to their frivolous wants are available in abundance these days through both domestic production and imports. As mentioned above, this is reinforced by the international demonstration effect which exercises a strong influence on the consumption behaviour of the richer sections of the Indian society. However, too high marginal rates of income tax will encourage tax evasion. Therefore, in order to ensure tax compliance on the one hand and to achieve equity in distribution of tax burden on the other, marginal tax rates *should be moderately high.*

Besides, private savings, private investment can be directly encouraged through taxation. Firstly, in order to stimulate private investment, the *retained profits* which are reinvested by the business firms instead of distributing them among the shareholders can be exempted from taxation or taxed at preferential rates. Secondly, to boost private investment *liberal depreciation and investment allowances* have also to be allowed to the business firms which will be used for purposes of investment in new plant, equipment and machinery. Further, "subsidies on investment can also be provided by the Government which generally prove to be a very effective way of promoting private investment".

Another important fiscal method of stimulating private investment in developing countries is *granting of tax holidays or relief from tax on the profits of new enterprises* for some specified period of time. Further, indirect taxes can also be manipulated in a variety of ways to promote private investment in certain selected fields of industrial activity. Thus exmption or lowering of sales tax or excise duties on some domestically produced important raw materials or lowering of import duties on raw materials and capital goods from abroad can provide a boost to private investment.

It needs to be stressed that various incentives to promote private saving and investment will prove effective only if they are kept as simple, certain and stable as possible. A complicated schemes of incentives with frequent and arbitrary changes are likely to defeat the very purpose of these incentive schemes. Prof. Prest rightly points out, "*If the main purpose of investment incentives is to raise the long-term level of investment rather than offset cyclical downturns and this clearly is the case in underdeveloped countries ... the emphasis should be on the stability of these tax arrangements rather than their variability.*"[5]

It is important to note that private investment depends upon several factors such as size of the market, cost of inputs, availability of infrastructural facilities such as power, coal, oil, transport, availability of technical know-how. Tax incentives will prove effective only if conditions regarding these other factors are not unfavourable. Further, unless there is an efficient and competent system of tax administration it is very likely that incentives become tax loopholes. The businessmen in the developing countries tend to take advantages of these tax exemptions on bogus basis without fulfilling and carrying out the underlying intent of such concessions. An honest and efficient administrative machinery, therefore, remains the basic precondition for the purposeful use of incentives.[6]

---

5. See Prest, A.R. Fiscal Measures and Capital Accumulation in Agarwala and Singh (ed.), *Accelerating Investment in Developing Countries*, Oxford University Press.
6. A.R. Prest. *op. cit., p.* 445.

GOVERNMENT BORROWING AND RESOURCE MOBILISATION FOR ECONOMIC DEVELOPMENT

Government borrowing is another fiscal method by which savings of the community may be mobilised for economic development. In developing economies, the Governments resort to borrowing in order to finance schemes of economic development. Government or what is also called public borrowing becomes necessary because taxation alone cannot provide sufficient funds for economic development. Besides, too heavy taxation has an adverse effect on private saving and investment. It may be noted that when there is fiscal deficit (*i.e.*, budget deficit). It can be financed in two ways. First, by borrowing by the Government from the market and this borrowing leads to the increase in public debt. Borrowing as a means to finance the budget deficit is therefore also called **debt-financing of budget deficit**.

Under borrowing the government issues bonds and sells it to the public. Generally, sale of interest-bearing bonds to the public is indirect through financial intermediarises such as banks. Banks buy the bonds floated by the government with the currency deposits of the public. Therefore, *debt-financing of budget deficit* is also known as *bond-financing of budget deficit*. With the borrowed money in this way the government is able to expand its expenditure but at the same time it adds to public debt which has both short-run and long-run consequences. It may also be noted that budget deficit also comes about when taxes are reduced, keeping government expenditure constant. This type of budget deficit can also be financed through incurring debt by selling bonds to the banks or public. The government has not only to pay annually interest on borrowed funds but has also to pay back the principal sum borrowed for which it may levy higher taxes in future.

The Keynesians have emphasised the expansionary effect of debt-financing of government expenditure or budget deficit. In the Keynesian model with a fixed price level, the increase in government expenditure through use of borrowed money causes an upward shift in aggregate expenditure $(C+I+G)$ curve. If the economy is working at less than full-employment level of national income so that output gap exists in the economy, the increase in debt-financed government expenditure will bring about expansion in output or income. With the increase in income at the given tax rate, tax revenue collected will rise which will over time reduce the budget deficit or even ultimately eliminate it so that budget becomes balanced.

However, critics have pointed out that debt-financed government expenditure is largely offset by the ***crowding-out effect*** of debt financing on private investment. The crowding-out effect on private investment takes place in a variety of ways. First, it has been pointed out that government's borrowing funds to finance budget deficit will lead to the increase in demand for lendable funds which will cause the rate of interest to rise. The rise in interest rate will cause private investment to decline. Thus debt-financed increase in government expenditure crowds out private investment. According to this view, due to crowding-out effect on private investment net expansionary effect of increase in government expenditure is negligible. On the other hand, the society will have to bear the burden of increase in public debt as a result of debt-financed expansion in government expenditure. If budget deficit arises due to reduction in taxes, keeping government expenditure constant, this will also lead to rise in interest rate and will therefore cause crowding-out effect on private investment. This happens because reduction in taxes stimulates consumption expenditure of the people which reduces savings. The decline in savings causes interest rate to rise resulting in fall in private investment.

Government borrowing takes two forms : (*a*) *market loans* and (*b*) *small savings*. In the case of market borrowing, the Government sells to the public negotiable Government securities of varying terms and duration and treasury bills. For financing capital projects long-term Government bonds are floated in the capital market. This form of public borrowing is more important for mobilising resources for development. The treasury bills which represent short-term borrowing are intended to meet only the current Government expenditure. New bonds may be issued for meeting old maturing bonds. The small savings represent public borrowing which are not negotiable and are not bought and sold in the capital market. For mobilising small savings, various types of saving certificates are issued, e.g., National Savings Certificates, National Development Certificates, Rural Development Bonds, Postal Certificates and Postal Accounts, mutual funds, etc. A widespread campaign is necessary to attract small savings.

Borrowing is the quickest mode of raising funds. Tax finance is not so expeditious because passing of tax laws, assessment of taxes based on those laws and their collection involves considerable delay. Besides, *public debt does not involve any burden if it is devoted to productive works.* The subscribers to Government loans are able to find remunerative investment whereas the Government can pay the principal and interest out of the income yielded by investment financed from loans. Thus public borrowing is not only necessary but also desirable.

There is another advantage of Government borrowing. *Government borrowing is anti-inflationary*. The underdeveloped countries are victims of inflation since they have to resort to money financing (that is, printing of new money) for finding funds for economic development. Since money financing is inflationary, public borrowing is preferable to money financing. Public borrowing mops up the surplus purchasing power with the people. It thus checks consumption and so a rise in prices. At the same time idle balances are absorbed in productive activity.

Public borrowing generates additional productive capacity. The funds raised by public borrowing can be utilised for building up economic infrastructure for the economy through schemes for the development of irrigation, transport, power and communication. They can help also in building up of the agricultural and industrial base of the economy. All such investments facilitate further economic growth. There is no doubt, therefore, that the public borrowing plays a very useful and important role in accelerating economic growth of developing economies. Public debt promotes saving and investment, the two most crucial determinants of economic growth.

But there exist a number of obstacles which hinder the success of borrowing policy in developing countries. In many such countries, there are no organised money and capital markets and in those where such markets exist, they constitute a very small proportion of total money market of the country. There may not, besides, exist any organic relationship between the organised and unorganised parts of the money market.

Moreover, the resources of the organised money market may be too inadequate to fulfil the needs of both the private and public sectors. Further, in the financial market the competition for funds between the government and the private sector will raise rate of interest and this will have a highly disincentive effect on the expansion of investment in the private sector. More borrowing by the Government leads to the rise in market rates of interest. The higher interest rates tends to reduce private investment. Therefore, it is often asserted that the *higher borrowing target by the Government 'crowds out' private investment*. In India the rates of interest on loans (on bonds or securities) of Government have been raised quite substantially. Since banks and others prefer to invest in Government securities because they are safe (*i.e.*, riskless). This has reduced funds for private investment.

For the success of government's borrowing policy, it is necessary that financial institutions be developed and extended into the rural areas of the economy in order to inculcate the habit of thrift in the population and to mobilise for productive purposes the amount of savings originating in this sector. Besides, for the mobilisation of savings it will be necessary to check and regulate the diversion of savings into unproductive investment such as real estate, gold and jewellery and inventory accumulation.

Suitable techniques of borrowing must also be devised. For example, bonds issued by the Government should be adjusted to the preferences of the general public; bonds of large denomination and long maturity may be offered to the institutional investors, whereas those of small denomination and short maturity may be reserved for the non-institutional public. If properly devised and conducted small savings campaign can mobilise a sizable amount of resources. Further, the mobilisation of the hoardings of gold and jewellery through government programmes constitutes a highly desirable source of resource mobilisation. Of course, suitable techniques of public borrowing for the mobilisation of these resources have to be evolved.

ROLE OF BORROWING : THE CASE OF INDIA

In India there has been a problem of persistent budget deficits which has been largely financed by borrowing from the banks and public and thus adding to the public debt. In 1991 as a measure of economic reforms IMF directed that fiscal deficit of the central government should be reduced to achieve economic stability. The economists associated with IMF and World Bank hold the view that large fiscal deficit raises inflation rate of the economy on the one hand and since it is financed largely by borrowing from the market, this raises rate of interest and therefore crowds out private investment and adversely affects economic growth. Besides, it has been pointed out that the persistent budget deficit year after year adds to public debt and as a result ratio of public debt to national income (Debt/GDP ratio) will greatly increase which will land the country in the debt trap[13].

In view of the above it is appropriate to discuss the above issues relating to borrowing or debt-financing of budget deficit in the light of the recent Indian experience. It is worth mentioning that from the years 1997 to 2002-03 and again in 2008 and 2009 the Indian economy experienced slowdown in economic growth due to lack of aggregate demand resulting mainly from the fall in public investment and poor performance in agriculture. In this situation *output gap* in the Indian economy emerged as the existing production capacity was not fully utilised. Besides, there has been lack of infrastructure facilities which stands in the way of raising private investment. Again in 2008-09 there had been slowdown in the Indian economy due to the global financial crises (2007-09) leading to a sharp fall in India's exports. An important factor for this is deficiency of aggregate demand

With their focus on reducing fiscal deficit the government reduces its capital expenditure (*i.e.* investment expenditure) because it fails to curb its consumption expenditure and subsidies. Thus, Mihir Rakshit, a leading Indian macroeconomist, rightly states. "With their focus on fiscal deficit, policy makers seem to think that what matters primarily is curbing government expenditure .... irrespective of changes in their composition. The period 1995-2000 was marked by 9.6 per cent and 12.6 per cent growth in government consumption and subsidies respectively, but government capital accumulation grew at snail's pace of 1.9 per cent and its two crucial constituents, namely, investment in agriculture and infrastructure actually declined by 5.6 per cent and 0.2 per cent respectively"[14]

The consequences of debt-financed budget deficit in the case of India depends on whether or not output gap, that is, underutilisation of productive capacity exists due to lack of demand and infrastructural facilities. If the output gap exists, then increase in government expenditure on consumption and subsidies will raise aggregate demand and help in utilising more fully the existing production capacity and over time will cause private investment to rise. But this will not raise public saving and public investment and therefore will not result in much higher growth of the economy. This may also raise ratio of public debt to GDP since due to slow growth in GDP, tax collection will not appreciably rise. Mihir Rakshit aptly points out that, "The *Indian economy since 1997*[15] *has also been characterised by output gap, high fiscal deficit and growing debt/GDP ratio. The mainstream*

13. For this view, see Shankar Acharya, former Chief Economic Advisor who puts forward this view in a forcefull manner in 'How Fiscal Deficit Hurts Economic Growth'.
14. Mihir Rakshit, "Some Macroeconomics of India's Reforms Experience" in *India's Emerging Economy* (*ed.*) Kaushik Basu, Oxford University Press, 2004, p,104.

view in India is that despite the output gap fiscal deficits crowds out private investment and are unsustainable"[15].

The mainstream view of debt-financed fiscal deficit is not correct and has been rightly challenged by some prominent Indian economists such as Mihir Rakshit, V.N. Pandit and Prabhat Patnaik, among others. Under the circumstances when there exists output-gap and under-utilisation of production capacity, the increase in government expenditure, especially of investment nature will *crowd in* private investment and speed up rate of economic growth. To quote Mihir Rakshit, "contrary to wide spread perception among commentators *budget deficits associated with closing the output gap in fact crowds in private investment*......... crowding in will be much more pronounced in countries like India where government's infrastructural investment favourably affects private investment even while projects are being executed : the fact that highways are being built in some area or that it will soon have abundant supply of power, communication facilities is likely to induce private investors to start setting up new units and expending existing ones even in the shrot run"[16].

When there is underutilisation of productive capacity in a developing economy such as India, even increase in Government's consumption expenditure will crowd in private investment through the former's demand effect. But, as has been pointed out by Dr. Mihir Rakshit, crowding-in effect of government's investment expenditure will be greater because it expands the infrastructural facilities (*i.e.*, supply-side factors) badly needed for increase in private investment.[17]

In our view, the expansionary effect of government's investment expenditure and also its crowding-in effect on private investment in a developing country like India is not confined to the situation when output gap and under-utilisation of capital stock exists due to demand deficiency but also when such an economy functions at its normal capacity. Besides, even in normal times, debt-financed government investment expenditure which brings about rapid economic growth, budget deficits and debt/GDP ratio over time can be reduced. An important rule of public finance, which is sometimes described as **a golden rule is that if borrowed money by the government is used for investment or developmental purposes,** it leads to growth in GDP or national income. Given the tax rate, this increase in income will ensure collection of more tax revenue possible. As a result, budget deficit or what is called fiscal deficit will be reduced and debt/GDP ratio will decline. This has actually happened in India. Thus, the viability and sustainability of debt-financed budget deficits in a growing economy must be based on the magnitude of Government investment expenditure in the total expenditure.

It is thus clear that sustainability of budget deficit and public debt depends on *shifting the composition of government expenditure towards investment*. To quote Mihir Rakshit, "Budgetary viability requires an improvement in revenue balances in the medium term and the long run....... public investment in agriculture aided by crowding-in effect, raises agricultural productivity and acts as a stimulant to a rural economy, brings down poverty and *enables the government to reduce over time expenditure on subsidies*. An increase in government investment in rural and urban infrastructural facilities will through increased revenue receipts and decreased subsidies will strengthen budgetary position not only in the medium term and the long run but in the short run as well"[18]. It is interesting to note that when with effect from year 2003 the Government investment expenditure in India was raised, tax revenue collection significantly rose and also fiscal deficit, revenue deficit and debt/GDP ratio declined. Besides, private investment also went up (*i.e.*, crowed in) rather than crowding out by increase in debt-financed increase in government expenditure.

15. Mihir Rakshit describes the situation that prevailed during 1997-2002-03.
16. Budget Deficit: Sustainability, Solvancy and Optimality, printed in Amaresh Bagchi, "*Readings in Public Finance*" Oxford University Press, 2005, pp. 342-343.
17. Mihir Rabshit, op. cit. p.345
18. Mihir Rakshit, op. cit. 2005 p.105

Thus, in the nineties when the focus in our strategy was to reduce fiscal deficit, no matter reducing capital expenditure of the government for this purpose, the Indian economy experienced slowdown in growth and our fiscal situation worsened. On the other hand, when during 2003-04 and 2007-08 we shifted the focus toward increase in government investment expenditure on power, ports, highways, rural roads in a big way, private investment also crowed in, generated higher economic growth which resulted in lower fiscal deficits and lower debt/GDP ratio.

MONEY FINANCING AND RESOURCE MOBILISATION FOR ECONOMIC GROWTH

Meaning of Money Financing. Money financing was earlier called **deficit financing** Deficit financing was variously defined but the one idea underlying all these definitions is clear viz., it refers to '*printing new money*', *i.e.*, creation of additional purchasing power in the form of currency notes. Money inancing or deficit financing is said to have been practised whenever Government expenditure exceeds the Government receipts from taxes, fees, surpluses from public undertakings, borrowings from the public. *Such an excess of expenditure is financed by borrowing from the Central Bank.*

When the Government borrows from the Central Bank which is a note-issuing authority, the Central Bank simply issues more notes and gives them to the Government against Government securities. Thus in the last analysis money financing means the creation of new currency. It may be noted that in India *Net Bank Credit from RBI* by the central Government is called deficit financing or money financing. fact when Central Government borrows from RBI and the latter issues new currency it is called *monetisation of fiscal deficit*. It is this monetisation of debt that leads to the expansion in money supply due to Government's fiscal deficit that was earlier called deficit financing. However, in the modern terminology it is now called **monetisation of fiscal deficit**.

Need for Money Financing. The developing countries keen to promote rapid economic growth, the resources required for development far exceeds the amount which can be raised by normal means of resource mobilisation, viz., taxation, borrowing, surpluses from public enterprises, etc. The uncovered gap is made up by money financing. Rapid economic development can be achieved only by stepping up the rate of investment. But where from are the developing countries to raise the additional resources? In the absence of sufficient foreign aid forthcoming from friendly countries and international organisations, the additional funds must come from domestic resources. For this purpose voluntary savings must be stepped up. These savings are then mopped up through national small savings schemes to add to the resources available to the government.

But in the country where a majority of the people are living at the subsistence level, the margin between income and consumption is very low so that voluntary savings, however welcome, cannot by themselves provide sufficient resources for development. The government may also attempt to increase the volume of resources by additional taxes. Yet because of extreme poverty of the great masses of the people, additional taxation beyond a point raises difficult problems, both economical and political. Therefore, in their anxiety to implement development schemes, the governments are compelled to resort to money financing.

Money Financing and Inflation. Since money financing involves expansion of money supply with the public, it has inflationary potential. But if the supply of output, especially that of consumer goods, is increasing when money financing is being done, there is no danger of inflation. Therefore, it should not be presumed that money financing necessarily leads to inflation. Deficit or money financing generates inflationary pressures only when the supply of output cannot be increased to match the increase in money supply which becomes available through money financing.

Money financing practised during the depression in the developed countries does not generate inflationary pressures because of the elastic nature of the supply curve of output. Additional govern-

ment expenditure leads to an increase in effective demand, depending upon the magnitude of the multiplier. Similarly, in developing countries when supply of output can be increased to match additional demand, there are no inflationary pressures. In the developed countries during the depression, there is a lot of excess capacity in the system so that an increase in output presents no difficult problems.

The situation in the developing countries is, however, different. Here an increase in investment does create additional demand but a corresponding increase in the supply of output cannot be taken for granted. First, a developing country suffers from the dearth of capital and there is no large excess capacity to be utilized for creating additional supply of consumer goods. Besides, the basic wage goods industry, *i.e.*, agriculture, suffers from an inelastic supply curve in the short run. The farmer's ability to increase his output is limited. His holding is a tiny one and often lies scattered all over the village; he lacks resources to buy more and better seeds and fertilizers; irrigation facilities are lacking so that even with the best of will in the world, unaided by any outside agency, the farmer's efforts to increase his output may not bear fruit. In the absence of elastic supply of consumer goods, money financing carries with it great inflationary bias.

In the early stages of development, the inflationary danger is very real indeed. This is because of the urgent need to invest large sums in long-term projects such as building of big dams, steel plants, machines making industry and other types of heavy and basic industries as well as in the development of transport and communication system. Investment in such long-term projects does create additional demand, but these projects do not add to the supply of consumer goods in the short run. Thus in the short run prices generally shoot up under the pressure of excessive demand for consumer goods. And once inflationary spiral starts operating, it is difficult to control it.

Reasonable Money Financing Helps Development

From above it should not be understood that every and any amount of money financing is harmful. Money financing of a reasonable amount is very useful. A reasonable dose of deficit financing helps the development of the economy. In a developing country like India, a huge amount of natural and human resources are lying unutilised and underutilised. With the help of money financing these unutilised and underutilised resources can be employed for productive purposes. If money financing is used to invest in those projects of schemes such as small irrigation works, land reclamation schemes which yield quick results, then the danger of inflation is not there. These quick-yielding projects will increase the supply of consumer goods in the immediate period and will therefore prevent the creation of inflationary pressures. Further, if, under the development plans, serious efforts are made by the government to help the farmers to increase agricultural production by providing the farmers with HYV seeds, fertilizers and irrigation facilities in time and in adequate quantities, then the supply of agricultural goods can be made elastic. To the extent we are able to increase agricultural production, we can safely do money financing. Since the income elasticity of demand for foodgrains is very high in the developing countries like India the incomes generated by investment outlay under the development plans are mostly directed to the purchase of foodgrains. But if we succeed in raising agricultural production, especially foodgrains, then a reasonable dose of money financing will not result in inflation.

Further, as the economy develops, the monetary sector expands. In other words, *as the economy grows, it becomes more monetized*. As a result of the expansion of monetary sector, needs for money increase. If new money is created to match this extra need for money, that will not prove inflationary. Moreover, with the general growth of the economy under development plans, the output of goods and services rises. There is no harm in creating new money which will match this additional output made possible by growth of the economy. Thus, if economic growth occurs at the rate of 8 per cent per annum, then money supply through deficit financing can be increased by 8 per cent without the risk of inflation.

It is worth repeating here that *the danger of money financing leading to inflation will be less only if resources raised through money financing are used for purposes of productive investment.* In the long run, productive investments made under the plans will increase the productive capacity and will therefore bear fruit in the form of greater supply of consumer goods. Thus inflation created by productive investment in the short run is likely to be self-destructive in the long run. But there is real danger of short-run inflation becoming self-cumulative rather than self-destructive if money financing is used for providing subsidies or for financing government consumption activities. If money financing is undertaken to make investments in quick-yielding projects in both agriculture and industry, then the danger of inflation can be avoided. For instance, if new money is created to invest in quick-yielding schemes like building of wells. tube-wells, tanks and conservation of soil to get quick returns, it will not prove inflationary.

Thus, within limits, money financing is not only desirable but essential as well. *It proves inflationary only when safe limit is crossed.* Money financing can serve as a useful instrument of economic development if a right dose of it is taken considering the growth of national output, especially that of foodgrains and if it is used for financing those schemes or projects which yield quick results.

FISCAL POLICY, EQUITY AND PRICE STABILITY

Fiscal Policy and Equitable Income Distribution

Let us now explain how fiscal policy can be used to achieve equitable distribution of income. Attainment of a wider measure of equality in incomes, wealth and opportunities must form an integral part of economic development and social advance. Existence of gross inequalities is a social evil and no measure of economic development will increase economic welfare unless an equitable distribution of the rising national product is assured. Instrument of taxation, therefore, must be used as a means of bringing about a redistribution of income in favour of the poorer sections of the society. A caution is, however, necessary. It is essential to strike a balance between the two objectives of lessening economic inequalities and that of sustaining and strengthening incentives to invest and increase production. Fiscal policy must maintain unimpaired the flow of savings and investment which makes for continued progress of productive enterprises. Larger production and greater equality are both objectives of high importance in relation to general economic and social policy. Higher incomes can be taxed without adverse repercussions on private productive effort and enterprise. Optimum rate of growth and maximum social welfare are not irreconcilable. It will be possible to reconcile these two objectives by the formulation of a well-balanced fiscal programme.

But lessening inequalities through taxing higher incomes is only one form of fiscal operations. A better and complementary fiscal policy consists of *increasing public expenditure for promoting welfare of the less privileged classes*. Increasing public expenditure on anti-poverty programmes such as construction of rural public works, employment guarantee schemes will ensure equity in income distribution. Stepping up of public expenditure on primary education and public health will greatly improve the economic conditions of the poor people. In fact, international experience shows that active public expenditure policies aimed at raising the consumption of the poor are far more effective in promoting equity as compared to tax policies aimed at containing the incomes of the rich.

Fiscal Policy for Achieving Price Stability

India as well as other developing countries have been experiencing the problem of rising prices or inflation. Inflation in them has been of both demand-pull and cost-push types. The main cause of demand-pull inflation has been the *fiscal deficit* in Government's budgets which has arisen because they have not been able to finance the mounting public expenditure through revenue from taxes and public sector surpluses In India in the year 1990-91, fiscal deficit rose to 8.3 per cent of GDP (Gross Domestic Product) and after 14 years of efforts, the Central Government was able to achieve about 50 per cent reduction in fiscal deficit. In 2004-05, fiscal deficit was estimated to be of the order of 4.0 per cent of GDP. However, to achieve price stabilisation IMF recommended its reduction to 3 per cent of GDP. A huge fiscal deficit in Government is financed in two ways: (1) by Government borrowing from the market, (2) by monetising the deficit which is commonly called money or deficit financing in India. A high degree of fiscal deficit leads to excess market borrowing by the Government which causes expansion in bank credit to the Government and therefore increase in money supply in the economy causing prices to rise.

Besides, excessive Government borrowing from the market leads to the rise in interest rate which discourages private investment. Further, a part of fiscal deficit is monetised through borrowing from Reserve Bank of India which issues new currency (which is called reserve or high powered money) for the Government. This causes greater expansion in money supply through the process of money multiplier and generates inflationary situation in the economy. Thus, to check the rate of inflation, fiscal deficit has to be reduced to the reasonable amount through both raising revenue of the Government and reducing Government non-developmental expenditure. In what follows we first explain the concepts of fiscal deficit, revenue deficit, primary deficit. We will then explain various measures in the Indian context that can be adopted to reduce fiscal deficit and thereby to reduce inflationary pressures in the economy.

CONCEPTS OF BUDGET DEFICITS IN INDIA

Government expenditure on goods and services and resources mobilised by it through taxes, etc., are important factors that determine aggregate demand in the economy. When there is a deficit in the budget of the government, it spends more than it collects resources through taxes and non-tax revenue. In recent years there have been huge budget deficits in India which have created large excess demand in the economy. This has resulted in inflation or sharp rise in the general level in prices. The deficit may occur either in the revenue budget or capital budget or in both taken together. When there is an overall budget deficit of the Government, it has to be financed by either borrowing from the market or from the Reserve Bank of India which is the nationalised central bank of the country. RBI has the power to create new money, that is, to issue new notes. Thus, to finance its budget deficit, the government may borrow from Reserve Bank of India against its own securities. This is only a technical way of creating new money because the government has to pay neither the rate of interest nor the original amount when it borrows from the Reserve Bank of India against its own securities. It is thus clear that budget deficit implies that government incurs more expenditure on goods and services than its normal receipts from taxes and non-tax revenue. This excess expenditure by the government is financed by either borrowing from the market or by newly created money which leads to the rise in incomes of the people. This causes the aggregate demand of the community to rise to a greater extent than the actual amount of money financing through the operation of what Keynes called *income multiplier.*

In the opinion of many economists, the expansion in money supply caused by monetisation of deficit, that is, deficit financing leads to the excess aggregate demand in the economy, especially when aggregate supply of output is inelastic. The excess aggregate demand causes rise in the price level or brings about inflation in the economy.

Revenue Deficit

As mentioned above, the budget has two parts : *Revenue Budget* and *Capital Budget.* Receipts in the revenue account come from such sources as various types of direct and indirect taxes and also from non-tax sources such as interest received on loans given, dividend and profits of public enterprises.

The items of expenditure in the revenue account are of the type that represents *collective consumption* of the society and therefore, creates no earning assets. The various types of expenditure on the revenue account are incurred on : (1) Interest payments on public debit, (2) Civil administration, (3) Defence, (4) Subsidies on food, fertilisers, oil and (5) Social services such as education, health, etc.

Revenue deficit refers to the excess of revenue expenditure over revenue receipts. Prudent management of public finance requires that receipts on revenue account should exceed expenditure on revenue account. In other words, there should be surplus on revenue account so that this surplus should be used for investment in development projects or building assets which yield return. In fact, surplus on revenue account of the budget represents *public or government savings* which can be used for financing developmental activities. However, in India, for the past several years, there has been deficit on the revenue account. That is, there has been *government dissaving* for the last some years in India. Therefore, borrowed funds from the capital account have been used to meet a part of revenue or consumption expenditure of the government. This has bad consequences for the economy. Revenue deficit as percentage of gross domestic product (GDP) had been quite high upto 2002-03. Revenue deficit of the central government of India for various years is given in Table 34.1.

Since revenue deficit represents negative savings of the Government, it lowers investment by the

Table 34.1: Trends in Budget Deficits of Central Government

Year	*Fiscal deficit*	*Revenue deficit*	*Primary deficit*	*Revenue deficit as per cent of fiscal deficit*
	(As per cent of GDP)			
1996-97	4.1	2.4	–0.2	58.2
1997-98	4.8	3.0	0.5	63.5
1998-99	5.1	3.8	0.7	74.8
1999-2000	5.4	3.5	0.7	64.6
2000-01	5.7	4.1	0.9	71.7
2001-02	6.2	4.4	1.5	71.1
2002-03	5.9	4.4	1.1	74.4
Enactment of FRBMA				
2003-04	4.5	3.6	0.0	79.7
2004-05	4.0	2.5	–0.1	62.3
2005-06	4.1	2.6	0.4	63.0
2006-07	3.4	1.9	–0.2	56.3
2007-08	2.7	1.4	–0.9	41.4
2008-09	6.0	4.5	2.6	75.2
2009-10	6.3	5.1	3.1	81.0
2010-11	4.8	3.5	1.7	67.5
2011-12	5.7	4.3	–	75.5
2012-13	5.1	3.9	–	68.2

Source: Economic Survey, 2010-11, 2011-12 and 2012-13

government and, therefore, slows down economic growth of the country. Therefore, every effort should be made to reduce revenue deficit. in 2003 Fiscal Responsibility Budget Management Act (FRBMA) was passed according to which revenue deficit was to be completely eliminated by 2008-09. It will be seen that after 2002-03 revenue deficit as per cent of GDP came down to 1.4 per cent of GDP in 2007-08 but again rose to 4.5 per cent in 2008-09 and to 4.3 per cent of GDP in 2011-12.

Fiscal Deficit

Fiscal deficit in the budget is an important measure of deficit. IMF and the World Bank generally prescribe targets for budget deficit in terms of fiscal deficit. *Fiscal deficit is the excess of total expenditure (both on revenue and capital accounts) over revenue receipts and only non-debt type of capital receipts such as recoveries of loans.*

Thus,

Fiscal Deficit = **(*Total Expenditure both on Revenue Account and Capital Account*) – (*Revenue Receipts + Non-debt Capital Receipts*)**

Fiscal deficit is a more comprehensive measure of budgetary imbalances. Thus, we see that when the government's total expenditure, both revenue and capital expenditure, exceeds its revenue from taxes and non-debt capital receipts, *fiscal deficit* is created. Now, this fiscal deficit can be financed in two ways. Firstly, through borrowing by the government from the market, both inside and outside the country. On this borrowing, the government has to pay rate of interest annually. Apart from this, it has to pay back the internal and external debt taken. Secondly, the government

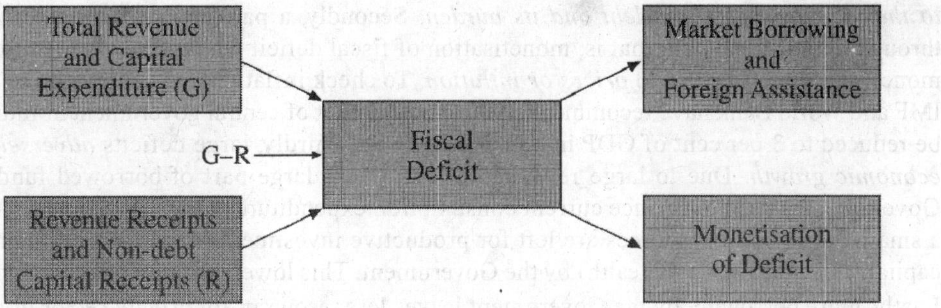

Fig. 34.1. *Financing of Fiscal Deficit*

can finance the fiscal deficit by borrowing from the Reserve Bank of India which issues new notes against government securities. Thus, borrowing from the Reserve Bank results in expansion of high powered money in the economy and is popularly called money financing. It is in fact *monetisation of fiscal deficit* which, if undertaken to an excessive degree, leads to inflation in the economy. On the other hand, Government borrowing from the market to finance fiscal deficit adds to the public debt and increases burden on future generations on whom heavy taxes have to be imposed for repaying the loans.

In the Table 34.1, fiscal deficit of the Central Government of India has been calculated for the last seventeen years. Fiscal deficit which was 4.7% of GDP in 1997-98 rose to 6.2% of GDP in 2001-2002 but it fell to 2.5% of GDP in 2007-08. It will be seen from this that in the Indian economy, fiscal deficit was quite large prior to 2003-04 which led to inflation or rise in prices in the economy on the one hand and increase in public debt on the other. Therefore, it was decided to reduce it to 3 per cent of GDP by the year 2008-09 and Fiscal Responsibility Budget Management (FRBM) Act was passed to discipline Government's fiscal policy and reduce fiscal deficit.

Accordingly, the government did not borrow directly from RBI through privately placing bonds with it since 2003 (That is, did not monetise the fiscal deficit since 2002). However, for the years 2008-09 and 2009-10, the Government planned to monetise the deficit to some extent as fiscal deficit greatly went up due to fiscal stimulus packages adopted to overcome recessionary conditions in the Indian economy created by global financial crisis of 2008-09 and it was not considered prudent to finance it fully through borrowing from the market which would have led to higher interest rates and crowded out private investment apart from raising the burden of public debt. In the budget for 2007-08, fiscal deficit of the Central government was brought down to 2.5 per cent of GDP. For 2008-09, actual fiscal deficit rose to 6 per cent of GDP and in 2009-10 to 6.3 per cent of GDP due to fiscal stimulus. In budget for 2010-11, the Finance Minister succeeded in to reducing it to 4.8 per of GDP (RE) (see Table 34.1). However, in 2011-12 due to adoption of several welfare schemes fiscal deficit again shot up to 5.7 per cent of GDP which caused much increase in aggregate demand and has been responsible for rise in inflation rate. For 2012-13 against the budget target of 4.6% of GDP it was feared that fiscal deficit would go up to even 6 per cent of GDP because of less than estimated collection of taxes due to slowdown of the economy and decline in estimated funds from 2G Spectrum and disinvestment of public sector. However, the Finance Minister succeeded in reducing government expenditure by cutting *planned expenditure* of over 91,000 crore though it was quite undesirable to do so. Again for the year 2013-14, by pruning plan expenditure to the extent of ₹ 75,000 crore and postponing the payment of subsidies to the oil companies, Finance Minister succeeded in reducing fiscal deficit to 4.6% of GDP as against the target of 4.8 per cent. The States in India also have fiscal deficit of around 2.2 to 3 per cent of GDP.

Implications of Large Fiscal Deficit. Thus, there are three implications of fiscal deficit. A good part of it is financed through borrowing from within and outside the country. This *leads* *to the increase in public debt and its burden.* Secondly, a part of fiscal deficit is financed through deficit financing, that is, monetisation of fiscal deficit which leads to creation of new money and therefore *rise in prices or inflation.* To check inflation and achieve price stability, IMF and World Bank have recommended that fiscal deficit of central government in India should be reduced to 3 per cent of GDP in a phased manner.Thirdly, large deficits *adversely affects economic growth.* Due to large revenue deficit, a very large part of borrowed funds by the Government is used to finance current consumption expenditure of the Government. As result, a smaller amount of resources are left for productive investment in infrastructure and social capital (*i.e.* education and health) by the Government. This lowers the rate of economic growth. Lastly, more borrowing by the Government leaves less resources for private sector investment.

To reduce the central fiscal deficit to 3 per cent requires drastic cut in non-productive revenue expenditure which is a difficult task. *In India, attempts have been made to reduce fiscal deficit by curtailing capital expenditure which is incurred on projects of capital formation and other developmental activities.* This is not a desirable way of reducing fiscal deficit because this adversely affects economic growth. For sound management of Government finance there is need to cut revenue expenditure and raise revenue receipts by mobilising resources through taxation. Attempts to reduce fiscal deficit by curtailing capital expenditure, as has been the practice in India so far, adversely affects economic growth and should therefore be avoided.

To reduce fiscal deficit in his budget speech for 2013-14, the finance minister presented a roadmap for reducing fiscal deficit to 3% of GDP in 2016-17 as shown in Fig. 33.2. However, as shall be discussed below fiscal deficit, to a reasonable degree, is not bad. In times of recessionary situation or slowdown in economic growth such as the one that prevails in 2008-09 and 2009-10, it is needed to fight recession and prevent slowdown in the economy. All over the world (including the US), the governments resort to a large dozes of fiscal deficit to stimulate the economy and prevent further deepening of recession and more losses of more jobs. It was for such a situation when private investment declines that J. M. Keynes recommended that Government should undertake deficit spending on a large scale to overcome recession and increase employment. In our view, though undertaking reasonable fiscal deficit in recessionary situation or showdown in economic growth is desirable but in a developing country such as ours borrowed money should be used for ***productive purposes*** and not frittered away in spending on useless and wasteful projects.

Primary Deficit

Primary deficit is another important concept of budgetary deficit. Primary deficit is a measure of budget deficit which is obtained by deducting interest payments from fiscal deficit. Thus,

Primary Deficit = Fiscal Deficit – Interest Payments

Interest payments on public debt are transfer payments made by the government. The difference between the fiscal deficit and primary deficit shows the importance of interest payments on public debt incurred in the past. Interest payments are very largely responsible for causing large fiscal deficit. A major part of Government borrowing to finance fiscal deficit is used for making interest payment on the past debt.

In India, in recent years, interest payments on public debt has increased very much. The higher interest payments on the past borrowings by the Government has greatly increased the fiscal deficit. Therefore, primary deficit is much lower than the fiscal deficit. In India, in the year 2001-02 primary deficit was 1.5 per cent of GDP, whereas fiscal deficit was 6.2 per of GDP. The primary deficit came down to zero in 2003-04 which implied that all the proceeds

19. See his article 'How Fiscal Deficits Hurt Economic Growth, *The Economic Times*, Nov-1, 2001 and 'Why Large Fiscal Deficits are bad for us, CNBC, January 2003
20. *Ibid.*

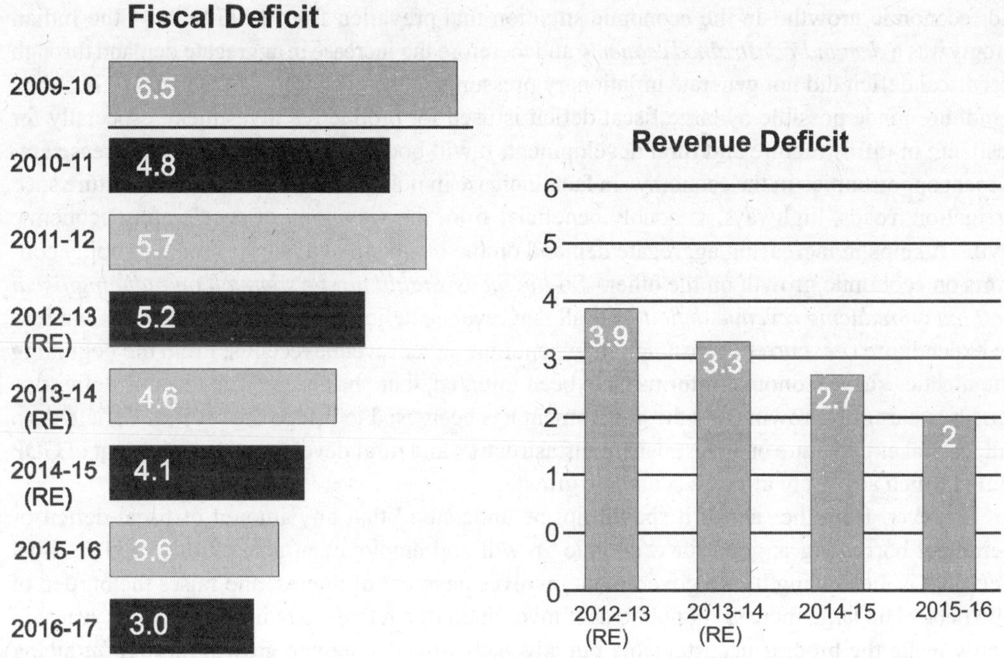

Fig. 34.2. *Roadmap of Reduction in Central Government's Fiscal and Revenue Deficits As Per Cent of GDP*

from government borrowing were used to spend on making interest payment on the past public debt. In the recent years 2006-07, 2007-08, primary deficit has been negative (– 0.2). This shows expenditure on interest payments exceeded borrowing by the Government. As mentioned above, interest payments is an item of liabilities in the revenue account of the budget. Therefore, if fiscal deficit has to be reduced, interest payments in the revenue account should be reduced which can be done if past public debt is quickly retired by mobilising more resources and curtailing non-developmental public expenditure.

Monetisation of Fiscal Deficit

It may be noted that budget deficit can financed by borrowing from the Reserve Bank of India by the central government against its own securities or treasury bills. The budget deficit is financed by borrowing from the Reserve Bank which issues new money or currency against government securities, which will lead to the expansion in money supply. In the old terminology, it was known as *deficit financing in India.* Financing the budget by issuing new money through borrowing from the Reserve Bank against securities in the new terminology is called *monetisation of fiscal deficit or money financing.* It may be noted that in the earlier years separate data regarding the budgetary deficit and therefore, the magnitude of deficit financing undertaken in a year were provided by the government. However, in recent years the data regarding budgetary deficit is not separately provided by the government and it has become a part of fiscal deficit which is shown to be financed by *government borrowing and other new liabilities.* Now the data regarding three deficits, namely, (1) revenue deficit, (2) fiscal deficit and (3) primary deficit are provided in the budget documents.

Fiscal Deficit and Economic Growth

How does fiscal deficit affect economic growth is a hotly debated issue. A number of Keynesian economists argue that fiscal deficit promotes growth. In India when in the past some years a good deal of industrial capacity was lying idle due to lack of aggregate demand, and there were enough stocks of foodgrains, it was asserted that fiscal deficit would stimulate demand and thereby ensure rapid economic growth. In the economic situation that prevailed from 1996 to 2004 the Indian economy was a *demand-constrained economy* and therefore the increase in aggregate demand through larger fiscal deficit did not generate inflationary pressures in the economy. If the increase in public expenditure made possible by large fiscal deficit is used for productive investment, especially for investment in infrastructure and rural development, it will boost production and help increase employment opportunities in the economy. In fact, increase in public investment in infrastructure such as irrigation, roads, highways, is doubly beneficial from the viewpoint of accelerating economic growth. It helps in increasing aggregate demand on the one hand and helps to reduce supply constraints on economic growth on the other. So *the focus should not be so much on reducing fiscal deficit but on reducing revenue deficit*. Recall that revenue deficit is the excess of government revenue expenditure (*i.e.* current consumption expenditure) over revenue receipts. From the beginning of the nineties since economic reforms have been initiated, there has been large revenue deficits so that a large part of borrowings by the government has been used to bridge the revenue deficit. As a result, capital expenditure on investment in infrastructure and rural development as a percent of GDP declined which adversely affected economic growth.

However, from the above it should not be understood that any amount of fiscal deficit or government borrowing is good for economic growth and employment generation. Higher fiscal deficit, that is, borrowing by the government involves payment of interest and raises the burden of public debt. The large increase in public debt involving large interest payments year after year will not only make the process unsustainable but adversely affect economic growth through reducing investible resources for spending on infrastructure such as power, irrigation, transport and social sectors (education and health) increased. The higher revenue deficits and large interest payments during the nineties caused a drastic decline in capital expenditure and public investment in physical infrastructure (irrigation + power + transport) as compared to the later half of the eighties (1985-86 to 1989-90) while current expenditure on social services (such as education, health, housing, anti-poverty schemes) remained almost stagnant. This shows fiscal and revenue deficits (especially revenue deficit) have worked to lower economic growth.

Another impact of fiscal deficit on economic growth has been its adverse effect on saving and investment in the Indian economy. Large revenue deficits increases dissaving of government which lowers the rate of saving in the economy.

It may be noted that the implementation during (1997-2000) of Eighth Pay Commission report enhancing the salaries of Government staff both at the Centre and States sharply increased the revenue expenditure of the governments and increased public dissavings. This adversely affected domestic rate of saving and investment and lowered rate of economic growth. The high and rising fiscal deficits which results in larger government borrowings from the market preempted the needed resources for investment by the private sector. This had an adverse effect on private investment and was mainly responsible for slowdown in economic growth.

However, it is important to note that in 2008 when as a result of global financial crisis there was economic slowdown in India which caused huge job losses relatively large fiscal deficit was necessary to prevent sharp slowdown of the economy. To prevent the situation from worsening further the Government came out with three fiscal stimulus packages to keep the growth momentum. In these stimulus packages Government raised its expenditure, especially on infrastructure on the one hand and cut taxes on the other to stimulate aggregate demand. To increase its expenditure Government borrowed from the market about ₹ 300,000 crore in 2008-09 ₹ 400,000 crore in 2009-10. As a result, its fiscal deficit went up from 2.7 per cent of GDP in 2007-08 to 6.0 per cent in 2008-09 and 6.4% of GDP in 2009-10. *But this did not produce bad results for the private sector investment, nor did it result in higher rate of interest*. Of course, RBI also reduced cash reserve ratio to increase liquidity in the banking system and lowered its repo rate to enable banks to lower the lending rates of interest. As a matter of fact, increased borrowing and expenditure by the Government in 2008-09 and 2009-10 led to the increase in demand for the products of private sector. Therefore, from May 2009 onward there were signs of revival of the Indian economy and in 2009-10 and 2010-11 it registered quite a high growth rate. Thus, despite 6.0 per cent fiscal deficit in 2008-09 and 6.4 % in 2009-10 and consequently heavy borrowing by the government in these two years manufacturing output recorded high growth.

It is because of the fiscal stimulus packages and increase in government expenditure made possible by heavy borrowing and fiscal deficit that India could achieve 6.8 per cent rate of economic growth in 2008-09 and 8.7% in 2009-10, 9.3 % in 2010-11 which is quite high, especially when there were recessionary conditions in the US and Europe. So in our view fiscal deficit of more than 3% in a year is not always bad. All depends on the economic situation in the country and the purposes for which borrowed funds are spent. If there is recession or slowdown in the economy, the fiscal deficit of 6 to 7 per cent of GDP is necessary to lift the economy out of recession or to prevent sharp slowdown in the growth of the economy. If borrowed funds are spent by the Government for investment or building durable assets, it will lead to the expansion in productive capacity and therefore ensure sustained economic growth.

It is evident from above that larger fiscal deficit at the time of recession or economic slowdown far from reducing private saving and investment is helpful for fighting recession or keeping growth momentum of the economy.

MEASURES FOR FISCAL CONSOLIDATION

By fiscal consolidation we mean raising more resource and reducing non-essential expenditure by the government so as to reduce fiscal deficit to a reasonable level. Reducing fiscal deficit is a formiddle challenge for control of inflation and achieving 8% growth in the 12th plan period (2012-17). Large fiscal deficit has two bad consequences. First, it leads to excessive Government borrowing from the market which causes rise in market interest rate. Higher market interest rate tends to reduce private investment. Further, it reduces the resources available for private sector investment. Second, the extent to which a large fiscal deficit is financed by borrowing from the Reserve Bank of India which issues new currency (which is called reserve money or high-powered money) for the government. This causes greater expansion in money supply through the process of money multiplier and generates inflationary situation in the economy. Thus, to check the rate of inflation, fiscal deficit has to be reduced through both raising revenue of the government and reducing government expenditure. In the Indian context, the following measures can be adopted to reduce fiscal deficit and thereby to reduce inflationary pressures in the economy. We first spell out the measures which may be adopted to reduce government expenditure and then describe measures for raising Government revenue.

Measures to Reducc Public Expenditure. In the context of the Indian economy, the following measures can be adopted to reduce public expenditure for reducing fiscal deficit and thereby check inflation.

1. A drastic reduction in expenditure on major subsidies such as food, fertilisers, and petroleum products is required to curtail public expenditure. A huge sum of money is spent on major subsidies on food, fertilisers, petroleum products by the central government. Without a drastic cut in subsidies over time it is difficult to reduce public expenditure to an appreciable degree. In June 2012, the government rightly decontrolled petrol so that its price is aligned with global price level. Besides, to reduce its expenditure on subsidies diesel prices were increased in September 2012 by ₹ 5 per litre and now it has been decided to increase diesel price by around 50 paise every month. As regards checking leakages the policy of direct cash transfers

to the beneficiaries has been adopted. To reduce subsidy on LPG, the supply of subsidised LPG cylinder to each consumer was capped at 6 per annum which together with hike in diesel prices was expected to lower government expenditure by ₹ 2300 crore. However, in the budget for 2013-14 expenditure on subsidies as per cent of GDP was reduced marginally to 2 per cent of GDP (RE) compared to 2.2% of GDP for the years 2009-10 and 2010-11.

2. The huge sum of money is spent by the government on LTC (Leave Travelling Concessions), bonus, leave encashment etc. A reduction in expenditure on these is necessary if the government is determined to cut public expenditure.
3. Another useful measure to cut public expenditure is to reduce interest payments on past debt. In India, interest payments account for about 40 per cent of expenditure on revenue account of the central government. In our view, *funds raised through disinvestment in the public sector should be used to retire a part of old public debt rather than financing current expenditure*. Retirement of public debt quickly will reduce burden of interest payments in future.
4. Budgetary support to public sector enterprises other than infrastructure projects should be substantially reduced. Further, public sector enterprises should be asked to raise funds from the market and banks.
5. Austerity measures should be adopted to curtail non-plan expenditure in all government departments.

Increasing Revenue from Taxation

To reduce fiscal deficit and thereby check rise in inflation rate, apart from reducing government expenditure, government revenue has to be raised. However, in recent years tax-GDP ratio has declined. In 2007-08, tax GDP ratio was 12 per cent which came down to 10.2 per cent for the year 2013-14. Continuing on the path of fiscal consolidation with a view to narrowing the gap in Government spending and resources, the tax-GDP ratio has been targeted at 10.9 per cent in the 2014-15 (BE). However, this is not enough for fiscal consolidation to reduce fiscal deficit to 3% of GDP. The Finance Minister has not made genuine efforts to raise more resources through taxation. He in his budget for 2013-14, only levied a surcharge of 10% on income of those earning ₹ 1 crore or more. This is too low to yield enough tax revenue. With current income tax rate of 30% in this income bracket, it will means a super rich person will pay only ₹ 3 lakh more tax on his or her income of ₹ one crore per annum which is too small.

1. As regards mobilising resources to increase public revenue, it may be noted that the policy of moderate taxes with simplified taxation structure should be followed. This will help to increase public revenue rather than reduce it. High marginal rates of taxes should be avoided as they serve as disincentives to work more, save more and invest more. Further, high marginal rates of direct taxes cause evasion of taxes. However, *in our view, the present marginal rate of tax in India is 30 per cent for above 10 lakh income per annum* is relatively small. Besides, due to various exemptions effective rate has been estimated to be around 20 per cent. Therefore, there is need for introducing a higher income tax slab with 35% rate of income tax.
2. In India, the *tax base is narrow for both direct and indirect taxes*; only about 2.7 per cent of population pays income tax. To increase revenue from taxation, tax base should be broadened by taxing agricultural incomes and incomes derived from unorganised industrial and services sectors. *The various exemptions and deductions provided in the income and wealth taxes should be withdrawn to broaden the tax base and collect more revenue*. It may be noted that

the Indian experience of the last 50 years reveals that these exemptions and deductions do not promote the intended objectives.

3. As is well known, there is a huge amount of black money in the Indian economy which has come into existence as a result of tax evasion. A good part of black money is parked in Swiss banks. In the last VDIS (Voluntary Disclosure Income Scheme) in 1997-98, more than, 10,000 crores of rupees were collected. However, there has been huge increase in the amount of black money since then. Not only the current black money has to be mopped up but also tax evasion that occurs every year has to be prevented by strict enforcement of the tax laws.

4. The past experience has shown that various tax concessions which have been given in income and indirect taxes for promoting employment, industrial development of backward regions and for other such social objectives do not actually serve the intended purposes and are largely used for evading taxes. These *concessions should therefore be withdrawn to collect more revenue from taxes and the social objectives should be served by adopting more effective policy instruments.* Long-term capital gains on equity shares are exempted from income tax. In the context of boom conditions in the stock market, their exemption should be withdrawn to increase public revenue. They represent *unearned incomes* and canon of equity in taxation demands that this exemption should be withdrawn

To sum up, with the adoption of above measures of reducing public expenditure and enhancing public revenue, it will be possible to reduce fiscal deficit to a safe limit. The reduction in fiscal deficit will prevent the emergence of excess demand in the economy and thereby help in controlling inflation and achieving price stability.

the books. Experience of the last [illegible] years suggests that these exemptions and [illegible] [illegible] [illegible] effective.

It is well known there is a large amount of "black money" in the [illegible] economy. [illegible] [illegible] of tax evasion [illegible] is placed in [illegible] [illegible] [illegible] [illegible] [illegible] [illegible] [illegible] [illegible] [illegible] [illegible] [illegible] [illegible]

The government has [illegible] tax concessions which have been given [illegible] [illegible] [illegible] [illegible] [illegible] [illegible] [illegible] [illegible] [illegible] [illegible] [illegible] [illegible] [illegible] [illegible] [illegible] exemption [illegible] in the stock [illegible] exemption should be withdrawn [illegible] [illegible] [illegible] exemption should be withdrawn.

To [illegible] [illegible] measures of reducing public expenditure and enhancing [illegible] [illegible] [illegible] [illegible] [illegible] in the economy and [illegible] of controlling [illegible] [illegible] [illegible]

PART – VIII
ECONOMIC GROWTH

- Economic Growth and its Determinants.
- Harrod-Domar Model of Growth
- Neoclassical Growth Model
- Sen vs Bhagwati : Debate on Growth and Distribution

CHAPTER

35

Economic Growth and its Determinants

Economic growth is another major concern of macroeconomics. Before explaining the factors which determine economic growth it is useful to describe how the terms economic growth and development are interpreted by the economists. In the fifties and sixties when the economics of growth and development were evolved, economic growth and development were considered to have the same meaning and therefore these two terms were used interchangeably. Today, however, an important distinction is drawn between economic growth and economic development. In what follows we first explain the meaning of these terms and the distinction between them.

Meaning of Economic Growth

Economic growth has been defined in two ways. In the first place, *economic growth is defined as a sustained annual increases in an economy's real national income over a long period of time*. In other words, economic growth means *rising trend of net national product at constant prices*. This definition has been criticized by some economists as inadequate and unsatisfactory. They argue that total national income may be increasing and yet the standard of living of the people may be falling. This can happen when the population is increasing at a faster rate than total national income. For instance, if national income is rising by 1% per year and population is increasing at 2% per year, the standard of living of the people will tend to fall. This is so because when population is increasing more rapidly than national income, per capita income will go on falling. Per capita income will rise when the national income increases faster than population.Therefore, the second and better way of defining economic growth is to do so in terms of per capita income. According to the second view, *"economic growth means the annual increase in real per capita income of a country over the long period.* Thus Professor Arthur Lewis says that *"economic growth means the growth of output per head of population."* Since the main aim of economic growth is to raise the standards of living of the people, therefore the second way of defining economic growth which runs in terms of per capita income or output is better.

Another point which is worth mentioning in regard to the definition of economic growth is that the increase in national income, or more correctly increase in per capita income or output, must be a 'sustained increase' if it is to be called economic growth. By sustained increase in per capita income we mean the upward or rising trend in per capita income over a long period of time. A mere short-period rise in per capita income, such as that occurs over a business cycle, cannot be validly called economic growth.

Now, almost universally, rates of economic growth are measured both in terms of increase in overall Gross National Product (GNP) or Net National Product (NNP) and increase in per capita income. While Gross National Product (GNP) measures the total output of goods and services which an economy is capable of producing, per capita income measures how much of real goods and services which an average person of the community will have for consumption and investment, that is, average level of living of a citizen of a country.

Thus, world organizations such as World Bank and IMF have been employing both these measures of economic growth in their annual World Development Reports for comparing growth and levels of living of the developed and the developing countries. In India also our Planning Commission, Central Statistical Organization (CSO), and Reserve Bank of India have been measuring economic growth on the basis of both overall GNP or NNP and per capita income. The recent estimates of annual growth in GNP and per capita income is given in Table 31.1. This table reveals an interesting feature *that economic growth achieved in recent years is higher in the developing countries than in the developed countries*. However, it should be noted that in the past several decades the present-day developed countries recorded much higher growth rates than the developing countries which remained static for a long period. As a result, per capita income and levels of living of the people of the developed countries are now much higher as compared to those of the developing countries. The problem of the developing countries is to catch up with the developed countries through attaining rapid economic growth so as to enjoy higher levels of living.

Table 35.1: GNP Per Capita, Growth Rate and Population in Some Developed and Developing Countries

Country	Population (millions) 2009	GNP Per Capita in 2009 (US Dollars)	Growth Rate of GNP 1980-90	1990-2000	2000-09
Developed Countries					
U.S.A.	307	46,360	3.0	3.5	2.0
Australia	22	43,770	3.5	3.9	3.3
U.K.	62	41,378	3.2	3.7	2.0
Canada	34	41,980	3.4	3.1	2.0
Japan	128	38,080	4.1	1.3	1.1
Developing Countries					
India	1155	1,230	5.8	6.0	7.9
China	1331	3,650	10.2	10.6	10.9
Pakistan	170	1,000	6.3	3.8	5.2
Bangladesh	162	580	4.3	4.8	5.9
Sri Lanka	20	1,990	4.2	5.3	5.8

Source: World Bank, *World Development Report*, 2011

Meaning of Economic Development : Traditional View

As mentioned above, no distinction was drawn between economic growth and development in the beginning of the evolution of economics of development. However, since the seventies it has been thought necessary to distinguish between economic growth and economic development. There are two views even about the concept of economic development. The traditional view has been to interpret it in terms of planned changes in the structure of national product and the occupational pattern of labour force and also the institutional and technological changes that bring about such changes or accompany such changes. It may be noted that Kuznets in his study of *Modern Economic Growth* interpreted the process of modern economic growth which involves these structural changes[1]. In this view during the process of economic growth share of agriculture in both national product and employment of labour force declines and that of industries and services increases. Various strategies of development which were suggested until 'seventies' generally focussed on rapid industrialization so that structural transformation could be achieved. For this purpose appropriate institutional and

1. It may be noted that Kuznets in his study of "*Modern Economic Growth*" interpreted the process of modern economic growth which involves these structural changes.

technological changes were recommended to bring about such structural changes. Thus C.P. Kindleberger writes, *"Economic growth means more output and economic development implies both more output and changes in the technical and institutional arrangements by which it is produced."*[2]

Thus, according to traditional view, economic development implies growth plus structural change. Structural change refers to changes in technological and institutional factors which cause shift of labour from agriculture to modern manufacturing and services sectors and also generate self-sustaining growth of output. An aspect of structural change which is of special mention is that during the process of economic development there occurs a shift of working population from low productivity employment in agriculture to the modern industrial and services sectors having higher levels of productivity of labour. That is, during the process of economic development percentage share of working population in agriculture sharply falls whereas percentage shares of working population employed in modern industrial and services sectors substantially increase. Along with this change in sectoral distribution of labour force there occurs a change in sectoral composition of national income in which percentage contribution of agriculture to national income declines and percentage contributions to national income of industrial and services sectors increase. This occurs due to the change in pattern of consumption of the people as economy grows and people's income increases as well as due to the changes in levels of productivity in the different sectors of the economy.

It is worth mentioning that in this view causal references were made to the role of some social factors such as growth of literacy, education and good health in economic development but they were considered to be of secondary importance. On the whole, in this view of economic development which generally prevailed till seventies, development was considered to be an economic phenomenon in which benefits from growth in overall GNP or per capita GNP and the structural changes accompanying it would trickle down to the poor and unemployed. No separate or special attention was paid to eliminate mass poverty and unemployment and to reduce inequalities in income distribution.

The Concept of Economic Development : The Modern View

The experience of the developing countries during the sixties and seventies showed that whereas target rates of economic growth were in fact achieved, trickle-down effect in the form of creation of more employment opportunities, rise in wages and improvement in income distribution did not operate. The problems of poverty, unemployment and income inequality further worsened instead of getting reduced during the process of growth in the Fifties and Sixties in the developing countries. For instance, in India Dandekar and Rath[3] found that 40 per cent of rural population in India lived below the poverty line in 1968-69. Using somewhat different approach, B.S. Mimhas[4] estimated that 37 per cent of rural population in India lived below the poverty line in 1967-68. Similarly, the magnitude of poverty and unemployment and the extent of income inequalities also increased in many other developing countries.

Thus, due to the failure of traditional strategies of development in solving the problems of poverty, unemployment and inequality, it was realised in the seventies that the concept of development should be broadened so that it should signify that well-being of the people has increased. This led to the view that economic development should not be judged on the basis of growth in GNP alone. Therefore, when we regard the well-being of the masses as the ultimate objective of development, we have to see whether poverty and unemployment are decreasing and how the increases in gross national product or national income are being distributed among the population. Economic development will take place in true terms only if the poor people are raised above the poverty line. Late Prof. Sukhamoy Chakravarty rightly writes, *"The rate of growth strategy is by itself an inad-*

2. C.P. Kindleberger, *Economic Development.*
3. Dandekar and Rath, *Poverty in India*, 1971.
4. B.S. Minhas, "Poverty, Land Redistribution and Development Strategy," *Indian Economic Review*, 1971

equate device to deal with the problems of generating employment opportunities and for reducing economic disparities. Much depends on the composition of the growth process and how growth is financed and how benefits from growth process are distributed.[5]

It is worth mentioning that there is no guarantee that when there is increase in GNP, employment will also increase. It can happen that with the use of more capital-intensive technique while production may be increasing at a rapid rate, employment may be falling instead of rising. According to the modern perception of economic development, rapid increase in GNP secured through displacing labour by machines and thus causing rise in unemployment and underemployment cannot be called true economic development. Professor Dudley Seers makes the meaning of economic development according to the new perception in the following words:

"The questions to ask about a country's development are therefore: What has been happening to poverty? What has been happening to unemployment? What has been happening to inequality? If all three of these have declined from high levels, then beyond doubt this has been a period of development for the country concerned. If one or two of these central problems have been growing worse, especially if all three have, it would be strange to call the result development even if per capita income doubled."[6]

Recently, the concept of economic development has been further widened so that it now involves not only reduction in poverty, inequality and unemployment but also requires improvement in *quality of life which includes cleaner environment, better education, good health and nutrition.* Thus World Development Report 1991, published by World Bank, asserts: "*The challenge of development is to improve the quality of life. Especially in the world's poor countries, a better quality of life generally calls for higher incomes but it involves much more. It encompasses as ends in themselves better education, higher standards of health and nutrition, less proverty, a cleaner environment, more equality of opportunity* ."[7] Thus the concept of economic development has been greatly broadened. Today economic development is interpreted as not only in more growth in economic well-being but also in terms of good quality of life which, according to Prof. Amartya Sen, consists in 'enlargement of opportunities for people and freedom of human choices'. This new concept of development includes achievement of freedom from servitude to ignorance and illiteracy. It also includes enjoyment of human rights. Thus United Nations '*Human Development Report*' of 1994 in the writting of which Prof Amartya Sen made a significant contribution, asserts, "Human beings are born with certain potential capabilities. The purpose of development is *to create an environment in which all people can expand their capabilities, and opportunities can be enlarged* for both present and future generations..... .Wealth is important for human life. but to concentrate on it exclusively is wrong for two reasons. First, accumulating wealth is not necessary for the fulfilment of some important human choices .... Second, human choices extend far beyond economic well-being." In his recent book, Amartya Sen writes: "Economic growth cannot be sensibly treated as an end in itself. Development has to be more concerned with enhancing the *lives we lead and the freedoms we enjoy.*"[8]

On the basis of various ingredients of good quality of life and other criteria such as enlargement of human choices and freedom, a human development index is prepared by United Nations Development Programme (UNDP). This human development index is considered as a better indicator of economic development.

5. Sukhamoy Charkravarty, "Some Observations on Growth Process", *Seminar*, 1971.
6. Dudley Seers, "The Meaning of Development" presented at the Eleventh World Conference of the Society for International Development. (New Delhi), 1969.
7. United Nations, *Measures for Economic Develpment of Underdeveloped Countries*, 1951
8. See Amartya Sen, *Development as Freedom,* Oxford University Press, 2001, p.175

FACTORS DETERMINING ECONOMIC GROWTH

The process of economic growth is a highly complex phenomenon and is influenced by numerous and varied factors such as economic, political, social and cultural factors. It is believed by some economists that the capital is the only requirement for growth and therefore the greatest emphasis be laid on capital formation to bring about economic development. But this is wrong. As Professor Nurkse r.ghtly remarks, *"Economic development has much to do with human endowments. social attitudes, political conditions and historical accidents, Capital is a necessary but not a sufficient condition of progress"*. The following are various factors which determine economic growth and development:

(*i*) Capital formation which depends upon the rate of domestic saving and investment and inflow of foreign capital;
(*ii*) Foreign aid and foreign investment;
(*iii*) Education and health ;
(*iv*) Technological progress; and
(*v*) Growth of population.

We examine below each of these factors in turn.

(i) Capital Formation

Labour is combined with capital to produce goods and services. Workers need machines, tools and factories to work. In fact. thc use of capital makes workers more productive. Setting up of more factories equipped with machines and tools raises the productive capacity of the economy. Therefore, in the opinion of many economists, capital formation is the very core of economic development. Whatever the type of economic system, without capital accumulation the process of economic growth cannot be accelerated. Levels of productivity in the United States of America are very high mainly because American people work with more and better type of capital goods built up over the last several years. Low productivity and poverty of developing countries is largely due to the scarcity or shortage of real physical capital in these countries. Economic growth cannot be speeded up without accumulating various types of capital goods, that is, without building factories, machines, tools, dams, bridges, roads, railways, ports, ships, irrigation works, fertilizers, etc., much economic development is not possible.

But capital formation requires saving, that is, the sacrifice of some current consumption. An increase in supplies of capital goods can only result from investment, and investment in turn is only possible if a portion of current income is saved. Thus saving is essential to economic growth. According to Professor Arthur Lewis, *"The central problem in the theory of economic growth is to understand the process by which a community is converted from being a 5 per cent saver to a 12 per cent saver with all the changes in attitudes, in institutions and in techniques which accompany this conversion."*[9] Underdeveloped economies generally save very little. For instance, saving in India on the eve of independence was about 6 per cent of the national income. On the other hand, rich countries save from 15 to 30 per cent of their national income. In order to bring about economic growth, rate of savings must be stepped up to over 15 per cent of national income. But in developing countries, the rate of saving has been low because income of the people has been low and that they are living at the level of subsistence. Thus, the lower the per capita income, the more difficult it is to forgo current consumption. It is difficult for people living at or near subsistence level to curtail current consumption. This in large part explains the low rate of saving in the poor, underdeveloped countries.

It may be noted that gross saving rate in India rose to 34 per cent of national income in 2009-10. However, for achieving 9 per cent rate of growth in GNP which is now the target of planning in India it is estimated that 36 per cent rate of saving is needed if capital-output ratio remains constant at 4 which was actually obtained in the 9th Plan period.

9. Arthur Lewis, "Economic Development with Unlimited Supplies of Labour," *Manchester School,* 1954.

It must be emphasized, however, that savings in itself do not contribute to economic growth. It is only when savings are invested and used productively that they contribute to economic growth. If savings are hoarded in the form of gold or precious jewels, or if they are used for buying land, they do not result in an increase in supplies of capital goods and thus make no contribution to economic growth. Studies conducted to examine the relationship between investment and growth in terms of increase in GDP have found that there exists a *strong correlation between the two* though it is not perfect. Countries that allocate a larger fraction of their GDP to investment such as Japan and Singapore achieved high growth rates, and countries that allocate a small share of GDP to investment such as Bangladesh and Nepal have low growth rates.

(ii) Foreign Aid and Foreign Investment

As domestic savings are not sufficient to make possible the necessary or desired accumulation of capital goods, borrowing from abroad may play an important role. Professor AJ. Brown rightly says that *"Development demands that people somewhere should refrain from spending a part of their incomes, thus allowing a part of the world's productive resources to be used for accumulation of capital goods. The people who can best afford to do this are generally those who live in countries of high average income. On the other hand, the countries where development is likely to alleviate suffering and promote welfare to the greatest extent are those where average incomes are low. There is a strong general case for the rich countries lending to the poor ones."*[10] Nearly every developed state obtained the foreign assistance to supplement its own small saving during the early stages of its development. England borrowed from Holland in the seventeenth and eighteenth centuries, and in turn came to lend to almost every other country in the world in the nineteenth and twentieth centuries. The United States of America, now the richest country in the world, borrowed heavily in the nineteenth century, and has now emerged as the major lender country of the twentieth century which is assisting the poor countries in their attempts to bring about economic growth. .

It should be noted that foreign capital does not flow into the developing countries in the form of *aid* alone (that is, loans at concessional rates of interest) but also through *direct investment* by foreign companies. Foreign direct investment (FDI) is an important way for a country to accelerate its economic growth. Though the foreign companies send back profits earned, their investments in factories *increase the rate of capital accumulation* in the developing countries leading to a higher rate of economic growth and higher productivity of labour. Besides, foreign direct investment enables the developing countries *to learn the new advanced technologies* developed and used in the rich developed countries.

The importance of foreign capital is reinforced by *the need of a developing country for foreign exchange to buy imports.* A developing country has to import huge quantities of capital goods, technical know-how and essential raw-materials which are required for industrial growth and building up of infrastructure such as power projects, roads, irrigation facilities, ports and telecommunication. For all these, foreign exchange is needed which can be obtained if foreign rich countries lend it to developing economies or if foreign companies make direct investment in the developing countries. If foreign assistance is not forthcoming in adequate quantity, then the developing countries will experience serious difficulties of balance of payments. In the absence of sufficient borrowing from abroad, or direct foreign investment, rapid economic development of the developing countries will turn their balance of payments seriously adverse.

Furthermore, developing countries suffer not only from a shortage of savings but also from a *lack of technical know-how, managerial ability,* etc. Foreign capital when it comes in the form of private investment in developing countries by foreign companies, especially the multinational corporations (MNCs), bring with it these complementary factors which are very essential for development.

10. AJ. Brown, *Introduction to the World Economy.*

Due to bad experience of the colonial rule in the past, the developing countries were generally against the foreign capital, especially against private foreign investment. However the fears of foreign investment and aid are now no longer there. Further, now *multilateral foreign aid* is available through World Bank and International Monetary Fund (IMF) which provide loans at concessional rates to the developing countries for accelerating growth. As far as private, foreign investment is concerned, the developing countries (induding China and India) are competing with each other to attract private foreign investors. In India, the Government has set the target of achieving annual inflow of $10 billion of foreign direct investment. It has now been realised that foreign investment will not only supplement domestic saving and thereby raise the rate of investment, bring better technology and managerial know-how, but will also ease the problem of foreign exchange. Through raising the rate of investment and providing foreign exchange resources, it will not only increase output but will also generate employment opportunities: Besides, like the domestic investment, *foreign investment also produces a multiplier effect on output, income and employment* in the developing countries.

In the last fifteen years, China's very high rate of economic growth which is generally described as *"Chinese growth miracle"* is due to higher inflow of foreign direct investment (FDI) as compared to India. Foreign direct investment flows to China grew from $3.5 billion from 1990 to $53 billion in 2002. On the other hand, FDI flow to India was a low $0.4 billion in 1990 and rose to $5.5 billion in 2002. Further, FDI has contributed significantly to the rapid growth of China's manufacturing exports. In India by contrast FDI has been much less important in driving India's export growth, except in information technology. For higher foreign direct investment flows to China World Investment Report 2003 mentions among other things that China has more business-oriented and FDI-friendly attitudes, its FDI procedures are easier and decisions are taken rapidly. Besides, China has more flexible labour laws, a better labour climate and better entry and exit procedures for business. It is therefore not unexpected that China has emerged at the top in attracting FDI flows. Against this, in 2002 India was 15th in the World's FDI destination.

(iii) Education And Health

Till recently economists have been considering physical capital as the most important factor determining economic growth and have been recommending that rate of physical capital formation in developing countries must be increased to accelerate the process of economic growth and raise the living standards of the people. But the last three decades of economic research has revealed the importance of education as a crucial factor in economic development. Education refers to the development of human skills and knolwedge of the labour force. It is not only the quantitative expansion of educational opportunities but also the qualitative improvement of the education which is imparted to the labour force that holds the key to economic development. Because of its significant contribution to economic development, education has been called as *human capital* and expenditure on education of the people as *investment in man or human capital*. Speaking of the importance of education or human capital. Prof. Harbison writes: "Human resources constitute the ultimate basis of production, human beings are the active agents who accumulate capital, exploit natural resources, build social, economic and political organisations; and carry forward national development. Clearly, a country which is unable to develop the skills and knowledge of its people and to utilise them effectively in the national economy will be unable to develop anything else."[11]

Prof. Amartya Sen gives greater importance to education and health for inclusive growth in the economy. He laments that India has not given enough importance to make investment in education and health.

11. Frederick Harbison, *Human Resources as the Wealth of Nations.* Oxford University Press, 1973.

Table 35.2 : Sources of US Economic Growth, 1929-1982 (per cent)

Annual growth of output (per cent)	2.9
(*a*) Growth in labour input	32
(*b*) Growth in labour productivity :	
(1) Education per worker	14
(2) Capital formation	19
(3) Technological change	28
(4) Economies of scale	9
(5) Other factors	–2

Source: Edward E. Denison, *Trends in American Economic Growth* (1929-82), The Brookings Institution, 1983, p. 30.

Several empirical studies made in developed countries, especially the U.S.A., regarding the sources of growth or, in other words, contributions made by various factors such as physical capital, man-hours, (i.e., physical labour), education etc. have shown that education or the development of human capital is a significant source of economic growth. Professor Solow[12] who was one of the first economists to measure the contribution of human capital to economic growth estimated that for United States between 1909 and 1949, 57.5 per cent of growth in output per manhour could be attributed to the *residual factor* which represents the effect of technological change and of the improvements in the quality of labour mainly as a consequence of education.

Denison, another American economist, made further refinement in estimating the contribution to economic growth of various factors. Denison tried to separate and measure the contributions of various elements of 'residual factor'. Denison's estimates for various sources of US growth during 1929-82 are given in Table 31.2 As will be seen from Table 31.2 Gross Domestic Product in the USA grew at the rate of 2.9 per cent per annum over this period. The factors determining growth in this period have been divided into two groups. It will be seen from the table that the *growth in the quantity of labour* accounted for 32 per cent of growth in GDP of the USA over this period. The other group consisting of *various variables determining growth in labour productivity has-been* divided into five factors. It is noteworthy that education per worker contributed 14 per cent to growth in output during this period, technological change contributed 28 per cent to the growth in output. Thus, growth in education per worker and technological change together accounted for 42 per cent of growth in the output in the USA over this period whereas capital formation contributed 19 per cent to the growth rate. This shows the great importance of education and technological change as determinants of economic growth.[13]

Another approach to measure the contribution of education is based upon the analysis of the relationship between expenditure on education and income. Using this approach Schultz studied the relationship between expenditure on education and individual income and also the relationship between expenditure on education and physical capital formation for the United States during the period 1900 to 1956. He found that when measured in constant dollars, "the resources allocated to education rose about three and a half times (*a*) relative to consumer income in dollars, (*b*) relative to the gross formation of physical capital in dollars.[14] This implies that the "income elasticity" of the demand for education was about 3.5 over the period or, in other words, education considered as an investment could be regarded as 3.5 times more attractive than investment in physical capital. It may,

12. Robert M. Solow, "Technical Change and Aggregate Production Function", *Review of Economics and Statistics,* Aug. 1957.
13. Edward E. Denison, *Trends in American Growth* (1929.82), The Brookings Institution, 1983, p. 30.
14. Schultz, "Education and Economic Growth, in Nelson B. Henry (ed.), *The Sixtieth Year Book of the National Society for the Study of Education.* University of Chicago Press, 1961.

however, be noted that these estimates of Schultz only indirectly reflect the contribution of education to economic growth.

In our above analysis we have explained that education is regarded as investment and like investment in physical capital, it raises productivity of labour and thus contributes to growth of national income. Some economists have argued that education is of crucial importance not only because education raises the productivity and therefore earnings of individual workers, but it creates *positive externalities, that is, beneficial external effects*. A positive *externality* occurs when the activity of a person provides benefits to *others.* For example, an educated person might generate new ideas which may lead to the improvement in methods of producing goods. When these ideas become a part of society's pool of knowledge *(i.e.* stock of human capital), everyone can use them and derive benefits from them. These ideas are therefore external benefits of education. One problem facing the developing countries, especially India, is of *brain drain,* that is, migration of a large number of highly educated persons (such as those trained by IIT, 11M and medical colleges) to the developed countries such as the USA to make higher earnings there. If education has positive external effects, then this brain drain will deprive the Indian economy of the beneficial effects which these educated people would have created here.

(iv) Technological Progress and Economic Growth

Another important factor in economic growth is progress in technology, Use of advanced techniques in production or *progress in technology brings about a significant increase in per capita output.* Technological advance refers to the discovery of new and better ways of doing things or an improvement in the old ways. Sometimes technological advances result in an increase in available supplies of natural resources. *But more generally technological advance results in increasing the productivity or effectiveness* with which natural resources, capital and labour are used and worked to produce goods. As a result of technological advance it becomes possible to produce more output with same resources or the same amount of product with less resources.

But the question arises as to how does the technological progress take place. The technological progress takes place through *inventions* and *innovations.* The word invention is used for the new scientific discoveries, whereas the innovations are said to take place only when the new scientific discoveries are used for actual production processes or commercial purposes. Some inventions may not be economically profitable to be used for actual production.

It is quite well known that improvements in technology greatly increase the effectiveness with which natural resources are used. In United States, for instance, increased use of mechanized power-driven farm equipment on land has greatly raised the agricultural productivity of land per hectare. It may also be noted that some technological improvements have resulted in the increased effectiveness with which capital goods are used. But, as stated above, technological change more generally results in higher productivity of resources. Technological change raises the productivity of workers through the provision of better machines, better methods and superior skills. By bringing about increase in productivity of resources the progress in technology makes it possible to produce more output with the same resources or the same amount of output with less resources.

Technical progress manifests itself in the change in production function. So a simple measure of the technical progress would be the comparison of the position of production function at two points of time. The technological change may operate upon the production function through improvements of various sorts such as a superior equipment, an improved material, and superior organisational efficiency. Also, the technological progress may express itself in making available new products. It is now widely accepted that technological change raises productivity and that a *continuous technological change will enable the economy to escape from being driven to the stationary state or economic stagnation.* Classical economists like Ricardo and J.S. Mill expressed fear that the increase in the stock of capital will sooner or later, because of the operation of diminishing returns, land the economy into stationary state beyond which economic growth will come to an end. *Classical economists remained occupied with the idea of a stationary state because they did not take into account technological progress that could postpone the occurrence of a stationary state and ensure continued economic growth.* Indeed, if technological progress continuously takes place, the demon of stationary state can be put off indefinitely.

It may be noted that Adam Smith viewed technological progress as a rise in productivity of workers as a result of increase in division of labour and specialisation. The rise in productivity leads to the growth in national income. *But it was J.A. Schumpeter who laid great stress on the role of technological innovations in bringing about economic growth.* He laid stress on the introduction of technical innovations in bringing about economic progress. It is the entrepreneur who carries out the innovations and organises the production structure more efficiently. As, according to Schumpeter, innovations occur in spurts rather than in a smooth flow, economic progress is not a smooth and an uninterrupted process. The pace of economic progress is punctuated by the pace of innovations.

Prof. Rostow proposed five stages in the development of an economy. These stages are : traditional society; (*ii*) preconditions for take off; (*iii*) take-off into self-sustaining growth; (*iv*) drive to maturity; and (*v*) stage of high mass consumption. It may be noted that the economic transformation of the society from one stage to another involves, along with other things, a change in the level and character of technology. In the present age of greater specialisation it is the technology factor that underlies all major aspects of the modern productive apparatus such as decision making, production programming, skill requirements and market strategy.

Productivity of workers depends upon the quantity and quality of capital tools with which the labourers work. For higher productivity the instruments of. production have to be technologically more efficient and superior. The technological options open to an economy determine the input-mix of production. A commodity can be produced by various technologies. The quantity and quality of capital, skills and other factors required for production are directly dependent on the efficiency of the technique of production being used. Also, the managerial and organisational expertise has to be in tune with the technological requirements of production. Viewed thus, technology in the present stage of economic development is an indispensable factor of production.

This is the age of technology. The developing countries are obsessed by the desire to make rapid progress in technology so as to catch up with the present-day developed countries. Strenuous efforts are being made to use improved technology in agriculture, industries, health, sanitation, education and, in fact, in all walks of human life. Indeed, the newly emerging nations have come to regard technology as a bastion of national autonomy and as a status symbol in the international community.

The process of technological progress is inseparably linked with the process of capital formation. In fact, both go hand in hand. Technological progress is virtually impossible without capital formation. It is because the introduction of superior or more efficient techniques requires building up of new capital equipment which incorporates new technology. In other words, new and superior technology can contribute to national product and its growth if it is first embodied in the new capital equipment. The new capital investment has,. therefore, been called the vehicle for the steady introduction of new technology into the economy.

The new inventions and innovations lead to new and more efficient techniques of production and new and better products. As is well known, it is the inventions and innovations in cotton textile industry that led to the industrial revolution in England. In the olden times inventions were the work of some individuals and innovations were introduced into the production process by the private entrepreneurs. Keeping in view the importance of technological progress in the economic growth of a country, the governments of various countries are spending a lot of money on *"research and development" (R & D),* which is carried on in various laboratories and institutes to promote technological progress.

Developing countries are using the technology imported from the developed countries because they have not yet made sufficient progress in technology, nor have they developed to an adequate extent capital goods industries which produce capital goods, embodying advanced technology. But imitation and use of the technology of the advanced countries by these underdeveloped countries has produced one unfavourable result. It is that the technology of the advanced countries is not in accordance with the factor endowments of these developing countries, since they have abundance of capital while the developing countries have surplus labour. As a result of the use of the capital-intensive technology, enough employment opportunities have not been created by the large-scale industries using imported technology. As a result, unemployment in developing countries like India has been increasing despite the progress in industrialisation of the economy. In view of this not so happy experience in regard to the creation of employment opportunities by industrial growth, an eminent English economist, Prof. Schumacher, has recommended the use of *intermediate technology* or what is also known as *appropriate technology* by the developing countries like India. *By intermediate or appropriate technology we mean the technology which is labour-intensive and yet highly productive so that with its use enough employment opportunities are created along with more production.* But in order to find out this appropriate technology for several industries, a good deal of research and development *(*R & D*)* activity is required to be carried out.

(v) The Growth of Population

The growth of population is another factor which determines the rate of economic growth. The growing population increases the level of output by increasing the number of working population or labour force provided all are absorbed in productive employment. We saw above that according to estimates of Denison, increase in the quantity of labour contributed to the extent of 32 per cent to economic growth of output in the USA during 1929-1982. Moreover, the increase in population leads to the increase in demand for goods. Thus, growing population means growing market for goods which facilitates the process of growth. When market for goods is enlarged, they can be produced on a large scale and thus economies of large-scale production can be reaped. The economic history of U.S.A. and European countries shows that population growth contributed greatly to the increase in their national output.

But what has been true of U.S.A. and European countries may not be true in case of the present-day developing countries. Whether or not the growth of population contributes to economic growth depends on the existing size of population; the available supplies of natural and capital resources, and the prevailing technology. In the United States, where supplies of natural and capital resources are comparatively abundant, the growth in population raises national output by increasing the quantity of labour. In India where supplies of other economic resources, especially capital equipment, are relatively scarce, increase in population hinders economic growth instead of promoting it.

Labour is combined with capital to produce goods and services. Therefore, increase in the quantity of labour force will contribute to economic growth when the cooperating factor capital is also increasing. In the modem times workers need machines, tools and factories to work. Since a developing country such as India has a lot of surplus labour but a small stock of capital, the workers cannot be productive unless they are employed in some activities. We thus see that a rapidly growing labour force by itself is no guarantee of economic growth. Increase in national output, that is, economic growth is pqssible only when the supplies of capital and other resources are increasing adequately along with the growth of labour force. If, on the other hand, when the supplies of capital and the other resources are meagre, the increase in the labour force (or population) will merely add to unemployment and will not bring about increase in national output.

As stated above, economic growth requires increasing supplies of capital goods. Increasing supplies of capital goods become possible only with higher rate of investment. And a higher rate of investment, in turn, is possible if rate of saving is high. Now, *increase in population by adding to number of mouths to be fed tends to raise consumption and, therefore, lowers both saving and investment.* Thus rapid growth of population by causing lower rate of saving and investment tends to hold down the rate of economic growth in developing countries. Thus, under conditions like those in India population growth actually impedes economic development rather than facilitates it

It is worth noting here that *changes in total* GDP which are used to measure rate of economic growth are not a good measure of economic well-being. For the purpose of evaluating changes in economic well-being or living standards of the people of a country GDP *per capita* is more important for it tells us the amount of goods and services that is available for an individual in the economy. But how does growth in population or labour force affect GDP per capita? The reason is that rapidly increasing labour force forces the economy *to spread more thinly* the other cooperating factors, especially capital and land. As a result, capital or land per worker declines causing decline in productivity or GDP per worker.

Further, rapid population growth nullifies out efforts to raise the living standards of our people. In other words, *a high rate of increase in population swallows up a large part of the increase in national income so that per capita income or living standard of the people does not rise much.* This is precisely what has happened during the planning era in India. Thus while the aggregate national income of India went up by 17.5 per cent in the First Plan period and 20 per cent in the Second Plan period, per capita income rose by only 8 per cent and 9 per cent respectively. Over the period of the Third Plan, as against an increase of 11.5 per cent in national income, per capita income improved by only 0.5 per cent. The relatively slow rate of rise in per capita income has been due to rapid population growth. The annual rate of population growth which was no more than 1.86 per cent in the First Plan period went up to 2.15 per cent in the Second Plan period.and further to 2.25 per cent in the Third and Fourth Plans.

Population Growth and Demographic Dividend. An aspect of population growth which is favourable for India has been called *demographic dividend. Demographic dividend refers to the increase in the ratio of working population* in the age-structure of the population of a country. Demographic dividend is beneficial in two ways. First, relatively more increase in working population can contribute to increase in *growth potential*. Thus, increase in workforce will ensure higher growth of output, if the additional workforce is employed in productive activities. Second, increase in the working population in the total population will reduce the *dependency burden* on the population which will not only raise levels of living of the families but also cause higher savings by them.

Now the recent census reports of India have projected that the proportion of working age population between 15 and 59 years is likely to increase from 58 per cent in 2001 to more than 64 per cent by 2021. In absolute numbers there will be approximately 63.5 million new entrants in the working age group between 2011 and 2016. Further, it is important to note that *bulk of this increase in working population is likely to take place in the relatively younger age group of 20-35 years*. Such a trend would make India one of the *youngest nations of the world*. In 2020 average Indian will be only 29 years old. The comparative figures for China and US are 37 years and for West Europe 45 and for Japan 48 years. *The higher proportion of young labour force in India has a great production potenial and has therefore been called demographic dividend.* However, its benefits will be realised only if our population is healthy, educated, appropriately skilled and gainfully employed. Therefore, greater focus on human and inclusive growth is necessary in India's plan strategy to best utilise its demographic dividend.

CAPITAL-OUTPUT RATIO

Capital-output ratio is an important concept of growth economics. Given other things, overall economic growth depends on rate of capital formation (or investment) and capital-output ratio. Capital-output ratio is determined by productivity of capital.

Capital-output ratio is the amount of capital required to produce output worth Re. 1. If Y stands for output or income and K for the stock of capital used to produce that output, then $\frac{K}{Y}$ represents capital-output ratio. It is useful to distinguish between marginal capital-output ratio and average capital-output ratio. Whereas average capital-output ratio describes the ratio of total capital to total output or income of the economy, marginal capital-output ratio is ratio of *increment* in the stock of capital to the *increment* in output. Therefore, marginal capital-output ratio can be written as $\frac{\Delta K}{\Delta Y}$ where ΔK is the increment in capital and ΔY is the resultant increase in income or output. Therefore, marginal capital-output ratio is also called *incremental capital-output ratio* (ICOR).

The rate of economic growth of a country depends upon the rate of capital formation and capital-output ratio. Capital-output ratio determines the rate at which output grows as a result of a given volume of capital investment. For example, a capital-output ratio of 4 would mean, in Indian rupees, that a capital investment of ₹ 4 results in the addition of output worth Re. 1. Hence, in order to produce a given level of output, smaller capital investment would be needed if the capital-output ratio is lower than when it is higher.

Factors Determining Capital-Output Ratio

It is difficult to estimate the capital-output ratio of an economy. The productivity of capital depends upon many factors such as the degree of technological development associated with capital investment, the efficiency of handling new types of equipment, the quality of managerial and organisational skill, the existence and the extent of the utilisation of economic overheads and the pattern and rate of investment. For instance, the higher the proportion of investment devoted to the production of light consumer goods, the lower the capital-output ratio; and higher the proportion of investment devoted to public utilities, *i.e.,* economic and social overheads, the higher will be the capital-output ratio, and *vice versa*. Likewise, the greater the investment devoted to basic heavy industries, the higher will be the capital-output ratio, and *vice versa*. The superior organising ability and the use of better technology will lower the capital-output ratio. The capital-output ratio also varies with the prices of inputs.

It is agreed that capital-output ratio in developing countries is generally higher, *i.e.,* the capital is less productive in them than in developed countries. This is so because there is a relative inefficiency of the industries which produce capital goods. There is the greater wastage of capital in the process of production due to low level of technical knowledge. Besides, owing to indivisibilities, certain kinds of investment are bound to be initially underutilised. As development proceeds in the developing countries the pattern of demand shifts towards the more capital-intensive industries.

In order to gain the most from capital formation, a country must also undergo technological and organizational progress, so that the capital-output ratio be reduced. Thus, the growth rate of output depends not only on the amount of capital accumulated but also on how much capital is required per unit increase in output (*i.e.,* incremental capital-output ratio). The lower the incremental capital-output ratio, the more accelerated is economic growth. A low capital-output ratio is, thus, as significant as large capital accumulation. But it must also be pointed out that a low increment capital-output ratio requires technological and organisational progress so that capital becomes more productive.

Limitations of Capital-Output Ratio

It may, however, be pointed out that the concept of capital-output ratio suffers from certain limitations. Its precise calculation presents some formidable difficulties. Hence, the quantitative relationship between capital investment and output, which the capital-output ratio suggests, may prove to be misleading. It would, therefore, be hazardous to base the estimates of capital requirements of an industry or economy on such ratios. Neither can the capital stock be assumed with any exactitude; nor is the other side of the ratio, *i.e.,* output capable of any precise measurement. Besides the index number problems, a clear distinction cannot be often made between capital goods and non-capital goods. Returns to social overheads, in particular, cannot be calculated accurately. Further, capital-output ratio is influenced by several variables, *e.g.,* technological improvements, better utilisation of equipment, organisational improvements, labour efficiency, and these factors elude quantitative measurement.

Hence, the concept of capital-output ratio has only a limited practical significance, because it cannot indicate the actual contribution of capital alone in a given scheme of investment. Great caution is, therefore, necessary in making use of a particular capital-output ratio in the adoption of actual investment policy.

CHAPTER 36

Harrod-domar Model of Growth

Introduction

Keynes in his General Theory was concerned with the determination of income and employment in the short run. He explained that since in the short-run situation of developed capitalist economies aggregate demand was deficient in relation to the aggregate supply of output, the equilibrium will be established at less than full employment level. Since the propensity to consume (and therefore saving propensity) is given and remains constant in the short run, if the amount of investment as determined by expected rate of profit and the market rate of interest is not equal to the amount of saving at the full-employment level of income, the economy will be in equilibrium at less than full capacity level (*i.e.* less than employment level) of output. He did not go into the question of the long-run growth of the economy. In fact, he overlooked the effect of investment in a given period on the increase in productive capacity. However, *investment has a dual effect.* Firstly, investment increases aggregate demand and income of the people through the multiplier process, and secondly, it raises the productive capacity of the economy through the addition it makes to the stock of capital. Indeed, investment by very definition means the addition to the stock of capital. While Keynes took into account the demand effect of investment, he ignored the capacity effect of investment.

Harrod[1] and Domar[2] extended the Keynesian analysis of income and employment to long-run problem of economic growth and therefore considered both the income and capacity effects of investment. Harrod and Domar models of economic growth explained at what rate investment should increase so that steady growth is possible in an advanced capitalist economy. In the growth models of Harrod and Domar, the rate of capital accumulation plays a crucial role in the determination of economic growth. The problem of present-day mature economies the late forties and early fifties lay in averting both secular stagnation and secular inflation. It were the pioneer works of Harrod and Domar that set the ball rolling in regard to this issue of conditions required for *i.e.*, the maintenance of steady economic growth in advanced industrialised countries. The *Harrod and Domar models seek to determine that unique rate at which investment and income must grow so that full employment level is maintained over a long period of time, i.e., equilibrium growth is achieved.*

Harrod and Domar developed their models of steady growth quite independently, though Harrod published his theory earlier than Domar. Although their models of steady growth differ in details, yet the underlying basic idea is essentially the same. Both of them assigned to capital accumulation a crucial role in the development process. But they emphasised the double role of the investment process, namely, generating income (increasing demand) and adding to the productive capacity of the economy. The classical economists confined their attention to the capacity-side only, whereas the earlier Keynesian economists studied the problem of demand only whereas Harrod and Domar consider both sides.

They start with full employment equilibrium level of income. According to them, to maintain full employment equilibrium, aggregate demand (total spending) generated by investment must be sufficient to be the additional output caused by this investment. To ensure steady growth with full

1. R.F. Harrod, *Towards a Dynamic Economics*, Macmillan & Co. London, 1930.
2. E. Domar, "Capital Expansion, Rate of Growth and Employment", *Economica,* Vol;. 14, 1946

employment the absolute amount of net investment must keep increasing and there must also be continuous growth of real national income. Because if demand and income did not increase while annual investment went on occurring, the additions made to the capital stock would remain unutilised and also employment could not be provided to the growing labour force which would result in unemployment of these two major resources. Obviously, such a situation is not conducive to steady economic growth.

DOMAR'S GROWTH MODEL

Fundamental Growth Equation

Let us first consider the supply side, that is, the capacity effect of investment. Increase in national output or national income of an economy during a period depends upon the increase in the stock of capital (which is represented by ΔK) during a period and the output-capital ratio or the productivity of capital. Assuming that both national income and the capital stock are measured in money, output-capital ratio can be written as $\Delta Y / \Delta K$, where ΔY stands for the increase in the national income and ΔK for the increase in the stock of capital. Thus if Rs. 4 worth of capital goods is required to produce one rupee worth of real output, marginal output-capital ratio $\left(\frac{\Delta Y}{\Delta K}\right)$ is equal to 1/4 or 0.25. Thus, the absolute increase in national income during a period (ΔY) can be obtained from increment in stock of capital ΔK multiplied by the output produced by a unit of capital $\left(i.e.\ \frac{\Delta Y}{\Delta K}\right)$. In symbolic terms we may express this as follows :

$$\Delta Y = \Delta K \cdot \frac{\Delta Y}{\Delta K} \quad ...(i)$$

Now, change in capital stock (ΔK) is nothing else but investment. Therefore, following Domar in place of ΔK we can write I. The marginal output-capital ratio $\Delta Y/\Delta K$ which is assumed to be constant as well as assumed to be equal to average output-capital ratio $\left(\frac{Y}{K}\right)$ by Domar and Harrod, can be denoted by σ. Thus, as Domar puts it, growth in capacity-output can be written as under:

$$\Delta Y = I\sigma \quad ...(ii)$$

It may be noted that *output-capital ratio* (σ) *is reciprocal of capital-output ratio i.e.* $\left(\frac{\Delta K}{\Delta Y} \text{ or } \frac{K}{Y}\right)$. Let us give an example. If ₹ 500 crores are invested in a year and capital-output ratio is 4 (*i.e.*, output-capital ratio will be 1/4), then growth in output in a year will be

$$\Delta Y = 500 \times \frac{1}{4}$$

$$= 125 \text{ crore}$$

Domar's Growth Equation in Terms of Rates of Growth

It is greatly helpful to express the above growth equation in terms of *rates of growth of income and capital*. That is, growth in income and capital should be expressed as ratios of total income. For doing so we divide both sides of equation (*i*) above by Y and obtain :

$$\frac{\Delta Y}{Y} = \frac{\Delta K}{Y} \cdot \frac{\Delta Y}{\Delta K} \quad ...(iii)$$

$\frac{\Delta Y}{Y}$ represents the rate of growth of income and is therefore written as simply G_y. Besides, ΔK stands for increment in capital during a given time period and is nothing else but investment. Therefore, for ΔK in the equation (*ii*) we can write I which represents investment. With these changes, we get the following equation :

$$G_y = \frac{I}{Y} \cdot \frac{\Delta Y}{\Delta K}$$

With the further assumption that output-capital ratio remains constant, then the marginal output-capital ratio $\left(\frac{\Delta Y}{\Delta K}\right)$ will be equal to average output-capital ratio $\left(\frac{Y}{K}\right)$. With this assumption and also expressing output-capital ratio by σ we can write the above equation as follows :

$$G_y = \frac{I}{Y} . \sigma \qquad \text{. . .}(iv)$$

where G_y = Growth rate of output or income

$\frac{I}{Y}$ = Rate of investment as ratio of national income

σ = Output-capital ratio

From the growth equation (*iv*) above, it is clear that, given the output-capital ratio, rate of growth of output depends upon the rate of investment; the greater the rate of investment, the greater the rate of growth of output or income. If the economy is inially is full-employment equilibrium as investment is equal to saving at full capacity output, then *to maintain full-employment equilibrium as the economy grows at a steady rate, savings (S) must remain equal to investment* (*I*). Therefore, in equation (*iv*) we can write $\frac{S}{Y}$ for $\frac{I}{Y}$. and rewriting equation (*iv*) we have

$$G_Y = \frac{S}{Y} . \sigma$$

Since $\frac{S}{Y}$ represents ratio of savings to national income (which is also simply called saving ratio), we can write it as *s*. With rewriting the above equation we have,

$$G_Y = s.\sigma \qquad \text{. . . }(v)$$

The above equation (*v*) represents the productive capacity effect of investment and saving and therefore represents the supply side of the growth problem.

The Condition for Equilibrium Growth

To achieve and maintain equilibrium or balanced growth, aggregate demand (*i.e.* productive aggregate expenditure) must increase at the rate which is large enough to use the increase in productive capacity which capital accumulation or investment generates. In his analysis Domar found that to remain on equlibrium growth path investment must increase at a rate large enough to absorb all savings which rising incomes make available.

Now, according to Domar, growth in capacity output will be realised only if aggregate demand or income of the people increases by a sufficient amount. The increase in aggregate demand or income is explained by the Keynesian theory of multiplier. Domar has based his analysis of demand or income effect of investment on the Keynesian theory of multiplier and income determination. According to this, *increase in income (or aggregate demand) is given by the increase in investment (ΔI) and the size of multiplier*, *i.e.* 1/*s* where *s* is the marginal propensity to save (assumed by Domar to be equal to the average propensity to save). Thus, according to income effect of investment,

$$\Delta Y = \frac{1}{s} . \Delta I \qquad \text{. . . }(vi)$$

Thus aggregate demand or income increases at the rate $\frac{1}{s} . \Delta I$ where *s* is propensity to save and

ΔI is the absolute increase in investment. On the other hand, as shown by equation(*ii*) above, the increase in capacity output occurs at the rate of $I\sigma$ where I is the absolute rate of investment and σ is the output-capital ratio. Thus, *steady equilibrium growth rate will be achieved only if rate of growth of aggregate expenditure (demand or income) equals the rate of growth in capacity output.*

Thus, it follows that to *maintain full-employment equilibrium growth of output* the following condition must hold :

$$\frac{1}{s}.\Delta I = I\sigma$$

$$\frac{\Delta I}{I} = s\sigma$$

where $\frac{\Delta I}{I}$ represents the rate of growth of investment.

As seen above in equation (*v*), rate of growth of income $\left(\frac{\Delta Y}{Y} \text{ or } G_Y\right)$ is also equal to $s\sigma$, it follows that for equilibrium growth $G_y = \frac{\Delta Y}{Y} = \frac{\Delta I}{I} = s\sigma$

Thus, the essential condition for maintaining a continuous equilibrium state of full employment is that investment and real income must both grow at a constant annual rate. This rate should be equal to the propensity to save (*s*) multiplied by output-capital ratio, (σ) *i.e.*, $s\sigma$.

It is evident from the basic equation $\frac{\Delta I}{I} = s\sigma$ that greater the saving rate(*s*), the greater will be the growth of investment needed to maintain the steady growth with full employment. Similarly, greater the value of σ (*i.e.* the output-capital ratio), the greater should be the increase in income to avoid emergence of excess capacity. But greater income is possibly only through greater investment. Hence, if income is to grow at a steady rate, investment must also grow at the annual steady rate given by $s\sigma$.

If $\frac{\Delta I}{I} < s\sigma$, *i.e.*, that is, if sufficient growth in investment does not take place, steady growth with full employment cannot be achieved. On the other hand, if today's investment is sufficient to achieve equilibrium growth with full employment, investment will have to be much more in the next period for generating sufficient increase in demand so as to utilise fully the expanded production capacity and to avoid the underutilisation of capital stock which will result in a fall in investment, and so cause depression. In other words, "*the economy must, so to speak, run faster and faster to stay in the same place, otherwise, it will slip downwards.*"[3]

HARROD'S GROWTH MODEL

Though Harrod's model of growth is similar to that of Domar, but it differs from the latter in details. Therefore we will explain below the essential features of Harrod's growth theory separately. In his essay "*Towards a Dynamic Economics*", Harrod put forward a theory which can be considered as truly dynamic. Explanation of secular trends is his main theme. He seeks to explain the secular causes of unemployment and inflation and the factors which determine the equilibrium and the actual rate of capital accumulation.

The classical economists considered economic development as a race between technological progress and capital accumulation on the one hand, and growing population and diminishing returns from land on the other. Harrod drops diminishing returns, regards technological progress and population growth as independent factors. In Harrod's analysis of economic growth there are three basic

3. Meir and Baldwin, *Economic Development*, 1966, p. 107.

elements: (a) population growth, (b) output per head as determined by level of technique or inventions and (c) capital accumulation. Inventions may be neutral, *i.e.*, leave the capital coefficient unchanged, or capital-saving, *i.e.*, reducing the capital coefficient, or 'labour-saving' which will increase the capital-output ratio. It may be noted that capital-output ratio is the reciprocal of output-capital ratio (σ), the concept used by Domar. It is important to mention that Harrod uses the concept of incremental capital-output ratio, which is the reciprocal of marginal output-capital ratio (σ) of Domar's model.

While arriving at the behaviour of income as a response to entrepreneurial decisions regarding investment, Harrod makes two assumptions: (*i*) Saving in any period of time is a constant proportion *s* of the income received during that period, and (*ii*) the investment is proportional to the rate of increase of income. The second assumption *is in fact the acceleration principle which states that the increase in output or income that occurs induces an increase in the stock of capital.*

Harrod begins his analysis of growth by marrying together acceleration principle and the theory of investment multiplier. As in Domar's model, Harrod explains that growth rate $\left(G_y \text{ or } \frac{\Delta Y}{Y}\right)$ depends on the rate of capital formation (or investment) and capital-output ratio which he defines as "the value of the capital goods required for the production of a unit increment of output". He put forward three growth equations. He takes saving as a fixed proportion of national output or income. Presenting a more elaborative analysis of growth than Domar, Harrod advanced three growth equations.

Harrod writes his first growth equation as follows:

$$G_y = \frac{s}{v} \qquad \ldots (i)$$

where G_y is the rate of growth in a period $\left(\frac{\Delta Y}{Y}\right)$, *s* is the rate of saving (*i.e.* proportion of saving to national income $\left(\frac{S}{Y}\right)$, and v is the capital-output ratio. It is important to note that capital-output ratio *v* in Harrod's growth equation (*i*) above is the one that is *actually obtained* from the extra capital accumulation (ΔK) and increase in production of goods and services in a year (ΔY). Harrod derives this growth equation as follows.

Following the Keynesian framework, Harrod takes that actual saving must be equal to actual investment. Further, since Harrod takes saving (*S*) as a constant proportion of national income (*Y*) in a period we have

$$S = sY_t$$

where *s* is propensity to save.

Investment (*I* or ΔK) in a period *t* depends on the rate of increase in production or income), that is, ΔY (*or* $Y_t - Y_{t-1}$) and the actual *capital-output ratio* (v). Thus we have

$$\Delta K \text{ or } I = v(Y_t - Y_{t-1})$$

Since in a period *actual* saving must be equal to *actual* investment, we have

$$v\,(Y_t - Y_{t-1}) = sY_t$$

Dividing both sides by *Y* we have

$$\frac{v(Y_t - Y_{t-1})}{Y_t} = s$$

or

$$\frac{(Y_t - Y_{t-1})}{Y_t} = \frac{s}{v}$$

Since $\frac{(Y_t - Y_{t-1})}{Y_t}$ represents actual growth of output or income we can denote it by G_y. Thus

$$G_y = \frac{s}{v}$$

G_y is the growth of output or income which *actually* occurs in a period. The above growth equation is in fact a truism as it is always true by definition depending as it is on the accounting identity that actual investment equals actual savings of a period.

Warranted Rate of Growth

Harrod proposes a second growth equation which he calls a fundamental growth equation to describe the *equilibrium geowth at a steady rate.* The warranted rate of growth is taken to be that rate of growth *which if it occurs will keep the entrepreneurs satisfied that they have produced neither more nor less than the right amount*. Being satisfied with the achievement of this growth rate, the entrepreneurs will maintain or perpetuate the same rate of growth. Warranted rate of growth is thus equilibrium rate of growth in the sense that producers, if they achieve it, will be induced to maintain it. The condition for warranted rate of growth is stated as under :

$$G_w = \frac{s}{v_r} \qquad \ldots (ii)$$

Harrod denotes capital-output ratio by the letter *C*, but following the modern practice we are using v for it.

G_w= "*Warranted rate of growth*", which is that rate of income growth of output or income. $(\Delta Y/Y)$, which will keep entrepreneurs satisfied with the amount of investment they have actually made, *i.e.*, it is in fact the full capacity rate of growth.

v_r= required incremental capital-output ratio to sustain the warranted rate of growth and is determined by the state of technology and the nature of goods constituting the increment in output.

s = average propensity to save, that is, $\frac{S}{Y}$.

The sort of entrepreneurial behaviour envisaged by Harrod means that *to maintain full employment, the desired (ex-ante) saving out of the full-employment income must be offset by an equal amount of desired investment*. But to induce this much investment, income must be growing.

In both the above equations *(i) and (ii) above* s is the same because Harrod assumes that the saving intentions are always realised so that ex-ante savings are always equal to ex-post savings.

Thus, Harrod is able to show that for dynamic equilibrium $G_w = \frac{s}{v_r}$.

It is important to note that v_r in growth equation (*ii*) is different from v of the growth equation (*i*), As noted above, v in Harrod's growth equation (*i*) shows the increment in the amount of new capital installed during a period divided by the *increase in output actually obtained* from it during that period. It shows what has been *actually* produced with the addition to the capital stock in a period and *not whether producers are satisfied with the increase in output actually realised.* For example, if there are boom conditions in the economy and as a result the increase in capital installed during the period is fully utilised, actual capital-output ratio (v) will be lower. On the other hand, if there is a demand recession in the economy, good amount of extra capital installed will not be utilised for production and consequently incremental capital-output ratio (v) will be higher.

But what determines the size of the required incremental capital-output ratio (v_r) which keeps entrepreneurs to perpetuate thangrund. The size of the v_r is determined by technological conditions and the nature of goods comprising the increment of output. *This warranted rate of growth will be achieved if sufficient increase in income takes place during the growth process.*

The proportion of investment to income being fixed, an increase in income would mean that in the next period both income and investment must be higher. In such a situation the producers would like to perpetuate the rate of growth which they have already realised. Under such circumstances the producers invest in the hope that they will be able to sell what they have planned to produce. In other words, the producers will desire to invest an amount required by $G_w v_r$, which will be equal in magnitude to *s*, *i.e.*, the given proportional investment rate.

Condition for Equilibrium Growth Rate

Now, what is the condition for equilibrium growth rate? *In Harrod's model, if incremental capital-output (v) actually realised happens to be equal to required capital-output ratio (v_r), warranted by technological and other conditions, then the actual rate of growth, G_Y is equal to the warranted rate of growth (G_w), the rate which the circumstances of the economy warrants, the economy will be growing at the equilibrium rate* ($G_y = G_w$). It may be noted that actual rate of growth will be equal to warranted rate of growth when investment is increasing at the rate high enough to generate adequate demand to ensure capacity growth rate (G_w).

Harrod lays down a condition for steady growth by saying that the actual rate of growth must be equal to the warranted rate of growth, *i.e.*, the rate of increase in output or income should be just so much as to keep the entrepreneurs satisfied with the actual investment they have made.

Thus, so long $v_r = v$, the producers would like to perpetuate a growth rate that is equal to the actual or realised rate. In other words, G_y (the actual growth rate) will be the same as that which the producers want to perpetuate, i.e., G_w. But we have seen above that G_w stands for the rate of growth which when realised leaves the entrepreneurs in a state of mind that they shall be prepared to undertake a similar advance in the future. Furthermore, if the income increases at this rate it will continue to increase at this rate. This is how a steady growth rate is assured. Income will have to grow faster and faster, if the entrepreneurs are to be convinced that the higher investment was desirable. In this way, both income and investment will go on increasing from one period to the next. There is thus a cumulative equilibrium growth of income and investment.

Natural Rate of Growth.

Expansion, however, cannot go on indefinitely. The availability of labour and natural resources would put the limit. In other words, it is not necessary that the warranted rate of growth G_w (which is also equal to the actual rate of growth G_y) is the maximum attainable rate of growth. With this view in mind, Harrod introduces yet another rate of growth called the '*natural rate of growth*', G_n which is the maximum rate of growth allowed by the increases of macro variables like population growth, technological improvements, and growth in natural resources. In fact, *G_n is the highest attainable growth rate which would bring about the fullest possible employment of the resources existing in the economy*. This may be considered as the ceiling rate of growth. Joan Robiuson calls it the maximum feasible rate of growth. If *l* stands for growth rate of population (or labour force) and *t* for technological progress (*i.e.* rate of increase of productivity), then natural rate of growth can be written as

$$G_n = l + t$$

Hence for the equilibrium growth rate at full employment of all existing resources, the following condition must be satisfied:

$$G_n = G_w = G_y$$

Any deviation from this path would bring about instability in the economy.

The Golden Age

The equality of three growth rates ($G_y = G_w = G_n$) ensures that economy is in moving or dynamic equilibrium. This is also called *balanced growth equilirbrium. Joan Robinson describes the equality of these three growth rates as a golden age as it represents a very satisfactory and happy situation.* This is a happy situation because the equality of these three growth rates

($G_y = G_w = G_n$) will ensure steady equilibrium growth rate along with full employment of labour and without creating excess productive capacity. However, Joan Robinson has emphasised that the golden age, namely, the equality of three growth rates, *"represents a mythical state of affairs not likely to obtain in any actual economy"*[4]. This is because the four key variables, namely, propensity to save (s), required capital-output ratio (v_r) of the warranted rate of growth, the rate of growth of population (l) and rate of technological change (t) are determined quite independently of each other. While the warranted rate of growth (G_w) is determined by the value of s and v_r, the natural rate of growth is determined by rate of population growth (l) and the rate of technological progress (t). The golden age or balanced growth equilibrium of $G_y = G_w = G_n$ will occur only when the four variables, s, v, l and t have appropriate values. But this seems to be very unlikely to occur. It is only by chance that these four variables will have right or appropriate values to guarantee the golden age equilibrium.

Relevance of Harrod-Domar Growth Model for Developing Countries

Despite the fact that Harrod-Domar model was not conceived with developing countries in mind it has nevertheless considerable influence in their development planning. An important aspect of the model is that it relates *rate of economic growth to investment which is often considered as a major limiting factor of economic growth*. Besides, it considers the level of savings which restricts investment in developing countries. The model has been used to answer the question as what rate of saving and therefore investment is required to achieve a certain target growth rate, given the assumed capital-output ratio. It has often been found that domestic resources or savings are inadequate to achieve target growth rate set for development plans of developing countries. Thus, there has been a saving gap in developing countries to achieve target growth rate. Therefore, the case of *foreign aid* or *foreign investment* has been made to supplement the domestic savings to achieve the planned growth rate.

However, there are some limitations of applying Harrod-Domar models to the conditions of developing countries. First, to assume away the role of government is to disown the realities completely. In fact, due to the vast structural changes to be effected government in these economies must step in a big way to initiate and accelerate economic development as an efficient manager of the whole economy, lest we may slip down the slope. Besides, the assumption of an initial full-employment level of income is not valid for the developing countries; disguised unemployment pervades these underdeveloped economies, especially the labour-surplus economies. It is a case of structural disequilibrium arising basically from the imbalance between labour and capital. Even if we make allowance for the entire savings to be invested, the growth of capital stock fails to match with the growth of labour force. Being based on fixed capital-output and capital-labour ratio, the Harrod and Domar models have only limited applicability for the developing world. Their peculiar problems demand a different solution from the one suggested by these models. *To absorb the surplus labour force, there is a need to bring down both the capital-output and capital-labour ratios through reducing capital intensity*. The Harrod-Domar models by assuming a constant capital coefficients rule out such a possibility.

Secondly, the usefulness of models based on the concept of capital-output ratio is of little operational significance in developing economies. Depending on the nature and degree of various shortages, bottlenecks and market imperfections, the productivity of invested capital is amenable to considerable fluctuations. It is indeed very difficult to have an accurate and valid estimate of a concept like capital-output ratio under such fluid conditions. Commenting in this regard, Prof. Hirschman[5] remarks that the predictive and operational significance of a model based on the concept of *capital-output* ratio is far less for a developing economy than for advanced economies.

4. Joan Robinson, *The Accumulation of Capital*, London, 1956.
5. Hirschman, *Strategy of Economic Development*, 1957.

Models such as these, therefore, cannot explain the mechanism through which economic growth can get under way and could be carried forward in the present-day developing economies.

Thirdly, the Harrod-Domar growth variables are aggregative in nature and, therefore, fail to show the sectorial interrelationship. The processes of development of the developing economies are, as is being increasingly acknowledged, fundamentally linked with structural and institutional changes. Their highly aggregative nature, comments Prof S. Chakravarty[6], '*prevents them from being used as a tool in detailed quantitative policy making and conceals many structural aspects of the problem of a steady rate of growth.*

Further, Harrod excludes autonomous investment as an explicit variable in his formulation of '*warranted*' saving-investment equality. But the exclusion of autonomous investment as an important factor in determining growth in developing countries by Harrod in his growth model renders Harrod's concept of 'warranted' growth rate analytically inadequate for the purpose of developing countries. He also ignored the role of public investment to which Keynes assigned a crucial role. But, autonomous investments, whether public or private, are of pivotal importance to the developing countries. Besides, Harrod-Domar growth models assume that propensity to save and the capital-output ratio are constant. But actually they are likely to change over the long-run. Further, if the proportion of factors can be changed as labour may be substituted for capital, then adjustment within the economy can be easily made and steady growth made possible without any rigid conditions.

In spite of the fact that these models are of limited applicability to the developing countries and fail to highlight the crucial issues involved in the development process of these economies, they nevertheless *are useful in fixing the overall targets of income, investment and savings* and in checking the consistency of such targets. Prof. Kurihara states that "Harrod and Domar have made the essential nature of the growth mechanism operationally significant, for they stress saving ratio and the capital-output ratio (or its reciprocal) as measurable strategic variables to investigate and possibly to manipulate for a desired rate of growth. Because of the universal character of these strategic variables, the growth mechanism discussed by Harrod and Domar is applicable to all economic systems, albeit with the modification".[7]

The use of Harrod-Domar model has actually been made in some countries. For instance, in the First Five Year Plan of India, the rate of saving was planned to be raised through keeping the marginal rate of saving above the average rate of saving. And the current rate of capital formation and therefore growth of the economy was sought to be maximised through raising the marginal rate of saving. Thus, these models served to guide the planners in determining the growth rate of the Indian economy. Commenting on these models, Prof. S. Chakravarty remarks that "*The great service that these models perform is to indicate very roughly the dimensions of the problem involved in raising the per capita income level in an underdeveloped country*".[8] Even India's Twelfth Five Year Plan points out that acceleration of economic growth requires increase in rate of investment and raising productivity of capital (*i.e.*, output-capital ratio).

As noted above, Harrod-Domar model brings out the crucial role for the continuous growth of investment to ensure sustained growth at a steady rate. If investment is not growing sufficiently, the problem of deficient demand will emerge which will bring about recesionary condition even in a developing country. The demand recession will result in rise in capital-output ratio due to the underutilisation of productive capacity. The Indian growth experience clearly brings out this fact. From the mide-sixties to the late seventies the Indian economy witnessed the problem of demand deficiency due to the fall in public investment resulting in lower industrial grwoth and increase in capital output-ratio. Again during 1997-2003 low industrial growth rate was achieved due to deficiency in demand resulting from stagnation in investment.

6. Sukhamoy Chakravarty, *The Logic of Investment Planning,* p.43.
7. K.K. Kurihara, *The Keynesian Theory of Development*, 1959. Ch. 9, pp.153-154
8. S. Chakravarty, *Op. cit.*

CHAPTER

37

Neoclassical Growth Model

Introduction

Having discussed Harrod-Domar growth model in the last chapter we will discuss neoclassical growth model in the present chapter. The neoclassical growth model was developed in the late 1950s and 1960s of the twentieth century as a result of intensive research in the field of growth economics. The American economist Robert Solow[1], who won a Nobel Prize in Economics and the British economist, J. E. Meade[2] are the two well known contributors to the neoclassical model of growth. This neoclassical growth model lays stress on capital accumulation and its related decision of saving as an important determinant of economic growth. Neoclassical growth model considered two factor production function with capital and labour as determinants of output. Besides, it added *exogenously determined factor, technology*, to the production function. Thus neoclassical growth model uses the following production function :

$$Y = AF(K, L) \qquad \dots (i)$$

where Y is Gross Domestic Product (GDP), K is the stock of capital, L is the amount of unskilled labour and *A is exogenously determined level of technology*. Note that change in this exogenous variable, technology, will cause a shift in the production function.

There are two ways in which technology parameter A is incorporated in the production function. One popular way of incorporating the technology parameter in the production function is to assume that technology is *labour augmenting* and accordingly the production function is written as

$$Y = F(K, AL) \qquad \dots (ii)$$

Note that *labour-augmenting technological change implies that it increases productivity of labour.*

The second important way of incorporating the technology factor in the production function is to assume that technological progress *augments all factors* (both capital and labour in our production function) and not just augmenting labour. It is in this way that we have written the production function equation (*i*) above. To repeat, in this approach production function is written as

$$Y = AF(K, L)$$

Considering in this way A represents *total factor productivity* (that is, productivity of both factor inputs). When we empirically estimate production function specified in this way, then contribution of A to the growth in total output is called *Solow residual* which means that total factor productivity really measures the increase in output *which is not accounted for by changes in factors, capital and labour.*

Unlike the *fixed proportion production function* of Harrod-Domar model of economic growth, neoclassical growth model uses *variable proportion production function,* that is, it considers unlimited *possibilities of substitution between capital and labour* in the production process. That is

1. Robert Solow, "A Contribution to the Theory of Economic Growth", *Quarterly Journal of Economics,* February 1956.
2. J. E. Meade, *Theory of Economic Growth.*

why it is called neoclassical growth model as the earlier neoclassicals considered such a variable proportion production function. The second important departure made by neoclassical growth model from Harrod-Domar growth model is that it assumes that *planned investment and saving are always equal* because of immediate adjustments in price (including interest). With these assumptions, neoclassical growth model focuses its attention on supply-side factors such as capital and technology for determining rate of economic growth of a country. Therefore, unlike Harrod-Domar growth model, it does not consider aggregate demand for goods limiting economic growth. Therefore, it is called '*classical*' along with '*neo*'. The growth of output in this model is achieved at least in the short run through higher rate of saving and therefore higher rate of capital formation, However, *diminishing returns to capital limit economic growth in this model*. Though the neoclassical growth model assumes *constant returns to scale* which exhibits *diminishing returns to capital and labour separately*.

We explain below how neoclassical growth model explains economic growth through capital accumulation (*i.e.*, saving and investment) and how this growth process ends in *steady state equilibrium. By steady state equilibrium for the economy we mean that growth rate of output equals growth rate of labour force and growth rate of capital* $\left(i.e. \frac{\Delta Y}{Y} = \frac{\Delta L}{L} = \frac{\Delta K}{K}\right)$ *so that per capita income and per capita capital are no longer changing*. Note that for income per capita and capital per worker to remain constant in this steady state equilibrium when labour force is growing implies that *income and capital must be growing at the same rate as labour force*. Since growth in labour force (or population) is generally denoted by letter 'n', in this steady state equilibrium, therefore, $\frac{\Delta Y}{Y} = \frac{\Delta K}{K} = \frac{\Delta N}{N} = n$. Neoclassic growth model explains the process of growth from any initial position to this steady state equilibrium.

Neoclassical Growth Model : Production Function and Saving

As stated above, neoclassical growth model uses following production function :

$$Y = AF(K, L)$$

However, the neoclassical theory explains the growth process using the above production function in its intensive form, that is, in per capita terms. To obtain the *above production function in per capita terms* we divide both sides of the given production function by L, the number of labour force. Thus

$$\frac{Y}{L} = AF\left(\frac{K}{L}, \frac{L}{L}\right)$$

$$= AF\left(\frac{K}{L}, 1\right) = AF\left(\frac{K}{L}\right) \quad \ldots (2)$$

To begin with, we assume that there is no technological progress. With this assumption then equation (2) is reduced to

$$\frac{Y}{L} = F\left(\frac{K}{L}\right) \quad \ldots (3)$$

The equation (3) states that output per head $\left(\frac{Y}{L}\right)$ is a function of capital per head $\frac{K}{L}$. We use lower-case letters to denote quantities per head (*i.e.*, per worker). Thus, writing y for $\frac{Y}{L}$ and k for $\frac{K}{L}$, equation (3) can be written as

$$y = f(k) \quad \ldots (4)$$

Now, in Figure 37.1 we represent the production function (4) in per capita terms. It will be noticed from Figure 37.1 that as capital per worker (k) increases output per worker increases, that is, marginal product of labour is positive. But, as will be seen from Figure 37.1, the slope of the production function curve decreases as capital per worker increases. This implies that marginal product of capital diminishes.

That is, the increase in capital per worker causes output per worker to increase but at a diminishing rate.

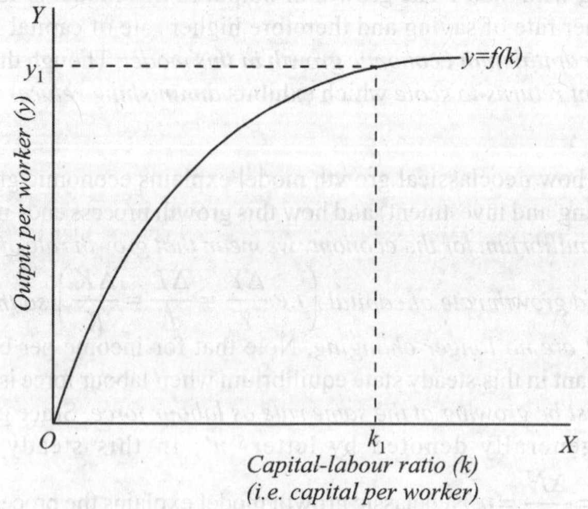

Fig. 37.1. *Production function relating output per worker to output per worker*

It will be seen from Figure 37.1 that at capital-labour ratio (*i. e.* capital per worker) equal to k_1, output per worker is y_1. Similarly, we can read from the production function curve: $y = f(k)$ the output per worker corresponding to any other capital per head.

Neoclassical Growth Model : Fundamental Growth Equation

According to neoclassical model, rate of saving plays an important role in the growth process of an economy. Like the Harrod-Domar model, neoclassical model considers saving as a *constant fraction of income*. Thus,

$$S = sY \qquad \ldots (5)$$

where S = saving

Y = income

s = propensity to save

Since s is a constant fraction of income, average propensity to save is equal to marginal propensity to save. Further, since national income equals national product, we can also write equation (5) as

$$sY = sF(K, L)$$

As in neoclassical model planned investment is always equal to planned saving, *net addition to the stock of capital* is (ΔK), which is the same thing as net investment (I), can be obtained by deducting *depreciation* of capital stock during a period from the planned saving. Thus,

$$\Delta K = I = sY - D \qquad \ldots (6)$$

where ΔK = net addition to the stock of capital, I stands for net investment and D for depreciation. Depreciation occurs at a certain percentage of the existing capital stock. The total depreciation (D) can be written as

$$D = dK$$

Substituting dK for D in equation (6) we have

$$\Delta K = sY - dK$$

or
$$sY = \Delta K + dK \qquad \ldots (7)$$

Now dividing and multiplying the first term of the right hand side of equation (7) by K we have

$$sY = K \cdot \frac{\Delta K}{K} + dK \qquad \ldots (8)$$

We have seen above, *for the steady state equilibrium, growth of capital* $\left(\frac{\Delta K}{K}\right)$ *must be equal to growth of labour force* $\left(\frac{\Delta L}{L}\right)$, *so that capital per worker and therefore income per worker remains constant*. If we denote growth rate of labour force $\left(\frac{\Delta L}{L}\right)$ by n, then in steady state $\frac{\Delta K}{K} = n$.

Substituting n for $\frac{\Delta K}{K}$ in equation (8) we have

$$sY = K.\, n + dK$$

or
$$sY = (n + d)\, K \qquad \ldots (9)$$

The above *equation (9) is a fundamental growth equation of the neoclassical growth model and states the condition for the steady state equilibrium when capital per worker and therefore income per capita remains constant even though population or labour force is growing*. Thus, for steady state growth equilibrium capital must be increasing equal to $(n + d)\, K$. Therefore, $(n + d)\, K$ represents the *required investment* (or change in capital stock) which ensures steady-state equilibrium when capital and income must be growing at the same rate as labour force (or population)

The Growth Process

From the growth equation (9) it is evident that if planned *saving sY is greater than the required investment, i.e. (n + d) K, to keep per capita income constant, capital for worker will increase*. This increase in capital per worker will cause increase in productivity of worker. As a result, the economy will grow at higher rate than the steady-state equilibrium growth rate. However, this higher growth rate will not occur endlessly because diminishing returns to capital will bring it down to the steady rate of growth, though at a higher level of per capita income and capital per worker.

In order to graphically show the growth process, the growth equation is conventionally used in *intensive form*, that is, in per capita terms (*i.e.*, per worker). In order to do so we divide both sides of equation (9) by L and have

$$\frac{sY}{L} = (n + d)\frac{K}{L}$$

where $\frac{Y}{L}$ represents income per worker and $\frac{K}{L}$ represents capital per worker (*i.e.* capital-labour ratio).

Writting y for $\frac{Y}{L}$ and k for $\frac{K}{L}$ we have

$$sy = (n + d)\, k \qquad \ldots (10)$$

The equation (10) represents fundamental neoclassical growth equation in per capita (*i.e.*, per worker) terms.

Growth Process and Steady Growth Rate. Figure 37.2 shows the growth process that moves the economy over time from an initial position to the steady state equilibrium growth rate. In the Figure 37.2 along with per capita production function ($y = f(k)$) we have also drawn per capita saving function curve *sy*. Besides, we have drawn $(n + d)k$ curve which depicts required investment per worker to keep constant the level of capital per capita when population or labour force is growing at a given rate n.

In Figure 37.2 $y = f(k)$ is per worker production function curve as in Figure 37.1. Since per capita saving is a constant fraction of per capita output (*i.e.* income), the curve *sy* depicting per capita saving function is drawn below the per capita output function curve ($y = f(k)$) with

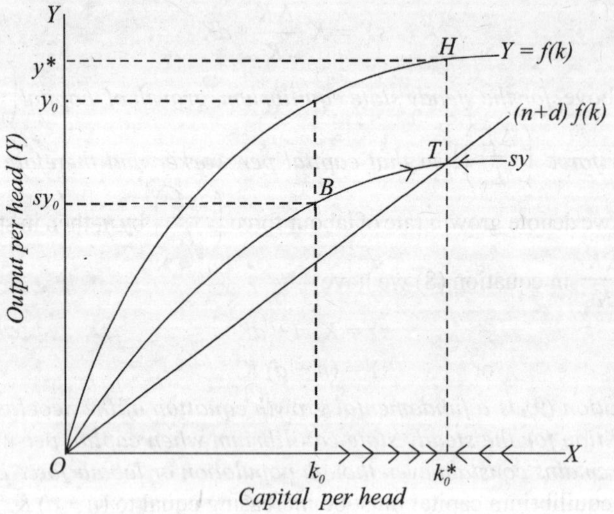

Fig. 37.2. *Neoclassical Model : Growth Process and Steady State Equilibrium*

the same shape. Another straight line curve labelled as $(n + d)k$, is drawn which depicts the *required investment* to keep capital per head (*i.e* capital-labour ratio) constant at various levels of capital per head.

Now, let us assume the current capital per head is k_o at which per capita income (or output) is y_0 and per capita saving is sy_0. It will be seen from Figure 37.2 that at capital per head k_0, per capita saving *sy* exceeds investment required to maintain capital per head equal to k_0, ($sy_0 > (n + d)k$). As a result, capital per head (k) will rise (as indicated by horizontal arrows) which will lead to increase in per capita income and the economy moves to the right. This adjustment process will continue so long as $sy > (n + d)\ k$. It will be seen from Fig. 37.2, when the economy reaches at capital per head equal to k^* and per capita income equal to y^* corresponding to which saving curve *sy* intersects the $(n + d)\ k$ curve at point *T*.

It will be noticed from Figure 37.2 that the adjustment process comes to rest at capital per head equal to k^* because saving and investment corresponding to this state is equal to the investment required to maintain capital per head at k^*. *Thus point T and its associated capital per head equal to k* and income or output per head equal to y* represent the steady state equilibrium.* It is worth noting that whether the economy is initially at the left or right of k^*, the adjustment process leads to the steady-state equilibrium at point *T*. It may however be noted that in steady-state equilibrium, the economy is growing at the same rate as labour force (that is, equal to n or $\Delta L/L$).

It will be seen from Figure 37.2 that although growth of economy comes down to the steady growth rate, its levels of per capita capital and per capita income at point *T* are greater as compared to the initial state at point *B*.

An important economic implication of the above growth process visualised in neoclassical growth model is that *different countries having same saving rate and population growth rate and access to the same technology will ultimately converge to same per capita income although this convergence process* may take different times in different countries.

Impact of Increase in the Saving Rate

As has been explained above that in steady state, both capital per head (k) and income per head (y) remain constant when economy is growing at the rate of growth of population or labour force ($i.e.$ n). In other words, in steady state equilibrium $\Delta k = 0$ and $\Delta Y = 0$. It follows from this that steady state growth rate or long-run growth rate which is equal to population or labour force growth rate n is not affected by changes in the saving rate. Changes in the saving rate affect only the *short-run growth rate* of the economy. This is an important implication of neoclassical growth model.

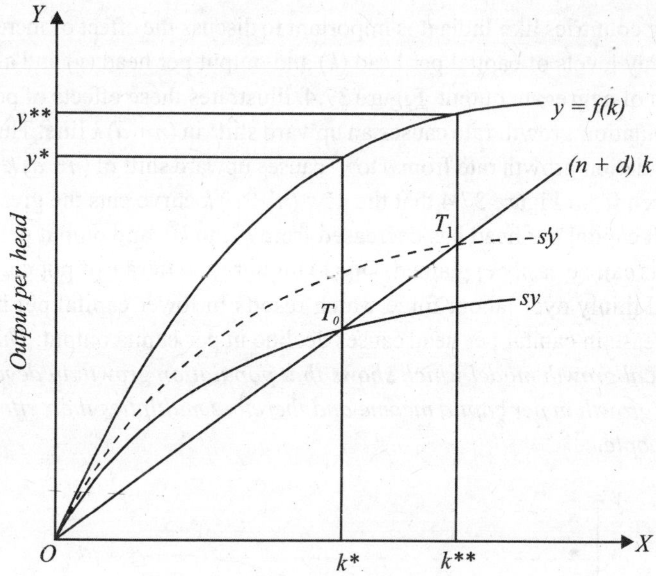

Fig. 37.3. *Impact of Increase in Saving Rate*

Now an important question is why do we get this apparently incredible result from the neoclassical growth model. Impact of increase in the saving is illustrated in Figure 37.3. It will be seen from this figure that initially with the saving curve sy, the economy is in steady state at point T_0 where the saving curve sy intersects required investment curve $(n + d)\,k$ with k^* as capital per head and y^* as income (output) per capita. Now suppose that saving rate increases, that is, individuals in the society decide to save a higher fraction of their income. As a result, saving curve shifts to the new higher position s'y (dotted). This higher saving curve $s'y$ intersects the $(n + d)k$ curve at point T_1 which therefore represents the new steady state. We thus see that increase in saving rate moves the steady state equilibrium to the right and causes both capital per head and income per head to rise to k^{**} and y^{**} respectively Note that in the new steady state the economy grows at the same rate as the growth rate of labour force (or population) which is denoted by n. It therefore follows that long-run growth rate of the economy remains unaffected by the increase in the saving rate though the steady state position has moved to the right.

Two points are worth noting here. First, though long-run growth rate of the economy remains the same as a result of increase in the saving rate, capital per head (k) and income per capita (y) have risen with the upward shift in the saving curve to $s'y$ and consequently the change in steady state from T_0 to T_1, capital per head has increased from k^* to k^{**} and income per head has risen from y^* to y^{**}.

It is worth mentioning that starting from initial steady state at time T_0 the increase in saving rate and capital formation leads to growth rate in total output higher than the steady growth rate n in the period from T_0 to T_1 but in period T_1 it returns to the steady growth rate path n. It is thus evident that the higher saving rate leads to a higher growth rate in the short run only, while *long-run growth rate* in output remains unaffected. *The increase in the saving rate raises the growth rate of output in the short run due to faster growth in capital and therefore in output.* As more capital is accumulated, the growth rate decreases due to the diminishing returns to capital and eventually falls back to the population or labour force growth rate (n).

Effect of Population Growth

For developing countries like India it is important to discuss the effect of increase in population growth rate on steady levels of capital per head (k) and output per head (y) and also on the steady-state rate of growth of aggregate output. Figure 37.4. illustrates these effects of population growth. An increase in population growth rate causes an upward shift in $(n + d) k$ line. Thus in Figure 37.4, the increase in population growth rate from n to n' causes upward shift of $(n + d) k$ to $(n' + d) k$ curve dotted. It will be seen from Figure 37.4 that the new $(n' + d) k$ curve cuts the given saving curve sy at point T' at which capital per head has decreased from k^*_1 to k^*_2 and output per capita has fallen from y^*_1 to y^*_2. This can be easily explained. Due to higher growth rate of population a given stock of capital is spread thinly over labour force which results in lower capital per head (*i.e.* capital-labour ratio). Decrease in capital per head causes decline in per capita output. *This is an important result of neoclassical growth model which shows that population growth in developing countries like India impedes growth in per capita income and therefore multiplies their efforts to raise living standards of the people.*

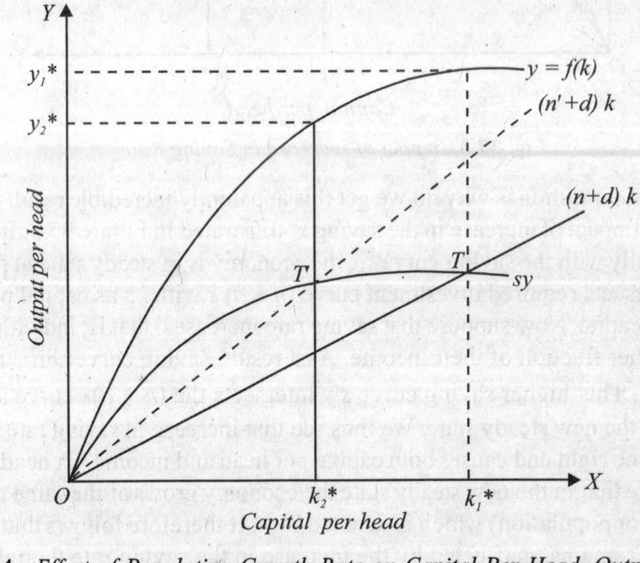

Fig. 37.4 *Effect of Population Growth Rate on Capital Per Head, Output Per Head, and Steady Growth Rate*

Figure 37.4 also shows that *higher growth rate of population raises the steady-state growth rate*. It will be seen from this figure that increase in population growth rate from n to n' causes $(n + d) k$ curve to shift upward to the new position $(n' + d) k$ (dotted) which intersects the saving curve at new steady-state equilibrium point T'. The steady state growth rate has therefore risen to n', that is, equal to the new growth rate of population. **It may however be noted that *higher steady rate of growth* is not a desirable thing.** As a matter of fact, a *higher steady growth means that to maintain a certain given capital-labour ratio and per capita income the economy has to save and invest more.* This implies that a higher rate of population acts as an obstacle to raise per capita income and therefore living standards of the people. Thus, this result provides a significant lesson for the developing countries like India, that is, if they want to achieve higher living standards for its people they should make efforts to control their population growth rate.

Long-run Economic Growth and Technological Change

Let us now analyse the effect of technological change on long-run economic growth of an economy. It is important to note that neoclassical growth model considers technological change as an *exogenous variable*. By exogenous technological change we mean it is determined outside the model, that is, it is independent of the values of other factors, capital and labour. That is why neoclassical production function is written as

$$Y = AF(K,L)$$

where A represents exogenous technological change and appears outside the bracket.

In the foregoing analysis of neoclassical growth model for the sake of simplification we have assumed that the technological change is absent, that is, $\frac{\Delta A}{A} = 0$. However, by assuming zero technological change we ignored the important factor that determines long-term growth of the economy. We now consider the effect of exogenous technological improvement over time, that is, when $\frac{\Delta A}{A} > 0$ over time.

We have seen above that in the absence of technological change in the basic solow model eventually the economy reaches a steady state in which output per person (Y) remains constant. However, in certain economies such as Japan output per person has grown at a sustained rate for many years. Solow model explains this with technological change (or what is also called increase in *total factor productivity*). The improvement in technology may occur as a result of research and innovations leading to increased productively of labour or higher efficient machines with greater

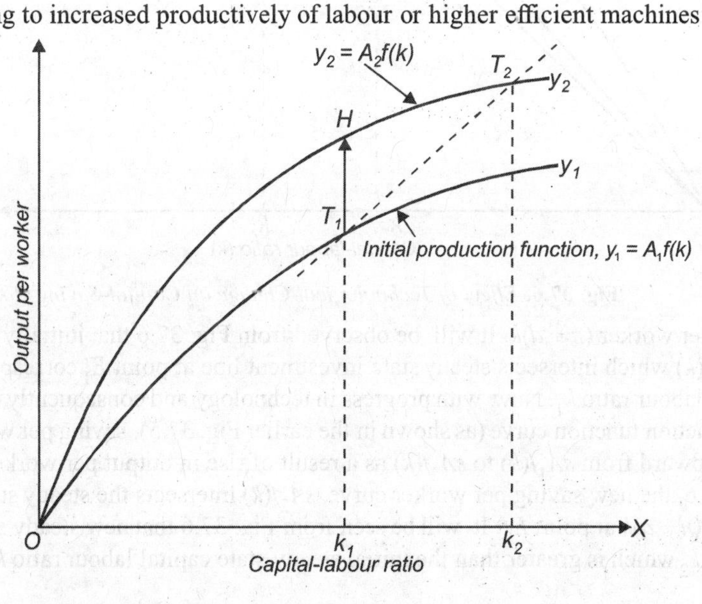

Fig. 37.5. *Effect of Technological Change on Output per Worker*

productivity. The effect of increase in productivity as a result of technological change is shown in Fig. 37.5, where per worker production function [$y = Af(k)$] shifts upward from $y_1 = A_1f(k)$ to $y_2 = A_2f(k)$ showing that at any given capital-labour ratio, a worker can produce more output which therefore leads to the increase in per capita income of the society. For example, at capital-labour ratio k_1, output per worker rises by T_1H as a result of improvement in productivity brought about by technological change. Similarly, rise in productivity per worker takes place at any other given capital-labour ratio (k). If there is further technological change resulting in more improvement in productivity per worker production function curve will further shift upward. In this way according to Solow, technological change can bring about increase in productivity per worker leading to the increase in per capita income in the society, that is, growth takes place in the economy.

Effect of Technological Change on the Steady-State Growth Rate

In Solow model the technological change causing improvement in productivity per worker (y) affects the steady state. As noted above, saving is proportional to output. Therefore, when technological change causes increase in output per worker, it also brings about rise in saving per worker leading to increase in steady-state capital-labour ratio. This is shown in Fig. 37.6. As explained above, steady state is determined by the intersection of saving per worker $sAf(k)$ and steady-state

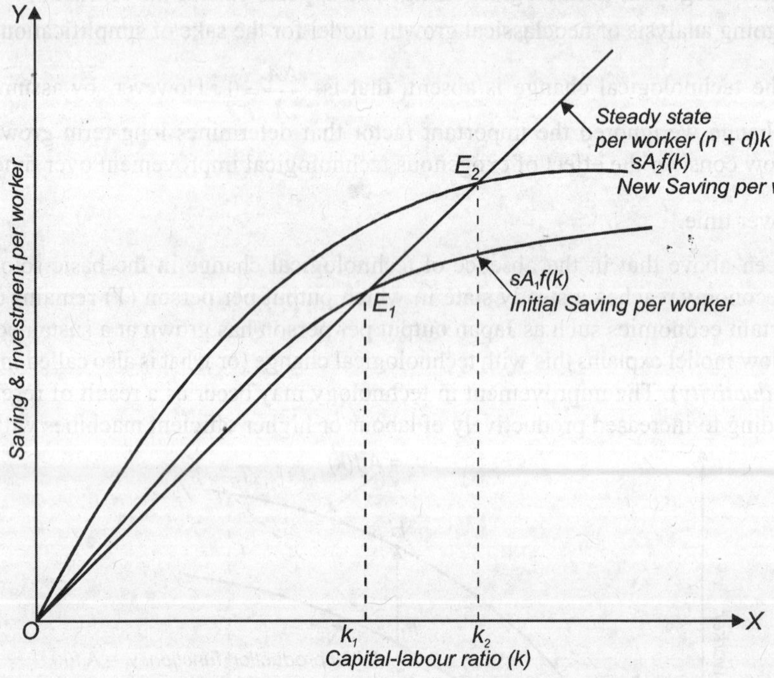

Fig. 37.6. *Effect of Technological Change on Capital-Saving Ratio*

investment per worker $(n + d)k$. It will be observed from Fig. 37.6 that initially saving per worker curve is $sA_1f(k)$ which intersects steady state investment line at point E_1 corresponding to steady-state capital-labour ratio k_1. Now, with progress in technology and consequently upward shift in per worker production function curve (as shown in the earlier Fig. 37.5), saving per worker curve in Fig. 37.6 shifts upward from $sA_1f(k)$ to $sA_2f(k)$ as a result of rise in output per worker. As will be seen from Fig. 37.6, the new saving per worker curve, $sA_2f(k)$ intersects the steady state investment per worker line, $(n + d)k$ at point E_2. It will be seen from Fig. 37.6 that new steady state capital-labour ratio rises to k_2 which is greater than the initial steady-state capital labour ratio k_1.

It is evident from above that technological change will lead to the increase in steady-state output and consumption per worker. This, takes place in two stages. First, as will be seen from Fig. 37.5, productivity improvement as a result of technological change *directly* raises output per worker and therefore consumption per person in the economy. Secondly, increase in output per worker, $y = Af(k)$ as a result of technological change will also raise the supply of saving which in the new steady-state equilibrium causes capital-labour ratio to rise which will further lead to the rise in output per person and consumption per head. Thus, in the previous Figure 37.5 as a result of productivity improvement due to technological change, production function shifts upward and at a given capital labour ratio k_1, output per worker rises from k_1T_1 to k_1 H. Further, as a result of increase in saving induced by technological change capital-labour ratio rises from k_1 to k_2 in Fig. 37.6. With this increase in capital-labour ratio,in Figure 37.5 output per worker increases from T_1 on initial production function y_1 to T_2 on the higher production function y_2 corresponding to increase in steady-state capital labour ratio from k_1 to k_2 due to higher saving. Thus, commenting on it, N. Gregory Mankiw writes, "With the addition of technological progress, neoclassical model can finally explain the sustained increases in standards of living that we observe. That is, ... technological progress can lead to sustained growth in output per worker. By contrast, a high rate of saving leads to a high rate of growth only until the steady state is reached. Once the economy is in steady state, the rate of growth of output per worker depends only on the rate of technological progress. *The Solow model shows that only technological progress can explain persistently rising living standards.*"[3]

SOURCES OF ECONOMIC GROWTH

An important issue in growth economics is what contributions of different factors, namely, capital, labour and technology make to economic growth. In other words, what is relative importance of these different factors as sources of economic growth. Robert Solow and Denison have attempted to study the relative importance of the various sources of economic growth by using the concept of production function. The rate of economic growth in an economy and differences in income levels of different countries and also their growth performance during a period can be explained in terms of the increase in these sources of economic growth.

It wll be recalled that the production function describes the amount of total output produced depends on the amount of different factors used and the state of technology. Capital-labour ratio rises from k_1 to k_2 in Fig. 37.6. With this increase in capital-labour ratio. The following production function has been used to measure the various sources of economic growth

$$Y = AF(K, L) \qquad \text{... (1)}$$

where Y = total national product
K = the quantity of physical capital used
L = the quantity of labour used
A = the state of technology

The production function equation (1) shows that increase in capital and labour and improvement in technology will lead to growth in national output.

Note that improvement in technology causes output increases with the given factor supplies. In other words, advancement in technology leads to the increase in productivity of factors used. Therefore, improvement in technology is generally measured by growth in **total factor productivity (TFP).**

It will also be noticed from the production function equation (1) that technology (A) has been taken to be a multiplicative factor. This implies that progress in technology increases the marginal productivity of both capital and labour uniformly. Such technological change is generally referred to

3. N. Gregory Mankiw, *Macroeconomics*, 2nd Edition, 1994, Worth Publishers, p.101 (italics in original)

as **neutral technological change**. Besides, we measure the sources of economic growth with the above production function by assuming *constant returns to scale.* Constant returns to scale implies that increase in inputs, that is, labour and capital, by a given percentage will lead to the same percentage increase in output. Further, the increase in improvement in technology (A) or what is also referred to as increase in total factor productivity causes a shift in the production function.

With the above assumptions it can be proved that the following factors represent the sources of economic growth.

$$\frac{\Delta Y}{Y} = \left(\theta \times \frac{\Delta K}{K}\right) + \left((1-\theta) \times \frac{\Delta L}{L}\right) + \frac{\Delta A}{A} \quad \ldots (2)$$

or, Growth of Output = (Share of Capital × Growth in Capital) + (Share of Labour × Growth in Labour) + Technical Progress

where θ denotes share of capital in national product, $1 - \theta$ denotes share of labour in national product.

The above equation, which is generally referred to as *growth accounting equation,* shows the various sources of growth which are summarised below :

1. The contribution of increase in capital to the growth in output (G or $\frac{\Delta Y}{Y}$) is given by increase in $\left(\frac{\Delta K}{K}\right)$ capital multiplied by the share (θ) of capital in national product;
2. The increase in labour force contributes to rate of economic growth equal to the labour share $(1 - \theta)$ in national product multiplied by the growth in labour force $\left(\frac{\Delta L}{L}\right)$; and
3. The technological improvement $\frac{\Delta A}{A}$ which is measured by the increase in total factor productivity also makes an important contribution to economic growth. As mentioned above, technological progress leads to the increase in total factor productivity (*TFP*) which implies that with the given resources (*i.e.* capital and labour) more output can be produced.

Proof

We can formally prove the growth accounting equation mentioned above. In the production function equation (1) the change in output (ΔY) depends on changes in various inputs or factors — capital and labour ΔK and ΔL and change in technology. This can be written as under :

$$\Delta Y = F(KL)\,\Delta A + MP_k \times \Delta K + MP_L \times \Delta L \quad \ldots (3)$$

where MP_k and MP_L represent marginal products of labour and capital respectively.

Dividing both sides of equation (3) by Y we have

$$\frac{\Delta Y}{Y} = \frac{F(K,L)\,\Delta A}{Y} + \frac{MP_K \cdot \Delta K}{Y} + \frac{MP_L \cdot \Delta L}{Y}$$

Since $Y = AF(K, L)$ we have

$$\frac{\Delta Y}{Y} = \frac{F(K,L)\,\Delta A}{AF(K,L)} + \frac{MP_K \cdot \Delta K}{Y} + \frac{MP_L \cdot \Delta L}{Y}$$

or

$$\frac{\Delta Y}{Y} = \frac{\Delta A}{A} + \frac{MP_K}{Y} \cdot \Delta K + \frac{MP_L}{Y} \cdot \Delta L \quad \ldots (4)$$

Now multiplying and dividing the second term of the left-hand side of equation (4) by K and also multiplying and dividing the third term of left-hand side of the equation by L we have

$$\frac{\Delta Y}{Y} = \frac{\Delta A}{A} + \frac{K.MP_K}{Y}.\frac{\Delta K}{K} + \frac{L.MP_L}{Y}.\frac{\Delta L}{L} \quad \ldots (5)$$

Now, if rewards of factors of production are determined by marginal products of factors as actually is the case under perfect competition in neoclassical model, then $\frac{K.MP_K}{Y}$ represents the share of capital in national product which we denote by θ and $\frac{L.MP_L}{Y}$ repersents the share of labour in national product (Y) which we denote by $1 - \theta$, then substituting these in equation (5) we have :

$$\frac{\Delta Y}{Y} = \frac{\Delta A}{A} + \theta\frac{\Delta K}{K} + (1-\theta)\frac{\Delta L}{L}$$

The above is the same as growth accounting equation (2) which indicates the sources of growth of output.

Table 37.1 Sources Of Economic Growth

	Growth of Output	Capital (%)	Labour	Total Factor Productivity
United States				
1960–73	4.0	4.0	1.7	1.6
1973–90	2.5	3.4	2.1	0.0
Japan				
1960–73	10.0	10.6	1.3	5.9
1973–90	4.0	5.80	1.0	1.8
Europe				
1960–73	4.9	5.7	(–)10.1	3.2
1973–90	2.3	3.1	0.1	1.3

Source : Kumiharu, Shigehra, "Causes of Declining Growth in Industrialised Countries" in *Policies For Long-run Economic Growth*". 1992.

In Table 37.1 we present the contributions made by capital, labour and total factor productivity (*i.e* technological improvement) in growth of output in the United States, Japan and the major countries of Europe in the two periods 1960-73 and 1973-90. It will be seen from the table that growth of capital and improvement in total factor productivity (*i.e.* technological progress) have been the important sources of economic growth, especially in case of economic growth in Japan and European countries. Table 37.1 further reveals that it is decline in total factor productivity (*i.e.* technological improvement) and in growth of capital that is responsible for slowdown of economic growth in the USA, Japan and European countries during the period 1973-90.

Knowledge or Education : the Missing Factor. In the above growth accounting equation, one factor, namely, knowledge or education, is missing which has been stressed among others by Nobel Laurette Prof. Amartya Sen as an important factor contributing to economic growth. It may be noted that increase in knowledge or education increases the productivity of workers by improving their productive skills and abilities. Besides, increased knowledge raises the productivity of capital and raises the return to investment in capital goods. Since investment in promotion of knowl-

1. See Dornbusch and Fischer, *Macroeconomics,* 6th edition McGraw Hill, pp. 265–266.

edge or education makes workers and machine more productive, the workforce equipped with knowledge and education is often called *human capital* which is regarded by modern economists as an important source of economic growth. Thus human capital or knowledge and education is the important missing factor in the growth equation of neoclassical economists, Solow and Denison. On including human capital as a separate factor which contributes to growth of output, the production function can be written as under.

$$Y = A\,F(K, L, H)$$

where H represents human capital which was omitted by Robert Solow in his growth accounting equation.

Economies of Scale and Economic Growth. Robert Solow in his study of sources of growth in real income also did not consider economies of scale as a factor contributing to growth. Solow assumed constrant returns to scale which implies if each factor in the production function increases by one per cent, output also increases by one per cent. However, some economists such as Denison and those associated with World Bank emphasise *economies of scale* or what is also called increasing returns to scale as a separate factor determining the rate of economic growth. In case of the United States, Denison estimated that of 2.92 per cent annual growth in national income recorded during the period 1929–1982, 0.26 per cent was due to economies of scale. However, whether there are increasing returns to scale or constant returns to scale is an empirical matter for investigation.

APPENDIX TO PART VIII

Sen Vs. Bhagwati: Debate on Growth and Distribution

Bhagwati's Approach

There is interesting ongoing debate between Sen and Bhagwati, two eminent India economists, about the issues of growth and distribution. Bhagwati focuses more on growth than distribution. He is one of the chief advocates of economic reforms involving liberalisation of economic controls (that is, removal of licensing and permits system and other restrictions on starting any industrial activity), the greater role of private sector in the growth process and globalisation, that is, liberalisation of foreign trade and foreign investment which he thinks will promote economic growth. However, Bhagwati also regards emphasis on economic growth as an instrument of poverty reduction and social advancement of the masses. He points out ways in which economic growth will cause reduction in poverty and increased welfare. First, economic growth would lead to increase in more gainful employment opportunities for the poor and thereby helping to lift them out of poverty. Higher incomes so earned by the poor from gainful employment would enable them to increase the personal spending on education and health and thereby to increase their welfare further.

Second, according to Bhagwati, economic growth leads to the increase in revenue for the government which means it can spend more on education, health and social welfare schemes for the poor. He has asserted that despite the growth-centred model having proved itself time and again to reduce poverty and increasing the living standards of the masses that critics of growth-centred model think that it is essential to redistribute income and wealth. He does not agree with the claim of Sen that the Indian state of Kerala and also Bangladesh are examples where redistribution rather than growth has led to rapid reduction in poverty compared to India as a whole. Bhagwati praises Gujarat model of development as he thinks it has generated a large employment opportunities by the private corporate companies helped by Modi government.

Commenting on alternative redistributive developmental model advanced by Prof. Amartya Sen he writes "In impoverished countries where the poor exceed the rich by a large margin redistribution would increase the consumption of the poor only minimally by, say a *Chapati* a day — and the increase would not be sustainable in the context of low income and high population growth. In short, for most developing countries the growth is the principal strategy for *inclusive development* — that is, development that consciously includes marginalist and poorest members of the society."[1]

It is worth mentioning that Bhagwati advocates ***market-oriented strategy of growth*** in which the private sector plays a dominant role and further that government should provide it incentives and remove stifling controls over it. For achieving rapid economic growth he has therefore been a chief supporter of market-friendly economic reforms involving liberalisation, privatisation and globalisation, initiated in India by Dr. Manmohan Singh. These economic reforms, according to Bhagwati, would eliminate poverty and unemployment by bringing about rapid economic growth.

Evaluation of Bhagwati's Approach

Before explaining Sen's view about economic growth, poverty and redistribution some comments on Prof. Bhagwati's market-oriented strategy of growth are in order. In our view as well as of Prof. Amartya Sen that though high rate of economic growth is necessary for tackling the problem of poverty and unemployment but not a sufficient condition for it. Whether a high rate of economic growth will help in reducing poverty depends on the composition of growth, the way growing output is produced as well as the distribution of benefits from it. Late Prof. Sukhamoy Chakratvarty rightly writes, "*the rate of growth strategy is by itself an inadequate device to deal with the problem of*

1. Jagdish Bhagwati, Redistribution and Poverty, *Economic Times,* Oct. 31, 2011

generating employment opportunities. Much depends on the composition of the growth process and how growth is financed and how benefits from growth process are distributed."[2]

Empirical evidence also confirms that growth of the modern industrial sector does not generate adequate employment opportunities. In the post-economic reforms period in India during which Bhagwati's policies of liberalisation and globalisation have been implemented, employment growth in the modern organised sector (both in the public and private sectors) grew by 0.05 per cent per annum during 1994-2008 despite 7.2 per cent average annual growth achieved during this period as against 1.20 per cent per annum in the pre-reform period in the eighties. Due to dilution of the role of public sector in industrial growth in the economic reforms initiated in India since 1991 there has been negative growth in employment in it that has not been made up by adequate employment opportunities generated in the private sector which has been given important and dominant role in the new industrial policy.

Besides, jobless nature of economic growth in India is also revealed by the recent 68th round of NSS conducted in 2011-12. According to this 68th round of NSS, overall employment rate in the Indian economy on the basis of usual states (both principal and subsidiary) has fallen from 38.6 per cent of population in 2011-12 from 39.2 per cent in 2009-10 and the absolute number of unemployed rose from 9.8 million persons in Jan 2010 to 10.8 million in January 2012, that is, one million increase in open unemployment in just two years.[3] This is despite the achievement of 8.9 per cent GDP growth rate in 2010-11 and 6.7 per cent in 2011-12 (revised estimates).

It is evident from above that it is not correct to say that rapid growth will necessarily generate employment opportunities and help in eradicating poverty. Much depends on what is being produced as to whether wage goods (especially food-grains and other essential goods, or luxury goods for those already well-off), and the techniques used for producing goods and services. If capital intensive techniques of production are employed for the production of industrial goods as has been the case in India, industrial growth will generate little employment opportunities and will therefore not lead to the reduction of poverty. As a matter of fact, in the first three decades of planning in India (1951-81) it was widely believed that benefits of growth would trickle down to the poor in the form of greater employment and higher wages. This is generally referred as **trickle-down theory**. After three decades of planning when it was realised that trickle-down effect did not work special employment and anti poverty schemes such as national rural employment scheme and Integrated Rural Development scheme were started.

The second way in which Bhagwati thinks that higher growth will help in eliminating poverty and unemployment is that higher growth would yield more revenue to the government which it can utilise it to spend more on schemes of promoting literacy, education, health care and other anti-poverty schemes such as MGNREGA (Mahatma Gandhi National Rural Employment Guarantee Act), Food Security Scheme). It is true that growth will yield more revenue through taxes but it does not follow that the extra revenue so obtained will be spent on social welfare and anti-poverty schemes and on building human resources through greater expenditure on education and health. For example, even after a substantial increase in revenue from direct taxes much of it is used to meet current revenue expenditure on non-productive activities and despite a large increase in tax revenue substantial amount of funds are borrowed from the market and thus incurring a *huge fiscal deficit*. And this huge fiscal deficit year after year has generated a persistent inflation which besides eroding the real incomes of the common man send many people below the poverty line.

Further, the strategy of growth suggested by Bhagwati gives dominant role to the private sector without much regulation and control over it and as the experience of post-reforms economic development reveals, this leads to glaring inequalities of income and wealth which are largely non-functional and *encourage conspicuous consumption* not conducive to promotion of economic growth. Strangely enough, Bhagwati advises the wealthy Indians to indulge less in conspicuous consumption, will the rich Indian entrepreneurs who have become bullionaires and spend several crores on the wedding of their children and lead a highly luxurious life listen to Bhagwati's advice? To quote Bhagwati "The political sustainability of the growth first model requires both symbolic and material effects. While growth does benefit the poor : it often benefits the rich disproportionately. So, to keep the poor committed to the system as their economic aspirations are aroused, the wealthy

2. Sukamoy Chakravarty "Some observation on Growth" *Seminar*, 1977
3. See 68th Round NSS Survey Report, July, 2013.

would be well advised to indulge less in conspicuous consumption"[4].

It follows from above that single-minded focus on growth without regard to its composition, technology used for production and distribution of its fruits brought about by unfettered free private enterprise is not an adequate answer to the problem of poverty and unemployment in India. This is not to deny that growth is important but equally important is its composition, its employment-generating potential and distribution of its fruits. It is on these grounds that Amartya Sen has criticized Bhagwati's growth-first approach. We now turn to examine Sen's Approach to growth, distribution and poverty.

Prof. Amartya Sen on Growth, Poverty and Distribution

Prof. Amartya Sen has been an advocate of the approach that consider *building of capabilities of the people* through more education and health care of the poor, Besides, he advocates for enlargement of job opportunities for the poor and freedom of human choice as a means of eliminating poverty and promoting well-being of the people. Unlike Bhagwati, he does not consider growth first and then redistribution to solve the problems of poverty and unemployment. In his latest look '*An Uncertain Glory : India and its Contradictions*' coauthored with Jean Dreze he points out that rapid growth in India has coexisted with grossly inadequate social services (education and health) and physical services (safe water, electricity, drainage and sanitation).

Despite significant economic growth achieved in the last two decades (1991–2012) there still prevails widespread poverty in India. The poor and underprivileged people suffer from undernourishment, poor health, illiteracy, lack of education and skills to get gainful employment. Freedom from hunger and undernourishment, freedom from illness and freedom from illiteracy are essential requirements of economic growth. It is building of the capabilities of the poor and gain freedom from illness and illiteracy that Sen views as economic development. To quote him, "*economic growth cannot be sensibly treated as an end in itself. Development has to be more concerned with enhancing the life we lead and freedom we enjoy*".[5]

Thus, according to him, the challenge of development is to improve the quality of life, especially in a developing countries such as ours. A better quality of life generally calls for high standards of health and nutrition, less poverty, more equality of opportunity[6]. In his latest book, 'An *Uncertain Glory. India and its Contradictions*', he cites successful countries like Korea and China to argue that fast economic growth is not sustainable without strong development of human capital and essential infrastructure. India lags behind many countries at a similar level of development and even behind poor Bangladesh. In an interview with *Times of India* at the time of publication of its above mentioned book in July, 2013 he says, "despite great success in many ways over the last two decades the fact is that India is in a dreadful state in many ways. *Inequality is the primary aspect of it*. About economic growth I think there are two things about it. First, the way the Indian dialogue has developed there seems to be basic involvement about how growth happens. *No country in the world with such a fast sustained rate of economic growth has done so little towards having* an *educated and healthy labour force.* The way the debate has come it is now just '*we now have growth so we have to make it inclusive*'. *Now, these are not two distinct things.* If growth happens it depends on how it is happening. *If it happens because you have an educated and healthy labour force, then a lot of people are better placed to earn more income*".

It is evident from the above that, according to Sen, the state should begin with investment in education and health-care of the people right away without waiting for first to become rich and then think of redistribution for achieving inclusive growth. He provides the example of Singapore, Taiwan, Korea, China which began with investment in education and health-care of the people without waiting for first becoming rich. In their case, according to him, growth happened along with the poor benefitting from it by making earnings from the education and health acquired by them in the process of growth and it this way become a productive part of the society. He further thinks that growth will generate more resources and if they are ploughed back for further investment in building human capabilities, it will still generate rapid economic growth. He bemoans the fact that even after 60 years of development India has not achieved universal education. In response to Bhagwati's criticism he says that he is not against liberalisation and globalisation and did not support the license-permit system.

4. Jagdish Bhagwati, Redistribution and Poverty, *The Economic Times,* Oct. 31, 2011
5. Amartys Sen, *Development as Freedom*, Oxford University Press, 2001, p.43.
6. Ibid p. 175.

But he emphasises that while economic reforms initiated by Dr. Manmohan Singh in 1991 *attempted to correct the over activity of government in some fields* (*i.e.,* removing license-permit system by undertaking liberalisation and privatisation), *the need to correct government underactivity* in other areas has not really been addressed. As back as in 1998, he wrote, "the success of liberalisation and closer integration with the world economy may be severely impaired by India's backwarders in basic education, elementary health-care, gender inequality and humilations".

It is because of absence of constructive activities of the state, namely, expansion in government spending on health-care and nutrition of the people that he has criticised 'Gujarat Model of Development' Sen and his coauthor. Jean Dreze have supported the starting of **MGNREGA Scheme** because it helps the poor to obtain gainful employment giving them income which they can use to end their undernourishment and contribute to the improvement of their health. Similarly, they have supported the passage of *food security bill* which would ensure the poor people adequate food to remove their hunger and unnourishment which will enhance their capability to participate in the process of development.

Thus Sen believes that the state *must directly* deliver food, employment, education and health-care rather than relying on trickle-down effect of economic growth achieved through the dominant role of private sector in a predominantly free-market economy. Besides, Sen is of the view that rapid economic growth achieved through liberalisation, privatisation and globalisation of the Indian economy has resulted in glaring income inequalities which besides being non-functional leads to conspicuous consumption of the few rich people. This has adversely affected resources available for growth and social spending by the government on food security, education, employment and health-care of the poor people. According to him, to rapid growth would have been brought about by investing in India's most abundant resource, that is, investing in education and health of its people and thereby building up their capabilities for productive work, the present glaring income inequalities would not have been there and inclusive growth in real terms would have been achieved.

Evaluation

Sen's view that a higher priority should have given to the investment in education and health and providing food and employment to the poor people in our growth strategy is a correct one and has been unjustly criticised by Bhagwati who believes in the efficiency of capitalism or free market economy to deliver rapid economic growth and enhanced welfare of the people.

However, Sen's present view of growth underplays the importance of investment in physical capital and infrastructure to promote growth. The expansion or accumulation of physical capital in both industry and agriculture is also crucial importance for increase in productivity of labour force and growth of employment. Besides, we need a growth strategy that ensures rapid growth of employment opportunities. For this we require the use of labour-intensive appropriate technologies for use in small and medium enterprises rather than labour-displacing capital-intensive technologies generally used by our big corporate enterprises. Even if there is expansion of educated and healthy people, if adequate opportunities for their employment are not created, the education and skills acquired by them will be of no avail and their growth potential will remain unutilised. There is a lot of even educated unemployment in India. Further, the special employment schemes such as Mahatma Gandhi National Rural Employment Guarantee Scheme (MGNREGS) which Sen strongly recommends have generally found to be not resulting in the creation of productive assets. Further, these special anti-poverty employment schemes cannot ensure employment generation on a sustainable basis. *What is required is employment-oriented strategy of development so that employment opportunities increase through the regular growth process.*

It is worth mentioning that for bringing about rapid growth in GDP and employment the private sector on which Bhagwati relies for bringing about growth will not make adequate investment in infrastructure such as power, coal, roads, ports, irrigation projects which create external economies and hold back economic growth. Therefore, the state has to play a crucial role for adequate investment in infrastructure projects.

To conclude, what is required is a balanced growth involving investment in education and health of the people as emphasised by Sen and adequate investment in expansion of physical capital goods and infrastructure. Besides, in India's growth strategy importance ought to be given to the growth of agriculture which produces *wage goods* and are essential for generation of employment opportunities and for ensuring price stability. Investment in agriculture has been neglected in India's growth strategy.

⊙⊙⊙